Mike Meyers'

CompTIA Network+®
Guide to Managing and
Troubleshooting Networks

Fourth Edition

(Exam N10-006)

Mike Meyers'

CompTIA Network+®
Guide to Managing and
Troubleshooting Networks

Fourth Edition

(Exam N10-006)

Mike Meyers

New York   Chicago   San Francisco
Athens   London   Madrid   Mexico City
Milan   New Delhi   Singapore   Sydney   Toronto

Cataloging-in-Publication Data is on file with the Library of Congress

McGraw-Hill Education books are available at special quantity discounts to use as premiums and sales promotions, or for use in corporate training programs. To contact a representative, please visit the Contact Us pages at www.mhprofessional.com.

Mike Meyers' CompTIA Network+® Guide to Managing and Troubleshooting Networks, Fourth Edition (Exam N10-006)

1234567890   QVS QVS   1098765

ISBN: Book p/n 978-0-07-184824-4 and CD p/n 978-0-07-184823-7
    of set 978-0-07-184827-5

MHID: Book p/n 0-07-184824-X and CD p/n 0-07-184823-1
    of set 0-07-184827-4

Sponsoring Editor
JEFF KELLUM

Editorial Supervisor
JODY MCKENZIE

Project Editor
HOWIE SEVERSON,
FORTUITOUS PUBLISHING

Acquisitions Coordinators
MARY DEMERY AND
AMY STONEBRAKER

Technical Editor
JONATHAN WEISSMAN

Copy Editor
BILL MCMANUS

Proofreader
PAUL TYLER

Indexer
JACK LEWIS

Production Supervisor
JEAN BODEAUX

Composition
CENVEO® PUBLISHING SERVICES

Illustration
CENVEO PUBLISHING SERVICES

Art Director, Cover
JEFF WEEKS

■ About the Author

Michael Meyers is the industry's leading authority on CompTIA Network+ certification. He is the president and founder of Total Seminars, LLC, a major provider of PC and network repair seminars for thousands of organizations throughout the world, and a member of CompTIA.

Mike has written numerous popular textbooks, including the best-selling *Mike Meyers' CompTIA A+® Guide to Managing & Troubleshooting PCs*, *Mike Meyers' CompTIA A+® Guide to Essentials*, and *Mike Meyers' CompTIA A+® Guide to Operating Systems*.

About the Contributor

Scott Jernigan wields a mighty red pen as Editor in Chief for Total Seminars. With a Master of Arts degree in Medieval History, Scott feels as much at home in the musty archives of London as he does in the crisp IPS glow of Total Seminars' Houston HQ. After fleeing a purely academic life, he dove headfirst into IT, working as an instructor, editor, and writer.

Scott has written, edited, and contributed to dozens of books on computer literacy, hardware, operating systems, networking, and certification, including *Computer Literacy—Your Ticket to IC³ Certification,* and co-authoring with Mike Meyers the *All-in-One CompTIA Strata® IT Fundamentals Exam Guide.*

Scott has taught computer classes all over the United States, including stints at the United Nations in New York and the FBI Academy in Quantico. Practicing what he preaches, Scott is a CompTIA A+ and CompTIA Network+ certified technician, a Microsoft Certified Professional, a Microsoft Office User Specialist, and Certiport Internet and Computing Core Certified.

About the Technical Editor

Jonathan S. Weissman has always listed teaching as his number one passion, since his very first class on September 4, 2001.

He is a tenured Associate Professor and IT Program Coordinator in the Computing Sciences Department at Finger Lakes Community College. In addition to teaching, Jonathan rewrote the FLCC IT degree, keeping it current with industry, and he designed the Networking Lab. He is also a full-time Lecturer in the Computing Security Department at Rochester Institute of Technology, teaching both graduate and undergraduate courses. The highlight of his career came in May 2014, when he was awarded the RIT Outstanding Teaching Award for Non-Tenure Track Faculty 2013–2014. Jonathan is also a Lecturer in the School of Management at Nazareth College where he teaches IT courses.

Jonathan has a Master's degree in Computer Science from Brooklyn College. He has 34 industry certifications, including Cisco's CCNP Routing and Switching, CCNA Routing and Switching, and CCNA Security; CompTIA's Security+, Network+, A+, and Linux+; EC-Council's Certified Ethical Hacker and Computer Hacking Forensic Investigator; and IPv6 Forum's Certified Network Engineer (Gold) and Certified Trainer (Gold).

Jonathan does computer networking and computer/network security industry consulting for area businesses and individuals, and also serves as technical editor for many industry textbooks.

He has taught over four dozen courses in networking, security, systems administration, ethical hacking, forensics, malware reverse engineering, programming, web design and scripting, database design, and many more.

Acknowledgments

I'd like to acknowledge the many people who contributed their talents to make this book possible:

To Jeff Kellum, my acquisitions editor at McGraw-Hill: So great to get a chance to work with you on this book. Your smooth desert vibe made a difficult task surprisingly enjoyable. Good luck!

To my in-house Editor-in-Chief, Scott Jernigan: I couldn't have done it without you, amigo. Truthfully, has there ever been a better combo than a wizard and a paladin?

To Jonathan S. Weissman, technical editor: Wait, how many more certifications did you get since the last edition? No wonder you keep me honest (and accurate)! Still, tossing in smiley faces after telling me, in perfect New Yorker, "you're totally wrong here!" doesn't actually stop the sting much. Ha!

To Bill McManus, copy editor: Astonishingly good work in a fast-paced timeframe. You rock!

To Shannon Murdoch, my right-hand for this book: Thanks for keeping me organized and on track with all those delightful and colorful sticky notes. (I still dread the neon pink ones . . . I'll remember, I promise!) Your work on discussions, proofing, and general awesomeness brightened the whole project.

To Michael Smyer, Total Seminars' resident tech guru and photographer: Your contributions continue to shine, from superb photographs to excellent illustrations and, in this edition, some nicely styled writing. Well done!

To Dave Rush, crack technologist and ridiculously talented person: How can I list the many contributions you've made to make this book—and all the crazy products that go with it—so awesome? Researching, writing, arguing, filming, arguing, researching some more . . . and the final product. All fun!

To Travis Everett, Internet guru and writer: Such a wonderful addition to the team this go-round, not just as a top-notch editor, but as a contributor as well. Your understanding of the Internet and the Cloud added excellent additions to the book. Looking forward to the next one to see what other talents you bring to the table!

To Ford Pierson, graphics maven and editor: I know you have a new prime directive with little Oliver, but thanks for pinch-hitting on some graphics and editing for the book. Much appreciated. And I'm really glad we do everything electronically nowadays. Diapers, yikes!

To Dudley Lehmer, my partner at Total Seminars: As always, thanks for keeping the ship afloat while I got to play on this book!

To Mary Demery and Amy Stonebraker, acquisitions coordinators at McGraw-Hill: Thanks for keeping track of everything and (gently) smacking Scott when *he* forgot things.

To Jody McKenzie and Howie Severson, project editors: It was a joy to work with you both again. I couldn't have asked for a better team. In fact, I asked for the best team and got exactly what I wanted!

To Paul Tyler, proofreader: You did a super job, thank you

To Cenveo, compositors: The layout was excellent, thanks!

To Tim Green: Thank you for all the years and projects you've worked on with me, and for your never-flagging professionalism and brilliance. And, yeah, thanks for putting up with me!

ABOUT THIS BOOK

■ Important Technology Skills

Information technology (IT) offers many career paths, leading to occupations in such fields as PC repair, network administration, telecommunications, Web development, graphic design, and desktop support. To become competent in any IT field, however, you need *certain basic computer skills.* Mike Meyers' CompTIA Network+® Guide to Managing and Troubleshooting Networks *builds a foundation for success in the IT field by introducing you to fundamental technology concepts and giving you essential computer skills.*

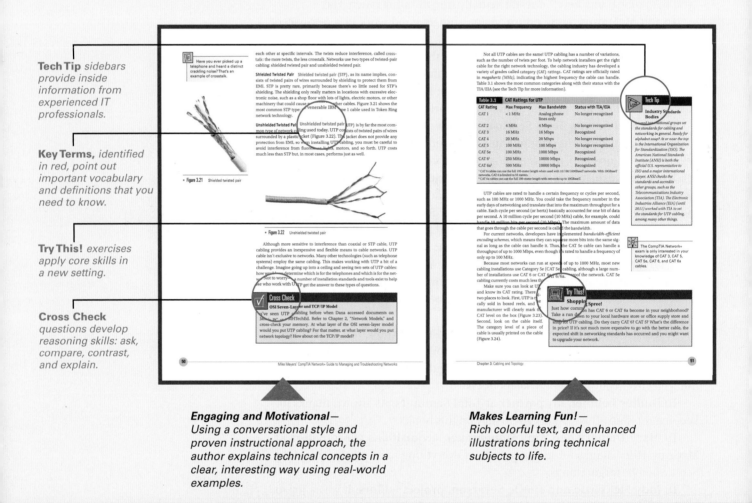

Tech Tip *sidebars provide inside information from experienced IT professionals.*

Key Terms, *identified in red, point out important vocabulary and definitions that you need to know.*

Try This! *exercises apply core skills in a new setting.*

Cross Check *questions develop reasoning skills: ask, compare, contrast, and explain.*

Engaging and Motivational—
Using a conversational style and proven instructional approach, the author explains technical concepts in a clear, interesting way using real-world examples.

Makes Learning Fun!—
Rich colorful text, and enhanced illustrations bring technical subjects to life.

Proven Learning Method Keeps You on Track

Mike Meyers' CompTIA Network+® Guide to Managing and Troubleshooting Networks *is structured to give you comprehensive knowledge of computer skills and technologies. The textbook's active learning methodology guides you beyond mere recall and—through thought-provoking activities, labs, and sidebars—helps you develop critical-thinking, diagnostic, and communication skills.*

■ Effective Learning Tools

This pedagogically rich book is designed to make learning easy and enjoyable and to help you develop the skills and critical-thinking abilities that will enable you to adapt to different job situations and troubleshoot problems.

Mike Meyers' proven ability to explain concepts in a clear, direct, even humorous way makes this book interesting, motivational, and fun.

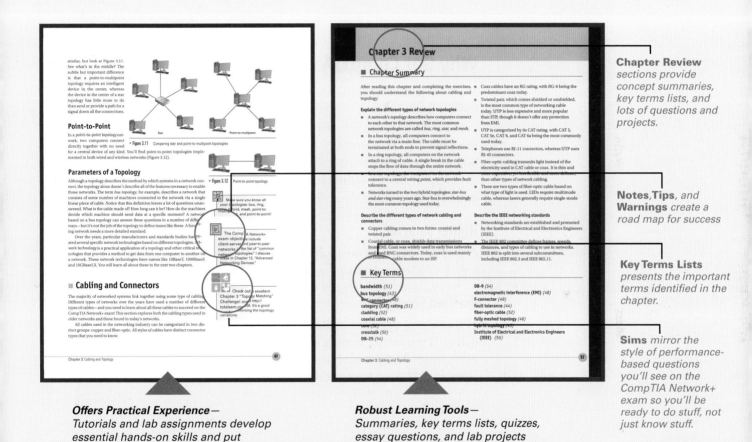

Chapter Review sections provide concept summaries, key terms lists, and lots of questions and projects.

Notes, Tips, and **Warnings** create a road map for success

Key Terms Lists presents the important terms identified in the chapter.

Sims mirror the style of performance-based questions you'll see on the CompTIA Network+ exam so you'll be ready to do stuff, not just know stuff.

Offers Practical Experience—
Tutorials and lab assignments develop essential hands-on skills and put concepts in real-world context.

Robust Learning Tools—
Summaries, key terms lists, quizzes, essay questions, and lab projects help you practice skills and measure progress.

Each chapter includes

■ **Learning Objectives** that set measurable goals for chapter-by-chapter progress

■ **Illustrations** that give you a clear picture of the technologies

■ **Tutorials** that teach you to perform essential tasks and procedures hands-on

■ **Try This!, Cross Check,** and **Tech Tip** sidebars that encourage you to practice and apply concepts in real-world settings

■ **Notes, Tips,** and **Warnings** that guide you through difficult areas

■ **Sims** links to practical simulations that prepare you for the performance-based questions on the CompTIA exams

■ **Chapter Summaries** and **Key Terms Lists** that provide you with an easy way to review important concepts and vocabulary

■ **Challenging End-of-Chapter Tests** that include vocabulary-building exercises, multiple-choice questions, essay questions, and on-the-job lab projects

▨ Becoming a CompTIA Certified IT Professional Is Easy

It's also the best way to reach greater professional opportunities and rewards.

Why Get CompTIA Certified?

Growing Demand

Labor estimates predict some technology fields will experience growth of more than 20% by the year 2020. (Source: CompTIA's *Ninth Annual Information Security Trends Study*, 2012: online survey of 500 U.S. IT and business executives responsible for information security policies and procedures.) CompTIA certification qualifies the skills required to join this workforce.

Higher Salaries

IT professionals with certifications on their resume command better jobs, earn higher salaries, and have more doors open to new multi-industry opportunities.

Verified Strengths

91% of hiring managers indicate CompTIA certifications are valuable in validating IT expertise, making certification the best way to demonstrate your competency and knowledge to employers. (Source: CompTIA's *Employer Perceptions of IT Training and Certification* study, 2011.)

Universal Skills

CompTIA certifications are vendor neutral—which means that certified professionals can proficiently work with an extensive variety of hardware and software found in most organizations.

Learn	Certify	Work
Learn more about what the exam covers by reviewing the following:	Purchase a voucher at a Pearson VUE testing center or at CompTIAstore.com.	Congratulations on your CompTIA certification!

Learn

Learn more about what the exam covers by reviewing the following:

- Exam objectives for key study points.
- Sample questions for a general overview of what to expect on the exam and examples of question format.
- Visit online forums, like LinkedIn, to see what other IT professionals say about CompTIA exams.

Certify

Purchase a voucher at a Pearson VUE testing center or at CompTIAstore.com.

- Register for your exam at a Pearson VUE testing center.
- Visit pearsonvue.com/CompTIA to find the closest testing center to you.
- Schedule the exam online. You will be required to enter your voucher number or provide payment information at registration.
- Take your certification exam.

Work

Congratulations on your CompTIA certification!

- Make sure to add your certification to your resume.
- Check out the CompTIA Certification Roadmap to plan your next career move.

Learn More: Certification.CompTIA.org/networkplus

CompTIA Disclaimer

CONTENTS AT A GLANCE

CONTENTS

Chapter 6
■ Installing a Physical Network   102

Chapter 7
■ TCP/IP Basics   144

Chapter 8
■ Routing   182

Chapter 9
■ TCP/IP Applications   222

Chapter 10
■ Network Naming   256

Chapter 11
■ Securing TCP/IP   288

Chapter 12
■ Advanced Networking Devices   326

Chapter 13
■ IPv6   358

Chapter 14
■ Remote Connectivity   380

Chapter 19
▓ Protecting Your Network   544

Chapter 20
▓ Network Monitoring   580

Chapter 21
▓ Network Troubleshooting   598

I was a teacher long before I was ever an author. I started writing computer books for the simple reason that no one wrote the kind of books I wanted to read. The books were either too simple (Chapter 1, "Using Your Mouse") or too complex (Chapter 1, "TTL Logic and Transistors") and none of them provided a motivation for me to learn the information. I guessed that there were geeky readers just like me who wanted to know *why* they needed to know the information in a computer book.

Good books motivate the reader to learn what he or she is reading. If a book discusses binary arithmetic but doesn't explain why I need to learn it, for example, that's not a good book. Tell me that understanding binary makes it easier to understand how an IP address works or why we're about to run out of IP addresses and how IPv6 can help, then I get excited, no matter how geeky the topic. If I don't have a good reason, a good motivation to do something, then I'm simply not going to do it (which explains why I haven't jumped out of an airplane!).

In this book, I teach you why you need to understand the wide world of networking. You'll learn everything you need to start building, configuring, and supporting networks. In the process, you'll gain the knowledge you need to pass the CompTIA Network+ certification exam.

Enjoy, my fellow geek.

For instructor and student resources, please visit:

http://mhprofessional.com/GuideToNetworks4e

Students will find chapter quizzes that will help them learn more about troubleshooting and fixing networks, and teachers can access the support materials outlined below.

■ Additional Resources for Teachers

McGraw-Hill Education connects instructors with their support materials and students with chapter assessments. The Online Learning Center provides resources for teachers in a format that follows the organization of the textbook.
This site includes the following:

- Answer keys to the end-of-chapter activities in the textbook
- Instructor's Manual that contains learning objectives, classroom preparation notes, instructor tips, and a lecture outline for each chapter
- Answer keys to the activities in Mike Meyers' Lab Manual (available separately)
- Access to test bank files and software that allow you to generate a wide array of paper- or network-based tests, and that feature automatic grading. The test bank includes:
  - Hundreds of practice questions and a wide variety of question types categorized by exam objective, enabling you to customize each test to maximize student progress
  - Test bank files available on EZ Test Online and as downloads from the Online Learning Center in these formats: Blackboard, Web CT, EZ Test, and Word
- Engaging PowerPoint slides on the lecture topics that include full-color artwork from the book

Please contact your McGraw-Hill Education sales representative for details.

CompTIA Network+ in a Nutshell

"Networking is an essential part of building wealth."

—Armstrong Williams

In this chapter, you will learn how to

- Describe the importance of CompTIA Network+ certification
- Illustrate the structure and contents of the CompTIA Network+ certification exam
- Plan a strategy to prepare for the exam

By picking up this book, you've shown an interest in learning about networking. But be forewarned. The term *networking* describes a vast field of study, far too large for any single certification, book, or training course to cover. Do you want to configure routers and switches for a living? Do you want to administer a large Windows network at a company? Do you want to install wide area network connections? Do you want to set up Web servers? Do you want to secure networks against attacks?

If you're considering a CompTIA Network+ certification, you probably don't yet know exactly what aspect of networking you want to pursue, and that's okay! You're going to love preparing for the CompTIA Network+ certification.

Attaining CompTIA Network+ certification provides you with four fantastic benefits. First, you get a superb overview of networking that helps you decide what part of the industry you'd like to pursue. Second, it acts as a prerequisite toward other, more advanced certifications. Third, the amount of eye-opening information you'll gain just makes getting CompTIA Network+ certified plain old fun. Finally, you'll significantly enhance your opportunity to get a job. Everything seems to be networked today, putting network techs in demand.

Nothing comes close to providing a better overview of networking than CompTIA Network+. The certification covers local area networks (LANs), wide area networks (WANs), the Internet (the world's largest WAN), security, cabling, and applications in a wide-but-not-too-deep fashion that showcases the many different parts of a network and hopefully tempts you to investigate the aspects that intrigue you by looking into follow-up certifications.

The process of attaining CompTIA Network+ certification will give you a solid foundation in the whole field of networking. Mastering the competencies will help fill in gaps in your knowledge and provide an ongoing series of "a-ha!" moments of grasping the big picture that make being a tech so much fun.

Ready to learn a lot, grab a great certification, and have fun doing it? Then welcome to CompTIA Network+ certification!

Who Needs CompTIA Network+? I Just Want to Learn about Networks!

Whoa up there, amigo! Are you one of those folks who either has never heard of the CompTIA Network+ exam or just doesn't have any real interest in certification? Is your goal only to get a solid handle on networks and a jump start on the basics? Are you looking for that "magic bullet" book that you can read from beginning to end and then start installing and troubleshooting a network? Do you want to know what's involved with running network cabling in your walls or getting your new wireless network working? Are you tired of not knowing enough about TCP/IP and how it works? If these types of questions are running through your mind, then rest easy—you have the right book. Like every book with the Mike Meyers name, you'll get solid concepts without pedantic details or broad, meaningless overviews. You'll look at real-world networking as performed by real techs. This is a book that understands your needs and goes well beyond the scope of a single certification.

If the CompTIA Network+ exam isn't for you, you can skip the rest of this chapter, shift your brain into learn mode, and dive into Chapter 2. But then, if you're going to have the knowledge, why *not* get the certification?

What Is CompTIA Network+ Certification?

CompTIA Network+ certification is an industry-wide, vendor-neutral certification program developed and sponsored by the Computing Technology Industry Association (CompTIA). The CompTIA Network+ certification shows that you have a basic competency in the physical support of networking systems and knowledge of the conceptual aspects of networking. To date, many hundreds of thousands of technicians have become CompTIA Network+ certified.

CompTIA Network+ certification enjoys wide recognition throughout the IT industry. At first, it rode in on the coattails of the successful CompTIA A+ certification program, but it now stands on its own in the networking industry and is considered the obvious next step after CompTIA A+ certification. (CompTIA A+ is the certification for PC technicians.)

What Is CompTIA?

CompTIA is a nonprofit, industry trade association based in Oakbrook Terrace, Illinois, on the outskirts of Chicago. Tens of thousands of computer resellers, value-added resellers, distributors, manufacturers, and training companies from all over the world are members of CompTIA.

CompTIA was founded in 1982. The following year, CompTIA began offering the CompTIA A+ certification exam. CompTIA A+ certification is now widely recognized as the *de facto* requirement for entrance into the PC industry. Because the CompTIA A+ exam initially covered networking only lightly, CompTIA decided to establish a vendor-neutral test covering basic networking skills. So, in April 1999, CompTIA unveiled the CompTIA Network+ certification exam.

CompTIA provides certifications for a variety of areas in the computer industry, offers opportunities for its members to interact, and represents its members' interests to government bodies. CompTIA certifications include CompTIA A+, CompTIA Network+, and CompTIA Security+, to name a few. Check out the CompTIA Web site at www.comptia.org for details on other certifications.

CompTIA is *huge*. Virtually every company of consequence in the IT industry is a member of CompTIA: Microsoft, Dell, Cisco… Name an IT company and it's probably a member of CompTIA.

The Current CompTIA Network+ Certification Exam Release

CompTIA constantly works to provide exams that cover the latest technologies and, as part of that effort, periodically updates its certification objectives, domains, and exam questions. This book covers all you need to know to pass the N10-006 CompTIA Network+ exam released in 2015.

How Do I Become CompTIA Network+ Certified?

To become CompTIA Network+ certified, you simply pass one computer-based exam. There are no prerequisites for taking the CompTIA Network+ exam, and no networking experience is needed. You're not required to take a training course or buy any training materials. The only requirements are that you pay a testing fee to an authorized testing facility and then sit for the exam. Upon completion of the exam, you will immediately know whether you passed or failed.

Once you pass, you become CompTIA Network+ certified for three years. After three years, you'll need to renew your certification by taking the current exam or completing approved Continuing Education activities. By completing these activities, you earn credits that (along with an annual fee) allow you to keep your CompTIA Network+ certification. For a full list of approved activities, check out CompTIA's Web site (www.comptia.org) and search for **CompTIA Continuing Education Program**.

The American National Standards Institute (ANSI) has accredited the CompTIA Network+ certification as compliant with the ISO 17024 Standard. That makes it special.

Now for the details: CompTIA recommends that you have at least nine to twelve months of networking experience and CompTIA A+ knowledge, but this is not a requirement. Note the word "recommends." You may not need experience or CompTIA A+ knowledge, but each helps! The CompTIA A+ certification competencies have a degree of overlap with the CompTIA Network+ competencies, such as types of connectors and how networks work.

As for experience, keep in mind that CompTIA Network+ is mostly a practical exam. Those who have been out there supporting real networks will find many of the questions reminiscent of the types of problems they have seen on LANs. The bottom line is that you'll probably have a much easier time on the CompTIA Network+ exam if you have some CompTIA A+ experience under your belt.

What Is the Exam Like?

The CompTIA Network+ exam contains 100 questions, and you have 90 minutes to complete the exam. To pass, you must score at least 720 on a scale of 100–900, at the time of this writing. Check the CompTIA Web site when you get close to testing to determine the current scale:

http://certification.comptia.org/getCertified/certifications/network.aspx

CompTIA uses two types of questions: multiple-choice and performance-based. *Multiple-choice questions* offer four or five answer options; you select the correct answer and proceed to the next question. The majority of the questions follow this format.

Performance-based questions require you to do something. You might need to arrange a wireless access point in an office for maximum coverage, for example, or properly align the colored wires on a network connector. You need to have appropriate command-line skills to respond at a command prompt. These are all things that good network techs should be able to do without blinking. I'll cover all the topics in the book, and you'll get practical experience as well in the various extra design elements and labs.

The exam questions are divided into five areas that CompTIA calls domains. This table lists the CompTIA Network+ domains and the percentage of the exam that each represents.

CompTIA Network+ Domain	Percentage
1.0 Network architecture	22%
2.0 Network operations	20%
3.0 Network security	18%
4.0 Troubleshooting	24%
5.0 Industry standards, practices, and network theory	16%

The CompTIA Network+ exam is extremely practical. Questions often present real-life scenarios and ask you to determine the best solution. The CompTIA Network+ exam loves troubleshooting. Let me repeat: many of the test objectives deal with direct, *real-world troubleshooting*. Be prepared to troubleshoot both hardware and software failures and to answer both "What do you do next?" and "What is most likely the problem?" types of questions.

CompTIA occasionally makes changes to the content of the exam, as well as the score necessary to pass it. Always check the Web site of my company, Total Seminars (www.totalsem.com), before scheduling your exam.

Although you can't take the exam over the Internet, Pearson VUE provides easy online registration. Go to www.vue.com to register online.

A qualified CompTIA Network+ certification candidate can install and configure a PC to connect to a network. This includes installing and testing a network card, configuring drivers, and loading all network software. The exam will test you on the different topologies, standards, and cabling.

Expect conceptual questions about the Open Systems Interconnection (OSI) seven-layer model. You need to know the functions and protocols for each layer to pass the CompTIA Network+ exam. You can also expect questions on most of the protocol suites, with heavy emphasis on the TCP/IP suite. If you've never heard of the OSI seven-layer model, don't worry! This book will teach you all you need to know.

How Do I Take the Test?

To take the test, you must go to an authorized testing center. You cannot take the test over the Internet. Pearson VUE administers the actual CompTIA Network+ exam. You'll find thousands of Pearson VUE testing centers scattered across the United States and Canada, as well as in over 75 other countries around the world. You may take the exam at any testing center. To locate a testing center and schedule an exam, call Pearson VUE at 877-551-7587. You can also visit their Web site at www.vue.com.

How Much Does the Test Cost?

CompTIA fixes the price, no matter what testing center you use. The cost of the exam depends on whether you work for a CompTIA member. At press time, the cost for non-CompTIA members is $246 (U.S.).

If your employer is a CompTIA member, you can save money by obtaining an exam voucher. In fact, even if you don't work for a CompTIA member, you can purchase a voucher from member companies (like mine) and take advantage of significant member savings. You simply buy the voucher and then use the voucher to pay for the exam. Vouchers are delivered to you on paper and electronically via e-mail. The voucher number is the important thing. That number is your exam payment, so protect it from fellow students until you're ready to schedule your exam.

If you're in the United States or Canada, you can visit www.totalsem.com or call 800-446-6004 to purchase vouchers. As I always say, "You don't have to buy your voucher from us, but for goodness' sake, get one from somebody!" Why pay full price when you have a discount alternative?

You must pay for the exam when you schedule, whether online or by phone. If you're scheduling by phone, be prepared to hold for a while. Have your Social Security number (or the international equivalent) ready and either a credit card or a voucher number when you call or begin the online scheduling process. If you require any special accommodations, Pearson VUE will be able to assist you, although your selection of testing locations may be a bit more limited.

International prices vary; see the CompTIA Web site for international pricing. Of course, prices are subject to change without notice, so always check the CompTIA Web site for current pricing!

How to Pass the CompTIA Network+ Exam

The single most important thing to remember about the CompTIA Network+ certification exam is that CompTIA designed it to test the knowledge of a technician with as little as nine months of experience—so keep it simple! Think in terms of practical knowledge. Read this book, answer the questions at the end of each chapter, take the practice exams on the media accompanying this book, review any topics you missed, and you'll pass with flying colors.

Is it safe to assume that it's probably been a while since you've taken an exam? Consequently, has it been a while since you've had to study for an exam? If you're nodding your head yes, you'll probably want to read the next sections. They lay out a proven strategy to help you study for the CompTIA Network+ exam and pass it. Try it. It works.

Obligate Yourself

The first step you should take is to schedule the exam. Ever heard the old adage that heat and pressure make diamonds? Well, if you don't give yourself a little "heat," you might procrastinate and unnecessarily delay taking the exam. Even worse, you may end up not taking the exam at all. Do yourself a favor. Determine how much time you need to study (see the next section), and then call Pearson VUE and schedule the exam, giving yourself the time you need to study—and adding a few extra days for safety. Afterward, sit back and let your anxieties wash over you. Suddenly, turning off the television and cracking open the book will become a lot easier!

Set Aside the Right Amount of Study Time

After helping thousands of techs get their CompTIA Network+ certification, we at Total Seminars have developed a pretty good feel for the amount of study time needed to pass the CompTIA Network+ exam. Table 1.1 will help you plan how much study time you must devote to the exam. Keep in mind that these are averages. If you're not a great student or if you're a little on the nervous side, add another 10 percent. Equally, if you're the type who can learn an entire semester of geometry in one night, reduce the numbers by 10 percent. To use this table, just circle the values that are most accurate for you and add them up to get the number of study hours.

A complete neophyte may need 120 hours or more of study time. An experienced network technician already CompTIA A+ certified should only need about 24 hours.

Study habits also come into play here. A person with solid study habits (you know who you are) can reduce the number by 15 percent. People with poor study habits should increase that number by 20 percent.

The total hours of study time you need is _____.

Study for the Test

Now that you have a feel for how long it's going to take to study for the exam, you need a strategy for studying. The following has proven to be an excellent game plan for cramming the knowledge from the study materials into your head.

Table 1.1	Determining How Much Study Time You Need				
		Amount of Experience			
Type of Experience		**None**	**Once or Twice**	**On Occasion**	**Quite a Bit**
Installing a SOHO wireless network		4	2	1	1
Installing an advanced wireless network (802.1X, RADIUS, etc.)		2	2	1	1
Installing structured cabling		3	2	1	1
Configuring a home router		5	3	2	1
Configuring a Cisco router		4	2	1	1
Configuring a software firewall		3	2	1	1
Configuring a hardware firewall		2	2	1	1
Configuring an IPv4 client		8	4	2	1
Configuring an IPv6 client		3	3	2	1
Working with a SOHO WAN connection (DSL, cable)		2	2	1	0
Working with an advanced WAN connection (Tx, OCx, ATM)		3	3	2	2
Configuring a DNS server		2	2	2	1
Configuring a DHCP server		2	1	1	0
Configuring a Web application server (HTTP, FTP, SSH, etc.)		4	4	2	1
Configuring a VLAN		3	3	2	1
Configuring a VPN		3	3	2	1
Configuring a dynamic routing protocol (RIP, EIGRP, OSPF)		2	2	1	1

This strategy has two alternate paths. The first path is designed for highly experienced technicians who have a strong knowledge of PCs and networking and want to concentrate on just what's on the exam. Let's call this group the Fast Track group. The second path, and the one I'd strongly recommend, is geared toward people like me: the ones who want to know why things work, those who want to wrap their arms completely around a concept, as opposed to regurgitating answers just to pass the CompTIA Network+ exam. Let's call this group the Brainiacs.

To provide for both types of learners, I have broken down most of the chapters into two parts:

- **Historical/Conceptual**   Although not on the CompTIA Network+ exam, this knowledge will help you understand more clearly what is on the CompTIA Network+ exam.

- **Test Specific**   These topics clearly fit under the CompTIA Network+ certification domains.

The beginning of each of these areas is clearly marked with a large banner that looks like the following.

Historical/Conceptual

If you consider yourself a Fast Tracker, skip everything but the Test Specific section in each chapter. After reading the Test Specific sections, jump immediately to the Chapter Review questions, which concentrate on information in the Test

Specific sections. If you run into problems, review the Historical/Conceptual sections in that chapter. After going through every chapter as described, take the free practice exams on the media that accompanies the book. First, take them in practice mode, and then switch to final mode. Once you start scoring in the 80–85 percent range, go take the test!

Brainiacs should first read the book—the whole book. Read it as though you're reading a novel, starting on Page 1 and going all the way through. Don't skip around on the first read-through, even if you are a highly experienced tech. Because there are terms and concepts that build on each other, skipping around might confuse you, and you'll just end up closing the book and firing up your favorite PC game. Your goal on this first read is to understand concepts—to understand the whys, not just the hows.

Having a network available while you read through the book helps a lot. This gives you a chance to see various concepts, hardware, and configuration screens in action as you read about them in the book. Plus, you'll need some gear to do all the hands-on exercises sprinkled throughout the book. Nothing beats doing it yourself to reinforce a concept or piece of knowledge!

You will notice a lot of historical information—the Historical/Conceptual sections—that you may be tempted to skip. Don't! Understanding how some of the older stuff worked or how something works conceptually will help you appreciate the reason behind current networking features and equipment, as well as how they function.

After you have completed the first read-through, cozy up for a second. This time, try to knock out one chapter per sitting. Concentrate on the Test Specific sections. Get a highlighter and mark the phrases and sentences that make major points. Look at the pictures and tables, noting how they illustrate the concepts. Then, answer the end of chapter questions. Repeat this process until you not only get all the questions right, but also understand *why* they are correct!

Once you have read and studied the material in the book, check your knowledge by taking the practice exams included on the media accompanying the book. The exams can be taken in practice mode or final mode. In practice mode, you are allowed to check references in the book (if you want) before you answer each question, and each question is graded immediately. In final mode, you must answer all the questions before you are given a test score. In each case, you can review a results summary that tells you which questions you missed, what the right answer is to each, and where to study further.

Use the results of the exams to see where you need to bone up, and then study some more and try them again. Continue retaking the exams and reviewing the topics you missed until you are consistently scoring in the 80–85 percent range. When you've reached that point, you are ready to pass the CompTIA Network+ exam!

 Be aware that you may need to return to previous chapters to get the Historical/Conceptual information you need for a later chapter.

If you have any problems or questions, or if you just want to argue about something, feel free to send an e-mail to me at michaelm@totalsem.com or to my editor, Scott Jernigan, at scottj@totalsem.com.

For additional information about the CompTIA Network+ exam, contact CompTIA directly at its Web site: www.comptia.org.

Good luck!

—Mike Meyers

Network Models

"First we thought the PC was a calculator. Then we found out how to turn numbers into letters with ASCII—and we thought it was a typewriter. Then we discovered graphics, and we thought it was a television. With the World Wide Web, we've realized it's a brochure."

—Douglas Adams

In this chapter, you will learn how to

- Describe how models such as the OSI seven-layer model and the TCP/IP model help technicians understand and troubleshoot networks
- Explain the major functions of networks with the OSI seven-layer model
- Describe the major functions of networks with the TCP/IP model

The CompTIA Network+ certification challenges you to understand virtually every aspect of networking—not a small task. Luckily for you, we use two methods to conceptualize the many parts of a network: the **Open Systems Interconnection (OSI) seven-layer model** and the **Transmission Control Protocol/Internet Protocol (TCP/IP) model**.

These models act as guidelines and break down how a network functions into discrete parts called layers. If you want to get into networking, you must understand both the OSI seven-layer model and the TCP/IP model in great detail.

These models provide two tools that make them critical for networking techs. First, the OSI and TCP/IP models provide powerful mental tools for diagnosing problems. Understanding the models enables a tech to determine quickly at what layer a problem can occur and helps him or her zero in on a solution without wasting a lot of time on false leads. Second, these models also provide a common language to describe networks—a way for us to communicate with each other about the functions of a network. Figure 2.1 shows a sample Cisco Systems Web page about configuring routing—a topic this book covers in detail later. A router operates at Layer 3 of the OSI seven-layer model, for example, so you'll hear techs (and Web sites) refer to it as a "Layer 3 switch."

The term "Layer 3 switch" has evolved over time and refers today to a variety of complex network boxes that I'll cover later in the book.

This chapter looks first at models in general and how models help conceptualize and troubleshoot networks. We'll then go into both the OSI seven-layer model and the TCP/IP model to see how they help clarify network architecture for techs.

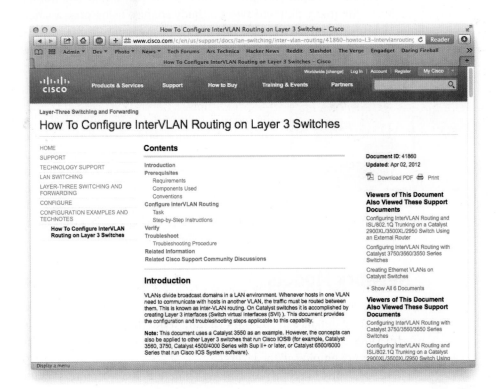

• **Figure 2.1**   Using the OSI terminology—Layer 3—in typical configuration documentation

Historical/Conceptual

■ Working with Models

Networking is hard. It takes a lot of pieces, both hardware and software, to get anything done. Just making Google appear in your Web browser requires millions of hours in research, development, and manufacturing. Whenever we encounter highly complex technologies, we need to simplify the overall process (making Google show up in your browser) by breaking it into discrete, simple, individual processes. We do this using models.

Modeling is critical in networking. We use models to understand and communicate with other techs about networks. Most beginning network techs, however, might have a very different idea of what modeling means.

Biography of a Model

What does the word "model" mean to you? Does the word make you think of a beautiful woman walking down a catwalk at a fashion show or some hunky guy showing off the latest style of blue jeans on a huge billboard? Maybe it makes you think of a plastic model airplane? What about those computer models that try to predict weather? We use the term "model" in a number of ways, but each use shares certain common themes.

All models are a simplified representation of the real thing. The human model ignores the many different types of body shapes, using only a single "optimal" figure. The model airplane lacks functional engines or the internal framework, and the computerized weather model might disregard subtle differences in wind temperatures or geology (Figure 2.2).

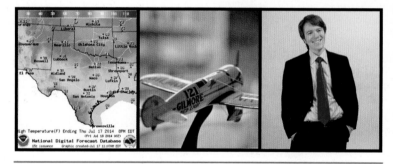

• **Figure 2.2** Types of models (images from left to right courtesy of NOAA, Mike Schinkel, and Michael Smyer)

Additionally, a model must have at least all the major functions of the real item, but what constitutes a major rather than a minor function is open to opinion. Figure 2.3 shows a different level of detail for a model. Does it contain all the major components of an airplane? There's room for argument that perhaps the model should have landing gear to go along with the propeller, wings, and tail.

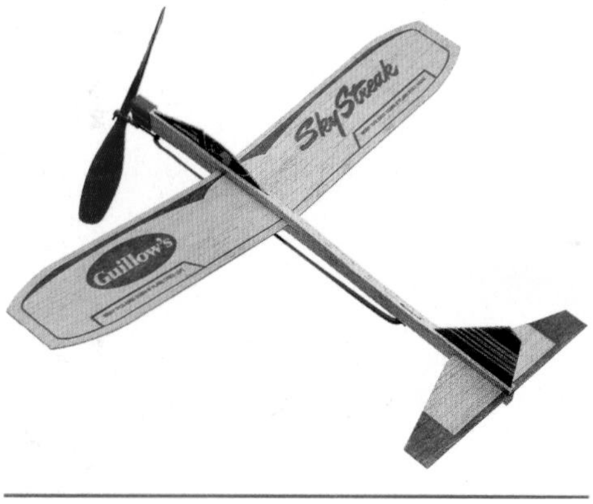

Network Models

Network models face similar challenges. What functions define all networks? What details can you omit without rendering the model inaccurate? Does the model retain its usefulness when describing a network that does not employ all the layers?

In the early days of networking, different manufacturers made unique types of networks that functioned fairly well. But each network had its own cabling, hardware, drivers, naming conventions, applications, and many other unique features. Back then, a single manufacturer provided everything for a customer when the customer purchased a network solution: cabling, NICs, hubs, drivers, and all the software in

• **Figure 2.3** Simple model airplane

one complete and expensive package. Although these networks worked fine as stand-alone networks, the proprietary nature of the hardware and software made it difficult—to put it mildly—to connect networks of multiple manufacturers. To interconnect networks and improve networking as a whole, someone needed to create a guide, a model that described the functions of a network, so that people who made hardware and software could work together to make networks that worked together well.

The granddaddy of network models came from the International Organization for Standardization, known as ISO. Their model, known as the Open Systems Interconnection (OSI) seven-layer model, works for almost every type of network, even extremely old and long-obsolete ones. On the other hand, the TCP/IP model only works for networks that use the now-dominant TCP/IP protocol suite. (Don't worry about what TCP/IP means yet—most of this book's job is to explain that in great detail.) Since most of the world uses TCP/IP, the TCP/IP model supplanted the OSI model in many cases, though most discussion that involves the word "layers" refers to the OSI model. A good tech can talk the talk of both models.

The best way to learn the OSI and TCP/IP models is to see them in action. For this reason, I'll introduce you to a small network that needs to copy a file from one computer to another. This example goes through each of the OSI and TCP/IP layers needed to copy that file, and I explain each step and why it is necessary. By the end of the chapter, you should have a definite handle on using either of these models as a tool to conceptualize networks. You'll continue to build on this knowledge throughout the book and turn your OSI and TCP/IP model knowledge into a powerful troubleshooting tool.

I'll begin by discussing the OSI seven-layer model. After seeing this small network through the lens of the OSI seven-layer model, we'll repeat the process with the TCP/IP model.

ISO may look like a misspelled acronym, but it's actually a word, derived from the Greek word *isos*, which means "equal." The International Organization for Standardization sets standards that promote *equality* among network designers and manufacturers, thus ISO.

■ The OSI Seven-Layer Model in Action

Each layer in the OSI seven-layer model defines an important function in computer networking, and the protocols that operate at that layer offer solutions to those functions. **Protocols** are sets of clearly defined rules, regulations, standards, and procedures that enable hardware and software developers to make devices and applications that function properly at a particular level. The OSI seven-layer model encourages modular design in networking, meaning that each layer has as little to do with the operation of other layers as possible. Think of it as an automobile assembly line. The guy painting the car doesn't care about the gal putting doors on the car—he expects the assembly line process to make sure the cars he paints have doors. Each layer on the model trusts that the other layers on the model do their jobs.

The OSI seven layers are:

- **Layer 7** Application
- **Layer 6** Presentation
- **Layer 5** Session
- **Layer 4** Transport
- **Layer 3** Network

Be sure to memorize both the name and the number of each OSI layer. Network techs use OSI terms such as "Layer 4" and "Transport layer" synonymously. Students have long used mnemonics for memorizing such lists. One of my favorites for the OSI seven-layer model is "Please Do Not Throw Sausage Pizza Away." Yum! Another great mnemonic that helps students to memorize the layers from the top down is "All People Seem To Need Data Processing." Go with what works for you.

This section is a conceptual overview of the hardware and software functions of a network. Your network may have different hardware or software, but it will share the same functions.

- **Layer 2** Data Link
- **Layer 1** Physical

The OSI seven layers are not laws of physics—anybody who wants to design a network can do it any way he or she wants. Although many protocols fit neatly into one of the seven layers, others do not.

Now that you know the names of the layers, let's see what each layer does. The best way to understand the OSI layers is to see them in action. Let's see them at work at the fictional company of MHTechEd, Inc.

Welcome to MHTechEd!

Mike's High-Tech Educational Supply Store and Post Office, or MHTechEd for short, has a small network of PCs running Windows, a situation typical of many small businesses today. Windows runs just fine on a PC unconnected to a network, but it also comes with all the network software it needs to connect to a network. All the computers in the MHTechEd network are connected by special network cabling.

As in most offices, virtually everyone at MHTechEd has his or her own PC. Figure 2.4 shows two workers, Janelle and Dana, who handle all the administrative functions at MHTechEd. Because of the kinds of work they do, these two often need to exchange data between their two PCs. At the moment, Janelle has just completed a new employee handbook in Microsoft Word, and she wants Dana to check it for accuracy. Janelle could transfer a copy of the file to Dana's computer by the tried-and-true Sneakernet method—saving the file on a flash drive and walking it over to her—but thanks to the wonders of computer networking, she doesn't even have to turn around in her chair. Let's watch in detail each piece of the process that gives Dana direct access to Janelle's computer, so she can copy the Word document from Janelle's system to her own.

Long before Janelle ever saved the Word document on her system—when the systems were first installed—someone who knew what they were doing set up and configured all the systems at MHTechEd to be part of a common network. All this setup activity resulted in multiple layers of hardware and software that can work together behind the scenes to get that Word document

• **Figure 2.4**   Janelle and Dana, hard at work

from Janelle's system to Dana's. Let's examine the different pieces of the network, and then return to the process of Dana grabbing that Word document.

Test Specific

Let's Get Physical—Network Hardware and Layers 1–2

Clearly the network needs a physical channel through which it can move bits of data between systems. Most networks use a cable like the one shown in Figure 2.5. This cable, known in the networking industry as unshielded twisted pair (UTP), usually contains four pairs of wires that can transmit and receive data.

Another key piece of hardware the network uses is a special box-like device that handles the flow of data from each computer to every other computer (Figure 2.6). This box is often tucked away in a closet or an equipment room. (The technology of the central box has changed over time. For now, let's just call it the "central box." I'll get to variations in a bit.) Each system on the network has its own cable that runs to the central box. Think of the box as being like one of those old-time telephone switchboards, where operators created connections between persons who called in wanting to reach other telephone users.

Layer 1 of the OSI model defines the method of moving data between computers, so the cabling and central box are part of the Physical layer (Layer 1). Anything that moves data from one system to another, such as copper cabling, fiber optics, even radio waves, is part of the OSI Physical layer. Layer 1 doesn't care what data goes through; it just moves the data from one system to another system. Figure 2.7 shows the MHTechEd network in the OSI seven-layer model thus far. Note that each system has the full range of layers, so data from Janelle's computer can flow to Dana's computer. (I'll cover what a "hub" is shortly.)

● **Figure 2.5** UTP cabling

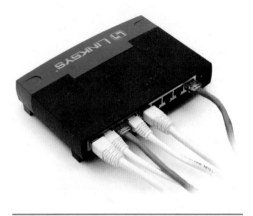

● **Figure 2.6** Typical central box

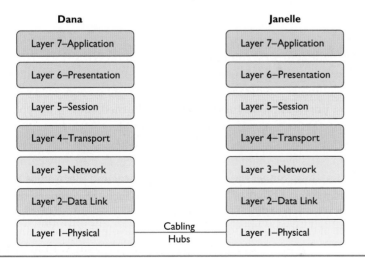

● **Figure 2.7** The network so far, with the Physical layer hardware installed

---

• **Figure 2.8** Typical NIC

• **Figure 2.9** NIC with cable connecting the PC to the wall jack

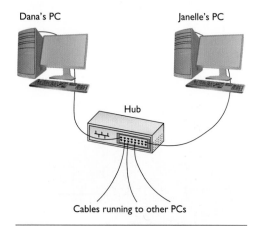

• **Figure 2.10** The MHTechEd network

Tech Tip

Hexadecimal

A hexadecimal numbering system uses base 16 for representing numbers—that is, 0–15. Contrast this with the more common decimal numbering system, numbered 0–9. Just as with decimal, people who work with hexadecimal need a single character to represent each number in the 16 values. Using 0–9 makes sense, but then hex is represented in letter form for the values 10–15 (A, B, C, D, E, F).

Hexadecimal works great with binary. Four bits provide the values of 0–15. 0001, for example, is the value 1; 1000 in binary is 8; 1111 is 15. When we work with MAC addresses, it's far easier to break each 4-bit section of the 48-bit address and translate that into hex. Humans work better that way!

The real magic of a network starts with the **network interface card**, or **NIC** (pronounced "nick"), which serves as the interface between the PC and the network. While NICs come in a wide array of shapes and sizes, the ones at MHTechEd look like Figure 2.8.

On older systems, a NIC truly was a separate card that snapped into a handy expansion slot, which is why they were called network interface *cards*. Even though they're now built into the motherboard, they are still called NICs.

When installed in a PC, the NIC looks like Figure 2.9. Note the cable running from the back of the NIC into the wall; inside that wall is another cable running all the way back to the central box.

Cabling and central boxes define the Physical layer of the network, and NICs provide the interface to the PC. Figure 2.10 shows a diagram of the network cabling system. I'll build on this diagram as I delve deeper into the network process.

You might be tempted to categorize the NIC as part of the Physical layer at this point, and you'd have a valid argument. The NIC clearly is necessary for the physical connection to take place. Many authors put the NIC in OSI Layer 2, the Data Link layer, though, so clearly something else is happening inside the NIC. Let's take a closer look.

The NIC

To understand networks, you must understand how NICs work. The network must provide a mechanism that gives each system a unique identifier—like a telephone number—so data is delivered to the right system. That's one of the NIC's most important jobs. Inside every NIC, burned onto some type of ROM chip, is special firmware containing a unique identifier with a 48-bit value called the **media access control address**, or **MAC address**.

No two NICs ever share the same MAC address—ever. Any company that makes NICs must contact the Institute of Electrical and Electronics Engineers (IEEE) and request a block of MAC addresses, which the company then burns into the ROMs on its NICs. Many NIC makers also print the MAC address on the surface of each NIC, as shown in Figure 2.11. Note that the NIC shown here displays the MAC address in hexadecimal notation. Count the number of hex characters—because each hex character represents 4 bits, it takes 12 hex characters to represent 48 bits.

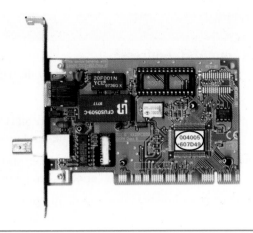

• **Figure 2.11** MAC address

The MAC address in Figure 2.11 is 004005-607D49, although in print, we represent the MAC address as 00–40–05–60–7D–49. The first six digits, in this example 00–40–05, represent the number of the NIC manufacturer. Once the IEEE issues those six hex digits to a manufacturer—referred to as the **Organizationally Unique Identifier (OUI)**—no other manufacturer may use them. The last six digits, in this example 60–7D–49, are the manufacturer's unique serial number for that NIC; this portion of the MAC is often referred to as the **device ID**.

Would you like to see the MAC address for your NIC? If you have a Windows system, type `ipconfig /all` from a command prompt to display the MAC address (Figure 2.12). Note that ipconfig calls the MAC address the **physical address**, which is an important distinction, as you'll see a bit later in the chapter.

Okay, so every NIC in the world has a unique MAC address, but how is it used? Ah, that's where the fun begins! Recall that computer data is binary,

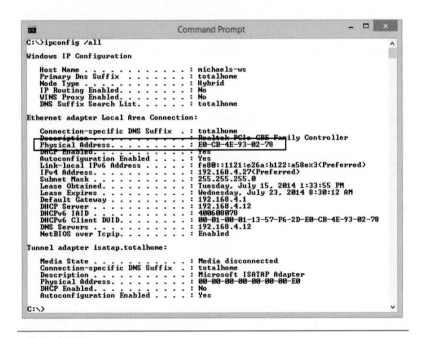

• **Figure 2.12** Output from `ipconfig /all`

which means it's made up of streams of ones and zeroes. NICs send and receive this binary data as pulses of electricity, light, or radio waves. The NICs that use electricity to send and receive data are the most common, so let's consider that type of NIC. The specific process by which a NIC uses electricity to send and receive data is exceedingly complicated but, luckily for you, not necessary to understand. Instead, just think of a *charge* on the wire as a *one* and *no charge* as a *zero*. A chunk of data moving in pulses across a wire might look something like Figure 2.13.

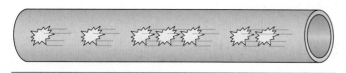

• **Figure 2.13**   Data moving along a wire

If you put an oscilloscope on the wire to measure voltage, you'd see something like Figure 2.14. An oscilloscope is a powerful tool that enables you to see electrical pulses.

Now, remembering that the pulses represent binary data, visualize instead a string of ones and zeroes moving across the wire (Figure 2.15).

Once you understand how data moves along the wire, the next question is how does the network get the right data to the right system? All networks transmit data by breaking whatever is moving across the Physical layer (files, print jobs, Web pages, and so forth) into discrete chunks called frames. A frame is basically a container for a chunk of data moving across a network. The NIC creates and sends, as well as receives and reads, these frames.

I like to visualize an imaginary table inside every NIC that acts as a frame creation and reading station. I see frames as those pneumatic canisters you see when you go to a drive-in teller at a bank. A little guy inside the network card—named Nic, naturally!—builds these pneumatic canisters (the frames) on the table and then shoots them out on the wire to the central box (Figure 2.16).

A number of different frame types are used in different networks. All NICs on the same network must use the same frame type, or they will not be able to communicate with other NICs.

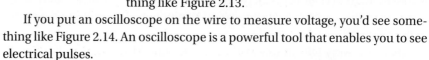

• **Figure 2.14**   Oscilloscope of data

1 0 1 0 1 1 1 0 1 1

• **Figure 2.15**   Data as ones and zeroes

• **Figure 2.16** Inside the NIC

Here's where the MAC address becomes important. Figure 2.17 shows a representation of a generic frame. Even though a frame is a string of ones and zeroes, we often draw frames as a series of rectangles, each rectangle representing a part of the string of ones and zeroes. You will see this type of frame representation used quite often, so you should become comfortable with it (even though I still prefer to see frames as pneumatic canisters).

Recipient's MAC address	Sender's MAC address	Type	Data	FCS

• **Figure 2.17** Generic frame

Note that the frame begins with the MAC address of the NIC to which the data is to be sent, followed by the MAC address of the sending NIC. Next comes the *Type* field, which indicates the specific network technology of the frame. Then comes the *Data* field, followed by a special bit of checking information called the **frame check sequence (FCS)**. The FCS uses a type of binary math called a **cyclic redundancy check (CRC)** that the receiving NIC uses to verify that the data arrived intact.

So, what's inside the data part of the frame? You neither know nor care. The data may be a part of a file, a piece of a print job, or part of a Web page. NICs aren't concerned with content! The NIC simply takes whatever data is passed to it via its device driver and addresses it for the correct system. Special software will take care of *what* data gets sent and what happens to that data when it arrives. This is the beauty of imagining frames as little pneumatic canisters (Figure 2.18). A canister can carry anything from dirt to diamonds—the NIC doesn't care one bit (pardon the pun).

Like a canister, a frame can hold only a certain amount of data. Different types of networks use different sizes of frames, but the frames used in most networks hold at most 1500 bytes of data.

This raises a new question: what happens when the data to be sent is larger than the frame size? Well, the sending system's software must chop the data up into nice, frame-sized chunks, which it then hands to the NIC for sending. As the receiving system begins to accept the incoming frames, the receiving system's software recombines the data chunks as they come in from

 CompTIA calls the use of the MAC address to get frames to the proper computer or node *MAC addressing.* This doesn't quite fit with the vast majority of networks, where you don't implement or configure MAC addresses. Ethernet simply uses the MAC addresses assigned to devices by manufacturers. Be aware of the term on the exam.

• **Figure 2.18** Frame as a canister

Tech Tip

FCS in Depth

Most FCSs are only 4 bytes long, yet the average frame carries at most 1500 bytes of data. How can 4 bytes tell you if all 1500 bytes in the data are correct? That's the magic of the math of the CRC. Without going into the grinding details, think of the CRC as just the remainder of a division problem. (Remember learning remainders from division back in elementary school?) The NIC sending the frame does a little math to make the CRC. Using binary arithmetic, it works a division problem on the data using a divisor called a key. *The result of this division is the CRC. When the frame gets to the receiving NIC, it divides the data by the same key. If the receiving NIC's answer is the same as the CRC, it knows the data is good.*

the network. I'll show how this disassembling and reassembling is done in a moment—first, let's see how the frames get to the right system!

Into the Central Box

When a system sends a frame out on the network, the frame goes into the central box. What happens next depends on the technology of the central box.

In the early days of networking, the central box was called a *hub*. A hub was a dumb device, essentially just a repeater. When it received a frame, the hub made an exact copy of that frame, sending a copy of the original frame to every other system on the network.

The interesting part of this process was when the copy of the frame came into all the other systems. I like to visualize a frame sliding onto the receiving NIC's "frame assembly table," where the electronics of the NIC inspected it. Here's where the magic took place: only the NIC to which the frame was addressed would process that frame—the other NICs simply erased it when they saw that it was not addressed to their MAC address. This is important to appreciate: with a hub, *every* frame sent on a network was received by *every* NIC, but only the NIC with the matching MAC address would process that particular frame (Figure 2.19).

Later networks replaced the hub with a smarter device called a switch. Switches, as you'll see in much more detail as we go deeper into networking, filter traffic by MAC address. Rather than sending all incoming frames to all network devices connected to it, a switch sends the frame only to the recipient MAC address.

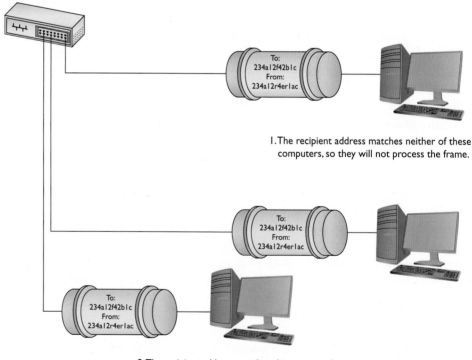

1. The recipient address matches neither of these computers, so they will not process the frame.

2. The recipient address matches this computer's address, so this computer will process the frame.

• **Figure 2.19** Incoming frame!

Mike Meyers' CompTIA Network+ Guide to Managing and Troubleshooting Networks

Getting the Data on the Line

The process of getting data onto the wire and then picking that data off the wire is amazingly complicated. For instance, what happens to keep two NICs from speaking at the same time? Because all the data sent by one NIC is read by every other NIC on the network, only one system may speak at a time. Networks use frames to restrict the amount of data a NIC can send at once, giving all NICs a chance to send data over the network in a reasonable span of time. Dealing with this and many other issues requires sophisticated electronics, but the NICs handle these issues completely on their own without our help. Thankfully, the folks who design NICs worry about all these details, so we don't have to!

Getting to Know You

Using the MAC address is a great way to move data around, but this process raises an important question. How does a sending NIC know the MAC address of the NIC to which it's sending the data? In most cases, the sending system already knows the destination MAC address because the NICs had probably communicated earlier, and each system stores that data. If it doesn't already know the MAC address, a NIC may send a broadcast onto the network to ask for it. The MAC address of FF-FF-FF-FF-FF-FF is the broadcast address—if a NIC sends a frame using the broadcast address, every single NIC on the network will process that frame. That broadcast frame's data will contain a request for a system's MAC address. Without knowing the MAC address to begin with, the requesting computer will use an IP address to pick the target computer out of the crowd. The system with the MAC address your system is seeking will read the request in the broadcast packet and respond with its MAC address. (See "IP—Playing on Layer 3, the Network Layer" later in this chapter for more on IP addresses and packets.)

The Complete Frame Movement

Now that you've seen all the pieces used to send and receive frames, let's put these pieces together and see how a frame gets from one system to another. The basic send/receive process is as follows.

First, the sending system's operating system hands some data to its NIC. The NIC builds a frame to transport that data to the receiving NIC (Figure 2.20).

After the NIC creates the frame, it adds the FCS, and then dumps it and the data into the frame (Figure 2.21).

Next, the NIC puts both the destination MAC address and its own MAC address onto the frame. It waits until no other NIC is using the cable, and then sends the frame through the cable to the network (Figure 2.22).

NIC receives the command to send data and starts to make the frame.

• **Figure 2.20**   Building the frame

• **Figure 2.21**   Adding the data and FCS to the frame

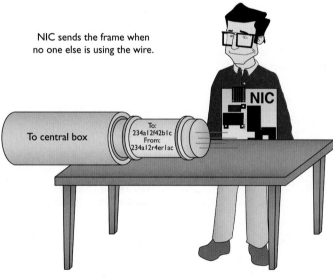

NIC sends the frame when
no one else is using the wire.

• **Figure 2.22**   Sending the frame

The frame propagates down the wire into the central box, which creates copies of the frame and sends it to every other system on the network (if the box is a hub). Every NIC receives the frame and checks the MAC address. If a NIC finds that a frame is addressed to it, it processes the frame (Figure 2.23); if the frame is not addressed to it, the NIC erases it.

So, what happens to the data when it gets to the *correct* NIC? First, the receiving NIC uses the FCS to verify that the data is valid. If it is, the receiving NIC strips off all the framing information and sends the data to the software—the operating system—for pro-

The frame has the
MAC address for this NIC.

• **Figure 2.23**   Reading an incoming frame

cessing. The receiving NIC doesn't care what the software does with the data; its job stops the moment it passes on the data to the software.

Any device that deals with a MAC address is part of the OSI **Data Link layer**, or Layer 2 of the OSI model. Let's update the OSI model to include details about the Data Link layer (Figure 2.24).

Note that the cabling and the central box are located in the Physical layer. The NIC is in the Data Link layer and the Physical layer.

The Two Aspects of NICs

Consider how data moves in and out of a NIC. On one end, frames move into and out of the NIC's network cable connection. On the other end, data moves back and forth between the NIC and the network operating system software. The many steps a NIC performs to keep this data moving—sending and receiving frames over the wire, creating outgoing frames, reading incoming frames, and attaching MAC addresses—are classically broken down into two distinct jobs.

The first job is called the **Logical Link Control (LLC)**. The LLC is the aspect of the NIC that talks to the system's operating system (usually via device drivers). The LLC handles multiple network protocols and provides flow control.

The second job is called the **Media Access Control (MAC)**, which creates and addresses the frame. It adds the NIC's own MAC address and attaches MAC addresses to the frames. Recall that each frame the LLC creates must include both the sender's and recipient's MAC addresses. The MAC sublayer adds or checks the FCS. The MAC also ensures that the frames, now complete with their MAC addresses, are then sent along the network cabling. Figure 2.25 shows the Data Link layer in detail.

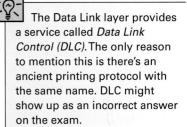

• **Figure 2.24**   Layer 1 and Layer 2 are now properly applied to the network.

 The Data Link layer provides a service called *Data Link Control (DLC)*. The only reason to mention this is there's an ancient printing protocol with the same name. DLC might show up as an incorrect answer on the exam.

The CompTIA Network+ exam tests you on the details of the OSI seven-layer model, so remember that the Data Link layer is the only layer that has any sublayers.

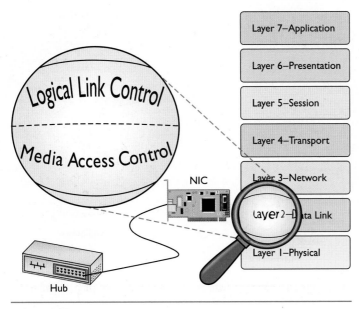

• **Figure 2.25**   LLC and MAC, the two parts of the Data Link layer

Tech Tip

NIC and Layers

Most networking materials that describe the OSI seven-layer model put NICs squarely into the Data Link layer of the model. It's at the MAC sublayer, after all, that data gets encapsulated into a frame, destination and source MAC addresses get added to that frame, and error checking occurs. What bothers most students with placing NICs solely in the Data Link layer is the obvious other duty of the NIC—putting the ones and zeroes on the network cable. How much more physical can you get?

Many teachers will finesse this issue by defining the Physical layer in its logical sense—that it defines the rules for the ones and zeroes—and then ignore the fact that the data sent on the cable has to come from something. The first question when you hear a statement like that—at least to me—is, "What component does the sending?" It's the NIC, of course, the only device capable of sending and receiving the physical signal.

Network cards, therefore, operate at both Layer 2 and Layer 1 of the OSI seven-layer model. If cornered to answer one or the other, however, go with the more common answer, Layer 2.

MAC addresses are also known as *physical addresses*.

Beyond the Single Wire—Network Software and Layers 3–7

Getting data from one system to another in a simple network (defined as one in which all the computers connect to one switch) takes relatively little effort on the part of the NICs. But one problem with simple networks is that computers need to broadcast to get MAC addresses. It works for small networks, but what happens when the network gets big, like the size of the entire Internet? Can you imagine millions of computers all broadcasting? No data could get through.

Equally important, data flows over the Internet using many technologies, not just Ethernet. These technologies, such as SONET, ATM, and others, don't know what to do with Ethernet MAC addresses. When networks get large, you can't use the MAC addresses anymore.

Large networks need a **logical addressing** method, like a postal code or telephone numbering scheme, that ignores the hardware and enables you to break up the entire large network into smaller networks called **subnets**. Figure 2.26 shows two ways to set up a network. On the left, all the computers connect to a single switch. On the right, however, the LAN is separated into two five-computer subnets.

To move past the physical MAC addresses and start using logical addressing requires some special software called a **network protocol**. Network protocols exist in every operating system. A network protocol not only has to create unique identifiers for each system, but also must create a set of communication rules for issues like how to handle data chopped up into multiple packets and how to ensure those packets get from one subnet to another. Let's take a moment to learn a bit about the most famous network protocol—TCP/IP—and its unique universal addressing system.

To be accurate, TCP/IP is really several network protocols designed to work together—better known as a *protocol suite*—but two protocols, TCP and IP, do

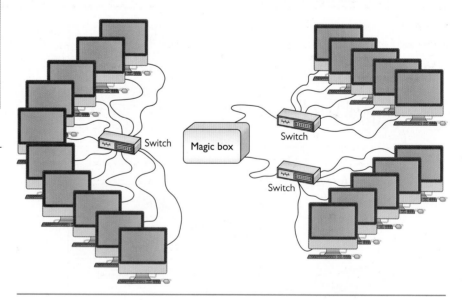

• **Figure 2.26**   Large LAN complete (left) and broken up into two subnets (right)

so much work that the folks who invented all these protocols named the whole thing TCP/IP. **TCP** stands for **Transmission Control Protocol**, and **IP** stands for **Internet Protocol**. IP is the network protocol I need to discuss first; rest assured, however, I'll cover TCP in plenty of detail later.

IP—Playing on Layer 3, the Network Layer

At the **Network layer**, Layer 3, containers called **packets** get created and addressed so they can go from one network to another. The Internet Protocol is the primary logical addressing protocol for TCP/IP. IP makes sure that a piece of data gets to where it needs to go on the network. It does this by giving each device on the network a unique numeric identifier called an **IP address**. An IP address is known as a **logical address** to distinguish it from the physical address, the MAC address of the NIC.

Every network protocol uses some type of naming convention, but no two protocols use the same convention. IP uses a rather unique dotted decimal notation (sometimes referred to as a dotted-octet numbering system) based on four 8-bit numbers. Each 8-bit number ranges from 0 to 255, and the four numbers are separated by periods. (If you don't see how 8-bit numbers can range from 0 to 255, don't worry—by the end of this book, you'll understand these naming conventions in more detail than you ever believed possible!) A typical IP address might look like this:

192.168.4.232

No two systems on the same network share the same IP address; if two machines accidentally receive the same address, unintended side effects may occur. These IP addresses don't just magically appear—they must be configured by the end user (or the network administrator).

Take a look at Figure 2.26. What makes logical addressing powerful is the magic box—called a **router**—that connects each of the subnets. Routers use the IP address, not the MAC address, to forward data. This enables networks to connect across data lines that don't use Ethernet, like the telephone network. Each network type (such as Ethernet, SONET, ATM, and others that we'll discuss later in the book) uses a unique frame. Figure 2.27 shows a typical router.

In a TCP/IP network, each system has two unique identifiers: the MAC address and the IP address. The MAC address (the physical address) is literally burned into the chips on the NIC, whereas the IP address (the logical address) is simply stored in the system's software. MAC addresses come with the NIC, so you don't configure MAC addresses, whereas you must configure IP addresses using software.

• **Figure 2.27**   Typical small router

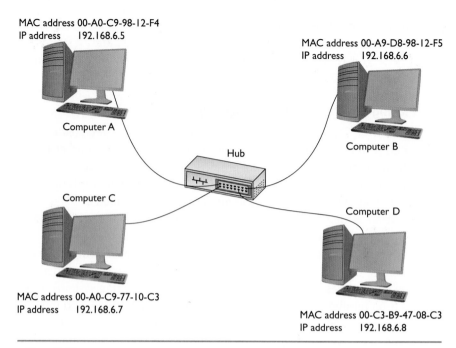

MAC address 00-A0-C9-98-12-F4
IP address   192.168.6.5

MAC address 00-A9-D8-98-12-F5
IP address   192.168.6.6

Computer A

Hub

Computer B

Computer C

Computer D

MAC address 00-A0-C9-77-10-C3
IP address   192.168.6.7

MAC address 00-C3-B9-47-08-C3
IP address   192.168.6.8

• **Figure 2.28**   MHTechEd addressing

Figure 2.28 shows the MHTechEd network diagram again, this time with the MAC and IP addresses displayed for each system.

Packets Within Frames

For a TCP/IP network to send data successfully, the data must be wrapped up in two distinct containers. A frame of some type enables the data to move from one device to another. Inside that frame is both an IP-specific container that enables routers to determine where to send data—regardless of the physical connection type—and the data itself. In TCP/IP, that inner container is the *packet*.

Figure 2.29 shows a typical IP packet; notice the similarity to the frames you saw earlier.

But IP packets don't leave their PC home without any clothes on! Each IP packet is handed to the NIC, which then encloses the IP packet in a regular frame, creating, in essence, a *packet within a frame*. I like to visualize the packet as an envelope, with the envelope in the pneumatic canister frame, as depicted in Figure 2.30. A more conventional drawing would look like Figure 2.31.

When you send data from one computer to another on a TCP/IP network such as the Internet, that data can go through

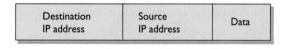

Destination IP address	Source IP address	Data

• **Figure 2.29**   IP packet

Data

To: 192.168.4.12
From: 192.168.4.75

• **Figure 2.30**   IP packet in a frame (as a canister)

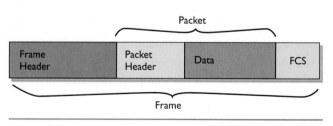

Packet

Frame Header	Packet Header	Data	FCS

Frame

• **Figure 2.31**   IP packet in a frame

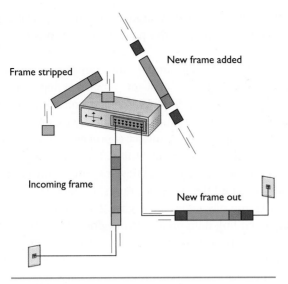

• Figure 2.32 Router removing network frame and adding one for the outgoing connection

many routers before it reaches its destination. Each router strips off the incoming frame, determines where to send the data according to the IP address in
the packet, creates a new frame, and then sends the packet within a frame
on its merry way. The new frame type will be the appropriate technology for
whatever connection technology connects to the next router. That could be a
cable or DSL network connection, for example (Figure 2.32). The IP packet, on
the other hand, remains unchanged.

Once the packet reaches the destination subnet's router, that router will
strip off the incoming frame—no matter what type—look at the destination IP
address, and then add a frame with the appropriate destination MAC address
that matches the destination IP address.

The receiving NIC strips away the Ethernet frame and passes the remaining
packet off to the software. The networking software built into your operating
system handles all the rest of the work. The NIC's driver software is the interconnection between the hardware and the software. The NIC driver knows
how to communicate with the NIC to send and receive frames, but it can't do
anything with the packet. Instead, the NIC driver hands the packet off to other
programs that know how to deal with all the separate packets and turn them
into Web pages, e-mail messages, files, and so forth.

The Network layer (Layer 3) is the last layer that deals directly with hardware.
All the other layers of the OSI seven-layer model work strictly within software.

Assembly and Disassembly—Layer 4, the Transport Layer

Because most chunks of data are much larger than a single packet, they must
be chopped up before they can be sent across a network. When a serving computer receives a request for some data, it must be able to chop the requested
data into chunks that will fit into a packet (and eventually into the NIC's
frame), organize the packets for the benefit of the receiving system, and hand
them to the NIC for sending. The receiving system must be able to recognize a
series of incoming packets as one data transmission, reassemble the packets

 Keep in mind that not all
networks are Ethernet networks.
Ethernet may dominate, but
IP packets fit in all sorts of
other connectivity options. For
example, cable modems use a
type of frame called DOCSIS.
The beauty of IP packets is that
they can travel unchanged in
many frame types. For more
about these technologies,
check out Chapter 14, "Remote
Connectivity."

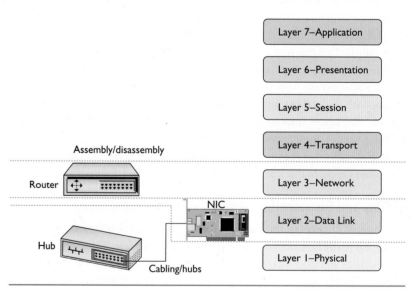

PARCEL ID: **32202273**

301-007

| PARCEL #: | 6 | OF | 50 |
| PARCEL WT: | 29 | LB. 6 | OZ. |

| ACCOUNT # | CONTROL # | SPECIAL INSTRUCTIONS: |
| CUSTOMER P.O. # | | |

ROW	BAY	LV	QTY	I N	ISBN # / DESCRIPTION
023	042	40	6		0-07-222991-8 A+ ALL-IN-ONE, 5E

• **Figure 2.33** Labeling the boxes

A lot of things happen on a TCP/IP network at the Transport layer. I'm simplifying here because the TCP/IP model does a way better job describing what happens with each TCP/IP-specific Transport layer protocol than does the OSI model.

correctly based on information included in the packets by the sending system, and verify that all the packets for that piece of data arrived in good shape.

This part is relatively simple—the transport protocol breaks up the data into chunks called **segments** or **datagrams** (depending on the specific transport protocol used) and gives each segment some type of sequence number. (Datagrams are simpler and don't get sequence numbers.)

I like to compare this sequencing process to the one that my favorite international shipping company uses. I receive boxes from UPS almost every day; in fact, some days I receive many, many boxes from UPS. To make sure I get all the boxes for one shipment, UPS puts a numbering system, like the one shown in Figure 2.33, on the label of each box. A computer sending data on a network does the same thing. Embedded into the data of each packet containing a segment is a sequencing number. By reading the sequencing numbers, the receiving system knows both the total number of segments and how to put them back together.

The MHTechEd network just keeps getting more and more complex, doesn't it? And the Word document still hasn't been copied, has it? Don't worry; you're almost there—just a few more pieces to go!

Layer 4, the **Transport layer** of the OSI seven-layer model, has a big job: it's the assembler/disassembler software. As part of its job, the Transport layer also initializes requests for packets that weren't received in good order (Figure 2.34).

Talking on a Network—Layer 5, the Session Layer

Now that you understand that the system uses software to assemble and disassemble data packets, what's next? In a network, any one system may be talking to many other systems at any given moment. For example, Janelle's PC has a printer used by all the MHTechEd systems, so there's a better than

Layer 7–Application

Layer 6–Presentation

Layer 5–Session

Layer 4–Transport

Layer 3–Network

Layer 2–Data Link

Layer 1–Physical

Assembly/disassembly

Router

NIC

Hub

Cabling/hubs

• **Figure 2.34** OSI updated

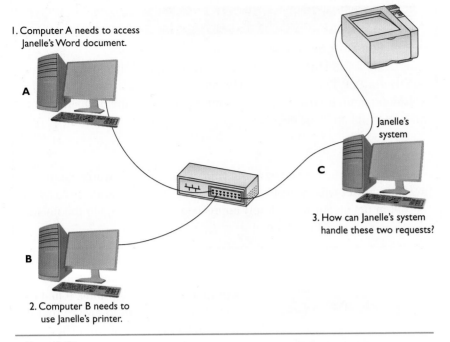

1. Computer A needs to access Janelle's Word document.

A

Janelle's system

C

3. How can Janelle's system handle these two requests?

B

2. Computer B needs to use Janelle's printer.

• **Figure 2.35** Handling multiple inputs

average chance that, as Dana tries to access the Word document, another system will be sending a print job to Janelle's PC (Figure 2.35).

Janelle's system must direct these incoming files, print jobs, Web pages, and so on, to the right programs (Figure 2.36). Additionally, the operating system must enable one system to make a connection to another system to verify that the other system can handle whatever operation the initiating system wants

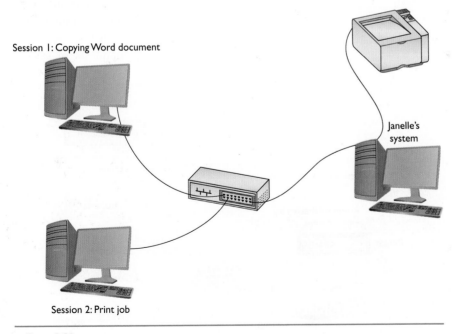

Session 1: Copying Word document

Janelle's system

Session 2: Print job

• **Figure 2.36** Each request becomes a session.

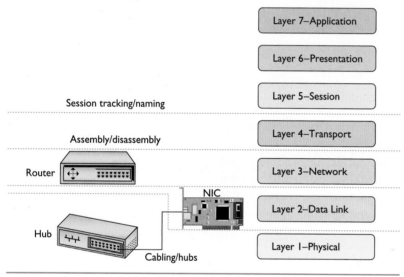

• **Figure 2.37**   OSI updated

to perform. If Bill's system wants to send a print job to Janelle's printer, it first contacts Janelle's system to ensure that it is ready to handle the print job. The session software handles this part of networking, connecting applications to applications.

Layer 5, the Session layer of the OSI seven-layer model, handles all the sessions for a system (Figure 2.37). The Session layer initiates sessions, accepts incoming sessions, and opens and closes existing sessions.

Translation—Layer 6, the Presentation Layer

The Presentation layer translates data from lower layers into a format usable by the Application layer, and *vice versa* (Figure 2.38). This manifests in several

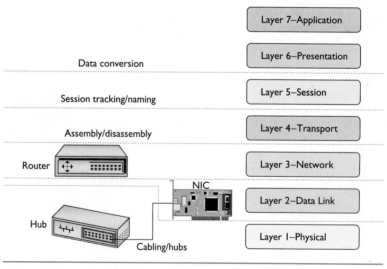

• **Figure 2.38**   OSI updated

ways and isn't necessarily clear cut. The messiness comes into play because TCP/IP networks don't necessarily map directly to the OSI model.

A number of protocols function on more than one OSI layer and can include Layer 6, Presentation. The two encryption protocols used in e-commerce, TLS and SSL, for example, initiate at Layer 5, then encrypt and decrypt at Layer 6. It makes for some confusion. Modern network discussions, therefore, work better using the TCP/IP model where the OSI Layers 5 through 7 are lumped together as the Application layer. We'll get there shortly.

Network Applications—Layer 7, the Application Layer

The last and most visible part of any network is the software applications that use it. If you want to copy a file residing on another system in your network, you need an application like Network in Windows 7 or 8 that enables you to access files on remote systems. If you want to view Web pages, you need a Web browser like Google Chrome or Mozilla Firefox. The people who use a network experience it through an application. A user who knows nothing about all the other parts of a network may still know how to open an e-mail application to retrieve mail (Figure 2.39).

Applications may include a number of additional functions, such as encryption, user authentication, and tools to control the look of the data. But these functions are specific to the given applications. In other words, if you want to put a password on your Word document, you must use the password functions in Word to do so.

The **Application layer** is Layer 7 in the OSI seven-layer model. Keep in mind that the Application layer doesn't refer to the applications themselves. It refers to the code built into all operating systems that enables network-aware applications. All operating systems have **Application Programming Interfaces (APIs)**

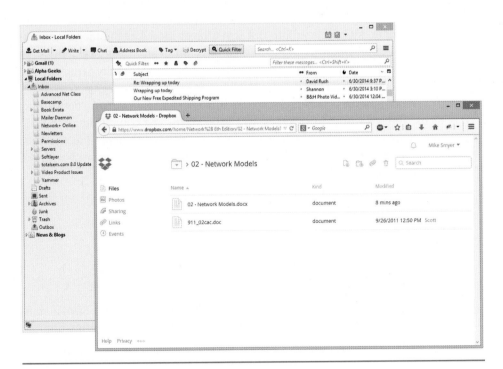

• **Figure 2.39** Network applications at work

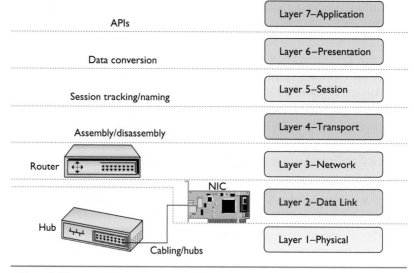

• **Figure 2.40**   OSI updated

that programmers can use to make their programs network aware (Figure 2.40). An API, in general, provides a standard way for programmers to enhance or extend an application's capabilities.

The TCP/IP Model

The OSI model was developed as a reaction to a world of hundreds, if not thousands, of different protocols made by different manufacturers that needed to play together. ISO declared the OSI seven-layer model as the tool for manufacturers of networking equipment to find common ground between multiple protocols, enabling them to create standards for interoperability of networking software and hardware.

The OSI model is extremely popular and very well known to all networking techs. Today's world, however, is a TCP/IP world. The complexity of the OSI model doesn't always make sense in a world with one protocol suite. Given its dominance, the aptly named TCP/IP model shares some popularity with the venerable OSI model.

The TCP/IP model consists of four layers:

- Application
- Transport
- Internet
- Link/Network Interface

It's important to appreciate that the TCP/IP model doesn't have a standards body to define the layers. Because of this, there are a surprising number of variations on the TCP/IP model.

A great example of this lack of standardization is the Link layer. Without a standardizing body, we can't even agree on the name. While "Link layer" is extremely common, the term "Network Interface layer" is equally popular. A good tech knows both of these terms and understands that they are interchangeable. Notice also that, unlike the OSI model, the TCP/IP model does not identify each layer with a number.

The version I use is concise, having only four layers, and many important companies, like Cisco and Microsoft, use it as well. The TCP/IP model gives each protocol in the TCP/IP protocol suite a clear home in one of the four layers.

The clarity of the TCP/IP model shows the flaws in the OSI model. The OSI model couldn't perfectly describe all the TCP/IP protocols. In fact, the OSI model couldn't perfectly describe any of the now-defunct alternative protocols, such as IPX/SPX and NetBIOS/NetBEUI.

The TCP/IP model fixes this ambiguity, at least for TCP/IP. Because of its tight protocol-to-layer integration, the TCP/IP model is a *descriptive* model, whereas the OSI seven-layer model is a *prescriptive* model.

The Link Layer

The TCP/IP model lumps together the OSI model's Layer 1 and Layer 2 into a single layer called the Link layer (or Network Interface layer), as seen in Figure 2.41. It's not that the Physical and Data Link layers are unimportant to TCP/IP, but the TCP/IP protocol suite really begins at Layer 3 of the OSI model. In essence, TCP/IP techs count on other techs to handle the physical connections in their networks. All of the pieces that you learned in the OSI model (cabling, hubs, physical addresses, and NICs) sit squarely in the Link layer.

A nice way to separate layers in the TCP/IP model is to think about packets and frames. Any part of the network that deals with complete frames is in the Link layer. The moment the frame information is stripped away from an IP packet, we move out of the Link layer and into the Internet layer.

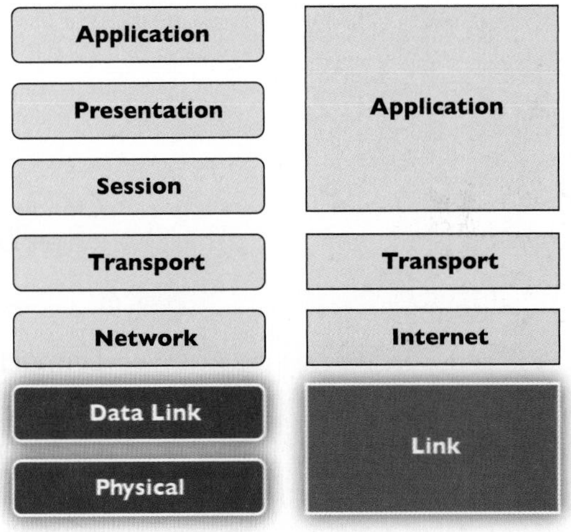

• **Figure 2.41** TCP/IP Link layer compared to OSI Layers 1 and 2

The Internet Layer

The Internet layer should really be called the "IP packet" layer (Figure 2.42). Any device or protocol that deals with pure IP packets—getting an IP packet to its destination—sits in the Internet layer. IP addressing itself is also part of the Internet layer, as are routers and the magic they perform to get IP packets to the next router. IP packets are created at this layer.

The Internet layer doesn't care about the type of data an IP packet carries, nor does it care whether the data gets there in good order or not. Those jobs are for the next layer: the Transport layer.

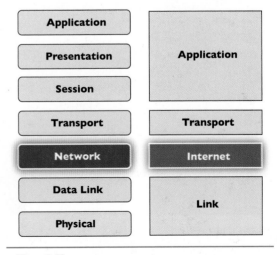

• **Figure 2.42** TCP/IP Internet layer compared to OSI Layer 3

The Transport Layer

The Transport layer combines features of the OSI Transport and Session layers with a dash of Application layer just for flavor (Figure 2.43). While the TCP/IP model is certainly involved with the assembly and disassembly of data, it also defines other functions, such as connection-oriented and connectionless communication.

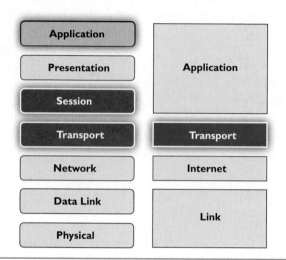

● **Figure 2.43** TCP/IP Transport layer compared to OSI Layers 4, 5, and part of 7

Connection-oriented vs. Connectionless Communication

Some protocols, like the popular Post Office Protocol (POP) used for sending e-mail messages, require that the e-mail client and server verify that they have a good connection before a message is sent (Figure 2.44). This makes sense because you don't want your e-mail message to be a corrupted mess when it arrives.

● **Figure 2.44** Connection between e-mail client and server

• **Figure 2.45**   Connectionless communication

Alternatively, a number of TCP/IP protocols simply send data without first waiting to verify that the receiving system is ready (Figure 2.45). When using Voice over IP (VoIP), for example, the call is made without verifying first whether another device is there.

The connection-oriented protocol is Transmission Control Protocol (TCP). The connectionless protocol is **User Datagram Protocol (UDP)**.

Everything you can do on the Internet, from Web browsing to Skype phone calls to playing World of Warcraft, is predetermined to be either connection-oriented or connectionless. It's simply a matter of knowing your applications.

 Chapter 7, "TCP/IP Basics," covers TCP, UDP, and all sorts of other protocols in detail.

Segments Within Packets

To see the Transport layer in action, strip away the IP addresses from an IP packet. What's left is a chunk of data in yet another container called a **TCP segment**. TCP segments have many other fields that ensure the data gets to its destination in good order. These fields have names such as Checksum, Flags, and Acknowledgement. Chapter 7 goes into more detail on TCP segments, but, for now, just know that TCP segments have fields that ensure the connection-oriented communication works properly. Figure 2.46 shows a typical (although simplified) TCP segment.

Data comes from the Application layer. The Transport layer breaks that data into chunks, adding port numbers and sequence numbers, creating the TCP segment. The Transport layer then hands the TCP segment to the Internet layer, which, in turn, creates the IP packet.

Destination port	Source port	Sequence number	Checksum	Flags	Acknowledgement	Data

• **Figure 2.46**   TCP segment

Although a lot of traffic on a TCP/IP network uses TCP at the Transport layer, like Yoda said in *The Empire Strikes Back,* "There is another," and that's UDP. UDP also gets data from the Application layer and adds port and length numbers plus a checksum to create a container called a **UDP datagram**. A UDP datagram lacks most of the extra fields found in TCP segments, simply because UDP doesn't care if the receiving computer gets its data. Figure 2.47 shows a UDP datagram.

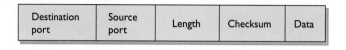

• **Figure 2.47**   UDP datagram

The Application Layer

The TCP/IP **Application layer** combines features of the top three layers of the OSI model (Figure 2.48). Every application, especially connection-oriented applications, must know how to initiate, control, and disconnect from a remote system. No single method exists for doing this. Each TCP/IP application uses its own method.

TCP/IP uses a unique port numbering system that gives each application a unique number between 1 and 65535. Some of these port numbers are very well known. The protocol that makes Web pages work, HTTP, uses port 80, for example.

Although we can say that the OSI model's Presentation layer fits inside the TCP/IP model's Application layer, no application requires any particular form of presentation as seen in the OSI model. Standard formats are part and parcel with TCP/IP protocols. For example, all e-mail messages use an extremely strict format called MIME. All e-mail servers and clients read MIME without exception.

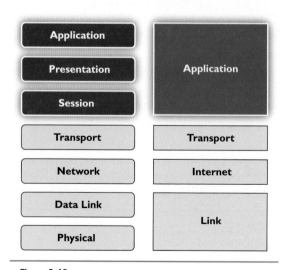

• **Figure 2.48**   TCP/IP Application layer compared to OSI Layers 5–7

In the OSI model, we describe the API—the smarts that make applications network-aware—as being part of the Application layer. While this is still true for the TCP/IP model, all applications designed for TCP/IP are, by definition, network-aware. There is no such thing as a "TCP/IP word processor" or a "TCP/IP image editor" that requires the added ability to know how to talk to a network—all TCP/IP applications can talk to the network, as long as they are part of a network. And every TCP/IP application must be a part of a network to function: Web browsers, e-mail clients, multiplayer games, and so on.

Don't think that the TCP/IP model is any simpler than the OSI model just because it only uses four layers. With the arguable exception of the Presentation layer, everything you saw in the OSI model is also found in the TCP/IP model (Figure 2.49).

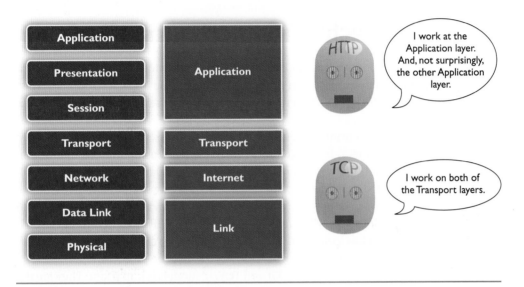

• **Figure 2.49** OSI model and TCP/IP model side by side

Frames, Packets, and Segments/Datagrams, Oh My!

The TCP/IP model shows its power in its ability to describe what happens at each layer to the data that goes from one computer to another. The Application layer programs create the data. The Transport layer breaks the data into chunks, putting those chunks into TCP segments or UDP datagrams. The Internet layer adds the IP addressing and creates the IP packets. The Link layer wraps the IP packet into a frame, with the MAC address information and a frame check sequence (FCS). Now the data is ready to hit the wire (or airwaves, if you're in a café). Figure 2.50 shows all this encapsulating goodness relative to the TCP/IP model.

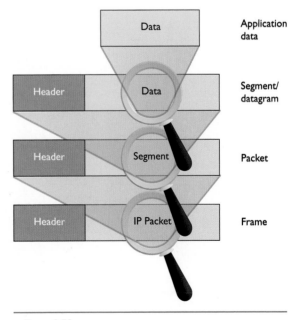

• **Figure 2.50** Data encapsulation in TCP/IP

Check out the "Network Models" Chapter 2 sim at **http://totalsem.com/006**. It's an excellent Challenge! game.

Knowing the layer at which each encapsulation takes place can assist in your troubleshooting. Table 2.1 shows the layers and the corresponding data structure.

Table 2.1	TCP/IP Model Layers and Corresponding Data Structures
TCP/IP Model Layer	**Data Structure**
Link	Frame
Internet	IP packet
Transport	TCP segment/UDP datagram
Application	(The data, or payload, starts and ends here)

■ The Tech's Troubleshooting Tools

The OSI seven-layer model and TCP/IP model provide you with a way to conceptualize a network to determine what could cause a specific problem when the inevitable problems occur. Good techs always use a model to troubleshoot their networks.

If Jane can't print to the networked printer, for example, a model can help solve the problem. If her NIC shows activity, then, using the OSI model, you can set aside both the Physical layer (Layer 1) and Data Link layer (Layer 2). If you're a TCP/IP model tech, you can look at the same symptoms and eliminate the Link layer. In either case, you'll find yourself moving up the layer ladder to the OSI model's Network layer (Layer 3) or the TCP/IP model's Internet layer. If her computer has a proper IP address, then you can set that layer aside too, and you can move on up to check other layers to solve the problem.

Understanding both the OSI and TCP/IP models is important. They are the primary diagnostic tools for troubleshooting networks and also the communication tools for talking with your fellow techs.

Chapter 2 Review

■ Chapter Summary

After reading this chapter and completing the exercises, you should understand the following about networking.

Describe how models such as the OSI seven-layer model and the TCP/IP model help technicians understand and troubleshoot networks

- Modeling is critical in networking. You use models to understand networks and to communicate with other techs about networks.

- All models are a simplified representation of the real thing. The human model ignores the many different types of body shapes, using only a single "optimal" figure. The model airplane lacks functional engines or the internal framework, and the computerized weather model might disregard subtle differences in wind temperatures or geology.

- In the early days of networking, different manufacturers made unique types of networks that functioned fairly well. But each network had its own cabling, hardware, drivers, naming conventions, applications, and many other unique features. To interconnect networks and improve networking as a whole, someone needed to create a guide—a model that described the functions of a network—so people who made hardware and software could work together to make networks that worked together well.

- The OSI seven-layer model defines the role played by each protocol. The OSI model also provides a common jargon that network techs can use to describe the function of any network protocol.

- The TCP/IP four-layer model applies only to networks that use the TCP/IP protocol suite, such as the Internet.

Explain the major functions of networks with the OSI seven-layer model

- OSI Layer 1, the Physical layer, includes anything that moves data from one system to another, such as cabling or radio waves.

- OSI Layer 2, the Data Link layer, defines the rules for accessing and using the Physical layer. The Data Link layer is divided into two sublayers: Media Access Control (MAC) and Logical Link Control (LLC).

- The LLC sublayer handles multiple network protocols and provides flow control. The MAC sublayer creates

and addresses the frame. It adds the NIC's own MAC address and attaches MAC addresses to the frames and adds or checks the FCS.

- OSI Layer 3, the Network layer, is the last layer to work directly with hardware. It creates and addresses packets. The IP addressing enables routers to make sure the packets get to the correct system without worrying about the type of hardware used for transmission. Anything having to do with logical addressing works at the Network layer.

- A network protocol creates unique identifiers for each system and also creates a set of communication rules for issues such as how to handle data chopped up into multiple packets and how to make sure those packets get from one subnet to another.

- OSI Layer 4, the Transport layer, breaks up data received from the upper layers into smaller pieces for transport and adds sequencing numbers for TCP segments to make sure the receiving computer can reassemble the data properly.

- Session software at OSI Layer 5 handles the process of differentiating between various types of connections on a PC. The Session layer initiates sessions, accepts incoming sessions, and opens and closes existing sessions. You can use the netstat program to view existing sessions.

- OSI Layer 6, the Presentation layer, translates data from the lower layers into formats usable by the Application layer; it also translates from the Application layer to lower layers. Several important functions occur here, including the encryption that makes e-commerce possible.

- OSI Layer 7, the Application layer, defines a set of tools that programs can use to access the network. Application layer programs provide services to the programs that the users see.

Describe the major functions of networks with the TCP/IP model

- The TCP/IP Link layer (or Network Interface layer) covers the first two layers of the OSI model—the physical components like hubs and cables as well as network frames.

- The TCP/IP Internet layer works just like the OSI model's Network layer. Anything involved with IP, including packets, addressing, and routing, happens at this layer.

- The TCP/IP Transport layer is similar to the OSI model's Transport layer, except that the TCP/IP version differentiates between connection-oriented communication and connectionless communication.

- In TCP/IP, the Transport layer takes data from the applications, splits the data into chunks called TCP segments or UDP datagrams, depending on the protocol used, and adds port and sequence numbers. The segments and datagrams get handed down to the Internet layer for IP to further encapsulate the data.

- The TCP/IP Application layer combines the top three layers of the OSI model into one super layer. The session component works similarly to the OSI model's Session layer. There is no presentation component that compares to the OSI model's Presentation layer, however. The TCP/IP Application layer is like the OSI model's version, except that TCP/IP connectivity is implied and not a separate program or function.

■ Key Terms

Application layer *(29, 34)*
Application Programming Interface (API) *(29)*
broadcast *(19)*
broadcast address *(19)*
cyclic redundancy check (CRC) *(17)*
Data Link layer *(21)*
datagram *(26)*
de-encapsulation *(30)*
device ID *(15)*
encapsulation *(30)*
EUI-48 *(15)*
frame *(16)*
frame check sequence (FCS) *(17)*
Internet layer *(31)*
Internet Protocol (IP) *(23)*
IP address *(23)*
Link layer *(31)*
logical address *(23)*
logical addressing *(22)*
Logical Link Control (LLC) *(21)*
MAC-48 *(15)*
MAC address *(14)*
Media Access Control (MAC) *(21)*
media access control address *(14)*
model *(10)*
network interface card (NIC) *(14)*

Network Interface layer *(31)*
Network layer *(23)*
network protocol *(22)*
Open Systems Interconnection (OSI) seven-layer model *(8)*
Organizationally Unique Identifier (OUI) *(15)*
packet *(24)*
payload *(36)*
physical address *(15)*
Physical layer *(13)*
Presentation layer *(28)*
protocol *(11)*
router *(23)*
segment *(26)*
Session layer *(28)*
session software *(28)*
subnet *(22)*
switch *(18)*
TCP segment *(33)*
Transmission Control Protocol (TCP) *(23)*
Transmission Control Protocol/Internet Protocol (TCP/IP) model *(8)*
Transport layer *(26, 32)*
UDP datagram *(34)*
unshielded twisted pair (UTP) *(13)*
User Datagram Protocol (UDP) *(33)*

Key Term Quiz

Use the Key Terms list to complete the sentences that follow. Not all terms will be used.

1. The _____ is an example of software that creates packets for moving data across networks.

2. Most often, the _____ provides the physical connection between the PC and the network.

3. Using the _____ enables a computer to send a packet that every other PC on the network will process.

4. You can connect two very different networks by using a(n) _____.

5. Every NIC has a hard-coded identifier called a(n) _____.

6. The _____ provides an excellent tool for conceptualizing how a TCP/IP network works. (Select the best answer.)

7. On a sending machine, data gets broken up at the _____ of the OSI seven-layer model.

8. NICs encapsulate data into a(n) _____ for sending that data over a network.

9. A(n) _____ enables multiple machines to connect over a network.

10. The _____ provides the key interface between the Physical and Network layers.

Multiple-Choice Quiz

1. Which of the following OSI layers converts the ones and zeroes to electrical signals and places these signals on the cable?

    A. Physical layer

    B. Transport layer

    C. Network layer

    D. Data Link layer

2. The term "unshielded twisted pair" describes which of the following network components?

    A. Cable

    B. Hub

    C. Router

    D. NIC

3. From the options that follow, select the one that best describes the contents of a typical (simplified) network frame.

    A. Sender's MAC address, recipient's MAC address, data, FCS

    B. Recipient's MAC address, sender's MAC address, data, FCS

    C. Recipient's IP address, sender's IP address, data, FCS

    D. Recipient's e-mail address, sender's e-mail address, data, FCS

4. Which of the following is most likely to be a MAC address assigned to a NIC?

    A. 192.168.1.121

    B. 24.17.232.7B

    C. 23.4F.17.8A.4C.10

    D. 713.555.1212

5. Which layer of the TCP/IP model involves routing?

    A. Link layer

    B. Transport layer

    C. Internet layer

    D. Application layer

6. How much data can a typical frame contain?

    A. 500 bytes

    B. 1500 bytes

    C. 1500 kilobytes

    D. 1 megabyte

7. Which of the following best describes an IP address?

    A. A unique dotted decimal notation burned into every NIC

    B. A unique 48-bit identifying number burned into every NIC

    C. A dotted decimal notation assigned to a NIC by software

    D. A 48-bit identifying number assigned to a NIC by software

8. Which layer of the OSI model makes sure the data is in a readable format for the Application layer?

   A. Application layer

   B. Presentation layer

   C. Session layer

   D. Transport layer

9. At which layer of the TCP/IP model are UDP datagrams created?

   A. Link/Network Interface

   B. Internet

   C. Transport

   D. Application

10. Which protocol creates the final IP packet?

   A. NIC

   B. IP

   C. TCP

   D. UDP

11. Which TCP/IP layer includes Layers 5–7 from the OSI seven-layer model?

   A. Application layer

   B. Transport layer

   C. Internet layer

   D. Link layer

12. What component of Layer 2 of the OSI seven-layer model creates and addresses the frame?

   A. MAC sublayer

   B. LLC sublayer

   C. CRC sublayer

   D. Data Link sublayer

13. Which components work at Layer 1 of the OSI seven-layer model? (Select two.)

   A. Cables

   B. Hub

   C. Network protocol

   D. Session software

14. Andalyn says complete 48-bit MAC addresses are allocated to NIC manufacturers from the IEEE. Buster says the IEEE only assigns the first 24 bits to manufacturers. Carlos says the IEEE assigns only the last 24 bits to manufacturers. Who is correct?

   A. Only Andalyn is correct.

   B. Only Buster is correct.

   C. Only Carlos is correct.

   D. No one is correct.

15. If a sending system does not know the MAC address of the intended recipient system, it sends a broadcast frame with what MAC address?

   A. 192.168.0.0

   B. FF-FF-FF-FF-FF-FF

   C. 11-11-11-11-11-11

   D. 00-00-00-00-00-00

■ Essay Quiz

1. Some new techs at your office are confused by the differences between a NIC's frame and an IP packet. Write a short essay describing the two encapsulations, including the components that do the encapsulating.

2. Your boss has received a set of files with the file extension .wp and is worried because he's never seen that extension before. He wants people to have access to the information in those files from anywhere in the network. Write a short memo describing how Microsoft Word can handle these files, including a discussion of how that fits with the OSI seven-layer model.

Lab Projects

• Lab Project 2.1

Examine your classroom network. What components does it have? How would you classify those components according to the OSI seven-layer model?

• Lab Project 2.2

Create a mnemonic phrase to help you remember the OSI seven-layer model. With two layers beginning with the letter *P*, how will you differentiate in your mnemonic between Presentation and Physical? How will you incorporate the two sublayers of the Data Link layer?

Cabling and Topology

"I'm not crazy. My mother had me tested!"

—SHELDON, *BIG BANG THEORY*

In this chapter, you will learn how to

- **Explain the different types of network topologies**
- **Describe the different types of network cabling and connectors**
- **Describe the IEEE networking standards**

Every network must provide some method to get data from one system to another. In most cases, this method consists of some type of cabling running between systems, although many networks skip wires and use wireless methods to move data. Stringing those cables brings up a number of critical issues you need to understand to work on a network. How do all these cables connect the computers? Does every computer on the network run a cable to a central point? Does a single cable snake through the ceiling, with all the computers on the network connected to it? These questions need answering!

Furthermore, manufacturers need standards so they can make networking equipment that works well together. While we're talking about standards, what about the cabling itself? What type of cable? What quality of copper? How thick should it be? Who defines the standards for cables so they all work in the network?

This chapter answers these questions in three parts. First, you will learn about the **network topology**—the way that cables and other pieces of hardware connect to one another. Second, you will tour the most common standardized cable types used in networking. Third, you will learn about the IEEE committees that create network technology standards.

Network Topologies

Computer networks employ many different *topologies,* or ways of connecting computers together. This section looks at both the historical topologies—bus, ring, and star—and the modern topologies—hybrid, mesh, point-to-multi-point, and point-to-point. In addition, we will look at what parameters are used to make up a network topology.

Bus and Ring

The first generation of wired networks used one of two topologies, both shown in Figure 3.1. A **bus topology** uses a single cable (the *bus*) that connects all of the computers in a line. A **ring topology** connects all computers on the network with a ring of cable.

 Note that topologies are diagrams, much like an electrical circuit diagram. Real network cabling doesn't go in perfect circles or perfect straight lines.

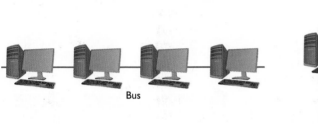

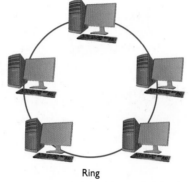

• **Figure 3.1**   Bus and ring topologies

Figure 3.2 shows a bus topology network that illustrates how the cable might appear in the real world.

Data flows differently between bus and ring networks, creating different problems and solutions. In bus topology networks, data from each computer simply goes out on the whole bus. A network using a bus topology needs termination at each end of the cable to prevent a signal sent from one computer from reflecting at the ends of the cable, quickly bringing the network down (Figure 3.3).

In a ring topology network, in contrast, data traffic moves in a circle from one computer to the next in the same direction (Figure 3.4). With no end to the cable, ring networks require no termination.

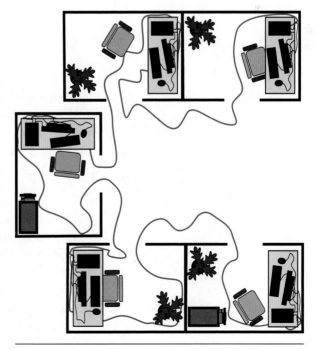

• **Figure 3.2**   Real-world bus topology

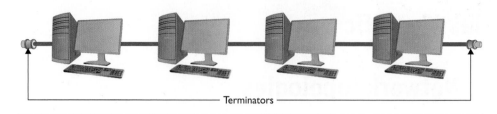

• **Figure 3.3**   Terminated bus topology

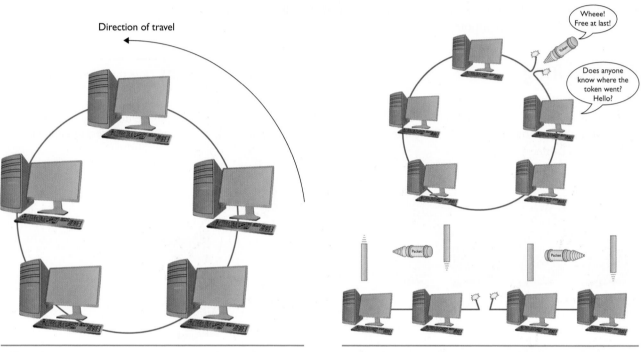

• **Figure 3.4**   Ring topology moving in a certain direction

• **Figure 3.5**   Nobody is talking!

Bus and ring topology networks work well but suffer from the same problem: the entire network stops working if the cable breaks at any point (Figure 3.5). The broken ends on a bus topology network don't have the required termination, which causes reflection between computers that are still connected. A break in a ring topology network simply breaks the circuit, stopping the data flow.

Star

The **star topology** uses a central connection box for all the computers on the network (Figure 3.6). Star topologies have a huge benefit over ring and bus topologies by offering **fault tolerance**—if one of the cables breaks, all of the other computers can still communicate. Bus and ring topology networks were popular and inexpensive to implement, however, so the old-style star topology networks weren't very successful. Network hardware designers couldn't easily redesign their existing networks to use a star topology.

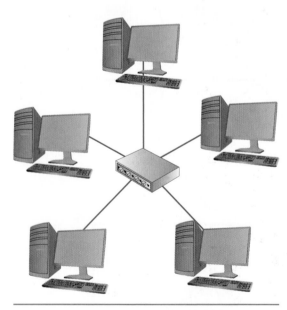

• **Figure 3.6**   Star topology

Hybrids

Even though network designers couldn't easily use a star topology, the benefits of star topologies were overwhelming, motivating smart people to come up with a way to use star topologies without requiring a major redesign—and the way they did so was ingenious. The ring topology network designers struck first by taking the entire ring and shrinking it into a small box, as shown in Figure 3.7.

This was quickly followed by the bus topology folks, who, in turn, shrunk their bus (better known as the **segment**) into their own box (Figure 3.8).

The most successful of the star ring topology networks was called *Token Ring*, manufactured by IBM.

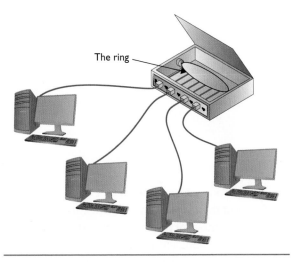

• **Figure 3.7** Shrinking the ring

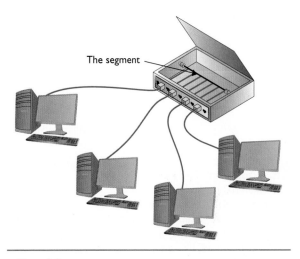

• **Figure 3.8** Shrinking the segment

Physically, they looked like a star, but if you examined them as an electronic schematic, the signals acted like a ring or a bus. Clearly the old definition of topology needed a little clarification. When we talk about topology today, we separate how the cables physically look (the **physical topology**) from how the signals travel electronically (the **signaling topology** or **logical topology**).

Any form of networking technology that combines a physical topology with a signaling topology is called a **hybrid topology**. Hybrid topologies have come and gone since the earliest days of networking. Only two hybrid topologies, **star-ring topology** and **star-bus topology**, ever saw any amount of popularity. Eventually star-ring lost market share, and star-bus reigned as the undisputed king of topologies.

Most techs refer to the signaling topology as the *logical topology* today. That's how you'll see it on the CompTIA Network+ exam as well.

Mesh and Point-to-Multipoint

Topologies aren't just for wired networks. Wireless networks also need topologies to get data from one machine to another, but using radio waves instead of cables involves somewhat different topologies. Almost all wireless networks use one of two different topologies: a mesh topology or a point-to-multipoint topology (Figure 3.9).

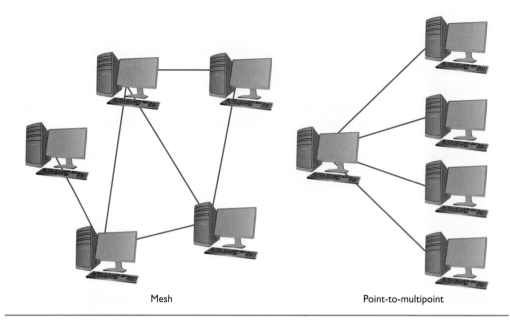

Mesh | Point-to-multipoint

• **Figure 3.9**   Mesh and point-to-multipoint topology

You won't find partial mesh networks in an office setting. You're more likely to see the term used to describe connections among networks over distance, like on a university campus. You won't see a full mesh network at all outside of the CompTIA Network+ exam.

Mesh

In a **mesh topology** network, every computer connects to every other computer via two or more routes. Some of the routes between two computers may require traversing through another member of the mesh network.

There are two types of meshed topologies: partially meshed and fully meshed (Figure 3.10). In a **partially meshed topology** network, at least two machines have redundant connections. Every machine doesn't have to connect to every other machine. In a **fully meshed topology** network, every computer connects directly to every other computer.

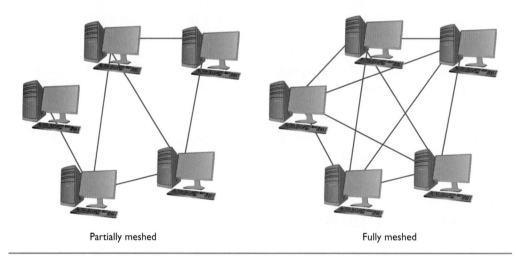

Partially meshed | Fully meshed

• **Figure 3.10**   Partially and fully meshed topologies

Point-to-Multipoint

In a **point-to-multipoint topology**, a single system acts as a common source through which all members of the point-to-multipoint network converse. If you compare a star topology to a slightly rearranged point-to-multipoint topology, you might be tempted to say they're the same thing. Granted, they're similar, but look at Figure 3.11. See what's in the middle? The subtle but important difference is that a point-to-multipoint topology requires an intelligent device in the center, whereas the device in the center of a star topology has little more to do than send or provide a path for a signal down all the connections.

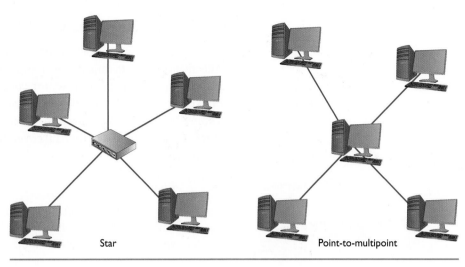

Star

Point-to-multipoint

• **Figure 3.11** Comparing star and point-to-multipoint topologies

Point-to-Point

In a **point-to-point topology** network, two computers connect directly together with no need for a central device of any kind. You'll find point-to-point topologies implemented in both wired and wireless networks (Figure 3.12).

• **Figure 3.12** Point-to-point topology

Parameters of a Topology

Although a topology describes the method by which systems in a network connect, the topology alone doesn't describe all of the features necessary to enable those networks. The term *bus topology,* for example, describes a network that consists of some number of machines connected to the network via a single linear piece of cable. Notice that this definition leaves a lot of questions unanswered. What is the cable made of? How long can it be? How do the machines decide which machine should send data at a specific moment? A network based on a bus topology can answer these questions in a number of different ways—but it's not the job of the topology to define issues like these. A functioning network needs a more detailed standard.

Over the years, particular manufacturers and standards bodies have created several specific network technologies based on different topologies. A **network technology** is a practical application of a topology and other critical technologies that provides a method to get data from one computer to another on a network. These network technologies have names like 10BaseT, 1000BaseF, and 10GBaseLX. You will learn all about these in the next two chapters.

Make sure you know all your topologies: bus, ring, star, hybrid, mesh, point-to-multipoint, and point-to-point!

The CompTIA Network+ exam objectives include client-server and peer-to-peer networks in the list of "common network topologies." I discuss these in Chapter 12, "Advanced Networking Devices."

■ Cabling and Connectors

The majority of networked systems link together using some type of cabling. Different types of networks over the years have used a number of different types of cables—and you need to learn about all these cables to succeed on the CompTIA Network+ exam! This section explores both the cabling types used in older networks and those found in today's networks.

All cables used in the networking industry can be categorized in two distinct groups: copper and fiber-optic. All styles of cables have distinct connector types that you need to know.

Check out the excellent Chapter 3 "Topology Matching" Challenge! over at http://totalsem.com/006. It's a good tool for reinforcing the topology variations.

Copper Cabling and Connectors

The most common form of cabling uses copper wire wrapped up in some kind of protective sheathing, thus the term *copper cables*. The two primary types of copper cabling used in the industry are coaxial and twisted pair.

Both cable types sport a variety of connector types, none of which are actually *copper connectors*, but that's the term used in the CompTIA Network+ objectives to lump them together. I'll cover the connector types as I discuss the cable varieties.

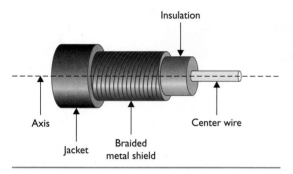

• **Figure 3.13**   Cutaway view of coaxial cable

Labels: Insulation, Axis, Jacket, Braided metal shield, Center wire

Coaxial Cable

Coaxial cable contains a central conductor wire (usually copper) surrounded by an insulating material, which, in turn, is surrounded by a braided metal shield. The cable is referred to as coaxial (coax for short) because the center wire and the braided metal shield share a common axis or centerline (Figure 3.13).

Coaxial cable shields data transmissions from electromagnetic interference (EMI). Many devices in the typical office environment generate magnetic fields, including lights, fans, copy machines, and refrigerators. When a metal wire encounters these magnetic fields, electrical current is generated along the wire. This extra current—EMI—can shut down a network because it is easily misinterpreted as a signal by devices like NICs. To prevent EMI from affecting the network, the outer mesh layer of a coaxial cable shields the center wire (on which the data is transmitted) from interference (Figure 3.14).

Early bus topology networks used coaxial cable to connect computers together. Back in the day, the most popular cable used special bayonet-style connectors called BNC connectors (Figure 3.15). Even earlier bus networks used thick cable that required vampire connections—sometimes called *vampire taps*—that literally pierced the cable.

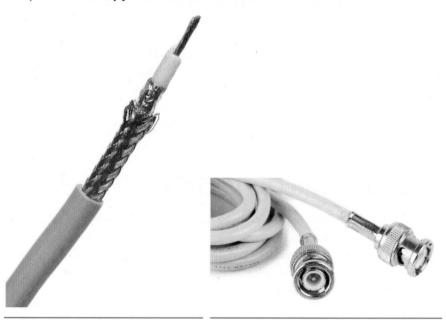

• **Figure 3.14**   Coaxial cable showing braided metal shielding

• **Figure 3.15**   BNC connector on coaxial cable

You'll find coaxial cable used today primarily to enable a cable modem to connect to an Internet service provider (ISP). Connecting a computer to the cable modem enables that computer to access the Internet. This cable is the same type used to connect televisions to cable boxes or to satellite receivers. These cables use an **F-connector** that screws on, making for a secure connection (Figure 3.16).

Cable modems connect using either RG-6 or, rarely, RG-59. RG-59 was used primarily for cable television rather than networking. Its thinness and the introduction of digital cable motivated the move to the more robust RG-6, the predominant cabling used today (Figure 3.17).

All coax cables have a **Radio Grade (RG) rating**. The U.S. military developed these ratings to provide a quick reference for the different types of coax. The only important measure of coax cabling is its **Ohm rating**, a relative measure of the resistance (or more precisely, characteristic impedance) on the cable. You may run across other coax cables that don't have acceptable Ohm ratings, although they look just like network-rated coax. Fortunately, most coax cable types display their Ohm ratings on the cables themselves (see Figure 3.18). Both RG-6 and RG-59 cables are rated at 75 Ohms.

• **Figure 3.16** F-type connector on coaxial cable

Coaxial cabling is also very popular with satellite dishes, over-the-air antennas, and even some home video devices. This book covers cable and other Internet connectivity options in great detail in Chapter 14, "Remote Connectivity."

The Ohm rating of a particular piece of cable describes the impedance of that cable. Impedance describes a set of characteristics that define how much a cable resists the flow of electricity. This isn't simple resistance, though. Impedance is also a factor in such things as how long it takes the wire to get a full charge—the wire's *capacitance*—and more.

• **Figure 3.17** RG-6 cable

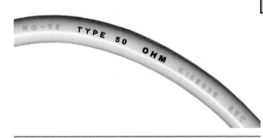

• **Figure 3.18** Ohm rating (on an older, RG-58 cable used for networking)

Given the popularity of cable for television and Internet in homes today, you'll run into situations where people need to take a single coaxial cable and split it. Coaxial handles this quite nicely with coaxial splitters like the one shown in Figure 3.19. You can also connect two coaxial cables together easily using a barrel connector when you need to add some distance to a connection (Figure 3.20).

Twisted Pair

The most common type of cabling used in networks consists of twisted pairs of cables, bundled together into a common jacket. Twisted-pair cabling for networks is composed of multiple pairs of wires, twisted around

• **Figure 3.19** Coaxial splitter

• **Figure 3.20** Barrel connector

Have you ever picked up a telephone and heard a distinct crackling noise? That's an example of crosstalk.

each other at specific intervals. The twists reduce interference, called **crosstalk**: the more twists, the less crosstalk. Networks use two types of twisted-pair cabling: shielded twisted pair and unshielded twisted pair.

Shielded Twisted Pair   Shielded twisted pair (STP), as its name implies, consists of twisted pairs of wires surrounded by shielding to protect them from EMI. STP is pretty rare, primarily because there's so little need for STP's shielding. The shielding only really matters in locations with excessive electronic noise, such as a shop floor with lots of lights, electric motors, or other machinery that could cause problems for other cables. Figure 3.21 shows the most common STP type: the venerable IBM Type 1 cable used in Token Ring network technology.

Unshielded Twisted Pair   Unshielded twisted pair (UTP) is by far the most common type of network cabling used today. UTP consists of twisted pairs of wires surrounded by a plastic jacket (Figure 3.22). This jacket does not provide any protection from EMI, so when installing UTP cabling, you must be careful to avoid interference from fluorescent lights, motors, and so forth. UTP costs much less than STP but, in most cases, performs just as well.

• **Figure 3.21**   Shielded twisted pair

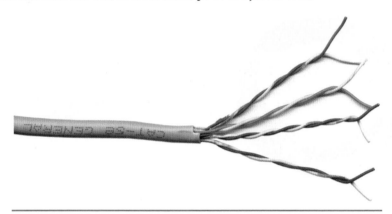

• **Figure 3.22**   Unshielded twisted pair

Although more sensitive to interference than coaxial or STP cable, UTP cabling provides an inexpensive and flexible means to cable networks. UTP cable isn't exclusive to networks. Many other technologies (such as telephone systems) employ the same cabling. This makes working with UTP a bit of a challenge. Imagine going up into a ceiling and seeing two sets of UTP cables: how would you determine which is for the telephones and which is for the network? Not to worry—a number of installation standards and tools exist to help those who work with UTP get the answer to these types of questions.

 Cross Check

OSI Seven-Layer and TCP/IP Model

You've seen UTP cabling before when Dana accessed documents on Janelle's PC at MHTechEd. Refer to Chapter 2, "Network Models," and cross-check your memory. At what layer of the OSI seven-layer model would you put UTP cabling? For that matter, at what layer would you put *network topology*? How about on the TCP/IP model?

Not all UTP cables are the same! UTP cabling has a number of variations, such as the number of twists per foot. To help network installers get the right cable for the right network technology, the cabling industry has developed a variety of grades called category (CAT) ratings. CAT ratings are officially rated in *megahertz (MHz)*, indicating the highest frequency the cable can handle. Table 3.1 shows the most common categories along with their status with the TIA/EIA (see the Tech Tip for more information).

Table 3.1	CAT Ratings for UTP		
CAT Rating	**Max Frequency**	**Max Bandwidth**	**Status with TIA/EIA**
CAT 1	< 1 MHz	Analog phone lines only	No longer recognized
CAT 2	4 MHz	4 Mbps	No longer recognized
CAT 3	16 MHz	16 Mbps	Recognized
CAT 4	20 MHz	20 Mbps	No longer recognized
CAT 5	100 MHz	100 Mbps	No longer recognized
CAT 5e	100 MHz	1000 Mbps	Recognized
CAT 6[1]	250 MHz	10000 Mbps	Recognized
CAT 6a[2]	500 MHz	10000 Mbps	Recognized

[1] CAT 6 cables can use the full 100-meter length when used with 10/100/1000BaseT networks. With 10GBaseT networks, CAT 6 is limited to 55 meters.
[2] CAT 6a cables can use the full 100-meter length with networks up to 10GBaseT.

UTP cables are rated to handle a certain frequency or cycles per second, such as 100 MHz or 1000 MHz. You could take the frequency number in the early days of networking and translate that into the maximum throughput for a cable. Each cycle per second (or hertz) basically accounted for one bit of data per second. A 10 million cycle per second (10 MHz) cable, for example, could handle 10 million bits per second (10 Mbps). The maximum amount of data that goes through the cable per second is called the bandwidth.

For current networks, developers have implemented *bandwidth-efficient encoding schemes,* which means they can squeeze more bits into the same signal as long as the cable can handle it. Thus, the CAT 5e cable can handle a throughput of up to 1000 Mbps, even though it's rated to handle a frequency of only up to 100 MHz.

Because most networks can run at speeds of up to 1000 MHz, most new cabling installations use Category 5e (CAT 5e) cabling, although a large number of installations use CAT 6 or CAT 6a to future-proof the network. CAT 5e cabling currently costs much less than CAT 6/6a.

Make sure you can look at UTP and know its CAT rating. There are two places to look. First, UTP is typically sold in boxed reels, and the manufacturer will clearly mark the CAT level on the box (Figure 3.23). Second, look on the cable itself. The category level of a piece of cable is usually printed on the cable (Figure 3.24).

• Figure 3.23   CAT level marked on box of UTP

• Figure 3.24   CAT level on UTP

Tech Tip

CAT 6a

The CAT 6a update doubles the bandwidth of CAT 6 to 500 MHz to accommodate 10-Gbps speeds up to 100 meters. (The 100-meter limitation, by the way, refers to the Ethernet standard, the major implementation of UTP in networks. Chapter 4 covers Ethernet in great detail.)

Other standards are in the works or already here, however, that go well beyond just Ethernet traffic. CAT 7a, for example, can handle 10GBaseT Ethernet or accommodate cable television, telephones, and Gigabit Ethernet at the same time. Sweet. Nothing beyond CAT 6 is on the exam.

Anyone who's plugged in a telephone has probably already dealt with the *registered jack (RJ)* connectors used with UTP cable. Telephones use **RJ-11** connectors, designed to support up to two pairs of wires. Networks use the four-pair **RJ-45** connectors (Figure 3.25).

Fiber-Optic Cabling and Connectors

Fiber-optic cable transmits light rather than electricity, making it attractive for both high-EMI areas and long-distance transmissions. Whereas a single copper cable cannot carry data more than a few hundred meters at best, a single piece of fiber-optic cabling will operate, depending on the implementation, for distances of up to tens of kilometers. A fiber-optic cable has four components: the glass fiber itself (the **core**); the **cladding**, which is the part that makes the light reflect down the fiber; *buffer* material to give strength; and the **insulating jacket** (Figure 3.26).

CompTIA uses the term *fiber cables* to describe the two varieties of fiber-optic cables discussed in this section. Just as copper cables don't have copper

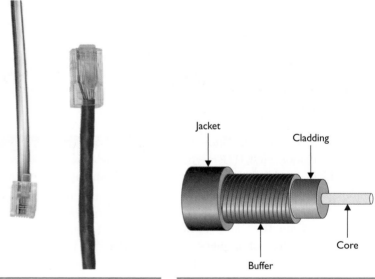

• Figure 3.25   RJ-11 (left) and RJ-45 (right) connectors

• Figure 3.26   Cross section of fiber-optic cabling

connectors, fiber cables don't have *fiber connectors*, but that's the term used in the CompTIA Network+ objectives. I'll discuss cables and connector types below.

Fiber-optic cabling is manufactured with many different diameters of core and cladding. In a convenient bit of standardization, cable manufacturers use a two-number designator to define fiber-optic cables according to their core and cladding measurements. The most common fiber-optic cable size is 62.5/125 μm. Almost all network technologies that use fiber-optic cable require pairs of fibers. One fiber is used for sending, the other for receiving. In response to the demand for two-pair cabling, manufacturers often connect two fibers together like a lamp cord to create the popular duplex fiber-optic cabling (Figure 3.27).

Fiber cables are pretty tiny! Light can be sent down a fiber-optic cable as regular light or as laser light. The two types of light require totally different fiber-optic cables. Most network technologies that use fiber optics use LEDs (light emitting diodes) to send light signals. A fiber-optic cable that uses LEDs is known as **multimode fiber (MMF)**.

A fiber-optic cable that uses lasers is known as **single-mode fiber (SMF)**. Using laser light and single-mode fiber-optic cables prevents a problem unique to multimode fiber optics called **modal distortion** (signals sent at the same time don't arrive at the same time because the paths differ slightly in length) and enables a network to achieve phenomenally high transfer rates over incredibly long distances.

Fiber optics also defines the wavelength of light used, measured in nanometers (nm). Almost all multimode cables transmit 850-nm wavelengths, whereas single-mode transmits either 1310 nm or 1550 nm, depending on the laser.

Fiber-optic cables come in a broad choice of connector types. There are over one hundred different connectors, but the four you need to know for the CompTIA Network+ exam are ST, SC, LC (Figure 3.28), and FC (Figure 3.29).

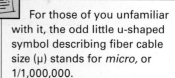
For those of you unfamiliar with it, the odd little u-shaped symbol describing fiber cable size (μ) stands for *micro,* or 1/1,000,000.

• **Figure 3.27** Duplex fiber-optic cable

A *nano*—abbreviated as *n*—stands for 1/1,000,000,000, or one-billionth of whatever. Here you'll see it as a nanometer (nm), one-billionth of a meter. That's one tiny wavelength!

• **Figure 3.28** From left to right: ST, SC, and LC fiber-optic connectors

• **Figure 3.29** FC connector

Although all fiber connectors must be installed in pairs, the ST and SC connectors traditionally have unique ends. The LC connector is always duplex, meaning both the send and receive cables are attached. You can certainly find SC connectors or sleeves to make them duplex too, so don't get too caught up with which can be which.

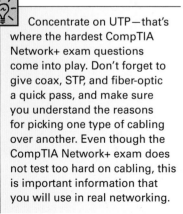

Other Cables

Fiber-optic and UTP make up almost all network cabling, but a few other types of cabling appear on the CompTIA Network+ exam: the ancient serial and parallel cables from the earliest days of PCs. These cables were used for networking, but have not been in use for many years.

Classic Serial

Serial cabling predates both networking and the personal computer. **RS-232**, the *recommended standard (RS)* upon which all serial communication takes places on your PC, dates from 1969 and hasn't substantially changed in around 40 years. When IBM invented the PC way back in 1980, serial connections were just about the only standard input/output technology available, so IBM included two serial ports on every PC. The most common serial port is a 9-pin, male D-subminiature (or **DB-9**) connector, as shown in Figure 3.30.

• **Figure 3.30**   Serial port

Serial ports offered a poor option for networking, with very slow data rates—only about 56,000 bps—and only point-to-point connections. Serial ports were last used for connecting to networking devices, such as high-end switches.

Parallel

Parallel connections are as ancient as serial ports. Parallel can run up to around 2 Mbps, although when used for networking, they tend to be much slower. Parallel is also limited to point-to-point topology but uses a 25-pin female—rather than male—DB type connector commonly called a **DB-25** (Figure 3.31). The **IEEE 1284** committee sets the standards for parallel communication. (See the section "Networking Industry Standards—IEEE," later in this chapter.)

Fire Ratings

Did you ever see the movie *The Towering Inferno?* Don't worry if you missed it—*The Towering Inferno* was one of the better disaster movies of the 1970s, although it was no *Airplane!* Anyway, Steve McQueen stars as the fireman who saves the day when a skyscraper goes up in flames because of poor-quality electrical cabling. The burning insulation on the wires ultimately spreads the fire to every part of the building. Although no cables made today contain truly flammable insulation, the insulation is made from plastic, and if you get any plastic hot enough, it will create smoke and noxious fumes. The risk of burning insulation isn't fire—it's smoke and fumes.

To reduce the risk of your network cables burning and creating noxious fumes and smoke, Underwriters Laboratories and the National Electrical Code (NEC) joined forces to develop cabling *fire ratings*. The two most common fire ratings are PVC and plenum. Cable with a **polyvinyl chloride (PVC)** rating has no significant fire protection. If you burn a PVC cable, it creates lots of smoke and noxious fumes. Burning **plenum**-rated cable creates much less smoke and fumes, but plenum-rated cable—often referred to simply as "plenum"—costs about three to five times as much as PVC-rated cable. Most city ordinances require the use of plenum cable for network installations. The bottom line? Get plenum!

The space between the acoustical tile ceiling in an office building and the actual concrete ceiling above is called the plenum—hence the name for the proper fire rating of cabling to use in that space. A third type of fire rating, known as **riser**, designates the proper cabling to use for vertical runs between floors of a building. Riser-rated cable provides less protection than plenum cable, though, so most installations today use plenum for runs between floors.

■ Networking Industry Standards—IEEE

The **Institute of Electrical and Electronics Engineers (IEEE)** defines industry-wide standards that promote the use and implementation of technology. In February 1980, a new committee called the 802 Working Group took over from the private sector the job of defining network standards. (Get it? 02/80?) The IEEE 802 committee defines frames, speeds, distances, and types of cabling to use in a network environment. Concentrating on cables, the IEEE recognizes that no single cabling solution can work in all situations and, therefore, provides a variety of cabling standards.

IEEE committees define standards for a wide variety of electronics. The names of these committees are often used to refer to the standards they publish. The IEEE 1284 committee, for example, sets standards for parallel communication. Have you ever seen a printer cable marked "IEEE 1284–compliant," as in Figure 3.32? This means the manufacturer followed the rules set by the IEEE 1284 committee.

• **Figure 3.32**   Parallel cable marked IEEE 1284–compliant

The IEEE 802 committee sets the standards for networking. Although the original plan was to define a single, universal standard for networking, it quickly became apparent that no single solution would work for all needs. The 802 committee split into smaller subcommittees, with names such as IEEE 802.3 and IEEE 802.5. Table 3.2 shows the currently recognized IEEE 802 subcommittees and their areas of jurisdiction. I've included the inactive subcommittees for reference. The missing numbers, such as 802.4 and 802.12, were used for committees long-ago disbanded. Each subcommittee is officially called a Working Group, except the few listed as a Technical Advisory Group (TAG) in the table.

Some of these committees deal with technologies that didn't quite make it, and the committees associated with those standards, such as IEEE 802.4, Token Bus, have become dormant. When preparing for the CompTIA Network+ exam, concentrate on the IEEE 802.3 and 802.11 standards. You will see these again in later chapters.

Table 3.2	IEEE 802 Subcommittees
IEEE 802	LAN/MAN Overview & Architecture
IEEE 802.1	Higher Layer LAN Protocols (with many subcommittees, like 802.11x for port-based network access control)
IEEE 802.2	Logical Link Control (LLC); now inactive
IEEE 802.3	Ethernet (with a ton of subcommittees, such as 802.3ae for 10-Gigabit Ethernet)
IEEE 802.5	Token Ring; now inactive
IEEE 802.11	Wireless LAN (WLAN); specifications, such as Wi-Fi, and many subcommittees
IEEE 802.15	Wireless Personal Area Network (WPAN)
IEEE 802.16	Broadband Wireless Access (BWA); specifications for implementing Wireless Metropolitan Area Networks (Wireless MANs); referred to also as WiMAX
IEEE 802.17	Resilient Packet Ring (RPR)
IEEE 802.18	Radio Regulatory Technical Advisory Group
IEEE 802.19	Coexistence Technical Advisory Group
IEEE 802.20	Mobile Broadband Wireless Access (MBWA)
IEEE 802.21	Media Independent Handover
IEEE 802.22	Wireless Regional Area Networks

Chapter 3 Review

■ Chapter Summary

After reading this chapter and completing the exercises, you should understand the following about cabling and topology.

Explain the different types of network topologies

■ A network's *topology* describes how computers connect to each other in that network. The most common network topologies are called *bus, ring, star,* and *mesh.*

■ In a bus topology, all computers connect to the network via a main line. The cable must be terminated at both ends to prevent signal reflections.

■ In a ring topology, all computers on the network attach to a ring of cable. A single break in the cable stops the flow of data through the entire network.

■ In a star topology, the computers on the network connect to a central wiring point, which provides fault tolerance.

■ Networks turned to the two hybrid topologies: *star-bus and star-ring* many years ago. Star-bus is overwhelmingly the most common topology used today.

■ In a mesh topology, each computer has a dedicated line to every other computer. Mesh networks can be further categorized as partially meshed or fully meshed, both of which require a significant amount of physical cable.

■ In a point-to-multipoint topology, a single system acts as a common source through which all members of the network converse.

■ Mesh and point-to-multipoint topologies are common among wireless networks.

■ In a point-to-point topology, two computers connect directly together.

Describe the different types of network cabling and connectors

■ Copper cabling comes in two forms: coaxial and twisted pair.

■ Coaxial cable, or coax, shields data transmissions from EMI. Coax was widely used in early bus networks and used BNC connectors. Today, coax is used mainly to connect a cable modem to an ISP.

■ Coax cables have an RG rating, with RG-6 being the predominant coax today.

■ Twisted pair, which comes shielded or unshielded, is the most common type of networking cable today. UTP is less expensive and more popular than STP, though it doesn't offer any protection from EMI.

■ UTP is categorized by its CAT rating, with CAT 5, CAT 5e, CAT 6, and CAT 6a being the most commonly used today.

■ Telephones use RJ-11 connectors, whereas UTP uses RJ-45 connectors.

■ Fiber-optic cabling transmits light instead of the electricity used in CAT cable or coax. It is thin and more expensive, yet less flexible and more delicate, than other types of network cabling.

■ There are two types of fiber-optic cable based on what type of light is used. LEDs require multimode cable, whereas lasers generally require single-mode cable.

■ All fiber-optic cable has three parts: the fiber itself; the cladding, which covers the fiber and helps it reflect down the fiber; and the outer insulating jacket. Additionally, there are over one hundred types of connectors for fiber-optic cable, but ST, SC, LC, and FC are the most common for computer networking.

■ Plenum-rated UTP is required by most cities for network installations.

■ Serial cables adhering to the RS-232 standard and parallel cables adhering to the IEEE-1284 standard may be used to network two computers directly together.

Describe the IEEE networking standards

■ Networking standards are established and promoted by the Institute of Electrical and Electronics Engineers (IEEE).

■ The IEEE 802 committee defines frames, speeds, distances, and types of cabling to use in networks. IEEE 802 is split into several subcommittees, including IEEE 802.3 and IEEE 802.11.

■ Key Terms

bandwidth *(51)*
bus topology *(43)*
BNC connector *(48)*
category (CAT) rating *(51)*
cladding *(52)*
coaxial cable *(48)*
core *(52)*
crosstalk *(50)*
DB-25 *(54)*
DB-9 *(54)*
electromagnetic interference (EMI) *(48)*
F-connector *(49)*
fault tolerance *(44)*
fiber-optic cable *(52)*
fully meshed topology *(46)*
hybrid topology *(45)*
Institute of Electrical and Electronics Engineers
   (IEEE) *(55)*
IEEE 1284 *(54)*
insulating jacket *(52)*
logical topology *(45)*
mesh topology *(46)*
modal distortion *(53)*
multimode fiber (MMF) *(53)*

network technology *(47)*
network topology *(42)*
Ohm rating *(49)*
partially meshed topology *(46)*
physical topology *(45)*
plenum *(55)*
point-to-multipoint topology *(46)*
point-to-point topology *(47)*
polyvinyl chloride (PVC) *(55)*
Radio Grade (RG) rating *(49)*
ring topology *(43)*
riser *(55)*
RJ-11 *(52)*
RJ-45 *(52)*
RS-232 *(54)*
segment *(45)*
shielded twisted pair (STP) *(50)*
signaling topology *(45)*
single-mode fiber (SMF) *(53)*
star topology *(44)*
star-bus topology *(45)*
star-ring topology *(45)*
unshielded twisted pair (UTP) *(50)*

■ Key Term Quiz

Use the Key Terms list to complete the sentences that follow. Not all terms will be used.

1. The _____ is a network topology that relies on a main line of network coaxial cabling.

2. The _____ of a cable will determine its speed.

3. A(n) _____ provides more fault tolerance than any other basic network topology.

4. When your network has all computers connected to a centrally located wiring closet, you have a physical _____ network.

5. _____ networks use more than one type of basic network topology.

6. CAT 5e cable is a type of _____ wiring.

7. Coaxial cable uses a braided metal shield to protect data from _____.

8. Network cabling can use either light or electricity to transmit data. The faster of these types uses light along _____.

9. _____-grade UTP must be installed in ceilings, whereas _____-grade UTP is often used to connect one floor to another vertically in a building.

10. The twisting of the cables in UTP and STP reduces _____.

■ Multiple-Choice Quiz

1. Which of the following are standard network topologies? (Select three.)

   A. Bus

   B. Star

   C. Ring

   D. Dual-ring

2. John was carrying on at the water cooler the other day, trying to show off his knowledge of networking. He claimed that the company had installed special cabling to handle the problems of crosstalk on the network. What kind of cabling did the company install?

   A. Coaxial

   B. Shielded coaxial

   C. Unshielded twisted pair

   D. Fiber-optic

3. Jill needs to run some UTP cable from one office to another. She found a box of cable in the closet and wants to make sure it's CAT 5 or better. How can she tell the CAT level of the cable? (Select two.)

   A. Check the box.

   B. Scan for markings on the cable.

   C. Check the color of the cable—gray means CAT 5, yellow means CAT 6e, and so on.

   D. Check the ends of the cable.

4. What topology provides the most fault tolerance?

   A. Bus

   B. Ring

   C. Star-bus

   D. Mesh

5. What organization is responsible for establishing and promoting networking standards?

   A. Institute of Electrical and Electronics Engineers (IEEE)

   B. International Networking Standards Organization (INSO)

   C. Federal Communications Commission (FCC)

   D. International Telecommunications Association (ITA)

6. What aspects of network cabling do the IEEE committees establish? (Select three.)

   A. Frame size

   B. Speed

   C. Color of sheathing

   D. Cable types

7. What types of coax cabling have been used in computer networking? (Select three.)

   A. RG-8

   B. RG-45

   C. RG-58

   D. RG-62

8. What applications are best suited for fiber-optic cabling? (Select two.)

   A. Short distances

   B. Wireless networks

   C. High-EMI areas

   D. Long distances

9. What are the main components of fiber-optic cabling? (Select three.)

   A. Cladding

   B. Insulating jacket

   C. Copper core

   D. Fiber

10. What is the most popular size fiber-optic cabling?

    A. 62.5/125 μm

    B. 125/62.5 μm

    C. 50/125 μm

    D. 125/50 μm

11. Most fiber-optic installations use LEDs to send light signals and are known as what?

    A. Single-mode

    B. Multimode

    C. Complex mode

    D. Duplex mode

12. Why must the main cable in a bus topology be terminated at both ends?

   A. To allow the signal to be amplified so it can reach both ends of the network

   B. To prevent the signal from dropping off the network before reaching all computers

   C. To prevent the signal from bouncing back and forth

   D. To convert the signal to the proper format for a bus network

13. Where are you most likely to encounter a mesh network?

   A. On any network using fiber-optic cable

   B. On any network using plenum cable

   C. On wireless networks

   D. On wired networks

14. You are asked by your boss to research upgrading all the network cable in your office building. The building manager requires the safest possible cabling type in case of fire, and your boss wants to future-proof the network so cabling doesn't need to be replaced when network technologies faster than 1 Gbps come on the market. You decide to use CAT 5e plenum cabling throughout the building. Which objective have you satisfied?

   A. Neither the building manager's nor your boss's requirements have been met.

   B. Only the building manager's requirement has been met.

   C. Only your boss's requirement has been met.

   D. Both the building manager's and your boss's requirements have been met.

15. Which committee is responsible for wireless networking standards?

   A. IEEE 802.2

   B. IEEE 802.3

   C. IEEE 802.5

   D. IEEE 802.11

■ Essay Quiz

1. You work in the computer training department at your company. A newly developed mobile training program is being planned. The plan requires setting up in a particular department five training computers you use to train on weekly. Write a short essay that describes which network topology would be quickest to set up and tear down for this type of onsite training.

2. Your boss has decided to have cable run to every computer in the office, but doesn't know which type to use. In an effort to help bring the company into the 21st century, write a short essay comparing the merits of UTP and fiber-optic cabling.

3. The NICs on your company's computers all have dual 10-Mbps and 100-Mbps capability, yet users complain that the network is slow. Write a brief essay that explains what could be the cause of the problem.

4. Your company has hired a group of new network techs, and you've been tasked to do their training session on networking standards organizations. Write a brief essay detailing the IEEE and its various committees.

Lab Projects

• Lab Project 3.1

This lab project requires you to demonstrate knowledge of the four basic network topologies. Obtain four blank pieces of paper. Proceed to draw six boxes on each page to represent six computers—neatness counts! At the top of each sheet, write one of the following: bus topology, mesh topology, ring topology, or star topology. Then draw lines to represent the physical network cabling required by each network topology.

• Lab Project 3.2

In your studies of network cabling for the CompTIA Network+ certification exam, you realize you could use a simplified chart to study from and memorize. Build a reference study chart that describes the features of network cabling. Create your completed chart using a spreadsheet program, or simply a sheet of paper, with the column headings and names shown in this table. If you wish, you can start by writing your notes here.

Cable Type	Description	Benefits	Drawbacks
CAT 5			
CAT 5e			
CAT 6			
CAT 6a			
Fiber-optic			

• Lab Project 3.3

In this lab project, you will demonstrate knowledge of the different IEEE committees that are most prevalent today. Use the Internet to research each of these subcommittees: IEEE 802.3, IEEE 802.5, and IEEE 802.11. Give an example of where each type of technology might best be used.

Ethernet Basics

"In theory there is no difference between theory and practice. In practice there is."

—YOGI BERRA

In this chapter, you will learn how to

- **Define and describe Ethernet**
- **Explain early Ethernet implementations**
- **Describe ways to extend and enhance Ethernet networks**

In the beginning, there were no networks. Computers were isolated, solitary islands of information in a teeming sea of proto-geeks who used clubs and wore fur pocket protectors. Okay, maybe it wasn't that bad, but if you wanted to move a file from one machine to another—and proto-geeks were as much into that as modern geeks—you had to use **Sneakernet**, which meant you saved the file on a disk, laced up your tennis shoes, and hiked over to the other system. All that walking no doubt produced lots of health benefits, but frankly, proto-geeks weren't all that into health benefits—they were into speed, power, and technological coolness in general. (Sound familiar?) It's no wonder, then, that geeks everywhere agreed on the need to replace Sneakernet with a faster and more efficient method of sharing data. The method they came up with is the subject of this chapter.

Historical/Conceptual

■ Ethernet

In 1973, Xerox answered the challenge of moving data without sneakers by developing **Ethernet**, a networking technology standard based on a bus topology. The Ethernet standard dominates today's networks and defines all of the issues involved in transferring data between computer systems. The original Ethernet used a single piece of coaxial cable in a bus topology to connect several computers, enabling them to transfer data at a rate of up to 3 Mbps. Although slow by today's standards, this early version of Ethernet was a huge improvement over Sneakernet methods and served as the foundation for all later versions of Ethernet.

Ethernet remained a largely in-house technology within Xerox until 1979, when Xerox decided to look for partners to help promote Ethernet as an industry standard. Xerox worked with Digital Equipment Corporation (DEC) and Intel to publish what became known as the Digital-Intel-Xerox (DIX) standard. Running on coaxial cable, the DIX standard enabled multiple computers to communicate with each other at a screaming 10 Mbps. Although 10 Mbps represents the low end of standard network speeds today, at the time it was revolutionary. These companies then transferred control of the Ethernet standard to the IEEE, which, in turn, created the **802.3 (Ethernet)** committee that continues to control the Ethernet standard to this day.

Ethernet's designers faced the same challenges as the designers of any network: how to send data across the wire, how to identify the sending and receiving computers, and how to determine which computer should use the shared cable at what time. The engineers resolved these issues by using data frames that contain MAC addresses to identify computers on the network and by using a process called CSMA/CD (discussed shortly) to determine which machine should access the wire at any given time. You saw some of this in action in Chapter 2, but now I need to introduce you to a bunch of new terms, so let's look at each of these solutions.

Tech Tip

IEEE

The source for all things Ethernet is but a short click away on the Internet. For starters, check out www.ieee802.org.

Tech Tip

Defining Ethernet

Providing a clear and concise definition of Ethernet has long been one of the major challenges in teaching networking. This difficulty stems from the fact that Ethernet has changed over the years to incorporate new and improved technology. Most folks won't even try to define Ethernet, but here's my best attempt at a current definition.

Ethernet is a standard for a family of network technologies that share the same basic bus topology, frame type, and network access method. Because the technologies share these essential components, you can communicate between them just fine. The implementation of the network might be different, but the frames remain the same. This is true for Ethernet running on a physical bus topology—the ancient 10Base5 and 10Base2—and a logical bus topology—10BaseT and later.

Topology

Every version of Ethernet invented since the early 1990s uses a hybrid star-bus topology. At the center of these early networks was a **hub**. A hub is nothing more than an electronic **repeater**—it interprets the ones and zeroes coming in from one port and repeats the same signal out to the other connected ports. Hubs do not send the same signal back down the port that originally sent it (Figure 4.1). Repeaters are not amplifiers! They read the incoming signal and send new copies of that signal out to every connected port on the hub.

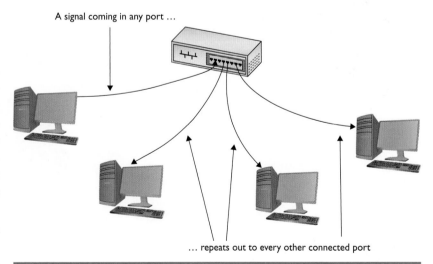
A signal coming in any port ...

... repeats out to every other connected port

• **Figure 4.1**   Ethernet hub

Test Specific

Ethernet Frames

All network technologies break data transmitted between computers into smaller pieces called **frames**, as you'll recall from Chapter 2. Using frames addresses two networking issues. First, frames prevent any single machine from monopolizing the shared bus cable. Second, they make the process of retransmitting lost data more efficient.

The process you saw in Chapter 2 of transferring a word processing document between two computers illustrates these two issues. First, if the sending computer sends the document as a single huge frame, the frame will monopolize the cable and prevent other machines from using the cable until the entire file gets to the receiving system. Using relatively small frames enables computers to share the cable easily—each computer listens on the **segment**, sending a few frames of data whenever it detects that no other computer is transmitting. Second, in the real world, bad things can happen to good data. When errors occur during transmission, the sending system must retransmit the frames that failed to get to the receiving system in good shape. If a word processing document were transmitted as a single massive frame, the sending system would have to retransmit the entire frame—in this case, the entire document. Breaking the file up into smaller frames enables the sending computer to retransmit only the damaged frames. Because of these benefits—shared access and more efficient retransmission—all networking technologies use frames, and Ethernet is no exception to that rule.

In Chapter 2, you saw a generic frame. Let's take what you know of frames and expand on that knowledge by inspecting the details of an Ethernet frame. A basic Ethernet frame contains six pieces of information: the MAC address of the frame's recipient, the MAC address of the sending system, the type of the data, the data itself, a pad (if needed), and a frame check sequence. Appended to the front of the frame is the preamble. Figure 4.2 shows these components.

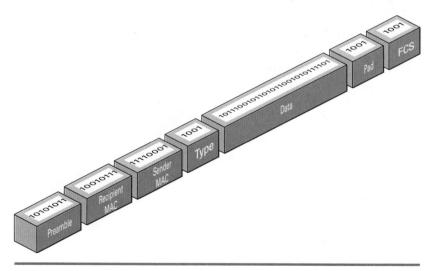

• **Figure 4.2** Ethernet frame

Preamble

All Ethernet frames begin with a **preamble**, a 7-byte series of alternating ones and zeroes followed by a 1-byte Start Frame. The preamble gives a receiving NIC time to realize a frame is coming and to know exactly where the frame starts. The preamble is added by the sending NIC.

The CompTIA Network+ exam might describe MAC addresses as 48-bit binary addresses or 6-byte binary addresses.

MAC Addresses

Each NIC, often referred to as a **node**, on an Ethernet network must have a unique identifying address. Ethernet identifies the NICs on a network using special 48-bit (6-byte) binary addresses known as **MAC addresses**.

 Cross Check

NICs and OSI

You learned about NICs and MAC addresses in Chapter 2, so check your memory with these questions. Where does the NIC get its MAC address? How does the MAC address manifest on the card? At what layer or layers of the OSI seven-layer model does the NIC operate?

MAC addresses give each NIC a unique address. When a computer sends out a data frame, it goes into the hub. The hub repeats an exact copy of that frame to every connected port, as shown in Figure 4.3. All the other computers on the network listen to the wire and examine the frame to see if it contains their MAC address. If it does not, they ignore the frame. If a machine sees a frame with its MAC address, it opens the frame and begins processing the data.

This system of allowing each machine to decide which frames it will process may be efficient, but because any device connected to the network cable can potentially capture any data frame transmitted across the wire, Ethernet networks carry a significant security vulnerability. Network diagnostic programs, commonly called **sniffers**, can order a NIC to run in **promiscuous mode**. When running in promiscuous mode, the NIC processes all the frames it sees on the cable, regardless of their MAC addresses. Sniffers are valuable troubleshooting tools in the right hands, but Ethernet provides no protections against their unscrupulous use.

There are many situations in which one computer might have two or more NICs, so one physical system might represent more than one node.

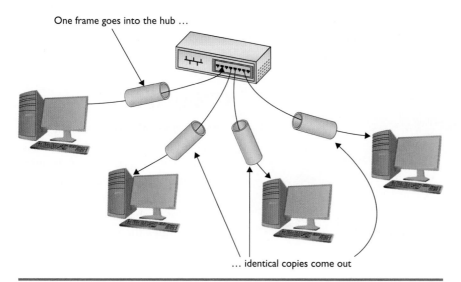

One frame goes into the hub ...

... identical copies come out

• **Figure 4.3**   Frames propagating on a network

Type

An Ethernet frame may carry one of several types of data. The Type field helps the receiving computer interpret the frame contents at a very basic level. This way the receiving computer can tell if the frame contains IPv4 data, for example, or IPv6 data. (See Chapter 7 for more details on IPv4; I cover IPv6 in Chapter 8.)

The Type field does *not* tell you if the frame carries higher-level data, such as an e-mail message or Web page. You have to dig deeper into the data section of the frame to find that information.

Data

The data part of the frame contains whatever payload the frame carries. If the frame carries an IP packet, that packet will include extra information, such as the IP addresses of both systems.

Pad

The minimum Ethernet frame is 64 bytes in size, but not all of that has to be actual data. If an Ethernet frame has fewer than 64 bytes of data to haul, the sending NIC will automatically add extra data—a **pad**—to bring the data up to the minimum 64 bytes.

Frame Check Sequence

The **frame check sequence (FCS)** enables Ethernet nodes to recognize when bad things happen to good data. Machines on a network must be able to detect when data has been damaged in transit. To detect errors, the computers on an Ethernet network attach a special code to each frame. When creating an Ethernet frame, the sending machine runs the data through a special mathematical formula and attaches the result, the frame check sequence, to the frame. The receiving machine opens the frame, performs the same calculation, and compares its answer with the one included with the frame. If the answers do not match, the receiving machine asks the sending machine to retransmit that frame.

At this point, those crafty network engineers have solved two of the problems facing them: they've created frames to organize the data to be sent, and put in place MAC addresses to identify machines on the network. But the challenge of determining which machine should send data at which time requires another solution: CSMA/CD.

> CSMA/CD is a network access method that maps to the IEEE 802.3 standard for Ethernet networks.

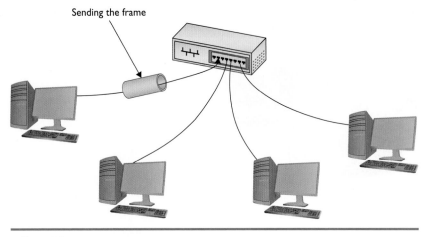

Sending the frame

• Figure 4.4   No one else is talking—send the frame!

CSMA/CD

Ethernet networks use a system called **carrier sense multiple access/collision detection (CSMA/CD)** to determine which computer should use a shared cable at a given moment. *Carrier sense* means that each node using the network examines the cable before sending a data frame (Figure 4.4). If another machine is using the network, the node detects traffic on the segment, waits a few milliseconds, and then rechecks.

If it detects no traffic—the more common term is to say the cable is "free"—the node sends out its frame.

Multiple access means that all machines have equal access to the wire. If the line is free, any Ethernet node may begin sending a frame. From Ethernet's point of view, it doesn't matter what function the node is performing: it could be a desktop system running Windows 8 or a high-end file server running Windows Server or Linux. As far as Ethernet is concerned, a node is a node is a node and access to the cable is assigned strictly on a first-come, first-served basis.

So what happens if two machines, both listening to the cable, simultaneously decide that it is free and try to send a frame? A collision occurs, and both of the transmissions are lost (Figure 4.5). A collision resembles the effect of two people talking at the same time: the listener hears a mixture of two voices and can't understand either one.

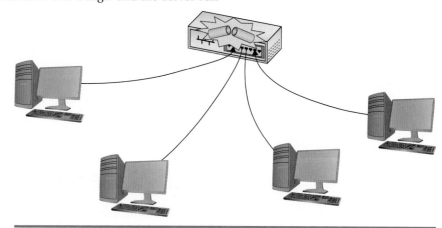

• **Figure 4.5**   Collision!

It's easy for NICs to notice a collision. When two NICs send at the same time, the hub sends out the overlapping signals, and the NICs immediately know that a collision has occurred. When they detect a collision, both nodes immediately stop transmitting.

They then each generate a random number to determine how long to wait before trying again. If you imagine that each machine rolls its magic electronic dice and waits for that number of seconds, you wouldn't be too far from the truth, except that the amount of time an Ethernet node waits to retransmit is much shorter than one second (Figure 4.6). Whichever node generates the lowest random number begins its retransmission first, winning the competition to use the wire. The losing node then sees traffic on the wire and waits for the wire to be free again before attempting to retransmit its data.

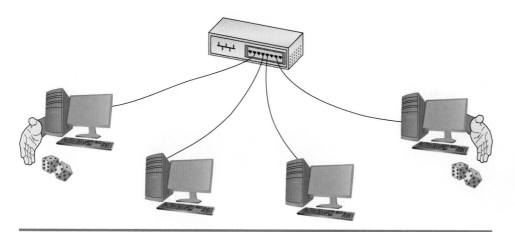

• **Figure 4.6**   Rolling for timing

Collisions are a normal part of the operation of an Ethernet network. Every Ethernet network wastes some amount of its available bandwidth dealing with these collisions. A properly running average Ethernet network has a maximum of 10 percent collisions. For every 20 frames sent, approximately 2 frames will collide and require a resend. Collision rates greater than 10 percent often point to damaged NICs or out-of-control software.

In an Ethernet network, a **collision domain** is a group of nodes that have the capability of sending frames at the same time as each other, resulting in collisions. A segment is certainly a collision domain, but there are ways to connect segments to create larger collision domains. If the collision domain gets too large, you'll start running into traffic problems that manifest as general network sluggishness. That's one of the reasons to break up networks into smaller groupings.

■ Early Ethernet Networks

Now we have the answers to many of the questions that faced those early Ethernet designers. MAC addresses identify each machine on the network. CSMA/CD determines when each machine should have access to the cable. But all this remains in the realm of theory—you still need to build the thing! Contemplating the physical network brings up numerous questions. What kind of cables should you use? What should they be made of? How long can they be? For these answers, turn to the IEEE 802.3 standard, both true bus and star bus versions.

Bus Ethernet

The original Ethernet networks employed a true bus topology, meaning every computer on a network connected to the same cable, the bus. In a Thicknet (10Base5) network, for example, devices tapped directly into a thick yellow cable that snaked throughout the network. Figure 4.7 shows a vampire tap used to pierce a Thicknet cable. Barbaric, but these networks worked.

The last true bus Ethernet standard, called **10Base2** or **Thinnet**, fudged on the single wire concept by having wires connect at a NIC into a **T connector** (Figure 4.8). The T connector enabled the bus to carry a single electrical signal that connected every device on the network.

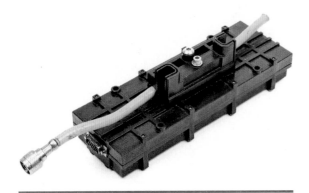

• **Figure 4.7**   Thicknet vampire tap

• **Figure 4.8**   10Base2 T connector in action

10Base2 networks—some are still in use today—use **RG-58** coaxial cable with **BNC connectors** on the end. The complete network is limited to 185 meters.

The big quirk with bus networks involves the signal. The ends of the bus *have* to be terminated, otherwise the signal reflects and the whole network goes down. Figure 4.9 shows a T connector connected to a BNC connector on one side and a terminating resistor on the other.

• **Figure 4.9** Terminating resistors and T connector

If you ever run into an installation where you have to support 10Base2, just remember to terminate the ends of the cable, the ends of the bus.

10BaseT

In 1990, the IEEE 802.3 committee created a new version of Ethernet called **10BaseT** to modernize the first generations of Ethernet. Very quickly 10BaseT became the most popular network technology in the world, replacing competing and now long-gone competitors with names like Token Ring and Apple-Talk. Over 99 percent of all networks use 10BaseT or one of its faster, newer, but very similar versions. The classic 10BaseT network consists of two or more computers connected to a central hub. The NICs connect with wires as specified by the 802.3 committee.

10BaseT hubs come in a variety of shapes and sizes to support different sizes of networks. The biggest differentiator between hubs is the number of **ports** (connections) that a single hub provides. A small hub might have only 4 ports, whereas a hub for a large network might have 48 ports. As you can imagine, the more ports on a hub, the more expensive the hub. Figure 4.10 shows two hubs. On the top is a small, 8-port hub for small offices or the home. It rests on a 12-port rack-mount hub for larger networks.

• **Figure 4.10** Two 10BaseT hubs

Regardless of size, all 10BaseT hubs need electrical power. Larger hubs will take power directly from a power outlet, whereas smaller hubs often come with an AC adapter. In either case, if the hub loses power, the entire segment will stop working.

 If you ever run into a situation on a 10BaseT or later network in which none of the computers can get on the network, always check the hub first!

✓ **Cross Check**

Physical vs. Logical

You might be tempted at this moment to define 10BaseT in terms of physical topology versus logical topology—after all, 10BaseT uses a physical star, but a logical bus. Refer to Chapter 3, however, and cross-check your memory. What's a physical topology? And a logical topology? What would you say if you walked into an office building that implemented a 10BaseT network? Yes, if you actually *walked into* it, you'd probably say "Ouch!" But beyond that, think about how you would describe the wires and connectors you would see in terms of physical or logical topology.

The names of two earlier physical bus versions of Ethernet, 10Base5 and 10Base2, gave the maximum length of the bus. 10Base5 networks could be up to 500 meters long, for example, whereas 10Base2 topped out at 185 meters. (What, you were expecting 200 meters?)

The name 10BaseT follows roughly the same naming convention used for earlier Ethernet cabling systems. The number *10* refers to the speed: 10 Mbps. The word *Base* refers to the signaling type: baseband. (*Baseband* means that the cable only carries one type of signal. Contrast this with *broadband*—as in cable television—where the cable carries multiple signals or channels.) The letter *T* refers to the type of cable used: twisted-pair. 10BaseT uses unshielded twisted-pair (UTP) cabling.

UTP

Officially, 10BaseT requires the use of CAT 3 (or higher), two-pair, unshielded twisted-pair (UTP) cable. One pair of wires sends data to the hub while the other pair receives data from the hub. Even though 10BaseT only requires two-pair cabling, everyone installs four-pair cabling to connect devices to the hub as insurance against the possible requirements of newer types of networking (Figure 4.11). Most UTP cables come with stranded Kevlar fibers to give the cable added strength, which, in turn, enables installers to pull on the cable without excessive risk of literally ripping it apart.

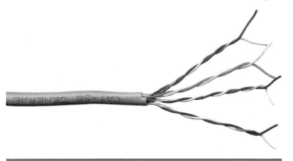

• **Figure 4.11**　A typical four-pair CAT 5e unshielded twisted-pair cable

10BaseT also introduced the networking world to the **RJ-45 connector** (Figure 4.12). Each pin on the RJ-45 connects to a single wire inside the cable; this enables devices to put voltage on the individual wires within the cable. The pins on the RJ-45 are numbered from 1 to 8, as shown in Figure 4.13.

The 10BaseT standard designates some of these numbered wires for specific purposes. As mentioned earlier, although the cable has four pairs, 10BaseT uses only two of the pairs. 10BaseT devices use pins 1 and 2 to send data, and pins 3 and 6 to receive data. Even though one pair of wires sends data and another receives data, a 10BaseT device connected to a hub cannot send and receive simultaneously. The

Cross Check

Check Your CATs!

You've already seen CAT levels in Chapter 3, so check your memory and review the different speeds of the various CAT levels. Could 10BaseT use CAT 2? Could it use CAT 6? What types of devices can use CAT 1?

• **Figure 4.12**　Two views of an RJ-45 connector

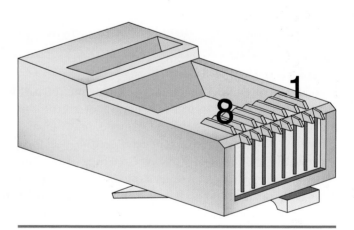

• **Figure 4.13**　The pins on an RJ-45 connector are numbered 1 through 8.

rules of CSMA/CD still apply: only one device can use the segment contained in the hub without causing a collision.

NICs that can communicate in only one direction at a time run in **half-duplex** mode. Later advances (as you'll see shortly) enabled NICs to send and receive at the same time, thus running in **full-duplex** mode.

An RJ-45 connector is usually called a *crimp*, and the act (some folks call it an art) of installing a crimp onto the end of a piece of UTP cable is called *crimping*. The tool used to secure a crimp onto the end of a cable is a *crimper*. Each wire inside a UTP cable must connect to the proper pin inside the crimp. Manufacturers color-code each wire within a piece of four-pair UTP to assist in properly matching the ends. Each pair of wires consists of a solid-colored wire and a striped wire: blue/blue-white, orange/orange-white, brown/brown-white, and green/green-white (Figure 4.14).

The Telecommunications Industry Association/Electronics Industries Alliance (TIA/EIA) defines the industry standard for correct crimping of four-pair UTP for 10BaseT networks. Two standards currently exist: **TIA/EIA 568A** and **TIA/EIA 568B**. Figure 4.15 shows the TIA/EIA 568A and TIA/EIA 568B color-code standards. Note that the wire pairs used by 10BaseT (1 and 2, 3 and 6) come from the same color pairs (green/green-white and orange/orange-white). Following an established color-code scheme, such as TIA/EIA 568A, ensures that the wires match up correctly at each end of the cable.

The ability to make your own Ethernet cables is a real plus for a network tech. With a reel of CAT 5e, a bag of RJ-45 connectors, a moderate investment in a crimping tool, and a little practice, you can kiss those mass-produced cables goodbye! You can make cables to your own length specifications, replace broken RJ-45 connectors that would otherwise mean tossing an entire cable—and, in the process, save your company or clients time and money.

 The real name for RJ-45 is "8 Position 8 Contact (8P8C) modular plug." The term RJ-45 is so prevalent, however, that nobody but the nerdiest of nerds calls it by its real name. Stick to RJ-45.

 TIA/EIA 568C, the current standard, includes the same wiring standards as TIA/EIA 568A and TIA/EIA 568B. It's all just wrapped up in a new name: *ANSI/TIA-568-C*. When the EIA left the planet in 2011, the names of the standards changed. CompTIA continues to use the older name on exams.

Tech Tip

568A and 568B
An easy trick to remembering the difference between 568A and 568B is the word "GO." The green and orange pairs are swapped between 568A and 568B, whereas the blue and brown pairs stay in the same place!

 For the CompTIA Network+ exam, you will be tested on the TIA/EIA 568A or 568B color codes. Memorize them.
You'll see the standards listed as EIA/TIA 568A, TIA/EIA 568A, T568A, or just 568A. Know the A and B and you'll be fine.

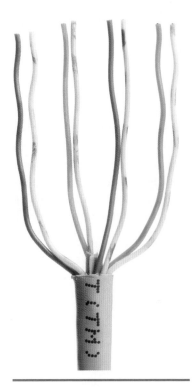

• **Figure 4.14**   Color-coded pairs

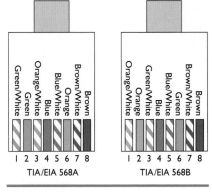

• **Figure 4.15**   The TIA/EIA 568A and 568B standards

10BaseT Limits and Specifications

Like any other Ethernet cabling system, 10BaseT has limitations, both on cable distance and on the number of computers. The key distance limitation for 10BaseT is the distance between the hub and the computer. The twisted-pair cable connecting a computer to the hub may not exceed 100 meters in length. A 10BaseT hub can connect no more than 1024 computers, although that limitation rarely comes into play. It makes no sense for vendors to build hubs that large—or more to the point, that *expensive*—because excessive collisions can easily bog down Ethernet performance with far fewer than 1024 computers.

10BaseT Summary

- **Speed** 10 Mbps
- **Signal type** Baseband
- **Distance** 100 meters between the hub and the node
- **Node limit** No more than 1024 nodes per hub
- **Topology** Star-bus topology: physical star, logical bus
- **Cable type** CAT 3 or better UTP cabling with RJ-45 connectors

 Check out the Chapter 4 Challenge! sim "T-568B" at http://totalsem.com/006. It's a great tool for getting the colors set in your head.

 10BaseFL is often simply called "10BaseF."

10BaseFL

Just a few years after the introduction of 10BaseT, a fiber-optic version, called **10BaseFL**, appeared. As you know from the previous chapter, fiber-optic cabling transmits data packets using pulses of light instead of using electrical current. Using light instead of electricity addresses the three key weaknesses of copper cabling. First, optical signals can travel much farther. The maximum length for a 10BaseFL cable is up to 2 kilometers, depending on how you configure it.

Second, fiber-optic cable is immune to electrical interference, making it an ideal choice for high-interference environments. Third, the cable is much more difficult to tap into, making it a good choice for environments with security concerns. 10BaseFL uses **multimode** fiber-optic and employs either an SC or an ST connector.

Figure 4.16 shows a typical 10BaseFL card. Note that it uses two fiber connectors—one to send and one to receive. All fiber-optic networks use at least two fiber-optic cables. Although 10BaseFL enjoyed some popularity for a number of years, most networks today are using the same fiber-optic cabling to run far faster network technologies.

10BaseFL Summary

- **Speed** 10 Mbps
- **Signal type** Baseband
- **Distance** 2000 meters between the hub and the node
- **Node limit** No more than 1024 nodes per hub

• **Figure 4.16** Typical 10BaseFL card

- **Topology**   Star-bus topology: physical star, logical bus
- **Cable type**   Multimode fiber-optic cabling with ST or SC connectors

So far you've seen two different flavors of star bus Ethernet, 10BaseT and 10BaseFL. Even though these use different cabling and hubs, the actual packets are still Ethernet frames. As a result, interconnecting flavors of Ethernet is common. Because 10BaseT and 10BaseFL use different types of cable, you can use a media converter (Figure 4.17) to interconnect different Ethernet types.

Extending and Enhancing Ethernet Networks

Once you have an Ethernet network in place, you can extend or enhance that network in several ways. You can install additional hubs to connect multiple local area networks, for example. A network bridge can connect two Ethernet networks. You can also replace the hubs with better devices to reduce collisions.

Couplers

You can easily extend an Ethernet segment by using a connection device called a *coupler*. The couplers—female connectors on both ends (Figure 4.18)—enable you to connect a machine in a location not originally envisioned when a network was installed. These simple connectors make working with older networks a snap. You can find couplers of all stripes: BNC couplers, UTP couplers, and so on. Get the one for the network you support.

Connecting Ethernet Segments

Sometimes, one hub is just not enough. Once an organization uses every port on its existing hub, adding more nodes requires adding hubs or a device called a bridge. Even fault tolerance can motivate an organization to add more hubs. If every node on the network connects to the same hub, that hub becomes a single point of failure—if it fails, everybody drops off the network. You can connect hubs in two ways: via an uplink port or a crossover cable. You can also connect Ethernet segments using a bridge.

Uplink Ports

Uplink ports enable you to connect two hubs using a straight-through cable. They're always clearly marked on the hub, as shown in Figure 4.19. To connect two hubs, insert one end of a cable to the uplink and the other cable to any one

• **Figure 4.17**   Typical copper-to-fiber Ethernet media converter (photo courtesy of TRENDnet)

• **Figure 4.18**   A BNC coupler

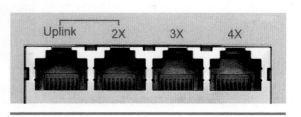

• **Figure 4.19**   Typical uplink port

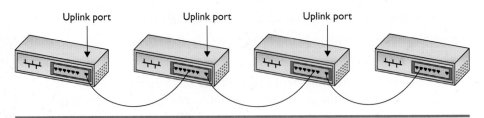

Uplink port   Uplink port   Uplink port

• **Figure 4.20**   Daisy-chained hubs

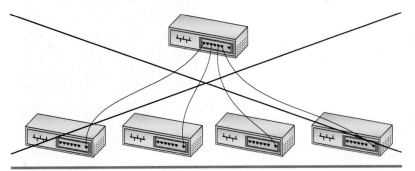

• **Figure 4.21**   A hierarchical hub configuration will not work!

of the regular ports. To connect more than two hubs, you must daisy-chain your hubs by using one uplink port and one regular port. Figure 4.20 shows properly daisy-chained hubs.

You cannot use a single central hub and connect multiple hubs to that single hub, as shown in Figure 4.21. It simply won't work.

Working with uplink ports is sometimes tricky, so you need to take your time. Messing up and using a central hub is easy. Hub makers give their uplink ports many different names, such as crossover, MDI-X, and OUT. There are also tricks to using uplink ports. Refer to Figure 4.19 again. See the line connecting the uplink port and the port labeled 2X? You may use only one of those two ports, not both at the same time. Additionally, some hubs place a switch on one of the ports; you press this switch to make it either a regular port or an uplink port (Figure 4.22). Pressing the button electronically reverses the wires inside the hub.

When connecting hubs, remember the following:

■ You can only daisy-chain hubs.

■ Take time to figure out the uplink ports.

■ If you plug hubs in incorrectly, no damage will occur—they just won't work.

Two terms you might see on hubs and switches and, consequently, on the exams are MDI and MDIX. A *media dependent interface (MDI)* is a regular port on a hub or switch. A *media dependent interface crossover (MDIX)* is an uplink port.

Crossover Cables

Hubs can also connect to each other via special twisted-pair cables called crossover cables. A standard cable cannot be used to connect two hubs without using an uplink port because both hubs will attempt to send data on the second pair of wires (3 and 6) and will listen for data on the first pair (1 and 2).

• **Figure 4.22**   Press-button port

• **Figure 4.23** A crossover cable reverses the sending and receiving pairs.

The CompTIA Network+ objectives compare three types of copper cables: straight-through vs. crossover vs. rollover. The first two you should have now, right? Straight-through uses the same standard for the RJ-45 on both ends; crossover uses 568A on one end and 568B on the other.

A *rollover cable* has an RJ-45 on one end and a class RS-232 serial port on the other. They're used to connect a laptop or other computer directly to a Cisco switch or router. A rollover cable, therefore, is completely different from the other two.

You'll see rollover cables in Chapter 8, "Routing," and the discussion of managed devices. Don't get fooled on the exam if rollover is added as possible answer for connecting computers.

A **crossover cable** reverses the sending and receiving pairs on one end of the cable. One end of the cable is wired according to the TIA/EIA 568A standard, whereas the other end is wired according to the TIA/EIA 568B standard (Figure 4.23). With the sending and receiving pairs reversed, the hubs can hear each other; hence the need for two standards for connecting RJ-45 jacks to UTP cables.

A crossover cable connects to a regular port on each hub. Keep in mind that you can still daisy-chain even when you use crossover cables. Interestingly, many hubs, especially higher-end hubs, do not come with any uplink ports at all. In these cases, your only option is to use a crossover cable.

In a pinch, you can use a crossover cable to connect two computers together using 10BaseT NICs with no hub between them at all. This is handy for quickie connections, such as for a nice little home network or when you absolutely, positively must chase down a friend in a computer game!

Be careful not to confuse crossover cables with uplink ports. First, never connect two hubs by their uplink ports with a straight-through cable. Take a straight-through cable; connect one end to the uplink port on one hub and the other end to any regular port on the other hub. Second, if you use a crossover cable, just plug each end into any handy regular port on each hub.

Bridges

The popularity and rapid implementation of Ethernet networks demanded solutions or workarounds for the limitations inherent in the technology. An Ethernet segment could only be so long and connect a certain number of computers. What if your network went beyond those limitations?

A **bridge** acts like a repeater or hub to connect two Ethernet networks, but it goes one step beyond—filtering and forwarding traffic between those segments based on the MAC addresses of the computers on those segments. This preserves precious bandwidth and makes a larger Ethernet network possible. To *filter* traffic means to stop it from crossing from one network to

Tech Tip

Crossing Crossovers

If you mess up your crossover connections, you won't cause any damage, but the connection will not work. Think about it. If you take a straight-through cable (that is, not a crossover cable) and try to connect two PCs directly, it won't work. Both PCs will try to use the same send and receive wires. When you plug the two PCs into a hub, the hub electronically crosses the data wires, so one NIC sends and the other can receive. If you plug a second hub to the first hub using regular ports, you essentially cross the cross and create a straight connection again between the two PCs! That won't work. Luckily, nothing gets hurt—except your reputation if one of your colleagues notes your mistake.

Try This!

Examine Your Uplink Ports

Although most hubs come with uplink ports, they all seem to have different ways to use them. Some hubs have dedicated uplink ports, and some have uplink ports that convert to regular ports at the press of a button. Take a look at some hubs and try to figure out how you would use an uplink port to connect it to another hub.

the next; to *forward* traffic means to pass traffic originating on one side of the bridge to the other.

A newly installed Ethernet bridge initially behaves exactly like a repeater, passing frames from one segment to another. Unlike a repeater, however, a bridge monitors and records the network traffic, eventually reaching a point where it can begin to filter and forward. This capability makes the bridge more "intelligent" than a repeater. A new bridge usually requires only a few seconds to gather enough information to start filtering and forwarding.

Although bridges offer a good solution for connecting two segments and reducing bandwidth usage, these days you'll mainly find bridges used in wireless, rather than wired, networks. (I cover those kinds of bridges in Chapter 15.) Most networks have now turned to a different magic box—a switch—to extend and enhance an Ethernet network.

Switched Ethernet

While plain-vanilla 10BaseT Ethernet performed well enough for first-generation networks (which did little more than basic file and print sharing), by the early 1990s networks used more-demanding applications, such as Lotus Notes, SAP business management software, and Microsoft Exchange, which quickly saturated a 10BaseT network. Fortunately, those crazy kids over at the IEEE kept expanding the standard, giving the network tech in the trenches a new tool that provided additional bandwidth—the switch.

The Trouble with Hubs

A classic 10BaseT network with a hub can only have one message on the wire at any time. When two computers send at the same time, the hub dutifully repeats both signals. The nodes recognize the collision and, following the rules of CSMA/CD, attempt to resend. Add in enough computers and the number of collisions increases, lowering the effective transmission speed for the whole network. A busy network becomes a slow network because all the computers share the same collision domain.

Switches to the Rescue

An Ethernet **switch** looks like a hub, because all nodes plug into it (Figure 4.24). But switches don't function like hubs inside. Switches come with extra smarts that enable them to take advantage of MAC addresses, effectively creating point-to-point connections between two conversing computers. This gives every conversation between two computers the full bandwidth of the network.

• **Figure 4.24**   Hub (top) and switch (bottom) comparison

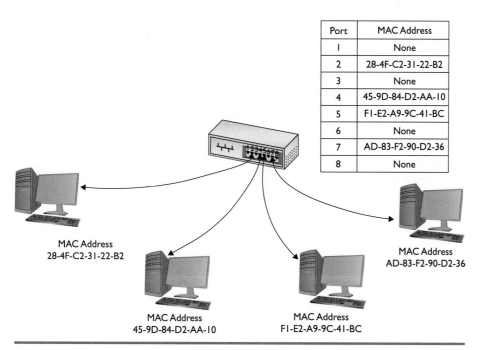

Port	MAC Address
1	None
2	28-4F-C2-31-22-B2
3	None
4	45-9D-84-D2-AA-10
5	F1-E2-A9-9C-41-BC
6	None
7	AD-83-F2-90-D2-36
8	None

MAC Address
28-4F-C2-31-22-B2

MAC Address
AD-83-F2-90-D2-36

MAC Address
45-9D-84-D2-AA-10

MAC Address
F1-E2-A9-9C-41-BC

• **Figure 4.25**   A switch tracking MAC addresses

To see a switch in action, check out Figure 4.25. When you first turn on a switch, it acts exactly as though it were a hub, passing all incoming frames right back out to all the other ports. As it forwards all frames, however, the switch copies the source MAC addresses and quickly creates an electronic table of the MAC addresses of each connected computer. The table is called a **Source Address Table (SAT)**.

As soon as this table is created, the switch begins to do something amazing. When a computer sends a frame into the switch destined for another computer on the same switch, the switch acts like a telephone operator, creating an on-the-fly connection between the two devices. While these two devices communicate, it's as though they are the only two computers on the network. Figure 4.26 shows this in action. Because the switch handles each conversation individually, each conversation runs at 10 Mbps.

 One classic difference between a hub and a switch is in the repeating of frames during normal use. Although it's true that switches initially forward all frames, they filter by MAC address in regular use. Hubs never learn and always forward all frames.

10 Mbps

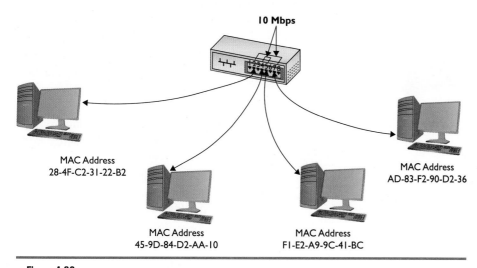

MAC Address
28-4F-C2-31-22-B2

MAC Address
AD-83-F2-90-D2-36

MAC Address
45-9D-84-D2-AA-10

MAC Address
F1-E2-A9-9C-41-BC

• **Figure 4.26**   A switch making two separate connections

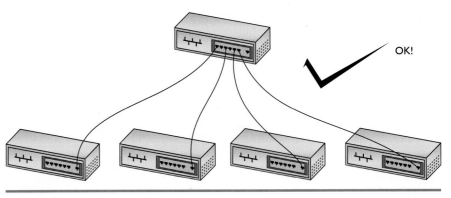

OK!

• **Figure 4.27**   Switches are very commonly connected in a tree organization.

Each port on a switch is in its own collision domain, plus the switch can buffer incoming frames. That means that two nodes connected to the switch can send data at the same time and the switch will handle it without any collision.

With half-duplex switches, collisions can occur and the rules of CSMA/CD apply. These collisions can only happen between the switch and a node, not between two nodes, if the switch tries to send a frame to a node at the same time as the node tries to send a frame to the switch.

Network developers eventually figured out how to make switches and NICs run in full-duplex mode, so they could send and receive data at the same time. With full-duplex Ethernet, CSMA/CD is disabled and no collisions can occur. Each node will always get the full bandwidth of the network.

With full-duplex switched Ethernet, you can ignore the old rules about daisy-chaining that applied to hubs. Feel free to connect your switches pretty much any way you wish (Figure 4.27).

Unicast messages always go only to the intended recipient when you use a switch. The switch will send all broadcast messages to all the ports. You'll commonly hear a switched network called a **broadcast domain** to contrast it to a hub-based network with its *collision domain*.

Spanning Tree Protocol

Because you can connect switches together in any fashion, you can create redundant connections in a network. These are called **bridging loops** (Figure 4.28).

In the early days of switches, making a bridging loop in a network setup would bring the network crashing down. A frame could get caught in the loop, so to speak, and not reach its destination.

The Ethernet standards body adopted the **Spanning Tree Protocol (STP)** to eliminate the problem of accidental bridge loops. Switches with STP enabled can detect loops, communicate with other switches, and set the looped port's state to blocking.

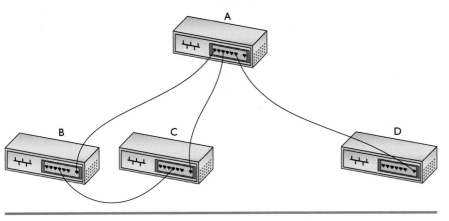

• **Figure 4.28**   A bridging loop

STP-enabled switches use a frame called a *Bridge Protocol Data Unit (BPDU)* to communicate with each other to determine things like the distances between them and to keep track of changes on the network.

When a change happens on the network, such as a switch getting replaced, the STP-enabled switches will receive frames from MAC addresses not contained in their MAC address table. At that point, they send out a query on every port to find the location of the new device, a process called *flooding*. Eventually, all the switches exchange information, update MAC address tables, set ports to *forwarding* or *blocking* traffic, and enter convergence, a stable state. At that point, the traffic to keep each switch up-to-date drops a lot.

Switches today all have STP enabled and network designers create bridging loops in their networks to provide fault tolerance. Ports set as blocking still listen to the traffic on the network. If a link fails, the blocking port can become a forwarding port, thus enabling traffic to flow properly.

The original Spanning Tree Protocol, introduced by IEEE as 802.1d, was replaced a long time ago (2001) by the Rapid Spanning Tree Protocol (RSTP), 802.1w. RSTP offers significantly faster convergence time following some kind of network change. STP could take up to 50 seconds to get back to a steady state, for example, whereas an RSTP network could return to convergence in 6 seconds.

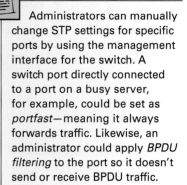
Administrators can manually change STP settings for specific ports by using the management interface for the switch. A switch port directly connected to a port on a busy server, for example, could be set as *portfast*—meaning it always forwards traffic. Likewise, an administrator could apply *BPDU filtering* to the port so it doesn't send or receive BPDU traffic.

Troubleshooting Hubs and Switches

The hubs and simple switches described in this chapter generally function flawlessly for years without any need for a tech to do more than wipe dust off the top. Very occasionally you'll run into a hub or switch that has problems. These problems fall into three categories:

- Obvious physical damage
- Dead ports
- General flakiness

Diagnosing any of these problems follows a similar pattern. First, you recognize that a hub or switch might have problems because a device you've plugged in can't connect to the network. Second, you examine the switch for obvious damage. Third, you look for link lights. If they're not flashing, try a different port. Fourth, you look at your cables. If anything looks bent, broken, or stepped on, you should replace it. A bad cable or improper cable type can lead to problems that point to a "failed" hub or switch when the true culprit is really the cable. Finally, you use the tried and true method of replacing the hub or switch or the cable with a known-good device.

When we get to modern higher-end switches in Chapter 12, you'll need to follow other procedures to do proper diagnostic work. We'll get there soon enough!

Chapter 4 Review

Chapter Summary

After reading this chapter and completing the exercises, you should understand the following about Ethernet.

Define and describe Ethernet

- Ethernet is based on a family of network technologies from a bus topology. Ethernet enables computers to send data across a network, identify sending and receiving computers, and determine which computer should use the cable at which time. Early Ethernet networks originally used a single coax cable as a physical bus.

- The IEEE 802.3 committee controls the Ethernet standard.

- Ethernet networks use a hybrid star-bus topology with a hub at the center. Hubs repeat the incoming signal to every connected port.

- Ethernet frames prevent any single computer from monopolizing the cable while making the retransmission of lost data efficient.

- Ethernet frames contain six basic parts: the MAC address of the destination computer, the MAC address of the sender, the type of data, the data itself, a pad, and a frame check sequence. Appended to the front of the frame is the preamble.

- CSMA/CD stands for carrier sense multiple access/collision detection. Carrier sense means that the node checks the network cable before sending to see if anyone else is transmitting. Multiple access means all computers have equal access to the network cable. Collision detection is when nodes detect that a transmission did not complete.

Explain early Ethernet implementations

- Early Ethernet networks used 10BaseT cabling.

- The physical topology of 10BaseT is a physical star; however, the data uses a logical bus topology with a central hub. Therefore, 10BaseT actually uses a hybrid star-bus topology to accomplish moving data frames through the network.

- 10BaseT supports speeds up to 10 Mbps over baseband.

- 10BaseT requires the use of CAT 3 or higher, two-pair, unshielded twisted-pair cable. These cables utilize RJ-45 connectors, which are crimped to the cable.

- Correct crimping follows either the TIA/EIA 568A or the TIA/EIA 568B color-code standard.

- A good network technician knows the limits and specifications of 10BaseT, such as the maximum speed and distance, maximum nodes per hub, and supported cabling types.

- 10BaseFL is a fiber-optic version of 10BaseT that uses multimode fiber-optic cable and SC or ST connectors. One major advantage of 10BaseFL is its increased maximum distance between hub and node.

Describe ways to extend and enhance Ethernet networks

- Because hubs act as repeaters, hubs can be used to connect multiple segments together. Most hubs also have a crossover port, sometimes labeled uplink, crossover, MDI-X, OUT, or another creative name.

- A crossover cable may be used to connect two hubs without an uplink port.

- A bridge filters and forwards traffic between Ethernet segments based on the MAC addresses of the computers on those segments. A bridge monitors and records the network traffic, eventually forwarding only the traffic that needs to go from one side of the bridge to the other. This helps reduce network bandwidth usage.

- Busy networks may suffer decreased bandwidth when using hubs. A switch solves this problem by managing the connection, based on MAC addresses, between the sending and receiving nodes.

- Switches break up collision domains. If full-duplex is used, collisions are eliminated and CSMA/CD is disabled.

- Connecting switches can lead to bridge loops, which caused early switched networks trouble. Switches that support the Spanning Tree Protocol are immune to bridge loops, even if wired in a physical loop.

- Hubs and switches fail from physical abuse or from electrical surges. Troubleshoot by checking link lights, trying different ports, or swapping out the hub, switch, or cable for a known-good replacement.

■ Key Terms

10Base2 *(68)*
10BaseFL *(72)*
10BaseT *(69)*
802.3 (Ethernet) *(63)*
BNC connector *(69)*
BNC coupler *(73)*
bridge *(75)*
bridging loop *(78)*
broadcast domain *(78)*
carrier sense multiple access/collision detection (CSMA/CD) *(66)*
collision domain *(68)*
crimper *(71)*
crossover cable *(75)*
Ethernet *(63)*
frame *(64)*
frame check sequence (FCS) *(66)*
full-duplex *(71)*
half-duplex *(71)*
hub *(63)*
MAC address *(65)*
media converter *(73)*

multimode *(72)*
node *(65)*
pad *(66)*
ports *(69)*
preamble *(65)*
promiscuous mode *(65)*
repeater *(63)*
RG-58 *(69)*
RJ-45 connector *(70)*
segment *(64)*
Sneakernet *(62)*
sniffer *(65)*
Source Address Table (SAT) *(77)*
Spanning Tree Protocol (STP) *(78)*
straight-through *(73)*
switch *(76)*
T connector *(68)*
Thinnet *(68)*
TIA/EIA 568A *(71)*
TIA/EIA 568B *(71)*
uplink port *(73)*
UTP coupler *(73)*

■ Key Term Quiz

Use the Key Terms list to complete the sentences that follow. Not all terms will be used.

1. The _____ is unique to each individual NIC.

2. When extra "filler" data is needed in a packet, a(n) _____ is added.

3. A network connection that can send or receive, but not send and receive, a signal is called a(n) _____ connection.

4. A NIC that is listening for all packets sent along the wire is said to be in _____.

5. Appended to the front of the frame is the _____.

6. A hub acts as a(n) _____ in that it copies all incoming signals to every connected port.

7. Connecting switches incorrectly can create a(n) _____, which can make the whole network stop working.

8. Hubs can be daisy-chained through their _____ or the use of a(n) _____.

9. _____ has a maximum distance between node and hub of 100 meters, whereas _____ has a maximum distance of 2000 meters.

10. A(n) _____ can be used to interconnect different Ethernet types.

1. How are the connectors wired on a crossover cable?

   A. One end is TIA/EIA 568A; the other end is TIA/EIA 568B.

   B. Both ends are TIA/EIA 568A.

   C. Both ends are TIA/EIA 568B.

   D. One end is an RJ-45; the other end is an RG-6.

2. What items make up the CSMA/CD system used in Ethernet networks? (Select three.)

   A. Collision avoidance

   B. Carrier sense

   C. Multiple access

   D. Collision detection

3. What happens when two computers transmit through a hub simultaneously?

   A. Nothing happens.

   B. The terminators prevent any transmission problems.

   C. Their signals are reflected back down the cable to their points of origin.

   D. A collision occurs.

4. What is a group of nodes that can at any point send messages at the same time, causing a collision?

   A. Collision domain

   B. Ethernet

   C. Fast Ethernet

   D. Sneakernet

5. Which committee is responsible for Ethernet standards?

   A. IEEE 803.2

   B. IEEE 803.3

   C. IEEE 802.2

   D. IEEE 802.3

6. What type of cabling did the first star-bus topology Ethernet networks use?

   A. 10Base2

   B. 10Base5

   C. 10BaseT

   D. 10Base-Cat5

7. What is the purpose of a preamble in an Ethernet frame?

   A. It gives the receiving NIC time to realize a frame is coming and to know when the frame starts.

   B. It provides the receiving NIC with the sending NIC's MAC address so communication can continue.

   C. It provides error-checking to ensure data integrity.

   D. It contains a description of the data that is to follow so the receiving NIC knows how to reassemble it.

8. What valuable network tool can you use to examine all frames on the network, regardless of their intended recipient?

   A. Repeater

   B. Media converter

   C. STP

   D. Sniffer

9. For what purpose is a crimping tool used?

   A. To splice a 10BaseT cable with a 10BaseFL cable

   B. To attach an RJ-45 connector to a UTP cable

   C. To attach a 10BaseT cable to a media converter

   D. To connect two hubs together

10. Which of the following is not a limitation on 10BaseT cable?

    A. Maximum speed of 10 Mbps

    B. Maximum distance between hub and node of 100 feet

    C. Maximum of 1024 nodes per hub

    D. Minimum CAT 3 or better UTP with RJ-45 connectors

11. Which of the following is not a limitation on 10BaseFL cable?

    A. Maximum speed of 10 Mbps

    B. Maximum distance between hub and node of 2000 meters

    C. Maximum of 1024 nodes per hub

    D. Minimum CAT 3 or better UTP with RJ-45 connectors

12. Upon looking at the front of a hub, you notice something labeled as MDI-X. What is this for?

   A. It is a special receptacle for the power cable.

   B. It is a regular port used to connect computers.

   C. It is an uplink port used to connect the hub to another hub.

   D. It is the brand name of the hub.

13. In a full-duplex switched network, when can collisions occur?

   A. A collision will occur when two nodes connected to the switch send frames at the same time.

   B. A collision will occur when a node tries to send to the switch at the same time the switch tries to send to the node.

   C. A collision will occur when two nodes send broadcast frames at the same time.

   D. A collision will never occur.

14. What feature of switches prevents the problem of bridging loops?

   A. STP

   B. TCP/IP

   C. IEEE 802.3

   D. UTP

15. What feature of switches keeps track of which MAC address goes to each port?

   A. FCS

   B. SAT

   C. STP

   D. UTP

■ Essay Quiz

1. Describe two ways that using frames helps move data along a network.

2. Define the term *CSMA/CD*, using simple descriptions to explain each of the three parts: CS, MA, and CD.

3. Describe what a hub does and some of its limitations. Then explain how a switch works to overcome the problems of a hub.

Lab Projects

• Lab Project 4.1

On a blank sheet of paper, use one side to list the basic facts you must know about 10BaseT for the CompTIA Network+ certification exam. Use the other side to list the essential facts you must know about 10BaseFL.

Double-check your work, either by yourself or with a classmate, to ensure its accuracy. Save this sheet to use as a quick-reference study aid when you're preparing to sit for your exam—it will help!

• Lab Project 4.2

In this chapter, you learned about the basic functionality of switches. Use the Internet to delve deeper and research the difference among a managed switch, an unmanaged switch, and a smart switch. Create a chart to compare their similarities and differences. In addition to the differences in features and functionality,

research and report on the pricing differences for similarly sized switches. For example, what is more expensive, a 24-port managed, unmanaged, or smart switch? What do you get for the extra money? Is it worth it?

• Lab Project 4.3

Use the Internet to research freeware or shareware programs that will "sniff" the data on your network. With your instructor's permission, download a program that you find, and then install it on your

classroom lab network. Try to sniff data going to and from your machine, as well as other traffic. Have fun, and document your findings.

Modern Ethernet

"To expect the unexpected shows a thoroughly modern intellect."

—OSCAR WILDE

In this chapter, you will learn how to

- **Describe the varieties of 100-megabit Ethernet**
- **Discuss copper- and fiber-based Gigabit Ethernet**
- **Discover and describe Ethernet varieties beyond Gigabit**

Within a few years of its introduction, 10BaseT proved inadequate to meet the growing networking demand for speed. As with all things in the computing world, bandwidth is the key. Even with switching, the 10-Mbps speed of 10BaseT, seemingly so fast when first developed, quickly found a market clamoring for even faster speeds. This chapter looks at the improvements in Ethernet since 10BaseT. You'll read about the 100-megabit standards and the Gigabit Ethernet standards. The chapter finishes with a look at Ethernet past Gigabit.

100-Megabit Ethernet

The quest to break 10-Mbps network speeds in Ethernet started in the early 1990s. By then, 10BaseT Ethernet had established itself as the most popular networking technology (although other standards, such as IBM's Token Ring, still had some market share). The goal was to create a new speed standard that made no changes to the actual Ethernet frames themselves. By doing this, the 802.3 committee ensured that different speeds of Ethernet could interconnect, assuming you had something that could handle the speed differences and a media converter if the connections were different.

Two of the defining characteristics of Ethernet—the frame size and elements, and the way devices share access to the bus (carrier sense multiple access [CSMA])—stay precisely the same when going from 10-megabit standards to 100-megabit (and beyond). This standardization ensures communication and scalability.

 CompTIA uses some seemingly sloppy language to describe CSMA in the objectives, calling it both C*D*MA (which is a completely different standard used for cell phones) and *carrier detect/sense*. You know what the technology means, so don't be thrown off if odd terminology appears on the exam.

> ### ☑ Cross Check
>
> **Interconnecting Ethernet Networks**
>
> You learned about the devices used to connect different types of Ethernet networks—hubs and switches—in Chapter 4, "Ethernet Basics." Check your memory now. What's the difference between the two devices? Which would you prefer for connections and why?

100BaseT

If you want to make a lot of money in the technology world, create a standard and then get everyone else to buy into it. For that matter, you can even give the standard away and still make tons of cash if you have the inside line on making the hardware that supports the standard.

When it came time to come up with a new standard to replace 10BaseT, network hardware makers forwarded a large number of potential standards, all focused on the prize of leading the new Ethernet standard. As a result, two twisted-pair Ethernet standards appeared: **100BaseT4** and **100BaseTX**. 100BaseT4 used CAT 3 cable, whereas 100BaseTX used CAT 5. By the late 1990s, 100BaseTX became the dominant 100-megabit Ethernet standard. 100BaseT4 disappeared from the market and today has been forgotten. As a result, we never say 100BaseTX, simply choosing to use the term **100BaseT**.

 100BaseT was at one time called Fast Ethernet. The term still sticks to the 100-Mbps standards even though there are now much faster versions of Ethernet.

100BaseTX (100BaseT) Summary

- **Speed**   100 Mbps
- **Signal type**   Baseband
- **Distance**   100 meters between the hub/switch and the node
- **Node limit**   No more than 1024 nodes per hub/switch

• **Figure 5.1**   Typical 100BaseT NIC

- **Topology**   Star-bus topology: physical star, logical bus
- **Cable type**   CAT 5 or better UTP or STP cabling with RJ-45 connectors

Upgrading a 10BaseT network to 100BaseT was not a small process. First, you needed CAT 5 cable or better. Second, you had to replace all 10BaseT NICs with 100BaseT NICs. Third, you needed to replace the 10BaseT hub or switch with a 100BaseT hub or switch. Making this upgrade cost a lot in the early days of 100BaseT, so people clamored for a way to make the upgrade a little easier and less expensive. This was accomplished via multispeed, auto-sensing NICs and hubs/switches.

Figure 5.1 shows a typical multispeed, auto-sensing 100BaseT NIC from the late 1990s. When this NIC first connected to a network, it negotiated automatically with the hub or switch to determine the other device's highest speed. If they both did 100BaseT, then you got 100BaseT. If the hub or switch only did 10BaseT, then the NIC did 10BaseT. All of this happened automatically (Figure 5.2).

Distinguishing a 10BaseT NIC from a 100BaseT NIC without close inspection is impossible. Look for something on the card to tell you its speed. Some NICs may have extra link lights to show the speed (see Chapter 6, "Installing a Physical Network," for the scoop on link lights). Of course, you can always simply install the card, as shown in Figure 5.3, and see what the operating system says it sees.

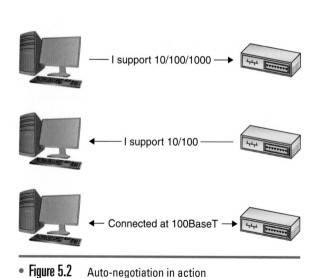

• **Figure 5.2**   Auto-negotiation in action

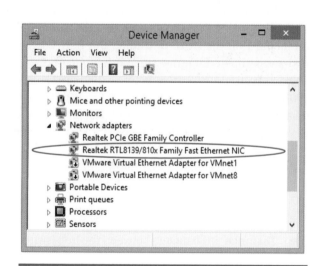

• **Figure 5.3**   Typical 100BaseT NIC in Windows 8.1

You'll also have trouble finding a true 10BaseT or 100BaseT NIC any longer because multispeed NICs have been around long enough to have replaced any single-speed NIC. All modern NICs are multispeed and auto-sensing.

100BaseFX

Most Ethernet networks use unshielded twisted pair (UTP) cabling, but quite a few use fiber-based networks instead. In some networks, using fiber simply makes more sense.

UTP cabling cannot meet the needs of every organization for three key reasons. First, the 100-meter distance limitation of UTP-based networks is inadequate for networks covering large buildings or campuses. Second, UTP's lack of electrical shielding makes it a poor choice for networks functioning in locations with high levels of electromagnetic interference (EMI)—disturbance in electrical signals caused by electrical radiation coming from nearby devices. Finally, the Maxwell Smarts and James Bonds of the world find UTP cabling (and copper cabling in general) easy to tap, making it an inappropriate choice for high-security environments. To address these issues, the IEEE 802.3 standard provides for a flavor of 100-megabit Ethernet using fiber-optic cable, called 100BaseFX.

The 100BaseFX standard saw quite a bit of interest for years, as it combined the high speed of 100-megabit Ethernet with the reliability of fiber optics. Outwardly, 100BaseFX looks exactly like 10BaseFL. Both use the same multimode fiber-optic cabling, and both use SC or ST connectors. 100BaseFX offers improved data speeds over 10BaseFL and equally long cable runs, supporting a maximum cable length of two kilometers.

100BaseFX Summary

- **Speed**   100 Mbps
- **Signal type**   Baseband
- **Distance**   Two kilometers between the hub/switch and the node
- **Node limit**   No more than 1024 nodes per hub/switch
- **Topology**   Star-bus topology: physical star, logical bus
- **Cable type**   Multimode fiber-optic cabling with ST or SC connectors

Full-Duplex Ethernet

Early 100BaseT NICs, just like 10BaseT NICs, could send and receive data, but not at the same time—a feature called half-duplex (Figure 5.4). The IEEE addressed this characteristic shortly after adopting 100BaseT as a standard.

There's no scenario where you'd deploy any 10-megabit networking hardware today, including 10Base2 or 10BaseT. Why the CompTIA Network+ exam objectives reference such old technologies in this fashion is unclear.

Tech Tip

Shielded Twisted Pair

Installing networks in areas of high EMI used to require the use of shielded twisted-pair (STP) *cabling rather than UTP. Even though you can still get STP cabling, its use is rare today. Most installations use fiber-optic cable in situations where UTP won't cut it. The exception to this rule is with relatively short cable runs through high-noise areas, like in a workshop. Swapping out a UTP cable with an STP cable is simpler and much less expensive than running fiber and changing NICs as well.*

The *Fiber Distributed Data Interface (FDDI)* flourished on college campuses during the 1990s because it could cover long distances and transfer data at the (then) blazing speed of 100 Mbps. FDDI used fiber-optic cables with a token bus network protocol over a ring topology. Fast Ethernet over UTP offered a much cheaper alternative when it became available, plus it was completely compatible with 10BaseT, so FDDI faded away.

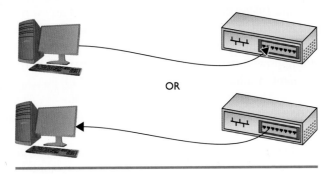

• **Figure 5.4**   Half-duplex: sending at the top, receiving at the bottom

• **Figure 5.5** Full-duplex

Full-duplex doesn't increase network speed directly, but it doubles network bandwidth. Imagine a one-lane road expanded to two lanes while keeping the speed limit the same. And if you recall from the previous chapter, going full-duplex disables CSMA/CD and eliminates collisions.

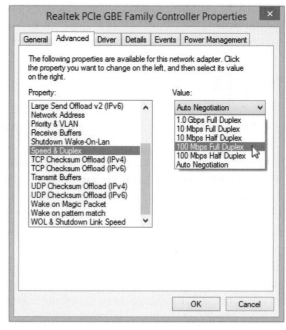

• **Figure 5.6** Forcing speed and duplex in Windows 8.1

Check out the two excellent Chapter 5 Sims over at http://totalsem.com/006. Both the Show and the Challenge titled "Manage Duplex Settings" help reinforce the concepts of full-duplex and half-duplex.

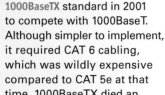

The TIA/EIA published the 1000BaseTX standard in 2001 to compete with 1000BaseT. Although simpler to implement, it required CAT 6 cabling, which was wildly expensive compared to CAT 5e at that time. 1000BaseTX died an early death, but still lives on, zombie-like, on the CompTIA Network+ exam.

By the late 1990s, most 100BaseT cards could auto-negotiate for full-duplex. With **full-duplex**, a NIC can send and receive at the same time, as shown in Figure 5.5.

Almost all NICs today can go full-duplex. The NIC and the attached switch determine full- or half-duplex during the auto-negotiation process. The vast majority of the time you simply let the NIC do its negotiation. Every operating system has some method to force the NIC to a certain speed/duplex, as shown in Figure 5.6.

Fast Ethernet at 100 Mbps makes sense for simple networks where you share small data, like documents and spreadsheets. Plenty of local area networks (LANs) around the world continue to soldier on at 100-megabit speeds. That's faster than the vast majority of Internet connections, after all. Still, Fast Ethernet is dead in new installations, so let's turn to the current standard.

Gigabit Ethernet

By the end of the 1990s, the true speed junkie needed an even more powerful version of Ethernet. In response, the IEEE created **Gigabit Ethernet**, which today is the most common type of Ethernet found on new NICs.

The IEEE approved two different versions of Gigabit Ethernet. The most widely implemented solution, published under the IEEE **802.3ab** standard, is called **1000BaseT**. The other version, published under the **802.3z** standard and known as **1000BaseX**, is divided into a series of standards, with names such as 1000BaseCX, 1000BaseSX, and 1000BaseLX.

1000BaseT uses four-pair UTP or STP cabling to achieve gigabit performance. Like 10BaseT and 100BaseT, 1000BaseT has a maximum cable length of 100 meters on a segment. 1000BaseT connections and ports look exactly like the ones on a 10BaseT or 100BaseT network. 1000BaseT is the dominant Gigabit Ethernet standard.

The 802.3z standards require a bit more discussion. Let's look at each of these solutions in detail to see how they work.

The term *Gigabit Ethernet* is more commonly used than *1000BaseT.*

1000BaseCX

1000BaseCX uses a unique cable known as twinaxial cable (Figure 5.7). Most techs shorten the cable name to *twinax.* Twinaxial cables are special shielded 150-Ohm cables with a length limit of only 25 meters. 1000BaseCX made little progress in the Gigabit Ethernet market.

• **Figure 5.7**   Twinaxial cable

1000BaseSX

Many networks upgrading to Gigabit Ethernet use the **1000BaseSX** standard. 1000BaseSX uses multimode fiber-optic cabling to connect systems, with a generous maximum cable length of 220 to 500 meters; the exact length is left up to the various manufacturers. 1000BaseSX uses an 850-nm (nanometer) wavelength LED to transmit light on the fiber-optic cable. 1000BaseSX devices look similar to 100BaseFX devices, and although both standards can use several types of connectors, 1000BaseSX devices commonly use LC, while 100BaseFX devices frequently use SC. (See "SFF Fiber Connectors" later in the chapter for the scoop on LC connectors.)

The **wavelength** of a particular signal (laser, in this case) refers to the distance the signal has to travel before it completes its particular shape and starts to repeat. The different colors of the laser signals feature different wavelengths.

Cross Check

SC and ST

You learned about the common fiber-optic cable SC and ST connectors in Chapter 3, so cross-check your knowledge here. What distinguishes the two connectors? Can 100BaseFX NICs use either one? Which do you need to twist like a bayonet?

1000BaseLX

1000BaseLX is the long-distance carrier for Gigabit Ethernet. 1000BaseLX uses lasers on single-mode cables to shoot data at distances up to 5 kilometers—and some manufacturers use special repeaters to increase that to distances as great as 70 kilometers! The Ethernet folks are trying to position this as the Ethernet backbone of the future, and already some large carriers are beginning to adopt 1000BaseLX. You may live your whole life and never see a 1000BaseLX device, but odds are good that you will encounter connections that use such devices in the near future. 1000BaseLX connectors look like 1000BaseSX connectors.

SFF Fiber Connectors

Around the time that Gigabit Ethernet first started to appear, two problems began to surface with ST and SC connectors. First, ST connectors are relatively large, twist-on connectors, requiring the installer to twist the cable

• **Figure 5.8** MT-RJ connector

• **Figure 5.9** LC-type connector

when inserting or removing it. Twisting is not a popular action with fiber-optic cables, as the delicate fibers may fracture. Also, big-fingered techs have a problem with ST connectors if the connectors are too closely packed: they can't get their fingers around them.

SC connectors snap in and out, making them much more popular than STs. SC connectors are also large, however, and the folks who make fiber networking equipment wanted to pack more connectors onto their boxes.

This brought about two new types of fiber connectors, known generically as **small form factor (SFF)** connectors. The first SFF connector—the **Mechanical Transfer Registered Jack (MT-RJ)**, shown in Figure 5.8—gained popularity with important companies like Cisco and is still quite common.

You read about the second type of popular SFF connector, the **LC**, in Chapter 3, "Cabling and Topology"—it's shown in Figure 5.9. LC-type connectors are very popular, particularly in the United States, and many fiber experts consider the LC-type connector to be the predominant fiber connector.

LC and MT-RJ are the most popular types of SFF fiber connectors, but many others exist, as outlined in Table 5.1. The fiber industry has no standard beyond ST and SC connectors, which means that different makers of fiber equipment may have different connections.

Table 5.1	Gigabit Ethernet Summary			
Standard	**Cabling**	**Cable Details**	**Connectors**	**Length**
1000BaseCX	Copper	Twinax	Twinax	25 m
1000BaseSX	Multimode fiber	850 nm	Variable, commonly LC	220–500 m
1000BaseLX	Single-mode fiber	1300 nm	Variable, commonly LC and SC	5 km
1000BaseT	CAT 5e/6 UTP	Four-pair/full-duplex	RJ-45	100 m

Mechanical Connection Variations

Aside from the various connection types (LC, MT-RJ, and so on), fiber connectors vary in the connection point. The standard connector type today is called a **Physical Contact (PC) connector** because the two pieces of fiber touch when inserted. These connectors replace the older **flat-surface connector** that left a little gap between the connection points due to imperfections in the glass. PC connectors are highly polished and slightly spherical, reducing the signal loss at the connection point.

Two technologies have dropped in price and have replaced PC connectors in some implementations: UPC and APC. **Ultra Physical Contact (UPC) connectors** are polished extensively for a superior finish. These reduce signal loss significantly over PC connectors. **Angled Physical Contact (APC) connectors** add an 8-degree angle to the curved end, lowering signal loss further. Plus, their connection does not degrade from multiple insertions, unlike earlier connection types.

Implementing Multiple Types of Gigabit Ethernet

Because Ethernet packets don't vary among the many flavors of Ethernet, network hardware manufacturers have long built devices capable of supporting more than one flavor right out of the box. Ancient hubs supported 10Base2 and 10BaseT at the same time, for example.

You can also use dedicated *media converters* to connect any type of Ethernet cabling together. Most media converters are plain-looking boxes with a port or dongle on either side. They come in all flavors:

- Single-mode fiber (SMF) to UTP/STP
- Multimode fiber (MMF) to UTP/STP
- Fiber to coaxial
- SMF to MMF

> The CompTIA Network+ exam objectives erroneously describe some media converters as single-mode fiber to Ethernet and multimode fiber to Ethernet. It's all Ethernet! Don't be surprised if you get one of those terms on the exam, however. Now you'll know what they mean.

Eventually, the Gigabit Ethernet folks created a standard for modular ports called a **gigabit interface converter (GBIC)**. With many Gigabit Ethernet switches and other hardware, you can simply pull out a GBIC module that supports one flavor of Gigabit Ethernet and plug in another. You can replace an RJ-45 port GBIC, for example, with an SC GBIC, and it'll work just fine. Electronically, the switch or other gigabit device is just that—Gigabit Ethernet—so the physical connections don't matter. Ingenious!

Current switches and other network equipment use a much smaller modular connector, called a **small form-factor pluggable (SFP)**. Hot-swappable like the GBICs, the SFPs take up a lot less space and support all the same networking standards. SFPs have replaced GBICs as the modular connector of choice.

> Interestingly, the CompTIA Network+ objectives mention SFPs and GBICs, but only when troubleshooting failed ones. I'll cover them in a little more detail, therefore, in Chapter 21, "Network Troubleshooting."

■ Ethernet Evolutions

The vast majority of wired networks today feature Gigabit Ethernet, which seems plenty fast for current networking needs. That has not stopped developers and manufacturers from pushing well beyond those limits. This last section looks at high-speed Ethernet standards: 10/40/100 gigabit.

10 Gigabit Ethernet

Developers continue to refine and increase Ethernet networking speeds, especially in the LAN environment and in backbones. **10 Gigabit Ethernet (10 GbE)** offers speeds of up to 10 gigabits per second, as its name indicates.

10 GbE has a number of fiber standards and two copper standards. While designed with fiber optics in mind, copper 10 GbE can still often pair excellent performance with cost savings. As a result, you'll find a mix of fiber and copper in data centers today.

Fiber-based 10 GbE

When the IEEE members sat down to formalize specifications on Ethernet running at 10 Gbps, they faced an interesting task in several ways. First, they had to maintain the integrity of the Ethernet frame. Data is king, after all, and the goal was to create a network that could interoperate with any other Ethernet network. Second, they had to figure out how to transfer those frames at such blazing speeds. This second challenge had some interesting ramifications because of two factors. They could use the traditional Physical layer mechanisms defined by the Ethernet standard. But a perfectly usable ~10-Gbps fiber network, called **SONET**, was already in place and being used for wide area networking (WAN) transmissions. What to do?

The IEEE created a whole set of 10 GbE standards that could use traditional LAN Physical layer mechanisms, plus a set of standards that could take advantage of the SONET infrastructure and run over the WAN fiber. To make the 10-Gbps jump as easy as possible, the IEEE also recognized the need for different networking situations. Some implementations require data transfers that can run long distances over single-mode fiber, for example, whereas others can make do with short-distance transfers over multimode fiber. This led to a lot of standards for 10 GbE.

The 10 GbE standards are defined by several factors: the type of fiber used, the wavelength of the laser or lasers, and the Physical layer signaling type. These factors also define the maximum signal distance.

The IEEE uses specific letter codes with the standards to help sort out the differences so you know what you're implementing or supporting. All the standards have names in the following format: "10GBase" followed by two other characters, what I'll call *xy*. The *x* stands for the type of fiber (usually, though not officially) and the wavelength of the laser signal; the *y* stands for the Physical layer signaling standard. The *y* code is always either *R* for LAN-based signaling or *W* for SONET/WAN-based signaling. The *x* differs a little more, so let's take a look.

10GBase*Sy* uses a short-wavelength (850 nm) signal over multimode fiber. The maximum fiber length is 300 meters, although this length will vary depending on the type of multimode fiber used. **10GBaseSR** is used for Ethernet LANs, and **10GBaseSW** is used to connect to SONET devices.

Standard	Fiber Type	Wavelength	Physical Layer Signaling	Maximum Signal Length
10GBaseSR	Multimode	850 nm	LAN	26–300 m
10GBaseSW	Multimode	850 nm	SONET/WAN	26–300 m

10GBase*Ly* uses a long-wavelength (1310 nm) signal over single-mode fiber. The maximum fiber length is 10 kilometers, although this length will vary

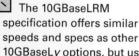
Chapter 14 covers SONET in great detail. For now, think of it as a data transmission standard that's different from the LAN Ethernet standard.

The 10GBaseLRM specification offers similar speeds and specs as other 10GBaseL*y* options, but uses multimode rather than single-mode fiber. This drops the distances down to 220 meters for most variations.

depending on the type of single-mode fiber used. **10GBaseLR** connects to Ethernet LANs and **10GBaseLW** connects to SONET equipment. 10GBaseLR is the most popular and least expensive 10 GbE media type.

Standard	Fiber Type	Wavelength	Physical Layer Signaling	Maximum Signal Length
10GBaseLR	Single-mode	1310 nm	LAN	10 km
10GBaseLW	Single-mode	1310 nm	SONET/WAN	10 km

10GBaseE*y* uses an extra-long-wavelength (1550 nm) signal over single-mode fiber. The maximum fiber length is 40 kilometers, although this length will vary depending on the type of single-mode fiber used. **10GBaseER** works with Ethernet LANs and **10GBaseEW** connects to SONET equipment.

Standard	Fiber Type	Wavelength	Physical Layer Signaling	Maximum Signal Length
10GBaseER	Single-mode	1550 nm	LAN	40 km
10GBaseEW	Single-mode	1550 nm	SONET/WAN	40 km

The 10 GbE fiber standards do not define the type of connector to use and instead leave that to manufacturers (see the upcoming section "10 GbE Physical Connections").

Copper-based 10 GbE

It took until 2006 for IEEE to come up with a standard for 10 GbE running on twisted pair cabling—called, predictably, 10GBaseT. **10GBaseT** looks and works exactly like the slower versions of UTP Ethernet. The only downside is that 10GBaseT running on CAT 6 has a maximum cable length of only 55 meters. The CAT 6a standard enables 10GBaseT to run at the standard distance of 100 meters. Table 5.2 summarizes the 10 GbE standards.

10 GbE Physical Connections

This hodgepodge of 10 GbE types might have been the ultimate disaster for hardware manufacturers. All types of 10 GbE send and receive the same signal; only the physical medium is different. Imagine a single router that had to come out in seven different versions to match all these types! Instead, the 10 GbE industry simply chose not to define the connector types and devised a very clever, very simple concept called **multisource agreements (MSAs)**: agreements among multiple manufacturers to make interoperable devices and standards. An transceiver based on an MSA plugs into your 10 GbE equipment, enabling

Tech Tip

The Other 10 GbE Fiber Standards
Manufacturers have shown both creativity and innovation in taking advantage of both existing fiber and the most cost-effective equipment. This has led to a variety of standards that are not covered by the CompTIA Network+ exam objectives, but that you should know about nevertheless. The top three as of this writing are 10GBaseL4, 10GBaseRM, and 10GBaseZR.

The 10GBaseL4 standard uses four lasers at a 1300-nanometer wavelength over legacy fiber. On FDDI-grade multimode cable, 10GBaseL4 can support up to 300-meter transmissions. The range increases to 10 kilometers over single-mode fiber.

The 10GBaseLRM standard uses the long wavelength signal of 10GBaseLR but over legacy multimode fiber. The standard can achieve a range of up to 220 meters, depending on the grade of fiber cable.

Finally, some manufacturers have adopted the 10GBaseZR "standard," which isn't part of the IEEE standards at all (unlike 10GBaseL4 and 10GBaseLRM). Instead, the manufacturers have created their own set of specifications. 10GBaseZR networks use a 1550-nanometer wavelength over single-mode fiber to achieve a range of a whopping 80 kilometers. The standard can work with both Ethernet LAN and SONET/WAN infrastructure.

Table 5.2	10 GbE Summary			
Standard	Cabling	Wavelength/Cable Details	Connectors	Length
10GBaseSR/SW	Multimode fiber	850 nm	Not defined	26–300 m
10GBaseLR/LW	Single-mode fiber	1310 nm	Variable, commonly LC	10 km
10GBaseER/EW	Single-mode fiber	1550 nm	Variable, commonly LC and SC	40 km
10GBaseT	CAT 6/6a UTP	Four-pair/full-duplex	RJ-45	55/100 m

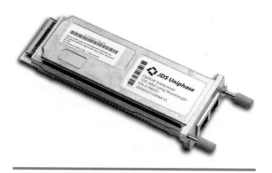

• **Figure 5.10**   XENPAK module

One of the most popular transceivers currently used in 10 GbE is called the *enhanced small form-factor pluggable (SFP+)*. But you won't see it on the current CompTIA Network+ exam.

you to convert from one media type to another by inserting the right transceiver. Figure 5.10 shows a typical module called XENPAK.

For now, 10 GbE equipment is the exclusive domain of high-bandwidth LANs and WANs, including parts of the big-pipe Internet connections.

Backbones

The beauty and the challenge of the vast selection of Ethernet flavors is deciding which one to use in your network. The goal is to give your users the fastest network response time possible while keeping costs reasonable. To achieve this balance, most network administrators find that a multispeed Ethernet network works best. In a multispeed network, a series of high-speed (relative to the rest of the network) switches maintain a backbone network. No computers, other than possibly servers, attach directly to this backbone. Figure 5.11 shows a typical backbone network. Each floor has its own switch that connects to every node on the floor. In turn, each of these switches also has a separate high-speed connection to a main switch that resides in the office's computer room.

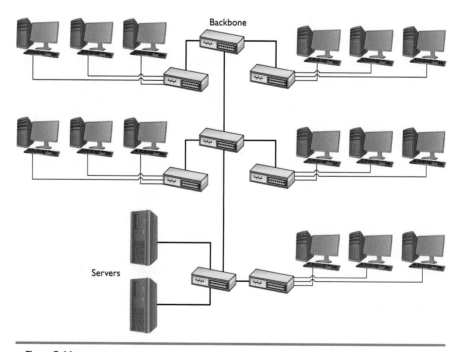

• **Figure 5.11**   Typical network configuration showing backbone

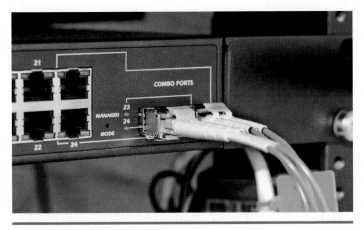

• **Figure 5.12**   Switches with dedicated, high-speed ports

To make this work, you need switches with separate, dedicated, high-speed ports like the ones shown in Figure 5.12. The ports (often fiber) on the switches run straight to the high-speed backbone switch.

Try This!

Shopping for Switches

Cisco, one of the industry leaders for Ethernet switches, has a great Web site for its products. Imagine that you are setting up a network for your school or business (keep it simple and pick a single building if you're in a large organization). Decide what type of switches you'd like to use, including both the backbone and local switches. If you're really motivated, decide where to locate the switches physically. Don't be afraid to try a fiber backbone—almost every Cisco switch comes with special ports to enable you to pick the type of Ethernet you want to use for your backbone.

■ Beyond Network+

IEEE 802.3ba

Way back in 2010, the IEEE 802.3ba committee approved standards for 40- and 100-Gb Ethernet, *40 Gigabit Ethernet (40 GbE)* and *100 Gigabit Ethernet (100 GbE)*, respectively. Both standards, in their many varieties, use the same frame as the slow-by-comparison earlier versions of Ethernet, so with the right switches, you've got perfect interoperability. Various committees are currently at work on expanding the 40 GbE and 100 GbE offerings, none of which you'll see on the CompTIA Network+ exam.

The 40 GbE and 100 GbE standards are primarily implemented in backbones and machine-to-machine connections. These standards aren't something you'll see in a LAN . . . yet.

Chapter 5 Review

■ Chapter Summary

After reading this chapter and completing the exercises, you should understand the following about Ethernet.

Describe the varieties of 100-megabit Ethernet

■ Fast Ethernet includes two UTP/STP variations, both arranged in a physical star, but operating in a logical bus—100BaseTX and 100BaseT4. The latter standard has disappeared into the dustbins of history.

■ In 100BaseTX Ethernet cabling systems, speeds are 100 Mbps, wires are twisted copper pairs, signals are baseband, and distance is limited to 100 meters from the node to the hub, with a limit of 1024 nodes per hub. The cabling used must be CAT 5 or better UTP/STP crimped with RJ-45 connectors.

■ Limitations of Fast Ethernet over UTP include distance (only 100 meters), inadequate shielding for some installations, and relative ease of intruder break-ins on the physical cable.

■ The fiber-optic variation of Fast Ethernet, 100BaseFX, overcomes these limitations, offering immunity to electrical interference and a range of up to two kilometers from node to hub.

■ A half-duplex NIC can only send or receive at any one time. Full-duplex NICs can send and receive at the same time, thereby doubling the bandwidth.

Discuss copper- and fiber-based Gigabit Ethernet

■ Two Gigabit Ethernet standards have been approved by the IEEE: 802.3z (1000BaseX) and 802.3ab (1000BaseT).

■ 1000BaseT uses four-pair UTP/STP cabling and has a maximum length of 100 meters.

■ 1000BaseX is divided into a number of standards: 1000BaseCX, 1000BaseSX, and 1000BaseLX.

■ 1000BaseCX uses twinaxial cable with a maximum length of 25 meters.

■ 1000BaseSX uses multimode fiber-optic cable with a maximum length between 220 and 500 meters, depending on the manufacturer.

■ 1000BaseLX uses single-mode fiber-optic cable with a maximum length of 5 kilometers. Some manufacturers use repeaters to extend the maximum length to 70 kilometers.

■ The small form factor (SFF) fiber connector includes the Mechanical Transfer Registered Jack (MT-RJ) and the LC, both of which were created to overcome problems with the ST and SC connectors.

■ Aside from the various connection types (LC, MT-RJ, and so on), fiber connectors vary in the connection point. The standard connector type today is called a Physical Contact (PC) connector because the two pieces of fiber touch when inserted. Ultra Physical Contact (UPC) connectors are polished extensively for a superior finish. These reduce signal loss significantly over PC connectors. Angled Physical Contact (APC) connectors add an 8-degree angle to the curved end, lowering signal loss further.

■ The gigabit interface converter (GBIC) is a standard for modular Gigabit Ethernet ports. With GBICs, you can switch out the module and replace it with a different Gigabit port type. Sweet.

Discover and describe Ethernet varieties beyond Gigabit

■ 10 Gigabit Ethernet (10 GbE) has several fiber standards and two copper standards.

■ SONET is the networking standard for long-distance optical connections that serve as the main backbone for the Internet.

■ 10 GbE is organized into six different standards: 10GBaseSR, 10GBaseSW, 10GBaseLR, 10GBaseLW, 10GBaseER, and 10GBaseEW.

■ 10GBaseSy uses multimode fiber with a maximum length of 300 meters. 10GBaseLR is used for Ethernet LANs, whereas 10GBaseSW is used to connect to SONET devices.

- 10GBaseL*y* uses single-mode fiber with a maximum length of 10 kilometers. 10GBaseLR is for Ethernet LANs, whereas 10GBaseLW is used to connect to SONET devices. 10GBaseLR is the most popular and least expensive 10 GbE media type.

- 10GBaseE*y* uses single-mode fiber with a maximum length of 40 kilometers. 10GBaseER is used for Ethernet LANs, whereas 10GBaseEW is used to connect to SONET devices.

- 10GBaseT defines 10 Gigabit Ethernet over UTP/STP cable. It is capable of a maximum distance of 55 meters with CAT 6; however, using CAT 6a, it can achieve 100 meters.

- All types of 10 GbE send and receive the exact same signal. Network devices, such as routers, that need to support different 10 GbE cable types use multisource agreements (MSAs) to enable the various cable types to connect.

■ Key Terms

10GBaseER *(93)*
10GBaseEW *(93)*
10GBaseLR *(93)*
10GBaseLW *(93)*
10GBaseSR *(92)*
10GBaseSW *(92)*
10GBaseT *(93)*
10 Gigabit Ethernet (10 GbE) *(92)*
100BaseFX *(87)*
100BaseT *(85)*
100BaseT4 *(85)*
100BaseTX *(85)*
1000BaseCX *(89)*
1000BaseLX *(89)*
1000BaseSX *(89)*
1000BaseT *(88)*
1000BaseTX *(88)*
1000BaseX *(88)*
802.3ab *(88)*
802.3z *(88)*

Angled Physical Contact (APC) connector *(91)*
baseband *(86)*
broadband *(86)*
electromagnetic interference (EMI) *(87)*
Fast Ethernet *(85)*
flat-surface connector *(91)*
full-duplex *(88)*
Gigabit Ethernet *(88)*
gigabit interface converter (GBIC) *(91)*
half-duplex *(87)*
LC *(90)*
Mechanical Transfer Registered Jack (MT-RJ) *(90)*
multisource agreement (MSA) *(93)*
Physical Contact (PC) connector *(91)*
Small form factor (SFF) *(90)*
Small form-factor pluggable (SFP) *(91)*
SONET *(92)*
Ultra Physical Contact (UPC) connector *(91)*
wavelength *(89)*

■ Key Term Quiz

Use the Key Terms list to complete the sentences that follow. Not all terms will be used.

1. When a network device can both send and receive data at the same time, it is said to be _____.

2. _____ has a maximum cable length of two kilometers and uses multimode fiber with ST or SC connectors.

3. 100BaseT is also known as _____.

4. _____ could use CAT 3, but _____ must use CAT 5 or better.

5. 802.3z and 802.3ab are both _____ standards.

6. _____ supports the longest maximum distance for Gigabit Ethernet.

7. The _____ and _____ IEEE standards support the longest maximum distance for 10 Gigabit Ethernet.

8. Many fiber experts consider the _____ to be the predominant fiber connector.

9. _____ is the least expensive and most popular 10 GbE media type.

10. Switches with a(n) _____ port can support a variety of Gigabit port types.

■ Multiple-Choice Quiz

1. Which of the following are 100BaseT cable types? (Select three.)
   A. CAT 3
   B. CAT 5
   C. CAT 5e
   D. 10BaseFL

2. What is the physical limit for the number of nodes on an Ethernet hub/switch?
   A. 24
   B. 256
   C. 512
   D. 1024

3. When a network device can only send data or receive data, but not both at the same time, it is operating in what mode?
   A. Duplex
   B. Full-duplex
   C. Half-duplex
   D. Halfplex

4. What important technology is also known as Gigabit Ethernet?
   A. 100BaseT
   B. 100BaseFL
   C. 100BaseFX
   D. 1000BaseT

5. What are the two major UTP variations of Fast Ethernet? (Select two.)
   A. 100BaseTL
   B. 100BaseTX
   C. 100BaseFL
   D. 100BaseT4

6. What are three limitations of Fast Ethernet over UTP? (Select three.)
   A. Distance is restricted to 100 meters from node to hub/switch.
   B. Shielding may be inadequate for some installations.
   C. Intrusion from outsiders may be possible without detection.
   D. The obsolete technology is insufficient for most networks.

7. Which standard defines Fast Ethernet using fiber cabling?
   A. 10BaseFL
   B. 100BaseFX
   C. 100BaseT4
   D. 100BaseTX

8. Which of the following are fiber connector types? (Select three.)
   A. LC
   B. LS
   C. MT-RJ
   D. ST

9. Which standard defines Gigabit Ethernet over twisted pair copper wire?

   A. 802.3ab

   B. 802.3e

   C. 802.3GbUTP

   D. 802.3z

10. You've lost the manual to your router. How can you tell the difference between a 1000BaseT port and a 100BaseT port on a router just by looking?

    A. The 1000BaseT ports are noticeably larger.

    B. The 100BaseT ports are green, whereas the 1000BaseT ports are gray.

    C. 1000BaseT ports are reversed with the clip on the top.

    D. You can't tell the difference by looking. They look exactly the same.

11. Which statement about Ethernet is correct?

    A. Only 10- and 100-megabit Ethernet may use a hub. Gigabit Ethernet must use a switch.

    B. 10- and 100-megabit Ethernet has a limit of 1024 nodes. Gigabit Ethernet has no limit.

    C. Gigabit Ethernet that uses UTP cabling has a maximum distance between the node and switch of 250–400 meters, depending on the manufacturer.

    D. All versions of 10 Gigabit Ethernet use the same cabling.

12. What will happen if you connect a 10BaseT NIC to an auto-sensing switch?

    A. The switch will operate in hub mode.

    B. The entire switch will operate at 10 megabits, even if 100-megabit devices are attached.

    C. The 10BaseT NIC will operate at 10 megabits while connected 100-megabit devices will operate at their full speed of 100 megabits.

    D. The 10BaseT NIC will overclock to run at 100 megabits.

13. What benefit does full-duplex offer?

    A. It allows all NICs on a hub to send signals at the same time without collisions.

    B. It doubles the bandwidth of the network.

    C. It doubles the speed of the network.

    D. It doubles both the bandwidth and the speed of the network.

14. What is the difference between the *R* and *W* designations in 10GBase standards, such as 10GBaseLR and 10GBaseLW, or 10GBaseER and 10GBaseEW?

    A. The *R* indicates "regular," or half-duplex. The *W* indicates "wide mode," which is the 10 Gigabit Ethernet version of full-duplex.

    B. The *R* indicates "read," or the ability to receive signals; the *W* indicates "write," or the ability to send signals.

    C. The *R* and *W* indicate differences in the circuitry, with the *W* versions used to connect to SONET equipment.

    D. The *R* indicates the use of UTP, whereas the *W* indicates the use of fiber optics.

15. Which of the following is a standard fiber connector type?

    A. AC

    B. BC

    C. EC

    D. PC

Essay Quiz

1. Which types of computer network cable connections are you familiar with already? Write a short paragraph describing your experience.

2. Your manager has just informed you that several departments at your company will be switching over to fiber-optic NICs. How many and what type of connectors will be needed for each node on the new segment? Document your recommendations.

3. Compose a letter to the network administrator of a nearby telecommunications company or ISP (Internet service provider). Introduce yourself in the top part of the letter as a networking student. Then ask if the company ever gives tours or holds open houses for the public. Close the letter by thanking the person reading it for his or her time. Spell-check and have others proofread your letter. Consider mailing the letter if you are serious about your visit and your instructor approves your final copy.

4. Prepare a list of questions you would ask a large organization's network administrator regarding cabling, connections, hubs, switches, and even routers. Use the situation described in Essay 3 to help you create your list of questions.

5. Prepare a thank-you note in advance for having been allowed to participate in a tour, as described in Essay 3. Mention some of the items you observed during the visit. If you would be interested in seeking employment at their facility, consider mentioning that and asking about the steps you would need to take to prepare for such a position. Sometimes a simple thank-you note can help land a job!

Lab Projects

• Lab Project 5.1

Find a hub or switch at your school or company. Examine the wiring closely to determine what cable connections it uses. Try to determine whether the cabling was placed neatly and in an organized manner, whether the ports are clearly labeled, and whether all the ends were crimped well. Be prepared to discuss your findings with the rest of the class.

• Lab Project 5.2

Use the Internet to research prices to order 100 each of the connectors from the following list. Don't forget to include basic shipping and handling to your organization's location, as these are a price factor in real life.

- RJ-45 connectors
- SC connectors
- ST connectors
- MT-RJ connectors
- LC connectors

From your research, which connectors would be the least costly?

• Lab Project 5.3

All these standards! How can you remember them?

Make a chart that compares the features (cabling, connectors, data throughput, and so on) of the following Ethernet technologies:

- 10BaseT
- 10BaseFL
- 100BaseTX
- 100BaseFX

- 1000BaseT
- 1000BaseCX
- 1000BaseLX
- 1000BaseSX
- 10GBaseSR/10GBaseSW
- 10GBaseLR/10GBaseLW
- 10GBaseER/10GBaseEW

Installing a Physical Network

"I am rarely happier than when spending an entire day programming my computer to perform automatically a task that it would otherwise take me a good ten seconds to do by hand."

—DOUGLAS ADAMS

In this chapter, you will learn how to

- **Recognize and describe the functions of basic components in a structured cabling system**
- **Explain the process of installing structured cable**
- **Install a network interface card**
- **Perform basic troubleshooting on a structured cable network**

A rmed with the knowledge of previous chapters, it's time to start going about the business of actually constructing a physical network. This might seem easy; after all, the most basic network is nothing more than a switch with a number of cables snaking out to all of the PCs on the network (Figure 6.1).

On the surface, such a network setup is absolutely correct, but if you tried to run a network using only a switch and cables running to each system, you'd have some serious practical issues. In the real world, you need to deal with physical obstacles like walls and ceilings. You also need to deal with those annoying things called *people*. People are incredibly adept at destroying physical networks. They unplug switches, trip over cables, and rip connectors out of NICs with incredible consistency unless you protect the network from their destructive ways. Although the simplified switch-and-a-bunch-of-cables type of network can function in the real world, the network clearly has some problems that need addressing before it can work safely and efficiently (Figure 6.2).

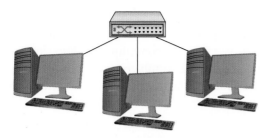

• **Figure 6.1**   What an orderly looking network!

This chapter takes the abstract discussion of network technologies from previous chapters into the concrete reality of real networks. To achieve this goal, it marches you through the process of installing an entire network system from the beginning. The chapter starts by introducing you to *structured cabling,* the critical set of standards used all over the world to install physical cabling in a safe and orderly fashion. It then delves into the world of larger networks—those with more than a single switch—and shows you some typical methods used to organize them for peak efficiency and reliability. Next, you'll take a quick tour of the most common NICs used in PCs, and see what it takes to install them. Finally, you'll look at how to troubleshoot cabling and other network devices, including an introduction to some fun diagnostic tools.

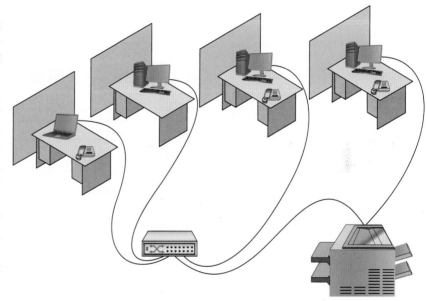

• **Figure 6.2**   A real-world network

Historical/Conceptual

■ Understanding Structured Cabling

If you want a functioning, dependable, real-world network, you need a solid understanding of a set of standards, collectively called **structured cabling**. These standards, defined by the Telecommunications Industry Association/ Electronic Industries Alliance (TIA/EIA)—yup, the same folks who tell you how to crimp an RJ-45 onto the end of a UTP cable—give professional cable installers detailed standards on every aspect of a cabled network, from the type of cabling to use to the position of wall outlets.

The CompTIA Network+ exam requires you to understand the basic concepts involved in designing a network and installing network cabling and to recognize the components used in a real network. The CompTIA Network+

> EIA ceased operations in 2011, but various groups (like TIA) maintain the standards. Expect to see EIA on the CompTIA Network+ exam.

A structured cabling system is useful for more than just computer networks. You'll find structured cabling defining telephone networks and video conferencing setups, for example.

Tech Tip

Integrating Wi-Fi

Many networks today have a wireless component in addition to a wired infrastructure. The switches, servers, and workstations rely on wires for fast networking, but the wireless component supports workers on the move, such as salespeople.

This chapter focuses on the wired infrastructure. Once we get through Wi-Fi in Chapter 15, "Wireless Networking," I'll add that component to our networking conversation.

exam does not, however, expect you to be as knowledgeable as a professional network designer or cable installer. Your goal is to understand enough about real-world cabling systems to communicate knowledgeably with cable installers and to perform basic troubleshooting. Granted, by the end of this chapter, you'll have enough of an understanding to try running your own cable (I certainly run my own cable), but consider that knowledge a handy bit of extra credit.

The idea of structured cabling is to create a safe, reliable cabling infrastructure for all of the devices that may need interconnection. Certainly this applies to computer networks, but also to telephone, video—anything that might need low-power, distributed cabling.

You should understand three issues with structured cabling. Cable basics start the picture, with switches, cabling, and PCs. You'll then look at the components of a network, such as how the cable runs through the walls and where it ends up. This section wraps up with an assessment of connections leading outside your network.

Cable Basics—A Star Is Born

This exploration of the world of connectivity hardware starts with the most basic of all networks: a switch, some UTP cable, and a few PCs—in other words, a typical physical star network (Figure 6.3).

No law of physics prevents you from installing a switch in the middle of your office and running cables on the floor to all the computers in your network. This setup works, but it falls apart spectacularly when applied to a real-world environment. Three problems present themselves to the network tech. First, the exposed cables running along the floor are just waiting for someone to trip over them, damaging the network and giving that person a wonderful lawsuit opportunity. Possible accidents aside, simply moving and stepping on the cabling will, over time, cause a cable to fail due to wires breaking or RJ-45 connectors ripping off cable ends. Second, the presence of other electrical devices close to the cable can create interference that confuses the signals going through the wire. Third, this type of setup limits your ability to make any changes to the network. Before you can change anything, you have to figure out which cables in the huge rat's nest of cables connected to the switch go to which machines. Imagine *that* troubleshooting nightmare!

"Gosh," you're thinking (okay, I'm thinking it, but you should be, too), "there must be a better way to install a physical network." A better installation would provide safety, protecting the star from vacuum cleaners, clumsy coworkers, and electrical interference. It would have extra hardware to organize and

• **Figure 6.3**   A switch connected by UTP cable to two PCs

protect the cabling. Finally, the new and improved star network installation would feature a cabling standard with the flexibility to enable the network to grow according to its needs and then to upgrade when the next great network technology comes along.

As you have no doubt guessed, I'm not just theorizing here. In the real world, the people who most wanted improved installation standards were the ones who installed cable for a living. In response to this demand, the TIA/EIA developed standards for cable installation. The TIA/EIA 568 standards you learned about in earlier chapters are only part of a larger set of TIA/EIA standards all lumped together under the umbrella of structured cabling.

Test Specific

Structured Cable Network Components

Successful implementation of a basic structured cabling network requires three essential ingredients: a telecommunications room, horizontal cabling, and a work area. Let's zero in on one floor of Figure 5.12 from the previous chapter. All the cabling runs from individual PCs to a central location, the **telecommunications room** (Figure 6.4). What equipment goes in there—a switch or a telephone system—is not the important thing. What matters is that all the cables concentrate in this one area.

All cables run horizontally (for the most part) from the telecommunications room to the PCs. This cabling is called, appropriately, **horizontal cabling**. A single piece of installed horizontal cabling is called a **run**. At the opposite end of the horizontal cabling from the telecommunications room is the work area. The **work area** is often simply an office or cubicle that potentially contains a PC

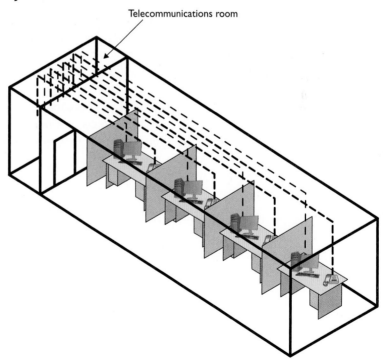

Telecommunications room

• **Figure 6.4** Telecommunications room

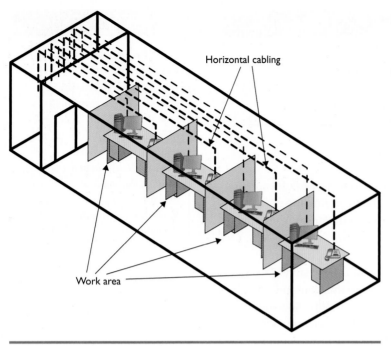

Horizontal cabling

Work area

• **Figure 6.5** Horizontal cabling and work area

A single piece of cable that runs from a work area to a telecommunications room is called a *run*.

and a telephone. Figure 6.5 shows both the horizontal cabling and work areas.

Each of the three parts of a basic star network—the telecommunications room, the horizontal cabling, and the work area(s)—must follow a series of strict standards designed to ensure that the cabling system is reliable and easy to manage. The cabling standards set by TIA/EIA enable techs to make sensible decisions on equipment installed in the telecommunications room, so let's tackle horizontal cabling first, and then return to the telecommunications room. We'll finish up with the work area.

Horizontal Cabling

A horizontal cabling run is the cabling that goes more or less horizontally from a work area to the telecommunications room. In most networks, this cable is CAT 5e or better UTP, but when you move into structured cabling, the TIA/EIA standards define a number of other aspects of the cable, such as the type of wires, number of pairs of wires, and fire ratings.

Solid Core vs. Stranded Core   All UTP cables come in one of two types: solid core or stranded core. Each wire in **solid core** UTP uses a single solid wire. With **stranded core**, each wire is actually a bundle of tiny wire strands. Each of these cable types has its benefits and downsides. Solid core is a better conductor, but it is stiff and will break if handled too often or too roughly. Stranded core is not quite as good a conductor, but it will stand up to substantial handling without breaking. Figure 6.6 shows a close-up of solid and stranded core UTP.

TIA/EIA specifies that horizontal cabling should always be solid core. Remember, this cabling is going into your walls and ceilings, safe from the harmful effects of shoes and vacuum cleaners. The ceilings and walls enable you to take advantage of the better conductivity of solid core without the risk of

• **Figure 6.6**   Solid and stranded core UTP

Mike Meyers' CompTIA Network+ Guide to Managing and Troubleshooting Networks

cable damage. Stranded cable also has an important function in a structured cabling network, but I need to discuss a few more parts of the network before I talk about where to use stranded UTP cable.

Number of Pairs Pulling horizontal cables into your walls and ceilings is a time-consuming and messy business, and not a process you want to repeat, if at all possible. For this reason, most cable installers recommend using the highest CAT rating you can afford. Many years ago, I would also mention that you should use four-pair UTP, but today, four-pair is assumed. Four-pair UTP is so common that it's difficult, if not impossible, to find two-pair UTP.

You'll find larger bundled UTP cables in higher-end telephone setups. These cables hold 25 or even 100 pairs of wires (Figure 6.7).

Unlike previous CAT standards, TIA/EIA defines CAT 5e and later as four-pair-only cables.

• **Figure 6.7**   25-pair UTP

 Cross Check

Fire Ratings

You saw another aspect of cabling way back in Chapter 3, "Cabling and Topology," so check your memory here. What are fire ratings? When should you use plenum-grade cabling and when should you use riser-grade cabling? What about PVC? What are the differences?

Choosing Your Horizontal Cabling In the real world, network people only install CAT 5e or CAT 6 UTP, although CAT 6a is also starting to show up as 10GBaseT begins to see acceptance. Installing higher-rated cabling is done primarily as a hedge against new network technologies that may require a more advanced cable. Networking *caveat emptor* (buyer beware): many network installers take advantage of the fact that a lower CAT level will work on most networks and bid a network installation using the lowest-grade cable possible.

The Telecommunications Room

The telecommunications room is the heart of the basic star. This room—technically called the **intermediate distribution frame (IDF)**—is where all the horizontal runs from all the work areas come together. The concentration of all this gear in one place makes the telecommunications room potentially one of the messiest parts of the basic star. Even if you do a nice, neat job of organizing the cables when they are first installed, networks change over time. People move computers, new work areas are added, network topologies are added or improved, and so on. Unless you impose some type of organization, this conglomeration of equipment and cables decays into a nightmarish mess.

The telecommunications room is also known as an *intermediate distribution frame (IDF)*, as opposed to the main distribution frame (MDF), which we will discuss later in the chapter.

Fortunately, the TIA/EIA structured cabling standards define the use of specialized components in the telecommunications room that make organizing a snap. In fact, it might be fair to say that there are too many options! To keep it simple, we're going to stay with the most common telecommunications room setup and then take a short peek at some other fairly common options.

Equipment Racks The central component of every telecommunications room is one or more equipment racks. An **equipment rack** provides a safe, stable platform for all the different hardware components. All equipment racks are 19 inches wide, but they vary in height from two- to three-foot-high models

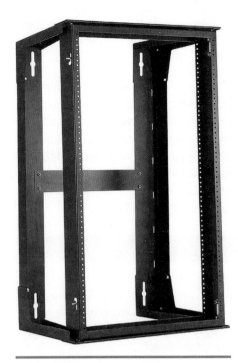

Equipment racks evolved out of the railroad signaling racks from the 19th century. The components in a rack today obviously differ a lot from railroad signaling, but the 19-inch width has remained the standard for well over a hundred years.

• **Figure 6.8**   A short equipment rack

• **Figure 6.9**   A free-standing rack

• **Figure 6.10**   A rack-mounted UPS

that bolt onto a wall (Figure 6.8) to the more popular floor-to-ceiling models, *free-standing racks* (Figure 6.9).

You can mount almost any network hardware component into a rack. All manufacturers make rack-mounted switches that mount into a rack with a few screws. These switches are available with a wide assortment of ports and capabilities. There are even rack-mounted servers, complete with slide-out keyboards, and rack-mounted uninterruptible power supplies (UPSs) to power the equipment (Figure 6.10).

All rack-mounted equipment uses a height measurement known simply as a **unit (U)**. A U is 1.75 inches. A device that fits in a 1.75-inch space is called a 1U; a device designed for a 3.5-inch space is a 2U; and a device that goes into a 7-inch space is called a 4U. Most rack-mounted devices are 1U, 2U, or 4U. The rack in Figure 6.10 is called a 42U rack to reflect the total number of Us it can hold.

The key when planning a rack system is to determine what sort of rack-mounted equipment you plan to have and then get the rack or racks for your space. For example, if your rack will only have patch panels (see the next section), switches, and routers, you can get away with a *two-post rack*. The pieces are small and easily supported.

If you're going to install big servers, on the other hand, then you need to plan for a *four-post rack* or a *server rail rack*. A four-post rack supports all four corners of the server. The server rail rack enables you to slide the server out so you can open it up. This is very useful for swapping out dead drives for new ones in big file servers.

When planning how many racks you need in your rack system and where to place them, take proper air flow into consideration. You shouldn't cram servers and gear into every corner. Even with good air conditioning systems, bad air flow can cook components.

Finally, make sure to secure the telecommunications room. Rack security is a must for protecting valuable equipment. Get a lock!

Patch Panels and Cables   Ideally, once you install horizontal cabling, you should never move it. As you know, UTP horizontal cabling has a solid core, making it pretty stiff. Solid core cables can handle some rearranging, but if you insert a wad of solid core cables directly into your switches, every time you move a cable to a different port on the switch, or move the switch itself, you will jostle the cable. You don't have to move a solid core cable many times before one of the solid copper wires breaks, and there goes a network connection!

Luckily for you, you can easily avoid this problem by using a patch panel. A **patch panel** is simply a box with a row of female ports in the front and permanent connections in the back, to which you connect the horizontal cables (Figure 6.11).

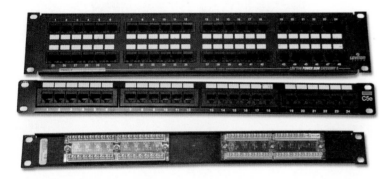

• **Figure 6.11**   Typical patch panels

The most common type of patch panel today uses a special type of connector called a **110 block**, or sometimes called a *110-punchdown block*. UTP cables connect to a 110 block using a **punchdown tool**. Figure 6.12 shows a typical punchdown tool, and Figure 6.13 shows the punchdown tool punching down individual strands.

• **Figure 6.12**   Punchdown tool

• **Figure 6.13**   Punching down a 110 block

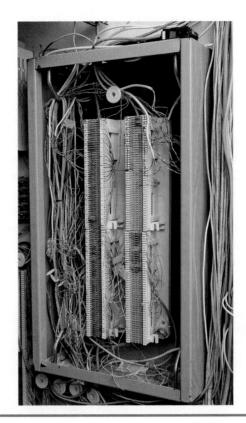

• Figure 6.14   66-block patch panels

 Make sure you insert the wires according to the same standard (TIA/EIA 568A or TIA/EIA 568B) on both ends of the cable. If you don't, you might end up swapping the sending and receiving wires (known as *TX/RX reversed*) and inadvertently creating a crossover cable.

The CompTIA Network+ exam uses the terms *110 block* and *66 block* exclusively to describe the punchdown blocks common in telecommunication. In the field, in contrast, and in manuals and other literature, you'll see the punchdown blocks referred to as *110-punchdown blocks* and *66-punchdown blocks* as well. Some manufacturers even split punchdown into two words: *punch down*. Be prepared to be nimble in the field, but expect 110 block and 66 block on the exam.

Tech Tip

Serious Labeling

The ANSI/TIA-606-B *standard covers proper labeling and documentation of cabling, patch panels, and wall outlets. If you want to know how the pros label and document a structured cabling system (and you've got some cash to blow), check out the ANSI/TIA-606-B naming conventions from TIA.*

The punchdown block has small metal-lined grooves for the individual wires. The punchdown tool has a blunt end that forces the wire into the groove. The metal in the groove slices the cladding enough to make contact.

At one time, the older 66-punchdown block patch panel, found in just about every commercial telephone installation (Figure 6.14), saw some use in PC networks. The 110 block introduces less crosstalk than 66 blocks, so most high-speed network installations use the former for both telephone service and LANs. Given their large installed base, it's still common to find a group of 66-block patch panels in a telecommunications room separate from the network's 110-block patch panels.

Not only do patch panels prevent the horizontal cabling from being moved, but they are also your first line of defense in organizing the cables. All patch panels have space in the front for labels, and these labels are the network tech's best friend! Simply place a tiny label on the patch panel to identify each cable, and you will never have to experience that sinking feeling of standing in the telecommunications room of your nonfunctioning network, wondering which cable is which. If you want to be a purist, there is an official, and rather confusing, TIA/EIA *naming convention* called **TIA/EIA 606**, but a number of real-world network techs simply use their own internal codes (Figure 6.15).

Patch panels are available in a wide variety of configurations that include different types of ports and numbers of ports. You can get UTP, STP, or fiber ports, and some manufacturers combine several different types on the same patch panel. Panels are available with 8, 12, 24, 48, or even more ports.

• **Figure 6.15**   Typical patch panels with labels

UTP patch panels, like UTP cables, come with CAT ratings, which you should be sure to check. Don't blow a good CAT 6 cable installation by buying a cheap patch panel—get a CAT 6 patch panel! A CAT 6 panel can handle the 250-MHz frequency used by CAT 6 and offers lower crosstalk and network interference. A higher-rated panel supports earlier standards, so you can use a CAT 6 or even CAT 6a rack with CAT 5e cabling. Most manufacturers proudly display the CAT level right on the patch panel (Figure 6.16).

Once you have installed the patch panel, you need to connect the ports to the switch through **patch cables**. Patch cables are short (typically two- to five-foot) straight-through UTP cables. Patch cables use stranded rather than solid cable, so they can tolerate much more handling. Even though you can make your own patch cables, most people buy premade ones. Buying patch cables enables you to use different-colored cables to facilitate organization (yellow for accounting, blue for sales, or whatever scheme works for you). Most prefabricated patch cables also come with a reinforced (booted) connector specially designed to handle multiple insertions and removals (Figure 6.17).

• **Figure 6.16**   CAT level on patch panel

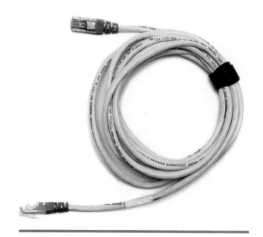

• **Figure 6.17**   Typical patch cable

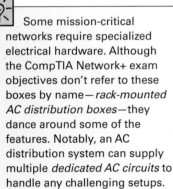

Cable runs

Rack 1

Rack 2

Some mission-critical networks require specialized electrical hardware. Although the CompTIA Network+ exam objectives don't refer to these boxes by name—*rack-mounted AC distribution boxes*—they dance around some of the features. Notably, an AC distribution system can supply multiple *dedicated AC circuits* to handle any challenging setups.

If you install such a box in your rack, make sure to add labels to both systems and circuits. Proper system labeling and circuit labeling can make life much easier in the event of problems later on.

• **Figure 6.18**   Network taking shape, with racks installed and horizontal cabling runs

A telecommunications room doesn't have to be a special room dedicated to computer equipment. You can use specially made cabinets with their own little built-in equipment racks that sit on the floor or attach to a wall, or you can use a storage room if the equipment can be protected from the other items stored there. Fortunately, the demand for telecommunications rooms has been around for so long that most office spaces have premade telecommunications rooms, even if they are no more than closets in smaller offices.

At this point, the network is taking shape (Figure 6.18). The TIA/EIA horizontal cabling is installed and the telecommunications room is configured. Now it's time to address the last part of the structured cabling system: the work area.

The Work Area

From a cabling standpoint, a work area is nothing more than a wall outlet that serves as the termination point for horizontal network cables: a convenient insertion point for a PC and a telephone. (In practice, of course, the term "work area" includes the office or cubicle.) A wall outlet itself consists of one or two female jacks to accept the cable, a mounting bracket, and a face-plate. You connect the PC to the wall outlet with a patch cable (Figure 6.19).

The female RJ-45 jacks in these wall outlets also have CAT ratings. You must buy CAT-rated jacks for wall outlets to go along with the CAT rating of the cabling in your network. In fact, many network connector manufacturers use the same connectors in the wall outlets that they use on the patch panels. These modular outlets significantly increase ease of installation. Make sure you

• **Figure 6.19**   Typical work area outlet

label the outlet to show the job of each connector (Figure 6.20). A good outlet will also have some form of label that identifies its position on the patch panel. Proper documentation of your outlets will save you an incredible amount of work later.

The last step is connecting the PC to the wall outlet. Here again, most folks use a patch cable. Its stranded cabling stands up to the abuse caused by moving PCs, not to mention the occasional kick.

You'll recall from Chapter 5, "Modern Ethernet," that 10/100/1000BaseT networks specify a limit of 100 meters between a hub or switch and a node. Interestingly, though, the TIA/EIA 568 specification allows only UTP cable lengths of 90 meters. What's with the missing 10 meters? Have you figured it out? Hint: the answer lies in the discussion we've just been having. Ding! Time's up! The answer is ... the patch cables! Patch cables add extra distance between the switch and the PC, so TIA/EIA compensates by reducing the horizontal cabling length.

The work area may be the simplest part of the structured cabling system, but it is also the source of most network failures. When a user can't access the network and you suspect a broken cable, the first place to look is the work area.

• Figure 6.20   Properly labeled outlet

Structured Cable—Beyond the Star

Thus far you've seen structured cabling as a single star topology on a single floor of a building. Let's now expand that concept to an entire building and learn the terms used by the structured cabling folks, such as the demarc and NIU, to describe this much more complex setup.

You can hardly find a building today that isn't connected to both the Internet and the telephone company. In many cases, this is a single connection, but for now, let's treat them as separate connections.

As you saw in the previous chapter, a typical building-wide network consists of a high-speed backbone that runs vertically through the building and connects to multispeed switches on each floor that, in turn, service the individual PCs on that floor. A dedicated telephone cabling backbone that enables the distribution of phone calls to individual telephones runs alongside the network cabling. While every telephone installation varies, most commonly you'll see one or more strands of 25-pair UTP cables running to the 66 block in the telecommunications room on each floor (Figure 6.21).

> Structured cabling goes beyond a single building and even describes methods for interconnecting multiple buildings. The CompTIA Network+ certification exam does not cover interbuilding connections.

Demarc

Connections from the outside world—whether network or telephone—come into a building at a location called a demarc, short for *demarcation point.* The term "demarc" refers to the physical location of the connection and marks the dividing line of responsibility for the functioning of the network. You take care of the internal functioning; the person or company that supplies the upstream service to you must support connectivity and function on the far side of the demarc.

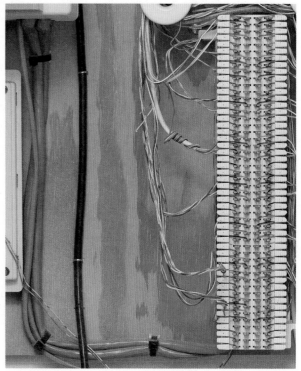

• Figure 6.21   25-pair running to local 66-block

• **Figure 6.22**   Typical home network interface box

In a private home, the DSL or cable modem supplied by your ISP is a **network interface unit (NIU)** that serves as a demarc between your home network and your ISP, and most homes have a network interface box, like the one shown in Figure 6.22, that provides the connection for your telephone.

In an office environment, the demarc is usually more complex, given that a typical building simply has to serve a much larger number of telephones and computers. Figure 6.23 shows the demarc for a midsized building, showing both Internet and telephone connections coming in from the outside.

One challenge to companies that supply ISP/telephone services is the need to diagnose faults in the system. Most of today's NIUs come with extra "smarts" that enable the ISP or telephone company to determine if the customer has disconnected from the NIU. These special (and very common) NIUs are known as **smart jacks**. Smart jacks also have the very handy capability to set up a remote loopback—critical for loopback testing when you're at one end of the connection and the other connection is blocks or even miles away.

Tech Tip

NIU=NIB=NID: Huh?

The terms used to describe the devices that often mark the demarcation point in a home or office get tossed about with wild abandon. Various manufacturers and technicians call them network interface units, network interface boxes, or network interface devices. (Some techs call them demarcs, just to muddy the waters further, but we won't go there.) By name or by initial—NIU, NIB, or NID—it's all the same thing, the box that marks the point where your responsibility begins on the inside.

The best way to think of a demarc is in terms of responsibility. If something breaks on one side of the demarc, it's your problem; on the other side, it's the ISP/phone company's problem.

• **Figure 6.23**   Typical office demarc

Mike Meyers' CompTIA Network+ Guide to Managing and Troubleshooting Networks

Connections Inside the Demarc

After the demarc, network and telephone cables connect to some type of box, owned by the customer, that acts as the primary distribution tool for the building. That box is called the **customer-premises equipment (CPE)**. Any cabling that runs from the NIU to whatever CPE is used by the customer is the **demarc extension**. For telephones, the cabling might connect to special CPE called a **multiplexer** and, on the LAN side, almost certainly to a powerful switch. This switch usually connects to a patch panel. This patch panel, in turn, leads to every telecommunications room in the building. This main patch panel is called a **vertical cross-connect**. Figure 6.24 shows an example of a fiber patch panel acting as a vertical cross-connect for a building.

• **Figure 6.24** LAN vertical cross-connect

Telephone systems also use vertical cross-connects. Figure 6.25 shows a vertical cross-connect for a telephone system. Note the large number of 25-pair UTP cables feeding out of this box. Each 25-pair cable leads to a telecommunications room on a floor of the building.

The combination of demarc, telephone cross-connects, and LAN cross-connects needs a place to live in a building. The room that stores all of this equipment is known as a **main distribution frame (MDF)** to distinguish it from the multiple IDF rooms (a.k.a., telecommunications rooms) that serve individual floors.

The ideal that every building should have a single demarc, a single MDF, and multiple IDFs is only that—an ideal. Every structured cabling installation is unique and must adapt to the physical constraints of the building provided. One building may serve multiple customers, creating the need for multiple NIUs each serving a different customer. A smaller building may combine

• **Figure 6.25** Telephone vertical cross-connect

a demarc, MDF, and IDF into a single room. With structured cabling, the idea is to appreciate the terms while, at the same time, appreciating that it's the actual building and the needs of the customers that determine the design of a structured cabling system.

■ Installing Structured Cabling

A professional installer always begins a structured cabling installation by first assessing your site and planning the installation in detail before pulling a single piece of cable. As the customer, your job is to work closely with the installer. That means locating floor plans, providing access, and even putting on old clothes and crawling along with the installer as he or she combs through your ceilings, walls, and closets. Even though you're not the actual installer, you must understand the installation process to help the installer make the right decisions for your network.

Structured cabling requires a lot of planning. You need to know if the cables from the work areas can reach the telecommunications room—is the distance less than the 90-meter limit dictated by the TIA/EIA standard? How will you route the cable? What path should each run take to get to the wall outlets? Don't forget that just because a cable looks like it will reach, there's no guarantee that it will. Ceilings and walls often include hidden surprises like firewalls—big, thick, concrete walls designed into buildings that require a masonry drill or a jackhammer to punch through. Let's look at the steps that go into proper planning.

Getting a Floor Plan

First, you need a blueprint of the area. If you ever contact an installer and he or she doesn't start by asking for a floor plan, fire them immediately and get one who does. The floor plan is the key to proper planning; a good floor plan shows you the location of closets that could serve as telecommunications rooms, alerts you to any firewalls in your way, and gives you a good over-all feel for the scope of the job ahead.

If you don't have a floor plan—and this is often the case with homes or older buildings—you'll need to create your own. Go get a ladder and a flashlight—you'll need them to poke around in ceilings, closets, and crawl spaces as you map out the location of rooms, walls, and anything else of interest to the installation. Figure 6.26 shows a typical do-it-yourself floor plan.

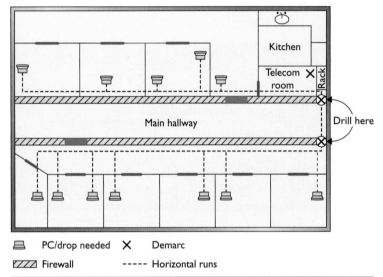

Symbol	Meaning	Symbol	Meaning
🖥	PC/drop needed	✕	Demarc
▨	Firewall	-----	Horizontal runs

• **Figure 6.26**   Network floor plan

Mapping the Runs

Now that you have your floor plan, you need to map the cable runs. Here's where you survey the work areas, noting the locations of existing or planned systems to determine where to place each cable drop. A **cable drop** is the location where the cable comes out of the wall in the workstation. You should also talk to users, management, and other interested parties to try to understand their plans for the future. Installing a few extra drops now is much easier than installing them a year from now when those two unused offices suddenly find themselves with users who immediately need networked computers!

At this point, cost first raises its ugly head. Face it: cables, drops, and the people who install them cost money! The typical price for a network installation is around US $50–150 per drop. Find out how much you want to spend and make some calls. Most network installers price their network jobs by quoting a per-drop cost.

While you're mapping your runs, you have to make another big decision: Do you want to run the cables in the walls or outside them? Many companies sell wonderful external **raceway** products that adhere to your walls, making for a much simpler, though less neat, installation than running cables in the

Mike Meyers' CompTIA Network+ Guide to Managing and Troubleshooting Networks

walls (Figure 6.27). Raceways make good sense in older buildings or when you don't have the guts—or the rights—to go into the walls.

Determining the Location of the Telecommunications Room

While mapping the runs, you should decide on the location of your telecommunications room. When deciding on this location, keep five issues in mind:

• **Figure 6.27**   A typical raceway

- ■ **Distance**   The telecommunications room must be located in a spot that won't require cable runs longer than 90 meters. In most locations, keeping runs under 90 meters requires little effort, as long as the telecommunications room is placed in a central location.

- ■ **Power**   Many of the components in your telecommunications room need power. Make sure you provide enough! If possible, put the telecommunications room on its own dedicated circuit; that way, when someone blows a circuit in the kitchen, it doesn't take out the entire network.

- ■ **Humidity**   Electrical components and water don't mix well. (Remind me to tell you about the time I installed a rack in an abandoned bathroom and the toilet that later exploded.) Remember that dryness also means low humidity. Avoid areas with the potential for high humidity, such as a closet near a pool or the room where the cleaning people leave mop buckets full of water. Of course, any well air-conditioned room should be fine—which leads to the next big issue...

- ■ **Cooling**   Telecommunications rooms tend to get warm, especially if you add a couple of server systems and a UPS. Make sure your telecommunications room has an air-conditioning outlet or some other method of keeping the room cool. Figure 6.28 shows how I installed an air-conditioning duct in my small equipment closet. Of course, I did this only after I discovered that the server was repeatedly rebooting due to overheating!

- ■ **Access**   Access involves two different issues. First, it means preventing unauthorized access. Think about the people you want and don't want messing around with your network, and act accordingly. In my small office, the equipment closet literally sits eight feet from me, so I don't concern myself too much with unauthorized access. You, on the other hand, may want to consider placing a lock on the door of your telecommunications room if you're concerned that unscrupulous or unqualified people might try to access it.

• **Figure 6.28**   An A/C duct cooling a telecommunications room

One other issue to keep in mind when choosing your telecommunications room is expandability. Will this telecommunications room be able to grow with your network? Is it close enough to be able to service any additional office

• **Figure 6.29**   Cable trays over a drop ceiling

space your company may acquire nearby? If your company decides to take over the floor above you, can you easily run vertical cabling to another telecommunications room on that floor from this room? While the specific issues will be unique to each installation, keep thinking "expansion" or *scalability* as you design—your network will grow, whether or not you think so now!

So, you've mapped your cable runs and established your telecommunications room—now you're ready to start pulling cable!

Pulling Cable

Pulling cable is easily one of the most thankless and unpleasant jobs in the entire networking world. It may not look that hard from a distance, but the devil is in the details. First of all, pulling cable requires two people if you want to get the job done quickly; having three people is even better. Most pullers like to start from the telecommunications room and pull toward the drops. In an office area with a drop ceiling, pullers will often feed the cabling along the run by opening ceiling tiles and stringing the cable via hooks or **cable trays** that travel above the ceiling (Figure 6.29). Professional cable pullers have an arsenal of interesting tools to help them move the cable horizontally, including telescoping poles, special nylon pull ropes, and even nifty little crossbows and pistols that can fire a pull rope long distances!

Cable trays are standard today, but a previous lack of codes or standards for handling cables led to a nightmare of disorganized cables in drop ceilings all over the world. Any cable puller will tell you that the hardest part of installing cables is the need to work around all the old cable installations in the ceiling (Figure 6.30).

• **Figure 6.31**   Nicely run cables

• **Figure 6.30**   Messy cabling nightmare

Local codes, TIA/EIA, and the National Electrical Code (NEC) all have strict rules about how you pull cable in a ceiling. A good installer uses either hooks or trays, which provide better cable management, safety, and protection from electrical interference (Figure 6.31). The faster the network, the more critical good cable management becomes.

• **Figure 6.32**   Cutting a hole

• **Figure 6.33**   Locating a dropped pull rope

Running cable horizontally requires relatively little effort, compared to running the cable down from the ceiling to a pretty faceplate at the work area, which often takes a lot of skill. In a typical office area with sheetrock walls, the installer first decides on the position for the outlet, generally using a stud finder to avoid cutting on top of a stud. Once the worker cuts the hole (Figure 6.32), most installers drop a line to the hole using a weight tied to the end of a nylon pull rope (Figure 6.33). They can then attach the network cable to the pull rope and pull it down to the hole. Once the cable is pulled through the new hole, the installer puts in an outlet box or a low-voltage **mounting bracket** (Figure 6.34). This bracket acts as a holder for the faceplate.

Back in the telecommunications room, the many cables leading to each work area are consolidated and organized in preparation for the next stage: making connections. A truly professional installer takes great care in organizing the equipment closet. Figure 6.35 shows a typical installation using special cable guides to bring the cables down to the equipment rack.

• **Figure 6.34**   Installing a mounting bracket

Making Connections

Making connections consists of connecting both ends of each cable to the proper jacks. This step also includes the most important step in the entire process: testing each cable run to ensure that every connection meets the requirements of the network that will use it. Installers also use this step to document and label each cable run—a critical step too often forgotten by inexperienced installers, and one you need to verify takes place!

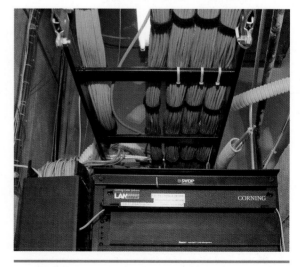

• **Figure 6.35**   End of cables guided to rack

Connecting the Work Areas

In the work area, the cable installer connects a cable run by crimping a jack onto the end of the wire and mounting the faceplate to complete the installation (Figure 6.36). Note the back of the jack shown in Figure 6.36. This jack uses the popular 110-punchdown connection just like the one shown earlier in the chapter for patch panels. All 110 connections have a color code that tells you which wire to punch into which connection on the back of the jack.

Rolling Your Own Patch Cables

Although most people prefer simply to purchase premade patch cables, making your own is fairly easy. To make your own, use stranded UTP cable that matches the CAT level of your horizontal cabling. Stranded cable also requires specific crimps, so don't use crimps designed for solid cable. Crimping is simple enough, although getting it right takes some practice.

Figure 6.37 shows the two main tools of the crimping trade: an RJ-45 crimper with built-in wire stripper and a pair of wire snips. Professional cable installers naturally have a wide variety of other tools as well.

Here are the steps for properly crimping an RJ-45 onto a UTP cable. If you have some crimps, cable, and a crimping tool handy, follow along!

1. Cut the cable square using RJ-45 crimpers or scissors.

2. Strip off ½ inch of plastic jacket from the end of the cable (Figure 6.38) with a dedicated wire stripper or the one built into the crimping tool.

3. Slowly and carefully insert each individual wire into the correct location according to either TIA/EIA 568A or B (Figure 6.39). Unravel as little as possible.

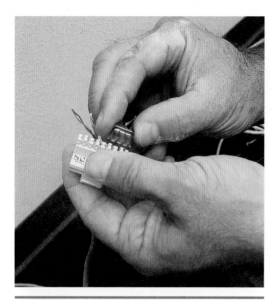

• **Figure 6.36**   Crimping a jack

• **Figure 6.37**   Crimper and snips

• **Figure 6.38**   Properly stripped cable

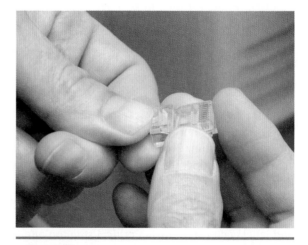

• **Figure 6.39**   Inserting the individual strands

Mike Meyers' CompTIA Network+ Guide to Managing and Troubleshooting Networks

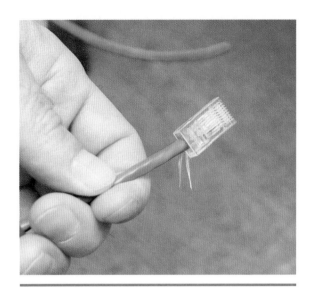

• **Figure 6.40**   Crimping the cable

• **Figure 6.41**   Properly crimped cable

4. Insert the crimp into the crimper and press (Figure 6.40). Don't worry about pressing too hard; the crimper has a stop to prevent you from using too much pressure.

Figure 6.41 shows a nicely crimped cable. Note how the plastic jacket goes into the crimp.

 Try This!

Crimping Your Own Cable

If you've got some spare CAT 5 lying around (and what tech enthusiast doesn't?) as well as a cable crimper and some crimps, go ahead and use the previous section as a guide and crimp your own cable. This skill is essential for any network technician. Remember, practice makes perfect!

A good patch cable should include a boot. Figure 6.42 shows a boot being slid onto a newly crimped cable. Don't forget to slide each boot onto the patch cable *before* you crimp both ends!

After making a cable, you need to test it to make sure it's properly crimped. Read the section on testing cable runs later in this chapter to see how to test them.

Connecting the Patch Panels

Connecting the cables to patch panels requires you to deal with three issues. The first issue is patch cable management. Figure 6.43 shows the front of a small network's equipment rack—note the complete lack of cable management!

Managing patch cables means using the proper cable management hardware. Plastic D-rings guide the patch cables neatly along the sides and front of the patch panel. Finger boxes

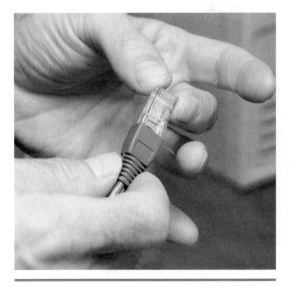

• **Figure 6.42**   Adding a boot

• **Figure 6.43**   Bad cable management

• **Figure 6.44**   Good cable management

are rectangular cylinders with slots in the front; the patch cables run into the open ends of the box, and individual cables are threaded through the fingers on their way to the patch panel, keeping them neatly organized.

Creativity and variety abound in the world of cable-management hardware—there are as many different solutions to cable management as there are ways to screw it up. Figure 6.44 shows a rack using good cable management—these patch cables are well secured using cable-management hardware, making them much less susceptible to damage from mishandling. Plus, it looks much nicer!

The second issue to consider when connecting cables is the overall organization of the patch panel as it relates to the organization of your network. Organize your patch panel so it mirrors the layout of your network. You can organize according to the physical layout, so the different parts of the patch panel correspond to different parts of your office space—for example, the north and south sides of the hallway. Another popular way to organize patch panels is to make sure they match the logical layout of the network, so the different user groups or company organizations have their own sections of the patch panel.

Finally, proper patch panel cable management means documenting everything clearly and carefully. This way, any competent technician can follow behind you and troubleshoot connectivity problems. Good techs draw diagrams!

Testing the Cable Runs

Well, in theory, your horizontal cabling system is now installed and ready for a switch and some systems. Before you do this, though, you must test each cable run. Someone new to testing cable might think that all you need to do is verify that each jack has been properly connected. Although this is an important and necessary step, the interesting problem comes after that: verifying that your cable run can handle the speed of your network.

Copper- and fiber-based network runs have different issues and potential problems, and thus require different tools to resolve. Let's look at copper, then fiber.

Before I go further, let me be clear: a typical network admin/tech cannot properly test a new cable run. TIA/EIA provides a series of incredibly complex and important standards for testing cable, requiring a professional cable installer. The testing equipment alone totally surpasses the cost of most smaller network installations. Advanced network testing tools easily cost over $5,000, and some are well over $10,000! Never fear, though—a number of lower-end tools work just fine for basic network testing.

 The test tools described here also enable you to diagnose network problems.

Copper Challenges

Most network admin types staring at a potentially bad copper cable want to know the following:

- How long is this cable? If it's too long, the signal will degrade to the point that it's no longer detectable on the other end.

- Are any of the wires broken or not connected in the crimp (open)? If a wire is broken or a connection is open, it no longer has **continuity** (a complete, functioning connection).

- Is there any place where two bare wires touch? This creates a *short*. Shorts can take place when cables are damaged, but you can also get a short when improperly crimping two cables into the same place on a crimp.

- If there is a break, where is it? It's much easier to fix if the location is detectable.

- Are all of the wires terminated in the right place in the plug or jack? Does each termination match to the same standard?

- Is there electrical or radio interference from outside sources? UTP is susceptible to electromagnetic interference.

- Is the signal from any of the pairs in the same cable interfering with another pair? This common problem in UTP installations is called a **split pair**.

To answer these questions you must verify that both the cable and the terminated ends are correct. Making these verifications requires a **cable tester**. Various models of cable testers can answer some or all of these questions, depending on the amount of money you are willing to pay. At the low end of the cable tester market are devices that only test for continuity. These inexpensive (under $100) testers are often called **continuity testers** (Figure 6.45).

• **Figure 6.45** Continuity tester

Many techs and network testing folks use the term *wiremap* to refer to the proper connectivity for wires, as in, "Hey Joe, check the wiremap!"

Many of these testers require you to insert both ends of the cable into the tester. Of course, this can be a bit of a problem if the cable is already installed in the wall!

Better testers can run a **wiremap** test that goes beyond mere continuity, testing that all the wires on both ends of the cable connect to the right spot. A wiremap test will pick up shorts, crossed wires, and more.

A multimeter works perfectly well to test for continuity, assuming you can place its probes on each end of the cable. Set the multimeter to its continuity setting if it has one (Figure 6.46) or to Ohms. With the latter setting, if you have a connection, you get zero Ohms, and if you don't have a connection, you get infinite Ohms.

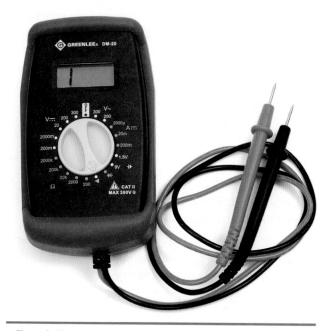

• **Figure 6.46**   Multimeter

Medium-priced testers (~$400) certainly test continuity and wiremap and include the additional capability to determine the length of a cable; they can even tell you where a break is located on any of the individual wire strands. This type of cable tester (Figure 6.47) is generically called a **time domain reflectometer (TDR)**. Most medium-priced testers come with a small loopback device to insert into the far end of the cable, enabling the tester to work with installed cables. This is the type of tester you want to have around!

If you want a device that fully tests a cable run to the very complex TIA/EIA standards, the price shoots up fast. These higher-end testers can detect things the lesser testers cannot, such as crosstalk and attenuation.

Crosstalk poses a threat to properly functioning cable runs. Today's UTP cables consist of four pairs of wires, all squished together inside a plastic tube. When you send a

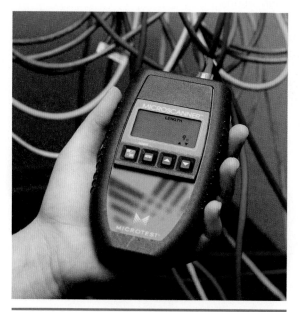

• **Figure 6.47**   A typical medium-priced TDR called a MicroScanner

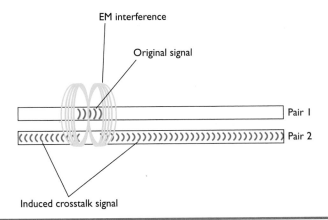

• **Figure 6.48** Crosstalk

signal down one of these pairs, the other pairs pick up some of the signal, as shown in Figure 6.48. This is called **crosstalk**.

Every piece of UTP in existence generates crosstalk. Worse, when you crimp the end of a UTP cable to a jack or plugs, crosstalk increases. A poor-quality crimp creates so much crosstalk that a cable run won't operate at its designed speed. To detect crosstalk, a normal-strength signal is sent down one pair of wires in a cable. An electronic detector, connected on the same end of the cable as the end emanating the signal, listens on the other three pairs and measures the amount of interference, as shown in Figure 6.49. This is called **near-end crosstalk (NEXT)**.

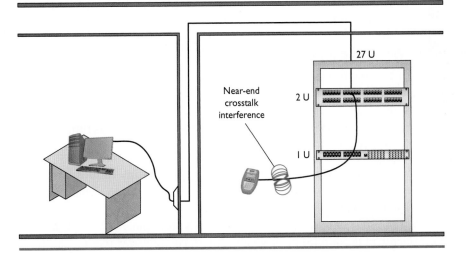

• **Figure 6.49** Near-end crosstalk

If you repeat this test, sending the signal down one pair of wires, but this time listening on the other pairs on the far end of the connection, you test for **far-end crosstalk (FEXT)**, as shown in Figure 6.50.

As if that's not bad enough, as a signal progresses down a piece of wire, it becomes steadily weaker: this is called **attenuation**. As a cable run gets longer, the attenuation increases, and the signal becomes more susceptible to crosstalk. A tester must send a signal down one end of a wire, test for NEXT and FEXT on the ends of every other pair, and then repeat this process for every pair in the UTP cable.

Both NEXT and FEXT are measured in decibels (dB). See the following Tech Tip for the scoop.

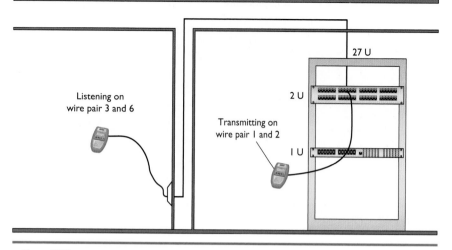

Listening on
wire pair 3 and 6

27 U

2 U

Transmitting on
wire pair 1 and 2

1 U

• **Figure 6.50**   Far-end crosstalk

• **Figure 6.51**   A typical cable certifier—a Microtest OMNIScanner (photo courtesy of Fluke Networks)

This process of verifying that every cable run meets the exacting TIA/EIA standards requires very powerful testing tools, generally known as **cable certifiers** or just certifiers. Cable certifiers can both do the high-end testing and generate a report that a cable installer can print out and hand to a customer to prove that the installed cable runs pass TIA/EIA standards.

Figure 6.51 shows an example of this type of scanner made by Fluke (www.fluke.com) in its Microtest line. Most network techs don't need these advanced testers, so unless you have some deep pockets or find yourself doing serious cable testing, stick to the medium-priced testers.

Fiber Challenges

Fiber cable runs offer similar challenges to copper cable runs, but there are also some very specific differences. Just like with copper, signal loss is important and measured in decibels. But the causes of loss can differ a lot. Also, the many competing standards can catch techs running fiber by surprise.

Signal Loss/Degradation   Just like with copper wire, various imperfections in the media—the glass fiber, in this case—cause signal loss over distance. A lot of factors come into play.

Broken cables or *open connections* obviously stop signals. The typical small form-factor pluggable (SFP) or gigabit interface converter (GBIC) can have problems. When you're checking for a *bad SFP/GBIC*, you'll need to check both the connector and the cable going into that connector. Either or both could cause the signal loss.

A *dirty connector* can cause pretty serious signal loss with fiber. It's important not to smudge the glass!

When you think about fiber-optic cables, you need to remember that the part that carries the signal is really tiny, only a few microns. When you're connecting two pieces of fiber, even a small *connector mismatch* in either the cladding (the outside) or the core (the inside) can cause serious losses.

• **Figure 6.52**   Light leakage—note the colored glow at the bends but the dark cable at the straight.

Attenuation is the weakening of a signal as it travels long distances. *Dispersion* is when a signal spreads out over long distances. Both attenuation and dispersion are caused when wave signals travel too far without help over fiber-optic media.

Every piece of fiber has a certain *bend radius limitation*. If you bend a fiber-optic cable too much, you get **light leakage**, as shown in Figure 6.52. Light leakage means that part of the signal goes out the cable rather than arriving at the end. That's not a good thing.

Physical or Signal Mismatch   Fiber networks have a relatively small number of connectors but offer a pretty wide variety of signal types that use those connectors. These variations come into play in several ways. First, just because you can connect to a particular SFC or GBIC, that doesn't mean the signal will work. Plugging a generic SFC into a Cisco switch might work in a physical sense, but if the switch won't play with anything but Cisco technology, you'll get a mismatch.

Likewise, you can find fiber connectors like SC or LC that will attach to single-mode or multimode fiber. Plugging a single-mode cable into a switch that expects multimode? Such a *cable mismatch* or *fiber mismatch* means your network—at least that portion of it—won't work.

Finally, different runs of fiber use different wavelength signals. You might be able to plug an LC connector into a switch just fine, for example, but if the signal starts at 1310 nm and the switch expects 1530 nm, that sort of *wavelength mismatch* will stop the transmission cold.

Fiber Tools   A fiber technician uses a large number of tools (Figure 6.53) and an almost artistic amount

• **Figure 6.53**   Older fiber termination kit

• **Figure 6.54**   An optical time domain reflectometer (photo courtesy of Fluke Networks)

of skill. Over the years, easier terminations have been developed, but putting an ST, SC, LC, or other connector on the end of a piece of fiber is still very challenging.

A fiber-optic run has problems that are both similar to and different from those of a UTP run. Fiber-optic runs don't experience crosstalk or interference (as we usually think of it) because they use light instead of an electrical current.

Fiber-optic cables still break, however, so a good tech always keeps an **optical time domain reflectometer (OTDR)** handy (Figure 6.54) for just such scenarios. OTDRs determine continuity and, if there's a break, tell you exactly how far down the cable to look for the break.

TIA/EIA has very complex requirements for testing fiber runs, and the cabling industry sells fiber certifiers to make sure a fiber will carry its designed signal speed.

The three big issues with fiber are attenuation, light leakage, and modal distortion. The amount of light propagating down the fiber cable diffuses over distance, which causes attenuation or **dispersion** (when the light signal spreads).

The process of installing a structured cabling system is rather involved, requires a great degree of skill, and should be left to professionals. By understanding the process, however, you can tackle most of the problems that come up in an installed structured cabling system. Most importantly, you'll understand the lingo used by the structured cabling installers so you can work with them more efficiently.

■ NICs

Now that the network is completely in place, it's time to turn to the final part of any physical network: the NICs. A good network tech must recognize different types of NICs by sight and know how to install and troubleshoot them. Let's begin by reviewing the differences between UTP and fiber-optic NICs.

All UTP Ethernet NICs use the RJ-45 connector. The cable runs from the NIC to a switch (Figure 6.55).

Tech Tip

Onboard NICs

Many motherboards these days include an onboard NIC. This, of course, completely destroys the use of the acronym "NIC" to represent network interface card *because no card is actually involved. But heck, we're nerds and, just as we'll probably never stop using the term "RJ-45" when the correct term is "8P8C," we'll keep using the term "NIC." I know! Let's just pretend it stands for* network interface connection!

• **Figure 6.55**   Typical UTP NIC

Fiber-optic NICs come in a wide variety; worse, manufacturers use the same connector types for multiple standards. You'll find a 100BaseFX card designed for multimode cable with an SC connector, for example, and an identical card designed for single-mode cable, also with an SC connector. You simply must see the documentation that comes with the two cards to tell them apart. Figure 6.56 shows a typical fiber-optic network card.

• **Figure 6.56**   Typical fiber NIC (photo courtesy of 3Com Corp.)

Buying NICs

Some folks may disagree with me, but I always purchase name-brand NICs. For NICs, I recommend sticking with big names, such as Intel. The NICs are better made, have extra features, and are easy to return if they turn out to be defective.

Plus, replacing a missing driver on a name-brand NIC is easy, and you can be confident the drivers work well. The type of NIC you should purchase depends on your network. Try to think about the future and go for multispeed cards if your wallet can handle the extra cost. Also, where possible, try to stick with the same model of NIC. Every different model you buy means another set of driver disks you need to haul around in your tech bag. Using the same model of NIC makes driver updates easier, too.

Physical Connections

I'll state the obvious here: If you don't plug the NIC into the computer, the NIC won't work! Many users happily assume some sort of quantum magic when it comes to computer communications, but as a tech, you know better. Fortunately, most PCs come with built-in NICs, making physical installation a nonissue. If you're buying a NIC, physically inserting the NIC into one of the PC's expansion slots is the easiest part of the job. Most PCs today have two types of expansion slots. The older, but still common, expansion slot is the Peripheral Component Interconnect (PCI) type (Figure 6.57).

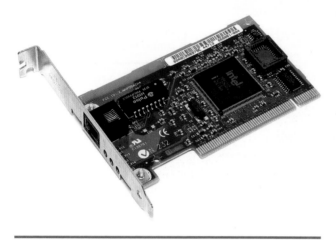

• **Figure 6.57**   PCI NIC

The newer PCI Express (PCIe) expansion slots are now more widely adopted by NIC suppliers. PCIe NICs usually come in either one-lane (×1) or two-lane (×2) varieties (Figure 6.58).

If you're not willing to open a PC case, you can get NICs with USB connections (Figure 6.59). USB NICs are handy to keep in your toolkit. If you walk up to a machine that might have a bad NIC, test your suspicions by inserting a USB NIC and moving the network cable from the potentially bad NIC to the USB one.

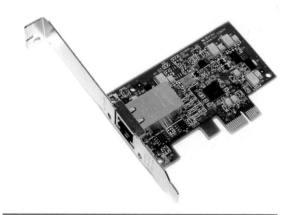

• **Figure 6.58**   PCIe NIC

• **Figure 6.59**   USB NIC

Drivers

Installing a NIC's driver into a Windows, OS X, or Linux system is easy: just insert the driver CD when prompted by the system. Unless you have a very offbeat NIC, the operating system will probably already have the driver preinstalled, but there are benefits to using the driver on the manufacturer's CD. The CDs that comes with many NICs, especially the higher-end, brand-name ones, include extra goodies such as enhanced drivers and handy utilities, but you'll only be able to access them if you install the driver that comes with the NIC.

Every operating system has some method to verify that the computer recognizes the NIC and is ready to use it. Windows systems have the Device Manager; Ubuntu Linux users have the Network applet under the Administration menu; and OS X users get the Network utility in System Preferences. Actually, most operating systems have multiple methods to show that the NIC is in good working order. Learn the various ways to verify the NIC for your OS, as this is the ultimate test of a good NIC installation.

Bonding

Most switches enable you to use multiple NICs for a single machine, a process called bonding or *link aggregation*. Bonding effectively doubles (or more) the speed between a machine and a switch. In preparing for this book, for example, I found that the connection between my graphics development computer and my file server was getting pounded by my constant sending and receiving of massive image files, slowing down everyone else's file access. Rather than upgrading the switches and NICs from Gigabit to 10 Gigabit Ethernet, I found that simply doubling the connections among those three machines—graphics computer, switch, and file server—increased performance all around. If you want to add link aggregation to your network to increase performance, use identical NICs and switches from the same companies to avoid incompatibility.

 The *Link Aggregation Control Protocol (LACP)* controls how multiple network devices send and receive data as a single connection.

Link Lights

All UTP NICs made today have some type of light-emitting diodes (LEDs) that give information about the state of the NIC's link to whatever is on the other end of the connection. Even though you know the lights are actually LEDs, get used to calling them link lights, as that's the term all network techs use. NICs can have between one and four different link lights, and the LEDs can be any color. These lights give you clues about what's happening with the link and are one of the first items to check whenever you think a system is disconnected from the network (Figure 6.60).

A link light tells you that the NIC is connected to a switch. Switches also have link lights, enabling you to check the connectivity at both ends of the cable. If a PC can't access a

• **Figure 6.60**   Mmmm, pretty lights!

• **Figure 6.61**   Multispeed lights

network and is acting disconnected, always check the link lights first. Multispeed devices usually have a link light that tells you the speed of the connection. In Figure 6.61, the light for port 2 in the top photo is orange, signifying that the other end of the cable is plugged into either a 10BaseT or 100BaseT NIC. The same port connected to a Gigabit NIC—that's the lower picture—displays a green LED.

A properly functioning link light is on and steady when the NIC is connected to another device. No flickering, no on and off, just on. A link light that is off or flickering indicates a connection problem.

Another light is the **activity light**. This little guy turns on when the card detects network traffic, so it intermittently flickers when operating properly. The activity light is a lifesaver for detecting problems, because in the real world, the connection light will sometimes lie to you. If the connection light says the connection is good, the next step is to try to copy a file or do something else to create network traffic. If the activity light does not flicker, there's a problem.

• **Figure 6.62**   Link lights on a switch

You might run into yet another light on some much older NICs, called a collision light. As you might suspect from the name, the **collision light** flickers when it detects collisions on the network. Modern NICs don't have these, but you might run into this phrase on the CompTIA Network+ certification exam.

Keep in mind that the device on the other end of the NIC's connection has link lights, too! Figure 6.62 shows the link lights on a modern switch. Most switches have a single LED per port to display connectivity and activity.

No standard governs how NIC manufacturers use their lights, and, as a result, they come in an amazing array of colors and layouts. When you encounter a NIC with a number of LEDs, take a moment to try to figure out what each one means. Although different NICs have various ways of arranging and using their LEDs, the functions are always the same: link, activity, and speed.

Many fiber-optic NICs don't have lights, making diagnosis of problems a bit more challenging. Nevertheless, most physical connection issues for fiber can be traced to the connection on the NIC itself. Fiber-optic cabling is incredibly delicate; the connectors that go into NICs are among the few places that anyone can touch fiber optics, so the connectors are the first thing to check when problems arise. Those who work with fiber always keep around a handy

• **Figure 6.63**   Optical connection tester

optical tester to enable them to inspect the quality of the connections. Only a trained eye can use such a device to judge a good fiber connection from a bad one—but once you learn how to use it, this kind of tester is extremely handy (Figure 6.63).

■ Diagnostics and Repair of Physical Cabling

"The network's down!" is easily the most terrifying phrase a network tech will ever hear. Networks fail for many reasons, and the first thing to know is that good-quality, professionally installed cabling rarely goes bad. Chapter 20, "Network Monitoring," covers principles of network diagnostics and support that apply to all networking scenarios, but let's take a moment now to discuss what to do when faced with a scenario that points to a problem with your physical network.

Diagnosing Physical Problems

Look for errors that point to physical disconnection. A key clue that you may have a physical problem is that a user gets a "No server is found" error, or tries to use the operating system's network explorer utility (like Network in Windows 7) and doesn't see any systems besides his or her own. First, try to eliminate software errors: if one particular application fails, try another. If the user can't browse the Internet, but can get e-mail, odds are good that the problem is with software, not hardware—unless someone unplugged the e-mail server!

Multiple systems failing to access the network often points to hardware problems. This is where knowledge of your network cabling helps. If all the systems connected to one switch suddenly no longer see the network, but all the other systems in your network still function, you not only have a probable hardware problem but also a suspect—the switch.

Check Your Lights

If you suspect a hardware problem, first check the link lights on the NIC and switch. If they're not lit, you know the cable isn't connected somewhere. If you're not physically at the system in question (if you're on a tech call, for

Not Connected

You are currently not
connected to any networks.

10:15 AM

• **Figure 6.64**   Disconnected NIC in Windows 7

example), you can have the user check his or her connection status through the link lights or through software. Every operating system has some way to tell you on the screen if it detects the NIC is disconnected. The network status icon in the Notification Area in Windows 7, for example, will display a little red × when a NIC is disconnected (Figure 6.64). A user who's unfamiliar with link lights (or who may not want to crawl under his or her desk) will have no problem telling you if the icon says "Not connected."

If your problem system is clearly not connecting, eliminate the possibility of a failed switch or other larger problem by checking to make sure other people can access the network, and that other systems can access the shared resource (server) that the problem system can't see. Make a quick visual inspection of the cable running from the back of the PC to the outlet.

Finally, if you can, plug the system into a known-good outlet and see if it works. A good network tech always keeps a long patch cable for just this purpose. If you get connectivity with the second outlet, you should begin to suspect bad wiring in structured cable running from the first outlet to the switch. Or, it could be a bad connector. Assuming the cable is installed properly and has been working correctly before this event, a simple continuity test will confirm your suspicion in most cases.

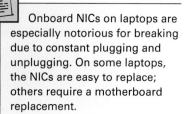
   Onboard NICs on laptops are especially notorious for breaking due to constant plugging and unplugging. On some laptops, the NICs are easy to replace; others require a motherboard replacement.

Check the NIC

Be warned that a bad NIC can also generate this "can't see the network" problem. Use the utility provided by your OS to verify that the NIC works. If you've got a NIC with diagnostic software, run it—this software will check the NIC's circuitry. The NIC's female connector is a common failure point, so NICs that come with diagnostic software often include a special test called a **loopback test**. A loopback test sends data out of the NIC and checks to see if it comes back. Some NICs perform only an internal loopback, which tests the circuitry that sends and receives, but not the actual connecting pins. A true external loopback requires a **loopback plug** inserted into the NIC's port (Figure 6.65). If a NIC is bad, replace it—preferably with an identical NIC so you don't have to reinstall drivers!

Cable Testing

The vast majority of network disconnect problems occur at the work area. If you've tested those connections, though, and the work area seems fine, it's time to consider deeper issues.

With the right equipment, diagnosing a bad horizontal cabling run is easy. Anyone with a network should own a midrange tester with TDR such as the Fluke MicroScanner.

With a little practice, you can easily determine not only whether a cable is disconnected but also where the disconnection takes place. Sometimes patience is required, especially if you've failed to label your cable runs, but you will find the problem.

• **Figure 6.65**   Loopback plug

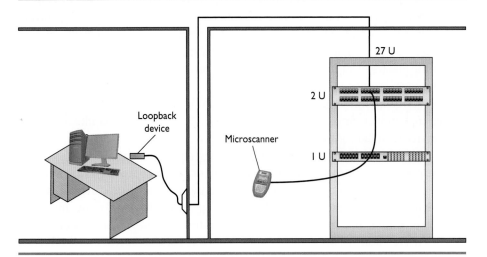

● **Figure 6.66**   Loopback plug in action

When you're testing a cable run, always include the patch cables as you test. This means unplugging the patch cable from the PC, attaching a tester, and then going to the telecommunications room. Here you'll want to unplug the patch cable from the switch and plug the tester into that patch cable, making a complete test, as shown in Figure 6.66.

Testing in this manner gives you a complete test from the switch to the system. In general, a broken cable must be replaced. Fixing a bad patch cable is easy, but what happens if the horizontal cable is to blame? In these cases, I get on the phone and call my local installer. If a cable's bad in one spot, the risk of it being bad in another is simply too great to try anything other than total replacement.

Finally, check the coupler if one is used to extend a cable run. *Couplers* are small devices with two female ports that enable you to connect two pieces of cable together to overcome *distance limitations*. UTP couplers are most common, but you can find couplers for every type of network: fiber couplers, even coaxial or BNC couplers. The plastic UTP couplers are relatively easily broken if exposed to humans.

Problems in the Telecommunications Room

Even a well-organized telecommunications room is a complex maze of equipment racks, switches, and patch panels. The most important issue to remember as you work is to keep your diagnostic process organized and documented. For example, if you're testing a series of cable runs along a patch panel, start at one end and don't skip connections. Place a sticker as you work to keep track of where you are on the panel.

Your biggest concerns in the telecommunications room are power and environmental issues.

All those boxes in the rack need good-quality power. Even the smallest rack should run off of a good **uninterruptible power supply (UPS)**, a battery backup that plugs into the wall. Make sure you get one that can handle the amount of wattage used by all the equipment in the rack.

Online vs. Standby Power Supplies

You can purchase two different types of UPSs—online and standby. An online UPS *continuously charges a battery that, in turn, powers the computer components. If the telecommunications room loses power, the computers stay powered up without missing a beat, at least until the battery runs out.*

A standby power supply (SPS) *also has a big battery but doesn't power the computer unless the power goes out. Circuitry detects the power outage and immediately kicks on the battery.*

A UPS provides several benefits. First, it acts as an inverter. It stores power as direct current in its battery, then inverts that power to alternating current as the servers and other boxes in the rack system require. A good UPS acts as a *power monitoring tool* so it can report problems when there's any fluctuation in the electrical supply. All UPS boxes can provide security from power spikes and sags.

A UPS enables you to shut down in an orderly fashion. It does *not* provide enough power for you to continue working. The device that handles the latter service is called a *generator*.

But what if the UPS reports lots of times when it's kicking on? Don't assume the power coming from your physical plant (or power company) is okay. If your UPS comes on too often, it might be time to install a voltage event recorder (Figure 6.67). As its name implies, a **voltage event recorder** plugs into your power outlet and tracks the voltage over time. These devices often reveal interesting issues. For example, a small network was having trouble sending an overnight report to a main branch—the uploading servers reported that they were not able to connect to the Internet. Yet in the morning the report could be run manually with no problems. After placing a voltage event recorder in the telecommunications room, we discovered that the building management was turning off the power as a power-saving measure. This would have been hard to determine without the proper tool.

The temperature in the telecommunications room should be maintained and monitored properly. If you lose the air conditioning, for example, and leave

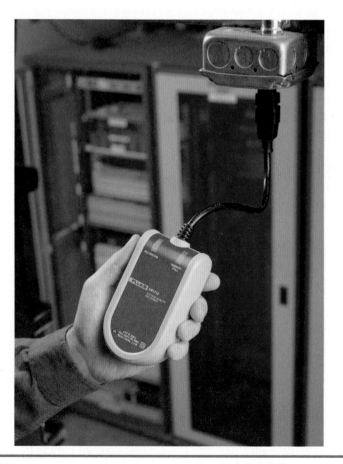

• **Figure 6.67** An excellent voltage event recorder (photo courtesy of Fluke Networks)

systems running, the equipment will overheat and shut down—sometimes with serious damage. To prevent this, all serious telecommunications rooms should have **temperature monitors** as part of their **rack monitoring system**.

Likewise, you need to control the level of humidity in a telecommunications room. You can install **environmental monitors** that keep a constant watch on humidity, temperature, and more, for just a few hundred dollars. The devices cost little in comparison to the equipment in the telecommunications room that you're protecting.

 Using a high-quality UPS and installing temperature and environmental monitors are safeguards that fall into a much larger discussion called "managing risk." Managing risk is a big topic, so I've devoted all of Chapter 18 to it.

Toners

It would be nice to say that all cable installations are perfect and that over the years they won't tend to grow into horrific piles of spaghetti-like, unlabeled cables. In the real world, though, you might eventually find yourself having to locate or *trace* cables. Even in the best-planned networks, labels fall off ports and outlets, mystery cables appear behind walls, new cable runs are added, and mistakes are made counting rows and columns on patch panels. Sooner or later, most network techs will have to be able to pick out one particular cable or port from a stack.

When the time comes to trace cables, network techs turn to a device called a toner for help. **Toner** is the generic term for two separate devices that are used together: a tone generator and a tone probe. The **tone generator** connects to the cable using alligator clips, tiny hooks, or a network jack, and it sends an electrical signal along the wire at a certain frequency. The **tone probe** emits a sound when it is placed near a cable connected to the tone generator (Figure 6.68). These two devices are often referred to by the brand-name Fox and Hound, a popular model of toner made by the Triplett Corporation.

You'll see a tone probe referred to on the CompTIA Network+ exam as a *toner probe*.

• **Figure 6.68** Fox and Hound

• **Figure 6.69**   Technician with a butt set

To trace a cable, connect the tone generator to the known end of the cable in question, and then position the tone probe next to the other end of each of the cables that might be the right one. The tone probe makes a sound when it's placed next to the right cable. Some toners have one tone probe that works with multiple tone generators. Each generator emits a separate frequency, and the probe sounds a different tone for each one. Even good toners are relatively inexpensive ($75); although inexpensive toners can cost less than $25, they don't tend to work well, so spending a little more is worthwhile. Just keep in mind that if you have to support a network, you'd do best to own a decent toner.

More advanced toners include phone jacks, enabling the person manipulating the tone generator to communicate with the person manipulating the tone probe: "Jim, move the tone generator to the next port!" These either come with their own headset or work with a *butt set,* the classic tool used by telephone repair technicians for years (Figure 6.69).

A good, medium-priced cable tester and a good toner are the most important tools for folks who must support, but not install, networks. A final tip: be sure to bring along a few extra batteries—there's nothing worse than sitting on the top of a ladder holding a cable tester or toner that has just run out of juice!

Chapter 6 Review

■ Chapter Summary

After reading this chapter and completing the exercises, you should understand the following about installing a physical network.

Recognize and describe the functions of basic components in a structured cabling system

■ Structured cabling refers to a set of standards established by the TIA/EIA regarding network cabling. The three basic structured cabling network components are the telecommunications room (a.k.a. server room), the horizontal cabling, and the work area (or the actual workers' office space).

■ Although wireless networks are popular, they lack the reliability and speed of wired networks.

■ All cabling should run from individual PCs to a telecommunications room.

■ A telecommunications room should have one or more sturdy equipment racks, used to hold mountable network devices (switches and routers); this space also houses server PCs, patch panels, UPSs, monitors, keyboards, mice, tape backup drives, and more.

■ Horizontal cabling usually refers to the cabling that runs from the telecommunications room out to the work areas of a single office building floor.

■ The work area is where PCs and printers connect to the ends of the horizontal cabling. In other words, the work area is the actual office space where the jacks should be located for connecting to the network.

■ UTP cable comes in one of two types: solid core and stranded core. Horizontal cabling should always be solid core.

■ Solid core UTP is a better conductor than stranded core but breaks easily if handled roughly. Stranded core holds up better to substantial handling.

■ Equipment racks are 19 inches wide and come in a variety of heights. Rack-mounted equipment is manufactured to fit in the 19-inch width, but the equipment height can vary.

■ Rack-mounted equipment heights are measured in units (Us), each U being equal to just under 1.75 inches.

■ UTP cables can be connected to a 110 block in a patch panel by using a punchdown tool.

■ The ANSI/TIA-606-B labeling standard can help a technician keep track of cables.

■ Patch cables are used to connect the ports on a patch panel to a switch. Although solid core horizontal runs typically connect to the 110 block, patch cables are usually stranded core.

■ Patch cables are also used in the work area to connect a PC to the RJ-45 wall jack.

■ TIA/EIA 568 limits horizontal runs to 90 meters, allowing 10 meters for patch cables before the 100-meter UTP cable limit is reached.

■ The demarc location is where the connection is made from the outside world to a private network. An Internet service provider or telephone company provides service through its demarc.

■ A network interface unit, such as a cable modem, may sit between the demarc and local network.

■ Demarcs and cross-connects typically reside in a room called the main distribution frame.

Explain the process of installing structured cable

■ A good installation entails planning the cabling runs with an actual floor plan, as well as poking around in walls and ceilings.

■ Raceway products may be used to run cable externally rather than inside walls.

■ When planning cable runs, keep five things in mind: distance, power, dryness, temperature, and access.

■ Cable trays may be used to aid in pulling cable within a drop ceiling.

■ If you make your own patch cables, be sure to use the correct crimp, as the crimps differ for solid core and stranded core UTP.

■ A variety of cable testers, including time domain reflectometers and optical time domain reflectometers, can be used to test for continuity, shorts, split pairs, attenuation, and crosstalk.

■ Big issues with fiber include signal degradation through broken, bad, or dirty connectors; attenuation, or light leakage; and physical or single mismatches.

Install a network interface card

- All UTP Ethernet NICs use an RJ-45 connector. Fiber-optic NICs use a variety of connectors, depending on the manufacturer.

- Many motherboards now include an onboard NIC.

- Using the same model of NIC for all the PCs on your network makes installing and updating drivers much easier.

- The most common type of expansion card for NICs is PCI express (PCIe), but legacy PCI cards are installed in many systems. USB NICs are convenient, and you don't have to open the computer case to install one.

- The link lights on a NIC indicate the status of the NIC, such as if it's connected to a network and if there is any network activity. Link lights may include the activity light and collision light.

Perform basic troubleshooting on a structured cable network

- A "No server is found" error is likely caused by a physical connection problem. If one program (such as a web browser) works but another (such as e-mail) does not, the problem is likely software related.

- If you suspect a hardware problem, check the link lights on the NIC and the switch. If the lights are not on, the cable is probably disconnected or the port may be faulty.

- A loopback test can check a NIC's circuitry, but not the actual connecting pins.

- When testing cables, be sure to test the entire run, including the patch cable in the work area, the cable leading from the work area wall back to the telecommunications room, and the patch cable from the patch panel to the switch.

- Tools that are helpful for troubleshooting a structured cable network include a voltage event recorder and a toner.

■ Key Terms

110 block *(109)*
activity light *(132)*
attenuation *(125)*
bonding *(131)*
cable certifier *(126)*
cable drop *(116)*
cable tester *(123)*
cable tray *(118)*
collision light *(132)*
continuity *(123)*
continuity tester *(123)*
crosstalk *(125)*
customer-premises equipment (CPE) *(115)*
demarc *(113)*
demarc extension *(115)*
dispersion *(128)*
environmental monitor *(137)*
equipment rack *(107)*
far-end crosstalk (FEXT) *(125)*
horizontal cabling *(105)*
intermediate distribution frame (IDF) *(107)*
light leakage *(127)*
link light *(131)*
loopback plug *(134)*
loopback test *(134)*
main distribution frame (MDF) *(115)*
mounting bracket *(119)*
multiplexer *(115)*

near-end crosstalk (NEXT) *(125)*
network interface unit (NIU) *(114)*
optical time domain reflectometer (OTDR) *(128)*
patch cables *(111)*
patch panel *(109)*
punchdown tool *(109)*
raceway *(116)*
rack monitoring system *(137)*
run *(105)*
smart jacks *(114)*
solid core *(106)*
split pair *(123)*
stranded core *(106)*
structured cabling *(103)*
telecommunications room *(105)*
temperature monitor *(137)*
TIA/EIA 606 *(110)*
time domain reflectometer (TDR) *(124)*
tone generator *(137)*
tone probe *(137)*
toner *(137)*
unit (U) *(108)*
uninterruptible power supply (UPS) *(135)*
vertical cross-connect *(115)*
voltage event recorder *(136)*
wiremap *(124)*
work area *(105)*

Key Term Quiz

Use the Key Terms list to complete the sentences that follow. Not all terms will be used.

1. All the cabling from individual work areas runs via _____ to a central location.

2. The central location that all cabling runs to is called the _____.

3. A single piece of installed horizontal cabling is called a(n) _____.

4. The set of standards established by the TIA/EIA regarding network cabling is called _____.

5. You use a(n) _____ to connect a strand of UTP to a 110 block or 66 block.

6. A short UTP cable that uses stranded, rather than solid, cable is called a(n) _____ and can tolerate much more handling near a patch panel.

7. The type of network interface unit (NIU) that enables an ISP or telephone company to determine if a home DSL box or cable router has been disconnected is called a(n) _____.

8. The spot where a cable comes out of the wall at the workstation is called a(n) _____.

9. The height measurement known as U is used for devices that fit into a(n) _____.

10. The term _____ describes the process of a signal weakening as it progresses down a piece of wire.

Multiple-Choice Quiz

1. Which item describes the length of cable installed within walls from a telecommunications room out to a jack?

   A. Cable drop

   B. Cable run

   C. Cable tester

   D. Cable tray

2. What is the term used to describe where the network hardware and patch panels are kept?

   A. Drop room

   B. Telecommunications room

   C. Routing room

   D. Telecloset room

3. Aside from outright breakage, what's the primary worry with bending a fiber-optic cable too much?

   A. Attenuation

   B. Bonding

   C. Light leakage

   D. Near-end crosstalk

4. When connecting a cable run onto a patch panel, which tool should you use?

   A. 110-punchdown tool

   B. Crimper

   C. TDR

   D. Tone generator

5. What is the structured cabling name for the end user's office space where network computers are set up?

   A. Backbone

   B. Building entrance

   C. Cable drop

   D. Work area

6. What type of twisted-pair cabling would work best within ceilings near lighting?

   A. Solid core plenum

   B. Solid core PVC

   C. Stranded core plenum

   D. Stranded core PVC

7. Why would network techs use stranded core cabling from a patch panel's ports to a switch?

   A. Cost

   B. Fire rating

   C. Flexibility

   D. Safety

8. What is the first thing a professional cable installer should do when providing an estimate at a site?

   A. Power on additional lighting.

   B. Put on a grounding wrist strap.

   C. Request a floor plan.

   D. Set up ladders.

9. What component best enables you to install more servers in the limited space of a telecommunications room?

   A. Cable tray

   B. Outlet box

   C. Patch panel

   D. Equipment rack

10. How tall is a network router that is 8U?

    A. 8 inches

    B. 8 centimeters

    C. 14 inches

    D. 14 centimeters

11. Your first day on the job, you get a call from the owner complaining that her network connection is down. A quick check of the central switch verifies that it's in good working order, as is the boss's PC. As luck would have it, your supervisor calls at just that time and tells you not to worry; she'll be by in a jiffy with her TDR to help root out the problem. What is she talking about?

    A. Tune domain resonator, her network tone generator

    B. Time detuning resonator, her network tester

    C. Time domain reflectometer, her network tester

    D. Time detail resource, her network schematic

12. Jenny's office building recently had sections renovated, and now some users are complaining that they can't see the network. She suspects that the workers might have inadvertently broken wires when they did ceiling work. George suggests she use a toner to figure out which wires go to the complaining users. Erin disagrees, saying that Jenny should use a Fox and Hound. Who's right?

    A. Only George is right.

    B. Only Erin is right.

    C. Both George and Erin are right.

    D. Neither George nor Erin is right.

13. What is generated by every piece of UTP cable in existence?

    A. Modal distortion

    B. Crosstalk

    C. EMI

    D. ESD

14. Which statement about structured cable is correct?

    A. The term "demarc" refers to a physical location, whereas the phrase "network interface unit" refers to a piece of equipment provided by an ISP.

    B. The term "demarc" refers to a piece of equipment provided by an ISP, whereas the phrase "network interface unit" refers to a piece of equipment provided by the customer.

    C. The terms "demarc" and "network interface unit" refer to pieces of equipment provided by an ISP.

    D. A demarc is used for fiber cabling, whereas a network interface unit is used for UTP.

15. Bill the fiber inspector comes back after reviewing a fiber run and says there's too much *attenuation*. What does he mean?

    A. The signal gets weak as it travels long distances.

    B. The signal spreads as it travels long distances.

    C. The signal amplifies as it travels long distances.

    D. He doesn't mean anything. "Attenuation" is technobabble.

■ Essay Quiz

1. Sketch a rough draft of your classroom, office, or the room you are in right now. Indicate any doors, windows, closets, lights, plumbing fixtures, desks or tables, and even any visible electrical wall outlets. Then indicate with a large letter *X* where you would place a new cable drop. Jot down some notes explaining why you would choose the location you did.

2. Your CompTIA A+ Certified coworker is listening in on a conversation you are having with your boss, and he thinks he knows what a "demarc" is. Write a quick note to him describing the true meaning of a structured cabling building entrance, so you can put it on his desk before you leave for the day.

3. The management team at your company wants to network five offices with low-cost PVC stranded

core cabling throughout the dropped ceiling in your offices. Compose a memo that justifies the cost of using more expensive cabling. Use any standard memo format that you are already familiar with.

4. The youth group at a local community organization has received funding to help with creating a computer network. They have already purchased the required number of PCI 10/100/1000 NICs. You have

been asked by one of the group's leaders to assist with installing the NICs. You want to help, but time doesn't permit you to volunteer any more hours in a week than you already do. It makes better sense to organize a step-by-step fact sheet that describes installing a NIC into an open slot on a computer. When you have finished, e-mail the fact sheet you created to your instructor (or a friend) for comments.

Lab Projects

• Lab Project 6.1

You are a recently hired network technician at a local business. During the interview phase with the company, some questions were raised about installing cable. You made it clear that professional cable installation was the way to go. You justified your statements and impressed the interviewers with your knowledge and honesty, so they hired you.

Now you need to research which professional cable installers are available in your area and what each charges as a "per drop" price. Use the Internet to gather research from at least two companies. Prepare a PowerPoint presentation to present your findings to management. Be sure to use color, graphics, and slide transitions (as time permits) to further impress your new bosses!

• Lab Project 6.2

You have become the de facto network administrator for your employer at a nearby tax preparation company. The owner of this small business closely monitors all expenses. She realizes that you could use additional tools to help with installing cable for her soon-to-be-expanded office network. You see this as the opportunity to purchase a cable tester and a tone generator. Your boss casually says to check out some

prices. You know that well-laid-out numbers could mean approval on the toys you'd like!

Prepare a spreadsheet that shows three levels, including prices, for each of these items. Arrange your spreadsheet in a "good/better/best" layout, with "best" listed on top for the most attention. Use the following chart as a guide:

"BEST"	Brand/Model	Price
Cable Tester A		$.
Tone Generator A		$.
Total for A Items		$.
"BETTER"	Brand/Model	Price
Cable Tester B		$.
Tone Generator B		$.
Total for B Items		$.
"GOOD"	Brand/Model	Price
Cable Tester C		$.
Tone Generator C		$.
Total for C Items		$.

chapter 7

TCP/IP Basics

"If it's sent by ship then it's a cargo, if it's sent by road then it's a shipment."

—DAVE ALLEN

In this chapter, you will learn how to

- **Describe how the TCP/IP protocol suite works**
- **Explain CIDR and subnetting**
- **Describe the functions of static and dynamic IP addresses**

The mythical MHTechEd network (remember that from Chapter 2?) provided an overview of how networks work. At the bottom of every network, at OSI Layers 1 and 2 (the Link/Network Interface layer of the TCP/IP model), resides the network hardware: the wires, network cards, switches, and more that enable data to move physically from one computer to another. Above the Physical and Data Link layers, the "higher" layers of the model—such as Network and Transport—work with the hardware to make the network magic happen.

Chapters 3 through 6 provided details of the hardware at the Physical and Data Link layers of the OSI model and the Link/Network Interface layer of the TCP/IP model. You learned about the network protocols, such as Ethernet, that create uniformity within networks, so that the data frame created by one NIC can be read properly by another NIC.

This chapter begins a fun journey into the software side of networking. You'll learn the details about the IP addressing scheme that enables computers on one network to communicate with each other and computers on other networks. You'll get the full story on how TCP/IP networks divide into smaller units—subnets—to make management of a large TCP/IP network easier. And you won't just get it from a conceptual standpoint. This chapter provides the details you've undoubtedly been craving—it teaches you how to set up a network properly. The chapter finishes with an in-depth discussion on implementing IP addresses.

Historical/Conceptual

Standardizing Networking Technology

The early days of networking software saw several competing standards that did not work well together. Novell NetWare, Microsoft Windows, and Apple Macintosh ran networking software to share folders and printers, while the UNIX/Linux world did crazy things like sharing terminals—handy for the UNIX/Linux users, but it made no sense to the Windows folks—and then there was this new thing called e-mail (like that was ever going to go anywhere). The Internet had just been opened to the public. The World Wide Web was merely a plaything for programmers and scientists. All of these folks made their own software, interpreting (or totally ignoring) the OSI model in various ways, and all trying (arguably) to become *the way* the whole world networked computers. It was an unpleasant, ugly world for guys like me who had the audacity to try to make, for example, a UNIX box work with a Windows computer.

The problem was that no one agreed on how a network should run. Everyone's software had its own set of Rules of What a Network Should Do and How to Do It. These sets of rules—and the software written to follow these rules—were broken down into individual rules called **protocols**. Each set of rules had many protocols lumped together under the term **protocol suite**. Novell NetWare called its protocol suite IPX/SPX; Microsoft's was called NetBIOS/NetBEUI; Apple called its AppleTalk; and the UNIX folks used this wacky protocol suite called TCP/IP.

Well, TCP/IP won. Sure, you may find the occasional network still running one of these other protocol suites, but they're rare these days. To get ahead today, to get on the Internet, and to pass the CompTIA Network+ exam, you only need to worry about TCP/IP. Novell, Microsoft, and Apple no longer actively support anything but TCP/IP. You live in a one-protocol-suite world, the old stuff is forgotten, and you kids don't know how good you got it!

 Even in the old days companies created methods to connect different operating systems together. Microsoft created software to enable a Windows client to connect to a NetWare server, for example. This software, called the *Microsoft IPX/SPX Protocol* or *NWLINK,* might show up as a possible answer on the CompTIA Network+ exam. This technology is long gone.

The software installed on a system that enables a specific protocol suite to function is called a *protocol stack*. When used for TCP/IP, you'll also hear the term *IP stack*, which means the same thing.

I feel so left out.

Link

• **Figure 7.1** The Link layer is important, but it's not part of the TCP/IP protocol suite.

The TCP/IP protocol suite consists of thousands of different protocols doing thousands of different things. For the most part, the rest of this book discusses TCP/IP protocols. Right now, my goal is to give you an idea of which protocols go where in the TCP/IP protocol suite.

Test Specific

▥ The TCP/IP Protocol Suite

Chapter 2 introduced you to the TCP/IP model. Let's take a second look, and this time examine some of the more critical protocols that reside at each layer. I'll also explore and develop the IP packet in more detail to show you how it organizes all of these protocols. Remember, TCP/IP is so powerful because IP packets can exist in almost any type of network technology. The Link layer, therefore, counts on technologies outside the TCP/IP protocol suite (like Ethernet, cable modem, or DSL) to get the IP packets from one system to the next (Figure 7.1).

When discussing the software layers of the TCP/IP protocol suite, let's focus on only the three top layers in the TCP/IP model: Internet, Transport, and Application (Figure 7.2). I'll revisit each of these layers and add representative protocols from the protocol suite so you gain a better understanding of "who's who" in TCP/IP.

• **Figure 7.2** The TCP/IP protocol suite redux

If you look at an IP packet, certain parts of that packet fit perfectly into layers of the TCP/IP model. The parts, conceptualized in Figure 7.3, consist of a series of nested headers with data. The header for a higher layer is part of the data for a lower layer. The packet's payload, for example, can be a TCP segment that consists of data from layers above and a sequence number. The higher you go up the model, more headers are stripped away until all you have left is the data delivered to the application that needs it.

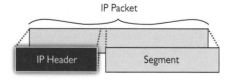

• **Figure 7.3** IP packet showing headers

Internet Layer Protocols

The **Internet Protocol (IP)** works at the Internet layer, taking data chunks from the Transport layer, adding addressing, and creating the final IP packet. IP then hands the IP packet to Layer 2 for encapsulation into a frame. Let's look at the addressing in more depth.

I think it's safe to assume that most folks have seen IP addresses before. Here's a typical example:

192.168.1.115

This type of address—four values ranging from 0 to 255, separated by three periods—is known officially as an **Internet Protocol version 4 (IPv4)** address.

This chapter introduces you to IPv4 addresses. You should understand the correct name for this older type of address because the world is moving to a newer, longer type of IP address called IPv6. Here's an example of an IPv6 address:

2001:0:4137:9e76:43e:2599:3f57:fe9a

IPv4 and IPv6 addresses aren't the only protocols that work at the Internet layer. A number of applications test basic issues at this layer, such as "Is there a computer with the IP address of 192.168.1.15?" These applications use the **Internet Control Message Protocol (ICMP)**. TCP/IP users rarely start a program that uses ICMP. For the most part, ICMP features are called automatically by applications as needed without your ever knowing. There is one very famous program that runs under ICMP, however: the venerable ping utility. Run ping from a command prompt to query if a host is reachable. Ping will show the *round trip time (RTT)*—some call this the *real transfer time*—for the ICMP packet, usually in seconds. If ping can't find the host, the packet will time out and ping will show you that information too.

When thinking about the Internet layer, remember the following three protocols:

 The TCP/IP model's Internet layer corresponds roughly to the OSI model's Network layer.

- IPv4 (sometimes you just say IP)

- IPv6

- ICMP

Figure 7.4 shows a highly simplified IP header.

The full IP packet header has 14 different fields. As you would expect, the destination and source IP addresses are part of the Network/Internet layer. Other fields include version, header length, and more. Dissecting the entire set of fields isn't important, but here are a few descriptions just to whet your appetite:

• **Figure 7.4**   Simplified IP header

- **Version**   The version (Ver) field defines the IP address type: 4 for IPv4, 6 for IPv6.

- **Header length**   The total size of the IP portion of the packet in words (32 bits) is displayed in the header length field.

- **Differentiated services code point (DSCP)**   The DSCP field contains data used by bandwidth-sensitive applications like Voice over IP. (Network techs with long memories will note that this field used to be called the *type of service* field.)

- **Time to live (TTL)** Routers on the Internet are not perfect and sometimes create loops. The TTL field prevents an IP packet from indefinitely spinning through the Internet by using a counter that decrements by one every time a packet goes through a router. This number cannot start higher than 255; many applications start at 128.

- **Protocol** In the vast majority of cases, the protocol field is either TCP or UDP and identifies what's encapsulated inside the packet. See the next section for more information.

Transport Layer Protocols

When moving data from one system to another, the TCP/IP protocol suite needs to know if the communication is connection-oriented or connection-less. When you want to be positive that the data moving between two systems gets there in good order, use a connection-oriented application. If it's not a big deal for data to miss a bit or two, then connectionless is the way to go. The connection-oriented protocol used with TCP/IP is called the **Transmission Control Protocol (TCP)**. The connectionless one is called the **User Datagram Protocol (UDP)**.

Let me be clear: you don't *choose* TCP or UDP. The people who developed the applications decide which protocol to use. When you fire up your Web browser, for example, you're using TCP because Web browsers use an Application layer protocol called HTTP. HTTP is built on TCP.

TCP

Over 95 percent of all TCP/IP applications use TCP—that's why we call the protocol suite "TCP/IP" and not "UDP/IP." TCP gets an application's data from one machine to another reliably and completely. As a result, TCP comes with communication rules that require both the sending and receiving machines to acknowledge the other's presence and readiness to send and receive data. We call this process ACK/NACK or just ACK (Figure 7.5). TCP also chops up data into **segments**, gives the segments a sequence number, and then verifies that all sent segments were received. If a segment goes missing, the receiving system must request the missing segments.

• **Figure 7.5** ACK in action

Figure 7.6 shows a simplified TCP header. Notice the source port and the destination port. Port numbers are values ranging from 1 to 65,535 and are used by systems to determine what application needs the received data. Each application is assigned a specific port number on which to listen/send. Web servers use

• **Figure 7.6** TCP header

port 80 (HTTP), for example, whereas port 110 is used to receive e-mail messages from e-mail servers (POP3). The client uses the source port number to remember which client application requested the data. The rest of this book dives much deeper into ports. For now, know that the TCP or UDP headers of an IP packet store these values.

Ports aren't the only items of interest in the TCP header. The header also contains these fields:

- **Sequence and ACK numbers**   These numbers enable the sending and receiving computers to keep track of the various pieces of data flowing back and forth.

- **Flags**   These individual bits give both sides detailed information about the state of the connection.

- **Checksum**   The checksum checks the TCP header for errors.

UDP

UDP is the "fire and forget" missile of the TCP/IP protocol suite. As you can see in Figure 7.7, a UDP **datagram** doesn't possess any of the extras you see in TCP to make sure the data is received intact. UDP works best when you have a lot of data that doesn't need to be perfect or when the systems are so close to each other that the chances of a problem occurring are too small to bother worrying about. A few dropped frames on a Voice over IP call, for example, won't make much difference in the communication between two people. So there's a good reason to use UDP: it's smoking fast compared to TCP. Two of the most important networking protocols, Domain Name System (DNS) and Dynamic Host Configuration Protocol (DHCP), use UDP.

You saw this back in Chapter 2, but I'll mention it again here. Data gets chopped up into chunks at the Transport layer when using TCP. The chunks are called *segments* with TCP. UDP *datagrams* don't get chopped up at the Transport layer; they just get a header.

| Source port | Destination port | Length | Checksum |

• **Figure 7.7**   UDP header

Application Layer Protocols

TCP/IP applications use TCP/IP protocols to move data back and forth between servers and clients. Because every application has different needs, I can't show you a generic application header. Instead, we'll look at one sample header from one function of possibly the most popular application protocol of all: HTTP.

As mentioned previously, Web servers and Web browsers use HTTP to communicate. Figure 7.8 shows a sample header for HTTP. Specifically, this header is a response segment from the Web server telling the remote system that the last set of data transfers is complete. This header begins with the value "HTTP/1.1" and the number "200" followed by "OK\r\n," which means "OK, go to the next line." The data (the contents of the Web page) begins below the header.

I'm simplifying the call and response interaction between a Web server and a Web client. The explanation here is only the first part of the process in accessing a Web page.

Super! Now that you're comfortable with how the TCP/IP protocols fit into clear points on the TCP/IP model, let's head back to the Internet layer and explore IP addressing.

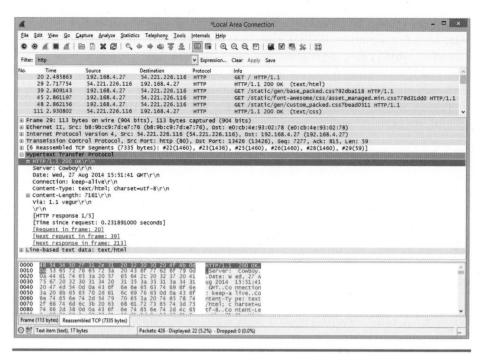

• **Figure 7.8** HTTP header

IP in Depth

TCP/IP supports simple networks and complex networks. You can use the protocol suite to connect a handful of computers to a switch and create a local area network (LAN). TCP/IP also enables you to interconnect multiple LANs into a wide area network (WAN).

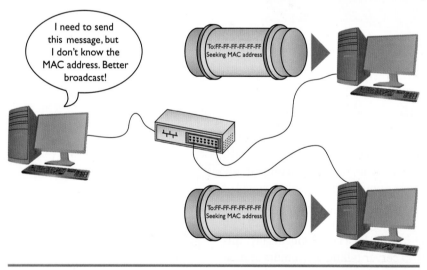

• **Figure 7.9** PC broadcasting for a MAC address

At the LAN level, all the computers use Ethernet, and this creates a hurdle for WAN-wide communication. For one computer to send a frame to another computer, the sending computer must know the MAC address of the destination computer. This begs the question: How does the sender get the recipient's MAC address?

In a small network this is easy. The sending computer simply *broadcasts* by sending a frame to MAC address FF-FF-FF-FF-FF-FF, the universal MAC address for broadcast. Figure 7.9 shows a computer broadcasting for another computer's MAC address.

✓ **Cross Check**

Broadcasting

You first ran into broadcasting in Chapter 2, so check your memory now. What happens to the broadcast frame? Does it reach all the computers on a LAN? How many computers actually process that broadcast frame?

• **Figure 7.10**   Broadcasting won't work for the entire Internet!

Broadcasting takes up some of the network bandwidth, but in a small network, the amount is acceptably small. But what would happen if the entire Internet used broadcasting (Figure 7.10)? In this case, the whole Internet would come to a grinding halt.

TCP/IP networks use **IP addressing** to overcome the limitations inherent in Ethernet networks. IP addresses provide several things. First, every machine on a TCP/IP network—small or large—gets a unique IP address that identifies the machine on that network. Second, IP addresses group together sets of computers into logical networks, so you can, for example, distinguish one LAN from another. Finally, because TCP/IP network equipment understands the IP addressing scheme, computers can communicate with each other *between* LANs, in a WAN, and without broadcasting for MAC addresses (other than for the default gateway). Chapter 2 touched on IP addresses briefly, but network techs need to understand them intimately. Let's look at the structure and function of the IP addressing scheme.

IP Addresses

The most common type of IP address (officially called IPv4, but usually simplified to just "IP") consists of a 32-bit value. Here's an example of an IP address:

    11000000101010000000010000000010

Whoa! IP addresses are just strings of 32 binary digits? Yes, they are, but to make IP addresses easier for humans to use, the 32-bit binary value is broken down into four groups of eight, separated by periods, or *dots,* like this:

    11000000.10101000.00000100.00000010

Tech Tip

Binary, Decimal, and Octal Numbering

We know binary numbering at heart is a single digit that represents on or off, a 1 or a 0. Another term for this numbering is base two. *How do you represent a 1 in binary? Well, "1" of course. But what's the next number? How do you display a 2? Add another column, just like in the preceding table: 10 equals the number 2 in binary.*

Base ten, or decimal numbering, is what humans use for the most part. We count from 0 to 9 and then add a second column, 10. So 10 equals the number 10 in decimal.

Base eight, or octal numbering, counts from 0 to 7 with a single digit and then adds a column. So how would you display the number 8? Right, 10 equals the number 8 in octal.

The only reason to use octal in computing is that it's easy to display all eight numbers using only three binary characters. Conveniently, really ancient computers (think IBM mainframes here) were 12-, 24-, or 36-bit systems, meaning their programming very easily divided into chunks of three.

Why did CompTIA decide to add octal numbering to the objectives? We may never know. We do know, however, that "octal" is very much not *the same as "octet." The latter refers to the groups of 8 bits in an IP address.*

Check out the two excellent Chapter 7 "Binary Calculator" sims over at http://totalsem.com/006. View the Show!, then practice on the Click!

Each of these 8-bit values is, in turn, converted into a decimal number between 0 and 255. If you took every possible combination of eight binary values and placed them in a spreadsheet, it would look something like the list in the left column. The right column shows the same list with a decimal value assigned to each.

00000000	00000000 = 0
00000001	00000001 = 1
00000010	00000010 = 2
00000011	00000011 = 3
00000100	00000100 = 4
00000101	00000101 = 5
00000110	00000110 = 6
00000111	00000111 = 7
00001000	00001000 = 8
(skip a bunch in the middle)	*(skip a bunch in the middle)*
11111000	11111000 = 248
11111001	11111001 = 249
11111010	11111010 = 250
11111011	11111011 = 251
11111100	11111100 = 252
11111101	11111101 = 253
11111110	11111110 = 254
11111111	11111111 = 255

Converted, the original value of 11000000.10101000.00000100.00000010 is displayed as 192.168.4.2 in IPv4's **dotted decimal notation** (also referred to as the *dotted octet numbering system*). Note that dotted decimal is simply a shorthand way for people to discuss and configure the binary IP addresses computers use.

People who work on TCP/IP networks must know how to convert dotted decimal to binary and back. You can convert easily using any operating system's calculator. Every OS has a calculator (UNIX/Linux systems have about 100 different ones to choose from) that has a scientific or programmer mode like the ones shown in Figure 7.11.

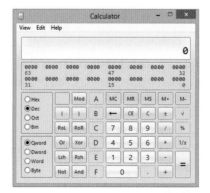

• **Figure 7.11** Windows 8.1 (left) and OS X (right) Calculators in Programmer mode

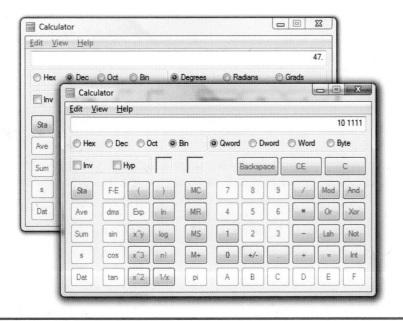

• **Figure 7.12**   Converting decimal to binary with Windows 7's Calculator

To convert from decimal to binary, just go to decimal view, type in the value, and then switch to binary view to get the result. To convert to decimal, just go into binary view, enter the binary value, and switch to decimal view to get the result. Figure 7.12 shows the result of Windows 7's Calculator converting the decimal value 47 into binary. Notice the result is 101111—the leading two zeroes do not appear. When you work with IP addresses, you must always have eight digits, so just add two more to the left to get 00101111.

Just as every MAC address must be unique on a network, every IP address must be unique as well. For logical addressing to work, no two computers on the same network may have the same IP address. In a small network running TCP/IP, every computer has both an IP address and a MAC address (Figure 7.13).

Every operating system comes with a utility (usually more than one utility) to display a system's IP address and MAC address. Figure 7.14 shows an OS X system's Network utility. Note the MAC address (00:14:51:65:84:a1) and the IP address (192.168.4.57).

Every operating system also has a command-line utility that gives you this information. In Windows, for example, you can use **ipconfig**

> Using a calculator utility to convert to and from binary/decimal is a critical skill for a network tech. Later on you'll do this again, but by hand!

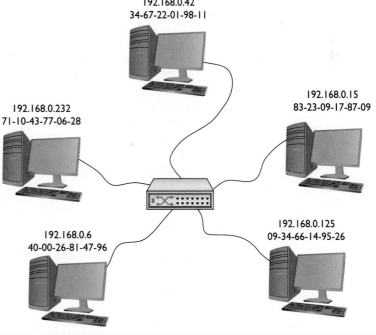

• **Figure 7.13**   A small network with both IP and MAC addresses

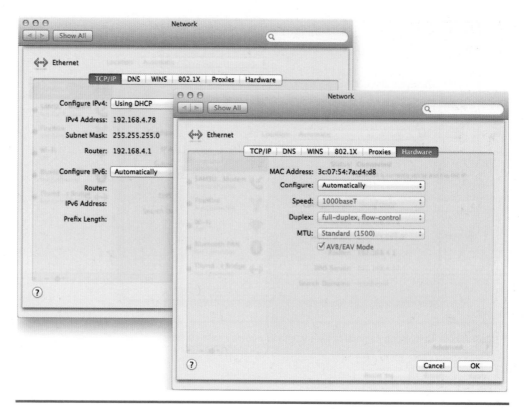

• **Figure 7.14** OS X Network utility

Make sure you know that ipconfig and ifconfig provide a tremendous amount of information regarding a system's TCP/IP settings.

to display the IP and MAC addresses. Run `ipconfig/all` to see the results shown in Figure 7.15.

In UNIX/Linux/OS X, you can run the very similar **ifconfig** command. Figure 7.16, for example, shows the result of running `ifconfig` ("eth0" is the NIC) in Ubuntu.

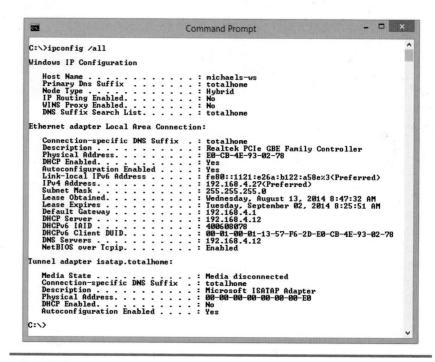

```
C:\>ipconfig /all

Windows IP Configuration

        Host Name . . . . . . . . . . . . : michaels-ws
        Primary Dns Suffix  . . . . . . . : totalhome
        Node Type . . . . . . . . . . . . : Hybrid
        IP Routing Enabled. . . . . . . . : No
        WINS Proxy Enabled. . . . . . . . : No
        DNS Suffix Search List. . . . . . : totalhome

Ethernet adapter Local Area Connection:

        Connection-specific DNS Suffix  . : totalhome
        Description . . . . . . . . . . . : Realtek PCIe GBE Family Controller
        Physical Address. . . . . . . . . : E0-CB-4E-93-02-78
        DHCP Enabled. . . . . . . . . . . : Yes
        Autoconfiguration Enabled . . . . : Yes
        Link-local IPv6 Address . . . . . : fe80::1121:e26a:b122:a58e%3(Preferred)
        IPv4 Address. . . . . . . . . . . : 192.168.4.27(Preferred)
        Subnet Mask . . . . . . . . . . . : 255.255.255.0
        Lease Obtained. . . . . . . . . . : Wednesday, August 13, 2014 8:47:32 AM
        Lease Expires . . . . . . . . . . : Tuesday, September 02, 2014 8:25:51 AM
        Default Gateway . . . . . . . . . : 192.168.4.1
        DHCP Server . . . . . . . . . . . : 192.168.4.12
        DHCPv6 IAID . . . . . . . . . . . : 400608078
        DHCPv6 Client DUID. . . . . . . . : 00-01-00-01-13-57-F6-2D-E0-CB-4E-93-02-78
        DNS Servers . . . . . . . . . . . : 192.168.4.12
        NetBIOS over Tcpip. . . . . . . . : Enabled

Tunnel adapter isatap.totalhome:

        Media State . . . . . . . . . . . : Media disconnected
        Connection-specific DNS Suffix  . : totalhome
        Description . . . . . . . . . . . : Microsoft ISATAP Adapter
        Physical Address. . . . . . . . . : 00-00-00-00-00-00-00-E0
        DHCP Enabled. . . . . . . . . . . : No
        Autoconfiguration Enabled . . . . : Yes

C:\>
```

• **Figure 7.15** `ipconfig/all` results

IP Addresses in Action

IP addresses support both LANs and WANs. This can create problems in some circumstances, such as when a computer needs to send data both to computers in its own network and to computers in other networks. How can this be accomplished?

To make all this work, IP must do three things:

- Create some way to use IP addresses so that each LAN has its own identification.

- Interconnect all of the LANs using routers and give those routers some way to use the network identification to send packets to the right network.

- Give each computer on the network some way to recognize if a packet is for the LAN or for a computer on the WAN so it knows how to handle the packet.

```
mike@michaels-moble: ~
mike@michaels-moble:~$ ifconfig
eth0      Link encap:Ethernet  HWaddr 00:25:64:5b:8a:0c
          inet addr:192.168.4.34  Bcast:192.168.4.255  Mask:255.255.255.0
          inet6 addr: fe80::225:64ff:fe5b:8a0c/64 Scope:Link
          UP BROADCAST RUNNING MULTICAST  MTU:1500  Metric:1
          RX packets:110 errors:0 dropped:0 overruns:0 frame:0
          TX packets:93 errors:0 dropped:0 overruns:0 carrier:0
          collisions:0 txqueuelen:1000
          RX bytes:20158 (20.1 KB)  TX bytes:14498 (14.4 KB)
          Interrupt:16

lo        Link encap:Local Loopback
          inet addr:127.0.0.1  Mask:255.0.0.0
          inet6 addr: ::1/128 Scope:Host
          UP LOOPBACK RUNNING  MTU:65536  Metric:1
          RX packets:706 errors:0 dropped:0 overruns:0 frame:0
          TX packets:706 errors:0 dropped:0 overruns:0 carrier:0
          collisions:0 txqueuelen:0
          RX bytes:69630 (69.6 KB)  TX bytes:69630 (69.6 KB)

mike@michaels-moble:~$ █
```

• **Figure 7.16** Results from running `ifconfig` in Ubuntu

Network IDs

To differentiate LANs from one another, each computer on a single LAN must share a very similar IP address. Some parts of the IP address will match all the others on the LAN. Figure 7.17 shows a LAN where all of the computers share the first three numbers of the IP address, with only the last number being unique on each system.

In this example, every computer has an IP address of 202.120.10.*x*. That means the **network ID** is 202.120.10.0. The *x* part of the IP address is the **host ID**.

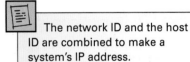 The network ID and the host ID are combined to make a system's IP address.

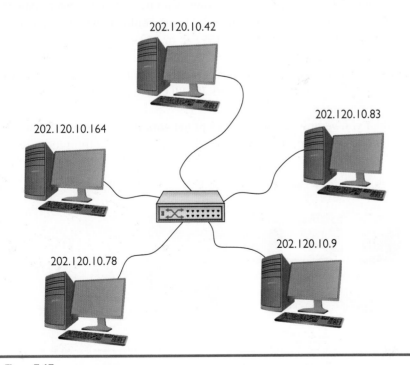

202.120.10.42

202.120.10.83

202.120.10.164

202.120.10.9

202.120.10.78

• **Figure 7.17** IP addresses for a LAN

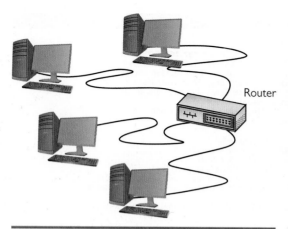

• **Figure 7.18**   LAN with router

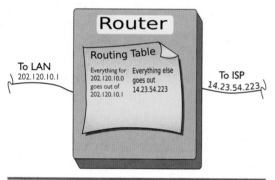

• **Figure 7.19**   Router diagram

Routing tables are covered in more detail in Chapter 8.

Combine the network ID (after dropping the ending 0) with the host ID to get an individual system's IP address. No individual computer can have an IP address that ends with 0 because that is reserved for network IDs.

Interconnecting

To organize all those individual LANs into a larger network, every TCP/IP LAN that wants to connect to another TCP/IP LAN must have a router connection. There is no exception to this critical rule. A router, therefore, needs an IP address on the LANs that it serves (Figure 7.18), so it can correctly route packets.

That router interface is known as the **default gateway**. When configuring a client to access the network beyond the router, you use the IP address for the default gateway.

Most network administrators give the LAN-side NIC on the default gateway the lowest host address in the network, usually the host ID of 1.

Routers use network IDs to determine network traffic. Figure 7.19 shows a diagram for a small, two-NIC router similar to the ones you see in many homes. Note that one port (202.120.10.1) connects to the LAN and the other port connects to the Internet service provider's network (14.23.54.223). Built into this router is a **routing table**, the actual instructions that tell the router what to do with incoming packets and where to send them.

Now let's add in the LAN and the Internet (Figure 7.20). When discussing networks in terms of network IDs, by the way, especially with illustrations in books, the common practice is to draw circles around stylized networks. Here, you should concentrate on the IDs—not the specifics of the networks.

Network IDs are very flexible, as long as no two interconnected networks share the same network ID. If you wished, you could change the network ID of the 202.120.10.0 network to 202.155.5.0, or 202.21.8.0, just as long as you can guarantee no other LAN on the WAN shares the same network ID. On the Internet, powerful governing bodies carefully allocate network IDs to ensure no two LANs share the same network ID. I'll talk more about how this works later in the chapter.

So far you've only seen examples of network IDs where the last value is zero. This is common for small networks, but it creates a limitation. With a

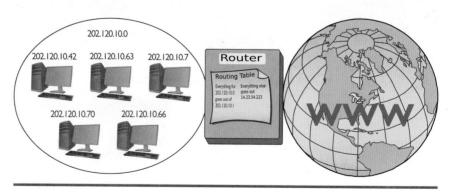

• **Figure 7.20**   LAN, router, and the Internet

Mike Meyers' CompTIA Network+ Guide to Managing and Troubleshooting Networks

network ID of 202.120.10.0, for example, a network is limited to IP addresses from 202.120.10.1 to 202.120.10.254. (202.120.10.255 is a broadcast address used to talk to every computer on the LAN.) This provides only 254 IP addresses: enough for a small network, but many organizations need many more IP addresses. No worries! You can simply use a network ID with more zeroes, such as 170.45.0.0 (for a total of 65,534 hosts) or even 12.0.0.0 (for around 16.7 million hosts).

Network IDs enable you to connect multiple LANs into a WAN. Routers then connect everything together, using routing tables to keep track of which packets go where. So that takes care of the second task: interconnecting the LANs using routers and giving those routers a way to send packets to the right network.

Now that you know how IP addressing works with LANs and WANs, let's turn to how IP enables each computer on a network to recognize if a packet is going to a computer on the LAN or to a computer on the WAN. The secret to this is something called the subnet mask.

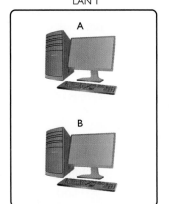

Subnet Mask

Picture this scenario. Three friends sit at their computers—Computers A, B, and C—and want to communicate with each other. Figure 7.21 illustrates the situation. You can tell from the drawing that Computers A and B are in the same LAN, whereas Computer C is on a completely different LAN. The IP addressing scheme can handle this communication, so let's see how it works.

• **Figure 7.21**   The three amigos, separated by walls or miles

The process to get a packet to a local computer is very different from the process to get a packet to a faraway computer. If one computer wants to send a packet to a local computer, it must send a broadcast to get the other computer's MAC address, as you'll recall from earlier in the chapter and Figure 7.9. (It's easy to forget about the MAC address, but remember that the network uses Ethernet and *must* have the MAC address to get the packet to the other computer.) If the packet is for some computer on a faraway network, the sending computer must send the packet to the default gateway (Figure 7.22).

In the scenario illustrated in Figure 7.21, Computer A wants to send a packet to Computer B. Computer B is on the same LAN as Computer A, but that begs a question: How does Computer A know this? Every TCP/IP computer needs a tool to tell the sending computer whether the destination IP address is local or long distance. This tool is the subnet mask.

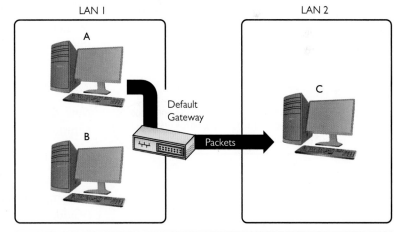

• **Figure 7.22**   Sending a packet remotely

A **subnet mask** is nothing more than a string of ones followed by some number of zeroes, always totaling exactly 32 bits, typed into every TCP/IP host. Here's an example of a typical subnet mask:

11111111111111111111111100000000

For the courtesy of the humans reading this (if any computers are reading this book, please call me—I'd love to meet you!), let's convert this to dotted decimal. First, add some periods:

11111111.11111111.11111111.00000000

Then convert each octet into decimal (use a calculator):

255.255.255.0

When you line up an IP address with a corresponding subnet mask in binary, the portion of the IP address that aligns with the ones of the subnet mask is the network ID portion of the IP address. The portion that aligns with the zeroes is the host ID. With simple IP addresses, you can see this with dotted decimal, but you'll want to see this in binary for a true understanding of how the computers work.

The IP address 192.168.5.23 has a subnet mask of 255.255.255.0. Convert both numbers to binary and then compare the full IP address to the ones and zeroes of the subnet mask:

	Dotted Decimal	Binary
IP address	192.168.5.23	11000000.10101000.00000101.00010111
Subnet mask	255.255.255.0	11111111.11111111.11111111.00000000
Network ID	192.168.5.0	11000000.10101000.00000101.x
Host ID	$x.x.x.23$	$x.x.x.$00010111

> The explanation about comparing an IP address to a subnet mask simplifies the process, leaving out how the computer uses its routing table to accomplish the goal. We'll get to routing and routing tables in Chapter 8. For now, stick with the concept of the node using the subnet mask to determine the network ID.

Before a computer sends out any data, it first compares the destination IP address to its own IP address using the subnet mask. If the destination IP address matches the computer's IP wherever there's a 1 in the subnet mask, then the sending computer knows the destination is local. The network IDs match. If even one bit of the destination IP address where the 1s are on the subnet mask is different, then the sending computer knows it's a long-distance call. The network IDs do not match.

> At this point, you should memorize that 0 = 00000000 and 255 = 11111111. You'll find knowing this very helpful throughout the rest of the book.

Let's head over to Computer A and see how the subnet mask works. Computer A's IP address is 192.168.5.23. Convert that into binary:

11000000.10101000.00000101.00010111

Now drop the periods because they mean nothing to the computer:

11000000101010000000010100010111

Let's say Computer A wants to send a packet to Computer B. Computer A's subnet mask is 255.255.255.0. Computer B's IP address is 192.168.5.45. Convert this address to binary:

11000000101010000000010100101101

Computer A compares its IP address to Computer B's IP address using the subnet mask, as shown in Figure 7.23. For clarity, I've added a line to show you where the ones end and the zeroes begin in the subnet mask. Computers certainly don't need the pretty red line!

Hmm. I want to send a packet to B, but is he local or remote? Better compare IPs.

Subnet mask: 11111111111111111111111|00000000
Computer A IP: 11000000101010000000101|00010111
Computer B IP: 11000000101010000000101|00101101

He's got the same subnet mask as me—he's local.

A

B

• Figure 7.23   Comparing addresses

Network-aware devices today have MAC addresses if they can connect to an Ethernet network. This includes NICs in PCs and Macs, network connections in tablets, phones, smart watches, and more. Because of the proliferation of such devices, a careful network administrator sometimes monitors the MAC addresses on the network. If he or she sees a MAC address with an unfamiliar prefix (that's the company signature part of the MAC address, as you'll recall from Chapter 2), the administrator can use one of the *MAC address lookup services* on the Internet. To see one in action, go to www.macaddresslookup.org/.

CompTIA specifically uses the term *mac address lookup table*, which probably refers to the *source address table (SAT)* that switches use to map MAC addresses to ports. Cisco calls SATs on their switches *MAC address tables*.

• **Figure 7.24**   Sending an ARP

A-ha! Computer A's and Computer B's network IDs match! It's a local call. Knowing this, Computer A can now send out an ARP request, which is a broadcast, as shown in Figure 7.24, to determine Computer B's MAC address. The **Address Resolution Protocol (ARP)** is how a TCP/IP network figures out the MAC address based on the destination IP address.

 **Cross Check**

ARP and the OSI Model

Remember the OSI model from way back in Chapter 2? Which layer does IP work on? How about MAC addresses? Where do you think ARP fits into the OSI model?

The addressing for the ARP frame looks like Figure 7.25. Note that Computer A's IP address and MAC address are included.

• **Figure 7.25**   Simplified ARP frame

Computer B responds to the ARP by sending Computer A an ARP response (Figure 7.26). Once Computer A has Computer B's MAC address, it starts sending packets.

The long-dead *Reverse Address Resolution Protocol (RARP)* was used to get a Layer 3 address when the computer's MAC address was known, thus, the reverse of an ARP. You'll see this sometimes as an incorrect answer on the CompTIA Network+ exam.

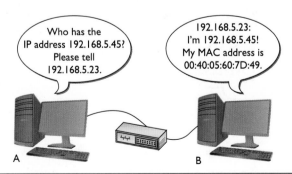

• **Figure 7.26**   Computer B responds.

Hmm. I want to send a packet to B, but is he local or remote? Better compare IPs.

Subnet mask: 11111111111111111111111|00000000
Computer A IP: 11000000101010000000101|00010111
Computer B IP: 10110110110110100000011|00101101

No match! It's a long-distance call !

A   B

• **Figure 7.27**   Comparing addresses again

But what happens when Computer A wants to send a packet to Computer C? First, Computer A compares Computer C's IP address to its own using the subnet mask (Figure 7.27). It sees that the IP addresses do not match in the 1s part of the subnet mask—meaning the network IDs don't match; therefore, this is a long-distance call.

Whenever a computer wants to send to an IP address on another LAN, it knows to send the packet to the default gateway. It still sends out an ARP to learn the MAC address for the default gateway (Figure 7.28). Once Computer A gets the default gateway's MAC address, it then begins to send packets.

Subnet masks are represented in dotted decimal like IP addresses—just remember that both are really 32-bit binary numbers. All of the following (shown in both binary and dotted decimal formats) can be subnet masks:

11111111111111111111111100000000 = 255.255.255.0
11111111111111110000000000000000 = 255.255.0.0
11111111000000000000000000000000 = 255.0.0.0

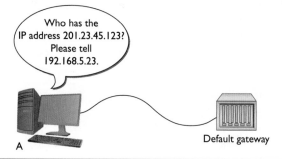

Who has the IP address 201.23.45.123? Please tell 192.168.5.23.

A   Default gateway

• **Figure 7.28**   Sending an ARP to the gateway

Most network folks represent subnet masks using special shorthand: a / character followed by a number equal to the number of ones in the subnet mask. Here are a few examples:

11111111111111111111111100000000 = /24 (24 ones)
11111111111111110000000000000000 = /16 (16 ones)
11111111000000000000000000000000 = /8 (8 ones)

An IP address followed by the / and number tells you the IP address and the subnet mask in one statement. For example, 201.23.45.123/24 is an IP address of 201.23.45.123 with a subnet mask of 255.255.255.0. Similarly, 184.222.4.36/16 is an IP address of 184.222.4.36 with a subnet mask of 255.255.0.0.

Fortunately, computers do all of this subnet filtering automatically. Network administrators need only to enter the correct IP address and subnet mask when they first set up their systems, and the rest happens without any human intervention.

If you want a computer to work in a routed internetwork (like the Internet), you absolutely must have an IP address that's part of its network ID, a subnet mask, and a default gateway. No exceptions!

 By definition, all computers on the same network have the same subnet mask and network ID.

Class IDs

The Internet is by far the biggest and the most complex TCP/IP internetwork. Numbering over half a billion computers way back in 2009, it has grown so quickly that now it's nearly impossible to find an accurate number. The single biggest challenge for the Internet is to make sure no two devices share the same public IP address. To support the dispersion of IP addresses, an organization called the **Internet Assigned Numbers Authority (IANA)** was formed to track and disperse IP addresses to those who need them. Initially handled by a single person (the famous Jon Postel) until 1998, IANA has grown dramatically and now oversees a number of Regional Internet Registries (RIRs) that parcel out IP addresses to large ISPs and major corporations. The RIR for North America is called the *American Registry for Internet Numbers (ARIN)*. The vast majority of end users get their IP addresses from their respective ISPs. IANA passes out IP addresses in contiguous chunks called **network blocks** (or just **blocks**), which are outlined in the following table:

	First Decimal Value	Addresses	Hosts per Network ID
Class A	1–126	1.0.0.0–126.255.255.255	16,277,214
Class B	128–191	128.0.0.0–191.255.255.255	65,534
Class C	192–223	192.0.0.0–223.255.255.255	254
Class D	224–239	224.0.0.0–239.255.255.255	Multicast
Class E	240–254	240.0.0.0–254.255.255.255	Experimental

A typical Class A network block, for example, has a network ID that starts between 1 and 126; hosts on that network have only the first octet in common, with any numbers for the other three octets. Having three octets to use for hosts means you have an enormous number of possible hosts, over 16 million different number combinations. The subnet mask for Class A network blocks is 255.0.0.0, which means you have 24 bits for host IDs.

CompTIA and many techs use the term *classful* to describe the traditional class blocks. Thus you'll see *classful A, B, C, and D addressing* on the exam. Keep reading and this will make sense.

Do you remember binary math? 2^{24} = 16,277,216. Because the host can't use all zeroes or all ones (those are reserved for the network ID and broadcast IP, respectively), you subtract two from the final number to get the available host IDs.

A Class B network block, with a subnet mask of 255.255.0.0, uses the first two octets to define the network ID. This leaves two octets to define host IDs, which means each Class B network ID can have up to 65,534 different hosts.

A Class C network block uses the first three octets to define only the network ID. All hosts in network 192.168.35.0, for example, would have all three first numbers in common. Only the last octet defines the host IDs, which leaves only 254 possible unique addresses. The subnet mask for a Class C block is 255.255.255.0.

Multicast class blocks are used for one-to-many communication, such as in streaming video conferencing. There are three types of ways to send a packet: a **broadcast**, which is where every computer on the LAN hears the message; a **unicast**, where one computer sends a message directly to another user; and a **multicast**, where a single computer sends a packet to a group of interested computers. Multicast is often used when routers talk to each other.

Experimental addresses are reserved and never used except for occasional experimental reasons. These were originally called Reserved addresses.

IP class blocks worked well for the first few years of the Internet but quickly ran into trouble due to the fact that they didn't quite fit for everyone. Early on, IANA gave away IP network blocks rather generously, perhaps too generously. Over time, unallocated IP addresses became scarce. Additionally, the IP class block concept didn't scale well. If an organization needed 2,000 IP addresses, for example, it either had to take a single Class B network block (wasting 63,000 addresses) or eight Class C blocks. As a result, a new method of generating blocks of IP addresses, called **Classless Inter-Domain Routing (CIDR)**, was developed.

CIDR and Subnetting

CIDR is based on a concept called **subnetting**: taking a single class of IP addresses and chopping it up into multiple smaller groups. CIDR and subnetting are virtually the same thing. Subnetting is done by an organization—it is given a block of addresses and then breaks the single block of addresses into multiple subnets. CIDR is done by an ISP—it is given a block of addresses, subnets the block into multiple subnets, and then passes out the smaller individual subnets to customers. Subnetting and CIDR have been around for quite a long time now and are a critical part of all but the smallest TCP/IP networks. Let's first discuss subnetting and then visit CIDR.

Subnetting

Subnetting enables a much more efficient use of IP addresses compared to class blocks. It also enables you to separate a network for security (separating a bank of public access computers from your more private computers) and for bandwidth control (separating a heavily used LAN from one that's not so heavily used).

The cornerstone to subnetting lies in the subnet mask. You take an existing /8, /16, or /24 subnet and extend the subnet mask by adding more ones (and taking away the corresponding number of zeroes). For example, let's say you have an Internet café with about 50 computers, 40 of which are for public use and 10 of which are used in the back office for accounting and such (Figure 7.29). Your network ID is 192.168.4.0/24. You want to prevent people who are using the public systems from accessing your private machines, so you decide to create subnets. You also have wireless Internet and want to separate wireless clients (never more than 10) on their own subnet.

You need to keep two things in mind about subnetting. First, start with the given subnet mask and move it to the right until you have the number of subnets you need. Second, forget the dots. They no longer define the subnets.

Never try to subnet without first converting to binary. Too many techs are what I call "victims of the dots." They are so used to working only with class blocks that they forget there's more to subnets

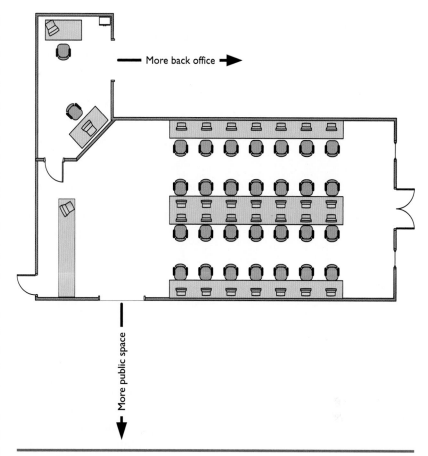

More back office ➡

More public space

• **Figure 7.29** Layout of the network

than just /8, /16, and /24 networks. There is no reason network IDs must end on the dots. The computers, at least, think it's perfectly fine to have subnets that end at points between the periods, such as /26, /27, or even /22. The trick here is to stop thinking about network IDs and subnet masks just in their dotted decimal format and instead return to thinking of them as binary numbers.

Let's begin subnetting the café's network of 192.168.4.0/24. Start by changing a zero to a one on the subnet mask so the /24 becomes a /25 subnet:

11111111111111111111111110000000

Calculating Hosts

Before going even one step further, you need to answer this question: On a /24 network, how many hosts can you have? Well, if you used dotted decimal notation you might say

192.168.4.1 to 192.168.4.254 = 254 hosts

But do this from the binary instead. In a /24 network, you have eight zeroes that can be the host ID:

00000001 to 11111110 = 254

There's a simple piece of math here: $2^x - 2$, where x represents the number of zeroes in the subnet mask.

$2^8 - 2 = 254$

If you remember this simple formula, you can always determine the number of hosts for a given subnet. This is critical! Memorize this!

If you have a /16 subnet mask on your network, what is the maximum number of hosts you can have on that network?

1. Because a subnet mask always has 32 digits, a /16 subnet means you have 16 zeroes left after the 16 ones.

2. $2^{16} - 2 = 65,534$ total hosts.

If you have a /26 subnet mask on your network, what is the maximum number of hosts you can have on that network?

1. Because a subnet mask always has 32 digits, a /26 subnet means you have 6 zeroes left after the 26 ones.

2. $2^6 - 2 = 62$ total hosts.

Excellent! Knowing how to determine the number of hosts for a particular subnet mask will help you tremendously, as you'll see in a moment.

Your First Subnet

You cannot subnet without using binary!

Let's now make a subnet. All subnetting begins with a single network ID. In this scenario, you need to convert the 192.168.4.0/24 network ID for the café into three network IDs: one for the public computers, one for the private computers, and one for the wireless clients.

The primary tool for subnetting is the existing subnet mask. Write it out in binary. Place a line at the end of the ones, as shown in Figure 7.30.

Now draw a second line one digit to the right, as shown in Figure 7.31. You've now separated the subnet mask into three areas that I call (from left to right) the default subnet mask (DSM), the network ID extension (NE), and the hosts (H). These are not industry terms so you won't see them on the CompTIA Network+ exam, but they're a handy Mike Trick that makes the process of subnetting a lot easier.

You now have a /25 subnet mask. At this point, most people first learning how to subnet start to freak out. They're challenged by the idea that a subnet mask of /25 isn't going to fit into one of the three pretty subnets of 255.0.0.0, 255.255.0.0, or 255.255.255.0. They think, "That can't be right! Subnet masks are made out of only 255s and 0s." That's not correct. A subnet mask is a string of ones followed by a string of zeroes. People only convert it into dotted decimal to enter things into computers. So convert /25 into dotted decimal.

Subnet mask |||||||||||||||||||||||||00000000

• **Figure 7.30**   Step 1 in subnetting

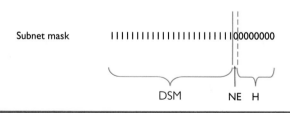

• **Figure 7.31**   Organizing the subnet mask

Mike Meyers' CompTIA Network+ Guide to Managing and Troubleshooting Networks

First write out 25 ones, followed by seven zeroes. (Remember, subnet masks are *always* 32 binary digits long.)

```
11111111111111111111111110000000
```

Insert the periods in between every eight digits:

```
11111111.11111111.11111111.10000000
```

Then convert them to dotted decimal:

```
255.255.255.128
```

Get used to the idea of subnet masks that use more than 255s and 0s. Here are some examples of perfectly legitimate subnet masks. Try converting these to binary to see for yourself.

```
255.255.255.224
255.255.128.0
255.248.0.0
```

Calculating Subnets

When you subnet a network ID, you need to follow the rules and conventions dictated by the good folks who developed TCP/IP to ensure that your new subnets can interact properly with each other and with larger networks. All you need to remember for subnetting is this: start with a beginning subnet mask and extend the subnet extension until you have the number of subnets you need. The formula for determining how many subnets you create is 2^y, where y is the number of bits you add to the subnet mask.

Let's practice this a few times. Figure 7.32 shows a starting subnet of 255.255.255.0. If you move the network ID extension over one, it's only a single digit, 2^1.

That single digit is only a zero or a one, which gives you two subnets. You have only one problem—the café needs three subnets, not just two! So let's take /24 and subnet it down to /26. Extending the network ID by two digits creates four new network IDs, $2^3 = 6$. To see each of these network IDs, first convert the original network ID—192.168.4.0—into binary. Then add the four different network ID extensions to the end, as shown in Figure 7.33.

Figure 7.34 shows all of the IP addresses for each of the four new network IDs.

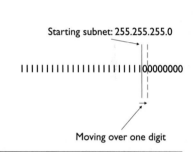

• **Figure 7.32** Organizing the subnet mask

```
11000000101010000000010000000001
11000000101010000000010000000010
11000000101010000000010000000011
11000000101010000000010000000100

11000000101010000000010001000001
11000000101010000000010001000010
11000000101010000000010001000011
11000000101010000000010001000100

11000000101010000000010010000001
11000000101010000000010010000010
11000000101010000000010010000011
11000000101010000000010010000100

11000000101010000000010011000001
11000000101010000000010011000010
11000000101010000000010011000011
11000000101010000000010011000100
```

Original network ID: 192.168.4.0 /24
Translates to this in binary:
11000000.10101000.00000100.00000000

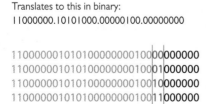

• **Figure 7.33** Creating the new network IDs

• **Figure 7.34** New network ID address ranges

Now convert these four network IDs back to dotted decimal:

Network ID	Host Range	Broadcast Address
192.168.4.0/26	(192.168.4.1–192.168.4.62)	192.168.4.63
192.168.4.64/26	(192.168.4.65–192.168.4.126)	192.168.4.127
192.168.4.128/26	(192.168.4.129–192.168.4.190)	192.168.4.191
192.168.4.192/26	(192.168.4.193–192.168.4.254)	192.168.4.255

Congratulations! You've just taken a single network ID, 192.168.4.0/24, and subnetted it into four new network IDs! Figure 7.35 shows how you can use these new network IDs in a network.

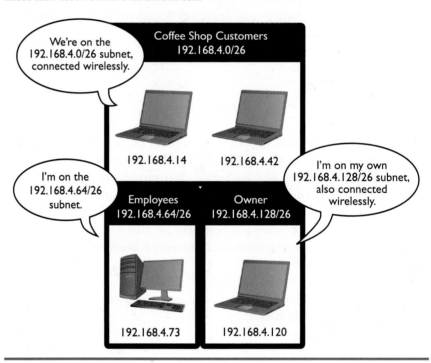

• Figure 7.35   Three networks using the new network IDs

You may notice that the café only needs three subnets, but you created four—you're wasting one. Because subnets are created by powers of two, you will often create more subnets than you need—welcome to subnetting.

For a little more subnetting practice, let's create eight subnets on a /27 network. First, move the NE over three digits (Figure 7.36).

If wasting subnets seems contrary to the goal of efficient use, keep in mind that subnetting has two goals: efficiency and making multiple network IDs from a single network ID. This example is geared more toward the latter goal.

```
Subnet mask        11111111111111111111111100000000
192.168.4.0        11000000101010000000010000000000


Add 000            11000000101010000000010000000000
Add 001            11000000101010000000010000100000
Add 010            11000000101010000000010001000000
Add 011            11000000101010000000010001100000
Add 100            11000000101010000000010010000000
Add 101            11000000101010000000010010100000
Add 110            11000000101010000000010011000000
Add 111            11000000101010000000010011100000
```

• Figure 7.36   Moving the network ID extension three digits

To help you visualize the address range, I'll calculate the first two subnets—using 000 and 001 (Figure 7.37). Please do the other six for practice.

Note that in this case you only get $2^5 - 2 = 30$ hosts per network ID! These better be small networks!

Converting these to dotted decimal, you get:

192.168.4.0/27 (192.168.4.1–192.168.4.30)
192.168.4.32/27 (192.168.4.33–192.168.4.62)
192.168.4.64/27 (192.168.4.65–192.168.4.94)
192.168.4.96/27 (192.168.4.97–192.168.4.126)
192.168.4.128/27 (192.168.4.129–192.168.4.158)
192.168.4.160/27 (192.168.4.161–192.168.4.190)
192.168.4.192/27 (192.168.4.193–192.168.4.222)
192.168.4.224/27 (192.168.4.225–192.168.4.254)

These two examples began with a Class C address. However, you can begin with any starting network ID. Nothing changes about the process you just learned.

```
11000000101010000000010000100000
11000000101010000000010000100001
11000000101010000000010000100010
        ⋮
11000000101010000000010000111101
11000000101010000000010000111110
11000000101010000000010000111111


11000000101010000000010001100000
11000000101010000000010001100001
11000000101010000000010001100010
        ⋮
11000000101010000000010001111101
11000000101010000000010001111110
11000000101010000000010001111111
```

• **Figure 7.37**   Two of the eight network ID address ranges

Manual Dotted Decimal to Binary Conversion

The best way to convert from dotted decimal to binary and back is to use a calculator. It's easy, fast, and accurate. There's always a chance, however, that you may find yourself in a situation where you need to convert without a calculator. Fortunately, manual conversion, although a bit tedious, is also fairly easy. You just have to remember a single number: 128.

Take a piece of paper and write the number **128** in the top-left corner. Now, what is half of 128? That's right, 64. Write **64** next to 128. Now keep dividing the previous number in half until you get to the number 1. The result will look like this:

```
128   64   32   16   8   4   2   1
```

Notice that you have eight numbers. Each of these numbers corresponds to a position of one of the eight binary digits. To convert an 8-bit value to dotted decimal, just take the binary value and put the numbers under the corresponding eight digits. Wherever there's a 1, add that decimal value.

Let's take the binary value 10010110 into decimal. Write down the numbers as shown, and then write the binary values underneath each corresponding decimal number:

```
128   64   32   16   8   4   2   1
 1     0    0    1   0   1   1   0
```

Add the decimal values that have a 1 underneath:

128+16+4+2 = 150

Converting from decimal to binary is a bit more of a challenge. You still start with a line of decimal numbers starting with 128, but this time, you place the decimal value above. If the number you're trying to convert is greater than or equal to the number underneath, subtract it and place a 1 underneath that value. If not, then place a 0 under it and move the number to the next position

CompTIA and many techs refer to a CIDR address as a *classless address,* meaning the subnet used does not conform to the big four on the classful side: A, B, C, or D. When you see that term on the exam, you'll know you should look for subnetting.

Tech Tip

ISPs and Classless Addresses

If you order real, unique, ready-for-the-Internet IP addresses from your local ISP, you'll invariably get a classless set of IP addresses. More importantly, when you order them for clients, you need to be able to explain why their subnet mask is 255.255.255.192, when all the books they read tell them it should be 255.255.255.0!

All this assumes you can get an IPv4 address by the time you're reading this book. See Chapter 13 for the scoop on IPv6, the addressing scheme of the future.

to the right. Let's give this a try by converting 221 to binary. Begin by placing 221 over the 128:

```
221
128    64    32    16    8    4    2    1
93
1
```

Now place the remainder, 93, over the 64:

```
       93
128    64    32    16    8    4    2    1
       29
1      1
```

Place the remainder, 29, over the 32. The number 29 is less than 32, so place a 0 underneath the 32 and move to 16:

```
                   29
128    64    32    16    8    4    2    1
                   13
 1      1     0     1
```

Then move to the 8:

```
                        13
128    64    32    16     8    4    2    1
                         5
 1      1     0     1     1
```

Then the 4:

```
                              5
128    64    32    16    8     4    2    1
                              1
 1      1     0     1    1     1
```

Then the 2. The number 1 is less than 2, so drop a 0 underneath and move to 1:

```
                                   1
128    64    32    16    8    4     2    1
 1      1     0     1    1    1     0    1
```

Make sure you can manually convert decimal to binary and binary to decimal.

Finally, the 1; 1 is equal to 1, so put a 1 underneath and you're done. The number 221 in decimal is equal to 11011101 in binary.

CIDR: Subnetting in the Real World

I need to let you in on a secret—there's a better than average chance that you'll never have to do subnetting in the real world. That's not to say that subnetting isn't important. It's a critical part of the Internet's structure. Subnetting most commonly takes place in two situations: ISPs that receive network blocks from IANA and then subnet those blocks for customers, and very large customers that take subnets (sometimes already subnetted class blocks from ISPs) and make their own subnets. Even if you'll never make a working subnet in the real world, there are a number of reasons to learn subnetting.

First and most obvious, the CompTIA Network+ exam expects you to know subnetting. For the exam, you need to be able to take any existing network ID and break it down into a given number of subnets. You need to know how many hosts the resulting network IDs possess. You need to be able to calculate the IP addresses and the new subnet masks for each of the new network IDs.

Second, even if you never do your own subnetting, you will most likely contact an ISP and get CIDR addresses. You can't think about subnet masks in terms of dotted decimal. You need to think of subnets in terms of CIDR values like /8, /22, /26, and so on.

Third, there's a better than average chance you'll look to obtain more advanced IT certifications. Most Cisco, many Microsoft, and a large number of other certifications assume you understand subnetting. Subnetting is a competency standard that everyone who's serious about networking understands in detail—it's a clear separation between those who know networks and those who do not.

You've done well, my little padawan. Subnetting takes a little getting used to. Go take a break. Take a walk. Play some World of Warcraft. Or fire up your Steam client and see if I'm playing Counter-Strike or Left 4 Dead (player name "desweds"). After a good mental break, dive back into subnetting and *practice*. Take any old network ID and practice making multiple subnets—lots of subnets!

■ IP Address Assignment

Whew! After all that subnetting, you've reached the point where it's time to start actually using some IP addresses. That is, after all, the goal of going through all that pain. There are two ways to give a computer an IP address, subnet mask, and default gateway: either by typing in all the information (called **static addressing**) or by having a server program running on a system that automatically passes out all the IP information to systems as they boot up on or connect to a network (called **dynamic addressing**). Additionally, you must learn about a number of specialty IP addresses that have unique meanings in the IP world to make this all work.

 The CompTIA Network+ exam objectives call the methods for setting up devices for IP addresses *IP address assignment*. Note that that term applies to both static and dynamic methods (discussed here).

Static IP Addressing

Static addressing means typing all of the IP information into each of your clients. But before you type in anything, you have to answer two questions: What are you typing in and where do you type it? Let's visualize a four-node network like the one shown in Figure 7.38.

To make this network function, each computer must have an IP address, a subnet mask, and a default gateway. First, decide what network ID to use. In the old days, your ISP gave you a block of IP addresses to use. Assume that's still the method and you've been allocated a Class C network block for 197.156.4.0/24. The first rule of Internet addressing is ... no one talks about Internet addressing. Actually, we can maul the *Fight Club* reference and instead say, "The first rule of Internet addressing is that you can do whatever you want with your own network ID." There are no rules other than to make sure every computer gets a legit IP address and subnet mask

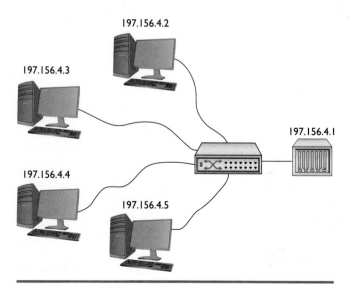

• **Figure 7.38** A small network

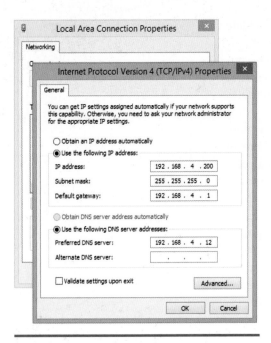

for your network ID and make sure every IP address is unique. You don't have to use the numbers in order, you don't have to give the default gateway the 192.156.4.1 address—you can do it any way you want. That said, most networks follow a common set of principles:

1. Give the default gateway the first IP address in the network ID.

2. Try to use the IP addresses in some kind of sequential order.

3. Try to separate servers from clients. For example, servers could have the IP addresses 197.156.4.10 to 197.156.4.19, whereas the clients range from 197.156.4.200 to 197.156.4.254.

4. Write down whatever you choose to do so the person who comes after you understands.

These principles have become unofficial standards for network techs, and following them will make you very popular with whoever has to manage your network in the future.

Now you can give each of the computers an IP address, subnet mask, and default gateway.

Every operating system has some method for you to enter in the static IP information. In Windows, you use the Internet Protocol Version 4 (TCP/IPv4) Properties dialog, as shown in Figure 7.39.

In OS X, run the Network utility in System Preferences to enter in the IP information (Figure 7.40).

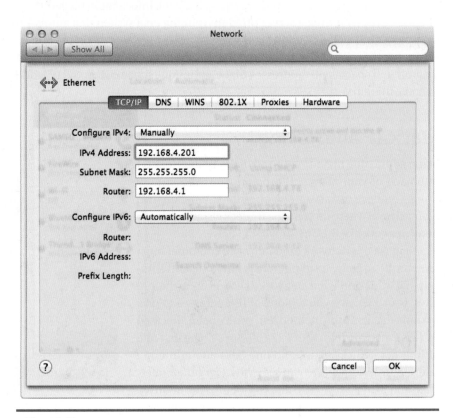

● **Figure 7.40** Entering static IP information in the OS X Network utility

```
●●●        mike@michaels-moble: ~
mike@michaels-moble:~$ sudo ifconfig eth0 192.168.4.202 netmask 255.255.255.0
[sudo] password for mike:
mike@michaels-moble:~$ ifconfig
eth0      Link encap:Ethernet  HWaddr 00:25:64:5b:8a:0c
          inet addr:192.168.4.202  Bcast:192.168.4.255  Mask:255.255.255.0
          inet6 addr: fe80::225:64ff:fe5b:8a0c/64 Scope:Link
          UP BROADCAST RUNNING MULTICAST  MTU:1500  Metric:1
          RX packets:911 errors:0 dropped:0 overruns:0 frame:0
          TX packets:302 errors:0 dropped:0 overruns:0 carrier:0
          collisions:0 txqueuelen:1000
          RX bytes:295866 (295.8 KB)  TX bytes:40908 (40.9 KB)
          Interrupt:16

lo        Link encap:Local Loopback
          inet addr:127.0.0.1  Mask:255.0.0.0
          inet6 addr: ::1/128 Scope:Host
          UP LOOPBACK RUNNING  MTU:65536  Metric:1
          RX packets:742 errors:0 dropped:0 overruns:0 frame:0
          TX packets:742 errors:0 dropped:0 overruns:0 carrier:0
          collisions:0 txqueuelen:0
          RX bytes:74000 (74.0 KB)  TX bytes:74000 (74.0 KB)

mike@michaels-moble:~$ ▮
```

• **Figure 7.41** Using the `ifconfig` command to set static IP addresses

The only universal tool for entering IP information on UNIX/Linux systems is the command-line `ifconfig` command, as shown in Figure 7.41. A warning about setting static IP addresses with `ifconfig`: any address entered will not be permanent and will be lost on reboot. To make the new IP address permanent, you need to find and edit your network configuration files. Fortunately, modern distributions (distros) make your life a bit easier. Almost every flavor of UNIX/Linux comes with some handy graphical program, such as Network Configuration in the popular Ubuntu Linux distro (Figure 7.42).

Once you've added the IP information for at least two systems, you should always verify using the `ping` command, as shown in Figure 7.43.

If you've entered an IP address and your ping is not successful, first check your IP settings. Odds are good you made a typo. Otherwise, check your connections, driver, and so forth. Static addressing has been around for a long time and is still heavily used for more critical systems on your network. Static addressing

Check out the excellent "Static IP in Linux" Show! over at http://totalsem.com/006. It'll take you through the process of setting up a static IP in a typical Linux distro.

• **Figure 7.42** Ubuntu's Network Configuration utility

```
CLI              Command Prompt             -  □  x

C:\>ping 192.168.4.8

Pinging 192.168.4.8 with 32 bytes of data:
Reply from 192.168.4.8: bytes=32 time<1ms TTL=128
Reply from 192.168.4.8: bytes=32 time<1ms TTL=128
Reply from 192.168.4.8: bytes=32 time<1ms TTL=128
Reply from 192.168.4.8: bytes=32 time<1ms TTL=128

Ping statistics for 192.168.4.8:
    Packets: Sent = 4, Received = 4, Lost = 0 (0% loss),
Approximate round trip times in milli-seconds:
    Minimum = 0ms, Maximum = 0ms, Average = 0ms

C:\>ping 192.168.4.8

Pinging 192.168.4.8 with 32 bytes of data:
Request timed out.
Request timed out.
Request timed out.
Reply from 192.168.5.200: Destination host unreachable.

Ping statistics for 192.168.4.8:
    Packets: Sent = 4, Received = 1, Lost = 3 (75% loss),

C:\>
```

• **Figure 7.43** Two pings (successful ping on top, unsuccessful ping on bottom)

Always verify with ping—it's too easy to make a typo when entering static IP addresses.

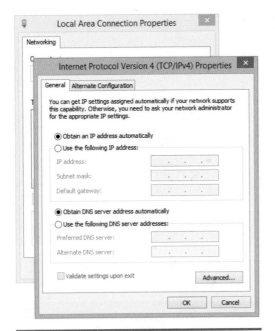

• **Figure 7.44**   Setting up for DHCP

DHCP uses *UDP* ports 67 and 68. And yes, memorize the numbers.

Check out the excellent Chapter 7 "DHCP Client Setup" Click! over at http://totalsem.com/006. It walks you through the process of setting up DHCP in Windows.

poses one big problem, however: making any changes to the network is a serious pain. Most systems today use a far easier and more flexible method to get their IP information: dynamic IP addressing.

Dynamic IP Addressing

Dynamic IP addressing, better known as **Dynamic Host Configuration Protocol (DHCP)** or the older (and long vanished) **Bootstrap Protocol (BOOTP)**, automatically assigns an IP address whenever a computer connects to the network. DHCP (and BOOTP, though for simplicity I'll just say DHCP) works very simply. First, configure a computer to use DHCP. Every OS has some method to tell the computer to use DHCP, as in the Windows example shown in Figure 7.44.

How DHCP Works

Once a computer is configured to use DHCP, we call it a *DHCP client*. When a DHCP client boots up, it automatically sends out a special DHCP Discover packet using the broadcast address.

This DHCP Discover message asks "Are there any DHCP servers out there?" (See Figure 7.45.)

For DHCP to work, one system on the LAN must be running special DHCP server software. This server is designed to respond to DHCP Discover requests with a DHCP Offer. The DHCP server is configured to pass out IP addresses from a range (called a *DHCP scope*) and a subnet mask (Figure 7.46). It also passes out other information, known generically as options, that cover an outrageously

• **Figure 7.45**   Computer sending out a DHCP Discover message

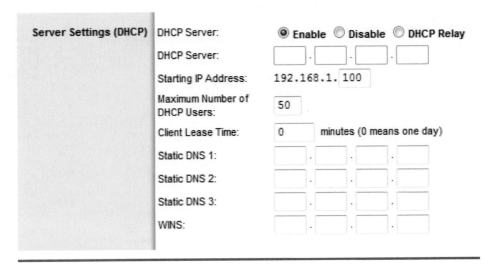

• **Figure 7.46**   DHCP server main screen

Mike Meyers' CompTIA Network+ Guide to Managing and Troubleshooting Networks

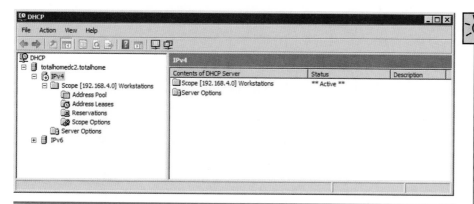

• **Figure 7.47** DHCP Server configuration screen

large number of choices, such as your default gateway, DNS server, Network Time server, and so on.

Figure 7.47 shows the configuration screen from the popular DHCP Server that comes with Windows Server 2012. Note the single scope. Figure 7.48 shows the same DHCP Server tool, in this case detailing the options screen. At this point, you're probably not sure what any of these options are for. Don't worry. I'll return to these topics in later chapters.

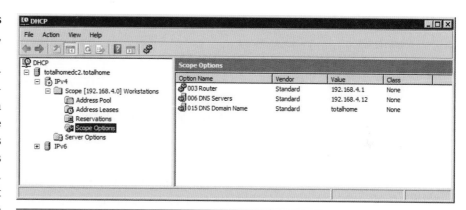

• **Figure 7.48** DHCP Server options screen

The DHCP client sends out a DHCP Request—a poor name choice as it is really accepting the offer. The DHCP server then sends a DHCP Acknowledgment and lists the MAC address as well as the IP information given to the DHCP client in a database (Figure 7.49).

At the end of the 4-step DHCP dance, the DHCP client gets a **DHCP lease**. A DHCP lease is set for a fixed amount of time, generally five to eight days. Near the end of the lease time, the DHCP client simply makes another DHCP Discover message. The DHCP server looks at the MAC address information and, unless another computer has taken the lease, always gives the DHCP client the same IP information, including the same IP address.

• **Figure 7.49** DHCP Request and DHCP Acknowledgment

Living with DHCP

DHCP is very convenient and, as such, very popular. It's so popular that you'll very rarely see a user's computer on any network using static addressing.

You should know how to deal with the problems that arise with DHCP. The single biggest issue is when a DHCP client tries to get a DHCP address and fails. You'll know when this happens because the operating system will post some

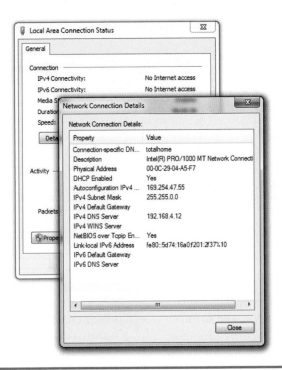

• **Figure 7.50**   DHCP error in Windows 7

form of error telling you there's a problem (Figure 7.50) and the DHCP client will have a rather strange address in the 169.254.0.0/16 network ID.

This special IP address is generated by a version of *zero-configuration networking (zeroconf)*. Microsoft's implementation is called **Automatic Private IP Addressing (APIPA)**. (That's the one you'll see on the exam.)

All DHCP clients are designed to generate an APIPA address automatically if they do not receive a response to a DHCP Discover message. The client only generates the last two octets of an APIPA address. This at least allows the dynamic clients on a single network to continue to communicate with each other because they are on the same network ID.

Unfortunately, APIPA cannot issue a default gateway, so you'll never get on the Internet using APIPA. That provides a huge clue to a DHCP problem: you can communicate with other computers on your network that came up *after* the DHCP server went down, but you can't get to the Internet or access computers that retain the DHCP-given address.

If you can't get to the Internet, use whatever tool your OS provides to check your IP address. If it's an APIPA address, you know instantly that you have a DHCP problem. First of all, try to reestablish the lease manually. Every OS has some way to do this. In Windows, you can type the following command:

```
ipconfig /renew
```

Systems that use static IP addressing can never have DHCP problems.

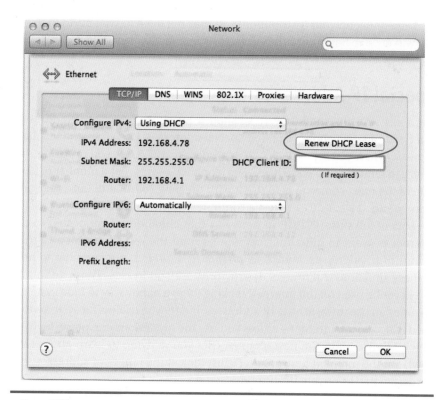

• **Figure 7.51** Network utility in System Preferences

With OS X, go to System Preferences and use the Network utility (Figure 7.51). Sometimes you might find yourself in a situation where your computer gets confused and won't grab an IP address no matter what you try. In these cases, you should first force the computer to release its lease. In Windows, get to a command prompt and type these two commands; follow each by pressing ENTER:

```
ipconfig /release
ipconfig /renew
```

In UNIX/Linux and OS X, use the `ifconfig` command to release and renew a DHCP address. Here's the syntax to release:

```
sudo ifconfig eth0 down
```

And here's the syntax to renew:

```
sudo ifconfig eth0 up
```

Tech Tip

Case Matters

With UNIX, Linux, and OS X command-line commands, case matters. If you run `sudo ifconfig eth0 down` *all in lowercase, for example, your Ethernet connection will drop as the DHCP or BOOTP lease is released. If you try running the same command in uppercase, on the other hand, the Linux et al. command prompt will look at you quizzically and then snort with derision. "What's this SUDO of which you speak?" And then it will give you a prompt for a "real" command. Watch your case with UNIX/Linux/OS X!*

CompTIA loves TCP and UDP port numbers, so make sure you know that DHCP and BOOTP servers use UDP port 67 and clients use port 68. You'll also see the term BOOTPS on the exam, which simply refers to a BOOTP server (as opposed to BOOTPC for a BOOTP client).

Check out the excellent Chapter 7 "ifconfig" Show! over at http://totalsem.com/006. You'll see ifconfig in all its glory.

Make sure you know how to configure your computers to use static IP addressing and know that you use ping to ensure they can communicate. For dynamic IP addressing, make sure you know the common protocol— DHCP—and the much older protocol—BOOTP. Understand that each client must have some way to "turn on" DHCP. Also understand the concept of a DHCP client and a DHCP server. Last but not least, be comfortable with APIPA and releasing and renewing a lease on a client.

Even though, by convention, you use 127.0.0.1 as the loopback address, the entire 127.0.0.0/8 subnet is reserved for loopback addresses! You can use any address in the 127.0.0.0/8 subnet as a loopback address.

Make sure you can quickly tell the difference between a private IP address and a public IP address for the CompTIA Network+ exam. The objectives mention the distinction as *private vs. public.*

Depending on your distribution, you may not need to type `sudo` first, but you will need to have root privileges to use ifconfig. Root privileges are Linux's version of administrative privileges in Windows.

Special IP Addresses

The folks who invented TCP/IP created a number of special IP addresses you need to know about. The first special address is 127.0.0.1—the **loopback address**. When you tell a device to send data to 127.0.0.1, you're telling that device to send the packets to itself. The loopback address has a number of uses. One of the most common is to use it with the ping command. I use the command `ping 127.0.0.1` to test a computer's network stack.

Lots of folks use TCP/IP in networks that either aren't connected to the Internet or want to hide their computers from the rest of Internet. Certain groups of IP addresses, known as *private IP addresses,* are available to help in these situations. All routers destroy private IP addresses. Those addresses can never be used on the Internet, making them a handy way to hide systems. Anyone can use these private IP addresses, but they're useless for systems that need to access the Internet—unless you use the mysterious and powerful NAT, which I'll discuss in the next chapter. (Bet you're dying to learn about NAT now!) For the moment, however, let's just look at the ranges of addresses that are designated as private IP addresses:

- 10.0.0.0 through 10.255.255.255 (1 Class A network block)
- 172.16.0.0 through 172.31.255.255 (16 Class B network blocks)
- 192.168.0.0 through 192.168.255.255 (256 Class C network blocks)

All other IP addresses are public IP addresses.

Chapter 7 Review

■ Chapter Summary

After reading this chapter and completing the exercises, you should understand the following about TCP/IP.

Describe how the TCP/IP protocol suite works

■ Whereas MAC addresses are physical addresses burned into the NIC, IP addresses are logical and are assigned via software.

■ An IP address consists of 32 binary digits, often written in dotted decimal notation to make it easier for humans to read.

■ Every IP address must be unique on its network.

■ The utilities ipconfig (Windows) and ifconfig (UNIX/Linux/OS X) can be used to view IP address information.

■ Every IP address contains both a network ID and a host ID. Computers on the same network will have the same network ID portion of an IP address, whereas the host ID portion will be unique.

■ The network's router's interface is called the default gateway. Its IP address is used by hosts to communicate off the network. The router uses an internal routing table and network IDs to determine where to send network packets.

■ A subnet mask helps to define the network ID of an IP address. All computers on a specific network share the same subnet mask.

■ An Address Resolution Protocol (ARP) broadcast is used to determine the MAC address of the destination computer or router based on its IP address.

■ Subnet masks are often written with the IP address in slash notation, such as 201.23.45.123/24. In this example, the IP address is 201.23.45.123 and the subnet mask consists of 24 ones, or 11111111.11111111.11111111.00000000 (255.255.255.0).

■ The Internet Assigned Numbers Authority (IANA) is the organization responsible for tracking and dispersing IP addresses to Internet service providers.

■ A broadcast is sent to every computer on the network. A unicast is sent from one node to one other node. A multicast is sent from one computer to multiple nodes.

Explain CIDR and subnetting

■ Subnet masks enable network adapters to determine whether incoming packets are being sent to a local network address or a remote network.

■ A subnet mask is similar in form to an IP address. Subnet masks consist of some number of ones, followed by zeroes, for a total of 32 bits.

■ Subnetting is done by organizations when they need to create multiple networks.

■ Classless Inter-Domain Routing (CIDR) is when an ISP subnets a block of addresses and passes them out to smaller customers.

■ Computers use subnet masks to distinguish (sub) network IDs from host IDs. Any bit on the full IP address that corresponds to a 1 on the subnet mask is part of the network ID. Any uncovered (turned off or = 0) bits show the host ID of an IP address.

■ Assignable IP addresses come in three basic classful address types: Class A, Class B, and Class C.

■ The Class A range of addresses has its first octet anywhere from 1 through 126. The default Class A subnet mask is 255.0.0.0.

■ A Class B address has its first octet anywhere from 128 through 191. Class B subnets use a mask of 255.255.0.0.

■ Class C addresses range from 192 through 223, with the standard Class C subnet mask set to 255.255.255.0.

■ Classless subnets do away with neat subnet masks. These subnet masks employ other binary representations in the masking process. For example, 255.255.255.0 is a standard Class C subnet mask, allowing for one subnet of 254 systems. Contrast that example with using subnet mask 255.255.255.240, which would allow for 14 subnets with 14 systems each.

Describe the functions of static and dynamic IP addresses

■ Static addressing requires the IP address, subnet mask, and default gateway to be entered manually.

■ Dynamic addressing uses the Dynamic Host Configuration Protocol (DHCP) to assign an IP address, subnet mask, and default gateway to a network client.

- A network client is assigned an IP address from a DHCP server by exchanging the following packets: DHCP Discover, DHCP Offer, DHCP Request, and DHCP Acknowledgement.
- The data accepted by the DHCP client is called the DHCP lease, which is good for a fixed period of time. The time varies based on how the DHCP server was configured.
- A DHCP client that fails to acquire a DHCP lease from a DHCP server self-generates an IP address and subnet mask via Automatic Private IP Addressing (APIPA). This address falls in the Class B range of 169.254.*x.x*/16.
- The 127.0.0.1 loopback address used in testing is a reserved IP address.
- Private IP addresses include the following ranges:
  10.0.0.0–10.255.255.255 (Class A)
  172.16.0.0–172.31.255.255 (Class B)
  192.168.0.0–192.168.255.255 (Class C)

Key Terms

Address Resolution Protocol (ARP) *(159)*
Automatic Private IP Addressing (APIPA) *(174)*
blocks *(161)*
Bootstrap Protocol (BOOTP) *(172)*
broadcast *(162)*
Classless Inter-Domain Routing (CIDR) *(162)*
datagram *(149)*
default gateway *(156)*
DHCP lease *(173)*
dotted decimal notation *(152)*
dynamic addressing *(169)*
Dynamic Host Configuration Protocol (DHCP) *(172)*
host ID *(155)*
ifconfig *(154)*
Internet Assigned Numbers Authority (IANA) *(161)*
Internet Control Message Protocol (ICMP) *(147)*
Internet Protocol (IP) *(147)*

Internet Protocol version 4 (IPv4) *(147)*
IP addressing *(151)*
ipconfig *(153)*
loopback address *(176)*
multicast *(162)*
network blocks *(161)*
network ID *(155)*
protocols *(145)*
protocol suite *(145)*
routing table *(156)*
segments *(148)*
static addressing *(169)*
subnet mask *(157)*
subnetting *(162)*
Transmission Control Protocol (TCP) *(148)*
unicast *(162)*
User Datagram Protocol (UDP) *(148)*

Key Term Quiz

Use the Key Terms list to complete the sentences that follow. Not all terms will be used.

1. The _____ resembles 192.168.17.0.

2. The _____ portion of an IP address assigned to a host computer consists of from one to three octets, with the final octet between 1 and 254.

3. The single organization that distributes IP addresses is called _____.

4. The IP address 10.11.12.13 is a valid _____ address.

5. The command _____ is a utility that comes with Microsoft Windows to show TCP/IP settings.

6. The command _____ is a utility for UNIX/Linux/OS X used to show TCP/IP settings.

7. _____ is used to translate IP addresses to MAC addresses.

8. Computers set for dynamic addressing that cannot locate a DHCP server use _____ to assign themselves an IP address.

9. The router interface on your subnet is commonly known as the _____.

10. The _____ is a 32-bit binary number common to all computers on a network that is used to determine to which network a computer belongs.

Multiple-Choice Quiz

1. What is the result of converting 11110000.10111001.
    00001000.01100111 to dotted decimal notation?

    A. 4.5.1.5

    B. 240.185.8.103

    C. 15.157.16.230

    D. 103.8.185.240

2. What does IANA stand for?

    A. International Association Numbers Authority

    B. International Association Numbering Authority

    C. Internet Assigned Numbering Authority

    D. Internet Assigned Numbers Authority

3. Which of the following describe IPv4? (Select three.)

    A. Uses decimal, not hexadecimal numbers

    B. Uses periods, not colons, as separators

    C. Uses four octets

    D. Uses eight sets of characters

4. What is the result of converting 192.168.0.1 to binary?

    A. 11000000.10101000.00000000.00000001

    B. 11000000.10101000.00000000.10000000

    C. 11000000.10101000.00000000.1

    D. 11.10101.0.1

5. Which of the following are *not* valid IP addresses to
    assign to a Windows-based system? (Select two.)

    A. 1.1.1.1/24

    B. 127.0.0.1/24

    C. 250.250.250.255/24

    D. 192.168.0.1/24

6. Which of the following is a valid assignable Class A
    IP address?

    A. 22.33.44.55

    B. 127.0.0.1

    C. 250.250.250.250

    D. 192.168.0.1

7. Which of the following is a valid Class B IP address?

    A. 10.10.10.253

    B. 191.254.254.254

    C. 192.168.1.1

    D. 223.250.250.1

8. Which of the following is a valid Class C
    IP address?

    A. 50.50.50.50

    B. 100.100.100.100

    C. 192.168.0.254

    D. 250.250.250.250

9. Which method sends a packet from a single
    computer to a group of interested computers?
    Select the best answer.

    A. Broadcast

    B. Unicast

    C. Multicast

    D. Omnicast

10. What processes are used to take a single class of
    IP addresses and chop it up into multiple smaller
    groups? (Select two.)

    A. CIDR

    B. ping

    C. Subnetting

    D. Subnitting

11. Which statements about subnet masks are true?
    (Select two.)

    A. Every network client has a unique subnet
        mask.

    B. Every client on a network shares the same
        subnet mask.

    C. A subnet mask consists of a string of zeroes
        followed by a string of ones.

    D. A subnet mask consists of a string of ones
        followed by a string of zeroes.

12. In which order are packets created and sent when a client requests an IP address from a DHCP server?

    A. DHCP Discover, DHCP Offer, DHCP Request, DHCP Acknowledgement

    B. DHCP Discover, DHCP Request, DHCP Offer, DHCP Acknowledgement

    C. DHCP Request, DHCP Offer, DHCP Discover, DHCP Acknowledgement

    D. DHCP Request, DHCP Offer, DHCP Acknowledgement, DHCP Discover

13. Which of the following is *not* a valid classful subnet mask?

    A. 255.0.0.0

    B. 255.255.0.0

    C. 255.255.255.0

    D. 255.255.255.255

14. Which command would you use to force a DHCP request on a Windows computer?

    A. ifconfig /all

    B. ifconfig /renew

    C. ipconfig /release

    D. ipconfig /renew

15. Which of the following IP addresses indicates a computer configured for dynamic addressing was unable to locate a DHCP server?

    A. 255.255.255.255

    B. 192.168.1.1

    C. 127.0.0.1

    D. 169.254.1.30

■ Essay Quiz

1. Use your Web browser to go to the www.webopedia.com Web site. Search for the full term TCP/IP. Write down its definition on a piece of paper, being sure to cite the exact Web site link to give credit to where you obtained the information.

2. You and a classmate are trying to calculate the number of possible IPv4 addresses versus IPv6 addresses. (The TCP/IP powers that be created the IPv6 addressing system to replace the IPv4 system discussed in this chapter. Because I feel IPv6 is going to be extremely important for all techs to understand in the future, this book devotes a full chapter to the subject—Chapter 13.) Research the Internet to discover exactly how many addresses are available for each of these numbering schemes. Document your findings in a short essay.

3. A new intern is confused about the CIDR notation for subnets, such as 192.168.1/24. In your own words, explain to him why the part in front of the slash represents only three of the four octets in an IP address and what the number after the slash is.

Lab Projects

• Lab Project 7.1

Use the Internet to research the components of what an individual TCP packet and an IP packet might look like. You can search on keywords such as "sample," "TCP," "IP," "session," and "packet." Create a reference document that has links to five sites with appropriate information. Save the document, so the links contain hyperlinks that you can click. Then write an additional paragraph describing your overall findings. Print one copy as well.

• Lab Project 7.2

Starting with the IP address 192.42.53.12, create a list of IP address ranges for six subnets.

• Lab Project 7.3

Log in to any available networked Windows computer. Select Start | Run or just Start, type **cmd**, and press ENTER to open a command prompt; from the command prompt, type **ipconfig /all**, and then press ENTER. Fill in as much information as you can from your screen onto a sheet like the following (or create one as directed by your instructor):

Host Name:
Primary DNS Suffix:
Node Type:
IP Routing Enabled:
WINS Proxy Enabled:
DNS Suffix Search List:
Connection-specific DNS Suffix:
Description: Physical Address:
DHCP Enabled:
Autoconfiguration Enabled:
IP Address:
Subnet Mask:
Default Gateway:
DHCP Server:
DNS Servers:
Primary WINS Server:
Lease Obtained:
Lease Expires:

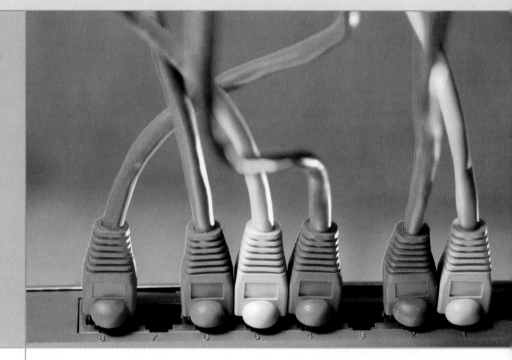

Routing

chapter

8

"Youngsters read it, grown men understand it, and old people applaud it."

—MIGUEL DE CERVANTES

In this chapter, you will learn how to

- **Explain how routers work**
- **Describe dynamic routing technologies**
- **Install and configure a router successfully**

The true beauty and amazing power of TCP/IP lies in one word: routing. Routing enables us to interconnect individual LANs into WANs. Routers, the magic boxes that act as the interconnection points, have all the built-in smarts to inspect incoming packets and forward them toward their eventual LAN destination. Routers are, for the most part, automatic. They require very little in terms of maintenance once their initial configuration is complete because they can talk to each other to determine the best way to send IP packets. The goal of this chapter is to take you into the world of routers and show you how they do this.

The chapter discusses how routers work, including an in-depth look at different types of Network Address Translation (NAT), and then dives into an examination of various dynamic routing protocols. You'll learn about vector protocols, including Routing Information Protocol (RIP) and Border Gateway Protocol (BGP), among others. The chapter finishes with the nitty-gritty details of installing and configuring a router successfully. Not only will you understand how routers work, you should be able to set up a basic home router and diagnose common router issues by the end of this chapter.

Historical/Conceptual

■ How Routers Work

A **router** is any piece of hardware or software that forwards packets based on their destination IP address. Routers work, therefore, at the Network layer of the OSI model and at the Internet layer of the TCP/IP model.

Classically, routers are dedicated boxes that contain at least two connections, although many routers contain many more connections. In a business setting, for example, you might see a Cisco 2600 Series device, one of the most popular routers ever made. These routers are a bit on the older side, but Cisco builds their routers to last. With occasional software upgrades, a typical router will last for many years. The 2611 router shown in Figure 8.1 has two connections (the other connections are used for maintenance and configuration). The two "working" connections are circled. One port leads to one network; the other leads to another network. The router reads the IP addresses of the packets to determine where to send the packets. (I'll elaborate on how that works in a moment.)

• **Figure 8.1**   Cisco 2611 router

• **Figure 8.2**   Business end of a typical home router

Most techs today get their first exposure to routers with the ubiquitous home routers that enable PCs to connect to a DSL modem or a cable modem (Figure 8.2). The typical home router, however, serves multiple functions, often combining a router, a switch, and other features like a firewall (for protecting your network from intruders), a DHCP server, and much more into a single box.

Figure 8.3 shows the electronic diagram for a two-port Cisco router, whereas Figure 8.4 shows the diagram for a Linksys home router.

Note that both boxes connect two networks. The big difference is that one side of the Linksys home router connects directly to a built-in switch. That's convenient! You don't have to buy a separate switch to connect multiple computers to the home router.

> See Chapter 19, "Protecting Your Network," for an in-depth look at firewalls and other security options.

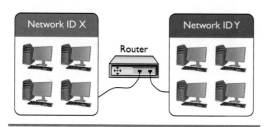

• **Figure 8.3**   Cisco router diagram

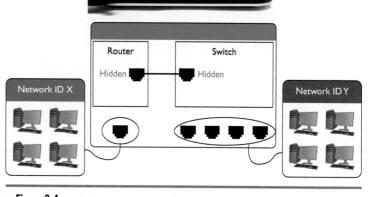

• **Figure 8.4**   Linksys home router diagram

All routers—big and small, plain or bundled with a switch—examine packets and then send the packets to the proper destination. Let's take a look at that process in more detail now.

Routing Tables

Routing begins as packets come into the router for handling (Figure 8.5). The router immediately strips off any of the Layer 2 information and drops the resulting IP packet into a queue (Figure 8.6). The important point to make here is that the router doesn't care where the packet originated. Everything is dropped into the same queue based on the time it arrived.

• **Figure 8.5**   Incoming packets

 Cross Check

What's Up with Layer 2?

You first read about routers stripping incoming frames of all their Layer 2 (OSI)/Link layer (TCP/IP) information way back in Chapter 2, "Network Models," so check your memory now. What defines the Layer 2 information? How is it assigned? Are there any differences between the TCP/IP model's Link layer and the OSI's Data Link layer?

The router inspects each packet's destination IP address and then sends the IP packet out the correct port. To perform this inspection, every router

• **Figure 8.6**   All incoming packets stripped of Layer 2 data and dropped into a common queue

comes with a **routing table** that tells the router exactly where to send the packets. This table is the key to understanding and controlling the process of forwarding packets to their proper destination. Figure 8.7 shows a very simple routing table for a typical home router. Each row in this routing table defines a single route. Each column identifies one of two specific criteria. Some columns define which packets are for the route and other columns define which port to send them out. (We'll break these down shortly.)

Routing Table Entry List Refresh

Destination LAN IP	Subnet Mask	Gateway	Interface
10.12.14.0	255.255.255.0	0.0.0.0	LAN
76.30.4.0	255.255.254.0	0.0.0.0	WAN
0.0.0.0	0.0.0.0	76.30.4.1	WAN

Close

• **Figure 8.7** Routing table from a home router

The router in this example has only two ports internally: one port that connects to a service provider, labeled as WAN in the Interface column of the table, and another port that connects to the router's built-in switch, labeled LAN in the table. Due to the small number of ports, this little router table has only four routes. Wait a minute: four routes and only two ports? No worries, there is *not* a one-to-one correlation of routes to ports, as you will soon see. Let's inspect this routing table.

Reading Figure 8.7 from left to right shows the following:

- **Destination LAN IP** A defined network ID. Every network ID directly connected to one of the router's ports is always listed here.
- **Subnet Mask** To define a network ID, you need a subnet mask (described in Chapter 7).

The router uses the combination of the destination LAN IP and subnet mask to see if a packet matches that route. For example, if you had a packet with the destination 10.12.14.26 coming into the router, the router would check the network ID and subnet mask. It would quickly determine that the packet matches the first route shown in Figure 8.8.

The other two columns in the routing table tell the router what to do with the packet:

- **Gateway** The IP address for the **next hop** router; in other words, where the packet should go. If the outgoing packet is for a network ID that's not directly connected to the router, the Gateway column tells the router the IP address of a router to which to send this packet. That router then handles the packet, and your router is done. (Well-configured routers ensure a packet will get to where it needs to go.) If the network ID is directly connected to the router, then you don't need a gateway. Based on what's needed, this is set to 0.0.0.0 or to the IP address of the directly connected port.

Destination LAN IP	Subnet mask	Gateway	Interface
10.12.14.0	255.255.255.0	0.0.0.0	LAN
76.30.4.0	255.255.254.0	0.0.0.0	WAN
239.0.0.0	255.0.0.0	0.0.0.0	LAN
0.0.0.0	0.0.0.0	76.30.4.1	WAN

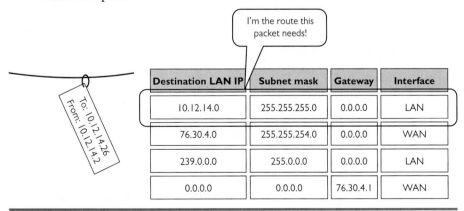

• **Figure 8.8** Routing table showing the route for a packet

- **Interface** Tells the router which of its ports to use. On this router, it uses the terms "LAN" and "WAN." Other routing tables use the port's IP address or some other type of abbreviation. Cisco routers, for example, use fa0/0, fa0/1, and so on.

A routing table looks like a table, so there's an assumption that the router will start at the top of the table and march down until it finds the correct route. That's not accurate. The router compares the destination IP address on a packet to every route listed in the routing table and only then sends the packet out. If a packet works for more than one route, the router will use the better route (we'll discuss this more in a moment).

The most important trick to reading a routing table is to remember that a zero (0) means "anything." For example, in Figure 8.7, the first route's destination LAN IP is 10.12.14.0. You can compare that to the subnet mask (255.255.255.0) to confirm that this is a /24 network. This tells you that any value (between 1 and 254) is acceptable for the last value in the 10.12.14/24 network ID.

A properly configured router must have a route for any packet it might encounter. Routing tables tell you a lot about the network connections. From just this single routing table, for example, the diagram in Figure 8.9 can be drawn.

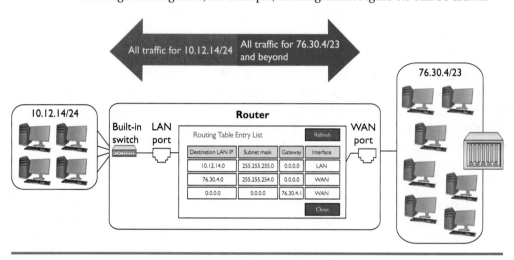

• **Figure 8.9** The network based on the routing table in Figure 8.7

Tech Tip

Top o' the Internet

There are two places where you'll find routers that do not have default routes: private (as in not on the Internet) internetworks, where every router knows about every single network, and the monstrous "Tier One" backbone, where you'll find the routers that make the main connections of the Internet.

Take another look at Figure 8.8. Notice the last route. How do I know the 76.30.4.1 port connects to another network? The third line of the routing table shows the default route for this router, and every router has one. (There's one exception to this. See the Tech Tip "Top o' the Internet.") This line says

> (*Any destination address*) (*with any subnet mask*) (*forward it to* 76.30.4.1) (*using my* WAN port)

```
Destination LAN IP    Subnet Mask         Gateway        Interface
0.0.0.0               0.0.0.0             76.30.4.1            WAN
```

The default route is very important because this tells the router exactly what to do with every incoming packet *unless* another line in the routing table gives another route. Excellent! Interpret the other two lines of the routing table in Figure 8.7 in the same fashion:

> (*Any packet for the* 10.12.14.0) (/24 *network ID*) (*don't use a gateway*) (*just ARP on the* LAN *interface to get the MAC address and send it directly to the recipient*)

```
Destination LAN IP    Subnet Mask     Gateway      Interface
10.12.14.0            255.255.255.0   0.0.0.0        LAN
```

(Any packet for the 76.30.4.0) (/23 network ID) (don't use a gateway)
(just ARP on the WAN interface to get the MAC address and send it
directly to the recipient)

```
Destination LAN IP    Subnet Mask     Gateway      Interface
76.30.4.0             255.255.254.0   0.0.0.0        WAN
```

I'll let you in on a little secret. Routers aren't the only devices that use routing tables. In fact, every node (computer, printer, TCP/IP-capable soda dispenser, whatever) on the network also has a routing table.

At first, this may seem silly—doesn't every computer only have a single Ethernet connection and, therefore, all data traffic has to go out that port? First of all, some computers have more than one NIC. But even if your computer has only a single NIC, how does it know what to do with an IP address like 127.0.0.1? Second, every packet sent out of your computer uses the routing table to figure out where the packet should go, whether directly to a node on your network or to your gateway. Here's an example of a routing table in Windows. This machine connects to the home router described earlier, so you'll recognize the IP addresses it uses.

Warning! The results screen of the `route print` command is very long, even on a basic system, so I've deleted a few parts of the output for the sake of brevity.

Tech Tip

Viewing Routing Tables in Linux and OS X
Every modern operating system gives you tools to view a computer's routing table. Most techs use the command line or terminal window interface— often called simply terminal— *because it's fast. To see your routing table in Linux or in OS X, for example, type this command at a terminal:*

`netstat -r`

The `netstat` *command works in Windows too, plus you can use* `route print` *as an alternative.*

```
C:\>route print
===========================================================================
Interface List
13 ...00 11 d8 30 16 c0......NVIDIA nForce Networking Controller
 1...........................Software Loopback Interface 1
57...00 00 00 00 00 00 00 e0 Microsoft ISATAP Adapter #15
56...00 00 00 00 00 00 00 e0 Teredo Tunneling Pseudo-Interface
===========================================================================
IPv4 Route Table
===========================================================================
Active Routes:
Network Destination        Netmask          Gateway       Interface  Metric
          0.0.0.0          0.0.0.0       10.12.14.1   10.12.14.201     25
        127.0.0.0        255.0.0.0         On-link       127.0.0.1    306
        127.0.0.1  255.255.255.255         On-link       127.0.0.1    306
  127.255.255.255  255.255.255.255         On-link       127.0.0.1    306
       10.12.14.0    255.255.255.0         On-link    10.12.14.201    281
     10.12.14.201  255.255.255.255         On-link    10.12.14.201    281
     10.12.14.255  255.255.255.255         On-link    10.12.14.201    281
        224.0.0.0        240.0.0.0         On-link       127.0.0.1    306
        224.0.0.0        240.0.0.0         On-link    10.12.14.201    281
  255.255.255.255  255.255.255.255         On-link       127.0.0.1    306
  255.255.255.255  255.255.255.255         On-link    10.12.14.201    281
===========================================================================
Persistent Routes:
None
```

Unlike the routing table for the typical home router you saw in Figure 8.7, this one seems a bit more complicated. My PC has only a single NIC, though, so it's not quite as complicated as it might seem at first glance. Take a look at the details. First note that my computer has an IP address of 10.12.14.201/24 and 10.12.14.1 as the default gateway.

You should note two differences in the columns from what you saw in the previous routing table. First, the interface has an actual IP address—10.12.14.201, plus the loopback of 127.0.0.1—instead of the word "LAN." Second—and this is part of the magic of routing—is something called the metric.

A **metric** is a relative value that defines the "cost" of using this route. The power of routing is that a packet can take more than one route to get to the same place. If a route were to suddenly cut off, then you would have an alternative. Figure 8.10 shows a networked router with two routes to the same place. The router has a route to Network B with a metric of 1 using Route 1, and a second route to Network B using Route 2 with a metric of 10.

Lowest routes always win. In this case, the router will always use the route with the metric of 1, unless that route suddenly stopped working. In that case, the router would automatically switch to the route with the 10 metric (Figure 8.11). This is the cornerstone of how the Internet works! The entire Internet is nothing more than a whole bunch of big, powerful routers connected to lots of other big, powerful routers. Connections go up and down all the time, and routers (with multiple routes) constantly talk to each other, detecting when a connection goes down and automatically switching to alternate routes.

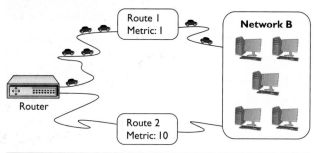

• **Figure 8.10**   Two routes to the same network

When a router has more than one route to the same network, it's up to the person in charge of that router to assign a different metric for each route. With dynamic routing protocols (discussed in detail later in the chapter in "Dynamic Routing"), the routers determine the proper metric for each route.

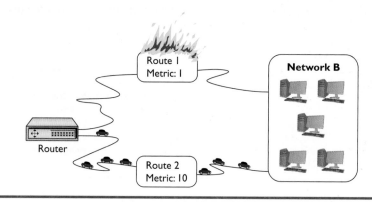

• **Figure 8.11**   When a route no longer works, the router automatically switches.

I'll go through this routing table one line at a time. Remember, every address is compared to every line in the routing table before it goes out, so it's no big deal if the default route is at the beginning or the end.

The top line defines the default route: (*Any destination address*) (*with any subnet mask*) (*forward it to my default gateway*) (*using my NIC*) (*Metric of 25 to use this route*). Anything that's not local goes to the router and from there out to the destination (with the help of other routers).

```
Network Destination      Netmask        Gateway      Interface   Metric
         0.0.0.0         0.0.0.0     10.12.14.1   10.12.14.201       25
```

The next three lines tell your system how to handle the loopback address. The second line is straightforward, but examine the first and third lines carefully. Earlier you learned that only 127.0.0.1 is the loopback, but according to the first route, any 127.0.0.0/8 address is the loopback. The third line is a little weird and is placed in the routing table to satisfy a loopback addressing requirement. Bottom line: no matter how you use a loopback address, as long as you start the address with 127, it will always go to 127.0.0.1.

Network Destination	Netmask	Gateway	Interface	Metric
127.0.0.0	255.0.0.0	On-link	127.0.0.1	306
127.0.0.1	255.255.255.255	On-link	127.0.0.1	306
127.255.255.255	255.255.255.255	On-link	127.0.0.1	306

The next line defines the local connection: (*Any packet for the* 10.12.14.0) (*/24 network ID*) (*don't use a gateway*) (*just ARP on the LAN interface to get the MAC address and send it directly to the recipient*) (*Cost of* 1 *to use this route*).

Network Destination	Netmask	Gateway	Interface	Metric
10.12.14.0	255.255.255.0	10.12.14.201	10.12.14.201	1

So, if a gateway of 10.12.14.201 here means "don't use a gateway," why put a number in at all? Local connections don't use the default gateway, although every routing table has a gateway column. The Microsoft folks had to put *something* there, thus they put the IP address of the NIC. That's why the gateway address is the same as the interface address. The NIC is the gateway between the local PC and the destination. Just pass it out the NIC and the destination will get it.

Okay, on to the next line. This one's easy. Anything addressed to this machine should go right back to it through the loopback (127.0.0.1).

Network Destination	Netmask	Gateway	Interface	Metric
10.12.14.201	255.255.255.255	127.0.0.1	127.0.0.1	1

The next line is the directed broadcast. Occasionally your computer needs to send a broadcast to the other computers on the same network ID. That's what this row signifies. This difference between a directed broadcast and a full broadcast is the former goes only to the targeted subnet, not the full broadcast domain.

Network Destination	Netmask	Gateway	Interface	Metric
10.12.14.255	255.255.255.255	0.12.14.201	10.12.14.201	1

The next two lines are for the multicast address range. Odds are good you'll never need it, but most operating systems put it in automatically.

Network Destination	Netmask	Gateway	Interface	Metric
224.0.0.0	240.0.0.0	On-link	127.0.0.1	306
224.0.0.0	240.0.0.0	On-link	10.12.14.201	281

The bottom lines define the default IP broadcast. If you send out an IP broadcast (255.255.255.255), your NIC knows to send it out to the local network.

Network Destination	Netmask	Gateway	Interface	Metric
255.255.255.255	255.255.255.255	On-link	127.0.0.1	306
255.255.255.255	255.255.255.255	On-link	10.12.14.201	281

 Try This!

Getting Looped

Try pinging any 127.0.0.0/8 address to see if it loops back like 127.0.0.1. What happens?

Just for fun, let's add one more routing table; this time from my old Cisco 2811, which is still connecting me to the Internet after all these years! I access the Cisco router remotely from my Windows system using a tool called PuTTY (you'll see more of PuTTY throughout this book), log in, and then run this command:

```
show ip route
```

Don't let all the text confuse you. The first part, labeled Codes, is just a help screen to let you know what the letters at the beginning of each row mean:

```
Gateway#show ip route

Codes: C - connected, S - static, R - RIP, M - mobile, B - BGP
       D - EIGRP, EX - EIGRP external, O - OSPF, IA - OSPF inter area
       N1 - OSPF NSSA external type 1, N2 - OSPF NSSA external type 2
       E1 - OSPF external type 1, E2 - OSPF external type 2
       i - IS-IS, su - IS-IS summary, L1 - IS-IS level-1, L2 - IS-IS level-2
       ia - IS-IS inter area, * - candidate default, U - per-user static route
       o - ODR, P - periodic downloaded static route

Gateway of last resort is 208.190.121.38 to network 0.0.0.0

C    208.190.121.0/24 is directly connected, FastEthernet0/1
C    192.168.4.0/24 is directly connected, FastEthernet0/0
S*   0.0.0.0/0 [1/0] via 208.190.121.38
```

These last three lines are the routing table. The router has two Ethernet interfaces called FastEthernet0/1 and FastEthernet0/0. This is how Cisco names router interfaces.

Reading from the top, you see that FastEthernet0/1 is directly connected (the C at the beginning of the line) to the network 208.190.121.0/24. Any packets that match 208.190.121.0/24 go out on FastEthernet0/1. Equally, any packets for the connected 192.168.4.0/24 network go out on FastEthernet0/0. The last route gets an S for static because I entered it in manually. The asterisk (*) shows that this is the default route.

In this section, you've seen three different types of routing tables from three different types of devices. Even though these routing tables have different ways to list the routes and different ways to show the categories, they all perform the same job: moving IP packets to the correct interface to ensure they get to where they need to go.

Freedom from Layer 2

Routers enable you to connect different types of network technologies. You now know that routers strip off all of the Layer 2 data from the incoming packets, but thus far you've only seen routers that connect to different Ethernet networks—and that's just fine with routers. But routers can connect to almost anything that stores IP packets. Not to take away from some very exciting upcoming chapters, but Ethernet is not the only networking technology out there. Once you want to start making long-distance connections, Ethernet disappears, and technologies with names like Data-Over-Cable Service Interface Specification (DOCSIS) (for cable modems), Frame Relay, and Asynchronous Transfer Mode (ATM) take over. These technologies are not Ethernet, and they all work very differently than Ethernet. The only common feature of these technologies is they all carry IP packets inside their Layer 2 encapsulations.

Most serious (that is, not home) routers enable you to add interfaces. You buy the router and then snap in different types of interfaces depending on your needs. Note the Cisco router in Figure 8.12. Like most Cisco routers, it comes with removable modules.

• **Figure 8.12**   Modular Cisco router

If you're connecting Ethernet to ATM, you buy an Ethernet module and an ATM module. If you're connecting Ethernet to a DOCSIS (cable modem) network, you buy an Ethernet module and a DOCSIS module.

Network Address Translation

The ease of connecting computers together using TCP/IP and routers creates a rather glaring security risk. If every computer on a network must have a unique IP address, and TCP/IP applications enable you to do something on a remote computer, what's to stop a malicious programmer from writing a program that does things on your computer that you don't want done? All he or she would need is the IP address for your computer and the attacker could target you from anywhere on the network. Now expand this concept to the Internet. A computer sitting in Peoria can be attacked by a program run from Bangkok as long as both computers connect directly to the Internet. And this happens all the time.

Security is one problem. The other is a deal breaker. Many regions of the world have depleted their available IPv4 addresses already and the end for everywhere else is in sight.

Although you can still get an IP address from an ISP, the days of easy availability are over. Routers running some form of **Network Address Translation (NAT)** hide the IP addresses of computers on the LAN but still enable those computers to communicate with the broader Internet. NAT extended the useful life of IPv4 addressing on the Internet for many years. NAT is extremely common and heavily in use, so learning how it works is important. Note that many routers offer NAT as a feature *in addition to* the core capability of routing. NAT is not routing, but a separate technology. With that said, you are ready to dive into how NAT works to protect computers connected by router technology and conserve IP addresses as well.

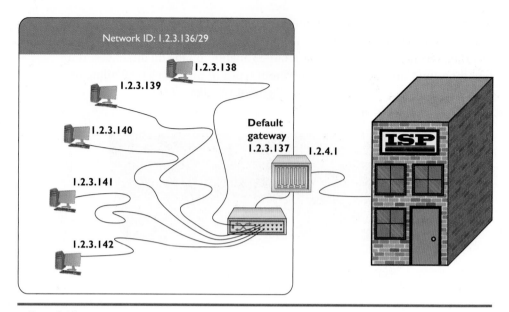

Network ID: 1.2.3.136/29

1.2.3.138

1.2.3.139

1.2.3.140

1.2.3.141

1.2.3.142

Default gateway
1.2.3.137

1.2.4.1

ISP

• **Figure 8.13**   Network setup

Many network techs and writers rail against the concept of NAT security, but base their arguments on what I consider a narrow interpretation of the word "security." In a very basic sense, NAT enables a computer inside a private network to access the Internet and, without express permission, does not allow a computer from the Internet to access the machines inside the local network. The protection afforded by anonymity has benefits.

It's quite arguable that security issues had *nothing* to do with NAT's *creation*. NAT addressed the problem of the limited IPv4 address space. Any other benefit was just a bonus.

NAT replaces the source IP address of a computer with the source IP address from the outside router interface on outgoing packets. NAT is performed by NAT-capable routers.

The Setup

Here's the situation. You have a LAN with five computers that need access to the Internet. With classic TCP/IP and routing, several things have to happen. First, you need to get a block of legitimate, unique, expensive IP addresses from an Internet service provider (ISP). You could call up an ISP and purchase a network ID, say 1.2.3.136/29. Second, you assign an IP address to each computer and to the LAN connection on the router. Third, you assign the IP address for the ISP's router to the WAN connection on the local router, such as 1.2.4.1. After everything is configured, the network looks like Figure 8.13. All of the clients on the network have the same default gateway (1.2.3.137). This router, called a **gateway router** (or simply a *gateway*), acts as the default gateway for a number of client computers.

This style of network mirrors how computers in LANs throughout the world connected to the Internet for the first 20 years, but the major problems of security and a finite number of IP addresses worsened as more and more computers connected.

NAT solved both of these issues for many years. NAT is a simple concept: The router replaces the source IP address of a computer with its outside interface address on outgoing packets. The simplest NAT, called **basic NAT**, does exactly that, translating the private or internal IP address to a global IP address on a one-to-one basis.

Port Address Translation

Most internal networks today don't have one machine, of course. Instead, they use a block of private IP addresses for the hosts inside the network. They connect to the Internet through one or more public IP addresses.

The most common form of NAT that handles this one-to-many connection—called **Port Address Translation (PAT)**—uses port numbers to map traffic from specific machines in the network. Let's use a simple example to make the process clear. John has a network at his office that uses the private

IP addressing space of 192.168.1.0/24. All the computers in the private network connect to the Internet through a single PAT router with the global IP address of 208.190.121.12/24. See Figure 8.14.

When an internal machine initiates a session with an external machine, such as a Web browser accessing a Web site, the source and destination IP addresses and port numbers for the TCP segment or UDP datagram are recorded in the PAT's translation table, and the private IP address is swapped for the public IP address on each packet. Plus, the port number used by the internal computer for the session is also translated into a unique port number and the router records this as well. See Figure 8.15.

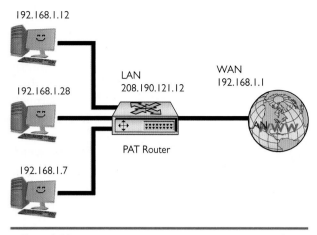

• **Figure 8.14** John's network setup

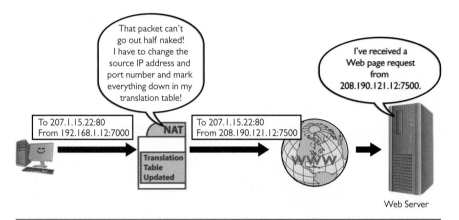

• **Figure 8.15** PAT in action—changing the source IP address and port number to something usable on the Internet

Table 8.1 shows a sample of the translation table inside the PAT router. Note that more than one computer translation has been recorded.

Table 8.1	Sample NAT Translation Table	
Source	**Translated Source**	**Destination**
192.168.1.12:7000	208.190.121.12:7500	
192.168.1.24:13245	208.190.121.12:15000	17.5.85.11:80

When the receiving system sends the packet back, it reverses the IP addresses and ports. The router compares the incoming destination port and source IP address to the entry in the **NAT translation table** to determine which IP address to put back on the packet. It then sends the packet to the correct computer on the network.

This mapping of internal IP address and port number to a translated IP address and port number enables perfect tracking of packets out and in. PAT can handle many internal computers with a single public IP address because the TCP/IP port number space is big, as you'll recall from Chapter 7, with values ranging from 1 to 65535. Some of those port numbers are used for common protocols, but many tens of thousands are available for PAT to work its magic.

Chapter 9, "TCP/IP Applications," goes into port numbers in great detail.

Tech Tip

Dynamic NAT

*With **dynamic NAT (DNAT)**, many computers can share a pool of routable IP addresses that number fewer than the computers. The NAT might have 10 routable IP addresses, for example, to serve 40 computers on the LAN. LAN traffic uses the internal, private IP addresses. When a computer requests information beyond the network, the NAT doles out a routable IP address from its pool for that communication. Dynamic NAT is also called pooled NAT. This works well enough—unless you're the unlucky 11th person to try to access the Internet from behind the company NAT—but has the obvious limitation of still needing many true, expensive, routable IP addresses.*

PAT takes care of all of the problems facing a network exposed to the Internet. You don't have to use legitimate Internet IP addresses on the LAN, and the IP addresses of the computers behind the routers are invisible and protected from the outside world.

Since the router is revising the packets and recording the IP address and port information already, why not enable it to handle ports more aggressively? Enter port forwarding, stage left.

Despite the many uses in the industry of the acronym SNAT, the CompTIA Network+ exam uses SNAT for static NAT exclusively.

Port Forwarding

The obvious drawback to relying exclusively on PAT for network address translation is that it only works for outgoing communication, not incoming communication. For traffic originating *outside* the network to access an *internal* machine, such as a Web server hosted inside your network, you need to use other technologies.

Static NAT (SNAT) maps a single routable (that is, not private) IP address to a single machine, enabling you to access that machine from outside the network. The NAT keeps track of the IP address or addresses and applies them permanently on a one-to-one basis with computers on the network.

With **port forwarding**, you can designate a specific local address for various network services. Computers outside the network can request a service using the public IP address of the router and the port number of the desired service. The port-forwarding router would examine the packet, look at the list of services mapped to local addresses, and then send that packet along to the proper recipient.

You can use port forwarding to hide a service hosted inside your network by changing the default port number for that service. To hide an internal Web server, for example, you could change the request port number to something other than port 80, the default for HTTP traffic. The router in Figure 8.16, for example, is configured to forward all port 8080 packets to the internal Web server at port 80.

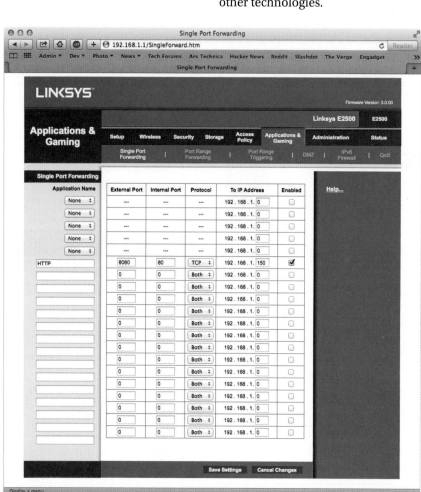

• **Figure 8.16** Setting up port forwarding on a home router

Most browsers require you to write out the full URL, including HTTP://, when using a nondefault port number.

To access that internal Web site from outside your local network, you would have to change the URL in the Web browser by specifying the port request number. Figure 8.17 shows a browser that has :8080 appended to the URL, which tells the browser to make the HTTP request to port 8080 rather than port 80.

Configuring NAT

Configuring NAT on home routers is a no-brainer as these boxes invariably have NAT turned on automatically. Figure 8.18 shows the screen on my home router for NAT. Note the radio buttons that say Gateway and Router.

By default, the router is set to Gateway, which is Linksys-speak for "NAT is turned on." If I wanted to turn off NAT, I would set the radio button to Router.

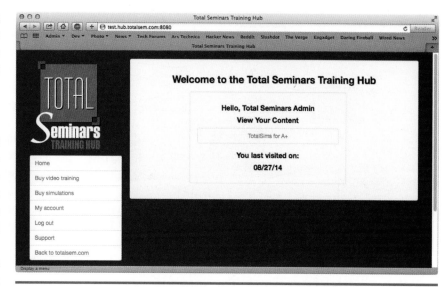

• **Figure 8.17**   Changing the URL to access a Web site using a nondefault port number

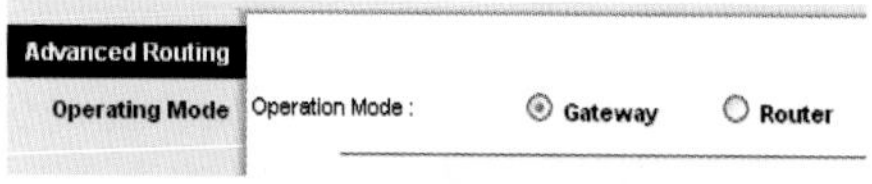

Figure 8.19 shows a router configuration screen on a Cisco router. Commercial routers enable you to do a lot more with NAT.

• **Figure 8.18**   NAT setup on home router

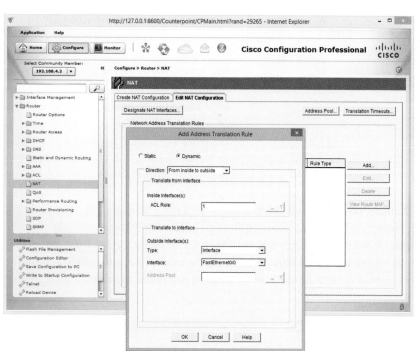

• **Figure 8.19**   Configuring NAT on a commercial-grade router

Dynamic Routing

Based on what you've read up to this point, it would seem that routes in your routing tables come from two sources: either they are manually entered or they are detected at setup by the router. In either case, a route seems to be a static beast, just sitting there and never changing. And based on what you've seen

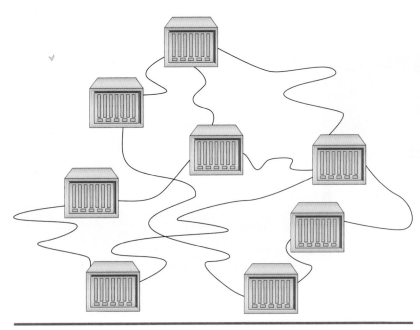

• Figure 8.20   Lots of routers

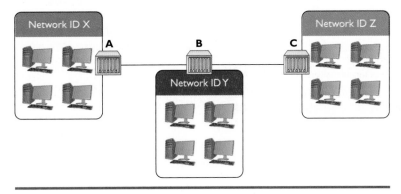

• Figure 8.21   Hopping through a WAN

so far, that is absolutely true. Routers have **static routes**. But most routers also have the capability to update their routes *dynamically,* assuming they're provided with the extra smarts in the form of **dynamic routing** protocols.

If you've been reading carefully, you might be tempted at this point to say, "Why do I need this dynamic routing stuff? Don't routers use metrics so I can add two or more routes to another network ID in case I lose one of my routes?" Yes, but metrics really only help when you have direct connections to other network IDs. What if your routers look like Figure 8.20?

Do you really want to try to set up all these routes statically? What happens when something changes? Can you imagine the administrative nightmare? Why not just give routers the brainpower to talk to each other so they know what's happening not only to the other directly connected routers but also to routers two or more routers away? A **hop** is defined as each time a packet goes through a router. Let's talk about hops for a moment. Figure 8.21 shows a series of routers. If you're on a computer in Network ID X and you ping a computer in Network ID Y, you go one hop. If you ping a computer in Network ID Z, you go two hops.

Routing protocols have been around for a long time, and, like any technology, there have been a number of different choices and variants over those years. CompTIA Network+ competencies break these many types of routing protocols into three distinct groups: distance vector, link state, and hybrid. CompTIA obsesses over these different types of routing protocols, so this chapter does too!

Routing Metrics

Earlier in the chapter, you learned that routing tables contain a factor called a *metric.* A metric is a relative value that routers use when they have more than one route to get to another network. Unlike the gateway routers in our homes, a more serious router will often have multiple connections to get to a particular network. This is the beauty of routers combined with dynamic protocols. If a router suddenly loses a connection, it has alternative routes to the same network. It's the role of the metric setting for the router to decide which route to use.

If a routing table has two or more valid routes for a particular IP address destination, it always chooses the route with the lowest value.

There is no single rule to set the metric value in a routing table. The various types of dynamic protocols use different criteria. Here are the most common criteria for determining a metric.

- **Hop**   The hop count is a fundamental metric value for the number of routers a packet will pass through on the way to its destination network. For example, if router A needs to go through three intermediate routers to reach a network connected to router C, the hop count is 4. The hop occurs when the packet is handed off to each subsequent router. (I'll go a lot more into hops and hop count in "Distance Vector and Path Vector," next.)

- **Bandwidth**   Some connections handle more data than others. An old dial-up connection theoretically tops out at 64 Kbps. A cable modem easily handles many millions of bits per second.

- **Latency**   Say you have a race car that has a top speed of 200 miles per hour, but it takes 25 minutes to start the car. If you press the gas pedal, it takes 15 seconds to start accelerating. If the engine runs for more than 20 minutes, the car won't go faster than 50 miles per hour. These issues prevent the car from doing what it should be able to do: go 200 miles per hour. Latency is like that. Hundreds of issues occur that slow down network connections between routers. These issues are known collectively as *latency*. A great example is a satellite connection. The distance between the satellite and the antenna causes a delay that has nothing to do with the speed of the connection.

- **Cost**   Some routing protocols use cost as a metric for the desirability of that particular route. A route through a low-bandwidth connection, for example, would have a higher cost value than one through a high-bandwidth connection. A network administrator can also manually add cost to routes to change the route selection.

Different dynamic routing protocols use one or more of these routing metrics to calculate their own routing metric. As you learn about these protocols, you will see how each of these calculates their own metrics differently.

Distance Vector and Path Vector

Distance vector routing protocols were the first to appear in the TCP/IP routing world. The cornerstone of all distance vector routing protocols is some form of total cost. The simplest total cost sums the hops (the hop count) between a router and a network, so if you had a router one hop away from a network, the cost for that route would be 1; if it were two hops away, the cost would be 2.

All network connections are not equal. A router might have two one-hop routes to a network—one using a fast connection and the other using a slow connection. Administrators set the metric of the routes in the routing table to reflect the speed. The slow single-hop route, for example, might be given the metric of 10 rather than the default of 1 to reflect the fact that it's slow. The total cost for this one-hop route is 10, even though it's only one hop. Don't assume a one-hop route always has a cost of 1.

Distance vector routing protocols calculate the total cost to get to a particular network ID and compare that cost to the total cost of all the other routes to get to that same network ID. The router then chooses the route with the lowest cost.

 The CompTIA Network+ objectives also list MTU as a routing metric, although that's not true in current routing protocols. The *maximum transmission unit (MTU)* determines the largest frame a particular technology can handle. Ethernet likes to use 1500-byte frames. Other technologies use smaller or larger frames.

If an IP packet is too big for a particular technology, that packet is broken into pieces to fit into the network protocol in what is called *fragmentation*. Fragmentation is bad because it slows down the movement of IP packets. By setting the optimal MTU size before IP packets are sent, you avoid or at least reduce fragmentation.

 Routers that use multiple routing protocols and thus can have multiple paths to the same destination use *administrative distance* as another metric for determining the best route at a particular moment. Administrative distance is a number assigned to a route/ protocol combination.

Shortest Path Bridging (SPB) is a routing metric standard to provide true shortest-path forwarding within an Ethernet mesh topology. Standardized by the IEEE 802.1aq committee, SPB supports large Layer 2 networks by providing fast convergence and improved usage of mesh networks with multiple, equal-cost paths.

For this to work, routers using a distance vector routing protocol transfer their entire routing table to other routers in the WAN. Each distance vector routing protocol has a maximum number of hops that a router will send its routing table to keep traffic down.

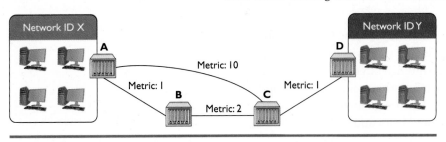

• **Figure 8.22**   Getting a packet from Network ID X to Network ID Y? No clue!

Assume you have four routers connected as shown in Figure 8.22. All of the routers have static routes set up between each other with the metrics shown. You add two new networks, one that connects to Router A and the other to Router D. For simplicity, call them Network ID X and Network ID Y. A computer on one network wants to send packets to a computer on the other network, but the routers in between Routers A and D don't yet know the two new network IDs. That's when distance vector routing protocols work their magic.

Because all of the routers use a distance vector routing protocol, the problem gets solved quickly. At a certain defined time interval (usually 30 seconds or less), the routers begin sending each other their routing tables (the routers each send their entire routing table, but for simplicity just concentrate on the two network IDs in question). On the first iteration, Router A sends its route to Network ID X to Routers B and C. Router D sends its route to Network ID Y to Router C (Figure 8.23).

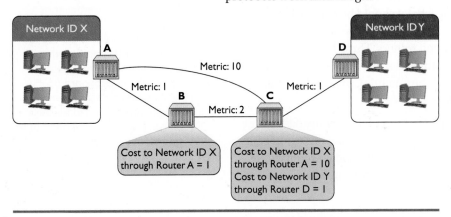

• **Figure 8.23**   Routes updated

This is great—Routers B and C now know how to get to Network ID X, and Router C can get to Network ID Y. There's still no complete path, however, between Network ID X and Network ID Y. That's going to take another interval. After another set amount of time, the routers again send their now updated routing tables to each other, as shown in Figure 8.24.

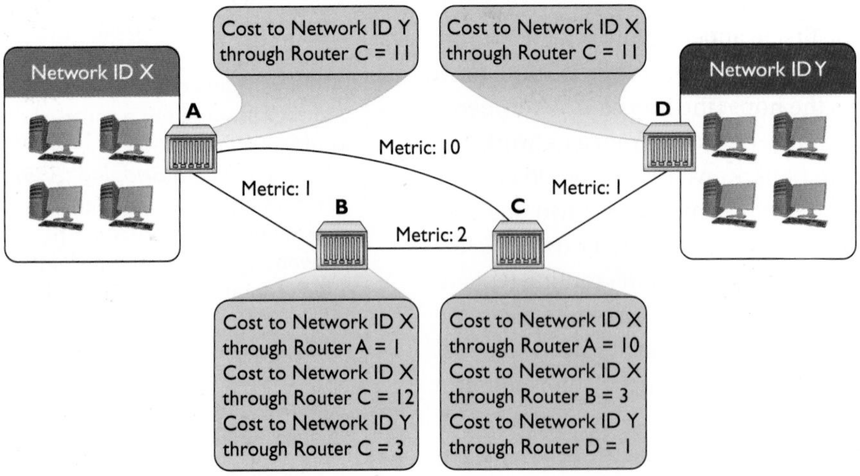

Router A knows a path now to Network ID Y, and Router D knows a path to Network ID X. As a side effect, Router B and Router C have two routes to Network ID X. Router B can get to Network ID X through Router A and through Router C. Similarly, Router C can get to Network ID X through Router A and through Router B. What to do? In cases where the router discovers multiple routes to the same network

• **Figure 8.24**   Updated routing tables

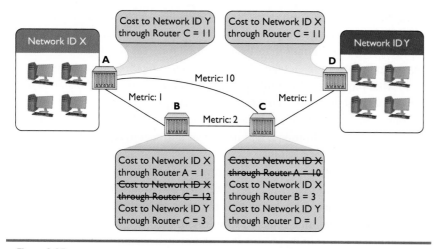

Figure 8.25 Deleting higher-cost routes

ID, the distance vector routing protocol deletes all but the route with the lowest total cost (Figure 8.25).

On the next iteration, Routers A and D get updated information about the lower total-cost hops to connect to Network IDs X and Y (Figure 8.26).

Just as Routers B and C only kept the routes with the lowest costs, Routers A and D keep only the lowest-cost routes to the networks (Figure 8.27).

Now Routers A and D have a lower-cost route to Network IDs X and Y. They've removed the higher-cost routes and begin sending data.

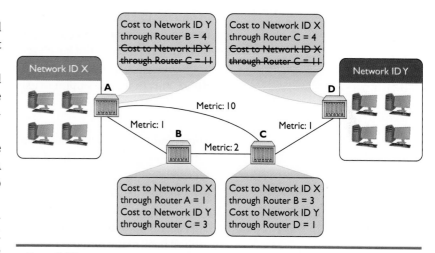

Figure 8.26 Argh! Multiple routes!

At this point, if routers were human they'd realize that each router has all the information about the network and stop sending each other routing tables. Routers using distance vector routing protocols, however, aren't that smart. The routers continue to send their complete routing tables to each other, but because the information is the same, the routing tables don't change.

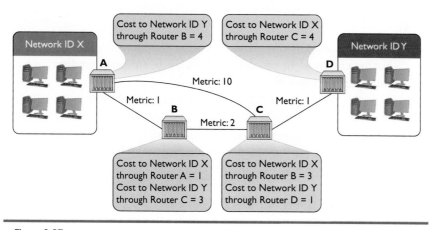

Figure 8.27 Last iteration

At this point, the routers are in **convergence** (also called *steady state*), meaning the updating of the routing tables for all the routers has completed. Assuming nothing changes in terms of connections, the routing tables will not change. In this example, it takes three iterations to reach convergence.

So what happens if the route between Routers B and C breaks? The routers have deleted the higher-cost routes, only keeping the lower-cost route that goes between Routers B and C. Does this mean Router A can no longer connect to Network ID Y and Router D can no longer connect to Network ID X? Yikes! Yes, it does. At least for a while.

Routers that use distance vector routing protocols continue to send to each other their entire routing table at regular intervals. After a few iterations, Routers A and D will once again know how to reach each other, although they will connect through the once-rejected slower connection.

Distance vector routing protocols work fine in a scenario such as the previous one that has only four routers. Even if you lose a router, a few minutes later the network returns to convergence. But imagine if you had tens of thousands of routers (the Internet). Convergence could take a very long time indeed. As a result, a pure distance vector routing protocol works fine for a network with a few (less than 10) routers, but it isn't good for large networks.

Routers can use one of two distance vector routing protocols: RIPv1 or RIPv2. Plus there's an option to use a path vector routing protocol, BGP.

RIPv1

The granddaddy of all distance vector routing protocols is the **Routing Information Protocol (RIP)**. The first version of RIP—called **RIPv1**—dates from the 1980s, although its predecessors go back all the way to the beginnings of the Internet in the 1960s. RIP (both versions) has a maximum hop count of 15, so your router will not talk to another router more than 15 routers away. This plagues RIP because a routing table request can literally loop all the way around back to the initial router.

RIPv1 sent out an update every 30 seconds. This also turned into a big problem because every router on the network would send its routing table at the same time, causing huge network overloads.

As if these issues weren't bad enough, RIPv1 didn't know how to use *variable-length subnet masking (VLSM),* where networks connected through the router use different subnet masks. Plus RIPv1 routers had no authentication, leaving them open to hackers sending false routing table information. RIP needed an update.

RIPv2

RIPv2, adopted in 1994, is the current version of RIP. It works the same way as RIPv1, but fixes many of the problems. VLSM has been added, and authentication is built into the protocol.

Most routers still support RIPv2, but RIP's many problems, especially the time to convergence for large WANs, makes it obsolete for all but small, private WANs that consist of a few routers. The growth of the Internet demanded a far more robust dynamic routing protocol. That doesn't mean RIP rests in peace! RIP is both easy to use and simple for manufacturers to implement in their routers, so most routers, even home routers, have the ability to use RIP (Figure 8.28). If your network consists of only two, three, or four routers, RIP's easy configuration often makes it worth putting up with slower convergence.

• **Figure 8.28**   Setting RIP in a home router

BGP

The explosive growth of the Internet in the 1980s required a fundamental reorganization in the structure of the Internet itself, and one big part of this reorganization was the call to make the "big" routers use a standardized dynamic routing protocol. Implementing this was much harder than you might think because the entities that govern how the Internet works do so in a highly decentralized fashion. Even the organized groups, such as the Internet Society (ISOC), the Internet Assigned Numbers Authority (IANA), and the Internet Engineering Task Force (IETF), are made up of many individuals, companies, and government organizations from across the globe. This decentralization made the reorganization process take time and many meetings.

What came out of the reorganization eventually was a multitiered structure. At the top of the structure sits many Autonomous Systems. An **Autonomous System (AS)** is one or more networks that are governed by a single dynamic routing protocol within that AS. Figure 8.29 illustrates the central structure of the Internet.

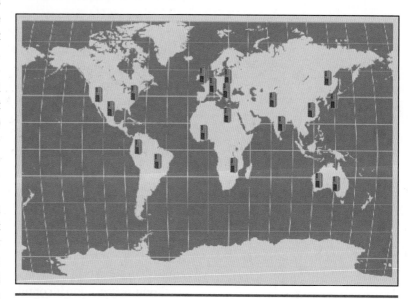

• **Figure 8.29**   The Internet

Autonomous Systems do not use IP addresses, but rather use a special globally unique Autonomous System Number (ASN) assigned by IANA. Originally a 16-bit number, the current ASNs are 32 bits, displayed as two 16-bit numbers separated by a dot. So, 1.33457 would be a typical ASN. Just as you would assign an IP address to a router, you would configure the router to use or be the ASN assigned by IANA. See Figure 8.30.

```
Router2811(config)#router bgp ?
  <1-65535>   Autonomous system number

Router2811(config)#router bgp 1902|
```

• **Figure 8.30**   Configuring a Cisco router to use an ASN

Autonomous Systems communicate with each other using a protocol, called generically an *Exterior Gateway Protocol (EGP)*. The network or networks within an AS communicate with protocols as well; these are called generically *Interior Gateway Protocols (IGPs)*.

Let me repeat this to make sure you understand the difference between EGP and IGP. Neither EGP nor IGP is a dynamic routing protocol; rather these are terms used by the large Internet service providers to separate their interconnected routers using ASNs from other interconnected networks that are not part of this special group of companies. The easy way to keep these terms separate is to appreciate that although many protocols are used *within*

Try This!

Discovering the Autonomous System Numbers

You can see the AS for most Web sites by using this handy little Firefox add-on:

www.asnumber.networx.ch

It doesn't work for every Web site, but it's still interesting.

Autonomous Systems, such as RIP, the Internet has settled on one protocol for communication between each AS: the **Border Gateway Protocol (BGP-4)**. BGP is the glue of the Internet, connecting all of the Autonomous Systems. Other dynamic routing protocols such as RIP are, by definition, IGP. The current version of BGP is BGP-4.

The CompTIA Network+ exam objectives list BGP as a *hybrid routing protocol*, but it's more technically a **path vector** routing protocol. BGP doesn't have the same type of routing table as you've seen so far. Instead, BGP routers are manually configured (these types of connections aren't the type that go down very often!) and advertise information passed to them from different Autonomous Systems' **edge routers**—that's what the AS-to-AS routers are called. BGP forwards these advertisements that include the ASN and other very non-IP items.

BGP also knows how to handle a number of situations unique to the Internet. If a router advertises a new route that isn't reliable, most BGP routers will ignore it. BGP also supports policies for limiting which and how other routers may access an ISP.

BGP implements and supports *route aggregation*, a way to simplify routing tables into manageable levels. Rather than trying to keep track of every other router on the Internet, the backbone routers track the location of routers that connect to subsets of locations.

Route aggregation is complicated, but an analogy should make its function clear. A computer in Prague in the Czech Republic sends a packet intended to go to a computer in Chicago, Illinois. When the packet hits one of the BGP routers, it doesn't have to know the precise location of the recipient. It knows the router for the United States and sends the packet there. The U.S. router knows the Illinois router, which knows the Chicago router, and so on.

BGP is an amazing and powerful dynamic routing protocol, but unless you're working deep in the router room of an AS, odds are good you'll never see it in action. Those who need to connect a few routers together usually turn to a family of dynamic routing protocols that work very differently from distance vector routing protocols.

> You can use BGP within an AS to connect networks, so you can and do run into situations where BGP is both the interior and exterior protocol for an AS. To distinguish between the two uses of the protocol, network folks refer to the BGP on the interior as the *internal BGP (iBGP)*; the exterior connection then becomes the *exterior BGP (eBGP)*.

> Please remember that in the earlier general distance vector routing example, I chose not to show that every update was an entire routing table! I only showed the changes, but trust me, the entire routing table is transmitted roughly every 30 seconds (with some randomization).

Link State

The limitations of RIP motivated the demand for a faster protocol that took up less bandwidth on a WAN. The basic idea was to come up with a dynamic routing protocol that was more efficient than routers that simply sent out their entire routing table at regular intervals. Why not instead simply announce and forward individual route changes as they appeared? That is the basic idea of a **link state** dynamic routing protocol. There are only two link state dynamic routing protocols: OSPF and IS-IS.

OSPF

Open Shortest Path First (OSPF) is the most commonly used IGP on the Internet. Most large Internet users (as opposed to ISPs) use OSPF on their internal networks. Even an AS, while still using BGP on its edge routers, will use OSPF internally because OSPF was designed from the ground up to work within a single AS. OSPF converges dramatically faster and is much more efficient than RIP. Odds are good that if you are using dynamic routing protocols, you're using OSPF.

Before you see OSPF in action, I need to warn you that OSPF is a complex protocol for routers. You won't find OSPF on inexpensive home routers because making it work takes a lot of computational firepower. But OSPF's popularity and CompTIA's coverage make this an important area for you to understand.

The description here, although more than enough to get you through the CompTIA Network+ exam successfully, is still only a light touch on OSPF.

Let's head back to the four-router setup used to explain RIP, but this time replace RIP with OSPF. Because OSPF is designed to work with the Internet, let's give Router B an upstream connection to the organization's ISP. When you first launch OSPF-capable routers, they send out *link state advertisements (LSAs),* called *Hello packets,* looking for other OSPF routers (Figure 8.31).

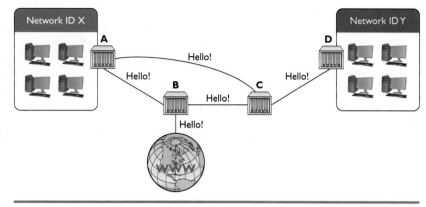

• **Figure 8.31**   Hello!

A new router sends a lot of LSAs when it first starts. This is called *flooding.*

One of the big differences between OSPF and RIP is the hop cost. Whereas single hops in RIP have a cost of 1 unless manually changed, the cost in OSPF is based on the speed of the link. The formula is

```
100,000,000/bandwidth in bps
```

A 10BaseT link's OSPF cost is 100,000,000/10,000,000 = 10. The faster the bandwidth, the lower the cost. You can override this manually if you wish.

To appreciate the power of OSPF, look at Figure 8.32. When OSPF routers send LSA Hellos, they exchange this information and update their link state databases.

These LSA Hellos are forwarded to every OSPF router in the network. Every router knows the link state for every other router. This happens in a few seconds.

Because every router in a network sends packets multiple times a minute, scaling up presents an issue. To cut down on excessive broadcast traffic,

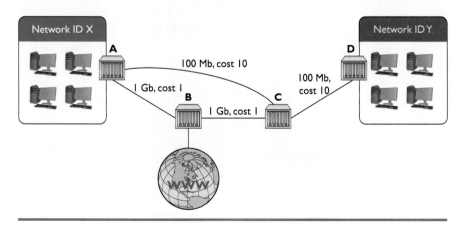

• **Figure 8.32**   Link states

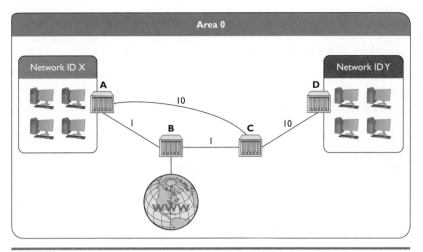

Area 0

• Figure 8.33   Area defined

you can group routers into **areas**, like the one illustrated in Figure 8.33. When you interconnect multiple areas, the central area—called the *backbone*—gets assigned the **Area ID** of 0 or 0.0.0.0. All traffic between areas has to go through the backbone. Special routers called *area border routers (ABRs)* interconnect areas.

OSPF areas almost instantly gain convergence compared to RIP. Once convergence is reached, all of the routers in the area send each other Hello LSAs every 30 minutes or so unless they detect a break in the link state. Also notice that OSPF routers keep alternate routes to the same network ID.

So what happens when something changes? For example, what if the connection between Routers A and B were to disconnect? In that case, both Routers A and B would almost instantly detect the break (as traffic between the two would suddenly stop). Each router would first attempt to reconnect. If reconnecting was unsuccessful (over a few seconds), the routers would then send out an LSA announcing the connection between the two was broken (Figure 8.34). We're talking about a single route, not the entire routing table. Each router updates its routing table to remove the route that no longer works.

OSPF isn't popular by accident. It scales to large networks quite well and is supported by all but the most basic routers. By the way, did I forget to mention that OSPF also supports authentication and that the shortest-path-first method, by definition, prevents loops?

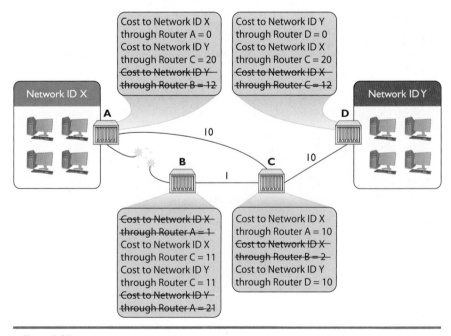

• Figure 8.34   Announcing a disconnect

Why would anyone use anything else? Well, OSPF had one problem that wasn't repaired until fairly recently: support for something called IPv6 (see Chapter 13 for details on IPv6). Not to preempt Chapter 13, but IPv6 is a new addressing system for IP that dumps the old 32-bit address, replacing it with a 128-bit address. IPv6 is quickly gaining popularity and will one day replace 32-bit IP addressing. Just for the record, I've been predicting the end of 32-bit IP addressing for so long I'm now afraid to predict anymore when it's going to happen—but it will eventually.

 OSPF corrects link failures and creates convergence almost immediately, making it the routing protocol of choice in most large enterprise networks. OSPF Version 2 is used for IPv4 networks, and OSPF Version 3 includes updates to support IPv6.

IS-IS

If you want to use a link state dynamic routing protocol and you don't want to use OSPF, your only other option is Intermediate System to Intermediate System (IS-IS). IS-IS is extremely similar to OSPF. It uses the concept of areas and send-only updates to routing tables. IS-IS was developed at roughly the same time as OSPF and had the one major advantage of working with IPv6 from the start. IS-IS is the *de facto* standard for ISPs. Make sure you know that IS-IS is a link state dynamic routing protocol, and if you ever see two routers using it, call me as I've never seen IS-IS in action.

EIGRP

There is exactly one protocol that doesn't really fit into either the distance vector or link state camp: Cisco's proprietary Enhanced Interior Gateway Routing Protocol (EIGRP). Back in the days when RIP was dominant, there was a huge outcry for an improved RIP, but OSPF wasn't yet out. Cisco, being the dominant router company in the world (a crown it still wears to this day), came out with the Interior Gateway Routing Protocol (IGRP), which was quickly replaced with EIGRP.

EIGRP has aspects of both distance vector and link state protocols, placing it uniquely into its own "hybrid" category. Cisco calls EIGRP an *advanced distance vector protocol*.

Dynamic Routing Makes the Internet

Without dynamic routing, the complex, self-healing Internet we all enjoy today couldn't exist. So many routes come and go so often that manually updating static routes would be impossible. Review Table 8.2 to familiarize yourself with the differences among the different types of dynamic routing protocols.

Table 8.2	Dynamic Routing Protocols		
Protocol	Type	IGP or BGP?	Notes
RIPv1	Distance vector	IGP	Old; only used variable subnets within an AS
RIPv2	Distance vector	IGP	Supports VLSM and discontiguous subnets
BGP-4	Distance vector	BGP	Used on the Internet, connects Autonomous Systems
OSPF	Link state	IGP	Fast, popular, uses Area IDs (Area 0/backbone)
IS-IS	Link state	IGP	Alternative to OSPF
EIGRP	Hybrid	IGP	Cisco proprietary

Route Redistribution

Wow, there sure are many routing protocols out there. It's too bad they can't talk to each other...or can they?

The routers cannot use different routing protocols to communicate with each other, but many routers can speak multiple routing protocols simultaneously. When a router takes routes it has learned by one method, say RIP or a statically set route, and announces those routes over another protocol such as OSPF, this is called route redistribution. This feature can come in handy when you have a mix of equipment and protocols in your network, such as occurs when you switch vendors or merge with another organization.

▪ Working with Routers

Understanding the different ways routers work is one thing. Actually walking up to a router and making it work is a different animal altogether. This section examines practical router installation. Physical installation isn't very complicated. With a home router, you give it power and then plug in connections. With a business-class router, you insert it into a rack, give it power, and plug in connections.

The complex part of installation comes with the specialized equipment and steps to connect to the router and configure it for your network needs. This section, therefore, focuses on the many methods and procedures used to access and configure a router.

The single biggest item to keep in mind here is that although there are many different methods for connecting, hundreds of interfaces, and probably millions of different configurations for different routers, the functions are still the same. Whether you're using an inexpensive home router or a hyper-powerful Internet backbone router, you are always working to do one main job: connect different networks.

Also keep in mind that routers, especially gateway routers, often have a large number of other features that have nothing to do with routing. Because gateway routers act as a separator between the computers and "The Big Scary Rest of the Network," they are a convenient place for all kinds of handy features like DHCP, protecting the network from intrusion (better known as firewalls), and NAT.

The term *Yost cable* comes from its creator's name, Dave Yost. For more information visit http://yost.com/computers/RJ45-serial.

• **Figure 8.35**   Cisco console cable

Connecting to Routers

When you take a new router out of the box, it's not good for very much. You need to somehow plug into that shiny new router and start telling it what you want to do. There are a number of different methods, but one of the oldest (yet still very common) methods is to use a special serial connection. This type of connection is almost completely unique to Cisco-brand routers, but Cisco's massive market share makes understanding this type of connection a requirement for anyone who wants to know how to configure routers. Figure 8.35 shows the classic Cisco console cable, more commonly called a *rollover* or Yost cable.

At this time, I need to make an important point: switches as well as routers often have some form of configuration interface. Granted, you have nothing to configure on a basic switch, but in later chapters, you'll discover a number of network features that you'll want to configure more advanced switches to use. Both routers and these advanced switches are called **managed devices**. In this section, I use the term *router*, but it's important for you to appreciate that all routers and many better switches are all managed devices. The techniques shown here work for both!

When you first unwrap a new Cisco router, you plug the rollover cable into the console port on the router (Figure 8.36) and a serial port on a PC. If you don't have a serial port, then buy a USB-to-serial adapter.

Once you've made this connection, you need to use a terminal emulation program to talk to the router. The two most popular programs are PuTTY (www.chiark.greenend.org.uk/~sgtatham/putty) and HyperTerminal (www.hilgraeve.com/hyperterminal). Using these programs requires that you to know a little about serial ports, but these basic settings should get you connected:

- 9600 baud
- 8 data bits
- 1 stop bit
- No parity

Every terminal emulator has some way for you to configure these settings. Figure 8.37 shows these settings using PuTTY.

Now it's time to connect. Most Cisco products run **Cisco IOS**, Cisco's proprietary operating system. If you want to configure Cisco routers, you must learn IOS. Learning IOS in detail is a massive job and outside the scope of this book.

• **Figure 8.36**   Console port

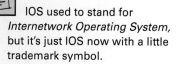
IOS used to stand for *Internetwork Operating System,* but it's just IOS now with a little trademark symbol.

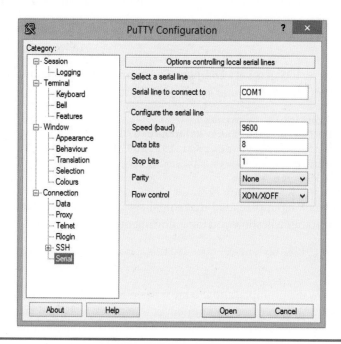

• **Figure 8.37**   Configuring PuTTY

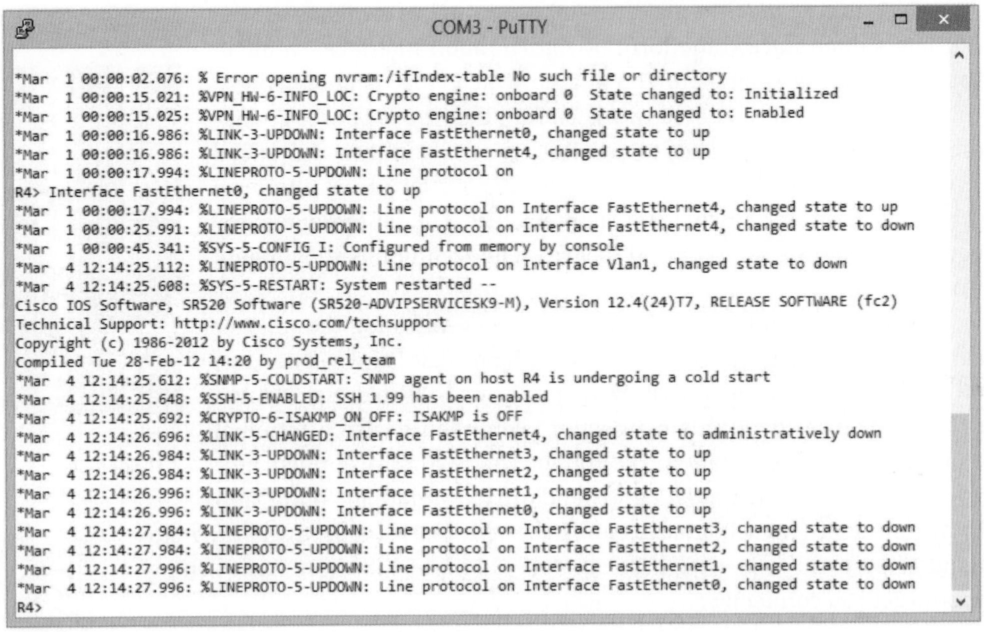

```
*Mar  1 00:00:02.076: % Error opening nvram:/ifIndex-table No such file or directory
*Mar  1 00:00:15.021: %VPN_HW-6-INFO_LOC: Crypto engine: onboard 0  State changed to: Initialized
*Mar  1 00:00:15.025: %VPN_HW-6-INFO_LOC: Crypto engine: onboard 0  State changed to: Enabled
*Mar  1 00:00:16.986: %LINK-3-UPDOWN: Interface FastEthernet0, changed state to up
*Mar  1 00:00:16.986: %LINK-3-UPDOWN: Interface FastEthernet4, changed state to up
*Mar  1 00:00:17.994: %LINEPROTO-5-UPDOWN: Line protocol on
R4> Interface FastEthernet0, changed state to up
*Mar  1 00:00:17.994: %LINEPROTO-5-UPDOWN: Line protocol on Interface FastEthernet4, changed state to up
*Mar  1 00:00:25.991: %LINEPROTO-5-UPDOWN: Line protocol on Interface FastEthernet4, changed state to down
*Mar  1 00:00:45.341: %SYS-5-CONFIG_I: Configured from memory by console
*Mar  4 12:14:25.112: %LINEPROTO-5-UPDOWN: Line protocol on Interface Vlan1, changed state to down
*Mar  4 12:14:25.608: %SYS-5-RESTART: System restarted --
Cisco IOS Software, SR520 Software (SR520-ADVIPSERVICESK9-M), Version 12.4(24)T7, RELEASE SOFTWARE (fc2)
Technical Support: http://www.cisco.com/techsupport
Copyright (c) 1986-2012 by Cisco Systems, Inc.
Compiled Tue 28-Feb-12 14:20 by prod_rel_team
*Mar  4 12:14:25.612: %SNMP-5-COLDSTART: SNMP agent on host R4 is undergoing a cold start
*Mar  4 12:14:25.648: %SSH-5-ENABLED: SSH 1.99 has been enabled
*Mar  4 12:14:25.692: %CRYPTO-6-ISAKMP_ON_OFF: ISAKMP is OFF
*Mar  4 12:14:26.696: %LINK-5-CHANGED: Interface FastEthernet4, changed state to administratively down
*Mar  4 12:14:26.984: %LINK-3-UPDOWN: Interface FastEthernet3, changed state to up
*Mar  4 12:14:26.984: %LINK-3-UPDOWN: Interface FastEthernet2, changed state to up
*Mar  4 12:14:26.996: %LINK-3-UPDOWN: Interface FastEthernet1, changed state to up
*Mar  4 12:14:26.996: %LINK-3-UPDOWN: Interface FastEthernet0, changed state to up
*Mar  4 12:14:27.984: %LINEPROTO-5-UPDOWN: Line protocol on Interface FastEthernet3, changed state to down
*Mar  4 12:14:27.984: %LINEPROTO-5-UPDOWN: Line protocol on Interface FastEthernet2, changed state to down
*Mar  4 12:14:27.996: %LINEPROTO-5-UPDOWN: Line protocol on Interface FastEthernet1, changed state to down
*Mar  4 12:14:27.996: %LINEPROTO-5-UPDOWN: Line protocol on Interface FastEthernet0, changed state to down
R4>
```

• **Figure 8.38** Initial router prompt

No worries, because Cisco provides a series of certifications to support those who wish to become "Cisco People." Although the CompTIA Network+ exam won't challenge you in terms of IOS, it's important to get a taste of how this amazing operating system works.

Once you've connected to the router and started a terminal emulator, you should see the initial router prompt, as shown in Figure 8.38. (If you plugged in and then started the router, you can actually watch the router boot up first.)

This is the IOS user mode prompt—you can't do too much here. To get to the fun, you need to enter privileged EXEC mode. Type **enable**, press ENTER, and the prompt changes to

```
Router#
```

From here, IOS gets very complex. For example, the commands to set the IP address for one of the router's ports look like this:

```
Router# configure terminal
Router(config)# interface Ethernet 0/0
Router(config-if)# ip address 192.168.4.10 255.255.255.0
Router(config-if)# ^Z
Router# copy run start
```

Cisco has long appreciated that initial setup is a bit of a challenge, so a brand-new router will show you the following prompt:

```
Would you like to enter the initial configuration dialog?
[yes/no]?
```

Simply follow the prompts, and the most basic setup is handled for you.

You will run into Cisco equipment as a network tech, and you will need to know how to use the console from time to time. For the most part, though, you'll access a router—especially one that's already configured—through Web access or network management software.

A new Cisco router often won't have a password, but all good admins know to add one.

Mike Meyers' CompTIA Network+ Guide to Managing and Troubleshooting Networks

Web Access

Most routers come with a built-in Web interface that enables you to do everything you need on your router and is much easier to use than Cisco's command-line IOS. For a Web interface to work, however, the router must have a built-in IP address from the factory, or you have to enable the Web interface after you've given the router an IP address. Bottom line? If you want to use a Web interface, you have to know the router's IP address. If a router has a default IP address, you will find it in the documentation, as shown in Figure 8.39.

Never plug a new router into an existing network! There's no telling what that router might start doing. Does it have DHCP? You might now have a rogue DHCP server. Are there routes on that router that match up to your network addresses? Then you see packets disappearing into the great bit bucket in the sky. Always fully configure your router before you place it online.

Most router people use a laptop and a crossover cable to connect to the new router. To get to the Web interface, first set a static address for your computer that will place your PC on the same network ID as the router. If, for example, the router is set to 192.168.1.1/24 from the factory, set your computer's IP address to 192.168.1.2/24. Then connect to the router (some routers tell you exactly where to connect, so read the documentation first), and check the link lights to verify you're properly connected. Open up your Web browser and type in the IP address, as shown in Figure 8.40.

Assuming you've done everything correctly, you almost always need to enter a default user name and password, as shown in Figure 8.41.

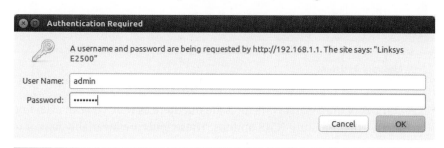

• **Figure 8.41** User name and password

The default user name and password come with the router's documentation. If you don't have that information, plenty of Web sites list this data. Do a Web search on *"default user name password"* to find one.

Once you've accessed the Web interface, you're on your own to poke around to find the settings you need. There's no standard interface—even between different versions of the same router make and model. When you encounter a new interface, take some time and inspect every tab and menu to learn about the router's capabilities. You'll almost always find some really cool features!

How to open the browser-based utility

For ALL

To access some advanced settings, you need to open the browser-based utility.

> **CAUTION**
> If you change settings in the browser-based utility, you might not be able to run Cisco Connect later.

To open the browser-based utility:

1. Run Cisco Connect, click **Change** under *Router settings*, click **Advanced settings**, then click **OK**.

   – or –

   Open a web browser on a computer connected to your network, then go to **192.168.1.1**. If your router is version 2 (look for **V2** on router's bottom label), you can go to **myrouter.local** instead.

   The router prompts you for a user name and password.

• **Figure 8.39** Default IP address

• **Figure 8.40** Entering the IP address

Many routers are also DHCP servers, making the initial connection much easier. Check the documentation to see if you can just plug in without setting an IP address on your PC.

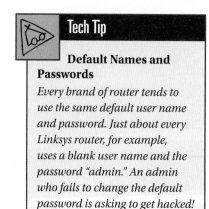

Tech Tip

Default Names and Passwords
Every brand of router tends to use the same default user name and password. Just about every Linksys router, for example, uses a blank user name and the password "admin." An admin who fails to change the default password is asking to get hacked!

Network Management Software

The idea of a "Web-server-in-a-router" works well for single routers, but as a network grows into lots of routers, administrators need more advanced tools that describe, visualize, and configure their entire network. These tools, known as **Network Management Software (NMS)**, know how to talk to your routers, switches, and even your computers to give you an overall view of your network. In most cases, NMS manifests as a Web site where administrators may inspect the status of the network and make adjustments as needed.

I divide NMS into two camps: proprietary tools made by the folks who make managed devices (OEM) and third-party tools. OEM tools are generally very powerful and easy to use, but only work on that OEM's devices. Figure 8.42 shows an example of Cisco Network Assistant, one of Cisco's NMS applications. Others include the Cisco Configuration Professional and Cisco Prime Infrastructure, an enterprise-level tool.

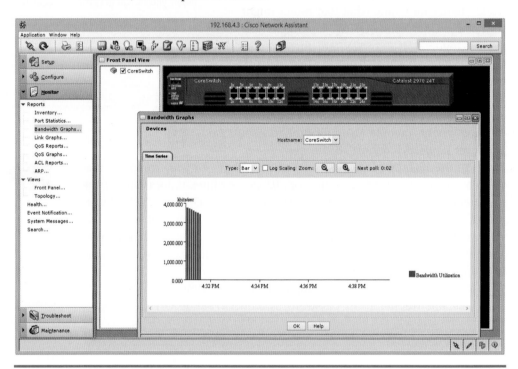

• **Figure 8.42**   Cisco Network Assistant

A number of third-party NMS tools are out there as well; you can even find some pretty good freeware NMS options. These tools are invariably harder to configure and must constantly be updated to try to work with as many devices as possible.

They usually lack the amount of detail you see with OEM NMS and lack interactive graphical user interfaces. For example, various Cisco products enable you to change the IP address of a port, whereas third-party tools will only let you see the current IP settings for that port. Figure 8.43 shows Open-NMS, a popular open source NMS.

Unfortunately, no single NMS tool works perfectly. Network administrators are constantly playing with this or that NMS tool in an attempt to give themselves some kind of overall picture of their networks.

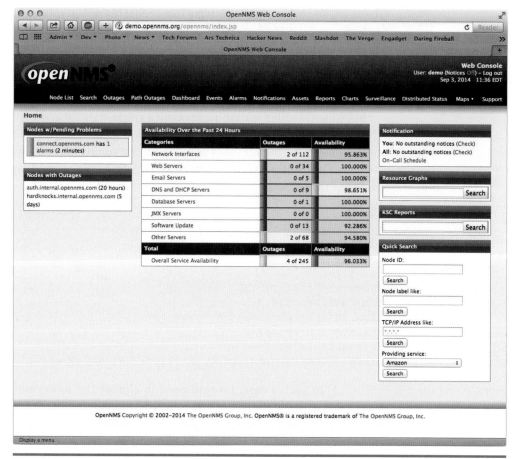

• Figure 8.43   OpenNMS

Other Connection Methods

Be aware that most routers have even more ways to connect. Many home routers come with USB ports and configuration software. More powerful routers may enable you to connect using the ancient Telnet protocol or its newer and safer equivalent Secure Shell (SSH). These are terminal emulation protocols that look exactly like the terminal emulators seen earlier in this chapter but use the network instead of a serial cable to connect (see Chapter 9 for details on these protocols).

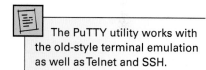

The PuTTY utility works with the old-style terminal emulation as well as Telnet and SSH.

Basic Router Configuration

A router, by definition, must have at least two connections. When you set up a router, you must configure every port on the router properly to talk to its connected network IDs, and you must make sure the routing table sends packets to where you want them to go. As a demonstration, Figure 8.44 uses an incredibly common setup: a single gateway router used in a home or small office that's connected to an ISP.

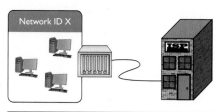

• Figure 8.44   The setup

Step 1: Set Up the WAN Side

To start, you need to know the network IDs for each side of your router. The WAN side invariably connects to an ISP, so you need to know what the ISP wants you to do. If you bought a static IP address, type it in now.

● Figure 8.45   WAN router setup

I'm ignoring a number of other settings here for the moment. I'll revisit most of these in later chapters.

However—brace yourself for a crazy fact—most home Internet connections use DHCP! That's right, DHCP isn't just for your PC. You can set up your router's WAN connection to use it too. DHCP is by far the most common connection to use for home routers. Access your router and locate the WAN connection setup. Figure 8.45 shows the setup for my home router set to DHCP.

But what if I called my ISP and bought a single static IP address? This is rarely done anymore, but virtually every ISP will gladly sell you one (although you will pay three to four times as much for the connection). If you use a static IP, your ISP will tell you what to enter, usually in the form of an e-mail message like the following:

```
Dear Mr. Meyers,
Thank you for requesting a static IP address from
totalsem.com!
Here's your new static IP information:
IP address: 1.151.35.55
Default Gateway: 1.151.32.132
Subnet Mask: 255.255.128.0
Installation instructions can be found at:
http://totalsem.com/setup/
Support is available at:
http://helpdesk.totalsem.com or by calling (281)922-4166.
```

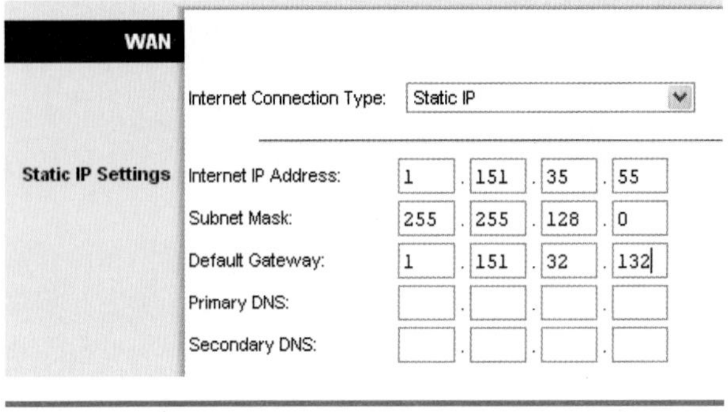

In such a case, I would need to change the router setting to Static IP (Figure 8.46). Note how changing the drop-down menu to Static IP enables me to enter the information needed.

Once you've set up the WAN side, it's time to head over to set up the LAN side of the router.

Step 2: Set Up the LAN

Unlike the WAN side, you usually have total control on the LAN side of the router. You need to choose a network ID, almost always some arbitrarily chosen private range unless you do not want to use NAT. This is why so many home networks have network IDs of 192.168.1/24, 192.168.0/24, and so forth. Once you decide on your LAN-side network ID, you need to assign the correct IP information to the LAN-side NIC. Figure 8.47 shows the configuration for a LAN NIC on my home router.

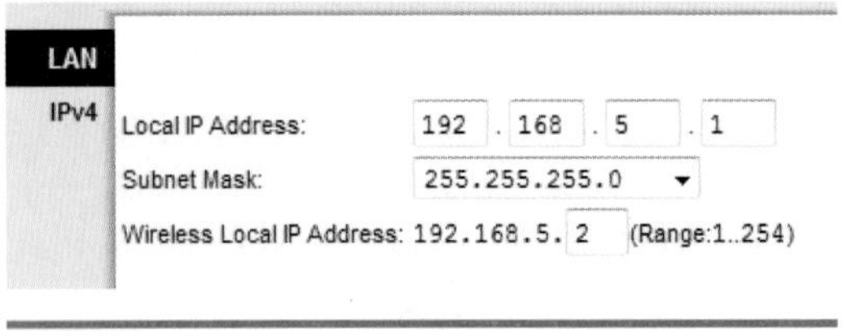

● Figure 8.46   Entering a static IP

Step 3: Establish Routes

Most routers are pretty smart and use the information you provided for the two interfaces to build a routing table automatically. If you need to add more routes, every router provides some method to add routes. The following shows the command entered on a Cisco router to add a route to one of its Ethernet interfaces. The term "fa0/0" is how Cisco describes Ethernet NICs in its device software. It is short for FastEthernet, which you may remember as being the common name (when you add a space) for 100BaseTX.

```
ip route 192.168.100.0 255.255.255.0 fa0/0 192.168.1.10
```

● Figure 8.47   Setting up an IP address for the LAN side

Step 4 (Optional): Configure a Dynamic Protocol

The rules for using any dynamic routing protocol are fairly straightforward. First, dynamic routing protocols are tied to individual NICs, not the entire router. Second, when you connect two routers together, make sure those two NICs are configured to use the same dynamic routing protocol. Third, unless you're in charge of two or more routers, you're probably not going to use any dynamic routing protocol.

The amazing part of a dynamic routing protocol is how easy it is to set up. In most cases you just figure out how to turn it on and that's about it. It just starts working.

Document and Back Up

Once you've configured your routes, take some time to document what you've done. A good router works for years without interaction, so by that time in the future when it goes down, odds are good you've forgotten why you added the routes. Last, take some time to back up the configuration. If a router goes down, it will most likely forget everything and you'll need to set it up all over again. Every router has some method to back up the configuration, however, so you can restore it later.

Router Problems

The CompTIA Network+ exam will challenge you on some basic router problems. All of these questions should be straightforward for you as long as you do the following:

- Consider other issues first because routers don't fail very often.
- Keep in mind what your router is supposed to do.
- Know how to use a few basic tools that can help you check the router.

Any router problem starts with someone not connecting to someone else. Even a small network has a number of NICs, computers, switches, and routers between you and whatever it is you're not connecting to. Compared to most of these, a router is a pretty robust device and shouldn't be considered as the problem until you've checked out just about everything else first.

In their most basic forms, routers route traffic. Yet you've seen in this chapter that routers can do more than just plain routing—for example, NAT. As this book progresses, you'll find that the typical router often handles a large number of duties beyond just routing. Know what your router is doing and appreciate that you may find yourself checking a router for problems that don't really have anything to do with routing at all.

Be aware that routers have some serious but rare potential problems. One place to watch is your routing table. For the most part, today's routers automatically generate directly connected routes, and dynamic routing takes care of itself, leaving one type of route as a possible suspect: the static routes. This is the place to look when packets aren't getting to the places you expect them to go. Look at the following sample static route:

```
Net Destination    Netmask           Gateway        Interface      Metric
22.46.132.0        255.255.255.255   22.46.132.1    22.46.132.11   1
```

No incoming packets for network ID are getting out on interface 22.46.132.11. Can you see why? Yup, the Netmask is set to 255.255.255.255, and there are no computers that have exactly the address 22.46.132.0. Entering the wrong network destination, subnet mask, gateway, and so on, is very easy. If a new static route isn't getting the packets moved, first assume you made a typo.

Make sure to watch out for missing routes. These usually take place either because you've forgotten to add them (if you're entering static routes) or, more commonly, there is a convergence problem in the dynamic routing protocols. For the CompTIA Network+ exam, be ready to inspect a routing table to recognize these problems.

When it comes to tools, networking comes with so many utilities and magic devices that it staggers the imagination. You've already seen some, like good old ping and route, but let's add two more tools: traceroute and mtr.

The **traceroute** tool, as its name implies, records the route between any two hosts on a network. On the surface, traceroute is something like ping in that it sends a single packet to another host, but as it progresses, it returns information about every router between them.

Every operating system comes with traceroute, but the actual command varies among them. In Windows, the command is `tracert` and looks like this (I'm running a traceroute to the router connected to my router—a short trip):

```
C:\>tracert 96.165.24.1

Tracing route to 96.165.24.1 over a maximum of 30 hops:

  1     1 ms     1 ms     1 ms     10.12.14.1
  2    10 ms    10 ms     8 ms     96.165.24.1
Trace complete.
```

The UNIX/Linux command is `traceroute` and looks like this:

```
michaelm@ubuntu:~$ traceroute 96.165.24.1
traceroute to 96.165.24.1 (96.165.24.1), 30 hops max, 40 byte
packets
1    10.12.14.1 (10.12.14.1)  0.763 ms 0.432 ms  0.233 ms
2    96.165.24.1 (96.165.24.1) 12.233 ms 11.255 ms 14.112 ms
michaelm@ubuntu:~$
```

The traceroute tool is handy, not so much for what it tells you when everything's working well, but for what it tells you when things are not working. Take a look at the following:

```
:\>tracert 96.165.24.1

Tracing route to 96.165.24.1 over a maximum of 30 hops
  1     1 ms     1 ms     1 ms   10.12.14.1
  2      *        *        *         Request timed out
  3  96.165.24.1  reports: Destination host unreachable.
```

If this traceroute worked in the past but now no longer works, you know that something is wrong between your router and the next router upstream. You don't know what's wrong exactly. The connection may be down; the router may not be working; but at least traceroute gives you an idea where to look for the problem and where not to look.

```
● ● ○                    mtr.totalsem.com — mtr — ssh — 99×28
                                My traceroute  [v0.85]
michaels-moble (0.0.0.0)                              Tue Sep  2 16:26:16 2014
Keys:  Help   Display mode   Restart statistics   Order of fields   quit
                                                          Pings
                                      Packets
 Host                                Loss%  Snt   Last   Avg  Best  Wrst StDev
 1. Router.totalhome                  0.0%   19    0.9   0.9   0.7   1.2   0.0
 2. ???
 3. xe-4-0-0-32767-sur02.airport.tx.houston.comcast.net  0.0%  19  9.2  13.7  7.5  50.6  11.0
 4. ae-4-0-ar01.bearcreek.tx.houston.comcast.net  0.0%  19  15.6  12.2   9.9  15.6   1.5
 5. 68.86.166.229                     0.0%   19   25.6  19.5  15.6  25.6   2.4
 6. pos-0-1-0-0-pe01.1950stemmons.tx.ibone.comcast.net  0.0%  19  21.2  21.8  16.5  62.0  10.0
 7. ae10.bbr01.eq01.dal03.networklayer.com  0.0%  19  19.4  17.1  15.0  26.3   2.3
 8. ae8.bbr01.sr02.hou02.networklayer.com  0.0%  19  22.2  22.5  20.0  31.8   3.1
 9. po31.dsr01.hstntx2.networklayer.com  0.0%  19  21.8  27.7  20.3 117.3  21.8
10. po1.car02.hstntx2.networklayer.com  0.0%  18  23.7  24.3  20.3  37.5   4.6
11. totalsem.com                      0.0%   18   22.0  22.8  20.1  31.2   2.3
```

• **Figure 8.48**   mtr in action

My traceroute (mtr) is very similar to traceroute, but it's dynamic, continually updating the route that you've selected (Figure 8.48). You won't find mtr in Windows; mtr is a Linux tool. Instead, Windows users can use pathping. This utility will ping each node on the route just like mtr, but instead of showing the results of each ping in real time, the pathping utility computes the performance over a set time and then shows you the summary after it has finished.

Chapter 8 Review

■ Chapter Summary

After reading this chapter and completing the exercises, you should understand the following about routing.

Explain how routers work

- A router is any piece of hardware that forwards network packets based on their destination IP addresses.

- A routing table is the chart of information kept on a router to aid in directing the flow of packets through computer networks.

- Some routers have only two ports—one to connect to the Internet and another to connect to a LAN switch. Some routers, however, have an integrated switch and thus have more than two ports.

- Routers learn new routes as they go, interacting with each other by exchanging routing table information. The routing tables are checked and can be updated dynamically as data flows across a network, with routers chatting with each other for the latest network and IP address information periodically.

- Routers can connect dissimilar networks, such as Ethernet, Frame Relay, ATM, and DOCSIS.

- NAT saves a table of information, so it knows which system is communicating with which external site. NAT solutions can be software based or included as part of a hardware device such as a router.

- PAT is the most common form of NAT that handles a one-to-many connection, using port numbers to map traffic from specific machines in the network.

- Dynamic NAT can share a pool of routable IP addresses with multiple computers.

- Static NAT maps a single IP address to a single machine, enabling you to access that machine from outside the network.

- Port forwarding hides port numbers from the public side of a network. The router simply forwards packets from one port number to another as the packet passes from the public to the private side of the router.

Describe dynamic routing technologies

- Routing table entries are entered manually on static routers and do not change. Dynamic routers, in contrast, automatically update their routing table. This is accomplished by using special routing protocols.

- There are three distinct groups of routing protocols: distance vector, link state, and hybrid.

- Routing tables are shared with other routers, and the complete route with the lowest cost is automatically chosen.

- Distance vector routing protocols are not recommended for networks with more than 10 routers because of the time it takes for the routers to reach convergence.

- Distance vector routing protocols include RIPv1 and RIPv2.

- RIPv1 has a maximum hop count of 15, with routing table updates sent every 30 seconds. Because RIPv1 lacked authentication and experienced network overloads as every router sent its routing table at the same time, the RIPv2 update was developed.

- RIPv2, which also has a maximum hop count of 15, supports VLSM and discontiguous subnets and provides authentication to prevent hackers from sending false routing table information. RIPv2's lengthy time to convergence for large networks led to the development of better routing protocols such as OSPF.

- An Autonomous System (AS) consists of one or more networks that are governed by a single protocol. Autonomous Systems do not use IP addresses, but instead use a special globally unique Autonomous System Number assigned by IANA.

- The protocol used by Autonomous Systems to communicate with each other is generically called an Exterior Gateway Protocol (EGP). Networks within an Autonomous System use an Interior Gateway Protocol (IGP). Edge routers connect an AS network to another AS network.

- Interior Gateway Protocols include RIP or other protocols. At this time, the Border Gateway Protocol (BGP) is the only Exterior Gateway Protocol used on the Internet. It connects all of the Autonomous Systems.

- BGP implements and supports route aggregation, a way to simplify routing tables into manageable levels.

- Link state protocols include OSPF and IS-IS. Link state protocols overcome the relatively slow and bandwidth-heavy usage of distance vector protocols.

- OSPF stands for the Open Shortest Path First routing protocol. It is the most commonly used Interior Gateway Protocol on the Internet. It is more efficient than RIP, converges dramatically faster than RIP, and supports IPv6 as of OSPF Version 3.

- OSPF broadcasts link state advertisements (Hello packets) when an OSPF-enabled router first boots up. Intermediate System to Intermediate System (IS-IS) is another link state dynamic routing protocol, similar to OSPF. It has supported IPv6 from the start. Enhanced Interior Gateway Routing Protocol (EIGRP) is a hybrid Cisco protocol that has aspects of both distance vector and link state protocols.

Install and configure a router successfully

- A Yost cable (rollover cable) is a special serial cable used to connect directly to a Cisco router for configuration purposes.

- Once a direct connection has been made to a router, use a terminal emulation program such as PuTTY or HyperTerminal to communicate.

- Most Cisco products run Cisco's proprietary operating system, Cisco IOS. Although not covered on the CompTIA Network+ certification exam, understanding IOS is a must for anyone who wants to become Cisco Certified.

- Most routers include a built-in Web interface for configuration. You must know the router's IP address to make this type of connection.

- Many techs use a laptop and a crossover cable to connect to a Web server–enabled router for the initial configuration. This method also requires setting a static IP address on the connected laptop, unless the router includes a DHCP server.

- Network Management Software (NMS) is used to describe, visualize, and configure an entire network. NMS is made both by the companies that make managed devices and by third-party companies.

- In general, NMS made by the companies that make managed devices is easy to use but only works on specific hardware. Much third-party NMS is available as freeware, but is typically harder to use and must be constantly updated to work with as many devices as possible.

- Some routers may be connected to via USB, Telnet, or SSH.

- When you set up a router, you must configure every port on the router properly to talk to its connected network IDs and to make sure the routing table sends packets to where you want them to go.

- Setting up a router can be broken down into five steps: set up the WAN side, set up the LAN, establish routes, optionally configure a dynamic routing protocol, and finally document and back up your settings.

- The traceroute utility records the route between any two hosts on a network and can be used to troubleshoot routing problems.

■ Key Terms

areas *(204)*
Area ID *(204)*
Autonomous System (AS) *(201)*
basic NAT *(192)*
Border Gateway Protocol (BGP-4) *(202)*
Cisco IOS *(207)*
convergence *(200)*
cost *(197)*
distance vector *(197)*
dynamic NAT (DNAT) *(193)*
dynamic routing *(196)*
edge routers *(202)*
Enhanced Interior Gateway Routing
   Protocol (EIGRP) *(205)*
gateway router *(192)*
hop *(196)*
hop count *(197)*
Intermediate System to Intermediate
   System (IS-IS) *(205)*
link state *(202)*
managed device *(207)*

metric *(188)*
My traceroute (mtr) *(215)*
NAT translation table *(193)*
Network Address Translation (NAT) *(191)*
Network Management Software (NMS) *(210)*
next hop *(185)*
Open Shortest Path First (OSPF) *(202)*
path vector *(202)*
Port Address Translation (PAT) *(192)*
port forwarding *(194)*
RIPv1 *(200)*
RIPv2 *(200)*
route redistribution *(206)*
router *(183)*
Routing Information Protocol (RIP) *(200)*
routing table *(185)*
static NAT (SNAT) *(194)*
static routes *(196)*
traceroute *(214)*
Yost cable *(206)*

■ Key Term Quiz

Use the Key Terms list to complete the sentences that follow. Not all the terms will be used.

1. A device called a(n) _____ is also called a Layer 3 switch.

2. The external routing protocol used on the Internet is _____.

3. The variety of _____ methods would include RIP, OSPF, BGP, and IGRP.

4. A(n) _____ is normally entered manually into a router.

5. A(n) _____ connects one Autonomous System to another Autonomous System.

6. _____ is a routing protocol that updates routing tables about every 30 seconds, resulting in overloaded network traffic.

7. When all routers can communicate with each other efficiently, they are said to have reached _____.

8. Multiple networks that do not use IP addresses and are governed by a single protocol are known as _____.

9. You can use the _____ utility to troubleshoot routing problems.

10. _____ uses IP addresses and port numbers to enable many internal computers to share a single public IP address.

■ Multiple-Choice Quiz

1. How many IP addresses should a router have?

   A. One

   B. One or more

   C. Two

   D. Two or more

2. Choose the Cisco Systems routing protocols from the following items. (Select two.)

   A. BGP-4

   B. EIGRP

   C. IGRP

   D. OSPF

3. If specialty accounting software being used at your company requires that packet headers remain unchanged, which item cannot be used on your network?

   A. RIP

   B. NAT

   C. OSPF

   D. traceroute

4. How does a router use a routing table to determine over which path to send a packet?

   A. The first line in the routing table is used if the path is available; otherwise, the router tries the next line down, and so on.

   B. The last line in the routing table is used if the path is available; otherwise, the router tries the next line up, and so on.

   C. After examining all rows in the routing table, the router sends the packet along the path with the highest metric.

   D. After examining all rows in the routing table, the router sends the packet along the path with the lowest metric.

5. Which version of NAT maps a single routable IP address to a single network node?

   A. Static NAT

   B. Dynamic NAT

   C. Pooled NAT

   D. SecureNAT

6. What technology enables you to designate a specific local address for various network services?

   A. Dynamic NAT

   B. Port Address Translation

   C. Port forwarding

   D. Port filtering

7. How is the distance between routers measured?

   A. In meters

   B. In hops

   C. In routes

   D. In segments

8. Distance vector routing protocols include which of the following?

   A. RIP

   B. OSPF

   C. BGP

   D. ASN

9. Which of the following are benefits of RIPv2 over RIPv1? (Select two.)

   A. Longer convergence times

   B. Support for authentication

   C. Support for VLSM

   D. Support for metrics

10. What is one way in which Autonomous Systems differ from typical Ethernet networks?

    A. They require a minimum of 10 nodes.

    B. They cannot exceed a maximum of 255 nodes.

    C. They are not able to interact with the Internet.

    D. They do not use IP addresses.

11. Why are link state protocols more efficient than RIP?

    A. Entire routing tables are updated on a stricter schedule.

    B. They forward only changes to individual routes instead of forwarding entire routing tables.

    C. Packets can be sent along multiple routes at the same time.

    D. Link state can send larger packets.

12. What happens when you first connect and turn on an OSPF router?

    A. It floods the network with Hello packets as it looks for other OSPF routers.

    B. It floods the network by requesting routing tables from every computer on the network.

    C. It is unavailable for several hours as it builds its default routing table.

    D. It runs a self-test to determine if it should run in hybrid mode (RIP and OSPF) or native mode (OSPF only).

13. Which of the following is a valid Area ID for an OSPF backbone?

    A. 0.1

    B. 0.0.0.0

    C. 1.0

    D. 255

14. How can you connect directly to a router for configuration purposes? (Select three.)

    A. Parallel cable

    B. USB cable

    C. Crossover cable

    D. Rollover cable

15. Once you have made a physical direct connection to a router, what utility/program can you use to issue commands and instructions? (Select three.)

    A. PuTTY

    B. HyperTerminal

    C. IOS

    D. Internet Explorer

Essay Quiz

1. You have been introduced to a lot more "alphabet soup" in this chapter. Quickly jot down what each of the following stands for: BGP-4, NAT, RIP, OSPF, NMS, PAT, EIGRP, IS-IS, AS, ASN, EGP, and IGP.

2. Explain why a router is sometimes called a Layer 3 switch.

3. Write a short essay about OSPF and its uses, as well as its benefits over using RIPv2.

Lab Projects

• Lab Project 8.1

A classmate of yours is all excited about some upcoming classes available at your school that will cover Cisco routing. He keeps talking about EIGRP and its importance in the workplace, as well as how much cash can be earned if you know EIGRP. Use the Internet to research EIGRP—its history, its uses, what devices run using EIGRP, and what salaries Cisco Certified professionals earn (possibly your next certification after passing the CompTIA Network+ exam). Then share this information with your instructor and your classmate to compare your findings. What does EIGRP do for corporate networks? What salaries are realistically possible? What were your sources?

• Lab Project 8.2

Start a command prompt at your computer and enter `netstat -nr` to view its routing table. Create a screenshot of the output and paste it into a word processing document. Under the pasted screenshot, briefly explain what each column is for. Compare your routing table to your classmates' routing tables and explain to each other what the differences are and why differences occur.

chapter 9

TCP/IP Applications

"The World Wide Web is the only thing I know of whose shortened form—www—takes three times longer to say than what it's short for."

—Douglas Adams

In this chapter, you will learn how to

- Describe common Transport and Network layer protocols
- Explain the power of port numbers
- Define common TCP/IP applications such as HTTP, HTTPS, Telnet, SSH, e-mail (SMTP, POP3, and IMAP4), and FTP

We network to get work done. Okay, sometimes that "work" involves a mad gaming session in which I lay some smack down on my editors, but you know what I mean. Thus far in the book, everything you've read about networking involves connecting computers together. This chapter moves further up the OSI seven-layer model and the TCP/IP model to look at applications such as Web browsers, e-mail messaging, and more.

To understand the applications that use TCP/IP networks, a tech needs to know the structures below those applications. Have you ever opened multiple Web pages on a single computer? Have you ever run multiple Internet apps, such as a Web browser, an e-mail client, and a remote connectivity app, all at the same time? Clearly, a lot of data is moving back and forth between your computer and many other computers. With packets coming in from two, three, or more computers, there has to be a mechanism or process that knows where to send and receive that data.

In this chapter, you'll discover the process used by TCP/IP networks to ensure the right data gets to the right applications on your computer. This process uses very important Transport and Network layer protocols—TCP, UDP, and ICMP—and port numbering. When used together, TCP and UDP along with port numbers enable you to get work done on a network.

■ Transport Layer and Network Layer Protocols

I hate to tell you this, but you've been lied to. Not by me. Even though I've gone along with this Big Lie, I need to tell you the truth.

There is no such thing as TCP/IP. *TCP over IP* is really many other things, such as *HTTP, DHCP, POP,* and about 500 more terms over *TCP,* plus *UDP* and *ICMP* over *IP.* Given that this overly complex but much more correct term is too hard to use, the people who invented this network protocol stack decided to call it *TCP/IP,* even though that term is way too simplistic to cover all the functionality involved. A common way to refer all the aspects and protocols that make up TCP/IP is to call it the **TCP/IP suite.** That's what you'll see on the CompTIA Network+ exam.

 There is a strong movement toward using the term *Internet Protocol* instead of the term *TCP/IP.* This movement has not yet reached the CompTIA Network+ certification.

So you can appreciate how TCP/IP applications work, this chapter breaks down the many unmentioned protocols and shows how they help make applications work. To start this process, let's consider how human beings communicate; you'll see some very interesting commonalities between computers and people.

How People Communicate

Imagine you walk into a school cafeteria to get some lunch. You first walk up to the guy making custom deli sandwiches (this is a great cafeteria!) and say, "Hello!" He says, "How may I help you?" You say, "I'd like a sandwich please." He says, "What kind of sandwich would you like?" and you order your sandwich. After you get your sandwich you say, "Thanks!" and he says, "You're welcome." What a nice guy! In the networking world, we would call this a **connection-oriented** communication. Both you and the lunch guy first acknowledge each other. You then conduct your communication; finally, you close the communication.

While you're in line, you see your friend Janet sitting at your usual table. The line is moving fast so you yell out, "Janet, save me a seat!" before you rush along in the line. In this case, you're not waiting for her to answer; you just yell to her and hope she hears you. We call this a **connectionless** communication. There is no acknowledgment or any closing.

In the networking world, any single communication between a computer and another computer is called a **session**. When you open a Web page, you make a session. When you call your buddy (using the Internet, not the cellular networks), you create a session. All sessions must begin and eventually end.

Test Specific

TCP

The **Transmission Control Protocol (TCP)** enables connection-oriented communication in networks that use the TCP/IP protocol suite. TCP is by far

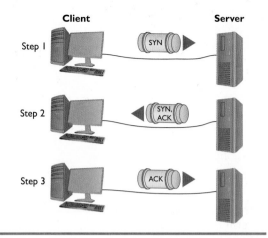

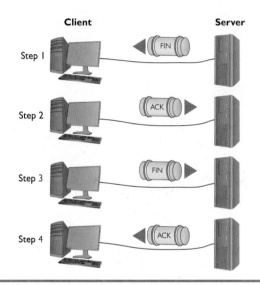

● **Figure 9.2** A connection-oriented session ending

● **Figure 9.3** DHCP steps

the most common type of session on a typical TCP/IP network. Figure 9.1 shows two computers. One computer (Server) runs a Web server and the other (Client) runs a Web browser. When you enter a computer's address in the browser running on Client, it sends a single SYN (synchronize) packet to the Web server. If Server gets that packet, it returns a single SYN, ACK (synchronize, acknowledge) packet. Client then sends Server a single ACK packet and immediately requests that Server begin sending the Web page. This process is called the **TCP three-way handshake**.

Once Server finishes sending the Web page, it sends a FIN (finished) packet. Client responds with an ACK (acknowledge) packet and then sends its own FIN packet. The server then responds with an ACK; now both parties consider the session closed (Figure 9.2).

Most TCP/IP applications use TCP because connection-oriented sessions are designed to check for errors. If a receiving computer detects a missing packet, it just asks for a repeat as needed.

UDP

User Datagram Protocol (UDP) runs a distant second place to TCP in terms of the number of applications that use it, but that doesn't mean UDP is not important. UDP is perfect for the types of sessions that don't require the overhead of all that connection-oriented stuff.

DHCP

Probably the best example of an application that uses UDP is the Dynamic Host Configuration Protocol (DHCP). DHCP can't assume another computer is ready on either side of the session, so each step of a DHCP session just sends the information for that step without any confirmation (Figure 9.3). Sending a connectionless packet also makes sense because the client won't have an IP address to begin the three-way handshake. Plus, if the server doesn't respond, the client can simply ask again.

As you learned in Chapter 7, "TCP/IP Basics," DHCP uses two port numbers. DHCP clients use port 67 for sending data to the DHCP server, and DHCP servers use port 68 for sending data to DHCP clients.

NTP/SNTP

Two popular applications that use UDP are Network Time Protocol (NTP) and his lightweight little brother, Simple Network Time Protocol (SNTP). These protocols synchronize the clocks of devices on a network. Computers need to use the same time so things like Kerberos authentication work properly. If a device requires NTP/SNTP, you will be able to enter the IP address for an NTP/SNTP server. NTP/SNTP uses port 123.

TFTP

You might also be tempted to think that UDP wouldn't work for any situation in which a critical data transfer takes place—untrue!

Trivial File Transfer Protocol (TFTP) enables you to transfer files from one machine to another. TFTP, using UDP, doesn't have any data protection, so you would never use TFTP between computers across the Internet. TFTP is popular for moving files between computers on the same LAN, where the chances of losing packets is very small. TFTP uses port 69.

ICMP

While TCP and UDP differ dramatically—the former connection-oriented and the latter connectionless—both manage and modify packets in the classic sense with a destination IP address, source IP address, destination port numbers, and source port numbers. A single session might be one packet or a series of packets.

On the other hand, sometimes applications are so simple that they're always connectionless and never need more than a single packet. The Internet Control Message Protocol (ICMP) works at Layer 3 to deliver connectionless packets. ICMP handles mundane issues such as disconnect messages (host unreachable) that applications use to let the other side of a session know what's happening.

Good old ping is one place where you'll see ICMP in action. Ping is an ICMP application that works by sending a single ICMP packet called an *echo request* to an IP address you specify. All computers running TCP/IP (assuming no firewall is involved) respond to echo requests with an *echo reply,* as shown in Figure 9.4.

```
○ ○ ○        ⌂ michaels@mediamac: ~ — ~ — zsh — 70×21
michaels@mediamac ~                                      [13:58:19]
> $ ping -c 4 www.totalsem.com
PING www.totalsem.com (216.40.231.195): 56 data bytes
64 bytes from 216.40.231.195: icmp_seq=0 ttl=54 time=20.913 ms
64 bytes from 216.40.231.195: icmp_seq=1 ttl=54 time=20.528 ms
64 bytes from 216.40.231.195: icmp_seq=2 ttl=54 time=20.398 ms
64 bytes from 216.40.231.195: icmp_seq=3 ttl=54 time=22.294 ms

--- www.totalsem.com ping statistics ---
4 packets transmitted, 4 packets received, 0.0% packet loss
round-trip min/avg/max/stddev = 20.398/21.033/22.294/0.752 ms

michaels@mediamac ~                                      [13:58:24]
> $
```

• **Figure 9.4** Ping in action

Ping provides a couple of responses that indicate problems locating the remote computer. If your computer has no route to the address listed, ping will display *destination host unreachable.* You might get the same message from a router upstream if that router can't go forward. If you ping a device and no echo reply comes back before the 1-second default time, ping will respond with *request timed out.* This can be caused by a slow network, excess traffic, a downed router, and more. Ping requests could be disabled on the target computer.

Many years ago, ping had a bug that allowed malicious users to send malformed ping packets to a destination. This *ping of death* would cause the recipient computer to crash. Ping was long ago fixed and you'll only hear this term from ancient techs—and you'll see it on the CompTIA Network+ exam.

IGMP

Do you remember the idea of IP multicast addresses, described in Chapter 7? The challenge to multicasting is determining who wants to receive the multicast and who does not. The Internet Group Management Protocol (IGMP) enables routers to communicate with hosts to determine a "group" membership. As you might remember from Chapter 7, multicast is in the Class D range (224/4). Multicast addresses only use a small subnet of the Class D range; specifically, they are assigned the network ID of 224.0.0.0/4. Multicast doesn't, however, assign IP addresses to individual hosts in the same manner as you've seen thus far. Instead, a particular multicast (called an *IGMP group*) is assigned

A *firewall* is a device or software that filters all the packets between two computers (or groups of computers) and acts like a club bouncer deciding who gets in and who gets blocked. Firewalls are vital for securing modern networks and will be discussed in Chapter 12, "Advanced Network Devices."

CompTIA uses the term *unreachable default gateway* as an ICMP-related issue. If you ping the default gateway and get a "Destination host unreachable" response, you could infer that the default gateway is unreachable.

• **Figure 9.5**   IGMP in action

to a 224.0.0.0/4 address, and those who wish to receive this multicast must tell their upstream router or switch (which must be configured to handle multicasts) that they wish to receive it. To do so, they join the IGMP group (Figure 9.5).

> ### ☑ Cross Check
>
> **Multicast**
>
> You first saw multicast in Chapter 7, "TCP/IP Basics," when you learned about classful IP addressing. Refer to that chapter and see if you can answer these questions. What IP numbers are reserved for multicast? What Class is that? What is the difference between unicast and multicast?

■ The Power of Port Numbers

If you want to understand the power of TCP/IP, you have to get seriously into port numbers. If you want to pass the CompTIA Network+ exam, you need to know how TCP/IP uses port numbers and you have to memorize a substantial number of common port numbers. As you saw in the previous chapter, port numbers make NAT work. As you progress through this book, you'll see a number of places where knowledge of port numbers is critical to protect your network, make routers work better, and address a zillion other issues. There is no such thing as a network administrator who isn't deeply into the magic of port numbers and who cannot manipulate them for his or her network's needs.

Let's review and expand on what you learned about port numbers in the previous chapter. Thus far, you know that every TCP/IP application requires a server and a client. Clearly defined port numbers exist for every popular or *well-known* TCP/IP application. A port number is a 16-bit value between 0 and 65535. Web servers, for example, use port number 80. Port numbers from 0 to 1023 are called **well-known port numbers** and are reserved for specific TCP/IP applications.

When a Web client (let's say your computer running Firefox) sends an HTTP ACK to a Web server to request the Web page, your computer's IP packet looks like Figure 9.6.

TCP/IP port numbers between 0 and 1023 are the well-known port numbers. You'll find them at every party.

Destination info:
147.58.201.183
Port: 80
Source info:
4.8.15.16

• **Figure 9.6**   HTTP ACK packet

As you can see, the destination port number is 80. The computer running the Web server reads the destination port number, telling it to send the incoming segment to the Web server program (Figure 9.7).

• **Figure 9.7**   Dealing with the incoming packet

The Web client's source port number is generated pseudo-randomly by the Web client computer. This value varies by operating system, but generally falls within the values 1024–5000 (the port numbers classically assigned as **ephemeral port numbers**) and 49152–65535 (the **dynamic port numbers** or **private port numbers**).

In the early days of the Internet, only ports 1024–5000 were used, but modern computers can use up all of those. More port numbers were added later. The Internet Assigned Numbers Authority (IANA) today recommends using only ports 49152–65535 as ephemeral port numbers. That's what current versions of Windows use as well. Let's redraw Figure 9.6 to show the more complete packet (Figure 9.8).

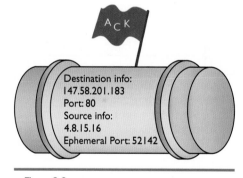

• **Figure 9.8**   A more complete IP packet

When the serving system responds to the Web client, it uses the ephemeral port number as the destination port to get the information back to the Web client running on the client computer (Figure 9.9).

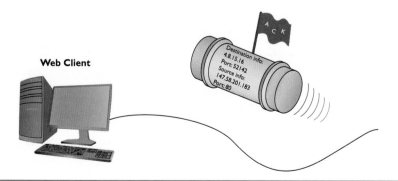

• **Figure 9.9**   Returning the packet

Registered Ports

The port numbers from 1024 to 49151 are called **registered ports**. Less-common TCP/IP applications can register their ports with the IANA. Unlike well-known ports, anyone can use these port numbers for their servers or for ephemeral numbers on clients. Most operating systems steer away (or are in the process of steering away) from using these port numbers for ephemeral ports, opting instead for the dynamic/private port numbers. Here's the full list of ports:

0–1023	Well-known port numbers
1024–49151	Registered ports
49152–65535	Dynamic or private ports

Each computer on each side of a session must keep track of the status of the communication. In TCP/IP, the session information (a combination of the IP address and port number) stored in RAM is called a **socket** or **endpoint**. When discussing the data each computer stores about the connection between two computers' TCP/IP applications, the term to use is **socket pairs** or **endpoints**. A *session* or **connection** refers to the connection in general, rather than anything specific to TCP/IP. Many people still use the term *session,* however. Here's a summary of the terms used:

- Terms for the session information (IP address and port number) stored on a single computer—*socket* or *endpoint*

- Terms for the connection data stored on two computers about the same connection—*socket pairs* or *endpoints*

- Terms for the whole interconnection—*connection* or *session*

 Even though almost all operating systems use netstat, there are subtle differences in options and output among the different versions.

As two computers begin to communicate, they store the information about the session—the endpoints—so they know where to send and receive data. At any given point in time, your computer probably has a large number of communications going on. If you want to know who your computer is communicating with, you need to see this list of endpoints. As you'll recall from Chapter 8, "Routing," Windows, Linux, and OS X come with **netstat**, the universal "show me the endpoint" utility. Netstat works at the command line, so open one up and type **netstat -n** to see something like this:

```
C:\>netstat -n
Active Connections
  Proto  Local Address         Foreign Address       State
   TCP   192.168.4.27:57913    216.40.231.195:80     ESTABLISHED
   TCP   192.168.4.27:61707    192.168.4.8:445       ESTABLISHED
C:\>
```

When you run netstat -n on a typical computer, you'll see many more than just two connections! The preceding example is simplified for purposes of discussing the details. It shows two connections: My computer's IP address is 192.168.4.27. The top connection is an open Web page (port 80) to a server at http://216.40.231.195. The second connection is an open Windows Network browser (port 445) to my file server (192.168.4.8). Looking on my Windows Desktop, you would certainly see at least these two windows open (Figure 9.10).

• **Figure 9.10**   Two open windows

Don't think that a single open application always means a single connection. The following example shows what `netstat -n` looks like when I open the well-known www.microsoft.com Web site (I took out the connections that were not involved with the Web browser's connections to www.microsoft.com):

```
C:\>netstat -n
Active Connections
  Proto  Local Address         Foreign Address       State
  TCP    192.168.4.27:50015    80.12.192.40:80       ESTABLISHED
  TCP    192.168.4.27:50016    80.12.192.40:80       ESTABLISHED
  TCP    192.168.4.27:50017    80.12.192.40:80       ESTABLISHED
  TCP    192.168.4.27:50018    80.12.192.40:80       ESTABLISHED
  TCP    192.168.4.27:50019    80.12.192.40:80       ESTABLISHED
  TCP    192.168.4.27:50020    80.12.192.51:80       ESTABLISHED
  TCP    192.168.4.27:50021    80.12.192.40:80       ESTABLISHED
  TCP    192.168.4.27:50022    80.12.192.40:80       ESTABLISHED
  TCP    192.168.4.27:50023    80.12.192.40:80       ESTABLISHED
  TCP    192.168.4.27:50024    80.12.192.40:80       ESTABLISHED
  TCP    192.168.4.27:50025    80.12.192.51:80       ESTABLISHED
  TCP    192.168.4.27:50027    80.12.192.40:80       ESTABLISHED
  TCP    192.168.4.27:50028    80.12.192.40:80       ESTABLISHED
  TCP    192.168.4.27:50036    80.12.192.75:80       ESTABLISHED
```

Netstat enables you to see active TCP/IP connections at a glance.

A single simple Web page needs only a single connection, but this Web page is very complex. Different elements in the Web page, such as advertisements, each have their own connection.

Netstat is a powerful tool, and you will see it used throughout this book. The CompTIA Network+ exam also tests your netstat skills. On the other hand, connections come and go constantly on your computer, and netstat, being a command-line utility, can't update to reflect changes automatically. All of the cool, hip, network techs use graphical endpoint tools. Take a moment right now and download the popular, powerful, and completely free TCPView, written by Mark Russinovich, the Guru of Windows utilities. Just type **TCPView** into your search engine to find it or try going here:

http://technet.microsoft.com /en-us/sysinternals/default.aspx

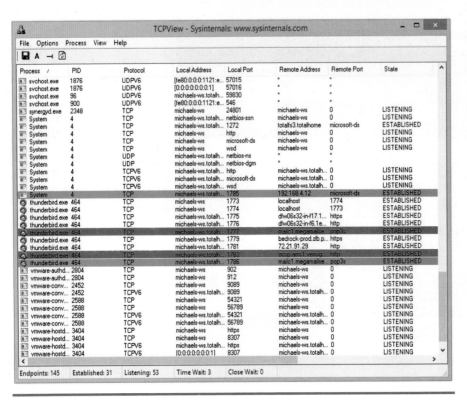

• **Figure 9.11** TCPView in action

Click the **Networking Utilities** icon to get the latest copy. Figure 9.11 shows TCPView in action. Note the red and green bars: red is for closing connections and green shows new connections as they appear.

TCPView won't work on anything but Windows, but other operating systems have equivalent programs. Linux folks often use the popular Net Activity Viewer (Figure 9.12), available here: http://netactview.source-forge.net

Connection Status

Connection states change continually, and it's helpful when using tools such as netstat or TCPView to understand the status of a connection at any given moment. Let's look at the various connection statuses so you understand what each means—this information is useful for determining what's happening on networked computers.

A socket that is prepared to respond to any IP packets destined for that socket's port number is called an **open port** or **listening port**. Every serving application has an open port. If you're running a Web server on a computer, for example, it will have an open port 80. That's easy enough to appreciate, but you'll be amazed at the number of open ports on just about *any* computer. Fire up a copy of netstat and type **netstat -an** to see all of your

The -a switch tells netstat to show all used ports. The -n switch instructs netstat to show raw port numbers and IP addresses.

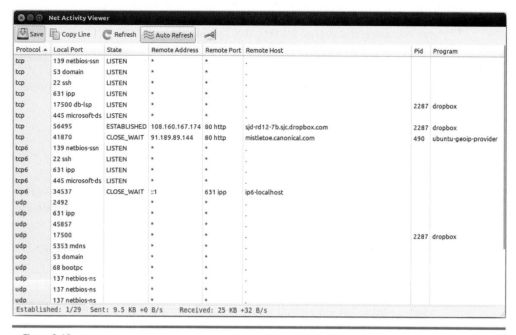

Protocol ▲	Local Port	State	Remote Address	Remote Port	Remote Host	Pid	Program
tcp	139 netbios-ssn	LISTEN	*	*	.		
tcp	53 domain	LISTEN	*	*	.		
tcp	22 ssh	LISTEN	*	*	.		
tcp	631 ipp	LISTEN	*	*	.		
tcp	17500 db-lsp	LISTEN	*	*	.	2287	dropbox
tcp	445 microsoft-ds	LISTEN	*	*	.		
tcp	56495	ESTABLISHED	108.160.167.174	80 http	sjd-rd12-7b.sjc.dropbox.com	2287	dropbox
tcp	41870	CLOSE_WAIT	91.189.89.144	80 http	mistletoe.canonical.com	490	ubuntu-geoip-provider
tcp6	139 netbios-ssn	LISTEN	*	*	.		
tcp6	22 ssh	LISTEN	*	*	.		
tcp6	631 ipp	LISTEN	*	*	.		
tcp6	445 microsoft-ds	LISTEN	*	*	.		
tcp6	34537	CLOSE_WAIT	::1	631 ipp	ip6-localhost		
udp	2492		*	*	.		
udp	631 ipp		*	*	.		
udp	45857		*	*	.		
udp	17500		*	*	.	2287	dropbox
udp	5353 mdns		*	*	.		
udp	53 domain		*	*	.		
udp	68 bootpc		*	*	.		
udp	137 netbios-ns		*	*	.		
udp	137 netbios-ns		*	*	.		
udp	137 netbios-ns		*	*	.		

Established: 1/29   Sent: 9.5 KB +0 B/s   Received: 25 KB +32 B/s

• **Figure 9.12**   Net Activity Viewer in action

listening ports. Running `netstat -an` gives a lot of information, so let's just look at a small amount:

```
C:\>netstat -an
Active Connections
   Proto  Local Address            Foreign Address          State
   TCP    0.0.0.0:7                0.0.0.0:0                LISTENING
   TCP    0.0.0.0:135              0.0.0.0:0                LISTENING
   TCP    0.0.0.0:445              0.0.0.0:0                LISTENING
   TCP    0.0.0.0:912              0.0.0.0:0                LISTENING
   TCP    0.0.0.0:990              0.0.0.0:0                LISTENING
   TCP    127.0.0.1:27015          0.0.0.0:0                LISTENING
   TCP    127.0.0.1:52144          127.0.0.1:52145          ESTABLISHED
   TCP    127.0.0.1:52145          127.0.0.1:52144          ESTABLISHED
   TCP    127.0.0.1:52146          127.0.0.1:52147          ESTABLISHED
   TCP    127.0.0.1:52147          127.0.0.1:52146          ESTABLISHED
   TCP    192.168.4.27:139         0.0.0.0:0                LISTENING
   TCP    192.168.4.27:52312       74.125.47.108:80         TIME_WAIT
   TCP    192.168.4.27:57913       63.246.140.18:80         CLOSE_WAIT
   TCP    192.168.4.27:61707       192.168.4.10:445         ESTABLISHED
```

First look at this line:

```
TCP    0.0.0.0:445              0.0.0.0:0                LISTENING
```

This line shows a listening port ready for incoming packets that have a destination port number of 445. Notice the local address is 0.0.0.0. This is how Windows tells you that the open port works on all NICs on this PC. In this case, my PC has only one NIC (192.168.4.27), but even if you have only one NIC, netstat still shows it this way. This computer is sharing some folders on the network. At this moment, no one is connected, so netstat shows the Foreign Address as 0.0.0.0. Incoming requests use port number 445 to connect to those shared folders. If another computer on my network (192.168.4.83) was accessing the shared folders, this line would look like

```
TCP    192.168.4.27:445          192.168.4.83:1073       ESTABLISHED
```

Established ports are active, working endpoint pairs. Over time all connections eventually close like this one:

```
TCP    192.168.4.27:57913        63.246.140.18:80        CLOSE_WAIT
```

This line shows a Web browser making a graceful closure, meaning each side of the conversation sees the session closing normally.

If data's going to move back and forth between computers, some program must always be doing the sending and/or receiving. Take a look at this line from `netstat -an`:

```
TCP    192.168.4.27:52312        74.125.47.108:80        ESTABLISHED
```

You see the 80 and might assume the connection is going out to a Web server. But what program on the computer is sending it? Enter the command **netstat -ano** (the -o switch tells netstat to show the process ID). Although you'll see many lines, the one for this connection looks like this:

```
Proto  Local Address        Foreign Address      State         PID
TCP    192.168.4.27:52312   74.125.47.108:80     ESTABLISHED   112092
```

Every running program on your computer gets a process ID (PID), a number used by the operating system to track all the running programs. Numbers aren't very helpful to you, though, because you want to know the name of the running program. In most operating systems, finding this out is fairly easy to do. In Windows, type **netstat -b**:

```
Proto      Local Address        Foreign Address      State
TCP        127.0.0.1:43543      Sabertooth:43544     ESTABLISHED
[firefox.exe]
```

In Linux, you can use the `ps` command:

```
michaelm@ubuntu:~$ ps
PID TTY          TIME CMD
3225 pts/1    00:00:00 bash
3227 pts/1    00:00:00 ps
```

If you want to find out the PID of a process, you can use the trusty Task Manager. The PIDs are hidden, by default, in versions of Windows prior to 8, but they are easy to enable. Simply fire up Task Manager, select the **Processes** tab, select the **View** menu, and click the **Select Columns...** option. The first option in the list will be PID (Process Identifier). Check the box and then click **OK**. Task Manager will now show you the PID for all running programs. In Windows 8 or later, open Task Manager and select **More Details** (if you haven't already), then jump over to the **Details** tab to see the PIDs.

Another great tool for discovering a PID (and a whole lot more) is Mark Russinovich's Process Explorer; it is a perfect tool for this. Figure 9.13 shows Process Explorer scrolled down to the bottom so you can see the program using PID 456—good old Firefox!

You might be tempted to say "Big whoop, Mike—what else would use port 80?" Then consider the possibility that you run netstat and see a line like the one just shown, but *you don't have a browser open!* You determine the PID and

To get Process Explorer, enter **"Process Explorer"** in your search engine to find it or try going here:

http://technet.microsoft.com/en-us/sysinternals/default.aspx

Click the **Process Utilities** icon to get the latest copy.

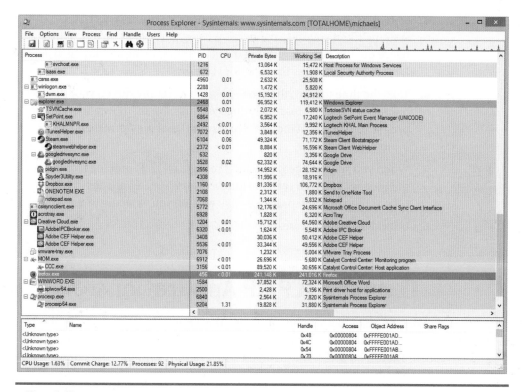

Process Explorer window:

Process Explorer - Sysinternals: www.sysinternals.com [TOTALHOME\michaels]

File   Options   View   Process   Find   Handle   Users   Help

Process	PID	CPU	Private Bytes	Working Set	Description
svchost.exe	1216		13,064 K	15,472 K	Host Process for Windows Services
lsass.exe	672		6,532 K	11,908 K	Local Security Authority Process
csrss.exe	4960	0.01	2,632 K	25,508 K	
winlogon.exe	2288		1,472 K	5,820 K	
dwm.exe	1428	0.01	15,192 K	24,912 K	
explorer.exe	2468	0.01	56,952 K	119,412 K	Windows Explorer
TSVNCache.exe	5548	< 0.01	2,072 K	6,580 K	TortoiseSVN status cache
SetPoint.exe	6864		6,952 K	17,240 K	Logitech SetPoint Event Manager (UNICODE)
KHALMNPR.exe	2492	< 0.01	3,564 K	9,992 K	Logitech KHAL Main Process
iTunesHelper.exe	7072	< 0.01	3,848 K	12,356 K	iTunesHelper
Steam.exe	6104	0.06	49,324 K	71,172 K	Steam Client Bootstrapper
steamwebhelper.exe	2372	< 0.01	8,884 K	16,596 K	Steam Client WebHelper
googledrivesync.exe	632		820 K	3,356 K	Google Drive
googledrivesync.exe	3528	0.02	62,332 K	74,644 K	Google Drive
pidgin.exe	2556		14,952 K	28,152 K	Pidgin
Spyder3Utility.exe	4308		11,996 K	18,916 K	
Dropbox.exe	1160	0.01	81,336 K	106,772 K	Dropbox
ONENOTEM.EXE	2108		2,312 K	1,880 K	Send to OneNote Tool
notepad.exe	7068		1,344 K	5,832 K	Notepad
csisyncclient.exe	5772		12,176 K	24,696 K	Microsoft Office Document Cache Sync Client Interface
acrotray.exe	6928		1,828 K	6,320 K	AcroTray
Creative Cloud.exe	1204	0.01	15,712 K	64,560 K	Adobe Creative Cloud
AdobeIPCBroker.exe	6320	< 0.01	1,624 K	5,548 K	Adobe IPC Broker
Adobe CEF Helper.exe	3408		30,036 K	50,412 K	Adobe CEF Helper
Adobe CEF Helper.exe	5536	< 0.01	33,344 K	49,556 K	Adobe CEF Helper
vmware-tray.exe	7076		1,232 K	5,004 K	VMware Tray Process
MOM.exe	6912	< 0.01	26,696 K	5,680 K	Catalyst Control Center: Monitoring program
CCC.exe	3156	< 0.01	89,520 K	30,656 K	Catalyst Control Center: Host application
firefox.exe	456	< 0.01	241,148 K	241,016 K	Firefox
WINWORD.EXE	1584		37,852 K	72,324 K	Microsoft Office Word
splwow64.exe	2500		2,428 K	6,156 K	Print driver host for applications
procexp.exe	6840		2,564 K	7,820 K	Sysinternals Process Explorer
procexp64.exe	5204	1.31	19,828 K	31,880 K	Sysinternals Process Explorer

Type	Name	Handle	Access	Object Address	Share Flags
<Unknown type>		0x48	0x00000804	0xFFFFE001AD...	
<Unknown type>		0x4C	0x00000804	0xFFFFE001AD...	
<Unknown type>		0x54	0x00000804	0xFFFFE001AB...	
<Unknown type>		0x70	0x00000804	0xFFFFE001AB...	

CPU Usage: 1.63%   Commit Charge: 12.77%   Processes: 92   Physical Usage: 21.85%

• **Figure 9.13**   Process Explorer

discover the name of the process is "Evil_Overlord.exe." Something is running on your computer that should not be there.

Understanding how TCP/IP uses ports is a base skill for any network tech. To pass the CompTIA Network+ exam, you need to memorize a number of different well-known ports and even a few of the more popular registered ports. You must appreciate how the ports fit into the process of TCP/IP communications and know how to use netstat and other tools to see what's going on inside your computer.

The biggest challenge is learning what's supposed to be running and what's not. No one on Earth can run a netstat command and instantly recognize every connection and why it's running, but a good network tech should know most of them. For those connections that a tech doesn't recognize, he or she should know how to research them to determine what they are.

Rules for Determining Good vs. Bad Communications

Here is the general list of rules I follow for determining good versus bad communications (as far as networking goes, at least!):

1. Memorize a bunch of known ports for common TCP/IP applications. The next section in this chapter will get you started.

2. Learn how to use netstat to see what's happening on your computer. Learn to use switches such as −a, −n, −o, and −b to help you define what you're looking for.

3. Take the time to learn the ports that normally run on your operating system. When you see a connection using ports you don't recognize, figure out the process running the connection using a utility such as Linux's `ps` or Process Explorer for Windows.

4. Take the time to learn the processes that normally run on your operating system. Most operating systems have their own internal programs (such as Windows' svchost.exe) that are normal and important processes.

5. When you see a process you don't recognize, just enter the filename of the process in a Web search. Hundreds of Web sites are dedicated to researching mystery processes that will tell you what the process does.

6. Get rid of bad processes.

Common TCP/IP Applications

Finally! You now know enough about the Transport layer, port numbering, and sockets to get into some of the gritty details of common TCP/IP applications. There's no pretty way to do this, so let's start with the big daddy of them all, the Web.

The World Wide Web

Where would we be without the World Wide Web? If you go up to a non-nerd and say "Get on the Internet," most of them will automatically open a Web browser, because to them the Web *is* the Internet. The Internet is the infrastructure that enables the Web to function, but it's certainly more than just the Web. I think it's safe to assume you've used the Web, firing up your Web browser to surf to one cool site after another, learning new things, clicking links, often ending up somewhere completely unexpected . . . it's all fun! This section looks at the Web and the tools that make it function, specifically the protocols that enable communication over the Internet.

The Web is composed of servers that store specially formatted documents using languages such as Hypertext Markup Language (HTML). Figure 9.14 shows the Web interface built into my wireless access point.

HTML has been around for a long time and, as a result, has gone

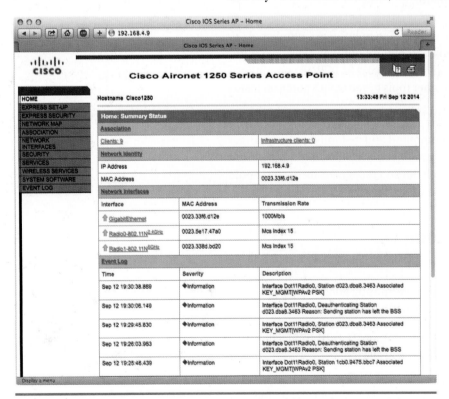

• **Figure 9.14**   My wireless access point's Web interface

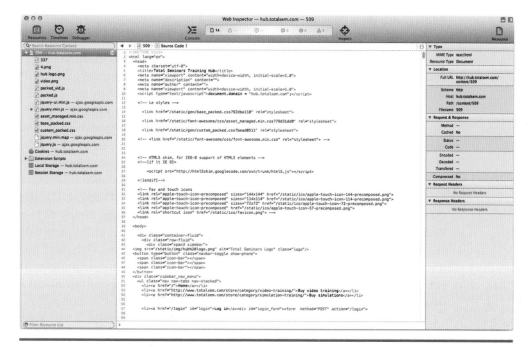

- **Figure 9.15** HTML5 source code

through many versions. Today many developers use the latest HTML version called HTML5. See Figure 9.15.

Web browsers are designed to request HTML pages from Web servers and then open them. To access a Web page, you enter **http://** plus the IP address of the Web server. When you type the address of a Web server, such as **http://192.168.4.1**, you tell the browser to go to 192.168.4.1 and ask for a Web page. All Web servers have a default Web page that they open unless you enter something more complex like **http://192.168.4.1/status**.

Granted, most people don't enter IP addresses into browsers, but rather enter text like www.totalsem.com or www.google.com. Memorizing text addresses is much easier than memorizing IP addresses. Web site text addresses use a naming protocol called Domain Name System (DNS), which you will learn about in the next chapter. For now, just enter the IP address as shown.

HTTP

The **Hypertext Transfer Protocol (HTTP)** is the underlying protocol used by the Web, and it runs, by default, on TCP port 80. When you enter **http://** at the beginning of a Web server's IP address, you are identifying how messages are formatted and transmitted, requesting and responding to the transfer of HTML-formatted files. HTTP defines what actions Web servers and browsers should take in response to various commands.

HTTP has a general weakness in its handling of Web pages: it relays commands executed by users without reference to any commands previously executed. The problem with this is that Web designers continue to design more complex and truly interactive Web pages. HTTP is pretty dumb when it comes to remembering what people have done on a Web site. Luckily for Web designers everywhere, other technologies exist to help HTTP relay commands and thus support more-interactive, intelligent Web sites. These technologies include JavaScript/AJAX, server-side scripting, Adobe Flash, and cookies.

HTML is the most well-known markup language, but many others roam the Web today, adding to HTML's capabilities. Expect to see the *Extensible Markup Language (XML)* on the exam. XML provides the basic format or markup language for everything from RSS feeds to Microsoft Office documents.

Most Web browsers are pretty forgiving. If you only type in **192.168.4.1**, forgetting the "http://" part, they just add it for you.

Before connections to the Web became fast, many people used a completely different Internet service for swapping information, ideas, and files. *USENET* enjoyed great popularity for some years, though it barely survives today. Clients used the *Network News Transfer Protocol (NNTP)* to access USENET over TCP port 119. It might show up as an incorrect answer on the exam.

Publishing Web Pages

Once you've designed and created an HTML document, you can share it with the rest of the world. To do so, you find a Web server that will "host" the page. You most certainly can install a Web server on a computer, acquire a public IP address for that computer, and host the Web site yourself. Self-hosting is a time-consuming and challenging project, though, so most people use other methods. Most Internet service providers (ISPs) provide Web servers of their own, or you can find relatively inexpensive Web hosting service companies. The price of Web hosting usually depends on the services and drive space offered. Web hosts typically charge around US$10 a month for simple Web sites.

One option that has been available for a while is free Web hosting. Usually the services are not too bad, but free Web hosts have limitations. Nearly all free Web hosts insist on the right to place ads on your Web page. Third-party ads are not as much of an issue if you are posting a basic blog or fan Web page, but if you do any sort of business with your Web site, ads can be most annoying to your customers. The worst sort of free Web host services place pop-up ads *over* your Web page. Beyond annoying!

Once you have uploaded your HTML pages to your Web host, the Web server takes over. What's a Web server? I'm glad you asked!

Web Servers and Web Clients

A Web server is a computer that delivers (or *serves up*) Web pages. Web servers listen on port 80, fetching requested HTML pages and sending them to browsers. You can turn any computer into a Web server by installing server software and connecting the machine to the Internet, but you need to consider the operating system and Web server program you'll use to serve your Web site. Microsoft's server is **Internet Information Services (IIS)**, shown in Figure 9.16.

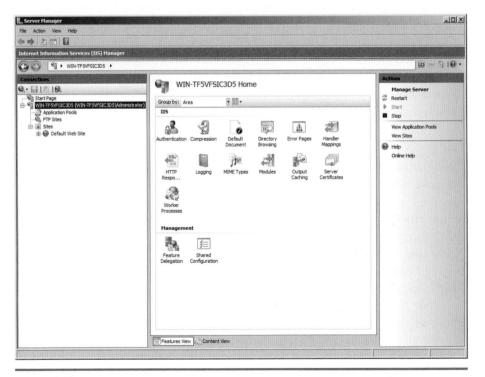

• **Figure 9.16**   IIS in action

IIS enables you to set a maximum connection limit on your Web server based on available bandwidth and memory. This enables you to protect your network against an overwhelming number of requests due to a particularly popular page or a type of malicious attack called a denial of service (DoS) attack (more on DoS attacks in Chapter 19, "Protecting Your Network").

Microsoft builds an artificial 20-connection limit into Windows client versions, so you should only run IIS on Server versions of Windows (unless you don't expect too many people to visit your Web site at one time).

A majority of UNIX/Linux-based operating systems run **Apache HTTP Server**. As of this writing, Apache serves ~50 percent of the active Web sites on the Internet. Apache is incredibly popular, runs on multiple operating systems (including Windows), and, best of all, is *free!* In comparison, even with the weight of Microsoft behind it, IIS only commands about 11 percent market share of active Web sites.

Apache is nothing more than an executable program and a bunch of text files, so it isn't much to look at. To ease configuration, most Web administrators use add-on graphical user interfaces (GUIs) such as Webmin that make administering Apache a breeze. Figure 9.17 illustrates the wonderful simplicity that is Webmin.

 An *active site* is a Web site that's functioning by serving Web pages. The percent of market share mentioned here changes a lot when you add in *parked sites*, domain names that have been registered but don't really do anything, like Web or e-mail servers.

• **Figure 9.17**   Webmin Apache module

Other common Web servers on the Internet include nginx, which is ranked second for active sites, and Google Web Server (GWS), which is in fourth place. GWS, used only by Google's servers, has about 8 percent of the total active Web server market! There are literally hundreds of other Web servers, but you'll rarely see them outside of small personal Web sites.

Web clients are the programs used to surf the Web. A client program (a Web browser) reads Web pages supplied by the Web server. To access a server, type either an IP address or, more commonly, the complete name of the Web server in the address bar. The complete name is often referred to as the *uniform resource locator (URL)*.

Most browsers handle multiple functions, from reading HTML documents to offering FTP services, and even serving as e-mail or newsgroup readers. (You'll learn all about these functions later in the chapter.) The most popular Web browsers are Microsoft Internet Explorer, Mozilla Firefox, Apple Safari, Opera, and Google Chrome.

HTTP is a perfect example of a common network vulnerability and threat, an unsecure protocol. Other vulnerabilities include open ports, like we discussed earlier, and other unsecure protocols that we'll hit next. For more in-depth coverage of vulnerabilities, see Chapter 19.

Secure Sockets Layer and HTTPS

Any nosy person who can plug into a network can see and read the HTTP packets moving between a Web server and a Web client. Less than nice people can easily create a fake Web site to trick people into thinking it's a legitimate Web site and then steal their user names and passwords.

For an Internet application to be secure, it must have the following:

- **Authentication**   User names and passwords
- **Encryption**   Stirring up the data so others can't read it
- **Nonrepudiation**   Source is not able to deny a sent message

While all of Chapter 11, "Securing TCP/IP," is dedicated to these concepts, I can't mention HTTP without at least touching on its secure counterpart, HTTPS. The Web has blossomed into a major economic player, requiring serious security for those who wish to do online transactions (e-commerce). In the early days of e-commerce, people feared that a simple credit card transaction on a less-than-secure Web site could transform their dreams of easy online buying into a nightmare of being robbed blind and ending up living in a refrigerator box. I can safely say that it was *never* as bad as all that.

Nowadays, many tools can protect your purchases *and* your anonymity. One such safeguard is called **Secure Sockets Layer (SSL)**. SSL is a protocol developed by Netscape for transmitting private documents over the Internet. SSL works by using a public key to encrypt communication. This encrypted communication is sent over an SSL connection and then decrypted at the receiving end using a private key. All the popular Web browsers and Web servers support SSL, and many Web sites use the protocol to obtain confidential user information, such as credit card numbers. One way to tell if a site is using SSL is by looking at the Web page address. By convention, Web pages that use an SSL connection start with *https* instead of *http*.

HTTPS stands for **Hypertext Transfer Protocol over SSL**. HTTPS uses TCP port 443. You can also look for a small lock icon in the address bar of your browser. Figure 9.18 shows a typical secure Web page. The *https:* in the address and the lock icon are circled.

The last few years have seen SSL replaced with the more powerful **Transport Layer Security (TLS)**. Your secure Web page still looks the same as with

Many techs refer to HTTPS as Hypertext Transfer Protocol *Secure,* probably because it's easier to explain to non-techs that way. Don't be surprised to see it listed this way on the CompTIA Network+ exam.

• Figure 9.18   Secure Web page

SSL, so only the folks setting this up really care. Just make sure you know that SSL and TLS are functionally the same with Web pages. Read Chapter 11 for more details on SSL and TLS.

HTTP enables you to access the Web, but HTTPS gets you there securely. HTTPS uses TLS to provide the security.

Telnet and SSH

Roughly one billion years ago, there was no such thing as the Internet or even networks... Well, maybe it was only about 40 years ago, but as far as nerds like me are concerned, a world before the Internet was filled with brontosauruses and palm fronds. The only computers were huge monsters called mainframes and to access them required a dumb terminal like the one shown in Figure 9.19.

A dumb terminal is a local system—generally a monitor, keyboard, and mouse—that enables you to access a distant system that has all the computing power. The dumb terminal can't do any work on its own, even though it might look like a personal computer.

• Figure 9.19   WANG dumb terminal

Operating systems didn't have windows and pretty icons. The interface to the mainframe was a command line, but it worked just fine for the time. Then the cavemen who first lifted their heads up from the computer ooze known as mainframes said to themselves, "Wouldn't it be great if we could access each other's computers from the comfort of our own caves?" That was what started the entire concept of a network. Back then the idea of sharing folders or printers or Web pages hadn't been considered yet. The entire motivation for networking was so people could sit at their dumb terminals and, instead of accessing only their local mainframes, access totally different mainframes. The protocol to do this was called the *Telnet Protocol* or simply **Telnet**.

```
CoreSwitch#sh ver
Cisco IOS Software, C2970 Software (C2970-LANBASE-M), Version 12.2(44)SE3, RELEA
SE SOFTWARE (fc2)
Copyright (c) 1986-2008 by Cisco Systems, Inc.
Compiled Sun 28-Sep-08 21:28 by nachen
Image text-base: 0x00003000, data-base: 0x00F00000

ROM: Bootstrap program is C2970 boot loader
BOOTLDR: C2970 Boot Loader (C2970-HBOOT-M) Version 12.1(14r)EA1a, RELEASE SOFTWA
RE (fc1)

CoreSwitch uptime is 33 weeks, 1 day, 23 hours, 59 minutes
System returned to ROM by power-on
System restarted at 14:26:51 CST Wed Jan 22 2014
System image file is "flash:c2970-lanbase-mz.122-44.SE3/c2970-lanbase-mz.122-44.
SE3.bin"

cisco WS-C2970G-24T-E (PowerPC405) processor (revision E0) with 122880K/8184K by
tes of memory.
Processor board ID CAT0832N5LZ
Last reset from power-on
1 Virtual Ethernet interface
24 Gigabit Ethernet interfaces
The password-recovery mechanism is enabled.

512K bytes of flash-simulated non-volatile configuration memory.
Base ethernet MAC Address       : 00:11:93:D3:35:80
Motherboard assembly number     : 73-8754-05
Power supply part number        : 341-0048-01
Motherboard serial number       : CAT083007K2
Power supply serial number      : DTH082517EK
Model revision number           : E0
Motherboard revision number     : A0
Model number                    : WS-C2970G-24T-E
System serial number            : CAT0832N5LZ
Top Assembly Part Number        : 800-23385-01
Top Assembly Revision Number    : H0
Hardware Board Revision Number  : 0x01


Switch Ports Model             SW Version          SW Image
------ ----- -----             ----------          --------
*    1  24   WS-C2970G-24T-E   12.2(44)SE3         C2970-LANBASE-M


Configuration register is 0xF

CoreSwitch#
```

• **Figure 9.20**   Telnet client

Modern PCs can (but shouldn't) use Telnet to connect remotely to another computer via the command line (Figure 9.20). Telnet runs on TCP port 23, enabling you to connect to a Telnet server and run commands on that server as if you were sitting right in front of it.

Telnet enables you to remotely administer a server and communicate with other servers on your network. As you can imagine, this is sort of risky. If you can remotely control a computer, what is to stop others from doing the same? Thankfully, Telnet does not allow just *anyone* to log on and wreak havoc with your network. You must enter a user name and password to access a Telnet server.

Unfortunately, Telnet does not have any form of encryption. If someone intercepted the conversation between a Telnet client and Telnet server, he or she would see all of the commands you type as well as the results from the Telnet server. As a result, you should never use Telnet on the Internet. Instead, use **Secure Shell (SSH)**, a terminal emulation program that looks exactly like Telnet but encrypts the data and the authentication.

Telnet/SSH Servers and Clients

The oldest Telnet server, found on UNIX and Linux systems, is telnetd. Like most UNIX/Linux servers, telnetd isn't much to look at, so let's move over to the Windows world. Since the halcyon days of Windows NT, Windows has come with a basic Telnet server. It is disabled, by default, in modern Windows systems, because Telnet is a gaping security hole. The built-in server is very limited and Microsoft discourages its use. I prefer to use a great little

Telnet only enables command-line remote access; it does not enable GUI access. If you want to access another computer's desktop remotely, you need another type of program.

• **Figure 9.21**   FreeSSHd

third-party server called freeSSHd (Figure 9.21). Note the name—freeSSHd, not "freeTelnet." As Telnet fades away and SSH becomes more dominant, finding a Telnet-only server these days is hard. All of the popular Telnet servers are also SSH servers.

A Telnet or SSH client is the computer from which you log into the remote server. Most operating systems have a built-in Telnet client that you run from a command prompt. Figure 9.22 shows the Telnet client built into OS X. Just open a terminal window and type `telnet` and the IP address of the Telnet server.

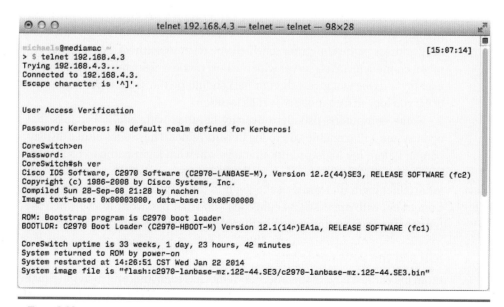

• **Figure 9.22**   OS X Telnet

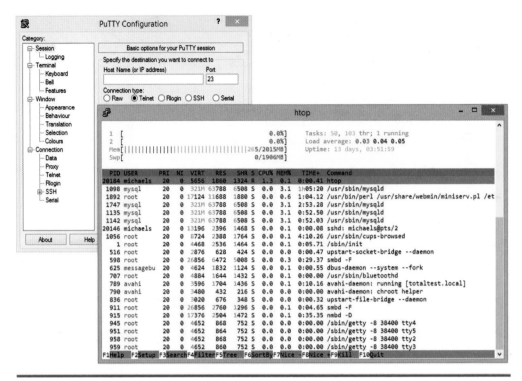

• Figure 9.23 PuTTY

Command-prompt clients lack a number of handy features. They can't, for example, remember the IP addresses, user names, or passwords for Telnet or SSH servers, so every time you use Telnet or SSH, you have to enter all that information again. Third-party Telnet/SSH clients, such as the very popular PuTTY, which you saw in Chapter 8, store all this information and much more (Figure 9.23).

Configuring a Telnet/SSH Client

When you configure a Telnet or SSH client, you must provide the host name, a valid login name, and the password. As I mentioned previously, you must have permission to access the server to use Telnet or SSH. A *host name* is the name or IP address of the computer to which you want to connect. For instance, you might connect to a Web server with the host name websrv.mhteched.com. The user *login name* you give Telnet or SSH should be the same login name you'd use if you logged into the server at its location.

Some computers, usually university libraries with online catalogs, have open systems that enable you to log in with Telnet. These sites either display a banner before the login prompt that tells you what login name to use, or they require no login name at all. As with the login name, you use the same password for a Telnet login that you'd use to log into the server directly. It's that simple. Computers with open access either tell you what password to use when they tell you what login name to use, or they require no login name/password at all.

> Telnet and SSH enable you to control a remote computer from a local computer over a network.

SSH and the Death of Telnet

From the earliest days of the Internet, Telnet has seen long and heavy use in the TCP world, but it suffers from lack of any security. Telnet passwords as well as data are transmitted in cleartext and are thus easily hacked. To that end, SSH has now replaced Telnet for any serious terminal emulation. In terms of what it does, SSH is extremely similar to Telnet in that it creates a terminal connection to a remote host. Every aspect of SSH, however, including both login and data transmittal, is encrypted. SSH uses TCP port 22 instead of Telnet's port 23.

SSH enables you to control a remote computer from a local computer over a network, just like Telnet. Unlike Telnet, SSH enables you to do it securely!

E-mail

Electronic mail (e-mail) has been a major part of the Internet revolution, and not just because it has streamlined the junk mail industry. E-mail provides an extremely quick way for people to communicate with one another, letting them send messages and attachments (like documents and pictures) over the Internet. It's normally offered as a free service by ISPs. Most e-mail client programs provide a rudimentary text editor for composing messages, but many can be configured to let you edit your messages using more sophisticated editors.

E-mail consists of e-mail clients and e-mail servers. When a message is sent to your e-mail address, it is normally stored in an electronic mailbox on your e-mail server until you tell the e-mail client to download the message. Most e-mail client programs can be configured to signal you in some way when a new message has arrived or to download e-mails automatically as they come to you. Once you read an e-mail message, you can archive it, forward it, print it, or delete it. Most e-mail programs are configured to delete messages from the e-mail server automatically when you download them to your local machine, but you can usually change this configuration option to suit your circumstances.

E-mail programs use a number of application-level protocols to send and receive information. Specifically, the e-mail you find on the Internet uses SMTP to send e-mail, and either POP3 or IMAP4 to receive e-mail.

SMTP, POP3, and IMAP4, Oh My!

The following is a list of the different protocols that the Internet uses to transfer and receive mail:

SMTP The Simple Mail Transfer Protocol (SMTP) is used to send e-mail. SMTP travels over TCP port 25 and is used by clients to send messages.

POP3 Post Office Protocol version 3 (POP3) is one of the two protocols that receive e-mail from SMTP servers. POP3 uses TCP port 110. POP3 is on its way out today, though you'll see it on the exam.

IMAP4 Internet Message Access Protocol version 4 (IMAP4) is a preferred alternative to POP3. Like POP3, IMAP4 retrieves e-mail from an e-mail server. IMAP4 uses TCP port 143 and supports some features that are not supported in POP3. For example, IMAP4 enables you to search through messages on the mail server to find specific keywords and select the messages you want to download onto your machine. IMAP4 also supports the concept of folders that you can place on the IMAP4 server to organize your e-mail. Some POP3 e-mail clients have folders, but that's not a part of POP3, just a nice feature added to the client.

Alternatives to SMTP, POP3, and IMAP4

Although SMTP, POP3, and IMAP4 are by far the most common and most traditional tools for sending and receiving e-mail, two other options are

The CompTIA Network+ objectives view Web-based e-mail as one of many **Web services**. Web services also include applications that you access on the Internet, like Google Docs and Google Sheets, online word processing and spreadsheet programs, respectively.

The major contrast between Web services and local services involves access. Web services offer access from any machine, as long as that machine is connected to the Internet. Local applications (usually) require local access, but don't need any other connectivity.

widely popular: Web-based e-mail and proprietary solutions. Web-based mail, as the name implies, requires a Web interface. From a Web browser, you simply surf to the Web-mail server, log in, and access your e-mail. The cool part is that you can do it from anywhere in the world where you find a Web browser and an Internet hookup! You get the benefit of e-mail without even needing to own a computer. Some of the more popular Web-based services are Google's Gmail (Figure 9.24), Microsoft's Windows Live Outlook, and Yahoo!'s Yahoo! Mail.

The key benefits of Web-based e-mail services are as follows:

- You can access your e-mail from anywhere.

- They're free.

- They're handy for throw-away accounts (like when you're required to give an e-mail address to download something, but you know you're going to get spammed if you do).

E-mail Servers

The e-mail server world is much more fragmented than the Web server world. The current leader is **sendmail** used on Linux and UNIX operating systems. Like Apache, sendmail doesn't really have an interface, but many different

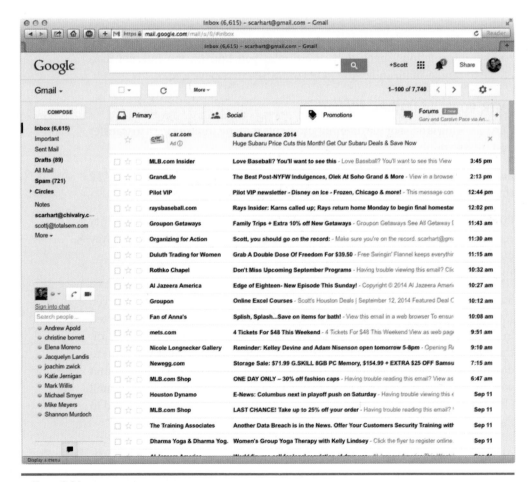

• **Figure 9.24**   Gmail in action

third-party interfaces are available to help configure sendmail, such as Webmin shown in Figure 9.25.

Sendmail controls about 20 percent of all e-mail servers but only uses SMTP. You must run a POP3 or IMAP4 server program to support e-mail clients. Programs like Eudora's Qpopper handle sending mail to POP3 e-mail clients. Microsoft, of course, has its own e-mail server, Microsoft Exchange Server, and like IIS, it only runs on Windows (Figure 9.26). Exchange Server is both an SMTP and a POP3 server in one package.

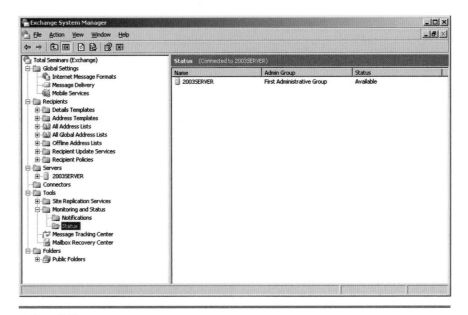

• **Figure 9.26**   Microsoft Exchange Server

E-mail servers accept incoming mail and sort out the mail for recipients into individual storage area mailboxes. These **mailboxes** are special separate holding areas for each user's e-mail. An e-mail server works much like a post office, sorting and arranging incoming messages, and kicking back those messages that have no known recipient.

E-mail servers are difficult to manage. E-mail servers store user lists, user rights, and messages, and are constantly involved in Internet traffic and resources. Setting up and administering an e-mail server takes a lot of planning, although it's getting easier. Most e-mail server software runs in a GUI, but even the command-line-based interface of e-mail servers is becoming more intuitive.

E-mail Client

An **e-mail client** is a program that runs on a computer and enables you to send, receive, and organize e-mail. The e-mail client program communicates with the SMTP e-mail server to send mail and communicates with the IMAP or POP e-mail server to download the messages from the e-mail server to the client computer. There are hundreds of e-mail programs, two of the most popular of which are Microsoft Outlook (Figure 9.27) and Mozilla Thunderbird.

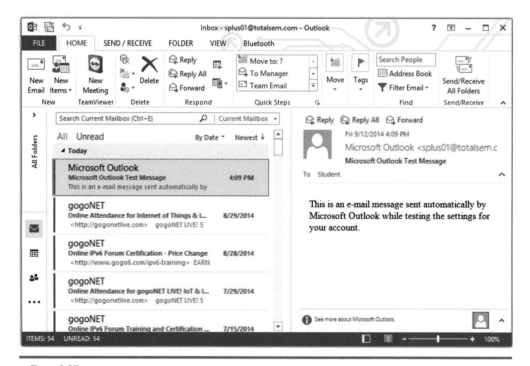

• **Figure 9.27**   Microsoft Outlook

Configuring an E-mail Client   Configuring a client is an easy matter. Your mail administrator will give you the server's domain name and your mailbox's user name and password. You need to enter the POP3 or IMAP4 server's domain name and the SMTP server's domain name to the e-mail client (Figure 9.28). Every e-mail client has a different way to add the server domain names or IP addresses, so you may have to poke around, but you'll find the option there somewhere! In many cases, this may be the same name or address for both

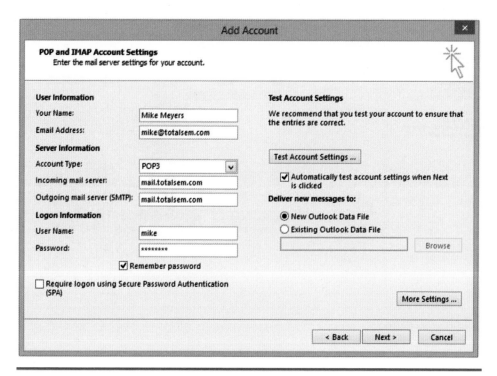

Add Account

POP and IMAP Account Settings
Enter the mail server settings for your account.

User Information

Your Name: Mike Meyers

Email Address: mike@totalsem.com

Server Information

Account Type: POP3

Incoming mail server: mail.totalsem.com

Outgoing mail server (SMTP): mail.totalsem.com

Logon Information

User Name: mike

Password: ********

☑ Remember password

☐ Require logon using Secure Password Authentication (SPA)

Test Account Settings

We recommend that you test your account to ensure that the entries are correct.

Test Account Settings ...

☑ Automatically test account settings when Next is clicked

Deliver new messages to:

⦿ New Outlook Data File

○ Existing Outlook Data File

Browse

More Settings ...

< Back   Next >   Cancel

• **Figure 9.28**   Entering server information in Microsoft Outlook

the incoming and outgoing servers—the folks administering the mail servers will tell you. Besides the e-mail server domain names or addresses, you must also enter the user name and password of the e-mail account the client will be managing.

FTP

File Transfer Protocol (FTP) is the original protocol used on the Internet for transferring files. Although HTTP can be used to transfer files as well, the transfer is often not as reliable or as fast as with FTP. In addition, FTP can do the transfer with security and data integrity. The old active FTP used TCP ports 21 and 20 by default, although passive FTP only uses port 21 for a default. See the discussion on active versus passive FTP later in this chapter.

FTP sites are either anonymous sites, meaning that anyone can log on, or secured sites, meaning that you must have a user name and password to access the site and transfer files. A single FTP site can offer both anonymous access and protected access, but you'll see different resources depending on which way you log in.

FTP Servers and FTP Clients

The FTP server does all the real work of storing the files, accepting incoming connections and verifying user names and passwords, and transferring the files. The client logs onto the FTP server (either from a Web site, a command line, or a special FTP application) and downloads the requested files onto the local hard drive.

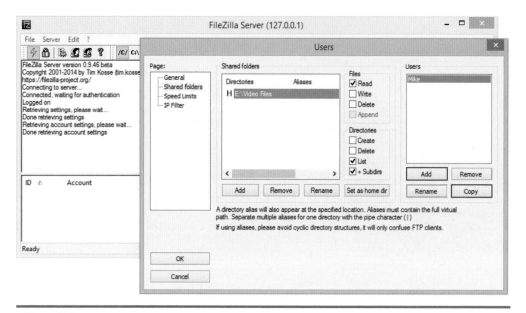

• **Figure 9.29** FileZilla Server

FTP Servers We don't set up servers for Internet applications nearly as often as we set up clients. I've set up only a few Web servers over the years, whereas I've set up thousands of Web browsers. FTP servers are the one exception, as we nerds like to exchange files. If you have a file you wish to share with a lot of people (but not the entire Internet), a reliable, old-school method is to put up a quick FTP server. Most versions of Linux/UNIX have built-in FTP servers, but many third-party applications offer better solutions. One of the simpler ones for Windows, especially for those "let me put up an FTP server so you guys can get a copy" type of situations, is the open source FileZilla Server (Figure 9.29).

FTP is not very secure because data transfers are not encrypted by default, so you don't want to use straight FTP for sensitive data. But you can add user names and passwords to prevent all but the most serious hackers from accessing your FTP server. I avoid using the anonymous login because unscrupulous people could use the server for exchanging illegal software.

Another thing to check when deciding on an FTP server setup is the number of clients you want to support. Most anonymous FTP sites limit the number of users who may download at any one time to around 500. This protects you from a sudden influx of users flooding your server and eating up all your Internet bandwidth.

> Most Web servers are also FTP servers. These bundled versions of FTP servers are robust but do not provide all the options one might want.

Try This!

Doing FTP

Never done FTP? Do a Web search for **"Public FTP servers"** and try accessing them from your Web browser. Then download a dedicated FTP client and try again! There are thousands of public FTP servers out there.

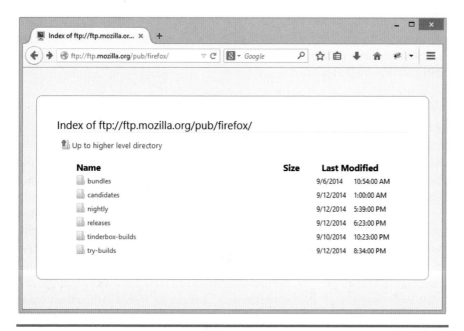

• **Figure 9.30**   FTP in a Web browser

FTP Clients   FTP clients, as noted before, can access an FTP server through a Web site, a command line, or a special FTP application. Usually special FTP applications offer the most choices for accessing and using an FTP site.

You have many choices when it comes to FTP clients. For starters, some Web browsers handle FTP as well as HTTP, although they lack a few features. For example, Firefox only supports an anonymous login. To use your Web browser as an FTP client, type **ftp://** followed by the IP address or domain name of the FTP server (Figure 9.30).

Every operating system has a command-line FTP client. I avoid using them unless I have no other choice, because they lack important features like the ability to save FTP connections to use again later.

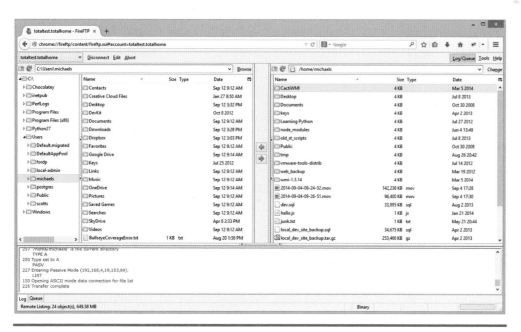

• **Figure 9.31**   Author's FireFTP hard at work

Tech Tip

Firefox Add-Ons

Firefox enables programmers to create add-ons, small programs that extend the capabilities of the browser with some pretty impressive results. Are you unfamiliar with Firefox add-ons? Start Firefox. Click **Firefox/ Add-ons** *(or* **Tools/Add-ons** *in older versions), and a whole new world will open for you. A couple of my favorites are Mouse Gestures—where you can flick the mouse left or right to navigate through windows and Web sites you've visited—and Speed Dial—quick access to your favorite sites.*

Trivial File Transfer Protocol (TFTP) is used for transferring files and has a similar-sounding name to FTP, but beyond that it is very different. TFTP uses UDP port 69 and does not use user names and passwords, although you can usually set some restrictions based on the client's IP address. TFTP is not at all secure, so never use it on any network that's less than trustworthy.

Check out the excellent Chapter 9 "Ports and Protocols" Challenge! over at http://totalsem .com/006. It'll help greatly in memorizing the port numbers that each protocol uses.

The best way to use FTP is to use a dedicated FTP client. So many good ones are available that I find myself using a different one all the time. FileZilla comes in a client version, but these days, I'm using an add-on to Firefox called FireFTP (Figure 9.31).

Active vs. Passive FTP

FTP has two ways to transfer data: *active* and *passive* FTP. Traditionally, FTP used the active process—let's see how this works. Remember that FTP uses TCP ports 20 and 21? Well, when your client sends an FTP request, it goes out on port 21. When your FTP server responds, however, it sends the data back using an ephemeral destination port and port 20 as a source port.

Active FTP works great unless your client uses NAT. Since your client didn't initiate the incoming port 20, your NAT router has no idea where to send this incoming packet. Additionally, any good firewall sees this incoming connection as something evil because it doesn't have anything inside the network that started the link on port 20. No problem! Good FTP clients all support passive FTP. With passive FTP, the server doesn't use port 20. Instead, the client sends an FTP request on port 21, just like active FTP. But then the server sends back a random port number, telling the client which port it's listening on for data requests. The client, in turn, sends data to the port specified by the FTP server. Because the client initiates all conversations, the NAT router knows where to send the packet.

The only trick to passive FTP is that the client needs to expect this other incoming data. When you configure an FTP client for passive, you're telling it to expect these packets.

Internet Applications

Use this table as a review tool to help you remember each Internet application:

Application	TCP/UDP	Port	Notes
HTTP	TCP	80	The Web
HTTPS	TCP	443	The Web, securely
Telnet	TCP	23	Terminal emulation
SSH	TCP	22	Secure terminal emulation
SMTP	TCP	25	Sending e-mail
POP3	TCP	110	E-mail delivery
IMAP4	TCP	143	E-mail delivery
FTP	TCP	20/21 (active) 21 (passive)	File transfer
TFTP	UDP	69	File transfer

Chapter 9 Review

Chapter Summary

After reading this chapter and completing the exercises, you should understand the following about the basics of TCP/IP.

Describe common Transport and Network layer protocols

- TCP/IP involves many more protocols other than just TCP over IP. HTTP, DHCP, POP, UDP, and ICMP are just a few of the hundreds of other protocols that operate over IP.

- Connections between computers are called sessions. If every communication requires an acknowledgment from the receiving computer, the session is said to be connection-oriented. Otherwise, the session is connectionless.

- TCP is a connection-oriented protocol, whereas UDP is connectionless. Most TCP/IP applications use TCP because connection-oriented sessions are designed to check for errors. If a receiving computer detects a missing packet, it just asks for a repeat as needed.

- ICMP works at Layer 3 to deliver connectionless packets. ICMP handles mundane issues such as disconnect messages (host unreachable) that applications use to let the other side of a session know what's happening.

- IGMP enables routers to forward multicast IP packets to IGMP groups.

Explain the power of port numbers

- Well-known port numbers fall within the range 0–1023. Web servers use port 80.

- Ephemeral port numbers fall within the range 1024–5000—the classic ephemeral ports—and 49152–65535—the dynamic or private ports. Most current operating systems use ports 49152–65535 for the ephemeral ports.

- Registered ports are those that have been registered with the Internet Assigned Numbers Authority and fall within the range 1024–49151.

- Information about a session is stored in RAM and is called a socket. The sockets stored by two computers in a session with each other are called socket pairs or endpoints.

- The netstat command-line utility, with the −n switch, is used to view a list of endpoints. It can't automatically update to display real-time information, however.

- An open port, or listening port, is a socket prepared to respond to incoming IP packets. You can type **netstat -an** to see all of your listening ports.

- You can use the netstat -ano command to identify which application is using a specific port, allowing you to identify malicious software.

- The netstat switches −a, −n, −b, and −o are important for any tech to know.

Define common TCP/IP applications, such as HTTP, HTTPS, Telnet, SSH, e-mail (SMTP, POP3, and IMAP4), and FTP

- HTTP stands for the Hypertext Transfer Protocol. HTTP uses port 80 to transmit the common data used in Web pages.

- To make Web pages available to the public, the Web pages must reside on a computer with Web server software installed and configured. Microsoft's Internet Information Services and Apache HTTP Server are the most common Web server software.

- A Web client is a program, such as a Web browser, that displays or reads Web pages.

- HTTPS stands for Hypertext Transfer Protocol over Secure Sockets Layer (SSL), which uses port 443. HTTPS protects sensitive data, like credit card numbers and personal information, by encrypting it.

- Telnet is a protocol that enables a user with the proper permissions to log onto a host computer, acting as a Telnet client. The user can then perform tasks on a remote computer, called a Telnet server, as if he or she were sitting at the remote computer itself.

- Telnet sends passwords and data in easily detected cleartext or plaintext, so most servers use Secure Shell (SSH) now.

- The term e-mail stands for electronic mail. E-mail is sent using the SMTP protocol on port 25 and is received using either POP3 (on port 110) or IMAP4 (on port 143).

- E-mail servers are needed to help forward, store, and retrieve e-mail messages for end users, who need a valid user name and password to gain access. E-mail can also contain attachments like pictures or small programs or data files.

- Sendmail is the leading e-mail server for Linux and UNIX, but it only supports SMTP. Exchange Server is the e-mail server software from Microsoft, and it supports both SMTP and POP.
- A mailbox is a storage area with an e-mail server that holds all the e-mail for a specific user.
- An e-mail client allows you to send, receive, and organize e-mail. Popular e-mail clients include Microsoft Outlook and Mozilla Thunderbird.
- FTP stands for File Transfer Protocol, which uses ports 20 and 21, and efficiently transmits large files.
- Active FTP uses both ports 20 and 21 and can be problematic if you are using NAT. The incoming connection from the server can appear to be unsolicited. This makes firewalls unhappy.
- Passive FTP uses only port 21 and works fine with NAT.
- Trivial FTP (TFTP) uses UDP port 69 and does not use user names or passwords, making it very insecure.
- A good network tech knows the port numbers for popular Internet applications and protocols such as HTTP, Telnet, SSH, SMTP, POP3, IMAP4, FTP, and TFTP.

Key Terms

Apache HTTP Server (237)
connection (228)
connectionless (223)
connection-oriented (223)
dynamic port numbers (227)
electronic mail (e-mail) (243)
e-mail client (246)
endpoint (228)
endpoints (228)
ephemeral port number (227)
File Transfer Protocol (FTP) (247)
Hypertext Transfer Protocol (HTTP) (235)
Hypertext Transfer Protocol over SSL (HTTPS) (238)
Internet Control Message Protocol (ICMP) (225)
Internet Group Management Protocol (IGMP) (225)
Internet Information Services (IIS) (236)
Internet Message Access Protocol version 4 (IMAP4) (243)
listening port (230)
mailbox (246)
netstat (228)

open port (230)
Post Office Protocol version 3 (POP3) (243)
private port number (227)
registered port (228)
Secure Shell (SSH) (240)
Secure Sockets Layer (SSL) (238)
sendmail (244)
session (223)
Simple Mail Transfer Protocol (SMTP) (243)
socket (228)
socket pairs (228)
TCP/IP suite (223)
TCP three-way handshake (224)
Telnet (240)
Transport Layer Security (TLS) (238)
Transmission Control Protocol (TCP) (223)
Trivial File Transfer Protocol (TFTP) (225)
unsecure protocol (238)
User Datagram Protocol (UDP) (224)
Web services (244)
well-known port number (226)

Key Term Quiz

Use the Key Terms list to complete the sentences that follow. Not all terms will be used.

1. A TCP port number that falls in the range of 0–1023 is called a(n) _____.

2. A TCP port number within the range of 1024–49151 is called a(n) _____.

3. The protocol used to transmit large files over the Web using both ports 20 and 21 is called _____.

4. The protocol that is much more popular than POP3 for receiving e-mail is _____.

5. Port 23 is used by _____ to emulate terminals on TCP/IP networks.

6. When you send out an e-mail message it uses the _____.

7. The quickest way to send information about an upcoming meeting to a few co-workers would be to send a(n) _____.

8. The _____ utility can be used to view the endpoints of your computer's sessions.

9. Telnet has largely been replaced by _____, which provides better security through data encryption.

10. TCP is _____ in that it requires computers to acknowledge each other, whereas UDP is _____ in that it provides no guarantee packets were successfully received.

■ Multiple-Choice Quiz

1. What port number is the well-known port used by Web servers to distribute Web pages to Web browsers?

  A. Port 20

  B. Port 21

  C. Port 25

  D. Port 80

2. What protocol handles large file transfers between Internet users?

  A. FTP

  B. IMAP

  C. POP3

  D. SMTP

3. How can you tell that a secure Web page transaction is taking place?

  A. The URL in the address bar starts with https.

  B. The URL in the address bar starts with http/ssl.

  C. The URL in the address bar starts with ssl.

  D. The URL in the address bar starts with tls.

4. Jane has been tasked to find and implement an application that will enable her boss to log into and control a server remotely and securely. Which of the following applications would work best?

  A. E-mail

  B. FTP

  C. Telnet

  D. SSH

5. SSH uses which port?

  A. TCP port 22

  B. TCP port 23

  C. UDP port 22

  D. UDP port 23

6. What is the session information—IP address and port number—stored in RAM called? (Select two.)

  A. Endpoint

  B. Port

  C. Session

  D. Socket

7. Which of the following are names of Web server software? (Select two.)

  A. Apache

  B. Exchange

  C. IIS

  D. Proxy server

8. Which of the following are names of Internet browser software? (Select two.)

  A. Internet Surfware

  B. Internet Explorer

  C. Firefox

  D. WS_FTP

9. Which of the following items does the *S* in HTTPS represent?

  A. Proxy server

  B. Secure Sockets Layer

  C. Subnet mask

  D. Switch

10. When using Windows, which command will show all used ports and the IP addresses using them?

  A. `telnet localhost 25`

  B. `telnet -ano`

  C. `netstat -an`

  D. `netstat -ao`

11. What is the main difference between TCP and UDP?

  A. TCP is connection-oriented, whereas UDP is connectionless.

  B. TCP supports HTTPS, whereas UDP supports SSL.

  C. TCP sessions can be encrypted, whereas UDP sessions cannot.

  D. TCP is used on Windows, whereas UDP is used on Linux/UNIX/OS X.

12. Which connectionless protocol handles chores such as disconnect messages?

    A. TCP

    B. UDP

    C. ICMP

    D. IGMP

13. John says he's concerned that open ports on the server make it vulnerable to attacks. What does he mean by "open ports"?

    A. An "open port" is a socket prepared to respond to any IP packets destined for that socket's port number.

    B. An "open port" is a socket prepared to respond to any IP packets on the network.

    C. An "open port" is a socket prepared to respond to any IP packets destined for an "open" command on port 80.

    D. An "open port" is a socket unavailable to respond to any IP packets destined for that socket's port number.

14. Which port does SMTP use?

    A. TCP port 22

    B. TCP port 25

    C. TCP port 80

    D. UDP port 81

15. What should you do if you are having difficulty transferring files with your FTP client when your router supports NAT?

    A. Configure your FTP client to use active FTP.

    B. Configure your FTP client to use passive FTP.

    C. Use SSH to transfer your files instead.

    D. Use Telnet to connect to the server and then use netstat to transfer the files.

■ Essay Quiz

1. Your company is interested in setting up secure Web pages for credit card transactions. The company currently does have a Web presence. Write two short paragraphs describing the two different port numbers that would be used on the company's improved Web site.

2. After checking various e-mail settings, a colleague of yours mentions port numbers. Write down some quick notes about which TCP ports would handle e-mail.

3. Write down a few notes explaining why some Web pages have an extra *s* after the http in their Web addresses. Be prepared to discuss your findings in class.

4. Write a paragraph that describes what a Web server does. Write a second paragraph that describes what an e-mail server does.

Lab Projects

• Lab Project 9.1

Start some Internet programs, such as a Web browser, an e-mail or FTP client, or an instant messenger. Open a command prompt and type `netstat -ano` or `netstat -b`. Make a list of the well-known ports in use and the process ID using the port. Then write the actual name of the application identified by the process ID. Linux users can type `ps` to learn the application name of a process ID, but Windows users have to use a third-party tool like Process Explorer.

• Lab Project 9.2

Using a word processing program or a spreadsheet program, create a chart that lists all the port numbers mentioned in this chapter, similar to the following list in the leftmost column. Use the Internet to look up other commonly used port numbers as well.

Fill in the Abbreviation column, the Full Name column, and the Brief Description column. Repeat this lab exercise several times until you have memorized it fully. This activity will help you pass the CompTIA Network+ exam!

Port #	Abbreviation	Full Name	Brief Description of What This Port Does...
20			
21			
22			
23			
25			
80			
110			
143			
443			

Network Naming

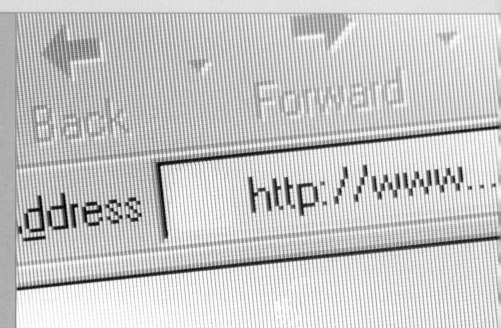

*What's in a name? That which
we call a rose
By any other name would smell
as sweet.*

—WILLIAM SHAKESPEARE

**In this chapter, you will learn
how to**

- Analyze and configure early
  name resolution solutions
- Describe the function and
  capabilities of DNS
- Use common TCP/IP utilities to
  diagnose problems with DNS

Did the last chapter seem a bit IP-address-heavy to you, compared to
your daily use of the Internet? When you open a Web page, for example,
do you type something like http://192.168.4.1, or do you type something
like www.totalsem.com? Odds are good you normally do the latter and only
rarely the former. Why do we use names when every resource on a TCP/IP
network is really an IP address? It's due to the fact that people are terrible at
memorizing numbers, but are pretty good at memorizing words. This creates
an interesting dilemma.

Although computers use IP addresses to communicate with each other over
a TCP/IP network, people prefer easy-to-remember names over IP addresses.
To solve this problem, long ago, even before TCP/IP and the Internet took
over, network developers created a process called **name resolution** that
automatically converts computer names to IP addresses (and *vice versa*) to
make it easier for people to communicate with computers (Figure 10.1).

Like any process that's been around for a long time, name resolution has
evolved over the years. Entire TCP/IP applications have been written, only
to be supplanted (but never totally abandoned) by newer name resolution
protocols.

Today, we use a name resolution protocol called **Domain Name System (DNS)**. DNS is a powerful, extensible, flexible system that supports name resolution on tiny in-house networks, as well as the entire Internet. Most of this chapter covers DNS, but be warned: your brand-new system, running the latest version of whatever operating system you prefer, still fully supports a number of older name resolution protocols that predate DNS. This makes name resolution in contemporary networks akin to a well-run house that's also full of ghosts; ghosts that can do very strange things if you don't understand how those ghosts think.

In this chapter, you'll take an in-depth tour of name resolution, starting with a discussion of two precursors to DNS: Microsoft's ancient NetBIOS/NetBEUI protocol and the infamous hosts file. We will then turn to DNS, learning how it works, and how DNS servers and clients are used today.

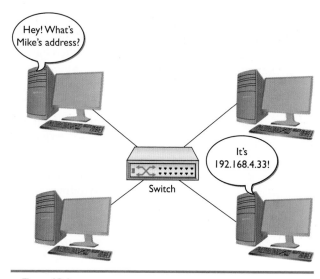

• **Figure 10.1** Turning names into numbers

Odds are good you have a system that is connected—or at least can connect—to the Internet. If I were you, I'd fire up that system and use it while you read this chapter. The vast majority of the programs you're going to learn about here come free with every operating system.

Test Specific

Before DNS

Early name resolution solutions offered simple but effective network naming. Surprisingly, these solutions continue to work in modern systems. Let's look at NetBIOS/NetBEUI first, and then explore hosts files.

NetBIOS/NetBEUI

Even though TCP/IP was available back in the 1980s, Microsoft developed and popularized a light and efficient networking protocol called **NetBIOS/NetBEUI**. It had a very simple naming convention (the NetBIOS part) that used broadcasts for name resolution. When a computer booted up, it broadcast its name (Figure 10.2) along with its MAC address. Every other NetBIOS/NetBEUI system heard the message and stored the information in a cache. Any time a system was missing a NetBIOS name, the broadcasting started all over again.

• **Figure 10.2** NetBIOS broadcast

For two reasons, NetBIOS/NetBEUI was suitable only for small networks. First, it provided no logical addressing like IP addresses; each system had to remember the NetBIOS name and the MAC address. Without a logical address, there was no way to support routing. Second, all of the broadcasting made it unacceptable for large networks.

But NetBIOS/NetBEUI wasn't invented for use in large networks. NetBIOS/NetBEUI was almost exclusively used to share folders and printers. There was no such thing as Telnet, e-mail, Minecraft, or the Web with NetBIOS/NetBEUI, but it worked well for what it did at the time.

Getting NetBIOS to play nicely with TCP/IP requires proper protocols. NetBIOS over TCP/IP uses TCP ports 137 and 139, and UDP ports 137 and 138.

By the mid-1990s, Microsoft realized the world was going with TCP/IP and DNS, and it needed to switch too. The problem was that there was a massive installed base of Windows networks that needed NetBIOS/NetBEUI.

Microsoft designed a new TCP/IP protocol that enabled it to keep using the NetBIOS names but dump the NetBEUI protocol. The new protocol, **NetBIOS over TCP/IP (NetBT)**, runs NetBIOS on top of TCP/IP. In essence, Microsoft created its own name resolution protocol that had nothing to do with DNS.

NetBT made things weird on Windows systems. Windows systems used NetBT names for local network jobs such as accessing shared printers or folders, but they also used DNS for everything else. It basically meant that every Windows computer had one name used on the local network—like MIKES-PC—and a DNS name for use on the Internet.

To be more accurate, NetBIOS/NetBEUI didn't actually do any of the resource sharing. Microsoft used another protocol called Server Message Block (SMB) that ran on top of NetBT to support sharing folders and files. SMB used NetBIOS names to support the sharing and access process. SMB isn't dependent on NetBIOS and today runs by itself using TCP port 445.

Try This!

Checking Out NetBIOS

Grab a handy Windows or Linux system and try running `netstat -a -n`. Can you find open or listening ports on port numbers 137, 138, 139, and 445? If you have a Windows system, you will see these. Systems listening on those ports show NetBT and SMB running just fine.

hosts

When the Internet was very young and populated with only a few hundred computers, name resolution was pretty simple. The original TCP/IP specification implemented name resolution using a special text file called hosts. A copy of this file was stored on every computer system on the Internet. The **hosts file** contained a list of IP addresses for every computer on the Internet, matched to the corresponding system names.

Remember, not only was the Internet a lot smaller then, but also there weren't yet rules about how to compose Internet names, such as that they must end in .com or .org, or start with www or ftp. Anyone could name their computer pretty much anything they wanted (there were a few restrictions on length and allowable characters) as long as nobody else had snagged the name first. Part of an old hosts file might look something like this:

```
192.168.2.1      fred
201.32.16.4      school2
23.54.122.103    bobs computer and feed store
123.21.44.16     server
```

If your system wanted to access the system called fred, it looked up the name fred in its hosts file and then used the corresponding IP address to contact fred. Every hosts file on every system on the Internet was updated every morning at 2 A.M.

This worked fine when the Internet was still the province of a few university geeks and some military guys, but when the Internet grew to about 5000 systems, it became impractical to make every system use and update a hosts file. This created the motivation for a more scalable name resolution process, but the hosts file did not go away.

Believe it or not, the hosts file is still alive and well in every computer. You can find the hosts file in \Windows\System32\Drivers\Etc in Windows 7/8/10.

On OS X and Linux systems, you usually find hosts in the /etc folder.

The hosts file is just a text file that you can open with any text editor. Here are a few lines from the default hosts file that comes with Windows:

```
# Additionally, comments (such as these) may be inserted on individual
# lines or following the machine name denoted by a '#' symbol.
#
# For example:
#
#          102.54.94.97    rhino.acme.com   # source server
#          38.25.63.10     x.acme.com  #     x client host
127.0.0.1           localhost
```

See the # signs? Those are remark symbols that designate lines as comments (for humans to read) rather than code. Windows ignores any line that begins with #. Remove the # and Windows will read the line and try to act on it. Although all operating systems continue to support the hosts file, it is rarely used in the day-to-day workings of most TCP/IP systems.

Even though the hosts file is rarely used, *every* operating system always looks first in the hosts file before anything else when attempting to resolve a name. To see the power of the hosts file, do the first Try This! sidebar in this chapter.

The Try This! sidebar example uses a Web browser, but keep in mind that a name in a hosts file resolves names for *every* TCP/IP application on that system. Go to a command prompt and type ping timmy. It works for ping too.

The Internet stopped using hosts files and replaced them with the vastly more powerful DNS. The hosts file still has a place today. Some folks place shortcut names in a hosts file to avoid typing long names in certain TCP/IP applications. It's also used by some of the more nerdy types as a tool to block adware/malware. There are a number of people who make hosts files you can copy and place into your own hosts file. Do a Google search for **"hosts file replacement"** and try a few.

 Try This!

Editing the hosts File

Every Windows computer has a hosts file that you can edit, so try this!

1. Go to a command prompt and type **ping www.totalsem.com**. You may or may not be successful with the ping utility, but you will get the IP address for my Web site. (You may get a different IP address from the one shown in this example.)

```
C:\>ping www.totalsem.com
Pinging www.totalsem.com [209.29.33.25] with 32 bytes of
data:
Reply from 209.29.33.25: bytes=32 time=60ms TTL=51
Reply from 209.29.33.25: bytes=32 time=60ms TTL=51
Reply from 209.29.33.25: bytes=32 time=60ms TTL=51
Reply from 209.29.33.25: bytes=32 time=60ms TTL=51
Ping statistics for 209.29.33.25:
    Packets: Sent = 4, Received = 4, Lost = 0 (0% loss),
Approximate round trip times in milli-seconds:
    Minimum = 60ms, Maximum = 60ms, Average = 60ms
```

2. Open your hosts file using any text editor and add this line (keep in mind you may have a different IP address from the one shown in this example). Just press the SPACEBAR a few times to separate the IP address from the word "timmy."

```
209.29.33.25  timmy
```

3. Save the hosts file and close the text editor.

4. Open your Web browser and type **timmy**. You can also type **http://timmy** if you'd like. What happens?

DNS

When the Internet folks decided to dump the hosts file for name resolution and replace it with something better, they needed a flexible naming system that worked across cultures, time zones, and different sizes of networks. They needed something that was responsive to thousands, millions, even billions of requests. They implemented DNS to solve these problems. This section looks at how DNS works, then examines the servers that make the magic happen. DNS wraps up with troubleshooting scenarios.

How DNS Works

So they fell back on that time-tested bureaucratic solution: delegation! The top-dog DNS system would delegate parts of the job to subsidiary DNS systems that, in turn, would delegate part of their work to other systems, and so on, potentially without end. These systems run a special DNS server program and are called, amazingly enough, **DNS servers**.

This is all peachy, but it raises another issue: they needed some way to decide how to divvy up the work. Toward this end, the Internet folks created a naming system designed to facilitate delegation. The top-dog DNS server is actually a bunch of powerful computers dispersed around the world. They work as a team and are known collectively as the **DNS root servers** (or simply as the *DNS root*). The Internet name of this computer team is "."—that's right, just "dot." Sure, it's weird, but it's quick to type, and they had to start somewhere.

DNS root has the complete definitive name resolution table, but most name resolution work is delegated to other DNS servers. Just below the DNS root in the hierarchy is a set of DNS servers—called the **top-level domain servers**—that handle what are known as the *top-level domain (TLD) names*. These are the famous com, org, net, edu, gov, mil, and int names (although many TLDs have been added since 2001). The top-level DNS servers delegate to thousands of second-level DNS servers; these servers handle the millions of names like totalsem.com and whitehouse.gov that have been created within each of the top-level domains. Second-level DNS servers support individual computers. For example, stored on the DNS server controlling the totalsem.com domain is a listing that looks like this:

```
www   209.29.33.25
```

This means the totalsem.com domain has a computer called *www* with the IP address of 209.29.33.25. Only the DNS server controlling the totalsem.com domain stores the actual IP address for *www*.totalsem.com. The DNS servers above this one have a hierarchical system that enables any other computer to find the DNS server that controls the totalsem.com domain.

Name Spaces

What does *hierarchical* mean in terms of DNS? Well, the DNS **hierarchical name space** is an imaginary tree structure of all possible names that could be used within a single system. By contrast, a hosts file uses a **flat name space**—basically just one big undivided list containing all names, with no grouping whatsoever. In a flat name space, all names must be absolutely unique—no two machines can ever share the same name under any circumstances. A flat name space

DNS servers primarily use UDP port 53 and sometimes TCP port 53.

The DNS root for the entire Internet consists of 13 powerful DNS server clusters scattered all over the world. Go to www.root-servers.org to see exactly where all the root servers are located.

The original top-level domain names were com, org, net, edu, gov, mil, and int.

The *Internet Corporation for Assigned Names and Numbers (ICANN)* has the authority to create new TLDs. Since 2001, they've added many TLDs, such as biz for businesses, info for informational sites, and pro for accountants, engineers, lawyers, and physicians in several Western countries.

Tech Tip

Going Beyond Three-Tier Names

The Internet DNS names are usually consistent with this three-tier system, but if you want to add your own DNS server(s), you can add more levels, allowing you to name a computer www.houston.totalsem.com if you wish. The only limit is that a DNS name can have a maximum of only 255 characters.

works fine on a small, isolated network, but not so well for a large organization with many interconnected networks. To avoid naming conflicts, all its administrators would need to keep track of all the names used throughout the entire corporate network.

A hierarchical name space offers a better solution, permitting a great deal more flexibility by enabling administrators to give networked systems longer, more fully descriptive names. The personal names people use every day are an example of a hierarchical name space. Most people address our town postman, Ron Samuels, simply as Ron. When his name comes up in conversation, people usually refer to him as Ron. The town troublemaker, Ron Falwell, and Mayor Jones's son, Ron, who went off to Toledo, obviously share first names with the postman.

In some conversations, people need to distinguish between the good Ron, the bad Ron, and the Ron in Toledo (who may or may not be the ugly Ron). They could use a medieval style of address and refer to the Rons as Ron the Postman, Ron the Blackguard, and Ron of Toledo, or they could use the modern Western style of address and add their surnames: "That Ron Samuels—he is such a card!" "That Ron Falwell is one bad apple." "That Ron Jones was the homeliest child I ever saw." You might visualize this as the People name space, illustrated in Figure 10.3. Adding the surname creates what you might fancifully call a *Fully Qualified Person Name*—enough information to prevent confusion among the various people named Ron.

A name space most of you are already familiar with is the hierarchical file name space used by hard drive volumes. Hard drives formatted using one of the popular file formats, like Windows' NTFS or Linux's ext3, use a hierarchical name space; you can create as many files named data.txt as you want, as long as you store them in different parts of the file tree.

In the example shown in Figure 10.4, two different files named data.txt can exist simultaneously on the same system, but only if they are placed in different directories, such as C:\Program1\Current\data.txt and C:\Program1\Backup\data.txt. Although both files have the same basic filename—data.txt—their fully qualified names are different: C:\Program1\Current\data.txt and C:\Program1\Backup\data.txt. Additionally, multiple subfolders can use the same name. Having two subfolders that use the name data is no problem, as long as they reside in different folders. Any Windows file system will happily let you create both C:\Program1\Data and C:\Program2\Data folders. Folks like this because they often want to give the same name to multiple folders doing the same job for different applications.

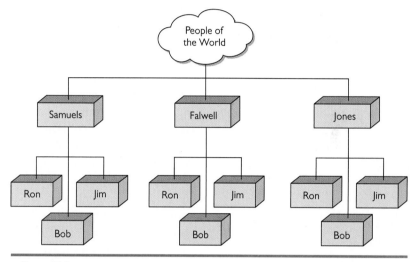

• **Figure 10.3** Our People name space

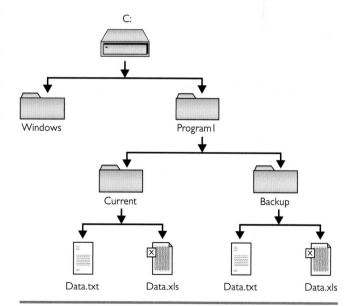

• **Figure 10.4** Two data.txt files in different directories on the same system

As hard as this may be to believe, some early file systems used a flat name space. Back in the late 1970s and early 1980s, operating systems such as CP/M and the early versions of DOS did not have the capability to use directories, creating a flat name space where all files resided on a single drive.

In contrast, imagine what would happen if your computer's file system didn't support folders/directories. Windows would have to store all the files on your hard drive in the root directory! This is a classic example of a flat name space. Because all your files would be living together in one directory, each one would have to have a unique name. Naming files would be a nightmare! Software vendors would have to avoid sensible descriptive names like *readme.txt* because they would almost certainly have been used already. You'd probably have to do what the Internet does for IP addresses: An organization of some sort would assign names out of the limited pool of possible filenames. With a hierarchical name space, on the other hand, which is what all file systems use (thank goodness!), naming is much simpler. Lots of programs can have files called readme.txt because each program can have its own folder and subfolders.

The DNS name space works in a manner extremely similar to how your computer's file system works. The DNS name space is a hierarchy of *DNS domains* and individual computer names organized into a tree-like structure that is called, rather appropriately, a *tree*. Each domain is like a folder—a domain is not a single computer, but rather a holding space into which you can add computer names.

At the top of a **DNS tree** is the root. The *root* is the holding area to which all domains connect, just as the root directory in your file system is the holding area for all your folders. Individual computer names—more commonly called **host names** in the DNS naming convention—fit into domains. In the PC, you can place files directly into the root directory. DNS also enables us to add computer names to the root, but with the exception of a few special computers (described in a moment), this is rarely done.

Even though you may use uppercase or lowercase, DNS does not differentiate between them.

Each domain can have subdomains, just as the folders on your PC's file system can have subfolders. You separate each domain from its subdomains with a period. Characters for DNS domain names and host names are limited to uppercase and lowercase letters (A–Z, a–z), numbers (0–9), and the hyphen (-). No other characters may be used.

Don't think DNS is only for computers on the Internet. If you want to make your own little TCP/IP network using DNS, that's fine, although you will have to set up at least one DNS server as the root for your little private *intranet*. Every DNS server program can be configured as a root; just don't connect that DNS server to the Internet because it won't work outside your little network. Figure 10.5 shows a sample DNS tree for a small TCP/IP network that is not attached to the Internet. In this case, there is only one domain: ABCDEF. Each computer on the network has a host name, as shown in the figure.

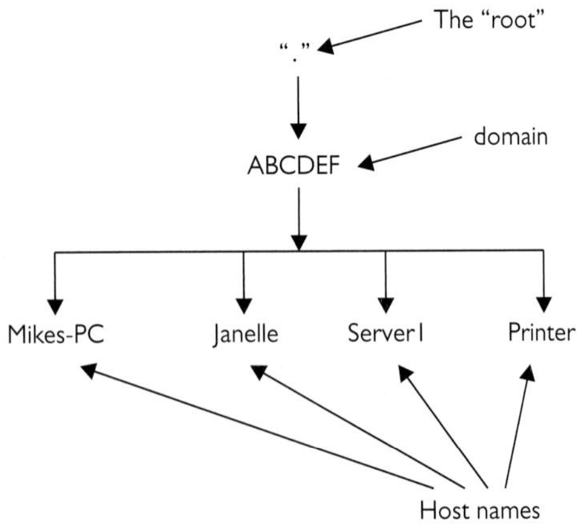

• **Figure 10.5** Private DNS network

When you write out the complete path to a file stored on your PC, the naming convention starts with the root directory on the left, followed by the first folder, then any subfolders (in order), and finally the name of the file—for example, C:\Sounds\Thunder\mynewcobra.wav.

The DNS naming convention is *exactly the opposite*. A complete DNS name, including the host name and all of its domains (in order), is called a **fully qualified domain name (FQDN)**, and it's written with the root on the far right, followed by the names of the domains (in order) added to the left of the root, and the host name on the far left. Figure 10.5 shows the

FQDNs for two systems in the ABCDEF domain. Note the period for the root is on the far *right* of each FQDN!

> Mikes-PC.ABCDEF.
> Janelle.ABCDEF.

Given that every FQDN will always have a period on the end to signify the root, it is commonplace to drop the final period when writing out FQDNs. To make the two example FQDNs fit into common parlance, therefore, you'd skip the last period:

> Mikes-PC.ABCDEF Janelle.ABCDEF

If you're used to seeing DNS names on the Internet, you're probably wondering about the lack of ".com," ".net," or other common DNS domain names. Those conventions are needed for computers that are visible on the Internet, such as Web servers, but they're not required on a private TCP/IP network. As long as you make a point never to make these computers visible on the Internet, you can use any naming convention you want.

Let's look at another DNS name space example, but make it a bit more complex. This network is not on the Internet, so I can use any domain I want. The network has two domains, Houston and Dallas, as shown in Figure 10.6. Note that each domain has a computer called Server1.

Because the network has two different domains, it can have two systems (one on each domain) with the same host name, just as you can have two files with the same name in different folders on your PC. Now, let's add some subdomains to the DNS tree, so that it looks like Figure 10.7.

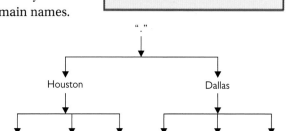

• **Figure 10.6** Two DNS domains

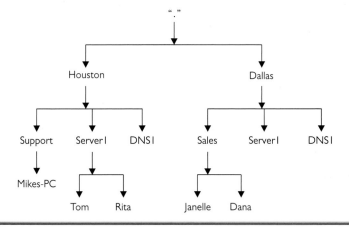

• **Figure 10.7** Subdomains added

You write out the FQDN from left to right, starting with the host name and moving up to the top of the DNS tree, adding all domains until you get to the top of the DNS tree:

> Mikes-PC.Support.Houston
> Tom.Server1.Houston
> Janelle.Sales.Dallas
> Server1.Dallas

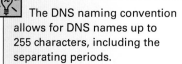

The DNS naming convention allows for DNS names up to 255 characters, including the separating periods.

Name Servers

So where does this naming convention reside and how does it work? The power of DNS comes from its incredible flexibility. DNS works as well on a small, private network as it does on the biggest network of all time—the Internet. Let's start with three key players:

- **DNS server** A *DNS server* is a computer running DNS server software.

- **Zone** A *zone* is a container for a single domain that gets filled with records.

- **Record** A *record* is a line in the zone data that maps an FQDN to an IP address.

Systems running DNS server software store the DNS information. When a system needs to know the IP address for a specific FQDN, it queries the DNS server listed in its TCP/IP configuration. Assuming the DNS server stores the zone for that particular FQDN, it replies with the computer's IP address.

A simple network usually has one DNS server for the entire network. This DNS server has a single zone that lists all the host names on the domain and their corresponding IP addresses. It's known as the authoritative name server for the domain.

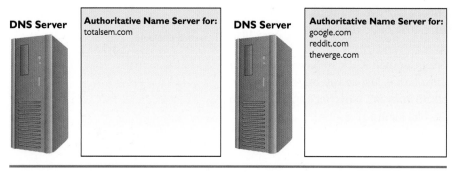

• **Figure 10.8** A single authoritative name server can support one or more domains.

If you've got a powerful computer, you can put lots of zones on a single DNS server and let that server support them all without a problem. A single DNS server, therefore, can act as the authoritative name server for one domain or many domains (Figure 10.8).

On the opposite end of the spectrum, a single domain can use more than one DNS server. Imagine how busy the google.com domain is—it needs lots of DNS servers to support all the incoming DNS queries. In this case a single DNS domain will still have a single authoritative name server but a number of other DNS servers, known simply as name servers, that are subordinate to the authoritative name server but all support the same domain, as shown in Figure 10.9.

If you have a lot of DNS servers all supporting the same domain, they need to be able to talk to each other frequently. If one DNS server gets a new record, that record must propagate to all the name servers on the domain. To support this, every DNS server in the domain knows the name and address

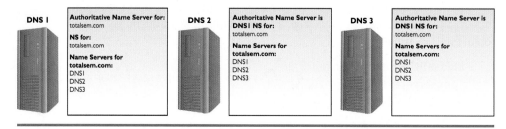

• **Figure 10.9** DNS flexibility

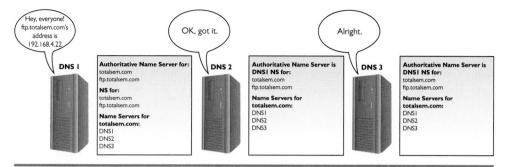

● **Figure 10.10**   New information passed out

of the authoritative name server as well as the name and address of every other name server in the domain. The authoritative name server's job is to make sure that all the other name servers are updated for changes. Let's say you add to the totalsem.com domain a new computer called ftp.totalsem.com with the IP address 192.168.4.22. As an administrator, you typically add this data to the authoritative name server. The authoritative name server then automatically distributes this information to the other name servers in the domain (Figure 10.10). This DNS feature is critical—you'll see more of this in detail later on in the "DNS Servers" section in this chapter. For now, appreciate that you can have multiple DNS servers for a single domain.

Now let's see how root servers work in DNS. What if Mikes-PC.Support.Houston needs the IP address of Server1.Dallas? Refer to Figure 10.11 for the answer. The network has two DNS servers: DNS1.Houston and DNS1.Dallas. DNS1.Dallas is the **authoritative DNS server** for the Dallas domain and DNS1.Houston is in charge of the Houston domain.

DNS1.Houston is also the root server for the entire network. As a root server, the Houston server has a listing for the authoritative name server in the Dallas domain. This does *not* mean it knows the IP address for every system in the Dallas network. As a root server, it only knows that if any system asks for an IP address from the Dallas side, it will tell that system the IP address of the Dallas server. The requesting system will then ask the Dallas DNS server (DNS1.Dallas) for the IP address of the system it needs. That's the beauty of DNS root servers—they don't know the IP addresses for all of the computers, but they know where to send the requests!

The hierarchical aspect of DNS has a number of benefits. For example, the vast majority of Web servers are called www. If DNS used a flat name space, only the first organization that created a server with the name www could use it. Because DNS naming appends domain names to the server names, however, the servers www.totalsem.com and www.microsoft.com can both exist simultaneously. DNS names like www.microsoft.com must fit within a worldwide hierarchical name space, meaning that no two machines should ever have the same FQDN.

● **Figure 10.11**   Root server in action

> In the early days of DNS, you had to enter manually into your DNS server the host name and IP address of every system on the network. See "Dynamic DNS," later in this chapter, for the way it's done today.

> Just because most Web servers are named www doesn't mean they must be named www! Naming a Web server www is etiquette, not a requirement.

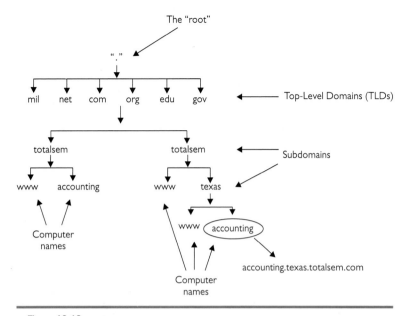

• **Figure 10.12** DNS domain

Technically, the texas.totalsem.com domain shown in Figure 10.12 is a subdomain of totalsem.com. Don't be surprised to see the terms "domain" and "subdomain" used interchangeably, as it's a common practice.

Figure 10.12 shows the host named accounting with an FQDN of accounting. texas.totalsem.com.

These domain names must be registered for Internet use with ICANN (www .icann.org). They are arranged in the familiar "second level.top level" domain name format, where the top level is com, org, net, and so on, and the second level is the name of the individual entity registering the domain name.

Name Resolution

In the early years of the Internet, DNS worked interchangeably with IP addressing. You could surf to a Web site, in other words, by typing in the FQDN or the IP address of the Web server. Figure 10.13 shows a browser accessing the awesome tech site AnandTech by IP address rather than by typing www.anandtech.com.

Modern Web sites don't really function well without DNS. The Web server that houses my company's domain name, for example, also hosts a dozen or more domain names. If you try to access my Web site by IP address, the Web server won't know what to do!

• **Figure 10.13** Accessing a Web site via IP address rather than name

You'll still find this 1:1 correlation of DNS name to IP address with simpler devices like IP security cameras. These are cameras with an Ethernet connection, a public IP address, and a built-in interface for viewing and control.

Once you get into how computers communicate on the Web, name resolution becomes an integral part of the process. When you type in a Web address, your browser must resolve that name to the Web server's IP address to make a connection to that Web server. It can resolve the name in three ways: by broadcasting, by consulting the locally stored hosts text file, or by contacting a DNS server.

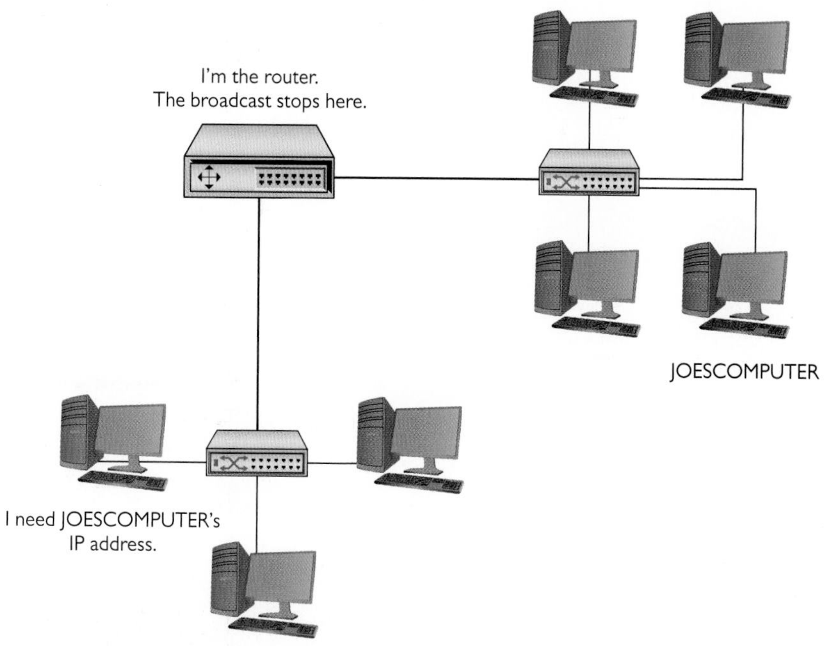

To *broadcast* for name resolution, the host sends a message to all the machines on the network, saying something like, "Hey! If your name is JOESCOMPUTER, please respond with your IP address." All the networked hosts receive that packet, but only JOESCOMPUTER responds with an IP address. Broadcasting works fine for small networks, but it is limited because it cannot provide name resolution across routers. Routers do not forward broadcast messages to other networks, as illustrated in Figure 10.14.

I'm the router.
The broadcast stops here.

JOESCOMPUTER

I need JOESCOMPUTER's IP address.

• **Figure 10.14** Routers don't forward broadcasts!

As discussed earlier, a hosts file functions like a little black book, listing the names and addresses of machines on a network, just like a little black book lists the names and phone numbers of people. A typical hosts file would look like this:

```
109.54.94.197      stephen.totalsem.com
138.125.163.17     roger.totalsem.com
127.0.0.1          localhost
```

Notice that the name `localhost` appears in the hosts file as an alias for the loopback address, 127.0.0.1.

The final way to resolve a name to an IP address is to use DNS. Let's say you type **www.microsoft.com** in your Web browser. To resolve the name www .microsoft.com, the host contacts its DNS server and requests the IP address, as shown in Figure 10.15.

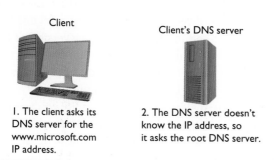

Client

Client's DNS server

1. The client asks its DNS server for the www.microsoft.com IP address.

2. The DNS server doesn't know the IP address, so it asks the root DNS server.

• **Figure 10.15** A host contacts its local DNS server.

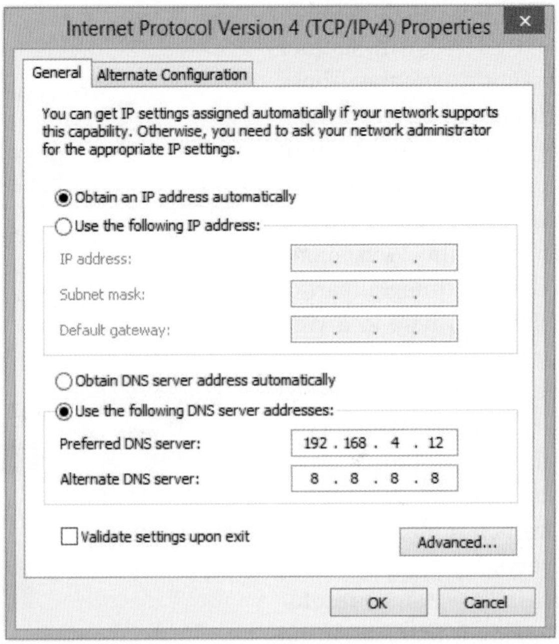

• **Figure 10.16**   DNS information in Windows

• **Figure 10.17**   Entering DNS information in Ubuntu

To request the IP address of www.microsoft .com, your PC needs the IP address of its DNS server. You must enter DNS information into your system. DNS server data is part of the critical basic IP information such as your IP address, subnet mask, and default gateway, so you usually enter it at the same time as the other IP information. You configure DNS in Windows Vista/7/8/10 using the Internet Protocol Version 4 (TCP/IPv4) Properties dialog box. Figure 10.16 shows the DNS settings for my system. Note that I have more than one DNS server setting; the second one is a backup in case the first one isn't working. Two DNS settings is not a rule, however, so don't worry if your system shows only one DNS server setting, or perhaps more than two.

Every operating system has a way for you to enter DNS server information. In Linux, you can directly edit the /etc/resolv.conf file using a text editor. Just about every version of Linux has some form of graphical editor as well to make this an easy process. Figure 10.17 shows Ubuntu's Network Configuration utility.

Every operating system also comes with a utility you can use to verify the DNS server settings. The tool in Windows, for example, is called **ipconfig**. You can see your current DNS server settings in Windows by typing **ipconfig / all** at the command prompt (Figure 10.18). In UNIX/Linux, type the following: **cat /etc/resolv.conf**.

Remember, the `ipconfig` command gives you a ton of useful IP information.

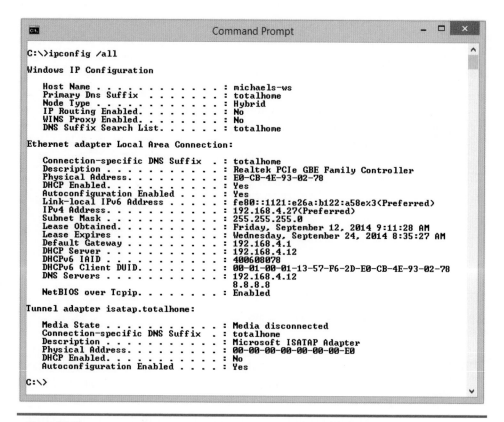

```
Command Prompt                                    _  □  ×

C:\>ipconfig /all

Windows IP Configuration

   Host Name . . . . . . . . . . . . : michaels-ws
   Primary Dns Suffix  . . . . . . . : totalhome
   Node Type . . . . . . . . . . . . : Hybrid
   IP Routing Enabled. . . . . . . . : No
   WINS Proxy Enabled. . . . . . . . : No
   DNS Suffix Search List. . . . . . : totalhome

Ethernet adapter Local Area Connection:

   Connection-specific DNS Suffix  . : totalhome
   Description . . . . . . . . . . . : Realtek PCIe GBE Family Controller
   Physical Address. . . . . . . . . : E0-CB-4E-93-02-78
   DHCP Enabled. . . . . . . . . . . : Yes
   Autoconfiguration Enabled . . . . : Yes
   Link-local IPv6 Address . . . . . : fe80::1121:e26a:b122:a58e%3(Preferred)
   IPv4 Address. . . . . . . . . . . : 192.168.4.27(Preferred)
   Subnet Mask . . . . . . . . . . . : 255.255.255.0
   Lease Obtained. . . . . . . . . . : Friday, September 12, 2014 9:11:28 AM
   Lease Expires . . . . . . . . . . : Wednesday, September 24, 2014 8:35:27 AM
   Default Gateway . . . . . . . . . : 192.168.4.1
   DHCP Server . . . . . . . . . . . : 192.168.4.12
   DHCPv6 IAID . . . . . . . . . . . : 400608078
   DHCPv6 Client DUID. . . . . . . . : 00-01-00-01-13-57-F6-2D-E0-CB-4E-93-02-78
   DNS Servers . . . . . . . . . . . : 192.168.4.12
                                       8.8.8.8
   NetBIOS over Tcpip. . . . . . . . : Enabled

Tunnel adapter isatap.totalhome:

   Media State . . . . . . . . . . . : Media disconnected
   Connection-specific DNS Suffix  . : totalhome
   Description . . . . . . . . . . . : Microsoft ISATAP Adapter
   Physical Address. . . . . . . . . : 00-00-00-00-00-00-00-E0
   DHCP Enabled. . . . . . . . . . . : No
   Autoconfiguration Enabled . . . . : Yes

C:\>
```

• **Figure 10.18**   The `ipconfig /all` command showing DNS information in Windows

Now that you understand how your system knows the DNS server's IP address, let's return to the DNS process.

The DNS server receives the request for the IP address of www.microsoft .com from your client computer. At this point, your DNS server checks a cache of previously resolved FQDNs to see if www.microsoft.com is there (Figure 10.19). In this case, www.microsoft.com is not in the cache.

Now your DNS server needs to get to work. The local DNS server may not know the address for www.microsoft.com, but it does know the addresses of the DNS root servers. The root servers, maintained by 12 root name server operators, know all the addresses of the top-level domain DNS servers. The

Yes, the 13 root name servers are maintained by 12 root name server operators. VeriSign, the company that handles security for a lot of the e-commerce on the Internet, maintains two root name server clusters.

The client asks its DNS server for the www.microsoft.com IP address.

Client's DNS server

Client

Cache		
Type	Name	IP
SOA	mail.totalsem.com	201.2.58.5
NS	ns1.fred.com	52.38.198.42
A	www.google.com	14.76.215.108
SOA	en.wikipedia.org	85.145.26.8
A	www.usa.gov	68.72.214.9
NS	ns1.blahblah.com	85.104.189.72

• **Figure 10.19**   Checking the DNS cache

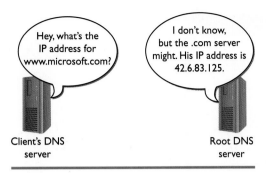

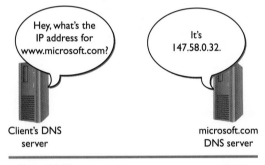

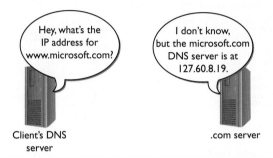

• **Figure 10.20** Talking to a root server

• **Figure 10.21** Talking to the .com server

• **Figure 10.22** Talking to the microsoft.com DNS server

root servers don't know the address of www.microsoft.com, but they do know the address of the DNS servers in charge of all .com addresses. The root servers send your DNS server an IP address for a .com server (Figure 10.20).

The .com DNS server also doesn't know the address of www.microsoft.com, but it knows the IP address of the microsoft.com DNS server. It sends that IP address to your DNS server (Figure 10.21).

The microsoft.com DNS server does know the IP address of www.microsoft.com and can send that information back to the local DNS server. Figure 10.22 shows the process of resolving an FQDN into an IP address.

Now that your DNS server has the IP address for www.microsoft.com, it stores a copy in its cache and sends the IP information to your PC. Your Web browser then begins the HTTP request to get the Web page.

 Cross Check

HTTP Process

You learned the specifics of HTTP in Chapter 9, "TCP/IP Applications," so check your memory now. Is the HTTP process connectionless or connection-oriented? At what OSI layers does the process happen?

Your computer also keeps a cache of recently resolved FQDNs. In Windows, for example, open a command prompt and type **ipconfig /displaydns** to see them. Here's a small part of the results of typing **ipconfig /displaydns**:

```
www.theverge.com

----------------------------------------
Record Name . . . . . : www.theverge.com
Record Type . . . . . : 1
Time To Live  . . . . : 259
Data Length . . . . . : 4
Section . . . . . . . : Answer
A (Host) Record . . . : 192.5.151.3
ftp.totalsem.com
_____
Record Name . . . . . : ftp.totalsem.com
Record Type . . . . . : 1
```

```
Time To Live  . . . . : 83733
Data Length . . . . . : 4
Section . . . . . . . : Answer
A (Host) Record . . . : 209.29.33.25
```
`C:\>`

DNS Servers

I've been talking about DNS servers for so long, I feel I'd be untrue to my vision of a Mike Meyers' book unless I gave you at least a quick peek at a DNS server in action. Lots of operating systems come with built-in DNS server software, including Windows Server and just about every version of UNIX/Linux. A number of third-party DNS server programs are also available for virtually any operating system. I'm going to use the DNS server program that comes with Microsoft Windows Server, primarily because (1) it takes the prettiest screen snapshots and (2) it's the one I use here at the office. You access the Windows DNS server by selecting **Start | Administrative Tools | DNS**. When you first open the DNS server, you won't see much other than the name of the server itself. In this case, Figure 10.23 shows a server, imaginatively named TOTAL-HOMEDC1.

 The most popular DNS server tool used in UNIX/Linux systems is called BIND.

The DNS server has (at least) three folder icons visible: Cached Lookups, Forward Lookup Zones, and Reverse Lookup Zones. Depending on the version of Windows Server you're running and the level of customization, your server might have more than three folder icons. Let's look at the three that are important for this discussion.

When you open the tree on a Windows DNS server, the first folder you see is called Cached Lookups. Every DNS server keeps a list of cached lookups—that is, all the IP addresses it has already resolved—so it won't have to re-resolve an

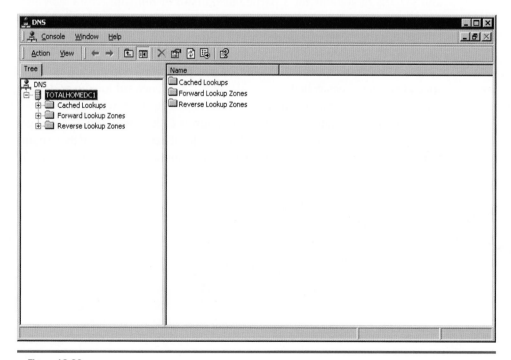

• **Figure 10.23**   DNS server main screen

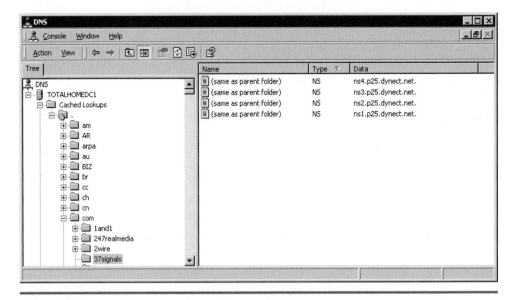

Name	Type ▽	Data
(same as parent folder)	NS	ns4.p25.dynect.net.
(same as parent folder)	NS	ns3.p25.dynect.net.
(same as parent folder)	NS	ns2.p25.dynect.net.
(same as parent folder)	NS	ns1.p25.dynect.net.

• **Figure 10.24**   Inspecting the DNS cache

FQDN it has already checked. The cache has a size limit, of course, and you can also set a limit on how long the DNS server holds cache entries. Windows does a nice job of separating these cached addresses by placing all cached lookups in little folders that share the first name of the top-level domain with subfolders that use the second-level domain (Figure 10.24). This sure makes it easy to see where folks have been Web browsing!

Now let's watch an actual DNS server at work. Basically, you choose to configure a DNS server to work in one of two ways: as an authoritative DNS server or as a cache-only DNS server. Authoritative DNS servers store IP addresses and FQDNs of systems for a particular domain or domains. **Cache-only DNS servers** are never the authoritative server for a domain. They are only used to talk to other DNS servers to resolve IP addresses for DNS clients. Then they cache the FQDN to speed up future lookups (Figure 10.25).

The IP addresses and FQDNs for the computers in a domain are stored in special storage areas called **forward lookup zones**. Forward lookup zones are the most important part of any DNS server. Figure 10.26 shows the DNS server for my small corporate network. My domain is called "totalhome." I can get away with a domain name that's not Internet legal because none of these computers are visible on the Internet. The totalhome domain only works on my

Microsoft DNS servers use a folder analogy to show lookup zones even though they are not true folders.

Cache		
Type	Name	IP
SOA	mail.totalsem.com	201.2.58.5
NS	ns1.fred.com	52.38.198.42
A	www.google.com	14.76.215.108
SOA	en.wikipedia.org	85.145.26.8
A	www.usa.gov	68.72.214.9
NS	ns1.blahblah.com	85.104.189.72

Authoritative   Cache-only

• **Figure 10.25**   Authoritative vs. cache-only DNS server

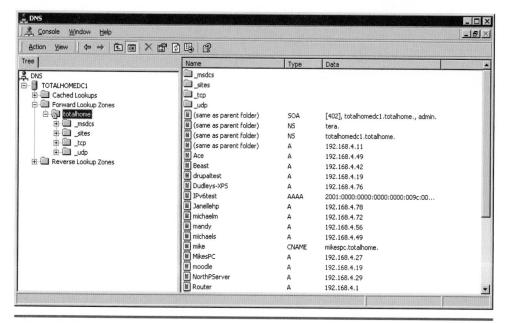

• **Figure 10.26**   Forward lookup zone totalhome

local network for local computers to find each other. I have created a forward lookup zone called totalhome.

Let's look at the contents of the totalhome domain. First, notice a number of folders: _msdcs, _sites, _tcp, and _udp. These folders are unique to Microsoft DNS servers, and you'll see what they do in a moment. For now, ignore them and concentrate on the individual computer listings. Every forward lookup zone requires a Start of Authority (SOA) record. The SOA record defines the single DNS server in charge of the forward lookup zone.

The SOA record in the folder totalhome, therefore, indicates that my server is the authoritative DNS server for a domain called totalhome.

You can even see a few of the systems in that domain (note to hackers: these are fake, so don't bother). A tech looking at this would know that totalhomedc1.totalhome is the authoritative DNS server for the totalhome domain. The **NS records** are all of the DNS servers for totalhome. Note that totalhome has two DNS servers: totalhomedc1.totalhome and tera. tera is not a member of the totalhome domain. In fact, tera isn't a member of *any* domain. A DNS server does not have to be a member of a domain to be a name server for that domain.

Having two DNS servers ensures that if one fails, the totalhome domain will continue to have a DNS server. The **A records** in the folder are the IPv4 addresses and names of all the systems on the totalhome domain.

Every DNS forward lookup zone will have one SOA and at least one NS record. In the vast majority of cases, a forward lookup zone will have some number of A records. But you may or may not see a number of other records in your standard DNS server. Look at Figure 10.27 for these less common types of DNS records: CNAME, MX, and AAAA.

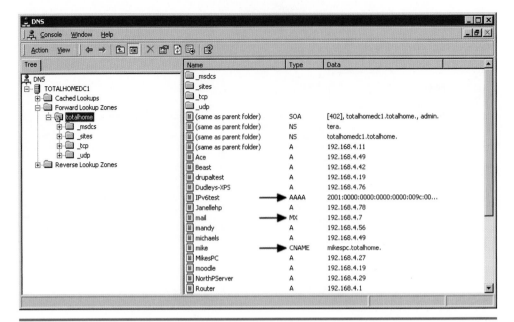

● **Figure 10.27** Less common DNS record types

A **canonical name (CNAME)** record acts like an alias. My computer's name is mikespc.totalhome, but you can also now use mike.totalhome to reference that computer. A ping of mike.totalhome returns the following:

```
C:\>ping mike.totalhome
Pinging mikespc.totalhome [192.168.4.27] with 32 bytes of data:
Reply from 192.168.4.27: bytes=32 time=2ms TTL=128
Reply from 192.168.4.27: bytes=32 time<1ms TTL=128

(rest of ping results deleted)
```

If your computer is a member of a domain and you are trying to access another computer in that domain, you can even skip the domain name, because your PC will simply add it back:

```
C:\>ping mike
Pinging mikespc.totalhome [192.168.4.27] with 32 bytes of data:
Reply from 192.168.4.27: bytes=32 time<1ms TTL=128
Reply from 192.168.4.27: bytes=32 time<1ms TTL=128

(rest of ping results deleted)
```

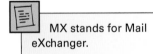

MX stands for Mail eXchanger.

MX records are used exclusively by SMTP servers to determine where to send mail. I have an in-house SMTP server on a computer I cleverly called mail. If other SMTP servers wanted to send mail to mail.totalhome (although they can't because the SMTP server isn't connected to the Internet and lacks a legal FQDN), they would use DNS to locate the mail server.

AAAA records are for a newer type of IP addressing called IPv6. You'll learn a lot more about IPv6 in Chapter 13, "IPv6."

There are two common types of forward lookup zones: a primary zone and a secondary zone. **Primary zones** are created on the DNS server that will act as the authoritative name server for that zone. **Secondary zones** are created on other DNS servers to act as backups to the primary zone. It's standard practice to have at least two DNS servers for any forward lookup zone: one primary and one secondary. Even in my small network, I have two DNS servers:

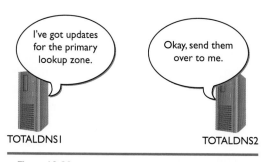

• Figure 10.28 Two DNS servers with updating taking place

• Figure 10.29 Reverse lookup zone

TOTALDNS1, which runs the primary zone, and TOTALDNS2, which runs a secondary zone (Figure 10.28). Any time a change is placed on TOTALDNS1, TOTALDNS2 is quickly updated.

A reverse lookup zone (Figure 10.29) enables a system to determine an FQDN by knowing the IP address; that is, it does the exact reverse of what DNS normally does! Reverse lookup zones take a network ID, reverse it, and add a unique domain called "in-addr-arpa" to create the zone. The record created is called a pointer record (PTR).

A few low-level functions (like mail) and some security programs use reverse lookup zones, so DNS servers provide them. In most cases, the DNS server asks you if you want to make a reverse lookup zone when you make a new forward lookup zone. When in doubt, make one. If you don't need it, it won't cause any trouble.

Microsoft added some wrinkles to DNS servers with the introduction of Windows 2000 Server, and each subsequent version of Windows Server retains the wrinkles. Windows Server can do cached lookups, primary and secondary forward lookup zones, and reverse lookup zones, just like UNIX/Linux DNS servers. But Windows Server also has a Windows-only type of forward lookup zone called an Active Directory–integrated zone.

> If you're looking at a Windows server and adding a new forward lookup zone, you'll see a third type called an Active Directory–integrated forward lookup zone. I'll cover that in just a moment.

Enter Windows

DNS works beautifully for any TCP/IP application that needs an IP address for another computer, but based on what you've learned so far, it has one glaring weakness: you need to add A records to the DNS server manually. Adding these can be a problem, especially in a world where you have many DHCP clients whose IP addresses may change from time to time. Interestingly, it was a throwback to the old Microsoft Windows NetBIOS protocol that fixed this and a few other problems all at the same time.

The solution was simple. Microsoft managed to crowbar the NetBIOS naming system into DNS by making the NetBIOS name the DNS name and by making the SMB protocol (which you learned about at the beginning of this chapter) run directly on TCP/IP without using NetBT.

Microsoft has used DNS names with the SMB protocol to provide folder and printer sharing in small TCP/IP networks. SMB is so popular that other operating systems have adopted support for SMB. UNIX/Linux systems come with the very popular Samba, the most popular tool for making non-Windows systems act like Windows computers (Figure 10.30).

> SMB running atop NetBIOS over TCP uses the same ports UDP 137 and 138, TCP 137 and 139. Without NetBIOS, SMB uses TCP port 445.

• Figure 10.30 Samba on Ubuntu (it's so common that the OS doesn't even use the term in the dialog)

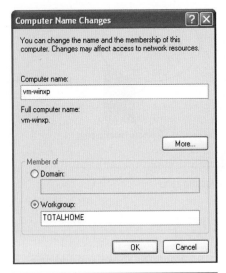

• **Figure 10.31**   Joining a workgroup

Living with SMB   SMB makes most small networks live in a two-world name resolution system. When your computer wants to access another computer's folders or files, it uses a simple SMB broadcast to get the name. If that same computer wants to do anything "Internety," it uses its DNS server. Both SMB and DNS live together perfectly well and, although many alternatives are available for this dual name resolution scheme, the vast majority of us are happy with this relationship.

Well, except for one little item we're almost happy: Windows continues to support an old organization of your computers into *groups*.

There are three types of groups: workgroup, Windows domain, and Active Directory. A **workgroup** is just a name that organizes a group of computers. A computer running Windows (or another operating system running Samba) joins a workgroup, as shown in Figure 10.31. When a computer joins a workgroup all the computers in the Network/My Network Places folder are organized, as shown in Figure 10.32.

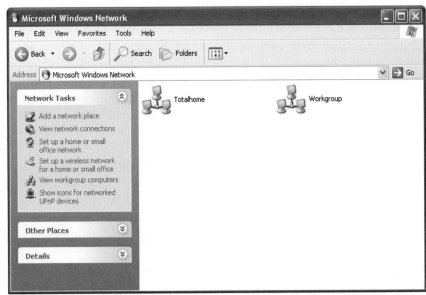

• **Figure 10.32**   Two workgroups in Network folder

A **Windows domain** is a group of computers controlled by a computer running Windows Server. This Windows Server computer is configured as a domain controller. You then have your computers join the domain.

• **Figure 10.33**   Logging into the domain

All the computers within a domain authenticate to the domain controller when they log in. Windows gives you this very powerful control over who can access what on your network (Figure 10.33).

Note that a Windows domain is not the same as a DNS domain. In the early days, a Windows domain didn't even have a naming structure that resembled the DNS hierarchically organized structure. Microsoft eventually revamped its domain controllers to work as part of DNS, however, and Windows domains now use DNS for their names. A Windows domain must have a true DNS name. DNS domains that are not on the Internet should use the top-level name .local (although you can cheat, as I do on my totalhome network, and not use it).

On a bigger scale, a Windows network can get complicated, with multiple domains connecting over long distances. To help organize this, Windows uses a type of super domain called Active Directory. An **Active Directory** is an organization of related computers that shares one or more Windows domains. Windows domain controllers are also DNS servers.

The beauty of Active Directory is that it has no single domain controller: all of the domain controllers are equal partners, and any domain controller can take over if one domain controller fails (Figure 10.34).

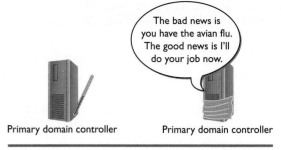

Primary domain controller   Primary domain controller

• **Figure 10.34** If one domain controller goes down, another automatically takes over.

Active Directory–Integrated Zones   Now that you have an understanding of Windows domains and Active Directory, let's return to forward lookup zones and DNS. A standard primary zone stores the DNS information in text files on the DNS server. You then use secondary zones on other DNS servers to back up that server. If the primary DNS server goes down, the secondary servers can resolve FQDNs, but you can't add any new records. Nothing can be updated until the primary DNS server comes back up.

In an Active Directory–integrated zone, all of the domain controllers (which are all also DNS servers) are equal and the whole DNS system is not reliant on a single DNS server. The DNS servers store their DNS information in a data structure called the Active Directory. The Active Directory is stored across the servers in the domain. All Active Directory–enabled DNS servers automatically send DNS information to each other, updating every machine's DNS information to match the others.

Dynamic DNS

In the early days of TCP/IP networks, DNS servers required manual updates of their records. This was not a big deal until the numbers of computers using TCP/IP exploded in the 1990s. Then every office had a network and every network had a DNS server to update. DHCP helped to some extent. You could add a special option to the DHCP server, which is generally called the *DNS suffix*. This way the DHCP clients would know the name of the DNS domain to which they belonged. It didn't help the manual updating of DNS records, but clients don't need records. No one accesses the clients! The DNS suffix helps the clients access network resources more efficiently.

All DHCP servers provide an option called *DNS server* that tells clients the IP address of the DNS server or servers.

Today, manual updating of DNS records is still the norm for most Internet-serving systems like Web servers and e-mail servers. DNS has moved beyond Internet servers; even the smallest Windows networks that run Active Directory use it. Whereas a popular Web server might have a phalanx of techs to adjust DNS settings, small networks in which most of the computers run DHCP need an alternative to old-school DNS. Luckily, the solution was worked out over a decade ago.

The TCP/IP folks came up with a new protocol called **Dynamic DNS (DDNS)** in 1997 that enabled DNS servers to get automatic updates of IP addresses of computers in their forward lookup zones, mainly by talking to the local DHCP server. All modern DNS servers support DDNS, and all but the most primitive DHCP servers support Dynamic DNS as well.

Windows leans heavily on DDNS. Windows networks use DDNS for the DHCP server to talk to the DNS server.

When a DHCP server updates its records for a DHCP client, it reports to the DNS server. The DNS server then updates its A records accordingly. DDNS simplifies setting up and maintaining a LAN tremendously. If you need to force a DNS server to update its records, use the `ipconfig /registerdns` command from the command prompt.

DNS Security Extensions

If you think about what DNS does, you can appreciate that it can be a big security issue. Simply querying a DNS server gives you a list of every computer name and IP address that it serves. This isn't the kind of information we want bad guys to have. It's easy to tell a DNS server not to respond to queries such as nslookup or dig, but DNS by definition is a public protocol that requires one DNS server to respond to another DNS server. (See "Troubleshooting DNS" later in the chapter for the scoop on nslookup and dig.)

The big fix is called *DNS Security Extensions (DNSSEC)*. DNSSEC is an authentication and authorization protocol designed to prevent bad guys from impersonating legitimate DNS servers. It's implemented through *extension mechanisms for DNS (EDNS)*, a specification that expanded several parameter sizes but maintained backward compatibility with earlier DNS servers.

Troubleshooting DNS

As I mentioned earlier, most DNS problems result from a problem with the client systems. This is because DNS servers rarely go down, and if they do, most clients have a secondary DNS server setting that enables them to continue to resolve DNS names. DNS servers have been known to fail, however, so knowing when the problem is the client system, and when you can complain to the person in charge of your DNS server, is important. All of the tools you're about to see come with every operating system that supports TCP/IP, with the exception of the `ipconfig` commands, which I'll mention when I get to them.

So how do you know when to suspect DNS is causing the problem on your network? Well, just about everything you do on an IP network depends on DNS to find the right system to talk to for whatever job the application does. E-mail clients use DNS to find their e-mail servers; FTP clients use DNS for their servers; Web browsers use DNS to find Web servers; and so on. The first clue something is wrong is generally when a user calls, saying he's getting a "server not found" error. Server not found errors look different depending on the application, but you can count on something being there that says in effect "server not found." Figure 10.35 shows how this error appears in an FTP client.

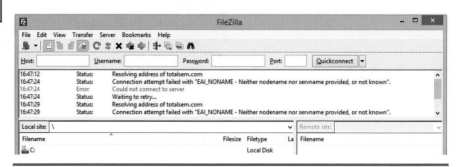

• **Figure 10.35** DNS error

Before you start testing, you need to eliminate any DNS caches on the local system. If you're running Windows, run the `ipconfig /flushdns` command now. In addition, most Web browsers also have caches, so you can't use a Web browser for any testing. In such cases, it's time to turn to the **ping** command.

Your best friend when testing DNS is ping. Run ping from a command prompt, followed by the name of a well-known Web site, such as `ping www.microsoft.com`. Watch the

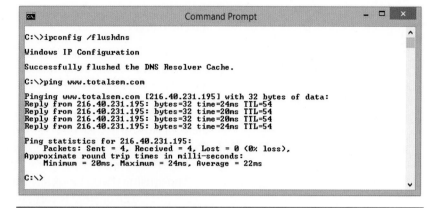

```
C:\>ipconfig /flushdns

Windows IP Configuration

Successfully flushed the DNS Resolver Cache.

C:\>ping www.totalsem.com

Pinging www.totalsem.com [216.40.231.195] with 32 bytes of data:
Reply from 216.40.231.195: bytes=32 time=24ms TTL=54
Reply from 216.40.231.195: bytes=32 time=20ms TTL=54
Reply from 216.40.231.195: bytes=32 time=20ms TTL=54
Reply from 216.40.231.195: bytes=32 time=24ms TTL=54

Ping statistics for 216.40.231.195:
    Packets: Sent = 4, Received = 4, Lost = 0 (0% loss),
Approximate round trip times in milli-seconds:
    Minimum = 20ms, Maximum = 24ms, Average = 22ms

C:\>
```

• **Figure 10.36** Using ping to check DNS

output carefully to see if you get an IP address. You may get a "request timed out" message, but that's fine; you just want to see if DNS is resolving FQDNs into IP addresses (Figure 10.36).

If you get a "server not found" error, you need to ping again using just an IP address. Most network techs keep the IP address of a known server in their heads. If you don't have one memorized, try 74.125.95.99 (Google). If ping works with the IP address but not with the Web site name, you know you have a DNS problem.

Once you've determined that DNS is the problem, check to make sure your system has the correct DNS server entry. Again, this information is something you should keep around. I can tell you the DNS server IP address for every Internet link I own—two in the office, one at the house, plus two dial-ups I use on the road. You don't have to memorize the IP addresses, but you should have all the critical IP information written down. If that isn't the problem, run `ipconfig /all` to see if those DNS settings are the same as the ones in the server; if they aren't, you may need to refresh your DHCP settings. I'll show you how to do that next.

If you have the correct DNS settings for your DNS server and the DNS settings in `ipconfig /all` match those settings, you can assume the problem is with the DNS server itself. The **nslookup** (name server lookup) command enables DNS server queries. All operating systems have a version of `nslookup`.

You run `nslookup` from a command prompt. With `nslookup`, you can (assuming you have the permission) query all types of information from a DNS server and change how your system uses DNS. Although most of these commands are far outside the scope of the CompTIA Network+ exam, you should definitely know `nslookup`. For instance, just running `nslookup` alone from a command prompt shows you some output similar to the following:

```
C:\>nslookup
Default Server:  totalhomedc2.totalhome
Address:  192.168.4.155
>
```

Running `nslookup` gives me the IP address and the name of my default DNS server. If I got an error at this point, perhaps a "server not found" error, I would know that either my primary DNS server is down or I might not have the correct DNS server information in my DNS settings. I can attach to any DNS

When troubleshooting, ping is your friend. If you can ping an IP address but not the name associated with that address, check DNS.

Make sure you know how to use `nslookup` to determine if a DNS server is active!

server by typing **server**, followed by the IP address or the domain name of the DNS server:

```
> server totalhomedc1
Default Server:  totalhomedc1.totalhome
Addresses:  192.168.4.157, 192.168.4.156
```

This new server has two IP addresses; it has two multihomed NICs to ensure there's a backup in case one NIC fails. If I get an error on one DNS server, I use nslookup to check for another DNS server. I can then switch to that server in my TCP/IP settings as a temporary fix until my DNS server is working again.

Those using UNIX/Linux have an extra DNS tool called **domain information groper (dig)**. The dig tool is very similar to nslookup, but it runs noninteractively. In nslookup, you're in the command until you type **exit**; nslookup even has its own prompt. The dig tool, on the other hand, is not interactive—you ask it a question, it answers the question, and it puts you back at a regular command prompt. When you run dig, you tend to get a large amount of information. The following is a sample of a dig command run from a Linux prompt:

```
[mike@localhost]$dig -x 13.65.14.4
; <<>> DiG 8.2 <<>> -x
;; res options: init recurs defnam dnsrch
;; got answer:
;; ->>HEADER<<- opcode: QUERY, status: NOERROR, id: 4
;; flags: qr aa rd ra; QUERY: 1, ANSWER: 1, AUTHORITY: 2,
ADDITIONAL: 2
;; QUERY SECTION:
;;   4.14.65.13.in-addr.arpa, type = ANY, class = IN
;; ANSWER SECTION:
4.14.65.13.in-addr.arpa.  4H IN PTR
server3.houston.totalsem.com.
;; AUTHORITY SECTION:
65.14.4.in-addr.arpa.  4H IN NS  kernel.risc.uni-linz.ac.at.
65.14.4.in-addr.arpa.  4H IN NS  kludge.risc.uni-linz.ac.at.
;; ADDITIONAL SECTION:
kernel.risc.uni-linz.ac.at.  4H IN A  193.170.37.225
kludge.risc.uni-linz.ac.at.  4H IN A  193.170.37.224
;; Total query time: 1 msec
;; FROM: kernel to SERVER: default — 127.0.0.1
;; WHEN: Thu Feb 10 18:03:41 2000
;; MSG SIZE  sent: 44  rcvd: 180
[mike@localhost]$
```

Check out the excellent Chapter 10 "Name Resolution" Type! over at http://totalsem.com/006. Working with the command line is cool!

■ Diagnosing TCP/IP Networks

I've dedicated all of Chapter 21, "Network Troubleshooting," to network diagnostic procedures, but TCP/IP has a few little extras that I want to talk about here. TCP/IP is a pretty robust protocol, and in good networks, it runs like a top for years without problems. Most of the TCP/IP problems you'll see come from improper configuration, so I'm going to assume you've run into problems with a new TCP/IP install, and I'll show you some classic screw-ups common in this situation. I want to concentrate on making sure you can ping anyone you want to ping.

I've done thousands of IP installations over the years, and I'm proud to say that, in most cases, they worked right the first time. My users jumped on the newly configured systems, fired up their My Network Places/Network, e-mail software, and Web browsers, and were last seen typing away, smiling from ear to ear. But I'd be a liar if I didn't also admit that plenty of setups didn't work so well. Let's start with the hypothetical case of a user who can't see something on the network. You get a call: "Help!" he cries. The first troubleshooting point to remember here: it doesn't matter *what* he can't see. It doesn't matter if he can't see other systems in his network or can't see the home page on his browser—you go through the same steps in any event.

Remember to use common sense wherever possible. If the problem system can't ping by DNS name, but all the other systems can, is the DNS server down? Of course not! If something—*anything*—doesn't work on one system, *always* try it on another one to determine whether the problem is specific to one system or affects the entire network.

One thing I always do is check the network connections and protocols. I'm going to cover those topics in greater detail later in the book, so, for now, assume the problem systems are properly connected and have good protocols installed. Here are some steps to take:

1. *Diagnose the NIC.* If you're lucky enough to own a higher-end NIC that has its own Control Panel applet (many Intel and 3COM NICs have this), use the diagnostic tool to see if the NIC is working.

2. *Check your NIC's driver.* Replace if necessary.

3. *Diagnose locally.* If the NIC's okay, diagnose locally by pinging a few neighboring systems, by both IP address and DNS name. If you're using NetBIOS, use the `net view` command to see if the other local systems are visible (Figure 10.37). If you can't ping by DNS, check your DNS settings. If you can't see the network using `net view`, you may have a problem with your NetBIOS settings.

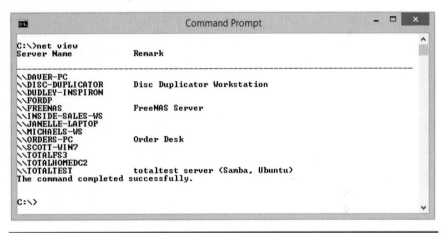

• **Figure 10.37** The `net view` command in action

4. *Check IP address and subnet mask.* If you're having a problem pinging locally, make sure you have the right IP address and subnet mask. Oh, if I had a nickel for every time I entered those incorrectly! If you're on DHCP, try renewing the lease—sometimes that does the trick. If DHCP fails, call the person in charge of the server.

5. *Run netstat.* At this point, another little handy program comes into play called **netstat**. The `netstat` program offers a number of options. The two handiest ways to run `netstat` are with no options at all and with the `-s` option. Running `netstat` with no options shows you all the current connections to your system. Look for a connection here that isn't working with an application—that's often a clue to an application problem, such as a broken application or a sneaky application running in the background. Figure 10.38 shows a `netstat` program running.

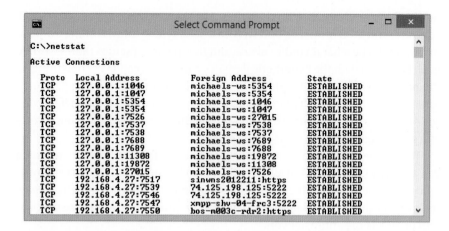

• **Figure 10.38** The `netstat` program in action

6. *Run netstat -s.* Running `netstat` with the `-s` option displays several statistics that can help you diagnose problems. For example, if the display shows you are sending but not receiving, you almost certainly have a bad cable with a broken receive wire.

7. *Diagnose to the gateway.* If you can't get on the Internet, check to see if you can ping the router. Remember, the router has two interfaces, so try both: first the local interface (the one on your subnet) and then the one to the Internet. You *do* have both of those IP addresses memorized, don't you? You should! If you can't ping the router, either it's down or you're not connected to it. If you can only ping the near side, something in the router itself is messed up, like the routing table.

8. *Diagnose to the Internet.* If you can ping the router, try to ping something on the Internet. If you can't ping one address, try another—it's always possible that the first place you try to ping is down. If you still can't get through, you can try to locate the problem using the **tracert** (trace route) command. Run `tracert` to mark out the entire route the ping packet traveled between you and whatever you were trying to ping. It may even tell you where the problem lies (see Figure 10.39).

```
C:\>tracert 216.40.231.195

Tracing route to totalsem.com [216.40.231.195]
over a maximum of 30 hops:

  1    <1 ms    <1 ms    <1 ms  Router.totalhome [192.168.4.1]
  2    11 ms     8 ms    10 ms  96.120.17.193
  3    66 ms     7 ms     8 ms  68.85.249.209
  4    10 ms     9 ms    10 ms  ae-4-0-ar01.bearcreek.tx.houston.comcast.net [68.85.87.145]
  5    20 ms    15 ms    15 ms  68.86.166.229
  6    17 ms    20 ms    18 ms  pos-0-1-0-0-pe01.1950stemmons.tx.ibone.comcast.net [68.86.86.94]

  7    20 ms    16 ms    17 ms  ae10.bbr01.eq01.dal03.networklayer.com [75.149.228.34]
  8    20 ms    19 ms    20 ms  ae0.bbr01.sr02.hou02.networklayer.com [173.192.18.219]
  9    22 ms    24 ms    19 ms  po31.dsr01.hstntx2.networklayer.com [173.192.18.233]
 10    21 ms    24 ms    20 ms  po1.car02.hstntx2.networklayer.com [74.55.252.70]
 11    20 ms    19 ms    19 ms  totalsem.com [216.40.231.195]

Trace complete.

C:\>
```

• **Figure 10.39** Using `tracert`

Chapter 10 Review

Chapter Summary

After reading this chapter and completing the exercises, you should understand the following about network naming.

Analyze and configure early name resolution solutions

■ Windows used a simple networking protocol for a long time, called NetBIOS/NetBEUI. It was designed primarily for sharing files and folders in a local network. The protocol didn't work when scaled up because it wasn't routable and relied too much on broadcasts.

■ Microsoft created a TCP/IP protocol called NetBT to support systems that relied on NetBIOS but needed to use DNS. Every Windows computer had one name used on the local network and a DNS name for use on the Internet.

■ The hosts file provided name resolution in the early days of TCP/IP networking. Even though the hosts file is rarely used, *every* operating system always looks first in the hosts file before anything else when attempting to resolve a name.

Describe the function and capabilities of DNS

■ A hosts file maps a computer name to an IP address. When the Internet was in its infancy, every Internet-connected computer had a copy of the same hosts file. Today, computers have their own unique hosts file, which is always checked before a computer tries to resolve a name using another method.

■ DNS is vital to IP networking, whether on the Internet or within the smallest of networks. DNS stands for Domain Name System, which functions as a hierarchical naming system for computers on a network. A DNS server resolves FQDNs (fully qualified domain names) to IP addresses.

■ The 13 DNS root servers for the Internet are logical servers composed of many DNS servers acting as a single monstrous server.

■ If one DNS domain name space cannot find out (resolve) the IP address of a computer, the request gets passed along to another DNS server. The process continues until the request reaches the destination computer.

■ Note that because not all computers are connected to the Internet, computer networks are not required to belong to a DNS domain. Administrators can set up their own DNS domain name spaces, however, without ever connecting to the Internet. These isolated internal intranets can be given elaborate naming structures of their own as well.

■ Name resolution can be accomplished through broadcasting by consulting the local hosts file or by contacting a DNS server.

■ Run `ipconfig /all` to view your DNS server settings. Run `ipconfig /displaydns` to display a cache of recently resolved FQDNs.

■ DNS servers store a list of cached lookups—all IP addresses the server has already resolved.

■ An authoritative DNS server stores IP addresses and FQDNs of all systems for a particular domain, whereas a cache-only DNS server is used to communicate with other DNS servers.

■ Forward lookup zones are the most important part of any DNS server because they contain the IP addresses and FQDNs.

■ Of the two types of forward lookup zones, primary zones are created on authoritative DNS servers while secondary zones are created on other DNS servers to act as a backup to the primary zone.

■ SOA records, A records, CNAME records, and MX records must be properly configured on any DNS server.

■ Reverse lookup zones resolve an IP address to an FQDN using PTR records.

■ Microsoft's Server Message Block (SMB) protocol is used primarily to share files and printers in small TCP/IP networks.

■ Windows organizes computers into one of three types of groups: workgroup, Windows domain, or Active Directory.

■ A Windows domain provides centralized management and user authentication via a computer acting as a domain controller.

■ An Active Directory is an organization of related computers that shares one or more Windows domains. There is no single domain controller in Active Directory because all domain controllers operate equally.

■ Under Active Directory, all domain controllers are also DNS servers.

- Because Active Directory domain controllers operate equally, there is no single point of failure throughout Active Directory's DNS system. All domain controllers hold primary zones.

- The Dynamic DNS (DDNS) protocol enables DNS servers to update their records automatically when they receive changed IP address information from a DHCP server or clients on the network.

- The command `ipconfig` is useful for troubleshooting TCP/IP settings. Running `ipconfig /flushdns` will clear the local cache of DNS entries.

- The `ping` command is essential in establishing connectivity to a destination PC. If you can ping a host computer by IP address (for example, `ping 192.168.4.55`), but not by name (`ping acctngpc2`), then you have a DNS resolution issue. Check cables, check the DNS servers listed under each network adapter card's settings, and finally, check to see that the DNS server is truly up and operational.

- The `nslookup` command enables you to research which name servers are being used by a particular computer. Advanced variations of the `nslookup` command can query information from a DNS server and even change how your system uses DNS.

- UNIX/Linux users have an additional DNS tool called dig, which is different from `nslookup` in that dig runs noninteractively.

Use common TCP/IP utilities to diagnose problems with DNS

- Always try to connect from another system to determine the extent of the problem. You can then begin the steps to diagnose TCP/IP errors on a single system.

- Remember to work "from the inside out"—that is, check for connectivity problems on the local system before moving on to check the larger network structure.

- On Windows systems, the `net view` command is worth trying. If you can't see the network using `net view`, you may have a problem with your NetBIOS settings.

- Running `netstat` shows all the current connections on your system. Running `netstat -s` displays useful statistical information.

- The `tracert` command allows you to mark the entire route a ping packet travels, telling you exactly where a problem lies.

■ Key Terms

A record *(273)*
Active Directory *(277)*
authoritative DNS server *(265)*
authoritative name server *(264)*
cached lookups *(271)*
cache-only DNS server *(272)*
canonical name (CNAME) *(274)*
DNS root server *(260)*
DNS server *(260)*
DNS tree *(262)*
domain information groper (dig) *(280)*
Domain Name System (DNS) *(257)*
Dynamic DNS (DDNS) *(277)*
flat name space *(260)*
forward lookup zone *(272)*
fully qualified domain name (FQDN) *(262)*
hierarchical name space *(260)*
host name *(262)*
hosts file *(258)*

ipconfig *(268)*
MX record *(274)*
name resolution *(256)*
name server *(264)*
NetBIOS over TCP/IP (NetBT) *(258)*
NetBIOS/NetBEUI *(257)*
netstat *(281)*
nslookup *(279)*
NS record *(273)*
ping *(279)*
pointer record (PTR) *(275)*
primary zone *(274)*
reverse lookup zone *(275)*
secondary zone *(274)*
top-level domain server *(260)*
tracert *(282)*
Windows domain *(276)*
workgroup *(276)*

Key Term Quiz

Use the Key Terms list to complete the sentences that follow. Not all the terms will be used.

1. The _____ command is used to establish connectivity.

2. The _____ protocol originally ran on top of NetBT, but today runs by itself and uses port 445.

3. The term _____ refers to networks that use DNS belonging to the same DNS system.

4. A helpful command that displays TCP/IP naming information is _____.

5. A DNS forward lookup zone uses a(n) _____ for individual host records.

6. To connect to systems on the Internet using domain names, your network needs the name of at least one _____.

7. The _____ gets precedence over DNS.

8. You can use the diagnostic utility called _____ to trace the progress of an ICMP packet between your system and a remote computer.

9. To avoid having to re-resolve an FQDN that it has already checked, a Windows DNS server keeps a list of IP addresses it has already resolved, called _____.

10. The single DNS server that has a list of all the host names on the domain and their corresponding IP addresses is the _____.

Multiple-Choice Quiz

1. Which of the following are needed for e-mail clients to find their e-mail servers, FTP clients to find their file servers, and Web browsers to find Web servers?

    A. DHCP servers

    B. DNS servers

    C. E-mail servers

    D. WINS servers

2. What do DNS servers use to help resolve IP addresses to DNS names?

    A. Authentication

    B. Authorization

    C. Backward lookup zones

    D. Reverse lookup zones

3. What do DNS servers use to help resolve DNS names to IP addresses?

    A. Accounting

    B. Administration

    C. Backward lookup zones

    D. Forward lookup zones

4. What type of DNS servers do not have any forward lookup zones and will resolve names of systems on the Internet for a network but are not responsible for telling other DNS servers the names of any clients?

    A. Cache-only servers

    B. Primary servers

    C. Secondary servers

    D. WINS servers

5. What command gives you the IP address and the name of your system's default DNS server?

    A. `nbtstat`

    B. `nslookup`

    C. `ping`

    D. `winword`

6. What file can override your DNS server?

    A. hosts

    B. SYSLOG

    C. SAM

    D. WIN

7. Which of the following ports are used by Windows to support pre-DNS naming protocols?

   A. TCP port 443

   B. TCP port 138

   C. UDP port 445

   D. TCP port 137

8. What does adding a caching-only DNS server enable you to accomplish on your network?

   A. Provides a backup DNS server

   B. Allows your hosts to broadcast DNS

   C. Speeds up DNS resolution

   D. Replaces your DHCP server

9. Folders with subfolders on a system, like domain names with subdomains, are said to have a structure resembling what?

   A. Branch

   B. Forest

   C. Root

   D. Tree

10. Which of the following commands clears the local cache of DNS entries?

    A. `ipconfig /clear`

    B. `ipconfig /cls`

    C. `ipconfig /flushdns`

    D. `ipconfig /renew`

11. What UDP and TCP port does DNS use?

    A. 53

    B. 137

    C. 138

    D. 445

12. Which of these terms are frequently used interchangeably? (Select two.)

    A. Domain

    B. Folder

    C. Subdomain

    D. Zone

13. Which of the following are valid DNS record entry types? (Select three.)

    A. A

    B. M

    C. NS

    D. SOA

14. Which of the following is an example of a top-level domain?

    A. .com

    B. totalsem.com

    C. support.totalsem.com

    D. houston.support.totalsem.com

15. How do authoritative DNS servers and cache-only DNS servers differ?

    A. Authoritative DNS servers contain forward lookup zones, whereas cache-only DNS servers contain only reverse lookup zones.

    B. Authoritative DNS servers store IP addresses and FQDNs of systems for a particular domain or domains, whereas cache-only DNS servers do not store any FQDNs because they are only used to talk to other DNS servers to resolve IP addresses.

    C. Authoritative DNS servers service requests for top-level domains, whereas cache-only DNS servers service requests for down-level domains.

    D. Authoritative DNS servers are found only in Windows Active Directory networks, whereas cache-only DNS servers are found universally throughout the Internet.

1. Your boss comes into your office in a panic. He can't reach the company's internal Web server from his office. It worked yesterday. Write an essay describing what you'd do to troubleshoot the situation. Which tool or tools would you use? Why?

2. After discussing flat versus hierarchical naming schemes in class, a feisty classmate proclaims that flat names should be used on individual systems as well as on the Internet for simplification.

Write a brief reason or two why he is wrong in his oversimplification.

3. Jot down some brief notes about how you would troubleshoot and diagnose a TCP/IP issue on one of the systems on your network. You can list the actual commands if you like, too. Choose an interesting Web site that you would ping on the Internet as your final step.

Lab Projects

• Lab Project 10.1

This chapter has presented many variations of common network troubleshooting commands. You have decided it would be beneficial to create an alphabetized chart of these commands, including their variations and what they do. Using either a word processing program or spreadsheet program, create a chart like the following—you fill in the rightmost column:

Command	Switch or Second-level Command	What It Does . . .
ipconfig	(blank)	
ipconfig	/all	
ipconfig	/release	
ipconfig	/renew	
ipconfig	/flushdns	
net	send	
net	view	
ping	127.0.0.1	
ping	disney.com	
ping	localhost	

• Lab Project 10.2

A request must potentially make many trips when trying to resolve a fully qualified domain name to an IP address. Aside from the hosts file, you have primary DNS servers, secondary DNS servers, authoritative DNS servers, cache-only DNS servers, DNS root servers, top-level DNS servers, and second-level domain servers.

On a piece of paper, sketch a diagram/flowchart showing how a request for www.example.com gets resolved to an IP address.

Securing TCP/IP

"Better to be despised for too anxious apprehensions than ruined by too confident a security."

—EDMUND BURKE

In this chapter, you will learn how to

- **Discuss the standard methods for securing TCP/IP networks**
- **Compare TCP/IP security standards**
- **Implement secure TCP/IP applications**

If you want to enter the minds of the folks who invented TCP/IP, Vint Cerf and Bob Kahn, look at TCP/IP from a security perspective. TCP/IP wasn't designed with any real security in mind. Oh sure, you can put user names and passwords on FTP, Telnet, and other TCP/IP applications, but everything else is basically wide open. Perhaps Cerf and Kahn thought the intent of the Internet was openness?

Sadly, today's world reveals a totally different perspective. Every device with a public IP address on the Internet is constantly bombarded with malicious code trying to gain some level of access to our precious data. Even data moving between two hosts is relatively easily intercepted and read. Bad guys make millions by stealing our data in any of a thousand different ways, and TCP/IP in its original form is all but powerless to stop them. Luckily for us, Cerf and Kahn gave TCP/IP a tremendous amount of flexibility, which over time has enabled developers to add substantial security to pretty much anything you want to send in an IP packet.

This chapter takes you on a tour of the many ways smart people have improved TCP/IP to protect our data from those who wish to do evil things to or with it. It's an interesting story of good intentions, knee-jerk reactions, dead ends, and failed attempts that luckily ends with a promise of easy-to-use protocols that protect our data.

This chapter examines the ways to make TCP/IP data and networks secure. I'll first give you a look at security concepts and then turn to specific standards and protocols used to implement security. The chapter wraps with a discussion on secure TCP/IP applications and their methods.

Test Specific

Making TCP/IP Secure

I break down TCP/IP security into five areas: encryption, integrity, nonrepudiation, authentication, and authorization.

Encryption means to scramble, mix up, or change data in such a way that bad guys can't read it. Of course, this scrambled-up data must also be easily descrambled by the person receiving the data.

Integrity is the process that guarantees that the data received is the same as originally sent. Integrity is designed to cover situations in which someone intercepts your data on-the-fly and makes changes.

Nonrepudiation is the process of making sure data came from the person or entity it was supposed to come from. This prevents others from pretending to be a different entity (like Mike Meyers or eBay.com) and doing evil things by impersonation (like posting threats of violence or stealing all your money).

Authentication means to verify that whoever is trying to access the data is the person you want accessing that data. The most classic form of authentication is the user name and password combination, but there are plenty more ways to authenticate.

Authorization defines what an authenticated person can do with that data. Different operating systems and applications provide different schemes for authorization, but the classic scheme for Windows is to assign permissions to a user account. An administrator, for example, can do a lot more after being authenticated than a limited user can do.

Encryption, integrity, nonrepudiation, authentication, and authorization may be separate issues, but they overlap a lot in TCP/IP security practices. If you send a user name and password over the Internet, wouldn't it be a good idea to encrypt the user name and password so others can't read it? Similarly, if you send someone a "secret decoder ring" over the Internet so she can unscramble the encryption, wouldn't it be a good idea for the recipient to know that the decoder ring actually came from you? In TCP/IP security, you have protocols that combine encryption, integrity, nonrepudiation (sometimes), authentication, and authorization to create complete security solutions for one TCP/IP application or another.

Encryption

All data on your network is nothing more than ones and zeroes. Identifying what type of data the strings of ones and zeroes in a packet represent usually

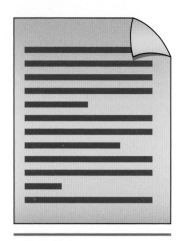

• **Figure 11.1**   Plaintext

is easy. A packet of data on the Internet always comes with a port number, for example, so a bad guy quickly knows what type of data he's reading.

All data starts as **plaintext**, a somewhat misleading term that simply means the data is in an easily read or viewed industry-wide standard format. Plaintext, often also referred to as **cleartext**, implies that all data starts off as text—untrue! Data often is text, but it also might be a binary file such as a photograph or an executable program. Regardless of the type of data, it all starts as plaintext. I'll use the image in Figure 11.1 as a universal figure for a piece of plaintext.

If you want to take some data and make figuring out what it means difficult for other people, you need a cipher. A **cipher** is a general term for a way to encrypt data. An **algorithm** is the mathematical formula that underlies the cipher.

Let's say you have a string of ones and zeroes that looks like this:

```
01001101010010010100101101000101
```

This string may not mean much to you, but if it was part of an HTTP segment, your Web browser would instantly know that this is Unicode—that is, numbers representing letters and other characters—and convert it into text:

```
01001101 01001001 01001011 01000101
M        I        K        E
```

So let's create a cipher to encrypt this cleartext. All binary encryption requires some interesting binary math. You could do something really simple such as add 1 to every value (and ignore carrying the 1):

```
0 + 1 = 1 and 1 + 1 = 0 10110010101101101011010010111010
```

No big deal; that just reversed the values. Any decent hacker would see the pattern and break this code in about three seconds. Let's try something harder to break by bringing in a second value (a key) of any eight binary numbers (let's use 10101010 for this example) and doing some math to every eight binary values using this algorithm:

If cleartext is...	And key value is...	Then the result is...
0	0	0
0	1	1
1	0	1
1	1	0

This is known as a binary *XOR (eXclusive OR)*. Line up the key against the first eight values in the cleartext:

```
10101010
01001101010010010100101101000101
11100111
```

Then do the next eight binary values:

```
1010101010101010
01001101010010010100101101000101
1110011111100011
```

Then the next eight:

```
1010101010101010101010
0100110101001001010010110100 0101
111001111110001111100001
```

Then the final eight:

```
10101010101010101010101010101010
010011010100100101001011 01000101
1110011111100011111000 0111101111
```

If you want to decrypt the data, you need to know the algorithm and the key. This is a very simple example of how to encrypt binary data. At first glance, you might say this is good encryption, but the math is simple, and a simple XOR is easy for someone to decrypt.

An XOR works with letters as well as numbers. See if you can crack the following code:

```
WKH TXLFN EURZQ IRA MXPSV RYHU WKH ODCB GRJ
```

This is a classic example of the Caesar cipher. You just take the letters of the alphabet and transpose them:

```
Real Letter: ABCDEFGHIJKLMNOPQRSTUVWXYZ
Code letter: DEFGHIJKLMNOPQRSTUVWXYZABC
```

Caesar ciphers are very easy to crack by using word patterns, frequency analysis, or brute force. The code "WKH" shows up twice, which means it's the same word (*word patterns*). The letters *W* and *H* show up fairly often too. Certain letters of the alphabet are used more than others, so a code-breaker can use that to help decrypt the code (*frequency analysis*). Assuming that you know this is a Caesar cipher, a computer can quickly go through every different code possibility and determine the answer (*brute force*). Incredibly, even though it's not as obvious, binary code also suffers from the same problem.

In computing, you need to make a cipher hard for anyone to break except the people you want to read the data. Luckily, computers do more complex algorithms very quickly (it's just math), and you can use longer keys to make the code much harder to crack.

Okay, let's take the information above and generate some more symbols to show this process. When you run cleartext through a cipher algorithm using a key, you get what's called **ciphertext** (Figure 11.2).

Over the years, computing people have developed hundreds of different complete algorithms for use in encrypting binary data. Of these, only a few were or still are commonly used in TCP/IP networks. The math behind all of these complete algorithms is incredibly complex and way beyond the scope of the CompTIA Network+ exam, but all of them have two items in common: a complex algorithm underlying the cipher and a key or keys used to encrypt and decrypt the text.

Any encryption that uses the same key for both encryption and decryption is called symmetric-key encryption or a **symmetric-key algorithm**. If you want someone to decrypt what you encrypt, you have to make sure they have some tool that can handle the algorithm and you have to give them the key. This is a

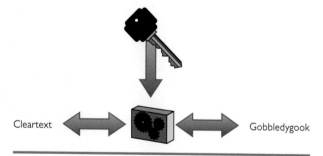

Cleartext   Gobbledygook

• **Figure 11.2** Encryption process

potential problem I will address later in this chapter. Any encryption that uses different keys for encryption and decryption is called asymmetric-key encryption or an **asymmetric-key algorithm**. Let's look at symmetric-key encryption first, and then turn to asymmetric-key encryption.

Symmetric-Key Algorithm Standards

There is one difference among symmetric-key algorithms. Most algorithms are called **block ciphers** because they encrypt data in single "chunks" of a certain length at a time. Let's say you have a 100,000-byte Microsoft Word document you want to encrypt. One type of encryption will take 128-bit chunks and encrypt each one separately (Figure 11.3). Block ciphers work well when data comes in clearly discrete chunks. Data crossing wired networks comes in IP packets, for example, so block ciphers are very popular with these sorts of packets.

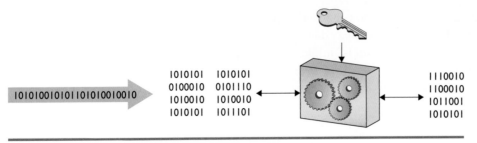

• **Figure 11.3**   Block cipher

The granddaddy of all TCP/IP symmetric-key algorithms is the **Data Encryption Standard (DES)**. DES was developed by the United States government in the late 1970s and was in widespread use in a variety of TCP/IP applications. DES used a 64-bit block and a 56-bit key. Over time, the 56-bit key made DES susceptible to brute-force attacks. The computing industry came up with a number of derivatives of DES to try to address this issue, with names such as 3DES, International Data Encryption Algorithm (IDEA), and Blowfish.

The alternative to a block cipher is the much quicker **stream cipher**, which takes a single bit at a time and encrypts on-the-fly (Figure 11.4). Stream ciphers were very popular whenever data came in long streams (such as with older wireless networks or cell phones).

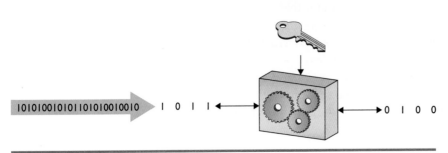

• **Figure 11.4**   Stream cipher

Very early on, back in the late 1980s, Ron Rivest invented a stream cipher called **Rivest Cipher 4 (RC4)**. RC4 was (and still is) pretty amazing: lighting fast, easy to use, and, most importantly, free. RC4 quickly became the dominant stream cipher, used in wireless, Web pages, remote desktops...the list goes on and on. Unfortunately, starting around 2001 and continuing to 2013, a number of weaknesses were discovered in RC4, making the security industry lose trust in RC4 and creating a move to block ciphers that continues to this day. So even though many encryptions (wireless, HTTP, RDP) still support RC4, it's quickly being looked at as a legacy cipher. As a result, almost all TCP/IP applications have moved to **Advanced Encryption Standard (AES)**.

AES is a block cipher created in the late 1990s. It uses a 128-bit block size and 128-, 192-, or 256-bit key size. AES is incredibly secure, practically uncrackable (for now at least), and so fast even applications that traditionally used stream ciphers are switching to AES.

Not at all limited to TCP/IP, you'll find AES used for many applications, from file encryption to wireless networking to some Web sites.

Many TCP/IP applications are still in the process of moving toward adoption.

When in doubt on a question about encryption algorithms, always pick AES. You'll be right most of the time.

Asymmetric-Key Algorithm Standards

Symmetric-key encryption has one serious weakness: anyone who gets a hold of the key can encrypt or decrypt data with it. The nature of symmetric-key encryption forces us to send the key to the other person in one way or another, making it a challenge to use symmetric-key encryption safely. As a result, folks have been strongly motivated to create a methodology that allows the encrypter to send a key to the decrypter without fear of interception (Figure 11.5).

• **Figure 11.5**　How do we safely deliver the key?

The answer to the problem of key sharing came in the form of using two different keys— one to encrypt and one to decrypt, thus, an asymmetric-key algorithm. Three men in the late 1970s—Whitfield Diffie, Martin Hellman, and Ralph Merkle— introduced what became known as **public-key cryptography**, with which keys could be exchanged securely.

Ron Rivest (along with Adi Shamir and Leonard Adleman) came up with some improvements to the Diffie-Hellman method of public-key cryptography by introducing a fully functional algorithm called **Rivest Shamir Adleman (RSA)** that enabled secure digital signatures.

Here's how public-key cryptography works. Imagine two people, Mike and Melissa, who wish to send each other encrypted e-mail messages (Figure 11.6). SMTP doesn't have any (popular) form of encryption, so Mike and Melissa must come up with some program that encrypts their messages. They will then send the encrypted messages as regular e-mail.

Before Melissa can send an encrypted e-mail to Mike, he first generates *two* keys. One of these keys is kept on his computer (the *private* key), and the other key is sent to anyone from whom he wants to receive encrypted e-mail

The public-key cryptography introduced by Diffie, Hellman, and Merkle became known as the *Diffie-Hellman key exchange*. Hellman, on the other hand, has insisted that if the scheme needs a name, it should be called the Diffie-Hellman-Merkle key exchange.

Public-key cryptography is the most popular form of e-mail encryption.

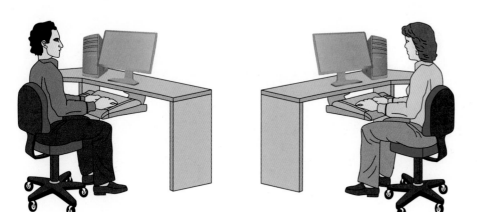
• **Figure 11.6**　Mike and Melissa, wanting to send encrypted e-mail messages

• **Figure 11.7**   Sending a public key

(the *public* key). These two keys—called a **key pair**—are generated at the same time and are designed to work together. He sends a copy of the public key to Melissa (Figure 11.7).

A public-key cryptography algorithm works by encrypting data with a public key and then decrypting data with a private key. The public key of the key pair encrypts the data, and only the associated private key of the key pair can decrypt the data. Since Melissa has Mike's public key, Melissa can encrypt and send a message to Mike that only Mike's private key can decrypt. Mike can then decrypt the message (Figure 11.8).

If Melissa wants Mike to send encrypted e-mail to her, she must generate her own key pair and send Mike the public key. In a typical public-key

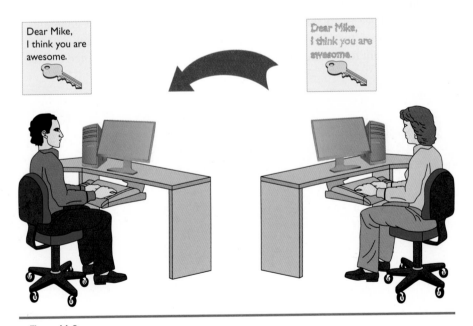

• **Figure 11.8**   Decrypting a message

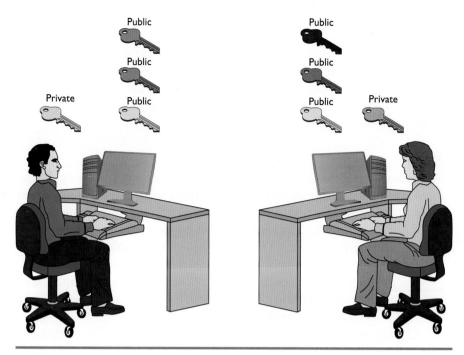

• **Figure 11.9**   Lots of keys

cryptography setup, everyone has their own private key plus a copy of the public keys for anyone with whom they wish to communicate securely (Figure 11.9).

The only problem with all these keys is the chance that someone pretending to be someone else might pass out a public key. Therefore, the recipients have a strong desire to know who is passing out a key. This issue falls under the banner of nonrepudiation.

> This simple description, while accurate, doesn't cover some big differences between Diffie-Hellman and RSA. The CompTIA Network+ exam doesn't go into those differences.

Encryption and the OSI Model

The process of encryption varies dramatically depending on what you want to encrypt. To make life a bit easier, let's look at how you encrypt using the OSI seven-layer model:

- **Layer 1**   No common encryption done at this layer.

- **Layer 2**   A common place for encryption using proprietary encryption devices. These boxes scramble all of the data in an Ethernet frame except the MAC address information. Devices or software encodes and decodes the information on-the-fly at each end.

- **Layer 3**   Only one common protocol encrypts at Layer 3: IPsec. IPsec is typically implemented via software that takes the IP packet and encrypts everything inside the packet, leaving only the IP addresses and a few other fields unencrypted.

- **Layer 4**   Neither TCP nor UDP offers any encryption methods, so little happens security-wise at Layer 4.

- **Layers 5, 6, and 7**   Important encryption standards (such as SSL and TLS used in e-commerce) happen within these layers, but don't fit cleanly into the OSI model.

Integrity

It's important to us that we receive the same data that was sent. It's not too terribly hard for bad luck and bad players to maul our data, however, so we need tools to ensure our data has the integrity we need. There are a number of tools to do this, but the one of greatest interest for the CompTIA Network+ exam is the hash function.

Hash

In computer security, a **hash** (or more accurately, a *cryptographic hash function*) is a mathematical function that you run on a string of binary digits of any length that results in a value of some fixed length (often called a *checksum* or a *message digest*). A cryptographic hash function is a one-way function. One-way means the hash is practically irreversible. You should not be able to re-create the data, even if you know the hashing algorithm and the checksum. A cryptographic hash function should also have a unique message digest for any two different input streams (Figure 11.10).

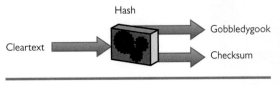

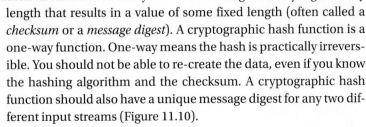

• **Figure 11.10**   A hash at work

Cryptographic hash functions have a huge number of uses, but a common one is for verifying file integrity. If I'm downloading a file from a reputable source, there are two main threats to its integrity: accidental damage caused by networking/storage issues, and tampering by an attack that has compromised the site or my connection.

When the download provider hashes the contents of the file and publishes the resulting message digest, I can hash the copy I downloaded and compare the digests to verify the file on my system is most-likely identical. This provides the best protection from accidental damage; an attacker capable of altering the file I download might also be able to alter the message digest published on the site. I can increase my confidence in its integrity by verifying the digest with more than one reputable source.

These days, **Secure Hash Algorithm (SHA)** is the primary family of cryptographic hash functions. It includes SHA-1, SHA-2 (which includes the popular SHA-256 and SHA-512 variants), and the soon-to-be-finalized SHA-3. One thing to keep in mind about cryptographic functions is that we err on the side of caution. Once someone demonstrates a practical attack against an algorithm, recommendations shift quickly to newer functions with improved security. Still, existing uses of the old functions can linger for a long time.

As the result of a number of attacks published in 2009, 2012, and 2013, two widely used hash functions, SHA-1 and *Message-Digest Algorithm version 5*—best known as **MD5** (Figure 11.11)—have both ended up on this list of hash functions that are no longer recommended as safe. Because of their popularity, you're likely to run into these in the wild or see them on the CompTIA Network+ exam.

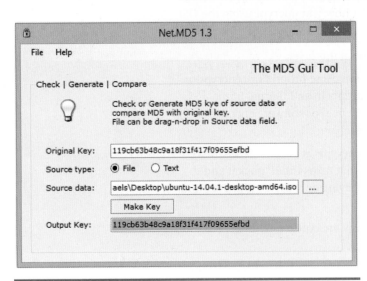

• **Figure 11.11**   Using MD5

 **Try This!**

Is This the File I Think It Is?

Let's download a common program—the latest version of Mozilla's Firefox browser—and use the trustworthy hash functions that come with our operating system to confirm our copy matches the hashes Mozilla has published. We'll use the SHA512 algorithm for this exercise.

1. Download a copy of the latest Firefox from https://www.mozilla .org/en-US/firefox/new/, but don't install it when the download completes.

2. Navigate to http://download.cdn.mozilla.net/pub/mozilla.org /firefox/releases/latest/ and look for the files ending with "SUMS". Each of these contains a long list of hashes computed using a given algorithm for all of the files in the directory. The part of the file name before "SUMS" specifies the algorithm used.

3. Click on the SHA512SUMS file. The left-hand column contains hashes, and the right-hand column contains relative file paths.

4. The way we actually calculate the hash varies a bit from platform to platform. Pick your platform below and type the appropriate command, replacing `<filename>` with the name or path of the file downloaded in step 1.

   a. Linux & OS/X:

      ■ Open a terminal window and navigate to the directory you downloaded the file to.

      ■ At the prompt, type this command:
      ```
      shasum -a 512 "<filename>"
      ```

      ■ This command will output a single line in the same format as the SHA512SUMS file. Select and copy the hash.

   b. Windows 8 or newer:

      ■ Open Windows PowerShell—not to be confused with the regular Windows command line—and navigate to the directory you downloaded the file to.

      ■ At the PowerShell prompt, type this sequence of commands:
      ```
      (Get-FileHash -Algorithm SHA512 '<filename>').hash | clip
      ```

      ■ This command generates and copies the hash directly to your clipboard.

5. Switch back to your browser and use **Find** to search the SHA512SUMS document for the hash you copied in step 4. If your file downloaded properly, you'll usually get a single match. Since there are unique installer files for different platforms and languages, the file path on the matched line should specify your platform, language, and the name of the file you downloaded in step 1 and hashed in step 4.

Many encryption and authentication schemes also use hashes. Granted, you won't actually see the hashes as they're used, but trust me: hashes are everywhere. For example, some SMTP servers use a special form of MD5, called *Challenge-Response Authentication Mechanism-Message Digest 5 (CRAM-MD5),* as a tool for server authentication. (See the discussion of CHAP later in the "User Authentication Standards" section for details on how challenge-response works.) Now that you understand hashes, let's return to public-key cryptography and see how digital signatures provide nonrepudiation and make public-key cryptography even more secure.

Nonrepudiation

Within networking, nonrepudiation simply means that the receiver of information has a very high degree of confidence that the sender of a piece of information truly is who the receiver thinks he or she or it should be. Nonrepudiation takes place all over a network. Is this truly the person who sent in the user name and password to log into my Windows domain? Is this really the eBay.com Web site I'm entering my credit card number into? Did this public key really come from Mike Meyers?

Digital Signatures

As mentioned earlier, public-key cryptography suffers from the risk that you might be getting a message or a public key from someone who isn't who they say they are. To avoid this problem, you add a digital signature. A **digital signature** is a hash of the message encrypted by the private key. The person with the matching public key decrypts the digital signature using the public key, generates their own hash, and compares it to the decrypted hash to verify it came from the intended sender. Digital signatures are very popular with e-mail users. Figure 11.12 shows an e-mail message being both encrypted and digitally signed in Mozilla Thunderbird.

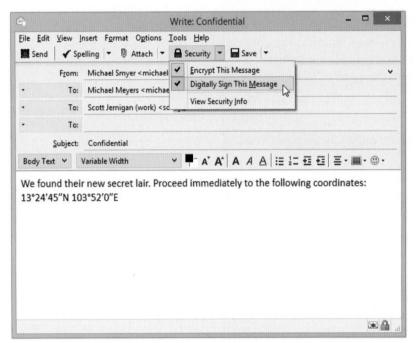

• **Figure 11.12**   Digitally signed

PKI

Digital signatures are great, but what happens when you want to do business with someone you do not know? Before you enter a credit card number to buy that new USB 3.0 Blu-ray Disc player, wouldn't you like to know that the Web site you are doing business with truly is eBay? To address that need the industry came up with the idea of certificates. A **certificate** is a standardized type of digital signature that includes the digital signature of a third party, a person or a company that guarantees that who is passing out this certificate truly is who they say they are. As you might imagine, certificates are incredibly common with secure Web pages. When you go to eBay to sign in, your browser redirects to a secure Web page. These are easy to identify by the lock icon at the bottom of the screen or in the address bar (Figure 11.13) or the https:// used (instead of http://) in the address bar.

In the background, several actions take place (all before the secure Web page loads). First, the Web server automatically sends a copy of its certificate. Built into that certificate is the Web server's public key and a signature from the third party that guarantees this is really eBay. Go to your national version of eBay (I'm in the United States, so I'll use eBay.com) and click **Sign In** (you don't even need an eBay account to do this). Now look at the certificate for the current session. Depending on the Web browser you use, you'll see it in different

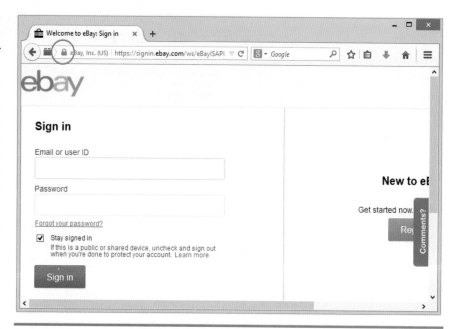

• **Figure 11.13**   Secure Web page

ways. Try clicking the little lock icon in the address bar as this usually works. Figure 11.14 shows the certificate for this session.

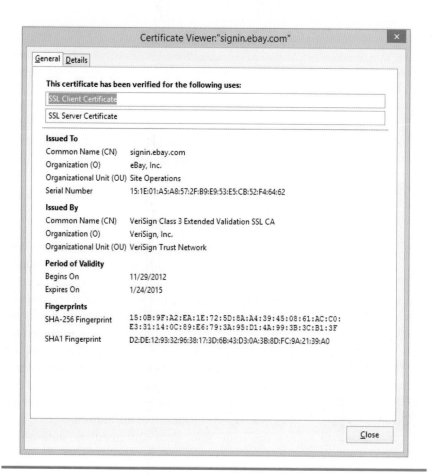

• **Figure 11.14**   eBay sign-in certificate

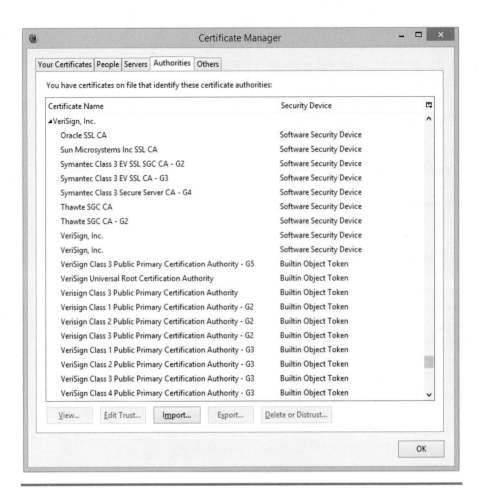

Figure 11.15 Certificate authority certificates on a system

> Becoming a root certificate authority with enough respect to have Web browsers install your certificate is very difficult!

So a company called VeriSign issued this certificate. That's great, but how does your computer check all this? VeriSign is a certificate authority (CA). Every Web browser keeps a list of certificate authority certificates that it checks against when it receives a digital certificate. Figure 11.15 shows the certificate authority certificates stored on my system.

When someone wants to create a secure Web site, he or she buys a certificate signed by a certificate authority, such as VeriSign (the biggest player in the market and the one I'll use for this example). VeriSign acts as the root, and the new Web site's certificate contains VeriSign's signature. For more advanced situations, VeriSign includes an intermediate certificate authority between VeriSign's root certificate authority and the user's certificate. This creates a tree of certificate authorization, with the root authorities at the top and issued certificates at the bottom.

You can also have intermediate authorities, although these are not as heavily used. Together, this organization is called a **public-key infrastructure (PKI)** (Figure 11.16).

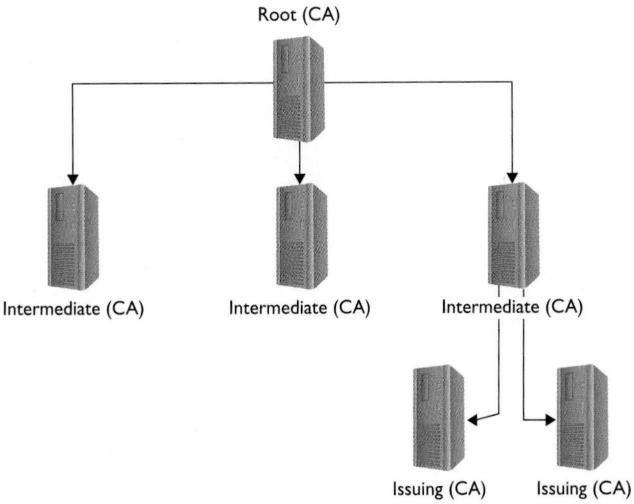

Figure 11.16 VeriSign's PKI tree

You don't have to use PKI to use certificates. First, you can create your own unsigned certificates. These are perfectly fine for lower-security situations (e-mail among friends, personal Web page, and so forth), but don't expect anyone to buy products on a Web site or send highly sensitive e-mail without a signed certificate from a well-known certificate authority like VeriSign, Thawte, or GoDaddy.

Digital certificates and asymmetric cryptography are closely linked because digital certificates are almost always used to verify the exchange of public keys. In many cases, this exchange takes place behind the scenes of e-mail, Web pages, and even in some very secure wireless networks. Though you may not see certificates in action very often, you now know that they are there.

Authentication

As mentioned at the beginning of this chapter, authentication is the process of positively identifying users trying to access data. The first exposure to authentication for most users is coming across a login screen prompting you to enter a user name and password, but there are many other ways to authenticate. A network technician should understand not only how different authentication methods control user names and passwords, but also some of the authentication standards used in today's TCP/IP networks.

Passwords offer significant security challenges. What happens after you type in a user name and password? How is this data transferred? Who or what reads this? What is the data compared to? A series of TCP/IP security standards that use combinations of user names, passwords, and sometimes certificates, all handled in a usually secure manner, address these issues, as described in the upcoming section "TCP/IP Security Standards."

But you can't stop with user names and passwords. What if someone gets a hold of your user name and password? To defeat those types of bad guys, some systems require a second form of authentication. These second forms of authentication include items you carry, like a smart card. They might also be something that uniquely identifies you, such as your retinal patterns or fingerprints. We call these *biometrics*. Whatever the case, when you use passwords and one or more other forms of authentication, we call this multifactor authentication (or sometimes two-factor authentication).

Authorization

A large part of the entire networking process involves one computer requesting something from another computer. A Web client might ask for a Web page, for example, or a Common Internet File System (CIFS) client might ask a file server for access to a folder. A computer far away might ask another computer for access to a private network. Whatever the case, you should carefully assign levels of access to your resources. This is authorization. To help define how to assign levels of access, you use an access control list.

An access control list (ACL) is nothing more than a clearly defined list of permissions that specifies what an authenticated user may perform on a shared resource. Over the years the way to assign access to resources has changed dramatically. To help you to understand these changes, the security industry likes to use the idea of *ACL access models*. There are three types of ACL access models: mandatory, discretionary, and role based.

In a mandatory access control (MAC) security model, every resource is assigned a label that defines its security level. If the user lacks that security level, he or she does not get access. MAC is used in many operating systems to define what privileges programs have to other programs stored in RAM. The MAC security model is the oldest and least common of the three.

Discretionary access control (DAC) is based on the idea that a resource has an owner who may at his or her discretion assign access to that resource. DAC is considered much more flexible than MAC.

Role-based access control (RBAC) is the most popular model used in file sharing. RBAC defines a user's access to a resource based on the roles the user plays in the network environment. This leads to the idea of creating groups. A group in most networks is nothing more than a name that has clearly defined accesses to different resources. User accounts are placed into various groups. A network might have a group called "Sales" on a Web server that gives any user account that is a member of the Sales group access to a special Web page that no other groups can see.

Keep in mind that these three types of access control are models. Every TCP/IP application and operating system has its own set of rules that sometimes follows one of these models, but in many cases does not. But do make sure you understand these three models for the CompTIA Network+ exam!

TCP/IP Security Standards

Now that you have a conceptual understanding of encryption, integrity, non-repudiation, authentication, and authorization, it's time to see how the TCP/IP folks have put it all together to create standards so you can secure just about anything in TCP/IP networks.

TCP/IP security standards are a rather strange mess. Some are authentication standards, some are encryption standards, and some are so unique to a single application that I'm not even going to talk about them in this section and instead will wait until the "Secure TCP/IP Applications" discussion at the end of this chapter. There's a reason for all this confusion: TCP/IP was never really designed for security. As you read through this section, you'll discover that almost all of these standards either predate the whole Internet, are slapped-together standards that have some serious issues, or, in the case of the most recent standards, are designed to combine a bunch of old, confusing standards. So hang tight—it's going to be a bumpy ride!

User Authentication Standards

Authentication standards are some of the oldest standards used in TCP/IP. Many are so old they predate the Internet itself. Once upon a time, nobody had fiber-optic, cable, or DSL connections to their ISPs. For the most part, if you wanted to connect to the Internet you had a choice: go to the computer center or use dial-up.

Dial-up, using telephone lines for the most part, predates the Internet, but the nerds of their day didn't want just anybody dialing into their computers. To prevent unauthorized access, they developed some excellent authentication methods that TCP/IP adopted for itself. A number of authentication methods

In the early days of dial-up, we used the *Serial Line Internet Protocol (SLIP)* to connect a modem to an Internet service provider (ISP). SLIP was a totally unsecure protocol and thus we migrated to PPP as soon as we could.

were used back in these early days, but, for the most part, TCP/IP authentication started with something called the Point-to-Point Protocol.

PPP

The **Point-to-Point Protocol (PPP)** enables two point-to-point devices to connect, authenticate with a user name and password, and negotiate the network protocol the two devices will use. Today that network protocol is almost always TCP/IP.

Note that point-to-point and dial-up are not Ethernet, but still can support TCP/IP. Many network technologies don't need Ethernet, such as telephone, cable modem, microwave, and wireless (plus a bunch more you won't even see until Chapter 14). In fact, once you leave a LAN, most of the Internet is just a series of point-to-point connections.

If you're nerdy enough to pull up RFC (Request for Comment) 1661, the RFC that defines how PPP works, you'll see there are five distinct phases to a PPP connection:

1. **Link dead** This is a nice way to say there isn't a link yet. The modem is turned off; no one is talking. This phase is when all PPP conversations begin. The main player at this (and later phases) is the *Link Control Protocol (LCP)*. The LCP's job is to get the connection going. As it starts up, we move into the...

2. **Link establishment** The LCP communicates with the LCP on the other side of the PPP link, determining a good link, which, in turn, opens the...

3. **Authentication** Here is where the authentication takes place. In most cases, authentication is performed by entering a simple user name/password. I'll go into more detail in the next section. For now, once the authentication is complete and successful, the PPP connection goes into...

4. **Network layer protocol** PPP works with a number of OSI Layer 3 network protocols. Today everyone uses TCP/IP, but PPP still supports long-dead protocols such as NetWare IPX/SPX and Microsoft NetBEUI. LCP uses yet another protocol called the **Network Control Protocol (NCP)** to make the proper connections for that protocol. You now have a good connection. To shut down, the LCP initiates a...

5. **Termination** When done nicely, the two ends of the PPP connection send each other a few termination packets and the link is closed. If one person is cut off, the LCP will wait for a certain timeout and then terminate on its own side.

PPP provided the first common method to get a server to request a user name and password. In such a point-to-point connection, the side asking for the connection is called the *initiator,* whereas the other side, which has a list of user names and passwords, is called the *authenticator* (Figure 11.17).

Initializing connection...

Users	Passwords
Mike	spork846z
stacey	hamsters
0cool	3141567

• **Figure 11.17** A point-to-point connection

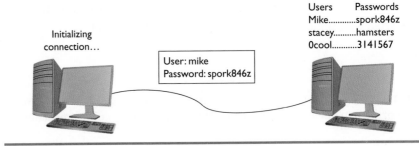

Initializing
connection...

Users   Passwords
Mike............spork846z
stacey.........hamsters
0cool...........3141567

User: mike
Password: spork846z

• **Figure 11.18**   PAP in action

PPP came with two methods of *user authentication*, the process of authenticating a user name and password. The original way—called **Password Authentication Protocol (PAP)**—simply transmits the user name and password over the connection in plaintext. Unfortunately, that means anyone who can tap the connection can learn the user name and password (Figure 11.18).

Fortunately, PPP also includes the safer **Challenge Handshake Authentication Protocol (CHAP)** to provide a more secure authentication routine. CHAP relies on hashes based on a shared secret, usually a password that both ends of the connection know. When the initiator of the connection makes the initial connection request, the authenticator creates some form of challenge message. The initiator then makes a hash using the password and sends that to the authenticator. The authenticator, in turn, compares that value to its own hash calculation based on the password. If they match, the initiator is authenticated (Figure 11.19).

Once the connection is up and running, CHAP keeps working by periodically repeating the entire authentication process. This prevents man-in-the-middle attacks, where a third party inserts an independent connection, intercepts traffic, reads or alters it, and then forwards it on without either the sender or recipient being aware of the intrusion.

CHAP works nicely because it never sends the actual password over the link. The CHAP standard leaves a number of issues undefined, however, like

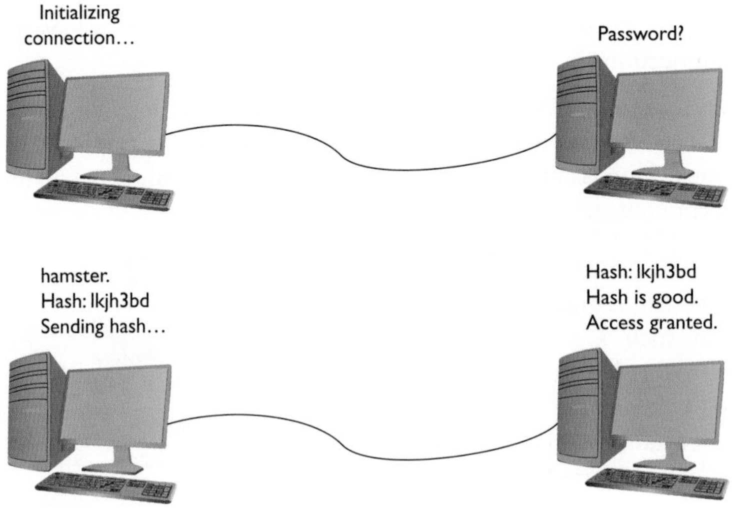

If you get a question on PAP, CHAP, and MS-CHAP on the CompTIA Network+ exam, remember that MS-CHAP offers the most security.

Initializing
connection...

Password?

hamster.
Hash: lkjh3bd
Sending hash...

Hash: lkjh3bd
Hash is good.
Access granted.

• **Figure 11.19**   CHAP in action

"If the hash doesn't match, what do I do?" The boom in dial-up connections to the Internet in the 1990s led Microsoft to invent a more detailed version of CHAP called **MS-CHAP**. (CompTIA drops the hyphen, so you might see it as *MSCHAP* on the exam.) The current version of MS-CHAP is called MS-CHAPv2. MS-CHAPv2 is still the most common authentication method for the few of us using dial-up connections. Believe it or not, dial-up is still being used, and even the latest operating systems support it. Figure 11.20 shows the dial-up connection options for Vista.

AAA

PPP does a great job of handling authentication for point-to-point connections, but it has some limitations. The biggest problem is that, in many cases, a network might have more than one point for an initiator to enter. PPP assumes that the authenticator at the endpoint has all the user name and password information, but that's not necessarily true. In traditional modem communication, for example, an ISP has a large bank of modems to support any number

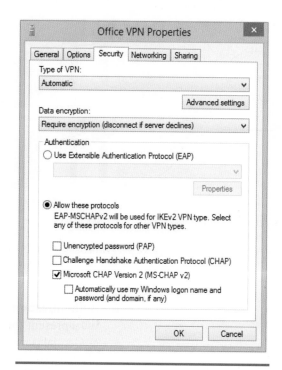

• **Figure 11.20**   MS-CHAP is alive and well.

of users. When a user dials in, the modem bank provides the first available connection, but that means that any modem in the bank has to support any of the users. You can't put the database containing all user names and passwords on every modem (Figure 11.21).

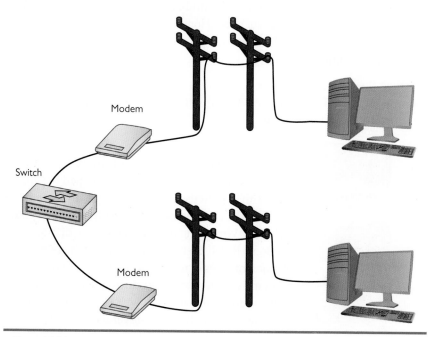

• **Figure 11.21**   Where do you put the user names and passwords?

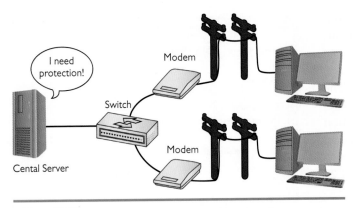

• **Figure 11.22** Central servers are vulnerable to attack

In this case, you need a central database of user names and passwords. That's simple enough, but it creates another problem—anyone accessing the network can see the passwords unless the data is somehow protected and encrypted (Figure 11.22). PPP is good at the endpoints, but once the data gets on the network, it's unencrypted.

Thus, the folks overseeing central databases full of user names and passwords needed to come up with standards to follow to protect that data. They first agreed upon a philosophy called Authentication, Authorization, and Accounting (AAA). AAA is designed for the idea of port authentication—the concept of allowing remote users authentication to a particular point-of-entry (a port) to another network.

- **Authentication** A computer that is trying to connect to the network must present some form of credential for access to the network. This credential is most commonly a user name and password, but it might also be a security token such as a smart card, retinal scan, or digital certificate. It might even be a combination of some of these. The authentication gives the computer the right to access the network.

- **Authorization** Once authenticated, the computer determines what it can or cannot do on the network. It might only be allowed to use a certain amount of bandwidth. It might be limited to working only certain times of day or might be limited to using only a certain set of applications.

- **Accounting** The authenticating server should do some form of accounting such as recording the number of times a user logs on and logs off. It might track unsuccessful logon attempts. It may track what services or resources the client system accessed. The number of items to be accounted is massive.

> NAS stands for either *Network Access Server* or *Network Attached Storage.* The latter is a type of dedicated file server used in many networks. Make sure you read the question to see which NAS it's looking for!

Once the idea of AAA took shape, those smart Internet folks developed two standards: RADIUS and TACACS+. Both standards offer authentication, authorization, and accounting.

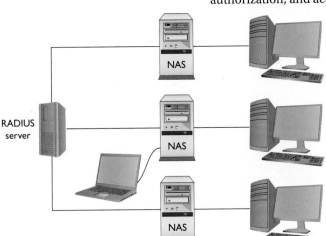

• **Figure 11.23** RADIUS setup

RADIUS Remote Authentication Dial-In User Service (RADIUS) is the better known of the two AAA standards and, as its name implies, was created to support ISPs with hundreds if not thousands of modems in hundreds of computers to connect to a single central database. While originally designed for dial-up connections, RADIUS still works hard in a huge number of different types of networks, both wired and wireless, and I'm sure there are a few ancient dial-up networks still working somewhere as well. RADIUS consists of three devices: the RADIUS server that has access to a database of user names and passwords, a number of Network Access Servers (NASs) that control the modems, and a group of systems that in some way connect to the network (Figure 11.23).

To use RADIUS, you need a RADIUS server. The most popular choice for Microsoft environments is Internet Authentication Service (IAS). IAS comes built in with most versions of Microsoft Windows Server operating systems. For the UNIX/Linux crowd, the popular (yet, in my opinion, hard to set up) FreeRADIUS is the best choice. If you prefer a more prepackaged server, you might look at Juniper Networks' Steel-Belted RADIUS line of powerful and somewhat easy-to-set-up servers that many people feel are well worth the price tag.

A single RADIUS server can support multiple NASs and provide a complete PPP connection from the requesting system, through the NAS, all the way to the RADIUS server. Like any PPP connection, the RADIUS server supports PAP, CHAP, and MS-CHAP. Even if you use PAP, RADIUS hashes the password so at no time is the user name/password exposed. Newer versions of RADIUS support even more authentication methods, as you will soon see. RADIUS performs this authentication on either UDP ports 1812 and 1813 or UDP ports 1645 and 1646.

TACACS+   Routers and switches need administration. In a simple network, you can access the administration screen for each router and switch by entering a user name and password for each device. When a network becomes complex, with many routers and switches, logging into each device separately starts to become administratively messy. The answer is to make a single server store the ACL for all the devices in the network. To make this secure, you need to follow the AAA principles.

Terminal Access Controller Access Control System Plus (TACACS+) is a protocol developed by Cisco to support AAA in a network with many routers and switches. TACACS+ is very similar to RADIUS in function, but uses TCP port 49 by default and separates authorization, authentication, and accounting into different parts. TACACS+ uses PAP, CHAP, and MD5 hashes, but can also use something called Kerberos as part of the authentication scheme.

Kerberos

Up to this point almost all the authentication schemes I've discussed either are based on PPP or at least take the idea of PPP and expand upon it. Of course, every rule needs an exception and Kerberos is the exception here.

Kerberos is an authentication protocol that has no connection to PPP. Twenty years ago, some Internet folks began to appreciate that TCP/IP was not secure and thus designed Kerberos. Kerberos is an authentication protocol for TCP/IP networks with many clients all connected to a single authenticating server—no point-to-point here! Kerberos works nicely in a network, so nicely that Microsoft adopted it as the authentication protocol for all Windows networks using a domain controller.

Kerberos is the cornerstone of the all-powerful Microsoft Windows domain. Be careful here—the use of domains I'm about to describe has nothing to do with DNS. A Windows domain is a group of computers that defers all authentication to a *domain controller,* a special computer running some version of Windows Server. The Windows domain controller stores a list of all user names and passwords. When you log on at a computer that is a member of a Windows domain, your user name and password go directly to the domain controller, which uses Kerberos for authentication.

The cornerstone of Kerberos is the Key Distribution Center (KDC), which has two processes: the Authentication Server (AS) and the Ticket-Granting

The original TACACS protocol was used for authentication in UNIX systems back in the mid-1980s. The CompTIA Network+ objectives pay homage to the ancient standard by not using the "plus" symbol with the acronym, but you need to know the current TACACS+ protocol for real-world networking.

Kerberos uses UDP or TCP port 88 by default.

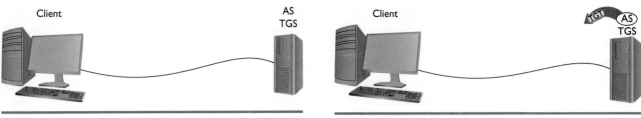

● **Figure 11.24**   Windows Kerberos setup

● **Figure 11.25**   AS sending a TGT back to client

Service (TGS). In Windows server environments, the KDC is installed on the domain controller (Figure 11.24).

When your client logs onto the domain, it sends a request that includes a hash of the user name and password to the AS. The AS compares the results of that hash to its own hash (as it also stores the user name and password) and, if they match, sends a **Ticket-Granting Ticket (TGT)** and a timestamp (Figure 11.25). The ticket has a default lifespan in Windows of ten hours. The client is now authenticated but not yet authorized.

The client then sends the timestamped TGT to the TGS for authorization. The TGS sends a timestamped service ticket (also called a *token* or *access token*) back to the client (Figure 11.26).

This token is the key that the client uses to access any single resource on the entire domain. This is where authorization takes place. The token authorizes the user to access resources without reauthenticating. Any time the client attempts to access a folder, printer, or service anywhere in the domain, the server sharing that resource uses the token to see exactly what access the client may have to that resource. If you try to access some other feature under Windows, such as retrieve your e-mail via Microsoft Exchange Server, you won't need to log in again. The ability to log in only one time and use the same token to access any resource (that you're allowed to access) on an entire network is called **single sign-on**.

> The TGT is sometimes referred to as *Ticket to Get Ticket*.

● **Figure 11.26**   TGS sending token to client

> In Windows, the security token is called a Security Identifier (SID).

Timestamping is important for Kerberos because it forces the client to request a new token every eight hours. This prevents third parties from intercepting the tokens and attempting to crack them. Kerberos tokens can be cracked, but it's doubtful this can be done in under eight hours.

Kerberos is very popular, but has some serious weaknesses. First, if the KDC goes down, no one has access. That's why Microsoft and other operating systems that use Kerberos always stress the importance of maintaining a backup KDC. In Windows, it is standard practice to have at least two domain controllers. Second, timestamping requires that all the clients and servers synchronize their clocks. This is fairly easy to do in a wired network (such as a Windows domain or even a bunch of connected routers using TACACS+), but it adds an extra level of challenge in dispersed networks (such as those connected across the country).

EAP

One of the great challenges to authentication is getting the two ends of the authentication process to handle the many different types of authentication options. Even though PPP pretty much owned the user name/password authentication business, proprietary forms of authentication using smartcards/tokens, certificates, and so on, began to show up on the market, threatening to drop practical authentication into a huge mess of competing standards.

The **Extensible Authentication Protocol (EAP)** was developed to create a single standard to allow two devices to authenticate. Despite the name, EAP is not a protocol in the classic sense, but rather it is a PPP wrapper that EAP-compliant applications can use to accept one of many types of authentication. Although EAP is a general-purpose authentication wrapper, its only substantial use is in wireless networks. (See Chapter 15, "Wireless Networking," to see where EAP is used.) EAP comes in various types, but currently only six types are in common use:

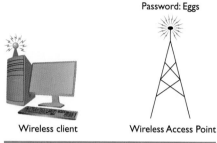

- **EAP-PSK**   Easily the most popular form of authentication used in wireless networks today, EAP-PSK (Personal Shared Key) is nothing more than a shared secret code that's stored on both the wireless access point and the wireless client, encrypted using the powerful AES encryption (Figure 11.27). See Chapter 15 for the scoop on wireless access points and EAP.

• **Figure 11.27**   EAP-PSK in action

- **EAP-TLS**   EAP with Transport Layer Security (TLS) defines the use of a RADIUS server as well as mutual authentication, requiring certificates on both the server and every client. On the client side, a smart card may be used in lieu of a certificate. EAP-TLS is very robust, but the client-side certificate requirement is an administrative challenge. Even though it's a challenge, the most secure wireless networks all use EAP-TLS. EAP-TLS is only used on wireless networks, but TLS is used heavily on secure Web sites (see the section "SSL/TLS" later in this chapter). Figure 11.28 shows a typical EAP-TLS setup for a wireless network.

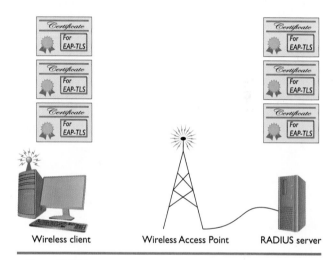

• **Figure 11.28**   EAP-TLS

- **EAP-TTLS**   EAP-TTLS (Tunneled TLS) is similar to EAP-TLS but only uses a single server-side certificate. EAP-TTLS is very common for more secure wireless networks (Figure 11.29).

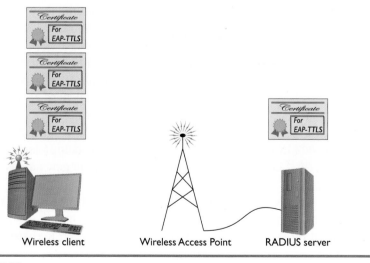

• **Figure 11.29**   EAP-TTLS

- **EAP-MS-CHAPv2** More commonly known as **Protected Extensible Authentication Protocol (PEAP)**, EAP-MS-CHAPv2 uses a password function based on MS-CHAPv2 with the addition of an encrypted TLS tunnel similar to EAP-TLS.

- **EAP-MD5** This is a very simple version of EAP that uses only MD5 hashes for transfer of authentication credentials. EAP-MD5 is weak and the least used of all the versions of EAP described.

- **LEAP** **Lightweight Extensible Authentication Protocol (LEAP)** is a proprietary EAP authentication used almost exclusively by Cisco wireless products. LEAP is an interesting combination of MS-CHAP authentication between a wireless client and a RADIUS server.

802.1X

EAP was a huge success and almost overnight gave those who needed point-to-point authentication a one-stop-shop methodology to do so. EAP was so successful that there was a cry to develop an EAP solution for Ethernet networks. This solution is called 802.1X. Whereas traditional EAP is nothing more than an authentication method wrapped in PPP, 802.1X gets rid of the PPP (Ethernet is not a point-to-point protocol!) and instead puts the EAP information inside an Ethernet frame.

802.1X is a port-based authentication network access control mechanism for networks. In other words, it's a complete authentication standard designed to force devices to go through a full AAA process to get anywhere past the interface on a gateway system. Before 802.1X, a system on a wired network could always access another system's port. Granted, an attacker wouldn't be able to do much until he gave a user name/password or certificate, but he could still send packets to any computer on the network. This wasn't good because it enabled attackers to get to the systems to try to do evil things. 802.1X prevented them from even getting in the door until they were authenticated and authorized.

The interesting part is that you already know about most of the parts of 802.1X because the standard worked hard to use existing technologies. From a distance, 802.1X looks a lot like a RADIUS AAA setup. 802.1X changes the names of some of the components, as shown in Figure 11.30. Compare this to Figure 11.23 to get the new names (the jobs don't change).

802.1X combines the RADIUS-style AAA with EAP versions to make a complete authentication solution. The folks who developed 802.1X saw it as a total replacement for every other form of authentication (even Kerberos), but the

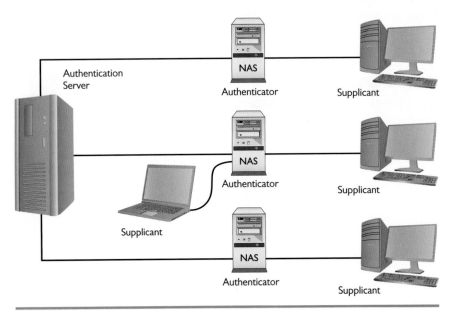

- **Figure 11.30** 802.1X components

Technically, wireless networks don't use EAP. They use 802.1X, which, in turn, uses EAP.

reality is that most people don't like changing something that already works. To that end, only wireless networking broadly adopted 802.1X.

I'm not done explaining authentication and authorization, but at least you now understand the basics of the popular authentication and authorization protocols and standards. You have more protocols to learn, but all of them are rather specialized for specific uses and thus are covered at various places throughout the book.

Encryption Standards

The Internet had authentication long before it had encryption. As a result, almost all encryption came out as a knee-jerk reaction to somebody realizing that his or her TCP/IP application wasn't secure. For years, there were new secure versions of just about every protocol in existence. New versions of all the classics started to appear, almost all starting with the word "Secure": Secure FTP, Secure SMTP, and even Secure POP were developed. They worked, but there were still hundreds of not-yet-secured protocols and the specter of redoing all of them was daunting. Fortunately, some new, all-purpose encryption protocols were developed that enabled a client to connect to a server in a secure way while still using their older, unsecure protocols—and it all started because of Telnet.

SSH

The broad adoption of the Internet by the early 1990s motivated programmers to start securing their applications. Telnet had a big problem. It was incredibly useful and popular, but it was a completely unsecure protocol. Telnet credentials were (and are) sent in cleartext, an obvious vulnerability.

Telnet needed to be fixed. As the story goes, Tatu Ylonen of the Helsinki University of Technology, reacting to an attack that intercepted Telnet user names and passwords on his network, invented a new secure replacement for Telnet called **Secure Shell (SSH)**. You've already seen SSH in action (in Chapter 9, "TCP/IP Applications") as a secure version of Telnet, but now that you know more about security, let's look at SSH in detail.

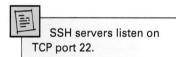

SSH servers listen on TCP port 22.

SSH servers use PKI in the form of an RSA key. The first time a client tries to log into an SSH server, the server sends its public key to the client (Figure 11.31).

After the client receives this key, it creates a session ID, encrypts it using the public key, and sends it back to the server. The server decrypts this session

• **Figure 11.31**   PuTTY getting an RSA key

ID and uses it in all data transfers going forward. Only the client and the server know this session ID. Next, the client and server negotiate the type of encryption to use for the session. These days, AES is popular, but older symmetric-key ciphers such as 3DES may still be used. The negotiation for the cipher is automatic and invisible to the user.

Using RSA and a cipher makes a very safe connection, but the combination doesn't tell the server who is using the client. All SSH servers, therefore, add user names and passwords to authenticate the client (Figure 11.32). Once a user logs in with a user name and password, he or she has access to the system.

In addition to using a password for authentication, SSH also can use public keys to identify clients. This opens up some interesting possibilities such as noninteractive logins. You can also turn off password login altogether, hardening your server even further. To use public/private keys for authentication, you must first generate a pair of RSA or Digital Signature Algorithm (DSA) keys with a tool such as PuTTYgen (Figure 11.33). The public key is then copied to the server, and the private key is kept safe on the client.

When you connect to the server, your client generates a signature using its private key and sends it to the server. The server then checks the signature with its copy of the public key, and if everything checks out, you will be authenticated with the server.

If SSH stopped here as a secure replacement for Telnet, that would be fantastic, but SSH has another trick up its sleeve: the capability to act as a *tunnel* for *any* TCP/IP application. Let's see what tunnels are and how they work.

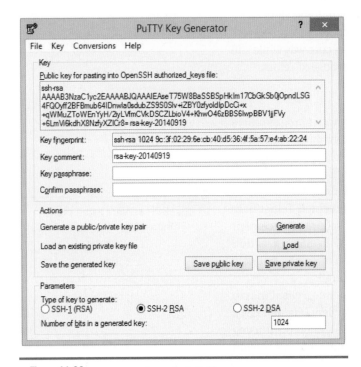

• **Figure 11.33**   Generated keys in PuTTYgen

Tunneling

Simply, a **tunnel** is an encrypted link between two programs on two separate computers. Let's take a look at an SSH link between a server and a client. Once established, anything you enter into the client application is encrypted, sent to the server, decrypted, and then acted upon (Figure 11.34).

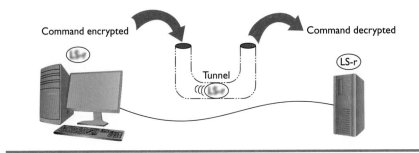

• **Figure 11.34**   SSH in action

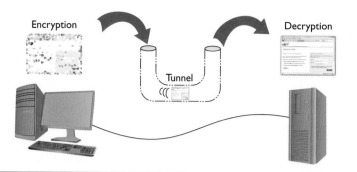

• Figure 11.35 Encrypting a Web client

The nature of SSH is such that it took very little to extend the idea of SSH to accept input from any source, even another program (Figure 11.35). As long as the program can redirect to the SSH client and then the SSH server redirect to the server application, anything can go through an SSH connection encrypted. This is an SSH tunnel.

SSH tunnels are wildly popular and fairly easy to set up. Equally, all of the popular SSH clients and servers are designed to go into tunnel mode, usually with no more than a simple click of a check box (Figure 11.36).

Many tunneling protocols and standards are used in TCP/IP. SSH is one of the simplest types of tunnels so it's a great first exposure to tunneling. As the book progresses, you'll see more tunneling protocols, and you'll get the basics of tunneling. For now, make sure you understand that a tunnel is an encrypted connection between two endpoints. Any packet that enters the encrypted tunnel, including a packet with unencrypted data, is automatically encrypted, goes through the tunnel, and is decrypted on the other endpoint.

SSH may be popular, but it's not the only option for encryption. All of the other encryption standards are built into combined authentication/encryption standards, as covered in the next section.

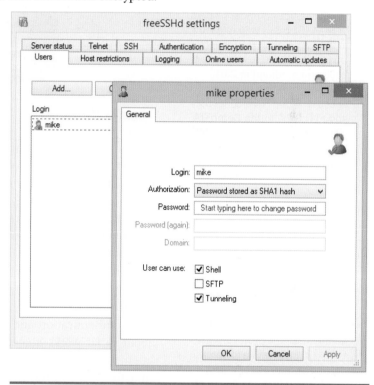

• Figure 11.36 Turning on tunneling in freeSSHd server

Combining Authentication and Encryption

The rest of the popular authentication and encryption standards are combined to include both authentication and encryption in a single standard. Lumping together authentication and encryption into the same standard does not make it weaker than the standards already discussed. These are some of the most popular standards on the Internet today, because they offer excellent security.

SSL/TLS

The introduction and rapid growth of e-commerce on the World Wide Web in the mid-1990s made it painfully obvious that some form of authentication and encryption was needed. Netscape Corporation took the first shot at a new standard. At the time, the dominant Web browser was Netscape Navigator. Netscape created a standard called Secure Sockets Layer (SSL). SSL requires a server with a certificate. When a client requests access to an SSL-secured server, the server sends to the client a copy of the certificate. The SSL client checks this certificate (all Web browsers come with an exhaustive list of CA root certificates preloaded), and if the certificate checks out, the server is authenticated and the client negotiates a symmetric-key cipher for use in the session (Figure 11.37). The session is now in a very secure encrypted tunnel between the SSL server and the SSL client.

• **Figure 11.37**   SSL at work

The Transport Layer Security (TLS) protocol was designed as an upgrade to SSL. TLS is very similar to SSL, working in almost the same way. TLS is more robust and flexible and works with just about any TCP application. SSL is limited to HTML, FTP, SMTP, and a few older TCP applications. TLS has no such restrictions and is used in securing Voice over IP (VoIP) and virtual private networks (VPNs), but it is still most heavily used in securing Web pages. Every Web browser today uses TLS for HTTPS-secured Web sites, and EAP-TLS is common for more-secure wireless networks.

IPsec

Every authentication and encryption protocol and standard you've learned about so far works *above* the Network layer of the OSI seven-layer model. Internet Protocol Security (IPsec) is an authentication and encryption protocol suite that works at the Internet/Network layer and should become the dominant authentication and encryption protocol suite as IPv6 continues to roll out and replace IPv4. (See Chapter 13 for details on IPv6.)

IPsec works in two different modes: Transport mode and Tunnel mode. In Transport mode, only the actual payload of the IP packet is encrypted: the destination and source IP addresses and other IP header information are still readable. In Tunnel mode, the entire IP packet is encrypted and then placed into an IPsec endpoint where it is encapsulated inside another IP packet. The mode you use depends on the application (Figure 11.38). IPv6 will use the IPsec Transport mode by default.

The IPsec protocol suite uses many open source protocols to provide both tight authentication and robust encryption. You do not need to know how each

SSL/TLS also supports mutual authentication, but this is relatively rare.

Developers have continued to refine TLS since the release of TLS 1.0 (SSL 3.1) in 1999. Each of the TLS versions is considered an upgrade from SSL 3.0, so you'll see both numbers listed. TLS 1.1 (SSL 3.2) was released in 2006. The most recent version is TLS 1.2 (SSL 3.3), released in 2008 and modified in 2011.

I only mention the numbers because CompTIA erroneously added TLS 2.0 to the CompTIA Network+ competencies. I think they must mean TLS 1.2. You do *not* need to memorize release dates or any other release number.

The *Internet Engineering Task Force (IETF)* specifies the IPsec protocol suite, managing updates and revisions. One of those specifications regards the acronym for the protocol suite, calling it *IPsec* with a lowercase "s" rather than IPS or IPSec, which you might imagine to be the initials or acronym. Go figure.

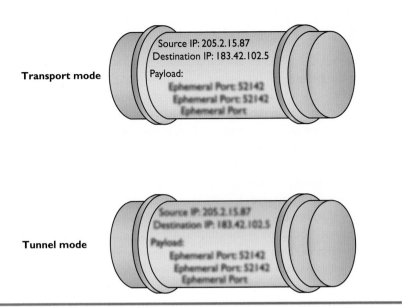

Transport mode

> Source IP: 205.2.15.87
> Destination IP: 183.42.102.5
>
> Payload:
>
> Ephemeral Port: 52142
> Ephemeral Port: 52142
> Ephemeral Port

Tunnel mode

> Source IP: 205.2.15.87
> Destination IP: 183.42.102.5
>
> Payload:
>
> Ephemeral Port: 52142
> Ephemeral Port: 52142
> Ephemeral Port

• **Figure 11.38**   IPsec's two modes

of the protocols works for the CompTIA Network+ exam, but you should recognize which protocols function within IPsec. Here are the main protocols:

- *Authentication Header (AH)* for authentication
- *Encapsulating Security Payload (ESP)* for implementing authentication and encryption
- *Internet Security Association and Key Management Protocol (ISAKMP)* for establishing security associations (SAs) that define things like the protocol used for exchanging keys
- *Internet Key Exchange (IKE and IKEv2)* and *Kerberized Internet Negotiation of Keys (KINK),* two widely used key exchanging protocols

Plus, IPsec can encrypt data using any number of encryption algorithms, such as MD5 and SHA that you read about earlier in this chapter.

IPsec is an incredibly powerful authentication/encryption protocol suite, but until IPv6 is widely implemented, its only common current use is creating secure tunnels between two computers: a job it performs very well. Keep an eye out for IPsec!

■ Secure TCP/IP Applications

I've covered quite a few TCP/IP security standards and protocols thus far in the chapter, but I really haven't put anything to work yet. Now is the time to talk about actual applications that use these tools to make secure connections. As mentioned earlier, this is in no way a complete list, as there are thousands of secure TCP applications; I'll stick to ones you will see on the CompTIA Network+ exam. Even within that group, I've saved discussion of some of the applications for other chapters that deal more directly with certain security aspects (such as remote connections).

HTTPS

You've already seen HTTPS back in Chapter 9, so let's do a quick review and then take the coverage a bit deeper. You know that HTTPS pages traditionally start with https:// and that most browsers also show a small lock icon in the lower-right corner or in the address bar. You also know that HTTPS uses SSL/TLS for the actual authentication and encryption process. In most cases, all of this works very well, but what do you do when HTTPS has trouble?

Since you won't get an HTTPS connection without a good certificate exchange, the most common problems are caused by bad certificates. When a certificate comes in from an HTTPS Web site, your computer checks the expiration date to verify the certificate is still valid and checks the Web site's URL to make sure it's the same as the site you are on. If either of these is not correct, you get an error such as the one shown in Figure 11.39.

If you get one of these errors, you need to decide what to do. Good certificates do go bad (this even happened on my own Web site once) and sometimes the URLs on the certificates are not exactly the same as the site using them. When in doubt, stop. On the other hand, if the risk is low (for example, you're not entering a credit card number or other sensitive information) and you know and trust the site, proceeding is safe in most cases. A courtesy e-mail or phone call to the Web site administrator notifying him or her about the invalid certificate is usually greatly appreciated.

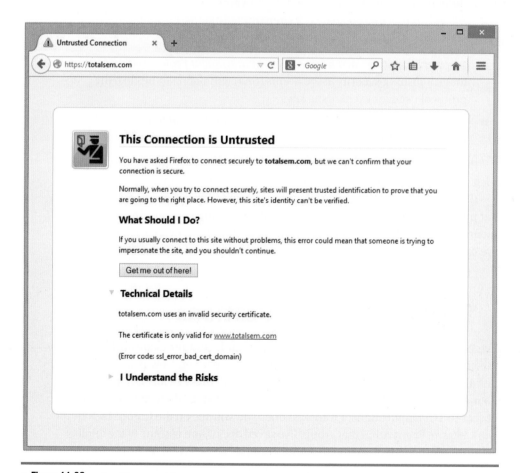

• Figure 11.39   Certificate problem

Invalid certificates aren't the only potential problems. After this basic check, the browser checks to see if the certificate has been revoked. Root authorities, like VeriSign, generate Certificate Revocation Lists (CRLs) that a Web browser can check against. Certificates are revoked for a number of reasons, but most of the time the reasons are serious, such as a compromised private key.

If you get a revoked certificate error, it's better to stay away from the site until they fix the problem.

SCP

One of the first SSH-enabled programs to appear after the introduction of SSH was the **Secure Copy Protocol (SCP)**. SCP was one of the first protocols used to transfer data securely between two hosts and thus might have replaced FTP. SCP works well but lacks features such as a directory listing. SCP still exists, especially with the well-known UNIX scp command-line utility, but it has, for the most part, been replaced by the more powerful SFTP.

Cross Check

FTP and TFTP

You saw FTP and TFTP back in Chapter 9, so check your memory now. How do they differ from SFTP? Do they use the same ports? Would you use FTP and TFTP in the same circumstances? Finally, what's the difference between active and passive FTP?

SFTP

Secure FTP (SFTP), also called *SSH FTP*, was designed as a replacement for FTP after many of the inadequacies of SCP (such as the inability to see the files on the other computer) were discovered. Although SFTP and FTP have similar names and perform the same job of transferring files, the way in which they do that job differs greatly.

The introduction of SSH made it easy to secure most TCP applications just by running them in an SSH tunnel. But FTP was a different case. FTP, at least active FTP, uses two ports, 20 and 21, creating a two-session communication. This makes FTP a challenge to run in its original form over SSH because SSH can only handle one session per tunnel. To fix this, a group of programmers from the OpenBSD organization developed a series of secure programs known collectively as **OpenSSH**. SFTP was one of those programs. SFTP looks like FTP, with servers and clients, but relies on an SSH tunnel. If you are on Windows and would like to connect with an SFTP server, WinSCP and FileZilla are two great client options.

SNMP

The **Simple Network Management Protocol (SNMP)** is a very popular method for querying the state of SNMP-capable devices. SNMP can tell you a number of settings like CPU usage, network utilization, and detailed firewall hits. SNMP uses *agents* (special client programs) to collect network information from

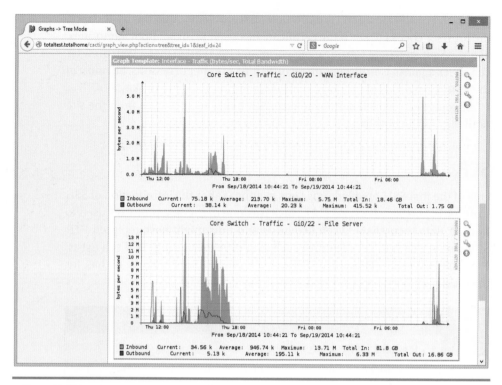

• **Figure 11.40**   Cacti at work

a **Management Information Base (MIB)**, SNMP's version of a server. To use SNMP, you need SNMP-capable devices and some tool to query them. One tool is Cacti (www.cacti.net), shown in Figure 11.40. Cacti, like most good SNMP tools, enables you to query an SNMP-capable device for hundreds of different types of information.

SNMP is a useful tool for network administrators, but the first version, SNMPv1, sent all data, including the passwords, unencrypted over the network. SNMPv2 had good encryption but was rather challenging to use. SNMPv3 is the standard version used today and combines solid, fairly easy-to-use authentication and encryption.

SNMP runs on UDP port 161.

LDAP

The **Lightweight Directory Access Protocol (LDAP)** is the tool that programs use to query and change a database used by the network. The networks today employ many different databases that are used in many different ways. I'm not talking about databases used by normal people to enter sales calls or to inventory trucks! These are databases used to track who is logged into the network, how many DHCP clients are currently DHCP active, or the location of all the printers in the local network.

One of the most complex and also most used databases is Windows Active Directory. Active Directory is the power behind single sign-on and network information (where's the closest printer to me?). Every Windows domain controller stores a copy of the Active Directory.

If a domain controller fails, another domain controller can and must instantly take over. To do this, every domain controller must have an identical copy of the Active Directory. That means if a single domain controller makes a change to the Active Directory, it must quickly send that change to other domain controllers.

Enter LDAP. LDAP is the tool used in virtually every situation where one computer needs to access another computer's database for information or to make an update. You will probably never use LDAP manually. Your domain controllers will use it automatically and transparently in the background to keep your databases in good order. LDAP uses TCP port 389 by default.

NTP

The **Network Time Protocol (NTP)** does one thing: it gives you the current time. NTP is an old protocol and isn't in and of itself much of a security risk unless you're using some timestamping protocol like Kerberos. Windows is by far the most common Kerberos user, so just make sure all of your computers have access to an NTP server so users don't run into problems when logging in. NTP uses UDP port 123.

Chapter 11 Review

■ Chapter Summary

After reading this chapter and completing the exercises, you should understand the following about securing TCP/IP.

Discuss the standard methods for securing TCP/IP networks

- TCP/IP security can be broken down into five areas: encryption, integrity, nonrepudiation, authentication, and authorization.

- Encryption means to scramble, mix up, or change the data in such a way that bad guys can't read the data.

- Integrity is the process that guarantees that the data received is the same as originally sent.

- Nonrepudiation is the process of making sure data came from the person or entity it was supposed to come from.

- Authentication means to verify that whoever is trying to access data is the person you want accessing that data.

- Authorization defines what an authenticated person can do with that data.

- All data starts as plaintext (also called cleartext), meaning the data is in an easily read or viewed industry-wide standard format.

- A cipher is a general term for a way to encrypt data, and an algorithm is the cipher's underlying mathematical formula.

- A symmetric-key algorithm is any encryption algorithm that uses the same key for both encryption and decryption. There are two types of symmetric-key algorithms: block ciphers and stream ciphers.

- Block ciphers encrypt data in single chunks of a certain length. Stream ciphers encrypt a single bit at a time.

- Data Encryption Standard (DES) is the oldest TCP/IP symmetric-key algorithm and uses a 64-bit block with a 56-bit key. DES is susceptible to brute-force attacks.

- Advanced Encryption Standard (AES) is the most secure TCP/IP symmetric-key algorithm and uses a 128-bit block with a 128-, 192-, or 256-bit key. AES is practically uncrackable.

- Symmetric-key encryption has one serious weakness: anyone who gets a hold of the key can encrypt or decrypt.

- Public-key cryptography is an implementation of asymmetric-key encryption, which uses one key to encrypt and a different key to decrypt.

- A key pair consists of a public key, which is shared and distributed to senders to use to encrypt data, and a private key, which is kept only by the recipient and used to decrypt data.

- A hash is a mathematical function that you run on a string of binary digits of any length that results in a value of some fixed length, often called a checksum or a message digest.

- A cryptographic hash function is a one-way function that produces a unique checksum that can be used to verify nonrepudiation. MD5 and SHA2 are popular hashes for this type of work.

- A digital signature is a hash of the message encrypted by the private key. It can only be generated from the unencrypted message and is another form of nonrepudiation.

- A certificate is a standardized type of digital signature used to verify the identity of someone (or something) you do not know, like a Web site. A certificate usually includes the digital signature of a third party, a person, or a company that guarantees that who is passing out this certificate truly is who they say they are. VeriSign and Thawte are popular certificate authorities.

- An access control list (ACL) is used to control authorization, or what a user is allowed to do once they have been authenticated. There are three types of ACL access modes: MAC, DAC, and RBAC.

- In a mandatory access control (MAC) security model, every resource is assigned a label that defines its security level. If the user lacks that security level, he or she does not get access.

- Discretionary access control (DAC) is based on the idea that a resource has an owner who may, at his or her discretion, assign access to that resource.

- Role-based access control (RBAC) is the most popular model used in file sharing and defines a user's access to a resource based on the user's group membership.

Compare TCP/IP security standards

- The Point-to-Point Protocol (PPP) enables two point-to-point devices to connect, authenticate with a user name and password, and negotiate the network protocol the two devices will use.

- PPP includes two methods to authenticate a user name and password: PAP and CHAP.

- The Password Authentication Protocol (PAP) transmits the user name and password over the connection in plaintext, which is not secure.

- The Challenge Handshake Authentication Protocol (CHAP) provides a more secure authentication routine because it relies on hashes based on a shared secret, usually a password that both ends of the connection know. Microsoft created its own version called MS-CHAP.

- Authentication, Authorization, and Accounting (AAA) is a philosophy applied to computer security. RADIUS and TACACS+ are standard implementations of AAA.

- Remote Authentication Dial-In User Service (RADIUS) is the better known of the two AAA standards and was created to support ISPs with hundreds if not thousands of modems in hundreds of computers to connect to a single central database.

- Microsoft's RADIUS server is called Internet Authentication Service (IAS) and comes built in with most versions of Microsoft Windows Server. FreeRADIUS is a popular RADIUS server for UNIX/Linux.

- Terminal Access Controller Access Control System Plus (TACACS+) is a proprietary protocol developed by Cisco to support AAA in a network with many routers and switches.

- Kerberos, unlike PPP, is an authentication protocol for TCP/IP networks with many clients all connected to a single authenticating server.

- Kerberos, which is the authentication protocol for all Windows networks using a domain controller, uses a Key Distribution Center (KDC) that has two processes: the Authentication Server (AS) and the Ticket-Granting Service (TGS).

- The Authentication Server authenticates users at login and, if successful, sends a Ticket-Granting Ticket (TGT) (good for ten hours by default) allowing the user to access network resources without having to reauthenticate.

- The timestamped TGT is sent to the TGS, which returns an access token used by the client for authorization to a network resource.

- The Extensible Authentication Protocol (EAP) was developed to help two devices negotiate the authentication process. It is used primarily in wireless networks. There are six commonly used types of EAP: EAP-PSK, EAP-TLS, EAP-TTLS, EAP-MS-CHAPv2 (PEAP), EAP-MD5, and LEAP.

- EAP Personal Shared Key (EAP-PSK) is the most popular form of authentication used in wireless networks today.

- Early wireless networks lacked any form of authentication, so the wireless community grabbed a preexisting authentication standard called 802.1X to use in their wireless networks. 802.1X combines the RADIUS-style AAA with EAP versions to make a complete authentication solution.

- Secure Shell (SSH) is a secure replacement for Telnet. SSH uses PKI in the form of an RSA key. At login, the SSH server sends its public key to the client. The client then encrypts data using the public key and transmits the data, which is subsequently decrypted on the server with the private key.

- Netscape created the Secure Sockets Layer (SSL) standard, which requires a server with a certificate. SSL has been updated to the Transport Layer Security (TLS) standard and is used for secure Web transactions, such as online credit card purchases.

- SSL is limited to HTML, FTP, SMTP, and a few older TCP applications, whereas TLS is less restrictive and is used for everything SSL does in addition to VoIP and VPNs.

- IPsec is an encryption protocol and is destined to become the dominant encryption protocol under IPv6. IPsec works in two different modes: Transport mode and Tunnel mode. IPv6 uses the IPsec Transport mode by default.

- In Transport mode, only the actual payload of the IP packet is encrypted; the destination and source IP addresses and other IP header information are still readable.

- In Tunnel mode, the entire IP packet is encrypted and then placed into an IPsec endpoint where it is encapsulated inside another IP packet.

Implement secure TCP/IP applications

- HTTPS uses SSL/TLS for the actual authentication and encryption process. Most browsers show a small lock icon in the lower-right corner or in the address bar when an HTTPS connection is established.

- The most common problems with HTTPS connections are caused by bad or outdated certificates.

- The Secure Copy Protocol (SCP) is an SSH-enabled program or protocol used to copy files securely between a client and a server. It has been replaced by Secure FTP (SFTP).

- The Simple Network Management Protocol (SNMP) is a method for querying the state of SNMP-capable devices. SNMP can tell you a number of settings like CPU usage, network utilization, and detailed firewall hits. SNMP uses agents and MIBs to capture and monitor network usage.

- SNMPv1 sent all data, including the passwords, unencrypted over the network. SNMPv2 had good encryption but was rather challenging to use. SNMPv3 is the standard version used today and combines solid, fairly easy-to-use authentication and encryption.

- Active Directory servers and other servers use the Lightweight Directory Access Protocol (LDAP) to keep important databases updated.

- The Network Time Protocol (NTP) gives you the current time. It isn't much of a security risk unless you're using some timestamping protocol like Kerberos.

■ Key Terms

802.1X *(310)*
access control list (ACL) *(301)*
Advanced Encryption Standard (AES) *(292)*
algorithm *(290)*
asymmetric-key algorithm *(292)*
authentication *(289)*
Authentication, Authorization, and Accounting (AAA) *(306)*
Authentication Server (AS) *(307)*
authorization *(289)*
block cipher *(292)*
certificate *(298)*
Challenge Handshake Authentication Protocol (CHAP) *(304)*
cipher *(290)*
ciphertext *(291)*
cleartext *(290)*
Data Encryption Standard (DES) *(292)*
digital signature *(298)*
discretionary access control (DAC) *(302)*
encryption *(289)*
Extensible Authentication Protocol (EAP) *(309)*
FreeRADIUS *(307)*
hash *(296)*

integrity *(289)*
Internet Authentication Service (IAS) *(307)*
Internet Protocol Security (IPsec) *(314)*
Kerberos *(307)*
Key Distribution Center (KDC) *(307)*
key pair *(294)*
Lightweight Directory Access Protocol (LDAP) *(318)*
Lightweight Extensible Authentication Protocol (LEAP) *(310)*
Management Information Base (MIB) *(318)*
mandatory access control (MAC) *(302)*
MD5 *(296)*
MS-CHAP *(305)*
multifactor authentication *(301)*
Network Access Server (NAS) *(306)*
Network Control Protocol (NCP) *(303)*
Network Time Protocol (NTP) *(319)*
nonrepudiation *(289)*
OpenSSH *(317)*
Password Authentication Protocol (PAP) *(304)*
plaintext *(290)*
Point-to-Point Protocol (PPP) *(303)*
Protected Extensible Authentication Protocol (PEAP) *(310)*

public-key cryptography *(293)*
public-key infrastructure (PKI) *(300)*
Remote Authentication Dial-In User
   Service (RADIUS) *(306)*
Rivest Cipher 4 (RC4) *(292)*
Rivest Shamir Adleman (RSA) *(293)*
role-based access control (RBAC) *(302)*
Secure Copy Protocol (SCP) *(317)*
Secure FTP (SFTP) *(317)*
Secure Hash Algorithm (SHA) *(296)*
Secure Shell (SSH) *(311)*

Secure Sockets Layer (SSL) *(314)*
Simple Network Management Protocol (SNMP) *(317)*
single sign-on *(308)*
stream cipher *(292)*
symmetric-key algorithm *(291)*
Terminal Access Controller Access Control System
   Plus (TACACS+) *(307)*
Ticket-Granting Ticket (TGT) *(308)*
Transport Layer Security (TLS) *(314)*
tunnel *(312)*
two-factor authentication *(301)*

■ Key Term Quiz

Use the Key Terms list to complete the sentences that follow. Not all the terms will be used.

1. _____ defines what a person accessing
   data can do with that data.

2. _____ is the act of verifying you are who
   you say you are.

3. _____ is the process of guaranteeing that
   data is as originally sent.

4. A(n) _____ encrypts data in fixed-length
   chunks at a time.

5. _____ is a secure replacement for Telnet.

6. A(n) _____ uses one key to encrypt data
   and a different key to decrypt the same data.

7. SSL has been replaced by the more robust
   _____.

8. SCP has been replaced by _____, a
   secure protocol for copying files to a server.

9. _____ is the default authentication
   protocol for Windows domains and is extremely
   time sensitive.

10. _____ uses a 128-bit block, up to a 256-
    bit key, and is a virtually uncrackable encryption
    algorithm.

■ Multiple-Choice Quiz

1. Justin wants his team to be able to send him
   encrypted e-mails. What should he do?

   A. Send each team member his private key.

   B. Send each team member his public key.

   C. Ask each team member for his or her private key.

   D. Ask each team member for his or her public key.

2. Which of the following are popular cryptographic
   hashing functions? (Select two.)

   A. MD5

   B. SHA2

   C. RADIUS

   D. TACACS+

3. A public and private key pair is an example of what?

   A. Symmetric-key algorithm

   B. Asymmetric-key algorithm

   C. Certificate

   D. RADIUS

4. Which authentication protocol is time sensitive and
   is the default authentication protocol on Windows
   domains?

   A. PPP

   B. MS-CHAP

   C. IPsec

   D. Kerberos

5. What helps to protect credit card numbers during online purchases? (Select two.)

   A. Certificates

   B. TLS

   C. SCP

   D. NTP

6. Emily wants to remotely and securely enter commands to be run at a remote server. What application should she use?

   A. Telnet

   B. SSH

   C. SFTP

   D. RSA

7. A hash function is by definition

   A. A complex function

   B. A PKI function

   C. A one-way function

   D. A systematic function

8. In order to have a PKI you must have a(n)

   A. Web server

   B. Web of trust

   C. Root authority

   D. Unsigned certificate

9. Which term describes the process of guaranteeing that the sender of the data cannot later deny having sent it?

   A. Authentication

   B. Authorization

   C. Encryption

   D. Nonrepudiation

10. If you saw some traffic running on TCP port 49, what AAA standard would you know was running?

    A. PPP

    B. RADIUS

    C. MS-CHAP

    D. TACACS+

11. What is the difference between RADIUS and TACACS+?

    A. RADIUS is the authentication control for Windows networks, whereas TACACS+ is the authentication control for UNIX/Linux networks.

    B. RADIUS is an implementation of an authentication control, whereas TACACS+ is an implementation of authorization control.

    C. RADIUS is a generic name for authentication control, and there are implementations for Windows, UNIX, and Linux servers. TACACS+ is authentication control for Cisco routers and switches.

    D. RADIUS supports encryption; TACACS+ does not and is, therefore, less desirable in a network.

12. AES is a(n) _____ cipher.

    A. Block

    B. Forwarding

    C. Stream

    D. Asymmetric

13. Which authentication protocol is broadly used on wireless networks?

    A. 802.1X

    B. PPP

    C. PAP

    D. MS-CHAP

14. Digital signatures and certificates help which aspect of computer security?

    A. Accounting

    B. Authentication

    C. Authorization

    D. Nonrepudiation

15. Which authorization model grants privileges based on the group membership of network users?

    A. MAC

    B. DAC

    C. RBAC

    D. GAC

■ Essay Quiz

1. Explain the difference between symmetric-key and asymmetric-key algorithms and give examples of each. Which is more secure? Why?

2. Access control lists help to control the authorization of network resources. Explain the differences among the three ACL access models.

3. You receive a call from a distressed user telling you she was in the middle of an online purchase (just entering her credit card number) when she noticed a certificate warning on the screen saying the Web site's certificate has expired. What advice would you give the user?

Lab Projects

● Lab Project 11.1

Download a copy of GnuPG from www.gnupg.org and one of the frontends from www.gnupg.org/related_software/frontends.en.html. Generate a key pair and share your public key with a classmate.

Have your classmate encrypt a file using your public key and e-mail it to you. Decrypt your file with your private key.

● Lab Project 11.2

You have learned many acronyms in this chapter! Make a list of the following acronyms, state what they stand for, and briefly describe them. Use this as a study sheet for the CompTIA Network+ certification exam: DES, AES, RSA, MD5, SHA, PKI, CRAM-MD5,

ACL, MAC, DAC, RBAC, PPP, PAP, CHAP, MS-CHAP, AAA, RADIUS, TACACS+, KDC, AS, TGT, SID, EAP, EAP-TLS, EAP-PSK, EAPTTLS, EAP-MS-CHAPv2, PEAP, EAP-MD5, LEAP, SSH, SSL, TLS, HTTPS, SCP, SFTP, SNMP, and NTP.

Advanced Networking Devices

"It followed from the special theory of relativity that mass and energy are both but different manifestations of the same thing. A somewhat unfamiliar conception for the average mind."

—ALBERT EINSTEIN

In this chapter, you will learn how to

- **Discuss client/server and peer-to-peer topologies**
- **Describe the features and functions of VPNs**
- **Define the capabilities and management of managed switches**
- **Configure and deploy VLANs**
- **Implement advanced switch features**

So far in this book we've looked at networks in a rather simplistic way. First, we explored network topologies. Ethernet networks employ a hybrid star-bus topology, for example, with a physical star and a logical bus. Second, we've seen a number of devices with very clear distinctions about their functions according to the OSI model. We had hubs humming along at Layer 1, switches at Layer 2, and routers at Layer 3, each performing specific services without overlap. This is a great way to learn about networking, but it's not a complete view of how many networks function. It's time to put everything together.

This chapter starts with connection concepts, looking at classic and current uses of terms like client, server, and peer. The second portion dives into virtual private networks: technology for connecting remote users to local resources. The chapter then turns to managing devices that handle switching, security, and more. The fourth portion examines switches that can segment a single network into multiple virtual networks. The chapter finishes with a discussion about multilayer switches—boxes that do pretty much everything from Layer 1 all the way to Layer 7.

Client/Server and Peer-to-Peer Topologies

To share data and services, networks place computers or services into the category of *server,* the provider of such things. Other computers act as *clients,* the users of services. Many networks today blend the two roles, meaning each computer can both serve and request. Let's look at classic usage of client/server and peer-to-peer topologies, and then examine how the terms have changed in modern networking.

Historical/Conceptual

Client/Server

The earliest networks used a client/server model. In that model, certain systems acted as dedicated servers. Dedicated servers were called "dedicated" because that's all they did. You couldn't go up to a dedicated server and run Word or Solitaire. Dedicated servers ran powerful server network operating systems that offered up files, folders, Web pages, and so on to the network's client systems. Client systems on a client/server network never functioned as servers. One client system couldn't access shared resources on another client system. Servers served and clients accessed, and never the twain . . . crossed over . . . in the old days of client/server!

Figure 12.1 shows one of these old-school client/server networks. As far as the clients are concerned, the only system on the network is the server system. The clients can neither see each other, nor share data with each other directly. They must save the data on the server, so that other systems can access it.

Back in the old days there was an operating system called Novell NetWare. Novell NetWare servers were true dedicated servers. You couldn't go up to a Novell NetWare server and write yourself a resume. There were no user applications that you ran on the server. The only thing Novell NetWare servers knew how to do was share their own resources, but they shared those resources extremely well! The Novell NetWare operating system was unique. It wasn't anything like Windows, Macintosh, or Linux. It required you to

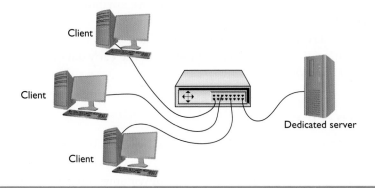

• **Figure 12.1**   A simple client/server network

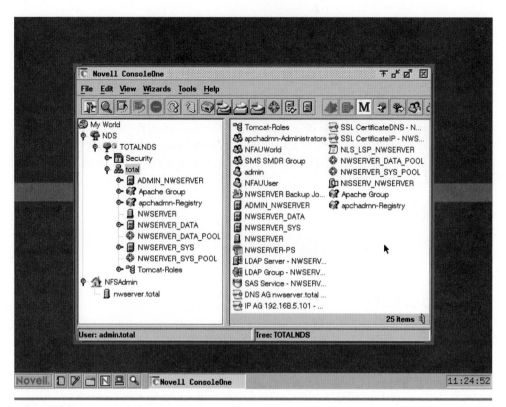

Novell ConsoleOne

File Edit View Wizards Tools Help

My World
 NDS
  TOTALNDS
   Security
   total
    ADMIN_NWSERVER
    Apache Group
    apchadmn-Registry
    NWSERVER
    NWSERVER_DATA
    NWSERVER_DATA_POOL
    NWSERVER_SYS
    NWSERVER_SYS_POOL
    Tomcat-Roles
  NFSAdmin
   nwserver.total

Tomcat-Roles
apchadmn-Administrators
NFAUWorld
SMS SMDR Group
admin
NFAUUser
NWSERVER Backup Jo...
ADMIN_NWSERVER
NWSERVER_DATA
NWSERVER_SYS
NWSERVER
NWSERVER-PS
LDAP Server - NWSERV...
LDAP Group - NWSERV...
SAS Service - NWSERV...
DNS AG nwserver.total ...
IP AG 192.168.5.101 - ...

SSL CertificateDNS - N...
SSL CertificateIP - NWS...
NLS_LSP_NWSERVER
NWSERVER_DATA_POOL
NWSERVER_SYS_POOL
NISSERV_NWSERVER
Apache Group
apchadmn-Registry

25 items

User: admin.total

Tree: TOTALNDS

Novell   Novell ConsoleOne   11:24:52

• **Figure 12.2**   Novell NetWare in action

learn an entirely different set of installation, configuration, and administration commands. Figure 12.2 shows a screen from Novell NetWare. Don't let the passing resemblance to Windows fool you—it was a completely different operating system!

Dedicated servers enabled Novell to create an entire feature set not seen before on personal computers. Each dedicated server had its own database of user names and passwords. You couldn't access any of the resources on the server without logging in. The server's administrator would assign "permissions" to a specific user account, such as Write (add files to a directory), File Scan (see the contents of a directory), and Erase (delete files).

By keeping the server functionality separate from the client systems, the Novell folks made very powerful, dedicated servers without overwhelming the client computers with tons of software. This was, after all, in the early days of personal computers and they didn't have anything near the power of a modern PC.

NetWare servers had tremendous power and great security because the only thing they did was run server software. In the early days of networking, client/server was king!

Novell NetWare as marketed today is a form of SUSE Linux. It is no longer a unique server-only operating system.

Peer-to-Peer

Novell NetWare was the first popular way to network PCs, but it wasn't too many years later that Microsoft introduced the first versions of network-capable Windows. The way in which these versions of Windows looked at networking, called peer-to-peer, was completely different from the client/server view of

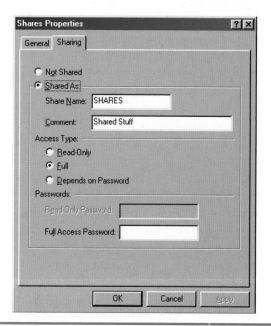

networking. In a **peer-to-peer** network, any system can act as a server, a client, or both, depending on how you configure that system. PCs on peer-to-peer networks frequently act as both clients and servers. One of the most common examples of a peer-to-peer network is the venerable Windows 9*x* series of operating systems. Figure 12.3 shows the sharing options for the ancient Windows 98 operating system, providing options to share a folder and thus turn that computer into a server.

At first glance, it would seem that peer-to-peer is the way to go—why create a network that doesn't allow the clients to see each other? Wouldn't it make more sense to give users the freedom to allow their systems both to share and access any resource? The problem was a lack of security. The early Windows systems did not have user accounts. You could apply only two permissions to a folder or file in these old versions: Read Only (read the folder or file but make no changes) and Full Control (do anything you want to do). So they made it easy to share but hard to control access to the shared resources. People wanted the freedom of peer-to-peer with the security of client/server.

 The "old school" client/server model means dedicated servers with strong security. Clients see only the server. In the peer-to-peer model, any system is a client, server, or both, but at the cost of lower security and additional demands on the system resources of each peer.

Test Specific

Client/Server and Peer-to-Peer Today

In response to demand, every modern operating system has dumped the classic client/server or peer-to-peer label. Windows, Linux, and OS X all have the capability to act as a server or a client while also providing robust security through user accounts, permissions, and the like.

Since the widespread adoption of TCP/IP and the Internet, client/server and peer-to-peer have taken on new or updated definitions and refer more to *applications* than to network operating systems. Consider e-mail for a moment.

I'm using the term "server" here to mean that you can share files and folders with other computers over a network, which is a server function. Don't confuse client versions of common operating systems, such as Windows 8.1, with specific server versions, such as Windows Server 2012 R2.

Chapter 12: Advanced Networking Devices

For traditional e-mail to work, you need an e-mail client like Microsoft Outlook. But you also need an e-mail server program like Microsoft Exchange to handle the e-mail requests from your e-mail client. Outlook is a *dedicated client*—you cannot use the Outlook client as a mail-serving program. Likewise, you cannot use Microsoft Exchange as an e-mail client. Exchange is a *dedicated server* program.

Peer-to-peer applications, often referred to simply as *P2P,* act as both client and server. The best examples of these applications are the now infamous file-sharing applications based on special TCP/IP protocols. The applications, with names like BitTorrent, LimeWire, and DC++, act as both clients and servers, enabling a user to share files and access shared files. BitTorrent is actually an entire protocol, not just a particular application. Many different applications use the BitTorrent standard. Figure 12.4 shows one such program, Transmission, in the process of simultaneously uploading and downloading files.

The terms *server, client,* and *peer* manifest in another way when discussing connecting to a local network from a remote site or connecting two networks together so they function as if they're one network. Let's turn now to a technology that makes these connection types possible: *virtual private networks.*

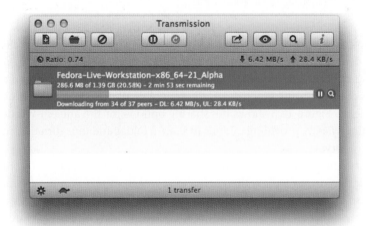

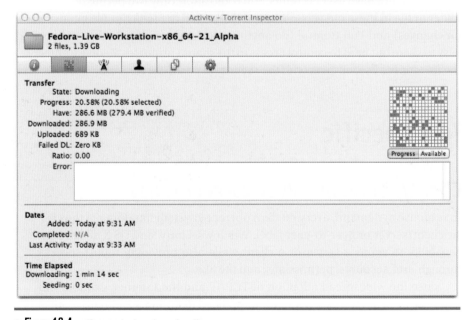

• **Figure 12.4**   Transmission downloading

Virtual Private Networks

Remote connections have been around for a long time, even before the Internet existed. The biggest drawback to remote connections was the cost to connect. If you were on one side of the continent and had to connect to your LAN on the other side of the continent, the only connection option was a telephone. Or, if you needed to connect two LANs across the continent, you ended up paying outrageous monthly charges for a private connection. The introduction of the Internet gave people wishing to connect to their home networks a very inexpensive connection option, but there was one problem—the whole Internet was (and is) open to the public. People wanted to stop using dial-up and expensive private connections and use the Internet instead, but they wanted to be able to do it securely.

If you read the previous chapter, you might think you could use some of the tools for securing TCP/IP to help, and you would be correct. Several standards use encrypted tunnels between a computer or a remote network and a private network through the Internet (Figure 12.5), resulting in what is called a **virtual private network (VPN)**.

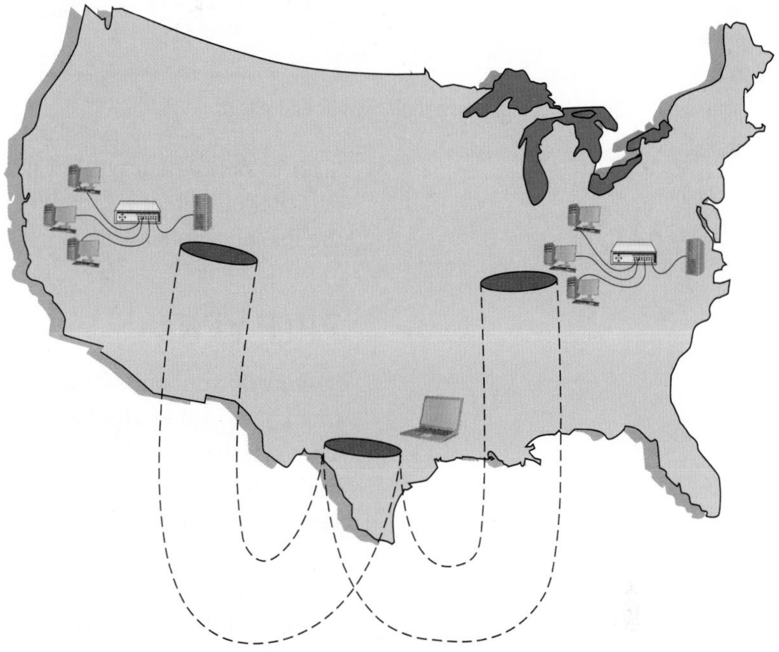

• **Figure 12.5**   VPN connecting computers across the United States

As you saw in the previous chapter, an encrypted tunnel requires *endpoints*—the ends of the tunnel where the data is encrypted and decrypted. In the tunnels you've seen thus far, the client for the application sits on one end and the server sits on the other. VPNs do exactly the same thing. Either some software running on a computer or, in some cases, a dedicated box must act as an endpoint for a VPN (Figure 12.6).

The key with the VPN is that all of the computers should be on the same network—and that means they must all have the same network ID. For example, you would want the laptop that you are using in an airport lounge to have the same network ID as all of the computers in your LAN back at the office. But there's no simple way to do this. If it's a single client trying to access a network, that client is going to take on the IP address from its local DHCP server. In the case of your laptop in the airport, your network ID and IP address come from the DHCP server in the airport, not the DHCP server back at the office.

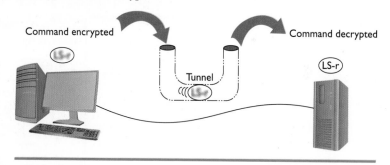

• **Figure 12.6**   Typical tunnel

To make the VPN work, you need a VPN client program protocol that uses one of the many tunneling protocols available. This remote client connects to the local LAN via its Internet connection, querying for an IP address from the local DHCP server. In this way, the VPN client will be on the same network ID as the local LAN. The remote computer now has two IP addresses. First, it has its Internet connection's IP address, obtained from the remote

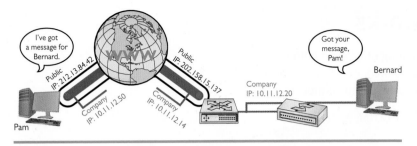

• **Figure 12.7** Endpoints must have their own IP addresses.

computer's ISP. Second, the VPN client creates a tunnel endpoint that acts like a NIC (Figure 12.7). This virtual NIC has an IP address that connects it to the local LAN.

Clever network engineers have come up with many ways to make this work, and those implementations function at different layers of the OSI model. PPTP and L2TP, for example, work at the Data Link layer. Many VPNs use IPsec at the Network layer to handle encryption needs. SSL and TLS VPNs don't really fit into the OSI model well at all, with some features in the Session layer and others in the Presentation layer.

PPTP VPNs

So how do you make IP addresses appear out of thin air? What tunneling protocol have you learned about that has the smarts to query for an IP address? That's right! Good old Point-to-Point Protocol (PPP)! Microsoft got the ball rolling with the **Point-to-Point Tunneling Protocol (PPTP)**, an advanced version of PPP that handles this right out of the box. The only trick is the endpoints. In Microsoft's view, a VPN is intended for individual clients to connect to a private network, so Microsoft places the PPTP endpoints on the client and the server. The server endpoint is a special remote access server program, originally only available on Windows Server, called **Routing and Remote Access Service (RRAS)**—see Figure 12.8.

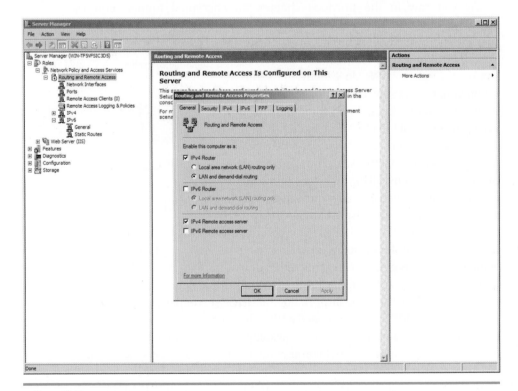

• **Figure 12.8** RRAS in action

On the Windows client side, you run **Create a New Connection**. This creates a virtual NIC that, like any other NIC, does a DHCP query and gets an IP address from the DHCP server on the private network (Figure 12.9).

When your computer connects to the RRAS server on the private network, PPTP creates a secure tunnel through the Internet back to the private LAN. Your client takes on an IP address of that network, as if your computer is directly connected to the LAN back at the office, even down to the default gateway. If you open your Web browser, your client will go across the Internet to the local LAN and then use the LAN's default gateway to get to the Internet! Using a Web browser will be much slower when you are on a VPN. Every operating system comes with some type of built-in VPN client that supports PPTP (among others). Figure 12.10 shows Network, the OS X VPN connection tool.

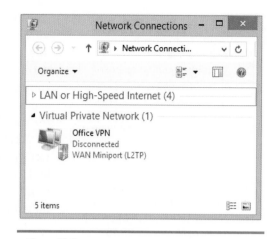

• **Figure 12.9**   VPN connection in Windows

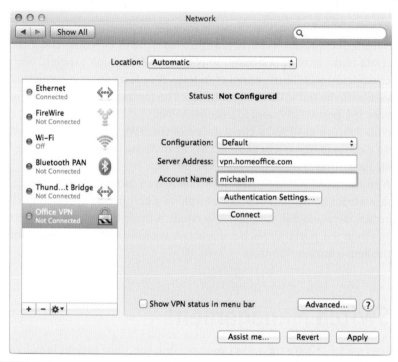

• **Figure 12.10**   VPN on an OS X system

> A system connected to a VPN looks as though it's on the local network, but performs much slower than if the system was connected directly back at the office because it's not local at all.

This type of VPN connection, where a single computer logs into a remote network and becomes, for all intents and purposes, a member of that network, is commonly called a **host-to-site** connection.

L2TP VPNs

The VPN protocol called **Layer 2 Tunneling Protocol (L2TP)** took all the good features of PPTP and a Cisco protocol called *Layer 2 Forwarding (L2F)* and added support to run on almost any type of connection possible, from telephones to Ethernet to ultra-high-speed optical connections. The endpoint on the local LAN went from a server program to a VPN-capable router, called a **VPN concentrator**, such as the Cisco 2811 Integrated Services Router shown in Figure 12.11.

> Cisco made hardware that supported PPP traffic using a proprietary protocol called *Layer 2 Forwarding (L2F)*. L2F did not come with encryption capabilities, so it was replaced by L2TP a long time ago. You'll sometimes see the term on the CompTIA Network+ exam as an incorrect answer.

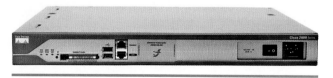

• **Figure 12.11**   Cisco 2811 Integrated Services Router

Tech Tip

Alternatives to PPTP, L2TP, and SSL

There are other popular VPN options beyond PPTP, L2TP, and SSL, such as OpenVPN and SSH. The most common VPN today offers pure (no L2TP) IPsec solutions. These VPN technologies use IPsec tunneling for VPNs, such as Cisco Easy VPN.

Another alternative is the Generic Routing Encapsulation (GRE) protocol. You can use GRE to make a point-to-point tunnel connection that carries all sorts of traffic over Layer 3, including multicast and IPv6 traffic.

Cisco provides free client software to connect a single faraway PC to a Cisco VPN. This creates a typical host-to-site connection. Network people often directly connect two Cisco VPN concentrators to connect two separate LANs permanently. It's slow, but inexpensive, compared to a dedicated high-speed connection between two faraway LANs. This kind of connection enables two separate LANs to function as a single network, sharing files and services as if in the same building. This is called a site-to-site VPN connection.

L2TP differs from PPTP in that it has no authentication or encryption. L2TP generally uses IPsec for all security needs. Technically, you should call an L2TP VPN an "L2TP/IPsec" VPN. L2TP works perfectly well in the single-client-connecting-to-a-LAN scenario, too. Every operating system's VPN client fully supports L2TP/IPsec VPNs.

SSL VPNs

Cisco has made a big push for companies to adopt VPN hardware that enables VPNs using Secure Sockets Layer (SSL). These types of VPN offer an advantage over Data Link– or Network-based VPNs because they don't require any special client software. Clients connect to the VPN server using a standard Web browser, with the traffic secured using SSL. The two most common types of SSL VPNs are SSL portal VPNs and SSL tunnel VPNs.

With SSL portal VPNs, a client accesses the VPN and is presented with a secure Web page. The client gains access to anything linked on that page, be it e-mail, data, links to other pages, and so on.

With tunnel VPNs, in contrast, the client Web browser runs some kind of active control, such as Java or Flash, and gains much greater access to the VPN-connected network. SSL tunnel VPNs create a more typical host-to-site connection than SSL portal VPNs, but the user must have sufficient permissions to run the active browser controls.

■ Switch Management

Managed switches have the extra programming and logic to handle switching, security, and many other functions, taking the concept of a switch well beyond the simple switches discussed so far in this book.

A managed switch, by definition, requires some configuration. You can connect to a managed switch to tell it what you want it to do. Exactly how you do this varies from switch to switch, but generally there are three ways:

1. Directly plug into a serial interface and use a virtual terminal program to connect to a command-line interface.

2. Get the switch on the network and then use a virtual terminal over SSH to connect to the same command-line interface.

3. Get the switch on the network and use the switch's built-in Web interface.

Let's look at the steps involved in each method.

First, many managed switches have a special serial port called a **console port**. Plug a laptop into the console port on the back of the switch (Figure 12.12). Then, run a terminal program like PuTTY to access the command-line interface on the switch. As long as you speak the language of the switch's command prompt, you're good to go. It's very common to use a console port for initial configuration of a new managed switch.

The second and third methods require the managed switch to be connected to the network and have an accessible IP address. Connect to the switch over the network and run some sort of software—either PuTTY or a Web browser—to manage the switch.

Wait! It's a switch. Switches that we've discussed in the book so far operate at Layer 2 of the OSI model. IP addresses don't show up until Layer 3. Here's the scoop in a nutshell. A managed switch needs an IP address to enable configuration on Layer 3.

This means a new, out-of-the-box managed switch has all the same configuration issues a new router would have. It's going to have a default IP address (but you should assign an IP address that's applicable to your network). It'll have a default user name and password (but you should change those!). And it'll have a bunch of other default settings that you'll probably want to change once you know what they mean.

Like any IP device, a managed switch needs good, basic maintenance. One example would be updating the firmware. Many managed switches support firmware updates over the Internet. That's a nice idea, but it means your switch needs a default gateway, a DNS server, and so forth to be able to access content over the Internet.

Armed with the IP address, configure your client or client software to connect to the managed switch. And now let's get serious.

As you might imagine, it would be scary to let unauthorized people have access to your switch management configuration. In the preceding examples, where you configure the switch over the network (**in-band management**), anyone who knows the IP addresses of your managed devices will be able to access them if they can get past the user name and password. To reduce exposure, it's common to dedicate one port on every managed device as a *management port*. You can do *interface configuration* only by directly connecting to that port.

Then, plug all those dedicated ports into a switch that's totally separate from the rest of the network, which will prevent unauthorized access to those ports. This is an example of **out-of-band management**.

Let's turn now to a technology that managed switches make possible: *virtual local area networks.*

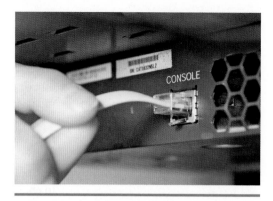

• **Figure 12.12** Plugging into a managed switch's console port using a serial cable

A managed switch enables you to configure every port on the switch in a lot of different ways, depending on the purpose and complexity of the switch. For example, it's easy to set the *speed and duplexing* of a port to match the client.

You configure a default gateway on a switch by telling the switch the IP address of the gateway router. For most implementations, type in the IP of your Internet connection box, such as DSL or cable modem.

Virtual LANs

Today's LANs are complex places. It's rare to see any serious network that doesn't have remote incoming connections, public Web or e-mail servers, wireless networks, as well as the basic string of connected switches. Leaving all of these different features on a single broadcast domain creates a tremendous amount of broadcast traffic and creates a security nightmare. You could separate the networks with multiple switches and put routers in between, but that's very inflexible and hard to manage. What if you could segment the network using the switches you already own? You can, and that's what a virtual local area network (VLAN) enables you to do.

To create a VLAN, you take a single physical broadcast domain made up of one or more switches and chop it up into multiple broadcast domains. This is most simply done by assigning each port to a specific VLAN.

VLANs require special switches loaded with extra programming to create the virtual networks.

Imagine a single switch with a number of computers connected to it. Up to this point, a single switch is always a single broadcast domain, but that's about to change. You've decided to take this single switch and turn it into two VLANs. VLANs typically get the name "VLAN" plus a number, like VLAN1 or VLAN275. The devices usually start at 1, although there's no law or rules on the numbering. In this example, I'll configure the ports on a single switch to be in one of two VLANs—VLAN1 or VLAN2 (Figure 12.13). I promise to show you how to configure ports for different VLANs shortly, but I've got a couple of other concepts to hit first.

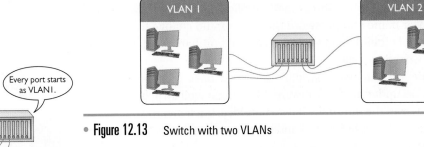

• **Figure 12.13**   Switch with two VLANs

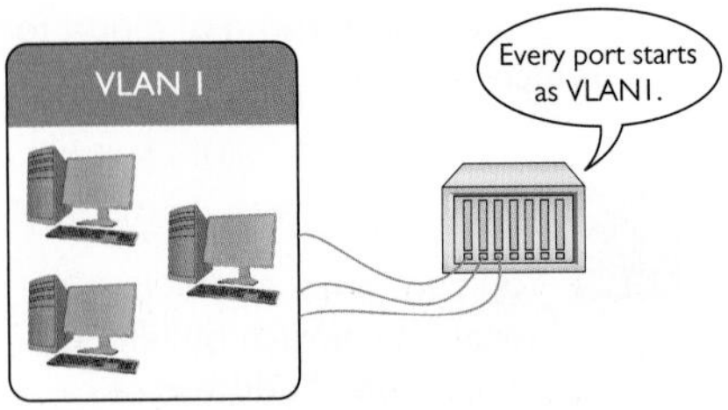

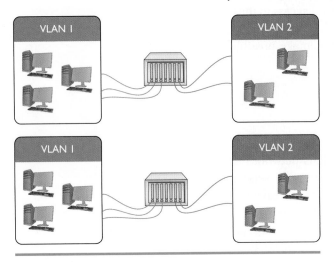

• **Figure 12.14**   Every port is VLAN1 by default.

Figure 12.14 shows a switch configured to assign individual ports to VLANs. Managed switches can handle any number of VLANs. Every port starts with the default VLAN, VLAN1, so even if you don't specify multiple VLANs, you get one by default.

When setting up a VLAN switch, we create one or more VLANs, then assign ports to those VLANs. Any host plugged into a port for VLAN1, therefore, would become part of the broadcast domain VLAN1.

A single switch configured into two VLANs is the simplest form of VLAN possible. More serious networks usually have more than one switch. Let's say you added a switch to a simple network. You'd like to keep VLAN1 and VLAN2 but use both switches. You can configure the new switch to use VLAN1 and VLAN2, but you've got to enable data to flow between the two switches, regardless of VLAN. That's where trunking comes into play.

Trunking

Trunking is the process of transferring VLAN traffic between two or more switches. Imagine two switches, each configured with a VLAN1 and a VLAN2, as shown in Figure 12.15.

You want all of the computers connected to VLAN1 on one switch to talk to all of the computers connected to VLAN1 on the other switch. Of course, you want to do this with VLAN2 also. To do this, you configure a port on each switch as a trunk port. A trunk port is a port on a switch configured to carry all traffic, regardless of VLAN number,

• **Figure 12.15**   Two switches, each with a VLAN1 and a VLAN2

between all switches in a LAN (Figure 12.16). The VLAN designation for a trunk port is its **native VLAN**. This becomes important when we discuss how data flows within a VLAN network. (See "Tagging" a bit later in the chapter.)

In the early days of VLANs, every switch manufacturer had its own way to make VLANs work. Cisco, for example, had a proprietary form of trunking called Inter-Switch Link (ISL). Today, every Ethernet switch uses the IEEE 802.1Q trunk standard that enables you to connect switches from different manufacturers.

Configuring a VLAN-capable Switch

If you want to configure a VLAN-capable switch, you need a method to perform that configuration. One method uses a serial (console) port like the one described in Chapter 3, "Cabling and Topology." The most common method is to log into the switch using SSH—not Telnet, because you need security—and use the command-line interface. The command line is going to be fast and precise. Alternatively, you can access the switch with a Web browser interface, like the one shown in Figure 12.17. Catalyst is a model name for a series of popular Cisco switches with advanced switching features.

Every switch manufacturer has its own interface for configuring VLANs, but the interface shown in Figure 12.18 is a classic example. This is Cisco Network Assistant, a GUI tool that enables you to configure multiple Cisco devices through the same interface. Note that you first must define your VLANs.

After you create the VLANs, you assign ports to VLANs. This process is called *VLAN assignment*. Assigning each port to a VLAN means that whatever computer plugs into that port, its traffic will get tagged with that port's VLAN. (See the following section, "Tagging.")

Figure 12.19 shows a port being assigned to a particular VLAN.

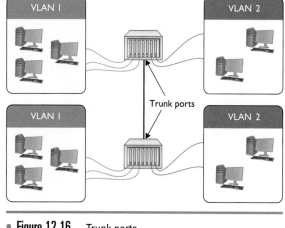

• **Figure 12.16** Trunk ports

Check out the excellent Chapter 12 Challenge! Sim, "Trunking," to test your understanding of trunking. You'll find it here: http://totalsem .com/006.

VLANs based on ports are the most common type of VLAN and are commonly known as *static VLANs*. VLANs based on MAC addresses are called *dynamic VLANs*. The latter method is never used these days.

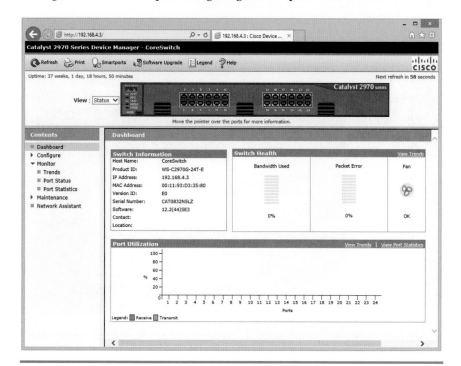

• **Figure 12.17** Catalyst 2970 Series Device Manager

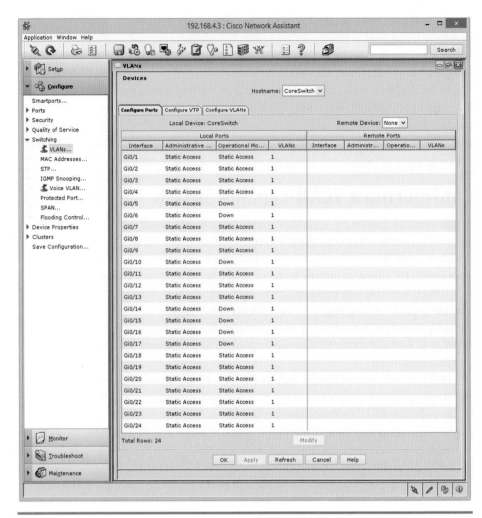

• Figure 12.18   Defining VLANs in Cisco Network Assistant

• Figure 12.19   Assigning a port to a VLAN

Tagging

When you have a busy network with multiple switches and multiple VLANs, how does a frame from a workstation in VLAN100 make it to a destination workstation in the same VLAN? What if the workstations are several switches apart? The key tool that makes this happen is *tagging*.

Workstations plug into **access ports**—regular ports that have been configured as part of a VLAN—that do the work of tagging traffic with the appropriate VLAN when frames enter the switch. Note that access ports are ports, just like trunk ports, but configured for the opposite purpose. Access ports connect to workstations; trunk ports connect to other trunk ports.

When the data enters the access port, the switch tags the frames with the appropriate VLAN. If the destination workstation is connected to the same switch, the frames flow to that workstation's access port. The tag is stripped off each frame and traffic flows as you would expect. If the destination workstation connects to a different switch, the initial switch sends the frames out its trunk port. What happens next is determined by how the trunk port is configured.

If the trunk port has a native VLAN that differs from the tag placed on the frame as it entered the access port, the switch leaves the tag on the frame and sends the tagged frame along to the next switch or switches. If the trunk port's native VLAN is the same as the access port's VLAN, then the switch drops the tag and sends the untagged frame out the trunk port.

Native VLANs exist to provide compatibility with older or simpler non-VLAN tagging switches, but there is a catch. The native VLAN opens your network to a nasty vulnerability called a *double-tagging attack* that lets the attacker access VLANs they should not be able to access. For this reason, in modern networks the native VLAN is set to an unused VLAN and the trunk port is configured to tag its native VLAN traffic as well.

VLAN Trunking Protocol

A busy network with many VLAN switches can require periods of intensive work to update. Imagine the work required to redo all the VLAN switches if you changed the VLAN configuration by adding or removing a VLAN. You'd have to access every switch individually, changing the port configuration to alter the VLAN assignment, and so on. The potential for errors is staggering. What if you missed updating one switch? Joe in Sales might wrongly have access to a sensitive accounting server or Phyllis in accounting might not be able to get her job done on time.

Cisco uses a proprietary protocol called **VLAN Trunking Protocol (VTP)** to automate the updating of multiple VLAN switches. With VTP, you put each switch into one of three states: server, client, or transparent. When you make changes to the VLAN configuration of the server switch, all the connected client switches update their configurations within minutes. The big job of changing every switch manually just went away.

When you set a VLAN switch to transparent, you tell it not to update but to hold onto its manual settings. You would use a transparent mode VLAN switch in circumstances where the overall VLAN configuration assignments did not apply.

 Clients can update servers the same way servers update clients. The difference is that VLAN info can only be changed on servers.

InterVLAN Routing

Once you've configured a switch to support multiple VLANs, each VLAN is its own broadcast domain, just as if the two VLANs were on two completely separate switches and networks. There is no way for data to get from one VLAN to another unless you use a router or a multilayer switch. (See "Multilayer Switches" later in the chapter for the scoop on these devices.)

The process of making a router work between two VLANs is called **interVLAN routing**. In the early days of interVLAN routing, you commonly used a router with multiple ports as a backbone for the network. Figure 12.20 shows one possible way to connect two VLANs with a single router. Note that the router has one port connected to VLAN 100 and another connected to VLAN 200. Devices on VLAN 100 may now communicate with devices on VLAN 200.

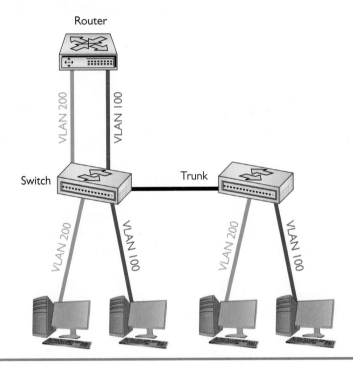

• **Figure 12.20** One router connecting multiple VLANs

Adding a physical router like this isn't a very elegant way to connect VLANs. This forces almost all traffic to go through the router, and it's not a very flexible solution if you want to add more VLANs in the future. As a result, many VLAN-capable switches also do routing.

Figure 12.21 shows an older interVLAN routing–capable switch, the Cisco 3550.

• **Figure 12.21** Cisco 3550

From the outside, the Cisco 3550 looks like any other switch. On the inside, it's a flexible device that not only supports VLANs, but also provides routing to

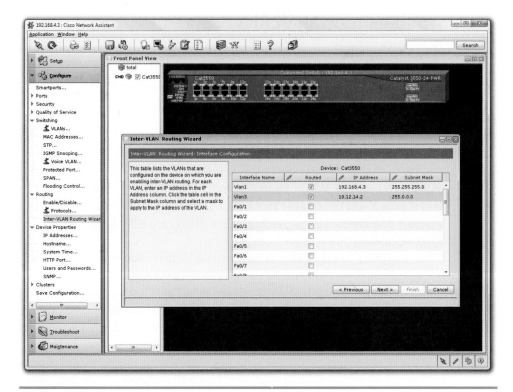

• **Figure 12.22** Setting up interVLAN routing

interconnect these VLANs. Figure 12.22 shows a GUI configuration screen for the 3550's interVLAN routing between two VLANs.

If the Cisco 3550 is a switch and a router, on what layer of the OSI seven-layer model does it operate? If it's a switch, then it works at Layer 2. But routers work at Layer 3. This isn't an ordinary switch. The Cisco 3550 works at both Layers 2 and 3 at the same time.

DHCP and VLANs

DHCP is an awesome tool to automate, track, and manage *IP address assignments*, as you know from previous chapters. Unfortunately, its native functions are limited to a single subnet. By default, DHCP requests can't pass through a router. So if you have a set of VLANs in a network, connected via routers, you need some method for getting IP addresses and other TCP/IP information to hosts.

When DHCP relay is enabled and configured within a router, the router will pass DHCP requests and responses across the router interfaces. So now we can use a single DHCP server to serve addresses to multiple networks or subnetworks.

Cisco implements DHCP relay through a configuration command called IP helper (the command is technically ip helper-address). IP helper enables DHCP relay support (ports 67 and 68). It also enables relaying for TFTP (port 69), Network Time Protocol (port 123), TACACS (port 49), DNS (port 53), NetBIOS (port 137), and NetBIOS Datagram (port 138).

Troubleshooting VLANs

At this level, troubleshooting a new VLAN is mostly about port assignment. If you give an incorrect VLAN assignment to a device, either you won't be able to see it or that device won't have access to resources it needs. Fix it.

■ Multilayer Switches

The Cisco 3550 is an amazing box in that it seems to defy the entire concept of a switch because of its support of interVLAN routing. Up to this point, I've said a switch works at Layer 2 of the OSI model, but now you've just seen a switch that clearly also works at Layer 3. The Cisco 3550 is one example of what we call a multilayer switch.

At this point you must stop thinking that a "switch" always works at Layer 2. A *Layer 2 switch* forwards traffic based on MAC addresses, whereas a *Layer 3 switch* forwards traffic based on IP addresses. A Layer 3 switch is a router that does what a traditional router does in software . . . in hardware. A Layer 3 switch, by definition, is a multilayer switch. From here on out, I will carefully address at what layer of the OSI seven-layer model a switch operates.

The challenge to multilayer switches comes with the ports. On a classic Layer 2 switch, individual ports don't have IP addresses. They don't need them. On a router, however, every port must have an IP address because the routing table uses the IP address to determine where to send packets.

A multilayer switch needs some option or feature for configuring ports to work at Layer 2 or Layer 3. Cisco uses the terms *switchport* and *router port* to differentiate between the two types of port. You can configure any port on a multilayer switch to act as a switchport or a router port, depending on your needs. Multilayer switches are incredibly common and support a number of interesting features, clearly making them part of what I call *advanced networking devices.*

I'm going to show you four areas where multilayer switches are very helpful: load balancing, quality of service, port bonding, and network protection. (Each term is defined in its respective section.) These three areas aren't the only places where multiplayer switches solve problems, but they are the most popular and the ones that the CompTIA Network+ exam covers.

> Any device that works at multiple layers of the OSI seven-layer model, providing more than a single service, is called a *multifunction network device.*

Load Balancing

Popular Internet servers are exactly that—popular. So popular that a single system cannot possibly support the thousands, if not millions, of requests per day that bombard them. But from what you've learned thus far about servers, you know that a single server has a single IP address. Put this to the test. Go to a command prompt and type **ping www.google.com**.

```
C:\>ping www.google.com

Pinging www.l.google.com [74.125.95.147] with 32 bytes of data:
Reply from 74.125.95.147: bytes=32 time=71ms TTL=242
Reply from 74.125.95.147: bytes=32 time=71ms TTL=242
Reply from 74.125.95.147: bytes=32 time=70ms TTL=242
Reply from 74.125.95.147: bytes=32 time=70ms TTL=242
```

Getting a definite number is tricky, but Google claims to have served *trillions* of search requests in 2014. Even at 2 trillion flat, the average is well over 5 billion search requests a day and 60,000 per second. Each request might require the Web server to deliver thousands of HTTP segments. A single, powerful, dedicated Web server (arguably) handles at best 2,000 requests/second. A busy Web site often needs more than one Web server to handle all the requests. Let's say a Web site needs three servers to handle the traffic. How does that one Web site, using three different servers, use a single IP address? The answer is found in something called *load balancing*.

Load balancing means making a bunch of servers look like a single server, creating a *server cluster*. Not only do you need to make them look like one server, you need to make sure that requests to these servers are distributed evenly so no one server is bogged down while another is idle. There are a few ways to do this, as you are about to see. Be warned, not all of these methods require an advanced network device called a *load balancer*, but it's common to use one. Employing a device designed to do one thing really well is always much faster than using a general-purpose computer and slapping on software.

Coming to a consensus on statistics like the number of requests/day or how many requests a single server can handle is difficult. Just concentrate on the concept. If some nerdy type says your numbers are way off, nicely agree and walk away. Just don't invite them to any parties.

DNS Load Balancing

Using DNS for load balancing is one of the oldest and still very common ways to support multiple Web servers. In this case, each Web server gets its own (usually) public IP address. Each DNS server for the domain has multiple "A" DNS records, each with the same fully qualified domain name (FQDN). The DNS server then cycles around these records so the same domain name resolves to different IP addresses. Figure 12.23 shows a Windows DNS server with multiple A records for the same FQDN.

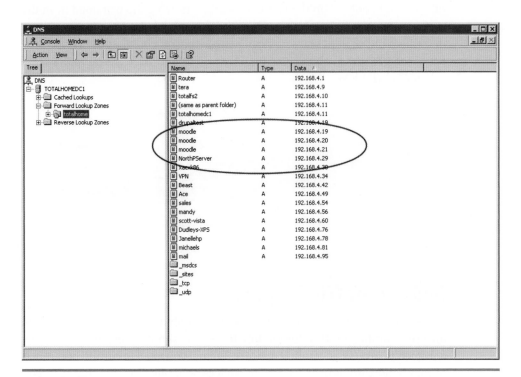

• **Figure 12.23**   Multiple IP addresses, same name

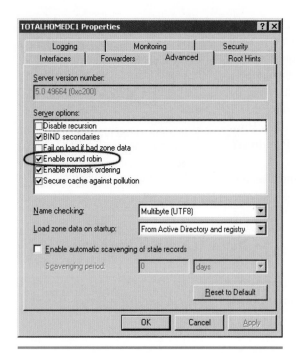

• Figure 12.24   Enabling round robin

The CompTIA Network+ exam refers to a content switch as a *content filter* network appliance.

Now that the A records have been added, you need to tell the DNS server to cycle around these names. With Windows DNS Server, you'll select a checkbox to do this, as shown in Figure 12.24.

When a computer comes to the DNS server for resolution, the server cycles through the DNS A records, giving out first one and then the next in a cyclic (round robin) fashion.

The popular BIND DNS server has a very similar process but adds even more power and features such as weighting one or more servers more than others or randomizing the DNS response.

Using a Multilayer or Content Switch

DNS is an easy way to load balance, but it still relies on multiple DNS servers, each with its own IP address. As Web clients access one DNS server or another, they cache that DNS server's IP address. The next time they access the server, they go directly to the cached DNS server and skip the round robin, reducing its effectiveness.

To hide all of your Web servers behind a single IP, you have two popular choices. First is to use a special multilayer switch that works at Layers 3 and 4. This switch is really just a router that performs NAT and port forwarding, but also has the capability to query the hidden Web servers continually and send HTTP requests to a server that has a lighter workload than the other servers.

The second option is to use a **content switch**. Content switches always work at Layer 7 (Application layer). Content switches designed to work with Web servers, therefore, are able to read the incoming HTTP and HTTPS requests. With this, you can perform very advanced actions, such as handling SSL certificates and cookies, on the content switch, removing the workload from the Web servers. Not only can these devices load balance in the ways previously described, but their HTTP savvy can actually pass a cookie to HTTP requesters—Web browsers—so the next time that client returns, it is sent to the same server (Figure 12.25).

• Figure 12.25   Layer 7 content switch

QoS and Traffic Shaping

Just about any router you buy today has the capability to block packets based on port number or IP address, but these are simple mechanisms mainly designed to protect an internal network. What if you need to control how much of your bandwidth is used for certain devices or applications? In that case, you need **quality of service (QoS)** policies to prioritize traffic based on certain rules.

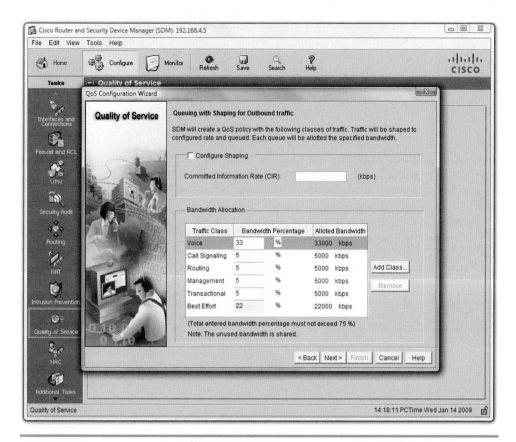

• **Figure 12.26**   QoS configuration on a router

These rules control how much bandwidth a protocol, PC, user, VLAN, or IP address may use (Figure 12.26).

On many advanced routers and switches, you can implement QoS through bandwidth management, such as *traffic shaping* where you control the flow of packets into or out of the network according to the type of packet or other rules.

Traffic shaping is very important when you must guarantee a device or application a certain amount of bandwidth and/or latency, such as with VoIP or video. Traffic shaping is also very popular in places such as schools, where IT professionals need to control user activities, such as limiting HTTP usage or blocking certain risky applications such as peer-to-peer file sharing.

Port Bonding

There are times when the data capacity of a connection between a switch and another device isn't enough to meet demand. Situations like these are encountered regularly in large data centers where tremendous amounts of data must be moved between racks of storage devices to vast numbers of users. Sometimes the solution is simple, like changing from a low-capacity standard like 100-megabit Ethernet to Gigabit Ethernet.

But there are other ways to achieve high-speed links between devices without having to upgrade the infrastructure. One of those ways is to join two or more connections' ports logically in a switch so that the resulting bandwidth is treated as a single connection and the throughput is multiplied by the number of linked connectors. All of the cables from the joined ports must go to the same

The CompTIA Network+ exam uses the generic term *traffic filtering,* which means *traffic shaping*—the filtering of traffic based on type of packet or other rules.

The term *bandwidth shaping* is synonymous with *traffic shaping.* The routers and switches that can implement traffic shaping are commonly referred to as *shapers.* The CompTIA Network+ exam refers to such devices as *bandwidth shapers.* Additionally, the exam uses the term *packet shaper* to describe a traffic shaping device that controls the flow based on packet rules.

device—another switch, a storage area network (SAN), a station, or whatever. That device must also support the logical joining of all of the involved ports. In CompTIA terms, this is called **port bonding**.

Elsewhere, port bonding goes by a pile of different names, including *link aggregation, NIC bonding, NIC teaming,* and a bunch of others. The Cisco protocol for accomplishing aggregation is called *Port Aggregation Protocol (PAgP).* You may also run across it in a very common implementation called **Link Aggregation Control Protocol (LACP)**, which is an IEEE specification. As it stands now, LACP is designated as IEEE 802.1AX-2008. LACP specifies a number of features and options to automate the negotiation, management, load balancing, and failure modes of aggregated ports.

Network Protection

The last area where you're likely to encounter advanced networking devices is network protection. *Network protection* is my term to describe four different areas:

- Intrusion protection/intrusion prevention
- Port mirroring
- Proxy serving
- AAA

Intrusion Detection/Intrusion Prevention

Intrusion detection and intrusion prevention detect that something has intruded into a network and then do something about it. Odds are good you've heard the term *firewall.* Firewalls are hardware or software tools that filter traffic based on various criteria, such as port number, IP address, or protocol. A firewall works at the border of your network, between the outside and the inside. (A *host-based firewall,* one installed on a single computer, similarly works on the border of that system.)

An **intrusion detection system (IDS)** is an application (often running on a dedicated IDS box) that inspects packets, looking for active intrusions. An IDS functions inside the network. A good IDS knows how to find attacks that a firewall might miss, such as viruses, illegal logon attempts, and other well-known attacks. Plus, because it inspects traffic inside the network, a good IDS can discover internal threats, like the activity of a vulnerability scanner smuggled in on a flash drive by a disgruntled worker planning an attack on an internal database server.

An IDS in promiscuous mode inspects a *copy* of every packet on a network. This placement outside the direct flow of traffic has three effects. First, there's a slight delay between something malicious hitting the network and the detection occurring. Second, there's no impact on network traffic flow. Third, if the IDS goes down, traffic keeps flowing normally.

An IDS always has some way to let the network administrators know if an attack is taking place: at the very least the attack is logged, but some IDSs offer a pop-up message, an e-mail, or even a text message to your phone.

An IDS can also respond to detected intrusions with action. The IDS can't stop the attack directly, but can request assistance from other devices—like a firewall—that can.

Modern IDS tools come in two flavors: network based or host based. A *network-based IDS (NIDS)* consists of multiple sensors placed around the network, often on one or both sides of the gateway router. These sensors report to a central application that, in turn, reads a signature file to detect anything out of the ordinary (Figure 12.27).

A *host-based IDS (HIDS)* is software running on individual systems that monitors for events such as system file modification or registry changes (Figure 12.28). More expensive IDSs do all this and can provide a single reporting source—very handy when one person is in charge of anything that goes on throughout a network.

A well-protected network uses both a NIDS and a HIDS. A NIDS monitors the incoming and outgoing traffic from the Internet, whereas the HIDS monitors the individual computers.

An **intrusion prevention system (IPS)** is very similar to an IDS, but an IPS sits directly in the flow of network traffic. This active monitoring has a trio of consequences. First, an IPS can stop an attack while it is happening. No need to request help from any other devices. Second, the network bandwidth and latency take a hit. Third, if the IPS goes down, the link might go down too.

Depending on what IPS product you choose, an IPS can block incoming packets on-the-fly based on IP address, port number, or application type. An IPS might go even further, literally fixing certain packets on-the-fly. As you

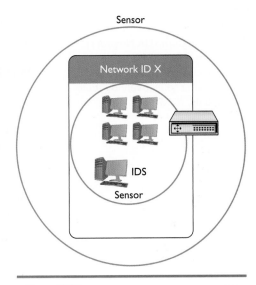

• **Figure 12.27**   Diagram of network-based IDS

The CompTIA Network+ exam can refer to an IDS system by either its location on the network—thus NIDS or HIDS—or by what the IDS system does in each location. The network-based IDS scans using signature files, thus it is a *signature-based IDS*. A host-based IDS watches for suspicious behavior on systems, thus it is a *behavior-based IDS*.

• **Figure 12.28**   OSSEC HIDS

The CompTIA Network+ exam refers to intrusion detection and prevention systems collectively by their initials, *IDPS*.

might suspect, you can roll out an IPS on a network and it gets a new name: a *network intrusion prevention system (NIPS)*.

Port Mirroring

Many managed switches have the capability to copy data from any or all physical ports on a switch to a single physical port. This is called port mirroring. It's as though you make a customized, fully configurable promiscuous port. Port mirroring is incredibly useful for any type of situation where an administrator needs to inspect packets coming to or from certain computers.

There are two forms of port mirroring: local and remote. Local port mirroring copies data from one or more ports on a single switch to a specific port on that switch. To monitor this data, you have to plug directly into the switch with ports being monitored. Remote port mirroring enables you to access data copied from one or more specific ports on a switch without plugging directly into that switch.

Proxy Serving

A proxy server sits in between clients and external servers, essentially pocketing the requests from the clients for server resources and making those requests itself. The client computers never touch the outside servers and thus stay protected from any unwanted activity. A proxy server usually *does something* to those requests as well. Let's see how proxy servers work using HTTP, one of the oldest uses of proxy servers.

Since proxy serving works by redirecting client requests to a proxy server, you first must tell the Web client not to use the usual DNS resolution to determine the Web server and instead to use a proxy. Every Web client comes with a program that enables you to set the IP address of the proxy server, as shown in the example in Figure 12.29.

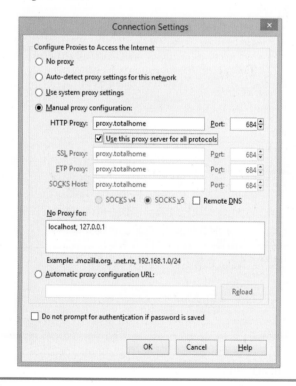

• **Figure 12.29** Setting a proxy server in Mozilla Firefox

Once the proxy server is configured, HTTP requests move from the client directly to the proxy server. Built into every HTTP request is the URL of the target Web server, so the Web proxy knows where to get the requested data once it gets the request. In the simplest format, the proxy server simply forwards the requests using its own IP address and then forwards the returning packets to the client (Figure 12.30).

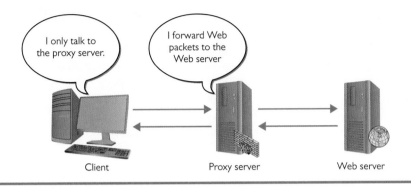

I only talk to the proxy server.

I forward Web packets to the Web server

Client   Proxy server   Web server

• **Figure 12.30**   Web proxy at work

This simple version of using a proxy server prevents the Web server from knowing where the client is located—a handy trick for those who wish to keep people from knowing where they are coming from, assuming you can find a public proxy server that accepts your HTTP requests (there are plenty!). There are many other good reasons to use a proxy server. One big benefit is caching. A proxy server keeps a copy of the served resource, giving clients a much faster response.

A **forward proxy server** acts on behalf of clients, getting information from various sources and handing that info to the clients. The sources (servers) don't know about the clients, only the proxy server.

A **reverse proxy server**, in contrast, acts on behalf of its servers. Clients contact the reverse proxy server, which gathers information from its associated server(s) and hands that information to the clients. The clients don't know about the servers behind the scenes. The reverse proxy server is the only machine with which they interact.

A proxy server might inspect the contents of the resource, looking for inappropriate content, viruses/malware, or just about anything else the creators of the proxy might desire it to identify.

HTTP proxy servers are the most common type of proxy server, but any TCP application can take advantage of proxy servers. Numerous proxy serving programs are available, such as Squid, shown in Figure 12.31. Proxy serving takes some substantial processing, so many vendors sell proxy servers in a box, such as the Blue Coat ProxySG.

Tech Tip

Proxy Caching

If a proxy server caches a Web page, how does it know if the cache accurately reflects the real page? What if the real Web page was updated? In this case, a good proxy server uses querying tools to check the real Web page to update the cache.

AAA

Authentication, authorization, and accounting (AAA), as you'll recall from Chapter 11, are vitally important for security on switches to support **port authentication**. Port authentication gives us a way to

Cross Check

AAA

You learned about AAA way back in Chapter 11, "Securing TCP/IP," so crosscheck your memory and answer these questions. I reminded you that the first A in AAA stands for authentication. What are the other two? Which jobs do they do to help lock down a TCP/IP network properly?

• **Figure 12.31**   Squid Proxy Server software

protect our network from unwanted people trying to access the network. Let's say that someone wants to bypass network security by bringing in a laptop and plugging the Ethernet connection straight into a switch port, or using that same laptop to connect wirelessly into one of the network WAPs. To prevent these types of intrusions, we use intelligent switches that support AAA.

When someone attempts a connection, he or she must have something at the point of connection to authenticate, and that's where advanced networking devices come into play. Many switches, and almost every wireless access point, come with feature sets to support port authentication. My Cisco 2811 router provides a great example. It supports RADIUS and 802.1X port authentication, as shown in Figure 12.32.

Configuring a switch for AAA is arguably one of the most complex configuration jobs a network tech may ever face. Before you get anywhere near the switch, you'll need to make a number of decisions, such as the version of AAA you want to use (RADIUS or TACACS+), the type of 802.1X authentication methods you will use (passwords?, certificates?, retina scanners?), deciding on and setting up the authentication database system, and opening up security polices to make sure it all works. This list is long, to say the least.

Once your AAA infrastructure is set up, you then configure a AAA-capable switch to support one or more methods of authentication. This is complicated too! There are ten flavors and "subflavors" of authentication supported by Cisco, for example, ranging from simple passwords to a local database to a RADIUS server and a TACACS+ server.

Configuring a switch for AAA—especially the first time—almost guarantees that you'll run into plenty of *TACAS+/RADIUS misconfiguration* issues.

Mike Meyers' CompTIA Network+ Guide to Managing and Troubleshooting Networks

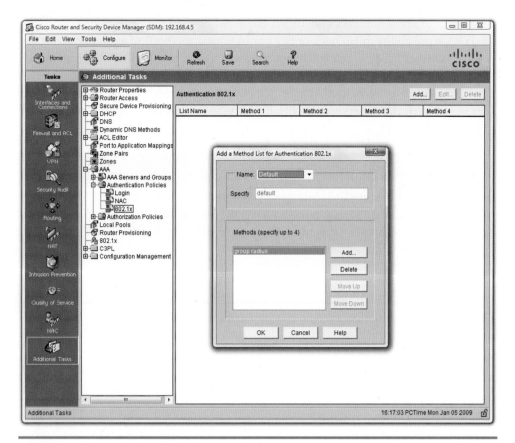

• **Figure 12.32** 802.1X configuration on a Cisco 2811

While it's impossible to name every possible misconfiguration issue, here's a list of some of the more common ones:

- *Failing to point the switch to the correct RADIUS/TACACS+ server.* You need to give the switch the right IP address. It's a simple issue, but one that often happens.

- *Improperly configuring the correct authentication method for the switch.* If you configure the switch for EAP-PEAP and the server is expecting EAP-TLS, it won't work properly. If you want to use a certificate-based authentication, you'll need a valid certificate that the server can use.

- *Failing to give the switch proper security policies on the server.* The switch won't be allowed to do its job.

Again, the list of misconfiguration issues setting up AAA is vast. The secret to dealing with these problems is locating and reading errors that come up on the switch and the AAA server. If a switch can get to the AAA server, then all the errors you need to know will be neatly listed for you on the server itself. How these errors manifest varies by the brand of AAA server you use. For example, Microsoft's RADIUS server (called Network Policy and Access Services) places all authentication errors in the Event Viewer. It's going to take some research and practice on your part, but once you have your misconfiguration issues handled, most AAA systems tend to run invisibly for years.

 CompTIA drops the + symbol when discussing TACACS+, as mentioned in Chapter 11. You'll see this subject on the exam as *TACACS/RADIUS misconfigurations*.

One of the really cool things about switch- and router-level authentication is the ability to fall back or failover to a "next method" of authentication. You can configure as many fallback methods as you like, as long as the method is supported by the switch you configure. The system attempts to authenticate using the first method in a list. If that first method isn't available (for instance, if the RADIUS server is down), it reverts to the second method in the list, and so forth.

 Try This!

Exploring Switch Capabilities

If you have access to a managed switch of any kind, now would be a great time to explore its capabilities. Use a Web browser of choice and navigate to the switch. What can you configure? Do you see any options for proxy serving, load balancing, or other fancy capability? How could you optimize your network by using some of these more advanced capabilities?

Chapter 12 Review

■ Chapter Summary

After reading this chapter and completing the exercises, you should understand the following about networking devices.

Discuss client/server and peer-to-peer logical topologies

■ In a client/server model, certain systems act as dedicated servers. A client never acts as a server, so one client can never access shared resources on another client.

■ In a peer-to-peer network, any system can act as a client, server, or both. This model first became popular in the 1990s with Microsoft Windows.

■ Today, the terms client/server and peer-to-peer refer more to applications than to network operating systems.

Describe the features and functions of VPNs

■ A VPN creates a tunnel that enables users to connect to remote LANs across the Internet.

■ RRAS, a program available only on Windows servers, allows VPN connections using PPTP. PPTP creates the secure tunnel through the Internet to your private LAN.

■ L2TP is a Cisco VPN protocol that was built on the best features of Microsoft's PPTP and Cisco's L2F. Rather than requiring special server software (such as Microsoft's RRAS), L2TP places a tunnel endpoint directly on a VPN-capable router.

■ L2TP provides no authentication or encryption. It usually relies on IPsec for this.

■ SSL VPNs come in two flavors: portal and tunnel. Both provide connectivity to the internal network through a standard Web browser and do not need special client software. SSL enables security.

Define the capabilities and management of managed switches

■ Managed switches enable you to go well beyond the simple capabilities of lesser switches.

■ Manage switches by directly connecting via a serial interface, or by accessing the terminal interface via a remote terminal or Web interface.

■ To configure a switch, you'll need an IP address and user name and password.

Configure and deploy VLANs

■ A VLAN takes a single physical broadcast domain and splits it into multiple virtual broadcast domains, thereby reducing broadcast traffic.

■ Trunking enables VLANs to work across multiple switches, so that multiple computers on the same LAN, but connected to different physical switches, can be members of the same VLAN.

■ A trunk port carries all traffic, regardless of VLAN number, between all switches on a LAN. Today, every Ethernet switch prefers the IEEE 802.1Q trunk standard, enabling you to connect switches from different manufacturers.

■ Many switches can be configured for VLANs via a serial port connection, but the most common method is to log into the switch using SSH and use the command-line interface.

■ Once the VLANs have been created on the switches, the next step is to assign switch ports to VLANs (static VLANs). This process is called VLAN assignment.

■ Tagging enables messages to get to their proper destination in more complicated VLAN setups. Tagging helps VLAN switches to know the appropriate ports to send frames.

■ Switches running Cisco VTP can be set in client mode to update automatically when a switch set to server mode is updated.

■ Many VLAN-capable switches also do routing, connecting different VLANs.

Implement advanced switch features

■ A multilayer switch is one that operates at multiple levels of the OSI model, such as the Cisco 3550 switch that functions at both Layer 2 and Layer 3.

■ Layer 2 switches forward frames based on MAC addresses, whereas Layer 3 switches (also called routers) forward packets based on IP addresses.

■ Load balancing involves configuring multiple servers to look like a single server, allowing multiple servers to handle requests sent to a single IP address. Additionally, load balancing spreads the requests evenly across all the servers so that no one system is bogged down.

- With DNS load balancing, each Web server receives a unique IP address because the DNS servers hold multiple A records, each with the same domain name, for each Web server. The DNS server then cycles around these records so the same domain name resolves to different IP addresses.

- DNS load balancing loses effectiveness when client computers cache the resolved IP address, bypassing the DNS server when connecting to a Web server.

- A content switch provides load balancing by reading the HTTP and HTTPS requests and acting upon them, taking the workload off the Web servers.

- Quality of service (QoS) sets priorities for how much bandwidth is used for certain protocols, PCs, users, VLANs, IP addresses, or other devices or applications. This is often implemented through traffic shaping.

- Port bonding or link aggregation enables you to join together two or more ports in a switch to improve bandwidth. A common implementation of port bonding is Link Aggregation Control Protocol (LACP).

- An intrusion detection system (IDS) inspects a copy of every packet on the network and actively monitors for attacks. A network-based IDS (NIDS) typically consists of sensors on one or both sides of the gateway router, whereas a host-based IDS (HIDS) consists of monitoring software installed on individual computers.

- An intrusion prevention system (IPS) proactively monitors for attacks and then reacts if an attack is identified. An IPS sits directly in the flow of network traffic.

- Port mirroring mirrors data from any or all physical ports on a switch to a single physical port, making it easy for administrators to inspect packets to or from certain computers.

- A proxy server intercepts client requests and acts upon them, usually by blocking the request or forwarding the request to other servers.

- Many switches support port authentication, a feature that requires network devices to authenticate themselves, protecting your network from rogue devices.

■ Key Terms

access port *(339)*
client/server *(327)*
console port *(335)*
content switch *(344)*
DHCP relay *(341)*
forward proxy server *(349)*
host-to-host *(334)*
host-to-site *(333)*
in-band management *(335)*
interVLAN routing *(340)*
intrusion detection system (IDS) *(346)*
intrusion prevention system (IPS) *(347)*
IP helper *(341)*
Layer 2 Tunneling Protocol (L2TP) *(333)*
Link Aggregation Control Protocol (LACP) *(346)*
load balancing *(343)*
managed switch *(334)*
multilayer switch *(342)*
native VLAN *(337)*

out-of-band management *(335)*
peer-to-peer *(329)*
Point-to-Point Tunneling Protocol (PPTP) *(332)*
port authentication *(349)*
port bonding *(346)*
port mirroring *(348)*
proxy server *(348)*
quality of service (QoS) *(344)*
reverse proxy server *(349)*
Routing and Remote Access Service (RRAS) *(332)*
site-to-site *(334)*
SSL VPN *(334)*
traffic shaping *(345)*
trunk port *(336)*
trunking *(336)*
virtual local area network (VLAN) *(336)*
virtual private network (VPN) *(331)*
VLAN Trunking Protocol (VTP) *(339)*
VPN concentrator *(333)*

Key Term Quiz

Use the Key Terms list to complete the sentences that follow. Not all terms will be used.

1. In a(n) _____ network, all computers can act in dual roles as clients or servers.

2. A(n) _____ services client requests and forwards them to the appropriate server.

3. In a(n) _____ network, client computers cannot share resources with each other or see each other. They can only connect to a server.

4. A VPN connection where a single computer logs into a remote network and becomes a member of that network is commonly called a(n) _____ connection.

5. _____ allows multiple VLANs to work across multiple switches.

6. The process of making a router work between two VLANs is called _____.

7. Routers that enable you to set QoS often use _____ to limit the amount of bandwidth used by certain devices or applications.

8. Creating a(n) _____ helps to reduce broadcast traffic on any one network by separating the one large network into smaller ones, but it requires the use of a special switch.

9. A(n) _____ is a network created by a secure tunnel from one network to another remote network.

10. _____ is a special program running on Microsoft servers that enables remote users to connect to a local Microsoft network.

Multiple-Choice Quiz

1. Which network model uses only truly dedicated servers?
   A. Client/server
   B. Peer-to-peer
   C. Virtual private network
   D. Virtual local area network

2. BitTorrent is an example of what kind of logical network topology?
   A. Peer-to-peer
   B. Client/server
   C. Multinode
   D. Server-to-server

3. Marcy is home sick, but she uses a VPN to connect to her network at work and is able to access files stored on the remote network just as if she were physically in the office. Which protocols make it possible for Marcy to receive an IP address from the DHCP server at work? (Select two.)
   A. PPTP
   B. IDS
   C. L2TP
   D. IPS

4. What is one benefit of a VLAN?
   A. It allows remote users to connect to a local network via the Internet.
   B. It reduces broadcast traffic on a LAN.
   C. It can create a WAN from multiple disjointed LANs.
   D. It provides encryption services on networks that have no default encryption protocol.

5. Where do you plug a workstation into a VLAN switch?
   A. Access port
   B. Proxy port
   C. Trunk port
   D. VLAN port

6. Rashan's company has multiple FTP servers, allowing remote users to download files. What should Rashan implement on his FTP servers so they appear as a single server with a guarantee that no single FTP server is receiving more requests than any other?
   A. Load balancing
   B. Port authentication
   C. Port mirroring
   D. Trunking

7. Which of the following describes a VPN?

   A. A remote connection using a secure tunnel across the Internet

   B. Segmenting a local network into smaller networks without subnetting

   C. A network that is protected from viruses

   D. A protocol used to encrypt L2TP traffic

8. To enable computers connected to different switches to be members of the same VLAN, what do the switches have to support?

   A. Content switching

   B. Port authentication

   C. Port mirroring

   D. Trunking

9. What is true of a multilayer switch?

   A. It can work at multiple OSI layers at the same time.

   B. It can work with one of several OSI layers at a time, depending on its configuration mode. Working at a different layer requires making a configuration change and resetting the switch.

   C. It can communicate with other switches that work at different OSI layers.

   D. It has twice the ports of a standard switch because it contains two regular switches, one stacked on top of the other.

10. Which statement about L2TP is true?

    A. It is more secure than PPTP.

    B. It was developed by Microsoft and is available by default on all Microsoft servers.

    C. It lacks security features and, therefore, relies on other protocols or services to handle authentication and encryption.

    D. It ensures router tables are kept synchronized across VLANs.

11. What's the most common method used to configure a VLAN-capable switch?

    A. Log into the switch using SSH and use the command-line interface.

    B. Plug into the switch with a serial cable and use the command-line interface.

    C. Log into the switch via a Web browser and use the GUI.

    D. Plug into the switch with a VLAN cable and use the command-line interface.

12. What are the benefits of caching on a Web proxy? (Select two.)

    A. Response time

    B. Virus detection

    C. Tracking

    D. Authentication

13. Which are effective methods of implementing load balancing? (Select two.)

    A. Content switching

    B. DNS round robin

    C. Traffic shaping

    D. Proxy serving

14. Employees in the sales department complain that the network runs slowly when employees in the art department copy large graphics files across the network. What solution might increase network speed for the sales department?

    A. DNS load balancing

    B. Content switching

    C. Traffic shaping

    D. 802.1z

15. Which of the following statements best applies to an IDS?

    A. An IDS inspects a copy of all traffic in a network and can respond to detected intrusions with actions.

    B. An IDS inspects all traffic as it enters a network and can respond to detected intrusions with actions.

    C. An IDS inspects a copy of all traffic in a network and reports intrusions to a configured user account.

    D. An IDS inspects all traffic as it enters a network and reports intrusions to a configured user account.

■ Essay Quiz

1. Your boss is becoming increasingly worried about hacking attempts on the company Web server. Write a letter explaining the various options for protecting against, and reacting to, attacks.

2. A coworker is constantly talking about VLANs and VPNs but rarely uses the terms correctly. Educate your coworker as to what VPNs and VLANs are, what they are for, and how they differ.

Lab Projects

• Lab Project 12.1

You have read quite a bit in this chapter about securing networks against attacks. Research at least three intrusion prevention systems and create a matrix comparing them. Include comparisons of features, cost, reliability, network/operating system support, and general user reviews.

• Lab Project 12.2

Your boss wants to reduce broadcast traffic and asks you to segment the network into multiple VLANs. Use your favorite e-commerce Web site for purchasing computer and networking devices and find at least three switches that support VLANs. Create a matrix comparing features and cost. Based on your research, which VLAN switch would you recommend to your employer and why?

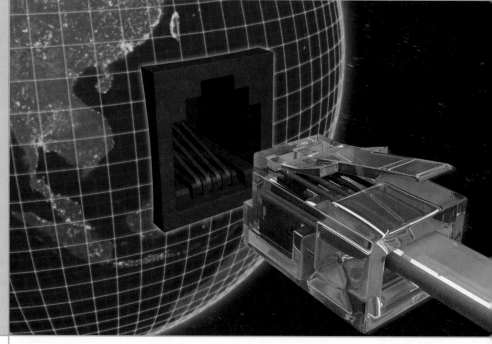

IPv6

chapter

13

> *"Give a man a fish and he will eat for a day. Teach a man to fish and he will eat for a lifetime. Teach a man to create an artificial shortage of fish and he will eat steak."*
>
> —JAY LENO

In this chapter, you will learn how to

- **Discuss the fundamental concepts of IPv6**
- **Describe IPv6 practices**
- **Implement IPv6 in a TCP/IP network**

The Internet developers wanted to make a networking protocol that had serious longevity, so they had to define a large enough IP address space to last well beyond the foreseeable future. They had to determine how many computers might exist in the future and then make the IP address space even bigger. But how many computers would exist in the future? Keep in mind that TCP/IP development took place in the early 1970s. There were fewer than 1000 computers in the entire world at the time, but that didn't keep the IP developers from thinking big! They decided to go absolutely crazy (as many people considered at the time) and around 1979 created the **Internet Protocol version 4 (IPv4)** 32-bit IP address space, creating about four billion IP addresses. That should have held us for the foreseeable future.

It didn't. First, the TCP/IP folks wasted huge chunks of IP addresses due to classful addressing and a generally easygoing, wasteful method of parceling out IP addresses. Second, the Internet reached a level of popularity way beyond the original developers' imaginations. By the late-1980s the rate of consumption for IP addresses started to worry the Internet people and the writing was on the wall for IPv4's 32-bit addressing.

As a result, the Internet Engineering Task Force (IETF) developed the **Internet Protocol version 6 (IPv6)** addressing system. IPv6 extended the 32-bit IP address space to 128 bits, allowing up to 2^{128} (that's close to 3.4×10^{38}) addresses. Take all the grains of sand on earth and that will give you an idea of how big a number that is.

But IPv6 wasn't just about expanding the IP address space. IPv6 also improves security by making the Internet Protocol Security (IPsec) protocol support a standard part of every IPv6 stack. That doesn't mean you actually have to use IPsec, just that manufacturers must support it. If you use IPsec, every packet sent from your system is encrypted, opening the possibility that IPv6 will eliminate most (but not all) of the many encryption methods currently in use today.

IPv6 also provides a more efficient routing scheme. Taking advantage of aggregation (see the section "Aggregation," later in this chapter), routing tables have shrunk dramatically, enabling fast routing.

It has taken a while, but IPv6 is here. This chapter breaks the process into three parts. First, you need the basic concepts, such as how the numbers work. Second, you need to learn how to enable or apply IPv6 in a variety of technologies, such as DHCP. Finally, you need answers on how to deploy IPv6 today.

If you really want to know how many IP addresses IPv6 provides, here's your number: 340,282,366,920,938,463,463,374, 607,431,768,211,456.

Test Specific

IPv6 Basics

Although they achieve the same function—enabling computers on IP networks to send packets to each other—IPv6 and IPv4 differ a lot when it comes to implementation. The addressing numbers work differently, for example, and don't look alike. IPv6 *always* uses link-local addressing. (The IPv4 version, APIPA—169.254.0.0/16—usually means something's wrong!) Subnetting works differently as well. You also need to understand the concepts of multicast, global addresses, and aggregation. Let's look at all six topics.

IPv6 Address Notation

The 32-bit IPv4 addresses are written as 197.169.94.82, using four octets. Well, IPv6 has 128 bits, so octets are gone. IPv6 addresses are written like this:

```
2001:0000:0000:3210:0800:200C:00CF:1234
```

IPv6 uses a colon as a separator, instead of the period used in IPv4's dotted decimal format. Each group—called a *quartet* or *hextet*—is a hexadecimal number between 0000 and FFFF.

A complete IPv6 address always has eight groups of four hexadecimal characters. If this sounds like you're going to type in really long IP addresses, don't worry, IPv6 offers a number of shortcuts.

First, leading zeroes can be dropped from any group, so 00CF becomes CF and 0000 becomes 0. Let's rewrite that IPv6 address using this shortcut:

```
2001:0:0:3210:800:200C:CF:1234
```

For those who don't play with hex regularly, one hexadecimal character (for example, F) represents 4 bits, so four hexadecimal characters make a 16-bit group.

CompTIA calls shortcuts for IPv6 addresses *address compression*.

To write IPv6 addresses containing strings of zeroes, you can use a pair of colons (::) to represent a string of consecutive groups with a value of zero. For example, using the :: rule, you can write the IPv6 address

`2001:0:0:3210:800:200C:CF:1234`

as

`2001::3210:800:200C:CF:1234`

Double colons are very handy, but you have to be careful when you use them. Take a look at this IPv6 address:

`FEDC:0000:0000:0000:00CF:0000:BA98:1234`

If I convert it to

`FEDC::CF:0:BA98:1234`

I may not use a second :: to represent the third-to-last group of four zeroes—only one :: is allowed per address! There's a good reason for this rule. If more than one :: was used, how could you tell how many sets of zeroes were in each group? Answer: you couldn't.

Here's an example of a very special IPv6 address that takes full advantage of the double colon, the IPv6 loopback address:

`::1`

Without using the double-colon notation, this IPv6 address would look like this:

`0000:0000:0000:0000:0000:0000:0000:0001`

 The unspecified address (all zeroes) can never be used, and neither can an address that contains all ones (all Fs in IPv6 notation).

> ✓ **Cross Check**
>
> **Loopback**
>
> You learned about the IPv4 loopback address in Chapter 7, "TCP/IP Basics," so check your memory as you read about the IPv6 loopback address here. What IP address or addresses could you use for a loopback address? When might you ping the loopback address? How would this differ from loopback testing discussed in Chapter 6, "Structured Cabling"?

IPv6 uses subnet masks, but you won't find a place to type in 255s anywhere. IPv6 uses the "/x" *prefix length* naming convention, similar to the Classless Inter-Domain Routing (CIDR) naming convention in IPv4. Here's how to write an IP address and subnet for a typical IPv6 host:

`FEDC::CF:0:BA98:1234/64`

Link-Local Address

The folks who created IPv6 worked hard to make it powerful and easy to use, but you pretty much have to forget all the rules you learned about IPv4 addressing. The biggest item to wrap your mind around is that you no longer have a single IP address unless your network isn't connected to a router.

When a computer running IPv6 first boots up, it gives itself a link-local address. Think of a link-local address as IPv6's equivalent to IPv4's APIPA address. The first 64 bits of a link-local address are always FE80::/10, followed by 54 zero bits. That means every address always begins with FE80:0000:0000:0000.

The second 64 bits of a link-local address, called the interface identifier, are generated in two ways. Windows clients since Windows Vista generate a 64-bit random number (Figure 13.1). Other operating systems, such as OS X, Linux, and Windows Server, use the random numbers. Very old operating systems, such as Windows XP and Windows Server 2003, use the device's MAC address to create a 64-bit number called an Extended Unique Identifier, 64-bit (EUI-64).

Although only the FE80::/10 denotes the link-local address, according to the Request for Comments that defined link-local addressing (RFC 4291), the next 54 bits have to be zeroes. That means in implementation, a link-local address will start with FE80::/64.

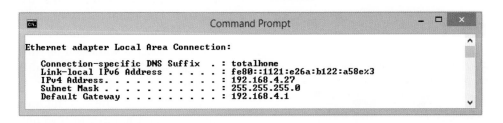

• **Figure 13.1**   Link-local address in Windows 8.1

The link-local address does all the hard work in IPv6, and, as long as you don't need an Internet connection, it's all you need. The old concepts of static and DHCP addressing don't really make much sense in IPv6 unless you have dedicated servers (even in IPv6, servers generally still have static IP addresses). Link-local addressing takes care of all your local network needs!

IPv6 Subnet Masks

IPv6 subnet masks function the same as IPv4 subnet masks, in that systems use them to determine whether to send packets to a local MAC address or to the default gateway to send the packets out to the Internet. But you need to know two new rules:

■   The last 64 bits of an IPv6 address are generated by the NIC, leaving a maximum of 64 bits for the subnet. Therefore, no subnet is ever longer than /64.

■   IANA passes out /48 subnets to big ISPs and end users who need large allotments. ISPs and others will borrow another 16 bits for subnetting and then pass out /64 subnets to end users.

With link-local addressing the subnet mask is defined as an address prefix of length /64.

Other types of IPv6 addresses get the subnet information automatically from their routers (described next).

The End of Broadcast

A system's IPv6 link-local address is a unicast address, a unique address that is exclusive to that system. IPv4 also relies on unicast addresses. But IPv6 completely drops the idea of broadcast addresses, replacing it with the idea of *multicast.*

Multicast isn't some new idea introduced with IPv6. Multicast addressing has been around for a long time and works well in IPv4 as well as in IPv6. A **multicast address** is a set of reserved addresses designed to go only to certain systems. As you've learned in previous chapters, any IPv4 address that starts with 224.0.0.0/4 (the old Class D network addresses) is reserved for multicast. Within that reserved range, individual addresses are assigned to specific applications that wish to use multicast. For example, if a system is configured to use the *Network Time Protocol (NTP)*, it will listen on multicast address 224.0.1.1 for time information.

Multicast works the same for IPv6, but brings in a number of IPv6-only multicast addresses to get specific jobs done. If an IPv6 system sends out a multicast to the address FF02::2, for example, only routers read the message while everyone else ignores it (Figure 13.2).

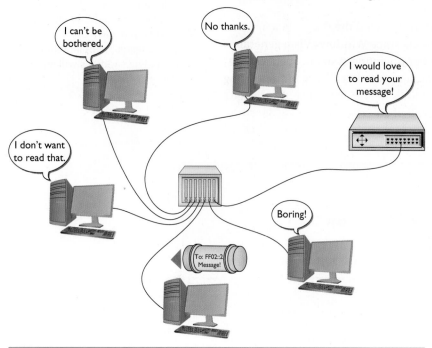

• **Figure 13.2** Multicast to routers

Multicast packets are encapsulated into Ethernet frames just like any other packet. Ethernet reserves the address 01-00-5E-*xx-xx-xx* for IPv4 multicast frame destination addresses. The Ethernet address 33-33-*xx-xx-xx-xx* is used on Ethernet frames that encapsulate IPv6 multicast packets.

Every computer sees the multicast frame, but only the computers specifically set up to process the frame process it. Table 13.1 shows some of the more useful IPv6 multicast addresses. You've just seen FF02::2; I'll explain the rest later in this chapter.

Table 13.1	IPv6 Multicast Addresses
Address	**Function**
FF02::1	All Nodes Address
FF02::2	All Routers Address
FF02::1:FFXX:XXXX	Solicited-Node Address

Looking at the first listing, FF02::1, you might ask: "How is that different from a broadcast?" The answer lies more in the definition of multicast than in what really takes place. A computer must be configured as a member of a particular group to read a particular multicast. In this case, if a computer is a member of "All Nodes," then it reads the message.

Beyond unicast and multicast, IPv6 uses a third type of addressing called **anycast**. An anycast address is a bit of a strange animal, so it's helpful to know why you need an anycast address before you try to understand what one is. The best place to learn how anycast works and why it is needed is the one place where its use is very common: DNS.

You learned in Chapter 10, "Network Naming," that the top of the DNS root structure consists of a number of root DNS servers. Every DNS server on the Internet keeps the IP addresses of the root servers in a file called *root hints*. Here's one part of the root hints file from my own DNS server:

```
                                NS    F.ROOT-SERVERS.NET.
F.ROOT-SERVERS.NET.             A     192.5.5.241
F.ROOT-SERVERS.NET.             AAAA  2001:500:2f::f
```

At first glance, you might think that this root server is a single physical box because it only has a single IPv4 address and a single IPv6 address. It's not. It is roughly 20 groups of server clusters strategically placed all over the world. In Chapter 12, "Advanced Network Devices," you saw how DNS can make a cluster of computers act as a single server, but none of those solutions can make a bunch of clusters all over the world act as a single server in an efficient way to make sure the DNS queries are answered as quickly as possible. To do this, we need anycasting.

Anycasting starts by giving a number of computers (or clusters of computers) the same IP address. Then routers (in the case of DNS, only the biggest, tier-one Internet routers) use the Border Gateway Protocol (BGP) to determine which computer in the cluster is closest. When that router gets a packet addressed to that IP address, it sends it only to the closest root DNS server, even though it may know where others are located. That is an anycast address.

An anycast address looks like a unicast address, and, in most cases, the computer sending the packet doesn't know or care to know that the address is anycast and not unicast. The only device that knows (and cares) is the top-tier router that has the smarts to send the packet only to the closest root DNS server.

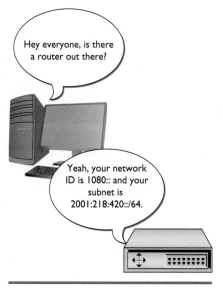

• **Figure 13.3**   Getting a global unicast address

Global Unicast Address

To get on the Internet, your system needs a second IPv6 address called a **global unicast address**, often referred to as a "global address." The only way to get a global unicast address is from your default gateway, which must be configured to pass out global IPv6 addresses. When your computer boots up, it sends out a router solicitation message on multicast address FF02::2 looking for a router. Your router hears this message and tells your computer the prefix. See Figure 13.3.

Once you have your prefix, your computer generates the rest of the global unicast address, the last 64 bits, just as it does to create the last 64 bits of a link-local address. You now have a legitimate public IP address as well as your link-local address. Figure 13.4 shows the IPv6 information on an Apple computer running OS X.

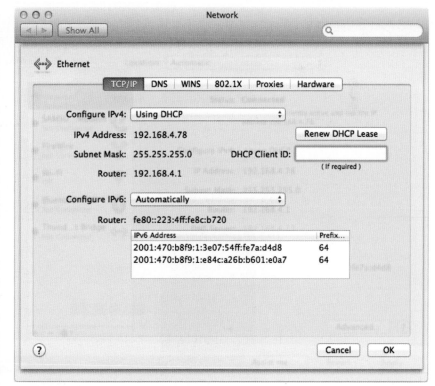

• **Figure 13.4**   IPv6 configuration on OS X

Let's look at this process in detail with an example:

1. An IPv6-capable computer boots up. As it boots, it sends out a router solicitation message (FF02::2).

2. An IPv6-configured router hears the request and then sends the prefix to the computer. In this example, let's say it is 2001:470:b8f9:1/64.

3. The computer takes the prefix and adds the interface identifier or EUI-64 address to the end of the prefix. If the MAC address is 00-0C-29-53-45-CA, for example, then the EUI-64 address is 20C:29FF:FE53:45CA.

4. Putting the prefix with the EUI-64 address, you get the global unicast address: 2001:470:b8f9:1:20C:29FF:FE53:45CA.

A global unicast address is a true Internet address. If another computer is running IPv6 and also has a global address, it can access your system unless you have some form of firewall.

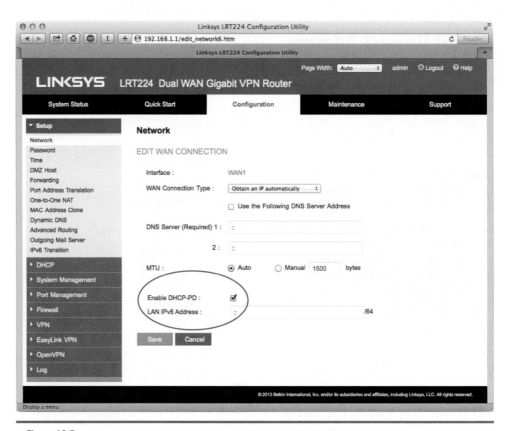

Computers using IPv6 need a global unicast address to access the Internet.

As routers make the transition from IPv4 to IPv6, one important feature to enable to allow router solicitation to work is called **prefix delegation** (Figure 13.5). Enabling it simply tells the router to go upstream and get a prefix to hand out to clients.

Aggregation

Routers need to know where to send every packet they encounter. Most routers have a default path on which they send packets that aren't specifically defined to go on any other route. As you get to the top of the Internet, the tier-one

• **Figure 13.5**   Enabling prefix delegation on a SOHO router (called DHCP-PD on this router)

Mike Meyers' CompTIA Network+ Guide to Managing and Troubleshooting Networks

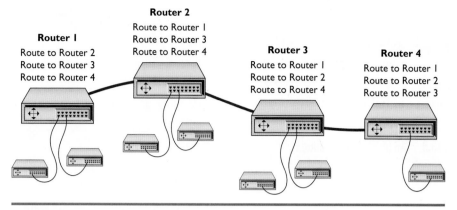

Router 2
Route to Router 1
Route to Router 3
Route to Router 4

Router 1
Route to Router 2
Route to Router 3
Route to Router 4

Router 3
Route to Router 1
Route to Router 2
Route to Router 4

Router 4
Route to Router 1
Route to Router 2
Route to Router 3

• **Figure 13.6**   No-default routers

routers that connect to the other tier-one routers can't have any default route (Figure 13.6). We call these the *no-default routers*.

The current state of the Internet's upper tiers is rather messy. A typical no-default router has somewhere around 500,000 routes in its routing table, requiring a router with massive firepower. But what would happen if the Internet was organized as shown in Figure 13.7? Note how every router underneath one router always uses a subset of that router's existing routes. This is called **aggregation**.

Aggregation would drastically reduce the size and complexity of routing tables and make the Internet faster. Aggregation would also give a more detailed, geographic picture of how the Internet is organized—you could get a good idea of where a person is physically located just by looking at the IP address.

It's way too late for IPv4 to use aggregation. Many organizations that received class licenses 20 to 30 years ago simply will not relinquish them, and the amount of effort necessary to make aggregation work would require a level of synchronization that would bring the entire Internet to its knees for days if not weeks.

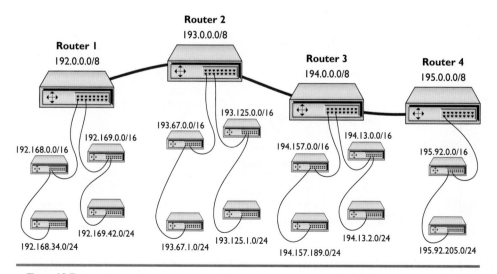

• **Figure 13.7**   Aggregation

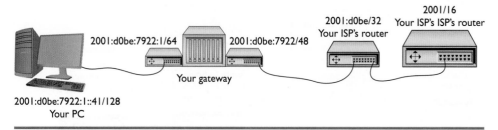

2001:d0be:7922:1/64   2001:d0be:7922/48   2001:d0be/32
Your ISP's router

2001/16
Your ISP's ISP's router

Your gateway

2001:d0be:7922:1::41/128
Your PC

• **Figure 13.8**   An IPv6 group of routers

Keep this formula in mind: A 48-bit prefix from upstream router + 16-bit subnet from default gateway + 64-bit unique number = 128-bit IPv6 address.

Tech Tip

Regional Internet Registries

The IANA doesn't actually pass out IPv6 prefixes. This job is delegated to the five Regional Internet Registries (RIRs):

- *American Registry for Internet Numbers (ARIN) supports North America.*

- *RIPE Network Coordination Centre (RIPE NCC) supports Europe, the Middle East, and Central Asia.*

- *Asia-Pacific Network Information Centre (APNIC) supports Asia and the Pacific region.*

- *Latin American and Caribbean Internet Addresses Registry (LACNIC) supports Central and South America and parts of the Caribbean.*

- *African Network Information Centre (AfriNIC) supports Africa.*

But aggregation is part and parcel with IPv6. Remember, your computer gets the first 64 bits of its Internet address from your default gateway. The router, in turn, gets a (usually) 48-bit prefix from its upstream router and adds its own 16-bit subnet.

This method allows the entire IPv6 network to change IP addresses on-the-fly to keep aggregation working. Imagine you have your default gateway connected to an upstream router from your ISP, as shown in Figure 13.8.

Your PC's IPv6 address is 2001:d0be:7922:1:fc2d:aeb2:99d2:e2b4. Let's cut out the last 64 bits and look at the prefix and see where this comes from:

Your network's prefix: 2001:d0be:7922:1/64

IPv6 addresses begin at the very top of the Internet with the no-default servers. We'll assume your ISP's ISP is one of those routers. Your ISP gets (usually) a 32-bit prefix from IANA or from its ISP if it is small.

In this case, the prefix is 2001:d0be/32. This prefix comes from the upstream router, and your ISP has no control over it. The person setting up the ISP's router, however, will add a 16-bit subnet to the prefix, as shown in Figure 13.9.

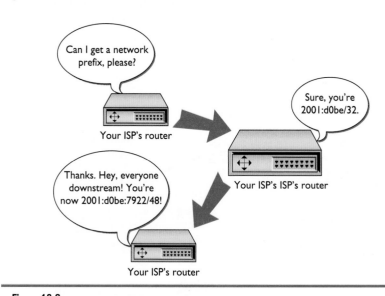

Can I get a network prefix, please?

Your ISP's router

Sure, you're 2001:d0be/32.

Your ISP's ISP's router

Thanks. Hey, everyone downstream! You're now 2001:d0be:7922/48!

Your ISP's router

• **Figure 13.9**   Adding the first prefix

Your router receives a 48-bit prefix (in this case, 2001:d0be:7922/48) from your ISP's router. Your router has no control over that prefix. The person setting

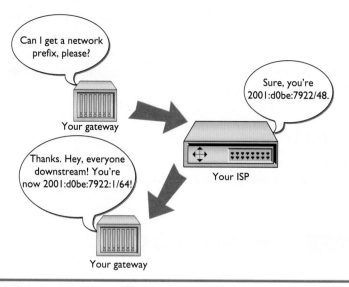

• **Figure 13.10** Adding the second prefix

up your gateway, however, adds your own 16-bit subnet (in this case, :0001 or :1) to the 48-bit prefix to make the 64-bit prefix for your network (Figure 13.10).

What makes all this particularly interesting is that any router upstream of anyone else may change the prefix it sends downstream, keeping aggregation intact. To see this in action, let's watch what happens if your ISP decides to change to another upstream ISP (Figure 13.11). In this case, your ISP moves from the old ISP (ISP1) to a new ISP (ISP2). When your ISP makes the new connection, the new ISP passes out a different 32-bit prefix (in this example, 2AB0:3C05/32). As quickly as this change takes place, all of the downstream routers make an "all nodes" multicast and all clients get new IP addresses.

Aggregation is an intrinsic but for the most part completely transparent part of IPv6. Know that your IPv6 Internet addresses may suddenly change from time to time and that the address changes are a fairly rare but normal aspect of using IPv6.

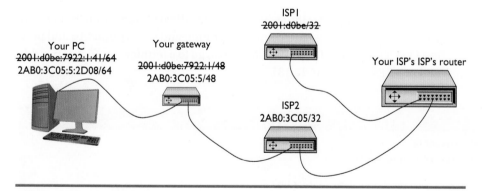

• **Figure 13.11** New IP address updated downstream

Using IPv6

Once IPv6 fully replaces IPv4, we will find ourselves in a very different world from the one we left in terms of configuration. In this section, you will see what it takes to turn on IPv6 for your network. This section also assumes you've turned off IPv4—which isn't a realistic option right now because IPv4 is still prevalent, but it makes understanding some aspects of using IPv6 much easier. You'll also learn how IPv6 works (or doesn't work, as the case may be) with NAT, DHCP, and DNS. We'll cover the idea of running IPv6 and IPv4 at the same time in the next section.

Enabling IPv6

Enabling IPv6 is very easy because, in most cases, it is already running on your operating system. Table 13.2 lists the popular operating systems and their IPv6 statuses.

Table 13.2	IPv6 Adoption by Operating System
Operating System	**IPv6 Status**
Windows 2000	Windows 2000 came with "developmental" IPv6 support. Microsoft does not recommend using Windows 2000 for IPv6.
Windows XP	Originally, Windows XP came with a rudimentary but fully functional IPv6 stack that had to be installed from the command prompt. SP1 added the ability to add the same IPv6 stack under the Install | Protocols menu.
Windows Vista/7/8/10	Complete IPv6 support. IPv6 is active on default installs.
Windows Server 2003	Complete IPv6 support. IPv6 is not installed by default but is easily installed via the Install | Protocols menu.
Windows Server 2008/2012	Complete IPv6 support. IPv6 is active on default installs.
Linux	Complete IPv6 support from Kernel 2.6. IPv6 is active on most default installs.
Mac OS X	Complete IPv6 support on all versions. IPv6 is active on default installs.

The fastest way to verify if your system runs IPv6 is to check the IP status for your OS. In Windows, go to a command prompt and type **ipconfig** and press ENTER (Figure 13.12). In Linux or Mac OS X, go to a terminal and type **ip addr** and press ENTER (Figure 13.13).

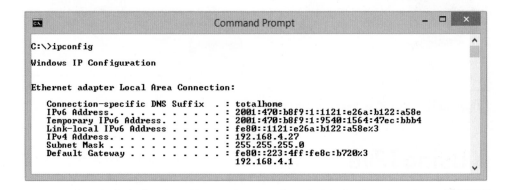

```
C:\>ipconfig

Windows IP Configuration


Ethernet adapter Local Area Connection:

   Connection-specific DNS Suffix  . : totalhome
   IPv6 Address. . . . . . . . . . . : 2001:470:b8f9:1:1121:e26a:b122:a58e
   Temporary IPv6 Address. . . . . . : 2001:470:b8f9:1:9540:1564:47ec:bbb4
   Link-local IPv6 Address . . . . . : fe80::1121:e26a:b122:a58e%3
   IPv4 Address. . . . . . . . . . . : 192.168.4.27
   Subnet Mask . . . . . . . . . . . : 255.255.255.0
   Default Gateway . . . . . . . . . : fe80::223:4ff:fe8c:b720%3
                                       192.168.4.1
```

• **Figure 13.12**   IPv6 enabled in Windows 8.1

```
michaels@michaels-moble: ~
michaels@michaels-moble ~                                            [13:19:09]
> $ ip add show dev eth0
2: eth0: <BROADCAST,MULTICAST,UP,LOWER_UP> mtu 1500 qdisc mq state UP group default qlen 1000
    link/ether 00:25:64:5b:8a:0c brd ff:ff:ff:ff:ff:ff
    inet 192.168.4.34/24 brd 192.168.4.255 scope global eth0
       valid_lft forever preferred_lft forever
    inet6 2001:470:b8f9:1:5158:4095:ce3d:1182/64 scope global temporary dynamic
       valid_lft 133sec preferred_lft 73sec
    inet6 2001:470:b8f9:1:225:64ff:fe5b:8a0c/64 scope global dynamic
       valid_lft 133sec preferred_lft 73sec
    inet6 fe80::225:64ff:fe5b:8a0c/64 scope link
       valid_lft forever preferred_lft forever

michaels@michaels-moble ~                                            [13:19:11]
> $ |
```

• **Figure 13.13**   IPv6 enabled in Ubuntu 14.10

NAT in IPv6

The folks pushing IPv6 forward are a vocal group with some pretty strong feelings about how IPv6 should work. If you want to get some really nasty e-mail, just go to one of the many IPv6 sites and ask this question: "How do I set up NAT on IPv6?" I know they will get mad because I asked that question. Here are some of the answers as I saw them:

> "NAT was developed a long time ago as a way to avoid running out of IP addresses. It was never meant to be a type of firewall."

> "NAT messes up IPsec."

> "Only jerks use NAT!"

If you're going to use IPv6, you're not going to use NAT. That means every one of your IP addresses will be exposed to the Internet, and that's not good. The answer is: count on IPv6 to make life hard on hackers and use a good firewall.

One big problem with IPv4 is how easy it is to sniff networks. Using tools like Anton Keks' popular Angry IP Scanner (http://angryip.org), you can scan an entire subnet looking for active IP addresses, as shown in Figure 13.14.

IPv6's huge address space makes such scanning programs obsolete. Let's say you knew my subnet was 2001:d0be:7922:1/64. There are 2^{64} different possible IP addresses on this subnet. Assuming a scanner could check one million addresses per second, it would take something like 580,000 years to check them all.

If a bad guy knows your address, the hope is that you're using IPsec to prevent other people from reading your information. You also have a number of other security options that aren't specific to IPv6 that you can use. You've seen some of these (like encryption) in earlier chapters. Others, like good firewalling, you'll see in later chapters.

 There was a proposed version of NAT for IPv6 called *NAPT-PT* (an earlier version was called NAT-PT). You might see this as an incorrect answer on the CompTIA Network+ exam.

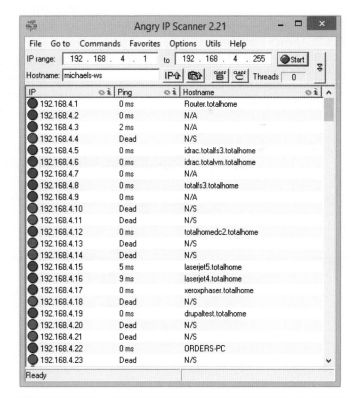

• **Figure 13.14**   Angry IP Scanner at work

DHCP in IPv6

DHCP is alive and well in the IPv6 world but works very differently than IPv4's DHCP. At first glance, you'd think you wouldn't need DHCP anymore. IPv6 clients get their IP address and subnet from their gateway router's advertisements (so they also know the default gateway). Although this is true, IPv6 router advertisements do not pass out a number of other very important bits of information that clients need, such as DNS and TFTP server information, giving DHCP a very important place in IPv6.

A fully functional DHCPv6 server works in one of two modes: stateful or stateless. A **stateful** DHCPv6 server works very similarly to an IPv4 DHCP server, passing out IPv6 addresses, subnet masks, and default gateways as well as optional items like DNS and TFTP server addresses. A **stateless** DHCPv6 server only passes out optional information. Figure 13.15 shows the DHCPv6 server on Windows Server.

 IPv6 DHCP servers use DHCPv6. This is not the sixth version of DHCP, mind you, just the name of DHCP for IPv6.

> ## Cross Check
>
> ### DHCP with IPv4
>
> You read about the IPv4 version of DHCP in Chapter 7, so check your memory now. How does DHCP work? What does a DHCP lease do for you? What happens if your computer can't get to a DHCP server but is configured for DHCP?

There's a push to get DNS server information added to IPv6 router advertisements. If this happens, the need for DHCPv6 might fall dramatically.

Most IPv6 installations should take advantage of IPv6's auto-configuration and only run stateless DHCPv6 servers. But if you really want to skip aggregation, you may certainly go stateful. Be careful about going stateful, however: as long as you're using an intranet or your upstream router knows what to do with your non-aggregated network ID, you're okay. Stateful DHCPv6 might be helpful for internal networks that do strange things like try to use subnets greater than /64, but, for the most part, expect stateless to be the norm.

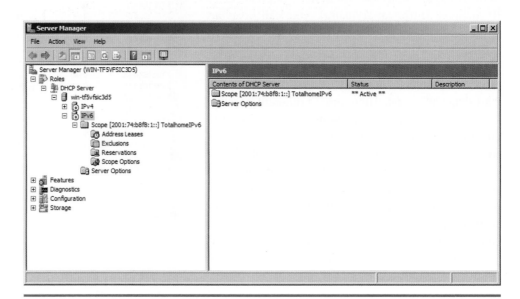

• **Figure 13.15**   DHCPv6 server in action

DNS in IPv6

Just about every DNS server today supports IPv6 addresses. So setting up DNS requires little from network administrators. All IPv6 addresses have a record type of AAAA. Figure 13.16 shows some IPv6 addresses in Windows Server.

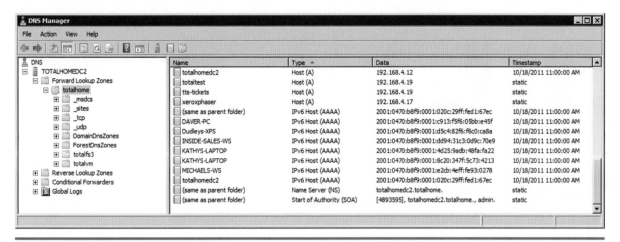

• Figure 13.16   IPv6 addresses on DNS server

■ Moving to IPv6

There's no reason for you *not* to try running IPv6 today—like right now! At the very least, a whole world of IPv6-only Web sites are out there for you to explore. At the most, you may very well become the IPv6 expert in your organization. You almost certainly have an operating system ready to do IPv6; the only trick is to get you connected to the rest of us fun-loving IPv6-capable folks.

This section is designed to help you get connected. If you can, grab an IPv6-capable system, fire up IPv6 as shown earlier, and make sure you're connected to the Internet. We are going someplace you've never been before: the IPv6 Internet.

IPv4 and IPv6

The first and most important point to make right now is that you can run both IPv4 and IPv6 on your computers and routers at the same time, just as my computer does, as shown in Figure 13.17. This ability is a critical part of the process enabling the world to migrate slowly from IPv4 to IPv6.

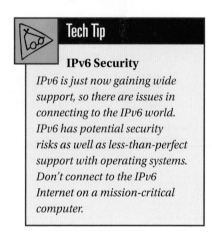

Check out the excellent pair of Sims for Chapter 13. You'll find both a Show! and a Click! called "IPv6 Configuration" that walk you through the process of configuring IPv6 in Windows.

Tech Tip

IPv6 Security

IPv6 is just now gaining wide support, so there are issues in connecting to the IPv6 world. IPv6 has potential security risks as well as less-than-perfect support with operating systems. Don't connect to the IPv6 Internet on a mission-critical computer.

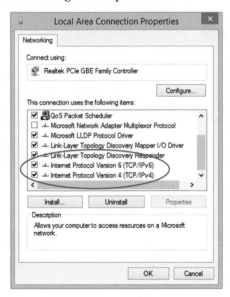

• Figure 13.17   IPv4 and IPv6 on one computer

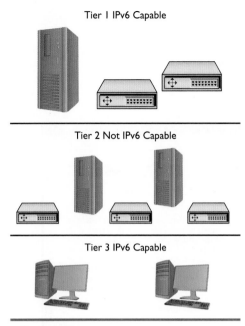

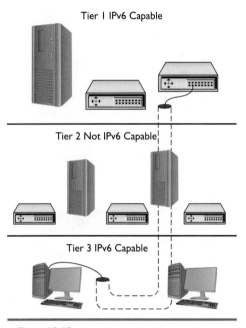

Tier 1 IPv6 Capable

Tier 2 Not IPv6 Capable

Tier 3 IPv6 Capable

• **Figure 13.18**   The IPv6 gap

Tier 1 IPv6 Capable

Tier 2 Not IPv6 Capable

Tier 3 IPv6 Capable

• **Figure 13.19**   The IPv4-to-IPv6 tunnel

Almost all operating systems support IPv6, and almost all serious routers support IPv6, but very few of the small home routers support IPv6. Plus not all routers on the Internet have their IPv6 support turned on.

In order for IPv6 to work, every router and every computer on the Internet needs to support IPv6, but the Internet is not yet there. Two critical parts of the Internet are ready, however:

■   All of the root DNS servers now support IPv6 resolution.

■   Almost all of the tier-one ISP routers properly forward IPv6 packets.

The problem is that the routers and DNS servers between your IPv6-capable computer and the other IPv6-capable computers to which you would like to connect are not yet IPv6-ready. How do you get past this IPv6 gap (Figure 13.18)?

Tunnels

To get on the IPv6 network, you need to leap over this gap, to implement an IPv4-to-IPv6 tunnel. The folks who developed IPv6 have a number of ways for you to do this using one of many IPv4-to-IPv6 tunneling standards, such as the one you'll see on the exam, **4to6**. An IPv4-to-IPv6 tunnel works like any other tunnel, encapsulating one type of data into another. In this case, you are encapsulating your IPv6 traffic into an IPv4 tunnel to get to an IPv6-capable router, as shown in Figure 13.19.

To make this tunnel, you are going to download a tunneling client and install it on your computer. You will then fire up the client and make the tunnel connection—it's very easy to do. Before you create this tunnel, however, you need to appreciate that this is only one way to make an IPv6 connection—I'll show you other ways in a moment. I describe four popular IPv4-to-IPv6 tunneling standards next.

6to4

6to4 is a tunneling protocol that enables IPv6 traffic to use the IPv4 Internet without having to set up explicit tunnels. 6to4 is generally used to connect two routers directly because it normally requires a public IPv4 address. 6to4 addresses always start with 2002::/16. If you have an IPv6-capable router, or if you have a computer directly connected to the Internet, you can set up a 6to4 tunnel. 6to4 uses public relay routers all around the world. Search the Web for **"public 6to4 relays"** to find one close to you. One IPv4 address, 192.88.99.1, is called the *6to4 anycast address* and works everywhere.

Setting up a 6to4 tunnel can be more challenging than setting up the tunnels that use tunnel brokers. If you're feeling adventurous, just do a Web search on **"6to4 setup"** and the name of your operating system. You'll find hundreds of Web sites to show you how to set up a 6to4 tunnel.

6in4

6in4 (also called IPv6-in-IPv4) is one of the most popular IPv6 tunneling standards and the one I'll use in the tunneling example. 6in4 is one of only two IPv6 tunneling protocols that can go through a NAT (called *NAT traversal*).

Teredo and Miredo

Teredo is the second NAT-traversal IPv6 tunneling protocol. Teredo is built into Microsoft Windows and, as a result, sees some adoption. Teredo addresses start with 2001:0000:/32. Most people prefer to skip Windows built-in support and instead get a third-party tool that supports 6to4 or 6in4.

Miredo is an open source implementation of Teredo for Linux and some other UNIX-based systems. (A version was briefly available for OS X, but that was a blip in terms of technology.)

 Try This!

Using Teredo

If you're using Windows XP (with Service Pack 1 or later) or later, you have nothing to lose but your chains, so try this! You can use Teredo to access the IPv6 Internet as long as you have access to the Internet normally and your computer is not part of a Windows domain; it's possible to use Teredo on a domain, but the process gets a little ugly in my opinion.

Beware! Some home routers can't handle Teredo, and many high-end routers are specifically designed to prevent this traffic (it's a great way to get around many network defenses), so if Teredo doesn't work, blame the router.

Here are the steps in Windows Vista or later:

1. Make sure the Windows Firewall is enabled. If you have a third-party firewall, turn it off.

2. Go to **Start** and type **cmd** in the Start Search box, but don't press ENTER yet. Instead, right-click the command prompt option above and select **Run as administrator**.

3. From the command prompt, type these commands, followed by ENTER each time:
   ```
   netsh
   interface
   teredo
   set state client
   exit
   ```

4. Test by typing `ipconfig /all`. You should see an adapter called "Tunnel adapter Teredo tunneling pseudo-interface" (or something close to that) with an IP address starting with 2001.

5. Type `ping ipv6.google.com` to make sure you can reach the Internet.

6. Open a Web browser and go to an IPv6 Web site, like www.sixxs. com or ipv6.google.com.

7. Remember, Microsoft loves to change things. If these steps don't work, search for new instructions on the Microsoft Web site.

You rarely have a choice of tunneling protocol. The tunneling protocol you use is the one your tunnel broker provides and is usually invisible to you.

ISATAP

Intra-Site Automatic Tunnel Addressing Protocol (ISATAP) is designed to work within an IPv4 network by actually adding the IPv4 address to an IPv6 prefix to create a rather interesting but nonstandard address for the endpoints. One example of an ISATAP address is 2001:DB8::98CA:200:131.107.28.9. ISATAP has a strong following, but other tunneling standards are gaining ground because they use a more common IPv6 addressing structure.

Tunnel Brokers

Setting up an IPv6 tunnel can be a chore. You have to find someone willing to act as the far endpoint; you have to connect to them somehow; and then you have to know the tunneling standard they use. To make life easier, those who provide the endpoints have created the idea of the **tunnel broker**. Tunnel brokers create the actual tunnel and (usually) offer a custom-made endpoint client for you to use, although more advanced users can often make a manual connection.

Many tunnel brokers take advantage of one of two automatic configuration protocols, called **Tunnel Setup Protocol (TSP)** and **Tunnel Information and Control (TIC) protocol**. These protocols set up the tunnel and handle configuration as well as login. If it wasn't for TSP and TIC, there would be no such thing as automatic third-party tunnel endpoint clients for you to use. Here's a good starting point for more information on tunneling and available resources: www.sixxs.net.

Setting Up a Tunnel

Every tunnel broker has its own setup, so you should always read the instructions carefully. In this example, you'll install the gogoCLIENT onto Windows 7. Go to www.gogo6.com and register for an account (look for the "Sign Up" link). You'll then be led to a download page where you can download the client. Gogo6 is always updating this client, so be sure to download the latest version. Install the client to see the screen shown in Figure 13.20. Enter the Gateway6 address and your user name and password. You can log on anonymously, as well, if the user name and password route doesn't work.

Click **Connect**, and, assuming you have a good connection, you should be on the IPv6 Internet. Go to the **Status** tab to see your IP information (Figure 13.21).

Excellent! Now let's check out the IPv6 Internet. Try these IPv6-only Web pages:

- www.ipv6.sixxs.net (click the **Enter website** hyperlink to see your IPv6 address on the bottom left of the page)

- http://ipv6.google.com

- http://ipv6.sunny.ch (shows your IPv6 address)

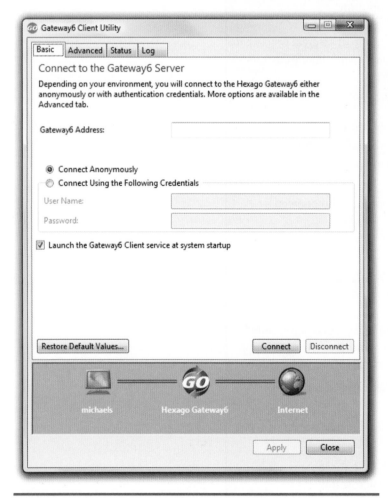

• **Figure 13.20**   Gateway6 Client Utility

Overlay Tunnels

An **overlay tunnel** enables two IPv6 networks to connect over an existing IPv4 infrastructure, such as the Internet. In more precise terms, the routers that connect the IPv6 networks to the IPv4 infrastructure run *dual stack*—both IPv4 and IPv6—and can encapsulate the traffic from the local network into IPv4 packets. Those IPv4 packets travel over the IPv4 infrastructure and the router at the other end of the tunnel strips the IPv4 stuff off the packet and sends the remaining IPv6 packet on its merry way.

Routers can use the same protocols used to connect an IPv4 client to an IPv6 network—6to4, ISATAP, and such (previously discussed)—or can be configured manually. A **manual tunnel** creates a simple point-to-point connection between the two IPv6 networks. Manual tunnels are good for regular, secure (via IPsec) communication between two networks.

IPv6 Is Here, Really!

Depending on who you talk to, IPv6 is either happening now or going to happen soon, and when it does happen, it'll happen very quickly. IPv4 addresses are already all but exhausted, and the time is coming when new devices simply will have to move to IPv6. The people who know IPv6 will be in a unique place to leap into the insanity of what will invariably be called "The Big Switchover" and will find themselves making a lot of money. Take some time to learn IPv6. You'll be glad you did.

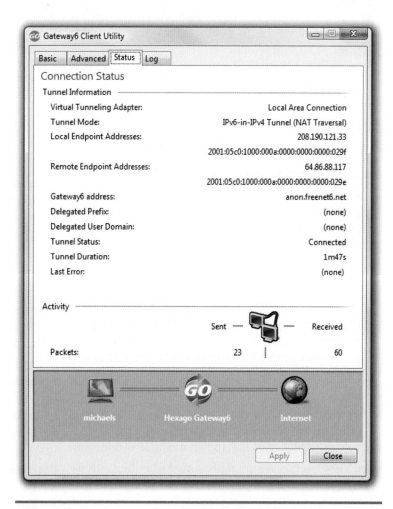

• **Figure 13.21**   Gateway6 Client Utility Status tab

Chapter 13 Review

Chapter Summary

After reading this chapter and completing the exercises, you should understand the following about IPv6.

Discuss the fundamental concepts of IPv6

- IPv4 supports only about 4 billion addresses, which is no longer enough for the future. IPv6 supports 2^{128} (or ~ 3.4×10^{38}) IP addresses.

- In addition to an expanded address space, IPv6 improves security by supporting IPsec out of the box.

- IPv6 provides a more efficient routing scheme because it uses aggregation.

- IPv6 addresses are composed of 128 bits written in hexadecimal notation. Every 4 bits are separated by a colon. 2001:0000:0000:3210:0800:200C:00CF:1234 is a valid IPv6 address.

- Leading zeroes can be dropped and double colons may be used to represent consecutive groups of zeroes in order to write an IPv6 address with fewer characters. 2001::3210:800:200C:CF:1234 is a valid IPv6 address.

- IPv6 subnet masks are represented with the /x prefix length naming convention. FEDC::CF:0:BA98:1234/64 translates to a 64-bit subnet mask.

- Computers using IPv6 that are on the Internet have (at least) two IPv6 addresses: a link-local address and a global unicast address.

- A link-local address is similar to an IPv4 APIPA address in that it is self-generated. The link-local address is guaranteed to be unique.

- A link-local address always starts with FE80::/10, followed by 54 zero bits.

- The last 64 bits of the link-local address are generated randomly in most operating systems.

- An IPv6 computer not on the Internet needs only the self-generated link-local address to participate on a local network. A server on such a network, however, still needs a static IP address, not a random self-generated link-local address.

- Link-local addresses always use /64 as the prefix length.

- IPv6 link-local addresses are unicast, or unique to a specific computer or network node.

- IPv6 relies heavily on multicasts.

- A multicast is a set of reserved addresses designed to go to only certain systems. Packets sent to addresses beginning with FF02::2 are only sent to routers.

- Multicasts, like broadcasts, can be sent to every computer on the network. Unlike broadcasts, though, only the target systems process the multicast packet.

- An IPv6 global unicast address is required for Internet access.

- Global unicast addresses are distributed by the default gateway, provided the router is configured to pass out global IPv6 addresses.

- The first half of a global unicast address is called the prefix and consists of the network ID and subnet mask. The prefix is passed out by the default gateway. The last half of the global unicast address is self-generated by the computer.

- Aggregation reduces the size and complexity of routing tables by allowing downstream routers to use a subset of an upstream router's routes to populate its routing table rather than tens or hundreds of thousands of disjointed routes.

Describe IPv6 practices

- IPv6 is active by default on every modern operating system, such as Windows 7/8, OS X, and most Linux distros.

- IPv6 does not support NAT.

- Although IPv6 global unicast addresses are passed out by the default gateway router (with a portion self-generated), DHCP servers are still important because they pass out DNS and TFTP server information.

- Stateful DHCPv6 servers pass out IPv6 addresses, subnet masks, default gateway addresses, and DNS server addresses, as well as other, optional information.

- Stateless DHCPv6 servers pass out only optional information. Stateless DHCPv6 servers are preferred to stateful servers because stateless servers support aggregation.

Implement IPv6 in a TCP/IP network

- Do not connect to the IPv6 Internet on a critical computer! Limited IPv6 support means potential security risks.

- Currently, all root DNS servers support IPv6 resolution and almost all tier-one ISP routers properly forward IPv6 packets. The routers between you and these root and tier-one servers, however, may not support IPv6 at the moment.

- An IPv4-to-IPv6 tunnel can be used to bridge the gap created by non-IPv6 routers, allowing you access to the root and tier-one routers that do support IPv6.

- There are several popular tunneling standards: 4to6, 6to4, 6in4, Teredo, Miredo, and ISATAP.

- 6to4 is a tunneling protocol that enables IPv6 traffic to use the IPv4 Internet without having to set up explicit tunnels. 6to4 addresses start with 2002::/16.

- Only 6in4 and Teredo can go through NAT.

- Teredo is built into Microsoft Windows. Teredo addresses always start with 2001:0000::/32. Miredo is the open source version used in Linux and UNIX systems.

- ISATAP adds an IPv4 address to an IPv6 prefix, for example, 2001:DB8:98CA:200:131.107.28.9.

- A tunnel broker is a service provider that creates the tunnel, acts as the far endpoint, and often provides a tunneling client for easier setup.

- TSP and TIC are two automatic configuration protocols for setting up IPv4-to-IPv6 tunnels.

- An overlay tunnel enables two IPv6 networks to connect over an existing IPv4 infrastructure, such as the Internet. Routers can use the same protocols used to connect an IPv4 client to an IPv6 network—6to4, ISATAP, and such—or can be configured manually A manual tunnel creates a simple, secure point-to-point connection between the two IPv6 networks.

■ Key Terms

4to6 *(372)*
6in4 *(373)*
6to4 *(372)*
aggregation *(365)*
anycast *(362)*
Extended Unique Identifier, 64-bit (EUI-64) *(361)*
global unicast address *(363)*
Internet Protocol version 4 (IPv4) *(358)*
Internet Protocol version 6 (IPv6) *(359)*
interface identifier *(361)*
Intra-Site Automatic Tunnel Addressing Protocol (ISATAP) *(374)*
link-local address *(361)*

manual tunnel *(375)*
Miredo *(373)*
multicast address *(362)*
overlay tunnel *(375)*
prefix delegation *(364)*
stateful *(370)*
stateless *(370)*
Teredo *(373)*
tunnel broker *(374)*
Tunnel Information and Control (TIC) protocol *(374)*
Tunnel Setup Protocol (TSP) *(374)*
unicast address *(361)*

■ Key Term Quiz

Use the Key Terms list to complete the sentences that follow. Not all the terms will be used.

1. A(n) _____ DHCPv6 server passes out only optional information.

2. A(n) _____ enables two IPv6 networks to connect over an existing IPv4 infrastructure.

3. It is the practice of _____ that greatly reduces the size of IPv6 routing tables by reducing them to a subnet of an upstream router.

4. You must have a(n) _____ to connect to the IPv6 Internet.

5. A(n) _____ address contains a total of 32 bits.

6. A packet sent to a(n) _____ is broadcast to all network nodes, but only the target nodes process the packet.

7. The _____ protocol can traverse NAT and is built into Windows.

8. The _____ appends an IPv4 address to the end of the IPv6 prefix.

9. Computers involved in a local network that has no Internet connectivity require only a(n) _____.

10. Employing the services of a(n) _____ automates the process of setting up an IPv6 tunnel.

■ Multiple-Choice Quiz

1. How many bits comprise an IPv6 address?

   A. 32

   B. 48

   C. 64

   D. 128

2. Which of the following is a valid IPv6 address?

   A. 192.168.0.1

   B. 2001:376:BDS:0:3378:BAAF:QR9:223

   C. 2541:FDC::ACDF:2770:23

   D. 0000:0000:0000:0000:0000:0000:0000:0000

3. Which of the following IPv6 addresses are equivalent to ACCB:0876:0000:0000:FD87:0000:0000:0064? (Select two.)

   A. ACCB:876::FD87:0:0:64

   B. ACCB:876::FD87::64

   C. ACCB:876:0:0:FD87::64

   D. ACCB:876:0:FD87:0:64

4. What is the only type of IPv6 address required to communicate with other computers on a local network?

   A. Link-local

   B. Global unicast

   C. EUI-64

   D. Multicast

5. Which of the following is a valid link-local address?

   A. 2001:2323:CCE:34FF:19:DE3:2DBA:52

   B. FE80::1994:33DD:22CE:769B

   C. FEFE:0:0:0:FEFE:0:0:0

   D. FFFF:FFFF:FFFF:FFFF:232D:0:DE44:CB2

6. What is true of link-local addresses?

   A. They are passed out by the default gateway router.

   B. They are completely randomly generated by each computer.

   C. All modern operating systems (post Windows XP) generate the second 64-bit portion randomly.

   D. They always start with 169.254.

7. What is a valid IPv6 prefix length?

   A. /64

   B. /72

   C. /255

   D. 255.255.255.0

8. How do IPv6 multicasts differ from broadcasts?

   A. Broadcasts are sent to all network nodes. Multicasts are sent only to specific network nodes.

   B. Both broadcasts and multicasts are sent to all network nodes, but in a multicast, only the destination nodes process the incoming packets.

   C. Broadcasts can cross over a router, whereas multicasts cannot.

   D. Broadcasts are used on local networks; multicasts are used on the Internet.

9. What type of address applies to a single unique network node?

   A. Unicast

   B. Unilateral

   C. Multicast

   D. Omnicast

10. A packet has been sent to the address FF02:0000:00 00:0002:0BCD:23DD:3456:0001. What will process the sent packet?

    A. The single computer with the address FF02:000 0:0000:0002:0BCD:23DD:3456:0001.

    B. Every network node.

    C. Every router on the network.

    D. Nothing will read the packet because it is an invalid address.

11. What must your computer have to access the IPv6 Internet?

    A. An IPv4 address

    B. A global multicast address

    C. A link-local address

    D. A global unicast address

12. What is true of current global unicast addresses?

    A. They always begin with 2001::, 2002::, 2003::, and so on.

    B. They always begin with FF02::1, FF02::2, FF03::3, and so on.

    C. They are only 64 bits long.

    D. They are only used by root and tier-one routers.

13. What is the main benefit of IPv6 aggregation?

   A. It allows users to combine multiple IPv6 addresses to increase their bandwidth and overall Internet speed exponentially.

   B. It is backward-compatible and can be directly applied to IPv4 networks.

   C. It reduces the size and complexity of routing tables, allowing routers to work more efficiently.

   D. Signals are increased with each router the packet travels through, allowing for greater distances over wireless networks.

14. Which protocol enables 6to4 tunneling in Linux?

   A. GOGO

   B. Miredo

   C. Teredo

   D. 6to4En

15. As IPv6 clients can get a portion of their IP address from the default gateway server, what purpose does a DHCPv6 server serve?

   A. DHCPv6 servers can still distribute DNS server information.

   B. DHCPv6 servers provide link-local addresses.

   C. DHCPv6 servers provide the other half of the IPv6 address.

   D. There is no such thing as a DHCPv6 server.

■ Essay Quiz

1. Explain to a colleague the difference between link-local and global IPv6 addresses. Be sure to include when each one is necessary.

2. Explain how aggregation reduces the size and complexity of routing tables.

3. NAT is not supported in IPv6, meaning that every computer with a global IPv6 address is exposed to the Internet. Why is this not a big concern?

Lab Projects

● Lab Project 13.1

Any decent network tech can work effectively with binary and hexadecimal notation. Get some practice by taking the following MAC addresses and calculating the EUI-64:

00-14-22-46-8A-77
BC-23-44-AB-A7-21
12-00-CF-C2-44-1A

Now use `ipconfig /all` to find your own MAC address and calculate the EUI-64.

● Lab Project 13.2

Choose one of the IPv4-to-IPv6 tunneling methods (6to4, 6in4, Teredo, or ISATAP) and configure a lab computer to connect to the Internet using IPv6. Document which method you used and the steps you took to get it working. Make your steps clear so someone else can follow them. Swap your steps with a classmate who used a different tunneling method and follow his or her steps to connect using the alternate method. Which method did you find more difficult? Why?

Remote Connectivity

"Gongs and drums, banners and flags, are means whereby the ears and eyes of the host may be focused on one particular point."

—Sun Tzu

In this chapter, you will learn how to

- **Describe WAN telephony technologies, such as SONET, T1, and T3**
- **Compare last-mile connections for connecting homes and businesses to the Internet**
- **Discuss and implement various remote access connection methods**
- **Troubleshoot various WAN scenarios**

Computers connect to other computers locally in a *local area network (LAN)*—you've read about LAN connections throughout this book—and remotely through a number of different methods. Interconnecting computers over distances, especially when the connections cross borders or jurisdictions, creates a **wide area network (WAN)**, though the term is pretty flexible. This chapter takes both an historical and a modern look at ways to interconnect a local computer or network with distant computers, what's called *remote connectivity*.

Historical/Conceptual

Remote connections have been around for a long time. Before the Internet, network users and developers created ways to take a single system or network and connect it to another faraway system or network. This wasn't the Internet! These were private interconnections of private networks. These connections were very expensive and, compared to today's options, pretty slow.

As the Internet developed, most of the same technologies used to make the earlier private remote connections became the way the Internet itself interconnects. Before the Internet was popular, many organizations used dedicated lines, called *T1 lines* (discussed in more detail later in this chapter), to connect far-flung offices. Some people still use T1 lines privately, but more often you'll see them used as an Internet connection to a company's local ISP. Private interconnections are only used today by organizations that need massive bandwidth or high security.

This chapter shows you all the ways you can make remote connections. You'll see every type of remote connection currently in popular use, from good-old telephone lines to advanced fiber-optic carriers, and even satellites. There are so many ways to make remote connections that this chapter is broken into four parts. The first part, "Telephony and Beyond," gives you a tour of the technologies that originally existed for long-distance voice connections that now also support data. The next part, "The Last Mile," goes into how we as individual users connect to those long-distance technologies and demonstrates how wireless technologies come into play in remote connectivity. Third, "Using Remote Access" shows you the many different ways to use these connections to connect to another, faraway computer. The chapter finishes with a section on troubleshooting various WAN scenarios. Let's get started!

 Even as you read this, more and more of the Internet interconnections are moving toward Gigabit and 10-Gigabit Ethernet. Telephone technologies, however, continue to dominate.

▪ Telephony and Beyond

We've already discussed the tier 1 ISPs of the Internet, but let's look at them once again in a different way. Describing the tier 1 Internet is always an interesting topic. Those of us in the instruction business invariably start this description by drawing a picture of the United States and then adding lines connecting big cities, as shown in Figure 14.1.

But what are these lines and where did they come from? If the Internet is just a big TCP/IP network, wouldn't these lines be Ethernet connections? Maybe copper, maybe fiber, but surely they're Ethernet? Well, traditionally they're not (with one exception; see the Note on this page). The vast majority of the long-distance connections that make up the Internet use a unique type of signal called SONET. SONET

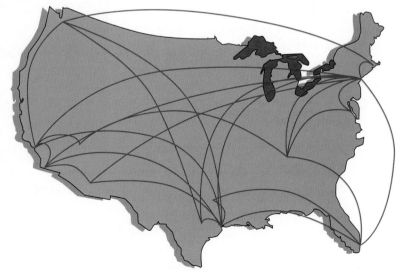

• **Figure 14.1**   The tier 1 Internet

Tech Tip

Telephony in Depth

This section is just the lightest of overviews to get you through the CompTIA Network+ exam. The full history of long-distance communication is an incredible story, full of good guys, bad guys, crazy technology, and huge fortunes won and lost.

was originally designed to handle special heavy-duty circuits with names like T1. Never heard of SONET or T1? Don't worry—you're about to learn quite a bit.

Most of the connections that make up the high-speed backbone of the Internet use technologies designed at least 20 years ago to support telephone calls. We're not talking about your cool, cell phone–type calls here, but rather the old-school, wire-runs-up-to-the-house, telephone-connected-to-a-phone-jack connections. (See "Public Switched Telephone Network" later in this chapter for more on this subject.) If you want to understand how the Internet connects, you have to go way back to the 1970s and 1980s, before the Internet really took off, and learn how the U.S. telephone system developed to support networks.

• **Figure 14.2** Old-time telephone operator (photo courtesy of the Richardson Historical and Genealogical Society)

The Dawn of Long Distance

Have you ever watched one of those old-time movies in which someone makes a phone call by picking up the phone and saying, "Operator, get me Mohawk 4, 3-8-2-5!" Suddenly, the scene changes to some person sitting at a switchboard like the one shown in Figure 14.2.

This was the telephone operator. The telephone operator made a physical link between your phone and the other phone, making your connection. The switchboard acted as a *circuit switch,* where plugging in the two wires created a physical circuit between the two phones. This worked pretty well in the first few years of telephones, but it quickly became a problem as more and more phone lines began to fill the skies overhead (Figure 14.3).

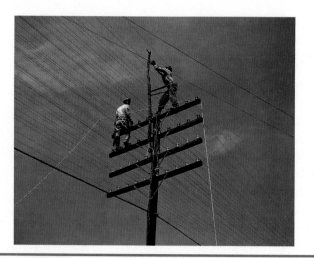

• **Figure 14.3** Now that's a lot of telephone lines!

These first generations of long-distance telephone systems (think 1930s here) used analog signals, because that was how your telephone worked—the higher and lower the pitch of your voice, the lower or greater the voltage. If you

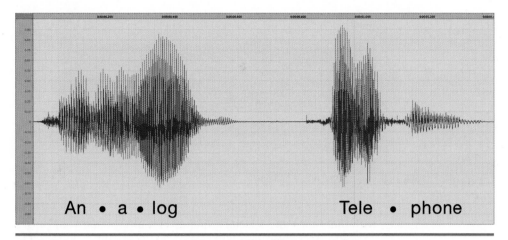

An • a • log   Tele • phone

• Figure 14.4   Another problem of early long-distance telephone systems

graphed out a voice signal, it looked something like Figure 14.4. This type of transmission had issues, however, because analog signals over long distances, even if you amplified them, lost sound quality very quickly.

The first problem to take care of was the number of telephone wires. Individual wires were slowly replaced with special boxes called multiplexers. A **multiplexer** took a circuit and combined it with a few hundred other circuits into a single complex circuit on one wire. A **demultiplexer** (devices were both multiplexers and demultiplexers) on the other end of the connection split the individual connections back out (Figure 14.5).

Over time, the entire United States was divided into hundreds, eventually thousands, of local exchanges. *Local exchanges* were a defined grouping of individual phone circuits served by a single multiplexer (calls within the exchange were handled first by human operators who were replaced,

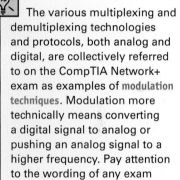

The various multiplexing and demultiplexing technologies and protocols, both analog and digital, are collectively referred to on the CompTIA Network+ exam as examples of modulation techniques. Modulation more technically means converting a digital signal to analog or pushing an analog signal to a higher frequency. Pay attention to the wording of any exam questions on modulation.

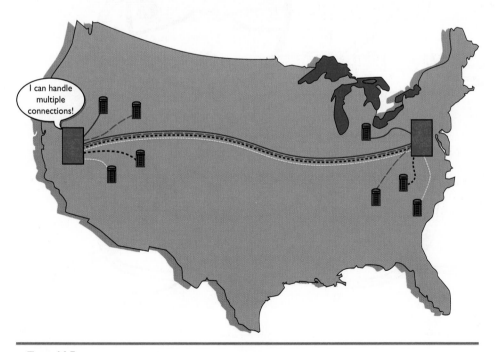

I can handle multiple connections!

• Figure 14.5   Multiplexers combine multiple circuits.

● Figure 14.6 A central office building

eventually, with dial tones and special switches that interpreted your pulses or tones for a number). One or more exchanges were (and still are) housed in a physical building called a **central office** (Figure 14.6) where individual voice circuits all came together. Local calls were still manually connected (although dial-up began to appear in earnest by the 1950s, after which many operators lost their jobs), but any connection between exchanges was carried over these special multiplexed trunk lines. Figure 14.7 shows a very stylized example of how this worked.

These old-style trunk lines were fascinating technology. How did they put a bunch of voice calls on a single piece of cable, yet still somehow keep them separate? To understand the trick you need to appreciate a little bit about frequency. A typical telephone only detects a fairly limited frequency range—

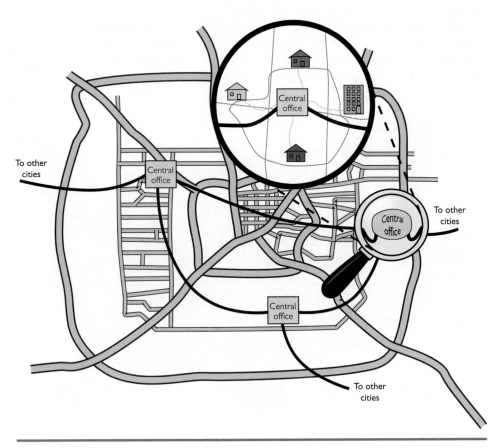

● Figure 14.7 Interconnected central offices

from around 350 Hz to around 4000 Hz. This range covers enough of the human speech range to make a decent phone call. As the individual calls came into the multiplexer, it added a certain frequency multiplier to each call, keeping every separate call in its own unique frequency range (Figure 14.8). This process is called **frequency division multiplexing (FDM)**.

This analog network still required a physical connection from one phone to the other, even if those phones were on opposite sides of the country. Long distance used a series of trunk lines, and at each intersection of those lines an operator had to connect the calls. When you physically connect two phones together on one circuit, you are using something called **circuit switching**. As you might imagine, circuit switching isn't that great for long distance, but it's your only option when you use analog.

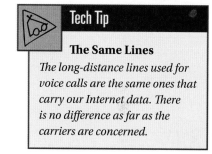

• **Figure 14.8**   Multiplexed FDM

This analog system worked pretty well through the 1930s to the 1950s, but telephones became so common and demand so heavy that the United States needed a new system to handle the load. The folks developing this new system realized that they had to dump analog and replace it with a digital system—sowing the seeds for the remote connections that eventually became the Internet.

Digital data transmits much easier over long distances than analog data because you can use repeaters. (You cannot use repeaters on analog signals.) If you remember from earlier chapters, a repeater is not an amplifier. An amplifier just increases the voltage and includes all the pops and hisses created by all kinds of interferences. A **repeater** takes the entire digital signal and re-creates it out the other end (Figure 14.9).

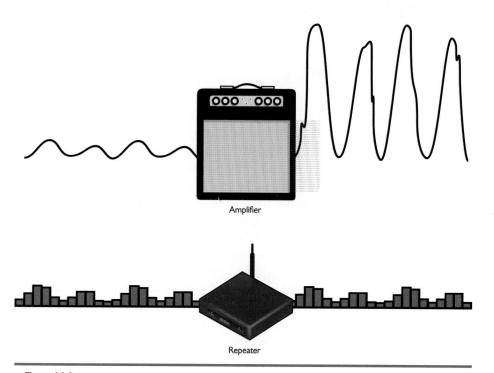

Amplifier

Repeater

• **Figure 14.9**   Repeater vs. amplifier

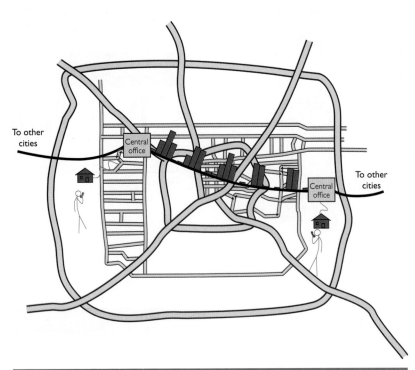

• **Figure 14.10** Analog and digital

Attempts were made to convert the entire telephone system, including your telephones, to digital, but these technologies never took off (except in a few niches). See "ISDN" later in this chapter.

The downside to adopting a digital system was that the entire telephone system was analog: every telephone, every switch, every multiplexer. The task of converting the entire analog voice system to digital was a massive undertaking. Luckily, virtually the entire U.S. phone system at that time was a monopoly run by a company called AT&T. A single company could make all of its own decisions and its own standards—one of the few times in history where a monopoly was probably a good thing. The AT&T folks had a choice here: completely revamp the entire U.S. phone system, including replacing every single telephone in the United States, or just make the trunk lines digital and let the central offices convert from analog to digital. They chose the latter.

Even today, a classic telephone line in your home or small office uses analog signals—the rest of the entire telephone system is digital. The telecommunications industry calls the connection from a central office to individual users the **last mile**. The telephone company's decision to keep the last mile analog has had serious repercussions that still challenge us even in the 21st century (Figure 14.10).

Test Specific

Digital Telephony

You'll find digital telephony easy to understand, because most of the aspects you've already learned about computer networking work roughly the same way in a telephone network. In fact, most of the concepts that created computer networking came from the telephone industry. For example, the telephone industry was the first technology to adopt heavily the idea of digital packets. It was the first to do what is now called switching. Heck, the telephone industry even made the first working topologies! Let's take advantage of what you already know about how networks work to learn about how the telephone industry invented the idea of digital networks.

When you learned about networks in the first few chapters of this book, you learned about cabling, frame types, speeds, switching, and so on. All of these are important for computer networks. Well, let's do it again (in a much simpler format) to see the cabling, frame types, speed, and switching used in telephone systems. Don't worry—unlike computer networks, in which a certain type of cable might run different types of frames at different speeds, most of the remote connections used in the telephony world tend to have one type of cable that only runs one type of frame at one speed.

Let's begin with the most basic data chunk you get in the telephone world: DS0.

It All Starts with DS0

When AT&T decided to go digital, it knew all phone calls had to be broken into a digital sample. AT&T determined that if it took an analog signal of a human voice and converted it into 8-bit chunks 8000 times a second, it would be good enough to re-create the sound later. Figure 14.11 shows an example of the analog human voice seen earlier being converted into a digital sample.

Converting analog sound into 8-bit chunks 8000 times a second creates a data stream (called a *digital signal*) of 8 × 8000 = 64 kilobits per second (Kbps). This digital signal rate, known as **DS0**, makes up the simplest data stream (and the slowest rate) of the digital part of the telephone system. Each analog voice call gets converted into a DS0 signal at the telephone company's central office. From there they are multiplexed into larger circuits.

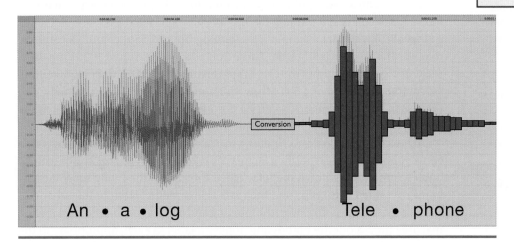

An • a • log   Tele • phone

• **Figure 14.11**   Analog to digital

Now that we have our voice calls converted to digital data, we need to get them to the right telephone. First, we need network technologies to handle the cabling, frames, and speed. Second, we need to come up with a method to switch the digital voice calls across a network. To handle the former, we need to define the types of interconnections, with names like T1 and OC-3. To handle the latter, we no longer connect via multiplexed circuit switching, as we did back with analog, but rather are now switching packets. I'll show you what I mean as I discuss the digital lines in use today.

Copper Carriers: T1 and T3

The first (and still popular) digital trunk carriers used by the telephone industry are called *T-carriers*. There are a number of different versions of T-carriers and the CompTIA Network+ exam expects you to know something about them.

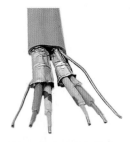

• **Figure 14.12**   T1 line

Let's begin with the most common and most basic, the venerable T-carrier level 1 (T1).

T1 has several meanings. First, it refers to a high-speed digital networking technology called a *T1 connection*. Second, the term **T1 line** refers to the specific, shielded, two-pair cabling that connects the two ends of a T1 connection (Figure 14.12). Two wires are for sending data and two wires are for receiving data. The cable ends with a modular jack called an *RJ-48C*, that looks a lot like the RJ-45 connector you're used to seeing with Ethernet cables.

At either end of a T1 line, you'll find an unassuming box called a **Channel Service Unit/Digital Service Unit (CSU/DSU)**. The CSU/DSU has a second connection that goes from the phone company (where the boxes reside) to a customer's equipment (usually a router). A T1 connection is point-to-point—you cannot have more than two CSU/DSUs on a single T1 line.

T1 uses a special signaling method called a **digital signal 1 (DS1)**.

DS1 uses a relatively primitive frame—the frame doesn't need to be complex because with point-to-point no addressing is necessary. Each DS1 frame has 25 pieces: a framing bit and 24 channels. Each DS1 channel holds a single 8-bit DS0 data sample. The framing bit and data channels combine to make 193 bits per DS1 frame. These frames are transmitted 8000 times/sec, making a total throughput of 1.544 Mbps (Figure 14.13). DS1 defines, therefore, a data transfer speed of 1.544 Mbps, split into 24 64-Kbps DS0 channels. The process of having frames that carry a portion of every channel in every frame sent on a regular interval is called **time division multiplexing (TDM)**.

When discussing T1 technology in class, I like to use an analogy of a conveyor belt in a milk-bottling factory. At regular intervals, big crates with 24 bottles come rolling down the belt. When they reach the filling machine, the bottles get filled with milk, and the crate keeps rolling down to the other end where two machines take over: the labeling and sorting machines. The labeling machine plucks out the bottles and applies a label to each, appropriate to the contents. The sorting machine sorts the bottles into cases of each type.

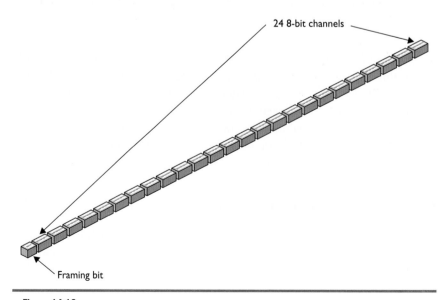

24 8-bit channels

Framing bit

• **Figure 14.13**   DS1 frame

This is pretty simple if the filling machine uses only one type of milk. All 24 bottles fill with whole milk; all are labeled as whole milk; and all go into the case marked "Whole Milk." Once enough full bottles of milk arrive, the case gets completed, and you have a product.

That's pretty much how an Ethernet frame works, right? The whole frame encapsulates a single set of data, such as an IP packet that, in turn, encapsulates a single type of TCP segment, UDP datagram, or ICMP packet. It generally takes multiple frames to get the data to the recipient, where the frames are removed, the IP packet is removed, and the segment or datagram gets put together to make the data transfer complete.

The cool thing about the DS1 frame, though, is that you don't have to use the whole frame for a single set of data. With the right CSU/DSU at either end, you can specify which channels go with a specific thread of data. Sloshing back into the analogy, the milk company produces four types of milk: whole milk, low-fat milk, chocolate milk, and strawberry milk. The strawberry milk is seasonal; the whole milk sells the most, followed by chocolate, and then low fat.

To accommodate the different products, the factory master might designate channels 1–10 for whole milk, 11–18 for chocolate milk, 19–22 for low-fat milk, and 23–24 for strawberry. Now the labeling and sorting machines are going to have to work for a living! When a crate reaches the filling machine, the bottles get filled with the various types of milk, and then the crate trundles on down the belt. The labeling machine knows the numbering system, so it labels bottles 1–10 as whole milk, 11–18 as chocolate, and so on. The sorting machine also knows the system and has four cases at hand, one for each product. As the bottles arrive, it places them into the appropriate cases. Note that the cases will fill at different rates of speed. The strawberry milk case will take longer to fill, especially compared to the whole milk case, because only two channels in each crate carry strawberry.

What happens if the cows temporarily stop producing chocolate milk? Will the whole factory need to be reordered so the filling machine's eight chocolate dispensers can dispense some other kind of milk? Not in this factory. The crates continue to roll down the conveyor belt at regular intervals. The filling machine fills the bottles in channels 1–10 with whole milk, leaves the bottles in channels 11–18 empty, and puts low fat and strawberry in channels 19–22 and 23–24, respectively.

DS1/T1 work the same way. The frame just keeps jetting down the line, even if some of the channels contain no data. The CSU/DSU at the other end collects the data streams and keeps them separate. To paraphrase the immortal words of Professor Egon, "Never cross the streams." (You have seen *Ghostbusters*, right?) Otherwise you'd lose data.

To bring the milk bottling–factory analogy completely into the realm of networking and T1 connections, keep in mind that two conveyor belts are running in opposite directions. Milk flows in; milk flows out. You can both send and receive on T1 connections.

A T1 line is a dedicated phone connection that you lease, usually on a monthly basis, from the telephone company. It has no telephone number, and it's always connected. An entire T1 bundle is expensive, so many telephone companies let you buy just some of these individual channels, a practice known as **fractional T1 access**.

Tech Tip

DS1 Gets No Respect!
People rarely use the term "DS1." Because T1 lines only carry DS1 signals, you usually just say T1 when describing the signal, even though the term DS1 is more accurate.

A **T3 line** supports a data rate of about 45 Mbps on a dedicated telephone connection. It consists of 672 individual DS0 channels. T3 lines (sometimes referred to as *DS3 lines*) are mainly used by regional telephone companies and ISPs connecting to the Internet.

Similar to the North American T1 line, E-carrier level 1 (**E1**) is the European format for digital transmission. An E1 line carries signals at 2.048 Mbps (32 channels at 64 Kbps), compared to the T1's 1.544 Mbps (24 channels at 64 Kbps). E1 and T1 lines can interconnect for international use. There are also **E3** lines, which carry 16 E1 lines, with a bandwidth of about 34 Mbps.

A CSU/DSU, as mentioned earlier, connects a leased T1 or T3 line from the telephone company to a customer's equipment. A CSU/DSU has (at least) two connectors, one that goes to the T1/T3 line running out of your demarc and another connection that goes to your router. It performs line encoding and conditioning functions and often has a loopback function for testing. Many newer routers have CSU/DSUs built into them.

 E1 and SONET use a derivative of the *High-Level Data Link Control (HDLC)* protocol as the control channel.

 Cross Check

Demarc

You first read about the *demarc*—the spot where connections from the outside world come into a building—way back in Chapter 6, "Installing a Physical Network," so check your memory and see if you can answer these questions. How does the demarc affect your wallet? What do you call the cable modem or DSL receiver that marks the demarc in many houses and offices?

Many routers feature two ports on one router, with the dual links providing redundancy if one link goes down. The CSU part of a CSU/DSU protects the T1 or T3 line and the user equipment from lightning strikes and other types of electrical interference. It also stores statistics and has capabilities for loopback testing. The DSU part supplies timing to each user port, taking the incoming user's data signals and converting the input signal into the specified line code and then framing the format for transmission over the provided line.

Make sure you know the four T-carriers shown in Table 14.1!

Table 14.1	T-carriers	
Carrier	**Channels**	**Speed**
T1	24	1.544 Mbps
T3	672	44.736 Mbps
E1	32	2.048 Mbps
E3	512	34.368 Mbps

Fiber Carriers: SONET/SDH and OC

T-carriers were a great start into the digital world, but in the early 1980s, fiber-optic cabling became the primary tool for long-distance communication all over the world. By now, AT&T as a monopoly was gone, replaced by a number of competing carriers (including a smaller AT&T). Competition was strong and everyone was making their own fiber transmission standards. In an incredible moment of corporate cooperation, in 1987, all of the primary fiber-optic carriers decided to drop their own standards and move to a new international standard called **Synchronous Optical Network (SONET)** in the United States and **Synchronous Digital Hierarchy (SDH)** in Europe.

All of these carriers adopting the same standard created a world of simple interconnections between competing voice and data carriers. This adoption defined the moment that truly made the Internet a universal network. Before SONET, interconnections happened, but they were outlandishly expensive, preventing the Internet from reaching many areas of the world.

SONET remains the primary standard for long-distance, high-speed, fiber-optic transmission systems. SONET, like Ethernet, defines interface standards at the Physical and Data Link layers of the OSI seven-layer model. The physical aspect of SONET is partially covered by the Optical Carrier standards, but it also defines a ring-based topology that most SONET adopters now use. SONET does not require a ring, but a SONET ring has fault tolerance in case of line loss. As a result, most of the big long-distance optical pipes for the world's telecommunications networks are SONET rings.

The real beauty of SONET lies in its multiplexing capabilities. A single SONET ring can combine multiple DS1, DS3, even European E1 signals, and package them into single, huge SONET frames for transmission. Clearly, SONET needs high-capacity fiber optics to handle such large data rates. That's where the Optical Carrier standards come into play!

The **Optical Carrier (OC)** standards denote the optical data-carrying capacity (in bps) of fiber-optic cables in networks conforming to the SONET standard. The OC standard describes an escalating series of speeds, designed to meet the needs of medium-to-large corporations. SONET establishes OC speeds from 51.8 Mbps (OC-1) to 39.8 Gbps (OC-768).

Still want more throughput? Many fiber devices use a very clever feature called *wavelength division multiplexing (WDM)* or its newer and more popular version, **dense wavelength division multiplexing (DWDM)**. DWDM enables an individual single-mode fiber to carry multiple signals by giving each signal a different wavelength by using different colors of laser light. The result varies, but a single DWDM fiber can support ~150 signals, enabling, for example, a 51.8-Mbps OC-1 line run at 51.8 Mbps × 150 signals = 7.6 *gigabits per second!* DWDM has become very popular for long-distance lines as it's usually less expensive to replace older SONET/OC-*x* equipment with DWDM than it is to add more fiber lines.

A related technology, **coarse wavelength division multiplexing (CWDM)**, also relies on multiple wavelengths of light to carry a fast signal over long distances. It's simpler than DWDM, which limits its practical distances to a mere 60 km. You'll see it used in higher-end LANs with 10GBase-LX4 networks, for example, where its lower cost (compared to direct competitors) offers benefits.

SONET uses the **Synchronous Transport Signal (STS)** signal method. The STS consists of two parts: the **STS payload** (which carries data) and the **STS overhead** (which carries the signaling and protocol information). When folks talk about STS, they add a number to the end of "STS" to designate the speed of the signal. For example, STS-1 runs a 51.85 Mbps signal on an OC-1 line. STS-3

Tech Tip

What's in a Name?
Students often wonder why two separate names exist for the same technology. In reality, SONET and SDH vary a little in their signaling and frame type, but routers and other magic boxes on the Internet handle the interoperability between the standards. The American National Standards Institute (ANSI) publishes the standard as SONET; the International Telecommunication Union (ITU) publishes the standard as SDH, but includes SONET signaling. For simplicity's sake, and because SONET is the more common term in the United States, this book uses SONET as the term for this technology.

SONET is one of the most important standards for making all WAN interconnections—and it's also the least likely standard you'll ever see because it's hidden away from all but the biggest networks.

DWDM isn't just upgrading SONET lines; DWDM works just as well on long-distance fiber Ethernet.

runs at 155.52 Mbps on OC-3 lines, and so on. Table 14.2 describes the most common optical carriers.

Table 14.2	Common Optical Carriers	
SONET Optical Level	**Line Speed**	**Signal Method**
OC-1	51.85 Mbps	STS-1
OC-3	155.52 Mbps	STS-3
OC-12	622.08 Mbps	STS-12
OC-24	1.244 Gbps	STS-24
OC-48	2.488 Gbps	STS-48
OC-192	9.955 Gbps	STS-192
OC-256	13.22 Gbps	STS-256
OC-768	39.82 Gbps	STS-768

Packet Switching

The first generation of packet-switching technology was called *X.25*. It enabled remote devices to communicate with each other across high-speed digital links without the expense of individual leased lines. CompTIA also refers to X.25 as the *CCITT Packet Switching Protocol*.

Machines that forward and store packets using any type of packet-switching protocol are called *packet switches.*

As its name would suggest, Frame Relay works at Layer 2 of the OSI model, using frames rather than packets. I don't know why no one invented the term "frame switching" to describe Frame Relay, but there you have it.

All of these impressive connections that start with *T*s and *O*s are powerful, but they are not in and of themselves a complete WAN solution. These WAN connections with their unique packets (DS0, STS, and so on) make up the entire mesh of long-range connections called the Internet, carrying both packetized voice data and TCP/IP data packets. All of these connections are point-to-point, so you need to add another level of devices to enable you to connect multiple T1s, T3s, or OC connections together to make that mesh. That's where packet switching comes into play.

Packets, as you know, need some form of addressing scheme to get from one location to another. The telephone industry came up with its own types of packets that run on T-carrier and OC lines to get data from one central office to another. These packet-switching protocols are functionally identical to routable network protocols like TCP/IP. Today's WAN connections predominantly use two different forms of packet switching: Frame Relay and ATM.

Frame Relay

Frame Relay is an extremely efficient packet-switching standard, designed for and used primarily with T-carrier lines. It works especially well for the off-again/on-again traffic typical of most LAN applications.

Frame Relay switches frames quickly, but without any guarantee of data integrity at all. You can't even count on it to deliver all the frames, because it will discard frames whenever there is network congestion. At first this might sound problematic—what happens if you have a data problem? In practice, however, a Frame Relay network delivers data quite reliably because T-carrier digital lines that use Frame Relay have very low error rates. It's up to the higher-level protocols to error-check as needed. Frame Relay was extremely popular in its day, but newer technologies such as ATM and especially MPLS are beginning to replace it. If you decide to go with a T1 line in the United States, you'll get a T1 line running Frame Relay, although many companies use the newer ATM standard as their packet-switching solution with T-carrier lines.

ATM

Don't think automatic teller machine here! **Asynchronous Transfer Mode (ATM)** is a network technology originally designed for high-speed LANs in the early 1990s. ATM only saw limited success in the LAN world but became extremely popular in the WAN world. In fact, until the recent advent of MPLS (see "MPLS" next), most of the SONET rings that moved voice and data all over the world used ATM for packet switching. ATM integrated voice, video, and data on one connection, using short and fixed-length frames called *cells* to transfer information. Every cell sent with the same source and destination traveled over the same route.

ATM existed because data and audio/video transmissions have different transfer requirements. Data tolerates a delay in transfer, but not signal loss (if it takes a moment for a Web page to appear, you don't care). Audio and video transmissions, on the other hand, tolerate signal loss but not delay (delay makes phone calls sound choppy and clipped). Because ATM transferred information in fixed-length cells (53 bytes long), it handled both types of transfers well. ATM transfer speeds ranged from 155.52 to 622.08 Mbps and beyond. If your location was big enough to order an OC line from your ISP, odds were good that OC line connected to an ATM switch.

ATM, like Frame Relay, works with frames at Layer 2, rather than packets at Layer 3. It, too, gets lumped into the category of a packet-switching technology.

Referring to ATM in the past tense might seem a bit premature. Plenty of ISPs still use ATM, but it's definitely on the way out due to MPLS.

MPLS

Frame Relay and ATM were both fantastic packet-switching technologies, but they were designed to support any type of traffic that might come over the network. Today, TCP/IP, the predominant data technology, has a number of issues that neither Frame Relay nor ATM addresses. For example, ATM uses a very small frame, only 53 bytes, which adds quite a bit of overhead to 1,500-byte Ethernet frames. To address this and other issues, many ISPs (and large ISP clients) use an improved technology called **Multiprotocol Label Switching (MPLS)** as a replacement for Frame Relay and ATM switching.

MPLS adds an MPLS label that sits between the Layer 2 header and the Layer 3 information. Layer 3 is always IP, so MPLS labels sit between Layer 2 and the IP headers. Figure 14.14 shows the structure of an MPLS header.

Label	CoS	S	TTL

• Figure 14.14   MPLS header

The MPLS header consists of four parts:

- **Label**   A unique identifier, used by MPLS-capable routers to determine how to move data.

- **Cost of Service (CoS)**   A relative value used to determine the importance of the labeled packet to be able to prioritize some packets over others.

- **S**   In certain situations, a single packet may have multiple MPLS labels. This single bit value is set to 1 for the initial label.

- **Time to Live (TTL)**   A value that determines the number of hops the label can make before it's eliminated

Figure 14.15 shows the location of the MPLS header.

• Figure 14.15   MPLS header inserted in a frame

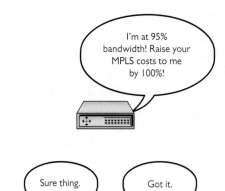

The original idea for MPLS was to give individual ISPs a way to move traffic through their morass of different interconnections and switches more quickly and efficiently by providing network-wide quality of service. MPLS-capable routers avoid running IP packets through their full routing tables and instead use the header information to route packets quickly. Where "regular" routers use QoS on an individual basis, MPLS routers use their existing dynamic routing protocols to send each other messages about their overhead, enabling QoS to span an entire group of routers (Figure 14.16).

• **Figure 14.16** MPLS routers talk to each other about their overhead.

 Cross Check

QoS

You learned about QoS back in Chapter 12, "Advanced Networking Devices," so see if you remember enough to answer these questions. What is the purpose of QoS? How does it speed up networks?

Let's see how the MPLS-labeled packets, combined with MPLS-capable routers, create improved throughput. To see this happen, I need to introduce a few MPLS terms:

- **Forwarding Equivalence Class (FEC)** FEC is a group of devices (usually computers) that tend to send packets to the same place, such as a single broadcast domain of computers connected to a router.

- **Label switching router (LSR)** An LSR looks for and forwards packets based on their MPLS label. These are the "MPLS routers" mentioned previously.

- **Label edge router (LER)** An LER is an MPLS router that has the job of adding MPLS labels to incoming packets that do not yet have a label.

- **Label Distribution Protocol (LDP)** LSRs and LERs use the LDP to communicate dynamic information about their state.

Figure 14.17 shows a highly simplified MPLS network. Note the position of the FECs, LERs, and LSRs.

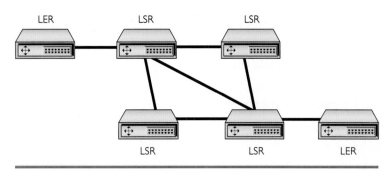

• **Figure 14.17** Sample MPLS network

When an MPLS network comes online, administrators will configure initial routing information, primarily setting metrics to routes (Figure 14.18).

LERs have the real power in determining routes. Because LERs are the entrances and exits for an MPLS network, they talk to each other to determine the best possible routes. As data moves from one FEC, the LERs add an MPLS label to every packet. LSRs strip away incoming labels and add their own. This progresses until the packets exit out the opposing LER (Figure 14.19).

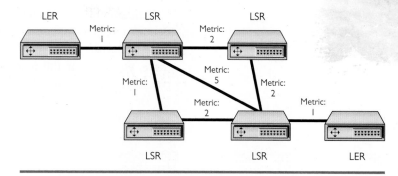

• **Figure 14.18**   MPLS initial routes added

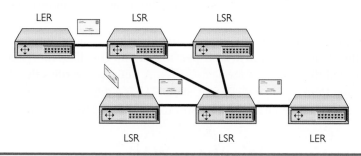

• **Figure 14.19**   Data routing through an MPLS network

Although MPLS was originally used just to move data quickly between LERs, MPLS's label-stacking ability makes it a perfect candidate for end-user VPNs. Instead of having to set up your own VPN, an ISP using MPLS can set up and lease you a fully functional connection to your network. The ISP makes the VPN for you; you just insert an RJ-45 plug into the switch in your office and it works. This feature of MPLS is called a *permanent virtual circuit (PVC)* and is a popular product sold by ISPs to connect two customer locations.

Real-World WAN

There are two reasons to use a telephony WAN connection: to get your LAN on the Internet or to make a private connection between two or more of your private LANs. How you go about getting one of these lines changes a bit depending on which you want to do. Let's start with connecting to the Internet.

Traditionally, getting a WAN Internet connection was a two-step process: you talked to the telephone company to get the line physically installed and then talked to an ISP to provide you with Internet access. Today, almost every telephone company is also an ISP, so this process is usually simple. Just go online and do a Web search of ISPs in your area and give them a call. You'll get a price quote, and, if you sign up, the ISP will do the installation.

You can use a few tricks to reduce the price, however. If you're in an office building, odds are good that a T1 or better line is already installed and that an ISP is already serving people in your building. Talk to the building supervisor. If there isn't a T1 or better line, you have to pay for a new line. If an interconnect is nearby, this option might be inexpensive. If you want the telephone company to run an OC line to your house, however, brace for a quote of thousands of dollars just to get the line.

The telephone company runs your T-carrier (or better) line to a demarc. This demarc is important because this is where the phone company's responsibility ends! Everything on "your" side of the demarc is your responsibility. From there, you or your ISP installs a CSU/DSU (for T-carriers) and that device connects to your router.

Depending on who does this for you, you may encounter a tremendous amount of variance here. The classic example (sticking with T-carrier) consists of a demarc, CSU/DSU, and router setup, as shown in Figure 14.20.

T-carriers have been around so long that many of these parts are combined. You'll often see a single box that combines the CSU/DSU and the router in one handy device.

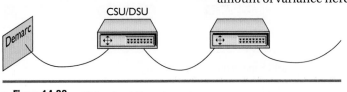

• **Figure 14.20**   Old-school T-carrier setup

WAN telephony carriers are incredibly dependable—far more dependable than inexpensive alternatives (like cable modems)—and that's one of the main reasons people still use them. But you should definitely know how to test your end of the connection if you ever suspect a problem. The single most important test is called the **Bit Error Rate Test (BERT)**. A BERT test verifies the T-carrier connection from end to end. Every CSU/DSU has a different way to perform a BERT test. Just make sure you know how to perform the test on yours!

Alternative to Telephony WAN

Telephony WANs were the first big connections. They're still the core of what makes up most of the Internet backbone and private connections, but they've given way to more advanced technologies. The biggest newer technology for WAN connectivity is Ethernet.

Over the last few years, many ISPs started replacing their T1, T3, and OC-*x* equipment with good-old Ethernet. Well, not "good-old" Ethernet—rather, superfast 10-Gbps Ethernet, 40-Gbps Ethernet, or 100-Gbps Ethernet running on single-mode fiber and connected to DWDM-capable switches. As a result, in many areas—especially metropolitan areas—you can get **metro Ethernet**— Ethernet throughout a city—right to your office. Anyone want a 10-, 40-, or 100-Gbps connection to their router? If you've got the money and you're in a lucky city, you can get it now.

These Ethernet connections also work great for dedicated connections. A good friend of mine leases a dedicated 10-Gbps Ethernet connection from his company's data center in Houston, Texas, to his office in London, England. It works great!

■ The Last Mile

Speed is the key to the Internet, but historically there's always been one big challenge: getting data from central offices to individual users. Although this wasn't a problem for larger companies that could afford their own WAN connections, what about individuals and small companies that couldn't or wouldn't pay hundreds of dollars a month for a T1? This area, the infamous last mile, was a serious challenge early on for both Internet connections and private connections because the only common medium was standard telephone lines. A number of last-mile solutions have appeared over the years, and the CompTIA Network+ exam tests you on the most popular ones—and a few obscure ones as well. Here's the list:

- Dial-up
- DSL
- Broadband cable
- Satellite
- Cellular WAN
- Fiber
- BPL

Dial-Up

Many different types of telephone lines are available, but all the choices break down into two groups: dedicated and dial-up. **Dedicated lines** are always off the hook (that is, they never hang up on each other).

A dedicated line (like a T1) does not have a phone number. In essence, the telephone company creates a permanent, hard-wired connection between the two locations, rendering a phone number superfluous. **Dial-up lines**, by contrast, have phone numbers; they must dial each other up to make a connection. When they're finished communicating, they hang up. Two technologies make up the overwhelming majority of dial-up connections: PSTN and ISDN.

Public Switched Telephone Network

The oldest, slowest, and most common original phone connection is the **public switched telephone network (PSTN)**. See Figure 14.21. PSTN is also known as **plain old telephone service (POTS)**. PSTN is just a regular phone line, the same line that used to run into everybody's home telephone jacks from the central office of your *Local Exchange Carrier (LEC)*. The LEC is the telephone company (telco) that provides local connections and usually the one that owns your local central office.

> A company that provides local telephone service to individual customers is called a *Local Exchange Carrier (LEC)*. A company that provides long-distance service is called an *Interexchange Carrier (IXC)*. Classically, LECs owned the central offices and IXCs owned the lines and equipment that interconnected them. Over time, the line between LECs and IXCs has become very blurred.

• **Figure 14.21**   Ancient telephone switchboard, just because

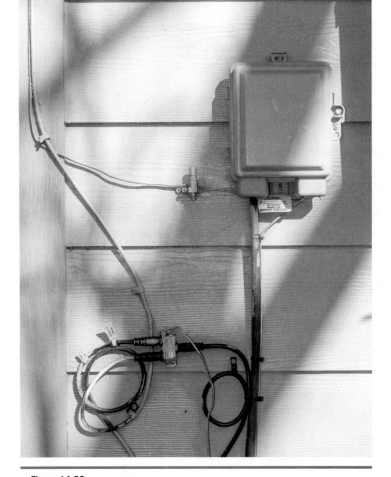

• **Figure 14.22** RJ-11 connectors (top and side views)

• **Figure 14.23** Typical home demarc

Internal modems are both a UART and a modem. External modems use a serial or USB port. The serial or USB port contains the UART, so the external modem truly is just a modem.

Because the PSTN was designed long before computers were common, it was designed to work with only one type of data: sound. Here's how it works. The telephone's microphone takes the sound of your voice and translates it into an electrical analog waveform. The telephone then sends that signal through the PSTN line to the phone on the other end of the connection. That phone translates the signal into sound on the other end using its speaker. Note the word *analog*. The telephone microphone converts the sounds into electrical waveforms that cycle 2400 times a second. An individual cycle is known as a **baud**. The number of bauds per second is called the **baud rate**. Pretty much all phone companies' PSTN lines have a baud rate of 2400. PSTN connections use a connector called RJ-11. It's the classic connector you see on all telephones (Figure 14.22).

When you connect your modem to a phone jack, the line then runs to either your **network interface unit (NIU)** or the demarc. The term "network interface unit" usually describes the small box on the side of a home that accepts the incoming lines from the telephone company and then splits them to the different wall outlets. "Demarc" more commonly describes large connections used in businesses. The terms always describe the interface between the lines the telephone company is responsible for and the lines for which you are responsible (Figure 14.23).

Computers, as you know, don't speak analog—only digital/binary (0 or 1) will do. In addition, the people who invented the way PCs communicate decided to divide any digital signal going in and out of your computer into 8 bits at a time. To connect over phone lines, PCs need two devices: one that converts this 8-bit-wide (parallel) digital signal from the computer into serial (1-bit-wide) digital data and then another device to convert (modulate) the data into analog waveforms that can travel across PSTN lines.

You already know that the device that converts the digital data to analog and back is called a **modulator-demodulator (modem)**. The modem in your PC (assuming you still have one) also contains a device called a **Universal Asynchronous Receiver/Transmitter (UART)**. The UART takes the 8-bit-wide digital data and converts it into 1-bit-wide digital data and hands it to the modem for conversion to analog. The process is reversed for incoming data.

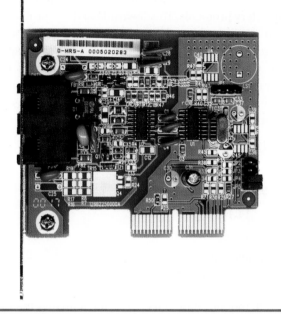

• Figure 14.24 Internal modem

Even though internal modems are actually both a UART and a modem, we just say the word "modem" (Figure 14.24).

Bit Rates vs. Baud Rate

Modems use phone lines to transmit data at various speeds. These speeds cause a world of confusion and problems for computer people. This is where a little bit of knowledge becomes dangerous. Standard modems you can buy for your home computer normally transmit data at speeds up to 56 Kbps. That's 56 kilobits per second, *not* 56 kilobaud! Many people confuse the terms *baud* and *bits per second*. This confusion arises because the baud rate and the bit rate are the same for modems until the data transfer rate surpasses 2400 bps.

A PSTN phone line takes analog samples of sound 2400 times a second. This standard *sampling size* was determined a long time ago as an acceptable rate for sending voice traffic over phone lines. Although 2400-baud analog signals are fine for voice communication, they are a big problem for computers trying to send data because computers only work with digital signals. The job of the modem is to take the digital signals it receives from the computer and send them out over the phone line in an analog form, using the baud cycles from the phone system. A 2400-bps modem—often erroneously called a 2400-baud modem—uses 1 analog baud to send 1 bit of data.

As technology progressed, modems became faster and faster. To get past the 2400-baud limit, modems modulated the 2400-baud signal multiple times in each cycle. A 4800-bps modem modulated 2 bits per baud, thereby transmitting 4800 bps. All PSTN modem speeds are a multiple of 2400, with the latest (and last) generation of modems achieving $2400 \times 24 = 57{,}600$ bps (56 Kbps).

V Standards

For two modems to communicate with each other at their fastest rate, they must modulate signals in the same fashion. The two modems must also negotiate with, or *query*, each other to determine the fastest speed they share. The modem manufacturers themselves originally standardized these processes as a set of proprietary protocols. The downside to these protocols was that unless you had two modems from the same manufacturer, modems often would not work together. In response, the International Telegraph and Telephone Consultative Committee (**CCITT**), a European standards body, established standards for modems. These standards, known generically as the **V standards**, define the speeds at which modems can modulate. The most common of these speed standards are as follows:

- **V.22** 1200 bps
- **V.22bis** 2400 bps
- **V.32** 9600 bps
- **V.32bis** 14,400 bps
- **V.34** 28,000 bps
- **V.90** 57,600 bps
- **V.92** 57,600 bps

The current modem standard now on the market is the **V.92 standard**. V.92 has the same download speed as the V.90, but upstream rates increase to as much as 48 Kbps. If your modem is having trouble getting 56-Kbps rates with V.90 in your area, you will not notice an improvement. V.92 also offers a Quick Connect feature that implements faster handshaking to cut connection delays. Finally, the V.92 standard offers a Modem On Hold feature that enables the modem to stay connected while you take an incoming call or even initiate an outgoing voice call. This feature only works if the V.92 server modem is configured to enable it.

In addition to speed standards, the CCITT, now known simply as the International Telecommunication Union (ITU), has established standards controlling how modems compress data and perform error checking when they communicate. These standards are as follows:

- **V.42** Error checking
- **V.42bis** Data compression
- **V.44** Data compression
- **MNP5** Both error checking and data compression

The beauty of these standards is that you don't need to do anything special to enjoy their benefits. If you want the theoretical 56-Kbps data transfers, for example, you simply need to ensure that the modems in the local system and the remote system both support the V.90 standard.

ISDN

PSTN lines traditionally just aren't that good. While the digital equipment that connects to a PSTN supports a full 64-Kbps DS0 channel, the combination of

Do not memorize these V standards—just know what they do.

One of the creative ways people way back in the day sped up Internet connections was by using more than one modem at the same time. This *link aggregation* could join a couple of 56-Kbps modems, for example, and run a protocol like multilink PPP to achieve blazing speeds at a fraction of the cost of ISDN . . . in the mid-1990s. You might see this protocol on the CompTIA Network+ exam.

the lines themselves and the conversion from analog to digital means that most PSTN lines rarely go faster than 33 Kbps—and, yes, that includes the 56-Kbps connections.

A PSTN telephone connection has many pieces. First, there's the modem in your computer that converts the digital information to analog. Then there's the phone line that runs from your phone out to your NIU and into the central office. The central office stores the modems that convert the analog signal back to digital and the telephone switches that interconnect multiple individual local connections into the larger telephone network. A central office switch connects to long-distance carriers via high-capacity *trunk lines* (at least a T1) and also connects to other nearby central offices. The analog last mile was an awful way to send data, but it had one huge advantage: most everyone owned a telephone line.

During this upgrade period, customers continued to demand higher throughput from their phone lines. The phone companies were motivated to come up with a way to generate higher capacities. Their answer was fairly straightforward: make the last mile digital. Since everything but the last mile was already digital, by adding special equipment at the central office and the user's location, phone companies felt they could achieve a true, steady, dependable throughput of 64 Kbps per line over the same copper wires already used by PSTN lines. This process of sending telephone transmission across fully digital lines end-to-end is called **Integrated Services Digital Network (ISDN)** service.

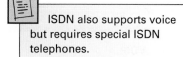

ISDN also supports voice but requires special ISDN telephones.

ISDN service consists of two types of channels: **Bearer channels (B channels)** carry data and voice information using standard DS0 channels (64 Kbps), whereas **Delta channels (D channels)** carry setup and configuration information at 16 Kbps. Most ISDN providers let the user choose either one or two B channels. The more common setup is two B/one D, called a **Basic Rate Interface (BRI)** setup. A BRI setup uses only one physical line, but each B channel sends 64 Kbps, doubling the throughput total to 128 Kbps.

Another type of ISDN is called **Primary Rate Interface (PRI)**. ISDN PRI is actually just a full T1 line, carrying 23 B channels.

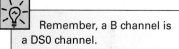

Remember, a B channel is a DS0 channel.

The physical connections for ISDN bear some similarity to PSTN modems. An ISDN wall socket is usually something that looks like a standard RJ-45 network jack. This line runs to your demarc. In home installations, many telephone companies install a second demarc separate from your PSTN demarc. The most common interface for your computer is a device called a **terminal adapter (TA)**. TAs look like regular modems and, like modems, come in external and internal variants. You can even get TAs that also function as hubs, enabling your system to support a direct LAN connection (Figure 14.25).

You generally need to be within approximately 18,000 feet of a central office to use ISDN. When you install an ISDN TA, you must configure the other ISDN telephone number you want to call, as well as a special number called the *Service Profile ID (SPID)*. Your ISP provides the telephone number, and the telephone company gives you the SPID. (In many

• **Figure 14.25**   A TeleWell ISDN terminal adapter

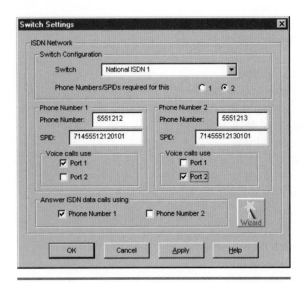

cases, the telephone company is also the ISP.) Figure 14.26 shows a typical installation screen for an internal ISDN TA in an old version of Windows. Note that each channel has a phone number in this case.

ISDN continues to soldier on in today's networking world, but with the exception of a few unique markets, such as automated teller machines (ATMs), ISDN has been replaced by faster and less expensive methods such as DSL and cable modems.

DSL

Many telephone companies offer a **digital subscriber line (DSL)** connection, a fully digital, dedicated (no phone number) connection. DSL represented the next great leap forward past ISDN for telephone lines. A physical DSL connection manifests as just another PSTN connection, using the same telephone lines and RJ-11 jacks as any regular phone line. DSL comes in a number of versions, but the two most important to know for the CompTIA Network+ exam are **symmetric DSL (SDSL)** and **asymmetric DSL (ADSL)**.

• **Figure 14.26** ISDN settings in an old version of Windows

SDSL lines provide the same upload and download speeds, making them excellent for those who send as much data as they receive, although SDSL is relatively expensive. ADSL uses different upload and download speeds. ADSL download speeds are much faster than the upload speeds. Most small office and home office (SOHO) users are primarily concerned with fast *downloads* for things like Web pages and can tolerate slower upload speeds. ADSL is always much less expensive than SDSL.

Tech Tip

VDSL

AT&T (along with other telecoms) uses a very fast DSL version in some of its U-verse offerings called very-high-bit-rate DSL (VDSL). *The current version, VDSL2, can provide simultaneous upload and download speeds in excess of 100 Mbps, though only at short distances (~300 meters). Typical U-verse speeds are a lot slower, in the range of 8 to 16 Mbps down and 1 to 2 Mbps up. You won't find VDSL (or U-verse) on the CompTIA Network+ exam, but it's certainly a growing concern in the real world.*

SDSL

SDSL provides equal upload and download speed and, in theory, provides speeds up to 15 Mbps, although the vast majority of ISPs provide packages ranging from 192 Kbps to 9 Mbps. A recent tour of some major DSL providers in my hometown of Houston, Texas, revealed the following SDSL speed options:

- 192 Kbps
- 384 Kbps
- 768 Kbps
- 1.1 Mbps
- 1.5 Mbps

As you might imagine, the pricing for the faster services was higher than for the lower services.

To use DSL, you must be within 18,000 feet of a central switch. The closer you are, the faster your connection will be.

ADSL

ADSL provides theoretical maximum download speeds up to 15 Mbps and upload speeds up to 1 Mbps. All ADSL suppliers "throttle" their ADSL speeds, however, and provide different levels of service. Real-world ADSL download speeds vary from 384 Kbps to 15 Mbps, and upload speeds go from as low as

128 Kbps to around 768 Kbps. Touring the same DSL providers in Houston, Texas, here are a few speed options:

- 384 Kbps download/128 Kbps upload
- 1.5 Mbps download/384 Kbps upload
- 6 Mbps download/768 Kbps upload

DSL Features

One nice aspect of DSL is that you don't have to run new phone lines. The same DSL lines you use for data can simultaneously transmit your voice calls.

All versions of DSL have the same central office–to–end user distance restrictions as ISDN—around 18,000 feet from your demarc to the central office. At the central office, your DSL provider has a device called a **DSL Access Multiplexer (DSLAM)** that connects multiple customers to the Internet.

Installing DSL

DSL operates using your preexisting telephone lines (assuming they are up to specification). This is wonderful but also presents a technical challenge. For DSL and your run-of-the-mill POTS line to coexist, you need to filter out the DSL signal on the POTS line. A DSL line has three information channels: a high-speed downstream channel, a medium-speed duplex channel, and a POTS channel.

Segregating the two DSL channels from the POTS channel guarantees that your POTS line will continue to operate even if the DSL fails. You accomplish this by inserting a filter on each POTS line, or a splitter mechanism that allows all three channels to flow to the DSL modem but sends only the POTS channel down the POTS line. The DSL company should provide you with a few POTS filters for your telephones. If you need more, most computer/electronics stores stock DSL POTS filters.

The most common DSL installation consist of a **DSL modem** connected to a telephone wall jack and to a standard network interface card (NIC) in your computer (Figure 14.27). The DSL line runs into a DSL modem via a standard phone line with RJ-11 connectors.

Tech Tip

Speed Guarantees

No DSL provider guarantees any particular transmission speed and will only provide service as a "best efforts" contract—a nice way to say that DSL lines are notorious for substantial variations in throughput.

Tech Tip

DSL POTS Filters

If you install a telephone onto a line in your home with DSL and you forget to add a filter, don't panic. You won't destroy anything, although you won't get a dial tone either! Just insert a DSL POTS filter and the telephone will work.

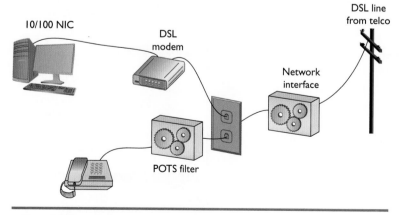

• **Figure 14.27** A DSL modem connection between a PC and telco

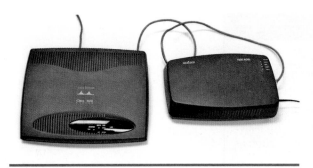

● Figure 14.28   DSL connection

The DSL modem connects to our gateway router with a CAT 5e patch cable, which, in turn, connects to the company's switch. Figure 14.28 shows an ADSL modem and a router.

Home users often connect the DSL modem directly to their PC's NIC. Either way, you have nothing to do in terms of installing DSL equipment on an individual system—just make sure you have a NIC. The person who installs your DSL will test the DSL line, install the DSL modem, connect it to your system, and verify that it all works.

The first generation of DSL providers used a **bridged connection**; once the DSL line was running, it was as if you had snapped an Ethernet cable into your NIC. You were on the network. Those were good days for DSL. You just plugged your DSL modem into your NIC and, assuming your IP settings were whatever the DSL folks told you to use, you were running.

The DSL providers didn't like that too much. There was no control—no way to monitor who was using the DSL modem. As a result, the DSL folks started to use **Point-to-Point Protocol over Ethernet (PPPoE)**, a protocol that was originally designed to encapsulate PPP frames into Ethernet frames. The DSL people adopted it to make stronger controls over your DSL connection. In particular, you could no longer simply connect; you now had to log on with an account and a password to make the DSL connection. PPPoE is now predominant on DSL. If you get a DSL line, your operating system has software to enable you to log onto your DSL network. Most SOHO routers come with built-in PPPoE support, enabling you to enter your user name and password into the router itself (Figure 14.29).

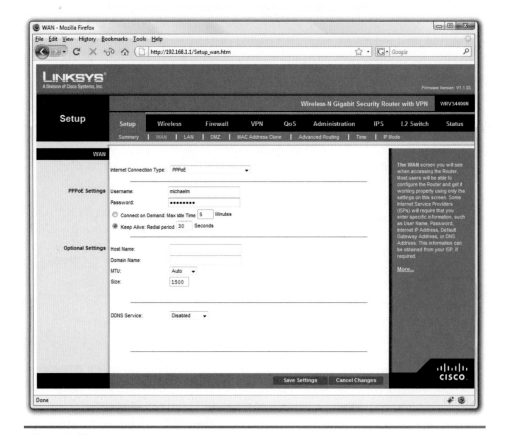

● Figure 14.29   PPPoE settings in SOHO router

Broadband Cable

The first big competition for ADSL came from the cable companies. A majority of houses in America has a coax cable running into it for cable TV. In a moment of genius, the cable industry realized that if it could put the Home Shopping Network and the History Channel into every home, why not provide Internet access? The entire infrastructure of the cabling industry had to undergo some major changes to deal with issues like bidirectional communication, but cable modem service quickly became common in the United States. Cable modems are now as common as cable TV boxes.

Cable modems have the impressive benefit of phenomenal top speeds. These speeds vary from cable company to cable company, but most advertise speeds in the 5 to 100 Mbps range. Many cable modems provide a throughput speed of 5 to 30 Mbps for downloading and 2 Mbps to 10 Mbps for uploading—there is tremendous variance among different providers.

In a cable modem installation, the cable modem connects to an outlet via a coaxial cable. It's separate from the one that goes to the television. It's the same cable line, just split from the main line as if you were adding a second cable outlet for another television. As with ADSL, cable modems connect to PCs using a standard NIC and UTP cabling (Figure 14.30).

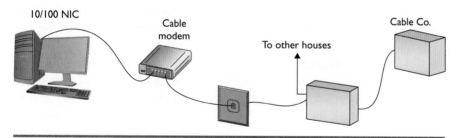

• **Figure 14.30**   Cable modem

Cable modems connect using coax cable to a head end, similar to a telephone company's central office. Head ends, in turn, connect to the cable company's network. This network uses a unique protocol called **Data Over Cable Service Interface Specification (DOCSIS)**. The current specification is DOCSIS 3.1.

You'll have a hard time telling a cable modem from a DSL modem. The only difference, other than the fact that one will have "cable modem" printed on it whereas the other will say "DSL modem," is that the cable modem has a coax F-connector and an RJ-45 connector; the DSL modem has an RJ-11 connector and an RJ-45 connector.

Cable companies aggressively market high-speed packages to business customers, making cable a viable option for businesses.

Satellite

Living in the countryside may have its charms, but you'll have a hard time getting high-speed Internet out on the farm. For those too far away to get anything else, satellite may be your only option. Satellite access comes in two types: one-way and two-way. *One-way* means that you download via satellite but you must use a PSTN/dial-up modem connection for uploads. *Two-way* means the satellite service handles both the uploading and downloading.

 The CompTIA Network+ objectives refer only to DOCSIS as an example of a *broadband standard.* You'll remember from Chapter 4 the distinction between broadband and baseband: multiple signals versus a single signal on some medium, like a wire. There are a lot of broadband standards out there now, though be prepared for DOCSIS on the exam.

 Companies that design satellite communications equipment haven't given up on their technology. At the time of this writing, at least one company, HughesNet, offered download speeds up to 15 Mbps. You can surf with that kind of speed!

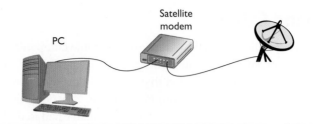

• **Figure 14.31**   Satellite connection

Satellite requires a small satellite antenna, identical to the ones used for satellite television. This antenna connects to a satellite modem, which, in turn, connects to your PC or your network (Figure 14.31).

Cellular WAN

Anyone with a smartphone these days appreciates the convenience of using wireless cellular technology on the road. Who doesn't love firing up an Android

phone or iPhone and cruising the Internet from anywhere? As cell-phone technology converges with Internet access technologies, competent techs need to understand what's happening behind the scenes. That means tackling an alphabet soup of standards.

Regardless of the standard, the voice and data you use on your smartphone (unless you have 802.11 wireless turned on) moves through a cellular wireless network with towers that now cover the world (Figure 14.32). All of these technologies are really nothing more than signaling standards that use basically the same cellular infrastructure in different ways to improve speed, latency, configuration, and dependability over the years.

Mobile data services started in the mid-1980s and, as you might imagine, have gone through a dizzying number of standards and protocols, all of which have been revised, improved, abandoned, and reworked. Instead of trying to advertise these fairly complex and intimidating technologies, the industry instead came up with the marketing term *generations,*

• **Figure 14.32**   Cellular tower

abbreviated by a number followed by the letter G: 2G, 3G, and 4G.

Salesmen and TV commercials use these terms to try to push mobile cellular services. These terms aren't generally used within the industry, and certainly not at a deeply technical level. As I go through the standards you'll see on the exam and encounter in real life, I'll mention both the technical name and the generation where applicable. I'll cover six common terms here:

- GSM and EDGE

- CDMA

- HSPA+

- WiMAX

- LTE

GSM and EDGE

The *Global System for Mobile (GSM),* the first group of networking technologies widely applied to mobile devices, relied on a type of time division multiplexing called *time division multiple access (TDMA).* TDMA enabled multiple users to share the same channel more or less at the same time, with the switching from one user to another happening so quickly no one would notice.

GSM introduced the handy SIM card that is now so ubiquitous in smartphones (Figure 14.33). The SIM card identifies the phone, enabling access to the cellular networks, and stores some other information (contents differ according to many factors, none relevant for this discussion).

The original GSM standard was considered a 2G technology. The standard continued to improve over the years, getting new names and better data speeds. One of the last of these (and one you might see on the exam) was *Enhanced Data rates for GSM Evolution (EDGE),* which offered data speeds up to 384 Kbps.

• **Figure 14.33**   SIM card in Dave's phone

CDMA

Code division multiple access (CDMA) came out not long after GSM, but used a spread-spectrum form of transmission that was totally incompatible with GSM's TDMA. Rather than enabling multiple users to share a single channel by splitting the channel into time slices, spread-spectrum transmission changes the frequencies used by each user.

The original CDMA was considered superior to the original GSM, and U.S. carriers adopted CDMA en masse, which created some problems. The rest of the world went GSM, for example. Plus, CDMA lacked some key features, like SIM cards.

The original CDMA was considered a 2G technology.

HSPA+

In the late 1990s the ITU forwarded a new standard called International Mobile Telecommunications-2000 (IMT-2000) to address a number of shortcomings in mobile technology. IMT-2000 defined higher speeds, support for full-time Internet connections, and a number of other critical functions. The standard pushed support for multimedia messaging system (MMS) (so you can send cat pictures in your text messages) and IP-based telephony.

Both GSM and CDMA went through a number of improvements in the late 1990s to the mid-2000s to address IMT-2000, all of which were marketed under probably the most confusing marketing term ever used: *3G.* Ideally, **3G** meant a technology that supported IMT-2000, although the industry was very lax in how companies used this term. (This time period is so confusing that many technologies in this period were given decimal generations to clarify the situation. One example is GSM EDGE being called 2.9G due to its lack of full IMT-2000 support.)

The CompTIA Network+ exam only addresses one truly 3G technology: **Evolved High-Speed Packet Access (HSPA+).** HSPA+ was the final 3G data standard, providing theoretical speeds up to 168 Mbps, although in reality most HSPA+ implementations rarely passed 10 Mbps.

WiMAX

Networks based on the **IEEE 802.16** wireless standard called **WiMAX** seemed poised to take the crown as the wireless service that replaced DSL and cable to provide high-speed Internet to the masses. With early speeds running upwards of 30 Mbps and subsequent developments pushing the speeds above 1 Gbps, plus data ranges of 50+ kilometers, the world seemed to have true 4G service.

Several major players in the telecom industry, such as Clear and Sprint, backed the technology and rolled out devices in the mid-to-late 2000s, but by 2011, most had stopped offering the service. Although some WiMAX networks around the world continue to operate (as of this writing), the end seems pretty near.

WiMAX provided the idea of wireless **metropolitan area networks (MANs)**, where cities could simply roll out fast Internet access to citizens at a fraction of the cost of physical connections. Despite good technology and a cool name, WiMAX ran into competition and lost.

LTE

Devices and networks using **Long Term Evolution (LTE)** technology rolled out world-wide in the early 2010s and now dominate wireless services. As early as 2013, for example, LTE already had ~20% market share in the United States and higher in parts of Asia. The numbers have only grown since then. Marketed as and now generally accepted as a true **4G** technology, LTE networks feature speeds (in theory) of up to 300 Mbps download and 75 Mbps upload.

Where WiMAX seemed to stumble was in seamless integration with other cell phone technologies. LTE offers voice and data and coexists just fine with slower technologies.

With excellent speed and the broad coverage of cell towers, LTE can readily replace wired network technology. To connect a computer to the Internet when out in the country, for example, you don't need a physical connection, such as DSL, cable, or fiber to an ISP. You can instead connect to a wireless **hotspot**—a device that connects via cellular and enables other devices to access the Internet—and be on your merry way. Hotspots can be dedicated devices, or simply a feature of a modern smartphone (Figure 14.34). Conversely, you could get an LTE NIC and just plug that into a convenient USB port (Figure 14.35).

• **Figure 14.34**   Hotspot

A common term describing a wireless network connected with cellular technology is *wireless wide area network (WWAN).* You won't see this on the CompTIA Network+ exam, though it's in common use today.

• **Figure 14.35**   Mobile wireless NIC

Fiber

DSL was the first popular last-mile WAN option, but over the years cable modems have taken the lead. In an attempt to regain market share, telephone providers rolled out fiber-to-the-home/fiber-to-the-premises options that are giving the cable companies a scare. In the United States, two companies, AT&T (U-verse) and Verizon (FiOS), offer Internet connectivity, television, and phone services at speeds that will eventually increase above 100 Mbps. Some markets also have Internet-only fiber offerings, such as Google Fiber, where users connect at 1 Gbps.

To make rollouts affordable, most fiber-to-the-home technologies employ a version of **passive optical network (PON)** architecture that uses a single fiber to the neighborhood switch and then individual fiber runs to each final destination. PON uses WDM to enable multiple signals to travel on the same fiber and then passively splits the signal at the switch to send traffic to its proper recipient.

Most municipalities in the United States have very tight deals in place with telephone and cable companies, allowing little room for any other high-speed Internet service. A few cities have bucked the regional monopolies and done pretty well, such as Chattanooga, Tennessee. Their publicly owned electric utility—EPB—rolled out fiber to every home and business by 2011 and currently offers Internet speeds up to 1 Gbps.

BPL

With the exception of fiber, most wired networks use electrical signaling to enable systems to interconnect. Rather than running all new wiring dedicated to networks, why not use the vast infrastructure of wiring already in place in just about every home and office in the developed world? Enterprising engineers have been working to provide networking over electrical power lines for many years now with varying degrees of success. The overall field is called *power line communications (PLC)* and encompasses everything from voice transmission to home automation to high-speed Internet access.

Broadband over Power Line (BPL) is one specific field of technologies that tries to bring usable Internet access to homes and businesses through the electrical power grid. The various companies that have rolled this out, such as Ambient Corporation, Current Technologies, and Motorola, have had some success, though the electrical grid poses serious challenges to networking because of noise and interference from other devices. Most BPL rollouts to date have failed, but companies continue to explore the possibilities.

Which Connection?

With so many connection options for homes and small offices, making a decision is often a challenge. Your first question is availability: Which services are available in your area? The second question is, how much bandwidth do you need? The latter is a question of great debate. Most services are more than

Try This

Going Connection Shopping

You've already checked the availability of DSL in your neighborhood, but now you have more choices! Try this! Do you have cable or satellite available? A great Web site to start your search is www.dslreports.com. It has a handy search feature that helps you determine the types of service and the costs for DSL, cable, and other services. Which one makes sense for you?

happy to increase service levels if you find that a certain level is too slow. I usually advise clients to start with a relatively slow level and then increase if necessary. After all, once you've tasted the higher speeds, going slower is hard, but the transition to faster is relatively painless!

Using Remote Access

Because most businesses are no longer limited to a simple little shop like you would find in a Dickens novel, many people need to be able to access files and resources over a great distance. Enter remote access. **Remote access** uses WAN and LAN connections to enable a computer user to log onto a network from the other side of a city, a state, or even the globe. As people travel, information has to remain accessible. Remote access enables users to connect a server at the business location and log into the network as if they were in the same building as the company. The only problem with remote access is that there are so many ways to do it! I've listed the six most common forms of remote access here:

- **Dial-up to the Internet**   Using a dial-up connection to connect to your ISP

- **Private dial-up**   Using a dial-up connection to connect to your private network

- **Virtual private network**   Using an Internet connection to connect to a private network

- **Dedicated connection**   Using a non-dial-up connection to another private network or the Internet

- **Remote terminal**   Using a terminal emulation program to connect to another computer

- **VoIP**   Voice over IP

In this section, I discuss the issues related to configuring these six types of connections. After seeing how to configure these types of remote connections, I move into observing some security issues common to every type of remote connection.

Dial-Up to the Internet

Dialing up to the Internet is the oldest and least expensive method to connect to the Internet, but it is rare today. Even with broadband and wireless so prevalent, every self-respecting network tech (or maybe just old network techs like me) keeps a dial-up account as a backup. You buy a dial-up account from an ISP (many wireless and broadband ISPs give free dial-up—just ask). All operating systems come with dial-up support programs, but you'll need to provide:

- A modem (most operating systems check for a modem before setting up a dial-up connection)

- The telephone number to dial (provided to you by the ISP)

- User name and password (provided to you by the ISP)

- Type of connection (dial-up always uses PPP)

- IP information (provided to you by the ISP—usually just DHCP)

You'll see the term *extranet* more in books than in the day-to-day workings of networks and network techs. So what is an extranet? Whenever you allow authorized remote users to access some part of your private network, you have created an extranet.

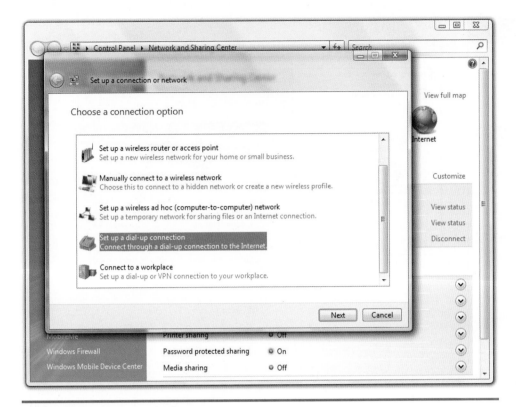

• **Figure 14.36**   Dial-up on Windows Vista

Every operating system comes with the software to help you set up a dial-up connection. In Windows Vista or Windows 7, you go to the **Set up a dial-up connection** option in the Network and Sharing Center (Figure 14.36). Whatever the name, this tool is what you use to create dial-up connections.

Private Dial-Up

A private dial-up connection connects a remote system to a private network via a dial-up connection. Private dial-up does not use the Internet! Private dial-up requires two systems. One system acts as a **remote access server (RAS)**. The other system, the client, runs a connection tool (usually the same tool you just read about in the previous section).

In Windows, a RAS is a server running the Routing and Remote Access Service (RRAS), dedicated to handling users who are not directly connected to a LAN but who need to access file and print services on the LAN from a remote location. For example, when a user dials into a network from home using an analog modem connection, she is dialing into a RAS. Once the user authenticates, she can access shared drives and printers as if her computer were physically connected to the office LAN.

You must set up a server in your LAN as a RAS server. That RAS server, which must have at least one modem, accepts incoming calls and handles password authentication. RAS servers use all the standard authentication methods (PAP, CHAP, EAP, 802.1X, and so on) and have separate sets of permissions for dial-in users and local users. You must also configure the RAS server to set the rights and permissions for all of the dial-in users. Configuring

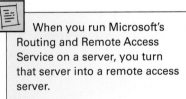

When you run Microsoft's Routing and Remote Access Service on a server, you turn that server into a remote access server.

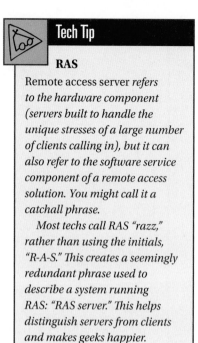
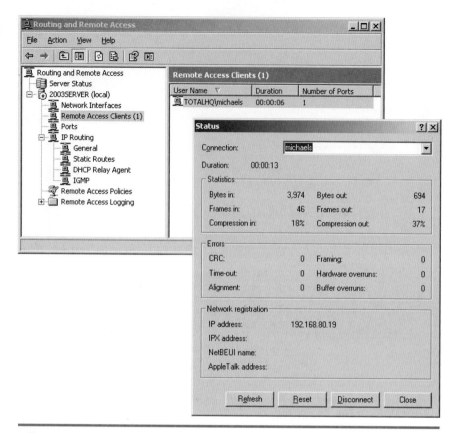

• **Figure 14.37**   Windows RRAS in action

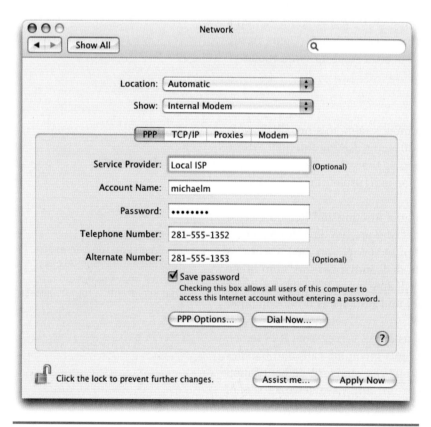

• **Figure 14.38**   Dial-up on OS X

a RAS server is outside the scope of this book, however, because each one is different. (Figure 14.37).

Creating the client side of a private dial-up connection is identical to setting up a dial-up connection to the Internet. The only difference is that instead of having an ISP tell you what IP settings, account name, and password to use, the person who sets up the RAS server tells you this information (Figure 14.38).

VPNs

A VPN enables you to connect through a tunnel from a local computer to a remote network securely, as you'll recall from the in-depth discussion in Chapter 12. Refer back to that chapter for the details.

Dedicated Connection

Dedicated connections are remote connections that are never disconnected. Dedicated connections can be broken

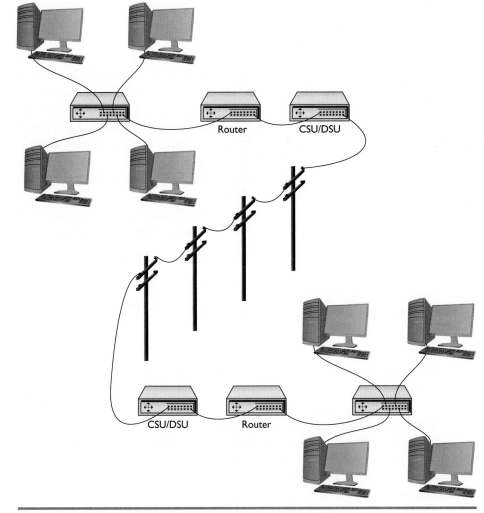

• **Figure 14.39** Dedicated private connection

into two groups: dedicated private connections between two locations and dedicated connections to the Internet. Dedicated private connections manifest themselves as two locations interconnected by a (usually high-speed) connection such as a T1 line (Figure 14.39).

Each end of the T1 line goes into a router (after going through a CSU/DSU, of course). Note that this connection does not use the Internet in any way—it is not a VPN connection. Private dedicated connections of this type are expensive and are only used by organizations that need the high bandwidth and high security these connections provide. These connections are invisible to the individual computers on each network. There is no special remote connection configuration of the individual systems, although you may have to configure DHCP, DNS, and WINS servers to ensure that the network runs optimally.

DSL and Cable

Dedicated connections to the Internet are common today. Cable modems and DSL have made dedicated connections to the Internet inexpensive and very popular. In most cases, you don't have to configure anything in these dedicated connections. Many cable and DSL providers give you a CD-ROM

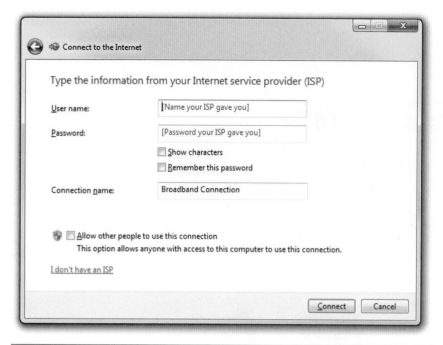

• **Figure 14.40**   PPPoE connection

that installs different items, such as testing software, PPPoE login support, and little extras like e-mail clients and software firewalls. Personally, I prefer not to use these (they add a lot of stuff you don't need) and instead use the operating system's tools or a hardware router. Figure 14.40 shows the DSL wizard built into Windows 7. This program enables you to connect by entering your PPPoE information for your ADSL connection. Once started, these programs usually stay running in the system tray until your next reboot.

Cable Issues

Dedicated cable connections provide the only exception to the "plug them in and they work" rule because most cable networks bring television and often voice communication into the same line. This complicates things in one simple way: *splitters.*

If you have a cable connection coming to your house and you have a television set in two rooms, how do you get cable in both rooms? Easy, right? Just grab a two-way splitter from Radio Shack and run an extra pair of cables, one to each room. The problem comes from the fact that every time you split a cable signal, the signal degrades by half. This is called, logically, a *split cable* problem.

The quality of a signal can be measured in **decibels (dB)**, a unit that describes a ratio between an ideal point—a reference point—and the current state of the signal. When discussing signal strength, a solid signal is 0 dB. When that signal degrades, it's described as a *dB loss* and a negative number. An increase in signal is *gain* and gets a positive number. Decibels are logarithmic units that, if you've forgotten the high school math, means that going up or down the scale in a simple number translates into a huge number in a percentage scale.

For example, when you split a cable signal into two, you get half the signal strength into each new cable. That's described as a –3 dB signal. Split it again and you've got a –6 dB signal. Although 6 isn't a big number in standard units, it's horribly huge in networking. You might have a 20-Mbps cable connection into your house, but split it twice and you're left with a 5-Mbps connection. Ouch!

The standard procedure with cable connections is to split them once: one cable goes to the cable modem and the other to the television. You can then split the television cable into as many connections as you need or can tolerate as far as reception quality.

Remote Terminal

You can use a terminal emulation program to create a **remote terminal**, a connection on a faraway computer that enables you to control that computer as if you were sitting in front of it, logged in. Terminal emulation has been a part of

TCP/IP from its earliest days, in the form of good-old Telnet. Because it dates from pre-GUI days, Telnet is a text-based utility; most modern operating systems are graphical, so there was a strong desire to come up with graphical remote terminal tools. Citrix Corporation made the first popular terminal emulation products—the *WinFrame/MetaFrame* products (Figure 14.41).

Remote terminal programs all require a server and a client. The server is the computer to be controlled. The client is the computer from which you do the controlling. Citrix created a standard called **Independent Computing Architecture (ICA)** that defined how terminal information was passed between the server and the client. Citrix made a breakthrough product—so powerful that Microsoft licensed the

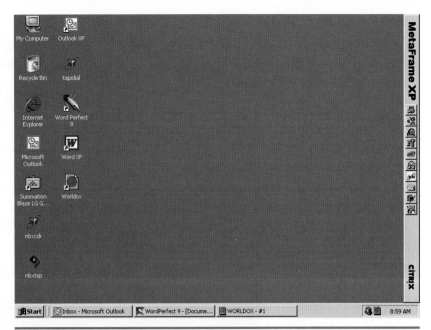

• **Figure 14.41**   Citrix MetaFrame

Citrix code and created its own product called Windows Terminal Services. Not wanting to pay Citrix any more money, Microsoft then created its own standard called **Remote Desktop Protocol (RDP)** and unveiled a new remote terminal called *Remote Desktop Connection (RDC)* starting with Windows XP. Figure 14.42 shows Windows Remote Desktop Connection running on a Windows 7 system, connecting to a Windows 2008 Server.

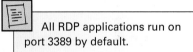
All RDP applications run on port 3389 by default.

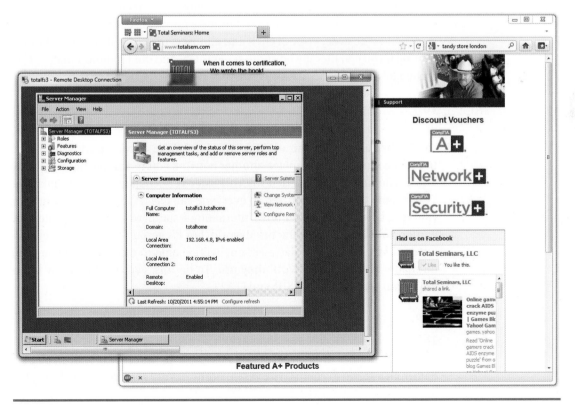

• **Figure 14.42**   RDC in action

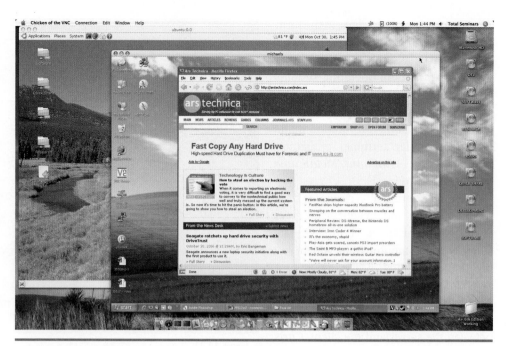

• **Figure 14.43**   VNC in action

Unfortunately, Terminal Services only works in the Windows environment; however, a number of third parties make absolutely amazing terminal emulation programs that run on any operating system. The best of these, *VNC* (VNC stands for Virtual Network Computing) doesn't let you share folders or printers because it is only a terminal emulator (Figure 14.43), but it runs on every operating system, is solid as a rock, and even runs from a Web browser. It works nicely in Secure Shell (SSH) tunnels for great security, plus it comes, by default, with every copy of OS X and almost every Linux distro. Why bother sharing if you can literally be at the screen? Oh, and did I mention that VNC is completely free?

VoIP

Voice over IP (VoIP) uses an IP network to transfer voice calls. VoIP works so well because it uses an existing network you're already paying for (your Internet connection) to replace another network you're also paying for (PSTN lines). The technology needed for VoIP isn't very challenging, but making a VoIP system that's standardized so everyone can use it (and still contact those who choose to use PSTN) requires international standards, making it quite a bit harder. VoIP is still a very fractured world, but it's getting closer to universally adopted standards—one day everyone will be able to contact everyone else, no matter what brand of VoIP they use. To do this, you need to know three important standards: RTP, SIP, and H.323.

RTP

The **Real-time Transport Protocol (RTP)**, the heavily adopted bedrock of VoIP standards, defines the type of packets used on the Internet to move voice or data from a server to clients. The vast majority of VoIP solutions available today use RTP.

SIP and H.323

Session Initiation Protocol (SIP) and H.323 handle the initiation, setup, and delivery of VoIP sessions. SIP and H.323 both run on top of RTP. Most VoIP solutions are either SIP/RTP or H.323/RTP. SIP uses TCP ports 5060 and 5061. H.323 uses port 1720. SIP and H.323 both have methods for handling multicasting.

Skype

Almost every VoIP solution available today uses SIP or H.323 running on top of RTP, with one huge exception: the very famous and incredibly popular Skype. Skype was unveiled in 2003 by Niklas Zennström, a Swedish computer guy famous for inventing the Kazaa peer-to-peer file-sharing system. Skype is completely different from and completely incompatible with any other type of VoIP solution: Skype doesn't use servers, but instead uses a peer-to-peer topology that is identical to the old Kazaa network. Skype calls are also encrypted using a proprietary encryption method. No one has a standard method for VoIP encryption at this time, although many smart people are working hard on the issue.

Streaming Media with RSTP

VoIP isn't the only thing that takes advantage of protocols such as RTP. Streaming video is now mainstream and many streaming video severs (Windows Media Player, QuickTime, and many others) use a popular protocol called Real Time Streaming Protocol (RTSP). Like SIP and H.323, RSTP runs on top of RTP. RSTP has a number of features that are perfect for video streaming such as the ability to run, pause, and stop videos. RSTP runs on TCP port 554.

■ WAN Troubleshooting Scenarios

Competent network techs can recognize and deal with typical remote connectivity issues in a WAN setting. Sometimes the problem lies well beyond the job description, but that's when the tech knows to escalate the problem. This section looks at four very important CompTIA Network+ problem areas: loss of Internet connectivity, interface errors, DNS issues, and interference.

Loss of Internet Connectivity

Given that the core reason to use all these forms of remote connectivity is to get to the Internet in the first place, I don't look at loss of Internet connectivity as a problem. It's more a symptom. Be sure to watch for WAN scenarios on the CompTIA Network+ exam that really aren't always WAN scenarios.

Ifyou want to connect a computer to the Internet, that computer needs a legitimate IP address, subnet mask, default gateway, and DNS address. These needs don't change whether you connect through a Gigabit Ethernet wired network or through a cable modem. Use the utilities already covered in the book in such a scenario, such as ping, ipconfig, netstat, nslookup, and so forth, to verify that the device has a solid IP connection.

Interface Errors

CompTIA loves to use the term *interface errors* as a catchall term to describe the many connections between your computer and the remote connection that enables you to get to the Internet. In a WAN scenario you'll have at least one more interface than in a native Ethernet world. Think about a typical office environment.

Local Ethernet Interface/LAN Interfaces

When you use DSL or cable or any other form of remote connection, it's very easy to forget all of the LAN connections that make connectivity possible. It's plausible, if you're anything like me, that you'll call an ISP like Comcast or AT&T and complain, only to find that you don't have a patch cable plugged into the right connection on the back of the computer. (Not that I've ever done this. Twice.)

Before you blame Comcast or AT&T for losing your connection, make sure to verify that everything on your end is in order. Is the computer properly connected to the LAN? If you are using a router, is it providing good IP information? Can you access the router and see if it is reporting that it has a proper upstream connection? Before you blame the WAN interface, always first confirm everything on the LAN.

Modem Interface

It doesn't really matter what type of remote connection you use. There's always a modem. Be careful here: "modem" is the term I use for any box that sits in your location and connects your LAN to the WAN, even if your ISP calls it something more lofty like: cable modem, router, or customer premises equipment (CPE). Everything said here that references "modem" works for whatever CPE device your ISP provides.

The modem's job is to connect your LAN to the WAN, so by definition it's going to have at least two interfaces: one to the LAN and one to the WAN. First of all, familiarize yourself with the lights on your modem, preferably before you have problems. Any modem is going to have a power LED, link LEDs to both the LAN and the WAN, and some form of activity LED. Study them first when you're looking for interface issues. In almost every case of a bad interface, you'll verify connections and reset the modem.

DNS Issues

I hate the fact that CompTIA places DNS issues under the WAN objectives. There really isn't such a thing as a WAN DNS issue that differs somehow from any other DNS issue. Refer back to the many chapters that reference DNS to make sure you know how to handle DNS issues and you'll be fine.

That said, there is one specific DNS issue that comes up in WANs: choosing what DNS server to use.

Every ISP has their own DNS server(s) and, in almost every case, your modem is going to propagate those DNS settings down to every device in your LAN. In most cases there isn't any problem with this, but there are two cases where you might want to consider manually adding DNS to your local devices or your local router. First, an ISP's DNS servers can fail.

Second, some ISPs notoriously use *DNS helpers,* DNS servers that redirect your browser to advertising when you type in an incorrect URL.

In either of these cases, the rules you learned back in Chapter 7, "TCP/IP Basics," still apply. Get yourself a fast public DNS IP address—I love the Google 8.8.8.8 and 8.8.4.4 addresses—and at the very least load one of those as a secondary DNS server.

Interference

Interference at the WAN level—that CompTIA Network+ techs can fix—generally implies the connection between the LAN and the WAN. The point at which the ISP's responsibility ends and the customer's begins is the demarc, as you'll recall from Chapter 6, "Installing a Physical Network." Let's look at both sides of the demarc for interference.

On the customer side, the CPE can create problems. In a busy office, building, for example, new installations or connections can add electromagnetic interference (EMI) and create disturbances. New things added to old environments, in other words, can create interference in existing networks.

When my company changed locations, for example, the building we moved into had several offices, connected to Internet and corporate WANs with several dedicated T1 lines (Figure 14.44). With the local cable company offering 100 Mbps connections, we opted to have cable installed in the building for us (T1 at 1.5 Mbps, not so much). If the cable company had not been careful or used properly shielded boxes and cables, this could have wreaked havoc on the other folks in the building.

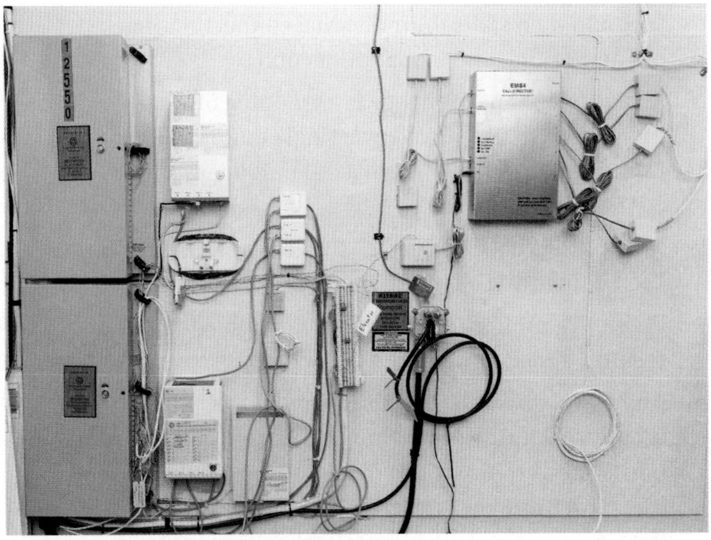

In a consumer space, the CPE doesn't run into interference that would block connectivity at the demarc, unless you overlybroaden the term "interference" to include "failure." Then you can point to the "modem" as the only major failure culprit.

Once you go to the ISP side of the demarc, there's not much interference involved, especially with existing, previously well-functioning networks. Again, WAN interference only happens

• **Figure 14.44**   Demarc at my office building

if you extend the definition to include failure. Then storms, downed power lines, extraterrestrial activity, and so on can cause problems.

In a home network, there are only two times you should worry about interference in a WAN outside the demarc: during installation and when changing the connection in any way. Every form of remote connection has very clear interference tolerances, and you should have the installation tech verify this. Cable and DSL self-installations are a big issue here as most people don't have access to the tools necessary to confirm their PSTN or coax cabling. If I'm installing a new DSL or cable modem, I refuse the self-install option and gladly pay the extra money to verify my cabling can handle the connection.

It's incredibly easy to introduce interference into an otherwise perfectly functioning wired WAN connection by adding splitters, noisy devices, splices, and so on. This is especially true for tech folks (like your humble author) who have learned this the hard way. In general, be conservative when disturbing your WAN connection and be ready to call support if needed.

Chapter Summary

After reading this chapter and completing the exercises, you should understand the following about remote connections.

Describe WAN telephony technologies, such as SONET, T1, and T3

- The majority of long-distance connections that make up the Internet use a unique type of signaling called SONET. The Internet backbone uses technologies designed more than 20 years ago to support telephone calls.

- A multiplexer combines multiple circuits at one end of a connection into a single complex circuit on one wire and then splits the individual connections back out at the other end of the connection.

- A local telephone exchange is a grouping of individual circuits served by a single multiplexer. Exchanges are housed in physical buildings called central offices.

- Multiplexers used frequency division multiplexing to keep individual calls separate.

- Physically connecting two phones on a single circuit is called circuit switching.

- Analog voice calls had to be converted to digital to accommodate travel over long distances. Central offices convert incoming analog calls to digital, transport the digital signal across trunk lines, and then convert the digital signal back to analog for delivery to the destination phone.

- The analog connection from the central office to individual users is called the last mile.

- Converting analog sound into 8-bit chunks 8000 times a second creates a 64-Kbps data stream known as DS0. Every analog voice call is converted to DS0 at the central office, where it is then multiplexed into larger circuits.

- A device that converts an analog signal to a digital signal is a modulator. A device that converts a digital signal to an analog signal is a demodulator. A device that does both is a modulator-demodulator, or modem.

- T1 refers to a high-speed digital networking technology, whereas T1 line refers to the physical shielded, two-pair cabling that connects the two ends of a T1 connection.

- A T1 line uses two pairs of wires, one pair to send data and one pair to receive data.

- A T1 line connects to a CSU/DSU at both ends. The CSU/DSU has a second connection connecting the phone company to a customer's equipment. You cannot have more than one CSU/DSU on a single T1 line because a T1 connection is point-to-point.

- Many new routers have a CSU/DSU built into them.

- T1 uses a signaling method called DS1. A DS1 frame is composed of one framing bit and 24 channels. Each DS1 channel holds a single 8-bit DS0, creating 193 bits per DS1 frame (192 bits from the 24 channels of 8-bit DS0 data samples plus the 1 framing bit).

- DS1 frames are transmitted 8000 times/sec for a T1 data transfer speed of 1.544 Mbps. This is split into 24 64-Kbps DS0 channels.

- The process of having frames carry a bit of every channel in every frame sent on a regular interval is called time division multiplexing.

- Because an entire T1 bundle is expensive, many telephone companies allow you to purchase fractional T1 access, or just some of the individual channels.

- A T3 line supports about 45 Mbps and consists of 672 individual DS0 channels. T3 lines are also known as DS3 lines and are used mainly by regional telephone companies and ISPs connecting to the Internet.

- An E1 is the European counterpart to a T1 but carries 32 channels at 64 Kbps for a total of 2.048 Mbps—slightly faster than a T1.

- E1 and T1 lines can be interconnected for international use.

- An E3 carries 16 E1 lines (512 channels) for a total bandwidth of roughly 34 Mbps—a little slower than an American T3.

- The CSU part of a CSU/DSU provides protection to the T1 or T3 lines from lightning strikes and other types of electrical interference. It also stores statistics and has loopback testing capability.

- The DSU part of a CSU/DSU supplies timing to each port, converts incoming signals to line code, and frames the format for transmission over the provided line.

- SONET is the primary standard for long-distance, high-speed, fiber-optic transmission in the United States. It is often implemented as a ring for redundancy. SDH is the European equivalent.

- SONET has extensive multiplexing capabilities, such as combining multiple DS1, DS3, and E1 signals into a single huge frame.

- The Optical Carrier (OC) specification defines speeds from 51.8 Mbps (OC-1) to 39.8 Gbps (OC-768) for fiber-optic cables used in networks conforming to the SONET standard.

- Many fiber devices utilize a very clever feature called wavelength division multiplexing (WDM) or its newer and more popular version, dense WDM (DWDM). DWDM enables an individual single-mode fiber to carry multiple signals by giving each signal a different wavelength. A single DWDM fiber can support ~150 signals, enabling, for example, a 51.8 Mbps OC-1 line to run at 51.8 Mbps × 150 signals = 7.6 *gigabytes per second.*

- A related technology, course WDM (CWSM) offers a simpler and less expensive solution to DWDM, though it offers much shorter distances (a mere 60 km).

- SONET uses the STS signal method in which the STS payload carries data and the STS overhead carries signaling and protocol information.

- The number at the end of STS, such as STS-1 or STS-3, indicates signal speed. For example, STS-1 runs on an OC-1 line at 51.85 Mbps, whereas STS-3 runs on an OC-3 line at 155.52 Mbps.

- Frame Relay is a packet-switching standard designed for and used primarily with T-carrier lines. Frames are switched quickly but with no guarantee of data integrity. Frame Relay actually discards frames whenever there is network congestion; however, T-carrier digital lines using Frame Relay have very low error rates.

- Most SONET rings that move voice and data used ATM for packet switching until the advent of MPLS. ATM integrates voice, video, and data on one connection using short, fixed-length cells to transfer information.

- ATM transfer speeds range from 155.52 to 622.08 Mbps and beyond.

- MPLS is a router feature that labels certain data to use a desired connection. For example, a network administrator can specify that all FTP traffic use the ATM connection rather than a secondary link that might be available on the network.

- There are two reasons to use a telephony WAN connection: to get your LAN on the Internet or to make a private connection between two or more of your private LANs.

- The first step to getting a WAN Internet connection is to have a line physically installed by the telephone company. The second step is to have an ISP provide Internet access via the line.

- The telephone company runs your line to a demarc. The other side of the demarc is where you (or your ISP) installs a CSU/DSU and your router.

- WAN telephony carriers are more dependable than less expensive alternatives, such as cable modem service. A BERT test, available on every CSU/DSU, can verify your T-carrier connection.

Compare last-mile connections for connecting homes and businesses to the Internet

- Dedicated lines are always connected, providing a permanent connection, and do not have an associated phone number. Dial-up lines have phone numbers and must dial to make a connection, hanging up when done.

- PSTN, also called POTS, is a regular phone line designed to work only with analog sound and uses an RJ-11 connector.

- Telephone microphones convert analog sounds into electrical waveforms that cycle 2400 times a second. Each individual cycle is a baud. The number of bauds per second is the baud rate.

- PC communications were designed to transmit data in and out of a computer 8 bits at a time.

- A UART converts 8-bit-wide parallel bits from the computer into 1-bit-wide serial bits to send to a modem for digital-to-analog conversion. The analog signal can then be sent over phone lines. The process is reversed for incoming signals.

- PSTN phone lines sample analog data 2400 times a second. By modulating the 2400-baud signal multiple times each second, faster transmission speeds are reached—up to 57,600 bps (56 Kbps).

- Modems must query each other to determine a common protocol with which to communicate.

The European CCITT developed the V standards, which define modem modulation speed and other features. The current standard is V.92.

- The conversion between analog and digital across the last mile resulted in reduced bandwidth. Making the last mile digital overcomes problems introduced by an analog last mile.

- ISDN lines provide a digital connection across the last mile, achieving dependable throughput of 64 Kbps over the same copper wires used by PSTN.

- ISDN consists of two channels: Bearer (B) and Delta (D) channels. B channels carry voice and data using standard DS0 channels. D channels carry setup and configuration information at 16 Kbps.

- A BRI setup includes two B channels and one D channel, providing a total throughput for voice and data of 128 Kbps.

- A PRI setup includes a full T1 line carrying 23 B channels for a total throughput for voice and data of 1472 Kbps (about 1.5 Mbps).

- A terminal adapter (TA) acts as the interface between a computer and the ISDN service.

- DSL provides a fully digital dedicated connection. Two versions of DSL are SDSL and ADSL.

- SDSL supports speeds up to 15 Mbps, but most ISPs only provide SDSL up to 9 Mbps. SDSL provides equal upload and download speeds.

- ADSL provides download speeds up to 15 Mbps and upload speeds up to 1 Mbps, although ISPs offer varying combinations of download/upload speeds.

- All versions of DSL are limited to a maximum distance of around 18,000 feet between a user's demarc and the central office. The central office houses a DSLAM connecting multiple customers to the Internet.

- Because DSL runs over normal POTS lines, filtering out the DSL signal on the POTS line is necessary. This guarantees your POTS line will continue to work if the DSL fails.

- A DSL modem connects the telephone jack (with the DSL signal) to your computer.

- RJ-11 connectors connect the telephone jack to the DSL modem, whereas RJ-45 connectors connect the DSL modem to the computer's NIC.

- Early DSL providers used bridged connections, but these connections have been replaced by PPPoE, so providers can monitor modem usage and require

users to log in with a valid account before they gain Internet access.

- Cable Internet providers offer plans ranging in speeds up to 100 Mbps.

- Download speeds are typically much faster than upload speeds.

- Cable modems use coaxial cable to connect to the head end and use regular UTP cabling to connect to the PC. The head end connects to the cable company's network using the DOCSIS protocol.

- Satellite access is available as one-way or two-way. With a one-way connection, you download over the satellite connection but upload over PSTN. Two-way satellite service accommodates both downloads and uploads over the satellite connection. It is sometimes the only option for remote or geographically challenging areas, however.

- Cell-phone technologies offer several options for connecting to the Internet. Many fall under the marketing term, generations, abbreviated by a number and a letter: 2G (very old), 3G, 4G. The technologies underlying the marketing vary a lot, but the most common you'll see today are HSPA+, WiMAX, and LTE.

- Evolved High-Speed Packet Access (HSPA+) was the final 3G data standard, providing theoretical speeds up to 168 Mbps, although in reality most HSPA+ implementations rarely passed 10 Mbps.

- 802.16, also called WiMAX, offered early promise in the 4G field, with speeds initially at 30 Mbps and subsequent developments up to 1 Gbps. Plus, WiMAX had a range of 50+ kilometers. WiMAX has been eclipsed in the marketplace by LTE.

- Long Term Evolution (LTE), a 4G technology, offers download speeds of up to 300 Mbps and upload speeds of up to 75 Mbps. LTE is very common on smartphones today for both mobile Internet and providing hotspots for other devices.

- In an attempt to regain their share of the market from cable providers, some phone companies offering DSL are now offering fiber-to-the-home connections in the form of U-verse (AT&T) or FiOS (Verizon).

Discuss and implement various remote access connections

- Remote access allows users to log onto networks remotely, making files and network resources available to users across the city, state, or globe.

- Dialing into the Internet over an analog phone line and modem is the oldest and least expensive means of connecting to the Internet. Many techs keep a dial-up account as a backup.

- A private dial-up connection, which does not use the Internet, connects a remote system to a private network via a dial-up connection. This requires a remote access server on one end and a client running a connection tool at the other end.

- Dedicated connections are remote connections that never disconnect and can be categorized as either dedicated private connections between two locations or dedicated connections to the Internet.

- Dedicated private connections are usually connected by a high-speed line such as a T1. This direct dedicated connection does not use the Internet.

- Remote terminal emulation allows a user to take over a remote computer as if he or she were sitting in front of it, as opposed to simply accessing remote resources. WinFrame/MetaFrame (made by Citrix) is a popular terminal emulator.

- Microsoft's terminal emulator is called Remote Desktop Connection, which uses its own Remote Desktop Protocol. VNC is a cross-platform terminal emulator that comes with OS X and many Linux distributions.

- VoIP uses an IP network to transfer voice calls. It depends on three standards: RTP, SIP, and H.323.

- RTP defines the type of packets used on the Internet to transfer voice or data between servers and clients. Most VoIP networks use RTP.

- SIP and H.323 both support multicasting on VoIP networks, allowing users to show a video to multiple people or hold conference calls.

Troubleshoot various WAN scenarios

- Competent network techs can recognize and deal with typical remote connectivity issues in a WAN setting. Issues include loss of Internet connectivity, interface errors, DNS problems, and interference.

- Loss of internet connectivity points to problems common to networks in general. Use standard command-line tools like ping and ipconfig to determine IP address, default gateway, and so on.

- Interface errors can be a lot of things. LAN settings can cause seemingly "WAN" errors, for example. The modem/cable box/CPE—i.e., the magic box that does routing as well as handling ingoing and outgoing traffic between the LAN and the WAN—can be the source of interface errors. Check the link lights, verify connections, and possibly reset the modem.

- DNS issues involve problems accessing an ISP's DNS servers. Keep a handy backup DNS server like 8.8.8.8 (Google) that you can plug in to bypass the local DNS servers if you experience problems.

- Interference at the WAN level generally falls into two categories: interference among the connectivity devices inside the demarc, the CPE, and changes to home cable or DSL installations outside the house (such as adding a splitter to a coaxial cable).

■ Key Terms

3G *(407)*
4G *(408)*
asymmetric DSL (ADSL) *(402)*
Asynchronous Transfer Mode (ATM) *(393)*
Basic Rate Interface (BRI) *(401)*
baud *(398)*
baud rate *(398)*
Bearer channel (B channel) *(401)*
Bit Error Rate Test (BERT) *(396)*
bridged connection *(404)*
CCITT *(400)*
central office *(384)*

Channel Service Unit/Digital Service Unit (CSU/DSU) *(388)*
circuit switching *(385)*
coarse wavelength division multiplexing (CWDM) *(391)*
Data Over Cable Service Interface Specification (DOCSIS) *(405)*
decibel (dB) *(414)*
dedicated line *(397)*
Delta channel (D channel) *(401)*
demultiplexer *(383)*
dense wavelength division multiplexing (DWDM) *(391)*
dial-up line *(397)*

digital signal 1 (DS1) *(388)*
digital subscriber line (DSL) *(402)*
DSL Access Multiplexer (DSLAM) *(403)*
DSL modem *(403)*
DS0 *(387)*
E1 *(390)*
E3 *(390)*
Evolved High-Speed Packet Access (HSPA+) *(407)*
fractional T1 access *(389)*
Frame Relay *(392)*
frequency division multiplexing (FDM) *(385)*
H.323 *(417)*
hotspot *(408)*
IEEE 802.16 *(408)*
Independent Computing Architecture (ICA) *(415)*
Integrated Services Digital Network (ISDN) *(401)*
last mile *(386)*
Long Term Evolution (LTE) *(408)*
metro Ethernet *(396)*
metropolitan area network (MAN) *(408)*
modulation techniques *(383)*
modulator-demodulator (modem) *(398)*
multilink PPP *(400)*
multiplexer *(383)*
Multiprotocol Label Switching (MPLS) *(393)*
network interface unit (NIU) *(398)*
Optical Carrier (OC) *(391)*
passive optical network (PON) *(409)*
plain old telephone service (POTS) *(397)*

Point-to-Point Protocol over Ethernet (PPPoE) *(404)*
Primary Rate Interface (PRI) *(401)*
public switched telephone network (PSTN) *(397)*
Real-time Transport Protocol (RTP) *(416)*
remote access *(410)*
remote access server (RAS) *(411)*
Remote Desktop Protocol (RDP) *(415)*
remote terminal *(414)*
repeater *(385)*
Session Initiation Protocol (SIP) *(417)*
symmetric DSL (SDSL) *(402)*
Synchronous Digital Hierarchy (SDH) *(391)*
Synchronous Optical Network (SONET) *(391)*
Synchronous Transport Signal (STS) *(391)*
STS overhead *(391)*
STS payload *(391)*
T1 *(388)*
T1 line *(388)*
T3 line *(390)*
terminal adapter (TA) *(401)*
time division multiplexing (TDM) *(388)*
Universal Asynchronous Receiver/Transmitter (UART) *(398)*
V standards *(400)*
V.92 standard *(400)*
Voice over IP (VoIP) *(416)*
wide area network (WAN) *(380)*
WiMAX *(408)*

■ Key Term Quiz

Use the Key Terms list to complete the sentences that follow. Not all the terms will be used.

1. A(n) _____ line has a maximum throughput of 1.544 Mbps.

2. A(n) _____ is a device that converts signals between analog and digital.

3. It is the job of the _____ to convert between 8-bit-wide digital data and 1-bit-wide digital data.

4. A(n) _____ signal is defined as a digital signal of 64 Kbps.

5. A(n) _____ combines individual circuits with hundreds of others, creating a complex circuit on a single wire.

6. _____ is the primary standard in the United States for long-distance, high-speed, fiber-optic transmission systems.

7. In the world of DSL, _____ provides equal upload and download speeds up to 15 Mbps.

8. _____ uses an IP network to transfer voice calls.

9. _____ lines consist of two digital channels over the same copper wire used by regular analog telephones.

10. _____ is a router feature that can help to optimize network traffic by labeling certain data to use a desired connection.

■ Multiple-Choice Quiz

1. When an analog sound is converted into 8-bit chunks 8000 times a second, this 64 kilobit per second data stream is created.

   A. DS0

   B. DS1

   C. E1

   D. T1

2. What exists at both ends of a T1 connection?

   A. A frame relay

   B. A CSU/DSU

   C. A digital trunk

   D. A multiplexer

3. This frame type consists of a single framing bit and 24 data channels, each holding an 8-bit DS0 sample, for a total of 193 bits.

   A. DS1

   B. T1

   C. T3

   D. SONET

4. Which line consists of 672 DS0 channels for a total throughput of around 45 Mbps?

   A. T1

   B. T3

   C. E1

   D. E3

5. Which standard supports a throughput of up to 39.8 Gbps?

   A. ISDN

   B. VDSL

   C. SONET

   D. MPLS

6. If you purchase a T1 line in the United States, how will packets be switched? (Select two.)

   A. OC

   B. Frame Relay

   C. ATM

   D. BERT

7. What describes the problem with "the last mile"?

   A. The connection from a central office to a user's home is analog, whereas the rest of the network is digital.

   B. Users must live within a mile of a central office in order to guarantee quality of service (QoS).

   C. SONET connections are limited to a maximum distance of one mile, and connecting central offices via multiplexers is expensive and difficult to maintain.

   D. Copper wires that carry analog telephone signals are limited to a maximum distance of one mile.

8. What terms describe a common telephone connection? (Select two.)

   A. ISDN

   B. POTS

   C. Fractional T1

   D. PSTN

9. What marks where the telephone company's responsibility ends and yours begins?

   A. Multiplexer

   B. Demarc

   C. Primary Rate Interface

   D. Bridges connection

10. The CCITT established which set of standards?

    A. Optical Carrier (OC)

    B. DSL (ADSL, SDSL, VDSL)

    C. Data Over Cable Service Interface Specification (DOCSIS)

    D. V standards

11. Which is the fastest ISDN connection?

    A. BERT

    B. BRI

    C. PRI

    D. ATM

12. Sinjay is 200 meters from his ISP's DSLAM. Which DSL version will provide him with, theoretically, up to 100 Mbps of both download and upload speed?

    A. DS3

    B. ADSL

    C. SDSL

    D. VDSL

13. Which protocol is used by cable companies?

    A. MPLS

    B. DOCSIS

    C. PSTN

    D. SIP

14. What is the benefit to using a satellite connection?

    A. It offers speeds faster than both DSL and cable.

    B. The upload and download speeds are always equal.

    C. It is often available in remote locations where DSL and cable are not.

    D. If offers better security than both DSL and cable.

15. Which protocols support multicasting on VoIP networks? (Select two.)

    A. SIP

    B. H.323

    C. RTP

    D. RAS

▪ Essay Quiz

1. Early DSL providers used bridged connections, but now they tend to use PPPoE instead. What is the difference between these connection types and why do you think DSL providers switched?

2. Upon tracing your company's physical T1 line, you find it connected to a box. It appears as though the box has another connection going to your router. What is this box and what does it do?

3. Briefly describe the six types of remote connections that enable users to connect to remote networks.

Lab Projects

• Lab Project 14.1

Many companies, such as Vonage, offer VoIP solutions for home users to replace their analog telephones. Other companies, such as Cisco, offer VoIP solutions for businesses. Research three VoIP solutions and compare them based on the following criteria: Are they targeting home users or businesses? Is long distance included? What is the startup cost? What is the monthly fee? What uptime guarantee is offered? Can emergency calls (911) be made if the network goes down?

• Lab Project 14.2

How much would a T1 cost you? How about a T3? Make a chart listing the provider from whom you could purchase a T1, fractional T1, or T3, and list the services included along with the costs. How do the providers compare to cable or DSL connections offered in your area?

Wireless Networking

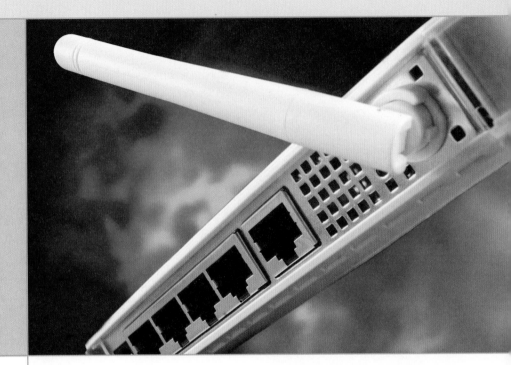

"It's...wireless!"

—Maurice Moss, The IT Crowd

In this chapter, you will learn how to

- Explain wireless networking standards
- Describe the process for implementing Wi-Fi networks
- Describe troubleshooting techniques for wireless networks

Every type of network covered thus far in the book assumes that your PCs connect to your network with some kind of physical cabling. Now it's time to cut the cord and look at the many technologies that collectively changed the way we use the Internet: wireless networking.

Historical/Conceptual

You need to be careful when talking about wireless networking. Wireless is everywhere. It's in our phones and our homes. It's at work and in our schools. Wireless is so transparent and handy we tend to forget that wireless isn't a single technology. There are a number of technologies that collectively make up wireless networking.

Let's start with the basics. Instead of a physical set of wires running among networked PCs, servers, printers, or what-have-you, a **wireless network** uses radio frequency (RF) waves to enable these devices to communicate with each other. Wireless technologies disconnected us from the wires that started the networking revolution and have given us incredible flexibility and mobility.

For all their disconnected goodness, wireless networks share more similarities than differences with wired networks. With the exception of the first two OSI layers, wireless networks use the same protocols as wired networks. The thing that differs is the type of media—radio waves instead of cables—and the protocols for transmitting and accessing data. Different wireless networking solutions have come and gone in the past, but the wireless networking market these days is dominated by the most common implementation of the IEEE 802.11 wireless Ethernet standard, **Wi-Fi**.

This chapter looks first at the standards for modern wireless networks and then turns to implementing those networks. The chapter finishes with a discussion on troubleshooting Wi-Fi.

Because the networking signal is freed from wires, you'll sometimes hear the term *unbounded media* to describe wireless networking.

The CompTIA Network+ objectives draw a clear distinction between wireless technologies that enable devices to *access the Internet*, such as WiMAX and LTE, and wireless technologies that you use to *create a network.* You read about the former in Chapter 14; now you're going to learn about the latter: Wi-Fi.

Test Specific

▪ Wi-Fi Standards

Wi-Fi is by far the most widely adopted wireless networking type today, especially for accessing the Internet. You'd be hard pressed to find a location, work or home, that doesn't have Wi-Fi. Millions of private businesses and homes have wireless networks, and most public places, such as coffee shops and libraries, offer Internet access through wireless networks.

Wi-Fi technologies have been around since the late 1990s, supported and standardized under the umbrella IEEE 802.11 standard. So in reality, Wi-Fi is really 802.11. The 802.11 standard has been updated continuously since then, manifested by a large number of amendments to the standard. These amendments have names such as 802.11g and 802.11ac. It's important for you to understand all of these 802.11 amendments in detail, as well as the original version, 802.11.

Wi-Fi originally stood for *wireless fidelity* to make it cutely equated with *high fidelity (Hi-Fi)*, but it doesn't really stand for anything anymore.

802.11

The **802.11** standard defines both how wireless devices communicate and how to secure that communication. The original 802.11 standard, now often referred to as *802.11-1997,* is no longer used, but it established the baseline features common to all subsequent Wi-Fi standards.

The 802.11-1997 standard defined certain features, such as a wireless network cards, special configuration software, and the capability to run in multiple styles of networks. In addition, 802.11-1997 defined how transmissions work, so we'll look at frequencies of radio signals, transmission methods, and collision avoidance.

Hardware

Wireless networking hardware serves the same function as hardware used on wired PCs. Wireless Ethernet NICs take data passed down from the upper OSI layers, encapsulate it into frames, send the frames out on the network media in streams of ones and zeroes, and receive frames sent from other computing devices. The only difference is that instead of charging up a network cable with electrical current or firing off pulses of light, these devices transmit and receive radio waves.

Wireless networking capabilities of one form or another are built into many modern computing devices. Almost all portable devices have built-in wireless capabilities. Desktop computers can easily go wireless by adding an expansion card. Figure 15.1 shows a wireless PCI Express (PCIe) Ethernet card.

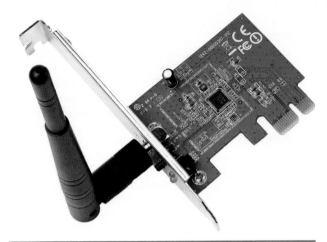

• **Figure 15.1**   Wireless PCIe NIC

You can also add wireless network capabilities using USB wireless network adapters, as shown in Figure 15.2. The USB NICs have the added benefit of being *placeable*—that is, you can move them around to catch the wireless signal as strongly as possible, akin to moving the rabbit ears on old pre-cable television sets.

Is the wireless network adapter in all your devices the only hardware you need to create a wireless network? Well, if your needs are simple—for example, if you're connecting a few laptops on a long train ride so you and your buddies can play a game together—then the answer is yes. If, however, you need to extend the capabilities of a wireless network—say, connecting a wireless network segment to a wired network—you need additional equipment. This typically means a wireless access point.

• **Figure 15.2**   External USB wireless NIC

A **wireless access point (WAP)** is a device designed to interconnect wireless network nodes with wired networks. A basic WAP operates like a hub and works at OSI Layer 1. Many WAP manufacturers combine multiple devices into one box, however, to create a WAP with a built-in switch and/or router, all rolled into one and working at several OSI layers. The Linksys device shown in Figure 15.3 is an example of this type of combo device.

Many manufacturers drop the word "wireless" from wireless access points and simply call them *access points.* Furthermore, many sources abbreviate both forms, so you'll see the former written as *WAP* and the latter as *AP.*

 Cross Check

Using Routers

You've seen wired routers before, and wireless routers function similarly, so cross-check your memory. Think way back to Chapter 2, "Network Models," and see if you can answer these questions. What can a router do for your network? Can you use a router to connect to the Internet? At what layer of the OSI seven-layer model do routers function? How do routers handle addressing?

● **Figure 15.3** Linksys device that acts as wireless access point, switch, and DSL router

Software

Every wireless network adapter needs two pieces of software to function with an operating system: a device driver to talk to the wireless NIC and a configuration utility. Installing drivers for wireless networking devices is usually automatic these days, but you should always consult your vendor's instructions before popping that card into a slot.

You also need a utility for configuring how the wireless hardware connects to other wireless devices. Every operating system has built-in wireless clients for configuring these settings, but these clients may lack advanced features for more complex wireless networks, requiring wireless clients provided by the wireless network adapter vendor or a third party. Figure 15.4 shows a typical wireless network adapter's client configuration utility. Using this utility, you can determine important things like the link state (whether your wireless device is connected) and the signal strength (a measurement of how well your wireless device is connecting to other devices). You can also configure items such as your wireless networking *mode,* security encryption, power-saving options, and so on. I'll cover each of these topics in detail later in this chapter.

You typically configure WAPs through browser-based setup utilities. The section "Implementing Wi-Fi" covers this process a bit later in this chapter. For now, let's look at the different modes that wireless networks use.

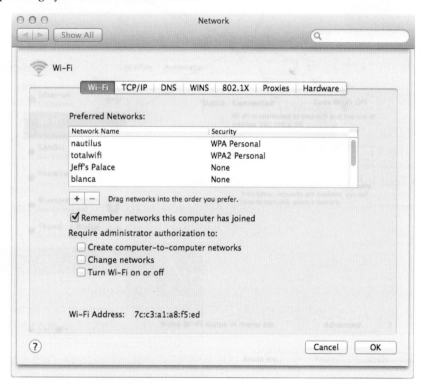

● **Figure 15.4** Wireless client configuration utility

Wireless Network Modes

802.11 networks operate in one of two modes. In the uncommon *ad hoc* mode, two or more devices communicate directly without any other intermediary hardware. The much more common *infrastructure* mode uses a WAP that, in essence, acts as a hub for all wireless clients. A WAP also bridges wireless network segments to wired network segments.

Ad Hoc Mode

Ad hoc mode is sometimes called **peer-to-peer mode**, with each wireless node in direct contact with each other node in a decentralized free-for-all, as shown in Figure 15.5. Ad hoc mode does not use a WAP and instead uses a *mesh* topology, as discussed in Chapter 3, "Cabling and Topology."

Two or more wireless nodes communicating in ad hoc mode form an **Independent Basic Service Set (IBSS)**. This is a basic unit of organization in wireless networks. If you think of an IBSS as a wireless workgroup, you won't be far off the mark.

Ad hoc mode networks work well for small groups of computers (fewer than a dozen or so) that need to transfer files or share printers. Ad hoc networks are also good for temporary networks, such as study groups or business meetings.

Hardly anyone uses ad hoc networks for day-to-day work, however, simply because you can't use an ad hoc network to connect to other networks (unless one of the machines is running Internet Connection Sharing [ICS] or some equivalent).

Infrastructure Mode

Wireless networks running in **infrastructure mode** use one or more WAPs to connect the wireless network nodes centrally, as shown in Figure 15.6. This configuration is similar to the physical *star* topology of a wired network. You also use infrastructure mode to connect wireless network segments to wired segments. If you plan to set up a wireless network for a large number of computing devices, or you need to have centralized control over the wireless network, use infrastructure mode.

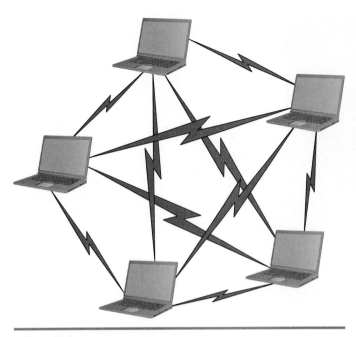

• **Figure 15.5**   Wireless ad hoc mode network

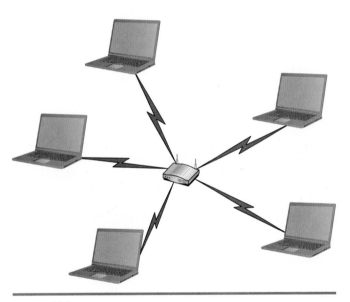

• **Figure 15.6**   Wireless infrastructure mode network

✓ Cross Check

Topologies

The physical topology of a network represents the connectivity between nodes. This seems as good a time as any to cross-check your knowledge of topologies, so recall Chapter 3 and answer these questions. What are the four standard topologies? What are the hybrid topologies? If you connect a wireless network in infrastructure mode to a wired Ethernet network, what topology would that combined network have?

A single WAP servicing a given area is called a **Basic Service Set (BSS)**. This service area can be extended by adding more access points. This is called, appropriately, an **Extended Service Set (ESS)**.

Wireless networks running in infrastructure mode require a little more planning—such as where you place the WAPs to provide adequate coverage—than ad hoc mode networks, and they provide a stable environment for permanent wireless network installations. Infrastructure mode is better suited to business networks or networks that need to share dedicated resources such as Internet connections and centralized databases. (See "Implementing Wi-Fi" later in this chapter.)

Range

Wireless networking range is hard to define. You'll see most descriptions listed with qualifiers such as "*around* 150 feet" and "*about* 300 feet." Wireless range is greatly affected by environmental factors. Interference from other wireless devices and solid objects affects range.

The maximum ranges listed in the sections that follow are those presented by wireless manufacturers as the *theoretical* maximum ranges. In the real world, you'll achieve these ranges only under the most ideal circumstances. Cutting the manufacturer's listed range in half is often a better estimate of the true effective range.

BSSID, SSID, and ESSID

Wireless devices connected together into a network, whether ad hoc or infrastructure, require some way to identify that network. Frames bound for computers within the network need to go where they're supposed to go, even when you have overlapping Wi-Fi networks. The jargon gets a little crazy here, especially because marketing has come into the mix. Stay with me.

The **Basic Service Set Identifier (BSSID)** defines the most basic infrastructure mode network—a BSS of one WAP and one or more wireless clients. With such a simple network, the Wi-Fi folks didn't see any reason to create some new numbering or naming scheme, so they made the BSSID the same as the MAC address for the WAP. Simple! Ah, but what do you do about ad hoc networks that don't have a WAP? The nodes that connect in an IBSS randomly generate a 48-bit string of numbers that looks and functions just like a MAC address, and that BSSID goes in every frame.

You could, if required, discover the MAC address for the WAP in a BSS and manually type that into the network name field when setting up a wireless computer. But that causes two problems. First, people don't want to remember strings of 48 binary digits, even if translated out as six hexadecimal octets, like A9–45–F2–3E–CA–12. People want names. Second, how do you connect two or more computers together into an IBSS when the BSSID has to be randomly generated?

The Wi-Fi folks created another level of naming called a **Service Set Identifier (SSID)**, a standard name applied to the BSS or IBSS to help the connection happen. The SSID—sometimes called a **network name**—is a 32-bit identification string that's inserted into the header of each frame processed by a WAP. Every Wi-Fi device must share the same SSID to communicate in a single network. By default, a WAP advertises its existence by sending out a continuous **SSID broadcast**. It's the SSID broadcast that lets you see the wireless networks that are available on your wireless devices.

Tech Tip

EBSS vs. ESS

Many techs have dropped the word "basic" from the Extended Basic Service Set, the early name for an infrastructure-mode wireless network with more than one WAP. Accordingly, you'll see the initials for the Extended Basic Service Set as ESS. Using either EBSS or ESS is correct.

To really see the power of 802.11 in action, let's take it one step further into a Wi-Fi network that has multiple WAPs: an ESS. How do you determine the network name at this level? You just use the SSID, only you apply it to the ESS as an **Extended Service Set Identifier (ESSID)**. In an ESS, every WAP connects to a central switch or switches to become part of a single broadcast domain.

With multiple WAPs in an ESS, clients will connect to whichever WAP has the strongest signal. As clients move through the space covered by the broadcast area, they will change WAP connections seamlessly, a process called **roaming**.

Most Wi-Fi manufacturers just use the term *SSID,* by the way, and not *ESSID.* When you configure a wireless device to connect to an ESS, you're technically using the ESSID rather than just the SSID, but the manufacturer often tries to make it simple for you by using only the term *SSID.*

The CompTIA Network+ certification exam uses the two terms—*SSID* and *ESSID*—interchangeably. Concentrate on these two terms for the exam.

Broadcasting Frequency

One of the biggest issues with wireless communication is the potential for interference from other wireless devices. To solve this, different wireless devices must operate in specific broadcasting frequencies. Knowing these wireless frequency ranges will assist you in troubleshooting interference issues from other devices operating in the same wireless band. The original 802.11 standards use either 2.4-GHz or 5.0-GHz radio frequencies.

Broadcasting Methods

The original IEEE 802.11 wireless Ethernet standard defined methods by which devices may communicate using *spread-spectrum* radio waves. Spread-spectrum broadcasts data in small, discrete chunks over the different frequencies available within a certain frequency range.

The 802.11 standard defines three different spread-spectrum broadcasting methods: **direct-sequence spread-spectrum (DSSS)**, **frequency-hopping spread-spectrum (FHSS)**, and **orthogonal frequency-division multiplexing (OFDM)**. DSSS sends data out on different frequencies at the same time, whereas FHSS sends data on one frequency at a time, constantly shifting (or *hopping*) frequencies. DSSS uses considerably more bandwidth than FHSS—around 22 MHz as opposed to 1 MHz. DSSS is capable of greater data throughput, but it's also more prone to interference than FHSS. OFDM is the latest of these three methods and is used on all but the earliest 802.11 networks.

Channels

Every Wi-Fi network communicates on a **channel**, a portion of the spectrum available. For the 2.4-GHz band, the 802.11 standard defines 14 channels of 20-MHz each, but different countries limit exactly which channels may be used. In the United States, for example, a WAP using the 2.4-GHz band may only use channels 1 through 11. These channels have some overlap, so two nearby WAPs should not use close channels like 6 and 7. Most WAPs use channels 1, 6, or 11 by default because these are the only non-overlapping channels. You can fine-tune a network by changing the channels on WAPs to avoid overlap with other nearby WAPs. This capability is especially important in environments with many wireless networks sharing the same physical space. See the section "Configuring the Access Point" later in this chapter for more details on channel utilization.

The 5.0-GHz band offers many more channels than the 2.4-GHz band. In general there are around 40 different channels in the spectrum, and different countries have wildly different rules for which channels may or may not be used. The versions of 802.11 that use the 5.0-GHz band use automatic channel switching, so from a setup standpoint we don't worry about channels when we talk about 5.0-GHz 802.11 standards.

CSMA/CA

Because only a single device can use any network at a time in a physical bus topology, network nodes must have a way to access the network media without stepping on each other's frames. Wired Ethernet networks use *carrier sense multiple access with collision detection (CSMA/CD)*, as you'll recall from previous chapters, but Wi-Fi networks use **carrier sense multiple access with collision avoidance (CSMA/CA)**. Let's compare both methods.

 Wired Ethernet networks use CSMA/CD. Wi-Fi networks use CSMA/CA. Cellular networks, as you'll recall from Chapter 14, "Remote Connectivity," use CDMA/CD. All three are close, letter-wise, so pay attention on the exam.

How do multiple devices share network media, such as a cable? Sharing is fairly simple: Each device listens in on the network media by measuring the level of voltage currently on the wire. If the level is below the threshold, the device knows that it's clear to send data. If the voltage level rises above a preset threshold, the device knows that the line is busy and it must wait before sending data. Typically, the waiting period is the length of the current frame plus a short, predefined silence period called an **interframe gap (IFG)**. So far, so good—but what happens when two devices both detect that the wire is free and try to send data simultaneously? As you probably guessed, frames transmitted on the network from two different devices at the same time will corrupt each other's signals. This is called a *collision*. Collisions are a fact of networking life. So how do network nodes deal with collisions? They both react to collisions after they happen, and take steps to avoid collisions in the first place.

Modern wired networks use switches running in full-duplex mode, so they don't have to worry about collisions. You'll recall that from back in Chapter 2. CSMA/CD is disabled with full-duplex. Wireless networks don't have this luxury.

With CSMA/CD, each sending node detects the collision and responds by generating a random timeout period for itself, during which it doesn't try to send any more data on the network—this is called a *backoff*. Once the backoff period expires (remember that I'm talking about only milliseconds here), the node goes through the whole process again. This approach may not be very elegant, but it gets the job done.

CSMA/CD won't work for wireless networking because wireless devices simply can't detect collisions, for two reasons. First, radio is a half-duplex transmission method. Wireless devices cannot listen and send at the same time. Second, if two wireless clients were to collide, there is no simple-to-detect electrical peak like there is with wired networks. Wireless networks need another way to deal with potential collisions. The CSMA/CA access method, as the name implies, proactively takes steps to avoid collisions, as does CSMA/CD. The difference comes in the collision avoidance.

The 802.11 standard defines two methods for collision avoidance: **Distributed Coordination Function (DCF)** and **Point Coordination Function (PCF)**. Currently, only DCF is implemented. DCF specifies rules for sending data onto the network media. For instance, if a wireless network node detects that the network is busy, DCF defines a backoff period on top of the normal IFG wait period before a node can try to access the network again. DCF also requires that receiving nodes send an acknowledgment (ACK) for every frame that they process. The ACK also includes a value that tells other wireless nodes to wait a certain duration before trying to access the network media. This period is calculated to be the time that the data frame takes to reach its destination based on the frame's length and data rate. If the sending node doesn't receive an ACK, it retransmits the same data frame until it gets a confirmation that the packet reached its destination.

The 802.11-1997 standard was the very oldest wireless standard (see Table 15.1). Over time, more detailed additions to 802.11 came along that improved speeds and took advantage of other frequency bands.

Table 15.1	802.11 Summary				
Standard	**Frequency**	**Spectrum**	**Speed**	**Range**	**Compatibility**
802.11-1997	2.4 GHz	DSSS	2 Mbps	~300'	802.11

802.11b

The first widely adopted Wi-Fi standard—**802.11b**—supports data throughput of up to 11 Mbps and a range of up to 300 feet under ideal conditions. The main downside to using 802.11b is its frequency. The 2.4-GHz frequency is a crowded place, so you're more likely to run into interference from other wireless devices. Table 15.2 gives you the 802.11b summary.

Table 15.2	802.11b Summary				
Standard	**Frequency**	**Spectrum**	**Speed**	**Range**	**Compatibility**
802.11b	2.4 GHz	DSSS	11 Mbps	~300'	802.11b

802.11a

The **802.11a** standard differs from the other 802.11-based standards in significant ways. Foremost is that it operates in a different frequency range, 5.0 GHz. The 5.0-GHz range is much less crowded than the 2.4-GHz range, reducing the chance of interference from devices such as telephones and microwave ovens. Too much signal interference can increase latency, making the network sluggish and slow to respond. Running in the 5.0-GHz range greatly reduces this problem.

The 802.11a standard also offers considerably greater throughput than 802.11b, with speeds up to 54 Mbps. Range, however, suffers somewhat and tops out at about 150 feet. Despite the superior speed of 802.11a, it has never enjoyed the popularity of 802.11b.

Although you can find NICs and WAPs that support both 802.11b and 802.11a, the standards are not compatible with each other because of the different frequency bands. A computer with an 802.11b NIC, for example, can't connect to a WAP that's only 802.11a, but it could connect to an 802.11a/b WAP. Table 15.3 gives you the 802.11a summary.

Table 15.3	802.11a Summary				
Standard	**Frequency**	**Spectrum**	**Speed**	**Range**	**Compatibility**
802.11a	5.0 GHz	DSSS	54 Mbps	~150'	802.11a

802.11g

The **802.11g** standard offers data transfer speeds equivalent to 802.11a—up to 54 Mbps—and the wider 300-foot range of 802.11b. More importantly, 802.11g is backward-compatible with 802.11b, so the same 802.11g WAP can service both 802.11b and 802.11g wireless nodes.

If an 802.11g network only has 802.11g devices connected, the network runs in *native mode*—at up to 54 Mbps—whereas when 802.11b devices connect, the network drops down to *mixed mode*—all communication runs up to only 11 Mbps. Table 15.4 gives you the 802.11g summary.

Table 15.4 802.11g Summary

Standard	Frequency	Spectrum	Speed	Range	Compatibility
802.11g	2.4 GHz	OFDM	54 Mbps	~300'	802.11b/g

Later 802.11g manufacturers incorporated **channel bonding** into their devices, enabling the devices to use two channels for transmission. Channel bonding is not part of the 802.11g standard, but rather proprietary technology pushed by various companies to increase the throughput of their wireless networks. Both the NIC and WAP, therefore, had to be from the same company for channel bonding to work.

802.11n

The **802.11n** standard brings several improvements to Wi-Fi networking, including faster speeds and new antenna technology implementations.

The 802.11n specification requires all but handheld devices to use multiple antennas to implement a feature called **multiple in/multiple out (MIMO)**, which enables the devices to make multiple simultaneous connections called streams. With up to four antennas, 802.11n devices can achieve amazing speeds. They also can implement channel bonding to increase throughput even more. (The official standard supports throughput of up to 600 Mbps, although practical implementation drops that down substantially.)

Many 802.11n WAPs employ **transmit beamforming**, a multiple-antenna technology that helps get rid of dead spots—or at least make them not so bad. The antennas adjust the signal once the WAP discovers a client to optimize the radio signal.

Like 802.11g, 802.11n WAPs can support earlier, slower 802.11b/g devices. The problem with supporting these older types of 802.11 is that 802.11n WAPs need to encapsulate 802.11n frames into 802.11b or 802.11g frames. This adds some overhead to the process. Worse, if any 802.11b devices join the network, traffic drops to 802.11b speeds. (802.11g devices don't cause this behavior on 802.11n networks.)

To handle these issues, 802.11 WAPs can transmit in three different modes: legacy, mixed, and greenfield. These modes are also sometimes known as connection types.

Legacy mode means the 802.11n WAP sends out separate packets just for legacy devices. This is a terrible way to utilize 802.11n, but it's been added as a stopgap measure if the other modes don't work. In **mixed mode**, also often called *high-throughput* or **802.11a-ht/802.11g-ht**, the WAP sends special packets that support the older standards yet also can improve the speed of those standards via 802.11n's wider bandwidth. Greenfield mode is exclusively for 802.11n-only wireless networks. The WAP will only process 802.11n frames. Dropping support for older devices gives greenfield mode the best goodput.

Table 15.5 gives you the 802.11n summary.

Table 15.5	802.11n Summary				
Standard	Frequency	Spectrum	Speed	Range	Compatibility
802.11n	2.4 GHz[1]	OFDM (QAM)	100+ Mbps	~300'	802.11b/g/n[2]

[1] Dual-band 802.11n devices can function simultaneously at both 2.4- and 5.0-GHz bands.
[2] Many dual-band 802.11n WAPs support 802.11a devices as well as 802.11b/g/n devices. This is not part of the standard, but something manufacturers have implemented.

802.11ac

802.11ac is a natural expansion of the 802.11n standard, incorporating even more streams, wider bandwidth, and higher speed. To avoid *device density* issues in the 2.4-GHz band, 802.11ac only uses the 5.0-GHz band. (See "What Wireless Is Already There?" later in this chapter for more on device density and how to deal with it.) Table 15.6 gives you the 802.11ac summary.

Table 15.6	802.11ac Summary				
Standard	Frequency	Spectrum	Speed	Range	Compatibility
802.11ac	5 GHz	OFDM (QAM)	Up to 1 Gbps	~300'	802.11a

The latest versions of 802.11ac include a new version of MIMO called *Multiuser MIMO (MU-MIMO)*. MU-MIMO gives a WAP the ability to broadcast to multiple users simultaneously.

WPS

By around 2006, 802.11 was everywhere and it was starting to get popular for non-PC devices such as printers, scanners, and speakers. The challenge with these devices was that they lacked any kind of interface to make it easy to configure the wireless settings.

To make configuration easier, the wireless industry created a special standard called Wi-Fi Protected Setup (WPS). WPS works in two modes: push button method or PIN method. (There were other modes, but they never were popular). With the push button method, you press a button on one device (all WPS-compatible devices have a physical or virtual push button) and then press the WPS button on the other device. That's it. The two devices automatically configure themselves on an encrypted connection.

The PIN method was for connecting a PC to a WPS device (usually a WAP). You press the button on the WAP, locate the SSID on your device, and then enter an eight-digit PIN number as the WPA personal shared key (more on WPA shortly). All WPS WAPs have the PIN printed on the device.

WPS is very easy to use, but is susceptible to different forms of *WPS attacks*. By design, the WPS PIN numbers are short. WPS attacks, therefore, concentrate on hacking the PIN number. By hacking the PIN, a bad actor can easily take control of the WAP, giving him or her access to the entire infrastructure. WPS has not been fixed, and since 2011 the wireless industry has told everyone to disable WPS on their WAPs.

Wi-Fi Security

One of the biggest problems with wireless networking devices is that right out of the box they provide *no* security. Vendors go out of their way to make setting up their devices easy, so usually the only thing that you have to do to join a wireless network is turn your wireless devices on and let them find each other. Sure, this is great from a configuration point of view—but from a security point of view, it's a disaster!

We need to use a number of techniques to make a wireless network secure, to *harden* it from malicious things and people. Wireless security is network hardening. (For details about network hardening techniques that apply to all kinds of networks, see Chapter 19, "Protecting Your Network.")

You also need to consider that your network's data frames float through the air on radio waves instead of zipping safely along wrapped up inside network cabling. What's to stop an unscrupulous network tech with the right equipment from grabbing those frames out of the air and reading that data?

To address these issues, 802.11 networks use three methods: MAC address filtering, authentication, and data encryption. The first two methods secure access to the network itself, and the third secures the data that's moving around the network. All three of these methods require you to configure the WAPs and wireless devices. Let's take a look.

All the methods used in wireless network security—authentication, encryption, MAC address filtering—can be considered network hardening techniques.

MAC Address Filtering

Most WAPs support **MAC address filtering**, a method that enables you to limit access to your network based on the physical addresses of wireless NICs. MAC address filtering creates a type of "accepted users" list to limit access to your wireless network. A table stored in the WAP lists the MAC addresses that are permitted to participate in the wireless network. Any network frames that don't contain the MAC address of a node listed in the table are rejected.

Many WAPs also enable you to deny specific MAC addresses from logging onto the network. This works great in close quarters, such as apartments or office buildings, where your wireless network signal goes beyond your perimeter. You can check the WAP and see the MAC addresses of every node that connects to your network. Check that list against the list of your computers, and you can readily spot any unwanted interloper. Putting an offending MAC address in the "deny" column effectively blocks that system from piggybacking onto your wireless connection.

Although address filtering works, a hacker can very easily *spoof* a MAC address—make the NIC report a legitimate address rather than its own—and access the network. Worse, a hacker doesn't have to connect to your network to grab your network traffic out of thin air! If you have data so important that a hacker would want to get at it, you should seriously consider using a wired network or separating the sensitive data from your wireless network in some fashion.

WAPs use an *access control list (ACL)* to enable or deny specific MAC addresses. Note that a WAP's ACL has *nothing* to do with ACL in NTFS; it's just the same term used for two different things.

MAC filtering with a *whitelist* means you allow only specific computers to join the network. When you deny specific computers, you create a *blacklist*. Whitelisting and blacklisting are labor-intensive processes, with whitelisting requiring far more work.

Wireless Authentication

Implementing authentication enables you to secure a network so only users with the proper credentials can access network resources. Authentication in a wired network, as you'll recall from Chapter 11, "Securing TCP/IP," generally takes the form of a centralized security database that contains user names, passwords, and permissions, like the Active Directory in a Windows Server environment. Wireless network clients can use the same security database as wired clients, but getting the wireless user authenticated takes a couple of extra steps.

The first real 802.11 security standard was known as 802.11i. 802.11i addressed both authentication and encryption, but for right now let's just discuss authentication under 802.11i. (Encryption under 802.11i is discussed a bit later in the "Data Encryption Using WPA" section.)

802.11i uses the IEEE **802.1X** standard to enable you to set up a network with some seriously secure authentication using a RADIUS server and passwords encrypted with **Extensible Authentication Protocol (EAP)**. Let's look at the components and the process.

A **RADIUS server** stores user names and passwords, enabling you to set a user's rights once in the network. A RADIUS server functions like a typical server, but the remote aspect of it requires you to learn new jargon. The terms "client" and "server" are *so* Active Directory, after all.

Here's how it works. The client wireless computer, called a **supplicant**, contacts the WAP, called a **Network Access Server (NAS)**, and requests permission to access the network. The NAS collects the supplicant's user name and password and then contacts the RADIUS server to see if the supplicant appears in the RADIUS server's security database. If the supplicant appears and the user name and password are correct, the RADIUS server sends a packet back to the supplicant, through the WAP, with an Access-Accept code and an Authenticator section that proves the packet actually came from the RADIUS server. Then the remote user gets access to the network resources. That's some serious security! See Figure 15.7.

> RADIUS stands for *Remote Authentication Dial In User Service*. Say that five times.

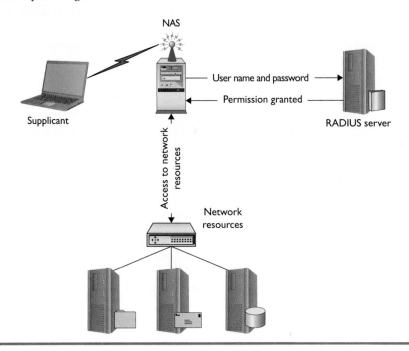

• **Figure 15.7**   Authenticating using RADIUS

But here's where it gets tricky. What are the points of potential security failure here? All over the place, right? The connection between each of these devices must be secure; several protocols make certain of that security. PPP, for example, provides a secure connection between the supplicant and the NAS. IPsec often provides the security between the NAS and the RADIUS server. We then need some form of authentication standard that encrypts all this authentication process. That's where 802.11i calls for the Extensible Authentication Protocol (EAP). See Figure 15.8.

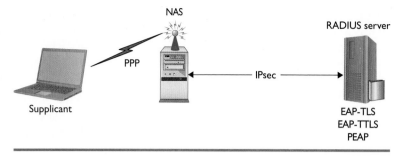

• Figure 15.8   Authentication using RADIUS with protocols in place

EAP defines a framework for authentication but does not specify how the authentication happens. Developers have, therefore, come up with many ways to handle the specifics, such as EAP-TLS, EAP-TTLS, and PEAP, to name just a few. (The CompTIA Network+ exam mentions implementing TLS/TTLS as network hardening. That happens in conjunction with EAP.)

The differences among the many flavors of EAP cause countless hours of argument among geeks, but from a technician's perspective, you simply use the scheme that your network hardware supports. Both the WAP and the wireless NICs have to use the same EAP authentication scheme. You set this in the firmware or software, as you can see in Figure 15.9.

EAP and RADIUS servers for authentication paint half the picture on 802.1X security implementation. The other half is WPA2, discussed shortly in "Data Encryption Using WPA2."

Data Encryption

The main way we secure a wireless network is by encrypting the data packets that are floating around. **Encryption** electronically scrambles data packets and locks them with a private encryption key before transmitting them onto the wireless network. The receiving network device has to possess the encryption key to unscramble the packet and process the data. Thus, a hacker who grabs any data frames out of the air can't read those frames unless he or she has the encryption key. Enabling wireless encryption through WPA2 provides a good level of security to data packets in transit.

Over the years there have been a number of encryption methods for wireless. There was the original 802.11 (which was so bad it doesn't even warrant discussion), WEP, WPA, and WPA2. There are additional features that tie encryption standards with authentication, such as WPA-PSK and WPA-Enterprise. Let's cover all of these.

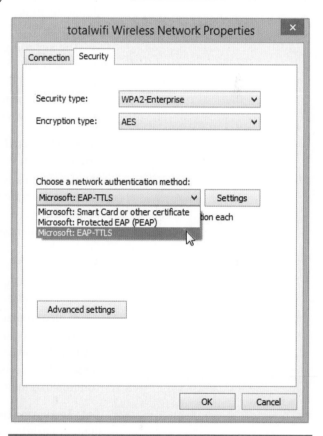

• Figure 15.9   Setting EAP authentication scheme

Data Encryption Using WEP   The granddaddy of wireless security, **Wired Equivalent Privacy (WEP)**, uses a 64- or 128-bit encryption algorithm to scramble data frames. But even with the strongest encryption enabled, WEP isn't a particularly robust security solution. In fact, WEP can be cracked in under a minute with just a regular laptop and open source software.

WEP is subject to many types of *WEP attacks*. Hackers can easily crack WEP, for two reasons: the size of the encryption key and the way the key is updated. First, the WEP keys were never really 64- and 128-bit. WEP uses an encryption cipher called *RC4*. There's nothing inherently wrong with RC4, but RC4 is a stream cipher and needs a little code to start the encryption process, just like a water pump needs some water in the pump before it works. This extra code is stored in the key in the form of what's called an *initialization vector (IV)*. The IV with WEP is 24 bits, which means the encryption part of a WEP key is only 40-bit or 104-bit.

The second problem with WEP is that the encryption key is both static (never changes from session to session) and shared (the same key is used by all network nodes). This means it's not that hard to crack assuming you can capture enough WEP-encrypted packets to figure out the code. WEP is simply a disaster.

WEP also fails to provide a mechanism for performing user authentication. That is, network nodes that use WEP encryption are identified by their MAC address, and no other credentials are offered or required. With just a laptop and some open source software, MAC addresses are very easy to sniff out and duplicate, thus opening you up to a possible spoofing attack. (See Chapter 19, "Protecting Your Network," for the scoop on spoofing and other common attacks.)

The key thing to remember about WEP is that it is outdated and should never be used. The only security WEP provides today is to prevent casual people from connecting to your WAP. Its encryption is so easily cracked that you might as well be transmitting plaintext. WEP is like a No Trespassing sign on a post, but without the fence.

Data Encryption Using WPA　The 802.11i standard was designed to address the problems with WEP and to provide proper authentication. The full standard took a while to complete, so the wireless industry implemented an intermediate fix. They invented a sales term called Wi-Fi Protected Access (WPA) that adopted most (not all) of the 802.11i standard, fixing some of the weaknesses of WEP. WPA offers security enhancements such as dynamic encryption key generation (keys are issued on a per-user and per-session basis) and an encryption key integrity-checking feature.

WPA works by using an extra layer of security, called the Temporal Key Integrity Protocol (TKIP), around the WEP encryption scheme. It's not, therefore, a complete replacement protocol for WEP. TKIP added a 128-bit encryption key that seemed unbreakable when first introduced. Within four years of introduction, however, researchers showed methods by which hackers could waltz through WPA security almost as quickly as through WEP security. Another solution had to be found.

Data Encryption Using WPA2　The IEEE 802.11i standard amended the 802.11 standard to add much-needed security features. I already discussed the 802.1X authentication measure using EAP to provide secure access to Wi-Fi networks. 802.11i also replaced the aging RC4 encryption with the much more robust Advanced Encryption Standard (AES), a 128-bit block cipher that's much tougher to crack than the TKIP used with WPA.

Implementing the full 802.11i standard took time because most of the installed Wi-Fi hardware couldn't be updated to handle AES encryption. WPA held the title of "most secure wireless" for a number of years.

Eventually, enough devices were made that could support AES that the full 802.11i standard was implemented under the sales term **Wi-Fi Protected Access 2 (WPA2)**. A "WPA2-compliant device" is really just a marketing term for a device that fully supports the 802.11i standard. WPA2 is the current top security standard used on 802.11 networks. WPA2 is not hack-proof, but it definitely offers a much tougher encryption standard that stops the casual hacker cold.

The most common way to set up WPA or WPA2 encryption is to use a simple version called WPA (or WPA2) Personal Shared Key, also called PSK or Personal. Basically, with these Personal versions, you create a secret key that must be added to any device that is going to be on that SSID. There is no authentication with WPA-PSK or WPA2-PSK.

WPA attacks and WPA2 attacks can happen, especially with wireless networks using WPA-Personal or WPA2-Personal passphrases. The attacks take place by using sophisticated methods that make a number of assumptions about the passphrase, and the fact that certain passphrases are used quite often. The most important thing to do to prevent these attacks from succeeding is to use long passphrases (16 or more characters), thus making the network hard to crack. Otherwise, you need authentication. If you want authentication you move into what most wireless folks will call an enterprise setup. For example, when you use a RADIUS server for authentication with WPA2 to create an amazingly secure wireless network, it gets a fancy name: **WPA2-Enterprise**. Let's talk about enterprise wireless a bit more.

> The CompTIA Network+ exam objectives refer to WPA-PSK and WPA2-PSK as hardening options, but call them *WPA-Personal* and *WPA2-Personal*. Be prepared for any of these terms.

Enterprise Wireless

A simple BSSID or ESSID is incredibly easy to set up. You can take a few cheap WAPs from your local electronics store, connect them to a switch, use a Web interface to configure each WAP, and start connecting clients. Inexpensive SOHO WAPs and wireless routers have been around so long—almost as long as 802.11 itself—that for many of us this is what we think a "wireless network" means.

But as a wireless networks becomes more important, complex, and busy, the cheap SOHO boxes just aren't going to work anymore. When you want dependable, robust, secure, administrable wireless networks, you need enterprise-class wireless equipment. In general, enterprise wireless differs from SOHO device in five areas: robust device construction, centralized management, VLAN pooling, Power over Ethernet, and bringing personal wireless devices into the enterprise environment.

Robust Device Construction

If you compare a typical SOHO WAP to an enterprise WAP, you'll notice immediately that the enterprise WAP is made of better materials (often metal instead of plastic). Enterprise WAPs for the most part will also be more configurable. Most enterprise WAPs enable you to swap out antennas and radios, so you can keep WAPs while upgrading them to the latest technologies. Figure 15.10 shows an enterprise WAP.

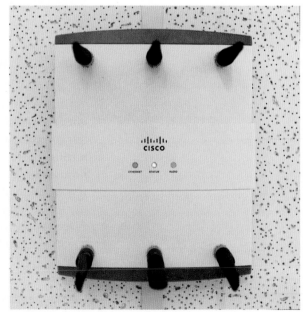

• **Figure 15.10** Cisco Enterprise WAP

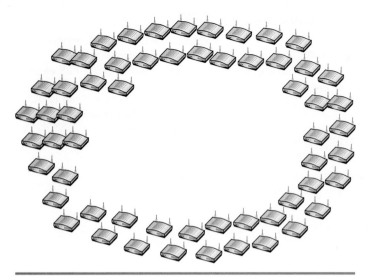

● **Figure 15.11**   Configuring WAPs

Wireless controllers have a number of other names, such as wireless switch, wireless LAN switch, and so forth.

Enterprise Wireless Administration

An enterprise wireless infrastructure is almost certainly going to consist of a large number of WAPs. It's impossible to administer a large number of WAPs when you have to access each WAP individually. Imagine something as simple as changing the password on a WPA2-encrypted ESSID on a wireless network with 50+ WAPs (Figure 15.11). The job would take forever!

The wireless industry long ago appreciated the complexity of enterprise-level wireless networks and created tools to make administration easier. The important point to any wireless network is that all of the WAPs, at least on a single SSID, connect to a single switch or group of switches. What if we offload the job of configuration to a switch that's designed to handle a number of WAPs simultaneously? We call these switches **wireless controllers** (Figure 15.12).

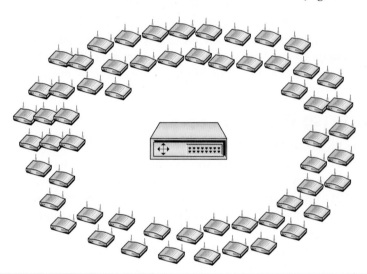

● **Figure 15.12**   Wireless controller

Any WAP that you can access directly and configure singularly via its own interface is called a **thick client**. A WAP that can only be configured by a wireless controller is called a **thin client**. For years, these centralized configuration methods were proprietary for each wireless manufacturer, making for little or no cross-brand interoperability. This incompatibility in thin and think clients was a common wireless issue back in the day. Today, most manufacturers use the *Lightweight Access Point Protocol (LWAPP)* to ensure interoperability. Given LWAPP's broad acceptance, most WAPs will accept commands from any wireless controller.

VLAN Pooling

One of the big challenges to larger enterprise networks is the large number of clients that might be on a single SSID at any given moment. As the number of devices grows, you get a huge amount of broadcasts on the network.

The traditional method to reduce this is to divide the wireless LAN (WLAN) into multiple broadcast domains and use routers to interconnect the domains. In many cases, though, the needs of the wireless network require a single domain; instead we create a pool of VLANs for a single SSID and randomly assign wireless clients to one of the VLANs. This is called **VLAN pooling**.

Power over Ethernet

Wireless access points need electrical power, but they're invariably placed in strange locations (like ceilings or high up on walls) where providing electrical power is not convenient. No worries! Better WAPs now support an IEEE standard (802.3af) called **Power over Ethernet (PoE)**, which enables them to receive their power from the same Ethernet cables that transfer their data. The switch that connects the WAPs must support PoE, but as long as both the WAP and the switches to which they connect support PoE, you don't have to do anything other than just plug in Ethernet cables. PoE works automatically. As you might imagine, it costs extra to get WAPs and switches that support PoE, but the convenience of PoE for wireless networks makes it a popular option.

The original PoE standard came out in 2003 with great response from the industry. Its popularity revealed a big problem: the original 802.3af standard only supported a maximum of 15.4 watts of DC power and many devices needed more. In 2009, 802.3af was revised to output as much as 25.5 watts. This new PoE amendment to 802.3 is called 802.3at, PoE plus, or PoE+.

Bring Your Own Device

Everybody seems to have a smartphone, a tablet, or both these days. Plus these devices rival desktop PCs in sheer computing power and functionality. Wouldn't it be cool to integrate these personal mobile devices into a corporate network? What could go wrong?

In truth, corporations have included mobile devices into their networking experience for a number of years. The BlackBerry Enterprise Service (BES) software enabled corporations to issue BlackBerrys to users and retain control over how those users could use the mobile device on their network. This enabled users to get and synchronize company e-mail, calendars, and more with mobile devices and workstations. Because of central control, network admins could allow or deny mobile devices access to network features, what's called *on-boarding and off-boarding mobile devices.*

The problem isn't so much with corporate-issued equipment, but rather with personal devices. How does John bring his Apple iPad to the office and take it on the road and get access to his company information at both locations? The network admins could install *mobile device management (MDM)* solutions (or have John install such on his iPad), but that creates problems. Once the device connects to the network, the network admins have control over a lot of personal information.

Apple and other big players in the mobile and portable device market have stepped up in recent years to provide more robust solutions for integrating all sorts of devices. These devices include cell phones, laptops, tablets, gaming devices, and media devices (like Apple TV). The more recent MDM solutions rely on tried-and-true protocols such as 802.1X to provide robust security and not restrict connectivity. This **bring your own device (BYOD)** movement has stormed the corporate world.

WLAN vs. PAN

What do you call the network at your local coffee shop? It's a local area network (LAN) for sure, but there's nowhere for ordinary customers to plug in. Thus, it's—in nontechnical terms—a **wireless LAN (WLAN)**. The thing to note here is that a WLAN is always going to be an 802.11-based network and will be able to serve a number of clients.

This is important because there are a number of other wireless LANs using technologies such as *Bluetooth*, *near field communication (NFC)*, and *infrared (IR)* that, while they all use some form of wireless communication, are designed to make a single point-to-point connection, and only at very short ranges. Bluetooth may go as far as 100 meters for the most powerful Bluetooth connections to as little as 5 cm for NFC devices. Any connections used by Bluetooth, NFC, or infrared are called **personal area networks (PANs)** to reflect their shorter distances and point-to-point nature.

■ Implementing Wi-Fi

Installing and configuring a Wi-Fi network requires a number of discrete steps. You should start with a site survey to determine any obstacles (existing wireless, interference, and so on) you need to overcome and to determine the best location for your access points. You'll need to install one or more access points, and then configure both the access point(s) and wireless clients. Finally, you should put the network to the test, verifying that it works as you intended.

Performing a Site Survey

As mentioned, the first step of installing a wireless network is the site survey. A **site survey** will reveal any obstacles to creating the wireless network, and will help determine the best possible location for your access points. The main components for creating a site survey are a floor plan of the area you wish to provide with wireless and a site survey tool such as Fluke Network's AirMagnet Survey Pro (Figure 15.13). **Wireless survey tools** help you discover any other wireless networks in the area and will integrate a drawing of your floor plan with interference sources clearly marked. This enables you to get the right kind of hardware you need and makes it possible to get the proper network coverage.

What Wireless Is Already There?

Discovering any wireless network signals other than your own in your space enables you to set both the SSID and channel to avoid networks that overlap. One part of any good site survey is a wireless analyzer. A **wireless analyzer** or **Wi-Fi analyzer** is any device that looks for and documents all existing wireless networks in the area. Wireless analyzers are handy tools that are useful for diagnosing wireless network issues and conducting site surveys. You can get dedicated, hand-held wireless analyzer tools or you can run site survey software on a laptop or mobile wireless device. Wireless survey tools like AirMagnet

Check out the excellent Chapter 15 Show! Sim about third-party wireless utilities at totalsem.com/006. It's a cool sim about non-Microsoft implementations.

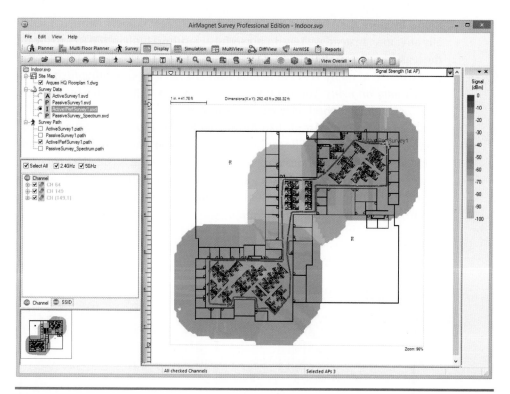

Survey Pro always include an analyzer as well. Figure 15.14 shows a screenshot of Acrylic Wi-Fi, a free and popular wireless analyzer.

Wireless networks send out radio signals on the 2.4- or 5.0-GHz spectrum using one of a number of discrete channels. In early wireless networks, a big part of the setup was to determine the channels used nearby in order to avoid

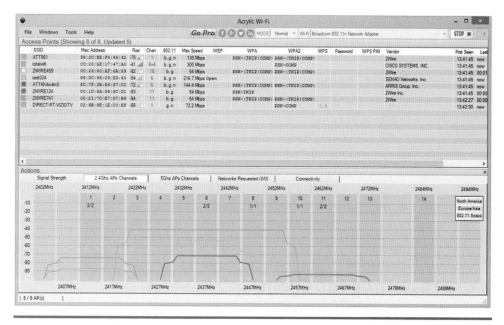

● Figure 15.14   Acrylic Wi-Fi

them. In more modern wireless networks, we rarely adjust channels manually anymore. Instead we rely on powerful algorithms built into WAPs to locate the least congested channels automatically. The bigger challenge today is the preexistence of many Wi-Fi networks with lots of clients, creating *high device density environments.* You need a wireless solution that handles many users running on the few wireless frequencies available.

There are plenty of tools like AirMagnet Survey Pro to support a wireless survey. All good survey utilities share some common ways to report their findings. One of the most powerful reports that they generate is called a heat map. A *heat map* is nothing more than a graphical representation of the RF sources on your site, using different colors to represent the intensity of the signal. Figure 15.15 shows a sample heat map.

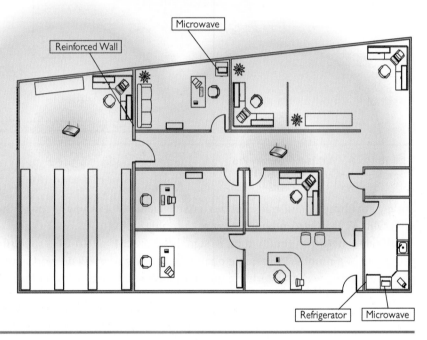

• **Figure 15.15**   Site survey with heat map

Interference Sources

It might seem like overkill in a small network, but any network beyond a simple one should have a sketched-out site survey with any potential interference sources clearly marked (Figure 15.16). Refrigerators, reinforced walls, metal plumbing, microwave ovens; all of these can create horrible dead spots where your network radio wave can't easily penetrate. With a difficult or high-interference area, you might need to move up to 802.11n or 802.11ac equipment with three or four antennas just to get the kind of coverage you want. Or you might need to plan a multiple WAP network to wipe out the dead zones. A proper site survey gives you the first tool for implementing a network that works.

Installing the Client

Because every Wi-Fi network needs clients (otherwise, what's the point?), you need to install Wi-Fi client hardware and software. Pretty much every type of

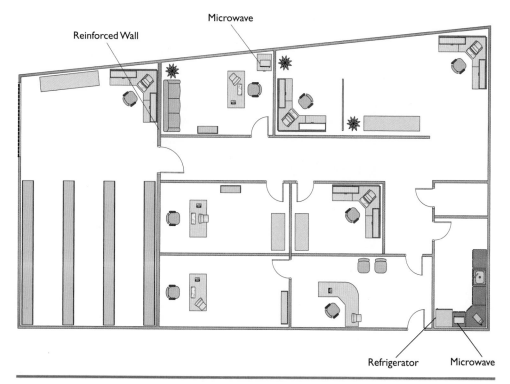

Reinforced Wall

Microwave

Refrigerator   Microwave

• **Figure 15.16**   Site survey with interference sources noted

mobile device (smartphones, laptops, tablets, and so forth) comes with a built-in client, usually part of the operating system.

Desktop systems are a different story. Most desktops don't have built-in wireless, so you'll need to install a wireless NIC. You have a choice between installing a PCIe card or a USB device. With a PCIe NIC, power down the PC, disconnect from the AC source, and open the case. Following good CompTIA A+ technician procedures, locate a free slot on the motherboard, remove the slot cover, remove the NIC from its antistatic bag, install the NIC, and affix the retaining screw. See Figure 15.17. Often you'll need to attach the antenna. Button everything up, plug it in, and start the computer. If prompted, put in the disc that came from the manufacturer and install drivers and any other software necessary.

With a USB NIC, you should install the drivers and software before you connect the NIC to the computer. This is standard operating procedure for any USB device, as you most likely recall from your CompTIA A+ certification training (or from personal experience).

• **Figure 15.17**   Wi-Fi NIC installed

Setting Up an Ad Hoc Network

Although ad hoc networks are rare, they are on the CompTIA Network+ exam. Plus, you might need to set one up in the real world, so let's look at the process.

Configuring NICs for ad hoc mode networking requires you to address four things: SSID, IP addresses, channel, and sharing. (Plus, of course, you have to set the NICs to function in ad hoc mode!) Each wireless node must be configured to use the same network name (SSID). It's common for one system

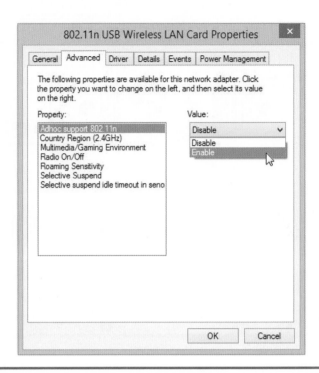

Figure 15.18   Selecting ad hoc mode in a wireless configuration utility

to set up an ad hoc node and then have other nodes attach to that node. Of course, no two nodes can use the same IP address, although this is unlikely because all operating systems use Automatic Private IP Addressing (APIPA). Finally, ensure that the File and Printer Sharing service is running on all nodes. Figure 15.18 shows a wireless network configuration utility with ad hoc mode selected.

Try This!

Ad Hoc-ing

If you have access to a Wi-Fi-enabled device and a friend or classmate has one as well, try this! Set up your Wi-Fi for ad hoc using the configuration utility, and then try to connect with your partner's device. Use default settings. Once you connect with the defaults, you can start playing with your ad hoc network! If you're in Windows 7, select Home for your network and set up a HomeGroup. Copy the sample images from one machine to another. Throw a big file into a Public folder and try copying that one, too. Then do it again, but with variations of distance and channels. How far can you separate your devices and still communicate? What happens if you change channels in the configuration utility, such as moving both devices from channel 6 to channel 4?

Setting Up an Infrastructure Network

Site survey in hand and Wi-Fi technology selected, you're ready to set up a wireless network in infrastructure mode. You need to determine the optimal location for your WAP, configure the WAP, and then configure any clients to access that WAP. Seems pretty straightforward, but the devil, they say, is in the details.

Placing the Access Points/Antennas

All wireless access points have antennas that radiate the 802.11 signal to the clients, so the optimal location for a WAP depends on the area you want to cover and whether you care if the signal bleeds out beyond the borders. You also need to use antennas that provide enough signal and push that signal in the proper direction. There are some interesting options here and you should know them both for modern networking and for the CompTIA Network+ exam.

Antenna placement on the WAPs is also very important. WAP antennas come in many shapes and sizes. In the early days it was common to see WAPs with two antennas (Figure 15.19). Some WAPs have only one antenna and some (802.11n and 802.11ac) have more than two. Even a WAP that doesn't seem to have antennas is simply hiding them inside the case.

There are three basic types of antennas common in 802.11 networks: omnidirectional, unidirectional, and patch. Each offers different solutions for coverage of specific wireless network setups. Let's look at all three.

• **Figure 15.19**   WRT54G showing two antennas

Omnidirectional   In general, an omnidirectional antenna radiates outward from the WAP in all directions. For a typical network, you want blanket coverage and would place a WAP with an omnidirectional antenna in the center of the area (Figure 15.20). This has the advantage of ease of use—anything within the signal radius can potentially access the network. The standard straight-wire antennas that provide the most omnidirectional function are called dipole antennas.

The famous little black antennas we see on older WAPs are all dipoles. A dipole antenna has two radiating elements that point in opposite directions. But if you look at a WAP antenna, it looks like it only points in one direction

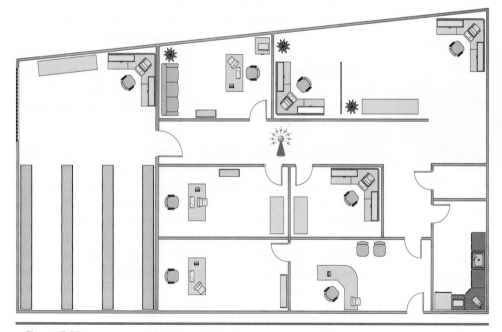

• **Figure 15.20**   Room layout with WAP in the center

• Figure 15.21 Typical WAP dipole antenna—where are the two elements?

Element   Element

• Figure 15.22 Same antenna from Figure 15.21 opened, showing the two elements

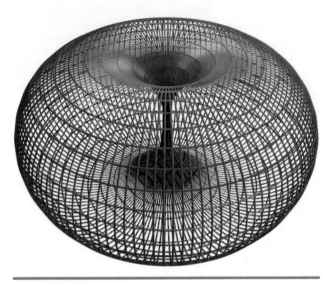

• Figure 15.23 Dipole radiation pattern

• Figure 15.24 Replacement antenna on a WAP

(Figure 15.21). If you open up one of these antennas, however, you'll see that it has two opposing radiating elements (Figure 15.22).

A dipole antenna doesn't radiate in a perfect ball. It actually is more of a doughnut shape, as shown in Figure 15.23. Note that this shape is great for outdoors or a single floor, but it doesn't send much signal above or below the WAP.

The omnidirectional and centered approach does not work for every network, for three reasons. First, if the signal exceeds the size of the network space, that signal bleeds out. The signal can bleed out a lot in some cases, particularly if your specific space doesn't allow you to put the WAP in the center, but rather off-center. This presents a security risk as well, because someone outside your network space could lurk, pick up the signal, and do unpleasant things to your network. Second, if your network space exceeds the signal of your WAP, you'll need to get some sort of signal booster. Third, any obstacles will produce glaring dead spots in network coverage. Too many dead spots make a less-than-ideal solution. To address these issues, you might need to turn to other solutions.

An antenna strengthens and focuses the RF output from a WAP. The ratio of increase—what's called **gain**—is measured in decibels (dB). The gain from a typical WAP is 2 dB, enough to cover a reasonable area, but not a very large room. Increasing the signal requires a bigger device antenna. Many WAPs have removable device antennas. To increase the signal in an omnidirectional and centered setup, simply replace the factory device antennas with one or more bigger device antennas (Figure 15.24). Get a big enough antenna and you can crank it all the way up to 11!

Unidirectional When you don't necessarily want to broadcast to the world, you can use one or more *directional antennas* to create a nicely focused network. A **unidirectional antenna**, as the name implies, focuses a radio wave into a beam of sorts. Unidirectional antennas come in a variety of flavors, such as parabolic, dish, and Yagi, to name a just a few. A *parabolic antenna* looks like a satellite dish. A *Yagi antenna* (named for one of its Japanese inventors) is often called a *beam antenna* and can enable a focused radio wave to travel a long way, even miles (Figure 15.25)! If you need to connect in a narrow beam (down a hallway or from one faraway point to another), unidirectional antennas are the way to go.

• **Figure 15.25**   Yagi antenna

• **Figure 15.26**   Patch antenna

Patch Antennas   *Patch antennas* are flat, plate-shaped antennas that generate a half-sphere beam. Patch antennas are always placed on walls. The half-sphere is perfect for indoor offices where you want to fill the room with a strong signal but not broadcast to the room behind the patch (Figure 15.26).

Optimal Antenna Placement   Optimal antenna placement varies according to the space to fill and security concerns. You can use the site survey and the same wireless analyzer tools to find dead spots, odd corners, and so on. Use the right kind of antenna on each WAP to fill in the space.

Configuring the Access Point

Wireless access points have a browser-based setup utility. Typically, you fire up the Web browser on one of your network client workstations and enter the access point's default IP address, such as 192.168.1.1, to bring up the configuration page. You need to supply an administrative password, included with your access point's documentation, to log in (Figure 15.27).

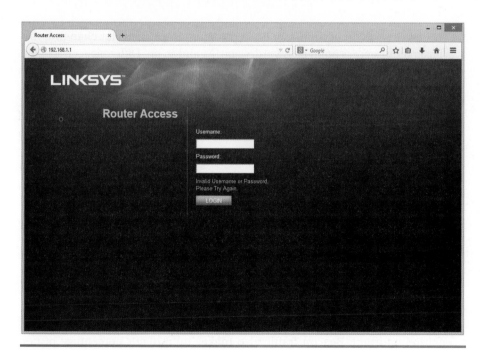

• **Figure 15.27**   Security login for Linksys WAP

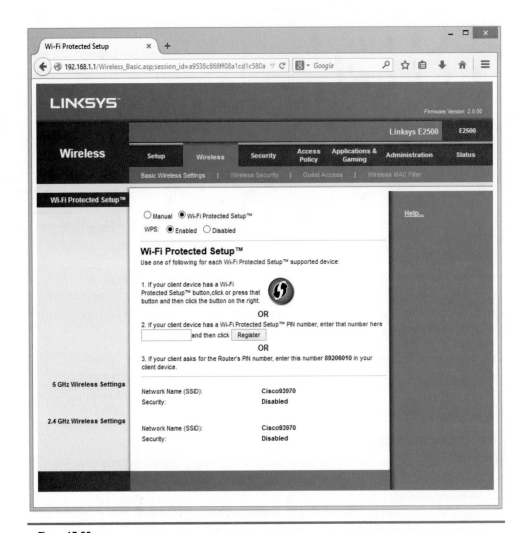

• **Figure 15.28**   Linksys WAP setup screen

Once you've logged in, you'll see configuration screens for changing your basic setup, access point password, security, and so on. Different access points offer different configuration options. Figure 15.28 shows the initial setup screen for a popular Linksys WAP/router.

Configuring the SSID (ESSID) and Beacon   The SSID option is usually located somewhere obvious on the configuration utility. On the Linksys model shown in Figure 15.28, this option is on the Setup tab. Configure your SSID to something unique.

The primary way we locate wireless networks is by using our clients to scan for SSIDs. All wireless networks have a function to turn off the SSID broadcast. You can choose not to broadcast the SSID, but this only stops casual users—sophisticated wireless intruders have tools to detect networks that do not broadcast their SSIDs. Turning off SSID broadcast forces users to configure the connection to a particular SSID manually.

Aside from the SSID (or ESSID in an extended network), broadcast traffic includes the *beacon,* essentially a timing frame sent from the WAP at regular intervals. The beacon frame enables Wi-Fi networks to function, so this is fairly important. Beacon traffic also makes up a major percentage of network traffic because most WAPs have beacons set to go off every 100 ms!

You can adjust the rate of the beacon traffic down and improve your network traffic speeds, but you lower the speed at which devices can negotiate to get on the network, among other things. Figure 15.29 shows the Beacon Interval setting on a Linksys router.

Beacon Period:	100	(20-4000 Kusec)	Data Beacon Rate (DTIM):	2	(1-100)
Max. Data Retries:	64	(1-128)	RTS Max. Retries:	64	(1-128)
Fragmentation Threshold:	2346	(256-2346)	RTS Threshold:	2347	(0-2347)

• **Figure 15.29**   Setting the beacon interval

Configuring MAC Address Filtering   Increase security even further by using MAC address filtering to build a list of wireless network clients that are permitted or denied access to your wireless network based on their unique MAC addresses. Figure 15.30 shows the MAC address filtering configuration screen on a Linksys WAP. Simply enter the MAC address of a wireless node that you want to allow or deny access to your wireless network.

Configuring Encryption   Enabling encryption ensures that data frames are secured against unauthorized access. To set up encryption, you turn on encryption at the WAP and generate a unique security key. Then you configure all connected wireless nodes on the network with the same key information. Figure 15.31 shows the WPA2 key configuration screen for a Linksys WAP.

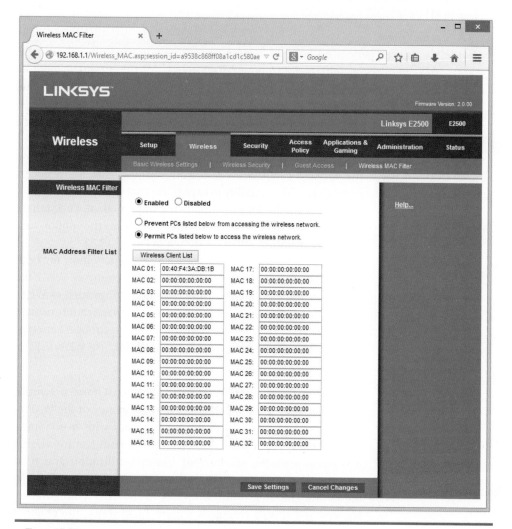

• **Figure 15.30**   MAC address filtering configuration screen for a Linksys WAP

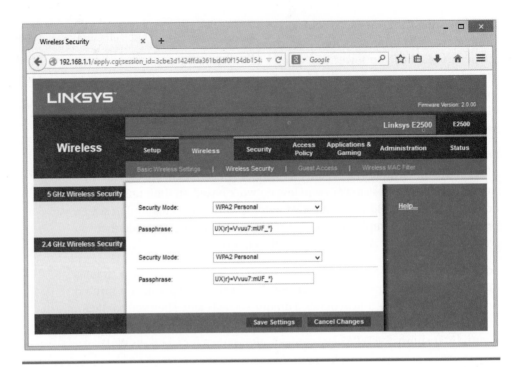

● **Figure 15.31**   Encryption key configuration screen on Linksys WAP

You can generate a set of encryption keys either automatically or manually. You can save yourself a certain amount of effort by using the automatic method. Select an encryption level—the usual choices are either 64-bit or 128-bit—and then enter a unique *passphrase* and click the **Generate** button (or whatever the equivalent button is called in your WAP's software). Then select a default key and save the settings.

The encryption level, key, and passphrase must match on the wireless client node or communication fails. Many access points have the capability to export the encryption key data onto removable media for easy importing onto a client workstation, or you can configure encryption manually using the vendor-supplied configuration utility, as shown in Figure 15.32.

If you have the option, choose WPA2 encryption for both the WAP and the NICs in your network. You configure WPA2 the same way you would WPA. Note that the settings such as WPA2 for the Enterprise assume you'll enable authentication using a RADIUS server (Figure 15.33). Always use the strongest encryption you can. If you have WPA2, use it. If not, use WPA. WEP is always a terrible choice.

Configuring Channel and Frequency   With most home networks, you can simply leave the channel and frequency of the WAP at the factory defaults, but in an environment with overlapping Wi-Fi signals, you'll want to adjust one or both features. Using a wireless analyzer, see current channel utilization and then change your channel to something that doesn't conflict. To adjust the channel, find the option in the WAP configuration screens and simply change it. Figure 15.34 shows the channel option in a Linksys WAP.

● **Figure 15.32**   Encryption screen on client wireless network adapter configuration utility

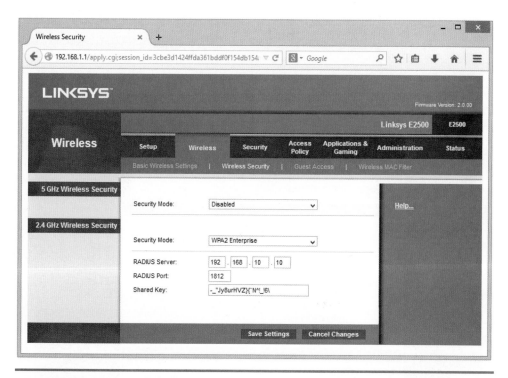

• Figure 15.33   Encryption screen with RADIUS option

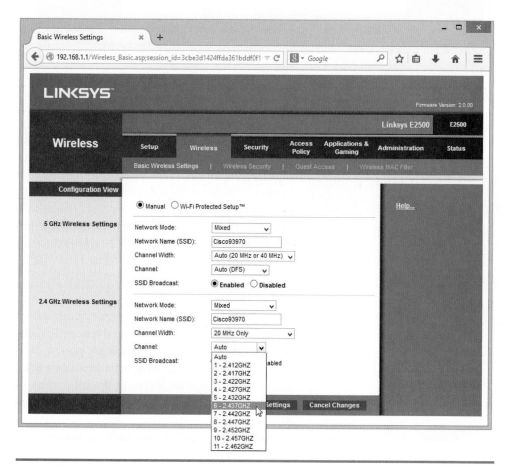

• Figure 15.34   Changing the channel

● **Figure 15.35**   Selecting frequency

With dual-band 802.11n WAPs, you can choose which band to put 802.11n traffic on, either 2.4 GHz or 5.0 GHz. In an area with overlapping signals, most of the traffic will be on the 2.4-GHz frequency because most devices are either 802.11b or 802.11g. You can avoid any kind of conflict with your 802.11n devices by using the 5.0-GHz frequency band instead. Figure 15.35 shows the configuration screen for a dual-band 802.11n WAP.

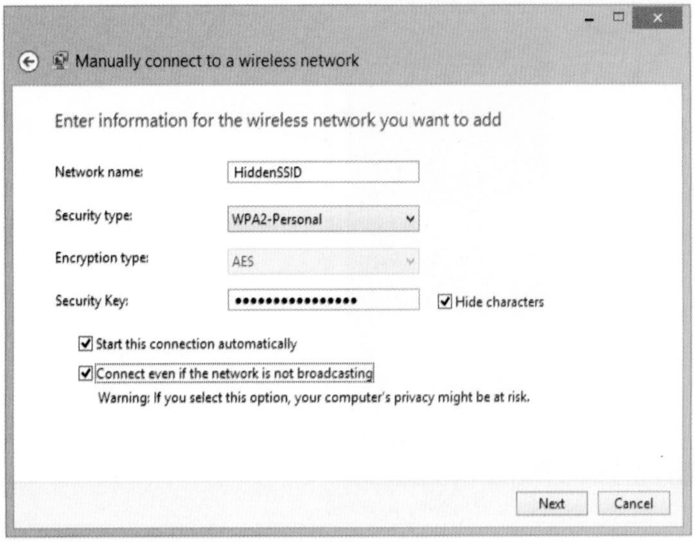

Configuring the Client

As with ad hoc mode wireless networks, infrastructure mode networks require that the same SSID be configured on all nodes and access points. Normally, the client would pick up a broadcast SSID and all you need to do is type in the security passphrase or encryption key. With nonbroadcasting networks, on the other hand, you need to type in a valid SSID as well as the security information (Figure 15.36).

● **Figure 15.36**   Typing in an SSID manually

The important thing to remember is that once you successfully connect to a wireless network, your client will store the settings for that client in a profile. From now on, whenever the client sees a particular SSID, your device will automatically try to connect to that SSID using the encryption and key stored in the profile. Of course, if the wireless network changes in any way—for example, if the encryption password is changed—you won't be able to access the network unless you delete the profile and reacquire the wireless network.

Extending the Network

Creating a Basic Service Set network with a single WAP and multiple clients works in a relatively small area, but you can extend a Wi-Fi network in a couple of ways if you have difficult spaces—with lots of obstructions, for example— or a need to communicate beyond the ~300-foot range of the typical wireless network. Most commonly, you'd add one or more WAPs to create an Extended Service Set. You can also install a wireless bridge to connect two or more wired networks.

Some manufacturers market special Wi-Fi extenders or repeaters that pick up the Wi-Fi signal wirelessly and repeat it into a wider space.

Adding a WAP

To add a WAP to a Wi-Fi network, you'll need to run a cable from a switch on the network to where you want to install it. Configuration is pretty straightforward. Both WAPs require the same ESSID, and if the WAPs are near each other, use separate channels.

Wireless Bridges

Dedicated **wireless bridges** are used to connect two wireless networks together, or to join wireless and wired networks together in the same way that wired switches do. You can also use wireless bridges to join wireless networks with other networked devices, such as printers.

Wireless bridges come in two different flavors: point-to-point and point-to-multipoint. **Point-to-point** bridges can only communicate with a single other bridge and are used to connect two wireless network segments. **Point-to-multipoint** bridges can talk to more than one other bridge at a time and can connect multiple network segments. Figure 15.37 shows a wireless bridge.

Verifying the Installation

• **Figure 15.37** Linksys wireless bridge device

Once you've completed the initial installation of a Wi-Fi network, test it. Move some traffic from one computer to another using the wireless connection. Never leave a job site without verifying the installation.

■ Troubleshooting Wi-Fi

Wireless networks are pretty magical when they work right, but the nature of no wires often makes them vexing things to troubleshoot when they don't.

As with any troubleshooting scenario, your first step in troubleshooting a wireless network is to break down your tasks into logical steps. First, figure out the scope of the wireless networking problem. I like to break wireless problems into three symptom types:

- You can't get on the wireless network. Your client (or clients) may or may not think it's connected, but you can't access shared resources (web pages, remote folders, and so on).

- Your wireless connections are way too slow. Your clients are accessing shared resources.

- Your wireless connection is doing weird things.

CompTIA Network+ objective 4.3 says "Given a scenario, troubleshoot and resolve common wireless issues" and then lists a large number of issues. You can bet good money that CompTIA will give you one or more scenario questions that mention one or more of these issues. Every one of these issues will fit into the three symptoms I just listed. So let's use these symptoms as a tool to organize how you will address these scenarios on the exam (and in the real world as well).

No Connection

Wi-Fi networks want to connect. You rarely if ever get an error on a device that says "You may not speak to WAP55 that is supporting SSID X." Instead, you get more subtle errors such as repeated prompts for passwords, APIPA addresses, and such.

Channel Problems

If you're working with one of the older 802.11 versions using the 2.4-GHz channel, you may have problems with channels. One issue is *overlapping channels.* All 2.4-GHz channels overlap with their nearest channel neighbors. For example, channel 3 overlaps with channels 1, 2, 4, and 5. Some folks make the mistake of configuring an ESSID and setting each WAP only one channel apart. This will lead to connection problems, so always try to stick to using channels 1, 6, and 11 only. *Mismatched channels,* where you set the SSID information correctly but a device is using a different channel than the WAP, may still take place. However, automatic channel selection is now the norm and mismatched channels are extremely rare. If you suspect this is a problem, set your wireless device to auto channel selection.

Wrong Encryption

The term *wrong encryption* can mean one of two things: either you've connected manually to a wireless network and have set up the incorrect encryption type, or you've entered the wrong encryption key. Entering the wrong encryption key is the classic no-errors-but-won't-work issue. In older operating systems, you often would only get one chance to enter a key and if you failed your only clue was that your client got an APIPA address. Pretty much every wireless NIC is set to DHCP and if you don't have the right

Be prepared for scenario questions that quiz you about the limits of the wireless standards, or what CompTIA calls *wireless standard related issues.* This includes throughput speeds (11-, 54-, 100+-Gbps), frequencies, distances, and channel usage. See the above standards discussions for the limitations of each standard.

You can use wireless scanning tools to check for *wireless channel utilization.* These are software tools that give you metrics and reports about nearby devices and which one is connected to which WAP. These tools enable you to discover overworked WAPs, saturated areas, and so on, so you can deploy WAPs to optimize your network.

password your client won't get past the WAP to talk to anything on the network, including the DHCP server.

- Symptoms: not on network, continual prompting for password, APIPA address

- Solution: Enter the correct password

Signal/Power

802.11 is a low-power radio and has a limited range. If the WAP doesn't have enough power, you'll have signal loss and you won't be able to access the wireless network. There are a number of issues that cause power levels to drop too low to connect beyond the obvious "you're too far away" from the WAP.

If you lack enough signal power you have five choices: get closer to the WAP, avoid dead spots, turn up the power, use a better antenna, or upgrade to a newer 802.11 version (like 802.11n or 802.11ac) with features that enable them to use the power they have more efficiently. I'm going to skip moving closer to the WAP as that's a bit obvious, but let's cover the other four.

A **dead spot** is what it sounds like, a place that should be covered by the network signal but where devices get no signal. Dead spots just happen in a wireless network due to environmental factors. When installing a network you must watch out for concrete walls, metal (especially metal studs), and the use of special RF-blocking window film. The solution is more careful planning of WAP placement and realizing that even in the best-planned environment it is not at all uncommon to move WAPs based on the need to clear dead spots.

Increasing the power is actually not that hard to do, depending on the wireless device. Most WAP manufacturers set their radio power levels relatively low out of the box. A few manufacturers—a great example is Cisco on

> Interference can also cause signal loss, but I choose to treat this as a separate issue later in this section. For now we are talking about simple signal loss due to insufficient power.

their high-end WAPs—enable you to increase or to decrease the power (Figure 15.38). Sadly, very few low-end/SOHO devices have a method to increase radio power using the OEM interface.

| Transmitter Power (Configured Power): | ○-1 ○2 ○5 ○8 ○11 ○14 ○17 ○20 ⊙Max | Power Translation Table (mW/dBm) |
| Client Power (dBm): | ○Local ○2 ○5 ○8 ○11 ○14 ○17 ○20 ⊙Max | |

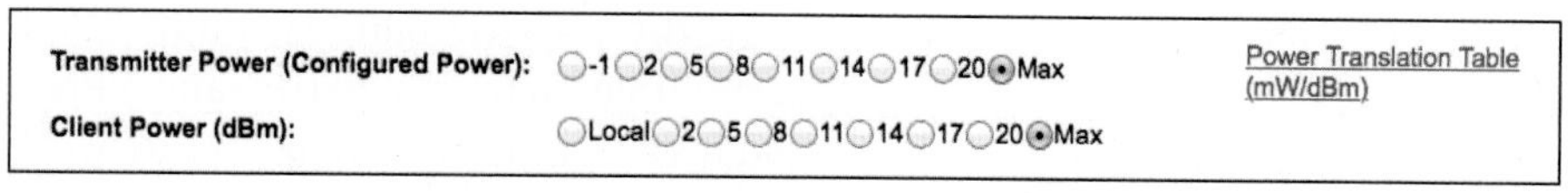

• **Figure 15.38**   Increasing power on a Cisco WAP

If you're willing to gamble, however, you should be able to find a third-party firmware such as OpenWRT which, on certain devices, gives you this capability.

Too many 802.11 installations ignore the antennas, dropping in WAPs using their default antennas. In most cases the omnidirectional antennas that come with WAPs are very good—which is why they are so often the default antennas—but in many cases they are simply the *wrong antenna type* and need to be replaced. If you're losing signal, don't forget to consider if the antenna is wrong for the wireless setup. Watch for scenarios on the CompTIA Network+ exam where replacing an omnidirectional antenna with one or more unidirectional antennas makes an easy fix.

The last power/signal issue is the fact that the MIMO features in 802.11n and 802.11ac are absolutely amazing in their ability to overcome dead spots and similar issues that on earlier versions of 802.11 can only be fixed with aggressive tweaking of WAP locations and antenna types. While MIMO and MU-MIMO aren't only to increase signal distance, it's almost certain you'll see a scenario where simply updating WAPs to 802.11n or 802.11ac will automatically fix otherwise tricky problems.

There are plenty of reasons for a device to run slowly that have nothing to do with wireless. Don't forget issues such as insufficient RAM, malware, and so forth.

Slow Connection

Slow wireless connections are far more difficult to troubleshoot than no connection at all. Unlike a disconnection, where you have obvious and clear clues, a slowdown is just . . . slow. In these situations you are clearly connected to an SSID, you have a good IP address, and the client itself runs well; but data transfer is slow: web pages load slowly, applications time out, and you sense a general, hard-to-measure, irritating slowness.

In general you can trace the cause of this slowness to one of two issues: either you have too many devices overworking your WAPs, or there is too much RFI on the network. Let's look at both of these issues.

Overworked WAPs

An individual WAP has a very specific amount of bandwidth that depends on the version of 802.11 and the way it is configured. Once you hit the maximum bandwidth, you're going to have network slowdowns as the overworked WAP tries to handle all of the incoming wireless connections.

We overwork WAPs in many different ways, but one of the most common is by attaching too many devices to a single SSID over time, what's called *device saturation*. Avoid device saturation by adding more capacity. Careful placement of extra WAPs in high-demand areas is a huge step in the right direction. Usually the best, but most expensive, method is to upgrade your hardware: leaping from the 802.11g to the 802.11ac standard alone makes a massive difference in eliminating device saturation.

Speaking of 802.11ac, the biggest single issue causing device saturation is the imbalance of many devices using the 2.4-GHz band vs. few devices using the 5.0-GHz band. In almost every midsized or larger wireless network, the 2.4-GHz band is simply filled to capacity, even with careful use of multiple channels, SSIDs, and VPNs. We call this **bandwidth saturation** and it's a huge issue with 802.11 networks. There is no answer other than to move to the 5.0-GHz band using primarily 802.11ac.

Another issue that causes WAPs to be overworked is **bounce**, which occurs when a signal sent by one device takes many different paths to get to the receiving systems. These multiple signals are hard for an 802.11 receiver to modulate. We minimize this issue first by trying to reduce anything that might reflect a signal. Secondly, we use WAPs with multiple antennas in a process called *multipath*.

Interference

Radio frequency interference (RFI) is an equally big problem when it comes to wireless network slowdowns. The 802.11 standard is pretty impressive in its ability to deal with noisy RF environments, but there's a point where any environment gets too noisy for 802.11. Interference comes from a number of sources, but basically we can break them down into two categories: RFI from non-Wi-Fi sources and RFI from Wi-Fi networks.

Non-Wi-Fi sources of RFI include lighting and low-power RF devices like Bluetooth, wireless phones, and microwaves. In general these devices can work nicely with 802.11 networks, but too many devices, especially devices too close to 802.11 equipment, can cause problems. The only way to eliminate this type of interference is to shut down or move the devices.

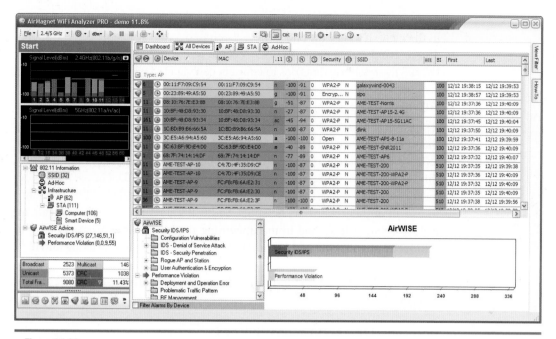

• Figure 15.39 SNR on AirMagnet

When it comes to 802.11-based interference, we are looking mainly at other WAPs generating signals that interfere with ours. The most common problem is that the limited number of 2.4-GHz channels and their natural overlap makes it easy to form overlapped channels.

A few years ago you could jump from one channel to another, using the classic channels 1, 6, or 11 in the United States, but today the most common method is to simply abandon the 2.4-GHz channel by avoiding 802.11g. The fix to interference (other than avoiding RF reflective surfaces) is to scan for RF sources using some form of RF scanner/analyzer. We measure RFI with the signal-to-noise ratio (SNR). Figure 15.39 shows the popular AirMagnet Wi-Fi Analyzer Pro reporting SNR. Use a channel that's not overwhelmed.

Weird Connection

There are a number of situations where devices are connected to a wireless network and run at a good speed but something is wrong—in some cases, dangerously wrong from a security perspective. Let's look at a few of these situations.

Open Networks

Open (non-encrypted) 802.11 networks are the bane of users and administrators. The two biggest challenges are how to avoid unintentionally logging into an open network with an SSID identical to one you have in another location, and how to provide security in an open network environment.

It's very common for your wireless device to access open networks with WAPs that use manufacturer default SSID names such as Linksys or D-Link. The danger with these is that bad guys know that most wireless devices, once they have created a profile to connect to one of these default, open SSIDs, will then automatically connect to them again should they ever see one—and bad guys love to use this as a tool to attack these devices.

The second issue with any open wireless is that all of the data is transferred in the clear. It's easy for bad guys to listen in on your transmissions. The only way to avoid this is either to use a VPN or to use a Web browser add-on, like HTTPS Everywhere, that tries to connect you via HTTPS to every Web page.

Wrong SSID

It's easy to access the wrong SSID. Some 802.11 clients are notorious for moving their list of discovered SSIDs in such a way that you think you are clicking one SSID when you are actually accidentally clicking the wrong one. The only fix to this is to practice diligence when logging onto a new SSID. For example, who hasn't seen SSIDs such as the infamous "attwifi"? This SSID is AT&T's attempt to use all of their clients as hotspots. Sadly, it's a simple process to create an evil twin SSID (described in the upcoming section "Rogue Access Point") to mimic the attwifi SSID and get otherwise unsuspecting people to log into it.

Manually entering an SSID can obviously result in a typo. Luckily, in these cases your typo won't accidentally land you onto another SSID. You'll just get an error.

Untested Updates/Incompatibilities

802.11 is an ever-evolving standard, and manufacturers learned a long time ago to work hard to ensure their devices could evolve with the standard. This means that anyone supporting any 802.11 network is going to find themselves continually updating client firmware/software and WAP firmware. These updates are almost always good, but you need to stay aware of problems.

First, always research and test any update, especially firmware updates as they aren't too easy to reverse. Untested updates that go into your production network can potentially wreak havoc. If at all possible, run updates on a test network first.

Incompatibilities are related to untested updates in that they tend to appear at the same time an update appears. Make sure you are extremely clear on backward compatibility of different 802.11 versions. Also be aware that even in the same type of network there might be incompatibilities. A few years ago I bought what I thought was a dual-band (2.4- and 5.0-GHz) 802.11n WAP. I invested serious money in upgrading my 802.11n NICs in a few clients to accept dual band. Sadly, it wasn't until I was installing the new WAP that I read in the instructions that the WAP only supported one of the two bands at a time, and was totally incompatible with my new, expensive wireless NICs. Ouch! Too bad I didn't test the WAP before I tried to run it in my production environment.

Rogue Access Point

A **rogue access point (rogue AP)** is simply an unauthorized access point. Rogue access points have tortured every wireless network since the day Linksys came out with the first cheap wireless router back in the early 2000s. Most rogue APs aren't evil: just a user wanting to connect to the network who installs a WAP in a handy location into the wired network. Evil rogue APs are far more nefarious, acting as a backdoor to a network or a man-in-the-middle attack, grabbing user names and passwords, among other items.

The most infamous form of rogue AP is called an evil twin. An **evil twin** is a rogue AP that intentionally mimics an existing SSID in order to get people to connect to it instead of the proper WAP. Evil twins work best in unsecured networks such as those you see in airports and hotels.

War Driving and War Chalking

We need to take a moment to discuss one of those weird CompTIA Network+ topics that covers very old issues that don't really exist anymore: war driving and war chalking. A long time ago—as late as around 2005—there weren't very many wireless networks around. Nerdy types would conduct *war driving*: looking for wireless networks by using omnidirectional antennas connected to laptops using wireless sniffing programs (this was well before every OS came with a client that located SSIDs). When a network was found, the war driver would place a special chalk mark on a nearby curb or sidewalk to tell other war drivers the location of the SSID. Figure 15.40 shows some of the more common war chalks.

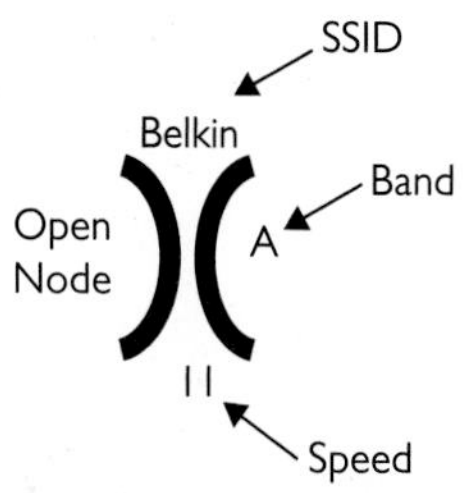

• **Figure 15.40** Sample war chalking mark with explanation

Feeling Blue

Bluetooth is an amazing form of wireless with plenty of good security. Basically, Bluetooth has two important tools to make using it more secure. First, all of today's Bluetooth devices are not visible unless they are manually set to *discovery* or *discoverable mode*. If you have a Bluetooth headset and you want to pair it to your smartphone, there is some place on the phone where you turn on this mode, as shown in Figure 15.41.

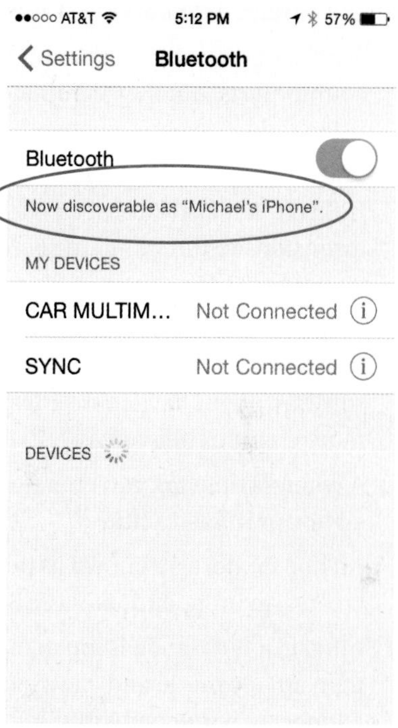

The beauty of discoverable mode is that you have a limited amount of time to make the connection, usually two minutes, before the device automatically turns it off and once again the device is no longer visible. Granted, there is radio communication between the two paired devices that can be accessed by powerful, sophisticated Bluetooth sniffers, but these sniffers are expensive and difficult to purchase and are only of interest to law enforcement and very nerdy people.

The second tool is the requirement of using a four-digit PIN during the pairing process. When one device initiates a discoverable Bluetooth device, the other device sees the request and generates a four-digit PIN. The first device must then enter that code and the pairing takes place.

• **Figure 15.41** Setting up discoverable mode

The problem with these two security tools is that they weren't required on the early generations of Bluetooth. From the time Bluetooth devices started coming out in the late 1990s up until around 2005, a number of devices skipped the discovery mode and/or using PINs. This resulted in several Bluetooth attacks, two of which show up in the CompTIA Network+ exam objectives: Bluejacking and Bluesnarfing. *Bluejacking* was the process of sending unsolicited messages to another Bluetooth device. These devices would pop up on your screen. Bluejacking wasn't considered anything more than irritating, but Bluesnarfing was another matter. *Bluesnarfing* used weaknesses in the Bluetooth standard to steal information from other Bluetooth devices.

The important thing to remember about Bluejacking and Bluesnarfing is that both of these cannot work unless you have a Bluetooth device that ignores both discover mode and PIN codes. These types of devices no longer exist, making these issues no longer viable.

■ Chapter Summary

After reading this chapter and completing the exercises, you should understand the following about wireless networking.

Explain wireless networking standards

- Wireless networks operate much like their wired counterparts, but they eliminate network cabling by using radio waves as a network medium.

- The most common wireless networking standard is IEEE 802.11, also known as Wi-Fi. 802.11 includes extensions to the standard such as 802.11a, 802.11b, 802.11g, 802.11n, and 802.11ac.

- Modern versions of Windows and OS X have wireless NIC configuration software built in. Third-party software might have more advanced features for more complex networks.

- A wireless network can operate in one of two modes: ad hoc or infrastructure.

- Ad hoc mode, also known as peer-to-peer mode, creates an Independent Basic Service Set (IBSS).

- Infrastructure mode is much more commonly used than ad hoc mode and allows wireless networks to connect to wired networks. A single wireless access point connecting computers in infrastructure mode is called a Basic Service Set (BSS). If multiple WAPs are used, an Extended Basic Service Set (EBSS) is created, although most techs simply refer to it as an Extended Service Set (ESS).

- Wireless networking ranges are also affected by environmental factors, interference from other wireless devices, and solid objects.

- The Basic Service Set Identifier (BSSID) identifies a single wireless network that acts as a broadcast domain.

- The Service Set Identifier (SSID) configuration parameter enables you to set a basic level of access security. Properly configured SSIDs, or network names, exclude any wireless network device that does not share the same SSID.

- A Wi-Fi network with multiple WAPs applies the SSID to the ESS, creating an Extended Service Set Identifier (ESSID).

- The original 802.11 standards use the 2.4-GHz frequency band, whereas later standards use either 2.4-GHz or 5.0-GHz frequency bands. These frequencies allow the wireless networks to operate with less chance of interference from other wireless devices that are not part of the network.

- Spread-spectrum radio waves distribute data in small chunks over different frequencies to reduce interference from other wireless devices that are not part of the network. 802.11 networks use different forms of spread spectrum.

- Wi-Fi channels use a portion of the available frequency spectrum to tune out potential interference further. At 2.4 MHz, most WAPs use channels 1, 6, or 11. The 5.0-GHz WAPs have a wider variety of channels, so overlap isn't a problem.

- Wi-Fi networks use carrier sense multiple access with collision avoidance (CSMA/CA) to send frames. CSMA/CA is both proactive and reactive in that it attempts to avoid collisions before they happen rather than simply detecting them when they occur, and it retransmits frames that weren't acknowledged.

- Currently, only the Distributed Coordination Function (DCF) method of CSMA/CA is implemented. DCF uses IFS wait periods, backoff periods, and acknowledgments (ACK) to detect and avoid collisions and resend frames that collided with other frames.

- Wireless networking speeds range from 2 Mbps to a theoretical limit of 600 Mbps. The speed is affected by the distance between wireless nodes, interference from other wireless devices such as wireless phones or baby monitors, and solid objects such as metal plumbing or air conditioning units.

- The 802.11b standard supports data throughput up to 11 Mbps over 300 feet on the 2.4-GHz frequency band.

- The 802.11a standard, which was released after 802.11b, supports data throughput up to 54 Mbps over 150 feet on the 5.0-GHz frequency band.

- The 802.11g standard supports data throughput up to 54 Mbps over 300 feet on the 2.4-GHz frequency band. 802.11g is also backward-compatible with 802.11b.

- The 802.11n standard supports data throughput up to 600 Mbps, theoretically, over 300 feet on the 2.4- or 5.0-GHz frequency band. 802.11n requires MIMO and transmit beamforming to achieve its greater data throughput. It is also backward-compatible with 802.11b, 802.11a, and 802.11g.

- 802.11n WAPs can transmit in three different modes: legacy, mixed, and greenfield. Legacy mode supports earlier standards; mixed enables some earlier devices to work better than expected. Greenfield mode means everything is running at the higher speed.

- The 802.11ac standard supports data throughput up to 1 Gbps over 300 feet on the 5.0-GHz frequency.

- Wireless networks may be secured with MAC address filtering, although this method can be easily hacked by spoofing.

- A RADIUS server stores user names and passwords, enabling you to set a user's rights once in the network. A supplicant contacts a NAS, which, in turn, contacts the RADIUS server.

- Data should be encrypted when being transferred across a wireless network. WEP offers no protection because it is easily hacked. WPA is better because it uses the Temporal Key Integrity Protocol (TKIP). WPA2, which uses the Advanced Encryption Standard (AES), is the strongest of the three.

- Better WAPs and switches can use Power over Ethernet (PoE) to provide electrical power to the WAP via the Ethernet cable that connects it with the switch. Both the WAP and the switch must have this capability built in for it to work.

Describe the process for implementing Wi-Fi networks

- The first step in creating a wireless network is to create a site survey, which identifies other wireless networks or objects that may cause interference and helps you to determine the best location for your WAPs.

- Wireless networking hardware must be installed in all the clients. Most laptops have wireless NICs built in, but a USB NIC can be used as an alternative. Desktop computers may use a PCIe card. Any computer with a USB port can use a USB wireless NIC.

- Configuring a NIC for ad hoc networking requires the SSID, IP address, channel, and sharing to be configured.

- Configuring a NIC for infrastructure networking requires planning the optimal placement of the WAP and its antennas. A replacement antenna can strengthen the wireless signal and extend the range. The WAP also needs to be configured with the proper settings for the SSID, security, and encryption options.

- A wireless network's range can be extended by adding multiple WAPs. The additional WAPs typically connect to each other via a hard cable.

- A wireless bridge connects two wireless networks together. A point-to-point bridge can only communicate with a single other bridge, whereas a point-to-multipoint bridge can communicate with more than one other bridge at the same time.

Describe troubleshooting techniques for wireless networks

- Troubleshooting Wi-Fi networks falls into three categories: you can't get on the network, the connection is slow, and the wireless connection is weird.

- When you can't get on a wireless network, the problem could be wrong encryption or insufficient signal. Many WAPs can increase their power. If your WAP does not do so natively, you might still be able to succeed with a third-party tool.

- Most modern operating systems inform you that you have the wrong encryption by prompting you to reenter information. This is not the case with older OSs.

- A slow wireless connection might be caused by overworked WAPs or interference from other sources. Solutions include adding more capacity with more WAPs and removing sources of interference. You can run a Wi-Fi analyzer to find such sources.

- Weird connections compromise security. Open networks, wrong SSIDs, and untested updates can create risk in Wi-Fi. Rogue access points are usually harmless, but some can be used to grab user names and passwords.

■ Key Terms

802.1X *(440)*
802.11 *(429)*
802.11a *(436)*

802.11a-ht *(437)*
802.11b *(436)*
802.11g *(437)*

802.11g-ht *(437)*
802.11i *(442)*
802.11n *(437)*
ad hoc mode *(432)*
Advanced Encryption Standard (AES) *(442)*
bandwidth saturation *(462)*
Basic Service Set (BSS) *(433)*
Basic Service Set Identifier (BSSID) *(433)*
bounce *(462)*
bring your own device (BYOD) *(445)*
carrier sense multiple access with collision avoidance (CSMA/CA) *(435)*
channel *(434)*
channel bonding *(437)*
dead spot *(461)*
dipole antenna *(451)*
direct-sequence spread-spectrum (DSSS) *(434)*
Distributed Coordination Function (DCF) *(435)*
encryption *(441)*
evil twin *(464)*
Extended Service Set (ESS) *(433)*
Extended Service Set Identifier (ESSID) *(434)*
Extensible Authentication Protocol (EAP) *(440)*
frequency-hopping spread-spectrum (FHSS) *(434)*
gain *(452)*
greenfield mode *(438)*
Independent Basic Service Set (IBSS) *(432)*
infrastructure mode *(432)*
interframe gap (IFG) *(435)*
latency *(436)*
legacy mode *(437)*
link state *(431)*
MAC address filtering *(439)*
mixed mode *(437)*
multiple in/multiple out (MIMO) *(437)*
Network Access Server (NAS) *(440)*
network name *(433)*

orthogonal frequency-division multiplexing (OFDM) *(434)*
peer-to-peer mode *(432)*
personal area network (PAN) *(446)*
Point Coordination Function (PCF) *(435)*
point-to-multipoint *(459)*
point-to-point *(459)*
Power over Ethernet (PoE) *(445)*
radio frequency interference (RFI) *(462)*
RADIUS server *(440)*
roaming *(434)*
rogue access point (rogue AP) *(464)*
Service Set Identifier (SSID) *(433)*
signal strength *(431)*
site survey *(446)*
SSID broadcast *(433)*
supplicant *(440)*
Temporal Key Integrity Protocol (TKIP) *(442)*
thick client *(444)*
thin client *(444)*
transmit beamforming *(437)*
unidirectional antenna *(452)*
VLAN pooling *(445)*
Wi-Fi *(429)*
Wi-Fi analyzer *(446)*
Wi-Fi Protected Access (WPA) *(442)*
Wi-Fi Protected Access 2 (WPA2) *(443)*
Wi-Fi Protected Setup (WPS) *(438)*
Wired Equivalent Privacy (WEP) *(441)*
wireless access point (WAP) *(430)*
wireless analyzer *(446)*
wireless bridge *(459)*
wireless controller *(444)*
wireless LAN (WLAN) *(446)*
wireless network *(429)*
wireless survey tool *(446)*
WPA2-Enterprise *(443)*

■ Key Term Quiz

Use the Key Terms list to complete the sentences that follow. Not all the terms will be used.

1. When a network uses the 802.11 standard, it is said to be a(n) _____.

2. Establishing a unique _____ or network name helps ensure that only wireless network

devices configured similarly are permitted access to the network.

3. Of the several wireless encryption protocols, _____ is least secure.

4. Of the three different spread-spectrum broadcasting methods, _____ sends data out on

different frequencies at the same time and, therefore, uses considerably more bandwidth.

5. WPA uses _____ to encrypt data, whereas WPA2 uses the more secure _____.

6. _____ allows devices on 802.11n networks to make multiple simultaneous connections, allowing for a theoretical throughput of 600 Mbps.

7. 802.11 implements _____, which proactively avoids network packet collisions rather than simply detecting them when they occur.

8. Connecting two Wi-Fi computers through a WAP uses _____, whereas connecting the two wirelessly together directly uses _____.

9. Some 802.11g and all 802.11n devices enable _____ to use two channels at the same time for transmission.

10. When you want to extend a wireless network, simply add another _____.

■ Multiple-Choice Quiz

1. With what technology can you avoid finding an AC outlet for a WAP?
   A. AES
   B. PoE
   C. Powered Wi-Fi
   D. TKIP

2. Where would wireless access points likely be found? (Select three.)
   A. Airport
   B. Café
   C. Historic buildings
   D. Secure facilities

3. Which of the following statements about SSIDs are true? (Select three.)
   A. All wireless networks use them.
   B. Only one wireless device uses them.
   C. They should be unique to your wireless LAN.
   D. They are broadcast, by default, by most wireless network devices.

4. What is the best way to connect multiple wireless segments together?
   A. Use an 802.11g network adapter.
   B. Use an 802.11i network adapter.
   C. Use a point-to-multipoint wireless bridge.
   D. Use a point-to-point wireless bridge.

5. What should you use when you want to limit access to your wireless network based on the physical, hard-coded address of each wireless network device?
   A. Bus scheduling
   B. Encoding
   C. Encryption
   D. MAC address filtering

6. What process secures a wireless network by protecting data packets being transmitted?
   A. Data packeting
   B. Pulse encoding
   C. Data encryption
   D. MAC broadcasting

7. What is the predefined silence period between data transmissions called?
   A. IEEE
   B. IFG
   C. ISM
   D. IPX

8. Which of the following networking standards operates at a frequency of 5.0 GHz?
   A. 802.11a
   B. 802.11b
   C. 802.11g
   D. 802.11i

9. Which of the following is the wireless network encryption method that is most secure?

   A. MAC address filtering

   B. WEP

   C. WPA

   D. WPA2

10. Which of the following is known as a Basic Service Set in infrastructure mode?

    A. A WAP

    B. A WPA

    C. A RADIUS server

    D. A TKIP

11. In an attempt to maximize your wireless throughput while minimizing interference on your brand new 802.11g WAP, which setting should you change?

    A. Change the WAP setting not to broadcast the SSID.

    B. Change the channel to 6.

    C. Change the channel to anything other than 6.

    D. Change the frequency to 5.0 GHz.

12. What innovation enables 802.11n networks to minimize dead spots?

    A. Channel bonding

    B. FIFO

    C. MIMO

    D. Transit beamforming

13. What's the optimal range for an 802.11n connection?

    A. 50'

    B. 150'

    C. 300'

    D. 600'

14. To achieve maximum Wi-Fi coverage in a room, where should you place the WAP?

    A. Place the WAP on the north side of the room.

    B. Place the WAP in the center of the room.

    C. Place the WAP near a convenient electrical outlet.

    D. It doesn't matter where you place the WAP.

15. Dave has set up a Wi-Fi network for his café that works well for most patrons but works poorly on the patio. What's the least expensive option for making Wi-Fi work for the patio customers?

    A. Replace the factory antennas on the WAP.

    B. Exchange his 802.11g WAP for an 802.11n WAP.

    C. Reverse the polarity on the WAP's antennas.

    D. Run another network drop to the patio and add a second WAP.

■ Essay Quiz

1. Some friends of yours insist that wireless network standard 802.11a was available before 802.11b. They also say 802.11a is "better" than 802.11b. Find the pages in this chapter that discuss these standards, and jot down some notes to explain the facts.

2. You are enrolled in a writing class at the local community college. This week's assignment is to write on a technical subject. Write a short paragraph about each of the wireless standards that can reach theoretical speeds of 54 Mbps.

3. Prepare a short memo to your instructor (or friend) that outlines the basic differences between the WEP, WPA, and WPA2 encryption methods. Use any standard memo format you are familiar with. Include a company or school logo on the top of the page to make the memo appear as if it were printed on company stationery (or "letterhead").

4. Write a few paragraphs describing the pros and cons of both wired and wireless networks. Specifically, compare 100BaseT to the 802.11g standard. (Review Chapter 5, "Modern Ethernet," for more details on 100BaseT.) Then conclude with a statement of your own personal preference.

Lab Projects

• Lab Project 15.1

You just received a nice tax return and want to expand your home network. Your current wired home network setup consists of two Intel Core 2 Duo-class desktop PCs with 10/100-Mbps NICs and a relative's older laptop with both an RJ-45 port and 802.11b wireless built in. The main Internet connection coming into your home enters your more powerful desktop system first and then spreads out to a 10-Mbps hub. Because you're spending your own money buying equipment, you seek a solution that will satisfy your needs for a long time.

You want to buy your new equipment locally, so you can set it up right away. Use the Internet to explore local stores' prices and equipment. Also check out reviews of the items you are interested in obtaining. After you have done sufficient research, prepare an itemized price list with your choices arranged like the following table:

ITEM	STORE/MODEL	PRICE	QUANTITY	TOTAL
Wireless NICs, PCIe				
Wireless NICs, Express Card				
Wireless Access Point				
Other				
TOTALS				

• Lab Project 15.2

You have been tasked with expanding your company's wireless network. Your IT Manager asked you to create a presentation that explains wireless routers and their functions. She specifically said to focus on the 802.11b and 802.11g wireless network standards. Create a brief, yet informative, PowerPoint presentation that includes comparisons of these two technologies. You may include images of actual wireless bridges from vendor Web sites as needed, being sure to cite your sources. Include any up-to-date prices from your research as well.

Virtualization and Cloud Computing

In this chapter, you will learn how to

- Describe the concepts of virtualization
- Explain why PC and network administrators have widely adopted virtualization
- Describe how virtualization manifests in modern networks
- Describe the service layers and architectures that make up cloud computing

For those of us used to the idea that a single computer system consists of one operating system running on its own hardware, virtualization challenges this definition. In the simplest terms, *virtualization* is the process of using powerful, special software running on a computer to create a complete environment that imitates (virtualizes) all of the hardware you'd see on a real computer. We can install and run an operating system in this virtual environment exactly as if it were installed on its own physical computer. That **guest** environment is called a **virtual machine (VM)**. Figure 16.1 shows one such example: a system running Windows 7 using a program called VMware Workstation to host a virtual machine running Ubuntu Linux.

In this chapter we'll explore virtualization in detail. We will see why we use it and how it influences the structure of modern networks. With this knowledge as a foundation, we'll examine important concepts in cloud computing (including the role virtualization plays), how cloud computing adds value to the Internet, and how cloud networks compare to and interface with both traditional networks and each other.

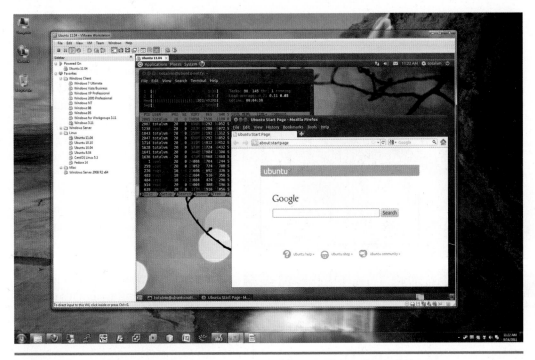

• Figure 16.1　VMware running Linux

Historical/Conceptual

What Is Virtualization?

Ask 100 people what the term *virtual* means and you'll get a lot of different answers. Most people define *virtual* with words like "fake" or "pretend," but these terms only begin to describe it. Let's try to zero in on virtualization using a term that hopefully you've heard: *virtual reality.* For most of us, the idea of virtual reality starts with someone wearing headgear and gloves, as shown in Figure 16.2.

The headgear and the gloves work together to create a simulation of a world or environment that appears to be real, even though the person wearing them is located in a room that doesn't resemble the simulated space. Inside this virtual reality you can see the world by turning your head, just as you do in the real world. Software works with the headset's inputs to emulate a physical world. At the same time, the gloves enable you to touch and move objects in the virtual world.

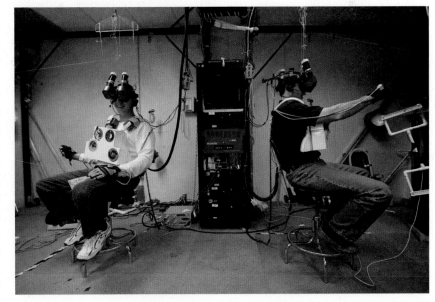

• Figure 16.2　Virtual reality training (Image courtesy of NASA)

To make virtual reality effective, the hardware and software need to work together to create an environment convincing enough for a human to work within it. Virtual reality doesn't have to be perfect—it has limitations—but it's pretty cool for teaching someone how to fly a plane or do a spacewalk without having to start with the real thing (Figure 16.3).

Virtualization on a computer is virtually (sorry, can't pass up the pun) the same as virtual reality for humans. Just as virtual reality creates an environment that convinces humans they're in a real environment, virtualization convinces an operating system it's running on its own hardware.

• **Figure 16.3**   Using virtual reality to practice spacewalking (Image courtesy of NASA)

Meet the Hypervisor

Because virtualization enables one machine—called the **host**—to run multiple operating systems simultaneously, full virtualization requires an extra layer of sophisticated programming called a **hypervisor** to manage the vastly more complex interactions.

A hypervisor has to handle every input and output that the operating system would request of normal hardware. With a good hypervisor like VMware Workstation you can easily add and remove virtual hard drives, virtual network cards, virtual RAM, and so on. Figure 16.4 shows the Hardware Configuration screen from VMware Workstation.

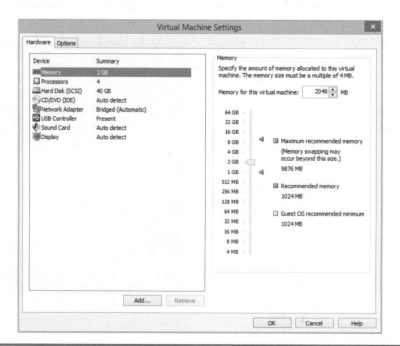

• **Figure 16.4**   Configuring virtual hardware in VMware Workstation

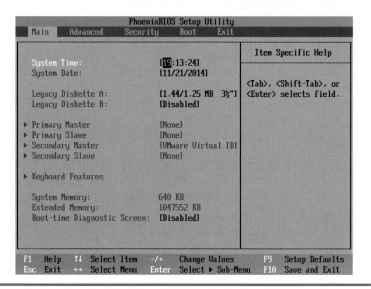

• **Figure 16.5**   System Setup in VMware Workstation

Virtualization even goes so far as to provide a virtualized BIOS and System Setup for every virtual machine. Figure 16.5 shows VMware Workstation displaying the System Setup, just like you'd see it on a regular computer.

Emulation vs. Virtualization

Virtualization takes the hardware of the host system and segments it into individual virtual machines. If you have an Intel system, a hypervisor creates a virtual machine that acts exactly like the host Intel system. It cannot act like any other type of computer. For example, you cannot make a virtual machine on an Intel system that acts like a Sony PlayStation 3. Hypervisors simply pass the code from the virtual machine to the actual CPU.

Emulation is very different from virtualization. An **emulator** is software or hardware that converts the commands to and from the host machine into an entirely different platform. Figure 16.6 shows a Super Nintendo Entertainment System emulator, Snes9X, running a game called Donkey Kong Country on a Windows system.

Desktop Virtualization

This chapter will show you a few of the ways you can perform virtualization, but before I go any further let's take the basic pieces you've learned about virtualization and put them together in one of its simplest forms. In this example, I'll use

• **Figure 16.6**   Super Nintendo emulator running on Windows

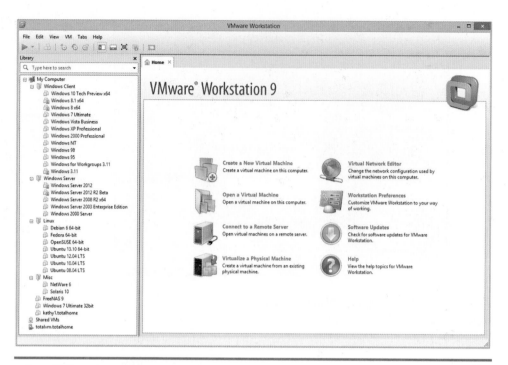

• **Figure 16.7** VMware Workstation

the popular VMware Workstation (Figure 16.7) on a Windows system and create a virtual machine running Ubuntu Linux.

Clicking **Create a New Virtual Machine** prompts you for a typical or custom setup (Figure 16.8). These settings are only for backward-compatibility with earlier versions of VMware, so just click **Next**.

The next dialog box is where the fun starts. Here, VMware Workstation asks for an operating system installation disc. Just because you're creating a virtual machine, don't think the operating system and applications aren't real. You need to install an operating system on that virtual machine. You can do this using some form of optical media, just as you would on a machine without virtualization. Would you like to use Microsoft Windows in your virtual machine? No problem, but know that every virtual machine on which you create and install Windows requires a separate, legal copy of Windows.

Because virtual machines are so flexible on hardware, VMware Workstation enables you to use either the host machine's optical drive or an ISO file. I'm installing Ubuntu,

• **Figure 16.8** Selecting a Typical or Custom setup

• **Figure 16.9** Selecting the installation media

• **Figure 16.10** Setting the virtual drive size

so I downloaded an ISO image from the Ubuntu website (www.ubuntu.com), and as Figure 16.9 shows, I've pointed the dialog box to that image.

If you look closely at Figure 16.9, you'll see that VMware reads the installation media and detects the operating system (note the "Ubuntu 64-bit 14.04.1 Detected"). Because VMware knows this operating system, it configures all of the virtual hardware settings automatically: amount of RAM, virtual hard drive size, and so on. You can change any of these settings, either before or after the virtual machine is created. Refer to Figure 16.5 to see these settings. Next, you need to accept the size of the virtual drive, as shown in Figure 16.10.

You also need to give the virtual machine a name. By default, VMware Workstation uses a simple name. For this overview, accept the default name: Ubuntu (plus some version-specific information). This dialog box also lets you decide where you want to store the files that comprise the virtual machine. Note that VMware uses a folder in the user's Documents folder called Virtual Machines (Figure 16.11).

• **Figure 16.11** Entering VM name and location

After you've gone through all the configuration screens, you can start using your virtual machine. You can start, stop, pause, add, or remove virtual hardware.

VMware is very convenient; it even configures the boot order in the virtual system setup to boot first from the installation media, making the Ubuntu installation automatic (Figure 16.12).

> Use descriptive names for virtual machines. This will save you a lot of confusion when you have multiple VMs on a single host.

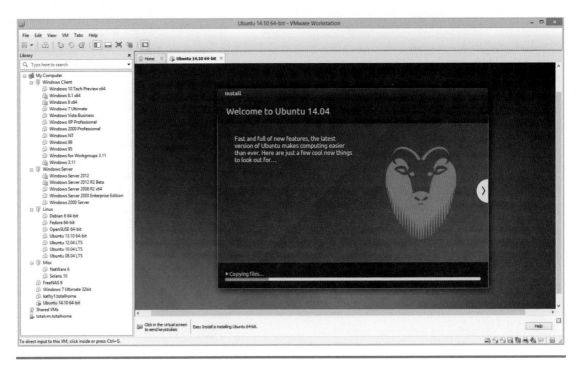

• **Figure 16.12**   Ubuntu installing into the new virtual machine

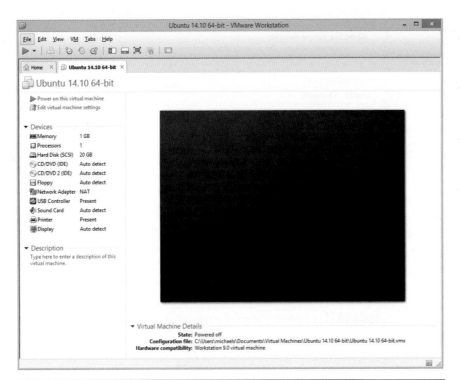

• **Figure 16.13**   VMware Workstation with a single VM

After the virtual machine installs, you then treat the VM exactly as though it were a real machine. The only big difference is that VMware Workstation replaces CTRL-ALT-DELETE with CTRL-ALT-INSERT by default. Figure 16.13 shows VMware Workstation with the single VM installed but not running. A VM goes through a POST process just like any computer, as shown in Figure 16.14. If you wish, you can even access a complete virtual System Setup by pressing the DELETE key just like on a real system.

Congratulations! You've just installed a *virtual desktop*. Virtual desktops were the first type of popular virtual machines seen in the PC world, championed by VMware and quickly copied by other virtualization programs.

There's a lot more to virtualization than just virtual desktops, however, but before I dive in too far, let's step back a moment and understand a very important question: Why do we virtualize?

• **Figure 16.14**   POST in a virtual machine

Test Specific

■ Why Do We Virtualize?

Virtualization has taken the networking world by storm, but for those who have never seen virtualization, the big question has got to be: Why? Let's talk about the benefits of virtualization. While you read this section, keep in mind two important things:

- A single hypervisor on a single system will happily run as many virtual machines as its RAM, CPU, and drive space allow. (RAM is almost always the limiting factor.)

- A virtual machine that's shut down is no more than a file or folder sitting on a hard drive.

Power Saving

Before virtualization, each server OS needed to be on a unique physical system. With virtualization, you can place multiple virtual servers on a single physical system, reducing electrical power use substantially. Rather than one machine running a Windows server and acting as a file server and DNS server, and a second machine running Linux for a DHCP server, for example, the same computer can handle both operating systems simultaneously. Apply this over an enterprise network or on a data server farm, and the savings—both in terms of dollars spent and electricity used—are tremendous.

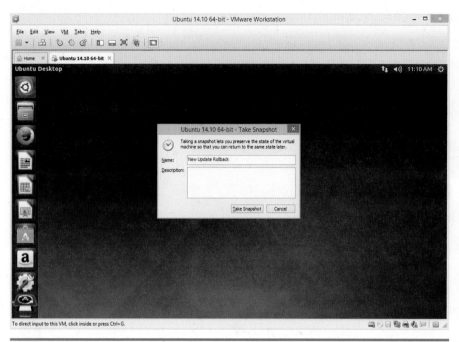

Similar to power saving, why buy a high-end server, complete with multiple processors, RAID arrays, redundant power supplies, and so on, and only run a single server? With virtualization, you can easily beef up the RAM and run a number of servers on a single box.

System Recovery

The most popular reason for virtualizing is probably to keep uptime percentage as high as possible. Let's say you have a Web server installed on a single system. If that system goes down—due to hacking, malware, or so on—you need to restore the system from a backup, which may or may not be easily at hand. With virtualization, you merely need to shut down the virtual machine and reload an alternate copy of it.

Most virtual machines let us take a **snapshot,** which saves the virtual machine's state at that moment, allowing us to quickly return to this state later. Snapshots are great for doing risky (or even not-so-risky) maintenance with a safety net. They aren't, however, a long-term backup strategy—each snapshot may reduce performance and should be removed as soon as the danger has passed. Figure 16.15 shows VMware Workstation saving a snapshot.

• **Figure 16.15**   Saving a snapshot

System Duplication

Closely tied to system recovery, system duplication takes advantage of the fact that VMs are simply files: like any other file, they can be copied. Let's say you want to teach 20 students about Ubuntu Linux. Depending on the hypervisor you choose (VMware does this extremely well), you can simply install a hypervisor on 20 machines and copy a single virtual machine to all the computers. Equally, if you have a virtualized Web server and need to add another Web server (assuming your physical box has the hardware to support it), why not just make a copy of the server and fire it up as well?

Research

The system shown in Figure 16.16 could obviously never run all those VMs at the same time.

Here's a great example that happens in my own company. I sell my popular Total Tester test banks: practice questions for you to test your skills on a broad number of certification topics. As with any distributed program, I tend to get a few support calls. Running a problem through the same OS, even down to the service pack, helps me solve it. In the pre-virtualization days, I usually had seven to ten multi-boot PCs just to keep active copies of specific Windows versions. Today, a single hypervisor enables me to support a huge number of Windows versions on a single machine (Figure 16.16)

Now that we know why virtualization is useful to us, let's take a look at how virtualization is implemented in networks.

Virtualization in Modern Networks

When it comes to servers, virtualization has pretty much taken over. Many of the servers we access, particularly web and email servers, are now virtualized. Like any popular technology, there are a lot of people continually working to make virtualization better. The VMware Workstation example shown earlier in this chapter is a very powerful desktop application, but it still needs to run on top of a single system that is already running an operating system—the host operating system. What if you could improve performance by removing the host operating system altogether and install nothing but a hypervisor? Well, you can! This is done all the time with another type of powerful hypervisor/OS combination called a *bare-metal* hypervisor. We call it bare metal because there's no other software between it and the hardware—just bare metal. The industry also refers to this class of hypervisors as *Type-1*, and applications such as VMware Workstation as *Type-2*.

In 2001 VMware introduced a bare-metal hypervisor, originally called ESX, that sheds the unnecessary overhead of an operating system. ESX has since been supplanted by ESXi in VMware's product lineup. ESXi is a free hypervisor that's powerful enough to replace the host operating system on a physical box, turning the physical machine into a system that does nothing but support virtual ones. ESXi, by itself, isn't much to look at; it's a tiny operating system/hypervisor that's often installed on something other than a hard drive. A host running its hypervisor from flash memory can dedicate all of its available disk space to VM storage, or even cut out the disks altogether and keep its VMs on a storage area network, which we'll discuss later in the chapter. Figure 16.17 shows how I loaded my copy of ESXi: via a small USB thumb drive. The server loads ESXi off the thumb drive when I power it up, and in short order a very rudimentary interface appears where I can input essential information, such as a master password and a static IP address.

Don't let ESXi's small size fool you. It's small because it only has one job: to host virtual machines. ESXi is an extremely powerful bare-metal hypervisor.

• **Figure 16.16** Lots of VMs used for research

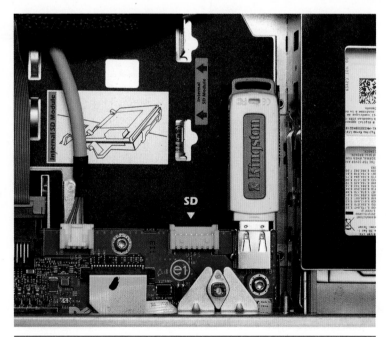

• **Figure 16.17** USB drive on server system

Hypervisors

While you have many choices when it comes to desktop virtualization, your choices for real bare-metal hypervisors on Intel-based systems are limited to VMware's ESXi, Microsoft's Hyper-V, and Citrix's XenServer. These embedded hypervisors scale readily and support common features like remote VM storage, live migration, and virtual network configuration.

- **VMware vSphere Hypervisor (ESXi)**   Industry-leading ESXi has a tiny disk footprint and easily scales from a single server up to a whole data center. ESXi often pioneers new features, has wide third-party support, and has a large community of established users.

- **Microsoft Hyper-V**   Hyper-V comes with Microsoft Server and Windows 8. Microsoft is investing heavily in Hyper-V, and it has captured substantial market share from VMware. It integrates well with Microsoft's server management software and can even run Linux VMs.

- **Citrix XenServer**   Based on the open source Xen project and built on Linux, XenServer is a powerful hypervisor that serves as the foundation for massive cloud offerings (which we'll discuss later in the chapter) by Amazon, IBM, and RackSpace. While Xen lacks the market share of VMware, its open source nature, low price (of free!), and popularity with cloud providers make it worth considering.

Administering a Hypervisor

Powerful hypervisors like ESXi and Hyper-V are rarely administered directly at the box. Instead you use tools like VMware's vSphere Client (Figure 16.18) or Microsoft's Hyper-V Manager to create, configure, and maintain virtual machines on the host from the comfort of a client computer running this program. Once the VM is up and running, you can close the vSphere Client or Hyper-V Manager and the VM will continue to run happily on the server. For example, let's say you create a VM and install a Web server on that VM. As long as everything is running well on the Web server, you will find yourself only using the vSphere Client or Hyper-V Manager for occasional maintenance and administration.

Scaling Virtualization

To understand the importance of virtualization fully, you need to get a handle on how it increases flexibility as the scale of an operation increases. Let's take a step back and talk about money. One of the really great things money does is give us

• **Figure 16.18**   VMware vSphere Client

common, easily divisible units we can exchange for the goods and services we need. When we don't have money, we have to trade goods and services to get it, and before we had money at all we had to trade goods and services for other goods and services.

Let's say I'm starving and all I have is a hammer, and you just so happen to have a chicken. I offer to build you something with my hammer, but all you really want is a hammer of your own. This might sound like a match made in heaven, but what if my hammer is actually worth at least five chickens, and you just have one? I can't give you a fifth of a hammer, and once I trade the hammer for your chicken, I can't use it to build anything else. I have to choose between going without food and wasting most of my hammer's value. If only my hammer was money.

In the same vein, suppose Mario has only two physical, non-virtualized servers; he basically has two really expensive hammers. If he uses one server to host an important site on his intranet, its full potential might go almost unused (especially since his intranet site will never land on the front page of reddit). But if Mario converts these machines into a small, centrally managed server cluster of virtual-machine hosts, he has taken a big step toward using his servers in a new, more productive way.

In this new model, Mario's servers become less like hammers and more like money. I still can't trade a fifth of my hammer for a chicken, but Mario can easily use a virtual machine to serve his intranet site and only allocate a fifth—or any other fraction—of the host's physical resources to this VM. As he adds hosts to his cluster, he can treat them more and more like a pool of common, easily divisible units used to solve problems. Each new host adds resources to the pool, and as Mario adds more and more VMs that need different amounts of resources, he increases his options for distributing them across his hosts to minimize unused resources (Figure 16.19).

As his cluster grows, Mario is going to be able to use some really exciting developments in data storage, virtual networking, and software-defined networking to increase the flexibility and efficiency of his hardware and network.

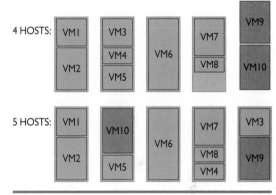

• **Figure 16.19**   No vacancy on these hosts

Data Storage

Storage (hard drives, basically) tends to be either highly under- or over-utilized on individual hosts. It's common to see situations where drives sit empty in one host while another runs out of space. Equally, maintenance of drives on individual hosts is a bit of a pain: even with RAID and backups, losing a drive on a host is at best an inconvenience and at worst the loss of critical services and data.

One of the ways to overcome these two issues is to take all the storage from all the hosts and consolidate the data in a single, separate system. In this section, you're going to learn about two popular methods: SAN and NAS. Both of these technologies predate virtualized systems, but given that hypervisors can boot from removable flash media, separating storage from virtualized systems is a comfortable fit. These technologies tend to be pricey so they generally aren't worthwhile for one or two servers. As our collection of virtualized hosts begins to grow, however, moving the storage out of the host starts making sense. Let's look at SAN and NAS and see how they are used to centralize storage outside of the hosts.

Storage Area Networks You might remember from CompTIA A+ that hard drive storage is broken up into tiny sectors, but you might not know that these sectors are also known as *blocks*. You might also remember that to access the hard drive, you have to plug it into an interface like SATA or maybe even SCSI, which your operating system uses to read and write to blocks on the disk. A **storage area network (SAN)** is a server that can take a pool of hard disks and present them over the network as any number of logical disks. The interface it presents to a client computer pretends to be a hard disk and enables the client's operating system to read and write blocks over a network.

Think of a drive accessed through the SAN as a virtual disk; much as the hypervisor convinces the operating system it runs on its own hardware, the SAN convinces the OS it is interacting with a physical hard drive. Just like with a traditional hard disk, we have to format a virtual disk before we can use it. But unlike a traditional hard disk, the virtual disk the SAN presents to us could be mapped to a number of physical drives in a number of physical locations, or even to other forms of storage.

One of the benefits of using a SAN is that, by just reading and writing at the block level, it avoids the performance costs of implementing its own file system. The SAN leaves it up to the client computers to implement their own file systems—these clients often use specialized shared file system software designed for high volume, performance, reliability, and the ability to support multiple clients using one drive.

When it comes to the infrastructure to support a SAN, there are two main choices: **Fibre Channel (FC)** and **Internet Small Computer System Interface (iSCSI)**.

- Fibre Channel is, for the most part, its own ecosystem designed for high-performance storage. It has its own cables, protocols, and switches, all increasing the costs associated with its use. While more recent developments like Fibre Channel over Ethernet (FCoE) make Fibre Channel a little more flexible within a local wired network, long-distance FC is still clumsy without expensive cabling and hardware.

- iSCSI is built on top of TCP/IP, enabling devices that use the SCSI protocol to communicate across existing networks using cheap, readily available hardware. Because the existing networks and their hardware weren't built as a disk interface, performance can suffer. Part of this performance cost is time spent processing frame headers. We can ease some of the cost of moving large amounts of data around the network at standard frame size by using **jumbo frames**. Jumbo frames are usually 9000 bytes long—though technically anything over 1500 qualifies—and they reduce the total number of frames moving through the network.

Network Attached Storage **Network attached storage (NAS)** is essentially a dedicated file server that has its own file system and typically uses hardware and software designed for serving and storing files. While a SAN shares a fast, low-level interface that the OS can treat just like it was a disk, the NAS—because it has its own internal file system—has to perform file-system work for all of its clients. While the simplicity and low price of a NAS make it attractive for some uses, these performance issues limit its utility in high-performance virtualization clusters.

Virtual Networking

I'll let you in on a secret: the software that runs network devices can also be run in a virtual machine. A network admin can create the virtual version of a network device on-the-fly without purchasing new hardware, or spending a Saturday at the office to move and re-cable existing hardware. These virtual networking components live on the hypervisor with the virtual servers they support. Let's take a look at the ones CompTIA wants you to know about.

Virtual Switches   Imagine for a moment that you have three virtual machines. You need all of these machines to have access to the Internet. Therefore, you need to give them all legitimate IP addresses. The physical server, however, only has a single NIC. There are two ways in which virtualization gives individual VMs valid IP addresses. The oldest and simplest way is to *bridge the NIC*. Each bridge is a software connection that passes traffic from the real NIC to a virtual one (Figure 16.20). This bridge works at Layer 2 of the OSI model, so each virtual NIC gets a legitimate, unique MAC address.

A subset of this type of bridging is to give every VM its own physical NIC (Figure 16.21). In this case, you're still bridging, but every virtual NIC goes straight to a dedicated physical NIC.

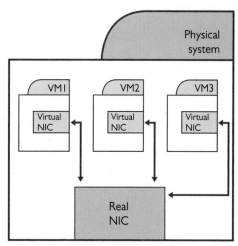

• **Figure 16.20**   Bridged NICs

> There is no difference between a virtual vs. a physical NIC, once properly configured. Virtual NICs have MAC addresses just like a physical NIC. You set up everything about a virtual NIC: IP address, subnet mask, etc., exactly as you do with a physical NIC.

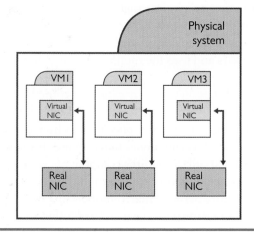

• **Figure 16.21**   Dedicated bridged NICs

The technology behind bridging NICs is a **virtual switch**, which is just software that does the same Layer 2 (Figure 16.22) switching a hardware switch does, including features like VLANs. The big difference is what it means to "plug" into the virtual switch. When the NICs are bridged, the VMs and the host's NIC are all connected to the virtual switch. In this mode, think of the NIC as the uplink port on a hardware switch. This makes virtual switches a very powerful component for networking your

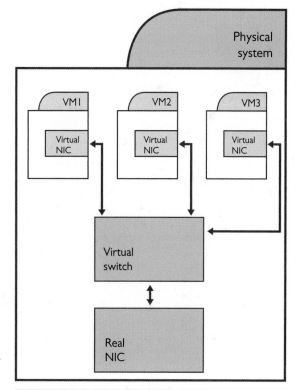

• **Figure 16.22**   Virtual switch

VMs—but just like physical networks, we need more than just Layer 2 switching. That's where virtual routers and firewalls come in.

> If you're interested in reading more about virtual routers and firewalls, a couple of interesting product lines to look at are Brocade's Vyatta vRouter and Cisco's Cloud Services Routers.

Virtual Routers and Firewalls   Similar to how virtual machines enable us to easily reallocate computing resources when demand changes, **virtual routers** let us dynamically reconfigure networks. This lets the network keep up when VMs are moved from host to host to meet demand or improve resource use. The virtual routers are just VMs like any other; we can allocate more resources to them as traffic grows, instead of having to buy bigger, better physical routers. When it comes to firewalls, the same rules apply: **virtual firewalls** can protect servers where it would be hard, costly, or impossible to insert a physical one.

Software Defined Networking

Traditionally, hardware routers and switches were designed with two closely integrated parts: a *control plane* that makes decisions about how to move traffic, and a *data plane* that is responsible for executing those decisions. The control plane on a router, for example, is what actually speaks the routing protocols like OSPF and BGP, discussed in Chapter 8, "Routing," and builds the routing tables that it gives to the data plane. The router's data plane reads incoming packets and uses the routing table to send them to their destination.

Software defined networking (SDN) cuts the control plane of individual devices out of the picture and lets an all-knowing program called a *network controller* dictate how both physical and virtual network components move traffic through the network (Figure 16.23). SDN requires components with data planes designed to take instructions from the network controller instead of their own control plane. While it's important enough that SDN allows for a master controller, the really revolutionary idea behind SDN is that the network controller is *programmable*: we can write code that controls how the entire network will behave.

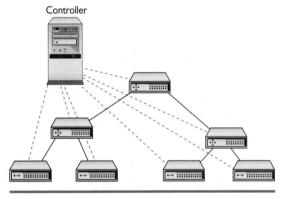

• **Figure 16.23**   A controller controls traffic to all the routers and switches

■ To the Cloud

While simple virtualization enabled Mario to optimize and reallocate his computing and networking resources in response to his evolving needs (as described earlier in the chapter), he can't exceed the capabilities of the hardware he owns, the networks he builds, and his ability to maintain them. Luckily, he's no longer stuck with just the hardware he owns. Because his virtual machines are just files running on a hypervisor, he can run them in *the cloud* on networks of servers worldwide. When we talk about the cloud, we're

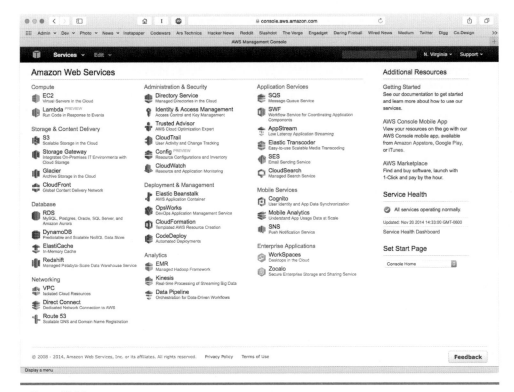

• **Figure 16.24**   Amazon Web Services Management Console

talking not just about friendly file-storage services like Dropbox or Google Drive, but also about simple interfaces to a vast array of on-demand computing resources sold by Amazon (Figure 16.24), Microsoft, and many other companies over the open Internet. The technology at the heart of these innovative services is virtualization.

The Service-Layer Cake

Service is the key to understanding the cloud. At the hardware level, we'd have trouble telling the difference between the cloud and the servers and networks that comprise the Internet as a whole. We use the servers and networks of the cloud through layers of software that add great value to the underlying hardware by making it simple to perform complex tasks or manage powerful hardware. As end users we generally interact with just the sweet software icing of the service-layer cake—Web applications like Dropbox, Gmail, and Facebook, which have been built atop it. The rest of the cake exists largely to support Web applications like these and their developers. Let's slice it open (Figure 16.25) and start at the bottom.

• **Figure 16.25**   A tasty three-layer cake

Infrastructure as a Service

Building on the ways virtualization allowed Mario to make the most efficient use of hardware in his local network, large-scale global **Infrastructure as a Service (IaaS)** providers use virtualization to minimize idle hardware, protect against data loss and downtime, and respond to spikes in demand. Mario can use big IaaS providers like Amazon Web Services (AWS) to launch new virtual servers

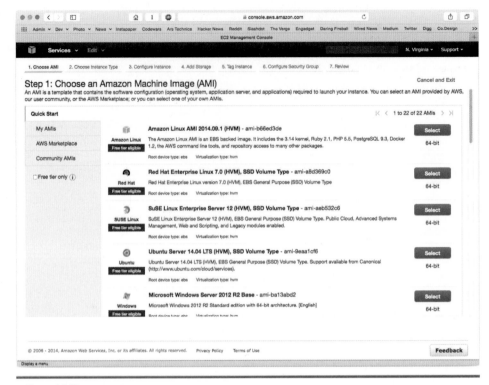

• Figure 16.26 Creating an instance on AWS EC2

using an operating system of his choice on demand (Figure 16.26) for pennies an hour. The beauty of IaaS is that you no longer need to purchase expensive, heavy hardware. You are using Amazon's powerful infrastructure as a service.

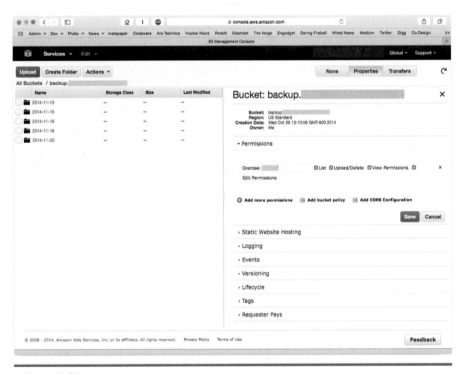

A huge number of websites are really more easily understood if you use the term Web applications. If you want to access Mike Meyers' videos, you go to hub. totalsem.com. This website is really an application (written in house) that you use to watch videos, practice simulation questions, etc. This web application is a great tool, but as more people access the application we often need to add more capacity so you won't yell at us for a slow server. Luckily, our application is designed to run distributed across multiple servers. If we need more servers, we just add as many more virtual servers as we need. But even this is just scratching the surface. AWS (Figure 16.27) provides many of the services needed to drive popular, complex

• Figure 16.27 Amazon S3

Web applications—unlimited data storage, database servers, caching, media hosting, and more—all billed by usage.

The hitch is that, while we're no longer responsible for the hardware, we are still responsible for configuring and maintaining the operating system and software of any virtual machines we create. This can mean we have a lot of flexibility to tune it for our needs, but it also requires knowledge of the underlying OS and time to manage it.

Platform as a Service

Web applications are built by programmers. Programmers do one thing really well: they program. The problem for programmers is that a web application needs a lot more than a just programmer. To develop a web application, we need people to manage the infrastructure: system administrators, database administrators, general network support, etc. A web application also needs more than just hardware and an operating system. It needs development tools, monitoring tools, database tools and potentially hundreds of other tools and services. Getting a web application up and running is a big job.

A **Platform as a Service (PaaS)** provider gives programmers all the tools they need to deploy, administer and maintain a web application. They have some form of infrastructure, which could be provided by an IaaS, but on top of that infrastructure the PaaS provider builds a platform: a complete deployment and management system to handle every aspect of a web application.

The important point of PaaS is that the infrastructure underneath the PaaS is largely invisible to the developer. The PaaS provider is aware of their infrastructure but the developer cannot control it directly, and doesn't need to think about its complexity. As far as the programmer is concerned, the PaaS is just a place to deploy and run their application.

Heroku, one of the earliest PaaS providers, creates a simple interface on top of the IaaS offerings of AWS, further reducing the complexity of developing and scaling Web applications. Heroku's management console (Figure 16.28) enables developers to increase or decrease the capacity of an application with a single slider, or easily set up add-ons that add a database, monitor your logs, track performance, and more. It could take days for a tech or developer unfamiliar with the software and services to install, configure, and integrate a set of these services with a running application; PaaS providers help cut this down to minutes or hours.

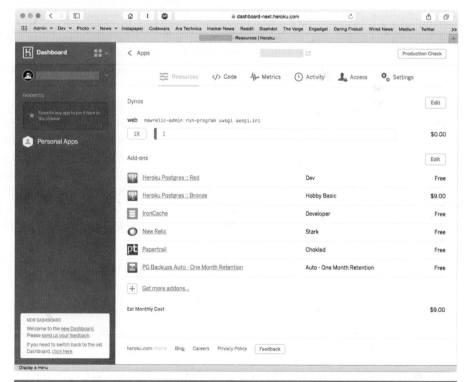

• **Figure 16.28**   Heroku's management console

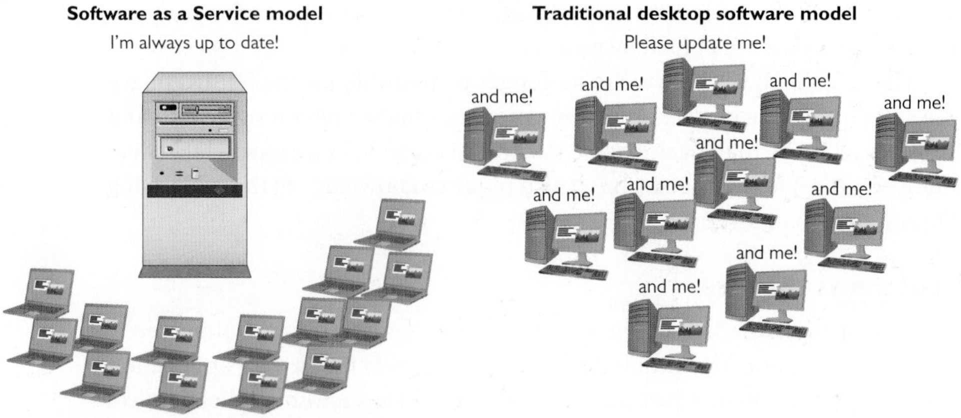

Software as a Service model
I'm always up to date!

Traditional desktop software model
Please update me!
and me! and me! and me! and me! and me! and me! and me! and me! and me! and me!

• **Figure 16.29** SaaS vs. every desktop for themselves

Software as a Service

Software as a Service (SaaS) sits at the top layer of the cake. SaaS shows up in a number of ways, but the best examples are the web applications we just discussed. Some Web applications, such as Total Seminars Training Hub, charge for access. Other Web applications, like Google Maps, are offered for free. Users of these Web applications don't own this software; you don't get an installation DVD, nor is it something you can download once and keep using. If you want to use a Web application you must get on the Internet and access the site. While this may seem like a disadvantage at first, the **Software as a Service (SaaS)** model provides access to necessary applications wherever you have an Internet connection, often without having to carry data with you or regularly update software. At the enterprise level, the subscription model of many SaaS providers makes it easier to budget and keep hundreds or thousands of computers up-to-date (Figure 16.29).

The challenge to perfectly defining SaaS is an argument that almost anything you access on the Internet could be called SaaS. A decade ago we would've called the Google search engine a website, but it provides a service (search) that you do not own and that you must access on the Internet. If you're on the Internet, you're arguably always using SaaS.

It isn't all icing, though. In exchange for the flexibility of using public, third-party SaaS, you often have to trade strict control of your data. Security might not be crucial when someone uses Google Drive to draft a blog post, but many companies are concerned about sensitive intellectual property or business secrets traveling through untrusted networks and being stored on servers they don't control.

Ownership and Access

Security concerns like those just discussed don't mean organizations have to forfeit all of the advantages of cloud computing, but they do make their management think hard about the trade-offs between cost, control, customization, and privacy. Some organizations also have unique capacity, performance, or other needs no existing cloud provider can meet. Each organization makes its own decisions about these trade-offs, but the result is usually a cloud network that can be described as public, private, community, or hybrid.

Public Cloud

Most folks usually just interact with a **public cloud**, a term used to describe software, platforms, and infrastructure delivered through networks that the general public can use. When we talk about *the* cloud, this is what we mean. Out on the open, public Internet, cloud services and applications can collaborate in ways that make it easier to think of them collectively as *the cloud* than as many public clouds. The public doesn't *own* this cloud—the hardware is often owned by companies like Amazon, Google, and Microsoft—but there's nothing to stop a company like Netflix from building its Web application atop the IaaS offerings of all three of these companies at once.

The public cloud sees examples of all the *x*aaS varieties, which give specific names to these *cloud concepts*:

- Public IaaS
- Public PaaS
- Public SaaS

Private Cloud

If a business wants some of the flexibility of the cloud, needs complete ownership of its data, and can afford both, it can build an internal cloud the business actually owns—a **private cloud**. A security-minded company with enough resources could build an internal IaaS network in an onsite data center. Departments within the company could create and destroy virtual machines as needed, and develop SaaS to meet collaboration, planning, or task and time management needs all without sending the data over the open Internet. A company with these needs but without the space or knowledge to build and maintain a private cloud can also contract a third party to maintain or host it.

Again, there are private versions of each of the cloud concepts:

- Private IaaS
- Private PaaS
- Private SaaS

Community Cloud

While a community center is usually a public gathering place for those in the community it serves, a **community cloud** is more like a private cloud paid for and used by more than one organization. Community clouds aren't run by a city or state for citizens' use; the community in this case is a group of organizations with similar goals or needs. If you're a military contractor working on classified projects, wouldn't it be nice to share the burden of defending your cloud against sophisticated attackers sponsored by foreign states with other military and intelligence contractors?

Just like with the public and private cloud, there are community cloud versions of all the *x*aaS varieties:

- Community IaaS
- Community PaaS
- Community SaaS

Hybrid Cloud

Sometimes we *can* have our cake and eat it too. Not all data is crucial, and not every document is a secret. Needs that an organization can only meet in-house might be less important than keeping an application running when demand exceeds what it can handle onsite. We can build a **hybrid cloud** by connecting some combination of public, private, and community clouds, allowing communication between them. Using a hybrid cloud model can mean not having to maintain a private cloud powerful enough to meet peak demand—an application can grow into a public cloud instead of grind to a halt, a technique called *cloud bursting*. But a hybrid cloud isn't just about letting one Web application span two types of cloud—it's also about integrating services across them. Let's take a look at how Mario could use a hybrid cloud to expand his business.

Mario runs a national chain of sandwich shops and is looking into drone-delivered lunch. He'll need a new application in his private cloud to calculate routes and track drones, and that application will have to integrate with the existing order-tracking application in his private cloud. But then he'll also need to integrate it with a third-party weather application in the public cloud to avoid sending drones out in a blizzard, and a flight-plan application running in a community cloud to avoid other drones, helicopters, and aircraft (and vice versa). The sum of these integrated services and applications *is* the hybrid cloud that will power Mario's drone-delivered lunch. Like the other three clouds, the hybrid cloud sees examples of all the *x*aaS varieties, which give specific names to these cloud concepts:

- Hybrid IaaS
- Hybrid PaaS
- Hybrid SaaS

Chapter 16 Review

■ Chapter Summary

After reading this chapter and completing the exercises, you should understand the following about virtualization and cloud computing.

Describe the concepts of virtualization

- Virtual reality creates a simulation of a world or environment that appears to be real, even though the person wearing the headgear and gloves is located in a room that doesn't resemble the simulated space. Virtual computing follows a similar concept.

- In virtual computing, software called a hypervisor creates one or more environments on a single machine. You can install an operating system into each environment, called a virtual machine (VM), that can run simultaneously.

- The hypervisor handles communication between the operating systems installed and the hardware. The hypervisor can easily add and remove hard drives, memory space, networking capabilities, and more.

- Emulation differs from virtualization: emulation software translates commands from an application into machine language the host computer can understand, whereas virtualization creates an environment that is native to the application—an operating system, in this case—requiring no translation.

Explain why PC and network administrators have widely adopted virtualization

- Going virtual enables companies to combine multiple servers onto fewer machines than in traditional computing. This offers tremendous savings in hardware purchases, electricity use, and in the space used for computing.

- Because a VM is only a single file or two, a hacked or corrupted server can rapidly be replaced with a snapshot (restore point) taken of the properly working server. This provides better uptime than in a traditional server setup. Likewise, the small number of files makes it easy to duplicate a VM.

- The ability to run many operating systems on a single physical machine makes multiplatform testing and research much easier and less costly than with traditional setups.

Describe how virtualization manifests in modern networks

- The simplest way virtualization manifests in networks is through one or more virtual machines performing chores that would have taken multiple physical boxes previously. VMware Workstation is the most common VM implementation tool in these sorts of networks.

- More aggressive network needs can use bare-metal virtualization software that requires no operating system on the VM-supporting machine. These hypervisors, such as VMware ESXi, take up minuscule space. You manage them remotely through client software, rather than at the server box.

- The more popular native hypervisors include VMware ESXi, Microsoft Hyper-V, and Citrix XenServer.

- Storage can be consolidated and centralized with a storage area network (SAN) or network attached storage (NAS). This can improve performance and makes maintaining, administering, and backing up the drives easier.

- Multiple VMs can share a single network connection through bridge or switch functions built into the hypervisor. You'll most commonly see these referred to as virtual switches.

- Virtual routers and firewalls are software-only versions of network components that can be created on demand and simplify restructuring the network.

- Software defined networking (SDN) allows a master controller to determine how network components will move traffic through the network.

Describe the service layers and architectures that make up cloud computing

- The cloud is the vast array of on-demand computing resources sold by Amazon, Microsoft, and many other companies over the open Internet.

- Virtual servers and virtual network components can be created in the cloud using Infrastructure as a Service (IaaS) providers, often at rates measured in pennies per hour.

- Platform as a Service (PaaS) providers combine the infrastructure needed to run a modern Web application with simple administrative controls. PaaS trades some of the flexibility of IaaS in order to drastically cut the time and knowledge needed to build and run a Web application.

- Centralized applications accessed over a network are known as Software as a Service (SaaS). They are often built on top of IaaS or PaaS offerings and are usually available as a subscription or for free.

- The public cloud is what we really mean when we talk about "the cloud." In reality, the public cloud is a number of large corporate-owned cloud networks that are open to the public for use and billed by usage.

- When a single organization owns a cloud network that is closed to outside use, we call it a private cloud. Private clouds require much space, money, and expertise to build and maintain, but can provide greater security and customization.

- Multiple organizations—usually with shared goals—can create a community cloud that is shared among the organizations. This community cloud can be tailored to the group's special needs and lets them share the burden of meeting those needs.

- A hybrid cloud is a combination of multiple private, public, or community clouds.

■ Key Terms

community cloud *(491)*

emulator *(475)*

Fibre Channel (FC) *(484)*

guest *(472)*

host *(474)*

hybrid cloud *(492)*

hypervisor *(474)*

Infrastructure as a Service (IaaS) *(487)*

Internet Small Computer System Interface (iSCSI) *(484)*

jumbo frame *(484)*

network attached storage (NAS) *(484)*

Platform as a Service (PaaS) *(489)*

private cloud *(491)*

public cloud *(491)*

snapshot *(480)*

Software as a Service (SaaS) *(490)*

software defined networking (SDN) *(486)*

storage area network (SAN) *(484)*

virtual firewall *(486)*

virtual machine (VM) *(472)*

virtual router *(486)*

virtual switch *(485)*

■ Key Term Quiz

Use the Key Terms list to complete the sentences that follow. Not all the terms will be used.

1. A(n) _____ is a complete environment for a guest operating system to function as though that operating system was installed on its own computer.

2. A program that runs multiple operating systems simultaneously is called a(n) _____.

3. John's hypervisor enables all five of the virtual machines on his system to communicate with each other through the _____ without going outside the host system.

4. You can create a(n) _____ as a restore point for a virtual machine.

5. _____ is a protocol for interfacing with a storage area network (SAN) over TCP/IP.

6. An Ethernet _____ is larger than 1500 bytes.

7. A(n) _____ is a virtual machine running on a hypervisor.

8. _____ is a competing protocol to iSCSI.

9. In _____, a controller is responsible for deciding how traffic will move through the network.

10. A computer that is using the SCSI protocol to write to a disk may actually be writing to a(n) _____.

■ Multiple-Choice Quiz

1. Tom is installing a Windows 10 virtual machine onto a copy of VMware Workstation. Which of the following does he need?

   A. A valid copy of Windows 10 installation media

   B. The IP address for the virtual machine host

   C. A disk image of another computer's installed Windows 10

   D. A valid ESXi key

2. The number of running virtual machines on a single host is limited by what factor?

   A. Physical RAM

   B. Virtual RAM

   C. Physical NICs

   D. Virtual NICs

3. When a virtual machine is not running, how is it stored?

   A. Firmware

   B. RAM drive

   C. Optical disc

   D. Files

4. The boss flies into your office yelling that the virtualized Web server has been hacked and now displays only purple dinosaurs. Which of the following would be the proper way to fix the problem?

   A. Restore from backup

   B. Run System Restore

   C. Reinstall Windows

   D. Load an earlier snapshot

5. Powerful hypervisors like ESXi are often booted from _____.

   A. Floppy diskettes

   B. Flash memory

   C. Firmware

   D. Windows

6. A _____ is a computer running multiple virtual machines.

   A. Hypervisor

   B. Host

   C. Platform

   D. Server

7. A network administrator can make a new subnet for a group of virtual machines without moving or re-cabling hardware by using a _____.

   A. Virtual NIC

   B. Virtual switch

   C. Virtual router

   D. Virtual firewall

8. Tom has a great idea for a new photo-sharing service for real pictures of Bigfoot, but he doesn't own any servers. Where can he quickly create a new server to build his dream?

   A. Public cloud

   B. Private cloud

   C. Community cloud

   D. Hybrid cloud

9. Ford logs into a site that continually selects and plays music for him based on how he has rated past selections. What is this type of service called?

   A. Software as a Service

   B. Infrastructure as a Service

   C. Platform as a Service

   D. Network as a Service

10. After the unforeseen failure of his Bigfoot-picture-sharing service, bgFootr—which got hacked when he failed to stay on top of his security updates—Tom has a great new idea for a new service to report UFO sightings. What service would help keep him from having to play system administrator?

    A. Software as a Service

    B. Infrastructure as a Service

    C. Platform as a Service

    D. Network as a Service

11. BigCorp is a successful Bigfoot-tracking company with an internal service to manage all of its automated Bigfoot surveillance stations. A Bigfoot migration has caused a massive increase in the amount of audio and video sent back from their stations. In order to add short-term capacity, they can create new servers in the public cloud. What model of cloud computing does this describe?

    A. Public cloud

    B. Private cloud

    C. Community cloud

    D. Hybrid cloud

12. A(n) _____ device allows you to read and write files over the network.

    A. iSCSI

    B. SMB

    C. Storage area network

    D. Network attached storage

13. A network of hospitals wants to create a centralized records service but has to observe serious governmental regulations on patient privacy. Which two of the following would best meet the network's needs?

    A. Public cloud

    B. Private cloud

    C. Community cloud

    D. Hybrid cloud

14. A _____ hypervisor improves the performance of virtualization by removing the underlying operating system.

    A. Hypervisor as OS

    B. Hardware abstraction layer

    C. Bare-metal

    D. Low-overhead

15. Which of the following are advantages of a virtual machine over a physical machine? (Select two.)

    A. Maximizes performance

    B. Capability to quickly add and remove hardware

    C. Consolidation of multiple physical machines

    D. Comes with an operating system

◼ Essay Quiz

1. A company has three discrete servers: a file server running Linux, a contact and e-mail server running Windows Server, and a DNS and DHCP server running an earlier version of Windows Server. Make a case for or against going virtual with this setup.

2. Write a short essay comparing Infrastructure as a Service with Platform as a Service.

Lab Projects

• Lab Project 16.1

Acquire a copy of VMware Workstation or another virtualization program and create some virtual machines. If you can add the VM host to a working network, then attempt to access the different VMs running and access other computers from any of the VMs. This should be a fun lab. Here are links to VM software:

www.vmware.com/products/workstation
www.virtualbox.org/wiki/Downloads

• Lab Project 16.2

Analyze the current server setup at your school or office. Does it use virtualization? If so, which programs does it use for which purposes? If not, discuss how virtualization could be implemented to make the network more efficient.

chapter 17

Building a Real-World Network

The currency of real networking is not greed but generosity.

—KEITH FERRAZZI

In this chapter, you will learn how to

- Explain the concepts of basic network design
- Describe unified communication features and functions
- Describe the function and major components of an ICS/SCADA network

A network tech with solid practical knowledge can handle just about any networking environment. You've seen so far in this book the processes and technologies for working with local area networks (LANs) and connecting to wide area networks (WANs). You've dealt with wired and wireless networks. And you've delved into the intricacies of TCP/IP.

This chapter lays out yet another kind of network, a medium-sized space spanning multiple buildings, in this case a **campus area network (CAN)**. Plus, it looks at the technologies that help organizations communicate and operate effectively in both commercial and industrial settings.

 Cross Check

MAN

We talked about another network type way back in Chapter 14, "Remote Connectivity," so check your knowledge here. What is a MAN? How does it differ from the CAN described here?

Here's the scenario we'll use in this chapter to describe a CAN. A company—the Bayland Widgets Corporation (BWC)—has just successfully crowd-funded to build and market its latest and greatest widget. They've gone from a startup operating in cafés to an established company operating in a new campus that has three buildings (Figure 17.1). One is the commercial office, where the sales and managerial staffs operate. The second is a factory space for building the new widget. The final building is the warehouse and shipping facility.

The commercial space houses the primary servers, but a fiber-based network connects all three buildings, all of which have communications equipment installed. Plus the factory and warehouse have robots and other mechanical systems that need computer-based controls.

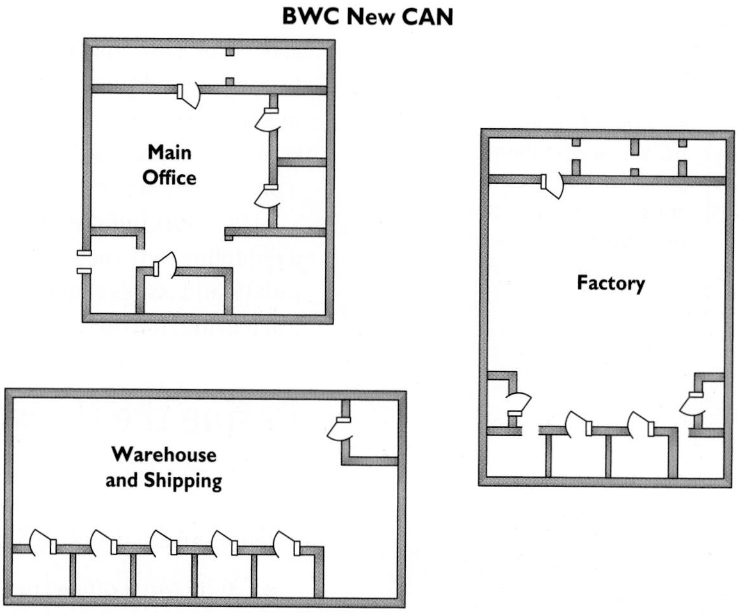

The discussion in this chapter starts with network design, then turns to the gear used for the unified communication systems that bind all the buildings together. The chapter wraps up with a look at the industrial control systems, such as SCADA, that run the factory and warehouse portions. Let's get to work.

BWC New CAN

• **Figure 17.1**   The new campus

Test Specific

■ Designing a Basic Network

Designing and building a network follows similar requirements, regardless of the scope of that network. The CompTIA Network+ exam objective 1.12 lists seven categories to consider:

1. **List of requirements**   Define the network's needs. Why are you installing this network? What primary features do you need?

2. **Device types/requirements**   What equipment do you need to build this network? How should you organize the network?

3. **Environment limitations**   What sort of building or buildings do you need to work with to install a network? Do you have access to the walls or ceiling?

4. **Equipment limitations**   Are you using existing equipment, applications, or cabling?

5. **Compatibility requirements**   What sort of compatibility issues do you have between old and new devices?

6. **Wired/wireless considerations**   What type of structured cabling do you need? Does this network need wireless? How do you connect to the Internet?

7. **Security considerations**   How will you deal with computer, data, and network security?

This list is workable, but seems a little too redundant in places. It also leaves out a few important considerations, like costs vs. budget. Plus, although I've numbered them here, these steps might come in any order. Even though network security is in the sixth position, for example, you might make a decision concerning the firewall as early as Step 2. Don't be afraid to jump around a bit as needed to construct the network.

Let's start building the Bayland Widgets CAN using this list somewhat as a guideline. For each point, I'll use a scenario or two to consider some of the pitfalls and issues that might pop up. Later chapters cover security in detail, so I'm leaving that out of the discussion in this chapter for the most part.

Define the Network Needs

What does a CAN need in a network? In this case, because Bayland Widgets has operations, manufacturing, and shipping, things can get a little complicated. Here are the most obvious points:

- Individual offices need workstations that can do specific jobs.
- The company needs servers that can handle anything thrown at them.
- The buildings need internal cabling.
- The buildings need intermediate distribution frames (IDFs) to provide connections . . .
- And the buildings need solid connectivity.

That seems to cover the hardware side of things, at least as far as the CAN goes. That leaves out the specific robotics or mechanical systems that handle production, warehousing, and shipping, but we can assume for now that those are all proprietary. Even if you end up working for such a company, you'd have to learn their specific systems. That's well beyond what a CompTIA Network+ tech knows right out of the box.

On the software side of things, the workstations and servers need appropriate operating systems. The network protocols need to be in place.

Once the hardware and software inside the network works, then the network needs connectivity beyond. That usually means connecting to the Internet today, though private networks within organizations continue to operate.

In the case of Bayland Widgets, on top of the standard network structures for a CAN, they need to add specific systems for unified communication and industrial controls. I'll cover those in the second and third major sections of this chapter.

Try This!

What Are *Your* Needs?

Imagine the coolest home network you've ever desired. What would that network look like? What would it do for you? Go ahead and sketch up a sample floor plan. Keep this floor plan handy for other "Try This!" sections in this chapter.

Documentation

Right here at the beginning of the network development process you should begin what will be an immediate and continual process: documentation. Every well-designed and maintained network documents every facet of that network in detail *to support configuration management*. Here are some of the areas of documentation.

- *Network diagrams.* You need pretty seriously detailed diagrams that describe both the *physical* network components and the *logical* components too. We talked about diagramming way back in Chapter 6, "Installing a Physical Network," so check there for details. (For the physical, think cabling runs, server locations, and workstations; for the logical, think about VLANs and network segmentation.)

- *Asset management.* The network needs a detailed list of all the software owned by the company installed on workstations and servers. This includes versions, upgrade paths, and the like. There are many good programs to facilitate this process.

- *IP address utilization.* We'll see this step later in the chapter, but I'll add a bit of foreshadowing here. You need to know which device—physical and virtual—has which allocated IP address.

- *Vendor documentation.* It's important to have printed or electronic versions of essential details about the hardware and software systems in use by the company. This includes up-to-date contact information for representatives of the products employed.

- *Internal operating procedures/policies/standards.* I'll cover this aspect of documentation more in Chapters 18, "Managing Risk," and 19, "Protecting Your Network," but suffice it to say for here that network policies on every aspect of network behavior—from acceptable use of equipment to standards for high-grade passwords—needs to be documented carefully and fully.

Network Design

Network design quantifies the equipment, operating systems, and applications used by the network. This task ties closely with the previously listed Steps 2 through 5 of designing a basic network.

You need to address the following equipment:

- Workstations
- Servers
- Equipment room
- Peripherals

Workstations

Most company workers need discrete workstations running a modern operating system, like Windows 8 or 10 or Mac OS X. What about the clichés that office workers, accountants, salespeople, and managers prefer Windows over OS X, while the graphics people and Web developers prefer OS X over Windows? Well, sometimes clichés have more than a grain of truth. But it's also a factor of application software.

A company like Bayland Widgets will have very definite needs depending on the department. The accounting department, for example, might run Sage 50 or QuickBooks Pro, the top competing applications. If they use the former, then clients and servers should run Windows; with the latter, I'd go OS X.

The graphics folks—who do images, brochure layouts, and Web design—have it a little easier today. With Adobe Creative Cloud dominating the graphics market, application choice is easy. The fact that Creative Cloud works equally well with Windows and OS X workstations means companies can choose the platform that most enhances worker productivity. (If most of your workers grew up in Windows, in other words, choose Windows. If they all grew up with OS X, stick with OS X.)

The most entrenched platform-specific employees might be the more standard office workers, simply because Microsoft has traditionally updated Microsoft Office for the PC a year or two ahead of the OS X version.

Servers

The network needs servers. In a small company, you'd traditionally have one or two servers to handle things like network authentication, file storage and redundancy, and so on. Once you get into a bigger network, though, you'll find life easier with a more robust server solution where most (or even all) the server functions are virtualized. You can adapt the server infrastructure to accommodate multiple client types, for example, and run the necessary server functions:

- Network authentication
- Network management
- Accounting
- File management (including redundancy)
- Intranet services, such as internal Wiki and document sharing (via Microsoft SharePoint, for example)
- Development environments (for product testing, Web development, and so on)
- Software repositories (where programmers handle software development and version management)

You have a lot of flexibility here. By going virtual for some or all server resources, you can reduce your power usage and increase uptime. It's a win for everyone, including the accountants handling the bottom line.

Equipment Room

An equipment room provides a centralized core for the network. This is where the main servers live, for example, and where you implement all the features you learned about way back in Chapter 6 (proper air flow, appropriate cable management, appropriate rack systems, and so on).

Because Bayland Widgets' servers go beyond a small office/home office (SOHO) setup, the equipment room would have much greater power needs and require better power management. A highly populated single floor-to-ceiling rack of servers, for example, can pull upward of 40 amps of power, enough to blow any standard circuit. Many routers and other equipment will run directly on DC rather than AC. To accommodate both higher-end and standard

Tech Tip

Network Attached Storage

Many small networks avoid using a full-blown file server and instead take advantage of inexpensive and reliable network attached storage (NAS) *devices. Technically, an NAS device is a computer that's preconfigured to offer file storage for just about any type of client. Many NAS systems use the* Common Internet File System (CIFS) *configuration to create a plug and play (PnP)–type of device. Others use* Network File System (NFS) *or* Hypertext Transfer Protocol (HTTP) *for a similar result. These devices include features such as RAID to make storage safer.*

equipment, therefore, you would run the higher-amperage circuits and then install one or more **power converters** to change from AC to DC.

The more-demanding equipment room also demands more robust power. A single, decent *uninterruptible power supply (UPS)* might adequately handle brief power fluctuations for a single rack, for example, but won't be able to deal with a serious power outage. For that kind of **power redundancy**—keeping the lights on and the servers rolling—you'd need to connect a *generator* or two to the equipment room.

Peripherals

The peripherals—such as printers, scanners, fax machines, and so on—that a company needs to plan for and implement depend very much on what that company does in house. Bayland Widgets might produce their own brochures and fliers, for example, and thus need good, robust, color laser printers for their graphics folks. They could house the printers in a central print room or attach them at various points in the network. The capability of the printers would fluctuate according to how many and what size documents they print.

Faxing might be handled by dedicated fax machines. Or, it could be a software function installed on the machines of the folks who need to fax regularly. All these features and peripherals would need to be unique to the company. (The foosball table, for example, simply must be a peripheral in my office.)

 Try This!

Your Network, Your Equipment

Continuing from the previous "Try This!" decide what equipment you want for your own home network. Surely you're going to add a home theater PC, but what about a separate media server? Do you want a computer in the kitchen? Would you like a rack in your house? Can you find a smaller rack online? Can you wall-mount it? Make a list similar to the one in this section and keep it handy for more "Try This!" sections.

Compatibility Issues

Although it doesn't necessarily apply in the scenario presented in this chapter, you need to take compatibility issues into consideration when upgrading a network in an existing space. Several issues apply. It might make huge financial sense to leave installed CAT 5e runs in place, for example, and only upgrade to CAT 6a for additional runs. The older standard can handle Gigabit Ethernet just fine, after all, and that might be sufficient for now.

If you're upgrading some systems and not others, security can become a concern. In recent years, for example, as Microsoft has pushed later, more powerful operating systems, many businesses stubbornly continue to use Windows XP. Upgrading some systems to Windows 10, but leaving others running Windows XP, presents a challenge. Microsoft isn't releasing security patches for the older OS anymore, which means Windows XP is more vulnerable by the day to hacking attacks.

If you find yourself having to deal with a mixed network of modern and legacy systems, you should isolate the legacy systems. Use VLANs to implement

Try This!

What's Compatible?

If you were building a new home network from scratch, which of your existing parts could work in the new network? Do you have older equipment that might have compatibility issues, like an old 100BaseT switch or router?

If you needed to use all of your old equipment, visualize your new network connecting to it and how you might get around some of these issues. Does your old printer have a way to connect to the network directly? Where would you connect your Xbox 360? What if you have older TVs? Will they work with an HDMI-equipped video card?

Create an inventory of your old equipment and jot down any compatibility issues you might imagine taking place.

Creative companies invented methods to use unshielded twisted pair (UTP) cabling to connect runs longer than Ethernet's 100-meter limit. These devices were called *copper line drivers/repeaters,* essentially special boxes at each end of the run to manage the much amplified signal. Line drivers enabled installers to avoid using fiber, which was wildly more expensive at the time.

network segmentation and get those old systems out of the main network. See the discussion on implementing VLANs later in the chapter for the specifics.

These kinds of considerations vary by location and scenario, so keep the step in mind if you find yourself in an upgrade situation. (It's a helpful step to remember if you run into such scenarios on the CompTIA Network+ exam, too!)

Internal Connections

Now that you have an idea of your equipment and what you want to do with it, you need to get everything properly connected using structured cabling. You should also begin to install your 802.11 network. Once you connect all your equipment, you're ready to configure your internal VLANs, IP address schemes, and so on.

Structured Cabling

The structured cabling for the Bayland Widgets CAN requires a little thought to accommodate the needs of the various campus buildings. Internally, each of the three buildings can efficiently be wired with CAT 6a to all the workstations. That would provide Gigabit throughout, with all the cabling terminating in the main equipment room (Figure 17.2).

To connect the buildings, the company could use faster pipes, thus providing adequate throughput for a lot of traffic. One option is fiber running some form of 10-Gigabit Ethernet, such as 10GBaseT. The fiber connections for all three buildings would terminate at intermediate distribution frames (IDFs), one in each building (Figure 17.3). (I'll talk about the SCADA systems in the factory later in this chapter, never fear!)

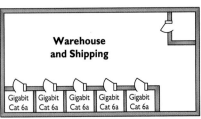
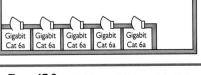
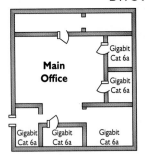

BWC New CAN

• **Figure 17.2**   Cabling within each building

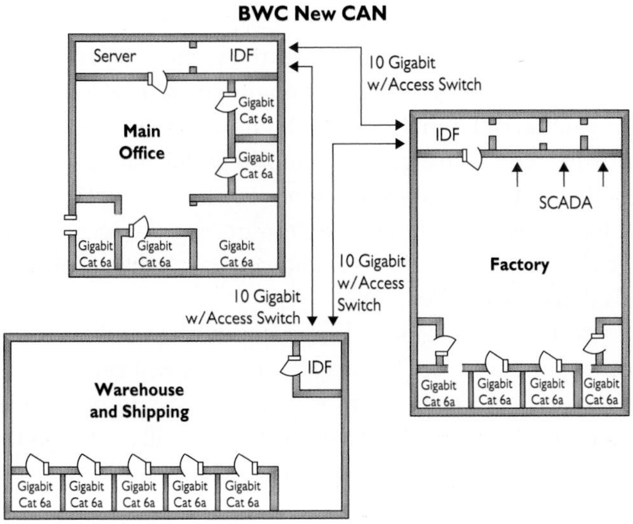

Figure 17.3 caption and preceding figure:

BWC New CAN

• Figure 17.3   Connecting the buildings

Wireless

A logical option for the Bayland Widgets CAN is to provide high-speed wireless throughout the area. Multiple 802.11ac units should be installed within each building and outside as well, all controlled by a central (or unified) wireless controller (Figure 17.4). This controller would in turn connect to the primary equipment room to provide connectivity with the wired networks.

✓ Cross Check

Install That Wireless!

Chapter 15, "Wireless Networking," went into great detail on the process of installing a wireless network. Generate a list of steps that the installer must go through to get the WAP properly configured. Keep in mind that this is a pure WAP, not a wireless router. Remember to include steps for dealing with PoE, SSIDs, VLANs, security, and so on. After that, go online and price out some serious "enterprise" WAPs. You'll have a lot to choose from, but the Cisco Aironet series has been reliable for a long time. Find the WAP that best fits your home network use.

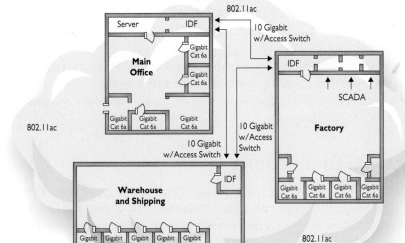

• Figure 17.4   Implementing wireless

VLANs

To provide a properly segmented network, the various departments and components in the CAN need to be placed into unique *virtual local area networks (VLANs)*. As you'll recall from Chapter 12, VLANs provide much better control over the network, with security and optimized performance.

Some of the VLANs are based on department. The *quality assurance (QA) lab* doesn't need access to all the same resources as the accounting folks, and vice versa, right? The *testing lab* tests software and firmware and has very different needs than other departments.

But take the network segmentation a step further and also create unique VLANs for network services. The wireless network will get its own VLAN, for example, plus we could split it into multiple VLANs to provide support for *separate private/public networks.* That way visitors will get access to what they need, but not to important internal systems.

We haven't talked about the phone connections (that's the next part of this chapter), but they'll invariably have their own VLAN. The same is true of the industrial control systems that take care of the internal functions of the factory and warehouse. This gets complicated fast!

Set Up the Network IP Address Scheme

Long before you start plugging in RJ-45s, you need to decide on your internal IP addressing scheme. For most SOHO networks, this means picking an arbitrary, unique, internal private IP network ID and then preassigning static IP addresses to servers and WAPs. Plus, pick a DHCP server and preassign DHCP scope IP address ranges.

Try to avoid the overused 192.168.1.0/24 network ID. Bad guys look for mistakes like these.

Try This!

Setting Up an IP Address Scheme

Now it's your turn to set up your dream home network's IP address scheme. List all of the IP address assignments for your network just like you did for Bayland Widgets. Here's the big question: Which computers get static addresses and which get DHCP? What would you use for a DHCP server?

Setting up the IP addressing scheme beforehand saves you a lot of time and effort once you start installing the systems. Be sure to make multiple copies of this scheme. Print out a copy and put it in the equipment room. Put a copy in your network documentation.

External Connections

No network is an island anymore. At the very least, Bayland Widgets needs an ISP so folks can Google and update their Facebook pages—err, I mean, get work done online. In a SOHO network like some of the ones you've seen earlier in this book, you don't have to deal with many of the issues you'd see in larger networks. A typical home-type ISP (DSL or cable) should be more than enough for a SOHO network in terms of bandwidth.

On the other hand, Bayland Widgets needs to be connected to the Internet all the time (or pay the price in lost business), so the company should consider a couple of options. First would be to have two ISPs, with the second ISP as a fallback in case the primary ISP fails. Another option is to pay up for a highly robust service like a metro Ethernet line.

A **metro Ethernet** connection is usually a dedicated fiber line from the ISP to an office. By using Ethernet rather than one of the remote connectivity options (like SONET or MPLS that you read about in Chapter 14), the installation is less expensive and syncs with the local network more easily.

Try This!

What's Available in Your Building?

Home networks won't have a preexisting ISP. You need to determine which ISPs provide service in your neighborhood. Fortunately, there's a great Web site designed to help you see what you can get: www.dslreports.com /reviews. Enter your ZIP code (sorry—USA only). Even if you already have an Internet connection at your house, see if you can find a better deal than the one you have. How much money can you save per month?

■ Unified Communication

Some years ago, TCP/IP-based communications began to replace the traditional PBX-style phone systems in most organizations. This switch enabled companies to minimize wire installation and enabled developers to get more creative with the gear. Technologies such as *Voice over IP (VoIP)* made it possible to communicate by voice right over an IP network, even one as big as the Internet. Today, TCP/IP communications encompass a range of technologies, including voice, video, and messaging. On the cutting edge (led by Cisco) is the field of **unified communication (UC)**. Rather than going old school, Bayland Widgets will implement UC throughout their CAN.

It Started with VoIP

Early VoIP systems usually required multiple cables running to each drop to accommodate the various services offered. Figure 17.5 shows a typical workstation VoIP phone that connects to a drop consisting of two RJ-45 connections, one for data and the other exclusively for VoIP.

These drops would often even go to their own separate switches, and from there into separate VoIP gateways that would interface with old-school PBX systems or directly into the telephone network.

As you'll recall from Chapter 14, "Remote Connectivity," virtually all

• **Figure 17.5**   Workstation drop

 Many VoIP systems, such as Skype, are complete Internet services that rely on nothing more than software installed on computers and the computers' microphone/speakers. All of the interconnections to the PSTN are handled in the cloud. While very popular for individuals, these systems, called **unified voice services**, are often considered unacceptable in office environments where people want a more classic "phone experience."

VoIP systems use the **Real-time Transport Protocol (RTP)** on TCP ports 5004 and 5005, as well as the **Session Initiation Protocol (SIP)** on TCP ports 5060 and 5061. This first-generation VoIP setup that required a separate wired network gave people pause. There really wasn't a critical need for physical separation of the data and the VoIP network, nor did these early VoIP systems handle video conferencing and text messaging. This prompted Cisco to develop and market its Unified Communications family of products.

Unified Communication Features

Of course, VoIP isn't the only communication game in town. As organizations were implementing VoIP, they realized a number of additional communications tasks would benefit from centralized management. Enter unified communication, which adds various additional services to the now-classic VoIP. These services include:

- Presence information
- Video conferencing/real-time video
- Fax
- Messaging
- Collaborate tools/workflow

Along with some other real-time communication-oriented tools, these are categorized as *real-time services (RTS)*.

Most of these services should be fairly self-explanatory, but I'd like to elaborate on two of them. *Presence information services* simply refers to technologies that enable users to show they are present for some form of communication. Think of presence as a type of flag that tells others that you are present and capable of accepting other forms of communication (such as a video conference). See Figure 17.6.

• **Figure 17.6**   Presence at work

It's also very important to differentiate between video conferencing and real-time video. **Video teleconferencing (VTC)** is the classic, multicast-based presentation where one presenter pushes out a stream of video to any number of properly configured and authorized multicast clients. These clients do not have a way (normally) to respond via video.

Unicast

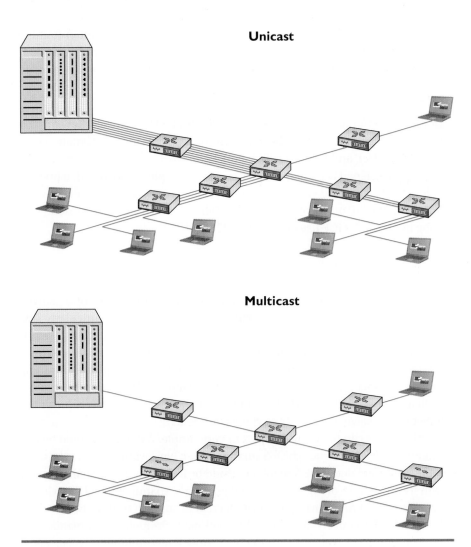

Multicast

• Figure 17.7   Multicast vs. unicast

Real-time video, in contrast, enables bidirectional communication via unicast messages. Real-time video offers both video and audio to communicate. Figure 17.7 compares the two types of video communication. Note that unicast traffic enables multiple unique signals.

UC Network Components

A typical UC network consists of three core components: UC devices, UC servers, and UC gateways. Let's take a quick peek at each of these.

A **UC device** is what we used to call the VoIP telephone. In a well-developed UC environment, the UC device handles voice, video, and more (Figure 17.8).

A **UC server** is typically a dedicated box that supports any UC-provided service. In small organizations this might be a single box, but in larger organizations there will be many UC servers. UC servers connect directly to every UC device on the LAN. It's not uncommon to see all the UC servers (as well as the rest of the UC devices) on a separate VLAN.

• Figure 17.8   Cisco Unified IP Phone

A **UC gateway** is an edge device, sometime dedicated but often nothing more than a few extra services added to an existing edge router. That router interfaces with remote UC gateways as well as with PSTN systems and services.

UC Protocols

Unified communication leans heavily on SIP and RTP protocols, but can also use H.323 or MGCP. **H.323** is the most commonly used video presentation protocol (or *codec*), and it runs on TCP port 1720. **Media Gateway Control Protocol (MGCP)** is designed from the ground up to be a complete VoIP or video presentation connection and session controller; in essence, taking over all the work from VoIP the SIP protocol used to do and all the work from video presentation done by H.323. MGCP uses TCP ports 2427 and 2727.

VTC and Medianets

All forms of communication over IP networks have some degree of sensitivity to disruption and slowdowns, but video teleconferencing is particularly susceptible. No one wants to sit in on a video conference that continually stops and jitters due to a poor or slow Internet connection. Medianets help to eliminate or reduce this problem. A **medianet** is a network of (typically) far-flung routers and servers that provide—via *quality of service (QoS)* and other tools—sufficient bandwidth for VTC. Plus, medianets work with UC servers (or sometime by themselves) to distribute video conferences.

Medianets can be wildly complex or very simple. A medianet could be two gateway routers with enough QoS smarts to open bandwidth for active VTCs as soon as they are detected. A medianet could be a huge multinational company with its own group of high-powered edge routers, spanning the globe with an MPLS-based VLAN, working with UC servers to support tens of thousands of voice and video conversations going on continually throughout its organization.

The CompTIA Network+ exam covers only a few rudimentary aspects of medianets, especially concentrating on a few protocols, so we don't need to dive too deeply. One aspect that the CompTIA Network+ exam does cover that is not too interesting is an early adoption of VTC using an ancient technology called ISDN.

ISDN vs. IP/SIP

Many organizations using VTC still rely on products based on the old *Integrated Services Digital Network (ISDN)* service that we discussed in Chapter 14. ISDN offers 128-Kbps bandwidth, which seems very slow by modern standards. But by using multiple ISDN channels, a special VTC over ISDN standard called **H.320** combined with aggressive compression enabled the VTC industry to roll out a number of not-too-shabby VTC systems all over the world. These were not based on IP addresses (so you couldn't connect via the Internet—which was OK back then because there wasn't an Internet), but they worked pretty well given the times.

With the Internet now dominant and IP/SIP-based VTC the norm, ISDN-based VTC is being replaced fairly quickly these days by high-speed Internet connections. However, it's important enough that CompTIA wants you to understand that ISDN-based VTC is still out there; and ISDN's 128-bps speed can be a real challenge to integrate into a typical high-speed Ethernet network.

QoS and Medianets

Medianets are all about the quality of service. But this isn't the simple QoS that you learned about back in Chapter 12. VTC is the ultimate real-time application and it needs a level of QoS that very few other applications need.

When we talk about QoS for medianets, we need to develop the concept of **differentiated services (DiffServ)**. DiffServ is the underlying architecture that makes all the QoS stuff work. The cornerstone of Diff-Serv is two pieces of data that go into every IP header on every piece of data: ECN and DSCP. ECN stands for *explicit congestion notification* and DSCP stands for *differentiated services code point*. These two comprise the differentiated services field (Figure 17.9).

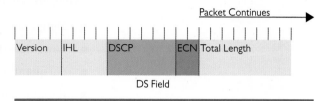

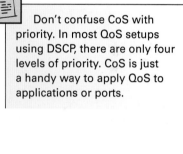

• **Figure 17.9**   DS field

ECN is a two-bit field where QoS-aware devices can place a "congestion encountered" signal to other QoS-aware devices. The following four values may show in that field:

00	Not QoS aware (default)
01	QoS aware, no congestion
10	QoS aware, no congestion
11	QoS aware, congestion encountered

The next six bits are DSCP, making a total of eight classes of service. A **class of service (CoS)** is just a value you may use (think of it like a group) to apply to services, ports, or whatever your QoS device might use. Figure 17.10 shows a sample from my home router. My router has four QoS priority queues and I can assign a CoS to every port.

> Don't confuse CoS with priority. In most QoS setups using DSCP, there are only four levels of priority. CoS is just a handy way to apply QoS to applications or ports.

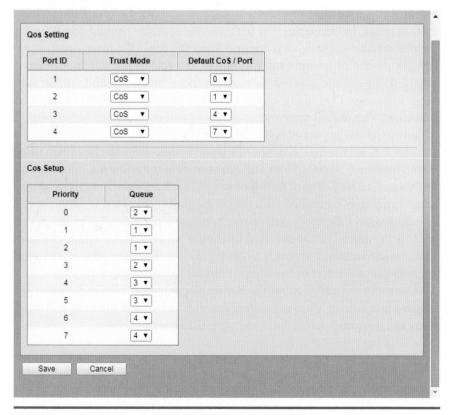

• **Figure 17.10**   CoS settings on router

■ ICS

Pretty much any industry that makes things, changes things, or moves things is filled with equipment to do the jobs that have to be done. From making mousetraps to ice cream, any given industrial plant, power grid, or pipeline is filled with stuff that needs to be monitored and stuff that needs to be controlled.

Here are some examples of things to monitor:

- Temperature
- Power levels
- Fill quantity
- Illumination
- Mass

And these are some examples of the things to control:

- Heaters
- Voltage
- Pumps
- Retractable roofs
- Valves

For Bayland Widgets, it's all about the robots that control the factory, the machines that help automate packing and shipping, and the air-conditioning controls for both buildings.

In the early days of automation, you might have a single person monitoring a machine that produced something. When the temperature hit a certain point, for example, that person—the operator—might open a valve or turn a knob to make changes and keep the machine functioning properly. As machines became more complex, the role of the operator likewise changed. He or she needed to monitor more functions and, sometimes, more machines. Eventually, computers were brought in to help manage the machines. The overall system that monitors and controls machines today is called an industrial control system (ICS).

The ICS isn't a new concept. It's been around for over 100 years using technology such as telescopes and horns to monitor and using mechanisms and pneumatics to control from a distance. But ICSs really started to take off when computers combined with digital monitors and controls. Over the last few years many ICSs have taken on more and more personal-computer aspects such as Windows- or Linux-based operating systems, Intel-style processors, and specialized PCs. Today, ICS is moving from stand-alone networks to interconnect with the Internet, bringing up serious issues for security.

CompTIA has added ICS to the Network+ exam objectives and expects you to know that it exists. Plus, competent network techs know the basic ICS variations and the components that make up those systems.

DCS

An ICS has three basic components: input/output (I/O) functions on the machine, a controller, and the interface for the operator. Input and output work through sensors and actuators. *Sensors* monitor things like temperature, for example, and the *actuator* makes changes that modify that temperature. The *controller,* some sort of computer, knows enough to manage the process, such as "keep the temperature between 50 and 55 degrees Fahrenheit." The operator watches some kind of monitor—the *interface*—and intervenes if necessary (Figure 17.11). Let's scale this up to a factory and add a little more complexity.

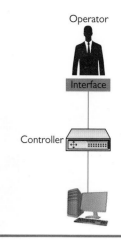

• **Figure 17.11**   A simple ICS

What if you have multiple machines that accomplish a big task, like in a factory that produces some finished product? The new widget at Bayland Widgets, for example, is produced in stages, with the machine at each stage needing monitoring and control. In the early days of computers, when computers were really expensive, the controller was a single computer. All the sensors from each of the machines had to provide feedback to that single controller. The controller would compute and then send signals to the various actuators to change things, managing the process. See Figure 17.12.

As computing power went up and costs when down, it made much more sense to put smaller controllers directly on each machine, to distribute the computing load. This is a **distributed control system (DCS)**.

In a modern DCS, each of the local controllers connects (eventually) to a centralized controller—what CompTIA calls the **ICS server**—where global changes can be made managed (Figure 17.13). Operators at the ICS server for Bayland Widgets, for example, could direct the controllers managing the robots to change production from green widgets to blue widgets.

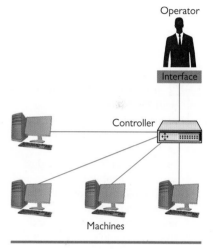

• **Figure 17.12**   An early computer-assisted ICS

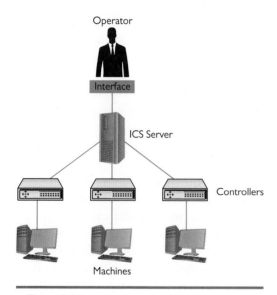

• **Figure 17.13**   A simple DCS

Operators interact with controllers through a control or computer called a **human machine interface (HMI)**. Early HMIs were usually custom-made boxes with gauges and switches. Today, an HMI is most likely a PC running a custom, touch-screen interface (Figure 17.14). It's important to appreciate that HMIs are not general purpose. You wouldn't run Microsoft Office on an HMI, even if the PC on which it is built is capable of such things. It's very common for an HMI to show a single interface that never changes.

• **Figure 17.14**   SIMATIC HMI Basic Panel with a touch screen (© Siemens AG 2014, All rights reserved)

PLC

A DCS makes sense for a process that requires a continuous flow. The sensors provide real-time feedback to the controllers; the controllers are sophisticated enough to keep the machines functioning properly, making changes via the actuators. In a process that follows specific, ordered steps, in contrast, a different kind of system would make more sense.

• **Figure 17.15** Siemens SIMATIC S7-1500 PLC

A classic **programmable logic controller (PLC)** is a computer that controls a machine according to a set of ordered steps (Figure 17.15). Take for example a machine that produces cakes. Each step in the process of producing a cake follows a certain pattern (add ingredients, mix, bake, etc.) that has to go in order and in the proper timing. The PLC monitors sensors (like timers and oven temperatures) and tells the machine when to do the next step in the process.

> ICS predates Ethernet and the TCP/IP protocols, but the predominance of Ethernet and TCP/IP has created a number of ICS solutions that use Ethernet and TCP/IP instead of proprietary cabling systems and communication protocols. If you were going to build an ICS from scratch today, odds are good that you would use Ethernet as your interconnection of choice.

SCADA

A **supervisory control and data acquisition (SCADA)** system is a subset of ICS. Generally, a SCADA system has the same basic components as a DCS, but differs in two very important ways. First, a SCADA system is designed for large-scale, distributed processes such as power grids, pipelines, and railroads. Second, due to the distance involved, a SCADA system must function with the idea that remote devices may or may not have ongoing communication with the central control.

Remote Terminal Unit

In general, a SCADA system is going to be a DCS using servers, HMIs, sensors, and actuators. The big difference is the replacement of controllers with devices called **remote terminal units (RTUs)**. RTUs provide the same function as a controller, but have two major differences. First, an RTU is designed to have some amount of autonomy in case it loses connection with the central control. Second, an RTU is designed to take advantage of some form of long-distance communication such as telephony, fiber optic, or cellular WANs (Figure 17.16). As you might imagine, the fear of interception is a big deal with SCADA systems these days, so let's discuss the need for network segmentation on a bigger scale than previously described in the chapter.

Network Segmentation

It's pretty easy to say that a network failure isn't a happy occurrence. On the lowest end, losing your network in your home is going to make someone very unhappy when they can't watch the latest episode of *Orange Is the New Black* on Netflix. Taking it to the other extreme, many ICSs are incredibly crucial for the

• **Figure 17.16** Substation Automation and RTUs

needs of everyday living. From the DCSs that run an oil refinery to the SCADA systems keeping our electrical infrastructure up and running, the potential downside of a catastrophic failure is far worse than that of missing a show!

Security isn't the only reason we segment networks. We also reduce network congestion and limit network problems through segmentation. We segment to optimize performance. We segment to be in compliance with standards, laws, or best practices. We also segment for easier troubleshooting.

Network segmentation is done for security, performance optimization, load balancing, and compliance.

One of the best tools to help us understand network segmentation is the OSI seven-layer model, in particular the first three layers:

- **Layer 1 (Physical)**   Physically separating your network from every other network. This is also known as an air gap.

- **Layer 2 (Data Link)**   Separating a physically connected network into separate broadcast domains. Think VLANs here.

- **Layer 3 (Network)**   Separating broadcast domains by blocking IP routes.

- **Above Layer 3**   VPNs, separate SSIDs, separate Windows domains, virtualization

The CompTIA Network+ covers a number of situations where network segmentation is important.

Segmentation and Industrial Control Systems

All forms of ICS are by definition closed networks. A *closed network* is any network that strictly controls who and what may connect to it. However, there are two places where we begin to see connectivity. In many SCADA systems, it is very convenient to use public wireless networks to connect RTUs, and, in some cases, we connect SCADA servers to the Internet to provide intranet access. The biggest single line of defense for these two scenarios are virtual private network connections. It's impossible to find any form of SCADA/ICS that doesn't use a VPN in the cases where it must be open to the public Internet.

Chapter 17 Review

■ Chapter Summary

After reading this chapter and completing the exercises, you should understand the following about building a real-world network.

Explain the concepts of basic network design

- When designing a basic network, you should consider the function of workstations, servers, peripherals, and equipment rooms.

- Workstations need connectivity based on the applications users will use.

- Even the smallest networks will probably need more than one server. Consider the following functions: network authentication, network management, file management, corporate accounting, intranet services, development environments, software repositories.

- Consider alternatives to complete servers such as network attached storage (NAS).

- An equipment room must have sufficient environmental support and access to sufficient electrical power to support equipment. Power converters and UPSs are common. Equipment rooms with mission-critical hardware use generators for power outages.

- When adding to an existing network, you need to consider compatibility issues at every step of the installation. Cabling types and network speeds are two examples.

- Once you have an idea of your needs, you can then develop a proper structured cabling system for your network.

- All but the simplest wireless networks should be configured for centralized administration using wireless controllers.

- All networks need VLANs. Good VLAN organization separates your network according to clear functions: private/public networks, wired/wireless, ICS, and so forth.

- You need to pick an ISP that provides the speeds and features your network needs. If available, metro Ethernet often provides the highest bandwidth. It's preferable to have a second ISP in case your first fails.

Describe unified communication features and functions

- Unified communication (UC) is the support of voice, video, and texting over IP networks. Unified communication is a natural evolution of VoIP technologies.

- VoIP uses Real-time Transport Protocol (RTP) on TCP ports 5004 and 5005, and Session Initiation Protocol (SIP) on TCP ports 5060 and 5061.

- UC improves over traditional VoIP by providing presence information, video conferencing/real-time video, fax, messaging, and collaborative tools/workflow.

- A UC network has UC devices, UC servers, and UC gateways.

- The most common UC protocols beyond RTP and SIP are H.323, which uses TCP port 1720, and MGCP, which uses ports 2427 and 2727.

- Video teleconferencing (VTC) is especially sensitive to network slowdowns. Medianets handle this problem using quality of service (QoS).

- Differentiated services are the underlying IP-level functions that make QoS work. There are two fields in every QoS-aware IP field: ECN (Explicit Congestion Notification) and DSCP (Differentiated Services Code Point). ECN is used to communicate congestion on sessions. DSCP is used to define a class of service (CoS) for the IP packet.

- The well-installed base of ISDN makes for a unique form of VTC called ISDN IP/SIP.

Describe the function and major components of an ICS/SCADA network

- ICS stands for industrial control system. An ICS consolidates the monitoring and control of a process into one or more control areas.

- An ICS has three basic components: input/output (I/O) functions on the machine, a controller, and the interface for the operator. A DCS has controllers distributed among the various machines to handle the I/O. The DCS controllers connect to the ICS server for managing global changes.

- The human machine interface (HMI) is how the ICS manifests itself to the operator(s) of the system.

- A programmable logic controller (PLC) has a parallel function to the controllers in a DCS, but works in a different way. A PLC controls a machine according to a set of ordered steps.
- A supervisory control and data acquisition (SCADA) system is designed for large-scale, distributed processes such as power grids.
- SCADA systems use remote terminal units (RTUs). An RTU uses some form of remote communication technology and is designed to have some amount of autonomy in case it loses connection with the central control.
- ICS/DCS/SCADA and other networks are traditionally good candidates for network segmentation.

Key Terms

air gap *(515)*
campus area network (CAN) *(498)*
class of service (CoS) *(511)*
compatibility requirements *(499)*
device types/requirements *(499)*
differentiated services (DiffServ) *(511)*
distributed control system (DCS) *(513)*
environment limitations *(499)*
equipment limitations *(499)*
H.320 *(510)*
H.323 *(510)*
human machine interface (HMI) *(513)*
ICS server *(513)*
industrial control system (ICS) *(512)*
list of requirements *(499)*
Media Gateway Control Protocol (MGCP) *(510)*
medianet *(510)*
metro Ethernet *(507)*

operator *(512)*
power converter *(503)*
power redundancy *(503)*
programmable logic controller (PLC) *(514)*
Real-time Transport Protocol (RTP) *(508)*
real-time video *(509)*
remote terminal unit (RTU) *(514)*
security considerations *(499)*
Session Initiation Protocol (SIP) *(508)*
supervisory control and data acquisition (SCADA) *(514)*
UC device *(509)*
UC gateway *(510)*
UC server *(509)*
unified communication (UC) *(507)*
unified voice services *(507)*
video teleconferencing (VTC) *(508)*
wired/wireless considerations *(499)*

Key Term Quiz

Use the Key Terms list to complete the sentences that follow. Not all the terms will be used.

1. Many better rack-based units plug into a(n) _____ rather than an AC outlet.

2. A(n) _____ connection is usually a dedicated fiber line from the ISP to an office.

3. The term _____ refers to technologies that include voice, video, and messaging.

4. _____ enables bidirectional communication via unicast messages.

5. The VTC over ISDN standard _____ combined with aggressive compression enabled early video teleconferencing to function well.

6. The _____ protocol supports video presentations and uses TCP port 1720.

7. A(n) _____ is a network of (typically) far-flung routers that provides sufficient bandwidth for VTC.

8. _____ is the underlying architecture for QoS in medianets.

9. A(n) _____ uses an HMI to manipulate DCS controllers.

10. A(n) _____ indicates physical separation of networks.

Multiple-Choice Quiz

1. What is a network composed of a number of geographically close buildings called?

   A. CAN

   B. LAN

   C. MAN

   D. PAN

2. Which of the following is considered a low-cost, simpler alternative to a full-blown file server?

   A. MAC

   B. NAS

   C. PC

   D. PLC

3. Scott wants to install six desktop systems with 10-Gigabit Ethernet cards into a legacy network. Which of the following should he consider? (Select two.)

   A. CAT rating on installed network cables

   B. Current ISP connection

   C. Current wireless speed

   D. Speed of installed switches

4. Bob's new coffee shop relies on wireless for both public and private networking. Which of the following examples would take advantage of VLANs to provide network segmentation?

   A. Assign MAC addresses of all devices on the private network to one VLAN, and all public to another.

   B. Create two SSIDs, one public, one private.

   C. Create two VLANs, one for servers and one for DHCP clients.

   D. VLANs should never be used on wireless networks.

5. RTP runs on which ports?

   A. ICMP ports 5004, 5005

   B. UDP ports 5004, 5005

   C. TCP ports 5004, 5005

   D. RTP is multicast and doesn't use ports.

6. SIP uses which ports? (Select two.)

   A. 4005

   B. 5060

   C. 4050

   D. 5061

7. Unified communication expands on which classic technology?

   A. VTC

   B. VoIP

   C. VPN

   D. VLAN

8. In a well-developed UC environment, what are the individual phones called?

   A. UC devices

   B. UC servers

   C. UC gateways

   D. UC nodes

9. MGCP replaces which of the following protocols? (Select two.)

   A. TCP

   B. SIP

   C. H.320

   D. H.323

10. In a medianet, what does DSCP define?

    A. Network congestion

    B. Differentiated services

    C. Explicit congestion notification

    D. Classes of service

11. Of the following, which would most likely have an industrial control system implementation?

    A. An apartment complex

    B. A coffee shop

    C. A city park

    D. A bottling company

12. Which of the following would most clearly differentiate a DCS from a SCADA system?

    A. Multiple control rooms

    B. Distances greater than 10 km

    C. Unified control room

    D. More than ten devices to be controlled

13. An ICS will commonly interface to the human operator via which service?

    A. RTU

    B. HMI

    C. Relay

    D. Control unit

14. Which of the following devices is unique to a SCADA system?

    A. RTU

    B. HMI

    C. Relay

    D. Control unit

15. Which of the following is a motivation for network segmentation? (Select two.)

    A. Load balancing

    B. Redundancy

    C. Ease of use

    D. Security

■ Essay Quiz

1. Using the examples of a milk bottling factory and a nuclear power plant, write a short essay describing the differences between DCS and PLC.

2. Using your classroom's infrastructure as an example, write an essay explaining how you would implement network segmentation.

Lab Projects

• Lab Project 17.1

Locate a small network, preferably a business with ten or fewer computers, and complete the following steps.

1. Document each computer and define its function: server, workstation, and so on.

2. Sketch out the wired topology for the network (if that applies).

3. Sketch the wireless topology for the network (if any). Include 802.11 version(s), WAP(s), and SSID(s). Be sure to connect any WAPs to the previous wired topology.

4. Using the IP addresses, determine the network ID(s) for the network, both wired and wireless.

5. Document all peripherals, including IP addresses if applicable.

6. If possible, determine all VLANs used in the network. Otherwise, speculate on how VLANs are used on the network.

• Lab Project 17.2

A small office network is running short of file space. Go online to compare the costs of adding hard drives to an existing server versus purchasing an NAS. Assume that the labor costs of installing drives to the existing server will take 2 hours at $100 per hour. Which option is cheaper?

Managing Risk

chapter
18

"There is no such thing as perfect security, only varying levels of insecurity."

—Salman Rushdie

In this chapter, you will learn how to

- **Describe the industry standards for risk management**
- **Discuss contingency planning**
- **Examine safety standards and actions**

Companies need to manage risk, to minimize the dangers posed by internal and external threats. They need policies in place for expected dangers and also procedures established for things that will happen eventually. This is contingency planning. Finally, every company needs proper safety policies. Let's look at all three facets of managing risk.

Risk Management

IT **risk management** is the process of how organizations deal with the bad things (let's call them attacks) that take place on their networks. The entire field of IT security is based on the premise that somewhere, at some time, something will attack some part of your network. The attack may take as many forms as your paranoia allows: intentional, unintentional, earthquake, accident, war, meteor impact . . . whatever.

What do we do about all these attacks? You can't afford to build up a defense for every possible attack—nor should you need to, for a number of reasons. First, different attacks have different probabilities of taking place. The probability of a meteor taking out your server room is very low. There is, however, a pretty good chance that some clueless user will eventually load malware on their company-issued laptop. Second, different attacks/potential problems have different impacts. If a meteor hits your server room, you're going to have a big, expensive problem. If a user forgets his password, it's not a big deal and is easily dealt with.

The CompTIA Network+ certification covers a number of issues that roughly fit under the idea of risk management. Let's run through each of these individually.

One of the scariest attacks is a data breach. A *data breach* is any form of attack where secured data is taken or destroyed. The many credit card hacks we've seen over the last few years are infamous examples of data breaches.

Security Policies

A **security policy** is a written document that defines how an organization will protect its IT infrastructure. There are hundreds of different security policies, but for the scope of the CompTIA Network+ certification exam we only need to identify just a few of the most common ones. These are found in almost every level of organization.

The CompTIA Network+ exam, is in my opinion, way too light in its coverage of security policies. The CompTIA Security+ exam does a much better job, but even it is a bit slim. Check out the Wikipedia entry for "security policy" to discover the many types of security policies in use today.

Acceptable Use Policy

The **acceptable use policy** defines what is and what is not acceptable to do on an organization's computers. It's arguably the most famous of all security policies as this is one document that pretty much everyone who works for any organization is required to read, and in many cases sign, before they can start work. The following are some provisions contained in a typical acceptable use policy:

- **Ownership**   Equipment and any proprietary information stored on the organization's computers are the property of the organization.

- **Network Access**   Users will access only information they are authorized to access.

- **Privacy/Consent to Monitoring**   Anything users do on the organization's computers is not private. The organization will monitor what is being done on computers at any time.

- **Illegal Use**   No one may use an organization's computers for anything that breaks a law. (This is usually broken down into many subheadings, such as introducing malware, hacking, scanning, spamming, and so forth.)

Many organizations require employees to sign an acceptable use policy, especially if it includes a consent to monitoring clause.

Network Policies

CompTIA uses the term "network policies" in a rather strange way, as there really aren't network policies. In all probability CompTIA means network access policies. Companies need a policy that defines who can do what on the company's network. The **network access policy** defines who may access the network, how they may access the network, and what they can access. Network access policies may be embedded into policies such as VPN policy, password policy, encryption policy, and many others, but they need to be in place.

Policies are the cornerstone of an organization's IT security. Policies help define what equipment is used, how data is organized, and what actions people take to ensure the security of an organization. Policies tell an organization how to handle almost any situation that might arise (such as disaster recovery, covered later in this chapter).

Adherence to Policies

Given the importance of policies, it's also imperative for an organization to adhere to its policies strictly. This can often be a challenge. As technologies change, organizations must review and update policies to reflect those changes.

 Try This!

Checking Out Real-World Security Policies

Security policies can be interesting, so try this! Go to the SANS institute Web site and check out all of their free, cool, sample security policies:

https://www.sans.org/security-resources/policies

Change Management

An IT infrastructure is an ever-changing thing. Applications are updated, operating systems change, server configurations adjust; change is a tricky part of managing an infrastructure. Change needs to happen, but not at the cost of losing security. The process of creating change in your infrastructure in an organized, controlled, safe way is called **change management**.

Change management usually begins with a **change management team**. This team, consisting of people from all over your organization, is tasked with the job of investigating, testing, and authorizing all but the simplest changes to your network.

Changes tend to be initiated at two levels: strategic-level changes, typically initiated by management and major in scope (for example, we're going to switch all the servers from Windows to Linux); and infrastructure-level changes, typically initiated by a department by making a request to the change management team. The CompTIA Network+ exam stresses the latter type of change, where *you* are the person who will go before the change management team. Let's go over what to expect when dealing with change management.

Initiating the Change

The first part of many change processes is a request from a part of the organization. Let's say you're in charge of IT network support for a massive art department. There are over 150 graphic artists, each manning a powerful OS X workstation. The artists have discovered a new graphics program that they claim will dramatically improve their ability to do what they do. After a quick read of the program's features on its Web site, you're also convinced that this a good idea. It's now your job to make this happen.

Create a change request. Depending on the organization, this can be a highly official document or, for a smaller organization, nothing more than a detailed e-mail message. Whatever the case, you need to document the reason for this change. A good change request will include the following:

- **Type of change**   Software and hardware changes are obviously part of this category, but this could also encompass issues like backup methods, work hours, network access, workflow changes, and so forth.

- **Configuration procedures**   What is it going to take to make this happen? Who will help? How long will it take?

- **Rollback process**   If this change in some way makes such a negative impact that going back to how things were before the change is needed, what will it take to roll back to the previous configuration?

- **Potential impact**   How will this change impact the organization? Will it save time? Save money? Increase efficiency? Will it affect the perception of the organization?

- **Notification**   What steps will be taken to notify the organization about this change?

Dealing with the Change Management Team

With your change request in hand, it's time to get the change approved. In most organizations, change management teams meet at fixed intervals, so there's usually a deadline for you to be ready at a certain time. From here, most organizations will rely heavily on a well-written change request form to get the details. The approval process usually consists of considering the issues listed in the change request, but also management approval and funding.

Making the Change Happen

Once your change is approved, the real work starts. Equipment, software, tools, and so forth must be purchased. Configuration teams need to be trained. The change committee must provide an adequate maintenance window: the time it will take to implement and thoroughly test the coming changes. As part of that process, the committee must *authorize downtime* for systems, departments, and so on. Your job is to provide *notification of the change* to those people who will be affected, if possible providing alternative workplaces or equipment.

Documenting the Change

The ongoing and last step of the change is documentation. All changes must be clearly documented, including but not limited to:

- Network configurations, such as server settings, router configurations, and so on

- Additions to the network, such as additional servers, switches, and so on

- Physical location changes, such as moved workstations, relocated switches, and so on

Patching and Updates

 CompTIA calls regularly updating operating systems and applications to avoid security threats *patch management*.

It's often argued whether applying patches and updates to existing systems fits under change management or regular maintenance. In general, all but the most major patches and updates are really more of a maintenance issue than a change management issue. But, given the similarity of patching to change management, it seems that here is as good a place as any to discuss patching.

When we talk about patching and updates, we aren't just talking about the handy tools provided to us by Microsoft Windows or Ubuntu Linux. Almost every piece of software and firmware on almost every type of equipment you own is subject to patching and updating: printers, routers, wireless access points, desktops, programmable logic controllers (PLCs) . . . everything needs a patch or update now and then.

> ## ✓ Cross Check
>
> ### PLC
>
> You'll remember PLCs from Chapter 17, "Building a Real-World Network," so cross check your memory now. What do these devices do for a modern network? How do they differ from a typical PC?

What Do We Update?

In general, specific types of updates routinely take place. Let's cover each of these individually, starting with the easiest and most famous, operating system (OS) updates.

OS updates are easily the most common type of update. Individuals install automatic updates on their OSs with impunity, but when you're updating a large number of systems, especially critical nodes like servers, it's never a good idea to apply all OS updates without a little bit of due diligence beforehand. Most operating systems provide some method of network server–based patching, giving administrators the opportunity to test first and then distribute patches when they desire.

All systems use device drivers, and they are another part of the system we often need to patch. In general, we only apply *driver updates* to fix an incompatibility, incorporate new features, or repair a bug. Since device drivers are only present in systems with full-blown operating systems, all OS-updating tools will include device drivers in their updates. Many patches will include feature changes and updates, as well as security vulnerability patches.

Feature changes/updates are just what they sound like: adding new functionality to the system. Remember back in the old days when a touchscreen phone only understood a single touch? Then some phone operating system came out to provide multi-touch. Competitors responded with patches to their own phone OSs that added the multi-touch feature.

All software of any complexity has flaws. Hardware changes, exposing flaws in the software that supports that hardware; newer applications create unexpected interactions; security standards change over time. All of these factors mean that responsible companies patch their products after they release them. How they approach the patching depends on scope: *major vs. minor updates* require different actions.

When a major vulnerability to an OS or other system is discovered, vendors tend to respond quickly by creating a fix in the form of a *vulnerability patch*. If the vulnerability is significant, that patch is usually made available as soon as it is complete. Sometimes, these high-priority security patches are even pushed to the end user right away.

Less significant vulnerabilities get patched as part of a regular patch cycle. You may have noticed that on the second Wednesday of each month, Microsoft-based computers reboot. Since October of 2003, Microsoft has sent out patches that have been in development and are ready for deployment on the second Tuesday of the month. This has become known as *Patch Tuesday*. These patches are released for a wide variety of Microsoft products, including operating systems, productivity applications, utilities, and more.

Firmware updates are far less common than software updates and usually aren't as automated (although a few motherboard makers might challenge this statement). In general, firmware patching is a manual process and is done in response to a known problem or issue. Keep in mind that firmware updates are inherently risky, because in many cases it's difficult to recover from a bad patch.

How to Patch

In a network environment, patching is a routine but critical process. Here are a few important steps that take place in almost every scenario of a network patch environment:

- **Research**   As a critical patch is announced, it's important to do some research to verify that the patch is going to do what you need it to do and that people who have already installed the patch aren't having problems.

- **Test**   It's always a good idea to test a patch on a test system when possible.

- **Configuration backups**   Backing up configurations is critical, especially when backing up firmware. The process of backing up a configuration varies from platform to platform, but almost all PCs can back up their system setups, and switches and routers have well-known "backup-config" style commands.

Keep in mind that a single system may have a number of patches over time. When necessary, you might find yourself having to perform a downgrade or rollback of the patch, returning to a patch that is one or two versions old. This is usually pretty easy on PCs because OSs track each update. With firmware, the best way to handle this is to track each upgrade and keep a separate copy for each patch in case a downgrade/rollback is needed.

Training

End users are probably the primary source of security problems for any organization. We must increase *end user awareness and training* so they know what to look for and how to act to avoid or reduce attacks. Training users is a critical piece of managing risk. While a formal course is preferred, it's up to the IT department to do what it can to make sure users have an understanding of the following:

- **Security policies**   Users need to read, understand, and, when necessary, sign all pertinent security policies.

- **Passwords**   Make sure users understand basic password skills, such as sufficient length and complexity, refreshing passwords regularly, and password control.

Tech Tip

Upgrading vs. Downgrading
Patches, whether major or minor, require thorough testing before techs or administrators apply them to clients throughout the network. Sometimes, though, a hot fix might slip through to patch a security hole that then breaks other things inadvertently. In those cases, by following good patch management procedures, you can roll back—the Windows terminology—or downgrade by removing the patch. You can then push an upgrade when a better patch is made available.

- **System and workplace security** Make sure users understand how to keep their workstations secure through screen locking and not storing written passwords in plain sight.

- **Social engineering** Users need to recognize typical social-engineering tactics and know how to counter them.

- **Malware** Teach users to recognize malware attacks and train them to deal with them.

Points of Failure

System failures happen; that's not something we can completely prevent. The secret to dealing with failures is to avoid a **single point of failure**: one system that, if it fails, will bring down an entire process, workflow, or, worse yet, an entire organization.

It's easy to say, "Oh, we will just make two of everything!" (This would create *redundancy* where needed.) But you can't simply make two of everything. That would create far too much unnecessary hardware and administration. Sure, redundancy is fairly easy to do, but the trick is to determine where the redundancy is needed to avoid single points of failure without too much complexity, cost, or administration. We do this process by identifying two things: critical assets and critical nodes.

Critical Assets

Every organization has assets that are critical to the operation of the organization. A bakery may have one PLC-controlled oven, a sales group might have a single database, or a Web server rack might only be connected to the Internet through one ISP. The process of determining critical assets is tricky and is usually a senior management process.

Critical Nodes

Unlike critical assets, critical nodes are very much unique to IT equipment: servers, routers, workstations, printers, and so forth. Identifying critical nodes is usually much clearer than identifying critical assets because of the IT nature of critical nodes and the fact that the IT department is always going to be painfully aware of what nodes are critical. Here are a few examples of critical nodes:

- A file server that contains critical project files
- A single Web server
- A single printer (assuming printed output is critical to the organization)
- An edge router

High Availability

Once you have identified the critical nodes in your network, it's important to ensure they keep working without interruption or downtime; in other words, to make sure critical systems have **high availability (HA)**. Core to building high availability into a network is *failover,* the ability for backup systems to detect when a master has failed and then to take over.

How does all the network traffic know to use the backup system? That's where the idea of a virtual IP comes in. A **virtual IP** is a single IP address shared by multiple systems. If that sounds a lot like what Network Address Translation

(NAT) does, well, you're right. The public IP address on NATed networks is a common implementation of a virtual IP, but virtual IPs are not limited to NAT. The way servers can fail over without dropping off the network is for all the servers in the cluster to accept traffic from a single, common IP—this common address is considered a virtual IP.

Building with high availability in mind extends to more than just servers; default gateway routers are another critical node that can be protected by adding redundant backups. The two protocols used to provide this redundancy are the open standard *Virtual Router Redundancy Protocol (VRRP)* and the Cisco proprietary *Hot Standby Router Protocol (HSRP)*. The nice thing about VRRP and HSRP is that, conceptually, they both perform the same function. They take multiple routers and gang them together into a single virtual router with a single virtual IP that clients use as a default gateway.

Standard Business Documents

Dealing with third-party vendors is an ongoing part of any organization. When you are dealing with third parties, you must have some form of agreement that defines the relationship between you and the third party. The CompTIA Network+ exam expects you to know about four specific business documents: a service level agreement, a memorandum of understanding, a multi-source agreement, and a statement of work. Let's review each of these documents.

Service Level Agreement

A service level agreement (SLA) is a document between a customer and a service provider that defines the scope, quality, and terms of the service to be provided. SLAs are common in the IT world, given the large number of services provided. Some of the more common SLAs in the IT world are provided by ISPs to customers. A typical SLA from an ISP contains the following:

- **Definition of the service provided** Defines the minimum and/or maximum bandwidth and describes any recompense for degraded services or downtime.

- **Equipment** Defines what equipment, if any, the ISP provides. It also specifies the type of connections to be provided.

- **Technical support** Defines the level of technical support that will be given, such as phone support, Web support, and in-person support. This also defines costs for that support.

Memorandum of Understanding

A memorandum of understanding (MOU) is a document that defines an agreement between two parties in situations where a legal contract wouldn't be appropriate. An MOU defines the duties the parties commit to perform for each other and a time frame for the MOU. An MOU is common between companies that have only occasional business relations with each other. For example, all of the hospitals in a city might generate an MOU to take on each other's patients in case of a disaster such as a fire or tornado. This MOU would define costs, contacts, logistics, and so forth.

Multi-source Agreement

Manufacturers of various network hardware agree to a multi-source agreement (MSA), a document that details the interoperability of their components. For example, two companies might agree that their gigabit interface converters (GBICs) will work in Cisco and Juniper switches.

Statement of Work

A **statement of work (SOW)** is in essence a legal contract between a vendor and a customer. An SOW defines the services and products the vendor agrees to supply and the time frames in which to supply them. A typical SOW might be between an IT security company and a customer. An SOW tends to be a detailed document, clearly explaining what the vendor needs to do. Time frames must also be very detailed, with milestones through the completion of the work.

Security Preparedness

Preparing for incidents is the cornerstone of managing risk. If you decide to take the next logical CompTIA certification, the CompTIA Security+, you'll find an incredibly detailed discussion of how the IT security industry spends inordinate amounts of time and energy creating a secure IT environment. But for the CompTIA Network+ certification, there are two issues that come up: vulnerability scanning and penetration testing.

Vulnerability Scanning

Given the huge number of vulnerabilities out there, it's impossible for even the most highly skilled technician to find them by manually inspecting your infrastructure. The best way to know your infrastructure's vulnerabilities is to run some form of program—a **vulnerability scanner**—that will inspect a huge number of potential vulnerabilities and create a report for you to then act upon.

There is no single vulnerability scanner that works for every aspect of your infrastructure. Instead, a good network tech will have a number of utilities that work for their type of network infrastructure. Here are a few of the more popular vulnerability scanners and where they are used.

Microsoft Baseline Security Analyzer (MBSA) is designed to test individual systems. It's getting a little old, but still does a great job of testing one Microsoft Windows system for vulnerabilities.

Nmap is a port scanner. Port scanners query individual nodes, looking for open or vulnerable ports and creating a report. Actually, it might be unfair to say that Nmap is *only* a port scanner, as it adds a number of other tools. Written by Gordon Lyon, Nmap is very popular, free, and well maintained. Figure 18.1 shows sample output from Nmap.

When you need to perform more serious vulnerability testing, it's common to

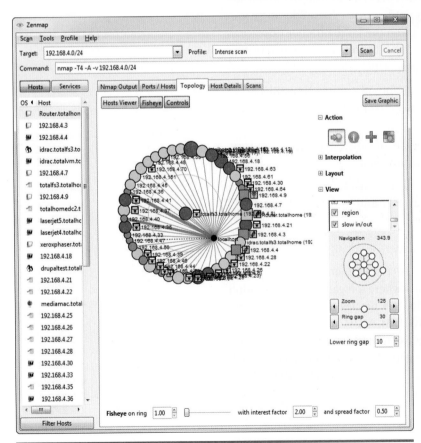

• **Figure 18.1**   Nmap output

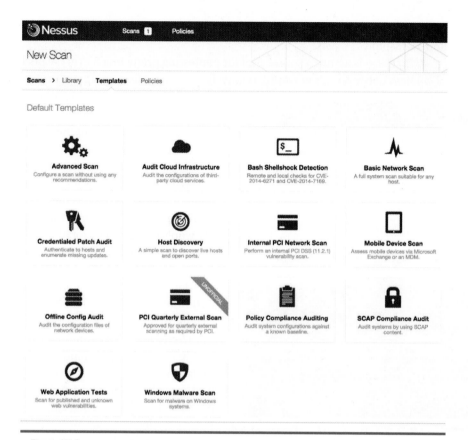

• **Figure 18.2**   Nessus output

turn to more aggressive and powerful comprehensive testers. There are plenty out there, but two dominate the field: Nessus and OpenVAS. **Nessus** (Figure 18.2), from Tenable Network Security, is arguably the first truly comprehensive vulnerability testing tool and has been around for almost two decades. Nessus is an excellent, well-known tool. Once free to everyone, Nessus is still free for home users, but commercial users must purchase a subscription.

OpenVAS is an open source fork of Nessus that is also extremely popular and, in the opinion of many security types, superior to Nessus.

You need to be careful not to use the term *vulnerability scanning* to mean "just running some program to find weaknesses." Vulnerability scanning is only a small part of a more strategic program called *vulnerability management.* **Vulnerability management** is an ongoing process of identifying vulnerabilities and dealing with them. The tools we use are a small but important part of the overall process.

Penetration Testing

Once you've run your vulnerability tools and hardened your infrastructure, it's time to see if your network can stand up to an actual attack. The problem with this is that you don't want *real* bad guys making these attacks. You want to be attacked by a "white hat" hacker, who will find the existing vulnerabilities and, instead of hurting your infrastructure, report findings so that you can further harden your network. This is called **penetration testing (pentest)**.

Unlike vulnerability testing, a good pentest requires a skilled operator who understands the target and knows potential vulnerabilities. To that end, there

A legal pentest requires lots of careful documentation that defines what the pentester is to test, the level of testing, time frames, and documentation.

are a number of tools that make this job easier. Two examples are Aircrack-ng and Metasploit.

Aircrack-ng is an open source tool for pentesting pretty much every aspect of wireless networks. It's powerful, relatively easy to use (assuming you understand 802.11 wireless networks in great detail), and completely free.

Metasploit is a unique tool that enables the pentester to use a massive library of attacks as well as tweak those attacks for unique penetrations. Metasploit is the go-to tool for vulnerability testing. You simply won't find a professional in this arena who does not use Metasploit. Metasploit isn't pretty, so many people now use the popular Armitage GUI front end to make it a bit easier (Figure 18.3).

There are also a number of highly customized Linux-based tools that incorporate many tools into a single bootable drive. One of the most famous packages is Kali Linux. It's hard to find a good security person who doesn't have a bootable Kali Linux USB drive.

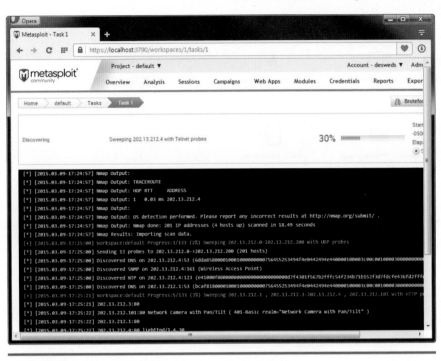

• **Figure 18.3**   Metasploit output

Contingency Planning

Despite the best efforts of competent techs, there will be times when the integrity of an infrastructure is compromised—an **incident**. Incidents can and will vary in size and scope, from something as simple as an attack that was caught and stopped to something serious such as a data breach or a hurricane wiping out a data center. Whatever the case, organizations should develop a set of **contingency plans**—documents about how to limit damage and recover quickly—to respond to these incidents.

The CompTIA Network+ exam covers only a few aspects of contingency planning (and those only lightly) which we can divide into three groups based on the severity and location of the incident: **incident response**, disaster recovery, and business continuity.

Incidents that take place within the organization that can be stopped, contained, and remediated without outside resources are handled by *incident response* planning. If an incident can no longer be contained, causing significant damage or danger to the immediate infrastructure, it is covered under *disaster recovery*. Last, if the disaster requires actions offsite from the primary infrastructure, it is under the jurisdiction of *business continuity*.

While related but not directly connected to contingency planning, we have forensics. Let's hit all these, but keep in mind that this is only the lightest touch on these very complex aspects of contingency planning. The goal of the

CompTIA Network+ certification is only to introduce you to these concepts so that you progress to the next level (hopefully CompTIA Security+).

Incident Response

The cornerstone of incident response is the incident response team—usually one or more trained, preassigned **first responders** with procedures in place for what to do. Depending on the type of event, the team may be responsible for things like: deciding whether it qualifies as an incident the team should address, ignore, or escalate; evaluating the scope and cause of the issue; preventing further disruption; resolving the cause; restoring order to affected systems; and identifying ways to prevent a recurrence. Most incidents are handled at this level. However, if an incident is so vast that the incident response team cannot stop, contain, or remediate it, disaster recovery comes into play.

Disaster Recovery

Disaster recovery is a critical part of contingency planning that deals directly with recovering your primary infrastructure from a disaster. A *disaster* is an event that disables or destroys substantial amounts of infrastructure, such as a hurricane or flood.

Disaster recovery starts with an organization developing a *disaster recovery plan*. An organization considers likely disasters and creates plans for how to deal with them. The actual plans vary by the type of disaster, but there are a few concepts you'll find in just about every situation.

First there is a *disaster recovery team,* whose goal is to get the IT infrastructure up and running at the primary business location(s). One of the big jobs here is creating data backups and making sure those backups are available quickly in the face of any negative event. Any company prepared for a disaster has one or more **backup** copies of essential data. The backed-up files comprise an **archive** of important data that the disaster recovery team can retrieve in case of some disaster.

In the early days of computing, such a backup was done via specific backup software onto some form of magnetic tape. Tape was cheap compared to hard drive space and was easy to move from one location to another. Backups followed fairly specific rotations, so that most of the essential data was always up to date in multiple locations.

Tape is slow and old these days, but hard drives and Internet connections are cheap and fast. Backups roll to removable hard drives and/or directly up into the *cloud.*

A proper assessment of a backup plan records how much data might by lost and how long it would take to restore. A **recovery point objective (RPO)** is the state of the backup when the data is recovered—in essence, how much data will be lost if a backup is used. Most restored systems have some amount of lost data based on when the last backup took place. Real-time backups, which are really just redundant servers, are the exception. The **recovery time objective (RTO)** is the amount of time needed to restore full functionality from when the organization ceases to function.

Disaster recovery handles everything from restoring hardware to backups, but only at the primary business location. Anything that requires moving part of the organization's business offsite until recovery is complete is a part of business continuity.

 I don't mean to make it sound as though tape backups are no longer used. They are. Many tape solutions still fully support the traditional incremental/differential style backups as well.

Business Continuity

When the disaster disables, wipes out, floods, or in some other way prevents the primary infrastructure from operating, the organization should have a plan of action to keep the business going at remote sites. The planning and processes necessary to make this happen are known as business continuity (BC). Organizations plan for this with **business continuity planning (BCP)**. Good BCP will deal with many issues, but one of the more important ones—and one that must be planned well in advance of a major disaster—is the concept of backup sites.

Every business continuity plan includes setting up some form of secondary location that enables an organization to continue to operate should its primary site no longer function. We tend to break these secondary sites into three different types: cold, warm, and hot.

- A **cold site** is a location that consists of a building, facilities, desks, toilets, parking—everything that a business needs . . . except computers. A cold site will generally take more than a few days to bring online.

- A **warm site** is the same as a cold site, but adds computers loaded with software and functioning servers—a complete hardware infrastructure. A warm site lacks current data and may not have functioning Internet/network links. Bringing this site up to speed may start with activating your network links, and it most certainly requires loading data from recent backups. A warm site should only take a day or two to bring online.

- A **hot site** has everything a warm site does, but also includes very recent backups. It might need just a little data restored from a backup to be current, but in many cases a hot site is a complete duplicate of the primary site. A proper hot site should only take a few hours to bring online.

Business continuity isn't just about backup sites, but this aspect is what the CompTIA Network+ exam focuses on. Another term related to continuity planning is **succession planning**: identifying people who can take over certain positions (usually on a temporary basis) in case the people holding those critical positions are incapacitated or lost in an incident.

Forensics

Computer forensics is the science of gathering, preserving, and presenting evidence stored on a computer or any form of digital media that is presentable in a court of law. Computer forensics is a highly specialized science, filled with a number of highly specialized skills and certifications. Three of the top computer forensic certifications are the Certified Forensic Computer Examiner (CFCE), offered by the International Association of Computer Investigative Specialists (IACIS); the Certified Computer Examiner (CCE) certification, from the International Society of Forensic Computer Examiners (ISFCE); and the GIAC Certified Forensic Analyst (GCFA), offered by the Global Information Assurance Certification (GIAC) organization. Achieving one of these challenging certifications gets you well on your way to a great career in forensics.

The CompTIA Network+ exam doesn't expect you to know all there is to know about computer forensics, but instead wants you, as the typical technician, to understand enough of forensics that you know what to do in the rare situation where you find yourself as the first line of defense.

In general, CompTIA sees you as either the first responder or the technician responsible for supporting the first responder. The first responder in a forensic situation is the person or robot whose job is to react to the notification of a computer crime by determining the severity of the situation, collecting information, documenting findings and actions, and providing the information to the proper authorities. In a perfect world, a first responder has a toolbox of utilities that enables him or her to capture the state of the system without disturbing it. At the very least they need to secure the state of the media (mainly hard drives) as well as any volatile memory (RAM) in a way that removes all doubt of tampering either intentionally or unintentionally.

One of the first mistakes any first responder can make is to turn off or reboot a computer.

Like so many aspects of computer security, there isn't a single school of thought on how exactly you should do computer forensics. There are, however, a number of basic attitudes and practices that every school of thought share, especially at the very basic level covered by the CompTIA Network+ exam.

In general, when you are in a situation where you are the first responder, you need to

- Secure the area
- Document the scene
- Collect evidence
- Interface with authorities

Secure the Area

The first step for a first responder is to secure the area. In most cases someone in authority has determined the person or persons who are allegedly responsible and calls you in to react to the incident. As a first responder, your job is to secure the systems involved as well as secure the immediate work areas.

The main way you secure the area is by your presence at the scene. If possible, you should block the scene from prying eyes or potential disturbance. If it's an office, lock the door, define the area of the scene, and mark it off in some way if possible.

Keep in mind that an incident is rarely anything as exciting (or scary) as catching a user committing a felony! In most cases an incident involves something as simple as trying to determine if a user introduced malware into a system or if a user was playing World of Warcraft during work hours. In these cases it's often easy to do your job. Simply observe the system and, if you identify an issue, provide that information in house. The rules for forensics still apply. If, however, you're responding to one of the more scary scenarios, it's important for you as a first responder to understand when you need to *escalate* an issue. Given that *you* were called in to react to a particular incident, most escalation situations involve you discovering something more serious than you expected.

Document the Scene

Once you have secured the area, it's time to *document the scene.* You need to preserve the state of the equipment and look for anything that you might need to inspect forensically.

It's always a good idea to use a camera to document the state of the incident scene, including taking pictures of the operating state of computers and switches and the location of media and other devices.

While it's obvious you'll want to locate computers, switches, WAPs, and routers, be sure to take copious notes, paying particular attention to electronic media. Here are a few items you will want to document:

- Smartphones
- Optical media

- External hard drives
- Thumb drives
- Cameras
- VoIP phones

Collect Evidence

With the scene secured and documented, it's time to start the *evidence/data collection*. The moment you take something away from an incident scene or start to handle or use any devices within the incident scene, there is a chance that your actions could corrupt the evidence you are collecting. You must handle and document all evidence in a very specific manner. **Chain of custody**, as the name implies, is the paper trail of who has accessed or controlled a given piece of evidence from the time it is initially brought into custody until the incident is resolved. From the standpoint of a first responder, the most important item to keep in mind about chain of custody is that you need to document what you took under control, when you did it, what you did to it, and when you passed it to the next person in line.

From a strict legal standpoint, the actual process of how you obtain evidence and collect data is a complex business usually left to certified forensic examiners. In general it boils down to using specialized utilities and tools, many of which are unique for the type of data you are retrieving. The tools used also differ depending on different OSs, platforms, and the personal tastes of the examiners. Every forensic examiner has a number of these tools in his or her unique forensic toolkit.

If you need to transport any form of evidence, make sure to document for chain of custody as well as inventory. In other words, make a list of who has what equipment/evidence at any one time. Pack everything carefully. You don't want a dropped case to destroy data! If you are transporting evidence, don't leave the evidence at any time. Delay your lunch break until after you hand the evidence over to the next person! Follow the proper procedures for *data transport* to avoid any problems with the evidence.

The end result of your forensics is a **forensics report**. In general, this is where you report your findings, if any. A good forensics report will include the following:

- Examiner's name and title
- Examiner's qualifications
- Objective for the forensics
- Any case or incident numbers
- Tools used
- Where the examination took place
- Files found
- Log file output
- Screen snapshots

There are two places where the forensic reports (and forensic evidence) might be used: legal holds and electronic discovery. A **legal hold** is the process of an organization preserving and organizing data in anticipation of or in reaction to a pending legal issue. For example, a company might discover that

your forensic report includes findings of criminal activity that requires reporting to the authorities. In that case the data and the reports must be preserved in such a way that, should a legal authority want access to that data, they can reasonably access it. **Electronic discovery** (or e-discovery) is the process of actually requesting that data and providing it in a legal way.

 As we go to press, the CompTIA Network+ objectives use the abbreviated term *eDiscovery* for electronic discovery. It means the same as e-discovery.

Safety

Managing risk to employee physical health falls into three broad categories: electrical safety, physical/installation safety, and emergency procedures. Let's wrap up this chapter with a discussion of these topics.

Electrical Safety

Electrical safety in a networking environment covers several topics: the inherent danger of electricity, grounding, and static.

As you'll recall from Science 101, electricity can shock you badly, damage you, or even kill you. Keep the networking closet or room clear of clutter. Never use frayed cords. Use the same skills you use to avoid getting cooked by electricity in everyday life.

It is very important with networking to use properly grounded circuits. This is more a data safety issue than a personal safety issue. Poorly grounded circuits can create a **ground loop**—where a voltage differential exists between two parts of your network. This can cause data to become unreadable. Improper grounding also exposes equipment to more risk from power surges.

Electrostatic discharge (ESD)—the passage of a static electrical charge from one item to another—can damage or destroy computing equipment. It's important to wear a properly connected anti-ESD wrist strap when replacing a NIC or doing anything inside a workstation (Figure 18.4).

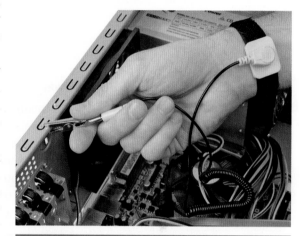

• **Figure 18.4** Anti-ESD wrist strap

The risks from ESD get a lot smaller when you stop opening up computing machines. Routers, switches, and other networking boxes are enclosed and thus protected from technician ESD. Even when you insert a module in a router or switch, the rack is metal and protected and the box should be attached to the rack and thus grounded too.

Physical/Installation Safety

IT techs live in a dangerous world. We're in constant danger of tripping, hurting our backs, and getting burned by hot components. You also need to keep in mind what you wear (in a safety sense). Let's take a moment to discuss these physical safety issues and what to do about them.

If you don't keep organized, hardware technology will take over your life. Figure 18.5 shows a corner of my office, a painful example of a cable "kludge."

• **Figure 18.5** Mike's cable kludge

• **Figure 18.6** What a long, strange trip it's been.

Cable messes such as these are dangerous tripping hazards. While I may allow a mess like this in my home office, all cables in a business environment are carefully tucked away behind computer cases, run into walls, or placed under cable runners. If you see a cable that is an obvious tripping hazard, contact the person in charge of the building (CompTIA calls these folks "building services") to take care of it immediately. The results of ignoring such hazards can be catastrophic (see Figure 18.6).

Another physical safety issue is lifting equipment. Computers, printers, routers—everything we use—all seem to come to us in heavy boxes. Remember never to lift with your back; lift with your legs, and always use a hand truck if available. You are never paid enough to risk your own well-being. Lifting is an important consideration in an important part of a network tech's life: working with racks.

Rack Installation and Maintenance

Installing components into a rack isn't too challenging of a process. Standard 19-inch equipment racks are designed to accept a tremendous amount of abuse, making it sometimes far too easy for people to use them in ways where failure is almost a guarantee. In general, you need to keep in mind three big areas when using rack-mounted equipment: power, mounting, and environment.

 Different rack manufacturers have specific rules and standards for rack electrical grounding. Refer to the installation instructions and consider hiring professional installers when placing your racks.

Power

Rack-mounted equipment has a number of special power needs. At an absolute minimum, start with a proper power source. A single small rack can get away with a properly grounded, 20-amp dedicated circuit. Larger installations will require larger, sometimes dedicated power transformers supplied by the local power grid.

When you get down to individual racks, it's always a good idea to provide each rack with its own rack-mounted UPS. You then connect every device to that UPS. If you're using power converters, always use a single power converter per rack.

 Cross Check

You learned about server room power needs way back in Chapter 17, so cross-check your knowledge now. Why would a server run on DC power rather than AC power?

Mounting

Installing gear into a safe, electrically sound, stable rack is a well-established process. For components that connect directly to a rack, such as switches, routers, and patch panels, hold them in place and secure them with four screws (Figure 18.7). The chassis are designed to support the weight of the devices.

• **Figure 18.7**   Directly connected devices in rack

Racks come in a number of styles, including enclosed, open frame, and "goal post." Best practices call for the rack to be secured to the surrounding facility structure to prevent movement or an off-balance situation from becoming a network disaster.

Bigger devices connect to the rack via a rail system. The standard procedure here is to install the rail system in the rack using locking brackets (Figure 18.8). Then install the device into the rail or tray.

Follow standard safety practices when installing gear, especially if you use power tools. *Tool safety* means, for example: use the properly sized screwdriver head; wear safety goggles when cutting wires; don't use a band saw to miter joints. The usual practices will both get you through any exam question and keep you safe in the workplace.

• **Figure 18.8**   Securing the rail system

Environment

Racks with servers, switches, routers, and such go into closets or server rooms and they dump heat. The environment within this space must be monitored and controlled for both temperature and humidity. Network components work better when cool rather than hot.

The placement of a rack should *optimize the airflow* in a server area. All racks should be placed so that components draw air in from a shared cool row and then exhaust the hot air into a hot row.

The **heating, ventilation, and air conditioning (HVAC)** system should be optimized to recirculate and purify the hot air into cool air in a continuous flow. What's the proper temperature and humidity level? The ideal for the room, regardless of size, is an average temperature of 68 degrees Fahrenheit and ~50% humidity. A proper *fire suppression system*—one that can do things like detect fire, cut power to protect sensitive equipment, displace oxygen with fire-suppressing gasses, alert relevant staff, and activate sprinklers in a pinch— is an absolute must for any server closet or room. You need to get any electrical spark out quickly to minimize server or data loss.

Finally, follow the guidelines in the **material safety data sheet (MSDS)** for the racks and network components to determine best practices for recycling and so forth. An MSDS, as you'll recall from both your CompTIA A+ studies and from previous chapters, details how you should deal with just about any component, including information on replacement parts, recycling, and more.

Emergency Procedures

A final step in managing risk in any company is to have proper *emergency procedures* in place before the emergencies happen. The CompTIA Network+ exam competencies list five essential aspects that should be covered:

■ Building layout

■ Fire escape plan

■ Safety/emergency exits

■ Fail open/fail close

■ Emergency alert system

Exit plans need to cover *building layout, fire escape plans,* and the locations of *emergency exits.* Exit signs should be posted strategically so people can quickly exit in a real emergency.

Secured spaces, such as server rooms, need some kind of default safety mechanism in case of an emergency. Locked doors need to fail open—doors default to open in case of emergency—or fail closed—doors lock in case of emergency.

Finally, nothing beats a properly loud *emergency alert system* blaring away to get people moving quickly. Don't forget to have annual fire drills and emergency alert mixers to make certain all employees know what they need to know.

标记

Chapter 18 Review

■ Chapter Summary

After reading this chapter and completing the exercises, you should understand the following about installing a physical network.

Describe the industry standards for risk management

- The field of IT security is based on the premise that there is a looming attack on some part of a network. Security attacks take many forms, including intentional, unintentional, accidental, natural disasters, acts of war, and others.

- A security policy is a document that defines how an organization will protect its IT infrastructure.

- An acceptable use policy specifies what is and is not permitted to be done on an organization's computers. Acceptable use policies cover topics including ownership of equipment and information, authorized access, privacy and monitoring consent, and illegal use.

- Network policies are really network access policies that define who can access the network, how it can be accessed, and what resources of the network can be accessed.

- Change management teams investigate, test, and authorize most IT changes. IT changes come from two major sources: major strategic-level changes, and areas of infrastructure that need localized changes that are dealt with by the change management team.

- Change management requests can be made with a formal document or via a less formal communication such as an e-mail message.

- Change requests should specify: the type of change, the configuration procedures, a rollback process, the potential impact, and a notification process.

- Most hardware and software requires occasional patches. Patches are issued for operating systems, device drivers, computers, and firmware. Before applying patches, research and test them. Keep configuration backups so equipment can be quickly reconfigured after a patch is applied.

- Effective risk management requires that users receive training in risk mitigation. Users should understand and follow security policies, use good password practices, maintain system and workplace security, recognize social-engineering tactics, and recognize malware.

- The key to dealing with failures is to avoid a single point of failure, where the failure of one system can bring down an entire process, workflow, or organization. Identify critical assets and critical nodes and supply redundancy where possible. Implement high availability for those assets and nodes by building in failover and redundant backups.

- There are four standard business documents defining relationships between an organization and its third-party vendors: a service level agreement, a memorandum of understanding, a multi-source agreement, and a statement of work.

- Preparation for incidents is a multifaceted process with the goal of analyzing IT vulnerabilities to prevent a security breach. Among other issues, security preparedness calls for vulnerability scanning and penetration testing. Popular vulnerability scanners include the Microsoft Baseline Security Analyzer, Nmap, Nessus, and Open VAS.

- Once vulnerabilities have been identified and secured, penetration testing, also called pentest, should be performed to further identify security holes. Pentest reports its findings, which can be used to further harden a network. Kali Linux is a popular collection of pentest tools used by security professionals to perform penetration analysis.

Discuss contingency planning

- An incident is an event in which the security of an IT infrastructure is compromised. Organizations must have contingency plans to respond to an incident in such a way that the organization can continue to function. Incidents that take place within the organization that can be stopped, contained, and remediated without outside resources are handled by incident response planning. Disaster recovery deals with providing methods of recovering your primary infrastructure from a disaster.

- Disaster recovery starts with a plan and includes data backups.

- Business continuity planning prepares for a disaster that requires the business to continue functioning at remote sites. The types of remote site are cold, warm, and hot.

标记

- Computer forensics is the science of gathering, preserving, and presenting computerized data. Technicians are often first responders or supporters of first responders to a security incident and should follow good forensic practices.

- In the event of an incident, secure the area, document the scene, collect evidence, and interface with authorities.

Examine safety standards and actions

- There are four broad categories to managing the physical safety of personnel: electrical safety, physical safety, installation safety, and emergency procedures.

- A clutter-free and well-grounded network environment is critical to human and infrastructure electrical safety. Following good anti-electrostatic discharge practices is necessary to prevent damage to or destruction of computing equipment.

- Physical safety calls for neat, uncluttered network layouts, safe lifting and carrying practices, and general awareness of surroundings.

- Use appropriate power sources and grounding techniques for equipment racks. Mount gear securely using shelves and rails where necessary. Place rack-mounted gear in environmentally friendly areas with good fire suppression protections.

- Have an emergency plan in place that covers: building layout, a fire escape plan, location of safety and emergency exits, which doors open or close upon system failure. Also have an emergency alert system.

■ Key Terms

acceptable use policy *(521)*

Aircrack-ng *(530)*

approval process *(523)*

archive *(531)*

backup *(531)*

business continuity planning (BCP) *(532)*

chain of custody *(534)*

change management *(522)*

change management team *(522)*

change request *(523)*

cold site *(532)*

computer forensics *(532)*

contingency plan *(530)*

disaster recovery *(531)*

documentation *(523)*

electronic discovery *(535)*

electrostatic discharge (ESD) *(535)*

exit plan *(538)*

fail closed *(538)*

fail open *(538)*

first responder *(531)*

forensics report *(534)*

ground loop *(535)*

heating, ventilation, and air conditioning (HVAC) *(537)*

high availability (HA) *(526)*

hot site *(532)*

incident *(530)*

incident response *(530)*

legal hold *(534)*

maintenance window *(523)*

material safety data sheet (MSDS) *(537)*

memorandum of understanding (MOU) *(527)*

Metasploit *(530)*

Microsoft Baseline Security Analyzer (MBSA) *(528)*

multi-source agreement (MSA) *(527)*

Nessus *(529)*

network access policy *(522)*

Nmap *(528)*

penetration testing (pentest) *(529)*

recovery point objective (RPO) *(531)*

recovery time objective (RTO) *(531)*

risk management *(521)*

security policy *(521)*

service level agreement (SLA) *(527)*

single point of failure *(526)*

statement of work (SOW) *(528)*

succession planning *(532)*

virtual IP *(526)*

vulnerability management *(529)*

vulnerability scanner *(528)*

warm site *(532)*

Key Term Quiz

Use the Key Terms list to complete the sentences that follow. Not all terms will be used.

1. A(n) _____ is a written statement that defines how an organization will protect its IT infrastructure.

2. A document or detailed communiqué submitted to the change management team to ask for a modification to the infrastructure is a(n) _____.

3. A(n) _____ is a document that defines the scope, quality, and terms of services to be provided by a service provider.

4. An event in which the security of an infrastructure is compromised is called a(n) _____.

5. The umbrella term that defines how an organization will continue to operate after a disaster is _____.

6. A person whose job it is to react to the notification of a computer crime is called a(n) _____.

7. _____ is the critical part of business continuity that deals with the aftermath of an event that destroys substantial amounts of infrastructure.

8. Should a primary facility fail, a(n) _____ provides all of the resources and computers, but not proper data, to bring an organization back to functionality.

9. _____ is the science of gathering, preserving, and presenting evidence stored on a computer that is acceptable in a court of law.

10. Among other things, _____ is a free utility that's primarily used as a port scanner.

Multiple-Choice Quiz

1. Risk management is a concept that would most likely address which of the following situations?

   A. A user needs to change a password.

   B. A power surge has damaged a switch.

   C. A file server is having more RAM installed.

   D. A user needs the access code to connect to the company wireless network.

2. What issues should be addressed in an acceptable use policy?

   A. ESD handling procedures

   B. Procedures to be followed if malware is detected

   C. How to operate the fire suppression system

   D. Ownership of data on company computers

3. As technologies change, what should organizations do?

   A. Encourage users to bring in new devices for immediate addition to the infrastructure.

   B. Reject new technologies generally in favor of the tried and true.

   C. Ask users to test new technologies in their areas and report their results to IT managers.

   D. Update policies to reflect changes in technologies.

4. Which of the following is true about change management?

   A. Change happens naturally over time as technologies improve.

   B. Once IT infrastructure is established and working, there is seldom need for change.

   C. Change needs to happen, but not at the cost of security.

   D. Change management should be handled by individual department heads for their own area of the network.

5. Before applying a major patch to a critical node, what should be done?

   A. The patch should be tested.

   B. The patch should be checked for malware.

   C. The patch should be applied to non-critical nodes and then, if no ill effects are encountered, installed on the critical nodes.

   D. Drivers should be updated in the critical node.

6. When selecting items to make redundant, which is the most important?

   A. UPS capacity.

   B. Critical nodes.

C. All servers should be made redundant.

D. All servers and switches should be made redundant.

7. Definition of service provided, equipment provided, and level of technical support are elements found in which document?

 A. Service level agreement (SLA)

 B. Memorandum of understanding (MOU)

 C. Statement of work (SOW)

 D. Privacy/consent to monitoring section of the security policy manual

8. As part of security preparedness planning, which two tasks should be performed?

 A. Configuration backup and patch testing

 B. Conduct fire drill and inspect the fire suppression system

 C. Vulnerability scanning and penetration testing

 D. Ensure the racks are grounded and issue ESD wrist straps

9. What is the next step after completing vulnerability scanning and hardening the infrastructure?

 A. Run Nmap to scan all ports.

 B. Run Nessus.

 C. Perform penetration testing.

 D. Run OpenVAS.

10. In terms of risk management, the compromising of an IT infrastructure's security is known as what?

 A. An accident

 B. An incident

 C. Malware

 D. An exploit

11. A cold backup site has which resources?

 A. Desks

 B. Computers

 C. Archived data

 D. Current data

12. The science of gathering, preserving, and presenting evidence stored on a computer is called what?

 A. Computer investigation

 B. Computer assurance

 C. Computer security

 D. Computer forensics

13. Which of the following tasks should be performed by first responders?

 A. Power down the computer and remove the RAM.

 B. Collect the birthdate and description of the user.

 C. Secure the area and document the scene.

 D. Plug the computer into a UPS to keep it running.

14. A paper trail of who has accessed or controlled a piece of evidence is called what?

 A. Legal hold

 B. Handoff trail

 C. Handling trail

 D. Chain of custody

15. Each rack of equipment should be provided with its own what?

 A. Rack-mounted UPS

 B. Optical drive

 C. Camera

 D. Demarc

■ Essay Quiz

1. From this list of forensic certifications, select two:

 ■ CFCE, CCE, GCFA

 Research the requirements of each and write an essay documenting the differences in requirements and benefits of achieving these two certifications.

2. Write a short essay comparing patch management with change management.

Lab Project

• Lab Project 18.1

Search Wikipedia for **"security policy"** and document five different types of security policies.

Protecting Your Network

"The superior man, when resting in safety, does not forget that danger may come."

—Confucius

In this chapter, you will learn how to

- **Discuss common security threats in network computing**
- **Discuss common vulnerabilities inherent in networking**
- **Describe methods for hardening a network against attacks**
- **Explain how firewalls protect a network from threats**

The very nature of networking makes networks vulnerable. By definition, a network must allow multiple users to access serving systems. At the same time, the network must be protected from harm. Doing so is a big business and part of the whole risk management issue touched on back in Chapter 18, "Managing Risk." This chapter concentrates on threats, vulnerabilities, network hardening, and firewalls.

Test Specific

■ Network Threats

A network **threat** is any form of *potential* attack against your network. Don't think only about Internet attacks here. Sure, hacker-style threats are real, but there are so many others. A threat can be a person sneaking into your offices and stealing passwords, or an ignorant employee deleting files they should not have access to in the first place.

Just by reading the word "potential" you should know that this list could go on for pages, but once again CompTIA breaks this down into a very specific list of common threats:

 Some writers use the term "threat agents" to describe the people who can carry out the threats.

- Spoofing
- Packet/protocol abuse
- Zero-day attack
- ARP cache poisoning
- Denial of service (with a lot of variations on a theme)
- Man-in-the-middle
- Session hijacking
- Brute force
- Compromised system
- Insider threat/malicious employee
- VLAN hopping
- Administrative access control
- Malware
- Social engineering
- And more!

It's quite a list, so let's get started.

Spoofing

Spoofing is the process of pretending to be someone or something you are not by placing false information into your packets. Any data sent on a network can be spoofed. Here are a few quick examples of commonly spoofed data:

- Source MAC address and IP address, to make you think a packet came from somewhere else
- E-mail address, to make you think an e-mail came from somewhere else
- Web address, to make you think you are on a Web page you are not on
- User name, to make you think a certain user is contacting you when in reality it's someone completely different

Generally, spoofing isn't so much a threat as it is a tool to make threats. If you spoof my e-mail address, for example, that by itself isn't a threat. If you use my e-mail address to pretend to be me, however, and to ask my employees to send to you their user names and passwords for network login? That's clearly a threat. (And also a waste of time; my employees would *never* trust me with their user names and passwords.)

Packet/Protocol Abuse

No matter how hard the Internet's designers try, it seems there is always a way to take advantage of a protocol by using it in ways it was never meant to be used. Anytime you do things with a protocol that it wasn't meant to do and that abuse ends up creating a threat, this is *protocol abuse*. A classic example involves the Network Time Protocol (NTP).

The Internet keeps time by using NTP servers. Without NTP providing accurate time for everything that happens on the Internet, anything that's time sensitive would be in big trouble.

Here's what happened. No computer's clock is perfect, so NTP is designed for each NTP server to have a number of peers. *Peers* are other NTP servers that one NTP server can compare its own time against to make sure its clock is accurate. Occasionally a person running an NTP server might want to query the server to determine what peers it uses. The command used on just about every NTP server to submit queries is called **ntpdc**. The ntpdc command puts the NTP server into interactive mode so that you can then make queries to the NTP server. One of these queries is called **monlist**. The monlist query asks the NTP server about the traffic going on between itself and peers. If you query a public NTP server with `monlist`, it makes a lot of output:

```
$ ntpdc -c monlist fake.timeserver5.org

remote address          port local address        count m ver rstr avgint  lstint
=================================================================================
time.apple.com           123 192.168.4.78            13 4   4   1d0   319     399
ntp.notreal.com          123 46.3.129.78           1324 4   4     1     0       0
123.212.32.44            123 32.42.77.82              0 0   0     0     0       0

<a few hundred more lines here>

ntpdc>
```

A bad guy can hit multiple NTP servers with the same little command—with a spoofed source IP address—and generate a ton of responses from the NTP server to that source IP. Enough of these requests will bring the spoofed source computer—now called the target or victim—to its knees. We call this a DoS attack (covered a bit later), and it's a form of protocol abuse.

If that's not sinister enough, hackers can also use evil programs that inject unwanted information into packets in an attempt to break another system. We call these *malformed packets*. Programs such as Metasploit give you the capability to custom-form (or should we say malform?) packets and send them to anyone. You can use this to exploit a server that isn't designed to handle such attacks. What will happen if you send a DHCP request packet into which you have placed totally incorrect information in the Option field? What, you didn't know DHCP request packets have an Option field? That's OK, most techs don't know that, but the guy doing this to your DHCP server is hoping that when your DHCP reads the request it will break the server somehow: giving root access, shutting down the DHCP server, whatever. This is an exploit created by packet abuse.

Zero-Day Attacks

The way (software or methods) an exploit takes advantage of a vulnerability is called an *attack surface*. The timeframe in which a bad guy can apply an attack surface against a vulnerability before patches are applied to prevent the exploit is called an *attack window*. New attacks using vulnerabilities that haven't yet been identified (or fixed) are called zero-day attacks.

ARP Cache Poisoning

ARP cache poisoning attacks target the ARP caches on hosts and switches. As we saw back in Chapter 7, "TCP/IP Basics," the process and protocol used in resolving an IP address to an Ethernet MAC address is called Address Resolution Protocol (ARP).

Every node on a TCP/IP network has an *ARP cache* that stores a list of known IP addresses and their associated MAC addresses. On a Windows system you can see the ARP cache using the arp -a command. Here's part of the result of typing arp -a on my system:

```
C:\Users\Mike>arp -a
Interface: 202.13.212.205 --- 0xc
  Internet Address      Physical Address      Type
  202.13.212.1          d0-d0-fd-39-f5-5e     dynamic
  202.13.212.100        30-05-5c-0d-ed-c5     dynamic
  202.13.212.101        00-02-d1-08-df-8d     dynamic
  202.13.212.208        00-22-6b-a0-a2-9b     dynamic
```

If a device wants to send an IP packet to another device, it must encapsulate the IP packet into an Ethernet frame. If the sending device doesn't know the destination device's MAC address, it sends a special broadcast called an *ARP request*. In turn, the device with that IP address responds with a unicast packet to the requesting device. Figure 19.1 shows a Wireshark capture of an ARP request and response.

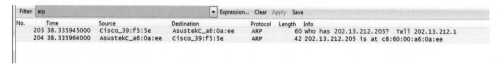

• **Figure 19.1**   ARP request and response

The problem with ARP is that there is no security. Any device that can get on a LAN can wreak havoc with ARP requests and responses. For example, ARP enables any device at any time to announce its MAC address without first getting a request. Additionally, ARP has a number of very detailed but relatively unused specifications. A device can just declare itself to be a "router." How that information is used is up to the writer of the software used by the device that hears this announcement. Fifteen years ago ARP poisoning caused a tremendous amount of trouble. The nature of ARP means it still has the same *ARP issues* today.

The Cisco **Dynamic ARP Inspection (DAI)** tool helps prevent ARP poisoning. DAI learns about your network's systems and their correct MAC and IP addresses, updating a database of trusted systems. DAI can then watch for false or suspicious ARP traffic and simply ignore it. Cisco's **DHCP snooping**, while not exactly an ARP feature, goes hand in hand with DAI as they are almost always configured at the same time (and they use the same database). *DHCP snooping* watches for incoming DHCP requests from unknown MAC addresses, especially any DHCP server requests it does not know, and again simply ignores them.

Denial of Service

Hundreds of millions of servers on the Internet provide a multitude of different services. Given the amount of security now built in at so many different levels, it's more difficult than ever for a bad guy to cripple any one particular service by exploiting a weakness in the servers themselves. So what's a bad guy (or gal, group, or government) to do to shut down a service he doesn't like, even if he is unaware of any exploits on the target servers? Why, denial of service, of course!

A **denial of service (DoS)** attack is a targeted attack on a server (or servers) that provides some form of service on the Internet (such as a Web site), with the goal of making that site unable to process any incoming server requests. DoS attacks come in many different forms. The simplest example is a *physical attack,* where a person physically attacks the servers. Bad guys could go to where the servers are located and shut them down or disconnect their Internet connections, in some cases permanently. Physical DoS attacks are good to know for the exam, but they aren't very common unless the service is very small and served in only a single location.

The most common form of DoS is when a bad guy uses his computer to flood a targeted server with so many requests that the service is overwhelmed and ceases functioning. These attacks are most commonly performed on Web and e-mail servers, but any Internet service's servers can be attacked via some DoS method.

The secret to a successful DoS attack is to send as many packets as possible to the victim. Not only do bad guys want to send a lot of packets, they want the packets to contain some kind of request that the target server must process as long as possible. The aspect of a DoS attack that makes a server do a lot of processing and responding is called **amplification**. A simple monlist command to an NTP server, like we discussed earlier, generates a big response from the server.

Internet-service servers are robust devices, designed to handle a massive number of requests per second. These robust servers make it tricky for a single bad guy at a single computer to send enough requests to slow them down. Far more menacing, and far more common than a simple DoS attack, are **distributed denial of service (DDoS)** attacks. A DDoS uses hundreds, thousands, or even millions of computers under the control of a single operator to launch a coordinated attack. DDoS operators don't own these computers, but instead use malware (discussed later) to take control of computers. A single computer under the control of an operator is called a **zombie**. A group of computers under the control of one operator is called a **botnet**.

Implementing Dynamic ARP Inspection (DAI) and DHCP snooping enhances *switchport security,* a key network hardening technique.

When Ethernet segments were made up of a single shared stretch of coaxial cable, or when stations were all attached to a simple hub, the network was susceptible to many more collisions than they are using current switching technology. When a collision occurred, one or both of the nodes involved in the collision would send out a *jam* signal on the segment. This signal would cause all stations to stop transmitting and begin their collision avoidance protocol. The intended result was that, eventually, all nodes would get a crack at sending their data on the medium.

A malicious user could take advantage of the process by sending out frequent (nonstop, actually!) artificial jam signals—what was called *jamming*—that effectively prevented any other station on the collision domain from transmitting its data onto the network. Think of jamming as an older cousin to DoS attacks.

The introduction of switches effectively rendered the process of jamming useless. You'll only find the term used now on a certain certification exam coming soon to you.

 Zombified computers aren't obvious. DDoS operators often wait weeks or months after a computer's been infected to take control of it.

To take control of your network's computers, someone has to install malware on the computer. Again, anti-malware, training, and procedures will keep your computers safe from zombification (as long as they aren't bitten by an already zombified computer).

The goal of a botnet operator conducting a DDoS attack is to send as many amplified requests as possible, but botnets are only one way to do this. Another tactic used in DDoS attacks is to send requests with the target server's IP address to otherwise normally operating servers, such as DNS or NTP servers. This is called **reflection** or a **reflective DDoS**. These servers then send massive numbers of amplified responses to the target. Such a huge increase in the number of packets—a **traffic spike**—will bring the target down.

DoS attacks come in many variations. Let's turn to three common types that you'll see on the CompTIA Network+ exam: smurf, unintentional, and permanent.

Smurf

A **smurf attack** is an early form of DoS. The attacker floods a network with ping packets sent to the broadcast address. The trick that makes this attack special is that the return address of the pings is spoofed to that of the intended victim. When all the computers on the network respond to the initial ping, they send their response to the intended victim. The attacker can then amplify the effect of the attack by the number of responding machines on the network. Due to modern network management procedures and controls built into modern operating systems, the danger of the smurf attack has been largely mitigated.

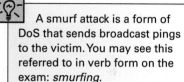
A smurf attack is a form of DoS that sends broadcast pings to the victim. You may see this referred to in verb form on the exam: *smurfing*.

Unintentional

A *friendly* or *unintentional DoS* is just as it's named: a system is brought down unintentionally. The most common form of friendly DoS occurs on a superbusy server: an organization's infrastructure isn't strong enough to keep up with legitimate demand. This is very common on the Web when a popular site makes a reference to a small site or someone mentions the small site on a radio or TV program, resulting in a massive increase in traffic to the small site. This "hug of death" goes by many names, such as **Slashdotting** or the **Reddit effect**.

Permanent DoS

A **permanent DoS (PDoS)** is an attack that damages the targeted machine—router, server, and so on—and renders that machine inoperable. The attacker gains control over the management interface of a router, for example, and makes malicious changes to brick that router. The router needs to be repaired or, worst case, replaced. PDoS attacks are sometimes referred to as *phlashing* attacks.

Man-in-the-Middle

In a **man-in-the-middle** attack, an attacker taps into communications between two systems, covertly intercepting traffic thought to be only between those systems, reading or in some cases even changing the data and then sending the data on. A classic man-in-the-middle attack would be a person using special software on a wireless network to make all the clients think his laptop is a WAP. He could then listen in on that wireless network, gathering up all the conversations and gaining access to passwords, shared keys, or other sensitive information. Man-in-the-middle attacks are commonly perpetrated using ARP poisoning.

Session Hijacking

Somewhat similarly to man-in-the-middle attacks, session hijacking tries to intercept a valid computer session to get authentication information. Unlike man-in-the-middle attacks, session hijacking only tries to grab authentication information, not necessarily listening in like a man-in-the-middle attack.

Brute Force

CompTIA describes brute force as a threat, but I think it's more of a method that threat agents use as opposed to a threat itself. Brute force is a method where a threat agent guesses every permutation of some part of data. Most of the time the term *brute force* refers to an attempt to crack a password, but the term applies to other attacks. You can brute force a search for open ports, network IDs, user names, and so on. Pretty much any attempt to guess the contents of some kind of data field that isn't obvious (or is hidden) is a considered a brute force attack.

Physical/Local Access

Not all threats to your network originate from faraway bad guys. There are many threats that lurk right in your LAN, inside your network. This is a particularly dangerous place as these threats don't need to worry about getting past your network edge defenses such as firewalls or WAPs. You need to watch out for problems with hardware, software and, worst of all, the people who are on your LAN.

Compromised System

Like any technology, computers can and will fail—usually when you can least afford for it to happen. Hard drives crash, servers lock up, the power fails—it's all part of the joy of working in the networking business. Because of this, you need to create redundancy in areas prone to failure (like installing backup power in case of electrical failure) and perform those all-important data backups. Beyond that, the idea is to deploy redundant hardware to provide fault tolerance. Take advantage of technologies like redundant array of inexpensive disks (RAID) to spread data across multiple drives. Buy a server case with multiple power supplies, or add a second NIC.

Insider Threats

The greatest hackers in the world will all agree that being inside an organization, either physically or by access permissions, makes evildoing much easier. Malicious employees are a huge threat because of their ability to directly destroy data, inject malware, and initiate attacks.

Trusted and Untrusted Users   A worst-case scenario from the perspective of security is *unsecured access to private resources*. A couple of terms come into play here. There are trusted users and untrusted users. A trusted user is an account that has been granted specific authority to perform certain or all administrative tasks. An untrusted user is just the opposite; an account that has been granted no administrative powers.

Trusted users with poor password protection or other security leakages can be compromised. Untrusted users can be upgraded "temporarily" to accomplish a particular task and then forgotten. Consider this situation: A user accidentally copied a bunch of files to several shared network repositories. The administrator does not have time to search for and delete all of the files. The user is granted deletion capability and told to remove the unneeded files. Do you feel a disaster coming? The newly created trusted user could easily remove the wrong files. Careful management of trusted users is the simple solution to these types of threats.

Every configurable device, like a multilayer switch, has a default password and default settings, all of which can create an inadvertent insider threat if not addressed. People sometimes can't help but be curious. A user might note the IP address of a switch on his network, for example, and run Telnet or SSH "just to see." Because it's so easy to get the default passwords/settings for devices with a simple Google search, that information is available to the user. One change on that switch might mean a whole lot of pain for the network tech or administrator who has to fix things.

Dealing with such authentication issues is pretty straightforward. Before bringing any system online, change any default accounts and passwords. This is particularly true for administrative accounts. Also, disable or delete any "guest" accounts (make sure you have another account created first!).

Malicious Users Much more worrisome than accidental accesses to unauthorized resources are those who consciously attempt to access, steal, or damage resources. CompTIA calls these folks **malicious users**, but they go by many names, often including the term "actors." Malicious actors may represent an external or internal threat.

What does a malicious user want to do? If they are intent on stealing data or gaining further access, they may try *packet sniffing*. This is difficult to detect, but as you know from previous chapters, encryption is a strong defense against sniffing. One of the first techniques that malicious users try is to probe hosts to identify any open ports. There are many tools available to poll all stations on a network for their up/down status and for a list of any open ports (and, by inference, all closed ports too). Angry IP Scanner is a great tool for troubleshooting hosts, but can be used for these types of malevolent activities.

Having found an open port, another way for a malicious user to gain information and additional access is to probe a host's open ports to learn details about running services. This is known as **banner grabbing**. For instance, a host may have a running Web server installed. Using a utility like Telnet or Netcat, a malicious user can send an invalid request to port 80 of the server. The server may respond with an error message indicating the type and version of Web server software that is running. With that information, the malicious actor can then learn about vulnerabilities of that product and continue their pursuit. The obvious solution to port scanning and banner grabbing is to not run unnecessary services (resulting in an open port) on a host and to make sure that running processes have current security patches installed.

In the same vein, a malicious user may attempt to exploit known vulnerabilities of certain devices attached to the network. MAC addresses of Ethernet NICs have their first 24 bits assigned by the IEEE. This is a unique number assigned to a specific manufacturer and is known as the **organizationally unique identifier (OUI)**, sometimes called the vendor ID. By issuing certain ICMP messages such as broadcasted ARP and RARP packets, a malicious user can collect all of the OUI numbers of the wired and wireless nodes attached to a network or subnetwork. Using common lookup tools, the malicious user can identify devices by OUI numbers assigned to particular manufactures, such as those assigned to Apple and used in a certain generation of iPads.

VLAN Hopping

An older form of attack that still comes up from time to time is called **VLAN hopping**. The idea behind VLAN hopping is to take a system that's connected to one VLAN and, by abusing VLAN commands to the switch, convince the switch to change your switchport connection to a trunk link. VLAN hopping is almost never seen anymore because modern switches are all designed to prevent this.

Administrative Access Control

All operating systems and many TCP applications come with some form of access control list (ACL) that defines what users can do with the server's shared resources. CompTIA also refers to this as an *access list*. An access control might be a file server giving a user read-only privileges to a particular folder, or a firewall only allowing certain internal IP addresses to access the Internet. ACLs are everywhere in a network. In fact, you'll see more of them from the standpoint of a firewall later in this chapter.

Every operating system—and many Internet applications—are packed with administrative tools and functionality. You need these tools to get all kinds of work done, but by the same token, you need to work hard to keep these capabilities out of the reach of those who don't need them.

Make sure you know the **administrative accounts** native to Windows (administrator), Linux (root), and OS X (root). You must carefully control these accounts. Clearly, giving regular users administrator/root access is a bad idea, but far more subtle problems can arise. I once gave a user the Manage Documents permission for a busy laser printer in a Windows network. She quickly realized she could pause other users' print jobs and send her print jobs to the beginning of the print queue—nice for her but not so nice for her co-workers. Protecting administrative programs and functions from access and abuse by users is a real challenge and one that requires an extensive knowledge of the operating system and of users' motivations.

The CompTIA Network+ exam does not test you on the details of file system access controls. In other words, don't bother memorizing details like NTFS permissions, but do appreciate that you have fine-grained controls available.

Administering your super accounts is only part of what's called *user account control*. See "Controlling User Accounts" later in this chapter for more details.

Malware

The term **malware** defines any program or code (macro, script, and so on) that's designed to do something on a system or network that you don't want to have happen. Malware comes in many forms, such as viruses, worms, macros, Trojan horses, rootkits, adware, and spyware. We'll examine all these malware flavors in this section. Stopping malware, by far the number one security problem for just about everyone, is so important that we'll address that topic in its own section later in this chapter, "Anti-Malware Programs."

Virus

A **virus** is a program that has two jobs: to replicate and to activate. *Replication* means it makes copies of itself, often as code stored in boot sectors or as extra code added to the end of executable programs. A virus is not a stand-alone program, but rather something attached to a host file, kind of like a human virus. *Activation* is when a virus does something like erase the boot sector of a drive. A virus only replicates to other applications on a drive or to other drives, such as thumb drives or optical media. It does not replicate across networks. Plus, a virus needs human action to spread.

Worm

A **worm** functions similarly to a virus, though it replicates exclusively through networks. A worm, unlike a virus, doesn't have to wait for someone to use a removable drive to replicate. If the infected computer is on a network, a worm will immediately start sending copies of itself to any other computers it can locate on the network. Worms can exploit inherent flaws in program code like *buffer overflows,* where a buffer cannot hold all the data sent to it. Worms, unlike viruses, do not need host files to infect.

Macro

A **macro** is any type of virus that exploits application macros to replicate and activate. A *macro* is also programming within an application that enables you to control aspects of the application. Macros exist in any application that has a built-in macro language, such as Microsoft Excel, that users can program to handle repetitive tasks (among other things).

Trojan Horse

A **Trojan horse** is a piece of malware that looks or pretends to do one thing while, at the same time, doing something evil. A Trojan horse may be a game, like poker, or a free screensaver. The sky is the limit. The more "popular" Trojan horses turn an infected computer into a server and then open TCP or UDP ports so a remote user can control the infected computer. They can be used to capture keystrokes, passwords, files, credit card information, and more. Trojan horses do not replicate.

Rootkit

For a virus or Trojan horse to succeed, it needs to come up with some method to hide itself. As awareness of malware has grown, anti-malware programs make it harder to find new locations on a computer to hide. A **rootkit** takes advantage of very low-level operating system functions to hide itself from all but the most aggressive of anti-malware tools. Worse, a rootkit, by definition, gains privileged access to the computer. Rootkits can strike operating systems, hypervisors, and even firmware.

Adware/Spyware

There are two types of programs that are similar to malware in that they try to hide themselves to an extent. **Adware** is a program that monitors the types of Web sites you frequent and uses that information to generate targeted advertisements, usually pop-up windows. Many of these programs use Adobe Flash. Adware isn't, by definition, evil, but many adware makers use sneaky methods to get you to use adware, such as using deceptive-looking Web pages ("Your computer is infected with a virus—click here to scan NOW!"). As a result, adware is often considered malware. Some of the computer-infected ads actually install a virus when you click them, so avoid these things like the plague.

    Spyware is a function of any program that sends information about your system or your actions over the Internet. The type of information sent depends on the program. A spyware program will include your browsing history. A more aggressive form of spyware may send keystrokes or all of the contacts in your e-mail. Some spyware makers bundle their product with ads to make them look innocuous. Adware, therefore, can contain spyware.

Social Engineering

A considerable percentage of attacks against your network fall under the heading of social engineering—the process of using or manipulating people inside the networking environment to gain access to that network from the outside. The term "social engineering" covers the many ways humans can use other humans to gain unauthorized information. This unauthorized information may be a network login, a credit card number, company customer data—almost anything you might imagine that one person or organization may not want a person outside of that organization to access.

Social engineering attacks aren't considered hacking—at least in the classic sense of the word—although the goals are the same. Social engineering is where people attack an organization through the people in the organization or physically access the organization to get the information they need.

The most classic form of social engineering is the telephone scam in which someone calls a person and tries to get him or her to reveal his or her user name/password combination. In the same vein, someone may physically enter your building under the guise of having a legitimate reason for being there, such as a cleaning person, repair technician, or messenger. The attacker then snoops around desks, looking for whatever he or she has come to find (one of many good reasons not to put passwords on your desk or monitor). The attacker might talk with people inside the organization, gathering names, office numbers, or department names—little things in and of themselves, but powerful tools when combined later with other social engineering attacks.

These old-school social engineering tactics are taking a backseat to a far more nefarious form of social engineering: phishing.

> All these attacks are commonly used together, so if you discover one of them being used against your organization, it's a good idea to look for others.

Phishing

In a phishing attack, the attacker poses as some sort of trusted site, like an online version of your bank or credit card company, and solicits you to update your financial information, such as a credit card number. You might get an e-mail message, for example, that purports to be from PayPal telling you that your account needs to be updated and provides a link that looks like it goes to http://www.paypal.com. Upon clicking the link, however, you end up at a site that resembles the PayPal login but is actually http://100.16.49.21/2s82ds.php, a phishing site.

Physical Intrusion

You can't consider a network secure unless you provide some physical protection to your network. I separate physical protection into two different areas: protection of servers and protection of clients.

Server protection is easy. Lock up your servers to prevent physical access by any unauthorized person. Large organizations have special server rooms, complete with card-key locks and tracking of anyone who enters or exits. Smaller organizations should at least have a locked closet. While you're locking up your servers, don't forget about any network switches! Hackers can access networks by plugging into a switch, so don't leave any switches available to them.

Physical server protection doesn't stop with a locked door. One of the most common mistakes made by techs is to walk away from a server while still logged in. Always log off from your server when you're not actively managing the server. As a backup, add a password-protected screensaver (Figure 19.2).

Locking up all of your client systems is difficult, but your users should be required to perform some physical security. First, all users should lock their computers when they step away from their desks. Instruct them to press the WINDOWS KEY-L combination to perform the lock. Hackers take advantage of unattended systems to get access to networks.

Second, make users aware of the potential for dumpster diving and make paper shredders available. Last, tell users to mind their work areas. It's amazing how many users leave passwords readily available. I can go into any office, open a few desk drawers, and invariably find little yellow sticky notes with user names and passwords. If users must write down passwords, tell them to put them in locked drawers!

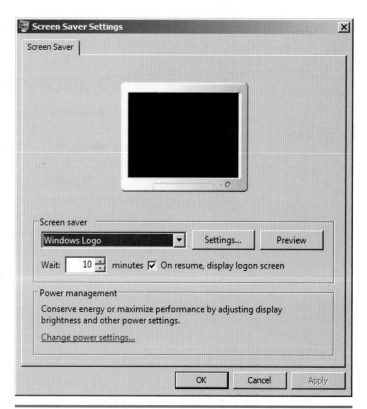

• **Figure 19.2** Applying a password-protected screensaver to a server

 Cross Check

Wireless Threats

You've just read about some threats common to all networks, but back in Chapter 15, "Wireless Networking," you learned about some threats specific to wireless networks, so cross check this out. Do you remember what a rogue access point (AP) does? What about war driving or war chalking? Are these common wireless threats today?

 Tech Tip

Lock Them Down
A Windows PC should be locked down when it's not actively being used. The simplest thing to teach your users to do is to press the WINDOWS KEY-L combination when they get up from their desks. The effects from the key combination vary according to both the version of Windows and whether a system is a member of a workgroup or domain, but all will require the user to log in to access his or her account (assuming the account is password protected in the first place, of course!).

▣ Common Vulnerabilities

If a threat is an action that threat agents do to try to compromise our networks, then a **vulnerability** is a potential weakness in our infrastructure that a threat might exploit. Note that I didn't say that a threat will take advantage of the vulnerability: only that the vulnerability is a weak place that needs to be addressed. Some vulnerabilities are obvious, such as connecting to the Internet without an edge firewall or not using any form of account control for user files. Other vulnerabilities are unknown or missed, and that makes the study of vulnerabilities very important for a network tech.

If you really want to specialize in threats and vulnerabilities, you need to look into gaining CompTIA Security+ certification and studying risk

If you want to get an idea as to the depth of vulnerabilities, check out the Common Vulnerabilities and Exposures (CVE) database hosted by MITRE Corporation here: https://cve.mitre.org/.

management at a far more structured level. For the CompTIA Network+, you only need to respond to a number of specific objectives.

Unnecessary Running Services

A typical system running any OS is going to have a large number of important programs running in the background, called **services**. Services do the behind-the-scenes grunt work that users don't need to see, such as wireless network clients, DHCP clients, Web servers, and so forth.

As a Windows user, I've gotten used to seeing zillions of services running on my system, and in most cases I can only recognize only about 50% of them—and I'm good at this! In a typical system, not all these services are necessary, so you should *disable unneeded network services.*

From a security standpoint, there are two reasons it's important not to run any unnecessary services. First, most OSs use services to listen on open TCP or UDP ports, potentially leaving systems open to attack. Second, bad guys often use services as a tool for the use and propagation of malware.

The problem with trying not to run unnecessary services is the fact that there are just so many of them. It's up to you to research services running on a particular machine to determine if they're needed or not. It's a rite of passage for any tech to review the services running on a system, going through them one at a time. Over time you will become familiar with many of the built-in services and get an eye for spotting the ones that just don't look right. There are tools available to do the job for you, but this is one place where you need skill and practice.

Closing unnecessary services closes TCP/UDP ports. Every operating system has some tool for you to see exactly what ports are open. Figure 19.3 shows an example of the `netstat` command in Windows.

• **Figure 19.3**   netstat in action

Unpatched/Legacy Systems

Unpatched systems—including operating systems and firmware—and legacy systems present a glaring security threat. You need to deal with such problems on live systems on your network. When it comes to unpatched OSs, well, patch or isolate them! There's a number of areas in the book that touch on proper patching, so we won't go into more detail here.

Unpatched firmware presents a little more of a challenge. Most firmware never needs to be or gets patched, but once in a while you'll run into devices that have a discovered flaw or security hole. These you'll need to patch.

The process of patching device firmware varies from device to device, so you'll need to do some research on each. In general, you'll download a patch from the manufacturer and run it on the device. Make sure you have good power before you start the patch. If something goes wrong in the update, you'll brick whatever device you're trying to patch. There's no undo or patch rollback with firmware, so patch only when necessary.

Legacy systems are a different issue altogether. By *legacy* we mean systems that are no longer supported by the OS maker and are no longer patched. In that case you need to consider the function of the system, update if possible, and if not possible, you need to isolate the legacy systems behind some type of firewall that will give them the support they need. Equally, you need to be extremely careful about adding any software or hardware to the systems as doing so might create even more vulnerabilities.

Unencrypted Channels

The open nature of the Internet has made it fairly common for us to *use secure protocols* or channels such as VPNs, SSL/TLS, and SSH. It never ceases to amaze me, however, how often people use unencrypted channels—especially in the most unlikely places. It was only a few years ago I stumbled upon a tech using Telnet to do remote logins into a very critical router for an ISP.

In general, look for the following insecure protocols and unencrypted channels:

- Using Telnet instead of SSH for remote terminal connections.

- Using HTTP instead of HTTPS on Web sites.

- Using insecure remote desktops like VNC.

- Using any insecure protocol in the clear. Run them through a VPN!

Cleartext Credentials

Older protocols offer a modicum of security—you often need a valid user name and password, for example, when connecting to a File Transfer Protocol (FTP) server. The problem with such protocols (FTP, Telnet, POP3) is that user names and passwords are sent from the user to the server in cleartext. Credentials can be captured and, because they're not encrypted, cleartext credentials can be readily discovered.

There are many other places where cleartext turns up, such as in third-party applications and improperly configured applications that would normally have encrypted credentials.

The problem with third-party applications using cleartext credentials is that there's no way for you to know if they do so or not. Luckily, we live in a world filled with people who run packet sniffers on just about everything. These vulnerabilities are often discovered fairly quickly and reported. Most likely, you'll get an automatic patch.

The last place where cleartext credentials can still come through is poor configuration of applications that would otherwise be well protected. Almost any remote control program has some form of "no security" level setting. This might be as obvious as a "turn off security" option or it could be a setting such as PAP (which, for those who are not aware, means cleartext passwords).

The answer here is understanding your applications and knowing ahead of time how to configure the application to ensure good encryption of credentials.

RF Emanation

Radio waves can penetrate walls, to a certain extent, and accidental spill, called RF emanation, can lead to a security vulnerability. Avoid this by placing some form of filtering between your systems and the place where the bad guys are going to be using their super high-tech Bourne Identity spy tools to pick up on the emanations.

To combat these emanations, the U.S. National Security Agency (NSA) developed a series of standards called TEMPEST. TEMPEST defines how to shield systems and manifests in a number of different products, such as coverings for individual systems, wall coverings, and special window coatings. Unless you work for a U.S. government agency, the chance of you seeing TEMPEST technologies is pretty small.

■ Hardening Your Network

Once you've recognized threats and vulnerabilities, it's time to start applying security hardware, software, and processes to your network to prevent bad things from happening. This is called hardening your network. Let's look at three aspects of network hardening: physical security, network security, and host security.

Physical Security

There's an old saying: "The finest swordsman in all of France has nothing to fear from the second finest swordsman in all of France." It means that they do the same things and know the same techniques. The only difference between the two is that one is a little better than the other. There's a more modern extension of the old saying that says: "On the other hand, the finest swordsman in all of France can be defeated by a kid with a rocket launcher!" Which is to say that the inexperienced, when properly equipped, can and will often do something totally unexpected.

Proper security must address threats from the second finest swordsman as well as the kid. We can leave no stone unturned when it comes to hardening the network, and this begins with physical security. Physical threats manifest themselves in many forms, including property theft, data loss due to natural damage such as fire or natural disaster, data loss due to physical access, and property destruction resulting from accident or sabotage.

Let's look at physical security as a two-step process. First, prevent and control access to IT resources to appropriate personnel. Second, track the actions of those authorized (and sometimes unauthorized) personnel.

Prevention and Control

The first thing we have to do when it comes to protecting the network is to make the network resources accessible only to personnel who have a legitimate need to fiddle with them. Start with the simplest approach: a locked door.

Locking the door to the **network closet** or equipment room that holds servers, switches, routers, and other network gear goes a long way in protecting the network. Key control is critical here and includes assigning keys to appropriate staff, tracking key assignments, and collecting the keys when they are no longer needed by individuals who move on. This type of access must be guarded against circumvention by ensuring policies are followed regarding who may have or use the keys. The administrator who assigns keys should never give one to an unauthorized person without completing the appropriate procedures and paperwork.

And it's not just the server room that we need to lock up. How about the front door? There are a zillion stories of thieves and saboteurs coming in through the front (or sometimes back) door and making their way straight to the corporate treasure chest. A locked front door can be opened by an authorized person, and an unauthorized person can attempt to enter through that already opened door, what's called **tailgating**. While it is possible to prevent tailgating with policies, it is only human nature to "hold the door" for that person coming in behind you. Tailgating is especially easy to do when dealing with large organizations in which people don't know everyone else. If the tailgater dresses like everyone else and maybe has a badge that looks right, he or she probably won't be challenged. Add an armload of gear, and who could blame you for helping that person by holding the door?

There are a couple of techniques available to foil a tailgater. The first is a **security guard**. Guards are great. They get to know everyone's faces. They are there to protect assets and can lend a helping hand to the overloaded, but authorized, person who needs in. They are multipurpose in that they can secure building access, secure individual room and office access, and perform facility patrols. The guard station can serve as central control of security systems such as video surveillance and key control. Like all humans, security guards are subject to attacks such as social engineering, but for flexibility, common sense, and a way to take the edge off of high security, you can't beat a professional security guard or two.

For areas where an entry guard is not practical, there is another way to prevent tailgating called a mantrap. A **mantrap** is an entryway with two successive locked doors and a small space between them providing one-way entry or exit. After entering the first door, the second door cannot be unlocked until the first door is closed and secured. Access to the second door may be a simple key or may require approval by someone else who watches the trap space on video. Unauthorized persons remain trapped until they are approved for entry, let out the first door, or held for the appropriate authorities.

Brass keys aren't the only way to unlock a door. This is the 21st century, after all. Twenty-five years ago, I worked in a campus facility with a lot of interconnected buildings. Initial access to buildings was through a security guard and then we traveled between the buildings with connecting tunnels. Each end of the tunnels had a set of sliding glass doors that kind of worked like the doors on the starship *Enterprise*. We were assigned badges with built-in radio frequency ID (RFID) chips. As we neared a door, the RFID chip was queried by circuitry in the door frame called a **proximity reader**, checked against a database for authorization, and then the door slid open electromechanically.

It was so cool and so fast that people would jog the hallways during lunch hours and not even slow down for any of the doors. A quarter century later, the technology has only gotten better. The badges in the old days were a little larger than a credit card and about three times as thick. Today, the RFID chip can be implanted in a small, unobtrusive **key fob**, like the kind you use to unlock your car.

If there is a single drawback to all of the physical **door access controls** mentioned so far, it is that access is generally governed by something that is in the possession of someone who has authorization to enter a locked place. That something may be a key, a badge, a key fob with a chip, or some other physical token. The problem here, of course, is that these items can be given or taken away. If not reported in a timely fashion, a huge security gap exists.

To move from the physical possession problem of entry access, physical security can be governed by something that is known only to authorized persons. A code or password that is assigned to a specific individual for a particular asset can be entered on an alphanumeric **keypad** that controls an electric or electromechanical door lock. There is a similar door lock mechanism called a cipher lock. A **cipher lock** is a door unlocking system that uses a door handle, a latch, and a sequence of mechanical push buttons. When the buttons are pressed in the correct order, the door unlocks and the door handle works. Turning the handle opens the latch or, if you pressed the wrong order of buttons, clears the unlocking mechanism so you can try again. Care must be taken by staff who are assigned a code to protect that code.

This knowledge-based approach to access control may be a little better than a possession-based system because information is more difficult to steal than a physical token. However, poor management of information can leave an asset vulnerable. Poor management includes writing codes down and leaving the notes easily accessible. Good password/code control means memorizing information where possible or securing written notes about codes and passwords.

Well-controlled information is difficult to steal, but it's not perfect because sharing information is so easy. Someone can loan out his or her password to a seemingly trustworthy friend or co-worker. While most times this is probably not a real security risk, there is always a chance that there could be disastrous results. Social engineering or over-trusting can cause someone to share a private code or password. Systems should be established to reassign codes and passwords regularly to deal with the natural leakage that can occur with this type of security.

The best way to prevent loss of access control is to build physical security around a key that cannot be shared or lost. **Biometric** access calls for using a unique physical characteristic of a person to permit access to a controlled IT resource. Doorways can be triggered to unlock using fingerprint readers, facial recognition cameras, voice analyzers, retinal blood vessel scanners, or other, more exotic characteristics. While not perfect, biometrics represent a giant leap in secure access. For even more effective access control, *multifactor authentication* can be used, where access is granted based on more than one access technique. For instance, in order to gain access to a secure server room, a user might have to pass a retinal scan and have an approved security fob.

Let me point out something related to all of this door locking and unlocking technology. Physical asset security is important, but generally not as important as the safety of people. Designers of these door-locking systems must take into account safety features such as what happens to the state of a lock in an emergency like a power failure or fire. Doors with electromechanical locking controls can respond to an emergency condition and lock or unlock automatically, respectively called **fail close** or **fail open**. Users and occupants of facilities should be informed about what to expect in these types of events.

Monitoring

Okay, the physical assets of the network have been secured. It took guards, locks, passwords, eyeballs, and a pile of technology. Now, the only people who have access to IT resources are those who have been carefully selected, screened, trained, and authorized. The network is safe, right? Maybe not. You see, here comes the old problem again: people are human. Humans make mistakes, humans can become disgruntled, and humans can be tempted. The only real solution is heavily armored robots with artificial intelligence and bad attitudes. But until that becomes practical, maybe what we need to do next is to ensure that those authorized people can be held accountable for what they do with the physical resources of the network.

Enter video surveillance. With video surveillance of facilities and assets, authorized staff can be monitored for mistakes or something more nefarious. Better still, our kid with a rocket launcher (remember him?) can be tracked and caught after he sneaks into the building.

For the purposes of the CompTIA Network+ objectives, let's look at two video concepts. **Video monitoring** entails using remotely monitored visual systems and covers everything from identifying a delivery person knocking on the door at the loading dock, to looking over the shoulder of someone working on the keyboard of a server. **IP cameras** and **closed-circuit televisions (CCTVs)** are specific implementations of video monitoring. CCTV is a self-contained, closed system in which video cameras feed their signal to specific, dedicated monitors and storage devices. CCTV cameras can be monitored in real time by security staff, but the monitoring location is limited to wherever the video monitors are placed. If real-time monitoring is not required or viewing is delayed, stored video can be reviewed later as needed.

IP cameras have the benefit of being a more open system than CCTV. IP video streams can be monitored by anyone who is authorized to do so and can access the network on which the cameras are installed. The stream can be saved to a hard drive or network storage device. Multiple workstations can simultaneously monitor video streams and multiple cameras with ease.

Network Security

Protecting network assets is more than a physical exercise. Physically speaking, we can harden a network by preventing and controlling access to tangible network resources through things like locking doors and video monitoring. Next we will want to protect our network from malicious, suspicious, or potential threats that might connect to or access the network. This is called **access control** and it encompasses both physical security and network security. In this section we look at some technologies and techniques to implement network access control, including user account control, edge devices, posture assessment, persistent and non-persistent agents, guest networks, and quarantine networks.

Controlling User Accounts

A user account is just information: nothing more than a combination of a user name and password. Like any important information, it's critical to control who has a user account and to track what these accounts can do. Access to user accounts should be restricted to the assigned individuals (no sharing, no stealing), and those accounts should have permission to access only the

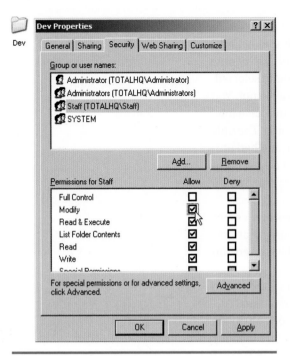

• Figure 19.4 Giving a group permissions for a folder in Windows

resources they need, no more. This control over what a legitimate account can do is called the *principle of least privilege* approach to network security and is, by far, the most common approach used in networks.

Tight control of user accounts helps prevent unauthorized access or improper access. *Unauthorized access* means a person does something beyond his or her authority to do. *Improper access* occurs when a user who shouldn't have access gains access through some means. Often the improper access happens when a network tech or administrator makes a mistake.

Disabling unused accounts is an important first step in addressing these problems, but good user account control goes far deeper than that. One of your best tools for user account control is to implement groups. Instead of giving permissions to individual user accounts, give them to groups; this makes keeping track of the permissions assigned to individual user accounts much easier.

Figure 19.4 shows an example of giving permissions to a group for a folder in Windows Server. Once a group is created and its permissions are set, you can then add user accounts to that group as needed. Any user account that becomes a member of a group automatically gets the permissions assigned to that group.

Figure 19.5 shows an example of adding a user to a newly created group in the same Windows Server system.

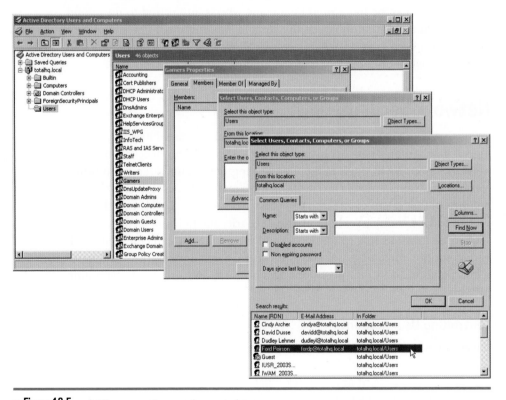

• Figure 19.5 Adding a user to a newly created group

You should always put user accounts into groups to enhance network security. This applies to simple networks, which get local groups, and to domain-based networks, which get domain groups. Do not underestimate the importance of properly configuring both local groups and domain groups.

Groups are a great way to get increased complexity without increasing the administrative burden on network administrators because all network operating systems combine permissions. When a user is a member of more than one group, which permissions does he or she have with respect to any particular resource?

In all network operating systems, the permissions of the groups are *combined,* and the result is what is called the **effective permissions** the user has to access the resource. Let's use an example from Windows Server. If Timmy is a member of the Sales group, which has List Folder Contents permission to a folder, and he is also a member of the Managers group, which has Read and Execute permissions to the same folder, Timmy will have List Folder Contents *and* Read and Execute permissions to that folder.

Combined permissions can also lead to *conflicting permissions,* where a user does not get access to a needed resource because one of his groups has Deny permission to that resource. Deny always trumps any other permission.

Watch out for *default* user accounts and groups—they can grant *improper access* or secret *backdoor access* to your network! All network operating systems have a default Everyone group, and it can easily be used to sneak into shared resources. This Everyone group, as its name implies, literally includes anyone who connects to that resource. Some versions of Windows give full control to the Everyone group by default. All of the default groups—Everyone, Guest, Users—define broad groups of users. Never use them unless you intend to permit all those folks to access a resource. If you use one of the default groups, remember to configure it with the proper permissions to prevent users from doing things you don't want them to do with a shared resource!

All of these groups only do one thing for you: they enable you to keep track of your user accounts. That way you know resources are only available for users who need those resources, and users only access the resources you want them to use.

Before I move on, let me add one more tool to your kit: diligence. Managing user accounts is a thankless and difficult task, but one that you must stay on top of if you want to keep your network secure. Most organizations integrate the creating, disabling/enabling, and deleting of user accounts with the work of their human resources folks. Whenever a person joins, quits, or moves, the network admin is always one of the first to know!

The administration of permissions can become incredibly complex—even with judicious use of groups. You now know what happens when a user account has multiple sets of permissions to the same resource, but what happens if the user has one set of permissions to a folder and a different set of permissions to one of its subfolders? This brings up a phenomenon called **inheritance**. I won't get into the many ways different network operating systems handle inherited permissions. Luckily for you, the CompTIA Network+ exam doesn't test you on all the nuances of combined or inherited permissions—just be aware they exist. Those who go on to get more advanced certifications, on the other hand, must become extremely familiar with the many complex permutations of permissions.

 The CompTIA Network+ objectives call the proper setup of groups *domain/local group configurations.* Kind of a mouthful, but it gets the point across.

Edge

Access control can be broadly defined as exactly what it sounds like: one or more methods to govern or limit entry to a particular environment. Historically, this was accomplished and enforced with simply communicated rules and policies and human oversight. As systems grew in size and sophistication, it became possible to enforce the governing rules using automated technology, relieving managers to focus on other tasks. These control technologies began their developmental life as a central control system with peripheral actuators.

Let me show you what I mean. Take the example of the *Star Trek*-like security door system I talked about in the *"Physical Security" section* a little while ago. That system worked by having a computer with a database of doors, staff, and a decision matrix. Because it controlled many doors, it was centrally located and had wires running to and from it to every controlled door on the campus. Each door had two peripherals installed: a proximity reader with a status indicator, and a door open/close actuator. The proximity reader would read the data from the RFID chip carried by someone and send the data over a sometimes very long data cable to the control computer.

The computer would take the data and the door identifier and check to see it the data was valid, current, and authorized to pass through the door. If it did not meet authorization criteria, a data signal was sent back down the data line to cause a red LED to blink on the proximity reader. Of course, the door would not open. If all of the criteria were met for authorization, a good signal was sent down the data line to make a green LED glow, and power was sent down the line to operate the door actuator.

We've talked about the benefits of this system, so let's look at a few drawbacks. First, the system was proprietary. As systems like these were introduced, competition stymied any effort to create industry standards. Central control meant that large, powerful boxes had to be developed as central controllers. Expandability became an issue as controllers maxed out the number of security doors they could support. Finally, the biggest problem was the large amount of cabling needed to support large numbers of doors and potentially great distances from the central controller. The problem was made worse when facilities had to retrofit non-secure doors for secure ones.

A lot of time and technology has passed since those days. Today's automated secure entry systems take advantage of newer technologies by leveraging existing network wiring. By using IP traffic and Power over Ethernet (PoE), the entire system can usually run over the existing wiring. Applications and protocols have been standardized so they can run on existing server hardware.

Also contributing to the simplification and standardization of these security systems are *edge* devices. An **edge** device is a piece of hardware that has been optimized to perform a task. Edge devices work in coordination with other edge devices and controllers.

The primary defining characteristic of an edge device is that it is installed closer to a client device, such as a workstation or a security door, than to the core or backbone of a network. In this instance, a control program that tracks entries, distributes and synchronizes copies of databases, and tracks door status can be run on a central server. In turn, it communicates with edge devices. The edge devices keep a local copy of the database and make their own decisions about whether or not a door should be opened.

Posture Assessment

Network access control (NAC) is a standardized approach to verify that a node meets certain criteria before it is allowed to connect to a network. Many product vendors implement NAC in different ways. Network Admission Control (also known as NAC) is Cisco's version of network access control.

Cisco's NAC can dictate that specific criteria must be met before allowing a node to connect to a secure network. Devices that do not meet the required criteria can be shunted with no connection or made to connect to another network. The types of criteria that can be checked are broad ranging and can be tested for in a number of ways. For the purposes of this text, we are mostly concerned about verifying that a device attempting to connect is not a threat to network security.

Cisco uses **posture assessment** as one of the tools to implement NAC. Posture assessment is a feature of certain advanced Cisco network appliances. A switch or router that has posture assessment enabled and configured will query network devices to confirm that they meet minimum security standards before being permitted to connect to the production network.

Posture assessment includes checking things like type and version of anti-malware, level of QoS, and type/version of operating system. Posture assessment can perform different checks at succeeding stages of connection. Certain tests can be applied at the initial physical connection. After that, more checks can be conducted prior to logging in. Prelogin assessment may look at the type and version of operating system, detect whether keystroke loggers are present, and check whether the station is real or a virtual machine. The host may be queried for digital certificates, anti-malware version and currency, whether the machine is real or virtual, and a large list of other checks.

If everything checks out, the host will be granted a connection to the production network. If posture assessment finds a deficiency or potential threat, the host can be denied a connection or connected to a non-production network until it has been sufficiently upgraded.

Persistent and Non-persistent Agents

How does a host respond to a posture assessment query? Like a lot of things, the answer depends on the environment. Let's focus on a workstation to answer this question. A workstation requires something called an *agent* to answer a posture assessment query. An **agent** is a process or program running within the computer that scans the computer to create an inventory of configuration information, resources, and assets. When the workstation attempts to connect to the network through a posture assessment–enabled device, it is the agent that answers the security query.

Agents come in two flavors. The first is a small scanning program that, once installed on the computer, stays installed and runs every time the computer boots up. These agents are composed of modules that perform a thorough inventory of each security-oriented element in the computer. This type of agent is known as a **persistent agent**. If there is no agent to respond to a posture assessment query, the node is not permitted to connect to the production network.

Sometimes a computer needs to connect to a secure network via a Web site portal. Some portals provide VPN access to a corporate network, while others provide a less-robust connection. In either case, it is important that these kinds of stations meet the appropriate security standards before they are granted access to the network, just as a dedicated, onsite machine must. To that end, a posture assessment is installed at the endpoint. The endpoint in this instance is the device that actually creates a secure attachment to the production network. At the workstation, a small agent that scans only for the queried conditions is downloaded and run. If the query is satisfied that the station needing access is acceptable, connection is granted and the node can access the production network. When the node disconnects from the network and leaves

Although CompTIA uses the term "non-persistent agent" in its objectives, Cisco uses the term "dissolvable agent." You may see either term on the exam.

the portal site, the agent is released from memory. This type of agent is known as a **non-persistent agent**.

It is worthwhile to note a couple of things here that, while not necessarily critical to the CompTIA Network+ exam, can be useful to know in the real world. First, the Cisco network admission control process does not consist solely of the posture assessment module in an edge device and the node agent. There is also the Cisco **Access Control Server (ACS)**. It is within this program/ process/server that the actual decision to admit or deny a node is made. From there, the ACS directs the edge access device to allow a connection or to implement a denial or redirect. There are additional components and configurations required to create a complete network access control system.

Also useful to know is that Cisco is not the only player in town (although they are decidedly the biggest in this arena) and using an agent is not the only way to check a node for security compliance. To paraphrase Shakespeare: "There are more things in heaven and earth, Horatio . . . and they aren't all workstations." There are tablets, smartphones, other bring-your-own devices (BYOD), switches, printers, and plenty of other things that can connect to a network. For this reason, there needs to be a flexible, cross-platform method of checking for node security before granting access to a secure network. For these platforms, an 802.1X supplicant, in the form of either an agent or a client, can be installed in the device. You'll remember 802.1X from *Chapter 11, "Securing TCP/IP."*

Further, a number of vendors have implemented **agent-less** posture assessment capability. Using a variety of techniques, hosts can be checked for things like a device fingerprint (set of characteristics that uniquely identifies a particular device), a CVE ID (from http://cve.mitre.org), or other agent-less responses. These techniques are easily implemented on a large variety of platforms and they work in a wide array of network environments.

Whether a station responds to a posture assessment query with or without an agent, the result is still one of three options: clearance into the network, connection denied, or redirect to a non-production network. Let's talk about those non-production networks

Guest Networks and Quarantine Networks

It may be desirable for an organization to provide a connection to the Internet as a service to visitors and clients. Envision a coffee shop that welcomes its patrons to check e-mail on their portable devices while enjoying an iced latte with two pumps of white cacao mocha. As you turn on your laptop to scan for Wi-Fi networks, two SSIDs appear. One SSID is labeled CustomerNet and the other is called CorpNet. Some might try to hack into CorpNet, but clearly the intent is for consumers to attach to CustomerNet and gain access to the Internet through that connection. The CustomerNet network is an example of a **guest network**.

A guest network can contain or allow access to any resource that management deems acceptable to be used by insecure hosts that attach to the guest network. Those resources might include an Internet connection, a local Web server with a company directory or catalog, and similar assets that are nonessential to the function of the organization.

In the preceding example, access to the guest network results from a user selecting the correct SSID. More in line with the goals of this book would be a scenario where a station attempts to connect to a network but is refused access because it does not conform to an acceptable level of security. In this case, the station might be assigned an IP address that only enables it to connect to the guest network. If the station needs access to the production network, the station could be updated to meet the appropriate security requirements. If it only requires the resources afforded by the guest network, then it's good to go.

Whenever a node is *denied* a connection to the production network, it is considered to be quarantined. It is common practice for suspicious nodes or nodes with active threats detected to be denied a connection or sent to a **quarantine network**.

So let's put it all together. An organization may have a multitude of production networks, a guest network, and a quarantine network. Who gets to go where? Stations that pass a profile query performed by an edge device with posture assessment features can connect to a production network. From there, access to the various networks and resources is determined by privileges granted to the login credentials.

If a station does not pass the posture query but does not appear to pose a threat, it will likely be connected to the guest network. Stations with active malware or that display a configuration that is conducive to hacking will be quarantined with no connection or connected to a quarantine network.

Host Security

The first and last bastion of defense for an entire infrastructure's security is at the individual hosts. It's the first bastion for preventing dangerous things that users do from propagating to the rest of the network. It's the last bastion in that anything evil coming from the outside world must be stopped here.

We've talked about local security issues several times in this book and even in this chapter. User accounts and strong passwords, for example, obviously provide a first line of defense at the host level. So let's look at another aspect of host security: malware prevention and recovery.

Malware Prevention and Recovery

The only way to protect your PC permanently from getting malware is to disconnect it from the Internet and never permit any potentially infected software to touch your precious computer. Because neither scenario is likely these days, you need to use specialized anti-malware programs to help stave off the inevitable assaults. Even with the best anti-malware tools, there are times when malware still manages to strike your computer. When you discover infected systems, you need to know how to stop the spread of the malware to other computers, how to fix infected computers, and how to remediate (restore) the system as close to its original state as possible.

Malware Prevention   If your PC has been infected by malware, you'll bump into some strange things before you can even run an anti-malware scan. Like a medical condition, malware causes unusual symptoms that should stand out from your everyday computer use. You need to become a PC physician and understand what each of these symptoms means.

Malware's biggest strength is its flexibility: it can look like anything. In fact, a lot of malware attacks can feel like normal PC "wonkiness"— momentary slowdowns, random one-time crashes, and so on. Knowing when a weird application crash is actually a malware attack is half the battle.

A slow PC can mean you're running too many applications at once or you've been hit with malware. How do you tell the difference? In this case, it's the frequency. If it's happening a lot, even when all of your applications are closed,

While it's not necessarily a malware attack, watch out for hijacked e-mail accounts, too, belonging either to you or to someone you know. Hackers can hit both e-mail clients and Webmail users. If you start receiving some fishy (or phishy) e-mail messages, change your Web-based e-mail user name and password or scan your PC for malware.

you've got a problem. This goes for frequent lockups, too. If Windows starts misbehaving (more than usual), run your anti-malware application right away.

Malware, however, doesn't always jump out at you with big system crashes. Some malware tries to rename system files, change file permissions, or hide files completely. Most of these issues are easily caught by a regular anti-malware scan, so as long as you remain vigilant, you'll be okay.

Some malware even fights back, defending itself from your many attempts to remove it. If your Windows Update feature stops working, preventing you from patching your PC, you've got malware. If other tools and utilities throw up an "Access Denied" road block, you've got malware. If you lose all Internet connectivity, either the malware is stopping you or removing the malware broke your connection. In this case, you might need to reconfigure your Internet connection: reinstall your NIC and its drivers, reboot your router, and so on.

Even your browser and anti-malware applications can turn against you. If you type in one Web address and end up at a different site than you anticipated, a malware infection might have overwritten your hosts file. The hosts file overrules any DNS settings and can redirect your browser to whatever site the malware adds to the file. Most browser redirections point you to phishing scams or Web sites full of free downloads (that are, of course, covered in malware). In fact, some free anti-malware applications are actually malware—what techs call a *rogue anti-malware* program. You can avoid these rogue applications by sticking to the recommended lists of anti-malware software found online.

Watch for security alerts in Windows, either from Windows' built-in security tools or from your third-party anti-malware program. Windows includes a tool called Action Center (see Figure 19.6). You don't actually configure much using these applets; they just tell you whether or not you are protected. Both of these tools place an icon and pop up a notification in the notification area whenever Windows detects a problem.

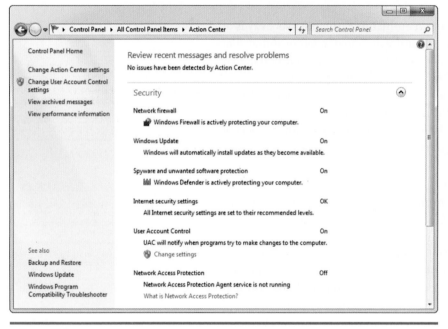

• **Figure 19.6**   Windows 7 Action Center

Symptoms of a Compromised System   A system hit by malware will eventually show the effects, although in any number of ways. The most common symptoms of malware on a *compromised system* are general sluggishness and random crashes. In some cases, Web browsers might default to unpleasant or unwanted Web sites. Frequently, compromised systems increase network outflow a lot.

If you get enough compromised systems in your network, especially if those systems form part of a botnet or DDoS attack force, your network will suffer. The amount of traffic specifically doing the bidding of the malware on the systems can hog network bandwidth, making the network sluggish.

Watch for *top talkers*—systems with very high network output—and a network that doesn't seem nearly as fast as the specs say it should be. Monitor employee complaints about sluggish machines or poor network performance carefully and act as soon as you think you might have infected systems. You need to deal with malware—hopefully catching it before it strikes, but dealing with it swiftly when it does. Let's go there next.

Dealing with Malware You can deal with malware in several ways: anti-malware programs, training and awareness, patch management, and remediation.

At the very least, every computer should run an anti-malware program. If possible, add an appliance that runs anti-malware programs against incoming data from your network. Also remember that an anti-malware program is only as good as its updates—keep everyone's definition file (explained a bit later) up to date with, literally, nightly updates! Users must be trained to look for suspicious ads, programs, and pop-ups, and understand that they must not click these things. The more you teach users about malware, the more aware they'll be of potential threats. Your organization should have policies and procedures in place so everyone knows what to do if they encounter malware. Finally, a good tech maintains proper incident response records to see if any pattern to attacks emerges. He or she can then adjust policies and procedures to mitigate these attacks.

Anti-Malware Programs An anti-malware program such as a classic antivirus program protects your PC in two ways. It can be both sword and shield, working in an active seek-and-destroy mode and in a passive sentry mode. When ordered to seek and destroy, the program scans the computer's boot sector and files for viruses and, if it finds any, presents you with the available options for removing or disabling them. Anti-malware programs can also operate as virus shields that passively monitor a computer's activity, checking for viruses only when certain events occur, such as a program executing or a file being downloaded.

Anti-malware programs use different techniques to combat different types of malware. They detect boot sector viruses simply by comparing the drive's boot sector to a standard boot sector. This works because most boot sectors are basically the same. Some anti-malware programs make a backup copy of the boot sector. If they detect a virus, the programs use that backup copy to replace the infected boot sector. Executable viruses are a little more difficult to find because they can be on any file in the drive. To detect executable viruses, the anti-malware program uses a library of signatures. A signature is the code pattern of a known virus. The anti-malware program compares an executable file to its library of signatures. There have been instances where a perfectly clean program coincidentally held a virus signature. Usually the anti-malware program's creator provides a patch to prevent further alarms.

Anti-malware software comes in multiple forms today. First is the classic host-based anti-malware that is installed on individual systems. Host-based anti-malware works beautifully, but is hard to administer when you have a number of systems. An alternative used in larger networks is network-based anti-malware. In this case a single anti-malware server runs on a number of systems (in some cases each host has a small client). These network-based programs are much easier to update and administer. Last is cloud/server-based anti-malware. These servers store the software on a remote location (in the cloud or on a local server), but it's up to each host to access the software and run it. This has the advantage of storing nothing on the host system and making updating easier, but suffers from lack of administration as it's still up to the user on each host to run the anti-malware program.

One of the most important malware mitigation procedures is to keep systems under your control patched and up to date through proper patch management. Microsoft does a very good job of putting out bug fixes and patches as soon as problems occur. Microsoft isn't perfect, and sometimes new exploits are found in the patches they release. Still, at the end of the day, a patched system will likely be more secure than an unpatched one. If your systems aren't set up to update automatically, then perform manual updates regularly.

The term *antivirus* is becoming obsolete (as are *anti-spyware* and similar terms). Viruses are only a small component of the many types of malware. Many people continue to use the term as a synonym for anti-malware.

■ Firewalls

Firewalls are devices or software that protect an internal network from unauthorized access by acting as a filter. That's right; all a firewall does is filter traffic that flows through its ports. Firewalls are essential tools in the fight against malicious programs on the Internet.

The most basic job of the firewall is to look at each packet and decide based on a set of *rules* whether to **block** or **allow** the traffic. This traffic can be either **inbound traffic**, packets coming from outside the network, or **outbound traffic**, packets leaving the network.

Types of Firewalls

Firewalls come in many different forms. The types covered in this section are the common ones CompTIA wants you to be familiar with.

Software vs. Hardware Firewalls

The **network-based firewall** is often implemented in some sort of **hardware appliance** or is built into the router that is installed between the LAN and the wilds of the Internet. Most network techs' first encounter with a network-based firewall is the small office/home office **(SOHO) firewall** built in to most consumer-grade routers. These firewalls form the first line of defense, providing protection for the whole network. While they do a great job of protecting whole networks, they can't provide any help if the malicious traffic is originating from inside the network itself. That is why we have host-based firewalls.

A **host-based firewall** is a *software* firewall installed on a "host" that provides firewall services for just that machine. A great example of this type of firewall is the Windows Firewall (Figure 19.7) that has shipped with every version of Windows since XP. This makes the host-based firewall probably one of the most common types of firewalls you will encounter in your career as a network tech.

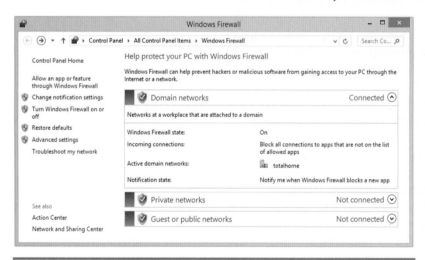

• **Figure 19.7**   Windows Firewall in Windows 8.1

Advanced Firewall Techniques and Features

Knowing that a firewall can live in the network or on a host is all well and good, but firewalls are very sophisticated these days and CompTIA wants you to be familiar with the features that separate a modern firewall from a dumb *packet filter*. One of the first modern techniques added to firewalls is **stateful inspection**, or the capability to tell if a packet is part of an existing connection. In other words, the firewall is aware of the packet's state, as it relates to other packets. This is an upgrade to the older **stateless inspection** model where the firewall looked at each packet fresh, with no regard to the state of the packet's relation to any other packet.

Building on the stateful firewall, firewalls that are **application/context aware** operate at Layer 7 of the OSI model and use *Deep Packet Inspection (DPI)* to filter based on the application or service that originated the traffic. This makes context-aware firewalls invaluable in stopping port-hopping applications such as BitTorrent from overloading your network.

Finally, modern, dedicated security appliances implement **unified threat management (UTM)**, marrying traditional firewalls with other security services, such as network-based IPS, load balancing, and more. UTM mitigates aggressive attacks such as *advanced persistent threats (APTs)*—organized, ongoing attacks on a specific entity. (A good example of an APT is a terrorist organization trying to hack into government security agency computers.)

Implementing and Configuring Firewalls

Now that you have a solid understanding of what a firewall is and how it works, let's delve into the details of installing and configuring a hardware firewall on a network. We'll start with the now familiar Bayland Widgets network and their gateway (Figure 19.8).

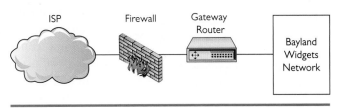

• **Figure 19.8**   Bayland Widgets network gateway

The location of the firewall in the Bayland Widgets network is one of the most common locations for a firewall. By placing the firewall between the trusted internal network and the Internet, it can see all the traffic flowing between the two networks. This also means that the firewall's performance is critical for our connection speed. If the firewall becomes overloaded, it can easily bring a 1-Gbps Internet connection down to 100 Mbps or slower speeds—yikes! In this case, Bayland Widgets has chosen a powerful Cisco ASA security appliance to provide the firewall.

Physically installing a firewall is just like installing other networking equipment such as routers and switches. The entry-level or SOHO models usually have a fixed number of ports, often with a fixed-purpose function (like dedicated ports for WAN traffic). Enterprise-grade hardware (typically supporting 200+ users) often is built around the idea of a flexible function that supports having cards added for different interface types and that can be reconfigured as the network changes. Once the hardware is plugged in, it's time to start configuring your firewall's settings.

Access Control Lists

Modern firewalls come with a massive number of features, and configuring them can be a daunting task for any network tech. But at its core, configuring a firewall is about defining which traffic can flow and which traffic shall not pass. This rule often takes the form of a humble **access control list (ACL)**. An ACL is a rule applied to an interface that allows or *denies* traffic based on things like source or destination IP addresses.

Now that we know what an ACL is, let's take a look at one that you might find on a Cisco router or firewall:

```
access-list 10 deny 10.11.12 0.0.0.255
access-list 20 permit any
```

That looks rather cryptic at first glance, but what it's doing is very simple. The beginning of the first line, `access-list 10`, tells IOS that we want to create an ACL and its number is 10 (back in the day, IOS ACLs only had numbers, not names). The end of the first line, `deny 10.11.12.0 0.0.0.255`, is the actual rule we want the firewall to apply. In this case, it means deny (or *block* as CompTIA says) all traffic from the 10.11.12.0/24 subnet.

 A common theme with network-based firewalls is how closely they are tied to routers. That's no coincidence, as firewalls often come with routers or ship with routing features. CompTIA refers to these as *routed firewalls*. An alternative to traditional routed firewalls is called a *Virtual Wire* firewall. Virtual Wire (VWire) is a feature of firewalls from Palo Alto Networks that allows traffic to pass through the firewall with absolutely no routing or even Layer 2 switching occurring on the packets.

CompTIA refers to the contrast between these two implementations as *Virtual Wire vs. routed firewalls*.

 A basic ACL can be thought of as a stateless firewall. In fact, many of the early firewalls were just ACLs on routers.

That's all well and good; any traffic coming from the 10.11.12.0/24 subnet will be dropped like a bad habit. But what's up with that second line, `access-list 20 permit any`? Well, that's there because of a very important detail about ACLs: they have an **implicit deny any**, or *automatically deny any packets that don't match a rule.* So in this case, if we stopped after the first line, no traffic would get through because we don't have a rule that explicitly permits it! So to make our ACL be a firewall instead of a brick wall, the last rule in this list will permit through any traffic that wasn't dropped by the first rule.

Once the ACL has been created, it must be assigned to an interface to be of any use. One interesting feature of ACLs is that they don't just get plugged in to an interface. You must specify the rules that apply to each *direction* the traffic flows. Traffic flowing through an interface can be thought of as either *inbound*, traffic entering from the network, or *outbound*, traffic flowing from the firewall out to the network. This is an important detail because you can and often want to have different rules for traffic entering and leaving through an interface.

ACLs are but one method for configuring a firewall. While they may seem primitive, we've only scratched the surface of what they can do. More advanced ACLs provide the interface to many of the advanced stateful features of a modern firewall. But don't discount the simple ones we've looked at here. They are still very important in modern network security, providing the critical filtering to keep traffic flowing where it should and, maybe more importantly, where it shouldn't.

DMZ and Firewall Placement

The use of a single firewall between the network and the ISP in the example shown in Figure 19.8 is just one approach to firewall placement. That configuration works well in simple networks or when you want strong isolation between all clients on the inside of the firewall. But what happens when we have servers, like a Web server, that need less restricted access to the Internet? That's where the concepts of the DMZ and internal/external firewalls come in.

A **demilitarized zone (DMZ)** is an area of the network carved out by a single or multiple firewalls to provide a special place (a zone) on the network for any servers that need to be publicly accessible from the Internet.

It's important to understand that, unlike with the little SOHO gateway routers, all traffic destined for the DMZ in non-SOHO networks is still very much being looked at and filtered by the firewall. Just because you placed a server in the DMZ does not mean it shouldn't have or need firewall protection.

The simplest type of DMZ is a single system that separates the public servers from the internal network. In this case the public servers are all located on a separate security zone and network ID from the internal network (Figure 19.9).

As you can see by looking at Figure 19.9, the DMZ isolates the public servers from our internal network. Of course, even with a well-configured firewall in front of your servers in the DMZ, the public nature of the DMZ means that the servers are under constant attack from the Internet. Should the worst happen and any of the machines in the DMZ become compromised (and I've seen how fast this can happen), the isolation provided by the DMZ means the hackers don't have a beachhead inside your internal network.

An alternative to the single-firewall DMZ design is to create a DMZ by using multiple firewalls to create a perimeter network. With a perimeter network

(Figure 19.10), the two firewalls carve out areas with different levels of trust. The firewall that sits between the perimeter network and the Internet is known as an **external firewall** and is responsible for bearing the brunt of the attacks from the Internet. This firewall still allows plenty of traffic through because behind it sit all the public-facing servers.

These servers are still publicly accessible, though, and are still more vulnerable to attack and takeover. That's where the **internal firewall** comes in; it sits between the perimeter network and the trusted network that houses all the organization's private servers and workstations.

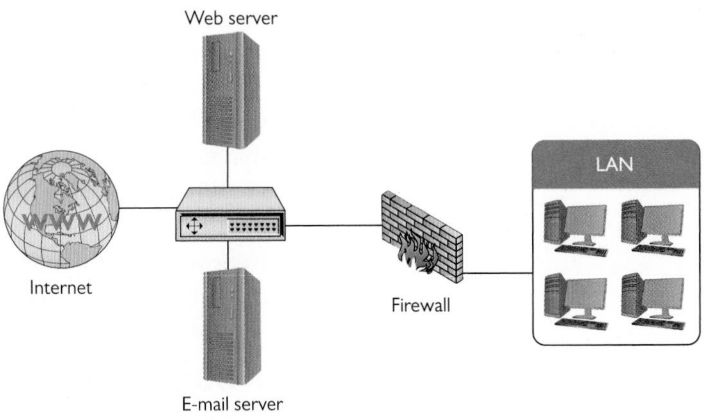

Honeypots and Honeynets

As described, firewalls are bidirectional "filter" systems that can prevent access into a network or out of a network. It's a good system, but nothing is foolproof. Any high-value network resource provides sufficient motivation for a nefarious actor to work through the hoops to get at your goodies. Remember that malicious hackers have three primary weapons to gain access to computer assets: expertise, time, and money (to pay others with more expertise and to buy time).

• **Figure 19.9**   A simple DMZ using one firewall

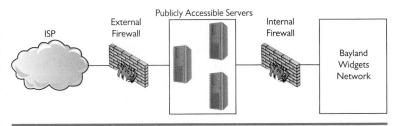

• **Figure 19.10**   Tasty firewall sandwich

To protect our network from expert hackers with too much time on their hands, we layer roadblocks to exhaust their time. We upgrade those roadblocks, and add more where practical, to defeat a hacker's expertise. We can also use something from our own arsenal that works in conjunction with our roadblocks: a detour.

Have you ever seen one of those sports-type movies where a ragtag team of misfits is playing a pro team? In the beginning of the game the pros are beating the brains out of the misfits. Then, when the misfits have had enough of a drubbing, the captain calls a play to "Let 'em through." The bad guy comes through and gets a pasting or two of his own. The network security equivalents to "Let 'em through" are honeypots and honeynets.

Now, "letting them through" is about choices. A network administrator may elect to make access to honeypots and honeynets an easy thing. Or, the network administrator may lay them out as a reward to a hacker after breaking through the normal protection barriers. This is a choice that depends on a lot of variables. In either case, a **honeypot** is a computer that presents itself as a sweet, tempting target to a hacker but, in reality, is a decoy. Honeypots can be as simple as a "real" network machine with decoy files in it. A text file called PASSWORDS.TXT with fake contents makes for an enticing objective.

Of course, there are much more sophisticated products that can run on a computer as a program or within a virtual machine. These products can mimic all of the features of a real computer asset, including firewalls and other roadblocks to keeping a hacker occupied and wasting time on a resource that will yield no value in the end.

Scale up a honeypot to present a complete network as a decoy and you have a **honeynet**. A honeynet, like a honeypot, could be built by constructing an actual network, but that wouldn't be very cost effective. Honeynets can run on a single computer or within a virtual machine and can look like a simple network or a vast installation.

Honeypots and honeynets are useful tools not just in their diversionary value, but in that they can also monitor and report the characteristics of attacks that target them.

When deploying honeypots and honeynets, it is critical that they be segmented from any live or production networks. Pure isolation is the ideal goal. Network segmentation can be achieved by creating a disconnected network or assigning them to an isolated VLAN.

Troubleshooting Firewalls

The firewalls used in modern networks are essential and flexible tools that are critical for securing our networks. Yet, this flexibility means a *misconfigured firewall* becomes more likely, and with it a security breach. You should be familiar with a couple of issues that can crop up, *misconfigured ACLs* and *misconfigured applications.*

When troubleshooting firewalls, a common place for misconfigurations to pop up is in the ACLs. Because of implicit deny, all nonmatching traffic is blocked by default. So if a newly installed firewall refuses to pass any traffic, check to see if it's missing the *permit any* ACL rule.

Another item to look for is ACL rule order. ACLs are numbered and processed from lowest to highest, and when a matching rule is found, the firewall either allows or drops the packet without looking at the rest of the rules. Here is an example of ACLs that shows what can happen if the order is wrong:

```
access-list 10 deny 10.11.12 0.0.0.255
access-list 20 permit host 10.11.12.10
access-list 30 permit any
```

In this example, the tech has added a rule to explicitly allow traffic from the host at 10.11.12.10. The issue is that the lower-numbered rule states that all traffic from that host's subnet is denied. To fix this misconfiguration, the rules need to be reconfigured to give the *permit host* the lowest number so that it will be processed first.

The other source of firewall misconfigurations you should know about concerns applications. With firewalls, "application" means two different things depending on whether you are configuring a network-based firewall or a host-based firewall.

With a network-based firewall, "application," in most situations, can be read as "protocol." Because ACLs on modern firewalls can use protocols as well as addresses and ports, a careless entry blocking an application/protocol can drop access to an entire class of applications on the network.

With a host-based firewall, "application" has its traditional meaning. A host-based firewall is aware of the actual applications running on the machine it's protecting, not just the traffic's protocol. With this knowledge, the firewall can be configured to grant or deny traffic to individual applications, not just protocols, ports, or addresses. When dealing with a misconfiguration here, symptoms are most likely to pop up when an application has been accidentally added to the deny list. When this happens, the application will no longer be able to communicate with the network. Fortunately, on a single system the fix is easy: open the firewall settings, look for the application's name or executable, and change the deny to allow.

Chapter Summary

After reading this chapter and completing the exercises, you should understand the following about network protection.

Describe common security threats in network computing

- Spoofing is the process of pretending to be someone or something you are not by placing false information into your packets. An attacker spoofs by replacing the attacker's MAC addresses, IP addresses, user names, e-mail addresses, and so forth with some other values.

- Abusing protocols is a common form of threat. A protocol is abused by forming communication in a way the protocol is not supposed to be used.

- ARP cache poisoning is a threat that confuses switches and nodes by sending false ARP comments to the system. ARP poisoning is a common method for man-in-the-middle attacks. Tools such as DHCP snooping and Dynamic ARP Inspection help negate ARP poisoning.

- A denial of service (DoS) attack is a targeted attack by one or more systems against a server or servers that provides some form of service on the Internet. A distributed denial of service (DDoS) uses a vast number of zombified systems (called a botnet) to attack a more robust target.

- In a man-in-the-middle attack, an attacker taps into communications between two systems, covertly intercepting traffic thought to be only between those systems, reading or in some cases even changing the data and then sending it on.

- Brute force means to try every permutation of some form of data in an attempt to discover protected information. Brute force is most commonly used on password cracking but can be used in other places such as guessing user names.

- Physical/local access threats are particularly dangerous as they take place inside your network. These threats include compromised systems, insider threats, VLAN hopping, and administrative access controls.

- Malware is probably the single greatest threat to our networks. Malware comes in a number of different forms such as viruses, worms, macros, Trojan horses, rootkits, and adware/spyware.

- Social engineering is the process of using or manipulating people inside the networking environment to gain access to that network from the outside. *Phishing*, using false e-mails and Web sites to collect user names and passwords, is a particularly notorious form of social engineering. Techniques like *tailgating* can be used to gain physical entry into a secure location.

Discuss common vulnerabilities inherent in networking

- Unneeded running services give attackers opportunities to attack by exploiting open ports and propagating malware. Shut them down.

- Any open ports on a system give attackers a potential attack vector. Close the ports by shutting down the associated service.

- Unpatched systems should be patched. Legacy systems should be isolated behind firewalls to protect them from attacks.

- Be careful about using any protocols over unencrypted channels and use VPN or SSH tunnels whenever possible.

- Using protocols or applications with cleartext credentials simply isn't done anymore. The industry often discovers applications that use cleartext credentials that are hard to discover on your own.

- RF emanation from systems can potentially be exploited by sophisticated detectors to read information from a distance. The NSA defines a series of standards called TEMPEST to block RF emanation.

Describe methods for hardening a network against attacks

- Our infrastructures must be physically secured. This includes the following: security guards, IP cameras, door locks with good access controls (key pads, biometrics, RFID readers), and mantraps.

- Hardening a network requires securing both the edges of the network and the internal network.
- Network access control (NAC) is a standardized approach to verify that a node meets certain criteria before it is allowed to connect to the network.
- A safe network includes both persistent and non-persistent agents.
- A compromised system will exhibit traffic spikes and system slowdowns.
- We prevent malware by using anti-malware software.

Explain how firewalls protect a network from threats

- All firewalls can be placed into one of two categories: network-based (usually hardware) and host-based (usually software).

- Firewalls may inspect packets in two ways: stateful and stateless. Stateful inspection is aware of the connection the packets are using. Stateless inspection means to inspect a packet alone without any other reference.
- The cornerstone of a firewall is its access control list (ACL). The ACL defines what packets will or will not be filtered. Almost any aspect of a packet can be part of an ACL.
- ACLs consider traffic as either inbound or outbound.
- A demilitarized zone (DMZ) normally consists of two firewalls: an external and an internal.
- A honeypot or honeynet presents attackers with a false target on which to waste their time and resources.

■ Key Terms

access control *(561)*
access control list (ACL) *(571)*
Access Control Server (ACS) *(566)*
administrative account *(552)*
adware *(553)*
agent *(565)*
agent-less *(566)*
allow *(570)*
amplification *(548)*
anti-malware program *(569)*
antivirus *(569)*
application/context aware *(570)*
ARP cache poisoning *(547)*
banner grabbing *(551)*
biometric *(560)*
block *(570)*
botnet *(548)*
brute force *(550)*
cipher lock *(560)*
cleartext credential *(557)*
closed-circuit television (CCTV) *(561)*
cloud/server-based *(569)*
demilitarized zone (DMZ) *(572)*
denial of service (DoS) *(548)*
DHCP snooping *(548)*
distributed denial of service (DDoS) *(548)*
door access control *(560)*

Dynamic ARP Inspection (DAI) *(548)*
edge *(564)*
effective permission *(563)*
external firewall *(573)*
fail close *(560)*
fail open *(560)*
fault tolerance *(550)*
firewall *(570)*
guest network *(566)*
hardening *(558)*
hardware appliance *(570)*
honeynet *(573)*
honeypot *(573)*
host-based anti-malware *(569)*
host-based firewall *(570)*
implicit deny any *(572)*
inbound traffic *(570)*
inheritance *(563)*
internal firewall *(573)*
IP camera *(561)*
key fob *(560)*
keypad *(560)*
macro *(553)*
malicious employee *(550)*
malicious user *(551)*
malware *(552)*
man-in-the-middle *(549)*

mantrap *(559)*
monlist *(546)*
network access control (NAC) *(564)*
network-based anti-malware *(569)*
network-based firewall *(570)*
network closet *(559)*
non-persistent agent *(566)*
ntpdc *(546)*
organizationally unique identifier (OUI) *(551)*
outbound traffic *(570)*
permanent DoS (PDoS) *(549)*
persistent agent *(565)*
phishing *(554)*
posture assessment *(565)*
proximity reader *(559)*
quarantine network *(567)*
Reddit effect *(549)*
reflection *(549)*
reflective DDoS *(549)*
RF emanation *(558)*
rootkit *(553)*
security guard *(559)*
services *(556)*
session hijacking *(550)*
signature *(569)*

Slashdotting *(549)*
social engineering *(554)*
SOHO firewall *(570)*
smurf attack *(549)*
spoofing *(545)*
spyware *(553)*
stateful inspection *(570)*
stateless inspection *(570)*
tailgating *(559)*
TEMPEST *(558)*
threat *(545)*
traffic spike *(549)*
Trojan horse *(553)*
trusted user *(550)*
unencrypted channel *(557)*
unified threat management (UTM) *(571)*
untrusted user *(550)*
video monitoring *(561)*
virus *(552)*
virus shield *(569)*
VLAN hopping *(552)*
vulnerability *(555)*
worm *(553)*
zero-day attack *(547)*
zombie *(548)*

■ Key Term Quiz

Use the Key Terms list to complete the sentences that follow. Not all terms will be used.

1. We use a number of different camera technologies for physical security. CCTV is an older technology, whereas a(n) _____ is much more modern.

2. _____ is a standardized approach to verify that a node meets certain criteria before it is allowed to connect to the network.

3. An edge firewall usually manifests as a(n) _____.

4. _____ is the process of pretending to be someone or something you are not by placing false information into your packets.

5. A(n) _____ is a potential attack on your network. A(n) _____ is a weakness of your network that might be used to make the attack.

6. A(n) _____ can attack firmware.

7. Phishing is a form of _____.

8. The process of applying security hardware, software, and processes to a network in defense of attacks is called _____.

9. A(n) _____ and a(n) _____ both help prevent tailgating.

10. In a Network Admission Control (NAC) environment, a(n) _____ is continually running on a client.

1. A hacker who sends an e-mail but replaces his return e-mail address with a fake one is _____ the e-mail address.

   A. hardening

   B. malware

   C. spoofing

   D. emulating

2. Which of the following is a tool to prevent ARP cache poisoning?

   A. DHCP

   B. DAI

   C. Edge firewall

   D. DNS snooping

3. A computer compromised with malware to support a botnet is called a _____.

   A. zombie

   B. reflection

   C. DDoS

   D. locked node

4. The goal of a DoS attack is to make the attacked system process each request for as long as possible. This is called _____.

   A. reflection

   B. rotation

   C. destruction

   D. amplification

5. Which is an ancient form of DoS attack?

   A. DDoS

   B. Ping

   C. Smurf

   D. Arrow

6. An attack where someone tries to hack a password using every possible password permutation is called what?

   A. Man-in-the-middle

   B. Spoofing

   C. Rainbow

   D. Brute force

7. Which Windows utility would most easily show you open ports on a host?

   A. netstat

   B. ping

   C. ipconfig

   D. nbtstat

8. Which of the following protocols are notorious for cleartext passwords? (Select two.)

   A. SSH

   B. Telnet

   C. HTTPS

   D. POP3

9. The NSA's TEMPEST security standards are used to combat which risk?

   A. RF emanation

   B. Spoofing

   C. DDoS

   D. Malware

10. Bob is told by his administrator to go to www .runthisantimalware.com and click the "Run the program" button on that site to check for malware. What form of anti-malware delivery is this called?

    A. Host-based

    B. Network-based

    C. Cloud-based

    D. FTP-based

1. Research three major computer hacking events that have occurred over the past year or two. Identify the type of attack, the impact to each company, its employees, and its customers, and any other significant effects.

2. There are a lot of anti-malware packages available. Research the benefits and features that a small (< 15 computers) organization might need. Select a package that best suits the organization you have in mind and write up a proposal to convince your boss why the organization should use this product.

3. The IT department has discovered that many employees are responding to phishing attack e-mails. These responses expose company information and employee personnel to ne'er-do-wells. Create a training document to teach staff how to identify phishing attacks and how to respond to them.

Lab Projects

• Lab Project 19.1

You are the boss and head nerd for a small office and you control the edge firewall. Your network ID for the entire network is 192.168.4/24. Your computer's IP address is 192.168.4.23. You want to prevent users from accessing a public Minecraft server and playing during company time (9 to 5, Monday through Friday). However, you don't want to prevent them from playing outside of company time. You, however, like to play Minecraft all day long. You are going to write in plain English some ACLs.

1. Research the port that Minecraft servers use.

2. Your routers are all set to UTC/GMT time. What is 9–5 in UTC/GMT in your time zone?

3. Write in plain English an ACL rule that blocks the Minecraft port from all computers on 192.168.4/24 from 9–5 UTC/GMT.

4. Write in plain English an ACL rule that will give your computer access at all times.

• Lab Project 19.2

You have a user who uses Valve's Steam to play his games. Research all the ports needed by a Steam client, and then use Windows Firewall to block all of them. If you do not have a Windows system, then just write all of the ports on a piece of paper.

• Lab Project 19.3

The CompTIA Network+ objectives give the concept of hardening your network only the lightest of touches. Do some research and list at least five aspects of network hardening that aren't listed in the CompTIA Network+ objectives.

chapter 20

Network Monitoring

In this chapter, you will learn how to

- **Explain how SNMP works**
- **Describe network monitoring tools**
- **Discuss a scenario that uses management and monitoring tools**

A modern network doesn't behave properly without regular or irregular intervention from network technicians. Techs need to install network management tools and then deploy other tools to monitor, troubleshoot, and optimize networks over time. Because IP networks dominate today, we have a standard set of free tools to accomplish these goals.

This chapter looks first at network management tools, then examines the monitoring tools available and in common use. The chapter finishes with scenarios that call for deploying specific tools, analyzing their output, and fixing problems. For that final section, we'll revisit the Bayland Widgets Corporation and their campus area network (CAN) first discussed back in Chapter 17, "Building a Real-World Network."

 Cross Check

CAN, MAN, LAN, WAN, WLAN

You encountered the acronym soup of networking terms back in Chapters 2, 4, 14, 15, 17 . . . so cross check your memory now. What do these terms mean? How do they differ? Do they all use Ethernet? How do they communicate if not?

Test Specific

■ SNMP

A quick Google search for **network monitoring tools** finds literally hundreds of products out there, ranging from complex and expensive to simple and free (Figure 20.1). One thing most of them have in common is the underlying protocol that enables them to work. The Simple Network Management Protocol (SNMP) is the de facto network management protocol for TCP/IP networks (and it comes dragging in a truckload full of jargon terms to describe the various components).

An SNMP system—which creates a managed network—consists of at least three components:

- SNMP manager
- Managed devices
- Management information bases

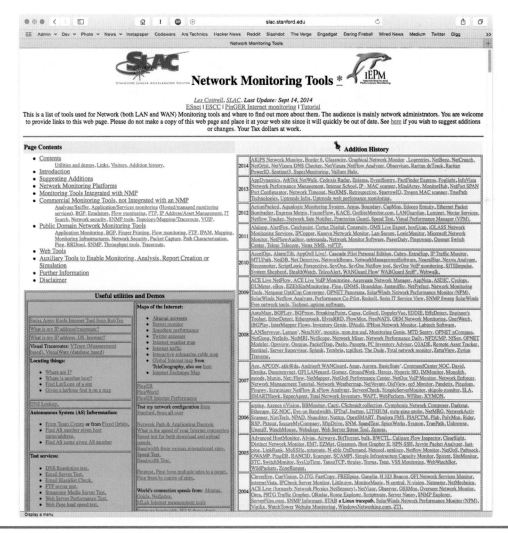

• **Figure 20.1**   Massive list of network monitoring tools maintained by the Stanford Linear Accelerator Center (SLAC)

"I'm running NMS to manage devices."

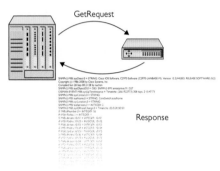

"We run agent software to respond to the NMS."

• **Figure 20.2** SNMP components

• **Figure 20.3** Simple SNMP process

The **SNMP manager** requests and processes information from the **managed devices**. The SNMP manager runs specialized software called a **network management station (NMS)**. Managed devices run specialized software called **agents**. Managed device types include workstations, printers, video cameras, routers, switches, and more. Figure 20.2 illustrates the basic SNMP hardware.

The kind of information the SNMP manager can get from managed devices varies a lot, primarily because SNMP is an *extensible protocol,* meaning it can be adapted to accommodate different needs. Developers can create software that queries pretty much any aspect of a managed device, from current CPU load on a workstation to how much paper is left in a printer. SNMP uses **management information bases (MIBs)** to categorize the data that can be queried (and subsequently analyzed).

Once set up properly, an SNMP managed network runs regular queries to managed devices and then gathers that information in a format usable by SNMP operators. We need to add a little more jargon to go through the steps of the process.

An SNMP system has up to eight core functions (depending on the version of SNMP), of which four merit discussion here: Get, Response, Set, and Trap. The common term for each of these functions is **protocol data unit (PDU)**.

When an SNMP manager wants to query an agent, it sends a **Get** request, such as *GetRequest* or *GetNextRequest*. An agent then sends a **Response** with the requested information. Figure 20.3 illustrates the typical SNMP process.

An NMS can tell an agent to make changes to the information it queries and sends, called **variables**, through a **Set** PDU, specifically *SetRequest*.

An agent can solicit information from an NMS with the **Trap** PDU. An agent can send a *Trap* with or without prior action from the SNMP manager, at least from SNMPv2 to the current SNMPv3.

I've just dropped a lot of jargon on you, so here's a scenario that will make the process and terms a little more understandable. The Bayland Widgets Art Department has a high-end color laser printer for producing brochures (Figure 20.4). Their CompTIA Network+ certified technicians maintain that laser printer, meaning they replace toner cartridges, change paper, and install the printer maintenance kits.

To manage this printer, nicknamed "Kitty," the techs use an SNMP network management system. At regular intervals, the NMS sends a *GetRequest* to the

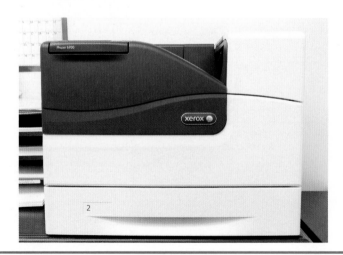

• **Figure 20.4** The Bayland Widgets art department printer

printer agent about the number of pages printed. According to the *Response* sent from the printer agent to the NMS, the techs can determine if the printer needs maintenance (that is, if it's at the point in its usage cycle where the printer maintenance kit parts need to be replaced).

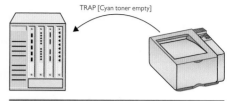

• **Figure 20.5** Trap in action

At irregular intervals, the printer agent has to tell the techs that the printer is out of toner or out of paper. Although this information could come from the Get/Response interaction, it makes more sense that it come from the printer agent without a query. Kitty needs to yell "Help!" when she's out of toner. Otherwise the techs have to deal with irate artists, and that's just never going to be pretty. Kitty yells for help by sending a *Trap* to the NMS. Figure 20.5 illustrates the interaction.

SNMP systems can use many additional utilities developed over the years. Some can automate various tasks. The **snmpwalk** utility, for example, tells the SNMP manager to perform a series of Get commands. Note that the CompTIA Network+ objectives shorten this utility name to *Walk*.

The BWC network techs don't sit at the SNMP manager, waiting for Kitty the printer to send messages about toner or ink. Instead, the manager software has the capability to send **alerts**, messages directly sent to the techs when their intervention is required. These alerts can have a variety of forms. When the SNMP system was initially rolled out, one snarky manager suggested using text messages via **Short Message Service (SMS) alerts** that would cause techs' smartphones to meow upon receipt. That idea was nixed pretty early in favor of **e-mail alerts** (without any lolcat pictures attached).

SNMP has (as of this writing) three major versions. SNMP version 1 (SNMPv1) appeared in three requests for proposals (RFPs) all the way back in 1988. SNMPv2 was a relatively minor tweak to version 1. SNMPv3 added additional security with support for encryption and robust authentication, plus it provided features to make administering a large number of devices easier.

SNMP uses User Datagram Protocol (UDP) ports 161 and 162 for unsecure communication. The NMS receives/listens on port 162. The agent receives/listens on port 161. When security is added via Transport Layer Security (TLS) the standard ports used are 10162 and 10161, respectively.

> SNMP managers listen on UDP ports 162 or 10162 (with TLS). Agents listen on ports 161 or 10161 (with TLS).

Monitoring Tools

The biggest trick to monitoring a network is to start by appreciating that even the smallest network has a dizzying amount of traffic moving though it every second. Even more, this traffic is moving through all kinds of different aspects of the network, from individual interfaces coming from a single NIC in a system to everything moving through a massive router on the edge of your infrastructure.

To be able to do the monitoring, the troubleshooting, and the optimizing necessary to keep our networks in top shape, we need the right monitoring tools at the right places looking for the right things. There are hundreds of different monitoring tools available, but for the scope of the CompTIA Network+ exam, we can break them down into four major types: packet sniffers, packet analyzers, interface monitors, and performance monitors.

> Check out the Chapter 20 "SNMP Monitoring" Show! and Click! sims at http://totalsem .com/006. The pair offer a great, practical introduction to SNMP tools.

Packet Sniffers

A **packet sniffer** is a program that queries a network interface and collects (captures) packets in a file called (surprisingly) a **capture file**. These programs might sit on a single computer, or perhaps on a router, a switch, or a dedicated piece of hardware.

Packet sniffers need to capture all the packets they can, so it's typical for them to connect to an interface in *promiscuous mode* or, in the case of a switch, a *mirrored port*. This ensures they get as much data as possible.

Packet sniffers by themselves aren't very useful, as we need a tool to let us analyze the captured packets. For this reason, you don't really see packet sniffers as a stand-alone product. Instead, they are usually packaged with a packet analyzer.

Clearly, not much is going to happen without packet sniffers, but given they are always built into packet analyzers, there's nothing to show you. They run silently and transparently in the background. But it's critical that you understand there's a difference between a packet sniffer and what you're about to be introduced to, a packet analyzer.

> Various names are used to describe utilities that analyze packets: *packet sniffer, packet analyzer, protocol analyzer, and network analyzer.* There's so much overlap here! That can be attributed to the fact that so many packet analyzers come with sniffers as well. Bottom line, don't rely on the name of the monitoring tool to determine all it can do. Read the tech specs.

Packet Analyzers

A **packet analyzer** is a program that reads capture files from packet sniffers and analyzes them based on our monitoring needs. A good packet analyzer can file and sort a capture file based on almost anything and create an output to help us do monitoring properly. A typical question a packet analyzer might answer is "What is the IP and MAC address of the device sending out DHCP Offer messages and when is it doing this?"

Packet Analyzing with Wireshark

There are plenty of protocol analyzers available out there, but you'd be hard pressed to find a network administrator/technician/whatever who isn't familiar with the powerful and free **Wireshark**. It was originally written by Gerald Combs, who still maintains the program with the help of hundreds of contributors. Wireshark is the perfect prototype of a protocol analyzer. (And it's also specifically mentioned in the CompTIA Network+ objectives. Know this amazing tool!)

 Try This!

Play Along with Wireshark

It's never too late to learn how to use packet analyzers, so try this! Download a copy of Wireshark (www.wireshark.org) and just play. There's no danger to doing so, and it's actually a lot of fun!

The default Wireshark screen has become the standard most other protocol analyzers are based on. You select an interface to begin the capture and let the capture begin (Figure 20.6).

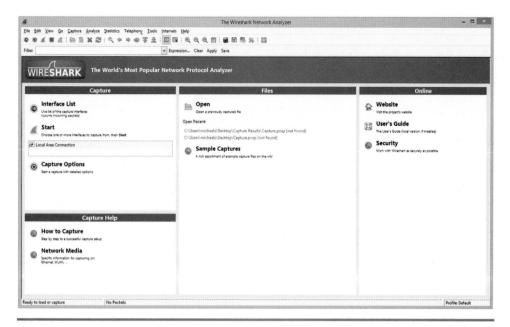

• **Figure 20.6**   Wireshark default window

When you stop the capture, you'll see something like Figure 20.7. Wireshark's screen breaks into three parts. The top part is a numbered list of all the packets in the capture file, showing some of the most important information. The second part is a very detailed breakdown of the packet that is currently highlighted in the top pane. The bottom pane is the hex representation and the ASCII representation of whatever part of the second pane is detailed.

The downside to a capture is that Wireshark is going to grab everything unless you filter the capture or filter the capture file after the capture. In many

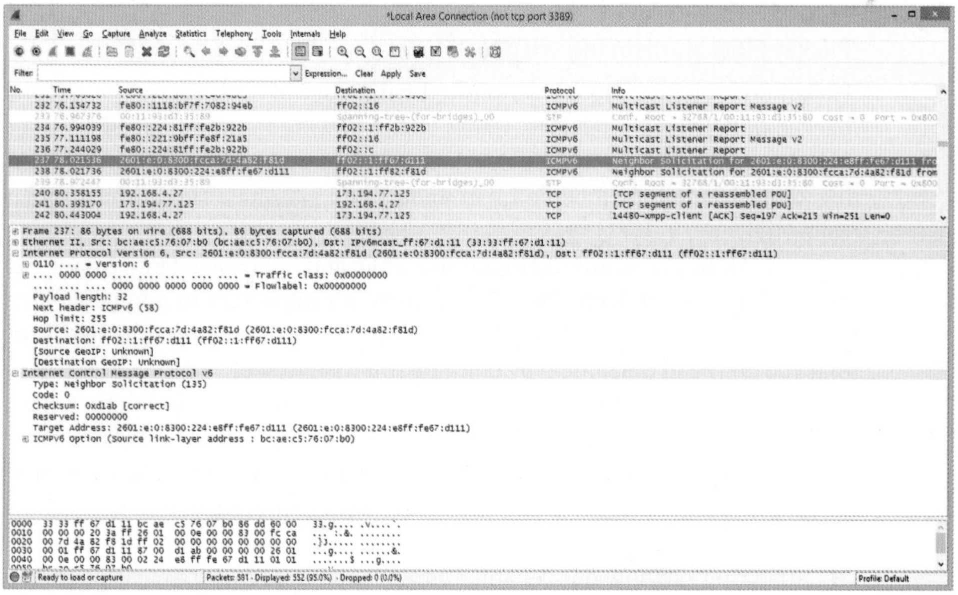

• **Figure 20.7**   Wireshark capturing packets

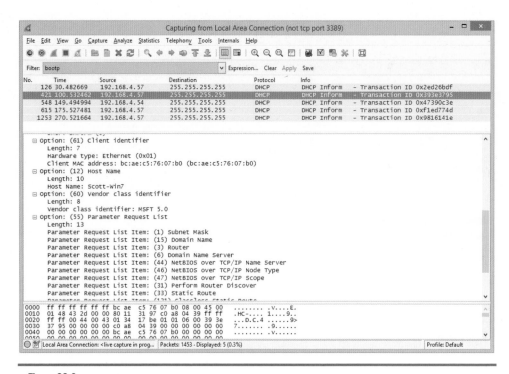

• **Figure 20.8** Wireshark filter

cases you'll find yourself doing both. The filter is the real challenge to Wireshark because it uses its own wonky syntax. Figure 20.8 shows a filter added to a capture file to only show DHCP packets. Note that the filter doesn't actually say "DHCP." Wireshark uses the term *bootp* (be careful, Wireshark is case sensitive).

Using Wireshark is like playing chess: it's easy to understand but takes a lifetime to master. We'll look at an example later in the chapter to see just how complex it really can be!

Packet Flow Monitoring with NetFlow

Packet flow monitoring, accomplished with a set of tools related to general packet sniffers and analyzers, tracks traffic flowing between specific source and destination devices. Cisco developed the concept of packet flow monitoring and subsequently included it in routers and switches. The primary tool is called **NetFlow**.

NetFlow has been around for quite a while and has evolved into a powerful tool that just about every Cisco house uses. It's important to appreciate that NetFlow is similar to SNMP but different. NetFlow is based on the idea of flows that you define to track the type of traffic you wish to see.

A single **flow** is a flow of packets from one specific place to another. Each of these flows is then cached in a **flow cache**. A single entry in a flow cache normally contains information such as destination and source addresses, destination and source ports, the source on the device running that flow, and total number of bytes of that flow.

Analyzing the flow data enables administrators to build a clear picture of the volume and flow of traffic on the network. This in turn enables them to optimize the network (by adding capacity where needed or other options).

To use NetFlow you must enable NetFlow on that device. If the device doesn't support NetFlow, you can use stand-alone probes that can monitor maintenance ports on the unsupported device and send the information to the NetFlow collector.

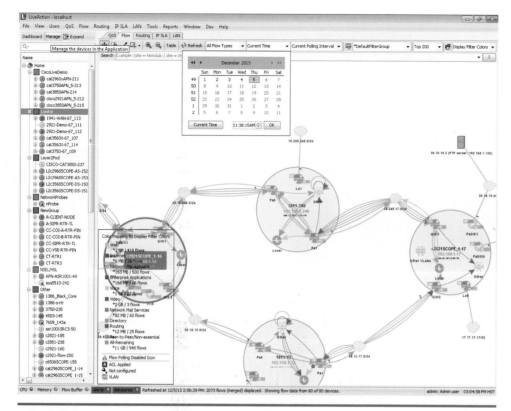

• **Figure 20.9** LiveAction in action!

Most of the heavy lifting of NetFlow is handled by the **NetFlow collectors**. NetFlow collectors store information from one or more devices' NetFlow caches, placing it into a table that can then be analyzed by NetFlow analysis tools.

There are many different companies selling different tools, and which tool you should choose is often a matter of features and cost. Figure 20.9 shows a screenshot of a popular tool called LiveAction.

Cisco's NetFlow started the idea of traffic flows that can then be collected and analyzed. Just about every other form of competing flow-monitoring concept (names like sFlow, Netstream, and IPFix) builds on the idea of the flow.

Interface Monitors

If you want to know how hard your network is working, turn to an interface monitor. **Interface monitors** track the bandwidth and utilization of one or more interfaces on one or more devices. Think of them as the traffic monitors for your network. A typical question you might ask an interface monitor is "How hard is the Gigabit Ethernet port 17 on our backbone switch working right now, in megabits per second?"

Interface monitors track the quantity and utilization of traffic through a physical port or ports on a single device. Interface monitoring will consist of, among other items, the following:

- **Speed and duplex** At what speed is the port set to run? What duplex is the port running?

- **Utilization** How much of the total bandwidth of the port is being used?

- **Packet drops** A port will drop a packet for one of two reasons: an error or a discard.

- **Errors** How many packets per second are errors? A port treats a packet as erroneous if the packet is malformed or unreadable.

- **Discards** How many frames are discarded per second? A *discard* is when a port intentionally drops a well-formed frame. A discard is not an error. There are many reasons for a port to discard a frame. If a port is trunking VLANs 1 and 2 and it gets a frame for VLAN 3, the port will discard the packet.

- **Interface resets** Is the interface being reset at any time? If so, how often is this taking place?

Interface monitors started as manufacturer-specific tools, and although there are plenty of interface monitors that work on just about any platform, the manufacturer-specific ones are still very common.

The Cisco Network Assistant (CNA) software enables you to monitor Cisco routers and switches. Figure 20.10 shows the percent of utilization for a specific port on a Catalyst 2970 switch. Figure 20.11 shows the packet drops and errors on that same port.

Contrast Figure 20.11 with Figure 20.12 showing CNA examining switch port 13 for drops and errors. That's a misbehaving port!

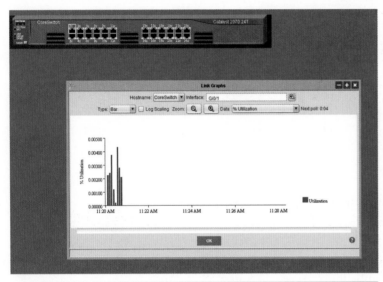

• **Figure 20.10** Percent of utilization of switch port 1

Limiting the description of CNA to an "interface monitor" completely sells the software short. It can monitor individual ports on a switch, but you can use the program to set up, manage, maintain, and troubleshoot all the functions of the switch. It's much more powerful a tool than just an interface monitor.

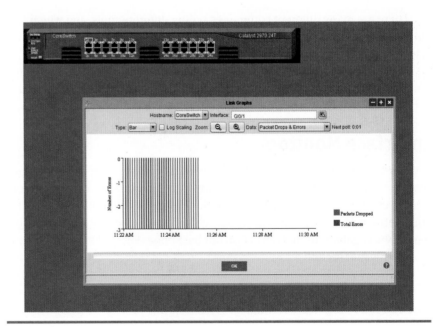

• **Figure 20.11** Hmm . . . looks pretty clean

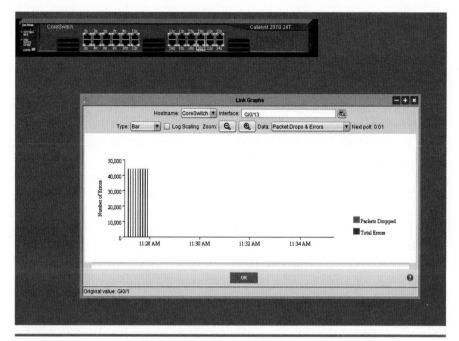

• **Figure 20.12**   Ouch. That's a lot of errors!

Performance Monitors

A **performance monitor** tracks the performance of some aspect of a system over time and lets you know when things aren't normal. Performance monitors are usually tied to a particular operating system or application, as the performance monitoring requires very detailed understanding of the low-level aspects of the system. A typical question you might ask a performance monitor is "How many hits per hour occurred on my Web server over the last two weeks?"

The two most common performance monitoring tools are Windows Performance Monitor (PerfMon) and Linux's syslog. Although they perform the same job, I want to introduce both tools to you because they do that job very differently . . . and use very different terms to describe the same things. As we next look at certain aspects that are common to any good performance monitor, I'll use the terminology for both tools.

Logs

Performance monitors use system log files to track performance over time. **Logs** store information about the performance of some particular aspect of a system. Different programs refer to the monitored aspect with different terms. Performance Monitor calls them *counters*; syslog calls them *facilities*. A log file might record the percentage of utilization over time of a specific Ethernet port, for example, or the average throughput of a network connection.

Baselines

The only way to know when a problem is brewing on your network is to know how things perform when all's well with the network. Part of any proper performance monitor is the facility to create a **baseline**: a log of performance indicators such as CPU usage, network utilization, and other values to give you a picture of your network and servers when they are working correctly. A major change in these values can point to problems on a server or the network as a whole.

All operating systems come with some form of baseline tools. Performance Monitor is the common tool used to create a baseline on Windows systems.

Log Management

Any system that generates electronic log files has two issues. First, is security. Log files are important for the information they provide. Second, is maintenance. Log files are going to continue to grow until they fill the mass storage they are stored on. The job of providing proper security and maintenance for log files is called log management.

Logs often contain private or sensitive data and thus must be protected. Access to active logs must be carefully controlled. It's very common to give read access rights only to specific users, to make sure only the correct users have access to the log files. In many cases it's not uncommon for the logging application to have only write access to the files—it's not a good idea to give root access to critical log files.

Generally log files by default simply grow until they fill the space they are stored on. To prevent this, it's common to make log files *cyclical*—when a file grows to a certain size, it begins to cycle. *Cycling* just means that as a new record appears in the file, the oldest record in the file is deleted. It's also common for log files to be re-created on a time basis. Depending on the utility, you can set a new log file to be created daily, weekly, hourly—whatever is most convenient for the administrators. These files can then be backed up.

There are many laws today that require retention of log files for a certain period of time. It's important to check with your legal department to see if any files need to be kept longer than your standard backup time frames.

Putting It All Together

Up to this point in the chapter, we've looked at management and monitoring tools as distinct things, easy to label and easy to differentiate. And in a small office/home office network, that kind of simplicity makes sense. If you have a Windows-based network with a single server running Windows Server, then of course you'd use Windows Performance Monitor to baseline and monitor your network over time. The CompTIA Network+ competencies lead to this modular thinking as well. Once you scale up past the one-server network, though, things get a lot more . . . *chaotic* isn't quite the right word . . . *nuanced* is better. Let's take a look.

Scenario: Monitoring and Managing

This scenario revisits the Bayland Widgets CAN and applies the network managing and monitoring tools to see how their techs would use these tools to manage, monitor, maintain, and troubleshoot their network.

Figure 20.13 shows the BWC campus layout with its three main buildings. The main office has servers and various individual offices. The factory houses the robots and control systems that produce the company's widgets. The warehouse and shipping building does exactly as it's named.

Internally, each building is wired with Gigabit Ethernet. In addition, the buildings interconnect with 10-Gigabit fiber into access switches. Add onto that a campus-wide Wi-Fi network (802.11ac) and, not pictured, the router that gives them access to the Internet.

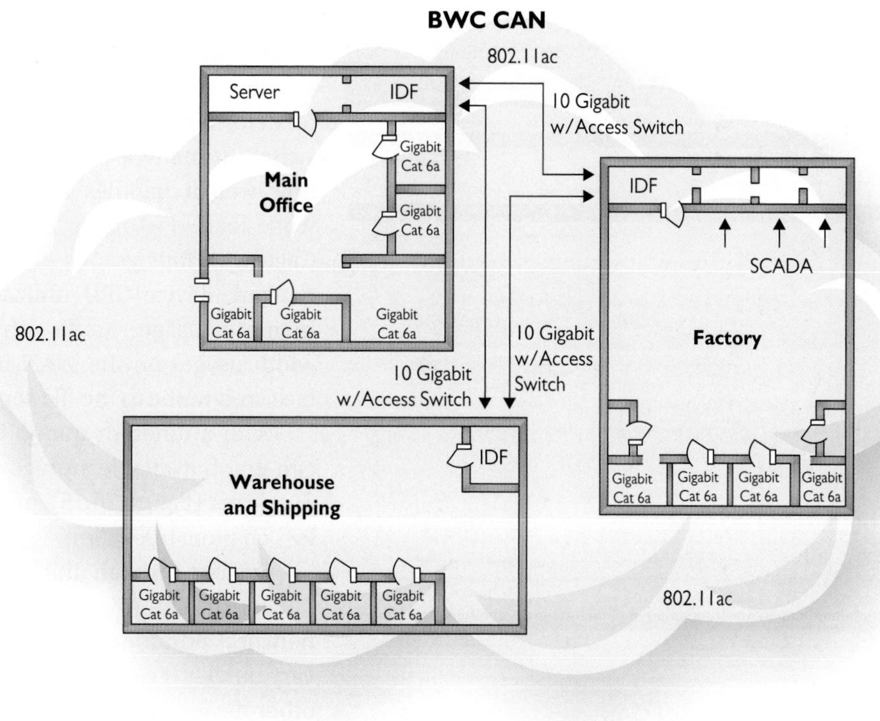

BWC CAN

• **Figure 20.13**   Diagram of Bayland Widgets' campus area network

Since we're talking about managing and monitoring the whole network here, let's list all the types of networked devices:

- Routers (wired and wireless)
- Switches
- Wireless access points
- Servers
- Workstations
- Printers
- Phones

Note that I've left out the industrial control systems that run the factory and shipping automation. Plus I've left out the security systems and other essential components of a functional CAN. This list focuses on the core networking devices that a CompTIA Network+ tech would encounter.

Modern networking tools enable skilled network administrators to manage networks as complex at Bayland Widgets' network fairly easily, after those tools have been set up properly. The tools used must be customized for the network. Plus, the various tools aren't really interchangeable. Just like you wouldn't use a hammer when you need to turn a screw, you wouldn't use a packet analyzer when you want to check toner levels in a laser printer.

Bayland Widgets could dedicate an area in the main office as a **network operations center (NOC)**, a centralized location for techs and administrators to manage all aspects of the network. From that NOC, they could use various programs on the SNMP-managed network to query devices. A **graphing** program could create graphs that display any set of the data received.

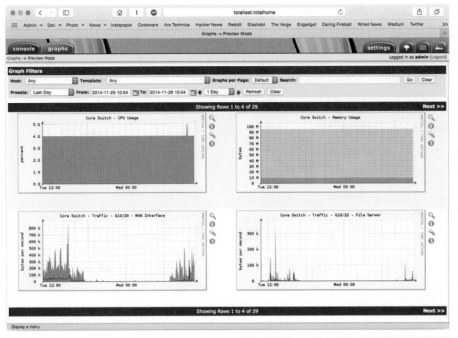

Graphing programs like **Cacti** would show everything about specific switches, for example, to determine utilization of that switch in many aspects—that is, how well it handles its current work load. Figure 20.14 shows Cacti with four graphs depicting network device CPU utilization, memory usage, traffic (bandwidth usage) on the WAN interface, and traffic to the file server.

With a different query, Cacti can graph available storage on a file server (Figure 20.15), or wireless channel utilization.

Cycling through the various network monitoring tools enables network administrators to see very quickly if a specific server or other device has problems. They could analyze the campus Wi-Fi

• **Figure 20.14** Cacti showing switch utilization graphs

Programs like Cacti enable you to see very quickly essential facts about your network hardware. You can see available storage, network device CPU usage, network device memory usage, and more. With wireless-aware tools, you can quickly spot problems with wireless channel usage or channel saturation. These tools are a tech's friend!

network and spot a problematic WAP. Going a little further up the food chain, BWC could add Nagios to their network toolboxes and, after proper configuration, have that system proactively send alerts via SMS or e-mail when problem areas were detected. If the **link status**—signifying how good the connection is between two systems—between the two access servers connecting the main office and the factory goes red, that's a whole different level of priority than if Kitty the art printer runs low on toner, right?

Each type of tool discussed in this chapter enables the network team at BWC to monitor and analyze all aspects of the network. The SNMP system

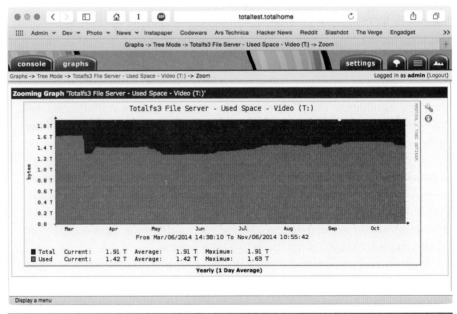

• **Figure 20.15** Cacti showing file server storage utilization graph

Mike Meyers' CompTIA Network+ Guide to Managing and Troubleshooting Networks

offers very specific information about managed devices, enabling techs to respond to problems.

Performance monitoring software enables the BWC techs to create baselines when the network is functioning correctly. If complaints about network performance come in from one portion of the network (Accounting, for example), that same software can be used to compare current network performance with the historical, normal performance. If there's a discrepancy, the techs can turn to other tools—packet flow analyzers and interface monitors—to figure out if the issue is excess traffic, failing devices, failing interfaces on a device, or an overworked **bottleneck** (a spot where traffic slows precipitously).

Network analyzers and packet flow analyzers can discover the busiest machines on the network, potentially sources of overall network slowdowns. **Top talkers** are the computers sending the most data, whereas **top listeners** are the ones receiving the most. If BWC is worried about a malware problem, finding that the computer assigned to Joe in Accounting is the top talker might track down that spam infestation.

The network techs turn to a packet sniffer/analyzer tool when they need to go deep into the traffic. Here's an example of when Wireshark might be the tool to start. BWC wants to move the network to IPv6 and turn off all IPv4 traffic. Turning off IPv4 on a test machine would be a good check on how ready the network is for IPv6. We did that the other day in my office, for example, and found that the test machine couldn't see anything on the network at all. Running Wireshark enabled us to see if the router was sending out IPv6 router advertisements with DNS. When we confirmed that information, the next step was more old-fashioned. Had we misconfigured the test workstation's IPv6 settings?

Accomplished techs use a variety of managing and monitoring tools to maintain a healthy network. Use each type of tool when that tool is appropriate. Often, you'll need to use multiple tools during a longer troubleshooting scenario.

SIEM

The Bayland Widgets people could use an approach called **security information and event management (SIEM)** to monitor and manage their network. SIEM is an industry-standard term, but there are many products of various types that are marketed as SIEM solutions. SIEM is a mashup of two processes: security event management (SEM) and security information management (SIM).

As the name would imply, SIEM is a two-part process that begins with the security event monitoring component. SEM is based on real-time monitoring of security events. The SEM framework calls for monitoring the entire enterprise, often through edge devices at monitor points, then saving the logged events to a location that supports single viewpoint review and analysis of the events. In addition to active event monitoring, another task of SEM is to collect and centralize otherwise disparately located security and event logs.

Once logs are created and saved, the second part of SIEM, security information management, kicks in: here, the log files are reviewed and analyzed by automated and human interpreters.

SIEM systems are complex solution suites that are found in large, enterprise environments. Depending on the organization, they may be self-implemented and managed or may be administered under contract by a vendor in the form of a managed security service provider (MSSP).

Chapter 20 Review

■ Chapter Summary

After reading this chapter and completing the exercises, you should understand the following about network monitoring.

Explain how SNMP works

- An SNMP managed network consists of three core components. The SNMP manager runs NMS software to work with managed devices that run agent software. Queries are categorized and stored for analysis in MIBs.

- An SNMP system has up to eight core functions, or PDUs. The Get, Response, Set, and Trap PDUs are used for queries to agents, responses from agents, setting of parameters, and actions from agents.

- An SNMP system can have all sorts of features. It can be set up to send SMS or e-mail alerts, for example, so techs will know when some part of the system needs maintenance.

- SNMP uses UDP ports 161 and 162 for unsecure communication. The NMS receives on port 162. The agent receives on port 161. When security is added via TLS, the standard ports used are 10162 and 10161, respectively.

Describe network monitoring tools

- Monitoring tools enable network techs and admins to gather information about all kinds of aspects of the network. This in turn enables them to manage, troubleshoot, and optimize network traffic.

- Packet sniffers, packet analyzers, and packet flow analyzers capture files and produce information on IP addresses, types of data flowing between connections, and much more. The prototypical tools in this category are Wireshark and NetFlow.

- Interface monitors track the bandwidth and utilization of one or more interfaces on one or more devices. They reveal information such as percentage of utilization, packet drops, errors, and more.

- Performance monitors track the performance of some aspect of a system over time and let you know when things aren't normal. They enable you to create baselines so you know how a system should run, then keep logs for analysis so that problem areas can be tracked down. Typical performance monitoring tools are Performance Monitor in Windows and syslog in OS X and Linux.

Discuss a scenario that uses management and monitoring tools

- SNMP tools enable network pros to manage just about any aspect of a network. Graphing programs like Cacti can display information as diverse as traffic on an individual switch port, to device CPU usage, to available file storage on a server. More powerful tools like Nagios can be customized to send alerts when monitored systems need help.

- The SIEM approach to monitoring and managing networks offers a range of tools for accomplishing its tasks. SIEM actively monitors at the enterprise level and makes log files available for analysis by automated and human interpreters.

■ Key Terms

agent *(582)*
alert *(583)*
baseline *(589)*
bottleneck *(593)*
Cacti *(592)*
capture file *(584)*
e-mail alert *(583)*

flow *(586)*
flow cache *(586)*
Get *(582)*
graphing *(591)*
interface monitor *(587)*
link status *(592)*
log *(589)*

log management *(590)*
managed device *(582)*
managed network *(581)*
management information base (MIB) *(582)*
NetFlow *(586)*
NetFlow collector *(587)*
network management station (NMS) *(582)*
network operations center (NOC) *(591)*
packet analyzer *(584)*
packet sniffer *(584)*
performance monitor *(589)*
protocol data unit (PDU) *(582)*
Response *(582)*

security information and event
   management (SIEM) *(593)*
Set *(582)*
Short Message Service (SMS) alert *(583)*
Simple Network Management Protocol (SNMP) *(581)*
SNMP manager *(582)*
snmpwalk *(583)*
top listener *(593)*
top talker *(593)*
Trap *(582)*
variable *(582)*
Wireshark *(584)*

■ Key Term Quiz

Use the Key Terms list to complete the sentences that follow. Not all the terms will be used.

1. A(n) _____ requests and processes information from managed devices.

2. An SNMP system uses _____ PDUs for querying agents.

3. An agent uses _____ PDUs to solicit information from an NMS.

4. The _____ utility tells the SNMP manager to perform a series of Get commands.

5. A packet sniffer queries a network interface and collects packets in a(n) _____.

6. A primary tool for capturing and analyzing the flow of packets from one device to another is called _____.

7. Use a(n) _____ program to track the quantity and utilization of traffic through a physical port or ports on a single device.

8. Raphael can compare the results of a current Performance Monitor output with the _____ to see if the network is performing correctly.

9. Performance monitors use a(n) _____ to store some form of performance information about a system.

10. Graphing programs like _____ can show everything about specific switches, such as bandwidth usage.

■ Multiple-Choice Quiz

1. In an SNMP managed network, which software does an SNMP manager run?

   A. Agent

   B. NMS

   C. SNMP manager

   D. MIB

2. In an SNMP managed network, which software does a managed device run?

   A. Agent

   B. NMS

   C. SNMP manager

   D. MIB

3. Which PDU enables a tech to change the variables queried of a managed device?

   A. Get

   B. Response

   C. Set

   D. Trap

4. How does an SNMP managed system categorize data that can be queried?

   A. MIBs

   B. PDUs

   C. UDP

   D. QoS

5. An analysis of a network shows a lot of traffic on one machine on port 162. What kind of machine is it?

   A. Managed device

   B. SNMP manager

   C. PDU

   D. MIB

6. A newly hired networking wiz works through the weekend and proudly announces at the Monday staff meeting, "Now you techs can't hide from your duties. All problems with managed devices will be reported to your cell phones." What did the wiz add to the SNMP managed system?

   A. PDU alerts

   B. Agent responses

   C. SMS alerts

   D. Trap alerts

7. The boss at a small business wants to implement a management system for his network, but due to the sensitive nature of the traffic flowing, that data needs to be secure. Which version of SNMP should he implement?

   A. SNMPv1

   B. SNMPv2

   C. SNMPv3

   D. SNMPv4

8. An SNMP agent listens on which port when used with TLS?

   A. 161

   B. 162

   C. 10161

   D. 10162

9. Jason is concerned about the communication between two workstations and wants to capture and analyze that traffic to see if anything illicit is going on. Which tool would best serve his needs?

   A. Interface monitor

   B. Packet flow monitor

   C. Packet sniffer

   D. Performance monitor

10. Jill suspects a switch on Level 12 has a bottlenecked port, with too much traffic. Which tool would enable her to check that port specifically?

    A. Interface monitor

    B. Packet sniffer

    C. Packet analyzer

    D. Packet flow monitor

11. Bart has a choice of tools to view his managed network, but he primarily wants to see graphs of various types of data, such as the overall traffic and the current capacities of the file servers. Which tool offers him the best option?

    A. Cacti

    B. CNA

    C. NetFlow

    D. Wireshark

12. Cindy's newly installed Windows network runs great! She needs to create a baseline now for later analysis. Which tool should she use?

    A. Cacti

    B. Performance Monitor

    C. Syslog

    D. Wireshark

13. What component in NetFlow stores information from NetFlow caches?

    A. Flow cache

    B. LiveAction

    C. NetFlow collectors

    D. NetFlow PDUs

14. Where does a packet sniffer put information it collects?

    A. Answer file

    B. Capture file

    C. Pocket file

    D. Sniffer file

15. John is conversing with another tech who consistently uses the term "network analyzer" when discussing network monitoring tools. What sort of tool is he using?

    A. Interface monitor

    B. Packet analyzer

    C. Performance analyzer

    D. Performance monitor

■ Essay Quiz

1. Write a short essay comparing a packet analyzer, like Wireshark, to an interface monitor, like CNA. Do they complement each other or overlap when you're trying to understand things such as overall network traffic? What about when assessing the performance of a specific network device, such as a managed switch?

2. Similarly to question 1, compare Wireshark with NetFlow and address the same questions. Do they complement or overlap?

Lab Projects

• Lab Project 20.1

Download a copy of Wireshark and run it. Capture packets for a few minutes, adding traffic by surfing various Web sites. Once you have a nice set of information, stop the capture and analyze the packets. How does the port 80 traffic manifest? Are there any errors?

• Lab Project 20.2

If you have access to a Cisco switch, download a copy of Cisco Network Assistant. (You'll need to register with Cisco if you haven't already.) Run it and log into the switch. Poke around. You can gather a ton of detailed information about that switch with CNA.

Network Troubleshooting

chapter 21

"This is the end / Beautiful friend / This is the end."

—JIM MORRISON

In this chapter, you will learn how to

- Describe appropriate troubleshooting tools and their functions
- Analyze and discuss the troubleshooting process
- Resolve common network issues
- Describe the Internet of Things

Have you ever seen a tech walk up to a network and seem to know all the answers, effortlessly typing in a few commands and magically making the system or network work? I've always been intrigued by how they do this. Observing such techs over the years, I've noticed that they tend to follow the same steps for similar problems—looking in the same places, typing the same commands, and so on.

When someone performs a task the same way every time, I figure they're probably following a plan. They understand what tools they have to work with, and they know where to start and what to do second and third and fourth until they find the problem.

This chapter's lofty goal is to consolidate my observations on how these "übertechs" fix networks. I'll show you the primary troubleshooting tools and help you formulate a troubleshooting process and learn where to look for different sorts of problems. Then you'll apply this knowledge to resolve common network issues.

At the end of the chapter, I'll look to the future and explore how these networks will weave into every aspect of our lives with the Internet of Things.

Test Specific

■ Troubleshooting Tools

While working through the process of finding a problem's cause, you sometimes need tools. These tools are the software and hardware tools that provide information about your network and enact repairs. I covered a number of tools already: hardware tools like cable testers and crimpers and software utilities like ping and tracert. The trick is knowing when and how to use these tools to solve your network problems.

Almost every new networking person I teach will, at some point, ask me: "What tools do I need to buy?" My answer shocks them: "None. Don't buy a thing." It's not so much that you don't need tools, but rather that different networking jobs require wildly different tools. Plenty of network techs never crimp a cable. An equal number never open a system. Some techs do nothing all day but pull cable. The tools you need are defined by your job.

This answer is especially true with software tools. Almost all the network problems I encounter in established networks don't require me to use any tools other than the classic ones provided by the operating system. I've fixed more network problems with ping, for example, than with any other single tool. As you gain skill in this area, you'll find yourself hounded by vendors trying to sell you the latest and greatest networking diagnostic tools. You may like these tools. All I can say is that I've never needed a software diagnostics tool that I had to purchase.

> No matter what the problem, always consider the safety of your data first. Ask yourself this question before performing any troubleshooting action: "Can what I'm about to do potentially damage my data?"

Hardware Tools

In multiple chapters in this book, you've read about tools used to configure a network. These hardware tools include cable testers, TDRs, OTDRs, certifiers, voltage event recorders, protocol analyzers, cable strippers, multimeters, tone probes/generators, line testers, butt sets, and punchdown tools. Some of these tools can also be used in troubleshooting scenarios to help you eliminate or narrow down the possible causes of certain problems. Let's review the tools as listed in the CompTIA Network+ exam objectives.

> Read this section! The CompTIA Network+ exam is filled with repair scenarios, and you must know what every tool does and when to use it.

Cable Testers, TDRs, and OTDRs

The vast majority of cabling problems occur when the network is first installed or when a change is made. Once a cable has been made, installed, and tested, the chances of it failing are pretty small compared to all of the other network problems that might take place. If you're having trouble connecting to a particular resource or experiencing performance problems after making a connection, a bad cable likely isn't the culprit. Broken cables don't make intermittent problems, and they don't slow down data. They make permanent disconnects.

Network techs define a "broken" cable in numerous ways. First, a broken cable might have an *open circuit,* where one or more of the wires in a cable simply don't connect from one end of the cable to the other. The signal lacks *continuity.* Second, a cable might have a *short,* where one or more of the wires

• **Figure 21.1** Typical cable tester

• **Figure 21.2** An EXFO AXS-100 OTDR (photo courtesy of EXFO)

in a cable connect to another wire in the cable. (Within a normal cable, no wires connect to other wires.)

Third, a cable might have a *wire map problem,* where one or more of the wires in a cable don't connect to the proper location on the jack or plug. This can be caused by improperly crimping a cable, for example. Fourth, the cable might experience *crosstalk,* where the electrical signal bleeds from one wire pair to another, creating interference.

Fifth, a broken cable might pick up *noise,* spurious signals usually caused by faulty hardware or poorly crimped jacks. Finally, a broken cable might have *impedance mismatch.* Impedance is the natural electrical resistance of a cable. When cables of different types—think thickness, composition of the metal, and so on—connect and the flow of electrons is not uniform, it can cause a unique type of electrical noise, called an *echo.*

Network technicians use three different devices to deal with broken cables. **Cable testers** can tell you if you have a continuity problem or if a wire map isn't correct (Figure 21.1). *Time domain reflectometers (TDRs)* and *optical time domain reflectometers (OTDRs)* can tell you where the break is on the cable (Figure 21.2). A TDR works with copper cables and an OTDR works with fiber optics, but otherwise they share the same function. If a problem shows itself as a disconnect and you've first checked easier issues that would manifest as disconnects, such as loss of permissions, an unplugged cable, or a server shut off, then think about using these tools.

Certifiers

Certifiers test a cable to ensure that it can handle its rated amount of capacity. When a cable is not broken but it's not moving data the way it should, turn to a certifier. Look for problems that cause a cable to underperform. A bad installation might increase crosstalk, attenuation, or interference. A certifier can pick up an impedance mismatch as well. Most of these problems show up at installation, but running a certifier to eliminate cabling as a problem is never a bad idea. Don't use a certifier for disconnects, only slowdowns. All certifiers need some kind of loopback on the other end of the cable run.

Light Meter

The extremely transparent fiber-optic cables allow light to shine but have some inherent impurities in the glass that can reduce light transmission. Dust, poor connections, and light leakage can also degrade the strength of light pulses as they travel through a fiber-optic run. To measure the amount of light loss, technicians use an **optical power meter**, also referred to as a **light meter** (see Figure 21.3).

The light meter system uses a high-powered source of light at one end of a run and a calibrated detector at the other end. This measures the amount of light that reaches the detector.

Voltage Event Recorder/Temperature Monitor

Networks need the proper temperature and adequate power, but most network techs tend to view these issues as outside of the normal places to look for problems. That's too bad, because both heat and power problems invariably manifest themselves as intermittent problems. Look for problems that might point to heat or power issues: server rooms that get too hot at certain times of the day, switches that fail whenever an air conditioning system kicks on, and so on. You can use a **voltage event recorder** and a **temperature monitor** to monitor server rooms over time to detect and record issues with electricity or heat, respectively. They're great for those "something happened last night" types of issues.

Protocol Analyzers

Protocol analyzers monitor the different protocols running at different layers on the network. A good protocol analyzer will give you Application, Session, Transport, Network, and Data Link layer information on every frame going through your network. Even though the CompTIA Network+ exam places protocol analyzers in a hardware category, they aren't necessarily always hardware. Some of the best and most useful protocol analyzers, like Wireshark, are software.

Use a protocol analyzer when being able to see the data on the network will help you answer these questions: Is something trying to start a session and not getting an answer? Maybe a DNS server isn't responding. Is some computer on the network placing confusing information on the network? Is a rogue DHCP server sending out responses to DHCP requests? In the same vein, a protocol analyzer helps you determine slowdowns on a network by giving you an idea of excess or unexpected traffic (see the "Packet Sniffer" subsection under "Software Tools" later in this chapter).

Cable Strippers/Snips

A **cable stripper** or **snip** (Figure 21.4) helps you to make UTP cables. Even though the CompTIA Network+ exam objectives don't mention crimpers, don't forget you'll need them too. You don't need these tools to punch down 66- or 110-blocks. You would use a punchdown tool for that.

• **Figure 21.4** A cable stripping and crimping tool

Multimeters

Multimeters test voltage (both AC and DC), resistance, and continuity. They are the unsung heroes of cabling infrastructures because no other tool can tell you how much voltage is on a line. They are also a great fallback for continuity testing when you don't have a cable tester handy.

Tone Probes and Tone Generators

Tone probes and their partners, **tone generators**, have only one job: to help you locate a particular cable. You'll never use a tone probe without a tone generator.

Butt Sets

Butt sets are the telephone person's best friend. Use a butt set to tap into a 66- or 110-block to see if a particular line is working.

Line Testers

Line testers are relatively simple devices used to check the integrity of telephone wiring. Use a line tester to check a twisted pair line to see if it is good, dead, reverse wired, or if there is AC voltage on the line.

• **Figure 21.3** Fiberlink® 6650 Optical Power Meter (photo courtesy of Communications Specialties, Inc.)

Tech Tip

Never Buy Cheap Tools

There's an old adage used by carpenters and other craftspeople that goes, "Never buy cheap tools." Cheap tools save you money at the beginning, but they often break more readily than higher-quality tools and, more importantly, make it harder to get the job done. This adage definitely applies to multimeters! You might be tempted to go for the $10 model that looks pretty much like the $25 model, but chances are the leads will break or the readings will lie on the cheaper model. Buy a decent tool, and you'll never have to worry about it.

The CompTIA Network+ exam and many techs refer to the probe as a *toner probe* rather than a *tone probe* or simply a *probe.* Don't be surprised by this terminology on the exam. You always need both a probe and a tone generator to use this tool properly.

• **Figure 21.5** A punchdown tool in action

Punchdown Tools

Punchdown tools (Figure 21.5) put UTP wires into 66- and 110-blocks. The only time you would use a punchdown tool in a diagnostic environment is a quick repunch of a connection to make sure all the contacts are properly set.

> **Try This!**
>
> ### Shopping Spree
>
> As more and more people have networks installed in their homes, the big-box hardware stores stock an increasing number of network-specific tools. Everybody loves shopping, right? So try this! Go to your local hardware store—big box, like Home Depot or Lowes, if there's one near you—and check out their tools. What do they offer? Write down prices and features and compare with what your classmates found.

Software Tools

Make the CompTIA Network+ exam (and real life) easier by separating your software tools into two groups: those that come built into every operating system and those that are third-party tools. Typical built-in tools are tracert/traceroute, ipconfig/ifconfig/ip, arp, ping, arping, pathping, nslookup/dig, hostname, route, nbtstat, and netstat/ss. Third-party tools fall into the categories of packet sniffers, port scanners, throughput testers, and looking glass sites.

> **Try This!**
>
> ### Playing Along
>
> This section contains many command-line tools that you've seen earlier in the book in various places. Now is a great time to refresh your memory about how each one works, so after I review each command, run it yourself. Then type **help** followed by the command to see the available switches for that command. Run the command with some of the switches to see what they do. Running the command is more fun than just reading about it; plus, you'll solidify the knowledge you need to master.

The CompTIA Network+ exam tests your ability to recognize the output from all of the built-in tools (except ss). Take some time to memorize example outputs from all of these tools.

The tracert/traceroute Commands

The **traceroute** command (the actual command in Windows is **tracert**) is used to trace all of the routers between two points. Use traceroute to diagnose where the problem lies when you have problems reaching a remote system. If a traceroute stops at a certain router, you know the problem is either the next router or the connections between them.

When sending a traceroute, it's important to keep a significant difference between Windows and UNIX/Linux/Cisco systems in mind. Windows tracert sends only ICMP packets, while UNIX/Linux/Cisco traceroute can send either ICMP packets or UDP packets, but sends UDP packets by default. Because many routers block ICMP packets, if your traceroute fails from a Windows system, running it on a Linux or UNIX system may return more complete results.

Here's sample `traceroute` output:

```
Tracing route to adsl-208-190-121-38.dsl.hstntx.swbell.net

[208.190.121.38] over a maximum of 30 hops:

  1     1 ms     <1 ms     1 ms    Router.totalhome
[192.168.4.1]

  2    38 ms     41 ms    70 ms    adsl-208-190-121-
38.dsl.hstntx.swbell.net [208.190.121.38]
```

The traceroute command defaults to IPv4, but also functions well in an IPv6 network. In Windows, use the command with the –6 switch: **tracert –6**. In UNIX/Linux, use **traceroute6** (or traceroute –6 in some variants of Linux).

The ipconfig/ifconfig/ip Commands

The **ipconfig** (Windows), **ifconfig** (UNIX), and **ip** (Linux) commands tell you almost anything you want to know about a particular computer's IP settings. Make sure you know that typing `ipconfig` alone only gives basic information. Typing `ipconfig /all` gives detailed information (like DNS servers and MAC addresses).

Here's sample `ipconfig` output:

```
Ethernet adapter Main:

   Connection-specific DNS Suffix  . :
   IPv6 Address. . . . . . . . . . . : 2001:470:bf88:1:fc2d:aeb2:99d2:e2b4
   Temporary IPv6 Address. . . . . . : 2001:470:bf88:1:5e4:c1ef:7b30:ddd6
   Link-local IPv6 Address . . . . . : fe80::fc2d:aeb2:99d2:e2b4%8
   IPv4 Address. . . . . . . . . . . : 192.168.4.27
   Subnet Mask . . . . . . . . . . . : 255.255.255.0
   Default Gateway . . . . . . . . . : fe80::223:4ff:fe8c:b720%8
                                       192.168.4.1

Tunnel adapter Local Area Connection* 6:

Media State . . . . . . . . . . . : Media disconnected
Connection-specific DNS Suffix  . :
```

And here's sample `ifconfig` output:

```
lo0: flags=8049<UP,LOOPBACK,RUNNING,MULTICAST> mtu 16384
        options=3<RXCSUM,TXCSUM>
        inet6 ::1 prefixlen 128
        inet 127.0.0.1 netmask 0xff000000
        inet6 fe80::1%lo0 prefixlen 64 scopeid 0x1
        nd6 options=1<PERFORMNUD>
gif0: flags=8010<POINTOPOINT,MULTICAST> mtu 1280
stf0: flags=0<> mtu 1280
en0: flags=8863<UP,BROADCAST,SMART,RUNNING,SIMPLEX,MULTICAST> mtu 1500
        options=10b<RXCSUM,TXCSUM,VLAN_HWTAGGING,AV>
        ether 3c:07:54:7a:d4:d8
        inet6 fe80::3e07:54ff:fe7a:d4d8%en0 prefixlen 64 scopeid 0x4
        inet 192.168.4.78 netmask 0xffffff00 broadcast 192.168.4.255
        inet6 2601:e::abcd:3e07:54ff:fe7a:d4d8 prefixlen 64 autoconf
        inet6 2601:e::abcd:b84e:9fad:3add:c73b prefixlen 64 autoconf temporary
        nd6 options=1<PERFORMNUD>
        media: autoselect (1000baseT <full-duplex,flow-control>)
        status: active
```

And finally, here's Linux's `ip addr` output:

```
1: lo: <LOOPBACK,UP,LOWER_UP> mtu 65536 qdisc noqueue state UNKNOWN group default
    link/loopback 00:00:00:00:00:00 brd 00:00:00:00:00:00
    inet 127.0.0.1/8 scope host lo
       valid_lft forever preferred_lft forever
    inet6 ::1/128 scope host
       valid_lft forever preferred_lft forever
2: eth0: <BROADCAST,MULTICAST,UP,LOWER_UP> mtu 1500 qdisc pfifo_fast state UNKNOWN group default qlen 1000
    link/ether 00:0c:29:e0:b2:85 brd ff:ff:ff:ff:ff:ff
    inet 192.168.4.19/24 brd 192.168.4.255 scope global eth0
       valid_lft forever preferred_lft forever
    inet6 2601:e:0:abcd:8cfb:6220:ec23:80a/64 scope global temporary dynamic

       valid_lft 86221sec preferred_lft 14221sec
    inet6 2601:e:0:abcd:20c:29ff:fee0:b285/64 scope global dynamic
       valid_lft 86221sec preferred_lft 14221sec
    inet6 fe80::20c:29ff:fee0:b285/64 scope link
       valid_lft forever preferred_lft forever
```

You get three for the price of one with sims in this chapter! Check out the Chapter 21, "Who Made That NIC" sims at http://totalsem.com/006. You'll find a Show!, a Click!, and a Challenge! on the subject that will help you solidify the usefulness of the tools for your technician's toolbox.

The CompTIA Network+ exam objectives refer to the ARP table as the MAC address lookup table, at least at the time this book went to press. Be prepared for either term.

The arp Command

Computers use the Address Resolution Protocol (ARP) to resolve IP addresses to MAC addresses. As the computer learns various MAC addresses on its LAN, it jots them down in the ARP table. When Computer A wants to send a message to Computer B, it determines B's IP address and then checks the ARP table for a corresponding MAC address.

The **arp** command enables you to view and change the ARP table on a computer. Here's sample output from `arp -a`:

```
Interface: 192.168.4.57 --- 0xc
  Internet Address      Physical Address      Type
  192.168.4.1           b8-9b-c9-7d-e7-76     dynamic
  192.168.4.2           00-87-b6-7e-ae-23     dynamic
  192.168.4.8           67-ab-cc-aa-fe-ed     dynamic
  192.168.4.12          23-b5-94-17-d7-33     dynamic
  192.168.4.13          4b-4b-4c-4d-4e-46     dynamic
  192.168.4.14          55-55-55-55-55-55     dynamic
```

The ping, pathping, and arping Commands

The **ping** command uses Internet Message Control Protocol (ICMP) packets to query by IP or by name. It works across routers, so it's generally the first tool used to check if a system is reachable. Unfortunately, many devices block ICMP packets, so a failed ping doesn't always point to an offline system.

The ping command defaults to IPv4, but also functions well in an IPv6 network. In Windows, use the command with the −6 switch: **ping −6**. In UNIX/ Linux, use **ping6**.

Here's sample `ping` output:

```
Pinging 192.168.4.19 with 32 bytes of data:
Reply from 192.168.4.19: bytes=32 time<1ms TTL=64
Reply from 192.168.4.19: bytes=32 time<1ms TTL=64
Reply from 192.168.4.19: bytes=32 time<1ms TTL=64
Reply from 192.168.4.19: bytes=32 time<1ms TTL=64
```

```
Ping statistics for 192.168.4.19:
    Packets: Sent = 4, Received = 4, Lost = 0 (0% loss),
Approximate round trip times in milli-seconds:
    Minimum = 0ms, Maximum = 0ms, Average = 0ms
```

If ping doesn't work, you can try **arping**, which uses ARP frames instead of ICMP. The only downside to arping is that ARP frames do not cross routers because they only consist of frames, and never IP packets, so you can only use arping within a broadcast domain. Windows does not have arping. UNIX and UNIX-like systems, on the other hand, support the arping utility.

Next is sample arping output:

```
ARPING 192.168.4.27 from 192.168.4.19 eth0
Unicast reply from 192.168.4.27 [00:1D:60:DD:92:C6]   0.875ms
Unicast reply from 192.168.4.27 [00:1D:60:DD:92:C6]   0.897ms
Unicast reply from 192.168.4.27 [00:1D:60:DD:92:C6]   0.924ms
Unicast reply from 192.168.4.27 [00:1D:60:DD:92:C6]   0.977ms
```

The ping and traceroute commands are excellent examples of *connectivity software*, applications that enable you to determine if a connection can be made between two computers.

Microsoft has a utility called **pathping** that combines the functions of ping and tracert and adds some additional functions.

Here is sample pathping output:

```
Tracing route to xeroxpaser.totalhome [182.168.4.17]
Over a maximum 30 hops:
  0  local-PC.totalhome [192.168.4.53]
  1  xrxphsr.totalhome [192.168.4.17]
Computing statistics for 25 seconds...
            Source to Here     This Node/Link
Hop  RTT    Lost/Sent - Pct    Lost/Sent - Pct Address
  0                                           local-PC.totalhome [192.168.4.53]
                                0/ 100 - 0%    :
  1   0ms    0/ 100 - 0%        0/ 100 - 0%  xrxphsr.totalhome [192.168.4.17] Trace complete
```

The ping command has the word Pinging in the output. The arping command has the word ARPING. Don't assume that the CompTIA Network+ exam will include those words in its sample outputs, however.

The nslookup/dig Commands

The **nslookup** (all operating systems) and **dig** (UNIX/Linux) commands are used to diagnose DNS problems. These tools are very powerful, but the CompTIA Network+ exam won't ask you more than basic questions, such as how to use them to see if a DNS server is working. When working on Windows systems, the nslookup command is your only choice by default. On UNIX/Linux systems, prefer the dig command. Both commands will help in troubleshooting your DNS issues, but dig provides more verbose output by default. You need to be comfortable working with both commands when troubleshooting modern networks.

Following is an example of the dig command:

```
dig mx totalsem.com
```

This command says, "Show me all the MX records for the totalsem.com domain."

Here's the output for that dig command:

```
; <<>> DiG 9.5.0-P2 <<>> mx totalsem.com
;; global options:  printcmd
;; Got answer:
```

```
;; ->>HEADER<<- opcode: QUERY, status: NOERROR, id: 6070
;; flags: qr rd ra; QUERY: 1, ANSWER: 3, AUTHORITY: 0, ADDITIONAL: 1
;; QUESTION SECTION:
;totalsem.com.                    IN      MX
;; ANSWER SECTION:
totalsem.com.  86400  IN  MX  10
mx1c1.megamailservers.com.
totalsem.com.  86400            IN      MX      100
mx2c1.megamailservers.com.
totalsem.com.  86400            IN      MX      110
mx3c1.megamailservers.com.
```

Running the networking commands several times will help you memorize the functions of the commands as well as the syntax. The CompTIA Network+ exam is also big on the switches available for various commands, such as ipconfig /all.

The hostname Command

The **hostname** command is the simplest of all the utilities shown here. When you run it, it returns with the host name of the computer you are on. Here's what it looked like when I ran it on my Windows 7 box:

```
C:\>
C:\>hostname
mike-win8beta
```

The mtr Command

My Traceroute (mtr) is a dynamic (keeps running) equivalent to traceroute. Windows does not support mtr.

Here's a sample of mtr output:

```
                                My traceroute  [v0.73]
totaltest (0.0.0.0)
Keys:  Help  Display mode  Restart statistics  Order of fields  quit
                                 Packets               Pings
Host                             Loss%  Snt  Last  Avg  Best  Wrst  StDev
1. Router.totalhome               0.0%    5   0.8  0.8   0.7   0.9   0.1
2. adsl-208-190-121-38.dsl.hstntx.s  0.0%    4   85.7  90.7  69.5  119.2  21.8
```

The route Command

The **route** command gives you the capability to display and edit the local system's routing table. To show the routing table, just type **route print** or **netstat -r**.

Here's a sample of route print output:

```
===========================================================================
Interface List


8 ...00 1d 60 dd 92 c6 ...... Marvell 88E8056 PCI-E Ethernet Controller
1 ........................ Software Loopback Interface 1
===========================================================================
IPv4 Route Table
===========================================================================
Active Routes:
Network Destination        Netmask          Gateway       Interface   Metric
0.0.0.0                    0.0.0.0      192.168.4.1    192.168.4.27       10
127.0.0.0                  255.0.0.0       On-link        127.0.0.1      306
127.0.0.1            255.255.255.255       On-link        127.0.0.1      306
127.255.255.255      255.255.255.255       On-link        127.0.0.1      306
169.254.0.0              255.255.0.0       On-link     192.168.4.27      286
169.254.214.185      255.255.255.255       On-link   169.254.214.185      276
169.254.255.255      255.255.255.255       On-link     192.168.4.27      266
```

```
192.168.4.0          255.255.255.0      On-link      192.168.4.27      266
192.168.4.27         255.255.255.255    On-link      192.168.4.27      266
192.168.4.255        255.255.255.255    On-link      192.168.4.27      266
224.0.0.0            240.0.0.0          On-link      127.0.0.1         306
224.0.0.0            240.0.0.0          On-link      169.254.214.185   276
224.0.0.0            240.0.0.0          On-link      192.168.4.27      266
255.255.255.255      255.255.255.255    On-link      127.0.0.1         306
255.255.255.255      255.255.255.255    On-link      169.254.214.185   276
255.255.255.255      255.255.255.255    On-link      192.168.4.27      266
========================================================================
Persistent Routes:

None
```

The nbtstat Command

The nbtstat command is a Windows-only program that can best be described as a command-line pseudo-equivalent to Window's My Network Places or Network icon. Always run nbtstat with a switch. The most useful switch is –n, which shows the local NetBIOS names. All versions of Windows include nbt-stat. Running nbtstat is a handy way to see what systems are on your Windows network. Any systems running Samba will also appear here.

Here's an example of running `nbtstat -n` from the command prompt:

```
Main:
Node IpAddress: [192.168.4.27] Scope Id: []
                        NetBIOS Local Name Table
         Name                Type            Status
    ---------------------------------------
    MIKESPC       <00>  UNIQUE       Registered
    TOTALHOME     <00>  GROUP        Registered
    MIKESPC       <20>  UNIQUE       Registered
    TOTALHOME     <1E>  GROUP        Registered
```

The netstat and ss Commands

The netstat command is a very handy tool that displays information on the current state of all of your running IP processes. It shows what sessions are active and can also provide statistics based on ports or protocols (TCP, UDP, and so on). Typing `netstat` by itself only shows current sessions. Typing `netstat -r` shows the routing table (100 percent identical to `route print`). If you want to know about your current sessions, netstat is the tool to use.

Here's sample `netstat` output:

```
Active Connections

  Proto   Local Address            Foreign Address         State
  TCP     127.0.0.1:27015          MikesPC:51090           ESTABLISHED
  TCP     127.0.0.1:51090          MikesPC:27015           ESTABLISHED
  TCP     127.0.0.1:52500          MikesPC:52501           ESTABLISHED
  TCP     192.168.4.27:54731       72-165-61-141:27039     CLOSE_WAIT
  TCP     192.168.4.27:55080       63-246-140-18:http      CLOSE_WAIT
  TCP     192.168.4.27:56126       acd4129913:https        ESTABLISHED
  TCP     192.168.4.27:62727       TOTALTEST:ssh            ESTABLISHED
  TCP     192.168.4.27:63325       65.54.165.136:https     TIME_WAIT
  TCP     192.168.4.27:63968       209.8.115.129:http      ESTABLISHED
```

Windows still comes with netstat, but the ss command has completely eclipsed it on the Linux side. The ss command is faster and more powerful than netstat. Unlike netstat, however, you won't find ss on the CompTIA Network+ exam. Here's sample output from `ss`, filtered to show only TCP connections:

```
State        Recv-Q Send-Q    Local Address:Port       Peer Address:Port
CLOSE-WAIT   28     0         10.0.2.15:52161          91.189.92.24:https
CLOSE-WAIT   28     0         10.0.2.15:46117          91.189.92.11:https
ESTAB        0      0         10.0.2.15:55542          74.125.239.40:http
```

Sometimes a GUI tool like Wireshark won't work because a server has no GUI installed. In situations like this, *tcpdump* is the go-to choice. This great command-line tool not only enables you to monitor and filter packets in the terminal, but can also create files you can open in Wireshark for later analysis. Even better, it's installed by default on most UNIX/Linux systems.

Packet Sniffer

Packet sniffer, *protocol analyzer,* or *packet analyzer*: All of these names are used to define a tool that intercepts and logs network packets. You have many choices when it comes to packet sniffers. Some sniffers come as programs you run on a computer, while others manifest as dedicated hardware devices. Arguably, the most popular GUI packet sniffer and analyzer is **Wireshark** (Figure 21.6). You've already seen Wireshark in the book, but here's a screen to jog your memory.

Port Scanners

As you'll recall from back in Chapter 18, "Managing Risk," a **port scanner** is a program that probes ports on another system, logging the state of the scanned ports. These tools are used to look for unintentionally opened ports that might make a system vulnerable to attack. As you might imagine, they also are used by hackers to break into systems.

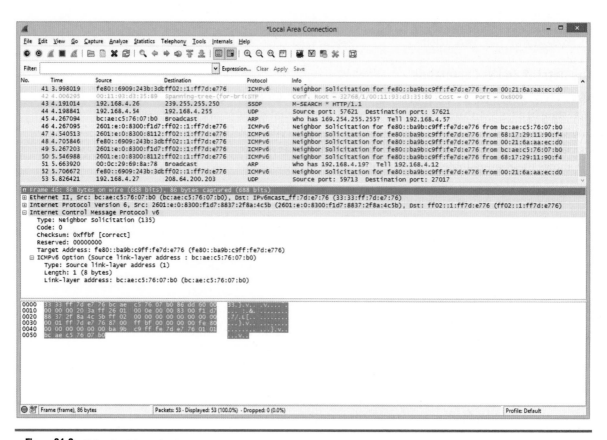

• **Figure 21.6**   Wireshark in action!

The most famous of all port scanners is probably the powerful and free Nmap. Nmap was originally designed to work on UNIX systems, so Windows folks used alternatives like Angry IP Scanner by Anton Keks (Figure 21.7). Nmap has been ported to just about every operating system these days, however, so you can find it for Windows.

Throughput Testers

Throughput testers enable you to measure the data flow in a network. Which tool is appropriate depends on the type of network throughput you want to test. Most techs use one of several **speed-test sites** for checking an Internet connection's throughput, such as MegaPath's Speakeasy Speed Test (Figure 21.8): www.speakeasy.net/speedtest.

Looking Glass Sites

Sometimes you need to perform a ping or traceroute from a location outside of the local environment. **Looking glass sites** are remote servers accessible with a browser that contain common collections of diagnostic tools such as ping and traceroute, plus some Border Gateway Protocol (BGP) query tools.

Most looking glass sites allow you to select where diagnostic process will originate from a list of locations, as well as the target destination, which diagnostic, and sometimes the version of IP to test. A Google search for "looking glass sites" will provide a large selection from which to choose.

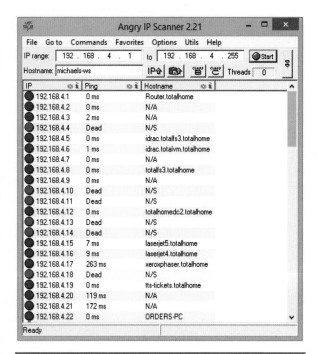

• **Figure 21.7** Angry IP Scanner

• **Figure 21.8** Speed Test results from Speakeasy

■ The Troubleshooting Process

Troubleshooting is a dynamic, fluid process that requires you to make snap judgments and act on them to try and make the network go. Any attempt to cover every possible scenario here would be futile at best, and probably also not in your best interest. If an exhaustive listing of all network problems is impossible, then how do you decide what to do and in what order?

Before you touch a single console or cable, you should remember two basic rules: To paraphrase the Hippocratic Oath, "First, do no harm." If at all possible, don't make a network problem bigger than it was originally. This is a rule I've broken thousands of times, and you will too.

But if I change the good doctor's phrase a bit, it's possible to formulate a rule you can actually live with: "First, do not trash the data!" My gosh, if I had a dollar for every megabyte of irreplaceable data I've destroyed, I'd be rich! I've learned my lesson, and you should learn from my mistakes.

The second rule is: "Always make good backups!" Computers can be replaced; data that is not backed up is, at best, expensive to recover and, at worst, gone forever.

No matter how complex and fancy, any troubleshooting process can be broken down into simple steps. Having a sequence of steps to follow makes the entire troubleshooting process simpler and easier, because you have a clear set of goals to achieve in a specific sequence.

The CompTIA Network+ exam objectives contain a detailed troubleshooting methodology that provides a good starting point for our discussion. Here are the basic steps in the troubleshooting process:

1. Identify the problem.

   a. Gather information.

   b. Duplicate the problem, if possible.

   c. Question users.

   d. Identify symptoms.

   e. Determine if anything has changed.

   f. Approach multiple problems individually.

2. Establish a theory of probable cause.

   a. Question the obvious.

   b. Consider multiple approaches:

      i. Top-to-bottom/bottom-to-top OSI model

      ii. Divide and conquer

3. Test the theory to determine cause.

   a. Once theory is confirmed, determine next steps to resolve the problem.

   b. If theory is not confirmed, reestablish new theory or escalate.

4. Establish a plan of action to resolve the problem and identify potential effects.

5. Implement the solution or escalate as necessary.

6. Verify full system functionality and, if applicable, implement preventative measures.

7. Document findings, actions, and outcomes.

Identify the Problem

First, *identify the problem*. That means grasping the true problem, rather than what someone tells you. A user might call in and complain that he can't access the Internet from his workstation, for example, which could be the only problem. But the problem could also be that the entire wing of the office just went down and you've got a much bigger problem on your hands. You need to gather information, duplicate the problem (if possible), question users, identify symptoms, determine if anything has changed on the network, and approach multiple problems individually. Following these steps will help you get to the root of the problem.

Gather Information, Duplicate the Problem, Question Users, and Identify Symptoms

Gather information about the situation. If you are working directly on the affected system and not relying on somebody on the other end of a telephone to guide you, you will *identify symptoms* through your observation of what is (or isn't) happening.

If you're troubleshooting over the telephone (always a *joy*, in my experience), you will need to *question users*. These questions can be *close-ended*, which is to say there can only be a yes-or-no-type answer, such as, "Can you see a light on the front of the monitor?" You can also ask *open-ended* questions, such as, "What have you already tried in attempting to fix the problem?"

The type of question you ask at any given moment depends on what information you need and on the user's knowledge level. If, for example, the user seems to be technically oriented, you will probably be able to ask more close-ended questions because they will know what you are talking about. If, on the other hand, the user seems to be confused about what's happening, open-ended questions will allow him or her to explain in his or her own words what is going on.

One of the first steps in trying to determine the cause of a problem is to understand the extent of the problem. Is it specific to one user or is it network-wide? Sometimes this entails trying the task yourself, both from the user's machine and from your own or another machine.

For example, if a user is experiencing problems logging into the network, you might need to go to that user's machine and try to use his or her user name to log in. In other words, try to *duplicate the problem*. Doing this tells you whether the problem is a user error of some kind, as well as enables you to see the symptoms of the problem yourself. Next, you probably want to try logging in with your own user name from that machine, or have the user try to log in from another machine.

In some cases, you can ask other users in the area if they are experiencing the same problem to see if the issue is affecting more than one user. Depending on the size of your network, you should find out whether the problem is occurring in only one part of your company or across the entire network.

What does all of this tell you? Essentially, it tells you how big the problem is. If nobody in an entire remote office can log in, you may be able to assume that

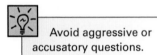
Eliminating variables is one of the first tools in your arsenal of diagnostic techniques.

the problem is the network link or router connecting that office to the server. If nobody in any office can log in, you may be able to assume the server is down or not accepting logins. If only that one user in that one location can't log in, the problem may be with that user, that machine, or that user's account.

Determine If Anything Has Changed

Determine if anything has changed on the network recently that might have caused the problem. You may not have to ask many questions before the person using the problem system can tell you what has changed, but, in some cases, establishing if anything has changed can take quite a bit of time and involve further work behind the scenes. Here are some examples of questions to ask:

- "What exactly was happening when the problem occurred?"
- "Has anything been changed on the system recently?"
- "Has the system been moved recently?"

Notice the way I've tactfully avoided the word *you,* as in "Have *you* changed anything on the system recently?" This is a deliberate tactic to avoid any implied blame on the part of the user. Being nice never hurts, and it makes the whole troubleshooting process more friendly.

You should also *internally* ask yourself some isolating questions, such as "Was that machine involved in the software push last night?" or "Didn't a tech visit that machine this morning?" Note you will only be able to answer these questions if *your* documentation is up to date. Sometimes, isolating a problem may require you to check system and hardware logs (such as those stored by some routers and other network devices), so make sure you know how to do this.

Avoid aggressive or accusatory questions.

Approach Multiple Problems Individually

If you encounter a complicated scenario, with various machines off the network and potential server room or wiring problems, break it down. *Approach multiple problems individually* to sort out root causes. Methodically tackle them and you'll eventually have a list of one or more problems identified. Then you can move on to the next step.

Establish a Theory of Probable Cause

Once you've identified one or more problems, try to figure out what could have happened. In other words, *establish a theory of probable cause.* Just keep in mind that a *theory is not a fact.* You might need to chuck the theory out the window later in the process and establish a revised theory.

This step comes down to experience—or good use of the support tools at your disposal, such as your knowledge base. You need to select the most *probable* cause from all the *possible* causes, so the solution you choose fixes the problem the first time. This may not always happen, but whenever possible, you want to avoid spending a whole day stabbing in the dark while the problem snores softly to itself in some cozy, neglected corner of your network.

Don't forget to *question the obvious.* If Bob can't print to the networked printer, for example, check to see that the printer is plugged in and turned on.

Consider multiple approaches when tackling problems. This will keep you from locking your imagination into a single train of thought. You can use the OSI seven-layer model as a troubleshooting tool in several ways to help with this process. Here's a scenario to work through.

Martha can't access the database server to start her workday. The problem manifests this way: She opens the database client on her computer, then clicks on recent documents, one of which is the current project that management has assigned to her team. Nothing happens. Normally, the database client will connect to the database that resides on the server on the other side of the network.

Try a *top-to-bottom* or *bottom-to-top OSI model* approach to the problem. Sometimes it pays to try both. Here are some ideas on how this might help.

7. Application: Could there be a problem with the API that enables the database application to connect to the database server? Sure.

6. Presentation: Could there be a problem with encryption between the application and the database server? Maybe, but Martha would probably see an error message rather than nothing.

5. Session: Could a database authentication failure be preventing access? Again, this could be the problem, but Martha would probably see an error message here as well.

4. Transport: Perhaps extreme traffic on the network could block an acknowledgment segment? This seems a bit of a reach, but worth considering.

3. Network: Someone might have changed the IP address of the database server.

2. Data Link: The MAC address of the database server or Martha's machine might be blacklisted.

1. Physical: A disconnected cable or dead NIC can make for a bad day.

You might imagine the reverse model in some situations. If the network was newly installed, for example, running through some of the basic connectivity at Layers 1 and 2 might be a good first approach.

Another option for tackling multiple options is to use the *divide and conquer* approach.

On its face, divide and conquer appears to be a compromise between top-to-bottom OSI troubleshooting and bottom-to-top OSI troubleshooting. But it's better than a compromise. If we arbitrarily always perform top-to-bottom troubleshooting, we'll waste a lot of time at Layers 7 through 3 to troubleshoot Data Link layer and Physical layer issues.

Divide and conquer is a time saver that comes into play as part of developing a theory of probable cause. As you gather information for troubleshooting, a general sense of where the problem lies should manifest. Place this likely cause at the appropriate layer of the OSI model and begin to test the theory and related theories at that layer. If the theory bears out, follow the appropriate troubleshooting steps. If the theory is wrong, move up or down the OSI model with new theories of probable causes.

Test the Theory to Determine Cause

With the third step, you need to *test the theory to determine the cause,* but do so without changing anything or risking any repercussions. If you have determined that the probable cause for Bob not being able to print is that the printer is turned off, go look. If that's the case, then you should plan out your next step to resolve the problem. Do not act yet! That comes next.

If the theory is not confirmed, you need to *reestablish a new theory or escalate the problem*. Go back to step two and determine a new probable cause. Once you have another idea, test it.

The reason you should hesitate to act at this third step is that you might not have permission to make the fix or the fix might cause repercussions you don't fully understand yet. For example, if you walk over to the print server room to see if the printer is powered up and online and find the door padlocked, that's a whole different level of problem. Sure, the printer is turned off, but management has done it for a reason. In this sort of situation, you need to escalate the problem.

To *escalate* has two meanings: either to inform other parties about a problem for guidance or to pass the job off to another authority who has control over the device/issue that's most probably causing the problem. Let's say you have a server with a bad NIC. This server is used heavily by the accounting department, and taking it down may cause problems you don't even know about. You need to inform the accounting manager to consult with them. Alternatively, you'll come across problems over which you have no control or authority. A badly acting server across the country (hopefully) has another person in charge to whom you need to hand over the job.

Regardless of how many times you need to go through this process, you'll eventually reach a theory that seems right. *Once the theory is confirmed, determine the next steps you need to take to resolve the problem.*

Establish a Plan of Action and Identify Potential Effects

By this point, you should have some ideas as to what the problem might be. It's time to "look before you leap" and *establish a plan of action to resolve the problem.* An action plan defines how you are going to fix this problem. Most problems are simple, but if the problem is complex, you need to write down the steps. As you do this, think about what else might happen as you go about the repair. *Identify the potential effects* of the actions you're about to take, especially the unintended ones. If you take out a switch without a replacement switch at hand, the users might experience excessive downtime while you hunt for a new switch and move them over. If you replace a router, can you restore all the old router's settings to the new one or will you have to rebuild from scratch?

Implement the Solution or Escalate as Necessary

Once you think you have isolated the cause of the problem, you should decide what you think is the best way to fix it and then *implement the solution,* whether that's giving advice over the phone to a user, installing a replacement part, or adding a software patch. Or, if the solution you propose requires either more skill than you possess at the moment or falls into someone else's purview, *escalate as necessary* to get the fix implemented.

If you're the implementer, follow these guidelines. All the way through implementation, try only one likely solution at a time. There's no point in installing several patches at once, because then you can't tell which one fixed the problem. Similarly, there's no point in replacing several items of hardware (such as a hard disk and its controller cable) at the same time, because then you can't tell which part (or parts) was faulty.

As you try each possibility, always *document* what you do and what results you get. This isn't just for a future problem either—during a lengthy trouble-shooting process, it's easy to forget exactly what you tried two hours before or which thing you tried produced a particular result. Although being methodical may take longer, it will save time the next time—and it may enable you to pin-point what needs to be done to stop the problem from recurring at all, thereby reducing future call volume to your support team—and as any support person will tell you, that's definitely worth the effort!

Then you need to test the solution. This is the part everybody hates. Once you think you've fixed a problem, you should try to make it happen again. If you can't, great! But sometimes you will be able to re-create the problem, and then you know you haven't finished the job at hand. Many techs want to slide away quietly as soon as everything seems to be fine, but trust me on this, it won't impress your customer when her problem flares up again 30 seconds after you've left the building—not to mention that you get the joy of another two-hour car trip the next day to fix the same problem, for an even more unhappy client!

In the scenario where you are providing support to someone else rather than working directly on the problem, you should have *her* try to re-create the problem. This tells you whether she understands what you have been telling her and educates her at the same time, lessening the chance that she'll call you back later and ask, "Can we just go through that one more time?"

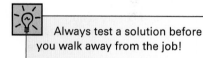
Always test a solution before you walk away from the job!

Verify Full System Functionality and Implement Preventative Measures

Okay, now that you have changed something on the system in the process of solving one problem, you must think about the wider repercussions of what you have done. If you've replaced a faulty NIC in a server, for instance, will the fact that the MAC address has changed (remember, it's built into the NIC) affect anything else, such as the logon security controls or your network man-agement and inventory software? If you've installed a patch on a client PC, will this change the default protocol or any other default settings that may affect other functionality? If you've changed a user's security settings, will this affect his or her ability to access other network resources? This is part of testing your solution to make sure it works properly, but it also makes you think about the impact of your work on the system as a whole.

Make sure you *verify full system functionality*. If you think you fixed the problem between Martha's workstation and the database server, have her open the database while you're still there. That way you don't have to make a second tech call to resolve an outstanding issue. This saves time and money and helps your customer do his or her job better. Everybody wins.

Also at this time, if applicable, *implement preventative measures* to avoid a repeat of the problem. If that means you need to educate the user to do or not do something, teach him or her tactfully. If you need to install software or patch a system, do it now.

Memorize these problem analysis steps:

1. Identify the problem.
   a. Gather information.
   b. Duplicate the problem, if possible.
   c. Question users.
   d. Identify symptoms.
   e. Determine if anything has changed.
   f. Approach multiple problems individually.
2. Establish a theory of probable cause.
   a. Question the obvious.
   b. Consider multiple approaches:
      i. Top-to-bottom/bottom-to-top OSI model
      ii. Divide and conquer
3. Test the theory to determine cause.
   a. Once theory is confirmed, determine next steps to resolve problem.
   b. If theory is not confirmed, reestablish new theory or escalate.
4. Establish a plan of action to resolve the problem and identify potential effects.
5. Implement the solution or escalate as necessary.
6. Verify full system functionality and, if applicable, implement preventative measures.
7. Document findings, actions, and outcomes.

Document Findings, Actions, and Outcomes

It is *vital* that you *document findings, actions, and outcomes* of all support calls, for two reasons: First, you're creating a support database to serve as a knowledge base for future reference, enabling everyone on the support team to identify new problems as they arise and know how to deal with them quickly, without having to duplicate someone else's research efforts. Second, documentation enables you to track problem trends and anticipate future workloads, or even to identify a particular brand or model of an item, such as a printer or a NIC, that seems to be less reliable or that creates more work for you than others. Don't skip this step—it *really* is essential!

■ Resolving Common Network Issues

Network problems fall into several basic categories, and most of these problems you or a network tech in the proper place can fix. Fixing problems at the workstation, work area, or server is a network tech's bread and butter. The same is true of connecting to resources on the LAN. Problems connecting to a WAN can often be resolved at the local level, but sometimes need to get escalated. The knowledge from the previous chapters combined with the tools and methods you've learned in this chapter should enable you to fix just about any network!

There are a couple of stumbling blocks when it comes to resolving network issues. First, at almost any level of problem, the result—as far as the end user is concerned—is the same. He or she can't access resources beyond the local machine. Whether a user tries to access the local file server or do a Google search, if the attempt fails, "the network is down!" You need to fall back on the most important question a tech can ask: What can cause this problem? Then methodically work through the troubleshooting steps and tools to narrow possibilities. Let's look at a scenario to illustrate the narrowing process.

"We Can't Access Our Web Server in Istanbul!"

Everyone in the local office appears to have full access to local and Internet Web sites. No one, however, can reach a company-operated server at a particular remote site in Istanbul. There has been a recent change to the firewall configuration, so it is up to technician Terry to determine if the firewall change is the culprit or if the problem lies elsewhere.

Terry has come up with three possible theories: the remote server is down, the remote site is inaccessible, or the local firewall is preventing communication with the server. He elects to test his theories with the "quickest to test" approach. His first test is to confirm that all of the local office workstations cannot reach the remote server. Using different hosts, he uses the ping and ping6 utilities. First he pings localhost to confirm the workstation has a working IP stack, then he attempts to ping the remote server and gets no response. Next, he tries the tracert and traceroute utilities on the different hosts. Traceroute shows a functional path to the router that connects the remote office to the Internet, but does not get a response from the server.

So far, everything seems to confirm that the local office cannot get to the remote server. Just to be able to say he tried everything, Terry runs the mtr utility from a Linux box and lets it run for an extended time. At the same time, he runs the pathping utility from a Windows computer. Neither utility can contact the server. He tries all of these utilities on some other company resources and Internet sites and has no problems connecting.

Confident that the reported symptom is confirmed, Terry puts in a call to the remote site to ask about the status. The virtual PBX sends Terry to voice-mail for every extension that he calls. This could point to a network disconnection at the site or to everyone being out of the office there. Since it is 3:00 A.M. at the remote site, Terry does not have a clear answer.

The next quick test to perform is to see if the site is reachable from outside of the local office. This will confirm or eliminate his theory of a local firewall configuration issue.

Terry sits down at a computer and searches on Google for a looking glass site. He selects one from the results list and browses to the site. Once in the site, he selects the location of a source router to perform a diagnostic test, and then he selects the type of test to run; in this case, he chooses a ping test. He enters the target server address of the company remote server and submits the test parameters. After a moment, the looking glass server sends a set of pings, none of which receives a response. He tries the test from a few other source router locations and gets the same results.

To complete his tests, Terry uses the looking glass site to ping some additional hosts at the remote site and is pleased to discover that they are all reachable. Now Terry knows that the site is accessible, so it must be that the server is down. When the office opens, he will contact the technician there and offer whatever help and information that he can. In the meantime, he informs the rest of the organization of the server's status.

Narrowing the problem to a single source—an apparently down server—doesn't get all the way to the bottom of the problem (although it certainly helps!). What could cause an unresponsive server?

- Local power outage, like a blown circuit breaker
- Failed NIC on the server
- Network cable disconnected
- Improper network configuration on the server
- A changed patch cable location in the rack
- Failed component in the server
- Server shutdown
- A whole lot of other possibilities

Let's look at some of the problems from a hands-on view first, then move to LAN and WAN issues.

Hands-On Problems

Hands-on problems refer to things that you can fix at the workstation, work area, or server. These include physical problems and configuration problems.

A *power failure* or *power anomalies,* such as dips and surges, can make a network device unreachable. We've addressed the fixes for such issues a couple of times already in this book: manage the power to the network device in question and install an uninterruptible power supply (UPS).

A *hardware failure* can certainly make a network device unreachable. Fall back on your CompTIA A+ training for troubleshooting. Check the link lights on the NIC. Try another NIC if the machine seems functional in every other aspect. Ping the localhost.

Hot-swappable *transceivers* (which you read about way back in Chapter 6) can go bad. The key when working with small form-factor pluggable (SFP) or the much older gigabit interface converter (GBIC) transceivers is that you need to check both the media and the module. In other words, a seemingly *bad SFP/ GBIC* could be *the cable connected to it or the transceiver.* As with other hardware issues, try known-good components to troubleshoot.

Outside invisible forces can cause problems with copper cabling. You've read about electromagnetic interference (EMI) and radio frequency interference (RFI) previously in the book. *EMI and RFI can disrupt signaling on a copper cable*, especially with the very low voltages used today on those cables. These are crazy things to troubleshoot.

An interference problem might manifest in a scenario like this one. John can use e-mail on his laptop successfully over the company's wireless network. When he plugs in at his desk in his cubicle, however, e-mail messages just don't get through.

Cross Check

Interference at the Demarc

You read about interference causing problems at the demarc in an office building back in Chapter 14, "Remote Connectivity," so cross check your knowledge now. What kind of interference could cause problems? How would you avoid the problems?

Typically, you'd test everything before suspecting EMI or RFI causing this problem. Test the NIC on the laptop by plugging into a known-good port. You'd use a cable tester on the cable. You'd check for continuity between the port in his office to the switch. You'd glance at the cabling certification documents to see that yes, the cable worked when installed.

Only then might a creative tech at their wit's end notice the recently installed, high-powered WAP on the wall outside Tom's office. RFI strikes!

If the installation is new and unproven, a perfectly fine network device might be unreachable because of *interface errors*, meaning that the installer didn't install the wall jack correctly. The resulting *incorrect termination* might be a mismatched standard (568A rather than 568B, for example). The cable from the wall to the workstation might be bad or might be a *crossover* cable rather than *straight-through* cable. Try another cable.

Aside from obvious physical problems, other hands-on problems you can fix manifest as some sort of misconfiguration. An *incorrect IP configuration*, such as setting a PC to a static IP address that's not on the same network ID as other resources, would result in a "dead-to-me" network. A similar fate would result from putting *incorrect default gateway IP address* information. The system will go nowhere, fast.

The fix for these sorts of problems should be pretty obvious to you at this point. Go into the network configuration for the device and put in correct numbers. Figure 21.9 shows TCP/IP settings for a Windows Server machine.

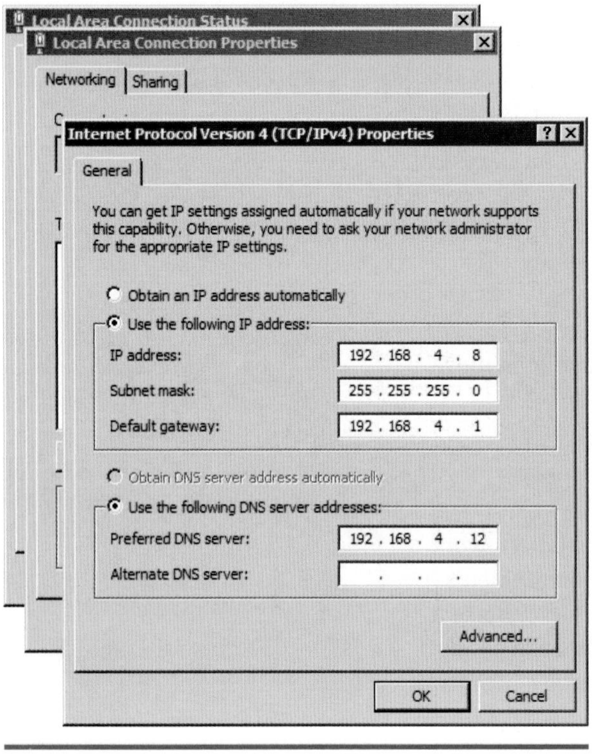

Some problems you can fix at the local machine don't point to messed-up hardware or invalid settings, but reflect

• **Figure 21.9** TCP/IP settings in Windows Server

the current mix of wired and wireless networks in the same place. Here's a scenario. Tina has a wireless network connection to the Internet. She gets a shiny new printer with an Ethernet port, but with no Wi-Fi capability. She wants to print from both her PC and her laptop, so she creates a small LAN: a couple of Ethernet cables and a switch. She plugs everything in, installs drivers, and all is well. She can print from both machines. Unfortunately, as soon as she prints, her Internet connection goes down.

The funny part is that the Internet connection didn't go anywhere, but her *simultaneous wired/wireless connections* created a network failure. The wired and wireless NICs can't actually operate simultaneously and, by default, the wired connection takes priority in the order in which devices are accessed by network services.

To fix this problem, open **Network Connections** in the Control Panel. Press the ALT key to activate the menu bar, then select **Advanced | Advanced Settings** (Figure 21.10). Change the connection priority in the Advanced Settings options by selecting the one Tina wants to take priority and clicking the up arrow to move it up the list.

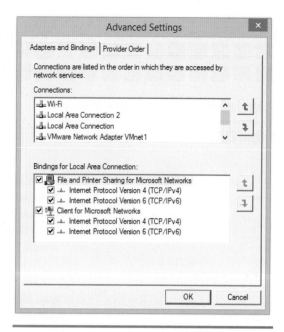

• **Figure 21.10** Network Connections Advanced Settings

LAN Problems

Incorrect configuration of any number of options in devices can stop a device from accessing resources over a LAN. These problems can be simple to fix, although tracking down the culprit can take time and patience.

One of the most obvious errors occurs when you're duplicating machines and using static IP addresses. As soon as you plug in the duplicated machine with its *duplicate IP* address, the network will howl. No two computers can have the same IP address on a broadcast domain. The fix for the problem—after the face-palm—is to change the IP address on the new machine either to an unused static IP or to DHCP.

Server Misconfigurations

Misconfigurations of server settings can block all or some access to resources on a LAN. *Misconfigured DHCP* settings on a host above can cause problems, but they will be limited to the host. If these settings are misconfigured on the DHCP server, however, many more machines and people can be affected. A *misconfigured DNS* server might direct hosts to incorrect sites or no sites at all. Misconfigured DNS settings on a client will stop name resolution altogether and cause the network to appear to be down for the user.

You'll be clued into such misconfiguration by using ping and other tools. If you can ping a file server by IP address but not by name, this points to *DNS issues.* Similarly, if a computer fails in *discovering neighboring devices/nodes,* like connecting to a networked printer, DHCP or DNS misconfiguration can be the culprit. To fix the issue, go into

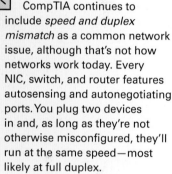 CompTIA continues to include *speed and duplex mismatch* as a common network issue, although that's not how networks work today. Every NIC, switch, and router features autosensing and autonegotiating ports. You plug two devices in and, as long as they're not otherwise misconfigured, they'll run at the same speed—most likely at full duplex.

It's important to note that if the speeds on the two NICs are mismatched, the link will not come up, but if it's just the duplex that's mismatched, the link will come up but the connection will be erratic. Look for this "common error" on the exam, but not in the real world.

Cross Check

DNS Settings

You learned about DNS in detail in Chapter 10, so dust off those memories and see if you can answer these questions. What might cause a DNS server to go down? What's a DNS root server? What are the authoritative top-level domain servers? Does DNS use a flat name space or a hierarchical name space? What's the difference?

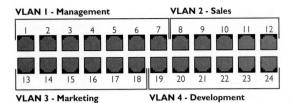

VLAN 1 - Management   VLAN 2 - Sales

| 1 | 2 | 3 | 4 | 5 | 6 | 7 | 8 | 9 | 10 | 11 | 12 |

| 13 | 14 | 15 | 16 | 17 | 18 | 19 | 20 | 21 | 22 | 23 | 24 |

VLAN 3 - Marketing   VLAN 4 - Development

• **Figure 21.11** Bill's VLAN assignments

the network configuration for the client or the server and find the misconfigured settings.

Adding VLANs

When you add VLANs into the network mix, all sorts of fun network issues can crop up. As an example, suppose Bill has a 24-port managed switch segmented into four VLANs, one for each group in the office: Management, Sales, Marketing, and Development (Figure 21.11).

Bill thought he'd assigned six ports to each VLAN when he set up the switch, but by mistake he assigned seven ports to VLAN 1 and only five ports to VLAN 2. Merrily plugging in the patch cables for each group of users, Bill gets called up by his boss asking why Cindy over in Sales suddenly can see resources reserved for management. This obviously points to an *interface misconfiguration* that resulted in an *incorrect VLAN assignment.*

Similarly, after fixing his initial mistake and getting the VLANs set up properly, Bill needs to plug the right patch cables into the right ports. If he messes up and plugs the patch cable for Cindy's computer into a VLAN 1 port, the intrepid salesperson would again have access to the management resources. Such *cable placement errors* show up pretty quickly and are readily fixed. Keep proper records of patch cable assignments and plug the cables into the proper ports.

Link Aggregation Problems

Ethernet networks (traditionally) don't scale easily. If you have a Gigabit Ethernet connection between the main switch and a very busy file server, that connection by definition can handle up to 1 Gbps bandwidth. If that connection becomes saturated, the only way to bump up the bandwidth cap on that single connection would be to upgrade both the switch and the server NIC to the next higher Ethernet standard, 10-Gigabit Ethernet. That's a big jump and an expensive one, plus it's an upgrade of 1000%! What if you needed to bump bandwidth up by only 20%?

The scaling issue became obvious early on, so manufacturers came up with ways to use multiple NICs in tandem to increase bandwidth in smaller increments, what's called **link aggregation** or **NIC teaming**. Numerous protocols enable two or more connections to work together simultaneously, such as the vendor-neutral IEEE 802.3ad specification *Link Aggregation Control Protocol (LACP)* and the Cisco-proprietary *Port Aggregation Protocol (PAgP).* Let's focus on the former for a common network issue scenario.

To enable LACP between two devices, such as the switch and file server just noted, each device needs two or more interconnected network interfaces configured for LACP. When the two devices interact, they will make sure they can communicate over multiple physical ports at the same speeds and form a single logical port that takes advantage of the full combined bandwidth (Figure 21.12).

Those ports can be in one of two modes: active or passive. *Active* ports want to use LACP and send special frames out trying to initiate creating an aggregated logical port. *Passive* ports wait for active ports to initiate the conversation before they will respond.

So here's the common network error with LACP setups. An aggregated connection set to active on both ends (*active-active*) automatically talks, negotiates, and works. One set to active on one

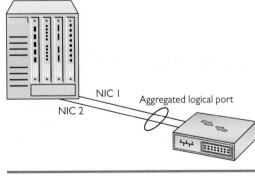

NIC 1

NIC 2

Aggregated logical port

• **Figure 21.12** LACP

end and passive on the other (*active-passive*) will talk, negotiate, and work. But if you set both sides to passive (passive-passive), neither will initiate the conversation and LACP will not engage. Setting both ends to passive when you want to use LACP is an example of *NIC teaming misconfiguration*.

NIC teaming provides many more benefits than just increasing bandwidth, such as redundancy. You can team two NICs in a logical unit, but set them up with one NIC as the primary—*live*—and the second as the hot spare—*standby*. If the first NIC goes down, the traffic will automatically flow through the second NIC. In a simple network setup for redundancy, you'd make one connection live and the other as standby on each device. Switch A has a live and a standby, Switch B has a live and a standby, and so on.

The key here is that multicast traffic to the various devices needs to be enabled on every device through which that traffic might pass. If Switch C doesn't play nice with multicast and it's connected to Switch B, this can cause multicast traffic to stop. One "fix" for this in a Cisco network is to turn off a feature called IGMP snooping, which is enabled by default on Cisco switches. IGMP snooping is normally a good thing, because it helps the switches keep track of devices that use multicast and filter traffic away from devices that don't.

The problem with turning off IGMP snooping is that the switches won't map and filter multicast traffic. Instead of only sending to the devices that are set up to receive multicast, the switches will treat multicast messages as broadcast messages and send them to everybody. This is a NIC teaming misconfiguration that can seriously degrade network performance.

A better fix would be to send a couple of network techs to change settings on Switch C and make it send multicast packets properly.

 The CompTIA Network+ exam objectives refer to this subset of *NIC teaming misconfiguration* as simply *multicast vs. broadcast*. It's not really one against the other, but there you have it.

WAN Problems

Problems that stop users from accessing content across a WAN, like the Internet, can originate at the local machine, switches within the LAN, routers that interconnect the WAN, switches within the distant network, and the distant machine itself. As you might infer from the opening scenario, some of these common network problems you can fix, and some you cannot. We discussed many remote connectivity problems and solutions way back in Chapter 14, "Remote Connectivity," so I won't rehash them here.

This section starts with router configuration issues, issues with ISPs and frame sizes, problems with misconfigured multi-layer network appliances, and company security policies. The following sections go into bigger problems that require escalation. The chapter wraps up with end-to-end connectivity.

Router Problems

Routers enable networks to connect to other networks, which you know well by now. Problems with routers simply make those connections not work. (Recall that physical problems with routers or router interface modules were covered in Chapter 9 and Chapter 14.) Loss of power or a bad module can certainly wreck a tech's day, but the fixes are pretty simple: provide power or replace the module.

Router configuration issues can be a bit trickier. The ways to mess up a router are many. You can specify the wrong routing protocol, for example, or misconfigure the right routing protocol.

> As you'll recall from Chapter 18, "Managing Risk," if you want to prevent downtime due to a failure on your default gateway, you should consider implementing *Virtual Router Redundancy Protocol (VRRP)* or, if you are a Cisco shop, *Hot Standby Router Protocol (HSRP)*.

An access control list (ACL) might include addresses to block that shouldn't be blocked or allow access to network resources for nodes that shouldn't have it. A misconfiguration can lead to *missing IP routes* so that some destinations just aren't there for users.

Improperly configured routers aren't going to send packets to the proper destination. The symptoms are clear: every system that uses the misconfigured router as a default gateway is either not able to get packets out or not able to get packets in, or sometimes both. Web pages don't come up, FTP servers suddenly disappear, and e-mail clients can't access their servers. In these cases, you need to verify first that everything in your area of responsibility works. If that is true, then escalate the problem and find the person responsible for the router.

The key tool for determining a router problem beyond your LAN is tracert /traceroute.

Run `traceroute` to your default gateway. If that fails, you know you have a local issue and can potentially do something about it. If the traceroute comes back positive, run it to a site on the Internet. A solid connection should return something like Figure 21.13. A failed route will return a failed response.

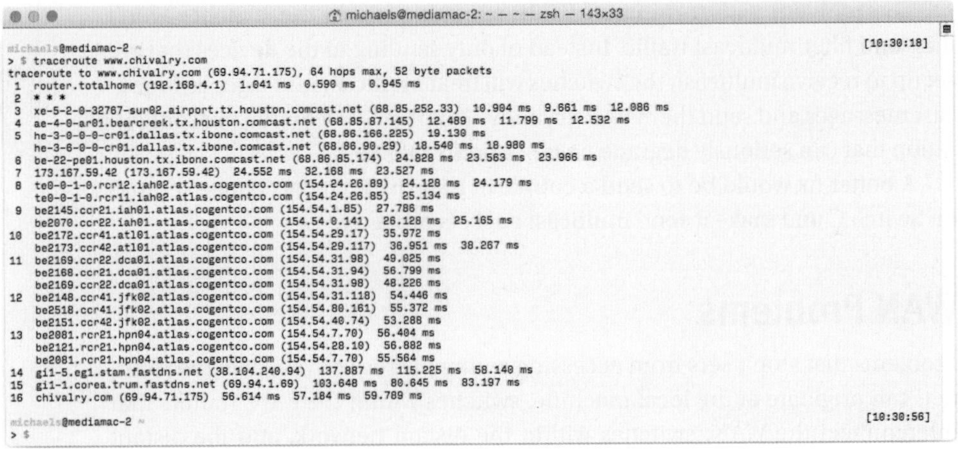

michaels@mediamac-2: ~ — ~ — zsh — 143×33
michaels@mediamac-2 ~
[10:30:18]
> $ traceroute www.chivalry.com
traceroute to www.chivalry.com (69.94.71.175), 64 hops max, 52 byte packets
1 router.totalhome (192.168.4.1) 1.041 ms 0.590 ms 0.945 ms
2 * * *
3 xe-5-2-0-32767-sur02.airport.tx.houston.comcast.net (68.85.252.33) 10.904 ms 9.661 ms 12.086 ms
4 ae-4-0-ar01.bearcreek.tx.houston.comcast.net (68.85.87.145) 12.489 ms 11.799 ms 12.532 ms
5 he-3-0-0-0-cr01.dallas.tx.ibone.comcast.net (68.86.166.225) 19.130 ms
he-3-6-0-0-cr01.dallas.tx.ibone.comcast.net (68.86.90.29) 18.540 ms 18.980 ms
6 be-22-pe01.houston.tx.ibone.comcast.net (68.86.85.174) 24.828 ms 23.563 ms 23.966 ms
7 173.167.59.42 (173.167.59.42) 24.552 ms 32.168 ms 23.527 ms
8 te0-0-1-0.rcr12.iah02.atlas.cogentco.com (154.24.26.89) 24.128 ms 24.179 ms
te0-0-1-0.rcr11.iah02.atlas.cogentco.com (154.24.26.85) 25.134 ms
9 be2145.ccr21.iah01.atlas.cogentco.com (154.54.1.85) 27.786 ms
be2070.ccr22.iah01.atlas.cogentco.com (154.54.0.141) 26.128 ms 25.165 ms
10 be2172.ccr41.atl01.atlas.cogentco.com (154.54.29.17) 35.972 ms
be2173.ccr42.atl01.atlas.cogentco.com (154.54.29.117) 36.951 ms 38.267 ms
11 be2169.ccr22.dca01.atlas.cogentco.com (154.54.31.98) 49.025 ms
be2168.ccr21.dca01.atlas.cogentco.com (154.54.31.94) 56.799 ms
be2169.ccr22.dca01.atlas.cogentco.com (154.54.31.98) 48.226 ms
12 be2148.ccr41.jfk02.atlas.cogentco.com (154.54.31.118) 54.446 ms
be2518.ccr41.jfk02.atlas.cogentco.com (154.54.80.161) 55.372 ms
be2151.ccr42.jfk02.atlas.cogentco.com (154.54.40.74) 53.288 ms
13 be2081.rcr21.hpn04.atlas.cogentco.com (154.54.7.70) 56.404 ms
be2121.rcr21.hpn04.atlas.cogentco.com (154.54.28.10) 56.882 ms
be2081.rcr21.hpn04.atlas.cogentco.com (154.54.7.70) 55.564 ms
14 gi1-5.eg1.stam.fastdns.net (38.104.240.94) 137.887 ms 115.225 ms 58.140 ms
15 gi1-1.corea.trum.fastdns.net (69.94.1.69) 103.648 ms 80.645 ms 83.197 ms
16 chivalry.com (69.94.71.175) 56.614 ms 57.184 ms 59.789 ms
michaels@mediamac-2 ~
[10:30:56]
> $

• **Figure 21.13** Good connection

ISPs and MTUs

I discussed the maximum transmission unit (MTU) in Chapter 8. Back in the dark ages (before Windows Vista), Microsoft users often found themselves with terrible connection problems because IP packets were too big to fit into certain network protocols. The largest Ethernet packet is 1500 bytes, so some earlier versions of Windows set their MTU size to a value less than 1500 to minimize the fragmentation of packets.

The problem cropped up when you tried to connect to a technology other than Ethernet, such as DSL. Some DSL carriers couldn't handle an MTU size greater than 1400. When your network's packets are so large that they must be fragmented to fit into your ISP's packets, we call it an *MTU mismatch*.

As a result, techs would tweak their MTU settings to improve throughput by matching up the MTU sizes between the ISP and their own network. This usually required a manual registry setting adjustment.

Around 2007, *Path MTU Discovery (PMTU)*, a method to determine the best MTU setting automatically, was created. PMTU works by adding a new feature called the "Don't Fragment (DF) flag" to the IP packet. A PMTU-aware operating system can automatically send a series of fixed-size ICMP packets (basically just pings) with the DF flag set to another device to see if it works. If it doesn't work, the system lowers the MTU size and tries again until the ping is successful. Imagine the hassle of incrementing the MTU size manually. That's the beauty of PMTU—you can automatically set your MTU size to the perfect amount.

Unfortunately, PMTU runs under ICMP; most routers have firewall features that, by default, are configured to block ICMP requests, making PMTU worthless. This is called a *PMTU* or *MTU black hole*. If you're having terrible connection problems and you've checked everything else, you need to consider this issue. In many cases, going into the router and turning off ICMP blocking in the firewall is all you need to do to fix the problem.

Appliance Problems

Many of the boxes that people refer to as "routers" contain many features, such as routing, Network Address Translation (NAT), switching, an intrusion detection system, a firewall, and more. These complex boxes, such as the *Cisco Adaptive Security Appliance (ASA)*, are called network appliances.

One common issue with network appliances is technician error. By default, for example, NAT rules take precedence over an appliance's routing table entries. If the tech fails to set the NAT rule order correctly, traffic that should be routed to go out one interface—like to the DMZ network—can go out an *incorrect interface*—like to the inside network.

Users on the outside would expect a response from something but instead get nothing, all because of a NAT *interface misconfiguration*.

The fix for such problems is to set up your network appliance correctly. Know the capabilities of the network appliance and the relationships among its services. Examine rules and settings carefully.

Company Security Policy

Implemented company security policies can make routine WAN connectivity actions completely fail. Here's a scenario.

Mike is the head of his company's IT department and he has a big problem: the amount of traffic running between the two company locations is on a dedicated connection and is blowing his bandwidth out of the water! It's so bad that data moving between the two offices will often drop to a crawl four to five times per day. Why are people using so much bandwidth?

As he inspects the problem, Mike realizes that the sales department is the culprit. Most of the data is composed of massive video files the sales department uses in their advertising campaign. He needs to make some security policy decisions. First, he needs to set up a throttling policy that defines in terms of megabits per second the maximum amount of bandwidth any single department can use per day. Second, he needs to add a *blocking policy*. If anyone goes over this limit, the company will block all traffic of that type for a certain amount of time (one hour). Third, he needs to update his company's *fair access policy* or *utilization limits* security policies to reflect these new limits. This lets employees, especially those pesky sales folks, know what the new rules are.

Beyond Local—Escalate

No single person is truly in control of an entire Internet-connected network. Large organizations split network support duties into very skill-specific areas: routers, cable infrastructure, user administration, and so on. Even in a tiny network with a single network support person, problems will arise that go beyond the tech's skill level or that involve equipment the organization doesn't own (usually it's their ISP's gear). In these situations, the tech needs to identify the problem and, instead of trying to fix it on his or her own, escalate the issue.

In network troubleshooting, problem escalation should occur when you face a problem that falls outside the scope of your skills and you need help. In large organizations, escalation problems have very clear procedures, such as who to call and what to document. In small organizations, escalation often is nothing more than a technician realizing that he or she needs help. The CompTIA Network+ exam objectives define some classic networking situations that CompTIA feels should be escalated. Here's how to recognize broadcast storms, switching loops, routing problems, routing loops, and proxy ARP.

Broadcast Storms

A broadcast storm is the result of one or more devices sending a nonstop flurry of broadcast frames on the network. The first sign of a broadcast storm is when every computer on the broadcast domain suddenly can't connect to the rest of the network. There are usually no clues other than network applications freezing or presenting "can't connect to..." types of error messages. Every activity light on every node is solidly on. Computers on other broadcast domains work perfectly well.

The trick is to isolate; that's where escalation comes in. You need to break down the network quickly by unplugging devices until you can find the one causing trouble. Getting a packet analyzer to work can be difficult, but at least try. If you can scoop up one packet, you'll know what node is causing the trouble. The second the bad node is disconnected, the network returns to normal. But if you have a lot of machines to deal with and a bunch of users who can't get on the network yelling at you, you'll need help. Call a supervisor to get support to solve the crisis as quickly as possible.

Switching Loops

Also known as a *bridging loop,* a switching loop is when you connect and configure multiple switches together in such a way that causes a circular path to appear. Switching loops are rare because all switches use the Spanning Tree Protocol (STP), but they do happen. The symptoms are identical to a broadcast storm: every computer on the broadcast domain can no longer access the network.

The good part about switching loops is that they rarely take place on a well-running network. Someone had to break something, and that means someone, somewhere is messing with the switch configuration. Escalate the problem, and get the team to help you find the person making changes to the switches.

Routing Loops

A routing loop occurs when interconnected routers loop traffic, causing the routers to respond slowly or not respond at all. The old RIP dynamic routing protocol could have issues with routing loops because of its slow convergence time, but most routing loops are caused by static routes. Your big clue is a huge amount of traffic—far more than your usual traffic—on the links between the routers. Routing loops never cause individual computers to stop responding (unless they happen to be on the same broadcast domain as the looping packets). As with any routing problem, be able to recognize the symptoms and escalate.

Proxy ARP

Proxy ARP is the process of making remotely connected computers truly act as though they are on the same LAN as local computers. Proxy ARP is done in a number of different ways, with a Virtual Private Network (VPN) as the classic example. If a laptop in an airport connects to a network through a VPN, that computer takes on the network ID of your local network. In order for all of this to work, the VPN concentrator needs to allow some very LAN-type traffic to go through it that would normally never get through a router. ARP is a great example. If your VPN client wants to talk to another computer on the LAN, it has to send an ARP request to get the IP address. Your VPN device is designed to act as a proxy for all that type of data.

Almost all proxy ARP problems take place on the VPN concentrator. With misconfigured proxy ARP settings, the VPN concentrator can send what looks like a denial of service (DoS) attack on the LAN. (A DoS attack is usually directed at a server exposed on the Internet, like a Web server. See Chapter 19 for more details on these and other malicious attacks.) If your clients start receiving a large number of packets from the VPN concentrator, assume you have a proxy ARP problem and escalate by getting the person in charge of the VPN to fix it.

End-to-End Connectivity

The **end-to-end principle** meant originally that applications and work should happen only at the endpoints in a network. In the early days of networking, this made a lot of sense. Connections weren't always fully reliable and thus were not good for real-time activity. So the work should get done by the computers at the ends of a network connection. The Internet was founded on the end-to-end principle.

With modern networks like the Internet, the end-to-end concept has had to evolve. Clearly, anything you do over the Internet goes through many different machines. So, perhaps end-to-end means that the intermediary devices simply don't change the essential data in packets that flow through them.

Add in today, though, the fact that plenty of intermediaries want to do a lot of things to your data as it flows through their devices. Thieves want to steal information. Merchants want to sell you things. Advertisers want to intrude on your monitor. Government agencies want to control what you can see or do, or simply want to monitor what you do for later, perhaps benign purposes. Other intermediaries help create trust bonds between your computer and a secure site so that e-commerce can function.

That dynamic between the fundamental principle of work only happening on the ends of the connection and all the intermediaries facilitating, pilfering, or punctuating is the current state of the Internet. It's the basic tension between ISP companies that want to build in tiered profit structures and the consumers and creators who want Net Neutrality.

In ancient times, when RIP ruled the routing roost, routers potentially could communicate a route back out the same interface it was learned through. So Router C might tell Router D that it was two hops away from Router A. Router D would pass along the information to Router E, saying it was three hops away from Router A. Because RIP was a pretty dumb protocol, Router E could respond back to Router D with the information that Router A was four hops away. Router D would then be pretty confused, thinking it was simultaneously three *and* five hops away from Router A!

That's where *split horizon* comes in: when a router learns a route through a certain interface, it will not communicate that route out the same interface. RIP has been gone a long time, but for some reason CompTIA keeps split horizon on the objectives. This is not a real-world issue; it's only a CompTIA Network+ exam issue.

From a technician's standpoint, there's not a lot you can do. So, why would CompTIA put end-to-end connectivity as a common network issue in the Network+ exam objectives?

As a common issue, *end-to-end connectivity* refers to connecting users with essential resources within a smaller network, such as a LAN or a private WAN. In such a scenario, the job of the tech is to ensure connections happen fully. Make sure the proper ports are open on an application server. Make sure the right people have the right permissions to access resources and that white list and black list ACLs are set up correctly.

Troubleshooting Is Fun!

The art of network troubleshooting can be a fun, frolicsome, and frequently frustrating feature of your network career. By applying a good troubleshooting methodology and constantly increasing your knowledge of networks, you too can develop into a great troubleshooting artist. Developing your artistry takes time, naturally, but stick with it. Begin the training. Use the Force. Learn new stuff, document problems and fixes, talk to other network techs about similar problems. Every bit of knowledge and experience you gain will make things that much easier for you when crunch time comes and a network disaster occurs—and as any experienced network tech can tell you, it will occur, even on the most robust network.

Internet of Things

People have been asking what-if questions about the future of technology for generations. What if cars could fly? What if we could teleport? In science-fiction and popular media, these what-if questions get transformed into radical visions of the future that capture the imagination. What if computers all over the globe could talk to each other? What if we could explore distant solar systems? What if our houses were automated and intelligent? Some of these big ideas turn into reality quicker than we could've ever imagined, but others always seem to be just out of reach.

For decades we've imagined a world where our homes could do a lot to take care of themselves and us—homes that could feed our pets, order groceries, turn on lights when we need them, and mow their own lawns. But even as we've continued to revise the wish list for these "smart" homes, cost and technological issues have kept them from becoming reality.

Not long after the cultural, economic, and day-to-day impact of the Internet on our lives became clear, another of these big ideas—everyday objects capable of communicating with each other—resurfaced with a new name: the Internet of Things (IoT).

So—what if everyday objects *could* communicate? What if my phone could talk to my watch, TV, car, stereo, and computer? Well, maybe that's not the best example. We're already living some of the earliest answers to this giant *what-if.* What if my phone could talk to my shoes and my glasses and my thermostat? These are all already happening. But the *idea* of the Internet of Things is really a lot bigger than these small examples, so let's take a longer look at the kinds of change the IoT promises to bring, the challenges in bringing the IoT about, and some of the technologies paving the way.

Utopia of Things

The preceding examples are still largely one person using a phone as a computing device to interact with these other "smart" objects one-on-one. The IoT is about a vast array of real-world smart objects collecting sensor data, communicating that data with other objects or computers, and making decisions based on it. To begin coming to grips with what excites technologists about the IoT, it helps to start with concrete examples of what we could do if there were sensors in everything.

Imagine a future like this: My phone collects data about my health and activity from a variety of devices and sensors in my home and clothing. I even use an app on my phone to establish the basics of the diet I'd like to follow and select recipes that both fit my diet and make my mouth water. My fridge communicates with my phone and converts these recipes into food orders from an online grocery service. The groceries arrive with sensors that enable the fridge to track each container.

When it's time to prepare my meals, the fridge asks my phone about my recent activity levels and other meals I've eaten away from home so it can adjust my portions—and the recipe—to keep me on-diet. My fridge knows when items will spoil, and can schedule recipes to make the best use of what expires soon. When I work too much, causing me to skip the gym for a week and burn fewer calories, these objects collaborate to order less food and rewrite recipes for smaller portions—and when I suddenly get back in the saddle they'll ramp up my caloric intake to help me get the most out of my workouts.

At the gym itself, my phone and the sensors in my clothes communicate over the network with computers, sensors, and transmitters in the equipment around me to learn how much work I'm doing, what impact it's having on my own biometrics, and how many calories I'm expending. My phone warns me when I push too hard, and encourages me when I'm not pushing hard enough. When I approach an empty machine or rack, it automatically adjusts its resistance to my workout routine—I won't even have to readjust it if I lose my spot when I run to the water fountain. Speaking of the water fountain—it and my water bottle can collaborate with my phone to make sure I'm drinking enough water.

But the future I described is just about me, and the IoT's potential is still much bigger than this. All of the sensors in my gym also track how much stress each piece of workout equipment has endured and help computers in the corporate office schedule preventative maintenance, order replacement parts before they are urgent, and track equipment failures.

Network sensors that track the location of each customer in the gym help management know if they have too many or too few of a certain machine. With permission to collect the biometric data I generate, they could even decide to replace the least effective machines with better alternatives. When the computers aggregating all of this data realize my gym is getting too busy and station wait-times are climbing, they automatically offer me a small monthly discount if I'll come an hour later or earlier.

Now think about the potential benefits we see here for just a few new smart objects in my home and gym, and start extrapolating them out to massive systems around the world. The IoT has the potential to revolutionize how we understand and manage systems like our homes, factories, the power grid, buildings, roads, shipping/distribution, cities, the atmosphere, geologic faults and plates, oceans, and even our networks themselves. But that's assuming it all works like we hope.

Challenges?

There's another thing we've been doing for as long as we've invented optimistic visions of future technology—and that's dreaming up tech-fueled nightmares. It might sound like a great idea at first to hook my toaster and coffee machine up to the Internet and let my alarm-clock app turn them both on shortly before I wake up—but it's good to be aware that we're imagining a best-case scenario (something few technologies ever live up to) and to think about challenges the IoT will have to overcome to get anywhere close to what we can imagine. These aren't little challenges, either—the IoT will be no exception when it comes to problems like bugs, hacking, and scale that plague our existing networks and computers. The IoT will also have to overcome some problems that aren't as familiar, too, like feedback loops, interoperability, waste/obsolescence, and power.

Bugs

A bug in a digital photo frame isn't a big deal in the grand scheme of things, but a bug in my networked toaster that causes it to run when I'm not around could be the end of my house, or even an entire apartment building. But this is trivial when we compare it to the problems that could be caused by bugs in sensors or control devices that help operate construction equipment, route air traffic, or manage the power grid.

Hacking

The even greater threat is that all of these networked devices, some of which are capable of real-world action, are vulnerable to exploitation over the network. The developers of the software operating my networked toaster might never even think someone might want to hack it—and even if they do, they probably can't dedicate the same resources to securing a toaster that might get dedicated to securing a large server. But depending on the vulnerabilities, one networked smart-object might be all an attacker needs to attack more secure members of the network.

Feedback Loops

When we start seriously designing objects that can make decisions and take actions that affect our world, we should prepare for the possibility that some smart objects will influence the decisions and actions of other smart objects by altering the inputs they use to make decisions. When a microphone recording ambient noise is too close to a speaker amplifying that noise, they get caught in a *feedback loop,* the speaker continually amplifying its own noise as the microphone captures it and feeds it back in. The tricky thing about predicting feedback loops with smart objects is that we'll never imagine all of the objects that could end up sharing the same environment.

Interoperability

Talking abstractly about a fridge that can communicate with other appliances, phones, computers, and Internet services makes it sound easy, but getting all of those technologies to play nice with each other is a lot of hard work—and making sure the fridge of today can talk with a replacement toaster eight years from now is even trickier. Having to buy a new fridge isn't a good solution.

Waste and Obsolescence

If the rate at which my phone becomes useless is any indication, many "smart" appliances won't age as gracefully as "dumb" counterparts that often have lifetimes measured in decades. Electronic waste is already a big problem—and that's without both vastly increasing the number of objects that have electronic components and decreasing their life spans.

Power

A lot of objects we might want to make smart aren't wired for power. How would electronics in something like a dumbbell have enough power to track useful information and report it over the network? It turns out there are a lot of potential answers—like batteries, renewable power, or power received wirelessly—but we don't really know which answers will win out yet.

Scale

The full vision for the IoT involves a drastic increase in the number of networked devices. Networks and networking equipment need to be able to handle a number of devices orders of magnitude larger than what they handle today. But scale isn't just about the number of connected devices. It's also about the ever-increasing amounts of traffic they could create when they're talking to each other of their own accord, and the task of storing, processing, and ultimately making sense of the mountains of data networked sensors promise to compile about our world.

Supporting Technologies

Much technological development has and will continue to be necessary to overcome these challenges and bring about a genuine Internet of Things. IPv6, for example, is essential for providing enough address space to handle a huge increase in the number of objects on the Internet. Ultra-low-power wireless radios will also be essential for communicating with vast networks of sensors in the natural environment or other places where traditional power infrastructure doesn't exist. When it comes to anticipating how our networks may change in the short term on the road to bringing about the IoT, it's useful to understand the IEEE 1905.1 standard. This standard is about supporting newer connectivity models, easier configuration, and making our networks flexible enough to incorporate dozens or scores of smart objects and appliances.

IEEE 1905.1

IEEE 1905.1 creates a hybrid networking standard with the goal of flexibly integrating a few types of wired and wireless networking technologies, including Wi-Fi, Ethernet, MoCA, and the powerline standard defined by IEEE 1901, allowing a network to span all four technologies. You already know all about Wi-Fi and Ethernet, so let's take a look at MoCA, and IEEE 1901—known commercially as HomePlug—before discussing how these four networking technologies will come together under the nVoy brand name.

> CompTIA may refer to the IEEE 1905.1 standard, which was ratified in 2013, as IEEE 1905.1-2013.

MoCA *Multimedia over Coax (MoCA)* provides Ethernet access through your existing coaxial cabling (even when it's being used for video) and is the technology used by Verizon's FiOS product to provide video, phone, and Internet service. If a home or office has coaxial cable and outlets in the right places, MoCA can make it easy to build a small wired network without any new cable.

HomePlug (IEEE 1901)   If you're faced with the daunting challenge of networking billions or trillions of new, real-world objects, it turns out things that are already plugged into electrical outlets are low-hanging fruit. They already have a steady power supply and can afford the extra juice for networking. In fact, they don't even need Wi-Fi radios. The IEEE 1901 standard, also known as *HomePlug* HD-PLC, provides high-speed home networking through a building's existing power infrastructure. We call this **Ethernet over power (EoP)**, but powerline technology can also provide Internet access itself, or *broadband over power lines (BPL)*.

Why can't we just use Wi-Fi for everything? Wi-Fi is great, but it has its share of problems—like low- or no-signal areas, disconnects, and exploits that trick naive devices into connecting by imitating their home network. And when the Wi-Fi network starts suffering from congestion, stationary devices are the most obvious candidates for wired connections. EoP is an even bigger boon when a wired connection is necessary but a building's layout or construction makes running Ethernet cable impractical.

nVoy   Much as the Wi-Fi trademark is branding that covers a variety of IEEE 802.11 standards, the branding for IEEE 1905.1 uses the name **nVoy**. nVoy-certified networking equipment will create a single network for devices spread across Ethernet, Wi-Fi, MoCA, and HomePlug connections. This by itself might not be earthshaking, but nVoy equipment can make intelligent decisions when it comes to communicating with devices that use more than one connection type.

For example, an nVoy router could make use of multiple connections to stream video to your TV, or seamlessly switch the data flowing to your wireless speakers from Wi-Fi to power line if the Wi-Fi connection stops working. These intelligent decisions can also include load balancing and rebalancing in response to network performance, or preferring lower-power interfaces when possible.

While features like these might be most interesting to those of us comfortable with building and configuring networks, the IEEE 1905.1 standard is also concerned with making nVoy equipment easy to configure, secure, and use. Acknowledging that networks can be difficult for the average consumer to set up and troubleshoot, nVoy equipment enables consumers to add, configure, and secure devices simply by pressing a button on the new device and a button on a device already in the network. In case there are issues, it also lets the service provider run advanced remote diagnostics on a customer's network—saving both parties the inconvenience of a service call.

We might not be that excited about these latter features, but making interoperable home networks so dead simple anyone can set one up is a big step on the path to making sure every device that needs to be online has network access. We can't expect Joe Average to buy a networked toaster if he suspects he'll need to be a certified network technician to set it up. In a way, the IEEE 1905.1 standard is a sign that networks are becoming as essential to modern life in this century as the appliances that spread to nearly every home in the last.

Looking Ahead

As an idea, the Internet of Things is already shaping our technologies and networks, but it's going to be a long transition. The IoT hasn't really changed the physical world and our knowledge of it all that much yet, even though that is one of its biggest promises. There won't be a clear finish line to cross or a switch to flip to announce its arrival. Much of the work of bringing it about—at least on the networking side of things—will be incremental change.

Day by day, more and more non-human users will crop up on our networks, chattering away about the weather or the power grid; we'll have to accommodate them. It's also almost inevitable that there will be headaches and lessons learned when these new members of our networks incite a crisis of one kind or another. Someday, probably while we're all busy upgrading network equipment, the combined traffic flowing across our networks between smart devices will quietly overtake the traffic generated by human users.

Chapter Summary

After reading this chapter and completing the exercises, you should understand the following about network troubleshooting.

Describe appropriate troubleshooting tools and their functions

- Before starting work on any problem, always ask yourself if what you are about to do can potentially harm your data.

- The vast majority of cabling problems take place when the network is first installed or when changes, if any, take place. Cables rarely go bad after they have been made, installed, and tested.

- Broken cables don't create intermittent problems— they make permanent disconnects. A TDR can tell you where a break is on a cable.

- Certifiers test a cable to ensure that it can handle its rated amount of capacity. If a cable isn't broken, yet isn't moving data the way it should, test it with a certifier. Use a certifier for slowdowns, not disconnects. With optical fiber, use an optical power meter (a light meter) to measure the amount of light loss.

- Heat and power problems manifest as intermittent network problems. Use a voltage event recorder to measure power, and use a temperature monitor to ensure proper temperature.

- A good protocol analyzer will give you the Application, Session, Transport, Network, and Data Link layer information on every frame going through your network. Protocol analyzers can be hardware or software.

- A multimeter tests voltage and can tell you how much voltage is on a line.

- Tone generators and tone probes work as a pair to help you locate a particular cable.

- A butt set is used to tap into a 66-block or 110-block to see if a particular line is working.

- Line testers enable you to check the integrity of telephone wiring.

- A punchdown tool places UTP wires into 66-blocks and 110-blocks. In a diagnostic environment, you'll find it useful to repunch a connection to make sure all the contacts are properly set.

- Software tools can be organized in two categories: those that come built into your operating system and those that are provided by a third party.

- The `traceroute` command (called `tracert` in Windows) is used to trace all the routers between two points. Use it to diagnose problems reaching a remote system.

- The `ipconfig` (Windows), `ifconfig` (UNIX), and `ip addr` (Linux) commands give you information about a computer's IP settings. Using `ipconfig` with the `/all` switch gives additional detailed information, including DNS server addresses and MAC addresses.

- The `ping` command uses ICMP packets to show you if you can simply reach a remote computer. Because some devices block the ICMP packets, `arping` can be used instead. However, `arping` is available only on UNIX/Linux systems—and it can't cross routers.

- The `nslookup` command is used to diagnose DNS problems and is the only utility on Windows by default.

- The `dig` tool is the preferred utility on UNIX/Linux systems, but Microsoft does not provide `dig` with Windows.

- The `hostname` command simply returns the host name of the local computer.

- The `mtr` command, which is not available on Windows, is similar to `traceroute` except that it keeps running until shut down.

- The `route` command enables you to display and edit the local system's routing table.

- The `nbtstat` command can show all the local NetBIOS names (Windows only) and is a command-line equivalent to My Network Places. You must run `nbtstat` with a switch.

- Running `netstat` or `ss` displays information on the current state of all the running IP processes on your computer. Use `netstat` or `ss` when you want to know about your current sessions.

- A packet sniffer intercepts and logs network packets. Wireshark and `tcpdump` are popular packet sniffers.

- A port scanner probes ports on another system, logging the state of scanned ports. It can be used to find an unintentionally open port so you can secure it. Hackers like to use port scanners to look for openings into machines. Once they have found these openings, they can attempt to exploit any vulnerabilities they have found.

■ Throughput testers and speed-test sites enable you to gauge the overall upload and download speeds of a connection.

■ Looking glass sites enable you to run various diagnostic tools from outside your network.

Analyze and discuss the troubleshooting process

■ There is no reference guide to troubleshooting every possible network problem because such a guide would be obsolete the moment it was created.

■ A basic troubleshooting model may include the following steps:

1. Identify the problem.
2. Establish a theory of probable cause.
3. Test the theory to determine cause.
4. Establish a plan of action to resolve the problem and identify potential effects.
5. Implement the solution or escalate as necessary.
6. Verify full system functionality and, if applicable, implement preventative measures.
7. Document findings, actions, and outcomes.

■ First, identify the problem. You need to gather information, duplicate the problem (if possible), question users, identify symptoms, determine if anything has changed on the network, and approach multiple problems individually. Following these steps will help you get to the root of the problem.

■ When establishing the symptoms, you may need to ask the user reporting the trouble both closed- and open-ended questions.

■ Isolating the cause of the problem includes identifying the scope of the problem, such as determining if it affects a single system or the entire network.

■ When trying to determine what recent changes may have caused the problem, it is important to recognize things that are not causes. Re-creating the problem yourself removes user error as a possible cause, and experiencing the problem on another computer removes the possibility of changed settings on the first computer as the cause.

■ Once you have determined possible causes, you should establish a theory of probable cause. The ability to identify the most probable cause improves with experience. Consider multiple approaches when tackling problems. Try a top-to-bottom or bottom-to-top OSI model approach.

■ With the third step, you need to test the theory to determine the cause, but do so without changing anything or risking any repercussions.

■ Next, establish a plan of action and identify potential effects. With complex problems, write down the steps you need to take. Review before implementing.

■ When implementing a solution, be sure to try only one thing at a time. If you perform multiple activities or make multiple changes, you won't know which action actually solved the problem—and you won't know which action made things worse.

■ Once a solution has been implemented, test it by trying to re-create the problem. If you can re-create the error, you haven't fixed the problem.

■ If you have fixed a problem, you need to recognize what potential problems you may have caused. For example, replacing a NIC in a server may get the server back online, but the new NIC has a different MAC address, which may introduce a whole new set of problems.

■ Problems, symptoms, and solutions should be documented so the solutions can be used later in a knowledge base. Additionally, the documentation will help you track problem trends.

■ Verify end-to-end connectivity on a local network. Users need connections to appropriate resources. Ports need to be open. ACLs need to be set up properly.

Resolve common network issues

■ Network problems fall into several basic categories, and most of these problems you or a network tech in the proper place can fix. You should know how to fix problems at the workstation, work area, and server. The same is true of connecting to resources on the LAN. Problems connecting to a WAN can often be resolved at the local level, but sometimes need to get escalated.

■ Hands-on problems refer to things that you can fix at the workstation, work area, or server. These include physical problems, such as power and hardware failures, and configuration problems, such as improper IP addressing or default gateway information, mixing wired and wireless networks, and more.

- Incorrect configuration of any number of options in devices can stop a device from accessing resources over a LAN. These run the gamut from server misconfigurations—DHCP or DNS settings—to VLAN assignment errors.

- On fancier networks, incorrectly setting up network devices to use link aggregation can cause that aggregation to fail. NIC teaming can cause all sorts of problems if combined with other misconfigurations, such as turning off IGMP snooping on Cisco switches.

- WAN issues include router configuration errors, and errors in complex network appliance settings causing traffic to flow in unintended ways. Company security policies can readily derail or stop common networking activity.

- Various networking problems that fall outside the scope of a tech's skill set should be escalated. These include broadcast storms, switching loops, route problems, routing loops, and proxy ARP.

Describe the Internet of Things

- The Internet of Things describes a category of networked objects capable of collecting, communicating, and making decisions with data, all without a person directly controlling them.

- Bringing all of these objects onto our networks will require adding enough capacity to support them, solving problems they may cause on our networks, and mitigating security risks they may pose.

- The always-on, ever-present connectivity needed to make the Internet of Things work will be enabled new networking technologies, like IEEE 1905.1. Also known as nVoy, the IEEE 1905.1 standard integrates Ethernet, Wi-Fi, Ethernet over power lines, and MoCA.

■ Key Terms

arp *(604)*

arping *(605)*

broadcast storm *(624)*

butt set *(601)*

cable stripper *(601)*

cable tester *(600)*

certifier *(600)*

dig *(605)*

end-to-end principle *(625)*

Ethernet over power (EoP) *(630)*

hardware tool *(599)*

HDMI Ethernet Channel (HEC) *(630)*

hostname *(606)*

IEEE 1905.1 *(629)*

ifconfig *(603)*

Internet of Things (IoT) *(626)*

ip *(603)*

ipconfig *(603)*

light meter *(600)*

line tester *(601)*

link aggregation *(620)*

looking glass site *(609)*

multimeter *(601)*

My Traceroute (mtr) *(606)*

nbtstat *(607)*

netstat *(607)*

network appliance *(623)*

NIC teaming *(620)*

nslookup *(605)*

nVoy *(630)*

optical power meter *(600)*

packet sniffer *(608)*

pathping *(605)*

ping *(604)*

ping –6 *(604)*

ping6 *(604)*

port scanner *(608)*

protocol analyzer *(601)*

proxy ARP *(625)*

punchdown tool *(602)*

route *(606)*

routing loop *(624)*

snip *(601)*

speed-test site *(609)*

switching loop *(624)*

temperature monitor *(601)*

tone generator *(601)*
tone probe *(601)*
traceroute *(602)*
traceroute6 *(603)*

tracert *(602)*
tracert –6 *(603)*
voltage event recorder *(601)*
Wireshark *(608)*

Key Term Quiz

Use the Key Terms list to complete the sentences that follow. Not all the terms will be used.

1. Use _____ to locate a problem between two routers.

2. Use a(n) _____ to put wires into 66- and 110-blocks.

3. A(n) _____ tests cables to ensure they can handle their rated capacity.

4. If ICMP packets are being blocked, you can use _____ to test connectivity to another system.

5. _____ is a popular packet sniffer/protocol analyzer/packet analyzer.

6. To view IP settings on a UNIX computer, use the _____ command.

7. Use a(n) _____ to test AC/DC voltage, resistance, and continuity.

8. Numerous protocols enable two or more connections to work together simultaneously, a process called NIC teaming or _____.

9. _____ uses ICMP packets to test connectivity between two systems.

10. IEEE 1905.1 devices use the _____ marketing name.

Multiple-Choice Quiz

1. Jordan says she can't access files on the server any more. No other user has reported this problem, and she can ping the server from another computer successfully. Typing `ping 127.0.0.1` from Jordan's computer is also successful. Using ping to try to reach the server or any other computer from Jordan's computer fails. A check of IP settings on Jordan's computer shows that her static IP address and other information is good. What is the most likely cause of the problem?

   A. The router that Jordan's computer connects to is down.

   B. Jordan's network card is bad.

   C. The DHCP server is down.

   D. Jordan's Ethernet cable has become unplugged from her computer.

2. You are trying to locate which patch cable in the main switch traces back to a particular computer. Which tool should you use?

   A. Tone probe

   B. Cable tester

   C. Punchdown tool

   D. Butt set

3. The Windows tracert tool fails sometimes because many routers block _____ packets.

   A. ping

   B. TCP

   C. UDP

   D. ICMP

4. What is the first step in the troubleshooting model?

   A. Implementing the solution

   B. Testing the solution

   C. Identifying the problem

   D. Establishing the symptoms

5. Kay's computer has lost all network access. Which tool should you use to test for a break on the cable?

   A. Certifier

   B. TDR

   C. Voltage event recorder

   D. Crimper

6. Which command shows you detailed IP information, including DNS server addresses and MAC addresses?

   A. `ipconfig`

   B. `ipconfig -a`

   C. `ipconfig /all`

   D. `ipconfig /dns`

7. Which tool uses ICMP packets to test connectivity between two systems?

   A. `arp`

   B. `arping`

   C. `netstat`

   D. `ping`

8. Which tools can you (and hackers) use to discover vulnerabilities on your network? (Select three.)

   A. Port scanner

   B. Nmap

   C. Angry IP Scanner

   D. `hostname`

9. Asking a user "Can you start your e-mail program?" is what type of question?

   A. Closed-ended

   B. Open-ended

   C. Leading

   D. Unprofessional

10. If you want to see which other computers on your network are currently connected to you, what command should you use?

    A. `ping`

    B. `nbtstat`

    C. `netstat`

    D. `tracert`

11. One of your users calls you with a complaint that she can't reach the site www.yahoo.com. You try and access the site and discover you can't connect either, but you can ping the site with its IP address. What is the most probable culprit?

    A. The workgroup switch is down.

    B. Yahoo! is down.

    C. The gateway is down.

    D. The DNS server is down.

12. A brand new employee is complaining on his second day of work that he can't log into his computer. What is the most probable cause?

    A. The server is down.

    B. His network card is bad.

    C. He forgot or is mistyping his password.

    D. A port on the switch is bad.

13. When should you use a cable tester to troubleshoot a network cable?

    A. When you have a host experiencing a very slow connection

    B. When you have an intermittent connection problem

    C. When you have a dead connection and you suspect a broken cable

    D. Never

14. Which tools should you use to diagnose problems with DNS?

    A. Nmap or Wireshark

    B. `nslookup` or `dig`

    C. `ping` or `pathping`

    D. `tracert` or `pathping`

15. Which Windows command displays the local system's routing table?

    A. `route print`

    B. `print route`

    C. `tracert /print`

    D. `tracert /p`

■ Essay Quiz

1. You and a co-worker are working late trying to fix a problem on the server. Your friend suggests applying three hot fixes and swapping out the network card for another. He wants to do all these things at the same time, however, to finish the job quicker. Explain to him why that's not a good idea.

2. Because of your outstanding troubleshooting skills, you have been selected by your supervisor to train a new intern. Explain to her the steps of a basic troubleshooting model.

3. You've read in this chapter: "First, do no harm." Explain in your own words what this phrase means to you. Then, think of a situation in which you were either the technician or the "victim" in a troubleshooting case where harm was done. What happened?

Lab Projects

● Lab Project 21.1

You've learned about many free software tools in this chapter—some available only for Windows, some only for UNIX/Linux, and some available for all. Make a chart with five columns: tool name, description, useful switches/options, supported operating system(s), built-in or third party. Fill in the chart with the tools from this chapter and use it as a study guide.

● Lab Project 21.2

Using the chart you created in the previous lab activity, run each of the tools to gain some familiarity with the interface, switches, and output. Do you use any of the tools in your chart on a regular (or semi-regular) basis? Which tools are the easiest for you to understand? Which tools do you not completely understand? If any tools are still unclear, ask your instructor or search the Internet for clarification on the tool's usage. Once you've run each of the tools, compare your findings with classmates or verify with your instructor to make sure your research resulted in correct information!

Objective Map: CompTIA Network+

Mike Meyers' CompTIA Network+ Guide to Managing and Troubleshooting Networks

Topic	Chapter(s)	Page(s)
Hybrid routing protocols	8	202
BGP	8	201–202, 205
Link state routing protocols	8	202–205
OSPF	8	202–204, 205–206
IS-IS	8	205
Interior vs exterior gateway routing protocols	8	201, 205
Autonomous system numbers	8	201
Route redistribution	8	206
High availability	18	526–527
VRRP	18	527
Virtual IP	18	526–527
HSRP	18	527
Route aggregation	8	202
Routing metrics	8	196–197
Hop counts	8	197, 200
MTU, bandwidth	8	197, 203
Costs	8	188–189, 197, 199–200, 203
Latency	8	197
Administrative distance	8	197
SPB	8	197
1.10 Identify the basics elements of unified communication technologies		
VoIP	17	507–510
Video	17	508–510
Real-time services	17	508
Presence	17	508
Multicast vs unicast	17	508–509
QoS	17	511
DSCP	17	511
COS	17	511
Devices	17	502, 504, 509–511
UC servers	17	509
UC devices	17	509
UC gateways	17	510
1.11 Compare and contrast technologies that support cloud and virtualization		
Virtualization	16	484–493
Virtual switches	16	485
Virtual routers	16	493
Virtual firewall	16	486
Virtual vs physical NICs	16	485
Software defined networking	16	486

Topic	Chapter(s)	Page(s)
2.2 Given a scenario, analyze metrics and reports from monitoring and tracking performance tools		
Baseline	20	589–590
Bottleneck	20	593
Log management	20	590
Graphing	20	591
Utilization	15, 20	587–588
Bandwidth	20	587, 592
Storage	20	592
Network device CPU	20	589, 592
Network device memory	20	592
Wireless channel utilization	15, 20	592
Link status	20	592
Interface monitoring	20	587
Errors	20	588
Utilization	20	587
Discards	20	588
Packet drops	20	588
Interface resets	20	588
Speed and duplex	20	587
2.3 Given a scenario, use appropriate resources to support configuration management		
Archives/backups	18	531
Baselines	20	593
On-boarding and off-boarding of mobile devices	15	445
NAC	11	301
Documentation	17	501, 506
Network diagrams (logical/physical)	17	501
Asset management	17	501
IP address utilization	17	501, 504, 506
Vendor documentation	17	501
Internal operating procedures/policies/standards	17	501
2.4 Explain the importance of implementing network segmentation		
SCADA systems/Industrial control systems	17	489–499, 514–515
Legacy systems	17	503
Separate private/public networks	17	500, 506
Honeypot/honeynet	19	573–574
Testing lab	17	506
Load balancing	17	515
Performance optimization	17	506, 515
Security	17	499, 506, 515
Compliance	17	515

Topic	Chapter(s)	Page(s)
Wireless bridge	15	459
Site surveys	15	446–448
Heat maps	15	48
Frequencies	15	430, 434
2.4 Ghz	15	436–438
5.0 Ghz	15	434–436
Channels	15	434–435, 437, 447–448, 456, 459
Goodput	15	436, 438
Connection types	15	437–438
802.11a-ht	15	437–438
802.11g-ht	15	437–438
Antenna placement	15	451, 453
Antenna types	15	451
Omnidirectional	15	451
Unidirectional	15	451–452
MIMO/MUMIMO	15	437–438
Signal strength	15	431
Coverage	15	431, 446, 448, 451–452
Differences between device antennas	15	451–452
SSID broadcast	16	433–434
Topologies	3, 15	43–47, 432
Ad hoc	15	432
Mesh	3, 15	46, 432
Infrastructure	15	432
Mobile devices	15	445, 449
Cell phones	15	445
Laptops	15	446, 449
Tablets	15	445, 449
Gaming devices	15	445
Media devices	15	445

3.0 Network security

3.1 Compare and contrast risk related concepts

Topic	Chapter(s)	Page(s)
Disaster recovery	18	530–531
Business continuity	18	530–531
Battery backups/UPS	18	536
First responders	18	531, 533–534
Data breach	18	521, 530
End user awareness and training	18	525

Topic	Chapter(s)	Page(s)
4.5 Given a scenario, troubleshoot and resolve common fiber cable issues		
Attenuation/Db loss	6	128
SFP/GBIC–cable mismatch	6	127
Bad SFP/GBIC–cable or transceiver	6	126
Wavelength mismatch	6	127
Fiber type mismatch	6	127
Dirty connectors	6	126
Connector mismatch	6	126
Bend radius limitations	6	127
Distance limitations	6	135
4.6 Given a scenario, troubleshoot and resolve common network issues		
Incorrect IP configuration/default gateway	21	618
Broadcast storms/switching loop	21	624
Duplicate IP	21	619
Speed and duplex mismatch	21	619
End-to-end connectivity	21	625
Incorrect VLAN assignment	12, 21	342, 620
Hardware failure	21	617
Misconfigured DHCP	21	619
Misconfigured DNS	21	619
Incorrect interface/interface misconfiguration	21	623
Cable placement	21	620
Interface errors	21	618
Simultaneous wired/wireless connections	21	619
Discovering neighboring devices/nodes	21	619
Power failure/power anomalies	21	617
MTU/MTU black hole	21	623
Missing IP routes	21	622
NIC teaming misconfiguration	21	621
Active-active vs active-passive	21	620–621
Multicast vs broadcast	21	621
4.7 Given a scenario, troubleshoot and resolve common security issues		
Misconfigured firewall	19	574
Misconfigured ACLs/applications	19	574
Malware	19	552
Denial of service	19	548
Open/closed ports	19	551
ICMP-related issues	9, 21	225, 623
Ping of death	9	225
Unreachable default gateway	9, 21	225

Create Your Study Plan

Congratulations on completing the Net+ Assessment test on the companion CD-ROM! You should now take the time to analyze your results with these two objectives in mind:

- Identifying the resources you should use to prepare for the CompTIA Network+ exam
- Identifying the specific topics you should focus on in your preparation

Review Your Overall Score

Use the following table to help you gauge your overall readiness for the CompTIA Network+ exam based on the number of questions you answered correctly on the Net+ Assessment test.

Number of Answers Correct	Recommended Course of Study
0–26	Spend a significant amount of time reviewing the corresponding chapters from this book to make sure you understand the topics completely.
27–39	Review your scores in the specific Exam Domains shown in the next table to identify the particular areas that require your focused attention, and then use this book to review that material.
40–50	Use this book to refresh your knowledge and prepare yourself mentally for the actual exam.

Review Your Score by CompTIA Network+ Exam Domain

Domain	Weight	Number of Questions in Assessment Test	High Priority for Additional Study	Medium Priority for Additional Study	Low Priority for Additional Study
1.0 Network architecture	22 percent	11	0–6 correct	7–9 correct	10–11 correct
2.0 Network operations	20 percent	10	0–5 correct	6–8 correct	9–10 correct
3.0 Network security	18 percent	9	0–5 correct	6–7 correct	8–9 correct
4.0 Troubleshooting	24 percent	12	0–6 correct	7–9 correct	10–12 correct
5.0 Industry standards, practices, and network theory	16 percent	8	0–4 correct	5–6 correct	7–8 correct

About the CD-ROM

appendix C

The CD-ROM included with this book comes with

- A video from author Mike Meyers introducing the CompTIA Network+ certification exam
- A link to the Total Tester practice exam software, which includes over 100 practice exam questions
- A link to over 20 sample simulations from Total Seminars' Total Sims
- A link to over an hour's worth of episodes from Mike Meyers' CompTIA Network+ Certification Video Training series
- Links to a collection of Mike's favorite tools and utilities for network troubleshooting
- An electronic copy of the book in PDF format

Playing the Mike Meyers Introduction Video

If your computer's optical drive is configured to auto-run, the menu will automatically start upon inserting the CD-ROM. If the auto-run feature does not launch the CD-ROM, browse to the disc and double-click the **Launch.exe** icon.

From the opening screen you can launch the video message from Mike by clicking the **Mike Meyers Introduction Video** button. This launches the video file using your system's default video player.

System Requirements

The software requires Windows XP or higher, in addition to a current or prior major release of Chrome, Firefox, or Internet Explorer. To run, the screen resolution must be set to 1024 × 768 or higher. The PDF files require Adobe Acrobat, Adobe Reader, or Adobe Digital Editions to view.

Total Tester Exam Software

Total Tester provides you with a simulation of the CompTIA Network+ exam. The exam can be taken in either Practice mode or Exam mode. Practice mode provides an assistance window with hints, references to the book, explanations of the correct and incorrect answers, and the option to check your answers as you take the test. Exam mode provides a simulation of the actual exam. Both Practice mode and Exam mode provide an overall grade and a grade broken down by certification objectives.

The link on the CD takes you to a Web download page. Click the download and follow the prompts to install the software. To take a test, launch the program and select **Network+ Demo** from the Installed Question Packs list. You can then select Practice Mode, Exam Mode, or Custom Mode. (In Custom mode, you can select the number of questions and the duration of the exam.) After making your selection, click **Start Exam** to begin.

Assessment Test

In addition to the sample exam questions, the Total Tester also includes a Network+ Assessment test to help you assess your understanding of the topics before reading the book. To launch the Assessment test, click **Net+ Assessment** from the Installed Question Packs list. The Network+ Assessment test is 50 questions and runs in Exam mode. When you complete the test, you can review the questions with answers and detailed explanation by clicking **See Detailed Results**. Once you've completed the Assessment test, refer to Appendix B, "Create Your Study Plan," to get a recommended study plan based on your results.

■ TotalSims for Network+

 The CD contains a link that takes you to Total Seminars Training Hub. Select **TotalSims for Network+ N10-006**. The simulations are organized by chapter, and there are over 20 free simulations available for reviewing topics referenced in the book, with an option to purchase access to the full TotalSims for Network+ N10-006 with over 120 simulations.

■ Mike's Video Training

The CD comes with links to training videos, starring Mike Meyers, for the first four chapters of the book. On the main page of the CD, click the **Software and Videos** link and then select **Mike Meyers Video Training Online**. Along with access to the videos from the first four chapters of the book, you'll find an option to purchase Mike's complete video training series.

■ Mike's Cool Tools

Mike loves freeware/open source networking tools! Most of the utilities mentioned in the text can be found via the CD. On the main page of the CD, click the **Software and Videos** link and then select **Mike's Cool Tools Online**. This will take you to the Total Seminars Web site, where you can download Mike's favorite tools.

■ PDF Copy of the Book

The entire contents of the book are provided as a PDF file on the CD-ROM. This file is viewable on your computer and many portable devices. Adobe Acrobat, Adobe Reader, or Adobe Digital Editions is required to view the file on your computer. The CD-ROM includes a link to Adobe's Web site, where you can download and install Adobe Reader.

To view the PDF copy of the book on a portable device, copy the PDF file to your computer from the CD-ROM, and then copy the file to your portable device using a USB or other connection. Adobe offers a mobile version of Adobe Reader, the Adobe Reader mobile app, which currently supports iOS and Android. For customers using Adobe Digital Editions and an iPad, you may have to download and install a separate reader program on your device. The Adobe Web site has a list of recommended applications, and McGraw-Hill Education recommends the Bluefire Reader.

 For more information on Adobe Reader and to check for the most recent version of the software, visit Adobe's Web site at www.adobe.com and search for the free Adobe Reader or look for Adobe Reader on the product page. Adobe Digital Editions can also be downloaded from the Adobe Web site.

■ Technical Support

Technical support information is provided in the following sections by feature.

Total Seminars Technical Support

For questions regarding the Total Tester software, the operation of the CD-ROM, the Mike Meyers videos, or Mike's Cool Tools, visit www.totalsem.com or e-mail support@totalsem.com.

McGraw-Hill Education Content Support

For questions regarding the PDF copy of the book, e-mail techsolutions@ mhedu.com or visit http://mhp.softwareassist.com.

For questions regarding book content, e-mail customer.service@mheducation.com. For customers outside the United States, e-mail international_cs@ mheducation.com.

3G Third generation wireless data standard for cell phones and other mobile devices. 3G matured over time until Evolved High-Speed Packet Access (HSPA+) became the final wireless 3G data standard. It transferred at theoretical maximum speeds up to 168 megabits per second (Mbps), although real-world implementations rarely passed 10 Mbps.

4G Most popularly implemented as Long Term Evolution (LTE), a wireless data standard with theoretical download speeds of 300 Mbps and upload speeds of 75 Mbps.

6in4 One of the most popular of all the IPv6 tunneling standards, and one of only two IPv6 tunneling protocols that can go through a NAT.

6to4 The dominant IPv6 tunneling protocol because it is the only IPv6 tunnel that doesn't require a tunnel broker. It is generally used to directly connect two routers because it normally requires a public IPv4 address.

10Base2 The last true bus-standard network where nodes connected to a common, shared length of coaxial cable.

10BaseFL Fiber-optic implementation of Ethernet that runs at 10 Mbps using baseband signaling. Maximum segment length is 2 km.

10BaseT An Ethernet LAN designed to run on UTP cabling. Runs at 10 Mbps and uses baseband signaling. Maximum length for the cabling between the NIC and the hub (or the switch, the repeater, and so forth) is 100 m.

10GBaseER/10GBaseEW A 10 GbE standard using 1550-nm single-mode fiber. Maximum cable length up to 40 km.

10GBaseLR/10GBaseLW A 10 GbE standard using 1310-nm single-mode fiber. Maximum cable length up to 10 km.

10GBaseSR/10GBaseSW A 10 GbE standard using 850-nm multimode fiber. Maximum cable length up to 300 m.

10GBaseT A 10 GbE standard designed to run on CAT 6a UTP cabling. Maximum cable length of 100 m.

10 Gigabit Ethernet (10 GbE) A very fast Ethernet designation, with a number of fiber-optic and copper standards.

100BaseFX An Ethernet LAN designed to run on fiber-optic cabling. Runs at 100 Mbps and uses baseband signaling. Maximum cable length is 400 m for half-duplex and 2 km for full-duplex.

100BaseT An Ethernet LAN designed to run on UTP cabling. Runs at 100 Mbps, uses baseband signaling, and uses two pairs of wires on CAT 5 or better cabling.

100BaseT4 An Ethernet LAN designed to run on UTP cabling. Runs at 100 Mbps and uses four-pair CAT 3 or better cabling. Made obsolete by 100BaseT.

100BaseTX The technically accurate but little-used name for 100BaseT.

110 Block Also known as a *110-punchdown block*, a connection gridwork used to link UTP and STP cables behind an RJ-45 patch panel.

110-Punchdown Block The most common connection used on the back of an RJ-45 jack and patch panels.

110-Punchdown Tool *See* Punchdown Tool.

802 Committee The IEEE committee responsible for all Ethernet standards.

802.1X A port-authentication network access control mechanism for networks.

802.3 (Ethernet) *See* Ethernet.

802.3ab The IEEE standard for 1000BaseT.

802.3z The umbrella IEEE standard for all versions of Gigabit Ethernet other than 1000BaseT.

802.11 *See* IEEE 802.11.

802.11a A wireless standard that operates in the frequency range of 5 GHz and offers throughput of up to 54 Mbps.

802.11a-ht Along with the corresponding 802.11g-ht standard, technical terms for mixed mode 802.11a/802.11g operation. In mixed mode, both technologies are simultaneously supported.

802.11b The first popular wireless standard, operates in the frequency range of 2.4 GHz and offers throughput of up to 11 Mbps.

802.11g Currently (2015) the wireless standard with the widest use, operates on the 2.4-GHz band with a maximum throughput of 54 Mbps.

802.11g-ht 802.11g-ht, and the corresponding 802.11a-ht standard, are technical terms for mixed mode 802.11a/802.11g operation. In mixed mode, both technologies are simultaneously supported.

802.11i A wireless standard that added security features.

802.11n An updated 802.11 standard that increases transfer speeds and adds support for multiple in/multiple out (MIMO) by using multiple antennas. 802.11n can operate on either the 2.4- or 5-GHz frequency band and has a maximum throughput of 400 Mbps.

802.16 *See* IEEE 802.16.

1000BaseCX A Gigabit Ethernet standard using unique copper cabling, with a 25-m maximum cable distance.

1000BaseLX A Gigabit Ethernet standard using single-mode fiber cabling, with a 5-km maximum cable distance.

1000BaseSX A Gigabit Ethernet standard using multimode fiber cabling, with a 220- to 500-m maximum cable distance.

1000BaseT A Gigabit Ethernet standard using CAT 5e/6 UTP cabling, with a 100-m maximum cable distance.

1000BaseTX Short-lived gigabit-over-UTP standard from TIA/EIA. Considered a competitor to 1000BaseT, it was simpler to implement but required the use of CAT 6 cable.

1000BaseX An umbrella Gigabit Ethernet standard. Also known as *802.3z*. Comprises all Gigabit standards with the exception of 1000BaseT, which is under the 802.3ab standard.

A Records A list of the IP addresses and names of all the systems on a DNS server domain.

AAA (Authentication, Authorization, and Accounting) *See* Authentication, Authorization, and Accounting (AAA).

Acceptable Use Policy A document that defines what a person may and may not do on an organization's computers and networks.

Access Control All-encompassing term that defines the degree of permission granted to use a particular resource. That resource may be anything from a switch port to a particular file to a physical door within a building.

Access Control List (ACL) A clearly defined list of permissions that specifies what actions an authenticated user may perform on a shared resource.

Access Control Server (ACS) Cisco program/process/server that makes the decision to admit or deny a node based on posture assessment. From there, the ACS directs the edge access device to allow a connection or to implement a denial or redirect.

Access Port Regular port in a switch that has been configured as part of a VLAN. Access ports are ports that hosts connect to. They are the opposite of a trunk port, which is only connected to a trunk port on another switch.

Active Directory A form of directory service used in networks with Windows servers. Creates an organization of related computers that share one or more Windows domains.

Activity Light An LED on a NIC, hub, or switch that blinks rapidly to show data transfers over the network.

Ad Hoc Mode A wireless networking mode where each node is in direct contact with every other node in a decentralized free-for-all. Ad hoc mode is similar to the mesh topology.

Address Resolution Protocol (ARP) A protocol in the TCP/IP suite used with the command-line utility of the same name to determine the MAC address that corresponds to a particular IP address.

Administrative Accounts Specialized user accounts that have been granted sufficient access rights and authority to manage specified administrative tasks. Some administrative accounts exist as a default of the system and have all authority throughout the system. Others must be explicitly assigned the necessary powers to administer given resources.

ADSL (Asymmetric Digital Subscriber Line) *See* Asymmetric Digital Subscriber Line (ADSL).

Advanced Encryption Standard (AES) A block cipher created in the late 1990s that uses a 128-bit block size and a 128-, 192-, or 256-bit key size. Practically uncrackable.

Adware A program that monitors the types of Web sites you frequent and uses that information to generate targeted advertisements, usually pop-up windows.

Agent   In terms of posture assessment, refers to software that runs within a client and reports the client's security characteristics to an access control server to be approved or denied entry to a system.

Agent-less   In terms of posture assessment, refers to a client that has its posture checked and presented by non-permanent software, such as a Web app program, that executes as part of the connection process. Agent-less software does not run directly within the client but is run on behalf of the client.

Aggregation   A router hierarchy in which every router underneath a higher router always uses a subnet of that router's existing routes.

Air Gap   The act of physically separating a network from every other network.

Aircrack-ng   An open source tool for penetration testing many aspects of wireless networks.

Alert   Proactive message sent from an SNMP manager as a result of a trap issued by an agent. Alerts may be sent as e-mail, SMS message, voicemail, or other avenue.

Algorithm   A set of rules for solving a problem in a given number of steps.

Allow   Permission for data or communication to pass through or to access a resource. Specific allowances through a firewall are called *exceptions*.

Amplification   The aspect of a DoS attack that makes a server do a lot of processing and responding.

Angled Physical Contact (APC)   Fiber-optic connector that makes physical contact between two fiber-optic cables. It specifies an 8-degree angle to the curved end, lowering signal loss. APC connectors have less connection degradation from multiple insertions compared to other connectors.

Anti-Malware Program   Software that attempts to block several types of threats to a client including viruses, Trojan horses, worms, and other unapproved software installation and execution.

Antivirus   Software that attempts to prevent viruses from installing or executing on a client. Some antivirus software may also attempt to remove the virus or eradicate the effects of a virus after an infection.

Anycast   A method of addressing groups of computers as though they were a single computer. Anycasting starts by giving a number of computers (or clusters of computers)

the same IP address. Advanced routers then send incoming packets to the closest of the computers.

Apache HTTP Server   An open source HTTP server program that runs on a wide variety of operating systems.

Application Layer   *See* Open Systems Interconnection (OSI) Seven-Layer Model.

Application/Context Aware   Advanced feature of some stateful firewalls where the content of the data is inspected to ensure it comes from, or is destined for, an appropriate application. Context-aware firewalls look both deeply and more broadly to ensure that the data content and other aspects of the packet are appropriate to the data transfer being conducted. Packets that fall outside these awareness criteria are denied by the firewall.

Application Log   Tracks application events, such as when an application opens or closes. Different types of application logs record different events.

Application Programming Interface (API)   Shared functions, subroutines, and libraries that allow programs on a machine to communicate with the OS and other programs.

Approval Process   One or more decision makers consider a proposed change and the impact of the change, including funding. If the change, the impact, and the funding are acceptable, the change is permitted.

Archive   The creation and storage of retrievable copies of electronic data for legal and functional purposes.

Archive Bit   An attribute of a file that shows whether the file has been backed up since the last change. Each time a file is opened, changed, or saved, the archive bit is turned on. Some types of backups turn off the archive bit to indicate that a good backup of the file exists on tape.

Area ID   Address assigned to routers in an OSPF network to prevent flooding beyond the routers in that particular network. *See also* Open Shortest Path First (OSPF).

Areas   Groups of logically associated OSPF routers designed to maximize routing efficiency while keeping the amount of broadcast traffic well managed. Areas are assigned a 32-bit value that manifests as an integer between 0 and 4294967295 or can take a form similar to an IP address, for example, "0.0.0.0."

ARP   *See* Address Resolution Protocol (ARP).

ARP Cache Poisoning   A man-in-the-middle attack, where the attacker associates his MAC address with someone else's IP address (almost always the router), so all traffic will be sent to him first. The attacker sends out unsolicited ARPs, which can either be requests or replies.

arping A command used to discover hosts on a network, similar to ping, but that relies on ARP rather than ICMP. The arping command won't cross any routers, so it will only work within a broadcast domain. *See also* Address Resolution Protocol (ARP) and ping.

Asset Management Managing each aspect of a network, from documentation to performance to hardware.

Asymmetric Digital Subscriber Line (ADSL) A fully digital, dedicated connection to the telephone system that provides download speeds of up to 9 Mbps and upload speeds of up to 1 Mbps.

Asymmetric-Key Algorithm An encryption method in which the key used to encrypt a message and the key used to decrypt it are different, or asymmetrical.

Asynchronous Transfer Mode (ATM) A network technology that runs at speeds between 25 and 622 Mbps using fiber-optic cabling or CAT 5 or better UTP.

Attenuation The degradation of signal over distance for a networking cable.

Authentication A process that proves good data traffic truly came from where it says it originated by verifying the sending and receiving users and computers.

Authentication, Authorization, and Accounting (AAA) A security philosophy wherein a computer trying to connect to a network must first present some form of credential in order to be authenticated and then must have limitable permissions within the network. The authenticating server should also record session information about the client.

Authentication Server (AS) In Kerberos, a system that hands out Ticket-Granting Tickets to clients after comparing the client hash to its own. *See also* Ticket-Granting Ticket (TGT).

Authoritative DNS Servers DNS servers that hold the IP addresses and names of systems for a particular domain or domains in special storage areas called *forward lookup zones*. They also have *reverse lookup zones*.

Authoritative Name Servers Another name for authoritative DNS servers. *See* Authoritative DNS Servers.

Authorization A step in the AAA philosophy during which a client's permissions are decided upon. *See also* Authentication, Authorization, and Accounting (AAA).

Automatic Private IP Addressing (APIPA) A networking feature in operating systems that enables DHCP clients to self-configure an IP address and subnet mask automatically when a DHCP server isn't available.

Autonomous System (AS) One or more networks that are governed by a single protocol, which provides routing for the Internet backbone.

Back Up To save important data in a secondary location as a safety precaution against the loss of the primary data.

Backup Designated Router (BDR) A second router set to take over if the designated router fails. *See also* Designated Router (DR).

Backup Generator An onsite generator that provides electricity if the power utility fails.

Bandwidth A piece of the spectrum occupied by some form of signal, whether it is television, voice, fax data, and so forth. Signals require a certain size and location of bandwidth to be transmitted. The higher the bandwidth, the faster the signal transmission, thus allowing for a more complex signal such as audio or video. Because bandwidth is a limited space, when one user is occupying it, others must wait their turn. Bandwidth is also the capacity of a network to transmit a given amount of data during a given period.

Bandwidth Saturation When the frequency of a band is filled to capacity due to the large number of devices using the same bandwidth.

Banner Grabbing When a malicious user gains access to an open port and uses it to probe a host to gain information and access, as well as learn details about running services.

Baseband Digital signaling that has only one signal (a single signal) on the cable at a time. The signals must be in one of three states: one, zero, or idle.

Baseline Static image of a system's (or network's) performance when all elements are known to be working properly.

Basic NAT A simple form of NAT that translates a computer's private or internal IP address to a global IP address on a one-to-one basis.

Basic Rate Interface (BRI) The basic ISDN configuration, which consists of two *B* channels (which can carry voice or data at a rate of 64 Kbps) and one *D* channel (which carries setup and configuration information, as well as data, at 16 Kbps).

Basic Service Set (BSS) In wireless networking, a single access point servicing a given area.

Basic Service Set Identifier (BSSID) Naming scheme in wireless networks.

Baud One analog cycle on a telephone line.

Baud Rate The number of bauds per second. In the early days of telephone data transmission, the baud rate was often analogous to bits per second. Due to advanced modulation of baud cycles as well as data compression, this is no longer true.

Bearer Channel (B Channel) A type of ISDN channel that carries data and voice information using standard DS0 channels at 64 Kbps.

Biometric Human physical characteristic that can be measured and saved to be compared as authentication in granting the user access to a network or resource. Common biometrics include fingerprints, facial scans, retinal scans, voice pattern recognition, and others.

Biometric Devices Devices that scan fingerprints, retinas, or even the sound of the user's voice to provide a foolproof replacement for both passwords and smart devices.

Bit Error Rate Test (BERT) An end-to-end test that verifies a T-carrier connection.

Block Access that is denied through to or from a resource. A block may be implemented in a firewall, access control server, or other secure gateway. *See also* Allow.

Blocks Contiguous ranges of IP addresses that are assigned to organizations and end users by IANA. Also called *network blocks*.

Block Cipher An encryption algorithm in which data is encrypted in "chunks" of a certain length at a time. Popular in wired networks.

BNC Connector A connector used for 10Base2 coaxial cable. All BNC connectors have to be locked into place by turning the locking ring 90 degrees.

BNC Coupler Passive connector used to join two segments of coaxial cables that are terminated with BNC connectors.

Bonding Two or more NICs in a system working together to act as a single NIC to increase performance.

Bootstrap Protocol (BOOTP) A component of TCP/IP that allows computers to discover and receive an IP address from a DHCP server prior to booting the OS. Other items that may be discovered during the BOOTP process are the IP address of the default gateway for the subnet and the IP addresses of any name servers.

Border Gateway Protocol (BGP-4) An exterior gateway routing protocol that enables groups of routers to share routing information so that efficient, loop-free routes can be established.

Botnet A group of computers under the control of one operator, used for malicious purposes. *See also* Zombie.

Bounce A signal sent by one device taking many different paths to get to the receiving systems.

Bps (Bits Per Second) A measurement of how fast data is moved across a transmission medium. A Gigabit Ethernet connection moves 1,000,000,000 bps.

Bridge A device that connects two networks and passes traffic between them based only on the node address, so that traffic between nodes on one network does not appear on the other network. For example, an Ethernet bridge only looks at the MAC address. Bridges filter and forward frames based on MAC addresses and operate at Layer 2 (Data Link layer) of the OSI seven-layer model.

Bridge Loop A negative situation in which bridging devices (usually switches) are installed in a loop configuration, causing frames to loop continuously. Switches using Spanning Tree Protocol (STP) prevent bridge loops by automatically turning off looping ports.

Bridged Connection An early type of DSL connection that made the DSL line function the same as if you snapped an Ethernet cable into your NIC.

Bridging Loop A physical wiring of a circuitous path between two or more switches, causing frames to loop continuously. Implementing Spanning Tree Protocol (STP) in these devices will discover and block looped paths.

Bring Your Own Device (BYOD) A trend wherein users bring their own network-enabled devices to the work environment. These cell phones, tablets, notebooks, and other mobile devices must be easily and securely integrated and released from corporate network environments using on-boarding and off-boarding technologies.

Broadband Analog signaling that sends multiple signals over the cable at the same time. The best example of broadband signaling is cable television. The zero, one, and idle states exist on multiple channels on the same cable. *See also* Baseband.

Broadcast A frame or packet addressed to all machines, almost always limited to a broadcast domain.

Broadcast Address The address a NIC attaches to a frame when it wants every other NIC on the network to read it. In TCP/IP, the general broadcast address is 255.255.255.255. In Ethernet, the broadcast MAC address is FF-FF-FF-FF-FF-FF.

Broadcast Domain A network of computers that will hear each other's broadcasts. The older term *collision domain* is the same but rarely used today.

Broadcast Storm The result of one or more devices sending a nonstop flurry of broadcast frames on the network.

Browser A software program specifically designed to retrieve, interpret, and display Web pages.

Brute Force A type of attack wherein every permutation of some form of data is tried in an attempt to discover protected information. Most commonly used on password cracking.

Building Entrance Location where all the cables from the outside world (telephone lines, cables from other buildings, and so on) come into a building.

Bus Topology A network topology that uses a single bus cable that connects all of the computers in a line. Bus topology networks must be terminated to prevent signal reflection.

Business Continuity Planning (BCP) The process of defining the steps to be taken in the event of a physical corporate crisis to continue operations. Includes the creation of documents to specify facilities, equipment, resources, personnel, and their roles.

Butt Set Device that can tap into a 66- or 110-punchdown block to see if a particular line is working.

Byte Eight contiguous bits, the fundamental data unit of personal computers. Storing the equivalent of one character, the byte is also the basic unit of measurement for computer storage. Bytes are counted in powers of two.

CAB Files Short for "cabinet files." These files are compressed and most commonly used during Microsoft operating system installation to store many smaller files, such as device drivers.

Cable Certifier A very powerful cable testing device used by professional installers to test the electrical characteristics of a cable and then generate a certification report, proving that cable runs pass TIA/EIA standards.

Cable Drop Location where the cable comes out of the wall at the workstation location.

Cable Modem A bridge device that interconnects the cable company's DOCSIS service to the user's Ethernet network. In most locations, the cable modem is the demarc.

Cable Stripper Device that enables the creation of UTP cables.

Cable Tester A generic name for a device that tests cables. Some common tests are continuity, electrical shorts, crossed wires, or other electrical characteristics.

Cable Tray A device for organizing cable runs in a drop ceiling.

Cache A special area of RAM that stores frequently accessed data. In a network there are a number of applications that take advantage of cache in some way.

Cache-Only DNS Servers (Caching-Only DNS Servers) DNS servers that do not have any forward lookup zones. They resolve names of systems on the Internet for the network, but are not responsible for telling other DNS servers the names of any clients.

Cached Lookup The list kept by a DNS server of IP addresses it has already resolved, so it won't have to re-resolve an FQDN it has already checked.

Caching Engine A server dedicated to storing cache information on your network. These servers can reduce overall network traffic dramatically.

Cacti Popular network graphing program.

Campus Area Network (CAN) A network installed in a medium-sized space spanning multiple buildings.

Canonical Name (CNAME) Less common type of DNS record that acts as a computer's alias.

Capture File A file in which the collected packets from a packet sniffer program are stored.

Capturing a Printer A process by which a printer uses a local LPT port that connects to a networked printer. This is usually only done to support older programs that are not smart enough to know how to print directly to a UNC-named printer; it's quite rare today.

Card   Generic term for anything that you can snap into an expansion slot.

Carrier Sense Multiple Access with Collision Avoidance (CSMA/CA)   *See* CSMA/CA (Carrier Sense Multiple Access with Collision Avoidance).

Carrier Sense Multiple Access with Collision Detection (CSMA/CD)   *See* CSMA/CD (Carrier Sense Multiple Access with Collision Detection).

CAT 3   Category 3 wire, a TIA/EIA standard for UTP wiring that can operate at up to 16 Mbps.

CAT 4   Category 4 wire, a TIA/EIA standard for UTP wiring that can operate at up to 20 Mbps. This wire is not widely used, except in older Token Ring networks.

CAT 5   Category 5 wire, a TIA/EIA standard for UTP wiring that can operate at up to 100 Mbps.

CAT 5e   Category 5e wire, a TIA/EIA standard for UTP wiring with improved support for 100 Mbps using two pairs and support for 1000 Mbps using four pairs.

CAT 6   Category 6 wire, a TIA/EIA standard for UTP wiring with improved support for 1000 Mbps.

Category (CAT) Rating   A grade assigned to cable to help network installers get the right cable for the right network technology. CAT ratings are officially rated in megahertz (MHz), indicating the highest-frequency bandwidth the cable can handle.

CCITT (Comité Consutatif Internationale Téléphonique et Télégraphique)   European standards body that established the V standards for modems.

Central Office   Building that houses local exchanges and a location where individual voice circuits come together.

Certificate   A public encryption key signed with the digital signature from a trusted third party called a *certificate authority (CA)*. This key serves to validate the identity of its holder when that person or company sends data to other parties.

Certifier   A device that tests a cable to ensure that it can handle its rated amount of capacity.

Chain of Custody   A document used to track the collection, handling, and transfer of evidence.

Challenge Handshake Authentication Protocol (CHAP)   A remote access authentication protocol. It has the serving system challenge the remote client, which must provide an encrypted password.

Change Management   The process of initiating, approving, funding, implementing, and documenting significant changes to the network.

Change Management Documentation   A set of documents that defines procedures for changes to the network.

Change Management Team   Personnel who collect change requests, evaluate the change, work with decision makers for approval, plan and implement approved changes, and document the changes.

Change Request   A formal or informal document suggesting a modification to some aspect of the network or computing environment.

Channel   A portion of the wireless spectrum on which a particular wireless network operates. Setting wireless networks to different channels enables separation of the networks.

Channel Bonding   Wireless technology that enables wireless access points (WAPs) to use two channels for transmission.

Channel Service Unit/Digital Service Unit (CSU/DSU)   *See* CSU/DSU (Channel Service Unit/Data Service Unit).

Chat   A multiparty, real-time text conversation. The Internet's most popular version is known as Internet Relay Chat (IRC), which many groups use to converse in real time with each other.

Checksum   A simple error-detection method that adds a numerical value to each data packet, based on the number of data bits in the packet. The receiving node applies the same formula to the data and verifies that the numerical value is the same; if not, the data has been corrupted and must be re-sent.

Cipher   A series of complex and hard-to-reverse mathematics run on a string of ones and zeroes in order to make a new set of seemingly meaningless ones and zeroes.

Cipher Lock   A door unlocking system that uses a door handle, a latch, and a sequence of mechanical push buttons.

Ciphertext   The output when cleartext is run through a cipher algorithm using a key.

Circuit Switching The process for connecting two phones together on one circuit.

Cisco IOS Cisco's proprietary operating system.

Cladding The part of a fiber-optic cable that makes the light reflect down the fiber.

Class of Service (CoS) A prioritization value used to apply to services, ports, or whatever a quality of service (QoS) device might use.

Class License Contiguous chunk of IP addresses passed out by the Internet Assigned Numbers Authority (IANA).

Classless Inter-Domain Routing (CIDR) Method of categorizing IP addresses in order to distribute them. *See also* Subnetting.

Classless Subnet A subnet that does not fall into the common categories such as Class A, Class B, and Class C.

Cleartext *See* Plaintext.

Cleartext Credentials Any login process conducted over a network where account names, passwords, or other authentication elements are sent from the client or server in an unencrypted fashion.

Client A computer program that uses the services of another computer program; software that extracts information from a server. Your autodial phone is a client, and the phone company is its server. Also, a machine that accesses shared resources on a server.

Client-to-Site A type of VPN connection where a single computer logs into a remote network and becomes, for all intents and purposes, a member of that network.

Client/Server A relationship in which client software obtains services from a server on behalf of a user.

Client/Server Application An application that performs some or all of its processing on an application server rather than on the client. The client usually only receives the result of the processing.

Client/Server Network A network that has dedicated server machines and client machines.

Closed-Circuit Television (CCTV) A self-contained, closed system in which video cameras feed their signal to specific, dedicated monitors and storage devices.

Cloud Computing Using the Internet to store files and run applications. For example, Google Docs is a cloud computing application that enables you to run productivity applications over the Internet from your Web browser.

Cloud/Server Based Remote storage and access of software, especially anti-malware software, where it can be singularly updated. This central storage allows users to access and run current versions of software easily, with the disadvantage of it not running automatically on the local client. The client must initiate access to and launching of the software.

Coarse Wavelength Division Multiplexing (CWDM) An optical multiplexing technology in which a few signals of different optical wavelength could be combined to travel a fairly short distance.

Coaxial Cable A type of cable that contains a central conductor wire surrounded by an insulating material, which in turn is surrounded by a braided metal shield. It is called coaxial because the center wire and the braided metal shield share a common axis or centerline.

Cold Site A location that consists of a building, facilities, desks, toilets, parking, and everything that a business needs except computers.

Collision The result of two nodes transmitting at the same time on a multiple access network such as Ethernet. Both frames may be lost or partial frames may result.

Collision Domain *See* Broadcast Domain.

Collision Light A light on some older NICs that flickers when a network collision is detected.

Command A request, typed from a terminal or embedded in a file, to perform an operation or to execute a particular program.

Common Internet File System (CIFS) The protocol that NetBIOS used to share folders and printers. Still very common, even on UNIX/Linux systems.

Community Cloud A private cloud paid for and used by more than one organization.

Compatibility Issue When different pieces of hardware or software don't work together correctly.

Compatibility Requirements With respect to network installations and upgrades, requirements that deal with how well the new technology integrates with older or existing technologies.

Complete Algorithm   A cipher and the methods used to implement that cipher.

Computer Forensics   The science of gathering, preserving, and presenting evidence stored on a computer or any form of digital media that is presentable in a court of law.

Concentrator   A device that brings together at a common center connections to a particular kind of network (such as Ethernet) and implements that network internally.

Configuration Management   A set of documents, policies, and procedures designed to help you maintain and update your network in a logical, orderly fashion.

Configuration Management Documentation   Documents that define the configuration of a network. These would include wiring diagrams, network diagrams, baselines, and policy/procedure/configuration documentation.

Configurations   The settings stored in devices that define how they are to operate.

Connection   A term used to refer to communication between two computers.

Connection-Oriented   Network communication between two hosts that includes negotiation between the hosts to establish a communication session. Data segments are then transferred between hosts, with each segment being acknowledged before a subsequent segment can be sent. Orderly closure of the communication is conducted at the end of the data transfer or in the event of a communication failure. TCP is the only connection-oriented protocol in the TCP/IP suite.

Connection-Oriented Communication   A protocol that establishes a connection between two hosts before transmitting data and verifies receipt before closing the connection between the hosts. TCP is an example of a connection-oriented protocol.

Connectionless   A type of communication characterized by sending packets that are not acknowledged by the destination host. UDP is the quintessential connectionless protocol in the TCP/IP suite.

Connectionless Communication   A protocol that does not establish and verify a connection between the hosts before sending data; it just sends the data and hopes for the best. This is faster than connection-oriented protocols. UDP is an example of a connectionless protocol.

Console Port   Connection jack in a switch used exclusively to connect a computer that will manage the switch.

Content Switch   Advanced networking device that works at least at Layer 7 (Application layer) and hides servers behind a single IP.

Contingency Planning   The process of creating documents that set out how to limit damage and recover quickly from an incident.

Continuity   The physical connection of wires in a network.

Continuity Tester   Inexpensive network tester that can only test for continuity on a line.

Convergence   Point at which the routing tables for all routers in a network are updated.

Copy Backup   A type of backup similar to Normal or Full, in that all selected files on a system are backed up. This type of backup does *not* change the archive bit of the files being backed up.

Core   The central glass of the fiber-optic cable that carries the light signal.

Cost   An arbitrary metric value assigned to a network route with OSFP capable routers.

Counter   A predefined event that is recorded to a log file.

CRC (Cyclic Redundancy Check)   A mathematical method used to check for errors in long streams of transmitted data with high accuracy.

Crimper   Also called a *crimping tool,* the tool used to secure a crimp (or an RJ-45 connector) onto the end of a cable.

Cross-Platform Support   Standards created to enable terminals (and now operating systems) from different companies to interact with one another.

Crossover Cable   A specially terminated UTP cable used to interconnect routers or switches, or to connect network cards without a switch. Crossover cables reverse the sending and receiving wire pairs from one end to the other.

Crosstalk   Electrical signal interference between two cables that are in close proximity to each other.

CSMA/CA (Carrier Sense Multiple Access with Collision Avoidance)   Access method used mainly on wireless networks. Before hosts send out data, they first listen for traffic. If the network is free, they send out a signal that reserves a certain amount of time to make sure the network is free of other signals. If data is detected on the wire, the hosts wait a random time period before trying again. If the wire is free, the data is sent out.

CSMA/CD (Carrier Sense Multiple Access with Collision Detection)   Access method that Ethernet systems use in wired LAN technologies, enabling frames of data to flow through the network and ultimately reach address locations. Hosts on CSMA/CD networks first listen to hear if there is any data on the wire. If there is none, they send out data. If a collision occurs, then both hosts wait a random time period before retransmitting the data.

CSU/DSU (Channel Service Unit/Data Service Unit)   A piece of equipment that connects a T-carrier leased line from the telephone company to a customer's equipment (such as a router). It performs line encoding and conditioning functions, and it often has a loopback function for testing.

Customer-Premises Equipment (CPE)   The primary distribution box and customer-owned/managed equipment that exists on the customer side of the demarc.

Cyclic Redundancy Check (CRC)   *See* CRC (Cyclic Redundancy Check).

Daily Backup   Also called a *daily copy backup,* makes a copy of all files that have been changed on that day without changing the archive bits of those files.

Daisy-chain   A method of connecting together several devices along a bus and managing the signals for each device.

Data Backup   The process of creating extra copies of data to be used in case the primary data source fails.

Data Encryption Standard (DES)   A symmetric-key algorithm developed by the U.S. government in the 1970s and formerly in use in a variety of TCP/IP applications. DES used a 64-bit block and a 56-bit key. Over time, the 56-bit key made DES susceptible to brute-force attacks.

Data Link Layer   *See* Open Systems Interconnection (OSI) Seven-Layer Model.

Data Over Cable Service Interface Specification (DOCSIS)   The unique protocol used by cable modem networks.

Datagram   A connectionless transfer unit created with User Datagram Protocol designed for quick transfers over a packet-switched network.

DB-25   A 25-pin, D-shaped subminiature connector, typically use in parallel and older serial port connections.

DB-9   A 9-pin, D-shaped subminiature connector, often used in serial port connections.

De-encapsulation   The process of stripping all the extra header information from a packet as the data moves up a protocol stack.

Dead Spot   A place that should be covered by the network signal but where devices get no signal.

Decibel (dB)   A measurement of the quality of a signal.

Dedicated Circuit   A circuit that runs from a breaker box to specific outlets.

Dedicated Line   A telephone line that is an always open, or connected, circuit. Dedicated telephone lines usually do not have telephone numbers.

Dedicated Server   A machine that does not use any client functions, only server functions.

Default   A software function or operation that occurs automatically unless the user specifies something else.

Default Gateway   In a TCP/IP network, the IP address of the router that interconnects the LAN to a wider network, usually the Internet. This router's IP address is part of the necessary TCP/IP configuration for communicating with multiple networks using IP.

Delta Channel (D Channel)   A type of ISDN line that transfers data at 16 Kbps.

Demarc   A device that marks the dividing line of responsibility for the functioning of a network between internal users and upstream service providers.

Demarc Extension   Any cabling that runs from the network interface to whatever box is used by the customer as a demarc.

Demilitarized Zone (DMZ)   A lightly protected or unprotected subnet network positioned between an outer firewall and an organization's highly protected internal network. DMZs are used mainly to host public address servers (such as Web servers).

Demultiplexer   Device that can extract and distribute individual streams of data that have been combined together to travel along a single shared network cable.

Denial of Service (DoS) An effort to prevent users from gaining normal use of a resource. *See also* Denial of Service (DoS) Attack.

Denial of Service (DoS) Attack An attack that floods a networked server with so many requests that it becomes overwhelmed and ceases functioning.

Dense Wavelength Division Multiplexing (DWDM) An optical multiplexing technology in which a large number of optical signals of different optical wavelength could be combined to travel over relatively long fiber cables.

Designated Router (DR) The main router in an OSPF network that relays information to all other routers in the area.

Destination Port A fixed, predetermined number that defines the function or session type in a TCP/IP network.

Device Driver A subprogram to control communications between the computer and some peripheral hardware.

Device ID The last six digits of a MAC address, identifying the manufacturer's unique serial number for that NIC.

Device Types/Requirements With respect to installing and upgrading networks, these determine what equipment is needed to build the network and how the network should be organized.

DHCP Lease Created by the DHCP server to allow a system requesting DHCP IP information to use that information for a certain amount of time.

DHCP Relay A router process that, when enabled, passes DHCP requests and responses across router interfaces. In common terms, DHCP communications can cross from one network to another within a router that has DHCP relay enabled and configured.

DHCP Scope The pool of IP addresses that a DHCP server may allocate to clients requesting IP addresses or other IP information like DNS server addresses.

DHCP Snooping Switch process that monitors DHCP traffic, filtering out DHCP messages from untrusted sources. Typically used to block attacks that use a rogue DHCP server.

Dial-up Lines Telephone lines with telephone numbers; they must dial to make a connection, as opposed to a dedicated line.

Differential Backup Similar to an incremental backup in that it backs up the files that have been changed since

the last backup. This type of backup does not change the state of the archive bit.

Differentiated Services (DiffServ) The underlying architecture that makes quality of service (QoS) work.

DIG (Domain Information Groper) *See* Domain Information Groper (DIG).

Digital Signal 1 (DS1) The signaling method used by T1 lines, which uses a relatively simple frame consisting of 25 pieces: a framing bit and 24 channels. Each DS1 channel holds a single 8-bit DS0 data sample. The framing bit and data channels combine to make 193 bits per DS1 frame. These frames are transmitted 8000 times/sec, making a total throughput of 1.544 Mbps.

Digital Signal Processor (DSP) *See* DSP (Digital Signal Processor).

Digital Signature An encrypted hash of a private encryption key that verifies a sender's identity to those who receive encrypted data or messages.

Digital Subscriber Line (DSL) A high-speed Internet connection technology that uses a regular telephone line for connectivity. DSL comes in several varieties, including Asymmetric (ADSL) and Symmetric (SDSL), and many speeds. Typical home-user DSL connections are ADSL with a download speed of up to 9 Mbps and an upload speed of up to 1 Kbps.

Dipole Antenna The standard straight-wire antenna that provides most omnidirectional function.

Direct Current (DC) A type of electric circuit where the flow of electrons is in a complete circle.

Direct-Sequence Spread-Spectrum (DSSS) A spread-spectrum broadcasting method defined in the 802.11 standard that sends data out on different frequencies at the same time.

Directional Antenna An antenna that focuses its signal more towards a specific direction; as compared to an omnidirectional antenna that radiates its signal in all directions equally.

Disaster Recovery The means and methods to recover primary infrastructure from a disaster. Disaster recovery starts with a plan and includes data backups.

Discretionary Access Control (DAC) Authorization method based on the idea that there is an owner of a resource who may at his or her discretion assign access to that resource. DAC is considered much more flexible than mandatory access control (MAC).

Disk Mirroring   Process by which data is written simultaneously to two or more disk drives. Read and write speed is decreased but redundancy, in case of catastrophe, is increased. Also known as *RAID level 1*. *See also* Duplexing.

Disk Striping   Process by which data is spread among multiple (at least two) drives. It increases speed for both reads and writes of data, but provides no fault tolerance. Also known as *RAID level 0*.

Disk Striping with Parity   Process by which data is spread among multiple (at least three) drives, with parity information as well to provide fault tolerance. The most commonly implemented type is RAID 5, where the data and parity information is spread across three or more drives.

Dispersion   Diffusion over distance of light propagating down fiber cable.

Distance Vector   Set of routing protocols that calculates the total cost to get to a particular network ID and compares that cost to the total cost of all the other routes to get to that same network ID.

Distributed Control System (DCS)   A small controller added directly to a machine used to distribute the computing load.

Distributed Coordination Function (DCF)   One of two methods of collision avoidance defined by the 802.11 standard and the only one currently implemented. DCF specifies strict rules for sending data onto the network media. *See also* Point Coordination Function (PCF).

Distributed Denial of Service (DDoS)   Multicomputer assault on a network resource that attempts, with sheer overwhelming quantity of requests, to prevent regular users from receiving services from the resource. Can also be used to crash systems.

DLL (Dynamic Link Library)   A file of executable functions or data that can be used by a Windows application. Typically, a DLL provides one or more particular functions, and a program accesses the functions by creating links to the DLL.

DNS Domain   A specific branch of the DNS name space. Top-level DNS domains include .com, .gov, and .edu.

DNS Resolver Cache   A cache used by Windows DNS clients to keep track of DNS information.

DNS Root Servers   The highest in the hierarchy of DNS servers running the Internet.

DNS Server   A system that runs a special DNS server program.

DNS Tree   A hierarchy of DNS domains and individual computer names organized into a tree-like structure, the top of which is the root.

Document   A medium and the data recorded on it for human use; for example, a report sheet or book. By extension, any record that has permanence and that can be read by a human or a machine.

Documentation   A collection of organized documents or the information recorded in documents. Also, instructional material specifying the inputs, operations, and outputs of a computer program or system.

Domain   A term used to describe a grouping of users, computers, and/or networks. In Microsoft networking, a domain is a group of computers and users that shares a common account database and a common security policy. For the Internet, a domain is a group of computers that shares a common element in their DNS hierarchical name.

Domain Controller   A Microsoft Windows Server system specifically configured to store user and server account information for its domain. Often abbreviated as "DC." Windows domain controllers store all account and security information in the *Active Directory* directory service.

Domain Information Groper (DIG)   Command-line tool in non-Windows systems used to diagnose DNS problems.

Domain Name System (DNS)   A TCP/IP name resolution system that resolves host names to IP addresses.

Domain Users and Groups   Users and groups that are defined across an entire network domain.

Door Access Controls   Methodology to grant permission or to deny passage through a doorway. The method may be computer-controlled, human-controlled, token-oriented, or many other means.

Dotted Decimal Notation   Shorthand method for discussing and configuring binary IP addresses.

Download   The transfer of information from a remote computer system to the user's system. Opposite of *upload*.

Drive Duplexing *See* Duplexing.

Drive Mirroring The process of writing identical data to two hard drives on the same controller at the same time to provide data redundancy.

DS0 The digital signal rate created by converting analog sound into 8-bit chunks 8000 times a second, with a data stream of 64 Kbps. This is the simplest data stream (and the slowest rate) of the digital part of the phone system.

DS1 The signaling method used by T1 lines, which uses a relatively simple frame consisting of 25 pieces: a framing bit and 24 channels. Each DS1 channel holds a single 8-bit DS0 data sample. The framing bit and data channels combine to make 193 bits per DS1 frame. These frames are transmitted 8000 times/sec, making a total throughput of 1.544 Mbps.

DSL Access Multiplexer (DSLAM) A device located in a telephone company's central office that connects multiple customers to the Internet.

DSL Modem A device that enables customers to connect to the Internet using a DSL connection. A DSL modem isn't really a modem—it's more like an ISDN terminal adapter—but the term stuck, and even the manufacturers of the devices now call them DSL modems.

DSP (Digital Signal Processor) A specialized microprocessor-like device that processes digital signals at the expense of other capabilities, much as the floating-point unit (FPU) is optimized for math functions. DSPs are used in such specialized hardware as high-speed modems, multimedia sound cards, MIDI equipment, and real-time video capture and compression.

Duplexing Also called *disk duplexing* or *drive duplexing,* similar to mirroring in that data is written to and read from two physical drives for fault tolerance. In addition, separate controllers are used for each drive, for both additional fault tolerance and additional speed. Considered *RAID level 1. See also* Disk Mirroring.

Dynamic Addressing A way for a computer to receive IP information automatically from a server program. *See also* Dynamic Host Configuration Protocol (DHCP).

Dynamic ARP Inspection (DAI) Cisco process that updates a database of trusted systems. DAI then watches for false or suspicious ARPs and ignores them to prevent ARP cache poisoning and other malevolent efforts.

Dynamic DNS (DDNS) A protocol that enables DNS servers to get automatic updates of IP addresses of computers in their forward lookup zones, mainly by talking to the local DHCP server.

Dynamic Host Configuration Protocol (DHCP) A protocol that enables a DHCP server to set TCP/IP settings automatically for a DHCP client.

Dynamic Link Library (DLL) *See* DLL (Dynamic Link Library).

Dynamic NAT (DNAT) Type of NAT in which many computers can share a pool of routable IP addresses that number fewer than the computers.

Dynamic Port Numbers Port numbers 49152–65535, recommended by the IANA to be used as ephemeral port numbers.

Dynamic Routing Process by which routers in an internetwork automatically exchange information with other routers. Requires a dynamic routing protocol, such as OSPF or RIP.

Dynamic Routing Protocol A protocol that supports the building of automatic routing tables, such as OSPF or RIP.

E-mail (Electronic Mail) Messages, usually text, sent from one person to another via computer. E-mail can also be sent automatically to a large number of addresses, known as a *mailing list.*

E-mail Alert Notification sent by e-mail as a result of an event. A typical use is a notification sent from an SNMP manager as a result of an out of tolerance condition in an SNMP managed device.

E-mail Client Program that runs on a computer and enables a user to send, receive, and organize e-mail.

E-mail Server Also known as a *mail server,* a server that accepts incoming e-mail, sorts the e-mail for recipients into mailboxes, and sends e-mail to other servers using SMTP.

E1 The European counterpart of a T1 connection that carries 32 channels at 64 Kbps for a total of 2.048 Mbps—making it slightly faster than a T1.

E3 The European counterpart of a T3 line that carries 16 E1 lines (512 channels), for a total bandwidth of 34.368 Mbps—making it a little bit slower than an American T3.

EAP-TLS (Extensible Authentication Protocol with Transport Layer Security) A protocol that defines the use of a RADIUS server as well as mutual authentication, requiring certificates on both the server and every client.

EAP-TTLS (Extensible Authentication Protocol with Tunneled Transport Layer Security) A protocol similar to *EAP-TLS* but only uses a single server-side certificate.

Edge A hardware device that has been optimized to perform a task in coordination with other edge devices and controllers.

Edge Router Router that connects one Autonomous System (AS) to another.

Effective Permissions The permissions of all groups combined in any network operating system.

Electromagnetic Interference (EMI) Interference from one device to another, resulting in poor performance in the device's capabilities. This is similar to having static on your TV while running a hair dryer, or placing two monitors too close together and getting a "shaky" screen.

Electronic Discovery The process of requesting and providing electronic and stored data and evidence in a legal way.

Electrostatic Discharge (ESD) *See* ESD (Electrostatic Discharge).

Emulator Software or hardware that converts the commands to and from the host machine to an entirely different platform. For example, a program that enables you to run Nintendo games on your PC.

Encapsulation The process of putting the packets from one protocol inside the packets of another protocol. An example of this is TCP/IP encapsulation in Ethernet, which places TCP/IP packets inside Ethernet frames.

Encryption A method of securing messages by scrambling and encoding each packet as it is sent across an unsecured medium, such as the Internet. Each encryption level provides multiple standards and options.

End-to-End Principle Early network concept that originally meant that applications and work should happen only at the endpoints in a network, such as in a single client and a single server.

Endpoint In the TCP/IP world, the session information stored in RAM. *See also* Socket.

Endpoints Correct term to use when discussing the data each computer stores about the connection between two computers' TCP/IP applications. *See also* Socket Pairs.

Enhanced Interior Gateway Routing Protocol (EIGRP) Cisco's proprietary hybrid protocol that has elements of both distance vector and link state routing.

Environment Limitations With respect to building and upgrading networks, refers to the degree of access to facilities and physical access to physical infrastructure. The type of building or buildings must be considered. Access to the walls and ceilings will factor in the construction of the network.

Environmental Monitor Device used in telecommunications rooms that keeps track of humidity, temperature, and more.

Ephemeral Port In TCP/IP communication, an arbitrary number generated by a sending computer that the receiving computer uses as a destination address when sending a return packet.

Ephemeral Port Number *See* Ephemeral Port.

Equipment Limitations With respect to installing and upgrading networks, the degree of usage of any existing equipment, applications, or cabling.

Equipment Rack A metal structure used in equipment rooms to secure network hardware devices and patch panels. Most racks are 19" wide. Devices designed to fit in such a rack use a height measurement called *units,* or simply *U.*

ESD (Electrostatic Discharge) The movement of electrons from one body to another. ESD is a real menace to PCs because it can cause permanent damage to semiconductors.

Ethernet Name coined by Xerox for the first standard of network cabling and protocols. Ethernet is based on a bus topology. The IEEE 802.3 subcommittee defines the current Ethernet specifications.

Ethernet over Power (EoP) The IEEE 1901 standard, also known as *HomePlug HD-PLC*, provides high-speed home networking through the building's existing power infrastructure.

Evil Twin An attack that lures people into logging into a rogue access point that looks similar to a legitimate access point.

Evolved High-Speed Packet Access (HSPA+) The final wireless 3G data standard, transferring theoretical maximum speeds up to 168 Mbps, although real-world implementations rarely passed 10 Mbps.

Executable Viruses Viruses that are literally extensions of executables and that are unable to exist by themselves. Once an infected executable file is run, the virus loads into memory, adding copies of itself to other EXEs that are subsequently run.

Exit Plan Documents and diagrams that identify the best way out of a building in the event of an emergency. It may also define other procedures to follow.

Extended Service Set (ESS) A single wireless access point servicing a given area that has been extended by adding more access points.

Extended Service Set Identifier (ESSID) An SSID applied to an Extended Service Set as a network naming convention.

Extended Unique Identifier, 48-bit (EUI-48) The IEEE term for the 48-bit MAC address assigned to a network interface. The first 24 bits of the EUI-48 are assigned by the IEEE as the organizationally unique identifier (OUI).

Extended Unique Identifier, 64-bit (EUI-64) The last 64 bits of the IPv6 address, which are determined based on a calculation based on a device's 48-bit MAC address.

Extensible Authentication Protocol (EAP) Authentication wrapper that EAP-compliant applications can use to accept one of many types of authentication. While EAP is a general-purpose authentication wrapper, its only substantial use is in wireless networks.

External Connections A network's connections to the wider Internet. Also a major concern when setting up a SOHO network.

External Data Bus (EDB) The primary data highway of all computers. Everything in your computer is tied either directly or indirectly to the EDB.

External Firewall The firewall that sits between the perimeter network and the Internet and is responsible for bearing the brunt of the attacks from the Internet.

External Network Address A number added to the MAC address of every computer on an IPX/SPX network that defines every computer on the network; this is often referred to as a *network number*.

External Threats Threats to your network through external means; examples include virus attacks and the exploitation of users, security holes in the OS, or weaknesses of the network hardware itself.

F-Connector A screw-on connector used to terminate small-diameter coaxial cable such as RG-6 and RG-59 cables.

Fail Close Defines the condition of doors and locks in the event of an emergency, indicating that the doors should close and lock.

Fail Open Defines the condition of doors and locks in the event of an emergency, indicating that the doors should be open and unlocked.

FAQ (Frequently Asked Questions) Common abbreviation coined by BBS users and spread to Usenet and the Internet. This is a list of questions and answers that pertains to a particular topic, maintained so that users new to the group don't all bombard the group with similar questions. Examples are "What is the name of the actor who plays X on this show, and was he in anything else?" or "Can anyone list all of the books by this author in the order that they were published so that I can read them in that order?" The common answer to this type of question is "Read the FAQ!"

Far-End Crosstalk (FEXT) Crosstalk on the opposite end of a cable from the signal's source.

Fast Ethernet Nickname for the 100-Mbps Ethernet standards. Originally applied to 100BaseT.

Fault Tolerance The capability of any system to continue functioning after some part of the system has failed. RAID is an example of a hardware device that provides fault tolerance for hard drives.

FDDI (Fiber Distributed Data Interface) *See* Fiber Distributed Data Interface (FDDI).

Federal Communications Commission (FCC) In the United States, regulates public airwaves and rates PCs and other equipment according to the amount of radiation emitted.

Fiber Distributed Data Interface (FDDI) Older technology fiber optic network used in campus-sized installations. It transfers data at 100Mbps and uses a token bus network protocol over a ring topology.

Fiber-Optic Cable A high-speed physical medium for transmitting data that uses light rather than electricity to transmit data and is made of high-purity glass fibers sealed within a flexible opaque tube. Much faster than conventional copper wire.

Fibre Channel (FC) A self-contained, high-speed storage environment with its own storage arrays, cables, protocols, cables, and switches. Fibre Channel is a critical part of storage addressed networking (SAN).

File Server A computer designated to store software, courseware, administrative tools, and other data on a local or wide area network (WAN). It "serves" this information to other computers via the network when users enter their personal access codes.

File Transfer Protocol (FTP) A set of rules that allows two computers to talk to one another as a file transfer is carried out. This is the protocol used when you transfer a file from one computer to another across the Internet.

Fire Ratings Ratings developed by Underwriters Laboratories (UL) and the National Electrical Code (NEC) to define the risk of network cables burning and creating noxious fumes and smoke.

Firewall A device that restricts traffic between a local network and the Internet.

FireWire An IEEE 1394 standard to send wide-band signals over a thin connector system that plugs into TVs, VCRs, TV cameras, PCs, and so forth. This serial bus developed by Apple and Texas Instruments enables connection of 60 devices at speeds ranging from 100 to 800 Mbps.

First Responder The person or robot whose job is to react to the notification of a possible computer crime by determining the severity of the situation, collecting information, documenting findings and actions, and providing the information to the proper authorities.

Flat Name Space A naming convention that gives each device only one name that must be unique. NetBIOS uses a flat name space. TCP/IP's DNS uses a hierarchical name space.

Flat-surface Connector Early fiber-optic connector that resulted in a small gap between fiber-optic junctions due to the flat grind faces of the fibers. It was replaced by Angled Physical Contact (APC) connectors.

Flow A stream of packets from one specific place to another.

Flow Cache Stores sets of flows for interpretation and analysis. *See also* Flow.

Forensics Report A document that describes the details of gathering, securing, transporting, and investigating evidence.

Forward Lookup Zone The storage area in a DNS server to store the IP addresses and names of systems for a particular domain or domains.

Forward Proxy Server Server that acts as middleman between clients and servers, making requests to network servers on behalf of clients. Results are sent to the proxy server, which then passes them to the original client. The network servers are isolated from the clients by the forward proxy server.

FQDN (Fully Qualified Domain Name) *See* Fully Qualified Domain Name (FQDN).

Fractional T1 Access A service provided by many telephone companies wherein customers can purchase a number of individual channels in a T1 line in order to save money.

Frame A defined series of binary data that is the basic container for a discrete amount of data moving across a network. Frames are created at Layer 2 of the OSI model.

Frame Check Sequence (FCS) A sequence of bits placed in a frame that is used to check the primary data for errors.

Frame Relay An extremely efficient data transmission technique used to send digital information such as voice, data, LAN, and WAN traffic quickly and cost-efficiently to many destinations from one port.

FreeRADIUS Free RADIUS server software for UNIX/Linux systems.

Freeware Software that is distributed for free with no license fee.

Frequency Division Multiplexing (FDM) A process of keeping individual phone calls separate by adding a different frequency multiplier to each phone call, making it possible to separate phone calls by their unique frequency range.

Frequency-Hopping Spread-Spectrum (FHSS) A spread-spectrum broadcasting method defined in the 802.11 standard that sends data on one frequency at a time, constantly shifting (or *hopping*) frequencies.

Frequently Asked Questions (FAQ) *See* FAQ (Frequently Asked Questions).

FUBAR Fouled Up Beyond All Recognition.

Full-Duplex Any device that can send and receive data simultaneously.

Fully Meshed Topology A mesh network where every node is directly connected to every other node.

Fully Qualified Domain Name (FQDN) The complete DNS name of a system, from its host name to the top-level

domain name. Textual nomenclature to a domain-organized resource. It is written left to right, with the host name on the left, followed by any hierarchical subdomains within the top-level domain on the right. Each level is separated from any preceding or following layer by a dot (.).

Gain The strengthening and focusing of radio frequency output from a wireless access point (WAP).

Gateway Router A router that acts as a default gateway in a TCP/IP network.

General Logs Logs that record updates to applications.

Get (SNMP) A query from an SNMP manager sent to the agent of a managed device for the status of a management information base (MIB) object.

Giga The prefix that generally refers to the quantity 1,073,741,824. One gigabyte is 1,073,741,824 bytes. With frequencies, in contrast, giga- often refers to one billion. One gigahertz is 1,000,000,000 hertz.

Gigabit Ethernet *See* 1000BaseT.

Gigabit Interface Converter (GBIC) Modular port that supports a standardized, wide variety of gigabit interface modules.

Gigabyte 1024 megabytes.

Global Unicast Address A second IPv6 address that every system needs in order to get on the Internet.

Grandfather, Father, Son (GFS) A tape rotation strategy used in data backups.

Graphing Type of software that creates visual representations and graphs of data collected by SNMP managers.

Greenfield Mode One of three modes used with 802.11n wireless networks wherein everything is running at higher speed.

Ground Loop A voltage differential that exists between two different grounding points.

Group Policy A feature of Windows Active Directory that allows an administrator to apply policy settings to network users *en masse*.

Group Policy Object (GPO) Enables network administrators to define multiple rights and permissions to entire sets of users all at one time.

Groups Collections of network users who share similar tasks and need similar permissions; defined to make administration tasks easier.

Guest In terms of virtualization, an operating system running as a virtual machine inside a hypervisor.

Guest Network A network that can contain or allow access to any resource that management deems acceptable to be used by insecure hosts that attach to the guest network.

H.320 A standard that uses multiple ISDN channels to transport video teleconferencing (VTC) over a network.

H.323 A VoIP standard that handles the initiation, setup, and delivery of VoIP sessions.

Hackers People who break into computer systems. Those with malicious intent are sometimes considered *black hat* hackers and those who do so with a positive intent (such as vulnerability testing) are regularly referred to as *white hat* hackers. Of course, there are middle-ground hackers: *gray hats*.

Half-Duplex Any device that can only send or receive data at any given moment.

Hardening Applying security hardware, software, and processes to your network to prevent bad things from happening.

Hardware Appliance Physical network device, typically a "box" that implements and runs software or firmware to perform one or a multitude of tasks. Could be a firewall, a switch, a router, a print server, or one of many other devices.

Hardware Tools Tools such as cable testers, TDRs, OTDRs, certifiers, voltage event recorders, protocol analyzers, cable strippers, multimeters, tone probes/generators, butt sets, and punchdown tools used to configure and troubleshoot a network.

Hash A mathematical function used in cryptography that is run on a string of binary digits of any length that results in a value of some fixed length.

HDMI Ethernet Channel (HEC) Ethernet-enabled HDMI ports that combine video, audio, and data on a single cable.

Heating, Ventilation, and Air Conditioning (HVAC) All of the equipment involved in heating and cooling the environments within a facility. These items include boilers, furnaces, air conditioners and ducts, plenums, and air passages.

Hex (Hexadecimal) Hex symbols based on a numbering system of 16 (computer shorthand for binary numbers), using 10 digits and 6 letters to condense 0s and 1s to binary numbers. Hex is represented by digits 0 through 9 and alpha *A* through *F*, so that 09h has a value of 9, and 0Ah has a value of 10.

Hierarchical Name Space A naming scheme where the full name of each object includes its position within the hierarchy. An example of a hierarchical name is www.totalseminars.com, which includes not only the host name, but also the domain name. DNS uses a hierarchical name space scheme for fully qualified domain names (FQDNs).

High Availability A collection of technologies and procedures that work together to keep an application available at all times.

High-Speed WAN Internet Cards A type of router expansion card that enables connection to two different ISPs.

History Logs Logs that track the history of how a user or users access network resources, or how network resources are accessed throughout the network.

Home Page Either the Web page that your browser is set to use when it starts up or the main Web page for a business, organization, or person. Also, the main page in any collection of Web pages.

Honeynet The network created by a honeypot in order to lure in hackers.

Honeypot An area of a network that an administrator sets up for the express purpose of attracting a computer hacker. If a hacker takes the bait, the network's important resources are unharmed and network personnel can analyze the attack to predict and protect against future attacks, making the network more secure.

Hop The passage of a packet through a router.

Hop Count An older metric used by RIP routers. The number of routers that a packet must cross to get from a router to a given network. Hop counts were tracked and entered into the routing table within a router so the router could decide which interface was the best one to forward a packet.

Horizontal Cabling Cabling that connects the equipment room to the work areas.

Host A single device (usually a computer) on a TCP/IP network that has an IP address; any device that can be the source or destination of a data packet. Also, a computer running multiple virtualized operating systems.

Host ID The portion of an IP address that defines a specific machine in a subnet.

Host Name An individual computer name in the DNS naming convention.

Host-Based Anti-Malware Anti-malware software that is installed on individual systems, as opposed to the network at large.

Host-Based Firewall A software firewall installed on a "host" that provides firewall services for just that machine, such as Windows Firewall.

Host-to-Host Type of VPN connection in which a single host establishes a link with a remote, single host.

Host-to-Site Type of VPN connection where a host logs into a remote network as if it were any other local resource of that network.

hostname Command-line tool that returns the host name of the computer it is run on.

Hosts File The predecessor to DNS, a static text file that resides on a computer and is used to resolve DNS host names to IP addresses. The hosts file is checked before the machine sends a name resolution request to a DNS name server. The hosts file has no extension.

Hot Site A complete backup facility to continue business operations. It is considered "hot" because it has all resources in place, including computers, network infrastructure, and current backups, so that operations can commence within hours after occupation.

Hotspot A wireless access point that is connected to a cellular data network, typically WiMAX, 3G, or 4G. The device can route Wi-Fi to and from the Internet. Hotspots can be permanent installations or portable. Many cellular telephones have the capability to become a hotspot.

HTML (Hypertext Markup Language) An ASCII-based script-like language for creating hypertext documents like those on the World Wide Web.

HTTP over SSL (HTTPS)   A secure form of HTTP in which hypertext is encrypted by SSL before being sent onto the network. It is commonly used for Internet business transactions or any time where a secure connection is required. *See also* Hypertext Transfer Protocol (HTTP) *and* Secure Sockets Layer (SSL).

Hub   An electronic device that sits at the center of a star topology network, providing a common point for the connection of network devices. In a 10BaseT Ethernet network, the hub contains the electronic equivalent of a properly terminated bus cable. Hubs are rare today and have been replaced by switches.

Human Machine Interface (HMI)   In a distributed control system (DCS), a computer or set of controls that exists between a controller and a human operator. The human operates the HMI, which in turn interacts with the controller.

Hybrid Cloud   A conglomeration of public and private cloud resources, connected to achieve some target result. There is no clear line that defines how much of a hybrid cloud infrastructure is private and how much is public.

Hybrid Topology   A mix or blend of two different topologies. A star-bus topology is a hybrid of the star and bus topologies.

Hypertext   A document that has been marked up to enable a user to select words or pictures within the document, click them, and connect to further information. The basis of the World Wide Web.

Hypertext Markup Language (HTML)   *See* HTML (Hypertext Markup Language).

Hypertext Transfer Protocol (HTTP)   Extremely fast protocol used for network file transfers on the World Wide Web.

Hypertext Transfer Protocol over SSL (HTTPS)   Protocol to transfer hypertext from a Web server to a client in a secure and encrypted fashion. SSL establishes a secure communication connection between hosts. It then encrypts the hypertext before sending it from the Web server and decrypts it when it enters the client. HTTPS uses port 443.

Hypervisor   In virtualization, a layer of programming that creates, supports, and manages a virtual machine. Also known as a *Virtual Machine Manager* (VMM).

ICS (Internet Connection Sharing)   Also known simply as *Internet sharing*, the technique of enabling more than one computer to access the Internet simultaneously using a single Internet connection. When you use Internet sharing, you connect an entire LAN to the Internet using a single public IP address.

ICS (Industrial Control System)   A centralized controller where the local controllers of a distributed control system (DCS) meet in order for global changes to be made.

IEEE (Institute of Electrical and Electronics Engineers)   The leading standards-setting group in the United States.

IEEE 802.2   IEEE subcommittee that defined the standards for Logical Link Control (LLC).

IEEE 802.3   IEEE subcommittee that defined the standards for CSMA/CD (a.k.a. *Ethernet*).

IEEE 802.11   IEEE subcommittee that defined the standards for wireless.

IEEE 802.14   IEEE subcommittee that defined the standards for cable modems.

IEEE 802.16   A wireless standard (also known as *WiMAX*) with a range of up to 30 miles.

IEEE 1284   The IEEE standard for the now obsolete parallel communication.

IEEE 1394   IEEE standard for FireWire communication.

IEEE 1905.1   Standard that integrates Ethernet, Wi-Fi, Ethernet over power lines, and Multimedia over Coax (MoCA).

IETF (Internet Engineering Task Force)   The primary standards organization for the Internet.

ifconfig   A command-line utility for Linux servers and workstations that displays the current TCP/IP configuration of the machine, similar to ipconfig for Windows systems. The newer command line utility, ip, is replacing ifconfig on most systems.

IMAP (Internet Message Access Protocol)   An alternative to POP3. Currently in its fourth revision, IMAP4 retrieves e-mail from an e-mail server like POP3, but has a number of features that make it a more popular e-mail tool. IMAP4 supports users creating folders on the e-mail server, for example, and allows multiple clients to access a single mailbox. IMAP uses TCP port 143.

Impedance The amount of resistance to an electrical signal on a wire. It is used as a relative measure of the amount of data a cable can handle.

Implicit Deny The blocking of access to any entity that has not been specifically granted access. May also be known as *implicit deny any*. An example might be a whitelist ACL. Any station that is not in the whitelist is implicitly denied access.

In-Band Management Technology that enables managed devices such as a switch or router to be managed by any authorized host that is connected to that network.

Inbound Traffic Packets coming in from outside the network.

Incident Response Reaction to any negative situations that take place within an organization that can be stopped, contained, and remediated without outside resources.

Incremental Backup Backs up all files that have their archive bits turned on, meaning they have been changed since the last backup. This type of backup turns the archive bits off after the files have been backed up.

Independent Basic Service Set (IBSS) A basic unit of organization in wireless networks formed by two or more wireless nodes communicating in ad hoc mode.

Industrial Control System (ICS) *See* ICS (Industrial Control System).

Infrastructure as a Service (IaaS) Providing servers, switches, and routers to customers for a set rate. IaaS is commonly done by large-scale, global providers that use virtualization to minimize idle hardware, protect against data loss and downtime, and respond to spikes in demand.

Infrastructure Mode Mode in which wireless networks use one or more wireless access points to connect the wireless network nodes centrally. This configuration is similar to the *star topology* of a wired network.

Inheritance A method of assigning user permissions, in which folder permissions flow downward into subfolders.

Institute of Electrical and Electronics Engineers (IEEE) *See* IEEE (Institute of Electrical and Electronics Engineers).

Insulating Jacket The external plastic covering of a fiber-optic cable.

Integrated Services Digital Network (ISDN) *See* ISDN (Integrated Services Digital Network).

Integrity Network process that ensures data sent to a recipient is unchanged when it is received at the destination host.

Interface Identifier The second half (64 bits) of an IPv6 address.

Interface Monitor A program that tracks the bandwidth and utilization of one or more interfaces on one or more devices in order to monitor traffic on a network.

Interframe Gap (IFG) A short, predefined silence originally defined for CSMA/CD; also used in CSMA/CA. Also known as an *interframe space (IFS)*.

Interframe Space (IFS) *See* Interframe Gap (IFG).

Intermediate Distribution Frame (IDF) The room where all the horizontal runs from all the work areas on a given floor in a building come together.

Intermediate System to Intermediate System (IS-IS) Protocol similar to, but not as popular as, OSPF, but with support for IPv6 since inception.

Internal Connections The connections between computers in a network.

Internal Firewall The firewall that sits between the perimeter network and the trusted network that houses all the organization's private servers and workstations.

Internal Network A private LAN, with a unique network ID, that resides behind a router.

Internal Threats All the things that a network's own users do to create problems on the network. Examples include accidental deletion of files, accidental damage to hardware devices or cabling, and abuse of rights and permissions.

Internet Assigned Numbers Authority (IANA) The organization originally responsible for assigning public IP addresses. IANA no longer directly assigns IP addresses, having delegated this to the five Regional Internet Registries. *See also* Regional Internet Registries (RIRs).

Internet Authentication Service (IAS) Popular RADIUS server for Microsoft environments.

Internet Connection Sharing (ICS) *See* ICS (Internet Connection Sharing).

Internet Control Message Protocol (ICMP) A TCP/IP protocol used to handle many low-level functions such as error reporting. ICMP messages are usually request and response pairs such as echo requests and responses, router solicitations and responses, and traceroute requests and responses. There are also unsolicited "responses" (advertisements) which consist of single packets. ICMP messages are connectionless.

Internet Engineering Task Force (IETF) *See* IETF (Internet Engineering Task Force).

Internet Group Management Protocol (IGMP) Protocol that routers use to communicate with hosts to determine a "group" membership in order to determine which computers want to receive a multicast. Once a multicast has started, IGMP is responsible for maintaining the multicast as well as terminating at completion.

Internet Information Services (IIS) Microsoft's Web server program for managing Web servers.

Internet Message Access Protocol Version 4 (IMAP4) *See* IMAP (Internet Message Access Protocol).

Internet of Things (IoT) The idea that everyday objects could be capable of communicating with each other. Although this is certainly true to an extent now, the future of this technology has much greater implications.

Internet Protocol (IP) The Internet standard protocol that handles the logical naming for the TCP/IP protocol using IP addresses.

Internet Protocol Security (IPsec) Network layer encryption protocol.

Internet Protocol Version 4 (IPv4) Protocol in which addresses consist of four sets of numbers, each number being a value between 0 and 255, using a period to separate the numbers (often called *dotted decimal* format). No IPv4 address may be all 0s or all 255s. Examples include 192.168.0.1 and 64.176.19.164.

Internet Protocol Version 6 (IPv6) Protocol in which addresses consist of eight sets of four hexadecimal numbers, each number being a value between 0000 and FFFF, using a colon to separate the numbers. No IP address may be all 0s or all FFFFs. An example is FEDC:BA98:7654:3210:0800:200C:00CF:1234.

Internet Small Computer System Interface (iSCSI) A protocol that enables the SCSI command set to be transported over a TCP/IP network from a client to an iSCSI-based storage system. iSCSI is popular with storage area network (SAN) systems.

InterVLAN Routing A feature on some switches to provide routing between VLANs.

Intra-Site Automatic Tunnel Addressing Protocol (ISATAP) An IPv6 tunneling protocol that adds the IPv4 address to an IPv6 prefix.

Intranet A private TCP/IP network inside a company or organization.

Intrusion Detection System (IDS)/Intrusion Prevention System (IPS) An application (often running on a dedicated IDS box) that inspects incoming packets, looking for active intrusions. The difference between an IDS and an IPS is that an IPS can react to an attack.

IP The core routing and addressing technology that makes up the modern Internet.

IP Address The numeric address of a computer connected to a TCP/IP network, such as the Internet. IPv4 addresses are 32 bits long, written as four octets of 8-bit binary. IPv6 addresses are 128 bits long, written as eight sets of four hexadecimal characters. IP addresses must be matched with a valid subnet mask, which identifies the part of the IP address that is the network ID and the part that is the host ID.

IP Addressing The processes of assigning IP addresses to networks and hosts.

IP Camera Still-frame or video camera with a network interface and TCP/IP transport protocols to send output to a network resource or destination.

IP Filtering A method of blocking packets based on IP addresses.

IP Helper Command used in Cisco switches and routers to enable, disable, and manage internetwork forwarding of certain protocols such as DHCP, TFTP, Time Service, TACACS, DNS, NetBIOS, and others.

ipconfig A command-line utility for Windows that displays the current TCP/IP configuration of the machine; similar to UNIX/Linux's ifconfig.

IRC (Internet Relay Chat) An online group discussion. Also called *chat*.

ISDN (Integrated Services Digital Network) The CCITT (Comité Consutatif Internationale Téléphonique et

Télégraphique) standard that defines a digital method for telephone communications. Originally designed to replace the current analog telephone systems. ISDN lines have telephone numbers and support up to 128-Kbps transfer rates. ISDN also allows data and voice to share a common phone line. Never very popular, ISDN is now relegated to specialized niches.

ISP (Internet Service Provider) An institution that provides access to the Internet in some form, usually for a fee.

IT (Information Technology) The business of computers, electronic communications, and electronic commerce.

Java A network-oriented programming language invented by Sun Microsystems and specifically designed for writing programs that can be safely downloaded to your computer through the Internet and immediately run without fear of viruses or other harm to your computer or files. Using small Java programs (called *applets*), Web pages can include functions such as animations, calculators, and other fancy tricks.

Jumbo Frames Usually 9000 bytes long, though technically anything over 1500 bytes qualifies, these frames make large data transfer easier and more efficient than using the standard frame size.

Just a Bunch of Disks (JBOD) An array of hard drives that are simply connected with no RAID implementations.

K- Most commonly used as the suffix for the binary quantity 1024. For instance, 640K means 640 × 1024 or 655,360. Just to add some extra confusion to the IT industry, *K* is often misspoken as "kilo," the metric value for 1000. For example, 10KB, spoken as "10 kilobytes," means 10,240 bytes rather than 10,000 bytes. Finally, when discussing frequencies, K means 1000. So, 1 KHz = 1000 kilohertz.

Kbps (Kilobits Per Second) Data transfer rate.

Kerberos An authentication standard designed to allow different operating systems and applications to authenticate each other.

Key Distribution Center (KDC) System for granting authentication in Kerberos.

Key Fob Small device that can be easily carried in a pocket or purse or attached to a key ring. This device is used to identify the person possessing it for the purpose of granting or denying access to resources such as electronic doors.

Key Pair Name for the two keys generated in asymmetric-key algorithm systems.

Keypad The device in which an alphanumeric code or password that is assigned to a specific individual for a particular asset can be entered.

Kilohertz (KHz) A unit of measure that equals a frequency of 1000 cycles per second.

LAN (Local Area Network) A group of PCs connected together via cabling, radio, or infrared that use this connectivity to share resources such as printers and mass storage.

Last Mile The connection between a central office and individual users in a telephone system.

Latency A measure of a signal's delay.

Layer A grouping of related tasks involving the transfer of information. Also, a particular level of the OSI seven-layer model, for example, Physical layer, Data Link layer, and so forth.

Layer 2 Switch Any device that filters and forwards frames based on the MAC addresses of the sending and receiving machines. What is normally called a "switch" is actually a "Layer 2 switch."

Layer 2 Tunneling Protocol (L2TP) A VPN protocol developed by Cisco that can be run on almost any connection imaginable. LT2P has no authentication or encryption, but uses IPsec for all its security needs.

Layer 3 Switch Also known as a *router,* filters and forwards data packets based on the IP addresses of the sending and receiving machines.

LC (Local Connector) A duplex type of Small Form Factor (SFF) fiber connector, designed to accept two fiber cables. *See also* Local Connector (LC).

LED (Light Emitting Diode) Solid-state device that vibrates at luminous frequencies when current is applied.

Leeching Using another person's wireless connection to the Internet without that person's permission.

Legacy Mode One of three modes used with 802.11n wireless networks where the wireless access point (WAP) sends out separate packets just for legacy devices.

Legal Hold The process of an organization preserving and organizing data in anticipation of or in reaction to a pending legal issue.

Light Leakage The type of interference caused by bending a piece of fiber-optic cable past its maximum bend radius. Light bleeds through the cladding, causing signal distortion and loss.

Light Meter An optical power meter used by technicians to measure the amount of light lost through light leakage in a fiber cable.

Lights-out Management Special "computer within a computer" features built into better servers, designed to give you access to a server even when the server itself is shut off.

Lightweight Directory Access Protocol (LDAP) A protocol used to query and change a database used by the network. LDAP uses TCP port 389 by default.

Lightweight Extensible Authentication Protocol (LEAP) A proprietary EAP authentication used almost exclusively by Cisco wireless products. LEAP is an interesting combination of MS-CHAP authentication between a wireless client and a RADIUS server.

Line Tester A device used by technicians to check the integrity of telephone wiring. Can be used on a twisted pair line to see if it is good, dead, or reverse wired, or if there is AC voltage on the line.

Link Aggregation Connecting multiple NICs in tandem to increase bandwidth in smaller increments. *See also* NIC teaming.

Link Aggregation Control Protocol (LACP) IEEE specification of certain features and options to automate the negotiation, management, load balancing, and failure modes of aggregated ports.

Link Light An LED on NICs, hubs, and switches that lights up to show good connection between the devices.

Link-Local Address The address that a computer running IPv6 gives itself after first booting. The first 64 bits of a link-local address are always FE80::/64.

Link Segments Segments that link other segments together but are unpopulated or have no computers directly attached to them.

Link State Type of dynamic routing protocol that announces only changes to routing tables, as opposed to entire routing tables. Compare to distance vector routing protocols. *See also* Distance Vector.

Linux The popular open source operating system, derived from UNIX.

List of Requirements A list of all the things you'll need to do to set up your SOHO network, as well as the desired capabilities of the network.

Listening Port A socket that is prepared to respond to any IP packets destined for that socket's port number.

LMHOSTS File A static text file that resides on a computer and is used to resolve NetBIOS names to IP addresses. The LMHOSTS file is checked before the machine sends a name resolution request to a WINS name server. The LMHOSTS file has no extension.

Load Balancing The process of taking several servers and making them look like a single server, spreading processing and supporting bandwidth needs.

Local Refers to the computer(s), server(s), and/or LAN that a user is physically using or that is in the same room or building.

Local Area Network (LAN) *See* LAN (Local Area Network).

Local Connector (LC) One popular type of Small Form Factor (SFF) connector, considered by many to be the predominant fiber connector. While there are several labels ascribed to the "LC" term, it is most commonly referred to as a *local connector*. *See also* LC (Local Connector).

Local User Accounts The accounts unique to a single Windows system. Stored in the local system's registry.

Localhost The hosts file alias for the loopback address of 127.0.0.1, referring to the current machine.

Log Information about the performance of some particular aspect of a system that is stored for future reference. Logs are also called *counters* in Performance Monitor or *facilities* in syslog.

Log Management The process of providing proper security and maintenance for log files to ensure the files are organized and safe.

Logical Address A programmable network address, unlike a physical address that is burned into ROM.

Logical Addressing As opposed to physical addressing, the process of assigning organized blocks of logically associated network addresses to create smaller manageable networks called subnets. IP addresses are one example of logical addressing.

Logical Link Control (LLC)   The aspect of the NIC that talks to the operating system, places outbound data coming "down" from the upper layers of software into frames, and creates the FCS on each frame. The LLC also deals with incoming frames by processing those addressed to the NIC and erasing ones addressed to other machines on the network.

Logical Network Diagram   A document that shows the broadcast domains and individual IP addresses for all devices on the network. Only critical switches and routers are shown.

Logical Topology   A network topology defined by signal paths as opposed to the physical layout of the cables. *See also* Physical Topology.

Long Term Evolution (LTE)   Better known as 4G, a wireless data standard with theoretical download speeds of 300 Mbps and upload speeds of 75 Mbps.

Looking Glass Site   Web sites that enable a technician to run various diagnostic tools from outside their network.

Loopback Address   Sometimes called the localhost, a reserved IP address used for internal testing: 127.0.0.1.

Loopback Plug   Network connector that connects back into itself, used to connect loopback tests.

Loopback Test   A special test often included in diagnostic software that sends data out of the NIC and checks to see if it comes back.

MAC-48   The unique 48-bit address assigned to a network interface card. This is also known as the *MAC address* or the *EUI-48*.

MAC (Media Access Control) Address   Unique 48-bit address assigned to each network card. IEEE assigns blocks of possible addresses to various NIC manufacturers to help ensure that each address is unique. The Data Link layer of the OSI seven-layer model uses MAC addresses for locating machines.

MAC Address Filtering   A method of limiting access to a wireless network based on the physical addresses of wireless NICs.

MAC Filtering   *See* MAC Address Filtering.

Macro   A specially written application macro (collection of commands) that performs the same functions as a virus. These macros normally autostart when the application is run and then make copies of themselves, often propagating across networks.

Mailbox   Special holding area on an e-mail server that separates out e-mail for each user.

Main Distribution Frame (MDF)   The room in a building that stores the demarc, telephone cross-connects, and LAN cross-connects.

Maintenance Window   The time it takes to implement and thoroughly test a network change.

Malicious User   A user who consciously attempts to access, steal, or damage resources.

Malware   Any program or code (macro, script, and so on) that's designed to do something on a system or network that you don't want to have happen.

Man in the Middle   A hacking attack where a person inserts him- or herself into a conversation between two others, covertly intercepting traffic thought to be only between those other people.

Managed Device   Networking devices, such as routers and advanced switches, that must be configured to use.

Managed Network   Network that is monitored by the SNMP protocol consisting of SNMP managed devices, management information base (MIB) items, and SNMP manager(s).

Managed Switch   *See* Managed Device.

Management Information Base (MIB)   SNMP's version of a server. *See* Simple Network Management Protocol (SNMP).

Mandatory Access Control (MAC)   A security model in which every resource is assigned a label that defines its security level. If the user lacks that security level, they do not get access.

Mantrap   An entryway with two successive locked doors and a small space between them providing one-way entry or exit. This is a security measure taken to prevent tailgating.

Manual Tunnel   A simple point-to-point connection between two IPv6 networks. As a tunnel, it uses IPsec encryption.

Material Safety Data Sheet (MSDS)   Document that describes the safe handling procedures for any potentially hazardous, toxic, or unsafe material.

Maximum Transmission Unit (MTU)   Specifies the largest size of a data unit in a communications protocol, such as Ethernet.

MB (Megabyte)   1,048,576 bytes.

MD5 (Message-Digest Algorithm Version 5)   Arguably the most popular hashing function.

Mechanical Transfer Registered Jack (MT-RJ)   The first type of Small Form Factor (SFF) fiber connector, still in common use.

Media Access Control (MAC)   The part of a NIC that remembers the NIC's own MAC address and attaches that address to outgoing frames.

Media Converter   A device that lets you interconnect different types of Ethernet cable.

Media Gateway Control Protocol (MGCP)   A protocol that is designed to be a complete VoIP or video presentation connection and session controller. MGCP uses TCP ports 2427 and 2727.

Medianet   A network of far-flung routers and servers that provides sufficient bandwidth for video teleconferencing (VTC) via quality of service (QoS) and other tools.

Mega-   A prefix that usually stands for the binary quantity 1,048,576. One megabyte is 1,048,576 bytes. One megahertz, however, is 1,000,000 hertz. Sometimes shortened to *meg*, as in "a 286 has an address space of 16 megs."

Memorandum of Understanding (MOU)   A document that defines an agreement between two parties in situations where a legal contract is not appropriate.

Mesh Topology   Topology in which each computer has a direct or indirect connection to every other computer in a network. Any node on the network can forward traffic to other nodes. Popular in cellular and many wireless networks.

Metasploit   A unique tool that enables a penetration tester to use a massive library of attacks as well as tweak those attacks for unique penetrations.

Metric   Relative value that defines the "cost" of using a particular route.

Metro Ethernet   A metropolitan area network (MAN) based on the Ethernet standard.

Metropolitan Area Network (MAN)   Multiple computers connected via cabling, radio, leased phone lines, or infrared that are within the same city. A perfect example of a MAN is the Tennessee city Chattanooga's gigabit network available to all citizens, the Chattanooga Gig.

MHz (Megahertz)   A unit of measure that equals a frequency of 1 million cycles per second.

Microsoft Baseline Security Analyzer (MBSA)   Microsoft-designed tool to test individual Windows-based PCs for vulnerabilities.

MIME (Multipurpose Internet Mail Extensions)   A standard for attaching binary files, such as executables and images, to the Internet's text-based mail (24-Kbps packet size).

Miredo   An open source implementation of Teredo for Linux and some other UNIX-based systems. It is a NAT-traversal IPv6 tunneling protocol.

Mirroring   Also called *drive mirroring*, reading and writing data at the same time to two drives for fault-tolerance purposes. Considered *RAID level 1*.

Mixed Mode   Also called *high-throughput*, or *802.11a-ht /802.11g-ht*, one of three modes used with 802.11n wireless networks wherein the wireless access point (WAP) sends special packets that support older standards yet can also improve the speed of those standards via 802.

Modal Distortion   A light distortion problem unique to multimode fiber-optic cable.

Model   A simplified representation of a real object or process. In the case of networking, models represent logical tasks and subtasks that are required to perform network communication.

Modem (Modulator-Demodulator)   A device that converts both digital bit streams into analog signals (modulation) and incoming analog signals back into digital signals (demodulation). Most commonly used to interconnect telephone lines to computers.

Modulation Techniques   The various multiplexing and demultiplexing technologies and protocols, both analog and digital.

Modulator-Demodulator (Modem)   *See* Modem (Modulator-Demodulator).

Monlist   A query that asks the NTP server about the traffic going on between itself and peers.

Mounting Bracket   Bracket that acts as a holder for a faceplate in cable installations.

MS-CHAP   Microsoft's dominant variation of the CHAP protocol, uses a slightly more advanced encryption protocol.

MTU (Maximum Transmission Unit) *See* Maximum Transmission Unit (MTU).

MTU Black Hole When a router's firewall features block ICMP requests, making MTU worthless.

MTU Mismatch The situation when your network's packets are so large that they must be fragmented to fit into your ISP's packets.

Multicast Method of sending a packet in which the sending computer sends it to a group of interested computers.

Multicast Addresses A set of reserved addresses designed to go from one system to any system using one of the reserved addresses.

Multifactor Authentication A form of authentication where a user must use two or more factors to prove his or her identity.

Multilayer Switch A switch that has functions that operates at multiple layers of the OSI seven-layer model.

Multilink PPP A communications protocol that logically joins multiple PPP connections, such as a modem connection, to aggregate the throughput of the links.

Multimeter A tool for testing voltage (AC and DC), resistance, and continuity.

Multimode Type of fiber-optic cable with a large-diameter core that supports multiple modes of propagation. The large diameter simplifies connections, but has drawbacks related to distance.

Multimode Fiber (MMF) Type of fiber-optic cable that uses LEDs.

Multiple In/Multiple Out (MIMO) A feature in 802.11 WAPs that enables them to make multiple simultaneous connections.

Multiplexer A device that merges information from multiple input channels to a single output channel.

Multiprotocol Label Switching (MPLS) A router feature that labels certain data to use a desired connection. It works with any type of packet switching (even Ethernet) to force certain types of data to use a certain path.

Multisource Agreement (MSA) A document that details the interoperability of network hardware from a variety of manufacturers.

MX Records Records within DNS servers that are used by SMTP servers to determine where to send mail.

My Traceroute (mtr) Terminal command in Linux that dynamically displays the route a packet is taking. Similar to traceroute.

Name Resolution A method that enables one computer on the network to locate another to establish a session. All network protocols perform name resolution in one of two ways: either via *broadcast* or by providing some form of *name server*.

Name Server A computer whose job is to know the name of every other computer on the network.

NAT (Network Address Translation) *See* Network Address Translation (NAT).

NAT Translation Table Special database in a NAT router that stores destination IP addresses and ephemeral source ports from outgoing packets and compares them against returning packets.

Native VLAN The specified VLAN designation that will be assigned to all untagged frames entering a trunk port in a switch.

nbtstat A command-line utility used to check the current NetBIOS name cache on a particular machine. The utility compares NetBIOS names to their corresponding IP addresses.

Near-End Crosstalk (NEXT) Crosstalk at the same end of a cable from which the signal is being generated.

Nessus Popular and extremely comprehensive vulnerability testing tool.

NetBEUI (NetBIOS Extended User Interface) Microsoft's first networking protocol, designed to work with NetBIOS. NetBEUI is long obsolesced by TCP/IP. NetBEUI did not support routing.

NetBIOS (Network Basic Input/Output System) A protocol that operates at the Session layer of the OSI seven-layer model. This protocol creates and manages connections based on the names of the computers involved.

NetBIOS Name A computer name that identifies both the specific machine and the functions that machine performs. A NetBIOS name consists of 16 characters: the first 15 are an alphanumeric name, and the 16th is a special suffix that identifies the role the machine plays.

NetBIOS over TCP/IP (NetBT)   A Microsoft-created protocol that enabled NetBIOS naming information to be transported over TCP/IP networks. The result is that Microsoft naming services can operate on a TCP/IP network without the need for DNS services.

NetFlow   The primary tool used to monitor packet flow on a network.

NetFlow Collector   Component process of NetFlow that captures and saves data from a NetFlow-enabled device's cache for future NetFlow analysis.

netstat   A universal command-line utility used to examine the TCP/IP connections open on a given host.

Network   A collection of two or more devices interconnected by telephone lines, coaxial cables, satellite links, radio, and/or some other communication technique. A computer *network* is a group of computers that are connected together and communicate with one another for a common purpose. Computer networks support "people and organization" networks, users who also share a common purpose for communicating.

Network Access Control (NAC)   Control over information, people, access, machines, and everything in between.

Network Access Policy   Rules that define who can access the network, how it can be accessed, and what resources of the network can be used.

Network Access Server (NAS)   System that controls the modems in a RADIUS network.

Network Address Translation (NAT)   A means of translating a system's IP address into another IP address before sending it out to a larger network. NAT manifests itself by a NAT program that runs on a system or a router. A network using NAT provides the systems on the network with private IP addresses. The system running the NAT software has two interfaces: one connected to the network and the other connected to the larger network.

The NAT program takes packets from the client systems bound for the larger network and translates their internal private IP addresses to its own public IP address, enabling many systems to share a single IP address.

Network Appliance   Feature-packed network box that incorporates numerous processes such as routing, network address translation (NAT), switching, intrusion detection systems, firewall, and more.

Network as a Service (NaaS)   The act of renting virtual server space over the Internet. *See also* Cloud Computing.

Network Attached Storage (NAS)   A dedicated file server that has its own file system and typically uses hardware and software designed for serving and storing files.

Network Blocks   Also called *blocks*, contiguous ranges of IP addresses that are assigned to organizations and end users by IANA.

Network Closet   An equipment room that holds servers, switches, routers, and other network gear.

Network Design   The process of gathering together and planning the layout for the equipment needed to create a network.

Network Diagram   An illustration that shows devices on a network and how they connect.

Network ID   A number used in IP networks to identify the network on which a device or machine exists.

Network Interface   A device by which a system accesses a network. In most cases, this is a NIC or a modem.

Network Interface Card (NIC)   Traditionally, an expansion card that enables a PC to link physically to a network. Modern computers now use built-in NICs, no longer requiring physical cards, but the term "NIC" is still very common.

Network Interface Unit (NIU)   Another name for a demarc. *See* Demarc.

Network Layer   Layer 3 of the OSI seven-layer model. *See also* Open Systems Interconnection (OSI) Seven-Layer Model.

Network Management Software (NMS)   Tools that enable you to describe, visualize, and configure an entire network.

Network Management Station (NMS)   SNMP console computer that runs the SNMP manager software.

Network Map   A highly detailed illustration of a network, down to the individual computers. A network map will show IP addresses, ports, protocols, and more.

Network Name   Another name for the SSID.

Network Operations Center (NOC)   A centralized location for techs and administrators to manage all aspects of a network.

Network Protocol Special software that exists in every network-capable operating system that acts to create unique identifiers for each system. It also creates a set of communication rules for issues like how to handle data chopped up into multiple packets and how to deal with routers. TCP/IP is the dominant network protocol today.

Network Share A shared resource on a network.

Network Technology The techniques, components, and practices involved in creating and operating computer-to-computer links.

Network Threat Any number of things that share one essential feature: the potential to damage network data, machines, or users.

Network Time Protocol (NTP) Protocol that gives the current time.

Network Topology Refers to the way that cables and other pieces of hardware connect to one another.

Network-Based Anti-Malware A single source server that holds current anti-malware software. Multiple systems can access and run the software from that server. The single site makes the software easier to update and administer than anti-malware installed on individual systems.

Network-Based Firewall Firewall, perhaps implemented in a gateway router or as a proxy server, through which all network traffic must pass inspection to be allowed or blocked.

Newsgroup The name for a discussion group on Usenet.

Next Hop The next router a packet should go to at any given point.

NFS (Network File System) A TCP/IP file system–sharing protocol that enables systems to treat files on a remote machine as though they were local files. NFS uses TCP port 2049, but many users choose alternative port numbers. Though still somewhat popular and heavily supported, NFS has been largely replaced by Samba/CIFS. *See also* Samba *and* Common Internet File System (CIFS).

NIC Teaming Connecting multiple NICs in tandem to increase bandwidth in smaller increments. *See also* link aggregation.

Nmap A network utility designed to scan a network and create a map. Frequently used as a vulnerability scanner.

Node A member of a network or a point where one or more functional units interconnect transmission lines.

Noise Undesirable signals bearing no desired information and frequently capable of introducing errors into the communication process.

Non-Discovery Mode A setting for Bluetooth devices that effectively hides them from other Bluetooth devices.

Non-Persistent Agent Software used in posture assessment that does not stay resident in client station memory. It is executed prior to login and may stay resident during the login session but is removed from client RAM when the login or session is complete. The agent presents the security characteristics to the access control server, which then decides to allow, deny, or redirect the connection.

Nonrepudiation The process of making sure data came from the person or entity it was supposed to come from.

Normal Backup A full backup of every selected file on a system. This type of backup turns off the archive bit after the backup.

Ns (Nanosecond) A billionth of a second. Light travels a little over 11 inches in 1 ns.

NS Records Records that list the DNS servers for a Web site.

nslookup A once-handy tool that advanced techs used to query the functions of DNS servers. Most public DNS servers now ignore all but the most basic nslookup queries.

NTFS (NT File System) A file system for hard drives that enables object-level security, long filename support, compression, and encryption. NTFS 4.0 debuted with Windows NT 4.0. Later Windows versions continue to update NTFS.

NTFS Permissions Groupings of what Microsoft calls special permissions that have names like Execute, Read, and Write, and that allow or disallow users certain access to files.

NTLDR A Windows NT/2000/XP/2003 boot file. Launched by the MBR or MFT, NTLDR looks at the BOOT.INI configuration file for any installed operating systems.

ntpdc A command that puts the NTP server into interactive mode in order to submit queries.

Object A group of related counters used in Windows logging utilities.

OEM (Original Equipment Manufacturer) Contrary to the name, does not create original hardware, but rather purchases components from manufacturers and puts them together in systems under its own brand name. Dell, Inc. and Gateway, Inc., for example, are for the most part OEMs. Apple, Inc., which manufactures most of the components for its own Mac-branded machines, is not an OEM. Also known as *value-added resellers (VARs)*.

Offsite The term for a virtual computer accessed and stored remotely.

Ohm Rating Electronic measurement of a cable's or an electronic component's impedance.

Onsite The term for a virtual computer stored at your location.

Open Port *See* Listening Port.

Open Shortest Path First (OSPF) An interior gateway routing protocol developed for IP networks based on the *shortest path first* or *link state algorithm*.

Open Source Applications and operating systems that offer access to their source code; this enables developers to modify applications and operating systems easily to meet their specific needs.

Open Systems Interconnection (OSI) An international standard suite of protocols defined by the International Organization for Standardization (ISO) that implements the OSI seven-layer model for network communications between computers.

Open Systems Interconnection (OSI) Seven-Layer Model An architecture model based on the OSI protocol suite, which defines and standardizes the flow of data between computers. The following lists the seven layers:

- **Layer 1** The *Physical layer* defines hardware connections and turns binary into physical pulses (electrical or light). Repeaters and hubs operate at the Physical layer.

- **Layer 2** The *Data Link layer* identifies devices on the Physical layer. MAC addresses are part of the Data Link layer. Bridges operate at the Data Link layer.

- **Layer 3** The *Network layer* moves packets between computers on different networks. Routers operate at the Network layer. IP and IPX operate at the Network layer.

- **Layer 4** The *Transport layer* breaks data down into manageable chunks. TCP, UDP, SPX, and NetBEUI operate at the Transport layer.

- **Layer 5** The *Session layer* manages connections between machines. NetBIOS and Sockets operate at the Session layer.

- **Layer 6** The *Presentation layer*, which can also manage data encryption, hides the differences among various types of computer systems.

- **Layer 7** The *Application layer* provides tools for programs to use to access the network (and the lower layers). HTTP, FTP, SMTP, and POP3 are all examples of protocols that operate at the Application layer.

OpenSSH A series of secure programs developed by the OpenBSD organization to fix SSH's limitation of only being able to handle one session per tunnel.

Operating System (OS) The set of programming that enables a program to interact with the computer and provides an interface between the PC and the user. Examples are Microsoft Windows 10, Apple Mac OS X, and SUSE Linux.

Operator In a distributed control system, the operator is a human who runs the computer-controlled resources through a human machine interface. *See also* Human Machine Interface (HMI).

Optical Carrier (OC) Specification used to denote the optical data carrying capacity (in Mbps) of fiber-optic cables in networks conforming to the SONET standard. The OC standard is an escalating series of speeds, designed to meet the needs of medium-to-large corporations. SONET establishes OCs from 51.8 Mbps (OC-1) to 39.8 Gbps (OC-768).

Optical Power Meter Device that measures light intensity of light pulses within or at the terminal ends of fiber-optic cables.

Optical Time Domain Reflectometer (OTDR) Tester for fiber optic cable that determines continuity and reports the location of cable breaks.

Organizationally Unique Identifier (OUI) The first 24 bits of a MAC address, assigned to the NIC manufacturer by the IEEE.

Orthogonal Frequency-Division Multiplexing (OFDM) A spread-spectrum broadcasting method that combines the multiple frequencies of DSSS with FHSS's hopping capability.

OS (Operating System) *See* Operating System (OS).

Oscilloscope   A device that gives a graphical/visual representation of signal levels over a period of time.

OSPF (Open Shortest Path First)   *See* Open Shortest Path First (OSPF).

Out-of-Band Management   Method to connect to and administer a managed device such as a switch or router that does not use a standard network-connected host as the administrative console. A computer connected to the console port of a switch is an example of out-of-band management.

Outbound Traffic   Packets leaving the network from within it.

Overlay Tunnel   Enables two IPv6 networks to connect over an IPv4 network by encapsulating the IPv6 packets within IPv4 headers, transporting them across the IPv4 network, then de-encapsulating the IPv6 data.

Packet   Basic component of communication over a network. A group of bits of fixed maximum size and well-defined format that is switched and transmitted as a complete whole through a network. It contains source and destination address, data, and control information. *See also* Frame.

Packet Analyzer   A program that reads the capture files from packet sniffers and analyzes them based on monitoring needs.

Packet Filtering   A mechanism that blocks any incoming or outgoing packet from a particular IP address or range of IP addresses. Also known as *IP filtering*.

Packet Sniffer   A tool that intercepts and logs network packets.

Pad   Extra data added to an Ethernet frame to bring the data up to the minimum required size of 64 bytes.

Partially Meshed Topology   A mesh topology in which not all of the nodes are directly connected.

Passive Optical Network (PON)   A fiber architecture that uses a single fiber to the neighborhood switch and then individual fiber runs to each final destination.

Password   A series of characters that enables a user to gain access to a file, a folder, a PC, or a program.

Password Authentication Protocol (PAP)   The oldest and most basic form of authentication and also the least safe because it sends all passwords in cleartext.

Patch Cables   Short (2 to 5 foot) UTP cables that connect patch panels to switches.

Patch Panel   A panel containing a row of female connectors (ports) that terminate the horizontal cabling in the equipment room. Patch panels facilitate cabling organization and provide protection to horizontal cabling. *See also* vertical cross-connect.

Path MTU Discovery (PMTU)   A method for determining the best MTU setting that works by adding a new feature called the "Don't Fragment (DF) flag" to the IP packet.

pathping   Command-line tool that combines the features of the ping command and the tracert/traceroute commands.

Payload   The primary data that is sent from a source network device to a destination network device.

PBX (Private Branch Exchange)   A private phone system used within an organization.

Peer-to-Peer   A network in which each machine can act as either a client or a server.

Peer-to-Peer Mode   *See* Ad Hoc Mode.

Penetration Testing (pentest)   An authorized, network hacking process that will identify real-world weaknesses in network security and document the findings.

Performance Monitor (PerfMon)   The Windows logging utility.

Peripherals   Noncomputer devices on a network; for example, fax machines, printers, or scanners.

Permanent DoS (PDoS)   An attack that damages a targeted machine, such as a router or server, and renders that machine inoperable.

Permissions   Sets of attributes that network administrators assign to users and groups that define what they can do to resources.

Persistent Connection   A connection to a shared folder or drive that the computer immediately reconnects to at logon.

Personal Area Network (PAN)   The network created among Bluetooth devices such as smartphones, tablets, printers, keyboards, mice, and so on.

Phishing A social engineering technique where the attacker poses as a trusted source in order to obtain sensitive information.

Physical Address An address burned into a ROM chip on a NIC. A MAC address is an example of a physical address.

Physical Contact (PC) Connector Family of fiber-optic connectors that enforces direct physical contact between two optical fibers being connected.

Physical Layer *See* Open Systems Interconnection (OSI) Seven-Layer Model.

Physical Network Diagram A document that shows all of the physical connections on a network. Cabling type, protocol, and speed are also listed for each connection.

Physical Topology The manner in which the physical components of a network are arranged.

ping (Packet Internet Groper) A small network message sent by a computer to check for the presence and response of another system. A ping uses ICMP packets. *See also* Internet Control Message Protocol (ICMP).

ping -6 Ping is a command-line utility to check the "up/down" status of an IP addressed host. The "-6" switch included on the command line, using the Windows version of ping, specifies that the host under test has an IPv6 address.

ping6 Linux command-line utility specifically designed to ping hosts with an IPv6 address.

Plain Old Telephone Service (POTS) *See* Public Switched Telephone Network (PSTN).

Plaintext Also called *cleartext*, unencrypted data in an accessible format that can be read without special utilities.

Platform Hardware environment that supports the running of a computer system.

Platform as a Service (PaaS) A complete deployment and management system that gives programmers all the tools they need to administer and maintain a Web application.

Plenum Usually a space between a building's false ceiling and the floor above it. Most of the wiring for networks is located in this space. Plenum is also a fire rating for network cabling.

Point Coordination Function (PCF) A method of collision avoidance defined by the 802.11 standard but has yet to be implemented. *See also* Distributed Coordination Function (DCF).

Point-to-Multipoint Topology Topology in which one device communicates with more than one other device on a network.

Point-to-Point Protocol (PPP) A protocol that enables a computer to connect to the Internet through a dial-in connection and to enjoy most of the benefits of a direct connection. PPP is considered to be superior to SLIP because of its error detection and data compression features, which SLIP lacks, and the capability to use dynamic IP addresses.

Point-to-Point Protocol over Ethernet (PPPoE) A protocol that was originally designed to encapsulate PPP frames into Ethernet frames. Used by DSL providers to force customers to log into their DSL connections instead of simply connecting automatically.

Point-to-Point Topology Network topology in which two computers are directly connected to each other without any other intervening connection components such as hubs or switches.

Point-to-Point Tunneling Protocol (PPTP) A protocol that works with PPP to provide a secure data link between computers using encryption.

Pointer Record (PTR) A record that points IP addresses to host names. *See also* Reverse Lookup Zone.

Polyvinyl Chloride (PVC) A material used for the outside insulation and jacketing of most cables. Also a fire rating for a type of cable that has no significant fire protection.

Port (Logical Connection) In TCP/IP, 16-bit numbers between 0 and 65535 assigned to a particular TCP/IP process or application. For example, Web servers use port 80 (HTTP) to transfer Web pages to clients. The first 1024 ports are called *well-known ports*. They have been pre-assigned and generally refer to TCP/IP processes and applications that have been around for a long time.

Port (Physical Connector) In general, the portion of a computer through which a peripheral device may communicate, such as video, USB, serial, and network ports. In the context of networking, the jacks found in computers, switches, routers, and network-enabled peripherals into which network cables are plugged.

Port Address Translation (PAT) The most commonly used form of Network Address Translation, where the NAT uses the outgoing IP addresses and port numbers (collectively known as a socket) to map traffic from specific machines in the network. *See also* Network Address Translation.

Port Authentication Function of many advanced networking devices that authenticates a connecting device at the point of connection.

Port Blocking Preventing the passage of any TCP segments or UDP datagrams through any ports other than the ones prescribed by the system administrator.

Port Bonding The logical joining of multiple redundant ports and links between two network devices such as a switch and storage array.

Port Filtering *See* Port Blocking.

Port Forwarding Preventing the passage of any IP packets through any ports other than the ones prescribed by the system administrator.

Port Mirroring The capability of many advanced switches to mirror data from any or all physical ports on a switch to a single physical port. Useful for any type of situation where an administrator needs to inspect packets coming to or from certain computers.

Port Number Number used to identify the requested service (such as SMTP or FTP) when connecting to a TCP/IP host. Some example port numbers include 80 (HTTP), 20 (FTP), 69 (TFTP), 25 (SMTP), and 110 (POP3).

Port Scanner A program that probes ports on another system, logging the state of the scanned ports.

Post Office Protocol Version 3 (POP3) One of the two protocols that receive e-mail from SMTP servers. POP3 uses TCP port 110. While historically most e-mail clients use this protocol, the IMAP4 e-mail protocol is now more common.

PostScript A language defined by Adobe Systems, Inc., for describing how to create an image on a page. The description is independent of the resolution of the device that will create the image. It includes a technology for defining the shape of a font and creating a raster image at many different resolutions and sizes.

Posture Assessment Process by which a client presents its security characteristics via an agent or agent-less interface to an access control server. The server checks the characteristics and decides whether to grant a connection, deny a connection, or redirect the connection depending on the security compliance invoked.

Power Converter Device that changes AC power to DC power.

Power over Ethernet (PoE) A standard that enables wireless access points (WAPs) to receive their power from the same Ethernet cables that transfer their data.

Power Redundancy Secondary source of power in the event that primary power fails. The most common redundant power source is an uninterruptible power supply (UPS).

Power Users A user account that has the capability to do many, but not all, of the basic administrator functions.

PPP (Point-to-Point Protocol) *See* Point-to-Point Protocol (PPP).

PPPoE (PPP over Ethernet) *See* Point-to-Point Protocol over Ethernet (PPPoE).

Preamble A 64-bit series of alternating 1s and 0s, ending with 11, that begins every Ethernet frame. The preamble gives a receiving NIC time to realize a frame is coming and to know exactly where the frame starts.

Prefix Delegation An IPv6 router configuration that enables it to request an IPv6 address block from an upstream source, then to disseminate it to local clients.

Presentation Layer *See* Open Systems Interconnection (OSI) Seven-Layer Model.

Primary Lookup Zone A *forward lookup zone* stored in a text file. *See also* Forward Lookup Zone.

Primary Rate Interface (PRI) A type of ISDN that is actually just a full T1 line carrying 23 B channels.

Primary Zone A *forward lookup zone* that is managed within and by the authoritative DNS server for that zone.

Private Cloud Software, platforms, and infrastructure that are delivered via the Internet and are made available to the general public.

Private Port Numbers *See* Dynamic Port Numbers.

Program A set of actions or instructions that a machine is capable of interpreting and executing. Used as a verb, it means to design, write, and test such instructions.

Programmable Logic Controller (PLC) A computer that controls a machine according to a set of ordered steps.

Promiscuous Mode A mode of operation for a NIC in which the NIC processes all frames that it sees on the cable.

Prompt A character or message provided by an operating system or program to indicate that it is ready to accept input.

Proprietary Term used to describe technology that is unique to, and owned by, a particular vendor.

Protected Extensible Authentication Protocol (PEAP) An authentication protocol that uses a password function based on MS-CHAPv2 with the addition of an encrypted TLS tunnel similar to *EAP-TLS*.

Protocol An agreement that governs the procedures used to exchange information between cooperating entities; usually includes how much information is to be sent, how often it is sent, how to recover from transmission errors, and who is to receive the information.

Protocol Analyzer A tool that monitors the different protocols running at different layers on the network and that can give Application, Session, Network, and Data Link layer information on every frame going through a network.

Protocol Data Unit (PDU) Specialized type of command and control packet found in SNMP management systems (and others).

Protocol Stack The actual software that implements the protocol suite on a particular operating system.

Protocol Suite A set of protocols that are commonly used together and operate at different levels of the OSI seven-layer model.

Proximity Reader Sensor that detects and reads a token that comes within range. The polled information is used to determine the access level of the person carrying the token.

Proxy ARP The process of making remotely connected computers act as though they are on the same LAN as local computers.

Proxy Server A device that fetches Internet resources for a client without exposing that client directly to the Internet. Most proxy servers accept requests for HTTP, FTP, POP3, and SMTP resources. The proxy server often caches, or stores, a copy of the requested resource for later use.

PSTN (Public Switched Telephone Network) *See* Public Switched Telephone Network (PSTN).

Public-Key Cryptography A method of encryption and decryption that uses two different keys: a public key for encryption and a private key for decryption.

Public-Key Infrastructure (PKI) The system for creating and distributing digital certificates using sites like VeriSign, Thawte, or GoDaddy.

Public Cloud Software, platforms, and infrastructure delivered through networks that the general public can use.

Public Switched Telephone Network (PSTN) Also known as *Plain Old Telephone Service (POTS)*. The most common type of phone connection, which takes your sounds, translated into an analog waveform by the microphone, and transmits them to another phone.

Punchdown Tool A specialized tool for connecting UTP wires to a 110-block. Also called a *110-punchdown tool*.

Quality of Service (QoS) Policies that control how much bandwidth a protocol, PC, user, VLAN, or IP address may use.

Quarantine Network Safe network to which are directed stations that either do not require or should not have access to protected resources.

Raceway Cable organizing device that adheres to walls, making for a much simpler, though less neat, installation than running cables in the walls.

Rack Monitoring System Set of sensors in an equipment closet or rack-mounted gear that can monitor and alert when an out-of-tolerance condition occurs in power, temperature, and/or other environmental aspects.

Radio Frequency Interference (RFI) The phenomenon where a Wi-Fi signal is disrupted by a radio signal from another device.

Radio Grade (RG) Ratings Ratings developed by the U.S. military to provide a quick reference for the different types of coaxial cables.

RADIUS Server A system that enables remote users to connect to a network service.

Real-Time Processing The processing of transactions as they occur, rather than batching them. Pertaining to an application, processing in which response to input is fast enough to affect subsequent inputs and guide the process, and in which records are updated immediately. The lag from input time to output time must be sufficiently small for acceptable timeliness. Timeliness is a function of the total system: missile guidance requires output within a few milliseconds of input, whereas scheduling of steamships requires a response time in days. Real-time systems are those with a response time of milliseconds; interactive systems respond in seconds; and batch systems may respond in hours or days.

Real-Time Transport Protocol (RTP) Protocol that defines the type of packets used on the Internet to move voice or data from a server to clients. The vast majority of VoIP solutions available today use RTP.

Real-Time Video Communication that offers both audio and video via unicast messages.

Recovery Point Objective (RPO) The state of the backup when the data is recovered. It is an evaluation of how much data is lost from the time of the last backup to the point that a recovery was required.

Recovery Time Objective (RTO) The amount of time needed to restore full functionality from when the organization ceases to function.

Reddit Effect The massive influx of traffic on a small or lesser-known Web site when it is suddenly made popular by a reference from the media. *See also* Slashdotting.

Redundant Array of Independent [or Inexpensive] Devices [or Disks] (RAID) A way to create a fault-tolerant storage system. RAID has six levels. Level 0 uses byte-level striping and provides no fault tolerance. Level 1 uses mirroring or duplexing. Level 2 uses bit-level striping. Level 3 stores error-correcting information (such as parity) on a separate disk and data striping on the remaining drives. Level 4 is level 3 with block-level striping. Level 5 uses block-level and parity data striping.

Reflection Used in DDoS attacks, requests are sent to normal servers as if they had come from the target server. The response from the normal servers are reflected to the target server, overwhelming it without identifying the true initiator.

Reflective DDoS *See* Reflection.

regedit.exe A program used to edit the Windows registry.

Regional Internet Registries (RIRs) Entities under the oversight of the Internet Assigned Numbers Authority (IANA), which parcels out IP addresses.

Registered Ports Port numbers from 1024 to 49151. The IANA assigns these ports for anyone to use for their applications.

Regulations Rules of law or policy that govern behavior in the workplace, such as what to do when a particular event occurs.

Remote Refers to the computer(s), server(s), and/or LAN that cannot be physically used due to its distance from the user.

Remote Access The capability to access a computer from outside a building in which it is housed. Remote access requires communications hardware, software, and actual physical links.

Remote Access Server (RAS) Refers to both the hardware component (servers built to handle the unique stresses of a large number of clients calling in) and the software component (programs that work with the operating system to allow remote access to the network) of a remote access solution.

Remote Authentication Dial-In User Service (RADIUS) An AAA standard created to support ISPs with hundreds if not thousands of modems in hundreds of computers to connect to a single central database. RADIUS consists of three devices: the RADIUS server that has access to a database of user names and passwords, a number of network access servers (NASs) that control the modems, and a group of systems that dial into the network.

Remote Copy Protocol (RCP) Provides the capability to copy files to and from the remote server without the need to resort to FTP or Network File System (NFS, a UNIX form of folder sharing). RCP can also be used in scripts and shares TCP port 514 with RSH.

Remote Desktop Protocol (RDP) A Microsoft-created remote terminal protocol.

Remote Installation Services (RIS) A tool introduced with Windows 2000 that can be used to initiate either a scripted installation or an installation of an image of an operating system onto a PC.

Remote Login (rlogin)   Program in UNIX that enables you to log into a server remotely. Unlike Telnet, rlogin can be configured to log in automatically.

Remote Shell (RSH)   Allows you to send single commands to the remote server. Whereas rlogin is designed to be used interactively, RSH can be easily integrated into a script.

Remote Terminal   A connection on a faraway computer that enables you to control that computer as if you were sitting in front of it and logged in. Remote terminal programs all require a server and a client. The server is the computer to be controlled. The client is the computer from which you do the controlling.

Remote Terminal Unit (RTU)   In a SCADA environment, has the same functions as a controller plus additional autonomy to deal with connection loss. It is also designed to take advantage of some form of long-distance communication.

Repeater   A device that takes all of the frames it receives on one Ethernet segment and re-creates them on another Ethernet segment. Repeaters operate at Layer 1 (Physical) of the OSI seven-layer model. They do not check the integrity of the Layer 2 (Data Link) frame so they may repeat incorrectly formed frames. They were replaced in the early 1980s by bridges which perform frame integrity checking before repeating a frame.

Replication   A process where multiple computers might share complete copies of a database and constantly update each other.

Resistance   The tendency for a physical medium to impede electron flow. It is classically measured in a unit called *ohms*. *See also* Impedance.

Resource   Anything that exists on another computer that a person wants to use without going to that computer. Also an online information set or an online interactive option. An online library catalog and the local school lunch menu are examples of information sets. Online menus or graphical user interfaces, Internet e-mail, online conferences, Telnet, FTP, and Gopher are examples of interactive options.

Response   Answer from an agent upon receiving a Get protocol data unit (PDU) from an SNMP manager.

Reverse Lookup Zone   A DNS setting that resolves IP addresses to FQDNs. In other words, it does exactly the reverse of what DNS normally accomplishes using forward lookup zones.

RF Emanation   The transmission, intended or unintended, of radio frequencies. These transmissions may come from components that are intended to transmit RF, such as a Wi-Fi network card, or something less expected, such as a motherboard or keyboard. These emanations may be detected and intercepted, posing a potential threat to security.

RG-58   A grade of small-diameter coaxial cable used in 10Base2 Ethernet networks. RG-58 has a characteristic impedance of 50 ohms.

Ring Topology   A network topology in which all the computers on the network attach to a central ring of cable.

RIP (Routing Information Protocol)   *See* Routing Information Protocol (RIP).

RIPv1   The first version of RIP, which had several shortcomings, such as a maximum hop count of 15 and a routing table update interval of 30 seconds, which was a problem because every router on a network would send out its table at the same time.

RIPv2   The last version of RIP. It fixed many problems of RIPv1, but the maximum hop count of 15 still applies.

Riser   Fire rating that designates the proper cabling to use for vertical runs between floors of a building.

Risk Management   The process of how organizations evaluate, protect, and recover from threats and attacks that take place on their networks.

Rivest Cipher 4 (RC4)   A popular streaming symmetric-key algorithm.

Rivest Shamir Adleman (RSA)   An improved asymmetric cryptography algorithm that enables secure digital signatures.

RJ (Registered Jack)   Connectors used for UTP cable on both telephone and network connections.

RJ-11   Type of connector with four-wire UTP connections; usually found in telephone connections.

RJ-45   Type of connector with eight-wire UTP connections; usually found in network connections and used for 10/100/1000BaseT networking.

Roaming   A process where clients seamlessly change wireless access point (WAP) connections, depending on whichever WAP has the strongest signal covered by the broadcast area.

Rogue Access Point (Rouge AP) An unauthorized wireless access point (WAP) installed in a computer network.

Role-Based Access Control (RBAC) The most popular authentication model used in file sharing, defines a user's access to a resource based on the roles the user plays in the network environment. This leads to the idea of creation of groups. A group in most networks is nothing more than a name that has clearly defined accesses to different resources. User accounts are placed into various groups.

ROM (Read-Only Memory) The generic term for nonvolatile memory that can be read from but not written to. This means that code and data stored in ROM cannot be corrupted by accidental erasure. Additionally, ROM retains its data when power is removed, which makes it the perfect medium for storing BIOS data or information such as scientific constants.

Root Directory The directory that contains all other directories.

Rootkit A Trojan horse that takes advantage of very low-level operating system functions to hide itself from all but the most aggressive of anti-malware tools.

route A command that enables a user to display and edit the local system's routing table.

Route Redistribution Occurs in a multiprotocol router. A multiprotocol router learns route information using one routing protocol and disseminates that information using another routing protocol.

Router A device that connects separate networks and forwards a packet from one network to another based only on the network address for the protocol being used. For example, an IP router looks only at the IP network number. Routers operate at Layer 3 (Network) of the OSI seven-layer model.

Routing and Remote Access Service (RRAS) A special remote access server program, originally only available on Windows Server, on which a PPTP endpoint is placed in Microsoft networks.

Routing Information Protocol (RIP) Distance vector routing protocol that dates from the 1980s.

Routing Loop A situation where interconnected routers loop traffic, causing the routers to respond slowly or not respond at all.

Routing Table A list of paths to various networks required by routers. This table can be built either manually or automatically.

RS-232 The recommended standard (RS) upon which all serial communication takes place on a PC.

Run A single piece of installed horizontal cabling.

Samba An application that enables UNIX systems to communicate using Server Message Blocks (SMBs). This, in turn, enables them to act as Microsoft clients and servers on the network.

SC Connector Fiber-optic connector used to terminate single-mode and multimode fiber. It is characterized by its push-pull, snap mechanical coupling, known as "stick and click." Commonly referred to as *Subscriber Connector, Standard Connector,* and sometimes, *square connector.*

Scalability The capability to support network growth.

Scanner A device that senses alterations of light and dark. It enables the user to import photographs, other physical images, and text into the computer in digital form.

Secondary Lookup Zone A backup lookup zone stored on another DNS server. *See also* Forward Lookup Zone.

Secondary Zone A backup of a primary zone. It is used to provide fault tolerance and load balancing. It gets its information from the primary zone and is considered authoritative. *See also* Primary Zone.

Secure Copy Protocol (SCP) One of the first SSH-enabled programs to appear after the introduction of SSH. SCP was one of the first protocols used to transfer data securely between two hosts and thus might have replaced FTP. SCP works well but lacks features such as a directory listing.

Secure FTP (SFTP) Designed as a replacement for FTP after many of the inadequacies of SCP (such as the inability to see the files on the other computer) were discovered.

Secure Hash Algorithm (SHA) A popular cryptographic hash.

Secure Shell (SSH) A terminal emulation program that looks exactly like Telnet but encrypts the data. SSH has replaced Telnet on the Internet.

Secure Sockets Layer (SSL) A protocol developed by Netscape for transmitting private documents over the Internet. SSL works by using a public key to encrypt sensitive data. This encrypted data is sent over an SSL connection and then decrypted at the receiving end using a private key.

Security A network's resilience against unwanted access or attack.

Security Considerations In network design and construction, planning how to keep data protected from unapproved access. Security of physical computers and network resources is also considered.

Security Guard Person responsible for controlling access to physical resources such as buildings, secure rooms, and other physical assets.

Security Information and Event Management (SIEM) A two-part process consisting of security event monitoring (SEM), which performs real-time monitoring of security events, and security information management (SIM), where the monitoring log files are reviewed and analyzed by automated and human interpreters.

Security Log A log that tracks anything that affects security, such as successful and failed logons and logoffs.

Security Policy A set of procedures defining actions employees should perform to protect the network's security.

Segment The bus cable to which the computers on an Ethernet network connect.

Sequential A method of storing and retrieving information that requires data to be written and read sequentially. Accessing any portion of the data requires reading all the preceding data.

Server A computer that shares its resources, such as printers and files, with other computers on the network. An example of this is a Network File System Server that shares its disk space with a workstation that has no disk drive of its own.

Server-Based Network A network in which one or more systems function as dedicated file, print, or application servers, but do not function as clients.

Server Message Block (SMB) *See* SMB (Server Message Block).

Service Level Agreement (SLA) A document between a customer and a service provider that defines the scope, quality, and terms of the service to be provided.

Service Set Identifier (SSID) A 32-bit identification string, sometimes called a *network name,* that's inserted into the header of each data packet processed by a wireless access point.

Services Background programs in an operating system that do the behind-the-scenes grunt work that users don't need to interact with on a regular basis.

Session A networking term used to refer to the logical stream of data flowing between two programs and being communicated over a network. Many different sessions may be emanating from any one node on a network.

Session Highjacking The interception of a valid computer session to get authentication information.

Session Initiation Protocol (SIP) A signaling protocol for controlling voice and video calls over IP. SIP competes with H.323 for VoIP dominance.

Session Layer *See* Open Systems Interconnection (OSI) Seven-Layer Model.

Session Software Handles the process of differentiating among various types of connections on a PC.

Set The PDU with which a network management station commands an agent to make a change to a management information base (MIB) object.

Share Level Security A security system in which each resource has a password assigned to it; access to the resource is based on knowing the password.

Share Permissions Permissions that only control the access of other users on the network with whom you share your resource. They have no impact on you (or anyone else) sitting at the computer whose resource is being shared.

Shareware Software that is protected by copyright, but the copyright holder allows (encourages!) you to make and distribute copies, under the condition that those who adopt the software after preview pay a fee. Derivative works are not allowed, and you may make an archival copy.

Shell Generally refers to the user interface of an operating system. A shell is the command processor that is the actual interface between the kernel and the user.

Shielded Twisted Pair (STP) A cabling for networks composed of pairs of wires twisted around each other at specific intervals. The twists serve to reduce interference (also called *crosstalk*). The more twists, the less interference. The cable has metallic shielding to protect the wires from external interference. *See also* Unshielded Twisted Pair (UTP) for the more commonly used cable type in modern networks.

Short Circuit Allows electricity to pass between two conductive elements that weren't designed to interact together. Also called a *short*.

Short Message Service (SMS) Alert A proactive message regarding an out-of-tolerance condition of an SNMP managed device sent as an SMS text.

Shortest Path First Networking algorithm for directing router traffic. *See also* Open Shortest Path First (OSPF).

Signal Strength A measurement of how well your wireless device is connecting to other devices.

Signaling Topology Another name for logical topology. *See* Logical Topology.

Signature Specific pattern of bits or bytes that is unique to a particular virus. Virus scanning software maintains a library of signatures and compares the contents of scanned files against this library to detect infected files.

Simple Mail Transfer Protocol (SMTP) The main protocol used to send electronic mail on the Internet.

Simple Network Management Protocol (SNMP) A set of standards for communication with network devices (switches, routers, WAPs) connected to a TCP/IP network. Used for network management.

Single-Mode Fiber (SMF) Fiber-optic cables that use lasers.

Single Point of Failure One component or system that, if it fails, will bring down an entire process, workflow, or organization.

Single Sign-on A process whereby a client performs a one-time login to a gateway system. That system, in turn, takes care of the client's authentication to any other connected systems for which the client is authorized to access.

Site Survey A process that enables you to determine any obstacles to creating the wireless network you want.

Site-to-Site A type of VPN connection using two Cisco VPN concentrators to connect two separate LANs permanently.

Slashdotting The massive influx of traffic on a small or lesser-known Web site when it is suddenly made popular by a reference from the media. *See also* Reddit Effect.

Small Form Factor (SFF) A description of later-generation, fiber-optic connectors designed to be much smaller than the first iterations of connectors. *See also* Local Connector (LC) *and* Mechanical Transfer Registered Jack (MT-RJ).

Small Form Factor Pluggable (SFP) A Cisco module that enables you to add additional features to its routers.

Small Office/Home Office (SOHO) *See* SOHO (Small Office/Home Office).

Smart Device Device (such as a credit card, USB key, etc.) that you insert into your PC in lieu of entering a password.

Smart Jack Type of NIU that enables ISPs or telephone companies to test for faults in a network, such as disconnections and loopbacks.

SMB (Server Message Block) Protocol used by Microsoft clients and servers to share file and print resources.

SMTP (Simple Mail Transfer Protocol) *See* Simple Mail Transfer Protocol (SMTP).

Smurf A type of hacking attack in which an attacker floods a network with ping packets sent to the broadcast address. The trick that makes this attack special is that the return address of the pings is spoofed to that of the intended victim. When all the computers on the network respond to the initial ping, they send their response to the intended victim.

Smurf Attack *See* Smurf.

Snap-Ins Small utilities that can be used with the Microsoft Management Console.

Snapshot A tool that enables you to save an extra copy of a virtual machine as it is exactly at the moment the snapshot is taken.

Sneakernet Saving a file on a portable medium and walking it over to another computer.

Sniffer Diagnostic program that can order a NIC to run in promiscuous mode. *See also* Promiscuous Mode.

Snip *See* Cable Stripper.

SNMP (Simple Network Management Protocol) *See* Simple Network Management Protocol (SNMP).

SNMP Manager Software and station that communicates with SNMP agents to monitor and manage management information base (MIB) objects.

Snmpwalk SNMP manager PDU that collects management information base (MIB) information in a tree-oriented hierarchy of a MIB object and any of its subordinate objects. The snmpwalk command queries the object and then automatically queries all of the objects that are subordinated to the root object being queried.

Social Engineering The process of using or manipulating people inside the networking environment to gain access to that network from the outside.

Socket A combination of a port number and an IP address that uniquely identifies a connection.

Socket Pairs *See* Endpoints.

Software Programming instructions or data stored on some type of binary storage device.

Software as a Service (SaaS) Centralized applications that are accessed over a network.

SOHO (Small Office/Home Office) Network Refers to a classification of networking equipment, usually marketed to consumers or small businesses, which focuses on low price and ease of configuration. SOHO networks differ from enterprise networks, which focus on flexibility and maximum performance.

SOHO Firewall Firewall, typically simple, that is built into the firmware of a SOHO router.

Solid Core A cable that uses a single solid wire to transmit signals.

SONET (Synchronous Optical Network) An American fiber carrier standard for connecting fiber-optic transmission systems. SONET was proposed in the mid-1980s and is now an ANSI standard. SONET defines interface standards at the Physical layer of the OSI seven-layer model.

Source Address Table (SAT) A table stored by a switch, listing the MAC addresses and port of each connected device.

Spanning Tree Protocol (STP) A protocol that enables switches to detect and prevent bridge loops automatically.

Speed-Test Site A Web site used to check an Internet connection's throughput, such as www.speakeasy.net /speedtest.

Split Pair A condition that occurs when signals on a pair of wires within a UTP cable interfere with the signals on another wire pair within that same cable.

Spoofing A security threat where an attacker makes some data seem as though it came from somewhere else, such as sending an e-mail with someone else's e-mail address in the sender field.

Spyware Any program that sends information about your system or your actions over the Internet.

SQL (Structured Query Language) A language created by IBM that relies on simple English statements to perform database queries. SQL enables databases from different manufacturers to be queried using a standard syntax.

SSID Broadcast A wireless access point feature that announces the WAP's SSID to make it easy for wireless clients to locate and connect to it. By default, most WAPs regularly announce their SSID. For security purposes, some entities propose disabling this broadcast.

SSL (Secure Sockets Layer) *See* Secure Sockets Layer (SSL).

SSL VPN A type of VPN that uses SSL encryption. Clients connect to the VPN server using a standard Web browser, with the traffic secured using SSL. The two most common types of SSL VPNs are SSL portal VPNs and SSL tunnel VPNs.

ST Connector Fiber-optic connector used primarily with 2.5mm, single-mode fiber. It uses a push on, then twist-to-lock mechanical connection commonly called stick-and-twist although ST actually stands for Straight Tip.

Star Topology A network topology in which all computers in the network connect to a central wiring point.

Star-Bus Topology A hybrid of the star and bus topologies that uses a physical star, where all nodes connect to a single wiring point (such as a hub) and a logical bus that maintains the Ethernet standards. One benefit of a star-bus topology is *fault tolerance*.

Stateful (DHCP) Describes a DHCPv6 server that works very similarly to an IPv4 DHCP server, passing out IPv6 addresses, subnet masks, and default gateways as well as optional items like DNS server addresses.

Stateful Filtering/Stateful Inspection   A method of filtering in which all packets are examined as a stream. Stateful devices can do more than allow or block; they can track when a stream is disrupted or packets get corrupted and act accordingly.

Stateless (DHCP)   Describes a DHCPv6 server that only passes out optional information.

Stateless Filtering/Stateless Inspection   A method of filtering where the device that does the filtering looks at each IP packet individually, checking the packet for IP addresses and port numbers and blocking or allowing accordingly.

Statement of Work (SOW)   A contract that defines the services, products, and time frames for the vendor to achieve.

Static Addressing   The process of assigning IP addresses by manually typing them into client computers.

Static NAT (SNAT)   A type of network address translation (NAT) that maps a single routable IP address to a single machine, allowing you to access that machine from outside the network.

Static Routes   Entries in a router's routing table that are not updated by any automatic route discovery protocols. Static routes must be added, deleted, or changed by a router administrator. Static routes are the opposite of dynamic routes.

Static Routing   A process by which routers in an internetwork obtain information about paths to other routers. This information must be supplied manually.

Storage   A device or medium that can retain data for subsequent retrieval.

Storage Area Network (SAN)   A server that can take a pool of hard disks and present them over the network as any number of logical disks.

STP (Spanning Tree Protocol)   *See* Spanning Tree Protocol (STP).

Straight-through Cable   UTP or STP cable segment that has the wire and pin assignments at one end of the cable match the wire and same pin assignments at the other end. Straight-through cables are used to connect hosts to switches and are the connective opposite of crossover cables.

Stranded Core   A cable that uses a bundle of tiny wire strands to transmit signals. Stranded core is not quite as good a conductor as solid core, but it will stand up to substantial handling without breaking.

Stream Cipher   An encryption method that encrypts a single bit at a time. Popular when data comes in long streams (such as with older wireless networks or cell phones).

Stripe Set   Two or more drives in a group that are used for a striped volume.

Structured Cabling   Standards defined by the Telecommunications Industry Association/Electronic Industries Alliance (TIA/EIA) that define methods of organizing the cables in a network for ease of repair and replacement.

STS Overhead   Carries the signaling and protocol information in Synchronous Transport Signal (STS).

STS Payload   Carries data in Synchronous Transport Signal (STS).

Subnet   Each independent network in a TCP/IP internetwork.

Subnet Mask   The value used in TCP/IP settings to divide the IP address of a host into its component parts: network ID and host ID.

Subnetting   Taking a single class of IP addresses and chopping it into multiple smaller groups.

Succession Planning   The process of identifying people who can take over certain positions (usually on a temporary basis) in case the people holding those critical positions are incapacitated or lost in an incident.

Supervisory Control and Data Acquisition (SCADA)   A system that has the basic components of a distributed control system (DCS), yet is designed for large-scale, distributed processes and functions with the idea that remote devices may or may not have ongoing communication with the central control.

Supplicant   A client computer in a RADIUS network.

Switch   A Layer 2 (Data Link) multiport device that filters and forwards frames based on MAC addresses.

Switching Loop   When you connect multiple switches together in a circuit causing a loop to appear. Better switches use spanning tree protocol (STP) to prevent this.

Symmetric DSL (SDSL)   Type of DSL connection that provides equal upload and download speed and, in theory, provides speeds up to 15 Mbps, although the vast majority of ISPs provide packages ranging from 192 Kbps to 9 Mbps.

Symmetric-Key Algorithm   Any encryption method that uses the same key for both encryption and decryption.

Synchronous   Describes a connection between two electronic devices where neither must acknowledge (ACK) when receiving data.

Synchronous Digital Hierarchy (SDH)   European fiber carrier standard equivalent to SONET.

Synchronous Optical Network (SONET)   *See* SONET (Synchronous Optical Network).

Synchronous Transport Signal (STS)   Signal method used by SONET. It consists of the STS payload and the STS overhead. A number is appended to the end of STS to designate signal speed.

System Log   A log file that records issues dealing with the overall system, such as system services, device drivers, or configuration changes.

System Restore   A Windows utility that enables you to return your PC to a recent working configuration when something goes wrong. System Restore returns your computer's system settings to the way they were the last time you remember your system working correctly—all without affecting your personal files or e-mail.

T Connector   A three-sided, tubular connector found in 10Base2 Ethernet networking. The connector is in the shape of a *T* with the "arms" of the *T* ending with a female BNC connector and the "leg" having a male BNC connector. The T connector is used to attach a BNC connector on a host between two cable segments.

T1   A leased-line connection capable of carrying data at 1,544,000 bps.

T1 Line   The specific, shielded, two-pair cabling that connects the two ends of a T1 connection.

T3 Line   A leased-line connection capable of carrying data at 44,736,000 bps.

Tailgating   When an unauthorized person attempts to enter through an already opened door.

TCP Segment   The connection-oriented payload of an IP packet. A TCP segment works on the Transport layer.

TCP/IP Model   An architecture model based on the TCP/IP protocol suite, which defines and standardizes the flow of data between computers. The following lists the four layers:

- **Layer 1**   The *Link layer (Network Interface layer)* is similar to OSI's Data Link and Physical layers. The Link layer consists of any part of the network that deals with frames.

- **Layer 2**   The *Internet layer* is the same as OSI's Network layer. Any part of the network that deals with pure IP packets—getting a packet to its destination—is on the Internet layer.

- **Layer 3**   The *Transport layer* combines the features of OSI's Transport and Session layers. It is concerned with the assembly and disassembly of data, as well as connection-oriented and connectionless communication.

- **Layer 4**   The *Application layer* combines the features of the top three layers of the OSI model. It consists of the processes that applications use to initiate, control, and disconnect from a remote system.

TCP/IP Suite   The collection of all the protocols and processes that make TCP over IP communication over a network possible.

TCP Three-way Handshake   A three-packet conversation between TCP hosts to establish and start a data transfer session. The conversation begins with a SYN request by the initiator. The target responds with a SYN response and an ACK to the SYN request. The initiator confirms receipt of the SYN ACK with an ACK. Once this handshake is complete, data transfer can begin.

Telecommunications Room   A central location for computer or telephone equipment and, most importantly, centralized cabling. All cables usually run to the telecommunications room from the rest of the installation.

Telephony   The science of converting sound into electrical signals, moving those signals from one location to another, and then converting those signals back into sounds. This includes modems, telephone lines, the telephone system, and any products used to create a remote access link between a remote access client and server.

Telnet   A program that enables users on the Internet to log onto remote systems from their own host systems.

Temperature Monitor Device for keeping a telecommunications room at an optimal temperature.

TEMPEST The NSA's security standard that is used to combat radio frequency (RF) emanation by using enclosures, shielding, and even paint.

Temporal Key Integrity Protocol (TKIP) The extra layer of security that Wi-Fi Protected Access (WPA) adds on top of Wired Equivalent Privacy (WEP).

Teredo A NAT-traversal IPv6 tunneling protocol, built into Microsoft Windows.

Terminal Access Controller Access Control System Plus (TACACS+) A proprietary protocol developed by Cisco to support authorization, authentication, and accounting (AAA) in a network with many routers and switches. It is similar to RADIUS in function, but uses TCP port 49 by default and separates AAA, and accounting into different parts.

Terminal Adapter (TA) The most common interface used to connect a computer to an ISDN line.

Terminal Emulation Software that enables a PC to communicate with another computer or network as if it were a specific type of hardware terminal.

TFTP (Trivial File Transfer Protocol) *See* Trivial File Transfer Protocol (TFTP).

Thick Client A wireless access point that is completely self-contained with a full set of management programs and administrative access ways. Each thick client is individually managed by an administrator who logs into the WAP, configures it, and logs out.

Thin Client A wireless access point with minimal configuration tools installed. Instead, it is managed by a central controller. An administrator can manage a large number of thin clients by logging into the central controller and performing management tasks on any thin client routers from there.

Thinnet Trade name for 10Base2 Ethernet technology. Thinnet is characterized by the use of RG-58 coaxial cable segments and BNC T connectors to attach stations to the segments.

Threat Any form of potential attack against a network.

TIA/EIA (Telecommunications Industry Association/Electronics Industry Association) The standards body that defines most of the standards for computer network cabling. Many of these standards are defined under the TIA/EIA 568 standard.

TIA/EIA 568A One of two four-pair UTP crimping standards for 10/100/1000BaseT networks. Often shortened to T568A. The other standard is *TIA/EIA 568B*.

TIA/EIA 568B One of two four-pair UTP crimping standards for 10/100/1000BaseT networks. Often shortened to T568B. The other standard is *TIA/EIA 568A*.

TIA/EIA 606 Official methodology for labeling patch panels.

Ticket-Granting Ticket (TGT) Sent by an Authentication Server in a Kerberos setup if a client's hash matches its own, signaling that the client is authenticated but not yet authorized.

Time Division Multiplexing (TDM) The process of having frames that carry a bit of every channel in every frame sent at a regular interval in a T1 connection.

Time Domain Reflectometer (TDR) Advanced cable tester that tests the length of cables and their continuity or discontinuity, and identifies the location of any discontinuity due to a bend, break, unwanted crimp, and so on.

TLS (Transport Layer Security) *See* Transport Layer Security (TLS).

Tone Generator *See* Toners.

Tone Probe *See* Toners.

Toners Generic term for two devices used together—a tone generator and a tone locator (probe)—to trace cables by sending an electrical signal along a wire at a particular frequency. The tone locator then emits a sound when it distinguishes that frequency. Also referred to as *Fox and Hound*.

Top Listener Host that receives the most data on a network.

Top Talker Host that sends the most data on a network.

Top-Level Domain Servers A set of DNS servers—just below the root servers—that handle the top-level domain names, such as .com, .org, .net, and so on.

Topology The pattern of interconnections in a communications system among devices, nodes, and associated input and output stations. Also describes how computers connect to each other without regard to how they actually communicate.

tracert (also traceroute)   A command-line utility used to follow the path a packet takes between two hosts.

tracert –6 (also traceroute6)   A command-line utility that checks a path from the station running the command to a destination host. Adding the –6 switch to the command line specifies that the target host uses an IPv6 address. tracerout6 is a Linux command that performs a traceroute to an IPv6 addressed host.

Traffic Analysis   Tools that chart a network's traffic usage.

Traffic Shaping   Controlling the flow of packets into or out of the network according to the type of packet or other rules.

Traffic Spike   Unusual and usually dramatic increase in the amount of network traffic. Traffic spikes may be the result of normal operations within the organization or may be an indication of something more sinister.

Transceiver   The device that transmits and receives signals on a cable.

Transmission Control Protocol (TCP)   Part of the TCP/IP protocol suite, operates at Layer 4 (Transport) of the OSI seven-layer model. TCP is a connection-oriented protocol.

Transmission Control Protocol/Internet Protocol (TCP/IP)   A set of communication protocols developed by the U.S. Department of Defense that enables dissimilar computers to share information over a network.

Transmit Beamforming   A multiple-antenna technology in 802.11n WAPs that helps get rid of dead spots.

Transport Layer   *See* Open Systems Interconnection (OSI) Seven-Layer Model.

Transport Layer Security (TLS)   A robust update to SSL that works with almost any TCP application.

Trap   Out-of-tolerance condition in an SNMP managed device.

Trivial File Transfer Protocol (TFTP)   A protocol that transfers files between servers and clients. Unlike FTP, TFTP requires no user login. Devices that need an operating system, but have no local hard disk (for example, diskless workstations and routers), often use TFTP to download their operating systems.

Trojan Horse   A virus that masquerades as a file with a legitimate purpose, so that a user will run it intentionally.

The classic example is a file that runs a game, but also causes some type of damage to the player's system.

Trunk Port   A port on a switch configured to carry all data, regardless of VLAN number, between all switches in a LAN.

Trunking   The process of transferring VLAN data between two or more switches.

Trusted User   An account that has been granted specific authority to perform certain or all administrative tasks.

Tunnel   An encrypted link between two programs on two separate computers.

Tunnel Broker   In IPv6, a service that creates the actual tunnel and (usually) offers a custom-made endpoint client for you to use, although more advanced users can often make a manual connection.

Tunnel Information and Control Protocol (TIC)   One of the protocols that sets up IPv6 tunnels and handles configuration as well as login.

Tunnel Setup Protocol (TSP)   One of the protocols that sets up IPv6 tunnels and handles configuration as well as login.

Twisted Pair   Twisted pairs of cables, the most overwhelmingly common type of cabling used in networks. The two types of twisted pair cabling are UTP (unshielded twisted pair) and STP (shielded twisted pair). The twists serve to reduce interference, called *crosstalk*; the more twists, the less crosstalk.

Two-Factor Authentication   A method of security authentication that requires two separate means of authentication; for example, some sort of physical token that, when inserted, prompts for a password.

U (Unit)   *See* Unit (U).

UART (Universal Asynchronous Receiver/Transmitter)   *See* Universal Asynchronous Receiver/Transmitter (UART).

UC Device   One of three components of a UC network, it is used to handle voice, video, and more.

UC Gateway   One of three components of a UC network, it is an edge device used to add extra services to an edge router.

UC Server   One of three components of a UC network, it is typically a dedicated box that supports any UC-provided service.

UDP (User Datagram Protocol) *See* User Datagram Protocol (UDP).

UDP Datagram A connectionless networking container used in UDP communication.

Ultra Physical Contact (UPC) Connector Fiber-optic connector that makes physical contact between two fiber-optic cables. The fibers within a UPC are polished extensively for a superior finish and better junction integrity.

UNC (Universal Naming Convention) Describes any shared resource in a network using the convention \\<*server name*>\<*name of shared resource*>.

Unencrypted Channel Unsecure communication between two hosts that pass data using cleartext. A Telnet connection is a common unencrypted channel.

Unicast A message sent from one computer to one other computer.

Unicast Address A unique IP address that is exclusive to a single system.

Unidirectional Antenna An antenna that focuses all of its transmission energy in a single, relatively narrow direction. Similarly, its design limits its ability to receive signals that are not aligned with the focused direction.

Unified Communication (UC) A system that rolls many different network services into one. Instant messaging (IM), telephone service, and video conferencing are a few examples.

Unified Threat Management (UTM) A firewall that is also packaged with a collection of other processes and utilities to detect and prevent a wide variety of threats. These protections include intrusion detection systems, intrusion prevention systems, VPN portals, load balancers, and other threat mitigation apparatus.

Unified Voice Services Complete self-contained Internet services that rely on nothing more than software installed on computers and the computers' microphone/speakers to provide voice telecommunication over the Internet. All of the interconnections to the Public Switched Telephone Network (PSTN) are handled in the cloud.

Uninterruptible Power Supply (UPS) A device that supplies continuous clean power to a computer system the whole time the computer is on. Protects against power outages and sags. The term *UPS* is often used mistakenly when people mean stand-by power supply or system (SPS).

Unit (U) The unique height measurement used with equipment racks; 1 U equals 1.75 inches.

Universal Asynchronous Receiver Transmitter (UART) A device inside a modem that takes the 8-bit-wide digital data and converts it into 1-bit-wide digital data and hands it to the modem for conversion to analog data. The process is reversed for incoming data.

UNIX A popular computer software operating system used on many Internet host systems.

Unsecure Protocol Also known as an *insecure protocol*, transfers data between hosts in an unencrypted, clear text format. If these packets are intercepted between the communicating hosts, their data is completely exposed and readable.

Unshielded Twisted Pair (UTP) A popular cabling for telephone and networks composed of pairs of wires twisted around each other at specific intervals. The twists serve to reduce interference (also called *crosstalk*). The more twists, the less interference. The cable has *no* metallic shielding to protect the wires from external interference, unlike its cousin, *STP*. 10BaseT uses UTP, as do many other networking technologies. UTP is available in a variety of grades, called categories, as defined in the following:

- **Category 1 UTP** Regular analog phone lines, not used for data communications.
- **Category 2 UTP** Supports speeds up to 4 Mbps
- **Category 3 UTP** Supports speeds up to 16 Mbps
- **Category 4 UTP** Supports speeds up to 20 Mbps
- **Category 5 UTP** Supports speeds up to 100 Mbps
- **Category 5e UTP** Supports speeds up to 100 Mbps with two pairs and up to 1000 Mbps with four pairs
- **Category 6 UTP** Improved support for speeds up to 10 Gbps
- **Category 6a UTP** Extends the length of 10-Gbps communication to the full 100 meters commonly associated with UTP cabling.

Untrusted User An account that has been granted no administrative powers.

Uplink Port Port on a switch that enables you to connect two switches together using a straight-through cable.

Upload The transfer of information from a user's system to a remote computer system. Opposite of *download*.

URL (Uniform Resource Locator) An address that defines the type and the location of a resource on the Internet. URLs are used in almost every TCP/IP application. An example HTTP URL is http://www.totalsem.com.

Usenet The network of UNIX users, generally perceived as informal and made up of loosely coupled nodes, that exchanges mail and messages. Started by Duke University and UNC-Chapel Hill. An information cooperative linking around 16,000 computer sites and millions of people. Usenet provides a series of "news groups" analogous to online conferences.

User Anyone who uses a computer. You.

User Account A container that identifies a user to the application, operating system, or network, including name, password, user name, groups to which the user belongs, and other information based on the user and the OS or NOS being used. Usually defines the rights and roles a user plays on a system.

User Datagram Protocol (UDP) A protocol used by some older applications, most prominently TFTP (Trivial FTP), to transfer files. UDP datagrams are both simpler and smaller than TCP segments, and they do most of the behind-the-scenes work in a TCP/IP network.

User-Level Security A security system in which each user has an account, and access to resources is based on user identity.

User Profile A collection of settings that corresponds to a specific user account and may follow the user, regardless of the computer at which he or she logs on. These settings enable the user to have customized environment and security settings.

UTP Coupler A simple, passive, double-ended connector with female connectors on both ends. UTP couplers are used to connect two UTP cable segments together to achieve longer length when it is deemed unnecessary or inappropriate to use a single, long cable.

V Standards Standards established by CCITT for modem manufacturers to follow (voluntarily) to ensure compatible speeds, compression, and error correction.

V.92 Standard The current modem standard, which has a download speed of 57,600 bps and an upload speed of 48 Kbps. V.92 modems have several interesting features, such as Quick Connect and Modem on Hold.

Variable Value of an SNMP management information base (MIB) object. That value can be read with a Get PDU or changed with a Set PDU.

Vertical Cross-Connect Main patch panel in a telecommunications room. *See also* Patch Panel.

Very High Bitrate DSL (VDSL) The latest form of DSL with download and upload speeds of up to 100 Mbps. VDSL was designed to run on copper phone lines, but many VDSL suppliers use fiber-optic cabling to increase effective distances.

Video Monitoring Security measures that use remotely monitored visual systems that include IP cameras and closed-circuit televisions.

Video Teleconferencing The classic, multicast-based presentation where one presenter pushes out a stream of video to any number of properly configured and properly authorized multicast clients.

View The different displays found in Performance Monitor.

Virtual Firewall A firewall that is implemented in software within a virtual machine in cases where it would be difficult, costly, or impossible to install a traditional physical firewall.

Virtual IP A single IP address shared by multiple systems. This is commonly the single IP address assigned to a home or organization that uses NAT to have multiple IP stations on the private side of the NAT router.

Virtual Local Area Network (VLAN) A common feature among managed switches that enables a single switch to support multiple logical broadcast domains. Not only is VLAN support a common feature of managed switches but VLAN installations take advantage of this feature and are very common today.

Virtual Machine (VM) A virtual computer accessed through a class of programs called a hypervisor or virtual machine manager. A virtual machine runs *inside* your actual operating system, essentially enabling you to run two or more operating systems at once.

Virtual Machine Manager (VMM) *See* Hypervisor.

Virtual PBX Software that functionally replaces a physical PBX telephone system.

Virtual Private Network (VPN) A network configuration that enables a remote user to access a private network via the Internet. VPNs employ an encryption methodology called *tunneling,* which protects the data from interception.

Virtual Router A router that is implemented in software within a virtual machine. The scalability of a virtual machine makes it easy to add capacity to the router when it is needed. Virtual routers are easily managed and are highly scalable without requiring the purchase of additional network hardware.

Virtual Switch Special software that enables virtual machines (VMs) to communicate with each other without going outside of the host system.

Virtual Trunk Protocol (VTP) A proprietary Cisco protocol used to automate the updating of multiple VLAN switches.

Virus A program that can make a copy of itself without your necessarily being aware of it. All viruses carry some payload that may or may not do something malicious.

Virus Definition or Data Files Enables the virus protection software to recognize the viruses on your system and clean them. These files should be updated often. Also called *signature files,* depending on the virus protection software in use.

Virus Shield Anti-malware program that passively monitors a computer's activity, checking for viruses only when certain events occur, such as a program executing or a file being downloaded.

VLAN Hopping Older technique to hack a switch to change a normal switch port from an access port to a trunk port. This allows the station attached to the newly created trunk port to access different VLANs. Modern switches have preventative measures to stop this type of abuse.

VLAN Pooling Used in wireless networking, a setup where multiple VLANs share a common domain. The multiple VLANs are used to keep broadcast traffic to manageable levels. Wireless clients are randomly assigned to different VLANs. Their common domain enables them all to be centrally managed.

VLAN Trunking Protocol (VTP) Cisco proprietary protocol to automate the updating of multiple VLAN switches.

Voice over IP (VoIP) Using an IP network to conduct voice calls.

Voltage The pressure of the electrons passing through a wire.

Voltage Event Recorder Tracks voltage over time by plugging into a power outlet.

Volt (V) Unit of measurement for voltage.

VPN Concentrator The new endpoint of the local LAN in L2TP.

Vulnerability A potential weakness in an infrastructure that a threat might exploit.

Vulnerability Scanner A tool that scans a network for potential attack vectors.

WAN (Wide Area Network) A geographically dispersed network created by linking various computers and LANs over long distances, generally using leased phone lines. There is no firm dividing line between a WAN and a LAN.

Warm Boot A system restart performed after the system has been powered and operating. This clears and resets the memory, but does not stop and start the hard drive.

Warm Site Facility with all of the physical resources, computers, and network infrastructure to recover from a primary site disaster. A warm site does not have current backup data and it may take a day or more to recover and install backups before business operations can recommence.

Wattage (Watts or W) The amount of amps and volts needed by a particular device to function.

Wavelength In the context of laser pulses, the distance the signal has to travel before it completes its cyclical oscillation and starts to repeat. Measured in nanometers, wavelength can be loosely associated with colors.

Web Server A server that enables access to HTML documents by remote users.

Web Services Applications and processes that can be accessed over a network, rather than being accessed locally on the client machine. Web services include things such as Web-based e-mail, network-shareable documents, spreadsheets and databases, and many other types of cloud-based applications.

Well-Known Port Numbers Port numbers from 0 to 1204 that are used primarily by client applications to talk to server applications in TCP/IP networks.

Wi-Fi   The most widely adopted wireless networking type in use today. Technically, only wireless devices that conform to the extended versions of the 802.11 standard—802.11a, b, g, n, and ac—are Wi-Fi certified.

Wi-Fi Analyzer   *See* Wireless Analyzer.

Wi-Fi Protected Access (WPA)   A wireless security protocol that addresses weaknesses and acts as an upgrade to WEP. WPA offers security enhancements such as dynamic encryption key generation (keys are issued on a per-user and per-session basis), an encryption key integrity-checking feature, user authentication through the industry-standard Extensible Authentication Protocol (EAP), and other advanced features that WEP lacks.

Wi-Fi Protected Access 2 (WPA2)   An update to the WPA protocol that uses the Advanced Encryption Standard algorithm, making it much harder to crack.

Wi-Fi Protected Setup (WPS)   Automated and semi-automated process to connect a wireless device to a WAP. The process can be as simple as pressing a button on the device or pressing the button and then entering a PIN code.

Wide Area Network (WAN)   *See* WAN (Wide Area Network).

WiMAX   *See* 802.16.

Windows Domain   A group of computers controlled by a computer running Windows Server, which is configured as a domain controller.

Windows Firewall   The firewall that has been included in Windows operating systems since Windows XP; originally named Internet Connection Firewall (ICF) but renamed in XP Service Pack 2.

Windows Internet Name Service (WINS)   A name resolution service that resolves NetBIOS names to IP addresses.

WINS Proxy Agent   A Windows Internet Name Service (WINS) relay agent that forwards WINS broadcasts to a WINS server on the other side of a router to keep older systems from broadcasting in place of registering with the server.

Wire Scheme   *See* Wiring Diagram.

Wired Equivalent Privacy (WEP)   A wireless security protocol that uses a 64-bit encryption algorithm to scramble data packets.

Wired/Wireless Considerations   The planning of structured cabling, determining any wireless requirements, and planning access to the Internet when building or upgrading networks.

Wireless Access Point (WAP)   Connects wireless network nodes to wireless or wired networks. Many WAPs are combination devices that act as high-speed hubs, switches, bridges, and routers, all rolled into one.

Wireless Analyzer   Any device that finds and documents all wireless networks in the area. Also known as a *Wi-Fi analyzer*.

Wireless Bridge   Device used to connect two wireless network segments together, or to join wireless and wired networks together in the same way that wired bridge devices do.

Wireless Controller   Central controlling device for thin client WAPs.

Wireless LAN (WLAN)   A complete wireless network infrastructure serving a single physical locale under a single administration.

Wireless Network   *See* Wi-Fi.

Wireless Survey Tool   A tool used to discover wireless networks in an area; it also notes signal interferences.

Wiremap   Term that techs use to refer to the proper connectivity of wires in a network.

Wireshark   A popular packet sniffer.

Wiring Diagram   A document, also known as a *wiring schematic,* that usually consists of multiple pages and that shows the following: how the wires in a network connect to switches and other nodes, what types of cables are used, and how patch panels are configured. It usually includes details about each cable run.

Wiring Schematic   *See* Wiring Diagram.

Work Area   In a basic structured cabling network, often simply an office or cubicle that potentially contains a PC attached to the network.

Workgroup   A convenient method of organizing computers under Network/My Network Places in Windows operating systems.

Workstation   A general-purpose computer that is small and inexpensive enough to reside at a person's work area for his or her exclusive use.

Worm   A very special form of virus. Unlike other viruses, a worm does not infect other files on the computer. Instead, it replicates by making copies of itself on other systems on a network by taking advantage of security weaknesses in networking protocols.

WPA2-Enterprise   A version of WPA2 that uses a RADIUS server for authentication.

WWW (World Wide Web)   A vast network of servers and clients communicating through the Hypertext Transfer Protocol (HTTP). Commonly accessed using graphical Web-browsing software such as Microsoft Internet Explorer and Google Chrome.

X.25   The first generation of packet-switching technology, it enables remote devices to communicate with each other across high-speed digital links without the expense of individual leased lines.

Yost Cable   Cable used to interface with a Cisco device.

Zero-Day Attack   New attack that exploits a vulnerability that has yet to be identified.

Zombie   A single computer under the control of an operator that is used in a botnet attack. *See also* Botnet.

INDEX

Application layer, TCP/IP, 34–35, 149–150
Application Programming Interfaces (APIs), 29–30, 34
applications, 329–330, 574
approval, from change management team, 523
APs (access points), 430
area border routers (ABRs), OSPF, 204
Area IDs, OSPF, 204
areas, OSPF, 204
ARIN (American Registry for Internet Numbers), 161, 366
ARP (Address Resolution Protocol)
    arp command, 604
    arping command, 605
    cache poisoning, 547–548
    overview of, 159
    troubleshooting proxy ARP, 625
    in Windows, 160
AS (Authentication Server), Kerberos, 307
AS (Autonomous Systems), 201–202
ASA (Adaptive Security Appliance), 623
Asia-Pacific Network Information Center (APNIC), 366
ASN (Autonomous System Number), 201–202
assembler/disassembler software, OSI Transport layer, 25–26
assets, redundancy for critical, 526
assignments, incorrect VLAN, 620
asymmetric DSL (ADSL), 402–403
asymmetric-key algorithms, 292, 293–295
Asynchronous Transfer Mode (ATM), 190–191, 393
AT&T, 386, 402, 409
ATM (Asynchronous Transfer Mode), 190–191, 393
ATMs (automated teller machines), and ISDN, 402
attack surface, zero-day attacks, 547
attack window, zero-day attacks, 547
attenuation, 125, 127–128
authentication
    defined, 289
    insider threats and, 552
    RAS servers for private dial-up, 411–412
    securing TCP/IP, 301
    in session hijacking, 550
    wireless, 440–441
Authentication, Authorization, and Accounting (AAA), 310, 349–352
Authentication Header (AH), IPsec, 315
Authentication Server (AS), Kerberos, 307
authentication standards
    802.1X, 310–311
    AAA port, 305–306, 349–352
    combined with encryption standards, 313–315
    EAP, 308–310
    Kerberos, 307–308
    overview of, 302–303
    PPP, 303–305
    RADIUS, 306–307
    TACACS+, 307
    WEP failure to perform wireless, 442
authenticator, point-to-point connections, 303
authoritative DNS server, 265, 272–273
authoritative name server, 264–265, 274

authorization
    ACL access models for, 301–302
    certificate, 300
    defined, 289
    DNSSEC authentication and, 278
    Kerberos token for, 308
    overview of, 301
    in physical security, 559–560
Authorization, AAA, 306–307
auto-negotiation, 100BaseT, 86
automated teller machines (ATMs), and ISDN, 402
Automatic Private IP Addressing (APIPA), 174, 460
Autonomous System Number (ASN), 201–202
Autonomous Systems (AS), 201–202
AWS (Amazon Web Service), IaaS in, 488–489

▪ B

B (Bearer) channels, ISDN, 400–402
backbone, 94–95, 204
backoff period, 435
backups
    configuring, 525
    for disaster recovery, 531
    high availability with failover, 526
    Kerberos, 309
    log file, 590
    router configuration, 213
    secondary zones acting as, 275
backward slash (/), binary masks, 161
bandwidth, 197, 344–345, 462, 587
bandwidth saturation, 462
bandwidth shaping (or shapers), 345
banner grabbing, 551
bare-metal hypervisors, 481
barrel connectors, coaxial cable, 49
base eight. See also dotted decimal notation, 152
base ten. See also decimal numbers, 152
base two. See also binary numbers, 152
baseband
    100BaseT, 85–87
    100BaseTx, 85
    10BaseFL, 72
    10BaseT, 70, 72
    broadband vs., 86, 406
    defined, 70, 86
baselines, performance monitor, 589–590
basic NAT, 192
Basic Rate Interface (BRI) setup, ISDN, 401
Basic Service Set (BSS), 433
Basic Service Set Identifier (BSSID), 433
bastion host, 572
batteries, cable tester/toner, 138
baud rate, 398, 399
BC (business continuity), 532
BCP (business continuity planning), 532
beacon traffic, configuring, 454–455

cabling and connectors (*cont.*)

    structured. *See* structured cabling

    troubleshooting. *See* troubleshooting tools, hardware

    UTP. *See* UTP (unshielded twisted pair) cabling

cache-only DNS servers, 272

cached lookups, 271–272, 275

caches, 270, 279, 547–548, 586–587

caching, proxy, 349

CACTI, 318, 592

Caesar cipher, 291

calculators, OS, 152–153, 167–168

CAN (campus area network), building. *See* building real-world network

canonical name (CNAME), 274

capacitance, 49

capture files, packet sniffers, 584

cards, 10BaseFL, 72

carrier sense multiple access/collision detection (CSMA/CD), 66–68, 78, 435

carrier sense multiple access (CSMA), 85

carrier sense multiple access with collision avoidance (CSMA/CA), Wi-Fi, 435–436

case sensitivity, 175, 262

CAT (category) ratings, UTP, 51–52, 86, 106–107, 111–113

`cat /etc/resolv.conf.` command, 268

categories, network design, 499–500

CCE (Certified Computer Examiner), 532

CCENT (Cisco Certified Entry Networking technician), 9

CCITT (International Telegraph and Telephone Consultative Committee), 400

CCITT Packet Switching Protocol (X.25), 392

CCTVs (closed-circuit televisions), 561

CDMA (code division multiple access), 407

cellular WAN, 406–408

central box, 13–14, 18, 20

Cerf, Vinton, 23

certificate authority (CA), 300–301

certificates, 298–301, 314, 316–317

certifications

    Cisco, 9, 208

    CompTIA Network+. *See* CompTIA Network+ certification

    computer forensic, 532

    professional cabling, 105

Certified Computer Examiner (CCE), 532

certifiers (cable certifiers), 125, 600

CFCE (Certified Forensic Computer Examiner), 532

chain of custody, computer forensic evidence, 534

Challenge Handshake Authentication Protocol. *See* CHAP (Challenge Handshake Authentication Protocol), PPP

Challenge-Response Authentication Mechanism-Message Digest 5 (CRAM-MD5), 298

challenges, Internet of Things, 628–629

change management, 522–523

change management team, 522, 523

change request, 523

changes, troubleshooting Wi-Fi, 612

channel bonding, and 802.11g, 437

Channel Service Unit/Digital Service Unit (CSU/DSU), 388–390

channels

    ad hoc network setup, 449–450

    configuring Wi-Fi, 456–457

    T-carrier, 390

    troubleshooting Wi-Fi connectivity, 460

    unencrypted, 557

    Wi-Fi, 434–435

    wireless site survey of, 446–448

CHAP (Challenge Handshake Authentication Protocol), PPP, 298, 304–307

Checksum field. TCP/UDP headers, 149

checksum, running hash on, 296

CIDR (Classless Inter-Domain Routing), 162–169

CIFS (Common Internet File System), NAS, 502

cipher locks, 560

ciphers, 290–293

ciphertext, 291

circuit switching, 382, 385

Cisco

    Catalyst 2970 Series Device Manager, 337

    certifications, 9

    Cisco 3550 switch, 340–342

    DHCP snooping, 548

    Dynamic ARP Inspection tool, 547–548

    Easy VPN, 334

    Network Assistant, 337–338

Cisco Certified Entry Networking technician (CCENT), 9

Cisco IOS (Internetwork Operating System), 207–211

Cisco Network Assistant (CNA), 588

Cisco routers

    configuring NAT on, 195

    connecting to, 206–208

    how they work, 183

    modular, 191

    routing table, 190

    supporting PPTP, 334

    as V concentrator, 333

Citrix, 415, 482

cladding, fiber-optic cable, 52

Class A-E blocks, IP addresses, 161–162

Class D, multicast in, 225

Class IDs, IP addresses, 161–162

class of service (CoS), QoS and medianets, 511

classful A, B, C, and D addressing, 161

classless addresses, 167

Classless Inter-Domain Routing (CIDR), 162–169

cleartext (plaintext), 242, 290, 557

client/server model. *See also* VPNs (virtual private networks), 327–330, 339

clients

    configuring Wi-Fi, 458–459

    DHCP, 172–176

    e-mail, 246–247

    FTP, 248–249

installing Wi-Fi, 448–449
protecting systems physically, 554–555
remote terminal, 415
Telnet/SSH, 240–242
troubleshooting DNS, 278
updating VLAN switches into, 339
Web, 238
clock synchronization, with NTP/SNTP, 224
closed-circuit televisions (CCTVs), 561
closed networks, ICS as, 515
cloud bursting, 492
cloud computing
chapter review, 493–497
to the cloud, 486–487
disaster recovery backup using, 531
hybrid cloud, 492
private/public/community clouds, 491
services in, 487–490
CNA (Cisco Network Assistant), 588
CNAME (canonical name), 274
coarse wavelength division multilplexing (CWDM), 391
coaxial cable, 48–49
code division multiple access (CDMA), 407
cold site, business continuity, 532
collaborate tools, unified communications, 508
collectors, NetFlow, 587
collision avoidance, in wireless networks, 435
collision domains, 68, 78
collision lights, NICs, 132
collisions, 66–68, 435
colon (:), IPv6, 359–360
color-coded pairs, UTP cabling, 71
Combs, Gerald, 584
command-line
displaying system's IP addresses, 153–154
FTP clients, 248
troubleshooting tools. *See* troubleshooting tools, software
comments (#), host file, 259
Common Internet File System (CIFS), NAS, 502
Common Vulnerabilities and Exposures (CVE), 556
communications, 32–33, 223–225
community cloud, 491
Comodo, 301
compatibility
in 802.11 versions, 436–438, 464
DNSSEC with backward, 278
ensuring in link aggregation, 131
in native VLANs, 339
in network design, 499, 503–504
settings for VMware backward, 476
using driver updates to fix, 524
using LWAPP for WAP, 444
compliance, network segmentation, 515
CompTIA A+ certification, 2–3, 5
CompTIA (Computing Technology Industry Association), 1–2

CompTIA Network+ certification
becoming certified, 2
exam, 3–4
how to pass exam, 5–7
overview of, 1–3
computer forensics, 532–535
Computing Technology Industry Association (CompTIA), 1–2
configuration backups, 525
configuration utility, wireless client, 431
conflicting permissions, user groups, 563
connection-oriented communication, 32–33, 223–224
connectionless communication, 32–33, 223–225
connections
10 GbE, 93–94
end-to-end, 625
how routers work, 183–184
inside demarc, 115
installing structured cabling, 119–122
LAN interconnections, 155–156
network design for, 504–507
to routers, 206–208
site-to-site VPN, 334
TCP/IP, 228–230
testing fiber cable runs, 125–126
throughput testers measuring, 609
troubleshooting Wi-Fi, 459–465
viewing status of, 230–233
VPN, 334
connectivity software, 605
connector mismatch, 125
console cables, 206–208
console, defined, 207
console (serial) ports, 207, 335, 337–338
content filtering, 572
content switches, 344
context aware firewalls, 570–571
contingency planning, 530–535
Continuing Education Program, CompTIA, 2
continuity, 123, 600
continuity testers, 123–124
control plane, routers, 486
controllers, 444, 595–598
controls, ICS. *See* ICS (industrial control system)
convergence (steady state), 200, 204–205, 214
conversion, IP address, 151–154
copper-based 10 GbE, 93
copper cabling and connectors
overview of, 48–52
testing cable runs, 123–126
troubleshooting, 618
types of, 75
core, fiber-optic cable, 52
CoS (class of service), QoS and medianets, 511
CoS (Cost of Service), MPLS header, 393
costs, vs. budget in network design, 500
counters, Performance Monitor, 589
couplers, UTP, 73, 135

hubs (*cont.*)

switches replacing, 18, 76

troubleshooting, 79

human machine interfaces. *See* HMIs (human machine interfaces), ICS

humidity, telecommunications room, 117

HVAC (heating, ventilation, and air conditioning), 537

hybrid cloud, 492

hybrid routing protocol, BGP as, 202

hybrid topology, 45, 63

Hyper-V, 482

HyperTerminal, 207

Hypertext Markup Language. *See* HTML (Hypertext Markup Language)

Hypertext Transfer Protocol. *See* HTTP (Hypertext Transfer Protocol)

hypervisors, 474–475, 481–482, 553

■ I

IaaS (Infrastructure as a Service), cloud computing, 487–489

IACIS (International Association of Computer Investigative Specialists), 532

IANA (Internet Assigned Numbers Authority), 161, 201, 227, 361

IAS (Internet Authentication Service), RADIUS, 307

iBGP (internal BGP), 202

IBM Type 1 cable, 50

IBSS (Independent Basic Service Set), 432, 433

ICA (Independent Computing Architecture), 415

ICANN (Internet Corporation for Assigned Names and Numbers), 260, 266

ICMP (Internet Control Message Protocol)

TCP/IP applications using, 225

at TCP/IP Internet layer, 264

traceroute and, 602

turning off in firewall, 623

ICS (industrial control system), 512–515, 595–596

ICS (Internet Connection Sharing), 432, 513

identify problem, in troubleshooting, 611–612

IDF (intermediate distribution frame), 107

IDS (intrusion detection system), 346–347

IEEE (Institute of Electrical and Electronics Engineers)

10 GbE, 92–93

1905.1, 628

802.16 (WiMAX), 408

802.3ba, 95

Ethernet, 63

HomePlug, 629

MAC addresses from, 14

networking industry, 55–56

IETF (Internet Engineering Task Force), 314, 359

`ifconfig` command, UNIX/Linux, 154–155, 171, 175, 603–604

IFG (interframe gap), wireless networks, 435

IGMP (Internet Group Management Protocol), 225–226, 621

IGP (Interior Gateway Protocol), 201

IIS (Internet Information Services), 236–237

IKE and IKEv2 (Internet Key Exchange), 315

illegal use, acceptable use policy, 521

IMAP4 (Internet Message Access Protocol version 4), 243–244, 246

impedance, 49

impedance mismatch, 600

implicit deny any rule, ACLs, 572

improper access, 562

IMT-2000 (International Mobile Telecommunications-2000) standard, 407

in-band management, managed switches, 335

inbound traffic, firewalls, 570, 572

incident response, 531, 569

incompatibilities, troubleshooting Wi-Fi, 464

Independent Basic Service Set (IBSS), 432, 433

Independent Computing Architecture (ICA), 415

industrial control system (ICS), 512–515, 595–596

information gathering, in troubleshooting, 611–612

infrared (IR) devices, as PANs, 446

Infrastructure as a Service (IaaS), cloud computing, 487–489

infrastructure-level changes, 522

infrastructure mode wireless networks

configuring client, 458–459

configuring WAPs, 453–458

overview of, 432–433

placing WAPs/antennas, 451–453

setting up, 450–451

inheritance, permission, 563

initiator, point-to-point connections, 303

Input/Output (IO), industrial control system, 512–513

insider threats, 550–552

insulating jacket, fiber-optic cable, 52

Integrated Services Digital Network (ISDN), 400–402, 510

integrity, 289, 296–298

Interchange Carrier (IXC), long-distance service, 397

Interface column, routing tables, 186–190

interface identifier, link-local address in IPv6, 361

interface monitors, 587–589

interface(s)

adding with routers, 191

distributed control system, 512–513

industrial control system, 513

troubleshooting, 418, 618

interference, 419, 448, 462–463

interframe gap (IFG), wireless networks, 435

Interior Gateway Protocol (IGP), 201

intermediate distribution frame (IDF), 107

Intermediate System to Intermediate System (IS-IS), 205

internal BGP (iBGP), 202

internal network connections, designing, 504–506

International Association of Computer Investigative Specialists (IACIS), 532

International Mobile Telecommunications-2000 (IMT-2000) standard, 407

International Organization for Standardization (ISO), 11, 30, 51

■ M

MSAs (multisource agreements), 93–94
MSDS (material safety data sheet), 537
MSSP (managed security service provider), 593
MT-RJ (Mechanical Transfer Registered Jack) connectors, SFF, 90
`mtr` command, 215, 606
MTU (maximum transmission unit), 197, 622–623
MU-MIMO (multiuser MIMO), 802.11ac, 438
multicast addresses, 162, 189, 225–226, 362–363
multicast vs. broadcast, 621
multifactor authentication, 301, 560
multifunction network device, 342
multilayer switches
    load balancing, 342–344
    network protection, 346–352
    overview of, 342
    port bonding, 345–346
    QoS and traffic shaping, 344–345
multilink PPP, 400
multimedia messaging system (MMS), IMT-2000, 407
multimeters, 124, 601
multimode fiber (MMF), 53, 72–73, 91
multiple-choice questions, CompTIA Network+ exam, 3
multiple input/multiple output (MIMO), 437, 438
multiplexers, 115, 383, 391
Multiprotocol Label Switching (MPLS), 393–395
multisource agreements (MSAs), 93–94
multispeed link lights, 132
MX records, SMTP servers, 274
Mytraceroute (mtr), 215

N

n (nano), 53
NAC (Network Access Control), 301, 564–565
NAC (Network Admission Control), Cisco, 564
name resolution, DNS, 257–259, 266–271
name servers, DNS, 264–266
name space, DNS, 260–263
naming conventions. *See also* network naming
    10BaseT Ethernet, 70
    DNS, 262–263
    IP, 23
    name servers, 264
    TIA/EIA 606 patch panel labels, 110
    virtual machines, 477
    Web servers, 265–266
nano (n), 53
nanometer (nm), 53, 89
NAPT-PT, 369
NAS (Network Access Server), RADIUS, 306–307
NAS (network attached storage) devices, 484–485, 502
NAT (Network Address Translation)
    implementing virtual IP, 527
    in IPv6, 369
    overview of, 191–195
    troubleshooting WANs, 623

NAT-PT, 369
National Electric Code (NEC), 55, 118
native VLANs, 337, 339
`nbstat` command, 607
NCP (Network Control Protocol), LCP, 303
near-end crosstalk (NEXT), 125
near field communication (NFC) devices, 446
NEC (National Electric Code), 55, 118
Nessus, vulnerability scanner, 529
Net Activity Viewer, Linux, 230
`net view` command, 281
NetBEUI, 275, 303
NetBIOS name, 275
NetBIOS/NetBEUI protocol, 257–258
NetBIOS over TCP/IP (NetBT), 258
NetFlow, 586–587
Netmask column, routing tables, 187–190
Netscape Navigator, 314
`netstat` command
    diagnosing NetBIOS, 258
    diagnosing TCP/IP networks, 281–282
    overview of, 230–233, 607–608
    viewing open ports, 556
    viewing routing tables, 187, 606–607
    viewing sessions, 28, 228–230
Netware, client/server model of, 327–328
Netware IPX/SPX, 303
network access, 521, 522
Network Access Control (NAC), 301, 564–565
Network Access Server (NAS), RADIUS, 306–307
Network Address Translation. *See* NAT (Network Address Translation)
Network Admission Control (NAC), Cisco, 564
network analyzer, 593
network appliances, troubleshooting, 623
Network Assistant, configuring VLANs, 337–338
network attached storage (NAS) devices, 484–485, 502
network-based anti-malware, 569
network-based firewalls, 570, 574
network-based IDS (NIDS), 347
network blocks, IP addresses in, 161–162
Network Connections, Control Panel, 619
Network Control Protocol (NCP), LCP, 303
network controller, 486
Network Destination column, routing tables, 187–190
Network File System (NFS), NAS, 502
network IDs, 163–170, 211–212, 331
network interface boxes (NIBs), 114
network interface cards. *See* NICs (network interface cards)
network interface devices (NIDs), 114
Network Interface (Link) layer, TCP/IP, 31, 76
network interface units (NIUs), 114, 398
network intrusion prevention system (NIPS), 348
Network layer (Layer 3), OSI
    encryption, 295
    ICMP, 225
    interVLAN routing, 341
    IPsec, 314

VPN connection in Windows with, 333
    wireless networking, 430
NIDS (network-based IDS), 347
NIDs (network interface devices), 114
NIPS (network intrusion prevention system), 348
NIUs (network interface units), 114, 398
nm (nanometer), 53, 89
Nmap port scanner, 528, 609
NMS (Network Management Software) tools, 210–211
NMS (network management station), SNMP, 582–583
NNTP (Network News Transfer Protocol), 235
no-default routers, 365
NOC (network operations center), 591
nodes
    creating redundancy for critical, 526
    NICs as, 65
    using routing tables, 187
noise, troubleshooting broken cables, 600
nonrepudiation, 289, 298–301
notation, IPv4/IPv6 address, 359–360
notification of change, in change management, 523
Novell Netware, as client/server model, 327–328
NS records, DNS forward lookup zones, 273
`nslookup` command, DNS, 279, 605–606
NTP (Network Time Protocol), 224, 319, 546–547
`ntpdc` command, 546
numbering system, subnet masks, 157–161
nVoy (1905.1 standard), 630
NWLink, 145

◼ O

obsolescence, IoT and, 628
OC (Optical Carrier) standards, SONET, 391–392
octet numbering system. *See* dotted decimal notation
OEM tools, network management, 211
OFDM (orthogonal frequency-division multiplexing)
    broadcasting, 434, 437–438
off-boarding mobile devices, 445
Ohm rating, cables, 49
omnidirectional antennas, wireless infrastructure networks, 451–452
on-boarding mobile devices, 445
onboard NICs, 129
one-way satellite, 405
online UPS, 136
open circuits, troubleshooting broken cables, 599–600
open networks, troubleshooting Wi-Fi, 463–464
open ports, 230
Open Shortest Path First (OSPF), 202–205
OpenNMS, 210–211
OpenSSH, 317
OpenVAS, vulnerability scanner, 529
OpenVPN, 334

operating systems
    avoiding single points of failure, 526
    installing NIC driver into, 131
    installing on VM, 476–479
    rootkit attacks on, 553
    updates, 524
    vulnerabilities of unpatched/legacy, 556
operators
    distributed control system, 512–513
    industrial control system, 512
Optical Carrier (OC) standards, SONET, 391–392
optical connection tester, 132–133
optical time domain reflectometers (OTDRs), 128, 600
Organizationally Unique Identifier (OUI), 15, 551–552
orthogonal frequency-division multiplexing (OFDM)
    broadcasting, 434, 437–438
OS X
    administrative account for, 552
    case sensitivity of commands in, 175
    converting IP addresses in, 152–153
    designing network workstations, **502**
    dial up on, **412**
    displaying IP addresses in, **153–154**
    enabling IPv6 in, **368–369**
    hosts file in, 259
    IPv6 configuration on, **363–364**
    link-local address in, 360
    NIC driver installation in, 131
    root account, **552**
    static IP addressing in, 170
    Telnet, 240
    troubleshooting DHCP in, **175**
    using netstat in, 228
    viewing routing tables in, 187, **187**
    VPN connection tool in, **333**
    workstations, 501–502
OSI (Open Systems Interconnection) model
    Application layer. *See* Application layer (Layer 7), OSI
    Data Link layer. *See* Data Link layer (Layer 2), OSI
    developed by ISO, 11
    encryption in, 295
    exam questions on, 4
    Layers 3-7 overview, 22–23
    layers of, 11–12
    MHTechEd and, 12–13
    Network layer. *See* Network layer (Layer 3), OSI
    network segmentation and, 515
    Physical layer. *See* Physical layer (Layer 1), OSI
    Presentation layer (Layer 6), OSI, 28–30, 295
    protocol analyzers for, 601
    Session layer (Layer 5), 26–28, 295
    as tech troubleshooting tool, 35
    Transport layer. *See* Transport layer (Layer 4), OSI
    troubleshooting using, 613
OSPF (Open Shortest Path First), 202–205
OTDRs (optical time domain reflectometers), 128, 600

network management software, 211
  Software as a Service using, 490
  terminal emulation programs, 416
  troubleshooting tools for, 609
threat agents, 545
threats
  administrative access control, 552
  adware, 553
  ARP cache poisoning, 547–548
  brute force, 550
  common vulnerabilities, 555–558
  denial of service, 548–549
  macro, 553
  malware, 552–554
  man-in-the-middle, 549
  overview of, 545
  packet/protocol abuse, 546–547
  phishing, 554
  physical/local access, 550–552
  rootkits, 553
  session hijacking, 550
  social engineering, 554
  spoofing, 545–546
  spyware, 553–554
  Trojan horse, 553
  virus, 552–553
  VLAN hopping, 635
  worm, 553
  zero day attacks, 547
throttling security policy, WANs, 623
throughput, 434
throughput testers, 609
TIA/EIA (Telecommunications Industry Association
  /Electronics Industries Alliance)
    568, color codes, 71
    568, crossover cables, 75
    568, inserting wires into patch panels, 110
    568, UTP cable length, 113
    606, patch panel labels, 110
    structured cabling standards, 103–105
    verifying copper cable runs, 125
TIA (Telecommunications Industry Association), 51
TIC (Tunnel Information and Control) protocol, 374
Ticket-Granting Service (TGS), Kerberos, 308
Ticket-Granting Ticket (TGT), Kerberos, 308
tier 1 Internet, long distance, 381–382
Time Division Multiple Access (TDMA), GSM, 407
Time Division Multiplexing (TDM), T1 lines, 388
time domain reflectometer (TDR), 124, 600
time, NTP giving current, 319
Time to Live (TTL), 148, 393
timestamped TGT, Kerberos, 308
TKIP (Temporal Key Integrity Protocol), WPA, 442
TLD (top-level domain) names, 260
TLS (Transport Layer Security)
  EAP-TLS, 309
  EAP-TTLS, 309

  HTTP using, 239
  SNMP using, 583
  SSL/TLS, 238–239, 314, 319
  upgrading SSL, 238–239, 314
token, Kerberos, 308
Token Ring networks, 45, 50
tone generators, 137
toners, 137–138, 601
top-level domain (TLD) names, 260
top talkers, in compromised system, 568–569
top-to-bottom OSI troubleshooting, 613
topologies. *See* network topology
`tracert` (traceroute) command
  as connectivity software, 605
  diagnosing TCP/IP networks, 282
  `mtr` command as dynamic, 606
  overview of, 214–215
  in `pathping` command, 605
  as troubleshooting tool, 602–603, 616
  using from looking glass sites, 609
  for WAN router problem, 622
tracing cables, 137–138
traffic shaping (filtering), using QoS, 344–345
traffic spikes, reflective DDoS, 549
training, 525–526, 569
Transmission program, 330
transmit beamforming, 802.11n WAPs, 437
transparent state, updating VLAN switches, 339
Transport layer (Layer 4), OSI
  load balancing, 344
  no encryption at, 295
  overview of, 25–26
  protocols, 223–226
  TCP/IP model vs., 32, 34
Transport Layer Security. *See* TLS (Transport Layer Security)
Transport layer, TCP/IP, 32–34, 148–149
Transport mode, IPsec, 314
Trap PDU, SNMP, 582–583
Trivial File Transfer Protocol (TFTP), 224–225, 250
Trojan horse, 553
troubleshooting
  AAA port authentication, 351
  cabling. *See* diagnostics/repair of physical cabling
  chapter review, 632–637
  CompTIA Network+ exam questions on, 3
  DHCP, 173–176
  DNS, 278–280
  end-to-end connectivity, 625–626
  Ethernet hubs and switches, 79
  firewalls, 574
  as fun, 626
  hands-on problems, 617–619
  LAN problems, 619–621
  OSI and TCP/IP models for, 35
  overview of, 598, 616
  physical cabling, 133–138
  port authentication with AAA, 351–352

wireless bridges, 459
wireless channel utilization, 460
wireless controllers, 444
wireless LANs (WLANs), vs. PANs, 446
wireless networking
    chapter review, 466–471
    design considerations, 499, 505
    mesh topology for, 46
    overview of, 428
    point-to-multipoint topology for, 46–47
    point-to-point topology for, 47
    range, 433
    Wi-Fi. *See* Wi-Fi
wireless survey tools, 446
wiremap test, 124
Wireshark
    ARP request/ response in, 547
    packet analyzing with, 584–586
    scenario using, 593
    as software protocol analyzer, 601
    troubleshooting with, 608
WLANs (wireless LANs), vs. PANs, 446
word patterns, cracking Caesar cipher, 291
work area
    connecting, 120
    defined, 105–106
    diagnosing physical cabling, 134–135
    overview of, 112–113
workflow, in unified communications, 508
workgroups, Windows, 276
workstations
    access ports connecting to, 339
    cable drops in wall of, 116

configuring WAPs on, 453
integrating Wi-Fi, 104
in network design, 500–502
VMware Workstation, 474–479
World Wide Web, 234–239
worms, 553
WPA 2 (Wi-Fi Protected Access 2), 442–443, 456
WPA (Wi-Fi Protected Access), 442, 456
WPA2- PSK (Personal Shared Key), 443
WPS (Wi-Fi Protected Setup), 438

X

X.25 (CCITT Packet Switching Protocol), 392
XenServer, hypervisor, 482
XML (Extensible Markup Language), 235

Y

Yagi antennas, 452
Yahoo! Mail, 244
Ylonen, Tatu, 311
Yost cables, 206–208

Z

zero (0), routing tables, 186
zero day attack, 547
zeroconf (zero-configuration) networking, 174
zombies, DDoS attacks, 548
zones
    Active Directory-integrated, 277
    as containers for single domains, 264

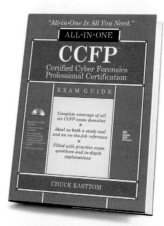
 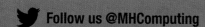